The Sporting News

THE
SERIES

The Sporting News

THE

SERIES

World Series Stories Written By
JOE HOPPEL

Editor/The Series
CRAIG CARTER

President-Chief Executive Officer
Richard Waters

Editor
Tom Barnidge

Director of Books and Periodicals
Ron Smith

ISSN: 0896-680X

ISBN: 0-89204-272-9

CONTENTS

WORLD SERIES

CHAMPIONSHIP SERIES

On the Cover: The Minnesota Twins were at the top of the baseball world after defeating the St. Louis Cardinals in Game 7 of the 1987 World Series. At the top of the pile is Al Newman with Gary Gaetti to the left and relief ace Jeff Reardon to the right hugging catcher Tim Laudner. Photo by Rich Pilling, Photo Editor of The Sporting News.

CONTENTS

INTRODUCTION

The World Series is Christy Mathewson tossing three shutouts in six days. It's Fred Snodgrass muffing a fly ball. And it's Bill Wambsganss making an unassisted triple play.

The Series is Grover Cleveland Alexander trudging out of the bullpen to strike out Tony Lazzeri. It's Babe Ruth calling his home run shot. And it's Joe Medwick being showered with debris from irate fans.

The Series is catcher Mickey Owen missing connections with a third strike. It's Enos Slaughter racing home from first base when everyone in the ball park (except Enos himself) assumed he'd hold up at third. And it's Cookie Lavagetto depriving Bill Bevens of no-hit glory.

The Series is a boy of yesteryear begging his science teacher to turn on the radio to find out how the Yankees and Dodgers are doing. It's Willie Mays making an incredible catch on Vic Wertz. And it's Johnny Podres bringing a championship to Brooklyn at last.

The Series is Don Larsen pitching perfectly. It's Bill Mazeroski homering in the bottom of the ninth to win it all. And it's Willie McCovey hitting a last-out line drive just within the reach of Bobby Richardson.

The Series is Bob Gibson striking out 17 batters. It's the fielding wizardry of Brooks Robinson and Graig Nettles. And it's Carlton Fisk homering off the foul pole.

The Series is Reggie Jackson clubbing three first-pitch homers in one game. It's the New York Mets down to their last strike against the Boston Red Sox. And it's Minnesota Twins fans raising the roof at the Metrodome.

The Series is crisp autumn air, Yankee dominance and families huddled around television sets, and it's an event that has been woven into the fabric of American life as much as any athletic endeavor possibly could be. Proof positive of the latter is the ever-familiar use of "The Series" to describe the annual October meeting of the National League and American League champions for baseball's top prize. The word "World" is missing and there is no clear-cut indication of the sport involved, but there never is any question about what is being discussed.

"The Series" does indeed say it all and, accordingly, it serves as a fitting title for this book.

The Sporting News' "The Series" brings together for the first time narrative reviews, game-by-game box scores, composite boxes and performance charts of both Championship Series play and World Series competition.

For 65 years, regular-season champions from one-divisional league alignments proceeded directly to the World Series. Then, in 1969, the majors realigned into four divisions and introduced Championship Series playoffs to determine the World Series participants.

The Championship Series has grown in stature, having attained best-of-seven status in 1985. A definitive book on the World Series must now include this vital steppingstone to the fall classic.

With 1988 marking the 20th year of Championship Series action and the 85th season of World Series play (exactly 500 World Series games had been played through 1987), this seems an appropriate time to unite the postseason extravaganzas in one volume. "The Series" achieves that objective.

1903 TO 1987

WORLD SERIES

From its meager beginning in 1903, the World Series grew into a major event that commanded national attention. President Franklin D. Roosevelt, with an assist above from Senators player-Manager Joe Cronin, throws out the first ball for Game 3 of the 1933 Series in Washington.

1903
BOSTON RED SOX
VS.
PITTSBURGH PIRATES

After going at each other with ax-wielding viciousness for two years, the established National League and fledgling American League buried the hatchet, at least temporarily, in 1903—thanks, in large part, to the owners of the N.L.'s Pittsburgh club and the A.L.'s Boston team.

With their clubs apparently headed toward pennants, Pittsburgh's Barney Dreyfuss and Boston's Henry Killilea agreed during the 1903 season to stage a best-of-nine postseason playoff for the "world championship." The accommodation came in the wake of open hostilities—punctuated by player raids—that had existed between the National League and American League since the junior league's entry upon the major league scene in 1901.

Dreyfuss' Pirates appeared to be stellar representatives for the National League, whose history dated to 1876. Pittsburgh had won its third consecutive pennant in '03. Boston also seemed a worthy competitor in this first modern World Series, having won the A.L. flag by 14½ games.

In Game 1, Pirates workhorse Deacon Phillippe pitched a six-hitter and right fielder Jimmy Sebring hit the first home run in Series history and drove in four runs as Pittsburgh scored a 7-3 victory. Third baseman Tommy Leach rapped two singles and two triples for the Pirates. Boston evened the Series, though, when Bill Dinneen threw a three-hitter and Patsy Dougherty walloped two homers in a 3-0 triumph.

Phillippe, pressed into heavy duty because of illness and injury to the Pittsburgh pitching staff, came back on just one day of rest to start Game 3. A 25-game winner during the season, Phillippe continued to excel. He allowed

Pittsburgh Owner Barney Dreyfuss was confident when he matched his National League Pirates against Boston of the upstart American League.

only four hits, won by a 4-2 score and, as it turned out, was just getting warmed up. When a travel day and rainout ensued, the Pirates turned to the good Deacon for Game 4 as well. Phillippe met the challenge with a complete-game 5-4 triumph—Leach knocked in three of the Pirates' runs, while Honus Wagner and Ginger Beaumont each collected three hits—and Pittsburgh led Boston, three games to one.

Cy Young, 36 years old but a 28-game winner for the 1903 Red Sox (also known as the Pilgrims, Puritans and Americans), was called upon to cool off the Pirates in Game 5—and did just that. Young yielded only six hits and drove in three runs in an 11-2 runaway. The next day, Dinneen was a 6-3 victor in a game that featured four hits, two RBIs and two stolen bases by the losers' Beaumont. After six games, it was the Red Sox 3, Phillippe 3.

Having won each time Phillippe had trudged to the mound, Pittsburgh sent the strong-armed righthander against Boston in Game 7. But this wasn't to be Phillippe's day. Jimmy Collins, the Red Sox's playing manager, and Chick Stahl touched him for first-inning triples and Boston bolted to a 2-0 lead en route to a 7-3 triumph. For the first time, the Red Sox had seized the Series lead. Ahead four games to three, Boston would attempt to nail down the championship on its Huntington Avenue Grounds.

The pitching matchup for Game 8 was a beauty—Dinneen against, yes, Deacon Phillippe. Working on two days of rest this time, Phillippe battled Dinneen to a scoreless tie through three innings. After Dinneen blanked Pittsburgh again in the fourth, the Red Sox broke through against the Deacon in their half of the inning. Buck Freeman led off

with a triple and Freddy Parent reached base on an error (with Freeman holding third). Candy LaChance then sacrificed Parent to second. Hobe Ferris followed with a single, putting Phillippe and the Pirates in a 2-0 hole.

The hole grew deeper two innings later when LaChance stroked a two-out triple and scored on Ferris' single.

Phillippe battled on and wound up pitching his fifth complete game in the Series, which lasted 13 days. But Dinneen bested him in climactic Game 8, tossing his second shutout of the Series and notching his third victory. The 3-0 decision was the Red Sox's fourth straight triumph and made the upstart Boston team champion of the first American League-vs.-National League World Series.

Dinneen and Young were bellwethers for Boston. Together, they pitched 69 of the 71 innings that Red Sox hurlers totaled in the fall classic (Tom Hughes lasted two-plus innings as Boston's third-game starter). Young, appearing in what would prove his only Series, won two of three decisions for Boston and recorded a 1.59 earned-run average.

With Phillippe, Dinneen and Young dominating play, hitters obviously had a tough time. The Red Sox batted .252 collectively, while Pittsburgh—despite the presence of N.L. batting champion Wagner in its lineup—showed a .237 mark. Wagner hit .222 in the Series, managing only one hit in the last four games. And the rival playing managers, third baseman Collins of Boston and left fielder Fred Clarke of Pittsburgh, drove in one run in a combined 70 at-bats.

Pittsburgh's Sebring, besides accounting for the first homer in Series history, also led all regulars with a .367 average.

Perhaps the main thing about the 1903 Series, though, was that it at least cooled tempers between baseball's warring factions. That the upstart American League buried the hatchet squarely in the back of the haughty National League—and did so with fiendish delight—was merely a sidelight.

Years later, former Pittsburgh workhorse Deacon Phillippe (above) could look back on his three victories in the inaugural World Series. Cy Young (below), at age 36, was a two-game Series winner for Boston.

Game 1

Thursday, October 1, At Boston

Pittsburgh	AB.	R.	H.	RBI.	PO.	A.
Beaumont, cf	5	1	0	0	3	0
Clarke, lf	5	0	2	0	4	0
Leach, 3b	5	1	4	1	0	1
Wagner, ss	3	1	1	1	1	2
Bransfield, 1b	5	2	1	0	7	0
Ritchey, 2b	4	1	0	0	1	2
Sebring, rf	5	1	3	4	1	0
Phelps, c	4	0	1	0	10	0
Phillippe, p	4	0	0	0	0	2
Totals	40	7	12	6	27	7

Boston	AB.	R.	H.	RBI.	PO.	A.
Dougherty, lf	4	0	0	0	1	1
Collins, 3b	4	0	0	0	2	3
Stahl, cf	4	0	1	0	2	0
Freeman, rf	4	2	2	0	2	0
Parent, ss	4	1	2	1	4	4
LaChance, 1b	4	0	0	2	8	0
Ferris, 2b	3	0	1	0	2	4
Criger, c	3	0	0	0	6	1
aO'Brien	1	0	0	0	0	0
Young, p	3	0	0	0	0	1
bFarrell	1	0	0	0	0	0
Totals	35	3	6	3	27	14

Pittsburgh...........................4 0 1 1 0 0 1 0 0—7
Boston...............................0 0 0 0 0 0 2 0 1—3

Pittsburgh	IP.	H.	R.	ER.	BB.	SO.
Phillippe (W)	9	6	3	2	0	10

Boston	IP.	H.	R.	ER.	BB.	SO.
Young (L)	9	12	7	3	3	5

aStruck out for Criger in ninth. bGrounded out for Young in ninth. E—Ferris 2, Criger 2, Leach, Wagner. LOB—Pittsburgh 9, Boston 6. 3B—Freeman, Parent, Leach 2, Bransfield. HR—Sebring. SB—Wagner, Bransfield, Ritchey. HBP—By Phillippe (Ferris). PB—Criger. U—O'Day (N.L.) and Connolly (A.L.). T—1:55. A—16,242.

Game 2

Friday, October 2, At Boston

Pittsburgh	AB.	R.	H.	RBI.	PO.	A.
Beaumont, cf	3	0	0	0	3	0
Clarke, lf	3	0	1	0	3	0
Leach, 3b	3	0	0	0	0	2

	AB.	R.	H.	RBI.	PO.	A.
Wagner, ss	3	0	0	0	3	3
Bransfield, 1b	3	0	0	0	9	1
Ritchey, 2b	3	0	1	0	3	3
Sebring, rf	3	0	1	0	1	0
Smith, c	3	0	0	0	2	1
Leever, p	0	0	0	0	0	0
Veil, p	2	0	0	0	0	0
aPhelps	1	0	0	0	0	0
Totals	27	0	3	0	24	10

Boston	AB.	R.	H.	RBI.	PO.	A.
Dougherty, lf	4	2	3	2	0	1
Collins, 3b	4	0	1	0	1	1
Stahl, cf	4	1	1	0	1	0
Freeman, rf	4	0	2	1	0	0
Parent, ss	3	0	1	0	3	3
LaChance, 1b	2	0	0	0	8	1
Ferris, 2b	4	0	0	0	3	0
Criger, c	3	0	0	0	11	0
Dinneen, p	2	0	1	0	0	3
Totals	30	3	9	3	27	9

Pittsburgh 0 0 0 0 0 0 0 0 0—0
Boston 2 0 0 0 0 1 0 0 x—3

Pittsburgh	IP.	H.	R.	ER.	BB.	SO.
Leever (L)	1	3	2	2	1	0
Veil	7	6	1	1	4	1

Boston	IP.	H.	R.	ER.	BB.	SO.
Dinneen (W)	9	3	0	0	2	11

aStruck out for Veil in ninth. E—Smith, Veil. DP—Pittsburgh 2, Boston 1. LOB—Pittsburgh 2, Boston 11. 2B—Stahl. HR—Dougherty 2. SB—Collins 2. SH—LaChance, Dinneen. HBP—By Veil (Dougherty). U—O'Day (N.L.) and Connolly (A.L.). T—1:47. A—9,415.

Game 3

Saturday, October 3, At Boston

Pittsburgh	AB.	R.	H.	RBI.	PO.	A.
Beaumont, cf	4	1	0	0	1	0
Clarke, lf	4	0	1	0	0	0
Leach, 3b	4	1	1	1	0	1
Wagner, ss	3	1	1	0	0	7
Bransfield, 1b	3	0	0	0	15	0
Ritchey, 2b	4	1	1	1	2	2
Sebring, rf	3	0	1	1	4	0
Phelps, c	4	0	2	1	5	1
Phillippe, p	4	0	0	0	0	4
Totals	33	4	7	4	27	15

Boston	AB.	R.	H.	RBI.	PO.	A.
Dougherty, lf	4	0	0	0	1	1
Collins, 3b	4	2	2	0	2	6
Stahl, cf	3	0	1	1	2	0
Freeman, rf	3	0	0	0	1	0
Parent, ss	4	0	0	1	0	7
LaChance, 1b	3	0	1	0	15	0
Ferris, 2b	4	0	0	0	2	2
Criger, c	3	0	0	0	4	1
Hughes, p	0	0	0	0	0	0
Young, p	3	0	0	0	0	2
Totals	31	2	4	2	27	19

Pittsburgh 0 1 2 0 0 0 0 1 0—4
Boston 0 0 0 1 0 0 0 1 0—2

Pittsburgh	IP.	H.	R.	ER.	BB.	SO.
Phillippe (W)	9	4	2	2	3	5

Boston	IP.	H.	R.	ER.	BB.	SO.
Hughes (L)	2*	4	3	2	2	0
Young	7	3	1	1	0	2

*Pitched to three batters in third.

E—Collins, Young. DP—Boston 1. LOB—Pittsburgh 6, Boston 5. 2B—Collins, LaChance, Clarke, Ritchey, Wagner, Phelps 2. SB—Leach. SH—Bransfield. HBP—By Young (Wagner). PB—Criger. U—O'Day (N.L.) and Connolly (A.L.). T—1:50. A—18,801.

Game 4

Tuesday, October 6, At Pittsburgh

Boston	AB.	R.	H.	RBI.	PO.	A.
Dougherty, lf	4	0	0	0	3	0
Collins, 3b	4	1	1	0	1	2
Stahl, cf	4	1	2	0	3	1
Freeman, rf	4	0	1	1	0	0
Parent, ss	4	1	1	1	1	3
LaChance, 1b	4	1	2	0	6	0
Ferris, 2b	4	0	1	0	2	0
Criger, c	3	0	1	1	8	1
aFarrell	1	0	0	1	0	0
Dinneen, p	3	0	0	0	0	1
bO'Brien	1	0	0	0	0	0
Totals	36	4	9	4	24	8

Pittsburgh	AB.	R.	H.	RBI.	PO.	A.
Beaumont, cf	4	2	3	0	3	0
Clarke, lf	4	1	1	0	1	0
Leach, 3b	4	1	2	3	2	5
Wagner, ss	4	0	3	1	1	1
Bransfield, 1b	4	0	1	1	9	1
Ritchey, 2b	3	0	0	0	5	5
Sebring, rf	4	0	0	0	1	0
Phelps, c	4	0	1	0	4	0
Phillippe, p	3	1	1	0	1	1
Totals	34	5	12	5	27	13

Boston 0 0 0 0 1 0 0 0 3—4
Pittsburgh 1 0 0 0 1 0 3 0 x—5

Boston	IP.	H.	R.	ER.	BB.	SO.
Dinneen (L)	8	12	5	5	1	7

Pittsburgh	IP.	H.	R.	ER.	BB.	SO.
Phillippe (W)	9	9	4	4	0	1

aFlied out for Criger in ninth, Parent scoring after the catch. bFlied out for Dinneen in ninth. E—Dougherty, Bransfield. DP—Boston 1, Pittsburgh 1. LOB—Boston 5, Pittsburgh 6. 3B—Beaumont, Leach. SB—Wagner. U—O'Day (N.L.) and Connolly (A.L.). T—1:30. A—7,600.

Game 5

Wednesday, October 7, At Pittsburgh

Boston	AB.	R.	H.	RBI.	PO.	A.
Dougherty, lf	6	0	3	3	3	0
Collins, 3b	6	0	2	0	0	4
Stahl, cf	5	2	1	0	2	0
Freeman, rf	4	2	2	1	2	0
Parent, ss	5	1	2	0	1	4
LaChance, 1b	4	2	1	1	13	0
Ferris, 2b	5	2	1	2	1	3
Criger, c	3	1	0	0	5	0
Young, p	5	1	2	3	0	2
Totals	43	11	14	10	27	13

Pittsburgh	AB.	R.	H.	RBI.	PO.	A.
Beaumont, cf	4	1	1	0	0	0
Clarke, lf	4	1	0	0	3	0
Leach, 3b	4	0	2	2	2	1
Wagner, ss	4	0	0	0	1	3
Bransfield, 1b	4	0	0	0	9	1
Ritchey, 2b	4	0	1	0	1	4
Sebring, rf	4	0	1	0	2	0
Phelps, c	3	0	0	0	9	0
Kennedy, p	2	0	1	0	0	1
Thompson, p	1	0	0	0	0	1
Totals	34	2	6	2	27	11

Boston 0 0 0 0 0 6 4 1 0—11
Pittsburgh 0 0 0 0 0 0 0 2 0— 2

Boston	IP.	H.	R.	ER.	BB.	SO.
Young (W)	9	6	2	0	0	4

Pittsburgh	IP.	H.	R.	ER.	BB.	SO.
Kennedy (L)	7	11	10	4	3	3
Thompson	2	3	1	1	0	1

E—Parent, LaChance, Clarke, Leach, Wagner 2. LOB—Boston 9, Pittsburgh 6. 2B—Kennedy. 3B—Leach, Dougherty 2, Collins, Stahl, Young. SB—Collins, Stahl. SH—Phelps, Criger. U—Connolly (A.L.) and O'Day (N.L.). T—2:00. A—12,322.

Game 6

Thursday, October 8, At Pittsburgh

Boston	AB.	R.	H.	RBI.	PO.	A.
Dougherty, lf	3	1	1	0	1	0
Collins, 3b	5	1	1	1	1	2
Stahl, cf	5	1	2	1	2	0
Freeman, rf	5	0	0	1	1	0
Parent, ss	4	2	1	0	5	2
LaChance, 1b	4	0	1	1	9	2
Ferris, 2b	4	0	2	1	1	3
Criger, c	4	0	1	0	6	0
Dinneen, p	4	1	1	0	1	2
Totals	38	6	10	5	27	11

Pittsburgh	AB.	R.	H.	RBI.	PO.	A.
Beaumont, cf	5	1	4	2	5	0
Clarke, lf	5	0	2	0	2	0
Leach, 3b	5	0	0	1	1	2
Wagner, ss	3	0	0	0	2	5
Bransfield, 1b	3	0	1	0	11	0
Ritchey, 2b	3	0	0	0	1	3
Sebring, rf	4	1	2	0	2	0
Phelps, c	4	1	1	0	3	0
Leever, p	4	0	0	0	0	2
Totals	36	3	10	3	27	12

Boston 0 0 3 0 2 0 1 0 0—6
Pittsburgh 0 0 0 0 0 0 3 0 0—3

Boston	IP.	H.	R.	ER.	BB.	SO.
Dinneen (W)	9	10	3	3	3	3

Pittsburgh	IP.	H.	R.	ER.	BB.	SO.
Leever (L)	9	10	6	5	2	2

E—Criger, Leach 2, Wagner. DP—Boston 1, Pittsburgh 1. LOB—Boston 8, Pittsburgh 9. 2B—Clarke, LaChance. 3B—Stahl, Parent. SB—Beaumont 2, Clarke, Leach, Stahl. HBP—By Leever (Parent). U—O'Day (N.L.) and Connolly (A.L.). T—2:02. A—11,556.

Game 7

Saturday, October 10, At Pittsburgh

Boston	AB.	R.	H.	RBI.	PO.	A.
Dougherty, lf	5	0	1	0	3	0
Collins, 3b	5	1	1	0	0	2
Stahl, cf	4	1	2	1	0	0
Freeman, rf	4	1	1	0	0	0
Parent, ss	4	2	2	1	3	6
LaChance, 1b	3	1	0	0	11	0
Ferris, 2b	3	1	2	0	4	4
Criger, c	4	0	2	3	6	2
Young, p	4	0	0	0	0	2
Totals	36	7	11	5	27	16

Pittsburgh	AB.	R.	H.	RBI.	PO.	A.
Beaumont, cf	5	0	1	0	2	0
Clarke, lf	5	1	1	0	1	0
Leach, 3b	5	0	0	0	0	1
Wagner, ss	3	0	0	1	2	6
Bransfield, 1b	4	1	3	0	13	2
Ritchey, 2b	4	0	0	1	5	8
Sebring, rf	4	1	2	0	1	0
Phelps, c	3	0	1	0	2	3
Phillippe, p	4	0	2	1	1	0
Totals	37	3	10	3	27	20

Boston 2 0 0 2 0 2 0 1 0—7
Pittsburgh 0 0 0 1 0 1 0 0 1—3

Boston	IP.	H.	R.	ER.	BB.	SO.
Young (W)	9	10	3	2	1	6

Pittsburgh	IP.	H.	R.	ER.	BB.	SO.
Phillippe (L)	9	11	7	5	0	2

E—Collins, Parent, LaChance 2, Wagner, Phelps, Phillippe. DP—Boston 1, Pittsburgh 1. LOB—Boston 4, Pittsburgh 9. 3B—Clarke, Bransfield, Collins, Stahl, Freeman, Parent, Ferris. SH—Wagner, LaChance, Ferris. WP—Phillippe. U—Connolly (A.L.) and O'Day (N.L.). T—1:45. A—17,038.

Game 8

Tuesday, October 13, At Boston

Pittsburgh	AB.	R.	H.	RBI.	PO.	A.
Beaumont, cf	4	0	0	0	5	0
Clarke, lf	4	0	1	0	3	0
Leach, 3b	3	0	0	0	0	3
Wagner, ss	4	0	1	0	3	0
Bransfield, 1b	3	0	0	0	7	1
Ritchey, 2b	2	0	0	0	2	1
Sebring, rf	3	0	1	0	1	1
Phelps, c	3	0	0	0	3	0
Phillippe, p	3	0	1	0	0	2
Totals	29	0	4	0	24	8

Boston	AB.	R.	H.	RBI.	PO.	A.
Dougherty, lf	4	0	0	0	3	0
Collins, 3b	4	0	1	0	0	2
Stahl, cf	4	0	0	0	2	0
Freeman, rf	4	1	1	0	2	0
Parent, ss	4	1	0	0	1	1
LaChance, 1b	3	1	1	0	11	0
Ferris, 2b	4	0	2	3	0	3
Criger, c	3	0	1	0	8	3
Dinneen, p	3	0	1	0	0	3
Totals	33	3	8	3	27	12

Pittsburgh 0 0 0 0 0 0 0 0 0—0
Boston 0 0 0 2 0 1 0 0 x—3

Pittsburgh	IP.	H.	R.	ER.	BB.	SO.
Phillippe (L)	8	8	3	3	0	2

Boston	IP.	H.	R.	ER.	BB.	SO.
Dinneen (W)	9	4	0	0	2	7

E—Wagner, Bransfield, Phelps. DP—Boston 1. LOB—Pittsburgh 4, Boston 7. 3B—Freeman, LaChance, Sebring. SB—Wagner. SH—LaChance. U—O'Day (N.L.) and Connolly (A.L.). T—1:35. A—7,455.

COMPOSITE BATTING AVERAGES

Boston Red Sox

Player-Position	G.	AB.	R.	H.	2B.	3B.	HR.	RBI.	BA.
Stahl, cf	8	33	6	10	1	3	0	3	.303
Ferris, 2b	8	31	3	9	0	1	0	6	.290
Freeman, rf	8	32	6	9	0	3	0	4	.281
Parent, ss	8	32	8	9	0	3	0	4	.281
Collins, 3b	8	36	5	9	1	2	0	1	.250
Dinneen, p	4	12	1	3	0	0	0	0	.250
Dougherty, lf	8	34	3	8	0	2	2	5	.235
Criger, c	8	26	1	6	0	0	0	4	.231
LaChance, 1b	8	27	5	6	2	1	0	4	.222
Young, p	4	15	1	2	0	1	0	3	.133
Farrell, ph	2	2	0	0	0	0	0	1	.000
O'Brien, ph	2	2	0	0	0	0	0	0	.000
Hughes, p	1	0	0	0	0	0	0	0	.000
Totals	8	282	39	71	4	16	2	35	.252

Pittsburgh Pirates

Player-Position	G.	AB.	R.	H.	2B.	3B.	HR.	RBI.	BA.
Kennedy, p	1	2	0	1	1	0	0	0	.500
Sebring, rf	8	30	3	11	0	1	1	5	.367
Leach, 3b	8	33	3	9	0	4	0	8	.273
Beaumont, cf	8	34	6	9	0	1	0	2	.265
Clarke, lf	8	34	3	9	2	1	0	0	.265
Phelps, ph-c	8	26	1	6	2	0	0	1	.231
Wagner, ss	8	27	2	6	1	0	0	3	.222
Phillippe, p	5	18	1	4	0	0	0	1	.222
Bransfield, 1b	8	29	3	6	0	2	0	1	.207
Ritchey, 2b	8	27	2	3	1	0	0	2	.111
Leever, p	2	4	0	0	0	0	0	0	.000
Smith, c	1	3	0	0	0	0	0	0	.000
Thompson, p	1	1	0	0	0	0	0	0	.000
Veil, p	1	2	0	0	0	0	0	0	.000
Totals	8	270	24	64	7	9	1	23	.237

COMPOSITE PITCHING AVERAGES

Boston Red Sox

Pitcher	G.	IP.	H.	R.	ER.	BB.	SO.	W.	L.	ERA.
Young	4	34	31	13	6	4	17	2	1	1.59
Dinneen	4	35	29	8	8	8	28	3	1	2.06
Hughes	1	2	4	3	2	2	0	0	1	9.00
Totals	8	71	64	24	16	14	45	5	3	2.03

Pittsburgh Pirates

Pitcher	G.	IP.	H.	R.	ER.	BB.	SO.	W.	L.	ERA.
Veil	1	7	6	1	1	4	1	0	0	1.29
Phillippe	5	44	38	19	16	3	20	3	2	3.27
Thompson	1	2	3	1	1	0	1	0	0	4.50
Kennedy	1	7	11	10	4	3	3	0	1	5.14
Leever	2	10	13	8	7	3	2	0	2	6.30
Totals	8	70	71	39	29	13	27	3	5	3.73

1905
NEW YORK GIANTS
VS.
PHILADELPHIA ATHLETICS

The New York Giants, having scuttled the 1904 World Series with an unmistakable air of disdain, were willing participants in the 1905 fall classic. And with righthanded sensation Christy Mathewson in tow, why not? The 25-year-old Mathewson had just reached the 30-victory plateau for the third consecutive season.

It's not that the 1904 Giants, National League champions by 13 games, had quaked in their cleats over thoughts of a Series date with the Boston Red Sox, repeat titlists in the American League. Instead, Giants Owner John T. Brush and Manager John McGraw had pent-up feelings against the American League—Brush being irate over the entry of an A.L. team (the Highlanders) into New York and McGraw still fuming over what he perceived as injustices meted out by A.L. President Ban Johnson when McGraw was plying his trade for the A.L.'s Baltimore Orioles.

"Why should we play this up-start club (Boston), or any other American League team, for any postseason championship?" McGraw had asked during the 1904 season. "When we clinch the National League pennant, we'll be champions of the only real major league."

So, the Giants turned down Boston's challenge for a World Series meeting in 1904, forcing the lone interruption in the history of the fall classic.

But 1905 was a different story. With the public expressing its indignation over the Giants' "thanks, but no thanks" Series attitude of the previous season, Brush, McGraw and company were ready to take on the American League champion Philadelphia Athletics after an N.L. race during which the Giants won 105

New York Giants great Christy Mathewson was phenomenal in the 1905 World Series, pitching three shutouts and allowing only 14 hits over a six-day span.

games. The Series would be contested under guidelines drawn up by the Giants' owner, who now was seeking to stabilize an event he earlier had torpedoed. Besides outlining a revenue formula, the John T. Brush Rules called for—among other things—a best-of-seven format in games.

The Athletics, reeling from the late-season loss of standout lefthander Rube Waddell, sidelined because of an injury, were faced with the prospect of going up against a Giants pitching rotation that featured Mathewson (31 victories), Joe McGinnity (21) and Red Ames (22) and also included Dummy Taylor (15) and Hooks Wiltse (14). New York wound up using only two of its "big five" as starters in the Series, but that twosome proved more than enough.

Lefthander Eddie Plank, a 25-game winner for the Athletics, was matched against Mathewson in the opening game. The contest was scoreless until the fifth inning when the Giants broke through for two runs—an outburst ignited by a Mathewson single. And with Mathewson contributing a key sacrifice in the ninth, New York added another run. Mathewson pitched masterfully throughout, finishing with a four-hit, 3-0 triumph. He did not walk a batter.

Athletics Manager Connie Mack called on Chief Bender in Game 2 and the righthander responded beautifully. Bender, supported by Bris Lord's run-scoring singles in the third and eighth innings, outdueled McGinnity, 3-0. Not only was the Series deadlocked, but a trend had developed. Two games, two shutouts.

Working with two days of rest, Mathewson trudged back to the mound for Game 3 and again baffled Philadelphia on four hits. This time, he issued only one base on balls. First baseman Dan McGann was the Giants' big gun in a 9-0 romp, collecting two singles and a double and driving in four runs.

As good as the pitching had been through the first three games of the 1905 Series, it

reached an even higher level in Game 4 when McGinnity and Plank hooked up in a contest that produced only one run and nine hits. The Giants notched the run, thanks to fourth-inning errors by Monte and Lave Cross, who manned the left side of the Athletics' infield. The 1-0 triumph increased New York's Series lead to three games to one.

Bender, only 21 years old but a three-season veteran of the major leagues, was Mack's choice to halt the Giants in Game 5. McGraw countered with the redoubtable Mathewson, who would be pitching with just one day of rest. Mathewson again was up to the challenge, allowing only six hits and walking no one. Bender was nearly as good, yielding just five hits, but he went down to a 2-0 defeat that made McGraw and company World Series champions.

Mathewson, the fabled Big Six, was merely phenomenal in his three outings against the Athletics. In the space of six days, he pitched three shutouts and permitted just 14 hits overall. The Giants' wheel horse struck out 18 batters and walked only one in 27 innings. Besides Matty and McGinnity, the only other Giants pitcher to see action was Ames, who worked all of one inning (as a reliever in Game 2).

The 1905 fall classic proved memorable not just because of Mathewson's heroics or the five shutouts in five games. The Series also was noteworthy because the Giants concentrated on scuttling the opposition instead of the event itself.

Game 1

Monday, October 9, At Philadelphia

New York	AB.	R.	H.	RBI.	PO.	A.
Bresnahan, c	3	1	1	1	6	1
Browne, rf	5	0	0	0	1	0
Donlin, cf	5	1	2	1	1	0
McGann, 1b	3	0	1	0	14	0
Mertes, lf	4	0	1	1	0	0
Dahlen, ss	4	0	0	0	3	5
Devlin, 3b	4	0	1	0	0	5
Gilbert, 2b	4	1	3	0	2	4
Mathewson, p	3	0	1	0	0	3
Totals	35	3	10	3	27	18

Philadelphia	AB.	R.	H.	RBI.	PO.	A.
Hartsel, lf	4	0	1	0	1	0
Lord, cf	4	0	0	0	2	0
Davis, 1b	4	0	1	0	14	0
L. Cross, 3b	4	0	0	0	0	2
Seybold, rf	3	0	0	0	0	0
Murphy, 2b	3	0	0	0	2	3
M. Cross, ss	3	0	0	0	3	7
Schreckengost, c	3	0	1	0	5	1
Plank, p	3	0	0	0	0	1
Totals	31	0	4	0	27	14

New York .... 0 0 0 0 2 0 0 0 1—3
Philadelphia .... 0 0 0 0 0 0 0 0 0—0

New York	IP.	H.	R.	ER.	BB.	SO.
Mathewson (W)	9	4	0	0	0	6

Philadelphia	IP.	H.	R.	ER.	BB.	SO.
Plank (L)	9	10	3	2	2	5

E—Donlin. DP—New York 1. LOB—New York 9, Philadelphia 4. 2B—McGann, Mertes, Schreckengost, Murphy, Davis. SB—Devlin, Gilbert, Bresnahan, Donlin. SH—Mathewson. HBP—By Plank (Bresnahan). U—Sheridan (A.L.) and O'Day (N.L.). T—1:46. A—17,955.

Game 2

Tuesday, October 10, At New York

Philadelphia	AB.	R.	H.	RBI.	PO.	A.
Hartsel, lf	4	1	2	0	0	0
Lord, cf	4	0	2	2	2	1
Davis, 1b	4	0	0	0	8	0
L. Cross, 3b	3	0	0	0	1	1
Seybold, rf	4	0	0	0	1	0
Murphy, 2b	4	0	1	0	4	3
M. Cross, ss	4	0	0	0	4	1
Schreckengost, c	4	2	1	0	10	2
Bender, p	2	0	0	0	1	0
Totals	33	3	6	2	27	8

New York	AB.	R.	H.	RBI.	PO.	A.
Bresnahan, c	4	0	1	0	3	1
Browne, rf	4	0	0	0	2	0
Donlin, cf	4	0	2	0	4	1
McGann, 1b	3	0	0	0	12	0
Mertes, lf	4	0	0	0	0	1
Dahlen, ss	3	0	0	0	1	6
Devlin, 3b	3	0	1	0	2	1
Gilbert, 2b	3	0	0	0	3	4
McGinnity, p	2	0	0	0	0	2
aStrang	1	0	0	0	0	0
Ames, p	0	0	0	0	0	0
Totals	31	0	4	0	27	17

Philadelphia .... 0 0 1 0 0 0 0 2 0—3
New York .... 0 0 0 0 0 0 0 0 0—0

Philadelphia	IP.	H.	R.	ER.	BB.	SO.
Bender (W)	9	4	0	0	3	9

New York	IP.	H.	R.	ER.	BB.	SO.
McGinnity (L)	8	5	3	0	0	2
Ames	1	1	0	0	1	1

aStruck out for McGinnity in eighth. E—Murphy, M. Cross, McGann, Devlin. LOB—Philadelphia 5, New York 7. 2B—Bresnahan, Donlin, Hartsel. SB—Dahlen, Devlin. SH—Bender. U—O'Day (N.L.) and Sheridan (A.L.). T—1:51. A—24,992.

Game 3

Thursday, October 12, At Philadelphia

New York	AB.	R.	H.	RBI.	PO.	A.
Bresnahan, c	3	2	0	0	8	3
Browne, rf	5	2	1	0	0	0
Donlin, cf	3	3	2	0	4	0
McGann, 1b	5	1	3	4	9	1
Mertes, lf	3	0	1	2	1	0
Dahlen, ss	3	1	0	1	2	1
Devlin, 3b	4	0	1	1	0	6
Gilbert, 2b	4	0	0	0	2	0
Mathewson, p	4	0	1	0	1	2
Totals	34	9	9	8	27	13

Philadelphia	AB.	R.	H.	RBI.	PO.	A.
Hartsel, lf	4	0	0	0	2	0
Lord, cf	4	0	0	0	2	0
Davis, 1b	4	0	1	0	10	0
L. Cross, 3b	4	0	1	0	2	1
Seybold, rf	3	0	1	0	1	1
Murphy, 2b	3	0	0	0	2	2
M. Cross, ss	3	0	1	0	4	2
Schreckengost, c	2	0	0	0	2	1
Powers, c	1	0	0	0	2	3
Coakley, p	2	0	0	0	0	2
Totals	30	0	4	0	27	12

New York .... 2 0 0 0 5 0 0 0 2—9
Philadelphia .... 0 0 0 0 0 0 0 0 0—0

New York	IP.	H.	R.	ER.	BB.	SO.
Mathewson (W)	9	4	0	0	1	8

Philadelphia	IP.	H.	R.	ER.	BB.	SO.
Coakley (L)	9	9	9	3	6	2

E—Devlin, Hartsel, L. Cross, Murphy 3. DP—Philadelphia 2. LOB—New York 4, Philadelphia 5. 2B—McGann. SB—Browne 2, Donlin, Dahlen, Devlin, Hartsel. HBP—By Mathewson (Coakley), by Coakley (Bresnahan). U—Sheridan (A.L.) and O'Day (N.L.). T—1:55. A—10,991.

Game 4

Friday, October 13, At New York

Philadelphia	AB.	R.	H.	RBI.	PO.	A.
Hartsel, lf	1	0	0	0	2	0
Lord, cf	4	0	0	0	2	0
Davis, 1b	4	0	1	0	8	1
L. Cross, 3b	4	0	1	0	2	1
Seybold, rf	3	0	0	0	3	0
Murphy, 2b	3	0	1	0	0	4
M. Cross, ss	3	0	0	0	1	1
Powers, c	3	0	0	0	6	0
aHoffman	1	0	0	0	0	0
Plank, p	3	0	1	0	1	5
Totals	30	0	5	0	24	8

New York	AB.	R.	H.	RBI.	PO.	A.
Bresnahan, c	2	0	1	0	5	0
Browne, rf	4	0	2	0	0	0
Donlin, cf	3	0	0	0	6	0
McGann, 1b	3	0	0	0	10	0
Mertes, lf	4	1	0	0	0	0
Dahlen, ss	3	0	0	0	1	2
Devlin, 3b	3	0	1	0	4	1
Gilbert, 2b	3	0	0	0	0	3
McGinnity, p	3	0	0	0	0	4
Totals	28	1	4	0	27	10

Philadelphia .... 0 0 0 0 0 0 0 0 0—0
New York .... 0 0 0 1 0 0 0 0 x—1

Philadelphia	IP.	H.	R.	ER.	BB.	SO.
Plank (L)	8	4	1	0	2	6

New York	IP.	H.	R.	ER.	BB.	SO.
McGinnity (W)	9	5	0	0	3	4

aStruck out for Powers in ninth. E—L. Cross, M. Cross, Donlin. LOB—Philadelphia 8, New York 7. 2B—Devlin. SB—Hartsel. SH—Donlin, McGann, Hartsel, Murphy. WP—Plank. U—O'Day (N.L.) and Sheridan (A.L.). T—1:55. A—13,598.

Game 5

Saturday, October 14, At New York

Philadelphia	AB.	R.	H.	RBI.	PO.	A.
Hartsel, lf	4	0	2	0	4	1
Lord, cf	4	0	0	0	3	0
Davis, 1b	4	0	1	0	10	0
L. Cross, 3b	4	0	0	0	1	2
Seybold, rf	3	0	1	0	0	0
Murphy, 2b	3	0	0	0	0	1
M. Cross, ss	3	0	1	0	1	3
Powers, c	3	0	1	0	5	1
Bender, p	3	0	0	0	0	6
Totals	31	0	6	0	24	14

New York	AB.	R.	H.	RBI.	PO.	A.
Bresnahan, c	4	0	2	0	5	2
Browne, rf	4	0	1	1	0	0
Donlin, cf	4	0	0	0	1	0
McGann, 1b	3	0	0	0	12	1
Mertes, lf	2	1	1	0	1	0
Dahlen, ss	2	0	0	0	3	5
Devlin, 3b	2	0	0	0	1	4
Gilbert, 2b	3	0	1	1	3	5
Mathewson, p	1	1	0	0	1	3
Totals	25	2	5	2	27	20

Philadelphia .... 0 0 0 0 0 0 0 0 0—0
New York .... 0 0 0 0 1 0 0 1 x—2

Philadelphia	IP.	H.	R.	ER.	BB.	SO.
Bender (L)	8	5	2	2	3	4

New York	IP.	H.	R.	ER.	BB.	SO.
Mathewson (W)	9	6	0	0	0	4

E—Mathewson. DP—New York 1. LOB—Philadelphia 4, New York 4. 2B—Bresnahan, Powers. SH—Devlin, Mathewson. U—Sheridan (A.L.) and O'Day (N.L.). T—1:35. A—24,187.

COMPOSITE BATTING AVERAGES
New York Giants

Player-Position	G.	AB.	R.	H.	2B.	3B.	HR.	RBI.	BA.
Donlin, cf	5	19	4	6	1	0	0	1	.316
Bresnahan, c	5	16	3	5	2	0	0	1	.313
Devlin, 3b	5	16	0	4	1	0	0	1	.250
Mathewson, p	3	8	1	2	0	0	0	0	.250
McGann, 1b	5	17	1	4	2	0	0	4	.235
Gilbert, 2b	5	17	1	4	0	0	0	2	.235
Browne, rf	5	22	2	4	0	0	0	1	.182
Mertes, lf	5	17	2	3	1	0	0	3	.176
Dahlen, ss	5	15	1	0	0	0	0	1	.000
McGinnity, p	2	5	0	0	0	0	0	0	.000
Strang, ph	1	1	0	0	0	0	0	0	.000
Ames, p	1	0	0	0	0	0	0	0	.000
Totals	5	153	15	32	7	0	0	13	.209

Philadelphia Athletics

Player-Position	G.	AB.	R.	H.	2B.	3B.	HR.	RBI.	BA.
Hartsel, lf	5	17	1	5	1	0	0	0	.294
Schreckengost, c	3	9	2	2	1	0	0	0	.222
Davis, 1b	5	20	0	4	1	0	0	0	.200
Murphy, 2b	5	16	0	3	1	0	0	0	.188
M. Cross, ss	5	17	0	3	0	0	0	0	.176
Plank, p	2	6	0	1	0	0	0	0	.167
Powers, c	3	7	0	1	1	0	0	0	.143
Seybold, rf	5	16	0	2	0	0	0	0	.125
L. Cross, 3b	5	19	0	2	0	0	0	0	.105
Lord, cf	5	20	0	2	0	0	0	2	.100
Bender, p	2	5	0	0	0	0	0	0	.000
Coakley, p	1	2	0	0	0	0	0	0	.000
Hoffman, ph	1	1	0	0	0	0	0	0	.000
Totals	5	155	3	25	5	0	0	2	.161

COMPOSITE PITCHING AVERAGES
New York Giants

Pitcher	G.	IP.	H.	R.	ER.	BB.	SO.	W.	L.	ERA.
Mathewson	3	27	14	0	0	1	18	3	0	0.00
McGinnity	2	17	10	3	0	3	6	1	1	0.00
Ames	1	1	1	0	0	1	1	0	0	0.00
Totals	5	45	25	3	0	5	25	4	1	1.00

Philadelphia Athletics

Pitcher	G.	IP.	H.	R.	ER.	BB.	SO.	W.	L.	ERA.
Coakley	1	9	9	9	0	5	2	0	1	0.00
Plank	2	17	14	4	2	4	11	0	2	1.06
Bender	2	17	9	2	2	6	13	1	1	1.06
Totals	5	43	32	15	4	15	26	1	4	0.84

CHICAGO WHITE SOX VS. CHICAGO CUBS

The 1906 fall classic appeared to be a classic mismatch. The intracity battle paired the Cubs, winners of a big-league-record 116 games, against a White Sox team that won the American League pennant despite a collective batting average of .228.

The Cubs, who finished 20 games ahead of the runner-up New York Giants in the National League race, boasted a crack pitching staff headed by Mordecai (Three Finger) Brown, Jack Pfiester, Ed Reulbach and Orval Overall and a standout infield featuring the Tinker-to-Evers-to-Chance double-play combination. The White Sox relied on pitchers Nick Altrock, Frank Owen, Big Ed Walsh and Doc White, parlaying their skills into a 19-game winning streak in August en route to a three-game edge over the runner-up New York Highlanders in the A.L. standings. No White Sox regular batted higher than .279.

Unquestionably, all of Chicago was abuzz over the World Series pairing. The South Side Sox against the West Side Cubs. (The National Leaguers' move to the North Side was another decade away.)

Manager Fielder Jones' White Sox played true to form in the first four games of the Series (Games 1 and 2, incidentally, were played amid periodic snow flurries), collecting only six runs and 11 hits in those contests. But the Hitless Wonders also showed their opportunistic nature, managing a 2-2 deadlock in games despite the meager offense.

After the White Sox captured the Series opener, 2-1, behind Altrock, the Cubs rebounded for a 7-1 victory that featured the one-hit pitching of Reulbach and the timely hitting of Harry Steinfeldt and Joe Tinker. A wild pitch and

George Rohe, a 31-year-old utilityman for the Chicago White Sox, was a big factor in his team's 1906 Series upset of the Cubs.

an error led to the White Sox's run in the fifth inning, but the A.L. titlists didn't collect their lone hit of the day until Jiggs Donahue singled in the seventh. Third baseman Steinfeldt, the "other" member of the Cubs' infield and a .327 hitter for the N.L.

kingpins in 1906 after his off-season acquisition from Cincinnati, went 3 for 3 and Tinker collected two hits and scored three runs.

In Game 3, Walsh allowed a single to Solly Hofman and a double to Frank Schulte in the first inning, then held the Cubs hitless

the rest of the way. The White Sox emerged as 3-0 winners, with Walsh striking out 12 batters and George Rohe tagging Pfiester for a bases-loaded triple in the sixth inning. Brown drew the Cubs even the next day, denying the White Sox a hit for the first 5⅔ innings on the way to a two-hit, 1-0 triumph.

Wonder of wonders, White Sox bats came alive in Games 5 and 6. In the fifth game, the Hitless Wonders drove Reulbach from the mound in the third inning, broke loose for four runs in the fourth and held on for an 8-6 victory. Frank Isbell paced the Sox's 12-hit attack with a Series-record four doubles, while George Davis knocked in three runs. In the sixth game, the American Leaguers chased Brown in the second inning and, led by another three-RBI effort from Davis and three runs batted in by Donahue, cruised to a stunning and Series-deciding 8-3 victory that was spiced by 14 White Sox hits.

The Sox had pulled off an upset of gigantic proportions despite hitting only .198 as a team in the Series. Three regulars—Patsy Dougherty, Billy Sullivan and Jones, the team's playing manager —combined for only four hits in 62 at-bats. Nevertheless, the Sox outhit the Cubs, who batted only .196. Manager Frank Chance epitomized the National Leaguers' futility at the plate. The cleanup hitter for the Cubs, first baseman Chance failed to drive in a run in the six games.

Little-known players had impact in this Series. Rohe, thrust into the White Sox's starting lineup because of an injury to shortstop Davis (regular third baseman Lee Tannehill took over at shortstop at the outset of the classic and Rohe manned third), was instrumental in his team's triumph. Besides delivering the decisive hit in Game 3, Rohe tripled and scored the first run in the opening-game pitchers' duel, went 3 for 4 in the fifth game and tacked on two more hits in Game 6. The 31-year-old utilityman and first baseman Donahue led the White Sox with .333 batting averages.

The Cubs' top hitter was center

The Chicago Cubs' legendary infield of 1906 featured (left to right) third baseman Harry Steinfeldt, shortstop Joe Tinker, second baseman Johnny Evers and first baseman Frank Chance. Righthander Ed Reulbach (below) was a key member of the Cubs' top-notch pitching staff.

fielder Hofman, who had appeared in only 64 games during the regular season. He played every inning of the Series and batted .304.

Game 1

Tuesday, October 9, At West Side Grounds

White Sox	AB.	R.	H.	RBI.	PO.	A.
Hahn, rf	3	0	0	0	1	0
Jones, cf	4	1	1	0	3	0
Isbell, 2b	4	0	1	1	0	1
Rohe, 3b	4	1	1	0	1	2
Donahue, 1b	4	0	0	0	12	2
Dougherty, lf	3	0	0	0	1	0
Sullivan, c	3	0	0	0	5	2
Tannehill, ss	3	0	0	0	1	4
Altrock, p	2	0	1	0	3	3
Totals	30	2	4	1	27	14

Cubs	AB.	R.	H.	RBI.	PO.	A.
Hofman, cf	3	0	0	0	1	1
Sheckard, lf	3	0	0	0	1	0
aMoran	1	0	0	0	0	0
Schulte, rf	4	0	1	0	1	0
Chance, 1b	4	0	1	0	11	0
Steinfeldt, 3b	4	0	0	0	0	2
Tinker, ss	3	0	0	0	2	3
Evers, 2b	3	0	0	0	1	3
Kling, c	2	1	1	0	9	1
Brown, p	2	0	1	0	1	6
Totals	29	1	4	0	27	16

White Sox	0 0 0 0 1 1 0 0 0—2
Cubs	0 0 0 0 0 1 0 0 0—1

White Sox	IP.	H.	R.	ER.	BB.	SO.
Altrock (W)	9	4	1	1	1	3

Cubs	IP.	H.	R.	ER.	BB.	SO.
Brown (L)	9	4	2	0	1	7

aFlied out for Sheckard in ninth. E—Isbell, Kling, Brown. LOB—White Sox 3, Cubs 4. 3B—Rohe. SB—Isbell, Dougherty. SH—Hahn, Hofman, Brown. WP—Brown, Altrock. PB—Kling 2. U—Johnstone (N.L.) and O'Loughlin (A.L.). T—1:45. A—12,693.

Game 2

Wednesday, October 10, At South Side Park

Cubs	AB.	R.	H.	RBI.	PO.	A.
Hofman, cf	4	0	1	1	2	0
Sheckard, lf	4	0	0	0	3	1
Schulte, rf	4	0	1	0	1	0
Chance, 1b	5	2	1	0	12	0
Steinfeldt, 3b	3	1	3	1	0	2
Tinker, ss	3	3	2	1	0	3
Evers, 2b	4	1	1	0	4	6
Kling, c	2	0	1	0	5	1
Reulbach, p	3	0	0	1	0	2
Totals	32	7	10	4	27	15

White Sox	AB.	R.	H.	RBI.	PO.	A.
Hahn, rf	3	0	0	0	0	0
Jones, cf	3	0	0	0	1	0
Isbell, 2b	4	0	0	0	6	2
Rohe, 3b	2	0	0	0	0	3
Donahue, 1b	3	0	1	0	10	1
Dougherty, lf	2	1	0	0	1	0
Sullivan, c	4	0	0	0	8	2
Tannehill, ss	3	0	0	0	0	3
White, p	0	0	0	0	0	1
aTowne	1	0	0	0	0	0
Owen, p	2	0	0	0	1	4
Totals	27	1	1	0	27	16

Cubs	0 3 1 0 0 1 0 2 0—7
White Sox	0 0 0 0 1 0 0 0 0—1

Cubs	IP.	H.	R.	ER.	BB.	SO.
Reulbach (W)	9	1	1	0	6	3

White Sox	IP.	H.	R.	ER.	BB.	SO.
White (L)	3	4	4	0	2	1
Owen	6	6	3	2	3	2

aFlied out for White in third. E—Tinker, Evers, Isbell, Sullivan. DP—Cubs 2. LOB—Cubs 6, White Sox 6. 2B—Kling. SB—Hofman, Chance 2, Tinker, Evers. SH—Sheckard, Steinfeldt, Reulbach. HBP—By Reulbach (Rohe). WP—Reulbach, Owens. U—O'Loughlin (A.L.) and Johnstone (N.L.). T—1:58. A—12,595.

Game 3

Thursday, October 11, At West Side Grounds

White Sox	AB.	R.	H.	RBI.	PO.	A.
Hahn, rf	2	0	0	0	0	0
aO'Neill, rf	1	1	0	0	1	0
Jones, cf	4	0	0	0	1	0
Isbell, 2b	4	0	0	0	1	4
Rohe, 3b	3	0	1	3	0	1
Donahue, 1b	3	0	2	0	14	0
Dougherty, lf	4	0	0	0	0	0
Sullivan, c	3	0	0	0	10	2
Tannehill, ss	3	1	1	0	0	5
Walsh, p	2	1	0	0	0	3
Totals	29	3	4	3	27	15

Cubs	AB.	R.	H.	RBI.	PO.	A.
Hofman, cf	4	0	1	0	1	0
Sheckard, lf	4	0	0	0	2	0
Schulte, rf	4	0	1	0	1	0
Chance, 1b	2	0	0	0	7	1
Steinfeldt, 3b	3	0	0	0	1	2
Tinker, ss	3	0	0	0	3	2
Evers, 2b	3	0	0	0	1	2
Kling, c	3	0	0	0	11	3
Pfiester, p	2	0	0	0	0	2
bGessler	1	0	0	0	0	0
Totals	29	0	2	0	27	12

White Sox	0 0 0 0 0 3 0 0 0—3
Cubs	0 0 0 0 0 0 0 0 0—0

White Sox	IP.	H.	R.	ER.	BB.	SO.
Walsh (W)	9	2	0	0	1	12

Cubs	IP.	H.	R.	ER.	BB.	SO.
Pfiester (L)	9	4	3	3	2	9

aRan for Hahn in sixth. bReached first on error for Pfiester in ninth. E—Isbell, Tinker, Pfiester. LOB—White Sox 4, Cubs 3. 2B—Schulte. 3B—Donahue, Rohe. SB—Rohe. SH—Donahue, Sullivan. HBP—By Pfiester (Hahn). WP—Walsh. U—Johnstone (N.L.) and O'Loughlin (A.L.). T—2:10. A—13,667.

Game 4

Friday, October 12, At South Side Park

Cubs	AB.	R.	H.	RBI.	PO.	A.
Hofman, cf	4	0	2	0	1	0
Sheckard, lf	3	0	0	0	1	0
Schulte, rf	4	0	0	0	1	0
Chance, 1b	4	1	2	0	13	1
Steinfeldt, 3b	2	0	1	0	1	1
Tinker, ss	1	0	0	0	1	4
Evers, 2b	3	0	1	1	2	4
Kling, c	3	0	0	0	6	3
Brown, p	3	0	1	0	1	5
Totals	27	1	7	1	27	18

White Sox	AB.	R.	H.	RBI.	PO.	A.
Hahn, rf	4	0	1	0	1	0
Jones, cf	3	0	0	0	0	0
Isbell, 2b	4	0	0	0	1	3
Rohe, 3b	3	0	0	0	0	4
Donahue, 1b	1	0	0	0	13	2
Dougherty, lf	3	0	1	0	2	0
Davis, ss	3	0	0	0	4	2
Sullivan, c	3	0	0	0	3	1
Altrock, p	2	0	0	0	3	8
aMcFarland	1	0	0	0	0	0
Totals	27	0	2	0	27	20

Cubs	0 0 0 0 0 0 1 0 0—1
White Sox	0 0 0 0 0 0 0 0 0—0

Cubs	IP.	H.	R.	ER.	BB.	SO.
Brown (W)	9	2	0	0	2	5

White Sox	IP.	H.	R.	ER.	BB.	SO.
Altrock (L)	9	7	1	1	1	2

aGrounded out for Altrock in ninth. E—Steinfeldt, Davis. DP—Cubs 1, White Sox 1. LOB—Cubs 5, White Sox 3. 2B—Hofman. SB—Sheckard. SH—Donahue, Steinfeldt 2, Tinker 3. PB—Kling. U—O'Loughlin (A.L.) and Johnstone (N.L.). T—1:36. A—18,385.

Game 5

Saturday, October 13, At West Side Grounds

White Sox	AB.	R.	H.	RBI.	PO.	A.
Hahn, rf	5	2	1	0	1	0
Jones, cf	4	1	1	0	1	0
Isbell, 2b	5	3	4	2	2	2
Davis, ss	5	2	2	3	2	8
Rohe, 3b	4	0	3	1	0	2
Donahue, 1b	3	0	1	1	15	2
Dougherty, lf	5	0	0	0	0	0
Sullivan, c	4	0	0	0	6	2
Walsh, p	2	0	0	0	0	2
White, p	0	0	0	0	0	0
Totals	37	8	12	7	27	18

Cubs	AB.	R.	H.	RBI.	PO.	A.
Hofman, cf	3	2	1	0	2	0
Sheckard, lf	4	0	0	0	1	0
Schulte, rf	5	1	3	2	2	1
Chance, 1b	4	0	1	0	8	0
Steinfeldt, 3b	5	1	1	1	1	2
Tinker, ss	4	1	0	0	2	2
Evers, 2b	3	0	0	0	2	5
aMoran	1	0	0	0	0	0
Kling, c	3	0	0	0	9	0
Reulbach, p	0	0	0	0	0	2
Pfiester, p	0	0	0	0	0	0
Overall, p	2	1	0	0	0	1
Totals	34	6	6	3	27	13

White Sox	1 0 2 4 0 1 0 0 0—8
Cubs	3 0 0 1 0 2 0 0 0—6

White Sox	IP.	H.	R.	ER.	BB.	SO.
Walsh (W)	6†	5	6	3	5	5
White	3	1	0	0	1	0

Cubs	IP.	H.	R.	ER.	BB.	SO.
Reulbach	2*	5	3	3	2	1
Pfiester (L)	1⅓	3	4	4	1	2
Overall	5⅔	4	1	1	1	5

*Pitched to two batters in third.
†Pitched to one batter in seventh.

aForced runner for Evers in ninth. E—Isbell 2, Davis, Rohe 2, Walsh. DP—Cubs 1. LOB—White Sox 8, Cubs 10. 2B—Isbell 4, Rohe, Davis 2, Donahue, Chance, Schulte, Steinfeldt. SB—Dougherty, Davis, Tinker, Evers. SH—Jones, Sheckard, Reulbach. HBP—By Walsh (Chance), by Pfiester (Donahue). WP—Overall. PB—Sullivan. U—Johnstone (N.L.) and O'Loughlin (A.L.). T—2:40. A—23,257.

Game 6

Sunday, October 14, At South Side Park

Cubs	AB.	R.	H.	RBI.	PO.	A.
Hofman, cf	5	1	2	1	3	0
Sheckard, lf	3	0	0	1	2	0
Schulte, rf	5	0	1	1	0	0
Chance, 1b	2	0	0	0	9	0
Steinfeldt, 3b	3	0	0	0	0	0
Tinker, ss	4	0	1	0	2	6
Evers, 2b	4	1	1	0	2	0
Kling, c	4	1	1	0	6	2
Brown, p	1	0	0	0	0	1
Overall, p	2	0	1	0	0	1
aGessler	0	0	0	0	0	0
Totals	33	3	7	3	24	10

White Sox	AB.	R.	H.	RBI.	PO.	A.
Hahn, rf	5	2	4	0	0	0
Jones, cf	3	2	0	0	3	0
Isbell, 2b	5	1	3	1	1	4
Davis, ss	5	2	2	3	1	4
Rohe, 3b	5	1	2	0	3	4
Donahue, 1b	4	0	2	3	15	1
Dougherty, lf	3	0	1	1	0	0
Sullivan, c	4	0	0	0	3	1
White, p	3	0	0	0	1	2
Totals	37	8	14	8	27	16

Cubs	1 0 0 0 1 0 0 0 1—3
White Sox	3 4 0 0 0 0 0 1 x—8

Cubs	IP.	H.	R.	ER.	BB.	SO.
Brown (L)	1⅔	8	7	7	1	0
Overall	6⅓	6	1	1	2	3

White Sox	IP.	H.	R.	ER.	BB.	SO.
White (W)	9	7	3	3	4	2

aBatted for Overall in ninth. E—Rohe, Donahue, Dougherty. DP—White Sox 1. LOB—Cubs 9, White Sox 9. 2B—Schulte, Overall, Evers, Davis, Donahue. SB—Rohe. SH—Sheckard, Jones. HBP—By White (Chance). U—O'Loughlin (A.L.) and Johnstone (N.L.). T—1:55. A—19,249.

COMPOSITE BATTING AVERAGES

Chicago White Sox

Player-Position	G.	AB.	R.	H.	2B.	3B.	HR.	RBI.	BA.
Rohe, 3b	6	21	2	7	1	2	0	4	.333
Donahue, 1b	6	18	0	6	2	1	0	4	.333
Isbell, 2b	6	26	4	8	4	0	0	4	.308
Davis, ss	3	13	4	4	3	0	0	6	.308
Hahn, rf	6	22	4	6	0	0	0	0	.273
Altrock, p	2	4	0	1	0	0	0	0	.250
Tannehill, ss	3	9	1	1	0	0	0	0	.111
Dougherty, lf	6	20	1	2	0	0	0	1	.100
Jones, cf	6	21	4	2	0	0	0	0	.095
Sullivan, c	6	21	0	0	0	0	0	0	.000
White, p	3	3	0	0	0	0	0	0	.000
Walsh, p	2	4	1	0	0	0	0	0	.000
Towne, ph	1	1	0	0	0	0	0	0	.000
Owen, p	1	2	0	0	0	0	0	0	.000
O'Neill, rf	1	1	1	0	0	0	0	0	.000
McFarland, ph	1	1	0	0	0	0	0	0	.000
Totals	6	187	22	37	10	3	0	19	.198

Chicago Cubs

Player-Position	G.	AB.	R.	H.	2B.	3B.	HR.	RBI.	BA.
Brown, p	3	6	0	2	0	0	0	0	.333
Hofman, cf	6	23	3	7	1	0	0	2	.304
Schulte, rf	6	26	1	7	3	0	0	3	.269
Overall, p	2	4	1	1	1	0	0	0	.250
Steinfeldt, 3b	6	20	2	5	1	0	0	2	.250
Chance, 1b	6	21	3	5	1	0	0	0	.238
Kling, c	6	17	2	3	1	0	0	0	.176
Tinker, ss	6	18	4	3	0	0	0	1	.167
Evers, 2b	6	20	2	3	1	0	0	1	.150
Sheckard, lf	6	21	0	0	0	0	0	1	.000
Moran, ph	2	2	0	0	0	0	0	0	.000
Reulbach, p	2	3	0	0	0	0	0	1	.000
Pfiester, p	2	2	0	0	0	0	0	0	.000
Gessler, ph	2	1	0	0	0	0	0	0	.000
Totals	6	184	18	36	9	0	0	11	.196

COMPOSITE PITCHING AVERAGES

Chicago White Sox

Pitcher	G.	IP.	H.	R.	ER.	BB.	SO.	W.	L.	ERA.
Altrock	2	18	11	2	2	2	5	1	1	1.00
Walsh	2	15	7	6	3	6	17	2	0	1.80
White	3	15	12	7	3	7	3	1	1	1.80
Owen	1	6	6	3	2	3	2	0	0	3.00
Totals	6	54	36	18	10	18	27	4	2	1.67

Chicago Cubs

Pitcher	G.	IP.	H.	R.	ER.	BB.	SO.	W.	L.	ERA.
Overall	2	12	10	2	2	3	8	0	0	1.50
Reulbach	2	11	6	4	3	8	4	1	0	2.45
Brown	3	19⅔	14	9	7	4	12	1	2	3.20
Pfiester	2	10⅓	7	7	7	3	11	0	2	6.10
Totals	6	53	37	22	19	18	35	2	4	3.23

1907
CHICAGO CUBS
VS.
DETROIT TIGERS

With the Detroit Tigers ahead, 3-2, in the ninth inning of Game 1 of the 1907 World Series, Del Howard was called upon to bat for Cubs shortstop Joe Tinker in a two-on, two-out situation. Harry Steinfeldt was on third base for Chicago and Johnny Evers was perched on second.

Bill Donovan was pitching for the Tigers, and the advantage clearly was with the American League champions. Donovan, after all, had fashioned a 25-4 season record. Howard, a June acquisition from the Boston Braves, had batted only .230 for the Cubs.

Sure enough, Donovan struck out Howard. Tiger fans couldn't have asked for more.

Except, maybe, for catcher Charlie Schmidt to hang on to the ball. Which Schmidt didn't. And as the ball got away from the second-year major leaguer, Steinfeldt raced home with the game-tying run.

Donovan retired the side without further damage, but the *real* damage had been done. The teams remained in a deadlock through three more innings, then the game was called because of darkness. Tigers 3, Cubs 3, 12 innings. Detroit had let certain victory—and almost-certain momentum—slip out of its grasp. And Manager Hugh Jennings' Tigers would pay dearly.

Given a reprieve, the Cubs proceeded to make short shrift of the Tigers. Detroit, which had edged the Philadelphia Athletics in a fiercely contested American League pennant race, failed to score more than one run in any of the remaining Series games. Chicago's Jack Pfiester handcuffed Detroit, 3-1, in Game 2 and Ed Reulbach stymied the A.L. champions, 5-1, the next day. The Tigers seized a 1-0 lead in

When Detroit catcher Charlie Schmidt let a ninth-inning pitch get away from him in Game 1 of the 1907 Series, the Cubs seized momentum and cruised past the outmanned Tigers.

the fourth inning of Game 4 as 20-year-old Ty Cobb, having just won his first big-league batting championship, slammed a triple and scored on Claude Rossman's single. But Detroit did nothing else of note against Orval Overall and went down to a 6-1 defeat. Overall himself put the Cubs ahead with a two-run single in the fifth inning. In Game 5, Mordecai

Brown spun a seven-hitter and the Cubs swept to a Series-clinching 2-0 triumph.

That the Cubs were primed to atone for their 1906 embarrassment at the hands of the Chicago White Sox was a given. That Frank Chance's team would make amends in such a dominant manner was not wholly anticipated.

But dominate the Cubs did.

They ran wild against the Tigers, stealing seven bases in Game 1 and finishing the Series with a total of 18 thefts. They got outstanding offensive production from Steinfeldt and Evers, who batted .471 and .350, respectively (with Steinfeldt getting seven hits in the last three games of the Series and Evers gathering seven in the first three contests). And, most of all, the Cubs exhibited exquisite pitching. Pfiester, Reulbach, Overall and Brown threw 43 scoreless innings out of a possible 48 and shut down the American League's two top hitters of 1907, Cobb and Sam Crawford. Cobb managed only a .200 average in the Series after batting .350 in the regular season, while Crawford hit .238 following a .323 season.

The Cubs, of course, had the potential to crush any opponent, as evidenced by their second consecutive runaway in the National League pennant race. In 1907, the Cubs won 107 games and finished 17 lengths in front of the second-place Pittsburgh Pirates. And, given a second chance in two years to demonstrate their apparent supremacy over the rest of major league baseball, the Cubs made the most of the opportunity this time.

Game 1

Tuesday, October 8, At Chicago

Detroit	AB.	R.	H.	RBI.	PO.	A.
Jones, lf	5	1	3	0	3	1
Schaefer, 2b	6	1	1	0	7	4
Crawford, cf	5	1	3	2	1	0
Cobb, rf	5	0	0	0	0	0
Rossman, 1b	4	0	0	1	9	3
Coughlin, 3b	5	0	0	0	1	0
Schmidt, c	5	0	2	0	12	3
O'Leary, ss	4	0	0	0	0	3
Donovan, p	5	0	0	0	3	2
Totals	44	3	9	3	36	16

Chicago	AB.	R.	H.	RBI.	PO.	A.
Slagle, cf	6	0	2	0	2	0
Sheckard, lf	5	0	1	0	2	0
Chance, 1b	4	2	1	0	15	0
Steinfeldt, 3b	3	1	1	0	2	2
Kling, c	4	0	2	1	7	4
Evers, 2b-ss	4	0	2	0	3	2
Schulte, rf	5	0	1	1	2	0
Tinker, ss	3	0	0	0	3	6
aHoward	1	0	0	0	0	0
Zimmermann, 2b	1	0	0	0	0	1
Overall, p	3	0	0	0	0	3
bMoran	0	0	0	0	0	0
Reulbach, p	2	0	0	0	0	0
Totals	41	3	10	2	36	18

Detroit	0 0 0 0 0 0 0 3 0 0 0 0—3
Chicago	0 0 0 1 0 0 0 0 2 0 0 0—3

(Game called at end of 12th inning on account of darkness.)

Detroit	IP.	H.	R.	ER.	BB.	SO.
Donovan	12	10	3	1	3	12

Chicago	IP.	H.	R.	ER.	BB.	SO.
Overall	9	9	3	1	2	5
Reulbach	3	0	0	0	0	2

aStruck out for Tinker in ninth, but reached first on missed third strike. bBatted for Overall in ninth, but side retired before his time at bat was completed. E—Coughlin, Schmidt 2, Kling, Evers 2, Schulte, Tinker. DP—Detroit 1, Chicago 1. LOB—Detroit 8, Chicago 9. SB—Slagle 2, Sheckard, Howard, Chance, Steinfeldt, Evers, Jones 2, Schaefer, Rossman. SH—Steinfeldt, Evers, O'Leary. HBP—By Donovan (Sheckard, Steinfeldt). U—O'Day (N.L.) and Sheridan (A.L.). T—2:40. A—24,377.

Game 2

Wednesday, October 9, At Chicago

Detroit	AB.	R.	H.	RBI.	PO.	A.
Jones, lf	4	0	2	0	1	0
Schaefer, 2b	4	0	1	0	2	3
Crawford, cf	4	0	0	0	1	1
Cobb, rf	3	0	1	0	0	0
Rossman, 1b	4	1	3	0	12	1
Coughlin, 3b	4	0	0	0	2	1
Payne, c	4	0	1	1	5	1
O'Leary, ss	2	0	1	0	0	6
Mullin, p	3	0	0	0	1	2
Totals	32	1	9	1	24	15

Chicago	AB.	R.	H.	RBI.	PO.	A.
Slagle, cf	3	1	2	1	3	0
Sheckard, lf	3	0	1	1	2	0
Chance, 1b	3	0	1	0	6	0
Steinfeldt, 3b	3	0	0	0	3	1
Kling, c	4	1	1	0	5	4
Evers, 2b	4	0	2	0	2	0
Schulte, rf	4	0	1	0	1	1
Tinker, ss	2	1	1	1	5	4
Pfiester, p	2	0	0	0	0	0
Totals	28	3	9	3	27	10

Detroit	0 1 0 0 0 0 0 0 0—1
Chicago	0 1 0 2 0 0 0 0 x—3

Detroit	IP.	H.	R.	ER.	BB.	SO.
Mullin (L)	8	9	3	3	3	5

Chicago	IP.	H.	R.	ER.	BB.	SO.
Pfiester (W)	9	9	1	1	1	3

E—Payne, Tinker. DP—Detroit 1, Chicago 2. LOB—Detroit 6, Chicago 7. 2B—Sheckard. 3B—Rossman. SB—Slagle 2, Chance, Tinker, Evers. SH—Sheckard, Pfiester. HBP—By Mullin (Steinfeldt), by Pfiester (Cobb). PB—Kling. U—Sheridan (A.L.) and O'Day (N.L.). T—2:13. A—21,901.

Game 3

Thursday, October 10, At Chicago

Detroit	AB.	R.	H.	RBI.	PO.	A.
Jones, lf	3	0	0	0	2	0
Schaefer, 2b	4	0	1	0	0	3
Crawford, cf	4	0	1	1	3	1
Cobb, rf	4	0	1	0	1	0
Rossman, 1b	4	0	2	0	9	0
Coughlin, 3b	3	0	0	0	4	1
Schmidt, c	3	0	0	0	1	2
O'Leary, ss	4	0	0	0	3	4
Siever, p	1	0	0	0	1	0
Killian, p	2	1	1	0	0	0
Totals	32	1	6	1	24	11

Chicago	AB.	R.	H.	RBI.	PO.	A.
Slagle, cf	4	0	0	0	3	0
Sheckard, lf	4	0	1	0	4	0
Chance, 1b	4	1	1	0	12	1
Steinfeldt, 3b	3	1	2	1	0	2
Kling, c	3	1	1	0	2	0
Evers, 2b	4	0	3	1	3	2
Schulte, rf	4	1	1	1	0	0
Tinker, ss	4	1	0	0	2	7
Reulbach, p	3	0	1	1	1	2
Totals	33	5	10	4	27	14

Detroit	0 0 0 0 0 1 0 0 0—1
Chicago	0 1 0 3 1 0 0 0 x—5

Detroit	IP.	H.	R.	ER.	BB.	SO.
Siever (L)	4	7	4	2	0	1
Killian	4	3	1	1	1	1

Chicago	IP.	H.	R.	ER.	BB.	SO.
Reulbach (W)	9	6	1	1	3	2

E—Jones, Evers. DP—Chicago 2. LOB—Detroit 7, Chicago 6. 2B—Sheckard, Chance, Evers 2, Steinfeldt. SH—Kling. U—O'Day (N.L.) and Sheridan (A.L.). T—1:35. A—13,114.

Game 4

Friday, October 11, At Detroit

Chicago	AB.	R.	H.	RBI.	PO.	A.
Slagle, cf	5	1	1	2	2	0
Sheckard, lf	5	0	2	1	1	0
Chance, 1b	3	0	0	0	11	0
Steinfeldt, 3b	4	0	2	0	3	2
Kling, c	4	0	0	0	6	0
Evers, 2b	4	1	0	0	0	2
Schulte, rf	3	2	1	0	2	1
Tinker, ss	1	2	0	0	2	3
Overall, p	2	0	1	2	0	3
Totals	31	6	7	5	27	11

Detroit	AB.	R.	H.	RBI.	PO.	A.
Jones, lf	2	0	0	0	3	0
Schaefer, 2b	3	0	0	0	2	3
Crawford, cf	4	0	0	0	2	0
Cobb, rf	4	1	1	0	4	0
Rossman, 1b	4	0	1	1	9	0
Coughlin, 3b	4	0	3	0	1	1
Schmidt, c	3	0	0	0	3	4
O'Leary, ss	4	0	0	0	3	2
Donovan, p	3	0	0	0	0	1
Totals	31	1	5	1	27	11

Chicago	0 0 0 0 2 0 3 0 1—6
Detroit	0 0 0 1 0 0 0 0 0—1

Chicago	IP.	H.	R.	ER.	BB.	SO.
Overall (W)	9	5	1	1	2	6

Detroit	IP.	H.	R.	ER.	BB.	SO.
Donovan (L)	9	7	6	3	2	4

E—Slagle, Tinker, O'Leary 2. DP—Chicago 1. LOB—Chicago 5, Detroit 7. 3B—Cobb. SB—Slagle, Chance. SH—Tinker 2, Overall 2, Jones, Schaefer. HBP—By Donovan (Chance). U—Sheridan (A.L.) and O'Day (N.L.). T—1:45. A—11,306.

Game 5

Saturday, October 12, At Detroit

Chicago	AB.	R.	H.	RBI.	PO.	A.
Slagle, cf	4	1	1	1	3	0
Sheckard, lf	4	0	0	0	1	0
Howard, 1b	4	0	1	0	10	1
Steinfeldt, 3b	4	0	3	1	2	0
Kling, c	4	0	0	0	5	1
Evers, 2b	4	1	0	0	1	6
Schulte, rf	4	0	1	0	1	0
Tinker, ss	3	0	1	0	3	3
Brown, p	3	0	0	0	1	1
Totals	34	2	7	2	27	12

Detroit	AB.	R.	H.	RBI.	PO.	A.
Jones, lf	3	0	1	0	1	1
Schaefer, 2b	4	0	0	0	1	8
Crawford, cf	4	0	1	0	0	0
Cobb, rf	4	0	1	0	4	0
Rossman, 1b	4	0	2	0	13	0
aPayne	0	0	0	0	0	0
Coughlin, 3b	4	0	2	0	1	2
Archer, c	3	0	0	0	4	1
bSchmidt	1	0	0	0	0	0
O'Leary, ss	3	0	0	0	3	3
Mullin, p	3	0	0	0	0	2
Totals	33	0	7	0	27	17

Chicago	1 1 0 0 0 0 0 0 0—2
Detroit	0 0 0 0 0 0 0 0 0—0

Chicago	IP.	H.	R.	ER.	BB.	SO.
Brown (W)	9	7	0	0	1	4

Detroit	IP.	H.	R.	ER.	BB.	SO.
Mullin (L)	9	7	2	1	3	2

aRan for Rossman in ninth. bFlied out for Archer in ninth. E—Schulte, Rossman, Coughlin. LOB—Chicago 8, Detroit 7. 2B—Crawford. 3B—Steinfeldt. SB—Slagle, Tinker, Evers, Schulte, Jones, Rossman, Coughlin. U—O'Day (N.L.) and Sheridan (A.L.). T—1:42. A—7,370.

COMPOSITE BATTING AVERAGES

Chicago Cubs

Player-Position	G.	AB.	R.	H.	2B.	3B.	HR.	RBI.	BA.
Steinfeldt, 3b	5	17	2	8	1	1	0	2	.471
Evers, 2b-ss	5	20	2	7	2	0	0	1	.350
Slagle, cf	5	22	3	6	0	0	0	4	.273
Schulte, rf	5	20	3	5	0	0	0	2	.250
Sheckard, lf	5	21	0	5	2	0	0	2	.238
Chance, 1b	4	14	3	3	1	0	0	0	.214
Kling, c	5	19	2	4	0	0	0	1	.211
Howard, ph-1b	2	5	0	1	0	0	0	0	.200
Overall, p	2	5	0	1	0	0	0	2	.200
Reulbach, p	2	5	0	1	0	0	0	1	.200
Tinker, ss	5	13	4	2	0	0	0	1	.154
Zimmerman, 2b	1	1	0	0	0	0	0	0	.000
Moran, ph	1	0	0	0	0	0	0	0	.000
Pfiester, p	1	2	0	0	0	0	0	0	.000
Brown, p	1	3	0	0	0	0	0	0	.000
Totals	5	167	19	43	6	1	0	16	.257

Detroit Tigers

Player-Position	G.	AB.	R.	H.	2B.	3B.	HR.	RBI.	BA.
Killian, p	1	2	1	1	0	0	0	0	.500
Rossman, 1b	5	20	1	8	0	1	0	2	.400
Jones, lf	5	17	1	6	0	0	0	0	.353
Coughlin, 3b	5	20	0	5	0	0	0	0	.250
Payne, c-pr	2	4	0	1	0	0	0	1	.250
Crawford, cf	5	21	1	5	1	0	0	3	.238
Cobb, rf	5	20	1	4	0	1	0	0	.200
Schmidt, c-ph	4	12	0	2	0	0	0	0	.167
Schaefer, 2b	5	21	1	3	0	0	0	0	.143
O'Leary, ss	5	17	0	1	0	0	0	0	.059
Donovan, p	2	8	0	0	0	0	0	0	.000
Mullin, p	2	6	0	0	0	0	0	0	.000
Siever, p	1	1	0	0	0	0	0	0	.000
Archer, c	1	3	0	0	0	0	0	0	.000
Totals	5	172	6	36	1	2	0	6	.209

COMPOSITE PITCHING AVERAGES

Chicago Cubs

Pitcher	G.	IP.	H.	R.	ER.	BB.	SO.	W.	L.	ERA.
Brown	1	9	7	0	0	1	4	1	0	0.00
Reulbach	2	12	6	1	1	3	4	1	0	0.75
Overall	2	18	14	4	2	4	11	1	0	1.00
Pfiester	1	9	9	1	1	1	3	1	0	1.00
Totals	5	48	36	6	4	9	22	4	0	0.75

Detroit Tigers

Pitcher	G.	IP.	H.	R.	ER.	BB.	SO.	W.	L.	ERA.
Donovan	2	21	17	9	4	5	16	0	1	1.71
Mullin	2	17	16	5	4	6	7	0	2	2.11
Killian	1	4	3	1	1	1	1	0	0	2.25
Siever	1	4	7	4	2	0	1	0	1	4.50
Totals	5	46	43	19	11	12	25	0	4	2.15

1908
CHICAGO CUBS
VS.
DETROIT TIGERS

After winning 223 games over the previous two National League seasons and building huge pennant-winning margins in those years, the Chicago Cubs went about the business of winning a league championship in a vastly different manner in 1908.

Oh, the Cubs had another outstanding season, all right, winning 99 games. But had it not been for a baserunning blunder by the New York Giants' Fred Merkle, Chicago would have finished with 98 victories—and been on the outside looking in.

In a September 23 Cubs-Giants game, Merkle failed to touch second base when Al Bridwell delivered an apparent game-winning hit in the bottom of the ninth inning. By the time the Cubs retrieved the ball and eventually forced Merkle at second, fans had swarmed the field. With order impossible to restore, the game was declared a 1-1 tie. As things turned out, Chicago and New York wound up with 98-55 records, meaning the "Merkle game" would have to be made up.

In an October 8 replay, the Cubs scored a 4-2 victory and left the Giants agonizing over what might have been. Or even what *should* have been. The Chicagoans, on the other hand, were reveling in what was.

Having repeated as N.L. titlists by the barest of margins (the Pirates, like the Giants, finished one game behind Chicago), the Cubs prepared for a second consecutive World Series date against the Detroit Tigers, who had won the American League championship on the final day of the regular season.

As was the case the previous year, the Tigers held the lead entering the ninth inning of the Series opener. And, as in 1907, De-

Righthander Orval Overall was splendid in Games 2 and 5 and the 1908 Cubs became the first team ever to win consecutive world championships.

troit frittered away the advantage. This time, the Tigers suffered a worse fate than being tied.

With his club ahead by a 6-5 score in the ninth, Detroit pitcher Ed Summers retired Johnny Evers to start the inning. Summers, a 24-game winner in 1908, then yielded six consecutive hits and five runs, the go-ahead runs scoring on a bases-loaded single by Solly Hofman. The Cubs pulled out all the stops en route to a 10-6 triumph, using Orval Overall and Mordecai Brown in relief roles behind Ed Reulbach.

The Tigers' Bill Donovan was paired against Overall in Game 2, and the righthanders put on quite a show. Through four innings,

neither pitcher had allowed a hit in a 0-0 standoff. After seven innings, the Tigers had three hits and the Cubs only one (and that was by Overall) as the game remained scoreless.

Overall proceeded to retire the Tigers in order in the top of the eighth, but Donovan ran into trouble in the bottom of the inning. Big trouble. After Harry Steinfeldt singled, Joe Tinker poked a home run to right field. And before the inning was over, the Cubs had collected four more hits and four more runs.

Ty Cobb delivered a run-scoring single in the ninth for Detroit, but Overall and Chicago prevailed, 6-1. The Cubs had won

their sixth consecutive Series game from the Tigers.

Detroit finally broke through against the Cubs in Game 3, with George Mullin checking the Chicagoans on seven hits in an 8-3 victory. Cobb had four hits and two runs batted in. Brown quieted any rising Tiger fervor, however, by recording a four-hit, 3-0 triumph in Game 4. And Overall, so magnificent three days earlier, was at the top of his game again in Game 5. The 27-year-old Californian allowed only three hits and struck out 10 batters and, backed by three hits and one RBI from both Evers and Manager Frank Chance, was a 2-0 winner. Only 6,210 fans witnessed the finale in Detroit, the smallest crowd in Series history.

The Cubs ruled major league baseball, having become the first team to win back-to-back World Series titles. And those championships had come on the heels of their record 116-victory season of 1906.

In the world of sports, the term "dynasty" just might have been bandied about for the first time in October 1908.

Game 1

Saturday, October 10, At Detroit

Chicago	AB.	R.	H.	RBI.	PO.	A.
Sheckard, lf	6	1	3	0	1	1
Evers, 2b	4	1	2	0	2	2
Schulte, rf	4	2	2	1	1	0
Chance, 1b	4	2	1	0	12	0
Steinfeldt, 3b	3	2	2	2	0	0
Hofman, cf	4	1	1	2	4	0
Tinker, ss	5	1	2	3	0	4
Kling, c	3	0	1	1	7	1
Reulbach, p	3	0	0	0	0	4
Overall, p	1	0	0	0	0	0
Brown, p	0	0	0	0	0	2
Totals	37	10	14	9	27	14

Detroit	AB.	R.	H.	RBI.	PO.	A.
McIntyre, lf	3	1	2	0	3	0
O'Leary, ss	4	0	1	0	1	3
bThomas	1	0	1	0	0	0
cWinter	0	0	0	0	0	0
Crawford, cf	4	1	0	0	4	0
Cobb, rf	4	2	2	1	0	0
Rossman, 1b	4	1	2	1	12	0
Schaefer, 3b	3	0	0	0	1	2
Schmidt, c	4	0	0	1	4	1
Downs, 2b	4	1	1	1	2	4
Killian, p	0	0	0	0	0	1
Summers, p	3	0	1	1	0	5
aJones	1	0	0	0	0	0
Totals	35	6	10	5	27	16

Chicago	0 0 4	0 0 0	1 0 5	—10
Detroit	1 0 0	0 0 0	3 2 0	— 6

Chicago	IP.	H.	R.	ER.	BB.	SO.
Reulbach	6⅔	8	4	4	0	5
Overall	⅓*	0	1	1	1	0
Brown (W)	2	2	1	0	1	1

Detroit	IP.	H.	R.	ER.	BB.	SO.
Killian	2⅓	5	4	3	3	1
Summers (L)	6⅔	9	6	5	1	2

*Pitched to one batter in eighth.

aStruck out for Summers in ninth. bSingled for O'Leary in ninth. cRan for Thomas in ninth. E—Evers, Chance, McIntyre, Cobb, Schaefer, Downs. LOB—Chicago 9, Detroit 7. 2B—Sheckard 2, Downs. SB—Chance 2, Hofman, McIntyre. SH—Evers, Schulte, Kling, Brown, Steinfeldt, Cobb, Schaefer. HBP—By Overall (McIntyre). WP—Brown. U—Sheridan (A.L.) and O'Day (N.L.). T—2:10. A—10,812.

Game 2

Sunday, October 11, At Chicago

Detroit	AB.	R.	H.	RBI.	PO.	A.
McIntyre, lf	4	0	0	0	3	0
O'Leary, ss	3	0	0	0	1	1
aJones	0	1	0	0	0	0
Crawford, cf	4	0	0	0	4	0
Cobb, rf	4	0	1	1	1	0
Rossman, 1b	4	0	0	0	8	1
Schaefer, 3b	3	0	2	0	0	1
Schmidt, c	3	0	1	0	7	0
Downs, 2b	2	0	0	0	0	4
Donovan, p	2	0	0	0	0	1
Totals	29	1	4	1	24	8

Chicago	AB.	R.	H.	RBI.	PO.	A.
Sheckard, lf	4	1	1	1	3	0
Evers, 2b	4	1	1	1	0	6
Schulte, rf	4	1	1	1	1	0
Chance, 1b	3	0	0	0	12	0
Steinfeldt, 3b	4	0	0	0	1	1
Hofman, cf	3	1	1	0	0	0
Tinker, ss	3	1	1	2	2	3
Kling, c	3	1	1	0	8	0
Overall, p	3	0	1	0	0	3
Totals	31	6	7	5	27	13

Detroit	0 0 0	0 0 0	0 0 1	—1
Chicago	0 0 0	0 0 0	0 6 x	—6

Detroit	IP.	H.	R.	ER.	BB.	SO.
Donovan (L)	8	7	6	6	1	7

Chicago	IP.	H.	R.	ER.	BB.	SO.
Overall (W)	9	4	1	1	2	5

aWalked for O'Leary in ninth. E—Donovan, Chance. DP—Detroit 1, Chicago 1. LOB—Detroit 4, Chicago 2. 2B—Kling. 3B—Schulte. HR—Tinker. SB—Sheckard, Evers, Chance. SH—Donovan. WP—Donovan. U—Klem (N.L.) and Connolly (A.L.). T—1:30. A—17,760.

Game 3

Monday, October 12, At Chicago

Detroit	AB.	R.	H.	RBI.	PO.	A.
McIntyre, lf	4	1	1	0	1	0
O'Leary, ss	4	2	0	0	1	3
Crawford, cf	5	1	2	1	3	0
Cobb, rf	5	1	4	2	0	0
Rossman, 1b	4	2	2	2	9	0
Schaefer, 2b	4	0	0	0	4	4
Thomas, c	3	0	1	1	9	2
Coughlin, 3b	3	0	0	1	0	1
Mullin, p	3	1	1	1	0	2
Totals	35	8	11	8	27	12

Chicago	AB.	R.	H.	RBI.	PO.	A.
Sheckard, lf	4	0	0	0	1	0
Evers, 2b	3	1	0	0	1	6
Schulte, rf	4	0	1	0	1	0
Chance, 1b	4	1	2	1	14	0
Steinfeldt, 3b	4	1	1	0	1	4
Hofman, cf	4	0	2	1	3	1
Tinker, ss	3	0	1	0	3	1
Kling, c	3	0	0	0	3	2
Pfiester, p	2	0	0	0	0	0
aHoward	1	0	0	0	0	0
Reulbach, p	0	0	0	0	0	1
Totals	32	3	7	2	27	15

Detroit	1 0 0	0 0 5	0 2 0	—8
Chicago	0 0 0	3 0 0	0 0 0	—3

Detroit	IP.	H.	R.	ER.	BB.	SO.
Mullin (W)	9	7	3	0	1	8

Chicago	IP.	H.	R.	ER.	BB.	SO.
Pfiester (L)	8	10	8	7	3	1
Reulbach	1	1	0	0	1	0

aGrounded out for Pfiester in eighth. E—O'Leary, Rossman 2, Coughlin, Chance, Steinfeldt. DP—Detroit 2, Chicago 2. LOB—Detroit 6, Chicago 3. 2B—Thomas, Cobb. 3B—Hofman. SB—Cobb 2, Rossman, Chance 2, Steinfeldt. SH—O'Leary, Coughlin. U—O'Day (N.L.) and Sheridan (A.L.). T—2:10. A—14,543.

Game 4

Tuesday, October 13, At Detroit

Chicago	AB.	R.	H.	RBI.	PO.	A.
Sheckard, lf	4	0	0	0	0	0
Evers, 2b	5	1	1	0	0	4
Schulte, rf	3	1	2	0	0	0
Chance, 1b	4	1	2	1	17	0
Steinfeldt, 3b	3	0	1	1	2	3
Hofman, cf	4	0	2	1	1	0
Tinker, ss	4	0	0	0	2	7
Kling, c	4	0	2	0	5	1
Brown, p	4	0	0	0	0	4
Totals	35	3	10	3	27	19

Detroit	AB.	R.	H.	RBI.	PO.	A.
McIntyre, lf	4	0	0	0	1	0
O'Leary, ss	4	0	2	0	2	3
Crawford, cf	4	0	2	0	2	0
Cobb, rf	3	0	0	0	1	0
Rossman, 1b	3	0	0	0	12	1
Schaefer, 2b	3	0	0	0	2	3
Schmidt, c	3	0	0	0	6	2
Coughlin, 3b	2	0	0	0	1	4
Summers, p	2	0	0	0	0	2
aJones	1	0	0	0	0	0
Winter, p	0	0	0	0	0	0
Totals	29	0	4	0	27	15

Chicago	0 0 2	0 0 0	0 0 1	—3
Detroit	0 0 0	0 0 0	0 0 0	—0

Chicago	IP.	H.	R.	ER.	BB.	SO.
Brown (W)	9	4	0	0	0	4

Detroit	IP.	H.	R.	ER.	BB.	SO.
Summers (L)	8	9	2	2	3	5
Winter	1	1	1	0	1	0

aGrounded out for Summers in eighth. E—Cobb. DP—Chicago 1. LOB—Chicago 10, Detroit 3. 2B—Crawford. SB—Schulte 2, Evers, Hofman. SH—Steinfeldt. HBP—By Brown (Coughlin). PB—Kling. Schmidt. U—Connolly (A.L.) and Klem (N.L.). T—1:35. A—12,907.

Game 5

Wednesday, October 14, At Detroit

Chicago	AB.	R.	H.	RBI.	PO.	A.
Sheckard, lf	3	0	1	0	2	0
Evers, 2b	4	1	3	1	2	3
Schulte, rf	3	0	1	0	0	0
Chance, 1b	4	0	3	1	11	0
Steinfeldt, 3b	2	0	0	0	0	3
Hofman, cf	4	0	0	0	2	0
Tinker, ss	4	0	1	0	1	4
Kling, c	3	1	0	0	9	2
Overall, p	2	0	1	0	0	0
Totals	29	2	10	2	27	12

Detroit	AB.	R.	H.	RBI.	PO.	A.
McIntyre, lf	3	0	1	0	2	0
O'Leary, ss	4	0	0	0	2	2
Crawford, cf	4	0	1	0	3	0
Cobb, rf	3	0	0	0	1	0
Rossman, 1b	4	0	0	0	7	3
Schaefer, 2b	3	0	0	0	3	1
Schmidt, c	4	0	0	0	5	4
Coughlin, 3b	3	0	1	0	2	1
Donovan, p	2	0	0	0	1	1
Totals	30	0	3	0	*26	12

Chicago	1 0 0	0 1 0	0 0 0	—2
Detroit	0 0 0	0 0 0	0 0 0	—0

Chicago	IP.	H.	R.	ER.	BB.	SO.
Overall (W)	9	3	0	0	4	10

Detroit	IP.	H.	R.	ER.	BB.	SO.
Donovan (L)	9	10	2	2	3	3

*Overall out; hit by batted ball. DP—Detroit 2. LOB—Chicago 6, Detroit 7. 2B—Evers, McIntyre. SB—Donovan. SH—Schulte, Steinfeldt, Overall. WP—Overall. U—Sheridan (A.L.) and O'Day (N.L.). T—1:25. A—6,210.

COMPOSITE BATTING AVERAGES

Chicago Cubs

Player-Position	G.	AB.	R.	H.	2B.	3B.	HR.	RBI.	BA.
Chance, 1b	5	19	4	8	0	0	0	3	.421
Schulte, rf	5	18	4	7	0	1	0	2	.389
Evers, 2b	5	20	5	7	1	0	0	2	.350
Overall, p	3	6	0	2	0	0	0	0	.333
Hofman, cf	5	19	2	6	0	1	0	4	.316
Tinker, ss	5	19	2	5	0	0	1	5	.263
Steinfeldt, 3b	5	16	3	4	0	0	0	3	.250
Kling, c	5	16	2	4	1	0	0	1	.250
Sheckard, lf	5	21	2	5	2	0	0	1	.238
Reulbach, p	2	3	0	0	0	0	0	0	.000
Brown, p	2	4	0	0	0	0	0	0	.000
Pfiester, p	1	2	0	0	0	0	0	0	.000
Howard, ph	1	1	0	0	0	0	0	0	.000
Totals	5	164	24	48	4	2	1	21	.293

Detroit Tigers

Player-Position	G.	AB.	R.	H.	2B.	3B.	HR.	RBI.	BA.
Thomas, ph-c	2	4	0	2	1	0	0	1	.500
Cobb, rf	5	19	3	7	1	0	0	4	.368
Mullin, p	1	3	1	1	0	0	0	1	.333
Crawford, cf	5	21	2	5	1	0	0	1	.238
McIntyre, lf	5	18	2	4	1	0	0	0	.222
Rossman, 1b	5	19	3	4	0	0	0	3	.211
Summers, p	2	5	0	1	0	0	0	1	.200
Downs, 2b	2	6	1	1	1	0	0	1	.167
O'Leary, ss	5	19	2	3	0	0	0	0	.158
Schaefer, 3b-2b	5	16	0	2	0	0	0	0	.125
Coughlin, 3b	3	8	0	1	0	0	0	1	.125
Schmidt, c	4	14	0	1	0	0	0	1	.071
Killian, p	1	0	0	0	0	0	0	0	.000
Jones, ph	3	2	1	0	0	0	0	0	.000
Donovan, p	2	4	0	0	0	0	0	0	.000
Winter, pr-p	2	0	0	0	0	0	0	0	.000
Totals	5	158	15	32	5	0	0	14	.203

COMPOSITE PITCHING AVERAGES

Chicago Cubs

Pitcher	G.	IP.	H.	R.	ER.	BB.	SO.	W.	L.	ERA.
Brown	2	11	6	1	0	1	5	2	0	0.00
Overall	3	18⅓	7	2	2	7	15	2	0	0.98
Reulbach	2	7⅔	9	4	4	1	5	0	0	4.70
Pfiester	1	8	10	8	7	3	1	0	1	7.88
Totals	5	45	32	15	13	12	26	4	1	2.60

Detroit Tigers

Pitcher	G.	IP.	H.	R.	ER.	BB.	SO.	W.	L.	ERA.
Mullin	1	9	7	3	0	1	8	1	0	0.00
Winter	1	1	1	1	0	1	0	0	0	0.00
Donovan	2	17	17	8	8	4	10	0	2	4.24
Summers	2	14⅔	18	8	7	4	7	0	2	4.30
Killian	1	2⅓	5	4	3	3	1	0	0	11.57
Totals	5	44	48	24	18	13	26	1	4	3.68

The hitting-on-all-cylinders machine known as the Chicago Cubs won 104 games in 1909 and lost only 49. Such a gaudy record by the National Leaguers surely instilled fear in the hearts of the World Series-bound American League representative.

Only thing is, the Cubs never made it to the Series in 1909. The Pittsburgh Pirates, led by veteran superstar Honus Wagner and three pitchers who combined for 66 victories, rolled to a pennant-winning 110-42 record and denied the Cubs a fourth consecutive appearance in the fall classic.

Wagner won his seventh N.L. batting championship in 1909 (he would add an eighth and last title two years later), hitting .339. Howie Camnitz and Vic Willis won 25 and 22 games, respectively, for the Pirates and Lefty Leifield posted 19 victories.

Detroit won its third straight A.L. flag in 1909, paced by the hitting of Ty Cobb and Sam Crawford and the pitching of George Mullin, Ed Willett and Ed Summers. Cobb captured his third straight A.L. batting crown with a .377 mark (he would finish his career with 12 titles), and Crawford hit .314. Mullin (29), Willett (22) and Summers (19) combined for 70 victories.

None of the Pirates' "big three" pitchers won a game in the Series, and only one of Detroit's standouts, Mullin, was victorious. Mullin won twice, 5-0 in Game 4 and 5-4 in Game 6.

While the Tigers solved Camnitz, Willis and Leifield, they couldn't handle rookie Babe Adams—and that tilted the Series in Pittsburgh's direction. Adams, who compiled a 12-3 record for the Pirates in 1909, drew the starting assignment in Game 1 and responded with a six-hitter. Playing

Veteran Pittsburgh star Honus Wagner (left) discusses hitting with Detroit's Ty Cobb during a break in the action of the 1909 World Series.

Manager Fred Clarke got the Pirates rolling with a game-tying home run in the fourth inning and the Pirates went on to win, 4-1.

Detroit's three-run outburst in the third inning of Game 2—an uprising spiced by Cobb's steal of

Player-Manager Fred Clarke (above) drove in seven runs and rookie Babe Adams won three times in Pittsburgh's 1909 triumph over Detroit.

home—paved the way for a Series-squaring 7-2 Tiger victory. Pittsburgh regained the lead, though, with an 8-6 decision that featured Wagner's three hits, three RBIs and three stolen bases.

Mullin brought the Tigers back the next day, though, tossing a five-hit shutout and striking out 10 Pirates.

The victory-swapping pattern continued unabated. In Game 5, Adams allowed only six hits—Crawford touched him for a single, double and home run—and Clarke hammered a tie-breaking three-run homer as Pittsburgh prevailed, 8-4. But the resilient Tigers found themselves back in business the next afternoon when Mullin, after being roughed up for three first-inning runs, surrendered only one more run and wound up with a seven-hit victory.

With the Series going down to a climactic seventh game—this was the first fall classic to go the limit —Pittsburgh's Clarke nominated Adams as his pitcher, while Detroit Manager Hugh Jennings decided on Bill Donovan, who was a complete-game winner in Game 2.

Donovan, known as Wild Bill, was just that. After hitting the game's first batter, Bobby Byrne, with a pitch, he proceeded to walk six batters in the first two innings. After three innings, Donovan was gone and Adams was holding a 2-0 lead.

Pittsburgh extended its advantage to 4-0 in the fourth when Dots Miller singled with the bases loaded and blew the game open in the sixth when Wagner tripled home two runs and then scored on an error. Adams continued to cruise, and he went on to nail down a six-hit, 8-0 victory that gave the Pirates their first World Series championship.

Wagner led Pirate hitters with a .333 mark against Detroit and drove in seven runs. He also accounted for six of Pittsburgh's 18 stolen bases. Clarke, despite batting only .211, also totaled seven RBIs and, in a one-for-the-book performance, drew four bases on balls in Game 7 (a contest he played from start to finish, going 0 for 0 officially at the plate).

Cobb, appearing in what would be his last Series, though he would be an active player through 1928, had his second sub-par classic out of three. He batted only .231, but did top Detroit in RBIs with six. Second baseman Jim Delahanty's .346 average led the Tigers.

Game 1

Friday, October 8, At Pittsburgh

Detroit	AB.	R.	H.	RBI.	PO.	A.
D. Jones, lf	3	0	2	0	5	0
Bush, ss	2	0	0	0	1	0
Cobb, rf	3	1	0	0	2	0
Crawford, cf	4	0	1	0	1	0
Delahanty, 2b	4	0	1	0	0	4
Moriarty, 3b	4	0	1	0	0	1
T. Jones, 1b	3	0	0	0	10	0
aMcIntyre	1	0	0	0	0	0
Schmidt, c	3	0	0	0	5	1
Mullin, p	4	0	1	0	0	4
Totals	31	1	6	1	24	10
Pittsburgh	AB.	R.	H.	RBI.	PO.	A.
Byrne, 3b	3	0	0	0	2	3
Leach, cf	3	0	0	1	4	0
Clarke, lf	4	1	1	1	2	0
Wagner, ss	3	1	1	0	0	6
Miller, 2b	4	0	1	0	6	0
Abstein, 1b	3	1	0	1	8	1
Wilson, rf	3	0	1	0	0	0
Gibson, c	3	1	1	1	4	0
Adams, p	3	0	0	0	0	2
Totals	29	4	5	4	*26	12

Detroit .... 1 0 0　0 0 0　0 0 0—1
Pittsburgh .... 0 0 0　1 2 1　0 0 x—4

Detroit	IP.	H.	R.	ER.	BB.	SO.
Mullin (L)	8	5	4	1	1	4
Pittsburgh	IP.	H.	R.	ER.	BB.	SO.
Adams (W)	9	6	1	1	4	2

*Delahanty out; hit by batted ball. aFlied out for T. Jones in ninth. E—Bush, Cobb, Delahanty, Schmidt. LOB —Detroit 8, Pittsburgh 5. 2B—Wagner, Gibson. HR— Clarke. SB—Cobb, Miller, Wilson. SH—Cobb. SF—Leach. HBP—By Mullin (Byrne, Wagner). PB—Schmidt. U— Johnstone (N.L.) and O'Loughlin (A.L.). T—1:55. A— 29,264.

Game 2

Saturday, October 9, At Pittsburgh

Detroit	AB.	R.	H.	RBI.	PO.	A.
D. Jones, lf	5	1	1	0	1	0
Bush, ss	3	1	1	0	0	2
Cobb, rf	3	1	1	0	0	0
Crawford, cf	4	1	1	0	3	0
Delahanty, 2b	3	1	1	2	3	1
Moriarty, 3b	3	1	1	0	3	1
T. Jones, 1b	3	1	1	0	8	1
Schmidt, c	4	0	2	4	9	1
Donovan, p	4	0	0	0	0	4
Totals	32	7	9	6	27	10

Pittsburgh	AB.	R.	H.	RBI.	PO.	A.
Byrne, 3b	3	1	0	0	4	3
Leach, cf	4	1	2	1	2	1
Clarke, lf	3	0	0	0	3	0
Wagner, ss	4	0	1	0	1	2
Miller, 2b	4	0	1	1	0	4
Abstein, 1b	4	0	1	0	12	1
Wilson, rf	4	0	0	0	0	0
Gibson, c	2	0	0	0	4	2
Camnitz, p	1	0	0	0	0	1
Willis, p	2	0	0	0	1	2
Totals	31	2	5	2	27	16

Detroit	0 2 3	0 2 0	0 0 0	—7
Pittsburgh	2 0 0	0 0 0	0 0 0	—2

Detroit	IP.	H.	R.	ER.	BB.	SO.
Donovan (W)	9	5	2	2	2	7

Pittsburgh	IP.	H.	R.	ER.	BB.	SO.
Camnitz (L)	2⅔	6	5	4	1	2
Willis	6⅓	3	2	2	4	2

E—Delahanty, Schmidt, Donovan, Abstein. DP—Detroit 1, Pittsburgh 1. LOB—Detroit 4, Pittsburgh 5. 2B—Schmidt, Crawford, Leach 2, Miller. SB—Cobb, Wagner, Gibson. SH—Bush, Clarke. U—Evans (A.L.) and Klem (N.L.). T—1:45. A—30,915.

Game 3

Monday, October 11, At Detroit

Pittsburgh	AB.	R.	H.	RBI.	PO.	A.
Byrne, 3b	5	1	2	0	2	2
Leach, cf	4	3	2	0	1	0
Clarke, lf	3	1	0	1	5	0
Wagner, ss	5	1	3	3	3	4
Miller, 2b	4	1	0	0	3	6
Abstein, 1b	4	1	2	0	8	0
Wilson, rf	4	0	1	1	0	0
Gibson, c	4	0	0	0	5	1
Maddox, p	4	0	0	0	0	1
Totals	37	8	10	5	27	14

Detroit	AB.	R.	H.	RBI.	PO.	A.
D. Jones, lf	5	2	1	0	0	0
Bush, ss	5	1	3	2	4	3
Cobb, rf	5	0	2	3	3	0
Crawford, cf	5	0	0	0	5	0
Delahanty, 2b	5	1	3	0	3	0
Moriarty, 3b	3	1	0	0	0	3
T. Jones, 1b	3	1	1	1	7	0
Schmidt, c	4	0	0	0	4	3
Summers, p	0	0	0	0	0	1
Willett, p	2	0	0	0	1	3
aMcIntyre	1	0	0	0	0	0
Works, p	0	0	0	0	0	1
bMullin	1	0	0	0	0	0
Totals	39	6	10	6	27	14

Pittsburgh	5 1 0	0 0 0	0 0 2	—8
Detroit	0 0 0	0 0 0	4 0 2	—6

Pittsburgh	IP.	H.	R.	ER.	BB.	SO.
Maddox (W)	9	10	6	0	2	4

Detroit	IP.	H.	R.	ER.	BB.	SO.
Summers (L)	⅓	3	5	0	1	0
Willett	6⅔	3	1	0	0	0
Works	2	4	2	2	0	2

aStruck out for Willett in seventh. bStruck out for Works in ninth. E—Byrne, Abstein 2, Bush 2, Crawford, Schmidt, Willett. LOB—Pittsburgh 6, Detroit 8. 2B—Abstein, Leach, Delahanty 2, Cobb. SB—Wagner 3. SF—Clarke. HBP—By Willett (Leach, Clarke). WP—Summers. U—O'Loughlin (A.L.), Johnstone (N.L.), Evans (A.L.) and Klem (N.L.). T—1:56. A—18,277.

Game 4

Tuesday, October 12, At Detroit

Pittsburgh	AB.	R.	H.	RBI.	PO.	A.
Byrne, 3b	4	0	1	0	0	2
Leach, cf	3	0	0	0	3	0
Clarke, lf	4	0	0	0	1	0
Wagner, ss	3	0	0	0	2	4
Miller, 2b	4	0	1	0	3	1
Abstein, 1b	4	0	1	0	12	1
Wilson, rf	4	0	1	0	0	0
Gibson, c	3	0	1	0	3	4
Leifield, p	1	0	0	0	0	5
aO'Connor	1	0	0	0	0	0
Phillippe, p	1	0	0	0	0	2
Totals	32	0	5	0	24	19

Detroit	AB.	R.	H.	RBI.	PO.	A.
D. Jones, lf	4	1	1	0	0	0
Bush, ss	5	1	1	1	0	1
Cobb, rf	3	0	1	2	1	0
Crawford, cf	4	0	1	0	2	0
Delahanty, 2b	3	0	0	0	1	3
Moriarty, 3b	4	1	2	0	1	3
T. Jones, 1b	3	1	1	0	13	0
Stanage, c	3	0	1	2	9	1
Mullin, p	3	1	0	0	0	4
Totals	32	5	8	5	27	12

Pittsburgh	0 0 0	0 0 0	0 0 0	—0
Detroit	0 2 0	3 0 0	0 0 x	—5

Pittsburgh	IP.	H.	R.	ER.	BB.	SO.
Leifield (L)	4	7	5	5	1	0
Phillippe	4	1	0	0	1	1

Detroit	IP.	H.	R.	ER.	BB.	SO.
Mullin (W)	9	5	0	0	2	10

aStruck out for Leifield in fifth. E—Miller 2, Abstein 2, Phillippe 2. DP—Pittsburgh 1. LOB—Pittsburgh 7, Detroit 9. 2B—Byrne, Cobb, Bush. SB—Byrne, Leach. SH—T. Jones, Stanage. HBP—By Leifield (Cobb, Delahanty). U—Klem (N.L.), Evans (A.L.), Johnstone (N.L.) and O'Loughlin (A.L.). T—1:57. A—17,036.

Game 5

Wednesday, October 13, At Pittsburgh

Detroit	AB.	R.	H.	RBI.	PO.	A.
D. Jones, lf	4	1	1	1	3	0
Bush, ss	3	0	0	0	1	4
Cobb, rf	4	1	1	0	0	0
Crawford, cf	4	2	3	2	1	0
Delahanty, 2b	4	0	0	0	1	1
Moriarty, 3b	4	0	0	0	1	3
T. Jones, 1b	4	0	1	0	11	0
Stanage, c	2	0	0	0	3	1
aMcIntyre	1	0	0	0	0	0
Summers, p	3	0	0	0	0	1
Schmidt, c	1	0	0	0	3	1
Willett, p	0	0	0	0	0	0
bMullin	1	0	0	0	0	0
Totals	35	4	6	3	24	11

Pittsburgh	AB.	R.	H.	RBI.	PO.	A.
Byrne, 3b	5	2	2	0	1	3
Leach, cf	4	1	2	0	3	0
Clarke, lf	2	2	2	3	2	0
Wagner, ss	2	1	1	0	1	2
Miller, 2b	4	0	0	1	0	1
Abstein, 1b	3	0	0	1	11	0
Wilson, rf	4	1	1	0	1	0
Gibson, c	4	1	2	1	8	0
Adams, p	3	0	0	0	0	1
Totals	31	8	10	6	27	7

Detroit	1 0 0	0 0 2	0 1 0	—4
Pittsburgh	1 1 1	0 0 0	4 1 x	—8

Detroit	IP.	H.	R.	ER.	BB.	SO.
Summers (L)	7*	10	8	7	3	4
Willett	1	0	0	0	0	1

Pittsburgh	IP.	H.	R.	ER.	BB.	SO.
Adams (W)	9	6	4	3	1	8

*Pitched to two batters in eighth.

aGrounded out for Stanage in seventh. bFlied out for Willett in ninth. E—Schmidt, Wagner 2. LOB—Detroit 5, Pittsburgh 5. 2B—Crawford, T. Jones, Wilson. HR—D. Jones, Crawford, Clarke. SB—Crawford, T. Jones, Wagner 2, Clarke, Gibson. SH—Clarke, Adams. HBP—By Summers (Wagner). WP—Summers. U—Johnstone (N.L.), O'Loughlin (A.L.), Klem (N.L.) and Evans (A.L.). T—1:46. A—21,706.

Game 6

Thursday, October 14, At Detroit

Pittsburgh	AB.	R.	H.	RBI.	PO.	A.
Byrne, 3b	4	1	1	0	2	4
Leach, cf	4	1	0	0	3	0
Clarke, lf	3	1	1	1	2	0
Wagner, ss	4	0	1	2	3	2
Miller, 2b	3	1	2	0	2	1
Abstein, 1b	4	0	1	0	9	1
Wilson, rf	3	0	0	0	0	1
Gibson, c	4	0	1	0	2	0
Willis, p	2	0	0	0	0	0
Camnitz, p	0	0	0	0	0	1
aHyatt	1	0	0	0	0	0
Phillippe, p	0	0	0	0	1	0
bAbbaticchio	1	0	0	0	0	0
Totals	33	4	7	3	24	10

Detroit	AB.	R.	H.	RBI.	PO.	A.
D. Jones, lf-cf	5	1	0	0	2	0
Bush, ss	2	2	1	0	2	3
Cobb, rf	4	0	1	1	1	0
Crawford, cf-1b	3	1	1	1	1	1
Delahanty, 2b	4	0	2	1	0	4
Moriarty, 3b	3	1	1	1	1	3
T. Jones, 1b	4	0	1	0	13	0
McIntyre, lf	0	0	0	0	0	0
Schmidt, c	3	0	1	0	7	3
Mullin, p	4	0	2	0	0	2
Totals	32	5	10	4	27	16

Pittsburgh	3 0 0	0 0 0	0 0 1	—4
Detroit	1 0 0	2 1 1	0 0 x	—5

Pittsburgh	IP.	H.	R.	ER.	BB.	SO.
Willis (L)	5	7	4	2	4	1
Camnitz	1	2	1	1	1	0
Phillippe	2	1	0	0	0	1

Detroit	IP.	H.	R.	ER.	BB.	SO.
Mullin (W)	9	7	4	3	1	5

aGrounded out for Camnitz in seventh. bStruck out for Phillippe in ninth. E—Clarke, Miller, Wilson, Bush, T. Jones, Schmidt. DP—Pittsburgh 1, Detroit 2. LOB—Pittsburgh 5, Detroit 9. 2B—Wagner, Cobb, Crawford, Delahanty, Mullin. SB—Miller, D. Jones, Bush. SH—Clarke, Wilson. HBP—By Willis (Bush). U—Evans (A.L.), Klem (N.L.), O'Loughlin (A.L.) and Johnstone (N.L.). T—2:00. A—10,535.

Game 7

Saturday, October 16, At Detroit

Pittsburgh	AB.	R.	H.	RBI.	PO.	A.
Byrne, 3b	0	0	0	0	0	0
Hyatt, cf	3	1	0	1	0	0
Leach, cf-3b	3	2	2	0	4	2
Clarke, lf	0	2	0	1	5	0
Wagner, ss	3	1	1	2	3	3
Miller, 2b	5	0	2	2	3	0
Abstein, 1b	4	1	1	0	10	0
Wilson, rf	4	1	0	0	0	0
Gibson, c	5	0	1	0	2	1
Adams, p	3	0	0	0	0	4
Totals	30	8	7	6	27	10

Detroit	AB.	R.	H.	RBI.	PO.	A.
D. Jones, lf	4	0	1	0	3	0
Bush, ss	3	0	0	0	2	5
Cobb, rf	4	0	0	0	1	0
Crawford, cf	4	0	0	0	4	0
Delahanty, 2b	3	0	2	0	3	3
Moriarty, 3b	1	0	1	0	1	0
O'Leary, 3b	3	0	0	0	1	1
T. Jones, 1b	4	0	1	0	9	0
Schmidt, c	3	0	1	0	3	2
Donovan, p	0	0	0	0	0	1
Mullin, p	3	0	0	0	0	2
Totals	32	0	6	0	27	14

Pittsburgh	0 2 0	2 0 3	0 1 0	—8
Detroit	0 0 0	0 0 0	0 0 0	—0

Pittsburgh	IP.	H.	R.	ER.	BB.	SO.
Adams (W)	9	6	0	0	1	1

Detroit	IP.	H.	R.	ER.	BB.	SO.
Donovan (L)	3	2	2	2	6	0
Mullin	6	5	6	4	4	1

E—D. Jones, Bush, Crawford. DP—Detroit 1. LOB—Pittsburgh 11, Detroit 7. 2B—Leach, Gibson, Abstein, Moriarty, Delahanty, Schmidt. 3B—Wagner. SB—Clarke 2, Miller, Abstein. SH—Leach, Clarke, Wilson, Adams. SF—Hyatt. HBP—By Adams (Bush), by Donovan (Byrne). U—O'Loughlin (A.L.), Johnstone (N.L.), Evans (A.L.) and Klem (N.L.). T—2:10. A—17,562.

COMPOSITE BATTING AVERAGES

Pittsburgh Pirates

Player-Position	G.	AB.	R.	H.	2B.	3B.	HR.	RBI.	BA.
Wagner, ss	7	24	4	8	2	1	0	7	.333
Leach, cf-3b	7	25	8	8	4	0	0	2	.320
Byrne, 3b	7	24	5	6	1	0	0	0	.250
Miller, 2b	7	28	2	7	1	0	0	4	.250
Gibson, c	7	25	2	6	2	0	0	2	.240
Abstein, 1b	7	26	3	6	2	0	0	2	.231
Clarke, lf	7	19	7	4	0	0	2	7	.211
Wilson, rf	7	26	2	4	1	0	0	1	.154
Adams, p	3	9	0	0	0	0	0	0	.000
Camnitz, p	2	1	0	0	0	0	0	0	.000
Willis, p	2	4	0	0	0	0	0	0	.000
Maddox, p	1	4	0	0	0	0	0	0	.000
Leifield, p	1	1	0	0	0	0	0	0	.000
O'Connor, ph	1	1	0	0	0	0	0	0	.000
Phillippe, p	2	1	0	0	0	0	0	0	.000
Hyatt, ph-cf	2	4	1	0	0	0	0	1	.000
Abbaticchio, ph	1	1	0	0	0	0	0	0	.000
Totals	7	223	34	49	13	1	2	26	.220

Detroit Tigers

Player-Position	G.	AB.	R.	H.	2B.	3B.	HR.	RBI.	BA.
Delahanty, 2b	7	26	2	9	4	0	0	4	.346
Moriarty, 3b	7	22	4	6	1	0	0	1	.273
Bush, ss	7	23	5	6	1	0	0	3	.261
Crawford, cf-1b	7	28	4	7	3	0	1	3	.250
T. Jones, 1b	7	24	3	6	1	0	0	1	.250
D. Jones, lf-cf	7	30	6	7	0	0	1	1	.233
Cobb, rf	7	26	3	6	3	0	0	6	.231
Schmidt, c	6	18	0	4	2	0	0	4	.222
Stanage, c	2	5	0	1	0	0	0	2	.200
Mullin, p-ph	6	16	1	3	1	0	0	0	.188
McIntyre, ph-lf	4	3	0	0	0	0	0	0	.000
Donovan, p	2	4	0	0	0	0	0	0	.000
Summers, p	2	3	0	0	0	0	0	0	.000
Willett, p	2	2	0	0	0	0	0	0	.000
Works, p	1	0	0	0	0	0	0	0	.000
O'Leary, 3b	1	3	0	0	0	0	0	0	.000
Totals	7	233	28	55	16	0	2	25	.236

COMPOSITE PITCHING AVERAGES

Pittsburgh Pirates

Pitcher	G.	IP.	H.	R.	ER.	BB.	SO.	W.	L.	ERA.
Phillippe	2	6	2	0	0	1	2	0	0	0.00
Maddox	1	9	10	6	0	2	4	1	0	0.00
Adams	3	27	18	5	4	6	11	3	0	1.33
Willis	2	11⅔	10	6	4	8	3	0	1	3.08
Leifield	1	4	7	5	5	1	0	0	1	11.25
Camnitz	2	3⅓	8	6	5	2	2	0	1	13.50
Totals	7	61	55	23	18	20	22	4	3	2.66

Detroit Tigers

Pitcher	G.	IP.	H.	R.	ER.	BB.	SO.	W.	L.	ERA.
Willett	2	7⅔	3	1	0	0	1	0	0	0.00
Mullin	4	32	22	14	8	8	20	2	1	2.25
Donovan	2	12	7	4	4	8	7	1	1	3.00
Summers	2	7⅓	13	13	7	4	4	0	2	8.59
Works	1	2	4	2	2	0	2	0	0	9.00
Totals	7	61	49	34	21	20	34	3	4	3.10

1910
PHILADELPHIA ATHLETICS
VS.
CHICAGO CUBS

The Chicago Cubs were back. Frank Chance's team returned to the top of the National League heap in 1910, winning the pennant by 13 games and increasing its total of N.L. flags to four in five seasons.

In ruling the National League, the Cubs won 104 games and ran their five-year victory total to 530, a startling figure.

The American League champion Philadelphia Athletics put up some pretty good numbers in 1910, too—collectively and individually. The young A's won 102 games and captured the A.L. pennant by 14½ games. They boasted .300 hitters in second baseman Eddie Collins and outfielders Rube Oldring and Danny Murphy and a 31-game winner in Jack Coombs, a 27-year-old righthander who had posted a 12-12 record the previous season.

Neither of the powerhouse teams was at full strength for the World Series, though. The Cubs lost second baseman Johnny Evers because of a broken ankle, and the Athletics played without Oldring (broken leg) and pitcher Eddie Plank (arm ailment).

While Philadelphia Manager Connie Mack appeared at a disadvantage because of the loss of Plank, he still had Coombs and Chief Bender. And that's all he needed.

Bender, coming off his first 20-victory season in the major leagues (he was 23-5), opposed the Cubs' Orval Overall in Game 1 of the Series. The matchup proved a mismatch, with Bender taking a one-hitter into the ninth inning and Overall departing after allowing three runs and six hits in the first three innings. The A's, getting three hits and two runs batted in from Frank Baker, scored a 4-1 victory as Bender wound up

Members of the Chicago Cubs and Philadelphia Athletics enjoyed a lighthearted get-together before the start of the 1910 Series. Talking things over (left to right) are Chicago Player-Manager Frank Chance, Philadelphia's Eddie Plank, Chicago's Mordecai Brown, Philadelphia's Harry Davis, Chicago's Jimmy Sheckard and Chicago's Jimmy Archer.

with a three-hitter and eight strikeouts. A bright spot for the Cubs was Harry McIntire's one-hit pitching in five innings of relief.

Coombs then gave the Athletics a 2-0 lead in the Series, although he was far from dazzling. Pitching a complete game, Coombs gave up eight hits and nine walks while staggering to a 9-3 triumph. The A's broke up a tight game with a six-run seventh, an inning that featured Murphy's two-run double off Cubs starter and loser Mordecai Brown.

Having teed off on two of Chicago's aces, Philadelphia went to work on another Cub stalwart. This time, the victim was Ed Reulbach, who left for a pinch-hitter in the second inning of Game 3 after yielding three runs. McIntire, so effective in the Series opener, took over in the third inning with the scored tied, 3-3, and was shelled for four runs—three scoring on Murphy's home run—in one-third inning. Before the in-

ning ended, the A's had tacked on a fifth run en route to a 12-5 romp. Coombs, pitching with only one day of rest, permitted six hits and helped himself at the plate with three hits and three RBIs. Shortstop Jack Barry also knocked in three Philadelphia runs.

The Cubs, on the brink of elimination, turned away from the "old breed" of their pitching staff and entrusted the club's immediate fate to the right arm of rookie Leonard (King) Cole, who had put together a 20-4 season. Cole performed admirably in Game 4, but Chicago trailed the A's, 3-2, when the 24-year-old pitcher left the contest for a pinch-hitter in the eighth inning. The Cubs, down to what seemed like their last gasp, gained new life in the ninth when Manager Chance tripled home Frank Schulte. Then, in the 10th, Chicago's Jimmy Sheckard came through with a two-out, game-winning single against Bender, who had gone the distance for

Mack's team.

Buoyed by their 4-3 victory, the Cubs sent 25-game winner Brown (the winner in relief in Game 4) against Coombs in Game 5. Through seven innings, pitching was the name of the game as Philadelphia held a 2-1 lead. But the A's struck for five runs in the eighth and came out on top, 7-2.

Using only two pitchers, Bender and three-time winner Coombs, in the entire Series, the A's had emerged as champions. And, considering the youth on this A's team, Philadelphia loomed as a team to be reckoned with for years to come.

Collins and Barry were only 23 years old, Baker was 24, Bender and Coombs were 27 and promising reserve Stuffy McInnis had just turned 20. Even the seemingly forever-old Mack was a mere stripling—47 years old—when he guided the A's to this World Series crown. One could only guess what might lie ahead for the Philadelphia Athletics.

Game 1

Monday, October 17, At Philadelphia

Chicago	AB.	R.	H.	RBI.	PO.	A.
Sheckard, lf	4	0	0	0	2	0
Schulte, rf	2	0	1	0	0	0
Hofman, cf	4	0	0	0	2	0
Chance, 1b	3	0	0	0	11	2
Zimmerman, 2b	3	0	0	0	2	3
Steinfeldt, 3b	3	0	0	0	0	3
Tinker, ss	3	1	1	0	3	2
Kling, c	3	0	1	1	4	3
Overall, p	1	0	0	0	0	0
McIntire, p	1	0	0	0	0	2
aBeaumont	1	0	0	0	0	0
Totals	28	1	3	1	24	15

Philadelphia	AB.	R.	H.	RBI.	PO.	A.
Strunk, cf	3	0	0	0	1	0
Lord, lf	4	1	1	0	0	0
Collins, 2b	2	1	1	0	2	5
Baker, 3b	4	1	3	2	3	2
Davis, 1b	3	0	0	0	11	0
Murphy, rf	3	1	1	1	1	0
Barry, ss	3	0	0	0	0	4
Thomas, c	1	0	0	0	8	2
Bender, p	3	0	1	1	1	0
Totals	26	4	7	4	27	13

Chicago	0 0 0 0 0 0 0 0 1—1
Philadelphia	0 2 1 0 0 0 0 1 x—4

Chicago	IP.	H.	R.	ER.	BB.	SO.
Overall (L)	3	6	3	3	1	1
McIntire	5	1	1	0	3	2

Philadelphia	IP.	H.	R.	ER.	BB.	SO.
Bender (W)	9	3	1	0	2	8

aGrounded out for McIntire in ninth. E—McIntire, Strunk, Thomas. LOB—Chicago 2, Philadelphia 4. 2B—Baker 2, Lord. SB—Murphy. SH—Davis, Collins. U—Connolly (A.L.), O'Day (N.L.), Rigler (N.L.) and Sheridan (A.L.) T—1:54. A—26,891.

Game 2

Tuesday, October 18, At Philadelphia

Chicago	AB.	R.	H.	RBI.	PO.	A.
Sheckard, lf	1	1	1	0	0	1
Schulte, rf	3	1	0	0	0	0
Hofman, cf	2	1	1	0	1	0
Chance, 1b	5	0	2	1	14	0
Zimmerman, 2b	3	0	1	2	1	2
Steinfeldt, 3b	5	0	1	0	0	2
Tinker, ss	4	0	2	0	3	4
Kling, c	4	0	0	0	5	2
Brown, p	3	0	0	0	0	2
aBeaumont	1	0	0	0	0	0
Richie, p	0	0	0	0	0	0
Totals	31	3	8	3	24	13

Philadelphia	AB.	R.	H.	RBI.	PO.	A.
Strunk, cf	5	1	2	1	4	0
Lord, lf	5	1	1	0	1	0
Collins, 2b	4	2	3	1	4	6
Baker, 3b	4	1	1	0	1	1
Davis, 1b	5	1	2	2	7	0
Murphy, rf	4	1	1	2	1	1
Barry, ss	3	0	1	0	3	1
Thomas, c	3	2	2	1	6	1
Coombs, p	4	0	1	0	0	1
Totals	37	9	14	7	27	11

Chicago	1 0 0 0 0 0 1 0 1—3
Philadelphia	0 0 2 0 1 0 6 0 x—9

Chicago	IP.	H.	R.	ER.	BB.	SO.
Brown (L)	7	13	9	7	4	6
Richie	1	1	0	0	0	0

Philadelphia	IP.	H.	R.	ER.	BB.	SO.
Coombs (W)	9	8	3	3	9	5

aStruck out for Brown in eighth. E—Sheckard, Steinfeldt 2, Davis 2, Coombs 2. DP—Chicago 1, Philadelphia 3. LOB—Chicago 14, Philadelphia 9. 2B—Collins 2, Davis, Murphy, Strunk, Tinker, Zimmerman, Sheckard, Steinfeldt. SB—Collins 2. SH—Schulte 2, Sheckard, Barry. SF—Zimmerman. U—Rigler (N.L.), Sheridan (A.L.), O'Day (N.L.) and Connolly (A.L.). T—2:25. A—24,597.

Game 3

Thursday, October 20, At Chicago

Philadelphia	AB.	R.	H.	RBI.	PO.	A.
Strunk, cf	5	1	1	0	3	0
Lord, lf	4	0	1	0	1	0
Collins, 2b	5	1	1	0	1	1
Baker, 3b	5	2	2	1	2	4
Davis, 1b	3	3	3	0	8	0
Murphy, rf	5	2	1	3	3	1
Barry, ss	5	3	3	3	1	2
Thomas, c	4	0	0	0	8	1
Coombs, p	5	0	3	3	0	0
Totals	41	12	15	10	27	9

Chicago	AB.	R.	H.	RBI.	PO.	A.
Sheckard, lf	1	2	0	0	2	0
Schulte, rf	4	0	2	2	2	0
Hofman, cf	3	1	1	1	2	0
Chance, 1b	1	0	0	0	3	0
Archer, 1b	3	0	0	0	9	0
Zimmerman, 2b	4	0	0	0	4	6
Steinfeldt, 3b	4	0	0	0	0	2
Tinker, ss	4	1	3	0	3	4
Kling, c	4	0	0	0	2	2
Reulbach, p	0	0	0	0	0	1
aBeaumont	0	1	0	0	0	0
McIntire, p	0	0	0	0	0	0
Pfiester, p	2	0	0	0	0	1
bNeedham	1	0	0	0	0	0
Totals	31	5	6	3	27	16

Philadelphia	1 2 5 0 0 0 4 0 0—12
Chicago	1 2 0 0 0 0 0 2 0— 5

Philadelphia	IP.	H.	R.	ER.	BB.	SO.
Coombs (W)	9	6	5	5	4	8

Chicago	IP.	H.	R.	ER.	BB.	SO.
Reulbach	2	3	3	2	2	0
McIntire (L)	⅓	3	4	4	0	0
Pfiester	6⅔	9	5	0	1	1

aWalked for Reulbach in second. bFouled out for Pfiester in ninth. E—Baker, Schulte, Hofman, Steinfeldt, Tinker 2. DP—Philadelphia 2, Chicago 1. LOB—Philadelphia 7, Chicago 4. 2B—Schulte 2, Tinker, Davis, Coombs, Barry 2. HR—Murphy. SB—Tinker. SH—Lord. SF—Hofman. HBP—By McIntire (Davis). WP—Coombs. U—O'Day (N.L.), Sheridan (A.L.), Rigler (N.L.) and Connolly (A.L.). T—2:07. A—26,210.

Game 4

Saturday, October 22, At Chicago

Philadelphia	AB.	R.	H.	RBI.	PO.	A.
Strunk, cf	5	0	2	1	2	0
Lord, lf	5	0	0	0	1	0
Collins, 2b	5	1	1	0	6	1
Baker, 3b	4	1	3	1	3	4
Davis, 1b	3	0	1	0	8	0
Murphy, rf	4	0	2	1	1	0
Barry, ss	4	0	0	0	2	1
Thomas, c	4	0	1	0	5	4
Bender, p	3	1	1	0	0	2
Totals	37	3	11	3	*28	12

Chicago	AB.	R.	H.	RBI.	PO.	A.
Sheckard, lf	4	1	1	1	3	1
Schulte, rf	4	2	2	0	2	0
Hofman, cf	3	0	2	1	1	0
Chance, 1b	4	0	2	2	10	2
Zimmerman, 2b	4	0	1	0	2	2
Steinfeldt, 3b	4	0	0	0	2	4
Tinker, ss	3	0	0	0	1	3
Archer, c	4	1	1	0	8	3
Cole, p	2	0	0	0	1	3
aKling	1	0	0	0	0	0
bKane	0	0	0	0	0	0
Brown, p	1	0	0	0	0	1
Totals	34	4	9	4	30	19

Philadelphia	0 0 1 2 0 0 0 0 0 0—3
Chicago	1 0 0 1 0 0 0 0 1 1—4

Two out when winning run scored.

Philadelphia	IP.	H.	R.	ER.	BB.	SO.
Bender (L)	9⅔	9	4	4	2	6

Chicago	IP.	H.	R.	ER.	BB.	SO.
Cole	8	10	3	3	3	5
Brown (W)	2	1	0	0	0	1

*Chance declared out for Hofman's interference. aReached first on error for Cole in eighth. bRan for Kling in eighth. E—Collins, Baker, Davis, Brown. DP—Philadelphia 1, Chicago 1. LOB—Philadelphia 10, Chicago 4. 2B—Baker, Murphy, Davis, Schulte, Archer. 3B—Strunk, Chance. SB—Sheckard. SH—Davis, Murphy, Hofman. HBP—By Cole (Barry). U—Connolly (A.L.), Rigler (N.L.), Sheridan (A.L.) and O'Day (N.L.). T—2:14. A—19,150.

Game 5

Sunday, October 23, At Chicago

Philadelphia	AB.	R.	H.	RBI.	PO.	A.
Hartsel, lf	5	2	1	0	2	0
Lord, cf	4	1	1	1	5	0
Collins, 2b	5	0	3	2	4	4
Baker, 3b	5	1	0	0	0	0
Davis, 1b	3	1	0	0	9	1
Murphy, rf	4	2	2	1	0	0
Barry, ss	2	0	0	0	2	4
Lapp, c	4	0	1	1	4	2
Coombs, p	4	0	1	0	1	3
Totals	36	7	9	5	27	14

Chicago	AB.	R.	H.	RBI.	PO.	A.
Sheckard, lf	4	1	2	0	1	0
Schulte, rf	4	0	1	0	0	0
Hofman, cf	3	0	0	0	1	0
Chance, 1b	4	1	2	1	13	0
Zimmerman, 2b	3	0	2	0	1	5
Steinfeldt, 3b	4	0	1	1	0	1
Tinker, ss	4	0	0	0	1	1
Archer, c	4	0	1	0	10	0
Brown, p	3	0	0	0	0	7
aKling	1	0	0	0	0	0
Totals	34	2	9	2	27	14

Philadelphia	1 0 0 0 1 0 0 5 0—7
Chicago	0 1 0 0 0 0 0 1 0—2

Philadelphia	IP.	H.	R.	ER.	BB.	SO.
Coombs (W)	9	9	2	2	1	4

Chicago	IP.	H.	R.	ER.	BB.	SO.
Brown (L)	9	9	7	4	3	7

aGrounded out for Brown in ninth. E—Baker, Zimmerman, Steinfeldt. LOB—Philadelphia 6, Chicago 7. 2B—Chance, Sheckard, Murphy, Lord, Collins 2. SB—Hartsel 2, Collins 2, Zimmerman. SH—Zimmerman, Barry. WP—Brown. U—O'Day (N.L.), Sheridan (A.L.), Rigler (N.L.) and Connolly (A.L.). T—2:06. A—27,374.

COMPOSITE BATTING AVERAGES

Philadelphia Athletics

Player-Position	G.	AB.	R.	H.	2B.	3B.	HR.	RBI.	BA.
Collins, 2b	5	21	5	9	4	0	0	3	.429
Baker, 3b	5	22	6	9	3	0	0	4	.409
Coombs, p	3	13	0	5	1	0	0	3	.385
Davis, 1b	5	17	5	6	3	0	0	2	.353
Murphy, rf	5	20	6	7	3	0	1	8	.350
Bender, p	2	6	1	2	0	0	0	1	.333
Strunk, cf	4	18	2	5	1	1	0	2	.278
Thomas, c	4	12	2	3	0	0	0	1	.250
Lapp, c	1	4	0	1	0	0	0	1	.250
Barry, ss	5	17	3	4	2	0	0	3	.235
Hartsel, lf	1	5	2	1	0	0	0	0	.200
Lord, lf-cf	5	22	3	4	2	0	0	1	.182
Totals	5	177	35	56	19	1	1	29	.316

Chicago Cubs

Player-Position	G.	AB.	R.	H.	2B.	3B.	HR.	RBI.	BA.
Chance, 1b	5	17	1	6	1	1	0	4	.353
Schulte, rf	5	17	3	6	3	0	0	2	.353
Tinker, ss	5	18	2	6	2	0	0	0	.333
Sheckard, lf	5	14	5	4	2	0	0	1	.286
Hofman, cf	5	15	2	4	0	0	0	2	.267
Zimmerman, 2b	5	17	0	4	1	0	0	2	.235
Archer, 1b-c	3	11	1	2	1	0	0	0	.182
Steinfeldt, 3b	5	20	0	2	1	0	0	1	.100
Kling, c-ph	5	13	0	1	0	0	0	1	.077
Overall, p	1	1	0	0	0	0	0	0	.000
McIntire, p	2	1	0	0	0	0	0	0	.000
Brown, p	3	7	0	0	0	0	0	0	.000
Richie, p	1	0	0	0	0	0	0	0	.000
Reulbach, p	1	0	0	0	0	0	0	0	.000
Pfiester, p	1	2	0	0	0	0	0	0	.000
Needham, ph	1	1	0	0	0	0	0	0	.000
Cole, p	1	2	0	0	0	0	0	0	.000
Kane, pr	1	0	0	0	0	0	0	0	.000
Beaumont, ph	3	2	1	0	0	0	0	0	.000
Totals	5	158	15	35	11	1	0	13	.222

COMPOSITE PITCHING AVERAGES

Philadelphia Athletics

Pitcher	G.	IP.	H.	R.	ER.	BB.	SO.	W.	L.	ERA.
Bender	2	18⅔	12	5	4	4	14	1	1	1.93
Coombs	3	27	23	10	10	14	17	3	0	3.33
Totals	5	45⅔	35	15	14	18	31	4	1	2.76

Chicago Cubs

Pitcher	G.	IP.	H.	R.	ER.	BB.	SO.	W.	L.	ERA.
Richie	1	1	1	0	0	0	0	0	0	0.00
Pfiester	1	6⅔	9	5	0	1	1	0	0	0.00
Cole	1	8	10	3	3	3	5	0	0	3.38
Brown	3	18	23	16	11	7	14	1	2	5.50
McIntire	2	5⅓	4	5	4	3	2	0	1	6.80
Overall	1	3	6	3	3	1	1	0	1	9.00
Reulbach	1	2	3	3	2	2	0	0	0	9.00
Totals	5	44	56	35	23	17	23	1	4	4.70

1911
PHILADELPHIA ATHLETICS
VS.
NEW YORK GIANTS

What could the defending World Series champion Philadelphia Athletics do for an encore in 1911?

Virtually what they did in their first Series-winning season, that's what. For starters, Connie Mack's team again ran roughshod over its competition in the American League, winning the pennant by 13½ games. The Athletics possessed the junior league's home run king in third baseman Frank Baker, who anchored the club's $100,000 infield (so called because of its purported worth). Not only did Baker sock 11 homers—a sizable total in that era—during the 1911 season, he also batted .334. Second baseman Eddie Collins hit .365 and first baseman Stuffy McInnis, seeing his first full-time duty in the majors, posted a .321 average. Shortstop Jack Barry

contributed a .265 mark and steadiness afield.

Outfielders Danny Murphy, Bris Lord and Rube Oldring batted a composite .312, while pitchers Jack Coombs, Eddie Plank, Chief Bender and Cy Morgan combined for 82 victories.

The Athletics' World Series opponents would be the New York Giants, setting up a rematch of the storied, shutout-punctuated 1905 fall classic that paired Mack's team against John McGraw's battlers. The Giants were a run-happy bunch in 1911, stealing a modern major league record of 347 bases. Christy Mathewson, who had thrown three shutouts against the A's in the Giants' earlier Series appearance, was still McGraw's pitching ace, as reflected by his 26-13 record in the recently concluded season. Just

emerging was 21-year-old Rube Marquard, a lefthander who had entered the season with a 9-18 career record in the majors but then proceeded to win 24 games. And the Giants had some heavy hitters, too, headed by Larry Doyle, Fred Merkle and Chief Meyers.

All was not rosy for the Giants, however. Their ball park, the Polo Grounds, burned to the ground in April and wasn't ready for reopening until late June. McGraw and company persevered, playing their home games at the park of the A.L.'s New York Highlanders and beginning their run at a 99-victory season.

Game 1 of the fall classic, played before a Series-record throng of 38,281 fans at the rebuilt Polo Grounds, pitted Bender against Mathewson. And Mathewson, a winner over Bender in the Series finale six years earlier, prevailed again. The A's seized a 1-0 lead in the second inning when Baker singled, moved to second on a groundout, advanced to third on a passed ball and scored on a single by veteran Harry Davis (who was filling in for the injured McInnis). After tying the game in the fourth without benefit of a hit, the Giants collected the game-winning run in the seventh when Meyers and Josh Devore cracked doubles. Mathewson finished with a six-hitter in New York's 2-1 conquest, while Bender yielded only five hits and struck out 11.

Marquard and Plank waged a magnificent pitchers' duel in Game 2. Neither walked a batter and hits were at a premium. The score was 1-1 when the A's came to bat in the bottom of the sixth inning, and Marquard showed no signs of weakening as he retired Lord and Oldring. However, Collins followed with a double and

Interested Philadelphians gathered outside Shibe Park in 1911 to get play-by-play accounts of the Athletics' World Series games in New York.

John McGraw and his New York Giants were dressed in black when the umpires went over the ground rules prior to Game 1 of the 1911 World Series. Flank- **ing McGraw (left to right) are Bill Dinneen, Tom Connolly, Philadelphia's Harry Davis, Bill Klem and Bill Brennan.**

cleanup hitter Baker was up next. Baker, playing only his third full season in the big leagues and thus still building his reputation as a power hitter, walloped a home run over the right-field wall. The smash proved the difference, with the A's holding on for a Series-evening 3-1 triumph.

It was more of the same the next day. With Philadelphia trailing Mathewson and the Giants, 1-0, with one out in the ninth inning, Baker strode to the plate and drilled a homer into the right-field stands.

Rescued from the abyss, the A's went on to score two runs in the 11th and wound up 3-2 winners. Coombs and Mathewson both pitched the distance, Coombs permitting only three hits and Mathewson giving up nine.

Then an unexpected force came into play. Mother Nature. For six days, it rained. And rained. And rained.

Game 4 finally was played on October 24, exactly a week after Game 3 had been contested and 10 days after the Series had begun (the late starting date was because the National League's regular-season schedule ran through Columbus Day). And, this time, Bender got the best of Mathewson in a 4-2 decision that gave Philadelphia a Series lead of three games to one.

New York escaped elimination in gritty fashion in Game 5, a contest in which Philadelphia, behind Coombs, held a 3-0 edge after six innings and a 3-1 lead with one out in the Giants' ninth. Art Fletcher then doubled for the National Leaguers, moved to third on a groundout and scored on reliever Doc Crandall's double. Devore followed with a game-tying single. Then, in the 10th, with Plank now on in relief for Philadelphia, Fred Snodgrass doubled

and later scored on a fly ball by Merkle. The Giants were 4-3 victors and clinging to life.

However, the never-say-die New Yorkers were left for dead in Game 6 when Philadelphia went on a four-run burst in the fourth inning and a seven-run spree in the seventh. With Bender stopping the Giants on four hits, the A's waltzed to a 13-2 victory and claimed their second successive World Series championship.

The Giants' offense had gone pfft in the Series, with six regulars batting .190 or less (cleanup man Red Murray was 0 for 21). And after running their N.L. opposition into the ground during the season, the Giants managed only four stolen bases against the Athletics.

The A's, meanwhile, had Bender, Coombs and Plank, who allowed New York only eight earned runs in six games. Perhaps

most of all, they had a young slugger who made a name for himself in this Series because of his timely long-ball hitting. Frank Baker was now *Home Run* Baker.

Game 1

Saturday, October 14, At New York

Philadelphia	AB.	R.	H.	RBI.	PO.	A.
Lord, lf	4	0	0	0	2	0
Oldring, cf	4	0	2	0	1	0
Collins, 2b	3	0	0	0	0	5
Baker, 3b	4	1	2	0	0	1
Murphy, rf	3	0	0	0	1	0
Davis, 1b	4	0	1	1	8	0
Barry, ss	3	0	0	0	0	1
Thomas, c	3	0	0	0	12	2
Bender, p	3	0	1	0	0	1
Totals	31	1	6	1	24	10

New York	AB.	R.	H.	RBI.	PO.	A.
Devore, lf	3	0	1	1	3	0
Doyle, 2b	3	0	1	0	1	0
Snodgrass, cf	2	1	0	0	2	0
Murray, rf	3	0	0	0	1	0
Merkle, 1b	4	0	1	0	11	1
Herzog, 3b	3	0	0	0	0	2
Fletcher, ss	4	0	0	0	2	3
Meyers, c	3	1	1	0	7	1
Mathewson, p	3	0	1	0	0	4
Totals	28	2	5	1	27	11

Philadelphia	0 1 0 0 0 0 0 0 0—1
New York	0 0 0 1 0 0 1 0 x—2

Philadelphia	IP.	H.	R.	ER.	BB.	SO.
Bender (L)	8	5	2	1	4	11
New York	**IP.**	**H.**	**R.**	**ER.**	**BB.**	**SO.**
Mathewson (W)	9	6	1	1	1	5

E—Collins, Baker. LOB—Philadelphia 5, New York 8. 2B—Oldring 2, Devore, Meyers. SB—Doyle. SH—Murphy, Murray. HBP—By Bender (Snodgrass). PB—Meyers. U—Klem (N.L.), Dinneen (A.L.), Brennan (N.L.) and Connolly (A.L.). T—2:12. A—38,281.

Game 2

Monday, October 16, At Philadelphia

New York	AB.	R.	H.	RBI.	PO.	A.
Devore, lf	4	0	0	0	5	0
Doyle, 2b	4	0	0	0	1	2
Snodgrass, cf	3	0	2	0	1	0
Murray, rf	4	0	0	0	0	0
Merkle, 1b	3	0	1	0	7	0
Herzog, 3b	3	1	1	0	1	1
Fletcher, ss	3	0	0	0	1	1
Meyers, c	3	0	1	1	8	1
Marquard, p	2	0	0	0	0	2
Crandall, p	1	0	0	0	0	0
Totals	30	1	5	1	24	7

Philadelphia	AB.	R.	H.	RBI.	PO.	A.
Lord, lf	4	1	1	0	2	1
Oldring, cf	3	0	0	0	1	0
Collins, 2b	3	1	2	0	2	4
Baker, 3b	3	1	1	2	1	1
Murphy, rf	3	0	0	0	0	0
Davis, 1b	3	0	0	0	10	0
Barry, ss	3	0	0	0	2	2
Thomas, c	3	0	0	0	9	0
Plank, p	3	0	0	0	0	2
Totals	28	3	4	2	27	10

New York	0 1 0 0 0 0 0 0 0—1
Philadelphia	1 0 0 0 0 2 0 0 x—3

New York	IP.	H.	R.	ER.	BB.	SO.
Marquard (L)	7	4	3	2	0	4
Crandall	1	0	0	0	0	2
Philadelphia	**IP.**	**H.**	**R.**	**ER.**	**BB.**	**SO.**
Plank (W)	9	5	1	1	0	8

E—Devore, Murray, Merkle. LOB—New York 3, Philadelphia 2. 2B—Herzog, Collins. HR—Baker. SH—Oldring. HBP—By Plank (Snodgrass). WP—Marquard. U—Connolly (A.L.), Brennan (N.L.), Klem (N.L.) and Dinneen (A.L.). T—1:52. A—26,286.

Game 3

Tuesday, October 17, At New York

Philadelphia	AB.	R.	H.	RBI.	PO.	A.
Lord, lf	5	0	0	0	5	0
Oldring, cf	5	0	0	0	0	0
Collins, 2b	5	1	2	0	5	4
Baker, 3b	5	2	2	1	2	1
Murphy, rf	5	0	0	1	2	0
Davis, 1b	5	0	2	1	10	0
Barry, ss	3	0	2	0	1	4
Lapp, c	4	0	1	0	8	6
Coombs, p	4	0	0	0	0	1
Totals	41	3	9	3	33	16

New York	AB.	R.	H.	RBI.	PO.	A.
Devore, lf	4	0	0	1	0	0
Doyle, 2b	4	0	0	0	5	5
Snodgrass, cf	3	0	0	0	3	0
Murray, rf	2	0	0	0	2	1
Merkle, 1b	3	0	0	0	11	1
Herzog, 3b	3	1	1	0	4	3
Fletcher, ss	4	0	0	0	3	4
Meyers, c	4	1	1	0	4	4
Mathewson, p	3	0	1	0	1	4
aBecker	1	0	0	0	0	0
Totals	31	2	3	1	33	22

Philadelphia	0 0 0 0 0 0 0 0 1 0 2—3
New York	0 0 1 0 0 0 0 0 0 0 1—2

Philadelphia	IP.	H.	R.	ER.	BB.	SO.
Coombs (W)	11	3	2	1	4	7
New York	**IP.**	**H.**	**R.**	**ER.**	**BB.**	**SO.**
Mathewson (L)	11	9	3	1	0	3

aReached first on error for Mathewson in eleventh. E—Collins 2, Herzog 3, Fletcher 2. DP—New York 1. LOB—Philadelphia 6, New York 1. 2B—Barry, Herzog. HR—Baker. SB—Collins, Barry. SH—Barry, Murray. U—Brennan (N.L.), Connolly (A.L.), Klem (N.L.) and Dinneen (A.L.). T—2:25. A—37,216.

Game 4

Tuesday, October 24, At Philadelphia

New York	AB.	R.	H.	RBI.	PO.	A.
Devore, lf	4	1	2	0	0	0
Doyle, 2b	3	1	1	1	2	0
Snodgrass, cf	3	0	0	1	0	0
Murray, rf	4	0	0	0	1	0
Merkle, 1b	4	0	1	0	12	2
Herzog, 3b	4	0	0	0	1	5
Fletcher, ss	4	0	2	0	0	4
Meyers, c	4	0	1	0	7	2
Mathewson, p	1	0	0	0	1	1
aBecker	1	0	0	0	0	0
Wiltse, p	0	0	0	0	0	0
Totals	32	2	7	2	24	14

Philadelphia	AB.	R.	H.	RBI.	PO.	A.
Lord, lf	4	0	1	0	2	0
Oldring, cf	3	0	0	0	3	0
Collins, 2b	3	1	2	0	2	4
Baker, 3b	3	1	2	1	4	3
Murphy, rf	4	1	2	1	0	0
Davis, 1b	4	1	1	1	10	0
Barry, ss	4	0	3	0	1	1
Thomas, c	3	0	0	1	5	2
Bender, p	4	0	0	0	0	1
Totals	32	4	11	4	27	11

New York	2 0 0 0 0 0 0 0 0—2
Philadelphia	0 0 0 3 1 0 0 0 x—4

New York	IP.	H.	R.	ER.	BB.	SO.
Mathewson (L)	7	10	4	4	1	5
Wiltse	1	1	0	0	0	1
Philadelphia	**IP.**	**H.**	**R.**	**ER.**	**BB.**	**SO.**
Bender (W)	9	7	2	2	2	4

aGrounded out for Mathewson in eighth. E—Murray, Fletcher, Mathewson, Baker. DP—Philadelphia 1. LOB—New York 6, Philadelphia 8. 2B—Merkle, Meyers, Baker 2, Murphy 2, Davis, Barry 2. 3B—Doyle. SH—Oldring, Collins. SF—Snodgrass, Thomas. U—Dinneen (A.L.), Klem (N.L.), Connolly (A.L.) and Brennan (N.L.). T—1:49. A—24,355.

Game 5

Wednesday, October 25, At New York

Philadelphia	AB.	R.	H.	RBI.	PO.	A.
Lord, lf	5	0	0	0	2	0
Oldring, cf	5	1	2	3	0	0
Collins, 2b	3	0	0	0	1	1
Baker, 3b	4	0	0	0	1	2
Murphy, rf	4	0	1	0	4	0
Davis, 1b	4	0	0	0	7	2
Barry, ss	4	0	1	0	3	4
Lapp, c	4	1	1	0	10	2
Coombs, p	4	1	2	0	1	1
bStrunk	0	0	0	0	0	0
Plank, p	0	0	0	0	0	0
Totals	37	3	7	3	29	12

New York	AB.	R.	H.	RBI.	PO.	A.
Devore, lf	5	0	1	1	3	0
Doyle, 2b	5	1	4	0	3	4
Snodgrass, cf	4	0	0	0	2	0
Murray, rf	5	0	0	0	0	0
Merkle, 1b	2	1	0	1	12	0
Herzog, 3b	4	0	1	0	1	3
Fletcher, ss	4	1	1	0	4	3
Meyers, c	3	0	1	1	5	3
Marquard, p	0	0	0	0	0	0
aBecker	1	0	0	0	0	0
Ames, p	1	0	0	0	0	0
Crandall, p	1	1	1	1	0	2
Totals	35	4	9	4	30	15

Philadelphia	0 0 3 0 0 0 0 0 0 0—3
New York	0 0 0 0 0 0 1 0 2 1—4

Two out when winning run scored.

Philadelphia	IP.	H.	R.	ER.	BB.	SO.
Coombs	9	8	3	2	2	9
Plank (L)	⅔	1	1	1	0	0
New York	**IP.**	**H.**	**R.**	**ER.**	**BB.**	**SO.**
Marquard	3	3	3	0	1	2
Ames	4	2	0	0	0	2
Crandall (W)	3	2	0	0	0	0

aFlied out for Marquard in third. bRan for Coombs in tenth. E—Collins, Doyle, Fletcher. DP—Philadelphia 1, New York 1. LOB—Philadelphia 5, New York 8. 2B—Doyle 2, Fletcher, Crandall. HR—Oldring. SB—Collins, Barry, Doyle, Herzog. SH—Snodgrass. SF—Merkle, Meyers. HBP—By Coombs (Merkle). WP—Crandall. U—Klem (N.L.), Dinneen (A.L.), Connolly (A.L.) and Brennan (N.L.). T—2:33. A—33,228.

Game 6

Thursday, October 26, At Philadelphia

New York	AB.	R.	H.	RBI.	PO.	A.
Devore, lf	4	0	0	0	5	0
Doyle, 2b	4	1	1	0	1	4
Snodgrass, cf	4	0	0	0	1	0
Murray, rf	3	0	0	0	0	0
Merkle, 1b	4	0	0	0	9	0
Herzog, 3b	4	1	1	0	0	0
Fletcher, ss	4	0	0	1	1	2
Meyers, c	3	0	1	0	6	1
Wilson, c	1	0	0	0	1	0
Ames, p	1	0	1	0	0	2
aCrandall	0	0	0	0	0	0
Wiltse, p	1	0	0	0	0	1
Marquard, p	0	0	0	0	0	0
Totals	33	2	4	1	24	10

Philadelphia	AB.	R.	H.	RBI.	PO.	A.
Lord, lf	5	1	3	1	1	0
Oldring, cf	5	1	1	0	3	0
Collins, 2b	4	1	0	1	2	4
Baker, 3b	5	2	2	1	2	2
Murphy, rf	4	3	4	1	1	0
Davis, 1b	4	2	1	2	9	1
McInnis, 1b	0	0	0	0	1	0
Barry, ss	2	2	1	2	2	1
Thomas, c	3	1	1	0	5	1
Bender, p	4	0	0	0	1	4
Totals	36	13	13	8	27	13

New York	1 0 0 0 0 0 0 0 1— 2
Philadelphia	0 0 1 4 0 1 7 0 x—13

New York	IP.	H.	R.	ER.	BB.	SO.
Ames (L)	4	4	5	2	1	4
Wiltse	2⅓	7	8	7	0	1
Marquard	1⅔	2	0	0	0	2
Philadelphia	**IP.**	**H.**	**R.**	**ER.**	**BB.**	**SO.**
Bender (W)	9	4	2	0	2	5

aWalked for Ames in fifth. E—Murray, Merkle, Ames, Oldring, Murphy, Barry 3. LOB—New York 6, Philadelphia 3. 2B—Doyle, Lord 2, Murphy, Barry. SB—Herzog. SH—Collins, Barry. SF—Barry. WP—Marquard, Bender. U—Connolly (A.L.), Brennan (N.L.), Klem (N.L.) and Dinneen (A.L.). T—2:12. A—20,485.

COMPOSITE BATTING AVERAGES

Philadelphia Athletics

Player-Position	G.	AB.	R.	H.	2B.	3B.	HR.	RBI.	BA.
Baker, 3b	6	24	7	9	2	0	2	5	.375
Barry, ss	6	19	2	7	4	0	0	2	.368
Murphy, rf	6	23	4	7	3	0	0	3	.304
Collins, 2b	6	21	4	6	1	0	0	1	.286
Lapp, c	2	8	1	2	0	0	0	0	.250
Coombs, p	2	8	1	2	0	0	0	0	.250
Davis, 1b	6	24	3	5	1	0	0	5	.208
Oldring, cf	6	25	2	5	2	0	1	3	.200
Lord, lf	6	27	2	5	2	0	0	1	.185
Bender, p	3	11	0	1	0	0	0	0	.091
Thomas, c	4	12	1	1	0	0	0	1	.083
Plank, p	2	3	0	0	0	0	0	0	.000
Strunk, ph	1	0	0	0	0	0	0	0	.000
McInnis, 1b	1	0	0	0	0	0	0	0	.000
Totals	6	205	27	50	15	0	3	21	.244

New York Giants

Player-Position	G.	AB.	R.	H.	2B.	3B.	HR.	RBI.	BA.
Ames, p	2	2	0	1	0	0	0	0	.500
Crandall, p-ph	3	2	1	1	1	0	0	1	.500
Doyle, 2b	6	23	3	7	3	1	0	1	.304
Meyers, c	6	20	2	6	2	0	0	2	.300
Mathewson, p	3	7	0	2	0	0	0	0	.286
Herzog, 3b	6	21	3	4	2	0	0	0	.190
Devore, lf	6	24	1	4	1	0	0	3	.167
Merkle, 1b	6	20	1	3	1	0	0	1	.150
Fletcher, ss	6	23	1	3	1	0	0	1	.130
Snodgrass, cf	6	19	1	2	0	0	0	1	.105
Murray, rf	6	21	0	0	0	0	0	0	.000
Marquard, p	3	2	0	0	0	0	0	0	.000
Becker, ph	3	3	0	0	0	0	0	0	.000
Wiltse, p	2	1	0	0	0	0	0	0	.000
Wilson, p	1	1	0	0	0	0	0	0	.000
Totals	6	189	13	33	11	1	0	10	.175

COMPOSITE PITCHING AVERAGES

Philadelphia Athletics

Pitcher	G.	IP.	H.	R.	ER.	BB.	SO.	W.	L.	ERA.
Bender	3	26	16	6	3	8	20	2	1	1.04
Coombs	2	20	11	5	3	6	16	1	0	1.35
Plank	2	9⅔	6	2	2	0	8	1	1	1.86
Totals	6	55⅔	33	13	8	14	44	4	2	1.29

New York Giants

Pitcher	G.	IP.	H.	R.	ER.	BB.	SO.	W.	L.	ERA.
Crandall	2	4	2	0	0	0	2	1	0	0.00
Marquard	3	11⅔	9	6	2	1	8	0	1	1.54
Mathewson	3	27	25	8	6	2	13	1	2	2.00
Ames	2	8	6	5	2	1	6	0	1	2.25
Wiltse	2	3⅓	8	8	7	0	2	0	0	18.90
Totals	6	54	50	27	17	4	31	2	4	2.83

The New York Giants had a storybook season in 1912. A storybook season capped by a horror-story ending, that is.

Manager John McGraw's Giants received an astonishing performance in 1912 from left-hander Rube Marquard, who established a modern major league record by winning his first 19 decisions of the season. Marquard finished with 26 victories. Christy Mathewson won 23 games. Rookie Jeff Tesreau was a key find, winning 17 games, leading the league in earned-run average with a 1.96 figure and tossing a no-hitter against Philadelphia in early September.

Offensively, New York got big seasons from second baseman Larry Doyle, who batted .330 and slugged 10 home runs; first baseman Fred Merkle, a .309 hitter who clubbed 11 homers; catcher Chief Meyers, who had a .358 batting average in 371 at-bats; and outfielder Red Murray, who knocked in a team-leading 92 runs.

Put it all together and you have a team that, despite a second-half slump, roared to 103 victories and outdistanced its closest National League rival by 10 games. Bring on the American League champions.

The A.L. titlists, of course, were expected to be the Philadelphia Athletics, World Series winners the previous two years. However, Connie Mack's A's never got fully cranked up and plunged to third place, 15 games behind the pennant-winning Boston Red Sox and one game in back of the runner-up Washington Senators. The Red Sox got a phenomenal year from 22-year-old righthander Smokey Joe Wood, who won 34 of 39 decisions and pitched 10 shutouts. Another young player,

Smokey Joe Wood won 34 regular-season games for the Red Sox and then added three more victories in the 1912 Series.

outfielder Tris Speaker, batted .383 in his fourth full season in the majors.

Wood was Boston Manager Jake Stahl's pitching selection for Game 1 of the 1912 World Series, while the Giants' John McGraw opted for newcomer Tesreau over either Marquard or Mathewson. Wood and the Red Sox prevailed, 4-3, with second baseman Steve Yerkes delivering a tie-breaking, two-run single in the seventh inning.

Game 2 was a stem-winder as the Giants overcame a 4-2 deficit with three runs in the top of the eighth inning, only to allow a tying run by the Red Sox in the bottom of the inning. New York regained the lead, 6-5, in the 10th, but Boston showed its pluck by rebounding once more in its half of the inning. With one out, Speaker drove a smash to deep center field and, running full steam, circled the bases when Giants reserve catcher Art Wilson (who had just entered the game) dropped the ball on a play at the plate. Speaker was credited with a triple. Neither club could score in the 11th, and darkness then put an end to the proceedings. The game went into the books as a 6-6 tie.

After Marquard deadlocked the Series the next day with a 2-1 victory, Wood and Tesreau renewed acquaintances in Game 4. Wood got the upper hand again, spacing nine hits in a 3-1 triumph. Then Red Sox rookie Hugh Bedient, a 20-game winner in 1912, outdueled Mathewson in a 2-1 decision that put the American Leaguers in command of the Series, three games to one (with one tie).

Their work obviously cut out for them, the Giants went to work—with a vengeance. They blasted Buck O'Brien for five first-inning runs in Game 6 and hammered Wood for six runs in the opening inning of Game 7. With Marquard pitching a seven-hitter and Tesreau then turning the tables on Wood, New York won those games by 5-2 and 11-4 scores. The best-of-seven battle would now require an *eighth* game.

Mathewson, winless in this Series after going the distance in the

Usually reliable center fielder Fred Snodgrass opened the door for Boston's 1912 victory with a costly error in the Series finale.

tie game and dropping Game 5, and the 22-year-old Bedient hooked up again in the finale. And, after nine tense innings, it was a 1-1 standoff. Mathewson was still pitching for New York, while Wood had taken over in the eighth for Bedient (who left the game in the seventh for a pinch-hitter, Olaf Henriksen, whose double tied the game).

In the 10th, New York's Murray laced a one-out double and scored on Merkle's single. While Wood retired the side without further damage, the Red Sox were faced with trying to rebound from a 2-1 deficit against the wily Mathewson, who had been his usual stingy self all afternoon.

A happy ending to New York's storybook campaign—a year featuring a spirited World Series comeback—appeared one out

closer when Boston pinch-hitter Clyde Engle began the bottom of the 10th by lofting a routine fly ball to center field. Fred Snodgrass camped under the ball—and dropped it. With Engle on second base after the misplay, Harry Hooper was robbed of a hit when Snodgrass made a great catch of his long drive. Engle advanced to third after Snodgrass' grab, and Yerkes followed with a walk. Speaker then hit a pop foul between a "frozen" Merkle and Meyers and, incredibly, the ball fell safely near the first-base coach's box. Given a reprieve, Speaker singled home Engle with the tying run.

With Yerkes stationed at third and Speaker on first with one out, Duffy Lewis was walked intentionally. Third baseman Larry Gardner then belted a deep fly

ball to Josh Devore in right field, and Yerkes tagged up and scored. The Red Sox, with more than a little help from the Giants' Snodgrass, had come back against the mighty Matty for a 3-2 victory and their second World Series championship.

For the stunned Giants, it was an unbelievable finish to what had been a make-believe season.

Game 1

Tuesday, October 8, At New York

Boston	AB.	R.	H.	RBI.	PO.	A.
Hooper, rf	3	1	1	1	1	0
Yerkes, 2b	4	0	1	2	0	1
Speaker, cf	3	1	1	0	0	1
Lewis, lf	4	0	0	1	2	0
Gardner, 3b	4	0	0	1	1	1
Stahl, 1b	4	0	0	0	6	1
Wagner, ss	3	1	2	0	5	3
Cady, c	3	0	1	0	11	1
Wood, p	3	1	0	0	1	1
Totals	31	4	6	4	27	9

New York	AB.	R.	H.	RBI.	PO.	A.
Devore, lf	3	1	0	0	0	0
Doyle, 2b	4	1	2	0	2	7
Snodgrass, cf	4	0	1	0	2	0
Murray, rf	3	0	1	2	1	0
Merkle, 1b	4	1	1	0	12	0
Herzog, 3b	4	0	2	0	1	1
Meyers, c	3	0	1	1	6	1
bBecker	0	0	0	0	0	0
Fletcher, ss	4	0	0	0	3	1
Tesreau, p	2	0	0	0	0	2
aMcCormick	1	0	0	0	0	0
Crandall, p	1	0	0	0	0	1
Totals	33	3	8	3	27	13

Boston...............0 0 0 0 0 1 3 0 0—4
New York.............0 0 2 0 0 0 0 0 1—3

Boston	IP.	H.	R.	ER.	BB.	SO.
Wood (W)	9	8	3	3	2	11

New York	IP.	H.	R.	ER.	BB.	SO.
Tesreau (L)	7	5	4	4	4	4
Crandall	2	1	0	0	0	2

aFlied out for Tesreau in seventh. bRan for Meyers in ninth. E—Wagner, Fletcher. DP—Boston 1. LOB—Boston 6, New York 6. 2B—Hooper, Wagner, Doyle. 3B—Speaker. SH—Hooper, Cady. HBP—By Wood (Meyers). U—Klem (N.L.), Evans (A.L.), Rigler (N.L.) and O'Loughlin (A.L.). T—2:10. A—35,730.

Game 2

Wednesday, October 9, At Boston

New York	AB.	R.	H.	RBI.	PO.	A.
Snodgrass, lf-rf	4	1	1	0	0	0
Doyle, 2b	5	0	1	0	2	5
Becker, cf	4	1	0	0	0	1
Murray, rf-lf	5	2	3	2	3	0
Merkle, 1b	5	1	1	0	19	0
Herzog, 3b	4	1	3	2	2	4
Meyers, c	4	0	2	1	5	0
aShafer, ss	0	0	0	0	0	3
Fletcher, ss	4	0	0	1	3	
bMcCormick	0	0	0	1	0	0
Wilson, c	0	0	0	0	1	0
Mathewson, p	5	0	0	0	1	6
Totals	40	6	11	6	33	23

Boston	AB.	R.	H.	RBI.	PO.	A.
Hooper, rf	5	1	3	0	3	0
Yerkes, 2b	5	1	1	1	3	4
Speaker, cf	5	2	2	0	2	0
Lewis, lf	5	2	2	0	2	0
Gardner, 3b	4	0	0	1	2	0
Stahl, 1b	5	0	2	2	10	0
Wagner, ss	5	0	0	0	5	5
Carrigan, c	5	0	0	0	6	4
Collins, p	3	0	0	0	0	1
Hall, p	1	0	0	0	0	0
Bedient, p	1	0	0	0	0	0
Totals	44	6	10	4	33	14

New York....................0 1 0 1 0 0 0 3 0 1 0—6
Boston........................3 0 0 0 1 0 0 1 0 1 0—6

(Game called at end of 11th inning on account of darkness.)

New York	IP.	H.	R.	ER.	BB.	SO.
Mathewson	11	10	6	2	0	4

Boston	IP.	H.	R.	ER.	BB.	SO.
Collins	7⅓	9	5	3	0	5
Hall	2⅔	2	1	1	4	0
Bedient	1	0	0	0	1	1

aRan for Meyers in tenth. bHit sacrifice fly for Fletcher in tenth. E—Merkle, Fletcher 3, Wilson, Lewis. DP—New York 1. LOB—New York 9, Boston 6. 2B—Snodgrass, Murray, Herzog, Lewis 2, Hooper. 3B—Murray, Merkle, Herzog, Yerkes, Speaker. SB—Snodgrass, Herzog, Hooper 2, Stahl. SH—Gardner. SF—Herzog, McCor-

mick. HBP—By Bedient (Snodgrass). U—O'Loughlin (A.L.), Rigler (N.L.), Klem (N.L.) and Evans (A.L.). T—2:38. A—30,148.

Game 3

Thursday, October 10, At Boston

New York	AB.	R.	H.	RBI.	PO.	A.
Devore, rf	4	0	2	0	2	0
Doyle, 2b	3	0	0	0	3	1
Snodgrass, cf	4	0	1	0	0	0
Murray, lf	4	1	1	0	5	0
Merkle, 1b	3	0	0	0	5	0
Herzog, 3b	2	1	1	1	1	3
Meyers, c	4	0	1	0	8	1
Fletcher, ss	3	0	1	1	3	2
Marquard, p	1	0	0	0	0	2
Totals	28	2	7	2	27	9

Boston	AB.	R.	H.	RBI.	PO.	A.
Hooper, rf	3	0	0	0	1	0
Yerkes, 2b	4	0	1	0	3	1
Speaker, cf	4	0	1	0	3	1
Lewis, lf	4	1	2	0	4	0
Gardner, 3b	3	0	1	1	0	2
Stahl, 1b	4	0	2	0	11	1
cHenriksen	0	0	0	0	0	0
Wagner, ss	4	0	0	0	1	3
Carrigan, c	2	0	0	0	3	1
aEngle	1	0	0	0	0	0
O'Brien, p	2	0	0	0	1	5
bBall	1	0	0	0	0	0
Cady, c	1	0	0	0	0	1
Bedient, p	0	0	0	0	0	0
Totals	33	1	7	1	27	15

New York .... 0 1 0 0 1 0 0 0 0—2
Boston .... 0 0 0 0 0 0 0 0 1—1

New York	IP.	H.	R.	ER.	BB.	SO.
Marquard (W)	9	7	1	1	1	6

Boston	IP.	H.	R.	ER.	BB.	SO.
O'Brien (L)	8	6	2	2	3	3
Bedient	1	1	0	0	0	0

aFlied out for Carrigan in eighth. bStruck out for O'Brien in eighth. cRan for Stahl in ninth. E—Merkle. DP—Boston 1. LOB—New York 6, Boston 7. 2B—Murray, Herzog, Stahl, Gardner. SB—Devore, Fletcher, Wagner. SH—Merkle, Marquard, Gardner. SF—Herzog. HBP—Bedient (Herzog). U—Evans (A.L.), Klem (N.L.), O'Loughlin (A.L.) and Rigler (N.L.). T—2:16. A—34,624.

Game 4

Friday, October 11, At New York

Boston	AB.	R.	H.	RBI.	PO.	A.
Hooper, rf	4	0	1	0	1	0
Yerkes, 2b	3	0	1	0	2	5
Speaker, cf	4	0	1	0	2	0
Lewis, lf	4	0	0	0	1	0
Gardner, 3b	3	2	2	0	0	2
Stahl, 1b	3	1	0	0	9	0
Wagner, ss	3	0	0	0	2	3
Cady, c	4	0	1	1	10	0
Wood, p	4	0	2	1	0	2
Totals	32	3	8	2	27	12

New York	AB.	R.	H.	RBI.	PO.	A.
Devore, lf	4	0	1	0	0	0
Doyle, 2b	4	0	1	0	4	1
Snodgrass, cf	4	0	0	0	2	0
Murray, rf	4	0	1	0	3	0
Merkle, 1b	4	0	1	0	8	0
Herzog, 3b	4	1	2	0	2	1
Meyers, c	4	0	0	0	5	1
Fletcher, ss	4	0	1	1	3	6
Tesreau, p	2	0	1	0	0	2
aMcCormick	1	0	1	0	0	0
Ames, p	0	0	0	0	0	1
Totals	35	1	9	1	27	12

Boston .... 0 1 0 1 0 0 0 0 1—3
New York .... 0 0 0 0 0 0 1 0 0—1

Boston	IP.	H.	R.	ER.	BB.	SO.
Wood (W)	9	9	1	1	0	8

New York	IP.	H.	R.	ER.	BB.	SO.
Tesreau (L)	7	5	2	2	2	5
Ames	2	3	1	1	1	0

aSingled for Tesreau in seventh. E—Wagner, Meyers. DP—New York 1. LOB—Boston 7, New York 7. 2B—Speaker, Fletcher. 3B—Gardner. SB—Stahl, Merkle. SH—Yerkes, Stahl. WP—Tesreau. U—Rigler (N.L.), O'Loughlin (A.L.), Evans (A.L.) and Klem (N.L.). T—2:06. A—36,502.

Game 5

Saturday, October 12, At Boston

New York	AB.	R.	H.	RBI.	PO.	A.
Devore, lf	2	0	0	0	0	0
Doyle, 2b	4	0	0	0	0	3
Snodgrass, cf	4	0	0	0	2	0
Murray, rf	3	0	0	0	0	1
Merkle, 1b	4	1	1	0	15	0
Herzog, 3b	4	0	0	0	2	3
Meyers, c	3	0	1	0	2	0
Fletcher, ss	2	0	0	0	2	2
aMcCromick	1	0	0	0	0	0
bShafer, ss	0	0	0	0	1	1
Mathewson, p	3	0	1	0	0	3
Totals	30	1	3	0	24	13

Boston	AB.	R.	H.	RBI.	PO.	A.
Hooper, rf	4	1	2	0	4	0
Yerkes, 2b	4	1	1	1	3	3
Speaker, cf	3	0	1	1	3	0
Lewis, lf	3	0	0	0	1	0
Gardner, 3b	3	0	0	0	3	2
Stahl, 1b	3	0	0	0	7	0
Wagner, ss	3	0	1	0	1	1
Cady, c	3	0	0	0	5	0
Bedient, p	3	0	0	0	0	0
Totals	29	2	5	2	27	6

New York .... 0 0 0 0 0 0 1 0 0—1
Boston .... 0 0 2 0 0 0 0 0 x—2

New York	IP.	H.	R.	ER.	BB.	SO.
Mathewson (L)	8	5	2	2	0	2

Boston	IP.	H.	R.	ER.	BB.	SO.
Bedient (W)	9	3	1	0	3	4

aReached first on error for Fletcher in seventh. bRan for McCormick in seventh. E—Doyle, Gardner. DP—Boston 1. LOB—New York 5, Boston 3. 2B—Merkle. 3B—Hooper, Yerkes. U—O'Loughlin (A.L.), Rigler (N.L.), Klem (N.L.) and Evans (A.L.). T—1:43. A—34,683.

Game 6

Monday, October 14, At New York

Boston	AB.	R.	H.	RBI.	PO.	A.
Hooper, rf	4	0	1	0	2	2
Yerkes, 2b	4	0	2	0	3	1
Speaker, cf	3	0	0	0	5	0
Lewis, lf	4	0	0	0	0	0
Gardner, 3b	4	1	0	0	0	1
Stahl, 1b	4	1	2	0	8	0
Wagner, ss	4	0	0	0	3	0
Cady, c	3	0	1	0	3	2
O'Brien, p	0	0	0	0	0	1
aEngle,	1	0	1	2	0	0
Collins, p	2	0	0	0	0	2
Totals	33	2	7	2	24	9

New York	AB.	R.	H.	RBI.	PO.	A.
Devore, lf	4	0	1	0	2	0
Doyle, 2b	4	1	1	0	1	1
Snodgrass, cf	4	0	1	0	6	0
Murray, rf	3	1	2	0	7	0
Merkle, 1b	3	1	2	1	4	1
Herzog, 3b	3	1	1	1	1	1
Meyers, c	3	1	2	0	6	0
Fletcher, ss	3	0	1	1	0	2
Marquard, p	3	0	0	0	0	2
Totals	30	5	11	3	27	7

Boston .... 0 2 0 0 0 0 0 0 0—2
New York .... 5 0 0 0 0 0 0 0 x—5

Boston	IP.	H.	R.	ER.	BB.	SO.
O'Brien (L)	1	6	5	3	0	1
Collins	7	5	0	0	0	1

New York	IP.	H.	R.	ER.	BB.	SO.
Marquard (W)	9	7	2	0	1	3

aDoubled for O'Brien in second. E—Yerkes, Cady, Devore, Marquard. DP—Boston 1, New York 1. LOB—Boston 5, New York 1. 2B—Engle, Merkle, Herzog. 3B—Meyers. SB—Speaker, Doyle, Herzog, Meyers. Balk—O'Brien. U—Klem (N.L.), Evans (A.L.), O'Loughlin (A.L.) and Rigler (N.L.). T—1:58. A—30,622.

Game 7

Tuesday, October 15, At Boston

New York	AB.	R.	H.	RBI.	PO.	A.
Devore, rf	4	2	1	0	3	1
Doyle, 2b	4	3	3	2	3	3
Snodgrass, cf	5	1	2	2	1	0
Murray, lf	4	0	0	0	1	0
Merkle, 1b	5	1	2	1	10	0
Herzog, 3b	4	2	1	0	0	2
Meyers, c	4	1	3	1	6	0
Wilson, c	1	0	1	0	2	0
Fletcher, ss	5	1	1	0	2	4
Tesreau, p	4	0	2	2	0	6
Totals	40	11	16	8	27	16

Boston	AB.	R.	H.	RBI.	PO.	A.
Hooper, rf	3	0	1	1	1	1
Yerkes, 2b	4	0	0	0	1	4
Speaker, cf	4	1	1	0	4	0
Lewis, lf	4	1	1	1	3	0
Gardner, 3b	4	1	1	1	2	0
Stahl, 1b	5	0	1	0	11	1
Wagner, ss	5	0	1	0	4	4
Cady, c	4	1	0	0	1	2
Wood, p	0	0	0	0	0	1
Hall, p	3	0	3	0	0	5
Totals	36	4	9	3	27	18

New York .... 6 1 0 0 0 2 1 0 1—11
Boston .... 0 1 0 0 0 0 2 1 0— 4

New York	IP.	H.	R.	ER.	BB.	SO.
Tesreau (W)	9	9	4	2	5	6

Boston	IP.	H.	R.	ER.	BB.	SO.
Wood (L)	1	7	6	4	0	0
Hall	8	9	5	3	5	1

E—Devore, Doyle 2, Merkle, Speaker, Gardner, Hall. DP—New York 1, Boston 1. LOB—New York 8, Boston 12. 2B—Snodgrass, Hall, Lewis. HR—Doyle, Gardner. SB—Devore 2, Doyle. SH—Murray. SF—Hooper. HBP—By Tesreau (Gardner). WP—Tesreau 2. U—Evans (A.L.), Klem (N.L.), O'Loughlin (A.L.) and Rigler (N.L.). T—2:21. A—32,694.

Game 8

Wednesday, October 16, At Boston

New York	AB.	R.	H.	RBI.	PO.	A.
Devore, rf	3	1	1	0	3	1
Doyle, 2b	5	0	0	0	1	5
Snodgrass, cf	4	0	1	0	4	1
Murray, lf	5	1	2	1	3	0
Merkle, 1b	5	0	1	1	10	0
Herzog, 3b	5	0	2	0	2	1
Meyers, c	3	0	0	0	4	1
Fletcher, ss	3	0	1	0	2	3
bMcCormick	1	0	0	0	0	0
Shafer, ss	0	0	0	0	0	0
Mathewson, p	4	0	1	0	0	3
Totals	38	2	9	2	29	15

Boston	AB.	R.	H.	RBI.	PO.	A.
Hooper, rf	5	0	0	0	3	0
Yerkes, 2b	4	1	1	0	0	3
Speaker, cf	4	0	2	1	2	0
Lewis, lf	4	0	0	0	1	0
Gardner, 3b	3	0	1	1	1	4
Stahl, 1b	4	1	2	0	15	0
Wagner, ss	3	0	1	0	3	5
Cady, c	4	0	0	0	5	3
Bedient, p	2	0	0	0	0	1
aHenriksen	1	0	1	1	0	0
Wood, p	0	0	0	0	0	2
cEngle	1	1	0	0	0	0
Totals	35	3	8	3	30	18

New York .... 0 0 1 0 0 0 0 0 0 1—2
Boston .... 0 0 0 0 0 0 1 0 0 2—3

Two out when winning run scored.

New York	IP.	H.	R.	ER.	BB.	SO.
Mathewson (L)	9⅔	8	3	1	5	4

Boston	IP.	H.	R.	ER.	BB.	SO.
Bedient	7	6	1	1	3	2
Wood (W)	3	3	1	1	1	2

aDoubled for Bedient in seventh. bFlied out for Fletcher in ninth. cReached second on error for Wood in tenth. E—Doyle, Snodgrass, Speaker, Gardner 2, Stahl, Wagner. LOB—New York 11, Boston 9. 2B—Murray 2, Herzog, Gardner, Stahl, Henriksen. SB—Devore. SH—Meyers. SF—Gardner. U—O'Loughlin (A.L.), Rigler (N.L.), Klem (N.L.) and Evans (A.L.). T—2:39. A—17,034.

COMPOSITE BATTING AVERAGES

Boston Red Sox

Player-Position	G.	AB.	R.	H.	2B.	3B.	HR.	RBI.	BA.
Henriksen, pr-ph	2	1	0	1	1	0	0	1	1.000
Hall, p	2	4	0	3	1	0	0	0	.750
Engle, ph	3	3	1	1	1	0	0	2	.333
Speaker, cf	8	30	4	9	1	2	0	2	.300
Hooper, rf	8	31	3	9	2	1	0	2	.290
Wood, p	4	7	1	2	0	0	0	1	.286
Stahl, 1b	8	32	3	9	2	0	0	2	.281
Yerkes, 2b	8	32	3	8	0	2	0	4	.250
Gardner, 3b	8	28	4	5	2	1	1	4	.179
Wagner, ss	8	30	1	5	1	0	0	0	.167
Lewis, lf	8	32	4	5	3	0	0	2	.156
Cady, c	7	22	1	3	0	0	0	1	.136
Carrigan, c	2	7	0	0	0	0	0	0	.000
Collins, p	2	5	0	0	0	0	0	0	.000
Bedient, p	4	6	0	0	0	0	0	0	.000
O'Brien, p	2	2	0	0	0	0	0	0	.000
Ball, ph	1	1	0	0	0	0	0	0	.000
Totals	8	273	25	60	14	6	1	21	.220

New York Giants

Player-Position	G.	AB.	R.	H.	2B.	3B.	HR.	RBI.	BA.
Wilson, c	2	1	0	1	0	0	0	0	1.000
Herzog, 3b	8	30	6	12	4	1	0	4	.400
Tesreau, p	3	8	0	3	0	0	0	2	.375
Meyers, c	8	28	2	10	0	1	0	3	.357
Murray, rf-lf	8	31	5	10	4	1	0	5	.323
Merkle, 1b	8	33	5	9	2	1	0	3	.273
McCormick, ph	5	4	0	1	0	0	0	1	.250
Devore, lf-rf	7	24	4	6	0	0	0	0	.250
Doyle, 2b	8	33	5	8	1	0	1	2	.242
Snod'ss, cf-lf-rf	8	33	2	7	2	0	0	2	.212
Fletcher, ss	8	28	1	5	1	0	0	3	.179
Mathewson, p	3	12	0	2	0	0	0	0	.167
Becker, pr-cf	2	4	1	0	0	0	0	0	.000
Crandall, p	1	1	0	0	0	0	0	0	.000
Shafer, pr-ss	3	0	0	0	0	0	0	0	.000
Marquard, p	2	4	0	0	0	0	0	0	.000
Ames, p	1	0	0	0	0	0	0	0	.000
Totals	8	274	31	74	14	4	1	25	.270

COMPOSITE PITCHING AVERAGES

Boston Red Sox

Pitcher	G.	IP.	H.	R.	ER.	BB.	SO.	W.	L.	ERA.
Bedient	4	18	10	2	1	7	7	1	0	0.50
Collins	2	14⅓	14	5	3	0	6	0	0	1.88
Hall	2	10⅔	11	6	4	9	1	0	0	3.38
Wood	4	22	27	11	9	3	21	3	1	3.68
O'Brien	2	9	12	7	5	3	4	0	2	5.00
Totals	8	74	74	31	22	22	39	4	3	2.68

New York Giants

Pitcher	G.	IP.	H.	R.	ER.	BB.	SO.	W.	L.	ERA.
Crandall	1	2	1	0	0	0	2	0	0	0.00
Marquard	2	18	14	3	1	2	9	2	0	0.50
Mathewson	3	28⅔	23	11	5	5	10	0	2	1.57
Tesreau	3	23	19	10	8	11	15	1	2	3.13
Ames	1	2	3	1	1	1	0	0	0	4.50
Totals	8	73⅔	60	25	15	19	36	3	4	1.83

1913 PHILADELPHIA ATHLETICS VS. NEW YORK GIANTS

Having undergone considerable mental anguish over their misfortunes in the 1911 and 1912 World Series, the New York Giants were hurting physically in the 1913 fall classic.

Fred Merkle was hobbled by a bad leg and was limited to 13 at-bats in the Series, while Fred Snodgrass, suffering from a severe charley horse, appeared in two games and made only three trips to the plate. And Chief Meyers went to the sidelines after suffering a finger fracture in practice preceding Game 2.

Giants Manager John McGraw, whose team had won the National League pennant by 12½ games, did have the services of pitching aces Rube Marquard, Christy Mathewson and Jeff Tesreau throughout the Series, which conceivably could have been enough to overcome Connie Mack's Philadelphia Athletics. Conceivably, yes; in fact, no.

The Athletics roughed up Marquard in the opener, shelling him for five runs and eight hits in five innings. Home Run Baker singled home a run in the fourth and launched a two-run homer in the fifth in support of Chief Bender, who yielded 11 hits while struggling to a 6-4 victory.

Mathewson, coming off his next-to-last 20-victory season in the majors (he posted a 25-11 record), was vintage Matty in Game 2. The old Bucknell University star, matched against former collegiate rival Eddie Plank (Gettysburg), broke a scoreless deadlock with a 10th-inning single and New York went on to a 3-0 victory. Mathewson permitted eight hits, and Plank gave up seven.

Bullet Joe Bush, a 20-year-old rookie who had won 14 games for Mack in 1913, shut down the Giants on five hits in Game 3 as

Frank (Home Run) Baker managed only one homer in the 1913 Series, but led the Philadelphia Athletics with a lusty .450 average.

Philadelphia battered Tesreau en route to an 8-2 triumph. The next day, catcher Wally Schang drove in three runs with two singles and helped Philadelphia to a 6-0 lead after five innings. Merkle then fueled a Giants comeback bid by poling a three-run homer in the seventh, but Bender and the A's held on for a 6-5 victory. The triumph was Bender's fourth straight in Series competition.

With the Athletics in control, three games to one, Plank and Mathewson went at it again in Game 5. This time, Plank was the master as he allowed only two hits—the first coming with one

out in the fifth—in a 3-1 decision. The Giants had been outmanned and outplayed, losing in the World Series for the third consecutive year.

Baker, whose homer in Game 1 was his third and last in Series play, led Philadelphia with a .450 batting average and seven runs batted in. Eddie Collins hit .421, while Schang contributed six RBIs and a .357 average.

Bender's conquests in Games 1 and 4 boosted his Series career victory total to six. Mathewson, pitching in what would be his final Series, wound up with a 5-5 lifetime mark in the fall classic—he was 4-0 at one point—after splitting two decisions in 1913.

Mathewson's Series slippage having mirrored the Giants' recent postseason problems, McGraw was fiercely determined to restore his club to fall-classic glory. But it would be another four years until McGraw's New Yorkers would take the field again for a World Series game.

Game 1

Tuesday, October 7, At New York

Philadelphia	AB.	R.	H.	RBI.	PO.	A.
E. Murphy, rf	4	0	1	0	2	0
Oldring, lf	4	0	1	0	2	0
Collins, 2b	3	3	3	0	4	6
Baker, 3b	4	1	3	3	1	3
McInnis, 1b	3	0	1	1	10	0
Strunk, cf	4	1	0	0	3	0
Barry, ss	4	1	1	0	1	3
Schang, c	4	0	1	2	4	1
Bender, p	4	0	0	0	0	2
Totals	34	6	11	6	27	15

New York	AB.	R.	H.	RBI.	PO.	A.
Shafer, cf	5	0	1	0	3	0
Doyle, 2b	4	1	2	2	2	2
Fletcher, ss	4	0	2	2	2	2
Burns, lf	4	0	1	0	3	0
Herzog, 3b	4	0	0	0	1	2
Murray, rf	4	0	2	0	1	0
Meyers, c	4	0	0	0	4	2
Merkle, 1b	4	2	2	0	11	0
Marquard, p	0	0	0	0	0	6
aMcCormick	1	1	1	0	0	0
Crandall, p	1	0	0	0	0	0
Tesreau, p	0	0	0	0	0	1
bMcLean	1	0	0	0	0	0
Totals	36	4	11	4	27	15

Philadelphia	0 0 0 3 2 0 0 1 0—6
New York	0 0 1 0 3 0 0 0 0—4

Philadelphia	IP.	H.	R.	ER.	BB.	SO.
Bender (W)	9	11	4	3	0	4

New York	IP.	H.	R.	ER.	BB.	SO.
Marquard (L)	5	8	5	5	1	1
Crandall	2*	3	1	1	0	1
Tesreau	2	0	0	0	1	1

*Pitched to three batters in eighth.

aSingled for Marquard in fifth. bPopped out for Tesreau in ninth. E—Barry. DP—Philadelphia 1. LOB—Philadelphia 4, New York 6. 2B—McInnis, Barry, Burns. 3B—Collins, Schang. HR—Baker. SB—Collins. SH—McInnis, Marquard. U—Klem (N.L.), Egan (A.L.), Rigler (N.L.) and Connolly (A.L.). T—2:06. A—36,291.

Game 2

Wednesday, October 8, At Philadelphia

New York	AB.	R.	H.	RBI.	PO.	A.
Herzog, 3b	5	1	0	0	1	4
Doyle, 2b	4	0	0	0	3	5
Fletcher, ss	5	0	2	2	1	3
Burns, lf	4	0	0	0	4	0
Shafer, cf	5	0	0	0	0	0
Murray, rf	4	0	0	0	0	0
McLean, c	4	0	2	0	5	1
bGrant	0	1	0	0	0	0
Wilson, c	0	0	0	0	1	0
Snodgrass, 1b	1	0	1	0	1	1
aWiltse, 1b	2	0	0	0	13	3
Mathewson, p	3	1	2	1	1	3
Totals	37	3	7	3	30	20

Philadelphia	AB.	R.	H.	RBI.	PO.	A.
E. Murphy, rf	5	0	0	0	5	0
Oldring, lf	5	0	1	0	4	0
Collins, 2b	4	0	1	0	2	2
Baker, 3b	5	0	2	0	0	0
McInnis, 1b	4	0	0	0	5	0
Strunk, cf	3	0	1	0	4	0
Barry, ss	4	0	1	0	2	1
Lapp, c	4	0	1	0	7	1
Plank, p	4	0	1	0	1	2
Totals	38	0	8	0	30	6

New York	0 0 0 0 0 0 0 0 0 3—3
Philadelphia	0 0 0 0 0 0 0 0 0 0—0

New York	IP.	H.	R.	ER.	BB.	SO.
Mathewson (W)	10	8	0	0	1	5

Philadelphia	IP.	H.	R.	ER.	BB.	SO.
Plank (L)	10	7	3	2	2	6

aRan for Snodgrass in third. bRan for McLean in tenth. E—Doyle 2, Collins, Baker. LOB—New York 8, Philadelphia 10. SH—Wiltse, Collins. HBP—By Plank (Doyle). U—Connolly (A.L.), Rigler (N.L.), Klem (N.L.) and Egan (A.L.). T—2:22. A—20,563.

Game 3

Thursday, October 9, At New York

Philadelphia	AB.	R.	H.	RBI.	PO.	A.
E. Murphy, rf	5	1	2	0	2	0
Oldring, lf	5	3	2	0	0	0
Collins, 2b	5	2	3	3	5	4
Baker, 3b	4	1	2	2	3	1
McInnis, 1b	4	0	0	0	9	0
Strunk, cf	4	0	0	0	1	0
Barry, ss	4	0	1	0	2	3
Schang, c	4	1	1	1	5	2
Bush, p	4	0	1	0	0	1
Totals	39	8	12	6	27	11

New York	AB.	R.	H.	RBI.	PO.	A.
Herzog, 3b	4	0	0	0	1	0
Doyle, 2b	4	0	1	0	5	1
Fletcher, ss	2	0	1	0	2	2
Burns, lf	4	0	0	0	3	0
Shafer, cf	3	1	1	0	2	0
Murray, rf	3	1	1	1	4	0
McLean, c	2	0	1	1	3	1
aCooper	0	0	0	0	0	0
Wilson, c	2	0	0	0	2	0
Merkle, 1b	2	0	0	0	3	0
bWiltse, 1b	0	0	0	0	2	0
Tesreau, p	2	0	0	0	0	0
Crandall, p	1	0	0	0	0	2
Totals	29	2	5	2	27	6

Philadelphia	3 2 0 0 0 0 2 1 0—8
New York	0 0 0 0 1 0 1 0 0—2

Philadelphia	IP.	H.	R.	ER.	BB.	SO.
Bush (W)	9	5	2	1	4	3

New York	IP.	H.	R.	ER.	BB.	SO.
Tesreau (L)	6⅓	11	7	6	0	3
Crandall	2⅔	1	1	1	0	1

aRan for McLean in fifth. bRan for Merkle in seventh. E—Schang, Fletcher. DP—Philadelphia 3, New York 1. LOB—Philadelphia 4, New York 5. 2B—Shafer. 3B—Collins. HR—Schang. SB—Oldring, Collins, Baker, Fletcher, Murray, Cooper. HBP—By Bush (Fletcher). U—Rigler (N.L.), Connolly (A.L.), Klem (N.L.) and Egan (A.L.). T—2:11. A—36,896.

Game 4

Friday, October 10, At Philadelphia

New York	AB.	R.	H.	RBI.	PO.	A.
Snodgrass, cf	2	0	0	0	2	0
Herzog, 3b	2	0	1	0	2	0
Doyle, 2b	4	0	0	0	2	4
Fletcher, ss	4	1	0	0	1	0
Burns, lf	4	2	2	1	2	0
Shafer, 3b-cf	4	0	1	1	1	0
Murray, rf	2	1	1	0	2	0
McLean, c	2	0	2	0	1	1
aCooper	0	0	0	0	0	0
Wilson, c	1	0	0	0	1	1
cCrandall	1	0	0	0	0	0
Merkle, 1b	4	1	1	3	10	1
Demaree, p	1	0	0	0	0	2
bMcCormick	1	0	0	0	0	0
Marquard, p	1	0	0	0	0	2
dGrant	1	0	0	0	0	0
Totals	34	5	8	5	24	11

Philadelphia	AB.	R.	H.	RBI.	PO.	A.
E. Murphy, rf	5	0	0	0	3	0
Oldring, lf	4	0	2	0	1	0
Collins, 2b	4	0	0	0	3	3
Baker, 3b	4	0	0	0	2	0
McInnis, 1b	4	1	1	0	7	0
Strunk, cf	2	2	1	0	3	0
Barry, ss	4	2	3	2	2	2
Schang, c	2	1	2	3	6	1
Bender, p	4	0	0	1	0	3
Totals	33	6	9	6	27	9

New York	0 0 0 0 0 0 3 2 0—5
Philadelphia	0 1 0 3 2 0 0 0 x—6

New York	IP.	H.	R.	ER.	BB.	SO.
Demaree (L)	4	7	4	2	1	0
Marquard	4	2	2	2	2	2

Philadelphia	IP.	H.	R.	ER.	BB.	SO.
Bender (W)	9	8	5	5	1	5

aRan for McLean in fifth. bFlied out for Demaree in fifth. cGrounded out for Wilson in ninth. dFouled out for Marquard in ninth. E—Merkle 2. LOB—New York 4, Philadelphia 7. 2B—Burns, Barry 2. 3B—Shafer, Oldring. HR—Merkle. SB—Burns, Murray, Collins. SH—Strunk. HBP—By Bender (Murray). PB—McLean. U—Egan (A.L.), Klem (N.L.), Connolly (A.L.) and Rigler (N.L.). T—2:09. A—20,568.

Game 5

Saturday, October 11, At New York

Philadelphia	AB.	R.	H.	RBI.	PO.	A.
E. Murphy, rf	3	1	2	0	3	0
Oldring, lf	4	2	0	0	3	0
Collins, 2b	3	0	1	0	2	3
Baker, 3b	3	0	2	2	0	2
McInnis, 1b	2	0	0	1	14	0
Strunk, cf	4	0	0	0	2	0
Barry, ss	4	0	0	0	2	7
Schang, c	4	0	1	0	1	0
Plank, p	3	0	0	0	0	1
Totals	30	3	6	3	27	13

New York	AB.	R.	H.	RBI.	PO.	A.
Herzog, 3b	4	0	0	0	1	2
Doyle, 2b	4	0	0	0	1	7
Fletcher, ss	3	0	0	0	2	3
Burns, lf	3	0	0	0	2	0
Shafer, cf	2	1	0	0	2	0
Murray, rf	3	0	0	0	2	0
McLean, c	3	0	1	1	3	1
Merkle, 1b	3	0	0	0	14	0
Mathewson, p	2	0	1	0	0	2
aCrandall	1	0	0	0	0	0
Totals	28	1	2	1	27	15

Philadelphia	1 0 2 0 0 0 0 0 0—3
New York	0 0 0 0 1 0 0 0 0—1

Philadelphia	IP.	H.	R.	ER.	BB.	SO.
Plank (W)	9	2	1	0	1	1

New York	IP.	H.	R.	ER.	BB.	SO.
Mathewson (L)	9	6	3	2	1	2

aGrounded out for Mathewson in ninth. E—Plank, Doyle, Burns. DP—Philadelphia 2. LOB—Philadelphia 5, New York 1. SH—Collins, McInnis. SF—Baker, McInnis. U—Klem (N.L.), Egan (A.L.), Rigler (N.L.) and Connolly (A.L.). T—1:39. A—36,632.

COMPOSITE BATTING AVERAGES

Philadelphia Athletics

Player-Position	G.	AB.	R.	H.	2B.	3B.	HR.	RBI.	BA.
Baker, 3b	5	20	2	9	0	0	1	7	.450
Collins, 2b	5	19	5	8	0	2	0	3	.421
Schang, c	4	14	2	5	0	1	1	6	.357
Barry, ss	5	20	3	6	3	0	0	2	.300
Oldring, lf	5	22	5	6	0	1	0	1	.273
Lapp, c	1	4	0	1	0	0	0	0	.250
Bush, p	1	4	0	1	0	0	0	0	.250
E. Murphy, rf	5	22	2	5	0	0	0	0	.227
Plank, p	2	7	0	1	0	0	0	0	.143
McInnis, 1b	5	17	1	2	1	0	0	2	.118
Strunk, cf	5	17	3	2	0	0	0	0	.118
Bender, p	2	8	0	0	0	0	0	1	.000
Totals	5	174	23	46	4	4	2	23	.264

New York Giants

Player-Position	G.	AB.	R.	H.	2B.	3B.	HR.	RBI.	BA.
Mathewson, p	2	5	1	3	0	0	0	1	.600
McCormick, ph	2	2	1	1	0	0	0	0	.500
McLean, ph-c	5	12	0	6	0	0	0	2	.500
Snodgrass, 1b-cf	2	3	0	1	0	0	0	0	.333
Fletcher, ss	5	18	1	5	0	0	0	4	.278
Murray, rf	5	16	2	4	0	0	0	1	.250
Merkle, 1b	4	13	3	3	0	0	1	3	.231
Shafer, cf-3b	5	19	2	3	1	1	0	1	.158
Burns, lf	5	19	2	3	2	0	0	1	.158
Doyle, 2b	5	20	1	3	0	0	0	2	.150
Herzog, 3b	5	19	1	1	0	0	0	0	.053
Meyers, c	1	4	0	0	0	0	0	0	.000
Marquard, p	2	1	0	0	0	0	0	0	.000
Crandall, p-ph	4	4	0	0	0	0	0	0	.000
Tesreau, p	2	2	0	0	0	0	0	0	.000
Grant, pr-ph	2	1	1	0	0	0	0	0	.000
Wilson, c	3	3	0	0	0	0	0	0	.000
Wiltse, pr-1b	2	2	0	0	0	0	0	0	.000
Cooper, pr	2	0	0	0	0	0	0	0	.000
Demaree, p	1	1	0	0	0	0	0	0	.000
Totals	5	164	15	33	3	1	1	15	.201

COMPOSITE PITCHING AVERAGES

Philadelphia Athletics

Pitcher	G.	IP.	H.	R.	ER.	BB.	SO.	W.	L.	ERA.
Plank	2	19	9	4	2	3	7	1	1	0.95
Bush	1	9	5	2	1	4	3	1	0	1.00
Bender	2	18	19	9	8	1	9	2	0	4.00
Totals	5	46	33	15	11	8	19	4	1	2.15

New York Giants

Pitcher	G.	IP.	H.	R.	ER.	BB.	SO.	W.	L.	ERA.
Mathewson	2	19	14	3	2	2	7	1	1	0.95
Crandall	2	4⅔	4	2	2	0	2	0	0	3.86
Demaree	1	4	7	4	2	1	0	0	1	4.50
Tesreau	2	8⅓	11	7	6	1	4	0	1	6.48
Marquard	2	9	10	7	7	3	3	0	1	7.00
Totals	5	45	46	23	19	7	16	1	4	3.80

1914
BOSTON BRAVES
VS.
PHILADELPHIA ATHLETICS

Make no mistake about it, the Boston Braves had pulled off a miracle during the 1914 season. In mid-July, Manager George Stallings' team was in last place in the National League. By season's end, the Braves not only had captured the N.L. pennant but had won the flag by *10½* games.

Miracle Braves, indeed.

However, most baseball people thought the miracle would cease once the Braves went head-to-head in the World Series against the Philadelphia Athletics, winners of three of the last four fall classics. Connie Mack's American League champions boasted a .344 hitter in Eddie Collins, a .319 batsman in Home Run Baker and a .314 producer in Stuffy McInnis, plus seven pitchers who won 10 or more games.

Dick Rudolph, a 27-game winner for the Braves, was chosen to start Game 1 of the Series against Chief Bender, whose .850 winning percentage (17 victories in 20 decisions) had led the majors in 1914. Rudolph spun a five-hitter and batterymate Hank Gowdy singled, doubled and tripled. Boston prevailed, 7-1.

The next day, Stallings called on his other ace, Bill James, who had won 26 games. Connie Mack countered with 39-year-old Eddie Plank. After eight innings, the Braves had no runs and five hits and the Athletics no runs and two hits.

In the top of the ninth, Boston's Charlie Deal hit a one-out double, stole third base and scored on a two-out single by Les Mann. In the last half of the inning, James walked two batters but got out of the jam by inducing Eddie Murphy to hit into a game-ending double play. James' two-hit, 1-0 victory gave Boston a Series lead of two games to none, and now

Four of Boston's 1914 miracle workers were (left to right) Hank Gowdy, 27-game winner Dick Rudolph, George (Lefty) Tyler and Joe Connolly.

the scene would shift to the Braves' home city. Their home *city*, not home ball park. The National Leaguers' home field was the South End Grounds, but the Braves opted to play their Series home games at the Boston Red Sox's Fenway Park, deemed a more attractive facility.

Game 3 was a wild one, the A's and Braves being tied, 2-2, through nine innings before Baker apparently settled matters with a two-run single in the 10th off Braves starter Lefty Tyler. But the Braves, still not out of miracles, struck for two runs in the bottom of the 10th when Gowdy led off with a home run and Joe Connolly produced a run-scoring

fly ball later in the inning.

James then took over for Tyler, who had retired for a pinch-hitter, and shut out Philadelphia in the next two innings. In the last of the 12th, Gowdy lashed a double off Bullet Joe Bush (who pitched all the way for the A's) and gave way to a pinch-runner, Mann. After an intentional walk to pinch-hitter Larry Gilbert, Herbie Moran followed with a bunt. Bush grabbed the ball and threw to third baseman Baker in an attempt to force Mann, but Bush's throw sailed past Baker. Mann darted home with the winning run. Braves 5, A's 4. Braves three victories, A's zero.

Having failed to win with

Bender, Plank and Bush, Mack turned to second-year major leaguer Bob Shawkey in an effort to get his team back into the Series —or at least to avoid the humiliation of a sweep. Shawkey held Boston scoreless for three innings, then permitted a fourth-inning run. The 23-year-old righthander helped his own cause with a game-tying double in the top of the fifth, only to surrender a two-run single to Johnny Evers in the bottom of the inning. Rudolph, who had pitched masterfully in Game 1, made the runs stand up and the Braves were 3-1 winners —and World Series champions.

Miracle Braves, indeed.

Gowdy, a .243 hitter during the regular season, performed miraculously in the Series. He slugged three doubles, a triple and a home run against A's pitching and batted .545. Evers hit .438. Rudolph and James, after accounting for 53 of the Braves' 94 regular-season victories, registered all four of Boston's Series triumphs.

No A's regular batted above .250 in the Series, and Philadelphia posted a .172 team hitting mark. No wonder Philadelphia had become the first team in Series history to be eliminated in four games (the 1907 Tigers also went winless, but Detroit managed to play a tie contest against the Chicago Cubs and thereby extended play to five games).

Stunned by his team's vanquishing, Mack soon began a dismantling of the Athletics. Collins was traded over the winter, Baker sat out the 1915 season in a dispute with Mack before eventually being sold to the New York Yankees and Plank and Bender went off to the Federal League (with whom they already had pledged allegiance at the time of the '14 Series). And by the middle of 1915, Barry, Murphy and Shawkey also had been traded or sold.

Game 1

Friday, October 9, At Philadelphia

Boston	AB.	R.	H.	RBI.	PO.	A.
Moran, rf	5	0	0	0	0	0
Evers, 2b	4	1	1	0	2	2
Connolly, lf	3	1	1	0	4	0
Whitted, cf	3	2	1	2	1	0
Schmidt, 1b	4	1	2	1	11	0
Gowdy, c	3	2	3	1	9	1
Maranville, ss	4	0	2	2	2	3
Deal, 3b	4	0	0	0	1	2
Rudolph, p	4	0	1	0	0	3
Totals	34	7	11	6	27	14

Philadelphia	AB.	R.	H.	RBI.	PO.	A.
Murphy, rf	4	0	1	0	0	0
Oldring, lf	3	0	0	0	2	0
Collins, 2b	3	0	0	0	2	2
Baker, 3b	4	0	1	0	3	4
McInnis, 1b	2	1	0	0	10	1
Strunk, cf	4	0	2	0	0	0
Barry, ss	4	0	0	0	3	3
Schang, c	2	0	0	0	3	0
Lapp, c	1	0	0	0	2	1
Bender, p	2	0	0	0	1	3
Wyckoff, p	1	0	1	0	1	0
Totals	30	1	5	0	27	14

Boston..................0 2 0 0 1 3 0 1 0—7
Philadelphia.........0 1 0 0 0 0 0 0 0—1

Boston	IP.	H.	R.	ER.	BB.	SO.
Rudolph (W)	9	5	1	0	3	8

Philadelphia	IP.	H.	R.	ER.	BB.	SO.
Bender (L)	5⅓	8	6	6	2	3
Wyckoff	3⅔	3	1	1	1	2

E—Moran, Evers. DP—Boston 1, Philadelphia 4. LOB—Boston 3, Philadelphia 6. 2B—Gowdy, Baker, Wyckoff. 3B—Gowdy, Whitted. SB—Moran, Schmidt, Gowdy. SH—Oldring. U—Dinneen (A.L.), Klem (N.L.), Byron (N.L.) and Hildebrand (A.L.). T—1:58. A—20,562.

Game 2

Saturday, October 10, At Philadelphia

Boston	AB.	R.	H.	RBI.	PO.	A.
Mann, rf	5	0	2	1	0	0
Evers, 2b	4	0	1	0	2	3
Cather, lf	5	0	0	0	2	0
Whitted, cf	3	0	0	0	1	0
Schmidt, 1b	4	0	1	0	12	1
Gowdy, c	2	0	0	0	8	1
Maranville, ss	2	0	1	0	2	4
Deal, 3b	4	1	1	0	2	2
James, p	4	0	0	0	0	3
Totals	33	1	7	1	27	14

Philadelphia	AB.	R.	H.	RBI.	PO.	A.
Murphy, rf	3	0	0	0	2	0
Oldring, lf	3	0	0	0	1	0
Collins, 2b	3	0	1	0	5	2
Baker, 3b	3	0	0	0	2	3
McInnis, 1b	3	0	0	0	7	0
Strunk, cf	3	0	0	0	4	0
Barry, ss	2	0	0	0	2	6
Schang, c	3	0	1	0	5	2
Plank, p	2	0	0	0	0	1
aWalsh	0	0	0	0	0	0
Totals	25	0	2	0	27	14

Boston..................0 0 0 0 0 0 0 0 1—1
Philadelphia.........0 0 0 0 0 0 0 0 0—0

Boston	IP.	H.	R.	ER.	BB.	SO.
James (W)	9	2	0	0	3	8

Philadelphia	IP.	H.	R.	ER.	BB.	SO.
Plank (L)	9	7	1	1	4	6

aWalked for Plank in ninth. E—Maranville, McInnis. DP—Boston 1. LOB—Boston 11, Philadelphia 1. 2B—Schang, Deal. SB—Deal 2, Barry. SH—Maranville. HBP—By Plank (Maranville). PB—Schang. U—Hildebrand (A.L.), Byron (N.L.), Klem (N.L.) and Dinneen (A.L.). T—1:56. A—20,562.

Game 3

Monday, October 12, At Boston

Philadelphia	AB.	R.	H.	RBI.	PO.	A.
Murphy, rf	5	2	2	0	2	0
Oldring, lf	5	0	0	0	1	0
Collins, 2b	4	0	1	1	1	4
Baker, 3b	5	0	2	2	4	4
McInnis, 1b	5	1	1	0	18	0
Walsh, cf	4	0	1	1	1	0
Barry, ss	5	0	0	0	0	7
Schang, c	4	1	1	0	6	1
Bush, p	5	0	0	0	0	5
Totals	42	4	8	4	33	21

Boston	AB.	R.	H.	RBI.	PO.	A.
Moran, rf	4	1	0	0	2	0
Evers, 2b	5	0	3	0	3	5
Connolly, lf	4	0	0	1	1	0
Whitted, cf	5	0	0	0	2	0
Schmidt, 1b	5	1	1	0	17	1
Deal, 3b	5	0	1	0	2	3
Maranville, ss	4	1	1	1	2	3
Gowdy, c	4	1	3	2	6	0
cMann	0	1	0	0	0	0
Tyler, p	3	0	0	0	1	5
aDevore	1	0	0	0	0	0
James, p	0	0	0	0	0	2
bGilbert	0	0	0	0	0	0
Totals	40	5	9	4	36	19

Philadelphia........1 0 0 1 0 0 0 0 0 2 0 0—4
Boston..................0 1 0 1 0 0 0 0 0 2 0 1—5
None out when winning run scored.

Philadelphia	IP.	H.	R.	ER.	BB.	SO.
Bush (L)	11	9	5	4	4	4

Boston	IP.	H.	R.	ER.	BB.	SO.
Tyler	10	8	4	4	3	4
James (W)	2	0	0	0	3	1

aStruck out for Tyler in tenth. bWalked for James in twelfth. cRan for Gowdy in twelfth. E—Schang, Bush, Connolly. DP—Boston 1. LOB—Philadelphia 10, Boston 8. 2B—Murphy 2, Gowdy 2, McInnis, Deal, Baker. HR—Gowdy. SB—Collins, Evers, Maranville 2. SH—Oldring, Moran. SF—Collins, Connolly. U—Klem (N.L.), Dinneen (A.L.), Byron (N.L.) and Hildebrand (A.L.). T—3:06. A—35,520.

Game 4

Tuesday, October 13, At Boston

Philadelphia	AB.	R.	H.	RBI.	PO.	A.
Murphy, rf	4	0	0	0	0	0
Oldring, lf	4	0	1	0	3	0
Collins, 2b	4	0	1	0	1	4
Baker, 3b	4	0	1	0	1	4
McInnis, 1b	4	0	1	0	15	0
Walsh, cf	2	0	1	0	1	0
Barry, ss	3	1	1	0	0	5
Schang, c	3	0	0	0	3	0
Shawkey, p	2	0	1	1	0	3
Pennock, p	1	0	0	0	0	1
Totals	31	1	7	1	24	18

Boston	AB.	R.	H.	RBI.	PO.	A.
Moran, rf	4	1	1	0	0	0
Evers, 2b	3	1	2	3	6	3
Connolly, lf	2	0	0	0	1	0
aMann, lf	2	0	0	0	1	0
Whitted, cf	3	0	2	0	1	0
Schmidt, 1b	4	0	1	1	12	0
Gowdy, c	2	0	0	0	8	2
Maranville, ss	3	0	0	0	1	3
Deal, 3b	3	0	0	0	1	4
Rudolph, p	2	1	1	0	0	4
Totals	28	3	6	3	27	16

Philadelphia........0 0 0 0 1 0 0 0 0—1
Boston..................0 0 0 1 2 0 0 0 x—3

Philadelphia	IP.	H.	R.	ER.	BB.	SO.
Shawkey (L)	5	4	3	3	2	0
Pennock	3	2	0	0	2	3

Boston	IP.	H.	R.	ER.	BB.	SO.
Rudolph (W)	9	7	1	1	1	7

aLined out for Connolly in sixth. DP—Boston 1. LOB—Philadelphia 4, Boston 5. 2B—Walsh, Shawkey, Moran. SB—Whitted. WP—Rudolph. PB—Schang. U—Byron (N.L.), Hildebrand (A.L.), Klem (N.L.) and Dinneen (A.L.). T—1:49. A—34,365.

COMPOSITE BATTING AVERAGES
Boston Braves

Player-Position	G.	AB.	R.	H.	2B.	3B.	HR.	RBI.	BA.
Gowdy, c	4	11	2	6	3	1	1	3	.545
Evers, 2b	4	16	2	7	0	0	0	2	.438
Rudolph, p	2	6	1	2	0	0	0	0	.333
Maranville, ss	4	13	1	4	0	0	0	3	.308
Schmidt, 1b	4	17	2	5	0	0	0	2	.294
Mann, rf-pr-ph	3	7	1	2	0	0	0	1	.286
Whitted, cf	4	14	2	3	0	1	0	2	.214
Deal, 3b	4	16	2	2	2	0	0	0	.125
Connolly, lf	3	9	1	1	0	0	0	1	.111
Moran, rf	3	13	2	1	1	0	0	0	.077
Cather, lf	1	5	0	0	0	0	0	0	.000
James, p	2	4	0	0	0	0	0	0	.000
Tyler, p	1	3	0	0	0	0	0	0	.000
Devore, ph	1	1	0	0	0	0	0	0	.000
Gilbert, ph	1	0	0	0	0	0	0	0	.000
Totals	4	135	16	33	6	2	1	14	.244

Philadelphia Athletics

Player-Position	G.	AB.	R.	H.	2B.	3B.	HR.	RBI.	BA.
Wyckoff, p	1	1	0	1	0	0	0	0	1.000
Shawkey, p	1	2	0	1	1	0	0	1	.500
Walsh, ph-cf	3	6	0	2	1	0	0	1	.333
Strunk, cf	2	7	0	2	0	0	0	0	.286
Baker, 3b	4	16	0	4	2	0	0	2	.250
Collins, 2b	4	14	0	3	0	0	0	1	.214
Murphy, rf	4	16	2	3	2	0	0	0	.188
Schang, c	4	12	1	2	1	0	0	0	.167
McInnis, 1b	4	14	2	2	1	0	0	0	.143
Barry, ss	4	14	1	1	0	0	0	0	.071
Oldring, lf	4	15	0	1	0	0	0	0	.067
Lapp, c	1	1	0	0	0	0	0	0	.000
Bender, p	1	2	0	0	0	0	0	0	.000
Plank, p	1	2	0	0	0	0	0	0	.000
Pennock, p	1	1	0	0	0	0	0	0	.000
Bush, p	1	5	0	0	0	0	0	0	.000
Totals	4	128	6	22	9	0	0	5	.172

COMPOSITE PITCHING AVERAGES
Boston Braves

Pitcher	G.	IP.	H.	R.	ER.	BB.	SO.	W.	L.	ERA.
James	2	11	2	0	0	6	9	2	0	0.00
Rudolph	2	18	12	2	1	4	15	2	0	0.50
Tyler	1	10	8	4	4	3	4	0	0	3.60
Totals	4	39	22	6	5	13	28	4	0	1.15

Philadelphia Athletics

Pitcher	G.	IP.	H.	R.	ER.	BB.	SO.	W.	L.	ERA.
Pennock	1	3	2	0	0	2	3	0	0	0.00
Plank	1	9	7	1	1	4	6	0	1	1.00
Wyckoff	1	3⅔	3	1	1	1	2	0	0	2.45
Bush	1	11	9	5	4	4	4	0	1	3.27
Shawkey	1	5	4	3	3	2	0	0	1	5.40
Bender	1	5⅓	8	6	6	2	3	0	1	10.13
Totals	4	37	33	16	15	15	18	0	4	3.65

1915
BOSTON RED SOX
VS.
PHILADELPHIA PHILLIES

Boston and Philadelphia, World Series opponents in 1914, met again in the 1915 fall classic and, once more, Boston's contingent made quick work of its Philadelphia counterpart.

This time, though, the competing teams were the Red Sox and Phillies, not the Braves and Athletics. And, in another strange twist, the Red Sox used the Braves' ball park in the 1915 fall classic whereas the Braves had "borrowed" the Red Sox's field a year earlier.

Five pitchers, including 20-year-old lefthander Babe Ruth, won 14 or more games in 1915 for Manager Bill Carrigan's Red Sox, whose 101 victories (against 50 losses) were just enough to stave off the Detroit Tigers (100-54) in the American League pennant race. The Phillies, meanwhile, rode the pitching of Grover Cleveland Alexander and the slugging of outfielder Gavvy Cravath to their first National League flag. Alexander tossed four one-hitters and won 31 games in 1915 (the first of three straight years in which he would reach the 30-victory mark), while Cravath slammed 24 home runs—a major league high thus far in the century—and drove in 115 runs.

Alexander opposed Ernie Shore in the Series opener, and the Phillies' Ol' Pete emerged as a 3-1 winner. With one on and one out in the ninth, Alexander had to dispose of Boston's leading home run hitter, pitcher Ruth, who despite his 18 regular-season victories was limited to this one appearance in the 1915 Series (as a pinch-hitter for Shore). Ruth, who had hit four homers in this dead-ball-era season, grounded out and Alexander then got Harry Hooper on a game-ending pop fly.

Philadelphia Phillies Manager Pat Moran presents his lineup card to umpire Bill Klem prior to Game 1 of the 1915 World Series.

Boston's Rube Foster was the story in Game 2. Not only did Foster shackle the Phillies on three hits at tiny Baker Bowl in Philadelphia, but he also drove in the winning run with a ninth-inning single. Erskine Mayer was the tough-luck 2-1 loser in a game witnessed by President Woodrow Wilson, whose appearance was the first by a Chief Executive at a Series contest.

With the Series deadlocked at a game apiece, the action moved to new Braves Field, whose seating capacity outstripped that of Fenway Park and thus proved enticing for the Red Sox. And, with a crowd of more than 42,000 looking on, lefthander Hubert (Dutch) Leonard was dazzling in a confrontation with Alexander. Leonard retired the last 20 Phillies batters he faced and notched a 2-1 victory when Duffy Lewis singled home Hooper in the ninth.

Manager Pat Moran's Phillies suffered their third consecutive 2-

1 setback the next day when Shore set down the National Leaguers on seven hits.

First baseman Fred Luderus and reliever Eppa Rixey kept Philadelphia in the hunt in Game 5, but to no avail. Luderus whacked a two-run double in the first inning and a bases-empty home run in the fourth, helping the Phils to a 4-2 lead; Rixey, pitching in relief of Mayer, took over with one out in the third inning and shut out the Red Sox through the seventh. In the eighth, however, Lewis hit a game-tying, two-run homer. Then, in the ninth, Hooper smashed his second homer of the game and, with Foster retiring the Phils in order in the bottom half of the inning, Boston pulled out a Series-clinching 5-4 victory.

As for those other Boston and Philadelphia teams, the Braves ran out of miracles and finished second in the N.L. in 1915 and the Athletics ran out of players and wound up last in the A.L. After their breakup by Connie Mack following a dismal showing in the 1914 World Series, the A's fielded a team that ended up 58½ games behind the Red Sox.

Game 1

Friday, October 8, At Philadelphia

Boston	AB.	R.	H.	RBI.	PO.	A.
Hooper, rf	5	0	1	0	0	0
Scott, ss	3	0	1	0	2	2
Speaker, cf	2	1	0	0	1	0
Hoblitzell, 1b	4	0	1	0	12	0
Lewis, lf	4	0	2	1	2	0
Gardner, 3b	3	0	1	0	0	1
Barry, 2b	4	0	1	0	4	4
Cady, c	2	0	0	0	3	2
aHenriksen	1	0	0	0	0	0
Shore, p	3	0	1	0	0	4
bRuth	1	0	0	0	0	0
Totals	32	1	8	1	24	13

Philadelphia	AB.	R.	H.	RBI.	PO.	A.
Stock, 3b	3	1	0	0	0	2
Bancroft, ss	4	1	1	0	4	1
Paskert, cf	3	1	1	0	1	0
Cravath, rf	2	0	0	1	1	0
Luderus, 1b	4	0	1	1	10	0
Whitted, lf	2	0	1	1	3	0
Niehoff, 2b	3	0	0	0	1	4
Burns, c	3	0	0	0	7	0
Alexander, p	3	0	1	0	0	5
Totals	27	3	5	3	27	12

Boston	0 0 0	0 0 0	0 1 0	—1
Philadelphia	0 0 0	1 0 0	0 2 x	—3

Boston	IP.	H.	R.	ER.	BB.	SO.
Shore (L)	8	5	3	3	4	2

Philadelphia	IP.	H.	R.	ER.	BB.	SO.
Alexander (W)	9	8	1	1	2	6

aReached first on error for Cady in ninth. bGrounded out for Shore in ninth. E—Shore, Luderus. LOB—Boston 9, Philadelphia 5. SB—Whitted, Hoblitzell. SH—Scott, Gardner, Cady, Cravath. U—Klem (N.L.), O'Loughlin (A.L.), Evans (A.L.) and Rigler (N.L.). T—1:58. A—19,343.

Game 2

Saturday, October 9, At Philadelphia

Boston	AB.	R.	H.	RBI.	PO.	A.
Hooper, rf	3	1	1	0	2	0
Scott, ss	3	0	0	0	0	3
aHenriksen	1	0	0	0	0	0
Cady, c	0	0	0	0	3	0
Speaker, cf	4	0	1	0	3	0
Hoblitzell, 1b	4	0	1	0	8	3
Lewis, lf	4	0	1	0	1	0
Gardner, 3b	4	1	2	0	0	2
Barry, 2b	4	0	1	0	0	3
Thomas, c	3	0	0	0	6	0
Janvrin, ss	1	0	0	0	1	0
Foster, p	4	0	3	1	3	0
Totals	35	2	10	1	27	11

Philadelphia	AB.	R.	H.	RBI.	PO.	A.
Stock, 3b	4	0	0	0	0	2
Bancroft, ss	4	0	1	0	2	2
Paskert, cf	4	0	0	0	1	0
Cravath, rf	3	1	1	0	1	0
Luderus, 1b	3	0	1	1	9	1
Whitted, lf	3	0	0	0	3	0
Niehoff, 2b	3	0	0	0	4	1
Burns, c	3	0	0	0	6	3
Mayer, p	3	0	0	0	1	3
Totals	30	1	3	1	27	12

Boston	1 0 0	0 0 0	0 0 1	—2
Philadelphia	0 0 0	0 1 0	0 0 0	—1

Boston	IP.	H.	R.	ER.	BB.	SO.
Foster (W)	9	3	1	1	0	8

Philadelphia	IP.	H.	R.	ER.	BB.	SO.
Mayer (L)	9	10	2	1	2	7

aPopped out for Scott in seventh. E—Burns. LOB—Boston 8, Philadelphia 2. 2B—Foster, Cravath, Luderus. U—Rigler (N.L.), Evans (A.L.), O'Loughlin (A.L.) and Klem (N.L.). T—2:05. A—20,306.

Game 3

Monday, October 11, At Boston

Philadelphia	AB.	R.	H.	RBI.	PO.	A.
Stock, 3b	3	0	1	0	1	0
Bancroft, ss	3	0	1	1	4	1
Paskert, cf	4	0	0	0	7	0
Cravath, rf	4	0	0	0	2	0
Luderus, 1b	3	0	0	0	3	1
Whitted, lf	3	0	0	0	2	0
Niehoff, 2b	3	0	0	0	0	2
Burns, c	3	1	1	0	5	2
Alexander, p	2	0	0	0	2	0
Totals	28	1	3	1	26	6

Boston	AB.	R.	H.	RBI.	PO.	A.
Hooper, rf	4	1	1	0	2	0
Scott, ss	3	0	0	0	2	1
Speaker, cf	3	1	2	0	2	0
Hoblitzell, 1b	3	0	0	1	9	0
Lewis, lf	4	0	3	1	1	0
Gardner, 3b	3	0	0	0	1	6
Barry, 2b	3	0	0	0	2	1
Carrigan, c	2	0	0	0	8	0
Leonard, p	3	0	0	0	0	2
Totals	28	2	6	2	27	10

Philadelphia	0 0 1	0 0 0	0 0 0	—1
Boston	0 0 0	1 0 0	0 0 1	—2

Two out when winning run scored.

Philadelphia	IP.	H.	R.	ER.	BB.	SO.
Alexander (L)	9	6	2	2	2	4

Boston	IP.	H.	R.	ER.	BB.	SO.
Leonard (W)	9	3	1	1	0	6

E—Hoblitzell. DP—Philadelphia 1. LOB—Philadelphia 3, Boston 4. 2B —Stock. 3B—Speaker. SH—Bancroft, Alexander, Stock, Scott. SF—Hoblitzell. U—O'Loughlin (A.L.), Klem (N.L.), Rigler (N.L.) and Evans (A.L.). T—1:48. A—42,300.

Game 4

Tuesday, October 12, At Boston

Philadelphia	AB.	R.	H.	RBI.	PO.	A.
Stock, 3b	4	0	1	0	0	3
Bancroft, ss	2	0	0	0	0	0
Paskert, cf	4	0	0	0	5	0
Cravath, rf	4	1	1	0	0	0
Luderus, 1b	4	0	3	1	5	0
aDugey	0	0	0	0	0	0
Becker, lf	0	0	0	0	0	0
Whitted, lf-1b	3	0	0	0	4	0
Niehoff, 2b	3	0	0	0	3	1
Burns, c	3	0	1	0	7	2
Chalmers, p	3	0	1	0	0	4
bByrne	1	0	0	0	0	0
Totals	31	1	7	1	24	10

Boston	AB.	R.	H.	RBI.	PO.	A.
Hooper, rf	4	0	1	1	2	0
Scott, ss	4	0	0	0	2	4
Speaker, cf	3	0	1	0	1	0
Hoblitzell, 1b	4	1	3	0	5	2
Lewis, lf	2	0	1	1	6	1
Gardner, 3b	4	0	0	0	2	2
Barry, 2b	2	1	0	0	3	1
Cady, c	3	0	2	0	6	1
Shore, p	2	0	0	0	0	1
Totals	28	2	8	2	27	12

Philadelphia	0 0 0	0 0 0	0 1 0	—1
Boston	0 0 1	0 0 1	0 0 x	—2

Philadelphia	IP.	H.	R.	ER.	BB.	SO.
Chalmers (L)	8	8	2	2	3	6

Boston	IP.	H.	R.	ER.	BB.	SO.
Shore (W)	9	7	1	1	4	4

aRan for Luderus in eighth. bFlied out for Chalmers in ninth. E—Barry. DP—Philadelphia 1, Boston 1. LOB—Philadelphia 8, Boston 7. 2B—Lewis. 3B—Cravath. SB—Dugey. SH —Whitted, Shore, Lewis. U—Evans (A.L.), Rigler (N.L.), O'Loughlin (A.L.) and Klem (N.L.). T—2:05. A—41,096.

Game 5

Wednesday, October 13, At Philadelphia

Boston	AB.	R.	H.	RBI.	PO.	A.
Hooper, rf	4	2	3	2	2	0
Scott, ss	5	0	0	0	2	2
Speaker, cf	5	0	1	0	3	0
Hoblitzell, 1b	1	0	0	0	1	0
aGainor, 1b	3	1	1	0	9	0
Lewis, lf	4	1	1	2	0	0
Gardner, 3b	3	1	1	0	2	3
Barry, 2b	4	0	1	1	1	0
Thomas, c	2	0	1	0	4	3
Cady, c	1	0	0	0	2	1
Foster, p	4	0	1	0	1	3
Totals	36	5	10	5	27	12

Philadelphia	AB.	R.	H.	RBI.	PO.	A.
Stock, 3b	3	0	0	0	1	1
Bancroft, ss	4	1	2	0	3	6
Paskert, cf	4	1	2	0	3	0
Cravath, rf	3	0	0	0	1	0
bDugey	0	0	0	0	0	0
Becker, rf	0	0	0	0	0	0
Luderus, 1b	2	1	2	3	13	2
Whitted, lf	4	0	0	0	2	0
Niehoff, 2b	4	1	1	0	1	2
Burns, c	4	0	1	0	2	2
Mayer, p	1	0	0	0	1	0
Rixey, p	2	0	1	0	0	1
cKillefer	1	0	0	0	0	0
Totals	32	4	9	3	27	14

Boston	0 1 1	0 0 0	0 2 1	—5
Philadelphia	2 0 0	2 0 0	0 0 0	—4

Boston	IP.	H.	R.	ER.	BB.	SO.
Foster (W)	9	9	4	3	2	5

Philadelphia	IP.	H.	R.	ER.	BB.	SO.
Mayer	2⅓	6	2	2	0	0
Rixey (L)	6⅔	4	3	3	2	2

aHit into double play for Hoblitzell in third. bRan for Cravath in eighth. cGrounded out for Rixey in ninth. E—Hooper, Bancroft. DP—Boston 1, Philadelphia 1. LOB—Boston 7, Philadelphia 5. 2B—Luderus. 3B—Gardner. HR—Hooper 2, Lewis, Luderus. HBP—By Foster (Stock, Luderus), by Rixey (Hooper). U—Klem (N.L.), O'Loughlin (A.L.), Evans (A.L.) and Rigler (N.L.). T—2:15. A—20,306.

COMPOSITE BATTING AVERAGES

Boston Red Sox

Player-Position	G.	AB.	R.	H.	2B.	3B.	HR.	RBI.	BA.
Foster, p	2	8	0	4	1	0	0	1	.500
Lewis, lf	5	18	1	8	1	0	1	5	.444
Hooper, rf	5	20	4	7	0	0	2	3	.350
Cady, c	4	6	0	2	0	0	0	0	.333
Gainor, 1b	1	3	1	1	0	0	0	0	.333
Hoblitzell, 1b	5	16	1	5	0	0	0	1	.313
Speaker, cf	5	17	2	5	0	1	0	0	.294
Gardner, 3b	5	17	2	4	0	1	0	0	.235
Shore, p	2	5	0	1	0	0	0	0	.200
Thomas, c	2	5	0	1	0	0	0	0	.200
Barry, 2b	5	17	1	3	0	0	0	1	.176
Scott, ss	5	18	0	1	0	0	0	0	.056
Janvrin, ss	1	1	0	0	0	0	0	0	.000
Carrigan, c	1	2	0	0	0	0	0	0	.000
Henriksen, ph	2	2	0	0	0	0	0	0	.000
Ruth, ph	1	1	0	0	0	0	0	0	.000
Leonard, p	1	3	0	0	0	0	0	0	.000
Totals	5	159	12	42	2	2	3	11	.264

Philadelphia Phillies

Player-Position	G.	AB.	R.	H.	2B.	3B.	HR.	RBI.	BA.
Rixey, p	1	2	0	1	0	0	0	0	.500
Luderus, 1b	5	16	1	7	2	0	1	6	.438
Chalmers, p	1	3	0	1	0	0	0	0	.333
Bancroft, ss	5	17	2	5	0	0	0	1	.294
Alexander, p	2	5	0	1	0	0	0	0	.200
Burns, c	5	16	1	3	0	0	0	0	.188
Paskert, cf	5	19	2	3	0	0	0	0	.158
Cravath, rf	5	16	2	2	1	1	0	1	.125
Stock, 3b	5	17	1	2	1	0	0	0	.118
Whitted, lf-1b	5	15	0	1	0	0	0	1	.067
Niehoff, 2b	5	16	1	1	0	0	0	0	.063
Mayer, p	2	4	0	0	0	0	0	0	.000
Dugey, pr	2	0	0	0	0	0	0	0	.000
Becker, lf	2	0	0	0	0	0	0	0	.000
Byrne, ph	1	1	0	0	0	0	0	0	.000
Killefer, ph	1	1	0	0	0	0	0	0	.000
Totals	5	148	10	27	4	1	1	9	.182

COMPOSITE PITCHING AVERAGES

Boston Red Sox

Pitcher	G.	IP.	H.	R.	ER.	BB.	SO.	W.	L.	ERA.
Leonard	1	9	3	1	1	0	6	1	0	1.00
Foster	2	18	12	5	4	2	13	2	0	2.00
Shore	2	17	12	4	4	8	6	1	1	2.12
Totals	5	44	27	10	9	10	25	4	1	1.84

Philadelphia Phillies

Pitcher	G.	IP.	H.	R.	ER.	BB.	SO.	W.	L.	ERA.
Alexander	2	17⅔	14	3	3	4	10	1	1	1.53
Chalmers	1	8	8	2	2	3	6	0	1	2.25
Mayer	2	11⅓	16	4	3	2	7	0	1	2.38
Rixey	1	6⅔	4	3	2	2	2	0	1	2.70
Totals	5	43⅔	42	12	10	11	25	1	4	2.06

1916
BOSTON RED SOX
VS.
BROOKLYN DODGERS

Brooklyn's Ebbets Field, site of many memorable moments in World Series history, played host to its first fall classic in 1916. Brooklyn fans would have little to cheer about in this Series, though, a postseason fate that the borough's burghers would have to endure for nearly 40 years.

The Boston Red Sox inflicted the initial Series disappointment on Brooklyn, beating the National Leaguers in five games. While they were without gifted outfielder Tris Speaker (traded to Cleveland in April after a contract dispute), the Red Sox still had Harry Hooper, Duffy Lewis and Larry Gardner. Most important, they had a young and talented pitching staff headed by lefthander Babe Ruth, who followed up his excellent rookie season of 1915 by winning 23 games in 1916 and leading the American League with a 1.75 earned-run average. Ruth, 21 years old, had sturdy support in Ernie Shore, 25, and Dutch Leonard and second-year major leaguer Carl Mays, both 24. Submarine pitcher Mays showed his vast potential by winning 18 games.

Manager Wilbert Robinson's Dodgers—they actually were known as the Robins at the time —had standout hitters in Zack Wheat and Jake Daubert, plus a formidable pitching staff led by Jeff Pfeffer (a 25-game winner), Larry Cheney and Sherry Smith, a threesome backed by retreads Rube Marquard and Jack Coombs of New York Giants and Philadelphia Athletics fame, respectively.

Robinson thought Brooklyn could get the upper hand in the Series by starting lefthanders in Games 1 and 2, so he nominated Marquard and Smith to pitch the opening games at Braves Field, which the Red Sox again chose as

The 1916 Boston Red Sox relied on a top-notch pitching staff that included (left to right) Rube Foster, Carl Mays, Ernie Shore, the up-and-coming Babe Ruth and Dutch Leonard.

their postseason home field over Fenway Park. Marquard and Shore were locked in a 2-1 battle through six innings—Boston was in front—before both clubs went on scoring flurries. The Red Sox jolted Marquard for three runs in the seventh and scored once more in the eighth off Pfeffer, while the Dodgers struck for four runs in the ninth. Shore held on for a 6-5 victory, with large assists from Mays and shortstop Everett Scott. Mays came on to get the last out, which was recorded when Scott made a great stop on Daubert's bases-loaded grounder.

Smith and Ruth hooked up in a double masterpiece in Game 2. After Brooklyn's Hy Myers hit an inside-the-park home run off Ruth in the first inning and Ruth delivered a run-scoring ground-out for Boston in the third, the teams traded zeros. More zeros. And even more zeros. Through 13 innings, both Smith and Ruth

had allowed only one run and six hits. In the 14th, Ruth kept it going by retiring Brooklyn in order. Boston's Dick Hoblitzell then led off the bottom of the inning by drawing his fourth base on balls of the day. After Lewis sacrificed Hoblitzell to second, Red Sox Manager Bill Carrigan inserted Mike McNally as a pinch-runner. Pinch-hitter Del Gainor followed with a single off Smith, giving Boston a 2-1 victory.

Having been foiled in his effort to win with lefthanders, Brooklyn's Robinson turned to righthander Coombs for Game 3, the first Series game ever contested at Ebbets Field. And Coombs, with standout relief help from Pfeffer (who retired all eight batters he faced), came out a 4-3 winner. But Boston came back for a 6-2 victory the next day as Leonard hurled a five-hitter and Gardner rapped a three-run home run.

The shot was Gardner's second homer in two days.

Shore wrapped up things in Game 5, stopping Brooklyn on only three hits and copping a 4-1 decision.

One thing Brooklyn fans did have to cheer about was the play of a 27-year-old outfielder, a man who later in his career would cause the borough considerable grief in his role as opposing World Series manager. The player's name? Casey Stengel. As Ol' Case, he would manage the New York Yankees to four Series conquests of the Brooklyn Dodgers. As young Case, he batted a Series-leading .364 for Brooklyn in 1916.

Game 1

Saturday, October 7, At Boston

Brooklyn	AB.	R.	H.	RBI.	PO.	A.
Myers, cf	5	0	2	1	1	0
Daubert, 1b	4	0	0	0	5	1
Stengel, rf	4	2	2	0	1	0
Wheat, lf	4	1	2	1	3	0
Cutshaw, 2b	3	1	0	0	5	2
Mowrey, 3b	3	1	1	1	1	2
Olson, ss	4	0	1	0	2	1
Meyers, c	4	0	1	0	6	3
Marquard, p	2	0	0	0	0	0
aJohnston	1	0	1	0	0	0
Pfeffer, p	0	0	0	0	0	0
bMerkle	0	0	0	1	0	0
Totals	34	5	10	4	24	9

Boston	AB.	R.	H.	RBI.	PO.	A.
Hooper, rf	4	2	1	0	1	1
Janvrin, 2b	4	1	2	0	2	8
Walker, cf	4	1	2	1	0	0
Hoblitzell, 1b	5	2	1	1	14	0
Lewis, lf	3	0	1	1	0	0
Gardner, 3b	4	0	1	1	1	3
Scott, ss	2	0	0	1	2	4
Cady, c	1	0	0	0	7	0
Thomas, c	0	0	0	0	0	0
Shore, p	4	0	0	0	0	3
Mays, p	0	0	0	0	0	0
Totals	31	6	8	5	27	19

Brooklyn .... 0 0 0 1 0 0 0 0 4—5
Boston .... 0 0 1 0 1 0 3 1 x—6

Brooklyn	IP.	H.	R.	ER.	BB.	SO.
Marquard (L)	7	7	5	4	4	6
Pfeffer	1	1	1	0	2	0

Boston	IP.	H.	R.	ER.	BB.	SO.
Shore (W)	8⅔	9	5	3	3	5
Mays	⅓	1	0	0	1	0

aSingled for Marquard in eighth. bWalked for Pfeffer in ninth. E—Stengel, Cutshaw, Olson 2, Janvrin. DP—Boston 4. LOB—Brooklyn 6, Boston 11. 2B—Lewis, Hooper, Janvrin, Wheat, Meyers. SH—Scott, Janvrin, Lewis. SF—Scott. HBP—By Shore (Cutshaw). PB—Meyers. U—Connolly (A.L.), O'Day (N.L.), Quigley (N.L.) and Dinneen (A.L.). T—2:16. A—36,117.

Game 2

Monday, October 9, At Boston

Brooklyn	AB.	R.	H.	RBI.	PO.	A.
Johnston, rf	5	0	1	0	1	0
Daubert, 1b	5	0	0	0	18	1
Myers, cf	6	1	1	1	4	1
Wheat, lf	5	0	0	0	2	0
Cutshaw, 2b	5	0	0	0	5	6
Mowrey, 3b	5	0	1	0	3	5
Olson, ss	2	0	1	0	2	4
Miller, c	5	0	1	0	4	1
Smith, p	5	0	1	0	1	7
Totals	43	1	6	1	40	25

Boston	AB.	R.	H.	RBI.	PO.	A.
Hooper, rf	6	0	1	0	2	1
Janvrin, 2b	6	0	1	0	4	5
Walker, cf	3	0	0	0	2	1
Walsh, cf	3	0	0	0	1	0
Hoblitzell, 1b	2	0	0	0	21	1
aMcNally	0	1	0	0	0	0
Lewis, lf	3	0	1	0	1	0
Gardner, 3b	5	0	0	0	3	7
bGainor	1	0	1	1	0	0
Scott, ss	4	1	2	0	1	8
Thomas, c	4	0	1	0	5	4
Ruth, p	5	0	0	1	2	4
Totals	42	2	7	2	42	31

Brooklyn .... 1 0 0 000 000 000 00—1
Boston .... 0 0 1 000 000 000 01—2
One out when winning run scored.

Brooklyn	IP.	H.	R.	ER.	BB.	SO.
Smith (L)	13⅓	7	2	2	6	2

Boston	IP.	H.	R.	ER.	BB.	SO.
Ruth (W)	14	6	1	1	3	4

aRan for Hoblitzell in fourteenth. bSingled for Gardner in fourteenth. E—Cutshaw, Mowrey, Gardner. DP—Brooklyn 2, Boston 1. LOB—Brooklyn 5, Boston 9. 2B—Smith, Janvrin. 3B—Scott, Thomas. HR—Myers. SH—Lewis 2, Thomas, Olson 2. U—Dinneen (A.L.), Quigley (N.L.), O'Day (N.L.) and Connolly (A.L.). T—2:32. A—41,373.

Game 3

Tuesday, October 10, At Brooklyn

Boston	AB.	R.	H.	RBI.	PO.	A.
Hooper, rf	4	1	2	1	1	0
Janvrin, 2b	4	0	0	0	1	0
Shorten, cf	4	0	3	1	0	0
Hoblitzell, 1b	4	0	1	0	12	2
Lewis, lf	4	0	0	0	1	1
Gardner, 3b	3	1	1	1	2	0
Scott, ss	3	0	0	0	1	7
Thomas, c	3	0	0	0	5	0
Mays, p	1	0	0	0	0	4
aHenriksen	0	1	0	0	0	0
Foster, p	1	0	0	0	1	2
Totals	31	3	7	3	24	16

Brooklyn	AB.	R.	H.	RBI.	PO.	A.
Myers, cf	3	0	0	0	3	0
Daubert, 1b	4	1	3	0	7	0
Stengel, rf	3	0	1	0	2	1
Wheat, lf	2	1	1	0	4	0
Cutshaw, 2b	4	0	1	1	4	0
Mowrey, 3b	3	1	0	0	2	1
Olson, ss	4	1	2	2	1	2
Miller, c	3	0	0	0	4	2
Coombs, p	3	0	1	1	0	2
Pfeffer, p	1	0	1	0	0	1
Totals	30	4	10	4	27	9

Boston .... 0 0 0 0 0 2 1 0 0—3
Brooklyn .... 0 0 1 1 2 0 0 0 x—4

Boston	IP.	H.	R.	ER.	BB.	SO.
Mays (L)	5	7	4	3	3	2
Foster	3	3	0	0	0	1

Brooklyn	IP.	H.	R.	ER.	BB.	SO.
Coombs (W)	6⅓	7	3	3	1	1
Pfeffer	2⅔	0	0	0	0	3

aWalked for Mays in sixth. E—Gardner. LOB—Boston 2, Brooklyn 9. 3B—Olson, Daubert, Hooper. HR—Gardner. SH—Wheat. SH—Stengel, Miller, Myers. HBP—By Mays (Myers). WP—Foster. U—O'Day (N.L.), Connolly (A.L.), Quigley (N.L.) and Dinneen (A.L.). T—2:01. A—21,087.

Game 4

Wednesday, October 11, At Brooklyn

Boston	AB.	R.	H.	RBI.	PO.	A.
Hooper, rf	4	1	2	0	3	0
Janvrin, 2b	5	1	0	0	1	2
Walker, cf	4	0	1	0	2	0
Hoblitzell, 1b	3	1	2	1	8	0
Lewis, lf	4	2	2	0	6	0
Gardner, 3b	3	1	1	3	1	3
Scott, ss	4	0	0	0	3	3
Carrigan, c	3	0	2	1	3	1
Leonard, p	3	0	0	0	0	1
Totals	33	6	10	5	27	10

Brooklyn	AB.	R.	H.	RBI.	PO.	A.
Johnston, rf	4	1	1	0	0	0
Myers, cf	4	1	1	1	1	0
Merkle, 1b	3	0	1	0	9	1
Wheat, lf	4	0	1	0	0	0
Cutshaw, 2b	4	0	1	1	3	2
Mowrey, 3b	3	0	0	0	1	4
Olson, ss	3	0	0	0	2	2
Meyers, c	3	0	0	0	11	3
cStengel	0	0	0	0	0	0
Marquard, p	1	0	0	0	0	2
aPfeffer	1	0	0	0	0	0
Cheney, p	0	0	0	0	0	0
bO'Mara	1	0	0	0	0	0
Rucker, p	0	0	0	0	0	0
dGetz	1	0	0	0	0	0
Totals	32	2	5	2	27	14

Boston .... 0 3 0 1 1 0 1 0 0—6
Brooklyn .... 2 0 0 0 0 0 0 0 0—2

Boston	IP.	H.	R.	ER.	BB.	SO.
Leonard (W)	9	5	2	1	4	3

Brooklyn	IP.	H.	R.	ER.	BB.	SO.
Marquard (L)	4	5	4	4	2	3
Cheney	3	4	2	1	1	5
Rucker	2	1	0	0	0	3

aStruck out for Marquard in fourth. bStruck out for Cheney in seventh. cRan for Meyers in ninth. dGrounded out for Rucker in ninth. E—Janvrin, Johnston, Merkle, Wheat, Cheney. LOB—Boston 5, Brooklyn 7. 2B—Lewis, Cutshaw, Hoblitzell. 3B—Johnston. HR—Gardner. SB—Hooper. SH—Carrigan, Gardner. WP—Leonard. PB—Meyers. U—Quigley (N.L.), Dinneen (A.L.), O'Day (N.L.) and Connolly (A.L.). T—2:30. A—21,662.

Game 5

Thursday, October 12, At Boston

Brooklyn	AB.	R.	H.	RBI.	PO.	A.
Myers, cf	4	0	0	0	0	0
Daubert, 1b	4	0	0	0	10	1
Stengel, rf	4	0	1	0	0	0
Wheat, lf	4	0	0	0	5	0
Cutshaw, 2b	3	1	0	0	2	3
Mowrey, 3b	3	0	1	0	1	3
Olson, ss	3	0	0	0	2	3
Meyers, c	3	0	1	0	4	2
Pfeffer, p	2	0	0	0	0	1
aMerkle	1	0	0	0	0	0
Dell, p	0	0	0	0	0	0
Totals	31	1	3	0	24	13

Boston	AB.	R.	H.	RBI.	PO.	A.
Hooper, rf	3	2	1	0	1	0
Janvrin, 2b	4	0	2	1	0	1
Shorten, cf	3	0	1	1	3	0
Hoblitzell, 1b	3	0	0	0	14	1
Lewis, lf	3	1	2	0	1	0
Gardner, 3b	2	0	0	1	0	5
Scott, ss	3	0	0	0	2	3
Cady, c	3	1	1	0	4	1
Shore, p	3	0	0	0	2	3
Totals	27	4	7	3	27	14

Brooklyn .... 0 1 0 0 0 0 0 0 0—1
Boston .... 0 1 2 0 1 0 0 0 x—4

Brooklyn	IP.	H.	R.	ER.	BB.	SO.
Pfeffer (L)	7	6	4	2	2	2
Dell	1	1	0	0	0	0

Boston	IP.	H.	R.	ER.	BB.	SO.
Shore (W)	9	3	1	0	1	4

aFlied out for Pfeffer in eighth. E—Mowrey, Olson 2, Scott 2. LOB—Brooklyn 5, Boston 4. 2B—Janvrin. 3B—Lewis. SH—Mowrey, Lewis, Shorten. SF—Gardner. WP—Pfeffer 2. PB—Cady. U—Connolly (A.L.), O'Day (N.L.), Quigley (N.L.) and Dinneen (A.L.). T—1:43. A—42,620.

COMPOSITE BATTING AVERAGES

Boston Red Sox

Player-Position	G.	AB.	R.	H.	2B.	3B.	HR.	RBI.	BA.
Gainor, ph	1	1	0	1	0	0	0	1	1.000
Carrigan, c	1	3	0	2	0	0	0	1	.667
Shorten, cf	2	7	0	4	0	0	0	2	.571
Lewis, lf	5	17	3	6	2	1	0	1	.353
Hooper, rf	5	21	6	7	1	1	0	1	.333
Walker, cf	3	11	1	3	0	1	0	1	.273
Cady, c	2	4	1	1	0	0	0	0	.250
Hoblitzell, 1b	5	17	3	4	1	1	0	2	.235
Janvrin, 2b	5	23	2	5	3	0	0	1	.217
Gardner, 3b	5	17	2	3	0	0	2	6	.176
Thomas, c	3	7	0	1	0	1	0	0	.143
Scott, ss	5	16	1	2	0	1	0	1	.125
Shore, p	2	7	0	0	0	0	0	0	.000
Mays, p	2	1	0	0	0	0	0	0	.000
Walsh, cf	1	3	0	0	0	0	0	0	.000
McNally, pr	1	0	1	0	0	0	0	0	.000
Ruth, p	1	5	0	0	0	0	0	1	.000
Henriksen, ph	1	0	1	0	0	0	0	0	.000
Foster, p	1	1	0	0	0	0	0	0	.000
Leonard, p	1	3	0	0	0	0	0	0	.000
Totals	5	164	21	39	7	6	2	18	.238

Brooklyn Dodgers

Player-Position	G.	AB.	R.	H.	2B.	3B.	HR.	RBI.	BA.
Stengel, rf-ph	4	11	2	4	0	0	0	0	.364
Coombs, p	1	3	0	1	0	0	0	1	.333
Johnston, ph-rf	3	10	1	3	0	1	0	0	.300
Olson, ss	5	16	1	4	0	1	0	2	.250
Pfeffer, p-ph	4	4	0	1	0	0	0	0	.250
Merkle, ph-1b	3	4	0	1	0	0	0	1	.250
Wheat, lf	5	19	2	4	0	1	0	1	.211
Meyers, c	3	10	0	2	0	1	0	0	.200
Smith, p	1	5	0	1	1	0	0	0	.200
Myers, cf	5	22	2	4	0	0	1	3	.182
Daubert, 1b	4	17	1	3	0	1	0	0	.176
Mowrey, 3b	5	17	2	3	0	0	0	1	.176
Miller, c	2	8	0	1	0	0	0	0	.125
Cutshaw, 2b	5	19	2	2	1	0	0	2	.105
Marquard, p	2	3	0	0	0	0	0	0	.000
O'Mara, ph	1	1	0	0	0	0	0	0	.000
Rucker, p	1	0	0	0	0	0	0	0	.000
Getz, ph	1	1	0	0	0	0	0	0	.000
Cheney, p	1	0	0	0	0	0	0	0	.000
Dell, p	1	0	0	0	0	0	0	0	.000
Totals	5	170	13	34	2	5	1	11	.200

COMPOSITE PITCHING AVERAGES

Boston Red Sox

Pitcher	G.	IP.	H.	R.	ER.	BB.	SO.	W.	L.	ERA.
Foster	1	3	3	0	0	0	1	0	0	0.00
Ruth	1	14	6	1	1	3	4	1	0	0.64
Leonard	1	9	5	2	1	4	3	1	0	1.00
Shore	2	17⅔	12	6	3	4	9	2	0	1.53
Mays	2	5⅓	8	4	3	3	2	0	1	5.06
Totals	5	49	34	13	8	14	19	4	1	1.47

Brooklyn Dodgers

Pitcher	G.	IP.	H.	R.	ER.	BB.	SO.	W.	L.	ERA.
Rucker	1	2	1	0	0	0	3	0	0	0.00
Dell	1	1	1	0	0	0	0	0	0	0.00
Smith	1	13⅓	7	2	2	6	2	0	1	1.35
Pfeffer	3	10⅔	7	5	2	4	5	0	1	1.69
Cheney	1	3	4	2	1	1	5	0	0	3.00
Coombs	1	6⅓	7	3	3	1	1	1	0	4.26
Marquard	2	11	12	9	8	6	9	0	2	6.55
Totals	5	47⅓	39	21	16	18	25	1	4	3.04

1917
CHICAGO WHITE SOX
VS.
NEW YORK GIANTS

Entering Game 6 of the 1917 World Series, the New York Giants hadn't exactly played exemplary baseball in some of the big games in franchise history.

Here was a team that paid dearly—in the form of the National League pennant—for a baserunning mistake by Fred Merkle in 1908; a club that had bungled a Series title in 1912 by making two crucial blunders in the 10th inning of the final game, the first being outfielder Fred Snodgrass'

Chicago White Sox ace Red Faber joined a select list of pitchers when he defeated the New York Giants three times in the 1917 World Series.

muff of a fly ball and the second a misplay of a catchable pop foul near the first-base coach's box; a franchise that, in fact, had wound up a loser in its last three Series appearances, which had come in succession from 1911 through 1913.

And Manager John McGraw's Giants, down three games to two in the 1917 Series, were back at their old tricks in Game 6. And it wasn't pretty.

Rube Benton of the Giants and Red Faber of the Chicago White Sox were engaged in a 0-0 struggle when the American Leaguers came to bat in the fourth inning. Eddie Collins led off and grounded to Giants third baseman Heinie Zimmerman, who made a two-base throwing error on the play. Joe Jackson's ensuing fly ball was dropped by right fielder Dave Robertson, leaving the White Sox with runners on third and first.

Happy Felsch then grounded back to Benton, who saw Collins break from third and threw to Zimmerman in an attempt to get Collins hung up. Zimmerman ran Collins toward home plate, but the White Sox star bounded past catcher Bill Rariden to make it a Zimmerman-Collins race to the plate. Collins won, with major assists from Rariden, Benton and first baseman Walter Holke, all of whom left the plate unattended as Zimmerman chased Collins across it. Jackson moved to third and Felsch to second during the rundown, and they scored on Chick Gandil's single. Faber already had enough runs to win.

The Giants cut the deficit to one with a two-run fifth, but the White Sox salted away the victory and their second World Series crown by adding an insurance run in the ninth and prevailing, 4-2.

New York Giants third baseman Heinie Zimmerman futilely chases Chicago's Eddie Collins across the un- **attended plate on a key Game 6 play during the 1917 World Series.**

Faber, besides winning Game 6, also was victorious in Games 2 and 5, the latter triumph coming in relief. But Faber had some off moments, too, as in the fifth inning of the second game when he tried to steal third base—which was occupied at the time by teammate Buck Weaver. And he was a 5-0 loser in Game 4, a contest in which the Giants' Ferdie Schupp hurled a seven-hitter and Benny Kauff slammed a pair of home runs.

Eddie Cicotte, a 28-game winner during the regular season, beat the Giants and pitching rival Slim Sallee, 2-1, in the Series opener and Felsch contributed a homer. After Faber's 7-2 conquest the next day pushed Manager Pants Rowland's White Sox into a two games-to-none lead, New York

tied the Series on the shutout pitching of Benton (a five-hit, 2-0 victory) and Schupp. But the White Sox regained the Series advantage in Game 5, breaking loose for three runs in both the seventh and eighth innings and taking an 8-5 decision. Five players had three hits in the game—Chicago's Collins, Jackson and Felsch and New York's Robertson and Rariden.

The chain of events had set the stage for Game 6—and another not-so-memorable moment in Giants history.

While Faber grabbed most of the headlines in the 1917 World Series, the Giants' Robertson was another notable performer. Despite his costly error in Game 6, Robertson won plaudits overall for his 11-for-22 performance at

the plate. Collins was a force, too, as evidenced by his .409 average for the White Sox.

In an oddity, famed Olympic Games athlete and football star Jim Thorpe made the only Series "appearance" of his major league career in Game 5—but never got onto the playing field. Listed as the Giants' starting right fielder for that game, the righthanded-hitting Thorpe, positioned sixth in the batting order, was removed for a lefthanded pinch-hitter, Robertson, in the top of the first inning after the White Sox had lifted lefthanded starter Reb Russell in favor of righthander Cicotte.

Still, nothing in this fall classic stood out quite like the Giants' knack for coming up with the big *mis*play. Again.

Game 1

Saturday, October 6, At Chicago

New York	AB.	R.	H.	RBI.	PO.	A.
Burns, lf	3	0	1	0	2	0
Herzog, 2b	4	0	1	0	3	1
Kauff, cf	4	0	0	0	0	0
Zimmerman, 3b	4	0	0	0	1	3
Fletcher, ss	4	0	0	0	2	3
Robertson, rf	4	0	1	0	0	1
Holke, 1b	3	0	2	0	14	0
McCarty, c	3	1	1	0	2	1
Sallee, p	3	0	1	1	0	6
Totals	32	1	7	1	24	15

Chicago	AB.	R.	H.	RBI.	PO.	A.
J. Collins, rf	4	1	3	0	1	0
McMullin, 3b	3	0	1	1	0	3
E. Collins, 2b	3	0	0	0	2	1
Jackson, lf	3	0	0	0	5	0
Felsch, cf	3	1	1	1	4	0
Gandil, 1b	3	0	1	0	10	1
Weaver, ss	3	0	0	0	2	1
Schalk, c	3	0	0	0	3	0
Cicotte, p	3	0	1	0	0	4
Totals	28	2	7	2	27	10

New York	0 0 0 0 1 0 0 0 0—1
Chicago	0 0 1 1 0 0 0 0 x—2

New York	IP.	H.	R.	ER.	BB.	SO.
Sallee (L)	8	7	2	2	0	2

Chicago	IP.	H.	R.	ER.	BB.	SO.
Cicotte (W)	9	7	1	1	1	2

E—McCarty, Weaver. DP—Chicago 1. LOB—New York 5, Chicago 3. 2B—McMullin, Robertson, J. Collins. 3B—McCarty. HR—Felsch. SB—Burns, Gandil. SH—McMullin. U—O'Loughlin (A.L.), Klem (N.L.), Rigler (N.L.) and Evans (A.L.). T—1:48. A—32,000.

Game 2

Sunday, October 7, At Chicago

New York	AB.	R.	H.	RBI.	PO.	A.
Burns, lf	3	0	1	0	0	0
Herzog, 2b	4	0	0	0	3	0
Kauff, cf	4	0	0	0	2	0
Zimmerman, 3b	4	0	0	0	4	2
Fletcher, ss	4	0	1	0	2	2
Robertson, rf	3	1	2	0	2	0
Holke, 1b	3	1	1	0	5	0
McCarty, c	1	0	1	1	5	0
Rariden, c	2	0	1	0	1	3
Schupp, p	1	0	0	0	0	1
Anderson, p	0	0	0	0	0	1
Perritt, p	1	0	1	0	0	0
bWilhoit	1	0	0	0	0	0
Tesreau, p	0	0	0	0	0	0
Totals	31	2	8	1	24	9

Chicago	AB.	R.	H.	RBI.	PO.	A.
J. Collins, rf	1	0	0	0	0	1
aLeibold, rf	3	1	1	1	0	0
McMullin, 3b	5	1	1	1	0	3
E. Collins, 2b	4	1	2	1	4	2
Jackson, lf	3	1	3	2	0	1
Felsch, cf	4	1	1	0	2	1
Gandil, 1b	4	0	1	1	12	1
Weaver, ss	4	1	3	1	7	6
Schalk, c	4	1	1	0	1	2
Faber, p	3	0	1	0	1	4
Totals	35	7	14	7	27	21

New York	0 2 0 0 0 0 0 0 0—2
Chicago	0 2 0 5 0 0 0 0 x—7

New York	IP.	H.	R.	ER.	BB.	SO.
Schupp	1⅓	4	2	2	1	2
Anderson (L)	2	5	4	4	0	3
Perritt	3⅔	5	1	1	1	0
Tesreau	1	0	0	0	1	1

Chicago	IP.	H.	R.	ER.	BB.	SO.
Faber (W)	9	8	2	2	1	1

aStruck out for J. Collins in second. bLined into double play for Perritt in eighth. E—Fletcher, Schalk. DP—New York 1, Chicago 3. LOB—New York 3, Chicago 7. SB—E. Collins 2, Jackson. PB—McCarty. U—Evans (A.L.), Rigler (N.L.), Klem (N.L.) and O'Loughlin (A.L.). T—2:13. A—32,000.

Game 3

Wednesday, October 10, At New York

Chicago	AB.	R.	H.	RBI.	PO.	A.
J. Collins, rf	4	0	0	0	1	0
McMullin, 3b	4	0	0	0	0	1
E. Collins, 2b	4	0	2	0	3	2
Jackson, lf	4	0	0	0	0	0
Felsch, cf	3	0	1	0	5	0
Gandil, 1b	3	0	0	0	6	0
Weaver, ss	3	0	2	0	0	2
Schalk, c	3	0	0	0	9	0
Cicotte, p	3	0	0	0	0	1
Totals	31	0	5	0	24	6

New York	AB.	R.	H.	RBI.	PO.	A.
Burns, lf	4	0	1	1	1	0
Herzog, 2b	4	0	1	0	1	1
Kauff, cf	4	0	0	0	0	0
Zimmerman, 3b	4	0	0	0	0	3
Fletcher, ss	4	0	0	0	1	4
Robertson, rf	4	1	3	0	1	0
Holke, 1b	4	1	1	1	15	0
Rariden, c	2	0	1	0	7	4
Benton, p	3	0	0	0	1	2
Totals	33	2	8	2	27	14

Chicago	0 0 0 0 0 0 0 0 0—0
New York	0 0 0 2 0 0 0 0 x—2

Chicago	IP.	H.	R.	ER.	BB.	SO.
Cicotte (L)	8	8	2	2	0	8

New York	IP.	H.	R.	ER.	BB.	SO.
Benton (W)	9	5	0	0	0	5

E—J. Collins 2, Cicotte, Fletcher, Holke. DP—New York 1. LOB—Chicago 4, New York 8. 2B—Holke, Weaver. 3B—Robertson. SB—Robertson. SH—Rariden. U—Klem (N.L.), O'Loughlin (A.L.), Evans (A.L.) and Rigler (N.L.). T—1:55. A—33,616.

Game 4

Thursday, October 11, At New York

Chicago	AB.	R.	H.	RBI.	PO.	A.
J. Collins, rf	4	0	2	0	0	0
McMullin, 3b	4	0	1	0	1	2
E. Collins, 2b	3	0	1	0	0	6
Jackson, lf	4	0	0	0	0	0
Felsch, cf	4	0	0	0	2	1
Gandil, 1b	4	0	1	0	15	0
Weaver, ss	3	0	0	0	0	1
Schalk, c	3	0	2	0	6	3
Faber, p	2	0	0	0	0	4
aRisberg	1	0	0	0	0	0
Danforth, p	0	0	0	0	0	1
Totals	32	0	7	0	24	18

New York	AB.	R.	H.	RBI.	PO.	A.
Burns, lf	4	0	1	0	2	0
Herzog, 2b	3	1	1	0	3	4
Kauff, cf	4	2	2	3	1	0
Zimmerman, 3b	4	0	1	0	2	2
Fletcher, ss	4	1	2	0	1	3
Robertson, rf	3	1	1	0	1	0
Holke, 1b	2	0	1	0	9	0
Rariden, c	3	0	0	1	7	1
Schupp, p	3	0	1	1	1	3
Totals	30	5	10	5	27	13

Chicago	0 0 0 0 0 0 0 0 0—0
New York	0 0 0 1 1 0 1 2 x—5

Chicago	IP.	H.	R.	ER.	BB.	SO.
Faber (L)	7	7	3	3	0	3
Danforth	1	3	2	2	0	2

New York	IP.	H.	R.	ER.	BB.	SO.
Schupp (W)	9	7	0	0	1	7

aFlied out for Faber in eighth. E—Herzog. DP—New York 1, Chicago 1. LOB—New York 3, Chicago 6. 2B—E. Collins. 3B—Zimmerman. HR—Kauff 2. SB—E. Collins. SH—Herzog. HBP—By Faber (Holke). WP—Faber. U—Rigler (N.L.), Evans (A.L.), O'Loughlin (A.L.) and Klem (N.L.). T—2:09. A—27,746.

Game 5

Saturday, October 13, At Chicago

New York	AB.	R.	H.	RBI.	PO.	A.
Burns, lf	4	2	1	1	3	0
Herzog, 2b	5	0	1	0	0	1
Kauff, cf	5	0	2	2	2	0
Zimmerman, 3b	5	1	1	0	1	2
Fletcher, ss	5	1	1	0	2	3
Thorpe, rf	0	0	0	0	0	0
aRobertson, rf	5	0	3	1	2	0
Holke, 1b	5	0	0	0	11	0
Rariden, c	3	1	3	1	3	1
Sallee, p	3	0	0	0	0	2
Perritt, p	0	0	0	0	0	0
Totals	40	5	12	5	24	9

Chicago	AB.	R.	H.	RBI.	PO.	A.
J. Collins, rf	5	1	1	0	1	0
McMullin, 3b	3	0	0	0	1	4
E. Collins, 2b	4	2	3	1	1	4
Jackson, lf	5	2	3	0	3	0
Felsch, cf	5	1	3	2	0	0
Gandil, 1b	5	1	1	2	10	2
Weaver, ss	4	1	1	0	2	2
Schalk, c	3	0	1	0	9	0
Russell, p	0	0	0	0	0	0
Cicotte, p	1	0	0	0	0	2
bRisberg	1	0	1	1	0	0
Williams, p	0	0	0	0	0	0
cLynn	1	0	0	0	0	0
Faber, p	0	0	0	0	0	1
Totals	37	8	14	6	27	15

New York	2 0 0 2 0 0 1 0 0—5
Chicago	0 0 1 0 0 1 3 3 x—8

New York	IP.	H.	R.	ER.	BB.	SO.
Sallee (L)	7⅓	13	8	7	4	2
Perritt	⅔	1	0	0	0	0

Chicago	IP.	H.	R.	ER.	BB.	SO.
Russell	0*	2	1	1	1	0
Cicotte	6	8	3	2	1	3
Williams	1	2	1	1	0	3
Faber (W)	2	0	0	0	0	1

*Pitched to three batters in first.

aSingled for Thorpe in first. bSingled for Cicotte in sixth. cStruck out for Williams in seventh. E—Herzog, Zimmerman, Fletcher, J. Collins, Gandil, Weaver 3, Williams. DP—Chicago 2. LOB—New York 11, Chicago 10. 2B—Kauff, Felsch, Fletcher, Gandil. SB—Kauff, Robertson, Schalk. SH—Sallee, McMullin. U—O'Loughlin (A.L.), Klem (N.L.), Rigler (N.L.) and Evans (A.L.). T—2:37. A—27,323.

Game 6

Monday, October 15, At New York

Chicago	AB.	R.	H.	RBI.	PO.	A.
J. Collins, rf	3	0	0	0	1	0
bLeibold, rf	2	0	1	1	1	0
McMullin, 3b	5	0	0	0	0	1
E. Collins, 2b	4	1	1	0	1	8
Jackson, lf	4	1	1	0	1	0
Felsch, cf	3	1	0	0	3	0
Gandil, 1b	4	0	2	2	14	0
Weaver, ss	4	1	1	0	2	2
Schalk, c	3	0	1	0	4	1
Faber, p	2	0	0	0	0	0
Totals	34	4	7	3	27	12

New York	AB.	R.	H.	RBI.	PO.	A.
Burns, lf	4	1	0	0	2	0
Herzog, 2b	4	0	2	2	2	5
Kauff, cf	4	0	0	0	2	0
Zimmerman, 3b	4	0	0	0	1	2
Fletcher, ss	4	0	1	0	1	2
Robertson, rf	3	0	1	0	0	1
Holke, 1b	4	0	1	0	12	0
Rariden, c	3	1	0	0	7	1
Benton, p	1	0	0	0	0	0
aWilhoit	0	0	0	0	0	0
Perritt, p	1	0	1	0	0	1
cMcCarty	1	0	0	0	0	0
Totals	33	2	6	2	27	12

Chicago	0 0 0 3 0 0 0 0 1—4
New York	0 0 0 0 2 0 0 0 0—2

Chicago	IP.	H.	R.	ER.	BB.	SO.
Faber (W)	9	6	2	2	2	4

New York	IP.	H.	R.	ER.	BB.	SO.
Benton (L)	5	4	3	0	1	3
Perritt	4	3	1	1	2	3

aWalked for Benton in fifth. bPopped out for J. Collins in seventh. cGrounded out for Perritt in ninth. E—Schalk, Kauff, Zimmerman, Robertson. LOB—Chicago 7, New York 7. 2B—Holke. 3B—Herzog. SH—Faber. HBP—By Faber (Robertson). PB—Schalk. U—Klem (N.L.), O'Loughlin (A.L.), Evans (A.L.) and Rigler (N.L.). T—2:18. A—33,969.

COMPOSITE BATTING AVERAGES

Chicago White Sox

Player-Position	G.	AB.	R.	H.	2B.	3B.	HR.	RBI.	BA.
Risberg, ph	2	2	0	1	0	0	0	1	.500
E. Collins, 2b	6	22	4	9	1	0	0	2	.409
Leibold, ph-rf	2	5	1	2	0	0	0	2	.400
Weaver, ss	6	21	3	7	1	0	0	1	.333
Jackson, lf	6	23	4	7	0	0	0	2	.304
J. Collins, rf	6	21	2	6	1	0	0	0	.286
Felsch, cf	6	22	4	6	1	0	1	3	.273
Schalk, c	6	19	1	5	0	0	0	0	.263
Gandil, 1b	6	23	1	6	1	0	0	5	.261
Cicotte, p	3	7	0	1	0	0	0	0	.143
Faber, p	4	7	0	1	0	0	0	0	.143
McMullin, 3b	6	24	1	3	1	0	0	2	.125
Danforth, p	1	0	0	0	0	0	0	0	.000
Russell, p	1	0	0	0	0	0	0	0	.000
Williams, p	1	0	0	0	0	0	0	0	.000
Lynn, ph	1	1	0	0	0	0	0	0	.000
Totals	6	197	21	54	6	0	1	18	.274

New York Giants

Player-Position	G.	AB.	R.	H.	2B.	3B.	HR.	RBI.	BA.
Perritt, p	3	2	0	2	0	0	0	0	1.000
Robertson, rf	6	22	3	11	1	1	0	1	.500
McCarty, c-ph	3	5	1	2	0	1	0	1	.400
Rariden, c	5	13	2	5	0	0	0	2	.385
Holke, 1b	6	21	2	6	2	0	0	1	.286
Herzog, 2b	6	24	1	6	0	1	0	2	.250
Schupp, p	2	4	0	1	0	0	0	1	.250
Burns, lf	6	22	3	5	0	0	0	2	.227
Fletcher, ss	6	25	2	5	1	0	0	0	.200
Sallee, p	2	6	0	1	0	0	0	1	.167
Kauff, cf	6	25	2	4	1	0	2	5	.160
Zimmerman, 3b	6	25	1	3	0	1	0	0	.120
Anderson, p	1	0	0	0	0	0	0	0	.000
Wilhoit, ph	2	1	0	0	0	0	0	0	.000
Tesreau, p	1	0	0	0	0	0	0	0	.000
Benton, p	2	4	0	0	0	0	0	0	.000
Thorpe, rf	1	0	0	0	0	0	0	0	.000
Totals	6	199	17	51	5	4	2	16	.256

COMPOSITE PITCHING AVERAGES

Chicago White Sox

Pitcher	G.	IP.	H.	R.	ER.	BB.	SO.	W.	L.	ERA.
Cicotte	3	23	23	6	5	2	13	1	1	1.96
Faber	4	27	21	7	7	3	9	3	1	2.33
Williams	1	1	2	1	1	0	3	0	0	9.00
Danforth	1	1	3	2	2	0	2	0	0	18.00
Russell	1	0	2	1	1	1	0	0	0	......
Totals	6	52	51	17	16	6	27	4	2	2.77

New York Giants

Pitcher	G.	IP.	H.	R.	ER.	BB.	SO.	W.	L.	ERA.
Benton	2	14	9	3	0	1	8	1	1	0.00
Tesreau	1	1	0	0	0	1	1	0	0	0.00
Schupp	2	10⅓	11	2	2	2	9	1	0	1.74
Perritt	3	8⅓	9	2	2	3	3	0	0	2.16
Sallee	2	15⅓	20	10	9	4	4	0	2	5.28
Anderson	1	2	5	4	4	0	3	0	1	18.00
Totals	6	51	54	21	17	11	28	2	4	3.00

1918
BOSTON RED SOX
VS.
CHICAGO CUBS

The *fall* classic this was not.

In the aftermath of the United States' entry into World War I the previous year, a U.S. government edict called for the end of major league baseball's 1918 regular season by Labor Day and the playing of the World Series immediately thereafter. Accordingly, the 1918 Series was a late-summer classic. It ran from September 5 through September 11.

Whatever its seasonal designation, baseball's big event was a big success story for the Boston Red Sox. Four times the Red Sox had appeared in the Series, and four times they had won it. Hopes of making it five for five rested on the strong right arms of Carl Mays, Sad Sam Jones and Bullet Joe Bush and the multi-talents of Babe Ruth.

Manager Ed Barrow's Red Sox got 21 victories from Mays, 16 from Jones and 15 from Bush in winning the shortened American League race with a 75-51 record. Ruth, seeing his first significant duty in the outfield while still making 19 pitching starts, chipped in with 13 victories, a .300 batting average and 11 home runs (which tied for the league lead).

First baseman Stuffy McInnis, outfielder Amos Strunk and catcher Wally Schang, obtained along with Bush in trades with the Philadelphia Athletics, were key additions for Boston.

The National League champions were the Chicago Cubs (84-45), who boasted 20-game winners in Hippo Vaughn (his 22 victories led the N.L.) and Claude Hendrix and received 19-victory production from Lefty Tyler. Charlie Hollocher, Chicago's rookie shortstop, was the fourth-best hitter in the league, batting .316.

Many big-league standouts, of

Chicago Cubs lefthander Hippo Vaughn pitched well in the 1918 World Series, but still lost twice to the opportunistic Boston Red Sox.

course, missed the 1918 season because of military duty. And while the Red Sox and Cubs, as a result, may not have quite measured up to previous Series teams, they put on a spirited battle for baseball's top prize.

The World Series opened at, of all places, Comiskey Park, home of the Chicago *White Sox.* While

the Red Sox had chosen Braves Field over their own Fenway Park as home grounds in their previous two Series appearances, it was the National League team that switched home bases in this go-round. The Cubs' decision to play Series games at Comiskey instead of Weeghman Park (later Wrigley Field) was based on

Boston righthander Sad Sam Jones started one game in the 1918 fall classic, but dropped a 3-0 decision to the Chicago Cubs.

greater seating capacity.

Ruth, having tossed 13 consecutive scoreless innings in his only previous Series pitching appearance two years earlier, extended his shutout streak to 22 innings in Game 1 by outdueling Vaughn, 1-0, in a contest that had only 11 hits—all singles. Tyler squared the Series the next day, hurling a six-hitter and collecting a two-run single in a 3-1 decision.

Vaughn was a hard-luck loser again in Game 3, dropping a 2-1 verdict to Mays and the Red Sox. The game's final out came when the Cubs' Charlie Pick was caught in a rundown between third and home while trying to score from second base on a passed ball. Boston then surged ahead by three games to one when Ruth increased his Series scoreless streak to 29 innings, a record, en route to a 3-2 triumph. Pitcher Ruth batted sixth in the Boston batting order and delivered the game's big hit, a two-run triple in the fourth inning.

Manager Fred Mitchell's Cubs received a big lift from Vaughn in Game 5. Having allowed only three runs and 12 hits in 18 innings in his previous two starts but possessor of a 0-2 record, Vaughn reached back for even a little more and baffled Boston, 3-0, on five hits. Dode Paskert's two-run double in the eighth provided Vaughn with some breathing room. But when all was said and done, the Cubs were done. Mays supplied the finishing touch in the form of a three-hit, 2-1 triumph in a game that was delayed as players haggled over gate receipts (Series shares would be reduced drastically because, for the first time, all first-division clubs would share in the revenue).

The Red Sox were now 5-0 in Series competition.

To say that pitching dominated the 1918 World Series would be a gross understatement. Neither team scored more than three runs in a game. The winning Red Sox batted a composite .186, while the Cubs managed a .210 mark. There were no home runs in the six contests. Boston pitchers combined for a 1.70 earned-run average; Chicago's staff, minus Grover

Cleveland Alexander (who went off to war early in the season), fashioned a 1.04 mark.

Considering the war-year scenario and the accompanying player depletion and shortened season, it wasn't a bad late-summer classic, after all.

Game 1

Thursday, September 5, At Chicago

Boston	AB.	R.	H.	RBI.	PO.	A.
Hooper, rf	4	0	1	0	4	0
Shean, 2b	2	1	1	0	0	3
Strunk, cf	3	0	0	0	2	0
Whiteman, lf	4	0	2	0	5	0
McInnis, 1b	2	0	1	1	10	0
Scott, ss	4	0	0	0	0	3
Thomas, 3b	3	0	0	0	1	1
Agnew, c	3	0	0	0	5	0
Ruth, p	3	0	0	0	0	1
Totals	28	1	5	1	27	8

Chicago	AB.	R.	H.	RBI.	PO.	A.
Flack, rf	3	0	1	0	2	0
Hollocher, ss	3	0	0	0	2	1
Mann, lf	4	0	1	0	0	0
Paskert, cf	4	0	2	0	2	0
Merkle, 1b	3	0	1	0	9	2
Pick, 2b	3	0	0	0	1	1
aO'Farrell	1	0	0	0	0	0
Deal, 3b	4	0	1	0	1	3
bMcCabe	0	0	0	0	0	0
Killefer, c	4	0	0	0	7	2
Vaughn, p	3	0	0	0	3	5
Totals	32	0	6	0	27	14

Boston	0 0 0 1 0 0 0 0 0—1
Chicago	0 0 0 0 0 0 0 0 0—0

Boston	IP.	H.	R.	ER.	BB.	SO.
Ruth (W)	9	6	0	0	1	4

Chicago	IP.	H.	R.	ER.	BB.	SO.
Vaughn (L)	9	5	1	1	3	6

aPopped out for Pick in ninth. bRan for Deal in ninth. LOB—Boston 5, Chicago 8. SH—Strunk, McInnis, Hollocher. HBP—By Ruth (Flack). U—O'Day (N.L.), Hildebrand (A.L.), Klem (N.L.) and Owens (A.L.). T—1:50. A—19,274.

Game 2

Friday, September 6, At Chicago

Boston	AB.	R.	H.	RBI.	PO.	A.
Hooper, rf	3	0	1	0	1	0
Shean, 2b	4	0	1	0	5	2
Strunk, cf	4	1	1	0	1	2
Whiteman, lf	3	0	1	1	3	0
McInnis, 1b	4	0	1	0	7	0
Scott, ss	3	0	0	0	3	2
Thomas, 3b	2	0	0	0	1	1
bDubuc	1	0	0	0	0	0
Agnew, c	2	0	0	0	2	4
aSchang, c	2	0	1	0	1	0
Bush, p	2	0	0	0	0	3
Totals	30	1	6	1	24	14

Chicago	AB.	R.	H.	RBI.	PO.	A.
Flack, rf	4	0	2	0	4	1
Hollocher, ss	4	0	1	0	5	4
Mann, lf	4	0	0	0	0	0
Paskert, cf	4	0	0	0	2	0
Merkle, 1b	2	1	1	0	6	1
Pick, 2b	2	1	1	0	4	4
Deal, 3b	2	0	0	0	1	1
Killefer, c	2	1	1	1	4	2
Tyler, p	3	0	1	2	1	2
Totals	27	3	7	3	27	15

Boston	0 0 0 0 0 0 0 0 1—1
Chicago	0 3 0 0 0 0 0 0 x—3

Boston	IP.	H.	R.	ER.	BB.	SO.
Bush (L)	8	7	3	3	3	0

Chicago	IP.	H.	R.	ER.	BB.	SO.
Tyler (W)	9	6	1	1	4	2

aSingled for Agnew in eighth. bStruck out for Thomas in ninth. E—Whiteman, Deal. DP—Chicago 2. LOB—Boston 7, Chicago 4. 2B—Killefer. 3B—Hollocher, Strunk, Whiteman. SH—Scott, Deal. U—Hildebrand (A.L.), Klem (N.L.), Owens (A.L.) and O'Day (N.L.). T—1:58. A—20,040.

Game 3

Saturday, September 7, At Chicago

Boston	AB.	R.	H.	RBI.	PO.	A.
Hooper, rf	3	0	1	0	3	0
Shean, 2b	4	0	0	0	1	2
Strunk, cf	4	0	0	0	1	0
Whiteman, lf	3	1	1	0	3	0
McInnis, 1b	4	1	1	0	12	0
Schang, c	4	0	2	1	6	3
Scott, ss	4	0	1	1	1	5
Thomas, 3b	3	0	1	0	0	2
Mays, p	3	0	0	0	0	2
Totals	32	2	7	2	27	14

Chicago	AB.	R.	H.	RBI.	PO.	A.
Flack, rf	3	0	0	0	3	1
Hollocher, ss	3	0	0	0	1	3
Mann, lf	4	0	2	0	1	0
Paskert, cf	4	0	1	0	1	0
Merkle, 1b	4	0	0	0	9	2
Pick, 2b	4	1	2	0	0	0
Deal, 3b	3	0	1	0	1	1
aBarber	0	0	0	0	0	0
Killefer, c	3	0	1	1	8	0
Vaughn, p	3	0	0	0	3	3
Totals	31	1	7	1	27	10

Boston	0 0 0 2 0 0 0 0 0—2
Chicago	0 0 0 0 1 0 0 0 0—1

Boston	IP.	H.	R.	ER.	BB.	SO.
Mays (W)	9	7	1	1	1	4

Chicago	IP.	H.	R.	ER.	BB.	SO.
Vaughn (L)	9	7	2	2	1	7

aAnnounced as batter for Deal in ninth. E—Hollocher. DP—Chicago 2. LOB—Boston 5, Chicago 5. 2B—Mann, Pick. SB—Whiteman, Schang, Pick. SH—Hollocher. HBP—By Vaughn (Whiteman). PB—Schang. U—Klem (N.L.), Owens (A.L.), O'Day (N.L.) and Hildebrand (A.L.). T—1:57. A—27,054.

Game 4

Monday, September 9, At Boston

Chicago	AB.	R.	H.	RBI.	PO.	A.
Flack, rf	4	0	1	0	3	0
Hollocher, ss	4	0	0	1	2	0
Mann, lf	4	0	1	1	2	0
Paskert, cf	4	0	0	0	3	0
Merkle, 1b	3	0	1	0	9	1
Pick, 2b	2	0	2	0	0	2
aZeider, 3b	0	0	0	0	1	2
Deal, 3b	2	0	1	0	1	3
bO'Farrell	1	0	0	0	0	0
Wortman, 2b	1	0	0	0	1	0
Killefer, c	2	1	0	0	1	0
eBarber	1	0	0	0	0	0
Tyler, p	0	0	0	0	1	4
cHendrix	1	0	1	0	0	0
dMcCabe	0	1	0	0	0	0
Douglas, p	0	0	0	0	0	0
Totals	29	2	7	2	27	21

Boston	AB.	R.	H.	RBI.	PO.	A.
Hooper, rf	3	0	0	0	1	0
Shean, 2b	3	0	1	0	4	4
Strunk, cf	4	0	0	0	0	0
Whiteman, lf	3	1	0	0	1	0
Bush, p	0	0	0	0	0	0
McInnis, 1b	3	1	1	0	16	1
Ruth, p-lf	2	0	1	2	0	4
Scott, ss	3	0	0	0	3	8
Thomas, 3b	3	0	0	0	2	3
Agnew, c	2	0	0	0	0	1
Schang, c	1	1	1	0	0	0
Totals	27	3	4	2	27	21

Chicago	0 0 0 0 0 0 0 2 0—2
Boston	0 0 0 2 0 0 0 1 x—3

Chicago	IP.	H.	R.	ER.	BB.	SO.
Tyler	7	3	2	2	2	1
Douglas (L)	1	1	1	0	0	0

Boston	IP.	H.	R.	ER.	BB.	SO.
Ruth (W)	8*	7	2	2	6	0
Bush	1	0	0	0	0	0

*Pitched to two batters in ninth.

aWalked for Pick in seventh. bHit into double play for Deal in seventh. cSingled for Tyler in eighth. dRan for Hendrix in eighth. eHit into double play for Killefer in ninth. E—Douglas. DP—Boston 3. LOB—Chicago 6, Boston 4. 2B—Shean. 3B—Ruth. SB—Shean. SH—Hooper, Ruth. WP—Ruth. PB—Killefer 2. U—Owens (A.L.), O'Day (N.L.), Hildebrand (A.L.) and Klem (N.L.). T—1:50. A—22,183.

Game 5

Tuesday, September 10, At Boston

Chicago	AB.	R.	H.	RBI.	PO.	A.
Flack, rf	2	1	0	0	1	0
Hollocher, ss	3	2	3	0	2	5
Mann, lf	3	0	1	1	2	0
Paskert, cf	3	0	1	2	3	0
Merkle, 1b	3	0	1	0	11	1
Pick, 2b	4	0	1	0	4	3
Deal, 3b	4	0	0	0	0	0
Killefer, c	4	0	0	0	4	0
Vaughn, p	4	0	0	0	0	3
Totals	30	3	7	3	27	12

Boston	AB.	R.	H.	RBI.	PO.	A.
Hooper, rf	4	0	1	0	1	0
Shean, 2b	3	0	1	0	3	2
Strunk, cf	4	0	1	0	4	0
Whiteman, lf	3	0	1	0	1	2
McInnis, 1b	3	0	0	0	9	0
Scott, ss	3	0	0	0	1	4
Thomas, 3b	3	0	1	0	1	1
Agnew, c	2	0	0	0	5	1
aSchang, c	1	0	0	0	1	0
Jones, p	1	0	0	0	1	3
bMiller	1	0	0	0	0	0
Totals	28	0	5	0	27	13

Chicago	0 0 1 0 0 0 0 2 0—3
Boston	0 0 0 0 0 0 0 0 0—0

Chicago	IP.	H.	R.	ER.	BB.	SO.
Vaughn (W)	9	5	0	0	1	4

Boston	IP.	H.	R.	ER.	BB.	SO.
Jones (L)	9	7	3	3	5	5

aStruck out for Agnew in eighth. bFlied out for Jones in ninth. DP—Chicago 3, Boston 1. LOB—Chicago 6, Boston 3. 2B—Mann, Paskert, Strunk. SB—Hollocher. SH—Mann, Shean. U—O'Day (N.L.), Hildebrand (A.L.), Klem (N.L.) and Owens (A.L.). T—1:42. A—24,694.

Game 6

Wednesday, September 11, At Boston

Chicago	AB.	R.	H.	RBI.	PO.	A.
Flack, rf	3	1	1	0	2	0
Hollocher, ss	4	0	0	0	0	4
Mann, lf	3	0	0	0	2	0
Paskert, cf	2	0	0	0	5	0
Merkle, 1b	3	0	1	1	8	2
Pick, 2b	3	0	1	0	3	1
Deal, 3b	2	0	0	0	2	1
aBarber	1	0	0	0	0	0
Zeider, 3b	0	0	0	0	0	0
Killefer, c	2	0	0	0	2	2
bO'Farrell, c	1	0	0	0	0	0
Tyler, p	2	0	0	0	0	3
cMcCabe	1	0	0	0	0	0
Hendrix, p	0	0	0	0	0	0
Totals	27	1	3	1	24	13

Boston	AB.	R.	H.	RBI.	PO.	A.
Hooper, rf	3	0	0	0	1	0
Shean, 2b	3	1	0	0	2	4
Strunk, cf	4	0	2	0	0	0
Whiteman, lf	4	0	0	0	2	0
Ruth, lf	0	0	0	0	1	0
McInnis, 1b	4	0	1	0	16	1
Scott, ss	4	0	1	0	3	3
Thomas, 3b	2	0	0	0	1	2
Schang, c	1	0	0	0	1	2
Mays, p	2	1	1	0	0	6
Totals	27	2	5	0	27	18

Chicago	0 0 0 1 0 0 0 0 0—1
Boston	0 0 2 0 0 0 0 0 x—2

Chicago	IP.	H.	R.	ER.	BB.	SO.
Tyler (L)	7	5	2	0	5	1
Hendrix	1	0	0	0	0	0

Boston	IP.	H.	R.	ER.	BB.	SO.
Mays (W)	9	3	1	1	2	1

aLined out for Deal in eighth. bPopped out for Killefer in eighth. cFouled out for Tyler in eighth. E—Flack, Tyler. LOB—Chicago 2, Boston 8. SB—Flack. SH—Hooper, Thomas. HBP—By Mays (Mann). U—Hildebrand (A.L.), Klem (N.L.), Owens (A.L.) and O'Day (N.L.). T—1:46. A—15,238.

COMPOSITE BATTING AVERAGES

Boston Red Sox

Player-Position	G.	AB.	R.	H.	2B.	3B.	HR.	RBI.	BA.
Schang, ph-c	5	9	1	4	0	0	0	1	.444
Whiteman, lf	6	20	2	5	0	1	0	1	.250
McInnis, 1b	6	20	2	5	0	0	0	1	.250
Shean, 2b	6	19	2	4	1	0	0	0	.211
Hooper, rf	6	20	0	4	0	0	0	0	.200
Ruth, p-lf	3	5	0	1	0	1	0	2	.200
Mays, p	2	5	1	1	0	0	0	0	.200
Strunk, cf	6	23	1	4	1	1	0	0	.174
Thomas, 3b	6	16	0	2	0	0	0	0	.125
Scott, ss	6	21	0	2	0	0	0	1	.095
Agnew, c	4	9	0	0	0	0	0	0	.000
Dubuc, ph	1	1	0	0	0	0	0	0	.000
Bush, p	2	2	0	0	0	0	0	0	.000
Jones, p	1	1	0	0	0	0	0	0	.000
Miller, ph	1	1	0	0	0	0	0	0	.000
Totals	6	172	9	32	2	3	0	6	.186

Chicago Cubs

Player-Position	G.	AB.	R.	H.	2B.	3B.	HR.	RBI.	BA.
Hendrix, ph	2	1	0	1	0	0	0	0	1.000
Pick, 2b	6	18	2	7	1	0	0	0	.389
Merkle, 1b	6	18	1	5	0	0	0	1	.278
Flack, rf	6	19	2	5	0	0	0	0	.263
Mann, lf	6	22	0	5	2	0	0	2	.227
Tyler, p	3	5	0	1	0	0	0	2	.200
Hollocher, ss	6	21	2	4	0	1	0	1	.190
Paskert, cf	6	21	0	4	1	0	0	2	.190
Deal, 3b	6	17	0	3	0	0	0	0	.176
Killefer, c	6	17	2	2	1	0	0	2	.118
Zeider, ph-3b	2	0	0	0	0	0	0	0	.000
Wortman, 2b	1	1	0	0	0	0	0	0	.000
O'Farrell, ph-c	3	3	0	0	0	0	0	0	.000
McCabe, pr-ph	3	1	1	0	0	0	0	0	.000
Barber, ph	2	2	0	0	0	0	0	0	.000
Vaughn, p	3	10	0	0	0	0	0	0	.000
Douglas, p	1	0	0	0	0	0	0	0	.000
Totals	6	176	10	37	5	1	0	10	.210

COMPOSITE PITCHING AVERAGES

Boston Red Sox

Pitcher	G.	IP.	H.	R.	ER.	BB.	SO.	W.	L.	ERA.
Mays	2	18	10	2	2	3	5	2	0	1.00
Ruth	2	17	13	2	2	7	4	2	0	1.06
Jones	1	9	7	3	3	5	5	0	1	3.00
Bush	2	9	7	3	3	3	0	0	1	3.00
Totals	6	53	37	10	10	18	14	4	2	1.70

Chicago Cubs

Pitcher	G.	IP.	H.	R.	ER.	BB.	SO.	W.	L.	ERA.
Douglas	1	1	1	1	0	0	0	0	1	0.00
Hendrix	1	1	0	0	0	0	0	0	0	0.00
Vaughn	3	27	17	3	3	5	17	1	2	1.00
Tyler	3	23	14	5	3	11	4	1	1	1.17
Totals	6	52	32	9	6	16	21	2	4	1.04

1919 CINCINNATI REDS VS. CHICAGO WHITE SOX

"... Any man who knows anything at all about base ball and base ball players knows absolutely that both the game and its exemplars are absolutely honest so far as its public presentation is concerned, and any man who insinuates that the 1919 World's Series was not honorably played by every participant therein not only does not know what he is talking about, but is a menace to the game quite as much as the gamblers would be if they had the ghost of a chance to get in their nefarious work ...."

—Editor,
1920 Reach Baseball Guide

Unfortunately, Francis C. Richter, editor of the Reach guide, was a little off the mark. The 1919 World Series was, in fact, *not* honorably played by every participant therein, as was disclosed late in the 1920 major league season when confessions were made confirming wrongdoing.

In fact, eight members of the 1919 White Sox—pitchers Eddie Cicotte and Claude (Lefty) Williams, outfielders Joe Jackson and Happy Felsch, first baseman Chick Gandil, shortstop Swede Risberg, third baseman Buck Weaver and reserve infielder Fred McMullin—eventually were charged with conspiring to fix the outcome of that year's fall classic against the Cincinnati Reds. The eight became forever known as the "Black Sox."

A sharp shift in the betting odds shortly before the start of the World Series—the highly favored White Sox suddenly became underdogs—aroused curiosity, as did swirling rumors that something might be amiss in certain players' on-field efforts. But, overall, fans and other observers accepted the "public presenta-tion" of the 1919 Series. Perhaps, as apparently was the case with Richter, they saw only what they wanted to see.

What everyone saw in Game 1 was a scintillating performance by the Reds' Dutch Ruether. Whatever "assists" he might have received from various members of the opposition, Ruether nevertheless was dazzling as he pitched a complete-game six-hitter and went 3 for 3 at the plate (two of his hits were triples) with three runs batted in. Outfielder Greasy Neale, who would lead the Reds in hitting in this Series with a .357 average and later become a noted football coach, and first baseman Jake Daubert also collected three hits apiece. The Reds were off and rolling, 9-1. The White Sox were off and rolling over.

Cincinnati's Slim Sallee stopped Chicago the next day, 4-2, with Larry Kopf's two-run triple in the fourth inning proving the telling blow. But White Sox rookie Dickey Kerr, left untouched by the fixing sphere but sensing something was wrong, was too tough for anyone—supposed friend or foe—to mess with in Game 3. The lefthander set down the Reds on three hits in a 3-0 triumph.

Manager Pat Moran's National League champions rebounded for 2-0 and 5-0 victories in Games 4 and 5, with Jimmy Ring and Hod Eller tossing the shutouts. In recording Cincinnati's fourth victory of the Series, Eller struck out six consecutive White Sox batters in one stretch.

Under normal circumstances, the World Series would have been over at this juncture. But these were not normal circumstances. Because of an intense postwar interest in the Series, baseball's bigwigs decided to make the 1919 classic a best-of-nine affair. What

The 1919 Chicago White Sox featured an infield of (left to right) third baseman Buck Weaver, shortstop Swede Risberg, second baseman Eddie Collins and first baseman Chick Gandil. All but Collins were suspended from baseball for their part in a World Series gambling fix.

Shoeless Joe Jackson, one of the great talents in baseball history, was banned forever from the game for his part in the 1919 Black Sox scandal.

timing. A "spectacular" was created just when baseball was about to make a spectacle of itself.

Chicago rebounded in the next two games as Kerr won a 10-inning, 5-4 struggle and Cicotte pitched a seven-hitter while prevailing, 4-1.

Cincinnati tore into Williams in Game 8, though, scoring four first-inning runs. The Reds expanded their lead to 10-1 on the way to a 10-5 victory that gave the team the World Series championship in its first-ever appearance in the competition.

That the "Black Sox" were selective in their misdeeds was apparent. Jackson, for instance, batted a Series-leading .375 but acknowledged that he had let up in key situations. Weaver contributed a .324 mark. Gandil supplied game-deciding hits in the third and sixth contests. And Cicotte, with his team one loss from elimination, pitched a one-run game for Manager Kid Gleason's Sox.

On the other hand, Williams, a 23-game winner during the regular season, lost all three of his Se-

ries starts. Cicotte made two errors in the fifth inning of Game 4, helping Cincinnati to the only two runs of the day. Plus, he hit the first Cincinnati batter of the Series, Morrie Rath, with a pitched ball, which supposedly was the signal to bettors that the fix was on. Gandil, despite some bright moments, hit only .233. Felsch and Risberg batted .192 and .080, respectively. McMullin made only two appearances in the Series, both as a pinch-hitter.

While the "Black Sox" were acquitted by the courts in 1921 despite their confessions (records of which were stolen from the prosecutor's office), they nevertheless were banned from Organized Baseball by Kenesaw Mountain Landis because of their undeniable link to gamblers. Not even a recanting of the players' confessions could sway Landis.

"Regardless of the verdict of juries," the baseball commissioner said in a statement, "no player that throws a ball game, no player that entertains proposals or promises to throw a game, no

player that sits in a conference with a bunch of crooked players and gamblers where the ways and means of throwing games are discussed, and does not promptly tell his club about it, will ever again play professional baseball."

While the infamy of the "Black Sox" lives on, so does the pluck of Dickey Kerr. Trying to win when the odds were stacked against him, Kerr compiled a 2-0 record and a 1.42 earned-run average in 19 innings of work during the 1919 Series. Francis C. Richter would call him an absolutely honest exemplar of the national pastime.

Game 1

Wednesday, October 1, At Cincinnati

Chicago	AB.	R.	H.	RBI.	PO.	A.
J. Collins, rf	4	0	1	0	0	0
E. Collins, 2b	4	0	1	0	3	3
Weaver, 3b	4	0	1	0	0	1
Jackson, lf	4	1	0	0	3	0
Felsch, cf	3	0	0	0	4	0
Gandil, 1b	4	0	2	1	7	0
Risberg, ss	2	0	0	0	5	6
Schalk, c	3	0	0	0	2	2
Cicotte, p	1	0	0	0	0	3
Wilkinson, p	1	0	0	0	0	0
aMcMullin	1	0	1	0	0	1
Lowdermilk, p	0	0	0	0	0	0
Totals	31	1	6	1	24	16
Cincinnati	AB.	R.	H.	RBI.	PO.	A.
Rath, 2b	3	2	1	1	4	2
Daubert, 1b	4	1	3	1	9	0
Groh, 3b	3	1	1	2	0	3
Roush, cf	3	0	0	0	8	0
Duncan, lf	4	0	2	1	1	0
Kopf, ss	4	1	0	0	1	3
Neale, rf	4	2	3	0	3	0
Wingo, c	3	1	1	1	1	2
Ruether, p	3	1	3	3	0	2
Totals	31	9	14	9	27	12

Chicago	0 1 0 0 0 0 0 0 0—1
Cincinnati	1 0 0 5 0 0 2 1 x—9

Chicago	IP.	H.	R.	ER.	BB.	SO.
Cicotte (L)	3⅔	7	6	6	2	1
Wilkinson	3⅓	5	2	1	0	1
Lowdermilk	1	2	1	1	1	0
Cincinnati	IP.	H.	R.	ER.	BB.	SO.
Ruether (W)	9	6	1	0	1	1

aSingled for Wilkinson in eighth. E—Gandil, Kopf. DP—Chicago 2. LOB—Chicago 5, Cincinnati 7. 2B—Rath. 3B—Ruether 2, Daubert. SB—Roush. SH—Felsch, Rath, Roush, Wingo. SF—Groh. HBP—By Cicotte (Rath), by Lowdermilk (Daubert). U—Rigler (N.L.), Evans (A.L.), Nallin (A.L.) and Quigley (N.L.). T—1:42. A—30,511.

Game 2

Thursday, October 2, At Cincinnati

Chicago	AB.	R.	H.	RBI.	PO.	A.
J. Collins, rf	4	0	0	0	2	0
E. Collins, 2b	3	0	0	0	2	3
Weaver, 3b	4	0	2	0	3	0
Jackson, lf	4	0	3	0	1	0
Felsch, cf	2	0	0	0	5	1
Gandil, 1b	4	0	1	0	7	0
Risberg, ss	4	1	1	0	2	2
Schalk, c	4	1	2	0	2	2
Williams, p	3	0	1	0	0	2
aMcMullin	1	0	0	0	0	0
Totals	33	2	10	0	24	10
Cincinnati	AB.	R.	H.	RBI.	PO.	A.
Rath, 2b	3	1	0	0	1	2
Daubert, 1b	3	0	0	0	12	0
Groh, 3b	2	1	0	0	0	1
Roush, cf	2	1	1	1	5	0
Duncan, lf	1	1	0	0	1	0
Kopf, ss	3	0	1	2	3	6
Neale, rf	3	0	1	1	1	0
Rariden, c	3	0	1	0	3	0
Sallee, p	3	0	0	0	1	3
Totals	23	4	4	4	27	14

Chicago	0 0 0 0 0 0 2 0 0—2
Cincinnati	0 0 0 3 0 1 0 0 x—4

Chicago	IP.	H.	R.	ER.	BB.	SO.
Williams (L)	8	4	4	4	6	1
Cincinnati	IP.	H.	R.	ER.	BB.	SO.
Sallee (W)	9	10	2	0	1	2

aGrounded out for Williams in ninth. E—Risberg, Daubert, Neale. DP—Chicago 2, Cincinnati 2. LOB—Chicago 7, Cincinnati 3. 2B—Jackson, Weaver. 3B—Kopf. SB—Gandil. SH—Felsch 2, Daubert, Duncan. Balk—Sallee. U—Evans (A.L.), Quigley (N.L.), Nallin (A.L.) and Rigler (N.L.). T—1:42. A—29,690.

Game 3

Friday, October 3, At Chicago

Cincinnati	AB.	R.	H.	RBI.	PO.	A.
Rath, 2b	4	0	0	0	3	3
Daubert, 1b	4	0	0	0	14	1
Groh, 3b	3	0	0	0	2	5
Roush, cf	3	0	0	0	0	0
Duncan, lf	3	0	1	0	0	0
Kopf, ss	3	0	1	0	1	1
Neale, rf	3	0	0	0	1	0
Rariden, c	3	0	0	0	2	3
Fisher, p	2	0	1	0	0	5
aMagee	1	0	0	0	0	0
Luque, p	0	0	0	0	1	0
Totals	29	0	3	0	24	18

Chicago	AB.	R.	H.	RBI.	PO.	A.
Leibold, rf	4	0	0	0	2	0
E. Collins, 2b	4	0	1	0	1	5
Weaver, 3b	4	0	1	0	0	4
Jackson, lf	3	1	2	0	1	0
Felsch, cf	2	1	0	0	1	0
Gandil, 1b	3	0	1	2	14	1
Risberg, ss	2	1	1	0	4	6
Schalk, c	3	0	1	1	4	0
Kerr, p	3	0	0	0	0	0
Totals	28	3	7	3	27	16

Cincinnati .... 0 0 0 0 0 0 0 0 0—0
Chicago .... 0 2 0 1 0 0 0 0 x—3

Cincinnati	IP.	H.	R.	ER.	BB.	SO.
Fisher (L)	7	7	3	2	2	1
Luque	1	0	0	0	0	1

Chicago	IP.	H.	R.	ER.	BB.	SO.
Kerr (W)	9	3	0	0	1	4

aFlied out for Fisher in eighth. E—Fisher. DP—Cincinnati 1, Chicago 1. LOB—Cincinnati 3, Chicago 3. 3B—Risberg. U—Quigley (N.L.), Nallin (A.L.), Rigler (N.L.) and Evans (A.L.). T—1:30. A—29,126.

Game 4

Saturday, October 4, At Chicago

Cincinnati	AB.	R.	H.	RBI.	PO.	A.
Rath, 2b	4	0	1	0	5	1
Daubert, 1b	4	0	0	0	9	1
Groh, 3b	4	0	0	0	2	3
Roush, cf	3	0	0	0	2	0
Duncan, lf	3	1	0	0	1	0
Kopf, ss	3	1	1	1	1	1
Neale, rf	3	0	1	1	4	0
Wingo, c	3	0	2	0	2	0
Ring, p	3	0	0	0	1	2
Totals	30	2	5	2	27	8

Chicago	AB.	R.	H.	RBI.	PO.	A.
Leibold, rf	5	0	0	0	0	0
E. Collins, 2b	3	0	0	0	3	5
Weaver, 3b	4	0	0	0	0	3
Jackson, lf	4	0	1	0	3	0
Felsch, cf	3	0	1	0	0	0
Gandil, 1b	4	0	1	0	14	0
Risberg, ss	3	0	0	0	3	4
Schalk, c	1	0	0	0	4	3
Cicotte, p	3	0	0	0	0	2
aMurphy	1	0	0	0	0	0
Totals	31	0	3	0	27	17

Cincinnati .... 0 0 0 0 2 0 0 0 0—2
Chicago .... 0 0 0 0 0 0 0 0 0—0

Cincinnati	IP.	H.	R.	ER.	BB.	SO.
Ring (W)	9	3	0	0	3	2

Chicago	IP.	H.	R.	ER.	BB.	SO.
Cicotte (L)	9	5	2	0	0	2

aFlied out for Cicotte in ninth. E—Rath, Groh, Cicotte 2. DP—Chicago 2. LOB—Cincinnati 1, Chicago 10. 2B—Jackson, Neale. SB—Risberg. SH—Felsch. HBP—By Ring (E. Collins, Schalk). U—Nallin (A.L.), Rigler (N.L.), Evans (A.L.) and Quigley (N.L.). T—1:37. A—34,363.

Game 5

Monday, October 6, At Chicago

Cincinnati	AB.	R.	H.	RBI.	PO.	A.
Rath, 2b	3	1	1	1	0	3
Daubert, 1b	2	0	0	0	11	0
Groh, 3b	3	1	0	0	1	2
Roush, cf	4	2	1	2	2	0
Duncan, lf	2	0	0	1	2	0
Kopf, ss	3	0	1	0	0	4
Neale, rf	4	0	0	1	1	0
Rariden, c	4	0	0	0	10	0
Eller, p	3	1	1	0	0	2
Totals	28	5	4	5	27	11

Chicago	AB.	R.	H.	RBI.	PO.	A.
Leibold, rf	3	0	0	0	1	0
E. Collins, 2b	4	0	0	0	1	2
Weaver, 3b	4	0	2	0	1	2
Jackson, lf	4	0	0	0	3	0
Felsch, cf	3	0	0	0	7	0
Gandil, 1b	3	0	0	0	8	1
Risberg, ss	3	0	0	0	1	2
Schalk, c	2	0	1	0	3	2
Lynn, c	1	0	0	0	1	0
Williams, p	2	0	0	0	1	0
aMurphy	1	0	0	0	0	0
Mayer, p	0	0	0	0	0	0
Totals	30	0	3	0	27	9

Cincinnati .... 0 0 0 0 4 0 0 1—5
Chicago .... 0 0 0 0 0 0 0 0 0—0

Cincinnati	IP.	H.	R.	ER.	BB.	SO.
Eller (W)	9	3	0	0	1	9

Chicago	IP.	H.	R.	ER.	BB.	SO.
Williams (L)	8	4	4	4	2	3
Mayer	1	0	1	0	1	0

aStruck out for Williams in eighth. E—E. Collins, Felsch, Risberg. LOB—Cincinnati 3, Chicago 4. 2B—Eller. 3B—Roush, Weaver. SB—Roush. SH—Daubert 2, Kopf. SF—Duncan. PB—Schalk. U—Rigler (N.L.), Evans (A.L.), Quigley (N.L.) and Nallin (A.L.). T—1:45. A—34,379.

Game 6

Tuesday, October 7, At Cincinnati

Chicago	AB.	R.	H.	RBI.	PO.	A.
J. Collins, rf	3	0	0	0	2	0
aLeibold, rf	1	0	0	0	0	0
E. Collins, 2b	4	0	0	1	4	6
Weaver, 3b	5	2	3	0	2	1
Jackson, lf	4	1	2	1	1	1
Felsch, cf	5	1	2	1	2	0
Gandil, 1b	4	0	1	1	11	0
Risberg, ss	4	1	0	0	3	5
Schalk, c	2	0	1	1	4	2
Kerr, p	3	0	1	0	1	4
Totals	35	5	10	5	30	19

Cincinnati	AB.	R.	H.	RBI.	PO.	A.
Rath, 2b	5	0	1	0	4	1
Daubert, 1b	4	1	2	0	8	0
Groh, 3b	4	0	1	0	2	2
Roush, cf	4	1	1	0	7	2
Duncan, lf	5	0	1	2	2	0
Kopf, ss	4	0	0	0	1	5
Neale, rf	4	1	3	0	3	0
Rariden, c	4	0	1	0	3	0
Ruether, p	2	1	1	1	0	0
Ring, p	2	0	0	0	0	1
Totals	38	4	11	3	30	11

Chicago .... 0 0 0 0 1 3 0 0 0 1—5
Cincinnati .... 0 0 2 2 0 0 0 0 0 0—4

Chicago	IP.	H.	R.	ER.	BB.	SO.
Kerr (W)	10	11	4	3	2	2

Cincinnati	IP.	H.	R.	ER.	BB.	SO.
Ruether	5*	6	4	4	3	0
Ring (L)	5	4	1	1	3	2

*Pitched to three batters in sixth.

aGrounded out for J. Collins in seventh. E—Felsch, Risberg 2. DP—Chicago 2, Cincinnati 3. LOB—Chicago 8, Cincinnati 8. 2B—Groh, Duncan, Ruether, Weaver 2, Felsch. 3B—Neale. SB—Leibold, Schalk, Rath, Daubert. SH—Daubert, Kerr. SF—E. Collins. HBP—By Kerr (Roush). U—Evans (A.L.), Quigley (N.L.), Nallin (A.L.) and Rigler (N.L.). T—2:06. A—32,006.

Game 7

Wednesday, October 8, At Cincinnati

Chicago	AB.	R.	H.	RBI.	PO.	A.
J. Collins, cf-rf	5	2	3	0	1	0
E. Collins, 2b	4	1	2	0	3	6
Weaver, 3b	4	1	0	0	2	2
Jackson, lf	4	0	2	2	3	0
Felsch, rf-cf	4	0	2	2	2	0
Gandil, 1b	4	0	0	0	9	0
Risberg, ss	4	0	0	0	3	2
Schalk, c	4	0	1	0	4	1
Cicotte, p	4	0	0	0	0	2
Totals	37	4	10	4	27	13

Cincinnati	AB.	R.	H.	RBI.	PO.	A.
Rath, 2b	5	0	1	0	3	3
Daubert, 1b	4	0	0	0	10	1
Groh, 3b	4	1	1	0	0	2
Roush, cf	4	0	0	0	3	1
Duncan, lf	4	0	1	1	1	1
Kopf, ss	4	0	1	0	2	5
Neale, rf	4	0	1	0	3	0
Wingo, c	1	0	1	0	5	1
Sallee, p	1	0	0	0	0	1
Fisher, p	0	0	0	0	0	1
aRuether	1	0	0	0	0	0
Luque, p	1	0	0	0	0	0
bMagee	1	0	1	0	0	0
cSmith	0	0	0	0	0	0
Totals	34	1	7	1	27	16

Chicago .... 1 0 1 0 2 0 0 0 0—4
Cincinnati .... 0 0 0 0 0 1 0 0 0—1

Chicago	IP.	H.	R.	ER.	BB.	SO.
Cicotte (W)	9	7	1	1	3	4

Cincinnati	IP.	H.	R.	ER.	BB.	SO.
Sallee (L)	4⅓	9	4	2	0	0
Fisher	⅔	0	0	0	0	1
Luque	4	1	0	0	0	5

aFouled out for Fisher in fifth. bSingled for Luque in ninth. cRan for Magee in ninth. E—E. Collins, Rath, Daubert, Groh, Roush. DP—Cincinnati 1. LOB—Chicago 7, Cincinnati 9. 2B—J. Collins, Groh. SH—E. Collins. U—Quigley (N.L.), Nallin (A.L.), Rigler (N.L.) and Evans (A.L.). T—1:47. A—13,923.

Game 8

Thursday, October 9, At Chicago

Cincinnati	AB.	R.	H.	RBI.	PO.	A.
Rath, 2b	4	1	2	0	2	2
Daubert, 1b	4	2	2	0	8	0
Groh, 3b	6	2	2	0	1	1
Roush, cf	5	2	3	4	3	0
Duncan, lf	4	1	2	3	1	0
Kopf, ss	3	1	1	0	1	3
Neale, rf	3	0	1	1	4	0
Rariden, c	5	0	2	2	7	0
Eller, p	4	1	1	0	0	0
Totals	38	10	16	10	27	6

Chicago	AB.	R.	H.	RBI.	PO.	A.
Leibold, cf	5	0	1	0	2	2
E. Collins, 2b	5	1	3	0	4	1
Weaver, 3b	5	1	2	0	1	5
Jackson, lf	5	2	2	3	1	0
Felsch, rf	4	0	0	0	2	0
Gandil, 1b	4	1	1	1	9	0
Risberg, ss	3	0	0	0	2	3
Schalk, c	4	0	1	0	6	3
Williams, p	0	0	0	0	0	0
James, p	2	0	0	0	0	0
Wilkinson, p	1	0	0	0	0	2
aMurphy	0	0	0	0	0	0
Totals	38	5	10	4	27	16

Cincinnati .... 4 1 0 0 1 3 0 1 0—10
Chicago .... 0 0 1 0 0 0 0 4 0— 5

Cincinnati	IP.	H.	R.	ER.	BB.	SO.
Eller (W)	9	10	5	4	1	6

Chicago	IP.	H.	R.	ER.	BB.	SO.
Williams (L)	⅓	4	4	4	0	0
James	4⅔*	8	4	3	3	2
Wilkinson	4	4	2	0	4	2

*Pitched to two batters in sixth.

aHit by pitcher for Wilkinson in ninth. E—Roush, Rariden, Schalk. LOB—Cincinnati 12, Chicago 8. 2B—Roush 2, E. Collins, Duncan, Weaver, Jackson. 3B—Kopf, Gandil. HR—Jackson. SB—Neale, Rath, Rariden, E. Collins. SH—Duncan, Daubert. HBP—By James (Eller), by Wilkinson (Roush), by Eller (Murphy). U—Quigley (N.L.), Nallin (A.L.), Rigler (N.L.) and Evans (A.L.). T—2:27. A—32,930.

COMPOSITE BATTING AVERAGES

Cincinnati Reds

Player-Position	G.	AB.	R.	H.	2B.	3B.	HR.	RBI.	BA.
Ruether, p-ph	3	6	2	4	1	2	0	4	.667
Wingo, c	3	7	1	4	0	0	0	1	.571
Fisher, p	2	2	0	1	0	0	0	0	.500
Magee, ph	2	2	0	1	0	0	0	0	.500
Neale, rf	8	28	3	10	1	1	0	4	.357
Eller, p	2	7	2	2	1	0	0	0	.286
Duncan, lf	8	26	3	7	2	0	0	8	.269
Daubert, 1b	8	29	4	7	0	1	0	1	.241
Rath, 2b	8	31	5	7	1	0	0	2	.226
Kopf, ss	8	27	3	6	0	2	0	3	.222
Roush, cf	8	28	6	6	2	1	0	7	.214
Rariden, c	5	19	0	4	0	0	0	2	.211
Groh, 3b	8	29	6	5	2	0	0	2	.172
Smith, pr	1	0	0	0	0	0	0	0	.000
Sallee, p	2	4	0	0	0	0	0	0	.000
Luque, p	2	1	0	0	0	0	0	0	.000
Ring, p	2	5	0	0	0	0	0	0	.000
Totals	8	251	35	64	10	7	0	34	.255

Chicago White Sox

Player-Position	G.	AB.	R.	H.	2B.	3B.	HR.	RBI.	BA.
McMullin, ph	2	2	0	1	0	0	0	0	.500
Jackson, lf	8	32	5	12	3	0	1	6	.375
Weaver, 3b	8	34	4	11	4	1	0	0	.324
Schalk, c	8	23	1	7	0	0	0	2	.304
J. Collins, rf-cf	4	16	2	4	1	0	0	0	.250
Gandil, 1b	8	30	1	7	0	1	0	5	.233
E. Collins, 2b	8	31	2	7	1	0	0	1	.226
Williams, p	3	5	0	1	0	0	0	0	.200
Felsch, cf-rf	8	26	2	5	1	0	0	3	.192
Kerr, p	2	6	0	1	0	0	0	0	.167
Risberg, ss	8	25	3	2	0	1	0	0	.080
Leibold, rf-ph	5	18	0	1	0	0	0	0	.056
Cicotte, p	3	8	0	0	0	0	0	0	.000
Wilkinson, p	2	2	0	0	0	0	0	0	.000
Lynn, c	1	1	0	0	0	0	0	0	.000
Murphy, ph	3	2	0	0	0	0	0	0	.000
Lowdermilk, p	1	0	0	0	0	0	0	0	.000
Mayer, p	1	0	0	0	0	0	0	0	.000
James, p	1	2	0	0	0	0	0	0	.000
Totals	8	263	20	59	10	3	1	17	.224

COMPOSITE PITCHING AVERAGES

Cincinnati Reds

Pitcher	G.	IP.	H.	R.	ER.	BB.	SO.	W.	L.	ERA.
Luque	2	5	1	0	0	0	6	0	0	0.00
Ring	2	14	7	1	1	6	4	1	1	0.64
Sallee	2	13⅓	19	6	2	1	2	1	1	1.35
Eller	2	18	13	5	4	2	15	2	0	2.00
Fisher	2	7⅔	7	3	2	2	2	0	1	2.35
Ruether	2	14	12	5	4	4	1	1	0	2.57
Totals	8	72	59	20	13	15	30	5	3	1.63

Chicago White Sox

Pitcher	G.	IP.	H.	R.	ER.	BB.	SO.	W.	L.	ERA.
Mayer	1	1	0	1	0	1	0	0	0	0.00
Kerr	2	19	14	4	3	3	6	2	0	1.42
Wilkinson	2	7⅓	9	4	2	4	3	0	0	2.45
Cicotte	3	21⅔	19	9	7	5	7	1	2	2.91
James	1	4⅔	8	4	3	3	2	0	0	5.79
Williams	3	16⅓	12	12	12	8	4	0	3	6.61
Lowdermilk	1	1	2	1	1	1	0	0	0	9.00
Totals	8	71	64	35	28	25	22	3	5	3.55

1920
CLEVELAND INDIANS
VS.
BROOKLYN DODGERS

The bare-bones final score of 8-1 gave no hint of anything dramatic. No clue that a noteworthy event or two might have unfolded.

But, in fact, Game 5 of the 1920 World Series was one of the most remarkable contests in the history of baseball's premier event.

When Brooklyn and Cleveland squared off on Sunday, October 10, the Series—another best-of-nine test—was tied at two victories apiece. Indians righthander Stan Coveleski had throttled the National League titlists on five hits in both Games 1 and 4, notching 3-1 and 5-1 decisions (in the latter contest, Leon Cadore, who had pitched the distance for Brooklyn in a 26-inning, 1-1 tie with Boston five months earlier, lasted just one inning in his lone Series start). Brooklyn sandwiched 3-0 and 2-1 Series triumphs between the Cleveland victories, with Burleigh Grimes tossing a seven-hit shutout and Sherry Smith stifling the Indians on three hits.

It didn't take long for the theatrics to begin in Game 5, which featured a rematch of second-game starters Grimes and Jim Bagby of Cleveland. In the bottom of the first inning, the Indians' Charlie Jamieson and Bill Wambsganss touched Grimes for singles and Tris Speaker, Cleveland's playing manager, bunted for a base hit. That brought Elmer Smith to the plate, and the 28-year-old outfielder proceeded to write his name into the record books and send the Cleveland crowd into a frenzy by smashing the first bases-loaded home run in Series history.

The score remained 4-0, Indians, until the fourth when Bagby became the first pitcher ever to hit a homer in the fall

Cleveland's Jim Bagby capped his 31-victory 1920 season by winning Game 5 of the World Series and becoming the first pitcher in Series history to hit a home run.

classic. And Bagby made it a particularly meaningful shot, connecting off Grimes with two runners on base.

Riding the landmark homers by Smith and Bagby to a 7-0 lead, Cleveland seemingly was in a position to coast—and to rest on its laurels. But the Indians left the record-keepers little time to regroup.

Pete Kilduff led off the Brooklyn fifth with a single and moved to second on Otto Miller's hit. At this point, Bagby had yielded eight hits in four-plus innings—but hadn't been scored upon. Relief pitcher Clarence Mitchell, who had entered the game in the fourth, was Brooklyn's next batter. Mitchell, sometimes used as a pinch-hitter and as an outfielder

or first baseman, lined to second baseman Wambsganss for one out. Wambsganss then stepped on second base, doubling off Kilduff, and wheeled around to tag Miller (who had broken for second) to complete a *triple play*. Never before had a triple play been pulled off in Series competition, and Cleveland's "Wamby" had accomplished it unassisted.

Manager Wilbert Robinson's Brooklyn club clearly was up against it this day. Mitchell, for one, could vouch for that. In his second and last trip to the plate in Game 5, he grounded into a double play. In two at-bats, Mitchell had accounted for five outs.

Furthermore, with one out in the ninth, Robinson's team had collected 12 hits—and still hadn't scored. Hit No. 13, a single by Ed Konetchy, finally cashed in a run. Bagby retired the side without further damage, though, and Cleveland emerged an 8-1 winner. The triumph proved the only victory of the Series for Bagby, who had won 31 games during the regular season.

Suitably inspired, Cleveland then dusted off the National Leaguers in Games 6 and 7, with late-season acquisition Walter (Duster) Mails and Coveleski throwing shutouts. Mails, a Dodger briefly in 1915 and 1916 and a minor leaguer for most of the 1920 season, blanked Brooklyn on three hits in a 1-0 decision and Coveleski, pitching his third five-hitter of the Series, won the decisive game by a 3-0 score. Cleveland pitchers had held Brooklyn to two runs in the final 43 innings of the fall classic.

For the second consecutive season, a first-time World Series entrant had made off with the title. Again, the champion hailed from Ohio as the Cleveland Indians supplanted the Cincinnati Reds as

Cleveland second baseman Bill Wambsganss (top left) wheels around and tags out Brooklyn's Otto Miller, completing an unassisted triple play in Game 5 of the 1920 World Series. Pete Kilduff, doubled off second base, is shown reaching third base as Indians third baseman Larry Gardner watches Wambsganss. In the same game, Cleveland's Elmer Smith (below) hit the first grand slam in Series history.

baseball's kingpins.

While "overcoming adversity" undeniably has evolved into a trite expression in sports, the phrase surely was little used at the time but fully applicable to the 1920 Indians. Speaker's team had to overcome the most traumatic adversity of all—the death of a teammate. In the heat of the pennant race, 29-year-old shortstop Ray Chapman was struck by a pitched ball in an August 16 game at New York and died the next day. Chapman was batting .303 and, as usual, supplying excellent defense and leadership.

Cleveland battled on, with newcomers Mails and Joe Sewell proving valuable additions. Mails, after posting an 18-17 record at Sacramento, went 7-0 in nine appearances with the Indians. Shortstop Sewell, obtained from New Orleans to replace Chapman, batted .329 in 22 games. Speaker hit .388 in the 1920 season and was ably supported by catcher Steve O'Neill (.321), out-

fielders Jamieson (.319) and Smith (.316) and third baseman Larry Gardner (.310). Coveleski backed Bagby's big season with 24 victories of his own, and Ray Caldwell won exactly 20.

The Indians captured the A.L. pennant by two games over the Chicago White Sox, who suffered in the late going from suspensions meted out to players implicated in the fixing scandal surrounding the 1919 World Series. Those suspensions came at the end of September in 1920, when names finally were named and misdeeds finally were exposed in the "Black Sox" episode of the previous year. The New York Yankees finished only three games back.

For Cleveland, it was an unforgettable season—tragic, yet triumphant.

Game 1

Tuesday, October 5, At Brooklyn

Cleveland	AB.	R.	H.	RBI.	PO.	A.
Evans, lf	2	0	0	0	1	0
bJamieson, lf	1	0	0	0	0	0
Wambsganss, 2b	3	0	0	0	0	2
Speaker, cf	4	0	0	0	4	0
Burns, 1b	3	1	1	0	9	1
eE. Smith, rf	1	0	0	0	0	0
Gardner, 3b	4	0	0	0	1	3
Wood, rf	2	2	1	0	4	0
fW. Johnston, 1b	1	0	0	0	0	1
Sewell, ss	3	0	1	0	3	4
O'Neill, c	3	0	2	2	3	0
Coveleski, p	3	0	0	0	2	2
Totals	30	3	5	2	27	13

Brooklyn	AB.	R.	H.	RBI.	PO.	A.
Olson, ss	3	0	2	0	0	3
J. Johnston, 3b	3	0	0	0	1	3
Griffith, rf	4	0	1	0	1	0
Wheat, lf	4	1	1	0	4	0
Myers, cf	4	0	0	0	1	0
Konetchy, 1b	4	0	0	1	12	1
Kilduff, 2b	3	0	0	0	1	3
Krueger, c	3	0	0	0	7	1
Marquard, p	1	0	0	0	0	0
aLamar	1	0	0	0	0	0
Mamaux, p	0	0	0	0	0	1
cMitchell	1	0	1	0	0	0
dNeis	0	0	0	0	0	0
Cadore, p	0	0	0	0	0	1
Totals	31	1	5	1	27	13

Cleveland............0 2 0 1 0 0 0 0 0—3
Brooklyn.............0 0 0 0 0 0 1 0 0—1

Cleveland	IP.	H.	R.	ER.	BB.	SO.
Coveleski (W)	9	5	1	1	1	3

Brooklyn	IP.	H.	R.	ER.	BB.	SO.
Marquard (L)	6	5	3	1	2	4
Mamaux	2	0	0	0	0	3
Cadore	1	0	0	0	0	0

aPopped out for Marquard in sixth. bGrounded out for Evans in eighth. cSingled for Mamaux in eighth. dRan for Mitchell in eighth. eGrounded out for Burns in ninth. fGrounded out for Wood in ninth. E—Konetchy. DP—Brooklyn 1. LOB—Cleveland 3, Brooklyn 5. 2B—O'Neill 2, Wood, Wheat. SH—Wambsganss, J. Johnston. U—Klem (N.L.), Connolly (A.L.), O'Day (N.L.) and Dinneen (A.L.). T—1:41. A—23,573.

Game 2

Wednesday, October 6, At Brooklyn

Cleveland	AB.	R.	H.	RBI.	PO.	A.
Jamieson, lf	4	0	1	0	2	0
Wambsganss, 2b	3	0	0	0	3	0
bBurns	0	0	0	0	0	0
Lunte, 2b	0	0	0	0	0	0
Speaker, cf	3	0	2	0	2	0
E. Smith, rf	4	0	0	0	3	0
Gardner, 3b	3	0	2	0	1	2
W. Johnston, 1b	4	0	0	0	3	3
Sewell, ss	4	0	0	0	1	1
O'Neill, c	4	0	1	0	7	2
Bagby, p	2	0	0	0	2	1
aGraney	1	0	0	0	0	0
Uhle, p	0	0	0	0	0	0
cNunamaker	1	0	1	0	0	0
Totals	33	0	7	0	24	9

Brooklyn	AB.	R.	H.	RBI.	PO.	A.
Olson, ss	4	1	1	0	3	2
J. Johnston, 3b	4	1	1	0	0	1
Griffith, rf	4	0	2	2	3	0
Wheat, lf	3	0	1	1	3	0
Myers, cf	3	0	1	0	2	0
Konetchy, 1b	3	0	0	0	10	1
Kilduff, 2b	3	0	0	0	2	3
Miller, c	3	0	0	0	3	1
Grimes, p	3	1	1	0	1	4
Totals	30	3	7	3	27	12

Cleveland ... 0 0 0 0 0 0 0 0 0—0
Brooklyn ... 1 0 1 0 1 0 0 0 x—3

Cleveland	IP.	H.	R.	ER.	BB.	SO.
Bagby (L)	6	7	3	2	1	0
Uhle	2	0	0	0	0	3

Brooklyn	IP.	H.	R.	ER.	BB.	SO.
Grimes (W)	9	7	0	0	4	2

aStruck out for Bagby in seventh. bWalked for Wambsganss in eighth. cSingled for Uhle in ninth. E—Bagby. DP—Cleveland 1. LOB—Cleveland 10, Brooklyn 4. 2B—Wheat, Gardner, Griffith, Speaker. SB—J. Johnston. U—Connolly (A.L.), O'Day (N.L.), Dinneen (A.L.) and Klem (N.L.). T—1:55. A—22,559.

Game 3

Thursday, October 7, At Brooklyn

Cleveland	AB.	R.	H.	RBI.	PO.	A.
Evans, lf	4	0	0	0	2	0
Wambsganss, 2b	3	0	0	0	2	2
Speaker, cf	4	1	1	0	2	0
Burns, 1b	3	0	0	0	12	0
Gardner, 3b	3	0	0	0	0	0
Wood, rf	3	0	0	0	1	0
Sewell, ss	2	0	0	0	2	3
O'Neill, c	3	0	2	0	2	2
bJamieson	0	0	0	0	0	0
Uhle, p	0	0	0	0	0	1
Caldwell, p	0	0	0	0	0	0
Mails, p	2	0	0	0	1	3
cNunamaker, c	1	0	0	0	0	0
Totals	28	1	3	0	24	11

Brooklyn	AB.	R.	H.	RBI.	PO.	A.
Olson, ss	2	1	1	0	0	6
J. Johnston, 3b	3	0	0	0	0	4
Griffith, rf	1	1	0	0	2	0
aNeis, rf	3	0	0	0	0	0
Wheat, lf	4	0	3	1	1	0
Myers, cf	4	0	2	1	1	0
Konetchy, 1b	3	0	0	0	17	2
Kilduff, 2b	1	0	0	0	2	6
Miller, c	1	0	0	0	2	0
S. Smith, p	3	0	0	0	2	2
Totals	25	2	6	2	27	20

Cleveland ... 0 0 0 1 0 0 0 0 0—1
Brooklyn ... 2 0 0 0 0 0 0 0 x—2

Cleveland	IP.	H.	R.	ER.	BB.	SO.
Caldwell (L)	⅓	2	2	1	1	0
Mails	6⅔	3	0	0	4	2
Uhle	1	1	0	0	0	0

Brooklyn	IP.	H.	R.	ER.	BB.	SO.
S. Smith (W)	9	3	1	0	2	2

aGrounded out for Griffith in third. bRan for O'Neill in eighth. cHit into double play for Mails in eighth. E—Sewell, Wheat. DP—Cleveland 2, Brooklyn 2. LOB—Cleveland 2, Brooklyn 7. 2B—Speaker. SH—J. Johnston, Kilduff, Miller. U—O'Day (N.L.), Dinneen (A.L.), Klem (N.L.) and Connolly (A.L.). T—1:47. A—25,088.

Game 4

Saturday, October 9, At Cleveland

Brooklyn	AB.	R.	H.	RBI.	PO.	A.
Olson, ss	4	0	1	0	1	3
J. Johnston, 3b	4	1	2	0	1	0
fNeis	0	0	0	0	0	0
Griffith, rf	4	0	1	1	1	0
Wheat, lf	4	0	0	0	0	0
Myers, cf	3	0	0	0	6	1
Konetchy, 1b	2	0	0	0	5	0
Kilduff, 2b	3	0	1	0	2	3
Miller, c	3	0	0	0	7	0
Cadore, p	0	0	0	0	1	0
Mamaux, p	1	0	0	0	0	0
Marquard, p	0	0	0	0	0	1
dLamar	1	0	0	0	0	0
Pfeffer, p	1	0	0	0	0	0
Totals	30	1	5	1	24	8

Cleveland	AB.	R.	H.	RBI.	PO.	A.
Jamieson, lf	2	0	0	0	1	0
cEvans, lf	3	0	1	0	0	0
Wambsganss, 2b	4	2	2	1	4	6
Speaker, cf	5	2	2	0	3	0
E. Smith, rf	1	0	1	1	1	0
aBurns, 1b	2	0	1	1	7	0
Gardner, 3b	3	0	1	1	2	3
W. Johnston, 1b	1	0	0	0	4	0
bWood, rf	2	0	0	0	0	0
eGraney, rf	1	0	0	0	0	0
Sewell, ss	4	0	2	0	1	7
O'Neill, c	2	0	1	0	4	0
Coveleski, p	4	1	1	0	0	2
Totals	34	5	12	4	27	18

Brooklyn ... 0 0 0 1 0 0 0 0 0—1
Cleveland ... 2 0 2 0 0 1 0 0 x—5

Brooklyn	IP.	H.	R.	ER.	BB.	SO.
Cadore (L)	1*	4	2	2	1	1
Mamaux	1†	2	2	2	0	1
Marquard	3	2	0	0	1	2
Pfeffer	3	4	1	1	2	1

Cleveland	IP.	H.	R.	ER.	BB.	SO.
Coveleski (W)	9	5	1	1	1	4

*Pitched to two batters in second.
†Pitched to two batters in third.

aSingled for E. Smith in third. bFlied out for W. Johnston in third. cFlied out for Jamieson in fourth. dGrounded out for Marquard in sixth. eForced runner for Wood in seventh. fRan for J. Johnston in ninth. E—Wheat, Burns, Sewell. DP—Brooklyn 1, Cleveland 2. LOB—Brooklyn 3, Cleveland 10. 2B—Griffith. SF—Gardner. WP—Pfeffer. PB—Miller. U—Dinneen (A.L.), Klem (N.L.), Connolly (A.L.) and O'Day (N.L.). T—1:45. A—25,734.

Game 5

Sunday, October 10, At Cleveland

Brooklyn	AB.	R.	H.	RBI.	PO.	A.
Olson, ss	4	0	2	0	3	5
Sheehan, 3b	3	0	1	0	1	1
Griffith, rf	4	0	0	0	0	0
Wheat, lf	4	1	2	0	3	0
Myers, cf	4	0	2	0	0	0
Konetchy, 1b	4	0	2	1	9	2
Kilduff, 2b	4	0	1	0	5	6
Miller, c	2	0	2	0	0	1
Krueger, c	2	0	1	0	2	1
Grimes, p	1	0	0	0	0	1
Mitchell, p	2	0	0	0	1	0
Totals	34	1	13	1	24	17

Cleveland	AB.	R.	H.	RBI.	PO.	A.
Jamieson, lf	4	1	2	0	2	1
aGraney, lf	1	0	0	0	0	0
Wambsganss, 2b	5	1	1	0	7	2
Speaker, cf	3	2	1	0	1	0
E. Smith, rf	4	1	3	4	0	0
Gardner, 3b	4	0	1	1	2	2
W. Johnston, 1b	3	1	2	0	9	1
Sewell, ss	3	0	0	0	2	4
O'Neill, c	2	1	0	0	3	1
Thomas, c	0	0	0	0	1	0
Bagby, p	4	1	2	3	0	2
Totals	33	8	12	8	27	13

Brooklyn ... 0 0 0 0 0 0 0 0 1—1
Cleveland ... 4 0 0 3 1 0 0 0 x—8

Brooklyn	IP.	H.	R.	ER.	BB.	SO.
Grimes (L)	3⅓	9	7	7	1	0
Mitchell	4⅔	3	1	0	3	1

Cleveland	IP.	H.	R.	ER.	BB.	SO.
Bagby (W)	9	13	1	1	0	3

aStruck out for Jamieson in eighth. E—Sheehan, Gardner, O'Neill. DP—Brooklyn 1, Cleveland 3. TP—Cleveland 1. LOB—Brooklyn 7, Cleveland 6. 3B—Konetchy, E. Smith. HR—E. Smith, Bagby. SH—Sheehan, W. Johnston. WP—Bagby. PB—Miller. U—Klem (N.L.), Connolly (A.L.), O'Day (N.L.) and Dinneen (A.L.). T—1:49. A—26,884.

Game 6

Monday, October 11, At Cleveland

Brooklyn	AB.	R.	H.	RBI.	PO.	A.
Olson, ss	4	0	1	0	4	1
Sheehan, 3b	4	0	0	0	0	3
Neis, rf	2	0	0	0	3	0
aKrueger	1	0	0	0	0	0
Griffith, rf	0	0	0	0	0	0
Wheat, lf	4	0	0	0	2	0
Myers, cf	4	0	1	0	1	0
Konetchy, 1b	3	0	1	0	9	0
bMcCabe	0	0	0	0	0	0
Kilduff, 2b	4	0	0	0	2	2
Miller, c	3	0	0	0	3	3
S. Smith, p	3	0	0	0	0	3
Totals	32	0	3	0	24	12

Cleveland	AB.	R.	H.	RBI.	PO.	A.
Evans, lf	4	0	3	0	4	0
Wambsganss, 2b	4	0	0	0	1	2
Speaker, cf	3	1	1	0	3	0
Burns, 1b	2	0	1	1	10	0
Gardner, 3b	3	0	0	0	2	2
Wood, rf	3	0	1	0	2	0
Sewell, ss	3	0	1	0	2	3
O'Neill, c	3	0	0	0	3	2
Mails, p	3	0	0	0	0	1
Totals	28	1	7	1	27	10

Brooklyn ... 0 0 0 0 0 0 0 0 0—0
Cleveland ... 0 0 0 0 0 1 0 0 x—1

Brooklyn	IP.	H.	R.	ER.	BB.	SO.
S. Smith (L)	8	7	1	1	1	1

Cleveland	IP.	H.	R.	ER.	BB.	SO.
Mails (W)	9	3	0	0	2	4

aForced runner for Neis in eighth. bRan for Konetchy in ninth. E—Gardner, Sewell 2. LOB—Brooklyn 7, Cleveland 4. 2B—Burns, Olson. U—Connolly (A.L.), O'Day (N.L.), Dinneen (A.L.) and Klem (N.L.). T—1:34. A—27,194.

Game 7

Tuesday, October 12, At Cleveland

Brooklyn	AB.	R.	H.	RBI.	PO.	A.
Olson, ss	4	0	0	0	1	1
Sheehan, 3b	4	0	1	0	2	1
Griffith, rf	4	0	0	0	3	0
Wheat, lf	4	0	2	0	3	0
Myers, cf	4	0	0	0	3	0
Konetchy, 1b	4	0	1	0	8	0
Kilduff, 2b	3	0	0	0	1	4
Miller, c	2	0	0	0	2	1
bLamar	1	0	0	0	0	0
Krueger, c	0	0	0	0	1	0
Grimes, p	2	0	1	0	0	2
cSchmandt	1	0	0	0	0	0
Mamaux, p	0	0	0	0	0	0
Totals	33	0	5	0	24	9

Cleveland	AB.	R.	H.	RBI.	PO.	A.
Jamieson, lf	4	1	2	1	3	0
Wambsganss, 2b	4	0	1	0	4	3
Speaker, cf	3	0	1	1	3	0
E. Smith, rf	3	0	0	0	3	1
Gardner, 3b	4	1	1	0	1	3
W. Johnston, 1b	2	0	1	0	11	1
Sewell, ss	4	0	0	0	0	6
O'Neill, c	4	0	1	0	1	0
Coveleski, p	3	1	0	0	0	1
Totals	31	3	7	2	a26	15

Brooklyn ... 0 0 0 0 0 0 0 0 0—0
Cleveland ... 0 0 0 1 1 0 1 0 x—3

Brooklyn	IP.	H.	R.	ER.	BB.	SO.
Grimes (L)	7	7	3	2	4	2
Mamaux	1	0	0	0	0	1

Cleveland	IP.	H.	R.	ER.	BB.	SO.
Coveleski (W)	9	5	0	0	0	1

aOlson out; hit by batted ball. bGrounded out for Miller in seventh. cGrounded out for Grimes in eighth. E—Sheehan, Grimes, Sewell 2, Coveleski. LOB—Brooklyn 6, Cleveland 8. 2B—O'Neill, Jamieson. 3B—Speaker. SB—W. Johnston, Jamieson. U—O'Day (N.L.), Dinneen (A.L.), Klem (N.L.) and Connolly (A.L.). T—1:55. A—27,525.

COMPOSITE BATTING AVERAGES

Cleveland Indians

Player-Position	G.	AB.	R.	H.	2B.	3B.	HR.	RBI.	BA.
Nunamaker, ph-c	2	2	0	1	0	0	0	0	.500
O'Neill, c	7	21	1	7	3	0	0	2	.333
Bagby, p	2	6	1	2	0	0	1	3	.333
Jamieson, ph-lf	6	15	2	5	1	0	0	1	.333
Speaker, cf	7	25	6	8	2	1	0	1	.320
E. Smith, ph-rf	5	13	1	4	0	1	1	5	.308
Evans, lf-ph	4	13	0	4	0	0	0	0	.308
Burns, 1b-ph	5	10	1	3	1	0	0	3	.300
W. Johnston, ph-1b	5	11	1	3	0	0	0	0	.273
Gardner, 3b	7	24	1	5	1	0	0	2	.208
Wood, rf-ph	4	10	2	2	1	0	0	0	.200
Sewell, ss	7	23	0	4	0	0	0	0	.174
Wambsganss, 2b	7	26	3	4	0	0	0	1	.154
Coveleski, p	3	10	2	1	0	0	0	0	.100
Lunte, 2b	1	0	0	0	0	0	0	0	.000
Graney, ph-rf-lf	3	3	0	0	0	0	0	0	.000
Uhle, p	2	0	0	0	0	0	0	0	.000
Caldwell, p	1	0	0	0	0	0	0	0	.000
Mails, p	2	5	0	0	0	0	0	0	.000
Thomas, c	1	0	0	0	0	0	0	0	.000
Totals	7	217	21	53	9	2	2	18	.244

Brooklyn Dodgers

Player-Position	G.	AB.	R.	H.	2B.	3B.	HR.	RBI.	BA.
Mitchell, ph-p	2	3	0	1	0	0	0	0	.333
Grimes, p	3	6	1	2	0	0	0	0	.333
Wheat, lf	7	27	2	9	2	0	0	2	.333
Olson, ss	7	25	2	8	1	0	0	0	.320
Myers, cf	7	26	0	6	0	0	0	1	.231
J. Johnston, 3b	4	14	2	3	0	0	0	0	.214
Griffith, rf	7	21	1	4	2	0	0	3	.190
Sheehan, 3b	3	11	0	2	0	0	0	0	.182
Konetchy, 1b	7	23	0	4	0	1	0	2	.174
Krueger, c-ph	4	6	0	1	0	0	0	0	.167
Miller, c	6	14	0	2	0	0	0	0	.143
Kilduff, 2b	7	21	0	2	0	0	0	0	.095
Lamar, ph	3	3	0	0	0	0	0	0	.000
Neis, pr-rf	4	5	0	0	0	0	0	0	.000
Marquard, p	2	1	0	0	0	0	0	0	.000
Mamaux, p	3	1	0	0	0	0	0	0	.000
Cadore, p	2	0	0	0	0	0	0	0	.000
S. Smith, p	2	6	0	0	0	0	0	0	.000
Pfeffer, p	1	1	0	0	0	0	0	0	.000
McCabe, pr	1	0	0	0	0	0	0	0	.000
Schmandt, ph	1	1	0	0	0	0	0	0	.000
Totals	7	215	8	44	5	1	0	8	.205

COMPOSITE PITCHING AVERAGES

Cleveland Indians

Pitcher	G.	IP.	H.	R.	ER.	BB.	SO.	W.	L.	ERA.
Mails	2	15⅔	6	0	0	6	6	1	0	0.00
Uhle	2	3	1	0	0	0	3	0	0	0.00
Covelski	3	27	15	2	2	2	8	3	0	0.67
Bagby	2	15	20	4	3	1	3	1	1	1.80
Caldwell	1	⅓	2	2	1	1	0	0	1	27.00
Totals	7	61	44	8	6	10	20	5	2	0.89

Brooklyn Dodgers

Pitcher	G.	IP.	H.	R.	ER.	BB.	SO.	W.	L.	ERA.
Mitchell	1	4⅔	3	1	0	3	1	0	0	0.00
S. Smith	2	17	10	2	1	3	3	1	1	0.53
Marquard	2	9	7	3	1	3	6	0	1	1.00
Pfeffer	1	3	4	1	1	2	1	0	0	3.00
Grimes	3	19⅓	23	10	9	9	4	1	2	4.19
Mamaux	3	4	2	2	2	0	5	0	0	4.50
Cadore	2	2	4	2	2	1	1	0	1	9.00
Totals	7	59	53	21	16	21	21	2	5	2.44

1921
NEW YORK GIANTS
VS.
NEW YORK YANKEES

In 1921, the newest first-time entrant in the World Series was a franchise that started out as the Baltimore Orioles and played under that banner in the American League's first two seasons, 1901 and 1902.

In 1903, the team moved to New York, became the Highlanders and went head-to-head with the National League's Giants club and Brooklyn franchise for the metropolitan area's baseball dollar. The Highlanders set up shop at Hilltop Park and while they showed they could contend with Brooklyn at the turnstiles, they quickly proved they were no match for the nearby Giants in the business of attracting fans. The A.L. club was such a non-factor, competition-wise, that the Giants—having nothing to fear and a few bucks to gain—took in the struggling team as a Polo Grounds tenant in 1913, a year in which the mighty men of John McGraw would win their third consecutive National League pennant.

For the American Leaguers, 1913 was both a season of change and here-we-go-again drudgery; the switch was in their nickname, from Highlanders to the stately title of *Yankees*; the constant came in the form of continued poor play, with the 50-102 Highlanders of 1912 becoming the 57-94 Yankees of 1913.

Gradually, though, the Yankees assembled a decent club. By 1919, they were more than decent— they were third-place finishers in the A.L. By early 1920, they had purchased an outfielder/pitcher who merely changed the face of the game. The acquisition: George Herman (Babe) Ruth, late of the Boston Red Sox.

Ruth, who had hammered 29 home runs (a major league rec-

Righthander Waite Hoyt was outstanding, but he couldn't keep the New York Yankees from losing their 1921 World Series debut.

ord) for Boston in 1919, brought the game into a new era in 1920 by pounding 54 homers for the Yankees. At the same time, he brought throngs to the Polo Grounds—as evidenced by the fact that he and the Yankees, playing their home games in the Giants' park, outdrew McGraw's team by more than 350,000 fans.

As amazing as Ruth was in '20, he was even better in 1921 and led the Yankees to their first A.L. pennant. The Bambino increased his homer output to a staggering 59, boosted his runs-batted-in total from 137 to 171 and inched his eye-catching batting average from .376 to .378. Ruth wasn't the whole story, though. Bob Meusel added 24 homers and 135 RBIs, and every Yankee regular batted .288 or higher. Carl Mays, obtained from Boston in mid-1919, was a 27-game winner for Manager Miller Huggins' team, which got 19 victories from Waite Hoyt (yet another acquisition from the Red Sox, coming over in December 1920) and 18 from Bob Shawkey.

The Giants were no slouches themselves. They had plenty of thump with such headliners as Frankie Frisch, Ross (Pep) Youngs, George Kelly and Irish Meusel (Bob's brother), and quality pitching in a staff featuring the foursome of Art Nehf, Fred Toney, Jesse Barnes and Phil Douglas.

In the first World Series to be played in its entirety at one stadium, the Yankees and Giants got things going with a Mays-vs.-Douglas matchup. The Yanks made their first-ever Series game a good one, blanking the Giants, 3-0, on Mays' five-hitter. Having gotten the hang of this postseason business in a hurry, Huggins' club went out and won by the same score the next day. This time, it was the two-hit pitching of Hoyt that turned the trick (loser Nehf allowed only three hits).

If the Giants' outlook in this best-of-nine battle appeared less than rosy at this point, it soon bordered on the bleak. With Game 3 scoreless after two innings, the Yankees hit the National Leaguers with four third-inning runs—two scoring on a single by Ruth. But McGraw's charges showed their mettle, rebounding with four runs of their own in the bottom half of the inning and then raking Yankees pitching for eight runs in a seventh-inning outburst that featured Youngs' bases-loaded triple. By game's end, the Giants had 20 hits and a

13-5 victory. And when Douglas beat the Yankees, 4-2, in the following game despite Ruth's first homer in Series play, the 1921 fall classic was deadlocked at two victories apiece.

Ruth, bothered by knee and arm ailments, nevertheless was a key figure in Game 5. Leading off the fourth inning of a 1-1 contest, the Yankees' slugger surprised the Giants by bunting for a base hit. He then scored what proved the game's winning run when Bob Meusel rapped a double. Hoyt, after yielding an unearned run in the first inning, held the Giants in check the rest of the way and the A.L. champions claimed a 3-1 victory. But while the Yankees had regained the Series lead, three games to two, all was not well with Huggins' crew: The hobbled Ruth couldn't continue.

Considering the overall strength of the Yankee team, the absence of Ruth from the starting lineup probably didn't doom the club's hopes. Or did it? The Giants, getting home runs from Irish Meusel and Frank Snyder, won the sixth game, 8-5, and Douglas was a 2-1 victor over Mays in Game 7.

In Game 8, the Giants scored an unearned run in the first inning and, with Nehf and Hoyt at the top of their games, it remained a 1-0 contest entering the bottom of the ninth. First baseman Wally Pipp, having an awful Series as reflected by his .154 batting average, was due to lead off the inning for the Yankees. Huggins went to his bench, though, and called on Ruth. The Babe grounded out to Kelly at first.

Aaron Ward then drew a walk. Home Run Baker followed with a ground ball, on which Giants second baseman Johnny Rawlings made a great stop. Rawlings, who fell down while lunging for the ball, was in a sitting position when he threw out Baker. On the play, Ward tried to advance all the way to third base, but Kelly's throw to Frisch cut down the baserunner and ended the Series in dramatic fashion. Nehf's first victory of the fall classic—a four-hit, 1-0 conquest—had sewn up the title for the Giants, five games

to three.

The Yankees, in their first World Series, had come up losers despite an extraordinary performance by Hoyt, who did not permit an earned run in 27 innings. Mays also was effective, achieving a 1.73 earned-run average over 26 innings. And Ruth batted .313 with one homer and four RBIs. (Replacement Chick Fewster homered in his first official at-bat after taking over for Ruth beginning in Game 6, but went 1 for 9 in the rest of the Series.)

For McGraw and the Giants, it was a return to glory they hadn't known since 1905, when the second fall classic was played. After four October failures in intervening years, the New York Giants once again were World Series champions.

Game 1

Wednesday, October 5, At Polo Grounds

Yankees	AB.	R.	H.	RBI.	PO.	A.
Miller, cf	4	1	1	0	0	0
Peckinpaugh, ss	3	1	1	0	1	9
Ruth, lf	3	0	1	1	4	0
R. Meusel, rf	4	0	1	1	0	0
Pipp, 1b	2	0	0	0	17	0
Ward, 2b	3	0	1	0	3	5
McNally, 3b	4	1	2	0	0	0
Schang, c	2	0	0	0	1	1
Mays, p	3	0	1	0	0	3
Totals	28	3	7	2	27	18

Giants	AB.	R.	H.	RBI.	PO.	A.
Burns, cf	4	0	0	0	0	0
Bancroft, ss	4	0	0	0	1	3
Frisch, 3b	4	0	4	0	1	4
Youngs, rf	3	0	0	0	0	0
Kelly, 1b	4	0	0	0	14	1
E. Meusel, lf	3	0	0	0	1	0
Rawlings, 2b	2	0	1	0	3	5
Snyder, c	3	0	0	0	7	1
Douglas, p	2	0	0	0	0	3
bSmith	1	0	0	0	0	0
Barnes, p	0	0	0	0	0	0
Totals	30	0	5	0	a26	18

Yankees			1 0 0	0 1 1	0 0 0	—3
Giants			0 0 0	0 0 0	0 0 0	—0

Yankees	IP.	H.	R.	ER.	BB.	SO.
Mays (W)	9	5	0	0	0	1

Giants	IP.	H.	R.	ER.	BB.	SO.
Douglas (L)	8	5	3	3	4	6
Barnes	1	2	0	0	0	1

aSchang out; hit by batted ball. bFlied out for Douglas in eighth. DP—Yankees 1, Giants 1. LOB—Yankees 5, Giants 5. 2B—McNally. 3B—McNally 2, Frisch. SH—Peckinpaugh, Pipp, Schang, Youngs. HBP—By Mays (Rawlings). PB—Snyder. U—Rigler (N.L.), Moriarty (A.L.), Quigley (N.L.) and Chill (A.L.). T—1:38. A—30,202.

Game 2

Thursday, October 6, At Polo Grounds

Giants	AB.	R.	H.	RBI.	PO.	A.
Burns, cf	3	0	0	0	1	0
Bancroft, ss	4	0	1	0	3	3
Frisch, 3b	4	0	1	0	3	2
Youngs, rf	2	0	0	0	2	0
Kelly, 1b	4	0	0	0	12	2
E. Meusel, lf	2	0	0	0	0	0
Rawlings, 2b	3	0	1	0	2	2
Smith, c	3	0	0	0	1	1
Nehf, p	2	0	0	0	0	3
Totals	27	0	2	0	24	13

Yankees	AB.	R.	H.	RBI.	PO.	A.
Miller, cf	3	0	0	0	1	0
Peckinpaugh, ss	3	0	0	0	3	1
Ruth, lf	1	1	0	0	0	0
R. Meusel, rf	4	1	1	0	1	0
Pipp, 1b	3	0	0	1	14	0
Ward, 2b	4	1	1	0	4	7
McNally, 3b	3	0	0	0	0	3
Schang, c	2	0	0	0	2	2
Hoyt, p	3	0	1	1	0	2
Totals	26	3	3	2	27	15

Giants	0 0 0 0 0 0 0 0 0—0
Yankees	0 0 0 1 0 0 0 2 x—3

Giants	IP.	H.	R.	ER.	BB.	SO.
Nehf (L)	8	3	3	1	7	0

Yankees	IP.	H.	R.	ER.	BB.	SO.
Hoyt (W)	9	2	0	0	5	5

E—Frisch, Smith Nehf. DP—Giants 2, Yankees 1. LOB—Giants 5, Yankees 6. SB—Ruth 2, R. Meusel. PB—Smith. U—Moriarty (A.L.), Quigley (N.L.), Chill (A.L.) and Rigler (N.L.). T—1:55. A—34,939.

Game 3

Friday, October 7, At Polo Grounds

Yankees	AB.	R.	H.	RBI.	PO.	A.
Miller, cf	5	1	1	1	2	0
Peckinpaugh, ss	3	1	0	0	4	2
Ruth, lf	3	0	1	2	1	0
aFewster, lf	0	1	0	0	0	0
R. Meusel, rf	3	0	2	0	1	0
Pipp, 1b	3	0	0	1	12	0
Ward, 2b	4	0	2	1	1	5
McNally, 3b	3	0	0	0	0	2
Schang, c	2	1	1	0	2	2
DeVormer, c	1	0	0	0	1	0
Shawkey, p	1	1	1	0	0	0
Quinn, p	2	0	0	0	0	1
Collins, p	0	0	0	0	0	0
Rogers, p	0	0	0	0	0	1
bBaker	1	0	0	0	0	0
Totals	31	5	8	5	24	13

Giants	AB.	R.	H.	RBI.	PO.	A.
Burns, cf	6	1	4	0	1	0
Bancroft, ss	5	1	1	1	3	2
Frisch, 3b	2	3	2	0	2	1
Youngs, rf	3	2	2	4	0	1
Kelly, 1b	3	1	0	1	7	1
E. Meusel, lf	5	2	3	3	2	0
Rawlings, 2b	5	0	2	3	3	5
Snyder, c	5	1	4	1	8	2
Toney, p	0	0	0	0	0	1
Barnes, p	5	2	2	0	1	1
Totals	39	13	20	13	27	14

Yankees	0 0 4 0 0 0 0 1 0— 5
Giants	0 0 4 0 0 0 8 1 x—13

Yankees	IP.	H.	R.	ER.	BB.	SO.
Shawkey	2⅓	5	4	4	4	0
Quinn (L)	3⅔†	8	4	4	2	2
Collins	⅔	4	4	4	1	0
Rogers	1⅓	3	1	1	0	1

Giants	IP.	H.	R.	ER.	BB.	SO.
Toney	2*	4	4	4	2	1
Barnes (W)	7	4	1	1	2	7

*Pitched to five batters in third.
†Pitched to five batters in seventh.

aRan for Ruth in eighth. bFlied out for Rogers in ninth. DP—Yankees 2. LOB—Yankees 5, Giants 10. 2B—R. Meusel, Youngs, E. Meusel, Burns. 3B—Burns, Youngs. SB—Burns, Frisch, E. Meusel. SH—Pipp, Bancroft. HBP—By Barnes (McNally). WP—Barnes. U—Quigley (N.L.), Chill (A.L.), Rigler (N.L.) and Moriarty (A.L.). T—2:40. A—36,509.

Game 4

Sunday, October 9, At Polo Grounds

Giants	AB.	R.	H.	RBI.	PO.	A.
Burns, cf	4	0	2	2	0	0
Bancroft, ss	4	0	0	0	4	1
Frisch, 3b	4	0	0	0	1	3
Youngs, rf	4	0	1	0	1	0
Kelly, 1b	4	1	1	0	9	0
E. Meusel, lf	4	1	2	1	0	0
Rawlings, 2b	4	1	2	1	1	4
Snyder, c	4	1	1	0	10	2
Douglas, p	2	0	0	0	1	2
Totals	34	4	9	4	27	12

Yankees	AB.	R.	H.	RBI.	PO.	A.
Miller, cf	4	0	0	0	1	0
Peckinpaugh, ss	4	0	1	0	2	6
Ruth, lf	4	1	2	1	2	0
R. Meusel, rf	4	0	0	0	1	0
Pipp, 1b	4	0	1	0	17	0
Ward, 2b	2	0	0	0	1	7
McNally, 3b	3	1	1	0	1	2
Schang, c	3	0	2	1	2	1
Mays, p	3	0	0	0	0	3
Totals	31	2	7	2	27	19

Giants	0 0 0 0 0 0 0 3 1—4
Yankees	0 0 0 0 1 0 0 0 1—2

Giants	IP.	H.	R.	ER.	BB.	SO.
Douglas (W)	9	7	2	2	0	8

Yankees	IP.	H.	R.	ER.	BB.	SO.
Mays (L)	9	9	4	4	0	1

E—Bancroft, McNally. DP—Yankees 1. LOB—Giants 4, Yankees 3. 2B—Burns, Kelly. 3B—Schang, E. Meusel. HR—Ruth. SH—Douglas, Ward. U—Chill (A.L.), Rigler (N.L.), Moriarty (A.L.) and Quigley (N.L.). T—1:38. A—36,372.

Game 5

Monday, October 10, At Polo Grounds

Yankees	AB.	R.	H.	RBI.	PO.	A.
Miller, cf	3	0	1	1	2	0
Peckinpaugh, ss	4	0	1	0	3	3
Ruth, lf	4	1	1	0	2	0
R. Meusel, rf	4	1	2	1	1	2
Pipp, 1b	3	0	0	0	6	1
Ward, 2b	3	0	0	1	5	3
McNally, 3b	2	1	0	0	1	1
Schang, c	3	0	1	0	7	1
Hoyt, p	3	0	0	0	0	1
Totals	29	3	6	3	27	12

Giants	AB.	R.	H.	RBI.	PO.	A.
Burns, cf	5	0	1	0	2	0
Bancroft, ss	4	1	1	0	3	1
Frisch, 3b	4	0	2	0	1	6
Youngs, rf	3	0	1	0	0	0
Kelly, 1b	4	0	3	1	11	1
E. Meusel, lf	4	0	1	0	3	0
Rawlings, 2b	4	0	1	0	0	2
Smith, c	3	0	0	0	6	1
Nehf, p	3	0	0	0	1	1
aSnyder	1	0	0	0	0	0
Totals	35	1	10	1	27	12

Yankees	0 0 1 2 0 0 0 0 0—3
Giants	1 0 0 0 0 0 0 0 0—1

Yankees	IP.	H.	R.	ER.	BB.	SO.
Hoyt (W)	9	10	1	0	2	6

Giants	IP.	H.	R.	ER.	BB.	SO.
Nehf (L)	9	6	3	3	1	5

aStruck out for Nehf in ninth. E—Ward, Frisch. DP—Yankees 1. LOB—Yankees 3. Giants 9. 2B—Schang, E. Meusel, R. Meusel, Miller, Rawlings. SH—Miller, Pipp, Ward. U—Rigler (N.L.), Moriarty (A.L.), Quigley (N.L.) and Chill (A.L.). T—1:50. A—35,758.

Game 6

Tuesday, October 11, At Polo Grounds

Giants	AB.	R.	H.	RBI.	PO.	A.
Burns, cf	3	1	1	0	0	0
Bancroft, ss	5	0	2	2	0	2
Frisch, 3b	4	2	0	1	1	2
Youngs, rf	5	0	1	0	2	0
Kelly, 1b	4	1	3	2	7	1
E. Meusel, lf	4	1	2	2	2	0
Rawlings, 2b	5	0	0	0	5	2
Snyder, c	4	2	2	1	10	0
Toney, p	0	0	0	0	0	0
Barnes, p	4	1	2	0	0	0
Totals	38	8	13	8	27	7

Yankees	AB.	R.	H.	RBI.	PO.	A.
Fewster, lf	3	2	1	2	5	0
Peckinpaugh, ss	5	0	0	0	3	1
Miller, cf	5	1	1	0	1	0
R. Meusel, rf	3	1	1	1	2	0
Pipp, 1b	4	0	1	0	2	0
Ward, 2b	4	0	1	2	3	1
McNally, 3b	4	0	0	0	3	0
Schang, c	2	0	1	0	8	3
Harper, p	0	0	0	0	0	0
Shawkey, p	3	1	1	0	0	0
aBaker	1	0	0	0	0	0
Piercy, p	0	0	0	0	0	0
Totals	34	5	7	5	27	5

Giants	0 3 0 4 0 1 0 0 0—8
Yankees	3 2 0 0 0 0 0 0 0—5

Giants	IP.	H.	R.	ER.	BB.	SO.
Toney	⅔	3	3	3	1	0
Barnes (W)	8⅓	4	2	2	4	10

Yankees	IP.	H.	R.	ER.	BB.	SO.
Harper	1⅓	3	3	3	2	1
Shawkey (L)	6⅔	8	5	3	2	5
Piercy	1	2	0	0	0	2

aGrounded out for Shawkey in eighth. E—Ward, McNally. DP—Yankees 2. LOB—Giants 8, Yankees 7. HR—E. Meusel, Snyder, Fewster. SB—Frisch, Pipp. SH—Burns. U—Moriarty (A.L.), Quigley (N.L.), Chill (A.L.) and Rigler (N.L.). T—2:31. A—34,283.

Game 7

Wednesday, October 12, At Polo Grounds

Yankees	AB.	R.	H.	RBI.	PO.	A.
Fewster, lf	4	0	1	0	0	0
Peckinpaugh, ss	4	0	2	0	0	4
Miller, cf	3	0	0	0	2	1
R. Meusel, rf	4	0	0	0	1	0
Pipp, 1b	4	1	1	0	13	0
Ward, 2b	3	0	0	0	0	4
McNally, 3b	1	0	1	1	0	2
Baker, 3b	3	0	2	0	1	0
aDeVormer	0	0	0	0	0	0
Schang, c	4	0	1	0	7	0
Mays, p	3	0	0	0	0	2
Totals	33	1	8	1	24	13

Giants	AB.	R.	H.	RBI.	PO.	A.
Burns, cf	4	0	2	0	2	0
Bancroft, ss	4	0	1	0	2	2
Frisch, 3b	4	0	0	0	2	3
Youngs, rf	3	1	1	0	2	0
Kelly, 1b	3	0	0	0	13	0
E. Meusel, lf	3	0	1	1	0	1
Rawlings, 2b	3	1	0	0	2	3
Snyder, c	3	0	1	1	3	0
Douglas, p	3	0	0	0	1	5
Totals	30	2	6	2	27	14

Yankees	0 1 0 0 0 0 0 0 0—1
Giants	0 0 0 1 0 0 1 0 x—2

Yankees	IP.	H.	R.	ER.	BB.	SO.
Mays (L)	8	6	2	1	0	7

Giants	IP.	H.	R.	ER.	BB.	SO.
Douglas (W)	9	8	1	1	1	3

aRan for Baker in ninth. E—Ward. LOB—Yankees 7, Giants 4. 2B—Peckinpaugh, Bancroft, Pipp, Burns 2, Snyder. SB—Youngs. SH—Ward. WP—Douglas. U—Quigley (N.L.), Chill (A.L.), Rigler (N.L.) and Moriarty (A.L.). T—1:40. A—36,503.

Game 8

Thursday, October 13, At Polo Grounds

Giants	AB.	R.	H.	RBI.	PO.	A.
Burns, cf	4	0	1	0	3	0
Bancroft, ss	3	1	0	0	0	4
Frisch, 3b	4	0	0	0	2	3
Youngs, rf	2	0	1	0	0	0
Kelly, 1b	4	0	0	0	13	1
E. Meusel, lf	4	0	1	0	1	0
Rawlings, 2b	4	0	3	0	4	4
Snyder, c	2	0	0	0	4	0
Nehf, p	4	0	0	0	0	0
Totals	31	1	6	0	27	12

Yankees	AB.	R.	H.	RBI.	PO.	A.
Fewster, lf	3	0	0	0	2	0
Peckinpaugh, ss	2	0	0	0	2	2
Miller, cf	4	0	1	0	1	0
R. Meusel, rf	4	0	0	0	2	0
Pipp, 1b	3	0	1	0	11	0
aRuth	1	0	0	0	0	0
Ward, 2b	3	0	1	0	0	2
Baker, 3b	3	0	0	0	1	3
Schang, c	3	0	0	0	8	1
Hoyt, p	3	0	1	0	0	3
Totals	29	0	4	0	27	11

Giants	1 0 0 0 0 0 0 0 0—1
Yankees	0 0 0 0 0 0 0 0 0—0

Giants	IP.	H.	R.	ER.	BB.	SO.
Nehf (W)	9	4	0	0	5	3

Yankees	IP.	H.	R.	ER.	BB.	SO.
Hoyt (L)	9	6	1	0	4	7

aGrounded out for Pipp in ninth. E—Peckinpaugh. DP—Giants 2. LOB—Giants 9, Yankees 7. 2B—Rawlings 2. SB—Youngs. SH—Snyder 2. WP—Nehf. U—Chill (A.L.), Rigler (N.L.), Moriarty (A.L.) and Quigley (N.L.). T—1:58. A—25,410.

COMPOSITE BATTING AVERAGES

New York Giants

Player-Position	G.	AB.	R.	H.	2B.	3B.	HR.	RBI.	BA.
Barnes, p	3	9	3	4	0	0	0	0	.444
Snyder, c-ph	7	22	4	8	1	0	1	3	.364
E. Meusel, lf	8	29	4	10	2	1	1	7	.345
Rawlings, 2b	8	30	2	10	3	0	0	4	.333
Burns, cf	8	33	2	11	4	1	0	2	.333
Frisch, 3b	8	30	5	9	0	1	0	1	.300
Youngs, rf	8	25	3	7	1	1	0	4	.280
Kelly, 1b	8	30	3	7	1	0	0	4	.233
Bancroft, ss	8	33	3	5	1	0	0	3	.152
Douglas, p	3	7	0	0	0	0	0	0	.000
Smith, ph-c	3	7	0	0	0	0	0	0	.000
Nehf, p	3	9	0	0	0	0	0	0	.000
Toney, p	2	0	0	0	0	0	0	0	.000
Totals	8	264	29	71	13	4	2	28	.269

New York Yankees

Player-Position	G.	AB.	R.	H.	2B.	3B.	HR.	RBI.	BA.
Shawkey, p	2	4	2	2	0	0	0	0	.500
Ruth, lf-ph	6	16	3	5	0	0	1	4	.313
Schang, c	8	21	1	6	1	1	0	1	.286
Baker, ph-3b	4	8	0	2	0	0	0	0	.250
Ward, 2b	8	26	1	6	0	0	0	4	.231
Hoyt, p	3	9	0	2	0	0	0	1	.222
McNally, 3b	7	20	3	4	1	0	0	1	.200
Fewster, pr-lf	4	10	3	2	0	0	1	2	.200
R. Meusel, rf	8	30	3	6	2	0	0	3	.200
Peckinpaugh, ss	8	28	2	5	1	0	0	0	.179
Miller, cf	8	31	3	5	1	0	0	2	.161
Pipp, 1b	8	26	1	4	1	0	0	2	.154
Mays, p	3	9	0	1	0	0	0	0	.111
DeVormer, c-pr	2	1	0	0	0	0	0	0	.000
Quinn, p	1	2	0	0	0	0	0	0	.000
Collins, p	1	0	0	0	0	0	0	0	.000
Rogers, p	1	0	0	0	0	0	0	0	.000
Harper, p	1	0	0	0	0	0	0	0	.000
Piercy, p	1	0	0	0	0	0	0	0	.000
Totals	8	241	22	50	7	1	2	20	.207

COMPOSITE PITCHING AVERAGES

New York Giants

Pitcher	G.	IP.	H.	R.	ER.	BB.	SO.	W.	L.	ERA.
Nehf	3	26	13	6	4	13	8	1	2	1.38
Barnes	3	16⅓	10	3	3	6	18	2	0	1.65
Douglas	3	26	20	6	6	5	17	2	1	2.08
Toney	2	2⅔	7	7	7	3	1	0	0	23.63
Totals	8	71	50	22	20	27	44	5	3	2.53

New York Yankees

Pitcher	G.	IP.	H.	R.	ER.	BB.	SO.	W.	L.	ERA.
Hoyt	3	27	18	2	0	11	18	2	1	0.00
Piercy	1	1	2	0	0	0	2	0	0	0.00
Mays	3	26	20	6	5	0	9	1	2	1.73
Shawkey	2	9	13	9	7	6	5	0	1	7.00
Rogers	1	1⅓	3	1	1	0	1	0	0	6.75
Quinn	1	3⅔	8	4	4	2	2	0	1	9.82
Harper	1	1⅓	3	3	3	2	1	0	0	20.25
Collins	1	⅔	4	4	4	1	0	0	0	54.00
Totals	8	70	71	29	24	22	38	3	5	3.09

1922
NEW YORK GIANTS
VS.
NEW YORK YANKEES

The 1922 major league season was not a majestic one for baseball's reigning box-office king and his court, Babe Ruth and the New York Yankees.

Oh, the Yankees had their moments, all right. Any team that earns its way into the World Series didn't exactly have a downer of a year and, sure enough, the Yanks were in the opposing dugout October 4 when Art Nehf of the defending Series champion New York Giants toed the rubber for Game 1 of the 1922 fall classic. The Yankees, though, had a real struggle getting there. They had won the American League pennant by a scant one game over the St. Louis Browns.

If the Yanks as a whole had a difficult time getting things going in 1922, consider Ruth's plight. The Bambino didn't even appear in a league game until May 20. He and Bob Meusel had been suspended by Commissioner Kenesaw Mountain Landis for making an unauthorized barnstorming tour following the 1921 Series. Later, the Babe was handed short suspensions following run-ins with umpires and other indiscretions. When the pennant chase roared to a finish, Ruth had appeared in only 110 of his club's 154 games. His batting average plummeted 63 points from the previous season, falling to .315, and, naturally, his home run and runs-batted-in totals suffered. Ruth's homer figure of 35 not only cost him the majors' seasonal crown, but it also dropped him to *third* in the American League. And his RBI output of 99 didn't even rank among the A.L.'s top five totals.

Miller Huggins' team persevered and won a Series rematch with the Giants, pennant winners by seven games in the National

Art Nehf provided the 1922 New York Giants with the World Series-clinching victory for the second year in a row.

League. The Yankees had fortified themselves with an off-season trade that netted pitchers Joe Bush and Sad Sam Jones and shortstop Everett Scott from the Boston Red Sox and the April purchase of outfielder Whitey Witt from the Philadelphia Athletics. The club further strengthened itself in a July deal with the Red Sox that made third baseman Joe Dugan a Yankee.

The Giants, too, made some good moves. Key additions were third baseman Heinie Groh and pitcher Jack Scott. Groh, acquired in a winter trade, had batted .331 in 97 games for Cincinnati in 1921. Scott was signed during the 1922 season after being released by the Reds.

Groh hit only .265 for the Giants in the regular season, but

went 3 for 3 in the first game of the World Series—which had reverted to a best-of-seven format—as John McGraw's club rallied for a 3-2 victory. Shut out by Bush through seven innings, the Giants rebounded from a 2-0 deficit in the eighth on Irish Meusel's two-run single and Ross (Pep) Youngs' sacrifice fly.

The Giants broke on top quickly in Game 2 as Meusel rocked Bob Shawkey for a three-run homer in the top of the first. But the Yankees battled back to tie the score with single runs in the first, fourth and eighth innings. Then, with the game still tied and at least a half-hour of daylight remaining, umpire George Hildebrand inexplicably called the game because of "darkness" after the 10th inning. Fans were furious, and Landis was nonplussed. The commissioner, trying to make the best of a bad public-relations situation, announced that receipts of the game would be turned over to charities.

At this juncture, Ruth was 2 for 8 at the plate with one RBI. A troublesome season wasn't getting any better—and it soon would deteriorate.

Jack Scott, who compiled an 8-2 record for the Giants while appearing in only 17 games, fired a four-hitter in Game 3 and beat the Yankees, 3-0. In Game 4, the National Leaguers' Dave Bancroft rapped a key two-run single and Hugh McQuillan notched a complete-game 4-3 victory. Nehf then applied the clincher (as he had done the year before), stopping the Yanks on five hits in a 5-3 triumph that featured a three-run Giants uprising in the eighth inning. Ruth was 0 for 9 in the three successive Yankee losses.

Groh batted .474 for the Giants in the Series and fiery teammate

Frankie Frisch was right behind at .471. As for Ruth, the Sultan of Swat he was not. The Bambino wound up with two hits in 17 at-bats and a .118 average. Aaron Ward, who hit only seven homers during the regular season, was transformed into the Yankees' muscle man in the Series. The Yanks' second baseman walloped his club's only two homers of the fall classic, but they were his only hits in the five games. (The Yankees not only exhibited little power, they batted only .203 as a team and also suffered offensively because of numerous baserunning blunders.)

The Giants' four victories-to-none triumph—with one tie, of course—would prove McGraw's third and last World Series championship. Ruth and company, frustrated by the events of 1922, were still seeking their first such crown.

Game 1

Wednesday, October 4, At Polo Grounds

Yankees	AB.	R.	H.	RBI.	PO.	A.
Witt, cf	4	0	1	0	1	0
Dugan, 3b	4	1	1	0	0	1
Ruth, rf	4	0	1	1	1	0
Pipp, 1b	4	0	1	0	10	0
R. Meusel, lf	4	1	2	0	0	0
Schang, c	2	0	1	0	7	1
Ward, 2b	1	0	0	1	5	4
Scott, ss	3	0	0	0	0	4
Bush, p	3	0	0	0	0	0
Hoyt, p	0	0	0	0	0	0
Totals	29	2	7	2	24	10

Giants	AB.	R.	H.	RBI.	PO.	A.
Bancroft, ss	4	1	1	0	3	2
Groh, 3b	3	1	3	0	2	3
Frisch, 2b	4	1	2	0	2	4
E. Meusel, lf	4	0	1	2	0	0
Youngs, rf	3	0	0	1	1	1
Kelly, 1b	4	0	2	0	9	0
Stengel, cf	4	0	1	0	4	0
Snyder, c	3	0	1	0	6	2
Nehf, p	2	0	0	0	0	1
aEarl Smith	1	0	0	0	0	0
Ryan, p	0	0	0	0	0	0
Totals	32	3	11	3	27	13

Yankees	0 0 0 0 0 1 1 0 0—2
Giants	0 0 0 0 0 0 0 3 x—3

Yankees	IP.	H.	R.	ER.	BB.	SO.
Bush (L)	7*	11	3	3	1	3
Hoyt	1	0	0	0	0	2

Giants	IP.	H.	R.	ER.	BB.	SO.
Nehf	7	6	2	1	1	3
Ryan (W)	2	1	0	0	0	2

*Pitched to four batters in eighth.

aHit into double play for Nehf in seventh. E—Youngs 2, Nehf. DP—Yankees 1, Giants 3. LOB—Yankees 4, Giants 7. 3B—Groh, Witt. SH—Schang 2, Ward, Youngs. PB—Schang. U—Klem (N.L.), Hildebrand (A.L.), McCormick (N.L.) and Owens (A.L.). T—2:08. A—36,514.

Game 2

Thursday, October 5, At Polo Grounds

Giants	AB.	R.	H.	RBI.	PO.	A.
Bancroft, ss	5	0	1	0	1	0
Groh, 3b	4	1	1	0	1	3
Frisch, 2b	4	1	2	0	1	4
E. Meusel, lf	4	1	1	3	0	0
Youngs, rf	3	0	1	0	1	0
Kelly, 1b	4	0	0	0	15	0
Stengel, cf	1	0	1	0	0	0
aCunningham, cf	2	0	0	0	2	0
bEarl Smith	1	0	0	0	0	0
King, cf	0	0	0	0	0	0
Snyder, c	4	0	1	0	9	1
J. Barnes, p	4	0	0	0	0	4
Totals	36	3	8	3	30	12

Yankees	AB.	R.	H.	RBI.	PO.	A.
Witt, cf	5	0	1	0	1	1
Dugan, 3b	5	1	2	0	3	0
Ruth, rf	4	1	1	0	5	0
Pipp, 1b	5	0	1	1	11	0
R. Meusel, lf	4	0	1	1	1	0
Schang, c	4	0	0	0	5	0
Ward, 2b	4	1	1	1	3	5
Scott, ss	4	0	1	0	1	3
Shawkey, p	4	0	0	0	0	2
Totals	39	3	8	3	30	11

Giants	3 0 0 0 0 0 0 0 0 0—3
Yankees	1 0 0 1 0 0 0 1 0 0—3

(Game called at end of 10th inning on account of darkness.)

Giants	IP.	H.	R.	ER.	BB.	SO.
J. Barnes	10	8	3	2	2	6

Yankees	IP.	H.	R.	ER.	BB.	SO.
Shawkey	10	8	3	3	2	4

aRan for Stengel in second. bStruck out for Cunningham in ninth. E—Bancroft. DP—Yankees 1. LOB—Giants 5, Yankees 8. 2B—Dugan, Ruth, R. Meusel. HR—E. Meusel, Ward. SB—Frisch. WP—Shawkey 2. U—Hildebrand (A.L.), McCormick (N.L.), Owens (A.L.) and Klem (N.L.). T—2:40. A—37,020.

Game 3

Friday, October 6, At Polo Grounds

Yankees	AB.	R.	H.	RBI.	PO.	A.
Witt, cf	3	0	0	0	1	0
Dugan, 3b	4	0	0	0	2	4
Ruth, rf	3	0	0	0	0	0
Pipp, 1b	4	0	1	0	10	1
R. Meusel, lf	4	0	1	0	1	1
Schang, c	3	0	1	0	2	2
Ward, 2b	2	0	0	0	2	4
aElmer Smith	1	0	0	0	0	0
McNally, 2b	0	0	0	0	1	1
E. Scott, ss	3	0	0	0	4	1
Hoyt, p	2	0	1	0	1	2
bBaker	1	0	0	0	0	0
Jones, p	0	0	0	0	0	1
Totals	30	0	4	0	24	17

Giants	AB.	R.	H.	RBI.	PO.	A.
Bancroft, ss	3	2	0	0	0	5
Groh, 3b	4	1	2	0	2	2
Frisch, 2b	2	0	2	2	1	5
E. Meusel, lf	4	0	1	1	1	0
Youngs, rf	4	0	3	0	2	0
Kelly, 1b	3	0	1	0	15	1
Cunningham, cf	3	0	1	0	3	0
Earl Smith, c	4	0	1	0	2	1
J. Scott, p	4	0	1	0	1	1
Totals	31	3	12	3	27	15

Yankees	0 0 0 0 0 0 0 0 0—0
Giants	0 0 2 0 0 0 1 0 x—3

Yankees	IP.	H.	R.	ER.	BB.	SO.
Hoyt (L)	7	11	3	1	2	2
Jones	1	1	0	0	1	0

Giants	IP.	H.	R.	ER.	BB.	SO.
J. Scott (W)	9	4	0	0	1	2

aStruck out for Ward in seventh. bGrounded out for Hoyt in eighth. E—Ward, Frisch. DP—Yankees 1. LOB—Yankees 5, Giants 9. 2B—Schang. SB—Pipp. SH—Frisch, Kelly. HBP—By J. Scott (Ruth). U—McCormick (N.L.), Owens (A.L.), Klem (N.L.) and Hildebrand (A.L.). T—1:48. A—37,620.

Game 4

Saturday, October 7, At Polo Grounds

Giants	AB.	R.	H.	RBI.	PO.	A.
Bancroft, ss	3	1	2	2	3	5
Groh, 3b	4	1	1	0	0	3
Frisch, 2b	3	0	0	0	4	3
E. Meusel, lf	4	0	1	1	1	0
Youngs, rf	4	0	2	1	3	0
Kelly, 1b	4	0	0	0	8	0
Cunningham, cf	3	0	0	0	3	2
Snyder, c	4	1	2	0	5	0
McQuillan, p	4	1	1	0	0	0
Totals	33	4	9	4	27	13

Yankees	AB.	R.	H.	RBI.	PO.	A.
Witt, cf	4	1	2	0	4	0
Dugan, 3b	4	1	1	0	0	3
Ruth, rf	3	0	0	0	1	0
Pipp, 1b	4	0	2	1	12	3
R. Meusel, lf	4	0	1	1	5	0
Schang, c	4	0	1	0	1	1
Ward, 2b	4	1	1	1	0	2
Scott, ss	2	0	0	0	4	2
Mays, p	2	0	0	0	0	4
aElmer Smith	1	0	0	0	0	0
Jones, p	0	0	0	0	0	0
Totals	32	3	8	3	27	15

Giants	0 0 0 0 4 0 0 0 0—4
Yankees	2 0 0 0 0 0 1 0 0—3

Giants	IP.	H.	R.	ER.	BB.	SO.
McQuillan (W)	9	8	3	2	2	4

Yankees	IP.	H.	R.	ER.	BB.	SO.
Mays (L)	8	9	4	4	2	1
Jones	1	0	0	0	0	0

aStruck out for Mays in eighth. E—Snyder. DP—Giants 1, Yankees 1. LOB—Giants 5, Yankees 4. 2B—McQuillan, Witt, Pipp. HR—Ward. SB—R. Meusel. SH—Frisch. U—Owens (A.L.), Klem (N.L.), Hildebrand (A.L.) and McCormick (N.L.). T—1:41. A—36,242.

Game 5

Sunday, October 8, At Polo Grounds

Yankees	AB.	R.	H.	RBI.	PO.	A.
Witt, cf	2	0	0	0	0	0
aMcMillan, cf	2	0	0	0	1	0
Dugan, 3b	3	1	1	0	0	1
Ruth, rf	3	0	0	0	2	0
Pipp, 1b	4	0	1	1	8	0
R. Meusel, lf	4	1	1	0	0	0
Schang, c	3	0	0	0	4	0
Ward, 2b	2	1	0	0	3	1
Scott, ss	2	0	1	1	5	5
Bush, p	3	0	1	1	1	3
Totals	28	3	5	3	24	10

Giants	AB.	R.	H.	RBI.	PO.	A.
Bancroft, ss	4	0	0	0	2	5
Groh, 3b	4	0	2	0	1	3
Frisch, 2b	4	1	2	0	2	4
E. Meusel, lf	4	2	1	0	1	0
Youngs, rf	2	2	0	0	2	1
Kelly, 1b	3	0	2	2	14	0
Cunningham, cf	2	0	1	2	2	0
bEarl Smith	1	0	0	0	0	0
King, cf	1	0	1	1	0	0
Snyder, c	4	0	1	0	3	2
Nehf, p	1	0	0	0	0	2
Totals	30	5	10	5	27	17

Yankees	1 0 0 0 1 0 1 0 0—3
Giants	0 2 0 0 0 0 0 3 x—5

Yankees	IP.	H.	R.	ER.	BB.	SO.
Bush (L)	8	10	5	5	4	3

Giants	IP.	H.	R.	ER.	BB.	SO.
Nehf (W)	9	5	3	3	2	3

aGrounded out for Witt in fifth. bStruck out for Cunningham in seventh. DP—Yankees 3. LOB—Yankees 4, Giants 6. 2B—Frisch. SH—Ruth, Scott, Kelly, Schang. HBP—By Nehf (Dugan). WP—Nehf. U—Klem (N.L.), Hildebrand (A.L.), McCormick (N.L.) and Owens (A.L.). T—2:00. A—38,551.

COMPOSITE BATTING AVERAGES

New York Giants

Player-Position	G.	AB.	R.	H.	2B.	3B.	HR.	RBI.	BA.
King, cf	2	1	0	1	0	0	0	1	1.000
Groh, 3b	5	19	4	9	0	1	0	0	.474
Frisch, 2b	5	17	3	8	1	0	0	2	.471
Stengel, cf	2	5	0	2	0	0	0	0	.400
Youngs, rf	5	16	2	6	0	0	0	2	.375
Snyder, c	4	15	0	5	0	0	0	0	.333
Kelly, 1b	5	18	0	5	0	0	0	2	.278
J. Scott, p	1	4	0	1	0	0	0	0	.250
McQuillan, p	1	4	1	1	1	0	0	0	.250
E. Meusel, lf	5	20	3	5	0	0	1	7	.250
Cunn'ham, pr-cf	4	10	0	2	0	0	0	2	.200
Bancroft, ss	5	19	4	4	0	0	0	2	.211
Ea. Smith, ph-c	4	7	0	1	0	0	0	0	.143
Nehf, p	2	3	1	0	0	0	0	0	.000
Ryan, p	1	0	0	0	0	0	0	0	.000
J. Barnes, p	1	4	0	0	0	0	0	0	.000
Totals	5	162	18	50	2	1	1	18	.309

New York Yankees

Player-Position	G.	AB.	R.	H.	2B.	3B.	HR.	RBI.	BA.
Hoyt, p	2	2	0	1	0	0	0	0	.500
R. Meusel, lf	5	20	2	6	1	0	0	2	.300
Pipp, 1b	5	21	0	6	1	0	0	3	.286
Dugan, 3b	5	20	4	5	1	0	0	0	.250
Witt, cf	5	18	1	4	1	1	0	0	.222
Schang, c	5	16	0	3	1	0	0	0	.188
Bush, p	2	6	0	1	0	0	0	1	.167
Ward, 2b	5	13	3	2	0	0	2	3	.154
E. Scott, ss	5	14	0	2	0	0	0	1	.143
Ruth, rf	5	17	1	2	1	0	0	1	.118
Shawkey, p	1	4	0	0	0	0	0	0	.000
El. Smith, ph	2	2	0	0	0	0	0	0	.000
McNally, 2b	1	0	0	0	0	0	0	0	.000
Baker, ph	1	1	0	0	0	0	0	0	.000
Jones, p	2	0	0	0	0	0	0	0	.000
Mays, p	1	2	0	0	0	0	0	0	.000
McMillan, ph-cf	1	2	0	0	0	0	0	0	.000
Totals	5	158	11	32	6	1	2	11	.203

COMPOSITE PITCHING AVERAGES

New York Giants

Pitcher	G.	IP.	H.	R.	ER.	BB.	SO.	W.	L.	ERA.
J. Scott	1	9	4	0	0	1	2	1	0	0.00
Ryan	1	2	1	0	0	0	2	1	0	0.00
J. Barnes	1	10	8	3	2	2	6	0	0	1.80
McQuillan	1	9	8	3	2	2	4	1	0	2.00
Nehf	2	16	11	5	4	3	6	1	0	2.25
Totals	5	46	32	11	8	8	20	4	0	1.57

New York Yankees

Pitcher	G.	IP.	H.	R.	ER.	BB.	SO.	W.	L.	ERA.
Jones	2	2	1	0	0	1	0	0	0	0.00
Hoyt	2	8	11	3	1	2	4	0	1	1.13
Shawkey	1	10	8	3	3	2	4	0	0	2.70
Mays	1	8	9	4	4	2	1	0	1	4.50
Bush	2	15	21	8	8	5	6	0	2	4.80
Totals	5	43	50	18	16	12	15	0	4	3.35

1923
NEW YORK YANKEES
VS.
NEW YORK GIANTS

It was the Giants vs. the Yankees again in 1923. The third consecutive all-New York World Series. Only this time, the fall classic would not be played entirely within the confines of the Polo Grounds.

After 10 seasons as co-tenants, the Yankees no longer shared the horseshoe-shaped Manhattan stadium with the Giants. The National Leaguers had served the suddenly prominent Yanks with an eviction notice, telling them to take their ball and find somewhere else to play.

"Somewhere else" turned out to be somethin' else. It was called *Yankee Stadium.* The ball park was hailed for its prime location, enormous seating capacity and stunning beauty. The location, much to the chagrin of the competition-wary Giants, was about a quarter-mile from the Polo Grounds and just across the Harlem River in the Bronx. The capacity was 62,000-plus, making Yankee Stadium significantly larger than any existing baseball structure (an expanded Polo Grounds now held approximately 50,000 patrons). And, of course, the glistening newness of the massive edifice was a gate attraction in itself.

That the addition of Yankee Stadium had enabled New York to corner the market on spacious and dazzling baseball facilities was not lost on the sporting public or the chroniclers of the day.

"...It is a thrilling thought that perhaps 2,500 years from now archeologists, spading up the ruins of Harlem and the lower Bronx, will find arenas that outsize anything that the ancient Romans and Greeks built," a Philadelphia newsman wrote. "In addition to the Colosseum of Rome, in the Old World are 11 ruins of ancient

Yankee slugger Bob Meusel (right) and brother Irish (left) were key figures in the 1923 all-New York World Series.

huge buildings where the seats for spectators surrounded the scene of the performance, and not one of these tops the capacity of New York's two great ball parks...."

The Giants, who in 1913 had no qualms about asking the struggling Highlanders/Yankees franchise to come in out of the cold and join them as Polo Grounds tenants, had more than a few qualms now. Once considered the "only game in town," despite the presence of the Brooklyn club and later the Yankees, the Giants had become the second game in town. While the Yanks had yet to win baseball's biggest prize, the World Series championship, the American Leaguers clearly were winning the battle for fans. After all, they had the game's No. 1 drawing card, Babe Ruth. And now they had the game's No. 1 arena.

Soon, the Yankees would demonstrate they had major league baseball's best team, too. A 16-game victory margin in the A.L. pennant race was an indication of this club's capabilities.

Ironically, the player who proved the biggest obstacle in the Yankees' path to World Series supremacy was Casey Stengel, who more than a quarter of a century later would win lasting fame as manager of the Bronx Bombers. A 34-year-old Giants outfielder, Stengel was the hero of the first Series game ever played at Yankee Stadium and also delivered the big blow in the second game contested there.

With two out in the top of the ninth inning of Game 1 and the score tied, 4-4, Stengel lined a Joe Bush pitch into left-center field. The ball got between Bob Meusel and Whitey Witt and rolled to the wall, and Stengel set sail around the bases. Well, he ran as hard as a sore-legged, veteran outfielder could. Arms flailing and one shoe half coming off, Stengel staggered home safely. The inside-the-park home run made Giants reliever Rosy Ryan the winner in a 5-4 decision.

The Yankees had now gone

Big and beautiful new Yankee Stadium provided a fitting backdrop for the ascension of the American **League's New Yorkers to the 1923 major league baseball throne.**

winless in their last nine Series games against the Giants, losing eight of the contests and tying the other. Ruth and Herb Pennock would put an end to this affront.

Ruth, coming off a season in which he hit a resounding .394 and shared the majors' home run title with the Philadelphia Phillies' Cy Williams (each rapped 41 homers), walloped fourth- and fifth-inning homers in Game 2 and Aaron Ward also connected for the Yankees. Pennock, another in a long and impressive line of standout players acquired from the Boston Red Sox, pitched the distance in a 4-2 Yankees triumph at the Polo Grounds.

With the action alternating between the Yankees' and Giants' home parks, Stengel was the man of the hour again in Game 3. Through six innings, the American Leaguers' Sad Sam Jones and the Nationals' Art Nehf were locked in a 0-0 battle. Then, with one out in the seventh, Stengel homered into the right-field stands at Yankee Stadium. Nehf made the run stand up, allowing five singles and a double in a 1-0 thriller.

The Yankees then went to work. They collected totals of 16 runs and 27 hits in the next two games and coasted to 8-4 and 8-1 victories. Witt had three hits and

two RBIs in Game 4, while Joe Dugan had four hits and three RBIs in support of Bush's three-hit pitching in Game 5, which produced the first Series triumph by the Yankees in their new stadium.

Miller Huggins' team finished off the Giants in Game 6. While Ruth drilled a bases-empty, upper-deck homer in the first inning, the Yankees needed a five-run eighth to overcome the Giants. Bob Meusel supplied the key hit in the big inning, a two-run single that enabled the Yanks to slip ahead, 5-4. The Yankees went on to win, 6-4, with Jones saving the victory for Pennock (who had left for a pinch-hitter in the eighth).

In helping his club reach the pinnacle of the baseball world, Ruth had a marvelous Series. He slugged three homers, a triple, a double and two singles, drew eights walks and batted .368. The rival second basemen, Ward and Frankie Frisch, also stood out. Each collected 10 hits. The Meusels also made their marks—the Yanks' Bob driving in eight runs overall and the Giants' Irish hitting a homer in Game 2 and collecting all three of his club's hits in Game 5.

The Giants did thwart the Yankees on one front. When Yanks

first baseman Wally Pipp was injured late in the season, the A.L. club sought permission to use a late-season call-up from Hartford in his stead. Giants Manager John McGraw blocked the request, and Pipp wound up starting all six games. Who was the youngster the Yanks wanted to play? A 20-year-old by the name of Lou Gehrig.

The 1923 World Series, which featured two Yankee Stadium crowds in excess of 62,000 fans and another surpassing the 55,000 mark, was the first to hit the $1 million figure in receipts. More significant, though, was the fact that this fall classic was the first ever won by the New York Yankees. Maybe, just maybe, this was a franchise to keep an eye on.

Game 1

Wednesday, October 10, At Yankee Stadium

Giants	AB.	R.	H.	RBI.	PO.	A.
Bancroft, ss	4	1	1	1	3	0
Groh, 3b	4	1	2	2	1	3
Frisch, 2b	4	0	1	1	2	2
Youngs, rf	3	0	0	0	1	0
E. Meusel, lf	4	0	0	0	6	0
Stengel, cf	3	1	2	1	2	0
Cunningham, cf	0	0	0	0	1	0
Kelly, 1b	4	1	1	0	5	2
Gowdy, c	0	0	0	0	1	0
aMaguire	0	0	0	0	0	0
Snyder, c	2	0	0	0	4	1
Watson, p	0	0	0	0	0	1
bBentley	1	0	1	0	0	0
cGearin	0	0	0	0	1	0
Ryan, p	2	0	0	0	1	2
Totals	31	5	8	5	27	11
Yankees	AB.	R.	H.	RBI.	PO.	A.
Witt, cf	5	0	1	2	5	0
Dugan, 3b	4	0	1	1	0	3
Ruth, rf	4	1	1	0	3	0
R. Meusel, lf	4	0	1	1	0	0
Pipp, 1b	4	0	2	0	10	0
Ward, 2b	4	1	2	0	6	3

	AB.	R.	H.	RBI.	PO.	A.
Schang, c	3	1	2	0	2	2
E. Scott, ss	2	0	0	0	1	6
dHendrick	1	0	0	0	0	0
Johnson, ss	0	0	0	0	0	1
Hoyt, p	1	0	0	0	0	0
Bush, p	3	1	2	0	0	2
Totals	35	4	12	4	27	17

Giants	0 0 4 0 0 0 0 0 1—5
Yankees	1 2 0 0 0 0 1 0 0—4

Giants	IP.	H.	R.	ER.	BB.	SO.
Watson	2	4	3	3	1	1
Ryan (W)	7	8	1	1	1	2

Yankees	IP.	H.	R.	ER.	BB.	SO.
Hoyt	2⅓	4	4	4	1	0
Bush (L)	6⅔	4	1	1	2	2

aRan for Gowdy in third. bSingled for Watson in third. cRan for Bentley in third. dFlied out for E. Scott in eighth. E—Schang. DP—Giants 2, Yankees 2. LOB—Giants 2, Yankees 7. 2B—R. Meusel, Bush, Schang. 3B—Groh, Ruth, Dugan. HR—Stengel. SB—Bancroft. SH—Scott. WP—Ryan. U—Evans (A.L.), O'Day (N.L.), Nallin (A.L.) and Hart (N.L.). T—2:05. A—55,307.

Game 2

Thursday, October 11, At Polo Grounds

Yankees	AB.	R.	H.	RBI.	PO.	A.
Witt, cf	5	0	0	0	1	0
Dugan, 3b	4	0	1	0	2	3
Ruth, rf	3	2	2	2	3	0
R. Meusel, lf	4	0	1	0	4	0
Pipp, 1b	3	1	1	0	13	0
Ward, 2b	4	1	2	1	3	4
Schang, c	4	0	1	0	1	0
E. Scott, ss	4	0	2	1	0	6
Pennock, p	3	0	0	0	0	1
Totals	34	4	10	4	27	14

Giants	AB.	R.	H.	RBI.	PO.	A.
Bancroft, ss	4	0	0	0	0	6
Groh, 3b	3	1	1	0	0	1
Frisch, 2b	4	0	2	0	2	6
Youngs, rf	4	0	2	1	0	0
E. Meusel, lf	4	1	2	1	4	0
Cunningham, cf	3	0	0	0	1	0
aGowdy	1	0	0	0	0	0
Stengel, cf	0	0	0	0	1	0
Kelly, 1b	4	0	1	0	16	1
Snyder, c	4	0	0	0	3	1
McQuillan, p	1	0	0	0	0	0
Bentley, p	2	0	1	0	0	2
bJackson	1	0	0	0	0	0
Totals	35	2	9	2	27	17

Yankees	0 1 0 2 1 0 0 0 0—4
Giants	0 1 0 0 0 1 0 0 0—2

Yankees	IP.	H.	R.	ER.	BB.	SO.
Pennock (W)	9	9	2	2	1	1

Giants	IP.	H.	R.	ER.	BB.	SO.
McQuillan (L)	3⅔	5	3	3	2	1
Bentley	5⅓	5	1	1	2	0

aFlied out for Cunningham in eighth. bFlied out for Bentley in ninth. E—Youngs 2. DP—Yankees 1, Giants 2. LOB—Yankees 8, Giants 7. 2B—Bentley, Dugan. HR—Ward, E. Meusel, Ruth 2. HBP—By Bentley (Pennock). U—O'Day (N.L.), Nallin (A.L.), Hart (N.L.) and Evans (A.L.). T—2:08. A—40,402.

Game 3

Friday, October 12, At Yankee Stadium

Giants	AB.	R.	H.	RBI.	PO.	A.
Bancroft, ss	3	0	0	0	3	5
Groh, 3b	4	0	0	0	1	5
Frisch, 2b	4	0	2	0	4	4
Youngs, rf	4	0	0	0	2	0
E. Meusel, lf	4	0	0	0	1	0
Stengel, cf	3	1	1	1	1	0
Kelly, 1b	3	0	0	0	10	0
Snyder, c	3	0	0	0	5	0
Nehf, p	3	0	1	0	0	1
Totals	31	1	4	1	27	15

Yankees	AB.	R.	H.	RBI.	PO.	A.
Witt, cf	4	0	1	0	3	0
Dugan, 3b	4	0	1	0	1	0
Ruth, rf-1b	2	0	1	0	4	0
R. Meusel, lf	4	0	0	0	5	0
Pipp, 1b	2	0	0	0	8	0
Haines, rf	1	0	0	0	0	0
Ward, 2b	4	0	1	0	0	3
Schang, c	4	0	1	0	3	0
E. Scott, ss	3	0	1	0	3	4
Jones, p	2	0	0	0	0	2
aHofmann	1	0	0	0	0	0
Bush, p	0	0	0	0	0	0
Totals	31	0	6	0	27	9

Giants	0 0 0 0 0 0 1 0 0—1
Yankees	0 0 0 0 0 0 0 0 0—0

Giants	IP.	H.	R.	ER.	BB.	SO.
Nehf (W)	9	6	0	0	3	4

Yankees	IP.	H.	R.	ER.	BB.	SO.
Jones (L)	8	4	1	1	2	3
Bush	1	0	0	0	0	0

aPopped out for Jones in eighth. E—E. Scott. DP—Giants 2, Yankees 1. LOB—Giants 5, Yankees 7. 2B—Dugan. HR—Stengel. U—Nallin (A.L.), Hart (N.L.), Evans (A.L.) and O'Day (N.L.). T—2:05. A—62,430.

Game 4

Saturday, October 13, At Polo Grounds

Yankees	AB.	R.	H.	RBI.	PO.	A.
Witt, cf	4	0	3	2	1	0
Dugan, 3b	5	1	0	0	2	3
Ruth, rf	3	2	1	0	2	0
R. Meusel, lf	5	0	1	2	3	0
Pipp, 1b	4	1	2	0	9	1
Ward, 2b	4	2	2	1	2	5
Schang, c	3	1	1	0	5	0
E. Scott, ss	5	1	2	2	2	1
Shawkey, p	3	0	1	1	1	2
Pennock, p	1	0	0	0	0	0
Totals	37	8	13	8	27	12

Giants	AB.	R.	H.	RBI.	PO.	A.
Bancroft, ss	5	0	1	0	2	3
Groh, 3b	3	0	0	0	1	2
Frisch, 2b	5	0	2	0	4	0
Youngs, rf	5	2	4	1	0	0
E. Meusel, lf	5	1	1	0	1	0
Stengel, cf	2	1	2	1	4	0
dCunningham	1	0	0	1	0	0
Kelly, 1b	5	0	2	0	7	0
Snyder, c	4	0	0	1	8	1
J. Scott, p	0	0	0	0	0	0
Ryan, p	0	0	0	0	0	0
McQuillan, p	2	0	0	0	0	1
aBentley	1	0	1	0	0	0
bMaguire	0	0	0	0	0	0
Jonnard, p	0	0	0	0	0	0
cO'Connell	0	0	0	0	0	0
Barnes, p	0	0	0	0	0	0
Totals	38	4	13	4	27	7

Yankees	0 6 1 1 0 0 0 0 0—8
Giants	0 0 0 0 0 0 0 3 1—4

Yankees	IP.	H.	R.	ER.	BB.	SO.
Shawkey (W)	7	12	3	3	4	2
Pennock	1	1	1	1	0	1

Giants	IP.	H.	R.	ER.	BB.	SO.
J. Scott (L)	1*	4	4	3	0	1
Ryan	⅔	2	2	0	1	0
McQuillan	5⅓	6	2	2	2	2
Jonnard	1	1	0	0	1	0
Barnes	1	0	0	0	0	2

*Pitched to four batters in second.

aSingled for McQuillan in seventh. bRan for Bentley in seventh. cHit by pitcher for Jonnard in eighth. dStruck out for Stengel in ninth. E—Ruth, J. Scott. DP—Yankees 2. LOB—Yankees 10, Giants 12. 2B—Witt 2, Ruth. 3B—R. Meusel. HR—Youngs. SH—Schang 2, Shawkey, Witt. HBP—By Shawkey (O'Connell). U—Hart (N.L.), Evans (A.L.), O'Day (N.L.) and Nallin (A.L.). T—2:32. A—46,302.

Game 5

Sunday, October 14, At Yankee Stadium

Giants	AB.	R.	H.	RBI.	PO.	A.
Bancroft, ss	4	0	0	0	2	3
Groh, 3b	4	0	0	0	0	2
Frisch, 2b	4	0	0	0	4	1
Youngs, rf	3	0	0	0	2	1
E. Meusel, lf	4	1	3	0	0	0
Stengel, cf	3	0	0	1	3	0
Kelly, 1b	2	0	0	0	6	1
Gowdy, c	3	0	0	0	6	0
Bentley, p	0	0	0	0	0	0
J. Scott, p	1	0	0	0	0	0
Barnes, p	1	0	0	0	1	2
aO'Connell	1	0	0	0	0	0
Jonnard, p	0	0	0	0	0	1
Totals	30	1	3	1	24	11

Yankees	AB.	R.	H.	RBI.	PO.	A.
Witt, cf	4	1	1	0	5	0
Dugan, 3b	5	3	4	3	0	3
Ruth, rf	4	2	1	0	4	0
R. Meusel, lf	5	1	3	3	1	0
Pipp, 1b	3	0	0	2	11	2
Ward, 2b	4	0	2	0	0	5
Schang, c	4	0	1	0	3	0
E. Scott, ss	4	0	1	0	1	1
Bush, p	4	1	1	0	2	1
Totals	37	8	14	8	27	12

Giants	0 1 0 0 0 0 0 0 0—1
Yankees	3 4 0 1 0 0 0 0 x—8

Giants	IP.	H.	R.	ER.	BB.	SO.
Bentley (L)	1⅓	5	7	6	2	1
J. Scott	2	5	1	1	1	1
Barnes	3⅔	4	0	0	0	2
Jonnard	1	0	0	0	0	1

Yankees	IP.	H.	R.	ER.	BB.	SO.
Bush (W)	9	3	1	1	2	3

aStruck out for Barnes in eighth. E—Frisch, Kelly. DP—Giants 1. LOB—Giants 4, Yankees 9. 2B—E. Meusel. 3B—E. Meusel, R. Meusel. HR—Dugan. SB—Ward. SH—Pipp. U—Evans (A.L.), O'Day (N.L.), Nallin (A.L.) and Hart (N.L.). T—1:55. A—62,817.

Game 6

Monday, October 15, At Polo Grounds

Yankees	AB.	R.	H.	RBI.	PO.	A.
Witt, cf	3	0	0	0	3	1
cBush	0	0	0	1	0	0
dJohnson	0	1	0	0	0	0
Jones, p	0	0	0	0	0	1
Dugan, 3b	3	1	0	1	2	1
Ruth, rf	3	1	1	1	1	0
R. Meusel, lf	4	0	1	2	1	0
Pipp, 1b	4	0	0	0	12	0
Ward, 2b	4	0	1	0	0	7
Schang, c	4	1	1	0	7	0
E. Scott, ss	4	1	1	0	1	2
Pennock, p	2	0	0	0	0	1
aHofmann	0	0	0	0	0	0
bHaines, cf	0	1	0	0	0	0
Totals	31	6	5	5	27	13

Giants	AB.	R.	H.	RBI.	PO.	A.
Bancroft, ss	4	0	0	0	1	7
Groh, 3b	4	1	1	0	1	2
Frisch, 2b	4	2	3	0	1	5
Youngs, rf	4	0	2	1	0	0
E. Meusel, lf	4	0	1	1	1	0
Cunningham, cf	3	0	1	1	0	0
eStengel, cf	1	0	0	0	0	0
Kelly, 1b	4	0	0	0	19	0
Snyder, c	4	1	2	1	4	0
Nehf, p	3	0	0	0	0	5
Ryan, p	0	0	0	0	0	0
fBentley	1	0	0	0	0	0
Totals	36	4	10	4	27	19

Yankees	1 0 0 0 0 0 0 5 0—6
Giants	1 0 0 1 1 1 0 0 0—4

Yankees	IP.	H.	R.	ER.	BB.	SO.
Pennock (W)	7	9	4	4	0	6
Jones	2	1	0	0	0	0

Giants	IP.	H.	R.	ER.	BB.	SO.
Nehf (L)	7	4	5	5	3	3
Ryan	1	1	1	0	1	1

aWalked for Pennock in eighth. bRan for Hofmann in eighth. cWalked for Witt in eighth. dRan for Bush in eighth. eFouled out for Cunningham in eighth. fGrounded out for Ryan in ninth. E—Cunningham. DP—Giants 1. LOB—Yankees 2, Giants 5. 3B—Frisch. HR—Ruth, Snyder. U—O'Day (N.L.), Nallin (A.L.), Hart (N.L.) and Evans (A.L.). T—2:05. A—34,172.

COMPOSITE BATTING AVERAGES

New York Yankees

Player-Position	G.	AB.	R.	H.	2B.	3B.	HR.	RBI.	BA.
Bush, p-ph	4	7	2	3	1	0	0	1	.429
Ward, 2b	6	24	4	10	0	0	1	2	.417
Ruth, rf-1b	6	19	8	7	1	1	3	3	.368
Shawkey, p	1	3	0	1	0	0	0	1	.333
Schang, c	6	22	3	7	1	0	0	0	.318
E. Scott, ss	6	22	2	7	0	0	0	3	.318
Dugan, 3b	6	25	5	7	2	1	1	5	.280
R. Meusel, lf	6	26	1	7	1	2	0	8	.269
Pipp, 1b	6	20	2	5	0	0	0	2	.250
Witt, cf	6	25	1	6	2	0	0	4	.240
Johnson, ss-pr	2	0	1	0	0	0	0	0	.000
Pennock, p	3	6	0	0	0	0	0	0	.000
Jones, p	2	2	0	0	0	0	0	0	.000
Haines, rf-cf-pr	2	1	1	0	0	0	0	0	.000
Hofmann, ph	2	1	0	0	0	0	0	0	.000
Hoyt, p	1	1	0	0	0	0	0	0	.000
Hendrick, ph	1	1	0	0	0	0	0	0	.000
Totals	6	205	30	60	8	4	5	29	.293

New York Giants

Player-Position	G.	AB.	R.	H.	2B.	3B.	HR.	RBI.	BA.
Bentley, ph-p	5	5	0	3	1	0	0	0	.600
Stengel, cf-ph	6	12	3	5	0	0	2	4	.417
Frisch, 2b	6	25	2	10	0	1	0	1	.400
Youngs, rf	6	23	2	8	0	0	1	3	.348
E. Meusel, lf	6	25	3	7	1	1	1	2	.280
Groh, 3b	6	22	3	4	0	1	0	2	.182
Kelly, 1b	6	22	1	4	0	0	0	1	.182
Nehf, p	2	6	0	1	0	0	0	0	.167
Cun'ham, cf-ph	4	7	0	1	0	0	0	1	.143
Snyder, c	5	17	1	2	0	0	1	2	.118
Bancroft, ss	6	24	1	2	0	0	0	1	.083
Ryan, p	3	2	0	0	0	0	0	0	.000
Gowdy, c-ph	3	4	0	0	0	0	0	0	.000
Maguire, pr	2	0	1	0	0	0	0	0	.000
McQuillan, p	2	3	0	0	0	0	0	0	.000
J. Scott, p	2	1	0	0	0	0	0	0	.000
Jonnard, p	2	0	0	0	0	0	0	0	.000
O'Connell, ph	2	1	0	0	0	0	0	0	.000
Barnes, p	2	1	0	0	0	0	0	0	.000
Watson, p	1	0	0	0	0	0	0	0	.000
Gearin, pr	1	0	0	0	0	0	0	0	.000
Jackson, ph	1	1	0	0	0	0	0	0	.000
Totals	6	201	17	47	2	3	5	17	.234

COMPOSITE PITCHING AVERAGES

New York Yankees

Pitcher	G.	IP.	H.	R.	ER.	BB.	SO.	W.	L.	ERA.
Jones	2	10	5	1	1	2	3	0	1	0.90
Bush	3	16⅔	7	2	2	4	5	1	1	1.08
Shawkey	1	7⅔	12	3	3	4	2	1	0	3.52
Pennock	3	17⅓	19	7	7	1	8	2	0	3.63
Hoyt	1	2⅓	4	4	4	1	0	0	0	15.43
Totals	6	54	47	17	17	12	18	4	2	2.83

New York Giants

Pitcher	G.	IP.	H.	R.	ER.	BB.	SO.	W.	L.	ERA.
Barnes	2	4⅔	4	0	0	0	4	0	0	0.00
Jonnard	2	2	1	0	0	1	1	0	0	0.00
Ryan	3	9⅓	11	4	1	3	3	1	0	0.96
Nehf	2	16⅓	10	5	5	6	7	1	1	2.76
McQuillan	2	9	11	5	5	4	3	0	1	5.00
Bentley	2	6⅔	10	8	7	4	1	0	1	9.45
J. Scott	2	3	9	5	4	1	2	0	1	12.00
Watson	1	2	4	3	3	1	1	0	0	13.50
Totals	6	53	60	30	25	20	22	2	4	4.25

1924
WASHINGTON SENATORS
VS.
NEW YORK GIANTS

First in war, first in peace and *first* in the American League. That was Washington, 1924.

The Washington Senators, under first-year Manager Bucky Harris, their 27-year-old second baseman, won the A.L. pennant by two games over the New York Yankees. The Senators' first-ever flag meant that longtime pitching star Walter Johnson finally would get a chance to pitch in the World Series—and Johnson himself played no small part in creating the opportunity. The 36-year-old righthander, who had not recorded a 20-victory season since 1919, showed his old form in '24 by winning 23 games, tossing six shutouts and fashioning a 2.72 earned-run average, all of which were league-leading figures. Not bad for a pitcher working his 18th big-league season.

For the eighth time in 14 years, the National League representative in the fall classic would be the New York Giants. Manager John McGraw's club, despite a .300 team batting average, had to scramble to win the N.L. pennant by 1½ games over the Brooklyn Dodgers.

Johnson and Series veteran Art Nehf were pitching opponents in Game 1 of the Series, and both went the distance in what turned out to be a 12-inning cliffhanger witnessed by, among others, President Calvin Coolidge. Backed by home runs off the bats of George Kelly and Bill Terry (a promising first baseman who had played only 80 regular-season games in the major leagues), Nehf took a 2-1 lead into the last of the ninth inning. However, Ossie Bluege's single and Roger Peckinpaugh's double sent the game into extra innings. In the 12th, Ross (Pep) Youngs' bases-loaded single and Kelly's run-scoring fly ball netted

two runs for the Giants, who then had to hold off a spirited Washington rally in the bottom of the inning to nail down a 4-3 victory.

Johnson didn't exactly flash his old form in this game, although he did strike out 12 New York batters. The Big Train allowed 14 hits and walked six batters.

While Washington won two of the next three games, Johnson was pounded again in Game 5. This time, he yielded 13 hits—including four by Fred Lindstrom and a home run by opposing pitcher Jack Bentley—as the Senators went down to a 6-2 defeat. Johnson was now 0-2 in his first Series, and Washington was one loss from elimination.

Harris and Tom Zachary brought the Senators back from the brink. Harris came through with a two-run single in the fifth inning of Game 6 and Zachary, after allowing a first-inning run, was in command the rest of way. Washington's 2-1 triumph squared the Series at three victories apiece.

Game 7 of the 1924 classic unfolded in a manner not unfamiliar to longtime Giants fans. Oh, the Giants and their supporters had enjoyed their share of ecstasy over the years, as reflected by three World Series championships. But they also had endured more than their share of agony, as the legacies of Merkle, Snodgrass and Zimmerman would suggest.

This time, though, the Giants didn't succumb to the errors of their ways. McGraw's athletes did make mistakes, all right; in fact, they had three errors in the final game of the '24 Series (Washington had four). But it was Lady Luck who really did them in.

The Giants guarded a 3-1 lead entering the bottom of the eighth inning of Game 7 at Griffith Sta-

dium, and a leadoff pop foul by Washington's Bluege drew New York within five outs of another Series crown. However, pinch-hitter Nemo Leibold drilled a double off the Giants' Virgil Barnes, Muddy Ruel collected an infield single and Bennie Tate, another pinch-hitter, walked. After Earl McNeely flied out (all three runners held), Harris hit a grounder that skipped over the head of 18-year-old third baseman Lindstrom. Two runs scored on the bad-hop single, tying the game. Nehf then relieved Barnes and induced Sam Rice to ground out.

Johnson came on in relief for the Senators in the ninth and, after retiring the first batter he faced, yielded a triple to Frankie Frisch. With the game on the line, Johnson issued an intentional walk to Youngs and then struck out Kelly and got Irish Meusel to ground out. The Giants had squandered a golden opportunity.

The 3-3 deadlock continued until the bottom of the 12th. With one out, Giants reliever Bentley got Ruel to hit a foul pop. But the "sure" second out of the inning never materialized as Hank Gowdy, World Series hero for the Boston Braves a decade earlier, stumbled over his mask and dropped the ball. Given a new life, Ruel cracked a double down the third-base line. Johnson then reached base on shortstop Travis Jackson's error, with Ruel holding second. McNeely grounded to third and, as happened four innings earlier, the ball took a sudden and inexplicable hop over Lindstrom's head and Ruel scurried home with the Series-deciding run.

Fittingly, Johnson, after tough sledding in his two Series starts and some anxious moments in a four-inning relief stint in this

Fred Lindstrom returned to Griffith Stadium in 1951 to re-enact the infamous bad-hop single, sometimes referred to as the "pebble hit," that cost the New York Giants the 1924 World Series. Bucky Harris (below) was the 27-year-old manager of the Senators when the Series opened.

climactic game, was the winning pitcher in the 4-3 contest that netted the Washington franchise its first World Series title.

First baseman Joe Judge batted .385 for Washington, while left fielder Goose Goslin and Harris provided the power by combining for five home runs and 14 runs batted in. Goslin hit a two-run home run and Harris socked a bases-empty shot in Game 2, which Washington won, 4-3, on Peckinpaugh's ninth-inning double. Goslin had four hits, including a three-run homer, in Washington's 7-4 triumph in the fourth game, and he also homered in Game 5, a 6-2 Giants victory.

Terry hit .429 for the Giants, while Frisch and Lindstrom, a fill-in for the injured Heinie Groh, each batted .333 for the National Leaguers. Frisch's performance marked the fourth consecutive Series in which he had batted .300 or higher. New York had four homers, half being struck by pitchers (reliever Rosy Ryan, who connected in New York's 6-4 victory in Game 3, pre-

ceded Bentley in the homer column).

While McGraw would preside over many more outstanding teams and manage the Giants into the 1932 season, this was the final World Series for Little Napoleon. And although he met his Waterloo a record six times in the postseason extravaganza (against three victories), only one man has surpassed the great McGraw in total Series managerial appearances—Casey Stengel, with 10.

Game 1

Saturday, October 4, At Washington

New York	AB.	R.	H.	RBI.	PO.	A.
Lindstrom, 3b	5	0	0	0	1	3
aBentley	0	0	0	0	0	0
bSouthworth, cf	0	1	0	0	1	1
Frisch, 2b-3b	5	0	2	0	3	3
Youngs, rf	6	0	2	1	2	0
Kelly, cf-2b	5	1	1	2	4	1
Terry, 1b	5	1	3	1	15	0
Wilson, lf	6	0	2	0	4	0
Jackson, ss	3	0	0	0	2	6
Gowdy, c	3	0	1	0	4	1
Nehf, p	5	1	3	0	0	2
Totals	43	4	14	4	36	17

Washington	AB.	R.	H.	RBI.	PO.	A.
McNeely, cf	5	1	1	0	4	0
Harris, 2b	6	0	2	1	3	3
Rice, rf	5	0	2	1	0	1
Goslin, lf	6	0	1	0	2	0
Judge, 1b	4	0	1	0	6	0
Bluege, 3b	5	1	1	0	2	2
Peckinpaugh, ss	5	0	2	1	4	4
Ruel, c	3	0	0	0	15	2
Johnson, p	4	0	0	0	0	1
cShirley	1	1	0	0	0	0
Totals	44	3	10	3	36	13

New York ....0 1 0 1 0 0 0 0 0 0 0 2—4
Washington ....0 0 0 0 0 1 0 0 1 0 0 1—3

New York	IP.	H.	R.	ER.	BB.	SO.
Nehf (W)	12	10	3	2	5	3

Washington	IP.	H.	R.	ER.	BB.	SO.
Johnson (L)	12	14	4	3	6	12

aWalked for Lindstrom in twelfth. bRan for Bentley in twelfth. cReached first on error for Johnson in twelfth. E—Jackson, McNeely. DP—New York 1, Washington 2. LOB—New York 11, Washington 10. 2B—Frisch, McNeely, Youngs, Peckinpaugh. HR—Kelly, Terry. SB—Frisch, Rice, Peckinpaugh. SH—Kelly, Jackson. PB—Ruel. U—Connolly (A.L.), Klem (N.L.), Dinneen (A.L.) and Quigley (N.L.). T—3:07. A—35,760.

Game 2

Sunday, October 5, At Washington

New York	AB.	R.	H.	RBI.	PO.	A.
Lindstrom, 3b	3	0	1	0	0	7
Frisch, 2b	3	1	1	0	2	2
Youngs, rf	4	0	1	0	0	0
Kelly, 1b	3	2	1	1	14	1
Meusel, lf	4	0	1	0	1	0
Wilson, cf	4	0	1	1	0	0
Jackson, ss	4	0	0	0	1	2
Gowdy, c	3	0	0	0	6	2
Bentley, p	3	0	0	0	1	2
Totals	31	3	6	2	25	16

Washington	AB.	R.	H.	RBI.	PO.	A.
McNeely, cf	4	0	0	0	0	0
Harris, 2b	3	1	1	1	3	5
Rice, rf	3	1	2	0	4	0
Goslin, lf	4	1	1	2	1	0
Judge, 1b	2	1	1	0	15	0
Bluege, 3b	3	0	0	0	0	5
Peckinpaugh, ss	4	0	1	1	2	6
Ruel, c	3	0	0	0	1	0
Zachary, p	2	0	0	0	1	2
Marberry, p	0	0	0	0	0	0
Totals	28	4	6	4	27	18

New York ....0 0 0 0 0 0 1 0 2—3
Washington ....2 0 0 0 1 0 0 0 1—4
One out when winning run scored.

New York	IP.	H.	R.	ER.	BB.	SO.
Bentley (L)	8⅓	6	4	4	4	6

Washington	IP.	H.	R.	ER.	BB.	SO.
Zachary (W)	8⅔	6	3	3	0	3
Marberry	⅓	0	0	0	0	1

E—Harris. DP—Washington 3. LOB—New York 4, Washington 5. 2B—Peckinpaugh. HR—Goslin, Harris. SB—Rice. SH—Rice, Bluege. PB—Gowdy. U—Klem (N.L.), Dinneen (A.L.), Quigley (N.L.) and Connolly (A.L.). T—1:58. A—35,922.

Game 3

Monday, October 6, At New York

Washington	AB.	R.	H.	RBI.	PO.	A.
Leibold, cf	4	0	0	0	2	0
Harris, 2b	5	1	1	0	2	4
Rice, rf	3	1	1	0	1	0
Goslin, lf	5	0	1	0	3	1
Judge, 1b	5	1	3	0	5	0
Bluege, 3b-ss	3	1	1	0	2	2
Peckinpaugh, ss	1	0	0	0	0	0
Miller, 3b	2	0	1	1	2	0
Ruel, c	3	0	0	0	7	0
Marberry, p	1	0	0	0	0	1
aTate	0	0	0	0	0	0
Russell, p	0	0	0	0	0	1
bMcNeely	1	0	0	0	0	0
Martina, p	0	0	0	0	0	0
cShirley	1	0	1	1	0	0
Speece, p	0	0	0	0	0	2
Totals	34	4	9	2	24	11

New York	AB.	R.	H.	RBI.	PO.	A.
Lindstrom, 3b	4	0	1	1	3	1
Frisch, 3b	4	0	2	0	4	6
Youngs, rf	4	0	1	0	2	0
Kelly, cf	4	1	2	0	2	0
Southworth, cf	0	0	0	0	0	0
Terry, 1b	4	1	2	0	10	0
Wilson, lf	4	0	0	0	4	0
Jackson, ss	4	2	1	0	0	1
Gowdy, c	4	0	2	2	2	0
McQuillan, p	0	1	0	0	0	2
Ryan, p	2	1	1	1	0	0
Jonnard, p	0	0	0	0	0	0
Watson, p	0	0	0	0	0	0
Totals	34	6	12	4	27	10

Washington	0 0 0 2 0 0 0 1 1—4
New York	0 2 1 1 0 1 0 1 x—6

Washington	IP.	H.	R.	ER.	BB.	SO.
Marberry (L)	3	5	3	1	2	4
Russell	3	4	2	1	0	0
Martina	1	0	0	0	0	1
Speece	1	3	1	1	0	0

New York	IP.	H.	R.	ER.	BB.	SO.
McQuillan (W)	3⅔	2	2	2	5	0
Ryan	4⅔	7	2	2	3	2
Jonnard	0*	0	0	0	1	0
Watson	⅔	0	0	0	0	0

*Pitched to one batter in ninth.

aWalked for Marberry in fourth. bFlied out for Russell in seventh. cSingled for Martina in eighth. E—Harris, Miller. DP—Washington 1, New York 1. LOB—Washington 13, New York 8. 2B—Judge, Lindstrom. HR—Ryan. SB—Jackson. SH—Miller, Ryan. HBP—By Marberry (Frisch). WP—Marberry. U—Dinneen (A.L.), Quigley (N.L.), Connolly (A.L.) and Klem (N.L.). T—2:25. A—47,608.

Game 4

Tuesday, October 7, At New York

Washington	AB.	R.	H.	RBI.	PO.	A.
McNeely, cf	5	2	3	0	3	0
Harris, 2b	5	2	2	0	2	8
Rice, rf	5	0	0	0	1	1
Goslin, lf	4	2	4	4	3	0
Judge, 1b	4	1	1	0	11	1
Bluege, ss	4	0	3	2	2	3
Ruel, c	3	0	0	0	5	0
Miller, 3b	4	0	0	0	0	2
Mogridge, p	4	0	0	0	0	0
Marberry, p	0	0	0	0	0	0
Totals	38	7	13	6	27	15

New York	AB.	R.	H.	RBI.	PO.	A.
Lindstrom, 3b	4	1	3	1	1	2
Frisch, 2b	4	0	0	0	3	3
Youngs, rf	4	1	0	1	0	0
Kelly, 1b	5	1	1	0	11	1
Meusel, lf	2	0	0	0	2	0
Wilson, cf	4	0	1	2	3	0
Jackson, ss	4	0	0	0	0	3
Gowdy, c	4	1	1	0	6	1
Barnes, p	0	0	0	0	1	1
aTerry	1	0	0	0	0	0
Baldwin, p	0	0	0	0	0	0
bSouthworth	1	0	0	0	0	0
Dean, p	0	0	0	0	0	0
cBentley	1	0	0	0	0	0
Totals	34	4	6	4	27	11

Washington	0 0 3 0 2 0 0 2 0—7
New York	1 0 0 0 0 1 0 1 1—4

Washington	IP.	H.	R.	ER.	BB.	SO.
Mogridge (W)	7⅓	3	3	2	5	2
Marberry	1⅔	3	1	0	1	2

New York	IP.	H.	R.	ER.	BB.	SO.
Barnes (L)	5	9	5	5	0	3
Baldwin	2	1	0	0	0	1
Dean	2	3	2	0	0	2

aGrounded out for Barnes in fifth. bReached first on error for Baldwin in seventh. cStruck out for Dean in ninth. E—Rice, Bluege, Miller, Meusel. LOB—Washington 5, New York 9. 2B—Kelly, McNeely, Wilson. HR— Goslin. SH—Ruel. WP— Barnes. U—Quigley (N.L.), Connolly (A.L.), Klem (N.L.) and Dinneen (A.L.). T—2:10. A—49,243.

Game 5

Wednesday, October 8, At New York

Washington	AB.	R.	H.	RBI.	PO.	A.
McNeely, cf	4	0	1	0	1	0
Harris, 2b	5	0	1	0	8	2
Rice, rf	4	0	0	0	1	2
Goslin, lf	4	1	2	1	1	0
Judge, 1b	4	1	3	0	3	2
Bluege, ss	3	0	0	0	0	2
Ruel, c	2	0	0	0	6	2
Miller, 3b	3	0	1	1	3	1
aLeibold	1	0	0	0	0	0
Johnson, p	3	0	1	0	1	2
bTate	0	0	0	0	0	0
cTaylor	0	0	0	0	0	0
Totals	33	2	9	2	24	13

New York	AB.	R.	H.	RBI.	PO.	A.
Lindstrom, 3b	5	0	4	2	1	1
Frisch, 2b	5	0	1	0	1	6
Youngs, rf	3	0	1	0	1	1
Kelly, cf	4	1	1	0	2	0
Terry, 1b	2	1	1	0	12	1
Wilson, lf	3	0	0	0	3	1
Jackson, ss	3	1	1	1	1	2
Gowdy, c	4	2	1	0	6	0
Bentley, p	3	1	2	2	0	1
McQuillan, p	1	0	1	1	0	0
Totals	33	6	13	6	27	13

Washington	0 0 0 1 0 0 0 1 0—2
New York	0 0 1 0 2 0 0 3 x—6

Washington	IP.	H.	R.	ER.	BB.	SO.
Johnson (L)	8	13	6	3	2	3

New York	IP.	H.	R.	ER.	BB.	SO.
Bentley (W)	7⅓	9	2	2	3	4
McQuillan	1⅔	0	0	0	1	1

aFlied out for Miller in ninth. bWalked for Johnson in ninth. cRan for Tate in ninth. E—Johnson. DP—Washington 2. LOB—Washington 9, New York 8. 2B—Frisch. 3B—Terry. HR—Bentley, Goslin. SH—Wilson, Jackson, Bluege. HBP—By Johnson (Youngs). U—Connolly (A.L.), Klem (N.L.), Dinneen (A.L.) and Quigley (N.L.). T—2:30. A—49,211.

Game 6

Thursday, October 9, At Washington

New York	AB.	R.	H.	RBI.	PO.	A.
Lindstrom, 3b	4	0	0	0	1	1
Frisch, 2b	4	0	2	0	1	2
Youngs, rf	4	1	0	0	1	0
Kelly, 1b	4	0	2	1	11	1
bSouthworth	0	0	0	0	0	0
Meusel, lf	4	0	0	0	1	0
Wilson, cf	4	0	2	0	1	0
Jackson, ss	3	0	0	0	3	2
Gowdy, c	3	0	1	0	5	1
Nehf, p	2	0	0	0	0	4
aSnyder	1	0	0	0	0	0
Ryan, p	0	0	0	0	0	1
Totals	33	1	7	1	24	12

Washington	AB.	R.	H.	RBI.	PO.	A.
McNeely, cf	2	1	0	0	1	0
Harris, 2b	4	0	1	2	4	5
Rice, rf	4	0	1	0	4	0
Goslin, lf	4	0	0	0	1	0
Judge, 1b	3	0	0	0	11	0
Bluege, 3b-ss	3	0	0	0	1	3
Peckinpaugh, ss	2	1	2	0	1	4
Taylor, 3b	0	0	0	0	0	0
Ruel, c	2	0	0	0	4	1
Zachary, p	3	0	0	0	0	2
Totals	27	2	4	2	27	15

New York	1 0 0 0 0 0 0 0 0—1
Washington	0 0 0 0 2 0 0 0 x—2

New York	IP.	H.	R.	ER.	BB.	SO.
Nehf (L)	7	4	2	2	4	4
Ryan	1	0	0	0	1	1

Washington	IP.	H.	R.	ER.	BB.	SO.
Zachary (W)	9	7	1	1	0	3

aFlied out for Nehf in eighth. bRan for Kelly in ninth. E—Kelly. DP—Washington 1. LOB—New York 5, Washington 7. 2B —Frisch 2. SB—McNeely, Bluege. SH—Ruel. U—Klem (N.L.), Dinneen (A.L.), Quigley (N.L.) and Connolly (A.L.). T—1:57. A—34,254.

Game 7

Friday, October 10, At Washington

New York	AB.	R.	H.	RBI.	PO.	A.
Lindstrom, 3b	5	0	1	0	0	3
Frisch, 2b	5	0	2	0	3	4
Youngs, rf-lf	2	1	0	0	2	0
Kelly, cf-1b	6	1	1	0	8	1
Terry, 1b	2	0	0	0	6	1
aMeusel, lf-rf	3	0	1	1	1	0
Wilson, lf-cf	5	1	1	0	4	0
Jackson, ss	6	0	0	0	1	4
Gowdy, c	6	0	1	0	8	0
Barnes, p	4	0	0	0	1	2
Nehf, p	0	0	0	0	0	0
McQuillan, p	0	0	0	0	0	0
eGroh	1	0	1	0	0	0
fSouthworth	0	0	0	0	0	0
Bentley, p	0	0	0	0	0	0
Totals	45	3	8	1	34	15

Washington	AB.	R.	H.	RBI.	PO.	A.
McNeely, cf	6	0	1	1	0	0
Harris, 2b	5	1	3	3	4	1
Rice, rf	5	0	0	0	2	0
Goslin, lf	5	0	2	0	3	0
Judge, 1b	4	0	1	0	11	1
Bluege, ss	5	0	0	0	1	7
Taylor, 3b	2	0	0	0	0	3
bLeibold	1	1	1	0	0	0
Miller, 3b	2	0	0	0	1	1
Ruel, c	5	2	2	0	13	0
Ogden, p	0	0	0	0	0	0
Mogridge, p	1	0	0	0	0	0
Marberry, p	1	0	0	0	1	0
cTate	0	0	0	0	0	0
dShirley	0	0	0	0	0	0
Johnson, p	2	0	0	0	0	1
Totals	44	4	10	4	36	14

New York	000 003 000 000—3
Washington	000 100 020 001—4

One out when winning run scored.

New York	IP.	H.	R.	ER.	BB.	SO.
Barnes	7⅔	6	3	3	1	6
Nehf	⅔	1	0	0	0	0
McQuillan	1⅔	0	0	0	0	1
Bentley (L)	1⅓	3	1	1	1	0

Washington	IP.	H.	R.	ER.	BB.	SO.
Ogden	⅓	0	0	0	1	1
Mogridge	4⅔*	4	2	1	1	3
Marberry	3	1	1	0	1	3
Johnson (W)	4	3	0	0	3	5

*Pitched to two batters in sixth.

aFlied out for Terry in sixth. bDoubled for Taylor in eighth. cWalked for Marberry in eighth. dRan for Tate in eighth. eSingled for McQuillan in eleventh. fRan for Groh in eleventh. E—Jackson 2, Gowdy, Judge, Bluege 2, Taylor. DP—New York 2, Washington 1. LOB—New York 14, Washington 8. 2B—Lindstrom, Leibold, Ruel, Goslin, McNeely. 3B—Frisch. HR—Harris. SB—Youngs. SH—Meusel, Lindstrom. U—Dinneen (A.L.), Quigley (N.L.), Connolly (A.L.) and Klem (N.L.). T—3:00. A—31,667.

COMPOSITE BATTING AVERAGES

Washington Senators

Player-Position	G.	AB.	R.	H.	2B.	3B.	HR.	RBI.	BA.
Shirley, ph-pr	3	2	1	1	0	0	0	1	.500
Peckinpaugh, ss	4	12	1	5	2	0	0	2	.417
Judge, 1b	7	26	4	10	1	0	0	0	.385
Goslin, lf	7	32	4	11	1	0	3	7	.344
Harris, 2b	7	33	5	11	0	0	2	7	.333
McNeely, cf-ph	7	27	4	6	3	0	0	1	.222
Rice, rf	7	29	2	6	0	0	0	1	.207
Bluege, 3b-ss	7	26	2	5	0	0	0	2	.192
Miller, 3b	4	11	0	2	0	0	0	2	.182
Leibold, cf-ph	3	6	1	1	1	0	0	0	.167
Johnson, p	3	9	0	1	0	0	0	0	.111
Ruel, c	7	21	2	2	1	0	0	0	.095
Marberry, p	4	2	0	0	0	0	0	0	.000
Taylor, pr-3b	3	2	0	0	0	0	0	0	.000
Tate, ph	3	0	0	0	0	0	0	0	.000
Zachary, p	2	5	0	0	0	0	0	0	.000
Mogridge, p	2	5	0	0	0	0	0	0	.000
Russell, p	1	0	0	0	0	0	0	0	.000
Martina, p	1	0	0	0	0	0	0	0	.000
Speece, p	1	0	0	0	0	0	0	0	.000
Ogden, p	1	0	0	0	0	0	0	0	.000
Totals	7	248	26	61	9	0	5	23	.246

New York Giants

Player-Position	G.	AB.	R.	H.	2B.	3B.	HR.	RBI.	BA.
Groh, ph	1	1	0	1	0	0	0	0	1.000
McQuillan, p	3	1	1	1	0	0	0	1	1.000
Ryan, p	2	2	1	1	0	0	1	1	.500
Terry, 1b-ph	5	14	3	6	0	1	1	1	.429
Nehf, p	3	7	1	3	0	0	0	0	.429
Frisch, 2b-3b	7	30	1	10	4	1	0	0	.333
Lindstrom, 3b	7	30	1	10	2	0	0	4	.333
Kelly, cf-2b-1b	7	31	7	9	1	0	1	4	.290
Bentley, ph-p	5	7	1	2	0	0	1	2	.286
Gowdy, c	7	27	3	7	0	0	0	2	.259
Wilson, lf-cf	7	30	1	7	1	0	0	3	.233
Youngs, rf-lf	7	27	3	5	1	0	0	2	.185
Meusel, lf-rf	4	13	0	2	0	0	0	1	.154
Jackson, ss	7	27	3	2	0	0	0	1	.074
So'wo'h, pr-cf-ph	5	1	1	0	0	0	0	0	.000
Barnes, p	2	4	0	0	0	0	0	0	.000
Jonnard, p	1	0	0	0	0	0	0	0	.000
Watson, p	1	0	0	0	0	0	0	0	.000
Baldwin, p	1	0	0	0	0	0	0	0	.000
Dean, p	1	0	0	0	0	0	0	0	.000
Snyder, ph	1	1	0	0	0	0	0	0	.000
Totals	7	253	27	66	9	2	4	22	.261

COMPOSITE PITCHING AVERAGES

Washington Senators

Pitcher	G.	IP.	H.	R.	ER.	BB.	SO.	W.	L.	ERA.
Martina	1	1	0	0	0	0	1	0	0	0.00
Ogden	1	⅓	0	0	0	1	1	0	0	0.00
Marberry	4	8	9	6	1	4	10	0	1	1.13
Zachary	2	17⅔	13	4	4	3	3	2	0	2.04
Johnson	3	24	30	10	6	11	20	1	2	2.25
Mogridge	2	12	7	4	3	6	5	1	0	2.25
Russell	1	3	4	2	1	0	0	0	0	3.00
Speece	1	1	3	1	1	0	0	0	0	9.00
Totals	7	67	66	27	16	25	40	4	3	2.15

New York Giants

Pitcher	G.	IP.	H.	R.	ER.	BB.	SO.	W.	L.	ERA.
Baldwin	1	2	1	0	0	0	1	0	0	0.00
Dean	1	2	3	2	0	0	2	0	0	0.00
Jonnard	1	0	0	0	0	1	0	0	0	0.00
Watson	1	⅔	0	0	0	0	0	0	0	0.00
Nehf	3	19⅔	15	5	4	9	7	1	1	1.83
McQuillan	3	7	2	2	2	6	2	1	0	2.57
Ryan	2	5⅔	7	2	2	4	3	0	0	3.18
Bentley	3	17⅔	18	7	7	8	10	1	2	3.57
Barnes	2	12⅔	15	8	8	1	9	0	1	5.68
Totals	7	67⅓	61	26	23	29	34	3	4	3.07

1925 PITTSBURGH PIRATES VS. WASHINGTON SENATORS

After four games of the 1925 World Series, Washington's Big Train was like a runaway locomotive. Unstoppable. And so, too, it appeared, were Walter Johnson's talented Senator teammates.

Johnson, who had encountered troubles as a starter in the 1924 Series, struck out 10 Pittsburgh batters in Game 1 of the '25 fall classic and gave up only five hits in a 4-1 triumph. In Game 4, the 37-year-old master permitted just six hits as the defending World Series champions downed the Pirates, 4-0, and stretched their lead to three games to one.

Pittsburgh had won the second game, 3-2, on Kiki Cuyler's two-run home run in the eighth inning, while the Senators had prevailed in the third contest, 4-3, thanks in large measure to Sam Rice's late-game circus catch in right-center field.

Vic Aldridge, who had pitched the distance in the Pirates' lone victory of the Series, was called upon by Manager Bill McKechnie to keep his club afloat in Game 5. Aldridge did just that, hurling his second straight complete-game, eight-hit victory. The 6-3 triumph —like his earlier success—had come at the expense of Stan Coveleski, the onetime Cleveland pitching great who had been obtained by Washington after the 1924 season.

Second baseman Eddie Moore, playing his first full season as an everyday player in the big leagues, then combined with second-year major leaguer Ray Kremer to lift Pittsburgh into a Series deadlock. Moore broke a 2-2 tie with a fifth-inning homer and Kremer set down the faltering Senators on six hits. The Pirates' 3-2 victory in Game 6 meant that it would all come down to one game at Pittsburgh's Forbes Field. And it

Walter Johnson, Washington's 37-year-old ace, is congratulated by brother Leslie after shutting out the Pirates in Game 4 of the 1925 classic.

would be that man, Johnson, going against Aldridge.

Johnson had reached the 20-victory plateau for the 12th and last time in 1925 and, in the process, climbed within four victories of the *400* mark in his big-league career. He had spent his entire professional career with the Washington Senators, and that career

dated to 1907. Aldridge, acquired from the Chicago Cubs after the '24 season, was coming off a 15-7 year with the Pirates. A right-hander, Aldridge was 10 days from his 32nd birthday.

An outstanding pitching matchup. At least on paper.

In fact, Aldridge lasted one-third of an inning. But Johnson,

given a 4-0 first-inning lead and a 6-3 edge in the fourth, couldn't contain the Pirates and was tagged for 15 hits in eight innings.

Despite Johnson's ineffectiveness, the Senators carried a 6-4 lead into the last of the seventh and seemed poised to ring up their second consecutive Series championship. The inning got off to a shaky start for Manager Bucky Harris' team, though, when shortstop Roger Peckinpaugh muffed Moore's pop fly. Moore reached second on the error—Peckinpaugh's *seventh* of the Series—and scored on Max Carey's third double of the game. Two outs later, Pie Traynor laced a game-tying triple off Johnson, but the Pirates' third baseman was out trying to stretch the hit into a home run.

With the Series tied at three victories apiece and Game 7 now deadlocked at 6-6, tension was high when Washington came to bat against Pirates reliever Kremer in the eighth. After Ossie Bluege grounded out, Peckinpaugh strode to the plate. At this point, the Series had been a nightmare for the 34-year-old veteran. He had made one error in Game 1, two in Game 2, one in Game 3, another in Game 5, one in Game 6 and, to this juncture, one in Game 7. And he had collected only five hits in 23 at-bats. Possessing very little power—he had hit 10 home runs in the last four seasons—Peckinpaugh, in a goat-to-hero turnaround, caught hold of a Kremer delivery and drilled it into the left-field seats. Washington was back on top, 7-6.

The prospect of Johnson holding on for his second Series-clinching victory in two seasons—after the superstar pitcher had toiled for one Washington also-ran after another for the bulk of his career—seemed the stuff of which baseball dreams are made. And the chances of same grew brighter as Johnson retired the first two Pittsburgh hitters in the bottom of the eighth, getting Glenn Wright to foul out and Stuffy McInnis to fly out.

Earl Smith and pinch-hitter Carson Bigbee followed with consecutive doubles, however, and

for the second straight inning Johnson had frittered away the lead. Moore walked and Carey reached base when Peckinpaugh made a poor throw while attempting to record a forceout at second. Cuyler then broke the 7-7 tie with a two-run ground-rule double, the Pirates' eighth two-base hit of the rainy afternoon.

The Big Train had jumped the tracks. And the Senators crashed with him, going down to a 9-7 defeat and losing a World Series they seemingly had locked up a few days earlier. The Pirates' comeback marked the first time that a team had rallied from a 3-1 deficit in games to win a best-of-seven Series.

While Carey batted a Series-leading .458 for Pittsburgh and Aldridge and Kremer each posted two pitching victories, the individual spotlight fell mainly on Washington players. Of particular note was the performance of the Senators' outfield, as Goose Goslin whacked three home runs in the Series for the second straight year, Joe Harris hit a robust .440 with three homers and Rice batted .364 and made an unforgettable defensive play.

With the Senators ahead by one run in the eighth inning of Game 3, Rice ran down a long drive by Smith at the wall in right-center and tumbled into the stands. There was no immediate indication whether Rice had speared the ball before falling into the crowd, and it took him approximately 15 seconds to get untangled from the fans and return to the field—at which time he held up the ball to signal he had made the catch. While the Pirates disputed the call, saying a Washington fan may well have stuffed the ball into Rice's glove, umpire Cy Rigler called Smith out.

Rice parried questions about the play for the rest of his life, but in a letter to Hall of Fame officials —a missive to be opened only after his death, which occurred in 1974—he tried to put an end to nearly 50 years of suspense. "At no time did I lose possession of the ball," Rice wrote.

Peckinpaugh, of course, was always losing possession of the ball.

The American League's Most Valuable Player in 1925, he suffered a stinging comedown against the Pirates by establishing a record for total errors in one Series (regardless of position) that still stands. Eight miscues.

And then there was Johnson, overpowering in his first two starts but underwhelming in the decisive seventh game.

For the Pirates, it was a return to a supremacy of the baseball world they had not enjoyed since 1909 when rookie pitcher Babe Adams led the club to the World Series crown by beating the Detroit Tigers three times. There was even a link to that previous title— Adams himself, who at age 43 pitched one inning of relief against Washington in Game 4.

Game 1

Wednesday, October 7, At Pittsburgh

Washington	AB.	R.	H.	RBI.	PO.	A.
Rice, cf-rf	4	0	2	2	3	0
S. Harris, 2b	3	0	0	1	0	0
Goslin, lf	4	1	1	0	0	0
Judge, 1b	3	0	0	0	5	2
J. Harris, rf	4	2	2	1	4	0
McNeely, cf	0	0	0	0	1	0
Bluege, 3b	4	1	2	1	0	2
Peckinpaugh, ss	4	0	1	0	3	2
Ruel, c	3	0	0	0	10	2
Johnson, p	3	0	0	0	0	0
Totals	32	4	8	4	27	8

Pittsburgh	AB.	R.	H.	RBI.	PO.	A.
Moore, 2b	4	0	0	0	1	1
Carey, cf	2	0	0	0	3	0
Cuyler, rf	4	0	1	0	0	0
Barnhart, lf	4	0	1	0	0	0
Traynor, 3b	4	1	2	1	1	3
Wright, ss	4	0	0	0	1	5
Grantham, 1b	3	0	0	0	15	1
Smith, c	3	0	1	0	5	0
aBigbee	0	0	0	0	0	0
Gooch, c	0	0	0	0	1	0
Meadows, p	1	0	0	0	0	2
bMcInnis	1	0	0	0	0	0
Morrison, p	0	0	0	0	0	1
Totals	30	1	5	1	27	13

Washington...........0 1 0 0 2 0 0 0 1—4
Pittsburgh............0 0 0 0 1 0 0 0 0—1

Washington	IP.	H.	R.	ER.	BB.	SO.
Johnson (W)	9	5	1	1	1	10

Pittsburgh	IP.	H.	R.	ER.	BB.	SO.
Meadows (L)	8	6	3	3	0	4
Morrison	1	2	1	1	0	1

aRan for Smith in eighth. bStruck out for Meadows in eighth. E—Peckinpaugh. DP—Washington 1, Pittsburgh 1. LOB—Washington 3, Pittsburgh 5. HR—J. Harris, Traynor. SB—Grantham, Bigbee. SH—Judge. HBP—By Johnson (Carey 2), by Meadows (S. Harris). U—Rigler (N.L.), Owens (A.L.), McCormick (N.L.) and Moriarty (A.L.). T—1:57. A—41,723.

Game 2

Thursday, October 8, At Pittsburgh

Washington	AB.	R.	H.	RBI.	PO.	A.
Rice, cf	5	0	2	0	2	0
S. Harris, 2b	3	0	0	0	4	4
Goslin, lf	4	0	0	0	0	0
Judge, 1b	4	1	1	1	11	0
J. Harris, rf	3	0	2	0	0	0
bMcNeely	0	0	0	0	0	0
Bluege, 3b	2	0	0	0	0	1
aMyer, 3b	1	0	1	0	1	0
Peckinpaugh, ss	3	0	1	0	1	7
Ruel, c	3	0	1	0	5	0
cVeach	0	0	0	1	0	0
Coveleski, p	2	0	0	0	0	2
dRuether	1	0	0	0	0	0
Totals	31	2	8	2	24	14

Pittsburgh	AB.	R.	H.	RBI.	PO.	A.
Moore, 2b	4	1	0	0	3	1
Carey, cf	4	0	2	0	4	0
Cuyler, rf	3	1	1	2	1	0
Barnhart, lf	4	0	1	0	3	0
Traynor, 3b	3	0	0	0	0	2

	AB.	R.	H.	RBI.	PO.	A.
Wright, ss	4	1	2	1	1	5
Grantham, 1b	4	0	0	0	9	1
Smith, c	3	0	1	0	6	2
Aldridge, p	3	0	0	0	0	2
Totals	32	3	7	3	27	13

Washington	0 1 0	0 0 0	0 0 1	—2
Pittsburgh	0 0 0	1 0 0	0 2 x	—3

Washington	IP.	H.	R.	ER.	BB.	SO.
Coveleski (L)	8	7	3	2	1	3

Pittsburgh	IP.	H.	R.	ER.	BB.	SO.
Aldridge (W)	9	8	2	2	2	4

aRan for Bluege in sixth. bRan for J. Harris in ninth. cSacrificed for Ruel in ninth. dStruck out for Coveleski in ninth. E—Peckinpaugh 2. LOB—Washington 8, Pittsburgh 7. HR—Judge, Wright, Cuyler. SH—S. Harris, Coveleski, Veach, Cuyler. HBP—By Aldridge (Bluege). PB—Ruel. Balk—Aldridge. U—Owens (A.L.), McCormick (N.L.), Moriarty (A.L.) and Rigler (N.L.). T—2:04. A—43,364.

Game 3

Saturday, October 10, At Washington

Pittsburgh	AB.	R.	H.	RBI.	PO.	A.
Moore, 2b	3	0	1	0	2	2
Carey, cf	4	0	2	0	3	0
Cuyler, rf	4	1	1	0	1	0
Barnhart, lf	5	0	1	1	2	0
Traynor, 3b	4	1	1	0	1	3
Wright, ss	3	1	0	1	1	2
Grantham, 1b	4	0	0	0	8	1
Smith, c	3	0	1	0	5	2
Kremer, p	3	0	1	1	0	1
dBigbee	1	0	0	0	0	0
Totals	34	3	8	3	a23	11

Washington	AB.	R.	H.	RBI.	PO.	A.
Rice, cf-rf	5	1	2	0	2	0
S. Harris, 2b	3	1	1	0	2	1
Goslin, lf	4	1	2	1	3	0
Judge, 1b	3	0	1	2	8	0
J. Harris, rf	4	0	2	1	0	0
Marberry, p	0	0	0	0	0	0
Myer, 3b	3	0	0	0	0	1
Peckinpaugh, ss	4	0	1	0	2	3
Ruel, c	3	0	1	0	8	2
Ferguson, p	2	0	0	0	0	0
bLeibold	0	0	0	0	0	0
cMcNeely, cf	0	1	0	0	2	0
Totals	31	4	10	4	27	7

Pittsburgh	0 1 0	1 0 1	0 0 0	—3
Washington	0 0 1	0 0 1	2 0 x	—4

Pittsburgh	IP.	H.	R.	ER.	BB.	SO.
Kremer (L)	8	10	4	4	3	5

Washington	IP.	H.	R.	ER.	BB.	SO.
Ferguson (W)	7	6	3	2	4	5
Marberry	2	2	0	0	0	2

aMyer out; hit by his own batted ball. bWalked for Ferguson in seventh. cRan for Leibold in seventh. dFlied out for Kremer in ninth. E—Carey, Wright, Smith, Peckinpaugh. DP—Pittsburgh 1, Washington 1. LOB—Pittsburgh 11, Washington 9. 2B—Judge, Cuyler, Carey. 3B—Traynor. HR—Goslin. SH—S. Harris, Marberry. SF—Wright, Judge. HBP—By Ferguson (Carey), by Marberry (Cuyler). PB—Smith. U—McCormick (N.L.), Moriarty (A.L.), Rigler (N.L.) and Owens (A.L.). T—2:10. A—36,495.

Game 4

Sunday, October 11, At Washington

Pittsburgh	AB.	R.	H.	RBI.	PO.	A.
Moore, 2b	4	0	1	0	3	3
Carey, cf	3	0	1	0	0	0
Cuyler, rf	4	0	0	0	0	0
Barnhart, lf	3	0	0	0	2	1
Traynor, 3b	4	0	2	0	0	3
Wright, ss	4	0	0	0	3	4
Grantham, 1b	3	0	2	0	10	3
Gooch, c	3	0	0	0	6	3
Yde, p	1	0	0	0	0	0
Morrison, p	1	0	0	0	0	2
aBigbee	1	0	0	0	0	0
C. Adams, p	0	0	0	0	0	0
Totals	31	0	6	0	24	19

Washington	AB.	R.	H.	RBI.	PO.	A.
Rice, cf	5	1	2	0	2	0
S. Harris, 2b	3	1	1	0	6	7
Goslin, lf	3	1	2	3	3	0
J. Harris, rf	4	1	1	1	2	0
Judge, 1b	3	0	0	0	9	0
Peckinpaugh, ss	4	0	1	0	0	2
Ruel, c	3	0	3	0	5	0
Myer, 3b	4	0	1	0	0	0
Johnson, p	4	0	1	0	0	1
Totals	33	4	12	4	27	10

Pittsburgh	0 0 0	0 0 0	0 0 0	—0
Washington	0 0 4	0 0 0	0 0 x	—4

Pittsburgh	IP.	H.	R.	ER.	BB.	SO.
Yde (L)	2⅓	5	4	3	3	1
Morrison	4⅔	5	0	0	1	4
C. Adams	1	2	0	0	0	0

Washington	IP.	H.	R.	ER.	BB.	SO.
Johnson (W)	9	6	0	0	2	2

aPopped out for Morrison in eighth. E—Wright. DP—Pittsburgh 1, Washington 2. LOB—Pittsburgh 6, Washington 9. 2B—Ruel. HR—Goslin, J. Harris. SB—Carey, Peckinpaugh. U—Moriarty (A.L.), Rigler (N.L.), Owens (A.L.) and McCormick (N.L.). T—2:00. A—38,701.

Game 5

Monday, October 12, At Washington

Pittsburgh	AB.	R.	H.	RBI.	PO.	A.
Moore, 2b	4	1	1	0	3	2
Carey, cf	4	2	2	0	0	0
Cuyler, rf	4	1	2	1	4	0
Barnhart, lf	4	1	2	2	1	0
Traynor, 3b	3	0	1	1	1	0
Wright, ss	5	1	2	1	1	3
McInnis, 1b	5	0	1	1	12	2
Smith, c	3	0	2	0	5	2
Aldridge, p	4	0	0	0	0	2
Totals	36	6	13	6	27	11

Washington	AB.	R.	H.	RBI.	PO.	A.
Rice, cf	5	1	2	1	3	0
S. Harris, 2b	3	0	0	0	2	3
Goslin, lf	4	0	1	1	5	0
Judge, 1b	3	0	0	0	11	0
J. Harris, rf	3	1	2	1	0	0
Peckinpaugh, ss	3	0	0	0	4	3
Ruel, c	3	0	1	0	1	1
Bluege, 3b	4	0	1	0	1	5
Coveleski, p	1	0	0	0	0	2
Ballou, p	0	0	0	0	0	0
aLeibold	1	1	1	0	0	0
Zachary, p	0	0	0	0	0	0
Marberry, p	0	0	0	0	0	0
bAdams	1	0	0	0	0	0
Totals	31	3	8	3	27	14

Pittsburgh	0 0 2	0 0 0	2 1 1	—6
Washington	1 0 0	1 0 0	1 0 0	—3

Pittsburgh	IP.	H.	R.	ER.	BB.	SO.
Aldridge (W)	9	8	3	3	4	5

Washington	IP.	H.	R.	ER.	BB.	SO.
Coveleski (L)	6⅓	9	4	4	4	0
Ballou	⅔	0	0	0	0	1
Zachary	1⅔	3	2	2	1	0
Marberry	⅓	1	0	0	0	0

aDoubled for Ballou in seventh. bGrounded out for Marberry in ninth. E—Peckinpaugh. DP—Pittsburgh 1, Washington 2. LOB—Pittsburgh 10, Washington 8. 2B—Goslin, Bluege, Leibold, Wright. HR—J. Harris. SB—Carey, Barnhart. SH—Traynor, E. Smith, S. Harris 2, Peckinpaugh. U—Rigler (N.L.), Owens (A.L.), McCormick (N.L.) and Moriarty (A.L.). T—2:26. A—35,899.

Game 6

Tuedsay, October 13, At Pittsburgh

Washington	AB.	R.	H.	RBI.	PO.	A.
Rice, cf	4	0	0	0	2	0
S. Harris, 2b	3	0	0	0	3	0
cVeach	1	0	0	0	0	0
Ballou, p	0	0	0	0	0	0
Goslin, lf	3	1	1	1	2	0
J. Harris, rf	4	0	1	0	2	0
Judge, 1b	4	0	1	0	9	0
Bluege, 3b	4	1	1	0	0	6
Peckinpaugh, ss	3	0	1	1	0	3
Severeid, c	3	0	1	0	6	0
aMcNeely	0	0	0	0	0	0
S. Adams, 2b	0	0	0	0	0	0
Ferguson, p	2	0	0	0	0	1
bLeibold	1	0	0	0	0	0
Ruel, c	0	0	0	0	0	0
Totals	32	2	6	2	24	10

Pittsburgh	AB.	R.	H.	RBI.	PO.	A.
Moore, 2b	3	2	2	1	2	4
Carey, cf	2	1	0	0	0	0
Cuyler, rf	3	0	0	0	2	0
Barnhart, lf	3	0	1	1	2	0
Traynor, 3b	4	0	2	1	1	4
Wright, ss	3	0	0	0	3	2
McInnis, 1b	4	0	1	0	12	1
Smith, c	4	0	1	0	3	1
Kremer, p	3	0	0	0	2	3
Totals	29	3	7	3	27	15

Washington	1 1 0	0 0 0	0 0 0	—2
Pittsburgh	0 0 2	0 1 0	0 0 x	—3

Washington	IP.	H.	R.	ER.	BB.	SO.
Ferguson (L)	7	7	3	3	2	6
Ballou	1	0	0	0	1	0

Pittsburgh	IP.	H.	R.	ER.	BB.	SO.
Kremer (W)	9	6	2	2	1	3

aRan for Severeid in eighth. bPopped out for Ferguson in eighth. cGrounded out for S. Harris in eighth. E—Peckinpaugh, Severeid, Kremer. DP—Washington 1. LOB—Washington 4, Pittsburgh 8. 2B—Peckinpaugh, Barnhart, J. Harris. HR—Goslin, Moore. SB—Traynor, McNeely. SH—Carey 2, Cuyler. U—Owens (A.L.), McCormick (N.L.), Moriarty (A.L.) and Rigler (N.L.). T—1:57. A—43,810.

Game 7

Thursday, October 15, At Pittsburgh

Washington	AB.	R.	H.	RBI.	PO.	A.
Rice, cf	5	2	2	0	3	0
S. Harris, 2b	5	0	0	0	6	3
Goslin, lf	4	2	1	0	2	0
J. Harris, rf	3	1	1	2	1	1
Judge, 1b	3	1	1	0	6	0
Bluege, 3b	4	0	1	1	0	0
xPeckinpaugh, ss	3	1	1	2	0	2
Ruel, c	4	0	0	1	6	0
Johnson, p	4	0	0	0	0	3
Totals	35	7	7	6	24	9

Pittsburgh	AB.	R.	H.	RBI.	PO.	A.
Moore, 2b	4	3	1	1	2	0
Carey, cf	5	3	4	2	4	0
Cuyler, rf	4	0	2	3	4	0
Barnhart, lf	5	0	1	1	2	0
Oldham, p	0	0	0	0	0	0
Traynor, 3b	4	0	1	1	1	3
Wright, ss	4	0	1	0	1	3
McInnis, 1b	4	0	2	0	7	0
Smith, c	4	0	1	0	4	0
bYde	0	1	0	0	0	0
Gooch, c	0	0	0	0	2	0
Aldridge, p	0	0	0	0	0	0
Morrison, p	1	1	1	0	0	0
aGrantham	1	0	0	0	0	0
Kremer, p	1	0	0	0	0	1
cBigbee, lf	1	1	1	1	0	0
Totals	38	9	15	9	27	7

Washington	4 0 0	2 0 0	0 1 0	—7
Pittsburgh	0 0 3	0 1 0	2 3 x	—9

Washington	IP.	H.	R.	ER.	BB.	SO.
Johnson (L)	8	15	9	5	1	3

Pittsburgh	IP.	H.	R.	ER.	BB.	SO.
Aldridge	⅓	2	4	4	3	0
Morrison	3⅔	4	2	2	0	2
Kremer (W)	4	1	1	1	0	1
Oldham	1	0	0	0	0	2

xAwarded first base on catcher's interference. aFlied out for Morrison in fourth. bRan for Smith in eighth. cDoubled for Kremer in eighth. E—Peckinpaugh 2, Moore, Cuyler. DP—Washington 1. LOB—Washington 5, Pittsburgh 7. 2B—Carey 3, Moore, J. Harris, Cuyler 2, Smith, Bigbee. 3B—Traynor. HR—Peckinpaugh. SB—Carey. SH—Cuyler. WP—Aldridge 2. U—McCormick (N.L.), Moriarty (A.L.), Rigler (N.L.) and Owens (A.L.). T—2:31. A—42,856.

COMPOSITE BATTING AVERAGES

Pittsburgh Pirates

Player-Position	G.	AB.	R.	H.	2B.	3B.	HR.	RBI.	BA.
Morrison, p	3	2	1	1	0	0	0	0	.500
Carey, cf	7	24	6	11	4	0	0	2	.458
Smith, c	6	20	0	7	1	0	0	0	.350
Traynor, 3b	7	26	2	9	0	2	1	4	.346
Bigbee, pr-ph-lf	4	3	1	1	1	0	0	1	.333
McInnis, ph-1b	4	14	0	4	0	0	0	1	.286
Cuyler, rf	7	26	3	7	3	0	1	6	.269
Barnhart, lf	7	28	1	7	1	0	0	5	.250
Moore, 2b	7	26	7	6	1	0	1	2	.231
Wright, ss	7	27	3	5	1	0	1	3	.185
Kremer, p	3	7	0	1	0	0	0	1	.143
Grantham, 1b-ph	5	15	0	2	0	0	0	0	.133
Aldridge, p	3	7	0	0	0	0	0	0	.000
Gooch, c	3	3	0	0	0	0	0	0	.000
Yde, p-pr	2	1	1	0	0	0	0	0	.000
Meadows, p	1	1	0	0	0	0	0	0	.000
C. Adams, p	1	0	0	0	0	0	0	0	.000
Oldham, p	1	0	0	0	0	0	0	0	.000
Totals	7	230	25	61	12	2	4	25	.265

Washington Senators

Player-Position	G.	AB.	R.	H.	2B.	3B.	HR.	RBI.	BA.
Leibold, ph	3	2	1	1	1	0	0	0	.500
J. Harris, rf	7	25	5	11	2	0	3	6	.440
Rice, cf-rf	7	33	5	12	0	0	0	3	.364
Severeid, c	1	3	0	1	0	0	0	0	.333
Ruel, c	7	19	0	6	1	0	0	1	.316
Goslin, lf	7	26	6	8	1	0	3	6	.308
Bluege, 3b	5	18	2	5	1	0	0	2	.278
Peckinpaugh, ss	7	24	1	6	1	0	1	3	.250
Myer, 3b	3	8	0	2	0	0	0	0	.250
Judge, 1b	7	23	2	4	1	0	1	3	.174
Johnson, p	3	11	0	1	0	0	0	0	.091
S. Harris, 2b	7	23	2	2	0	0	0	0	.087
McNeely, cf-pr	4	0	2	0	0	0	0	0	.000
Ferguson, p	2	4	0	0	0	0	0	0	.000
Veach, ph	2	1	0	0	0	0	0	1	.000
Coveleski, p	2	3	0	0	0	0	0	0	.000
Marberry, p	2	0	0	0	0	0	0	0	.000
Ballou, p	2	0	0	0	0	0	0	0	.000
S. Adams, ph-2b	2	1	0	0	0	0	0	0	.000
Ruether, ph	1	1	0	0	0	0	0	0	.000
Zachary, p	1	0	0	0	0	0	0	0	.000
Totals	7	225	26	59	8	0	8	25	.262

COMPOSITE PITCHING AVERAGES

Pittsburgh Pirates

Pitcher	G.	IP.	H.	R.	ER.	BB.	SO.	W.	L.	ERA.
C. Adams	1	1	2	0	0	0	0	0	0	0.00
Oldham	1	1	0	0	0	0	2	0	0	0.00
Morrison	3	9⅓	11	3	3	1	5	0	0	2.89
Kremer	3	21	17	7	7	4	9	2	1	3.00
Meadows	1	8	6	3	3	0	4	0	1	3.38
Aldridge	3	18⅓	18	9	9	9	9	2	0	4.42
Yde	1	2⅓	5	4	3	3	1	0	1	11.70
Totals	7	61	59	26	25	17	30	4	3	3.69

Washington Senators

Pitcher	G.	IP.	H.	R.	ER.	BB.	SO.	W.	L.	ERA.
Marberry	2	2⅓	3	0	0	0	2	0	0	0.00
Ballou	2	1⅔	0	0	0	1	1	0	0	0.00
Johnson	3	26	26	10	6	4	15	2	1	2.08
Ferguson	2	14	13	6	5	6	11	1	1	3.21
Coveleski	2	14⅓	16	7	6	5	3	0	2	3.77
Zachary	1	1⅔	3	2	2	1	0	0	0	10.80
Totals	7	60	61	25	19	17	32	3	4	2.85

ST. LOUIS CARDINALS
VS.
NEW YORK YANKEES

Bases loaded. Two out. Bottom of the seventh inning. Game 7 of the 1926 World Series. St. Louis Cardinals three victories, New York Yankees three victories. Yanks second baseman Tony Lazzeri approaching the plate. Cardinals trying to protect a 3-2 lead at Yankee Stadium and thereby win their first Series.

Unquestionably, it was a crucial, tension-filled situation. And it quickly became one of the most dramatic moments in Series history when Rogers Hornsby, the Cardinals' manager/second baseman, ambled to the mound and signaled to the bullpen for Grover Cleveland Alexander. Surely there must have been some mistake. The 39-year-old Alexander

had pitched a complete-game victory the day before. And, the story goes, Ol' Pete had celebrated well into the night, wholly confident (and why not?) that his aging right arm wouldn't get another workout until the spring of 1927. (Many years later, Alexander contended he didn't celebrate at all after Game 6 because Hornsby had advised him that "I may need you tomorrow.")

Hornsby's directive was no mistake. The battle-tested Alexander was the man Hornsby wanted to take over for Jesse Haines, who had shut out the Yankees in Game 3 and pitched reasonably well in this contest until the combination of a finger blister and a mounting New York threat brought about

his removal.

Lazzeri, 22 years old, had just completed an outstanding rookie season in the majors. He batted .275 for the Yankees with 18 home runs and 114 runs batted in. Alexander, on the other hand, was in the twilight of his career and had been obtained by the Cardinals on waivers from the Chicago Cubs in June. He won nine of 16 decisions for St. Louis.

With the Yankees' Earle Combs leading off third base, Bob Meusel stationed at second and Lou Gehrig on first, Alexander delivered his first pitch to Lazzeri. Ball one. The second pitch was a called strike. Lazzeri took a tremendous cut at Alexander's third offering and lined the ball down the third-base line—just foul. Amid a crescendo of crowd noise, Alexander readied himself once more and let fly. Lazzeri swung and missed. Ol' Pete had gotten the Cardinals out of a monumental jam.

After St. Louis threatened but failed to score in the eighth, Alexander retired the Yankees in order in their half of the inning. The Cardinals again were unable to add to their lead in the ninth, so it was up to Ol' Pete to protect the one-run margin one more time.

Combs started the Yankees' ninth by grounding out to third baseman Lester Bell, and Mark Koenig also was thrown out, Bell to first baseman Jim Bottomley. Only one batter stood between Alexander and a World Series championship for the Cardinals, but, oh, what a batter. George Herman (Babe) Ruth. The Bambino worked the count to 3 and 2, then drew his 11th walk of the Series. Up next was cleanup hitter Meusel, representing the winning run. Meusel, though, was denied his at-bat when Ruth, who had

St. Louis Cardinals second baseman Rogers Hornsby was a popular figure as the 1926 World Series opened in New York.

Yankee slugger Babe Ruth slides safely into second with a stolen base as Cardinal shortstop Tommy Thevenow takes the late throw in Game 6 of the 1926 fall classic. Ruth was not so successful in Game 7, when he was thrown out on the final play of the Series.

stolen second base in Game 6, daringly (some observers thought *foolishly*) tried to steal again. Catcher Bob O'Farrell's throw to Hornsby nailed the Yankees' slugger and ended the fall classic.

The Cardinals' decisive 3-2 triumph had been fashioned not only by Alexander's clutch relief stint, but also by the continued standout play of shortstop Tommy Thevenow. A .256 hitter during the regular season, Thevenow broke a 1-1 tie in Game 7 with a two-run single in the fourth inning. Overall, Thevenow was 10 for 24 against the Yankees, making him the Series' top hitter with a .417 mark.

New York got standout production from Combs and Gehrig, appearing in their first Series, and Ruth. Combs paced the Yankees with a .357 batting figure, while Gehrig hit .348 and knocked in the winning run in Game 1. Ruth bashed four homers in the Series, three coming in the Yanks' 10-5

romp in Game 4 at Sportsman's Park.

St. Louis' Haines and Alexander and New York's Herb Pennock were the top pitchers in the 1926 Series. Besides getting the victory in the finale, Haines allowed just five hits in a 4-0 triumph in the third game. Alexander retired the last 21 Yankees he faced in Game 2 and, backed by Billy Southworth's three-run homer, won a 6-2 decision. He then coasted, 10-2, in Game 6 as Bell homered and drove in four runs. Pennock was a 2-1 winner in the Series opener, yielding just three hits, and came back for a 3-2, 10-inning victory in Game 5, a contest that the Yankees tied in the ninth on Ben Paschal's pinch single and won in the 10th on Lazzeri's sacrifice fly.

The Cardinals were able to win the Series despite subpar performances from players instrumental in getting them to their first fall classic. Hornsby, a .317 hitter during the regular season (after

batting above .400 in three of the four previous years), was held to a .250 batting mark by Yankee pitching. And pitchers Flint Rhem and Bill Sherdel, St. Louis' biggest winners during the season with 20 and 16 victories, respectively, failed to win in the Series.

But there was Thevenow, whose hitting spree included an inside-the-park home run in Game 2 (Thevenow hit only two other homers in his 15-season career in the majors and, curiously, both came during the '26 regular season). Plus, the Cards had Bottomley and Southworth, both of whom hit at a .345 clip against New York, and O'Farrell, a .304 hitter in the Series.

Most of all, St. Louis had that wily veteran trudging in from the bullpen in the seventh inning of Game 7.

Game 1

Saturday, October 2, At New York

St. Louis	AB.	R.	H.	RBI.	PO.	A.
Douthit, cf	3	1	1	0	1	0
Southworth, rf	3	0	0	0	1	0
Holm, rf	1	0	0	0	0	0
Hornsby, 2b	4	0	0	0	3	2
Bottomley, 1b	4	0	2	1	10	0
L. Bell, 3b	3	0	0	0	1	1
Hafey, lf	4	0	0	0	5	1
O'Farrell, c	2	0	0	0	1	1
Thevenow, ss	2	0	0	0	1	7
Sherdel, p	2	0	0	0	1	2
aFlowers	1	0	0	0	0	0
Haines, p	0	0	0	0	0	0
Totals	29	1	3	1	24	14

New York	AB.	R.	H.	RBI.	PO.	A.
Combs, cf	3	1	1	0	2	0
Koenig, ss	4	0	1	0	0	4
Ruth, rf	3	1	1	0	1	0
Meusel, lf	1	0	0	0	3	0
Gehrig, 1b	4	0	1	2	14	0
Lazzeri, 2b	4	0	1	0	0	4
Dugan, 3b	3	0	1	0	1	3
Severeid, c	3	0	0	0	6	1
Pennock, p	2	0	0	0	0	3
Totals	27	2	6	2	27	15

| St. Louis | | | | | | 1 0 0 0 0 0 0 0 0—1 |
| New York | | | | | | 1 0 0 0 0 1 0 0 x—2 |

St. Louis	IP.	H.	R.	ER.	BB.	SO.
Sherdel (L)	7	6	2	2	3	1
Haines	1	0	0	0	1	0

New York	IP.	H.	R.	ER.	BB.	SO.
Pennock (W)	9	3	1	1	3	4

aFlied out for Sherdel in eighth. E—L. Bell. DP—St. Louis 1. LOB—St. Louis 5, New York 7. 2B—Douthit. SH—Pennock, Meusel, Thevenow. U—Dinneen (A.L.), O'Day (N.L.), Hildebrand (A.L.) and Klem (N.L.). T—1:48. A—61,658.

Game 2

Sunday, October 3, At New York

St. Louis	AB.	R.	H.	RBI.	PO.	A.
Douthit, cf	4	1	1	0	0	0
Southworth, rf	5	2	3	3	0	0
Hornsby, 2b	3	0	1	0	2	5
Bottomley, 1b	5	0	2	2	13	0
L. Bell, 3b	4	0	0	0	0	4
Hafey, lf	4	0	0	0	1	0
O'Farrell, c	4	1	2	0	10	1
Thevenow, ss	4	2	3	1	1	4
Alexander, p	4	0	0	0	0	4
Totals	37	6	12	6	27	18

New York	AB.	R.	H.	RBI.	PO.	A.
Combs, cf	3	0	1	0	1	0
Koenig, ss	4	0	0	0	1	3
Ruth, rf	4	0	0	0	1	0
Meusel, lf	4	1	1	0	3	0
Gehrig, 1b	3	0	0	0	12	0
Lazzeri, 2b	3	1	1	1	2	2
Dugan, 3b	3	0	1	0	1	1
Severeid, c	2	0	0	0	5	1
aPaschal	1	0	0	0	0	0
Collins, c	0	0	0	0	1	0

	AB.	R.	H.	RBI.	PO.	A.
Shocker, p	2	0	0	0	0	2
Shawkey, p	0	0	0	0	0	0
bRuether	1	0	0	0	0	0
Jones, p	0	0	0	0	0	0
Totals	30	2	4	1	27	9

St. Louis	0 0 2	0 0 0	3 0 1—6
New York	0 2 0	0 0 0	0 0 0—2

St. Louis	IP.	H.	R.	ER.	BB.	SO.
Alexander (W)	9	4	2	1	1	10

New York	IP.	H.	R.	ER.	BB.	SO.
Shocker	7*	10	5	5	0	2
Shawkey (L)	1	0	0	0	0	2
Jones	1	2	1	1	2	1

*Pitched to one batter in eighth.

aStruck out for Severeid in eighth. bGrounded out for Shawkey in eighth. E—Alexander. DP— St. Louis 1. LOB—St. Louis 7, New York 2. 2B—Hornsby, O'Farrell. HR—Southworth, Thevenow. SH—Hornsby. U—O'Day (N.L.), Hildebrand (A.L.), Klem (N.L.) and Dinneen (A.L.). T—1:57. A—63,600.

Game 3

Tuesday, October 5, At St. Louis

New York	AB.	R.	H.	RBI.	PO.	A.
Combs, cf	3	0	1	0	4	0
Koenig, ss	4	0	0	0	2	3
Ruth, lf	3	0	1	0	0	0
Meusel, rf	4	0	0	0	1	0
Gehrig, 1b	4	0	2	0	10	0
Lazzeri, 2b	4	0	0	0	4	6
Dugan, 3b	3	0	1	0	0	2
Severeid, c	2	0	0	0	3	0
Ruether, p	2	0	0	0	0	2
Shawkey, p	0	0	0	0	0	0
aPaschal	0	0	0	0	0	0
Thomas, p	0	0	0	0	0	0
Totals	29	0	5	0	24	13

St. Louis	AB.	R.	H.	RBI.	PO.	A.
Douthit, cf	3	0	0	0	1	0
Southworth, rf	3	1	2	0	2	0
Hornsby, 2b	4	0	1	0	1	5
Bottomley, 1b	4	0	1	1	13	0
L. Bell, 3b	4	1	1	0	0	4
Hafey, lf	3	0	1	0	4	0
O'Farrell, c	2	0	0	0	5	0
Thevenow, ss	3	1	0	0	1	2
Haines, p	3	1	2	2	0	2
Totals	29	4	8	3	27	13

New York	0 0 0	0 0 0	0 0 0—0
St. Louis	0 0 0	3 1 0	0 0 x—4

New York	IP.	H.	R.	ER.	BB.	SO.
Ruether (L)	4⅓	7	4	2	2	1
Shawkey	2⅔	0	0	0	0	1
Thomas	1	1	0	0	0	0

St. Louis	IP.	H.	R.	ER.	BB.	SO.
Haines (W)	9	5	0	0	3	3

aWalked for Shawkey in eighth. E—Koenig. DP—New York 1, St. Louis 2. LOB—New York 6, St. Louis 5. 2B—Hafey. HR—Haines. SH—Severeid, Southworth, Hafey. U—Hildebrand (A.L.), Klem (N.L.), Dinneen (A.L.) and O'Day (N.L.). T—1:41. A—37,708.

Game 4

Wednesday, October 6, At St. Louis

New York	AB.	R.	H.	RBI.	PO.	A.
Combs, cf	5	2	2	1	4	0
Koenig, ss	6	1	1	1	1	3
Ruth, lf	3	4	3	4	1	1
Meusel, rf	2	1	1	0	1	0
Gehrig, 1b	3	0	2	0	8	0
Lazzeri, 2b	3	1	1	1	1	3
Dugan, 3b	4	0	1	2	1	2
Severeid, c	4	1	3	0	10	0
Hoyt, p	4	0	0	0	0	0
Totals	34	10	14	9	27	9

St. Louis	AB.	R.	H.	RBI.	PO.	A.
Douthit, cf	5	1	2	1	2	2
Southworth, rf	5	0	3	0	1	2
Hornsby, 2b	5	1	2	1	3	4
Bottomley, 1b	4	0	1	0	6	1
L. Bell, 3b	4	0	1	1	3	0
Hafey, lf	5	1	1	0	0	0
O'Farrell, c	4	1	2	0	8	1
Thevenow, ss	4	1	2	1	3	2
Rhem, p	1	0	0	0	0	1
aToporcer	0	0	0	1	0	0
Reinhart, p	0	0	0	0	0	0
H. Bell, p	0	0	0	0	0	0
bFlowers	1	0	0	0	0	0
Hallahan, p	0	0	0	0	1	0
cHolm	1	0	0	0	0	0
Keen, p	0	0	0	0	0	1
Totals	39	5	14	5	27	14

New York	1 0 1	1 4 2	1 0 0—10
St. Louis	1 0 0	3 0 0	0 0 1— 5

New York	IP.	H.	R.	ER.	BB.	SO.
Hoyt (W)	9	14	5	2	1	8

St. Louis	IP.	H.	R.	ER.	BB.	SO.
Rhem	4	7	3	3	2	4
Reinhart (L)	0*	1	4	4	4	0
H. Bell	2	4	2	2	1	1
Hallahan	2	2	1	1	3	1
Keen	1	0	0	0	0	0

*Pitched to five batters in fifth.

aHit sacrifice fly for Rhem in fourth. bStruck out for H. Bell in sixth. cStruck out for Hallahan in eighth. E—Koenig. LOB—New York 10, St. Louis 10. 2B—Lazzeri, Dugan, Thevenow, Douthit, Koenig, Gehrig, Combs. HR—Ruth 3. SB—Hornsby. SH—Hoyt, Gehrig. SF—L. Bell, Lazzeri, Toporcer. Balk—H. Bell. U—Klem (N.L.), Dinneen (A.L.), O'Day (N.L.) and Hildebrand (A.L.). T—2:38. A—38,825.

Game 5

Thursday, October 7, At St. Louis

New York	AB.	R.	H.	RBI.	PO.	A.
Combs, cf	4	0	1	0	2	0
Koenig, ss	5	1	2	1	3	5
Ruth, lf	3	0	0	0	3	0
Meusel, rf	3	0	0	0	0	0
Gehrig, 1b	3	1	2	0	14	0
Lazzeri, 2b	4	0	2	1	3	2
Dugan, 3b	3	0	0	0	0	1
aPaschal	1	0	1	1	0	0
Gazella, 3b	0	0	0	0	1	2
Severeid, c	5	0	0	0	4	1
Pennock, p	4	1	1	0	0	2
Totals	35	3	9	3	30	13

St. Louis	AB.	R.	H.	RBI.	PO.	A.
Holm, cf	4	0	0	0	1	0
Southworth, rf	4	0	0	0	2	0
Hornsby, 2b	4	0	0	0	3	3
Bottomley, 1b	4	1	1	0	12	0
L. Bell, 3b	4	1	2	1	2	3
Hafey, lf	4	0	0	0	6	0
O'Farrell, c	4	0	3	1	2	3
Thevenow, ss	4	0	1	0	1	3
Sherdel, p	3	0	0	0	1	3
bFlowers	1	0	0	0	0	0
Totals	36	2	7	2	30	15

New York	0 0 0	0 0 1	0 0 1	1—3
St. Louis	0 0 0	1 0 0	1 0 0	0—2

New York	IP.	H.	R.	ER.	BB.	SO.
Pennock (W)	10	7	2	2	1	4

St. Louis	IP.	H.	R.	ER.	BB.	SO.
Sherdel (L)	10	9	3	2	5	2

aSingled for Dugan in ninth. bPopped out for Sherdel in tenth. E—Koenig, Thevenow. DP—New York 1, St. Louis 1. LOB—New York 11, St. Louis 5. 2B—Bottomley, Pennock, L. Bell, Gehrig. SB—Southworth. SH—Meusel 2. SF—Lazzeri. HBP— By Sherdel (Gazella). WP—Sherdel. PB—Severeid. U—Dinneen (A.L.), O'Day (N.L.), Hildebrand (A.L.) and Klem (N.L.). T—2:28. A—39,552.

Game 6

Saturday, October 9, At New York

St. Louis	AB.	R.	H.	RBI.	PO.	A.
Holm, cf	5	1	2	1	4	0
Southworth, rf	5	3	2	1	2	1
Hornsby, 2b	4	1	1	3	0	2
Bottomley, 1b	5	2	2	1	11	0
L. Bell, 3b	4	1	3	4	1	1
Hafey, lf	3	0	1	0	2	0
O'Farrell, c	4	0	0	0	6	0
Thevenow, ss	3	1	2	0	1	5
Alexander, p	2	1	0	0	0	2
Totals	35	10	13	10	27	11

New York	AB.	R.	H.	RBI.	PO.	A.
Combs, cf	5	0	2	1	2	0
Koenig, ss	5	0	0	0	3	2
Ruth, rf	3	0	0	0	0	1
Meusel, lf	3	1	2	0	2	0
Gehrig, 1b	4	0	1	1	9	1
Lazzeri, 2b	4	0	0	0	2	1
Dugan, 3b	4	1	2	0	3	2
Severeid, c	3	0	1	0	6	3
aAdams	0	0	0	0	0	0
Collins, c	1	0	0	0	0	0
Shawkey, p	2	0	0	0	0	1
Shocker, p	0	0	0	0	0	0
bPaschal	1	0	0	0	0	0
Thomas, p	0	0	0	0	0	2
cRuether	1	0	0	0	0	0
Totals	36	2	8	2	27	13

St. Louis	3 0 0	0 1 0	5 0 1—10
New York	0 0 0	1 0 0	1 0 0— 2

St. Louis	IP.	H.	R.	ER.	BB.	SO.
Alexander (W)	9	8	2	2	2	6

New York	IP.	H.	R.	ER.	BB.	SO.
Shawkey (L)	6⅓	8	7	6	2	4
Shocker	⅔	3	2	2	0	1
Thomas	2	2	1	1	0	0

aRan for Severeid in seventh. bStruck out for Shocker in seventh. cGrounded out for Thomas in ninth. E—L. Bell, Thevenow, Lazzeri. DP—St. Louis 1, New York 1. LOB—St. Louis 4, New York 9. 2B—Bottomley 2, Meusel, Southworth, Hafey, Combs. 3B—Meusel, Southworth. HR—L. Bell. SB—Ruth. SH—Hafey, Alexander 2. HBP—By Thomas (Thevenow). U—O'Day (N.L.), Hildebrand (A.L.), Klem (N.L.) and Dinneen (A.L.). T—2:05. A—48,615.

Game 7

Sunday, October 10, At New York

St. Louis	AB.	R.	H.	RBI.	PO.	A.
Holm, cf	5	0	0	0	2	0
Southworth, rf	4	0	0	0	0	0
Hornsby, 2b	4	0	2	0	4	1
Bottomley, 1b	3	1	1	0	14	0
L. Bell, 3b	4	1	0	0	0	4
Hafey, lf	4	1	2	0	3	0
O'Farrell, c	3	0	0	1	3	2
Thevenow, ss	4	0	2	2	1	3
Haines, p	2	0	1	0	0	4
Alexander, p	1	0	0	0	0	0
Totals	34	3	8	3	27	14

New York	AB.	R.	H.	RBI.	PO.	A.
Combs, cf	5	0	2	0	2	0
Koenig, ss	4	0	0	0	2	3
Ruth, rf	1	1	1	1	2	0
Meusel, lf	4	0	1	0	3	0
Gehrig, 1b	2	0	0	0	11	0
Lazzeri, 2b	4	0	0	0	2	1
Dugan, 3b	4	1	2	0	2	3
Severeid, c	3	0	2	1	3	1
aAdams	0	0	0	0	0	0
Collins, c	1	0	0	0	0	0
Hoyt, p	2	0	0	0	0	1
bPaschal	1	0	0	0	0	0
Pennock, p	1	0	0	0	0	1
Totals	32	2	8	2	27	10

St. Louis	0 0 0	3 0 0	0 0 0—3
New York	0 0 1	0 0 1	0 0 0—2

St. Louis	IP.	H.	R.	ER.	BB.	SO.
Haines (W)	6⅔	8	2	2	5	2
Alexander	2⅓	0	0	0	1	1

New York	IP.	H.	R.	ER.	BB.	SO.
Hoyt (L)	6	5	3	0	0	2
Pennock	3	3	0	0	0	0

aRan for Severeid in sixth. bGrounded out for Hoyt in sixth. E—Koenig, Meusel, Dugan. LOB—St. Louis 7, New York 10. 2B—Severeid. HR—Ruth. SH—Haines, Koenig, Bottomley. SF—O'Farrell. U—Hildebrand (A.L.), Klem (N.L.), Dinneen (A.L.) and O'Day (N.L.). T—2:15. A—38,093.

COMPOSITE BATTING AVERAGES

St. Louis Cardinals

Player-Position	G.	AB.	R.	H.	2B.	3B.	HR.	RBI.	BA.
Haines, p	3	5	1	3	0	0	1	2	.600
Thevenow, ss	7	24	5	10	1	0	1	4	.417
Bottomley, 1b	7	29	4	10	3	0	0	5	.345
Southworth, rf	7	29	6	10	1	1	1	4	.345
O'Farrell, c	7	23	2	7	1	0	0	2	.304
Douthit, cf	4	15	3	4	2	0	0	1	.267
L. Bell, 3b	7	27	4	7	1	0	1	6	.259
Hornsby, 2b	7	28	2	7	1	0	0	4	.250
Hafey, lf	7	27	2	5	2	0	0	0	.185
Holm, rf-ph-cf	5	16	1	2	0	0	0	1	.125
Alexander, p	3	7	1	0	0	0	0	0	.000
Flowers, ph	3	3	0	0	0	0	0	0	.000
Sherdel, p	2	5	0	0	0	0	0	0	.000
Rhem, p	1	1	0	0	0	0	0	0	.000
Toporcer, ph	1	0	0	0	0	0	0	1	.000
Reinhart, p	1	0	0	0	0	0	0	0	.000
H. Bell, p	1	0	0	0	0	0	0	0	.000
Hallahan, p	1	0	0	0	0	0	0	0	.000
Keen, p	1	0	0	0	0	0	0	0	.000
Totals	7	239	31	65	12	1	4	30	.272

New York Yankees

Player-Position	G.	AB.	R.	H.	2B.	3B.	HR.	RBI.	BA.
Combs, cf	7	28	3	10	2	0	0	2	.357
Gehrig, 1b	7	23	1	8	2	0	0	3	.348
Dugan, 3b	7	24	2	8	1	0	0	2	.333
Ruth, rf	7	20	6	6	0	0	4	5	.300
Severeid, c	7	22	1	6	1	0	0	1	.273
Paschal, ph	5	4	0	1	0	0	0	1	.250
Meusel, lf	7	21	3	5	1	1	0	0	.238
Lazzeri, 2b	7	26	2	5	1	0	0	3	.192
Pennock, p	3	7	1	1	1	0	0	0	.143
Koenig, ss	7	32	2	4	1	0	0	2	.125
Ruether, ph-p	3	4	0	0	0	0	0	0	.000
Collins, c	3	2	0	0	0	0	0	0	.000
Shawkey, p	3	2	0	0	0	0	0	0	.000
Hoyt, p	2	6	0	0	0	0	0	0	.000
Shocker, p	2	2	0	0	0	0	0	0	.000
Thomas, p	2	0	0	0	0	0	0	0	.000
Adams, pr	2	0	0	0	0	0	0	0	.000
Gazella, 3b	1	0	0	0	0	0	0	0	.000
Jones, p	1	0	0	0	0	0	0	0	.000
Totals	7	223	21	54	10	1	4	19	.242

COMPOSITE PITCHING AVERAGES

St. Louis Cardinals

Pitcher	G.	IP.	H.	R.	ER.	BB.	SO.	W.	L.	ERA.
Keen	1	1	0	0	0	0	0	0	0	.0.00
Haines	3	16⅔	13	2	2	9	5	2	0	1.08
Alexander	3	20⅓	12	4	3	4	17	2	0	1.33
Sherdel	2	17	15	5	4	8	3	0	2	2.12
Hallahan	1	2	2	1	1	3	1	0	0	4.50
Rhem	1	4	7	3	3	2	4	0	0	6.75
H. Bell	1	2	4	2	2	1	1	0	0	9.00
Reinhart	1	0	1	4	4	4	0	0	1	...
Totals	7	63	54	21	19	31	31	4	3	2.71

New York Yankees

Pitcher	G.	IP.	H.	R.	ER.	BB.	SO.	W.	L.	ERA.
Hoyt	2	15	19	8	2	1	8	1	1	1.20
Pennock	3	22	13	3	3	4	8	2	0	1.23
Thomas	2	3	3	1	1	0	0	0	0	3.00
Ruether	1	4⅓	7	4	2	2	1	0	1	4.15
Shawkey	3	10	8	7	6	2	7	0	1	5.40
Shocker	2	7⅔	13	7	7	0	3	0	1	8.22
Jones	1	1	2	1	1	2	1	0	0	9.00
Totals	7	63	65	31	22	11	28	3	4	3.14

NEW YORK YANKEES
VS.
PITTSBURGH PIRATES

The 1927 Pittsburgh Pirates were an outstanding team, as the presence of Pie Traynor, Paul and Lloyd Waner and Glenn Wright would indicate. The Pirates were talented enough, in fact, to win the National League pennant, finishing 1½ games ahead of the defending World Series champion St. Louis Cardinals and two in front of the New York Giants.

There was one major problem confronting Manager Donie Bush's Pirates, though, as they prepared for the World Series. Their postseason opposition would be a truly *great* team— quite possibly the best club ever fielded in the history of the sport. Leveling the opposition at virtually every turn, the New York Yankees had won the American League flag by a staggering 19 games.

Babe Ruth and Lou Gehrig were the biggest guns in the Yankees' shoot-first, ask-questions-later attack. In the regular season, they combined for 107 home runs and 339 runs batted in. The 32-year-old Ruth established a major league record with 60 homers, topping by one the figure he had attained six years earlier. Gehrig, in only his third full season as the Yankees' regular first baseman, set a big-league record with 175 RBIs.

Two other Yankees, Bob Meusel and Tony Lazzeri, exceeded the 100-RBI mark. Meusel drove in 103 runs, Lazzeri 102.

As murderous as the Yankees' row of sluggers was, Manager Miller Huggins' athletes also could hit for average. The outfield of Ruth, Meusel and Earle Combs combined for 597 hits and a .350 average (Ruth and Combs both hitting .356 and Meusel finishing at .337). Gehrig batted .373.

The Yankees could exhibit some speed, too—thanks largely to the presence of Combs, the gifted center fielder who whacked 23 triples in 1927. And the New Yorkers didn't play station-to-station baseball. Meusel stole 24 bases (the second-best total in the league), Lazzeri swiped 22 (good enough to tie for third in the A.L.) and Combs had 15 steals.

New York could get people out, too. Waite Hoyt tied for the league lead with 22 victories and was second in earned-run average with a 2.63 mark. Relief ace Wilcy Moore won 19 games and headed the A.L. with a 2.28 ERA, while Herb Pennock also won 19 and Urban Shocker collected 18 victories. Dutch Ruether and George Pipgras ranked fifth and sixth on the Yankees' list of winners, but they combined for a 23-9 record.

A many-faceted juggernaut, to be sure. One that rolled to 110 victories, an A.L. record that stood for more than a quarter of a century.

That the Pirates knew they had their hands full was a given. That the National Leaguers were beaten even before they started—the result of watching in awe as the Yankees displayed their long-ball proclivity in batting practice preceding Game 1—is baseball lore at its unsubstantiated best.

Nevertheless, the Yankees made short shrift of the Pirates in the 1927 Series. And they did it while flashing very little of their vaunted power.

In Game 1, two Pirate errors helped New York to three third-inning runs and Gehrig drove in two other runs as the Yankees prevailed, 5-4, at Forbes Field. Second-year major leaguer Paul Waner, the National League batting champion in '27 with a .380 average, had three hits for the losers. Ruth singled three times for the winners. Pipgras yielded a triple to the first batter (Lloyd Waner) he faced in Game 2 and a sacrifice fly to the second (Clyde Barnhart), then settled down and pitched New York to a 6-2 victory.

The third game of the Series belonged to Pennock, the 33-year-old lefthander who took a 4-0 career fall-classic record into the contest. Pennock gave a hint of things to come by retiring the Pirates in order in the first inning. It was more of the same in the second inning, and the third. In a groove now, Pennock mowed down the Bucs 1-2-3 again in the fourth, the fifth, the sixth. And the seventh. At that point, the Yankees were in front, 2-0, courtesy of Gehrig's first-inning triple that scored Combs and Mark Koenig.

The Yankees put the game away in their half of the seventh, scoring six times. Ruth capped the outburst by clubbing the first home run of the Series, a three-run shot.

Cleanup man Wright was Pittsburgh's first batter in the eighth, and he grounded out to shortstop Koenig. Twenty-two Pirates up, 22 down. Traynor, coming off a .342 season, was up next. The Bucs' third baseman elicited a groan from the Yankee Stadium throng of 60,695 fans by rapping a single to left field. Barnhart followed Traynor to the plate and further spoiled matters for Pennock by hitting a run-scoring double.

With one out in the ninth, Pennock allowed a third hit—a single by rookie sensation Lloyd Waner, who banged out 223 hits and batted .355 in the regular season. Hal Rhyne then flied out and Paul Waner popped out. Pennock's stirring performance in the 8-1

triumph left the Yankees one victory away from becoming the first A.L. club to sweep a Series.

Bush now turned to Carmen Hill, the man who had blossomed in 1927 as the ace of his pitching staff. In limited duty in six earlier seasons in the majors, Hill had never won more than three games. But in '27, he chalked up 22 victories. Huggins nominated Moore, a 30-year-old rookie who had made only 12 starts in his 50 regular-season appearances.

Hill allowed a run-scoring single to Ruth in the first inning and was victimized by the Bambino again in the fifth when the power king slugged a two-run homer. The Pirates' righthander left the game for a pinch-hitter in the seventh, an inning in which Pittsburgh scored twice off Moore to forge a 3-3 tie. The game was still deadlocked entering the last of the ninth when reliever John Miljus started his third inning of work for Pittsburgh.

Combs walked and Koenig beat out a bunt, and they advanced to third and second base when Miljus uncorked a wild pitch. Ruth then was issued an intentional walk, filling the bases with no one out and bringing Gehrig to the plate. Some predicament. Gehrig up, Meusel on deck and Lazzeri in the hole. And a fly ball would end the Series.

Miljus, reaching back for all he could muster, struck out Gehrig. Then he fanned Meusel. But with Lazzeri at the plate, he let loose with his second wild pitch of the inning and Combs danced across the plate with the winning run.

Game 1

Wednesday, October 5, At Pittsburgh

New York	AB.	R.	H.	RBI.	PO.	A.
Combs, cf	4	0	0	0	4	0
Koenig, ss	4	2	1	0	2	2
Ruth, rf	4	2	3	0	5	0
Gehrig, 1b	2	1	1	2	9	1
Meusel, lf	3	0	0	1	2	0
Lazzeri, 2b	4	0	1	1	2	5
Dugan, 3b	3	0	0	0	0	0
Collins, c	2	0	0	0	3	0
Hoyt, p	3	0	0	0	0	0
Moore, p	1	0	0	0	0	2
Totals	30	5	6	4	27	10

Pittsburgh	AB.	R.	H.	RBI.	PO.	A.
L. Waner, cf	4	2	1	0	1	0
Barnhart, lf	5	0	1	1	3	0
P. Waner, rf	4	0	3	1	3	0
Wright, ss	2	1	1	1	1	5
Traynor, 3b	4	0	1	0	1	2
Grantham, 2b	3	0	0	0	5	3
Harris, 1b	4	0	1	1	8	2
Smith, c	4	0	0	0	4	1
Kremer, p	2	1	1	0	0	0
Miljus, p	1	0	0	0	1	2
aBrickell	1	0	0	0	0	0
Totals	34	4	9	4	27	15

New York	1 0 3	0 1 0	0 0 0	—5
Pittsburgh	1 0 1	0 1 0	0 1 0	—4

New York	IP.	H.	R.	ER.	BB.	SO.
Hoyt (W)	7⅓	8	4	4	1	2
Moore	1⅔	1	0	0	0	0

Pittsburgh	IP.	H.	R.	ER.	BB.	SO.
Kremer (L)	5*	5	5	2	3	1
Miljus	4	1	0	0	1	3

*Pitched to one batter in sixth.

aGrounded out for Miljus in ninth. E—Meusel, Grantham, Smith. DP—New York 1, Pittsburgh 1. LOB—New York 4, Pittsburgh 7. 2B—Koenig, Lazzeri, L. Waner, P. Waner, Kremer. 3B—Gehrig. SH—Gehrig, Dugan, Wright 2. HBP—By Hoyt (L. Waner). U—Quigley (N.L.), Nallin (A.L.), Moran (N.L.) and Ormsby (A.L.). T—2:04. A—41,467.

Game 2

Thursday, October 6, At Pittsburgh

New York	AB.	R.	H.	RBI.	PO.	A.
Combs, cf	4	1	1	1	5	0
Koenig, ss	5	1	3	1	3	1
Ruth, rf	3	0	0	1	3	0
Gehrig, 1b	3	1	1	0	6	0
Meusel, lf	5	1	2	0	2	0
Lazzeri, 2b	4	0	2	1	2	2
Dugan, 3b	5	1	1	0	1	0
Bengough, c	3	1	0	0	4	0
Pipgras, p	3	0	1	0	1	2
Totals	35	6	11	4	27	5

Pittsburgh	AB.	R.	H.	RBI.	PO.	A.
L. Waner, cf	3	2	1	0	7	0
Barnhart, lf	3	0	2	1	1	0
P. Waner, rf	3	0	1	1	5	0
Wright, ss	4	0	0	0	0	0
Traynor, 3b	4	0	1	0	3	0
Grantham, 2b	4	0	2	0	1	2
Harris, 1b	4	0	0	0	3	0
Gooch, c	3	0	0	0	7	1
Aldridge, p	2	0	0	0	0	2
Cvengros, p	0	0	0	0	0	0
aSmith	1	0	0	0	0	0
Dawson, p	0	0	0	0	0	0
Totals	31	2	7	2	27	5

New York	0 0 3	0 0 0	0 3 0	—6
Pittsburgh	1 0 0	0 0 0	0 1 0	—2

New York	IP.	H.	R.	ER.	BB.	SO.
Pipgras (W)	9	7	2	2	1	2

Pittsburgh	IP.	H.	R.	ER.	BB.	SO.
Aldridge (L)	7⅓	10	6	6	4	4
Cvengros	⅔	1	0	0	0	0
Dawson	1	0	0	0	0	0

aGrounded out for Cvengros in eighth. E—L. Waner, Wright. DP—New York 1. LOB—New York 10, Pittsburgh 5. 2B—Gehrig, Traynor, Grantham. 3B—L. Waner. SB—Meusel. SH—Gehrig, Lazzeri, Ruth, Barnhart, P. Waner. HBP—By Cvengros (Combs). WP—Aldridge. U—Nallin (A.L.), Moran (N.L.), Ormsby (A.L.) and Quigley (N.L.). T—2:20. A—41,634.

Game 3

Friday, October 7, At New York

Pittsburgh	AB.	R.	H.	RBI.	PO.	A.
L. Waner, cf	4	0	1	0	1	1
Rhyne, 2b	4	0	0	0	0	6
P. Waner, rf	4	0	0	0	0	0
Wright, ss	3	0	0	0	3	2
Traynor, 3b	3	1	1	0	0	3
Barnhart, lf	3	0	1	1	0	1
Harris, 1b	3	0	0	0	11	0
Gooch, c	2	0	0	0	9	0
bSpencer, c	1	0	0	0	0	0
Meadows, p	2	0	0	0	0	1
Cvengros, p	0	0	0	0	0	0
cGroh	1	0	0	0	0	0
Totals	30	1	3	1	24	14

New York	AB.	R.	H.	RBI.	PO.	A.
Combs, cf	4	2	2	1	5	0
Koenig, ss	4	2	2	1	1	2
Ruth, rf	4	1	1	3	1	0
Gehrig, 1b	3	0	2	2	12	0
Meusel, lf	4	0	0	0	2	0
Lazzeri, 2b	4	1	1	0	1	7
Dugan, 3b	3	1	1	0	1	2
Grabowski, c	2	0	0	0	3	0
aDurst	1	0	0	0	0	0
Bengough, c	1	0	0	0	0	0
Pennock, p	4	1	0	1	1	1
Totals	34	8	9	8	27	12

Pittsburgh	0 0 0	0 0 0	0 1 0	—1
New York	2 0 0	0 0 0	6 0 x	—8

Pittsburgh	IP.	H.	R.	ER.	BB.	SO.
Meadows (L)	6⅓	7	7	7	1	6
Cvengros	1⅔	2	1	1	0	2

New York	IP.	H.	R.	ER.	BB.	SO.
Pennock (W)	9	3	1	1	0	1

aGrounded out for Grabowski in seventh. bGrounded out for Gooch in eighth. cPopped out for Cvengros in ninth. E—Traynor. LOB—Pittsburgh 2, New York 4. 2B—Barnhart, Koenig, Gehrig. 3B—Gehrig. HR—Ruth. SH—Dugan. U—Moran (N.L.), Ormsby (A.L.), Quigley (N.L.) and Nallin (A.L.). T—2:04. A—60,695.

Game 4

Saturday, October 8, At New York

Pittsburgh	AB.	R.	H.	RBI.	PO.	A.
L. Waner, cf	4	1	3	0	0	0
Barnhart, lf	5	0	1	1	2	0
P. Waner, rf	4	0	1	1	0	0
Wright, ss	4	0	1	1	1	6
Traynor, 3b	4	0	0	0	1	4
Grantham, 2b	4	0	2	0	0	2
Harris, 1b	4	0	2	0	13	0
Smith, c	3	0	0	0	6	0
aYde	0	1	0	0	0	0
Gooch, c	0	0	0	0	3	0
Hill, p	1	0	0	0	0	0
bBrickell	1	1	0	0	0	0
Miljus, p	1	0	0	0	0	0
Totals	35	3	10	3	26	12

New York	AB.	R.	H.	RBI.	PO.	A.
Combs, cf	4	3	2	0	2	0
Koenig, ss	5	0	3	0	0	3
Ruth, rf	4	1	2	0	1	0
Gehrig, 1b	5	0	0	3	14	2
Meusel, lf	5	0	0	0	2	0
Lazzeri, 2b	3	0	0	0	5	4
Dugan, 3b	4	0	1	0	1	4
Collins, c	3	0	3	0	2	1
Moore, p	4	0	1	0	0	3
Totals	37	4	12	3	27	17

Pittsburgh	1 0 0	0 0 0	2 0 0	—3
New York	1 0 0	0 2 0	0 0 1	—4

Two out when winning run scored.

Pittsburgh	IP.	H.	R.	ER.	BB.	SO.
Hill	6	9	3	3	1	6
Miljus (L)	2	3	1	1	3	3

New York	IP.	H.	R.	ER.	BB.	SO.
Moore (W)	9	10	3	1	2	2

aRan for Smith in seventh. bReached first on error for Hill in seventh. E—L. Waner, Lazzeri, Moore. DP—Pittsburgh 1, New York 2. LOB—Pittsburgh 9, New York 11. 2B—Collins. HR—Ruth. SB—Ruth. SH—L. Waner, P. Waner. WP—Miljus 2. U—Ormsby (A.L.), Quigley (N.L.), Nallin (A.L.) and Moran (N.L.). T—2:15. A—57,909.

COMPOSITE BATTING AVERAGES

New York Yankees

Player-Position	G.	AB.	R.	H.	2B.	3B.	HR.	RBI.	BA.
Collins, c	2	5	0	3	1	0	0	0	.600
Koenig, ss	4	18	5	9	2	0	0	2	.500
Ruth, rf	4	15	4	6	0	0	2	7	.400
Pipgras, p	1	3	0	1	0	0	0	0	.333
Combs, cf	4	16	6	5	0	0	0	2	.313
Gehrig, 1b	4	13	2	4	2	2	0	4	.308
Lazzeri, 2b	4	15	1	4	1	0	0	2	.267
Dugan, 3b	4	15	2	3	0	0	0	0	.200
Moore, p	2	5	0	1	0	0	0	0	.200
Meusel, lf	4	17	1	2	0	0	0	1	.118
Bengough, c	2	4	1	0	0	0	0	0	.000
Pennock, p	1	4	1	0	0	0	0	1	.000
Hoyt, p	1	3	0	0	0	0	0	0	.000
Grabowski, c	1	2	0	0	0	0	0	0	.000
Durst, ph	1	1	0	0	0	0	0	0	.000
Totals	4	136	23	38	6	2	2	19	.279

Pittsburgh Pirates

Player-Position	G.	AB.	R.	H.	2B.	3B.	HR.	RBI.	BA.
Kremer, p	1	2	1	1	1	0	0	0	.500
L. Waner, cf	4	15	5	6	1	1	0	0	.400
Grantham, 2b	3	11	0	4	1	0	0	0	.364
P. Waner, rf	4	15	0	5	1	0	0	3	.333
Barnhart, lf	4	16	0	5	1	0	0	4	.313
Traynor, 3b	4	15	1	3	1	0	0	0	.200
Harris, 1b	4	15	0	3	0	0	0	1	.200
Wright, ss	4	13	1	2	0	0	0	2	.154
Smith, c-ph	3	8	0	0	0	0	0	0	.000
Miljus, p	2	2	0	0	0	0	0	0	.000
Brickell, ph	2	2	1	0	0	0	0	0	.000
Gooch, c	3	5	0	0	0	0	0	0	.000
Aldridge, p	1	2	0	0	0	0	0	0	.000
Cvengros, p	2	0	0	0	0	0	0	0	.000
Dawson, p	1	0	0	0	0	0	0	0	.000
Rhyne, 2b	1	4	0	0	0	0	0	0	.000
Spencer, c	1	1	0	0	0	0	0	0	.000
Meadows, p	1	2	0	0	0	0	0	0	.000
Groh, ph	1	1	0	0	0	0	0	0	.000
Yde, pr	1	0	1	0	0	0	0	0	.000
Hill, p	1	1	0	0	0	0	0	0	.000
Totals	4	130	10	29	6	1	0	10	.223

COMPOSITE PITCHING AVERAGES

New York Yankees

Pitcher	G.	IP.	H.	R.	ER.	BB.	SO.	W.	L.	ERA.
Moore	2	10⅔	11	3	1	2	2	1	0	0.84
Pennock	1	9	3	1	1	0	1	1	0	1.00
Pipgras	1	9	7	2	2	1	2	1	0	2.00
Hoyt	1	7⅓	8	4	4	1	2	1	0	4.91
Totals	4	36	29	10	8	4	7	4	0	2.00

Pittsburgh Pirates

Pitcher	G.	IP.	H.	R.	ER.	BB.	SO.	W.	L.	ERA.
Dawson	1	1	0	0	0	0	0	0	0	0.00
Miljus	2	6⅔	4	1	1	4	6	0	1	1.35
Kremer	1	5	5	5	2	3	1	0	1	3.60
Cvengros	2	2⅓	3	1	1	0	2	0	0	3.86
Hill	1	6	9	3	3	1	6	0	0	4.50
Aldridge	1	7⅓	10	6	6	4	4	0	1	7.36
Meadows	1	6⅓	7	7	7	1	6	0	1	9.95
Totals	4	34⅔	38	23	20	13	25	0	4	5.19

1928
NEW YORK YANKEES
VS.
ST. LOUIS CARDINALS

The New York Yankees of 1928 didn't fold, spindle and mutilate the opposition like the '27 Yanks did. Well, not until the 25th World Series unfolded, anyway.

Miller Huggins' team had started off the season in scintillating fashion, boasting a 13-game lead over second-place Philadelphia on the morning of July 4. But the Athletics, who among their number had the likes of Al Simmons, Mickey Cochrane, Jimmie Foxx, Bing Miller, Jimmie Dykes, Lefty Grove, Rube Walberg and a couple of on-their-way-out veterans named Ty Cobb and Tris Speaker, caught fire and whittled away at the Yankees' advantage. Stunningly, Connie Mack's team slipped into the lead in September, only to drop right back out after a doubleheader loss to the New Yorkers.

When the season ground to a halt, the Yankees had withstood the Athletics' furious challenge and captured their third straight American League pennant. The margin was 2½ games.

The Yankees entered the World Series against the St. Louis Cardinals not only with wounded pride over their runaway-turned-close call, but also with wounded personnel. Pitcher Herb Pennock, who compiled a 17-6 record in 1928, was on the sidelines for the Series because of a sore arm. Center fielder Earle Combs, suffering from a broken finger, was available only for pinch-hitting duty, while second baseman Tony Lazzeri was a liability afield with a lame throwing arm (which resulted in rookie Leo Durocher serving as a late-game defensive replacement throughout the Series). And Babe Ruth was playing on a bad ankle.

Ruth, ankle injury and all, and slugging mate Lou Gehrig put on

Lou Gehrig and his Yankee teammates muscled up in 1928.

an astounding display in the Series. In the opener, Ruth rapped a single and two doubles and scored twice and Gehrig went 2 for 4 with two runs batted in as the Yankees beat Bill Sherdel and the Cardinals, 4-1. Bob Meusel socked a two-run home run for the Yankees, who received three-hit pitching from Waite Hoyt.

Facing their World Series nemesis of two years earlier, Grover Cleveland Alexander, in Game 2, the Yankees struck with a vengeance. Gehrig unloaded a three-run homer in the first inning and New York, collecting another run in the second and four more in the third, went on to a 9-3 romp. Ruth singled and doubled and scored two runs.

Gehrig stole the show in Game 3, and Ruth *was* the show in the fourth contest. Gehrig drilled two homers—the first a bases-empty shot and the second a two-run drive—as the Yankees assumed a three games-to-none lead with a 7-3 victory. Ruth had two more hits

for New York. Then, in Game 4, the Bambino walloped solo home runs in the fourth, seventh and eighth innings and Gehrig connected following Ruth's smash in the seventh. The Yankees had dispatched the Cardinals in four games, putting them away with another 7-3 conquest. New York hit a Series-record five homers in the decisive game, with Cedric Durst also banging one over the boards.

Ruth's homer parade was marvelous theater. For the second time in three World Series, he had crushed three home runs in one game—and each performance came in Game 4 at St. Louis' Sportsman's Park. In the '28 version of the prodigious feat, Ruth's second homer came after the Cardinals' Sherdel had thrown a third-strike quick pitch past the Bambino. However, umpire Cy Pfirman ruled against the delivery and Ruth subsequently slashed a Sherdel pitch over the right-field pavilion.

Together, Ruth and Gehrig went 16 for 27 at the plate—a .593 average—against the Cardinals and hammered seven homers with 13 runs batted in. Ruth established an overall Series record with a .625 average and set a four-game Series mark with 10 hits; Gehrig, who hit .545, knocked in a record nine runs for a four-game fall classic.

Incredibly, the other Yankees batted a composite .196. But the heroics of Ruth and Gehrig and solid pitching contributions by Hoyt, George Pipgras and Tom Zachary—the only three hurlers New York employed in the Series—were more than enough to handle the Cards. Hoyt won twice for the Yankees, following up his success in Game 1 by going the distance in the clincher despite al-

lowing 11 hits. Pipgras, who led the Yankee staff with 24 regular-season victories (one more than Hoyt), fired a four-hitter in the second game and Zachary, after a rough start, shut down St. Louis on one run in the final eight innings of Game 3.

Only one Cardinal regular batted .300 or higher in the Series, and just one Redbird had more than one RBI. Shortstop Rabbit Maranville hit .308 for St. Louis, and first baseman Jim Bottomley—who belted his club's lone home run of the Series—collected three RBIs.

The Series proved quite a turnaround from the '26 affair for St. Louis, which was now under the direction of Bill McKechnie (who had succeeded Bob O'Farrell as manager in 1928 after O'Farrell had filled the Cardinals' managerial void in 1927 following the Rogers Hornsby-for-Frankie Frisch trade with the New York Giants). Tommy Thevenow, the Cards' leading hitter in their first meeting with the Yankees, was now playing behind the 36-year-old Maranville and made just one brief appearance in the Series. And Alexander, who had a 1.33 earned-run average in 20⅓ innings of pitching in the '26 classic, collapsed to a *19.80* ERA in five innings of work this time around.

For the Yankees, the World Series was expiation for their late-season decline. And it was proof positive that Huggins' team—having swept the last two Series—was baseball's finest.

Game 1

Thursday, October 4, At New York

St. Louis	AB.	R.	H.	RBI.	PO.	A.
Douthit, cf	3	0	0	0	2	0
High, 3b	4	0	0	0	0	1
Frisch, 2b	4	0	0	0	1	6
Bottomley, 1b	3	1	2	1	10	0
Hafey, lf	4	0	0	0	3	0
Harper, rf	3	0	1	0	2	0
Wilson, c	3	0	0	0	3	0
Maranville, ss	2	0	0	0	2	0
aOrsatti	0	0	0	0	0	0
Thevenow, ss	0	0	0	0	1	0
Sherdel, p	2	0	0	0	0	3
bHolm	1	0	0	0	0	0
Johnson, p	0	0	0	0	0	0
Totals	29	1	3	1	24	10

New York	AB.	R.	H.	RBI.	PO.	A.
Paschal, cf	4	0	0	0	4	0
Durst, cf	0	0	0	0	0	0
Koenig, ss	4	1	1	0	2	3
Ruth, rf	4	2	3	0	3	0
Gehrig, 1b	4	0	2	2	6	0
Meusel, lf	4	1	1	2	2	0
Lazzeri, 2b	2	0	0	0	0	2
Durocher, 2b	1	0	0	0	0	0
Dugan, 3b	3	0	0	0	2	0
Bengough, c	3	0	0	0	8	1
Hoyt, p	3	0	0	0	0	1
Totals	32	4	7	4	27	7

St. Louis	0 0 0	0 0 0	1 0 0	—1
New York	1 0 0	2 0 0	0 1 x	—4

St. Louis	IP.	H.	R.	ER.	BB.	SO.
Sherdel (L)	7	4	3	3	0	2
Johnson	1	3	1	1	0	0

New York	IP.	H.	R.	ER.	BB.	SO.
Hoyt (W)	9	3	1	1	3	6

aWalked for Maranville in eighth. bLined out for Sherdel in eighth. E—Maranville. LOB—St. Louis 4, New York 4. 2B—Ruth 2, Gehrig. HR—Meusel, Bottomley. U—Owens (A.L.), Rigler (N.L.), McGowan (A.L.) and Pfirman (N.L.). T—1:49. A—61,425.

Game 2

Friday, October 5, At New York

St. Louis	AB.	R.	H.	RBI.	PO.	A.
Douthit, cf	4	0	0	1	2	1
High, 3b	3	0	0	0	0	1
Frisch, 2b	3	0	2	0	2	3
Bottomley, 1b	4	0	0	0	9	0
Hafey, lf	4	0	0	0	3	0
Harper, rf	3	1	0	0	1	0
Wilson, c	4	1	1	1	5	2
Maranville, ss	3	1	1	0	2	1
Alexander, p	1	0	0	1	0	1
Mitchell, p	2	0	0	0	0	1
cOrsatti	1	0	0	0	0	0
Totals	32	3	4	3	24	10

New York	AB.	R.	H.	RBI.	PO.	A.
Durst, cf	2	1	2	1	0	0
aPaschal, cf	2	0	1	1	1	0
Koenig, ss	5	0	0	0	1	2
Ruth, rf	3	2	2	0	1	0
Gehrig, 1b	3	2	1	3	9	0
Meusel, lf	3	2	1	1	2	0
Lazzeri, 2b	3	0	0	0	1	1
Durocher, 2b	0	0	0	0	0	0
Robertson, 3b	2	1	0	0	2	1
bDugan, 3b	0	0	0	1	1	0
Bengough, c	3	1	1	1	9	0
Pipgras, p	2	0	0	1	0	1
Totals	28	9	8	9	27	5

St. Louis	0 3 0	0 0 0	0 0 0	—3
New York	3 1 4	0 0 0	1 0 x	—9

St. Louis	IP.	H.	R.	ER.	BB.	SO.
Alexander (L)	2⅓	6	8	8	4	1
Mitchell	5⅔	2	1	1	2	2

New York	IP.	H.	R.	ER.	BB.	SO.
Pipgras (W)	9	4	3	3	4	8

aSingled for Durst in third. bHit sacrifice fly for Robertson in seventh. cGrounded out for Mitchell in ninth. E—Mitchell, Koenig, Lazzeri. DP—St. Louis 1, New York 1. LOB—St. Louis 6, New York 5. 2B—Ruth, Meusel, Wilson. HR—Gehrig. SB—Frisch 2, Meusel. SH—Lazzeri, Pipgras. SF—Dugan. HBP—By Mitchell (Pipgras). U—Rigler (N.L.), McGowan (A.L.), Pfirman (N.L.) and Owens (A.L.). T—2:04. A—60,714.

Game 3

Sunday, October 7, At St. Louis

New York	AB.	R.	H.	RBI.	PO.	A.
Durst, cf	5	1	0	0	3	0
Koenig, ss	5	0	1	0	1	4
Ruth, lf	4	2	2	1	2	1
Gehrig, 1b	2	2	2	3	11	0
Meusel, rf	3	1	0	0	1	0
Lazzeri, 2b	3	1	0	0	0	2
Durocher, 2b	0	0	0	0	1	1
Robertson, 3b	4	0	1	1	0	0
Bengough, c	4	0	1	0	8	0
Zachary, p	4	0	0	0	0	1
Totals	34	7	7	5	27	9

St. Louis	AB.	R.	H.	RBI.	PO.	A.
Douthit, cf	4	1	1	0	2	0
High, 3b	5	1	2	1	2	2
Frisch, 2b	2	1	1	0	2	3
Bottomley, 1b	4	0	1	2	6	1
Hafey, lf	4	0	2	0	1	0
Holm, rf	4	0	1	0	4	0
Wilson, c	4	0	0	0	6	0
Maranville, ss	4	0	1	0	4	1
Haines, p	2	0	0	0	0	1
Johnson, p	0	0	0	0	0	0
aBlades	1	0	0	0	0	0
Rhem, p	0	0	0	0	0	0
bOrsatti	1	0	0	0	0	0
Totals	35	3	9	3	27	8

New York	0 1 0	2 0 3	1 0 0	—7
St. Louis	2 0 0	0 1 0	0 0 0	—3

New York	IP.	H.	R.	ER.	BB.	SO.
Zachary (W)	9	9	3	3	1	7

St. Louis	IP.	H.	R.	ER.	BB.	SO.
Haines (L)	6	6	6	3	3	3
Johnson	1	1	1	0	1	1
Rhem	2	0	0	0	0	1

aStruck out for Johnson in seventh. bStruck out for Rhem in ninth. E—Lazzeri, Robertson, Hafey, Wilson 2. DP—New York 1, St. Louis 1. LOB—New York 4, St. Louis 8. 2B—High. 3B—Bottomley. HR—Gehrig 2. SB—Meusel, Lazzeri. SH—Frisch. HBP—By Zachary (Douthit). U—McGowan (A.L.), Pfirman (N.L.), Owens (A.L.) and Rigler (N.L.). T—2:09. A—39,602.

Game 4

Tuesday, October 9, At St. Louis

New York	AB.	R.	H.	RBI.	PO.	A.
Paschal, cf	4	0	1	0	3	0
Durst, cf	1	1	1	1	0	0
Koenig, ss	5	0	1	0	4	2
Ruth, lf	5	3	3	3	2	0
Gehrig, 1b	2	1	1	1	7	0
Meusel, rf	5	1	1	0	0	0
Lazzeri, 2b	4	1	3	0	1	2
Durocher, 2b	1	0	0	0	0	0
Dugan, 3b	3	0	1	0	0	0
aRobertson, 3b	2	0	0	1	0	0
Bengough, c	3	0	1	0	8	1
bCombs	0	0	0	1	0	0
Collins, c	1	0	1	0	2	0
Hoyt, p	4	0	1	0	0	2
Totals	40	7	15	7	27	7

St. Louis	AB.	R.	H.	RBI.	PO.	A.
Orsatti, cf	5	1	2	0	4	0
High, 3b	5	0	3	0	0	1
Frisch, 2b	4	0	0	1	3	1
Bottomley, 1b	3	0	0	0	11	1
Hafey, lf	3	0	1	0	1	0
Harper, rf	3	0	0	0	2	0
Smith, c	4	0	3	0	3	1
cMartin	0	1	0	0	0	0
Maranville, ss	4	1	2	0	3	1
Sherdel, p	3	0	0	0	0	0
Alexander, p	0	0	0	0	0	3
dHolm	1	0	0	1	0	0
Totals	35	3	11	2	27	8

New York	0 0 0	1 0 0	4 2 0	—7
St. Louis	0 0 1	1 0 0	0 0 1	—3

New York	IP.	H.	R.	ER.	BB.	SO.
Hoyt (W)	9	11	3	2	3	8

St. Louis	IP.	H.	R.	ER.	BB.	SO.
Sherdel (L)	6⅓	11	4	4	3	1
Alexander	2⅔	4	3	3	0	1

aHit into fielder's choice for Dugan in seventh. bHit sacrifice fly for Bengough in seventh. cRan for Smith in ninth. dGrounded out for Alexander in ninth. E—Koenig, Hoyt. DP—New York 1, St. Louis 1. LOB—New York 11, St. Louis 9. 2B—Lazzeri, Collins, Orsatti, High, Maranville. HR—Ruth 3, Durst, Gehrig. SB—Lazzeri, Maranville. SH—Hoyt. SF—Frisch, Combs. U—Pfirman (N.L.), Owens (A.L.), Rigler (N.L.) and McGowan (A.L.). T—2:25. A—37,331.

COMPOSITE BATTING AVERAGES

New York Yankees

Player-Position	G.	AB.	R.	H.	2B.	3B.	HR.	RBI.	BA.
Collins, c	1	1	0	1	1	0	0	0	1.000
Ruth, rf-lf	4	16	9	10	3	0	3	4	.625
Gehrig, 1b	4	11	5	6	1	0	4	9	.545
Durst, cf	4	8	3	3	0	0	1	2	.375
Lazzeri, 2b	4	12	2	3	1	0	0	0	.250
Bengough, c	4	13	1	3	0	0	0	1	.231
Paschal, cf-ph	3	10	0	2	0	0	0	1	.200
Meusel, lf-rf	4	15	5	3	1	0	1	3	.200
Dugan, 3b-ph	3	6	0	1	0	0	0	1	.167
Koenig, ss	4	19	1	3	0	0	0	0	.158
Hoyt, p	2	7	0	1	0	0	0	0	.143
Robertson, 3b-ph	3	8	1	1	0	0	0	2	.125
Durocher, 2b	4	2	0	0	0	0	0	0	.000
Zachary, p	1	4	0	0	0	0	0	0	.000
Pipgras, p	1	2	0	0	0	0	0	1	.000
Combs, ph	1	0	0	0	0	0	0	1	.000
Totals	4	134	27	37	7	0	9	25	.276

St. Louis Cardinals

Player-Position	G.	AB.	R.	H.	2B.	3B.	HR.	RBI.	BA.
Smith, c	1	4	0	3	0	0	0	0	.750
Maranville, ss	4	13	2	4	1	0	0	0	.308
High, 3b	4	17	1	5	2	0	0	1	.294
Orsatti, ph-cf	4	7	1	2	1	0	0	0	.286
Frisch, 2b	4	13	1	3	0	0	0	1	.231
Bottomley, 1b	4	14	1	3	0	1	1	3	.214
Hafey, lf	4	15	0	3	0	0	0	0	.200
Holm, ph-rf	3	6	0	1	0	0	0	1	.167
Harper, rf	3	9	1	1	0	0	0	0	.111
Douthit, cf	3	11	1	1	0	0	0	1	.091
Wilson, c	3	11	1	1	1	0	0	1	.091
Thevenow, ss	1	0	0	0	0	0	0	0	.000
Sherdel, p	2	5	0	0	0	0	0	0	.000
Johnson, p	2	0	0	0	0	0	0	0	.000
Alexander, p	2	1	0	0	0	0	0	1	.000
Mitchell, p	1	2	0	0	0	0	0	0	.000
Haines, p	1	2	0	0	0	0	0	0	.000
Blades, ph	1	1	0	0	0	0	0	0	.000
Rhem, p	1	0	0	0	0	0	0	0	.000
Martin, ph	1	0	1	0	0	0	0	0	.000
Totals	4	131	10	27	5	1	1	9	.206

COMPOSITE PITCHING AVERAGES

New York Yankees

Pitcher	G.	IP.	H.	R.	ER.	BB.	SO.	W.	L.	ERA.
Hoyt	2	18	14	4	3	6	14	2	0	1.50
Pipgras	1	9	4	3	3	4	8	1	0	3.00
Zachary	1	9	9	3	3	1	7	1	0	3.00
Totals	4	36	27	10	9	11	29	4	0	2.25

St. Louis Cardinals

Pitcher	G.	IP.	H.	R.	ER.	BB.	SO.	W.	L.	ERA.
Rhem	1	2	0	0	0	0	1	0	0	0.00
Mitchell	1	5⅔	2	1	1	2	2	0	0	1.59
Johnson	2	2	4	2	1	1	1	0	0	4.50
Haines	1	6	6	6	3	3	3	0	1	4.50
Sherdel	2	13⅓	15	7	7	3	3	0	2	4.73
Alexander	2	5	10	11	11	4	2	0	1	19.80
Totals	4	34	37	27	23	13	12	0	4	6.09

1929
PHILADELPHIA ATHLETICS
VS.
CHICAGO CUBS

It was the middle of the seventh inning of Game 4 of the 1929 World Series, and the outlook for the Chicago Cubs—so bleak a few days earlier—was brightening considerably.

The Cubs had dug a hole of massive proportions for themselves by dropping the first two games of the Series on their home grounds, but had rebounded for a 3-1 triumph over the Philadelphia Athletics in Game 3 at Shibe Park. Now, in Game 4 on the Athletics' field, the Cubs were coasting by an 8-0 score and Charlie Root was pitching a three-hitter. And with two of the next three games scheduled at Wrigley Field, Manager Joe McCarthy's Cubs seemingly had turned a bad situation into an encouraging one.

Seemingly.

Al Simmons, who had topped the American League in 1929 with 157 runs batted in, gave the Philadelphia faithful something to cheer about when he led off the last of the seventh with a home run to left. Jimmie Foxx and Bing Miller followed with singles as Connie Mack's club threatened to take a bite or two out of the Cubs' hefty lead. Jimmie Dykes was up next, and he, too, singled. With the score now 8-2 and two Athletics on base, the crowd began to stir. Joe Boley then delivered another run-scoring single, the fifth consecutive hit off Root, and now it was a five-run deficit. And, still, no one was out.

George Burns was sent up as a pinch-hitter for pitcher Ed Rommel and popped out, but Max Bishop kept things going with a base hit over Root's head. With the Cubs' edge now pared to 8-4 and Mule Haas strolling to the plate, McCarthy replaced Root with Art Nehf, the 37-year-old lefthander who had won games

for the New York Giants in four consecutive World Series earlier in the decade. Haas drove a Nehf pitch to center field, where the Cubs' Hack Wilson lost the ball in the sun. The ball shot past Wilson and rolled to the fence, and Boley, Bishop and even Haas scored on the play. The misplay-turned-home run sent the crowd into a frenzy. And it left the bewildered Cubs clinging to a *one*-run lead.

Mickey Cochrane coaxed a base on balls off Nehf, and Sheriff Blake then took over the Cub pitching duties. Simmons, up for the second time in the inning, came through with a single. Now, incredibly, the potential tying run rested at second base. But not for long. Foxx drilled his club's seventh single of the inning, scoring Cochrane and deadlocking the game at 8-8.

Pat Malone, the Cubs' pitching ace in 1929 with 22 victories and a starter in Game 2, was summoned by McCarthy. Malone got the Cubs into more trouble by hitting Miller with a pitch, loading the bases. That brought up Dykes, who rammed a double to the fence in left. Two runs scored. The ninth and 10th runs of the inning. Malone struck out Boley and Burns, ending the carnage. Simmons, Foxx and Dykes all had collected two hits in the inning.

The Cubs, understandably in a state of shock after blowing a seemingly insurmountable eight-run lead, went meekly in the rest of Game 4. Philadelphia's relief pitcher, one Robert Moses (Lefty) Grove, had something to do with that, no doubt. Grove retired Chicago in order in the eighth and ninth innings and struck out four consecutive batters in the process. The A's, staring at the likelihood of a 2-2 tie in games when they came to bat in seventh inning,

now boasted a three games-to-one lead after their unlikely 10-8 triumph and looked to close out the Cubs in Game 5.

Malone obviously had other ideas. Paired against first-game winner Howard Ehmke, he kept the Cubs' hopes alive with a tremendous pitching performance. Malone and Ehmke were locked in a 0-0 struggle until the fourth inning, when the Cubs struck for two runs and drove Ehmke from the game. Rube Walberg replaced Ehmke and matched Malone zero for zero on the scoreboard. Entering the bottom of the ninth, Chicago still had a 2-0 lead and Malone had yielded only two hits.

Pinch-hitter Walter French struck out, leaving the Cubs within two outs of sending the Series back to Wrigley Field. Bishop followed with a single, however, and Haas brought the crowd to its feet by slamming a Malone pitch over the right-field wall. Jolted by the game-tying homer, Malone nevertheless got Cochrane to hit a grounder for out No. 2. Simmons then doubled and Foxx was issued an intentional walk. Bing Miller was the next batter, and he hammered a Malone delivery off the scoreboard and Simmons chugged home with the winning run.

A three-run rally in the bottom of the ninth had dealt the Cubs another stinging defeat, and this time there was, in fact, no "tomorrow" for the National Leaguers. The 3-2 victory in Game 5 had made Mack's team the World Series champion for the first time since 1913.

And what a team Mack had. The A's compiled a 104-46 record in 1929 and won the A.L. pennant by 18 games over the New York Yankees, who had swept World Series in 1927 and 1928.

While six pitchers on Mack's staff won 11 or more games in 1929, the A's manager surprisingly named the 35-year-old Ehmke, a seven-game winner who had worked only 54⅔ innings, to start Game 1 of the Series. The crafty veteran responded by striking out a Series-record 13 Cubs and winning a 3-1 decision. In Game 2, Foxx belted a three-run homer and Simmons added a two-run shot as the A's frolicked, 9-3.

Kiki Cuyler's two-run single and Guy Bush's steady pitching featured the Cubs' third-game victory.

Game 1

Tuesday, October 8, At Chicago

Philadelphia	AB.	R.	H.	RBI.	PO.	A.
Bishop, 2b	4	0	0	0	2	1
Haas, cf	3	0	0	0	1	0
Cochrane, c	3	1	1	0	14	1
Simmons, lf	4	1	0	0	2	0
Foxx, 1b	4	1	2	1	4	0
Miller, rf	4	0	1	2	3	0
Dykes, 3b	4	0	1	0	1	1
Boley, ss	4	0	0	0	0	0
Ehmke, p	4	0	1	0	0	2
Totals	34	3	6	3	27	5

Chicago	AB.	R.	H.	RBI.	PO.	A.
McMillan, 3b	4	0	1	0	1	2
English, ss	4	0	2	0	1	3
Hornsby, 2b	4	0	0	0	1	3
Wilson, cf	4	0	0	0	3	0
Cuyler, rf	4	1	1	0	1	0
Stephenson, lf	4	0	2	1	4	0
Grimm, 1b	2	0	2	0	8	0
Taylor, c	2	0	0	0	6	0
aHeathcote	1	0	0	0	0	0
Gonzalez, c	0	0	0	0	2	0
cBlair	1	0	0	0	0	0
Root, p	2	0	0	0	0	0
bHartnett	1	0	0	0	0	0
Bush, p	0	0	0	0	0	2
dTolson	1	0	0	0	0	0
Totals	34	1	8	1	27	10

Philadelphia	0 0 0 0 0 0 1 0 2—3
Chicago	0 0 0 0 0 0 0 0 1—1

Philadelphia	IP.	H.	R.	ER.	BB.	SO.
Ehmke (W)	9	8	1	0	1	13

Chicago	IP.	H.	R.	ER.	BB.	SO.
Root (L)	7	3	1	1	2	5
Bush	2	3	2	0	0	0

aFlied out for Taylor in seventh. bStruck out for Root in seventh. cForced runner for Gonzalez in ninth. dStruck out for Bush in ninth. E—Dykes, English 2. DP—Chicago 1. LOB—Philadelphia 6, Chicago 8. 2B—English. HR—Foxx. SH—Grimm. U—Klem (N.L.), Dinneen (A.L.), Moran (N.L.) and Van Graflan (A.L.). T—2:03. A—50,740.

Game 2

Wednesday, October 9, At Chicago

Philadelphia	AB.	R.	H.	RBI.	PO.	A.
Bishop, 2b	4	0	0	0	0	4
Haas, cf	5	1	1	1	1	0
Cochrane, c	2	2	1	0	14	0
Simmons, lf	4	2	2	4	2	0
Foxx, 1b	5	2	3	3	7	0
Miller, rf	4	0	1	0	0	0
Dykes, 3b	4	1	3	1	1	1
Boley, ss	3	0	1	0	2	2
Earnshaw, p	3	1	0	0	0	0
Grove, p	2	0	0	0	0	1
Totals	36	9	12	9	27	8

Chicago	AB.	R.	H.	RBI.	PO.	A.
McMillan, 3b	4	0	0	0	1	0
English, ss	5	0	1	0	2	3
Hornsby, 2b	4	1	1	0	3	2
Wilson, cf	3	1	3	0	4	0
Cuyler, rf	4	0	0	0	1	0
Stephenson, lf	5	1	1	1	2	0
Grimm, 1b	4	0	2	1	6	1
Taylor, c	4	0	2	1	8	1
Malone, p	1	0	0	0	0	1
Blake, p	1	0	1	0	0	0
aHeathcote	0	0	0	0	0	0
bHartnett	1	0	0	0	0	0
Carlson, p	0	0	0	0	0	1
cGonzalez	1	0	0	0	0	0
Nehf, p	0	0	0	0	0	0
Totals	37	3	11	3	27	9

Philadelphia	0 0 3 3 0 0 1 2 0—9
Chicago	0 0 0 0 3 0 0 0 0—3

Philadelphia	IP.	H.	R.	ER.	BB.	SO.
Earnshaw (W)	4⅔	8	3	3	4	7
Grove	4⅓	3	0	0	1	6

Chicago	IP.	H.	R.	ER.	BB.	SO.
Malone (L)	3⅔	5	6	3	5	5
Blake	1⅓	2	0	0	0	1
Carlson	3	5	3	3	1	2
Nehf	1	0	0	0	0	0

aAnnounced for Blake in fifth. bStruck out for Heathcote in fifth. cStruck out for Carlson in eighth. E—English. DP—Philadelphia 1, Chicago 1. LOB—Philadelphia 9, Chicago 12. 2B— Foxx, English. HR—Simmons, Foxx. SH—Miller, Boley 2. U—Dinneen (A.L.), Moran (N.L.), Van Graflan (A.L.) and Klem (N.L.). T—2:29. A—49,987.

Game 3

Friday, October 11, At Philadelphia

Chicago	AB.	R.	H.	RBI.	PO.	A.
McMillan, 3b	4	0	0	0	1	1
English, ss	4	1	0	0	0	2
Hornsby, 2b	4	1	2	1	2	1
Wilson, cf	3	0	2	0	3	0
Cuyler, rf	4	0	1	2	3	0
Stephenson, lf	4	0	1	0	4	0
Grimm, 1b	4	0	0	0	9	0
Taylor, c	4	0	0	0	5	2
Bush, p	3	1	0	0	0	1
Totals	34	3	6	3	27	7

Philadelphia	AB.	R.	H.	RBI.	PO.	A.
Bishop, 2b	4	0	1	0	3	4
Haas, cf	5	0	2	0	0	0
Cochrane, c	3	1	2	0	12	0
Simmons, lf	3	0	0	0	0	0
Foxx, 1b	4	0	0	0	9	0
Miller, rf	4	0	1	1	2	0
Dykes, 3b	4	0	1	0	1	0
Boley, ss	4	0	2	0	0	2
Earnshaw, p	2	0	0	0	0	2
aSumma	1	0	0	0	0	0
Totals	34	1	9	1	27	8

Chicago	0 0 0 0 0 3 0 0 0—3
Philadelphia	0 0 0 0 1 0 0 0 0—1

Chicago	IP.	H.	R.	ER.	BB.	SO.
Bush (W)	9	9	1	1	2	4

Philadelphia	IP.	H.	R.	ER.	BB.	SO.
Earnshaw (L)	9	6	3	1	2	10

aStruck out for Earnshaw in ninth. E—English, Dykes. LOB—Chicago 6, Philadelphia 10. 2B—Hornsby, Stephenson. 3B—Wilson. SH—Simmons, Earnshaw. WP—Bush. U—Moran (N.L.), Van Graflan (A.L.), Klem (N.L.) and Dinneen (A.L.). T—2:09. A—29,921.

Game 4

Saturday, October 12, At Philadelphia

Chicago	AB.	R.	H.	RBI.	PO.	A.
McMillan, 3b	4	0	0	0	1	3
English, ss	4	0	0	0	2	1
Hornsby, 2b	5	2	2	0	1	1
Wilson, cf	3	1	2	0	3	0
Cuyler, rf	4	2	3	2	0	0
Stephenson, lf	4	1	1	1	2	1
Grimm, 1b	4	2	2	2	7	0
Taylor, c	3	0	0	1	8	1
Root, p	3	0	0	0	0	0
Nehf, p	0	0	0	0	0	0
Blake, p	0	0	0	0	0	0
Malone, p	0	0	0	0	0	0
bHartnett	1	0	0	0	0	0
Carlson, p	0	0	0	0	0	1
Totals	35	8	10	6	24	8

Philadelphia	AB.	R.	H.	RBI.	PO.	A.
Bishop, 2b	5	1	2	1	2	3
Haas, cf	4	1	1	3	2	0
Cochrane, c	4	1	2	0	9	0
Simmons, lf	5	2	2	1	0	0
Foxx, 1b	4	2	2	1	10	0
Miller, rf	3	1	2	0	3	0
Dykes, 3b	4	1	3	3	0	2
Boley, ss	3	1	1	1	1	5
Quinn, p	2	0	0	0	0	0
Walberg, p	0	0	0	0	0	0
Rommel, p	0	0	0	0	0	0
aBurns	2	0	0	0	0	0
Grove, p	0	0	0	0	0	0
Totals	36	10	15	10	27	10

Chicago	0 0 0 2 0 5 1 0 0— 8
Philadelphia	0 0 0 0 0 0 10 0 x—10

Chicago	IP.	H.	R.	ER.	BB.	SO.
Root	6⅓	9	6	6	0	3
Nehf	0†	1	2	2	1	0
Blake (L)	0†	2	2	2	0	0
Malone	⅔	1	0	0	0	2
Carlson	1	2	0	0	0	1

Philadelphia	IP.	H.	R.	ER.	BB.	SO.
Quinn	5*	7	6	5	2	2
Walberg	1	1	1	0	0	2
Rommel (W)	1	2	1	1	1	0
Grove	2	0	0	0	0	4

*Pitched to four batters in sixth.

†Pitched to two batters in seventh.

aPopped out and struck out for Rommel in seventh. bStruck out for Malone in eighth. E—Wilson, Cuyler, Miller, Walberg. DP—Philadelphia 1. LOB—Chicago 4, Philadelphia 6. 2B—Cochrane, Dykes. 3B—Hornsby. HR—Grimm, Haas, Simmons. SH—Taylor, Haas, Boley. HBP—By Malone (Miller). U—Van Graflan (A.L.), Klem (N.L.), Dinneen (A.L.) and Moran (N.L.). T—2:12. A—29,921.

Game 5

Monday, October 14, At Philadelphia

Chicago	AB.	R.	H.	RBI.	PO.	A.
McMillan, 3b	4	0	1	0	2	3
English, ss	4	0	1	0	3	3
Hornsby, 2b	4	0	0	0	2	4
Wilson, cf	4	0	1	0	1	0
Cuyler, rf	4	1	1	0	3	0
Stephenson, lf	2	1	1	0	1	0
Grimm, 1b	4	0	1	1	10	0
Taylor, c	4	0	1	1	4	0
Malone, p	3	0	1	0	0	0
Totals	33	2	8	2	26	10

Philadelphia	AB.	R.	H.	RBI.	PO.	A.
Bishop, 2b	4	1	1	0	2	1
Haas, cf	4	1	1	2	1	0
Cochrane, c	3	0	0	0	10	1
Simmons, lf	4	1	2	0	0	0
Foxx, 1b	3	0	0	0	8	1
Miller, rf	4	0	2	1	5	0
Dykes, 3b	3	0	0	0	0	1
Boley, ss	3	0	0	0	1	2
Ehmke, p	1	0	0	0	0	2
Walberg, p	1	0	0	0	0	1
aFrench	1	0	0	0	0	0
Totals	31	3	6	3	27	9

Chicago	0 0 0 2 0 0 0 0 0—2
Philadelphia	0 0 0 0 0 0 0 0 3—3

Two out when winning run scored.

Chicago	IP.	H.	R.	ER.	BB.	SO.
Malone (L)	8	6	3	3	2	4

Philadelphia	IP.	H.	R.	ER.	BB.	SO.
Ehmke	3	6	2	2	2	0
Walberg (W)	5	2	0	0	0	6

aStruck out for Walberg in ninth. E—Hornsby. DP—Chicago 2. LOB—Chicago 6, Philadelphia 4. 2B—Cuyler, Malone, Simmons, Miller. HR—Haas. SB—McMillan. U—Klem (N.L.), Dinneen (A.L.), Moran (N.L.) and Van Graflan (A.L.). T—1:42. A—29,921.

COMPOSITE BATTING AVERAGES

Philadelphia Athletics

Player-Position	G.	AB.	R.	H.	2B.	3B.	HR.	RBI.	BA.
Dykes, 3b	5	19	2	8	1	0	0	4	.421
Cochrane, c	5	15	5	6	1	0	0	0	.400
Miller, rf	5	19	1	7	1	0	0	4	.368
Foxx, 1b	5	20	5	7	1	0	2	5	.350
Simmons, lf	5	20	6	6	1	0	2	5	.300
Haas, cf	5	21	3	5	0	0	2	6	.238
Boley, ss	5	17	1	4	0	0	0	1	.235
Ehmke, p	2	5	0	1	0	0	0	0	.200
Bishop, 2b	5	21	2	4	0	0	0	1	.190
Earnshaw, p	2	5	1	0	0	0	0	0	.000
Grove, p	2	2	0	0	0	0	0	0	.000
Summa, ph	1	1	0	0	0	0	0	0	.000
Quinn, p	1	2	0	0	0	0	0	0	.000
Walberg, p	2	1	0	0	0	0	0	0	.000
Rommel, p	1	0	0	0	0	0	0	0	.000
Burns, ph	1	2	0	0	0	0	0	0	.000
French, ph	1	1	0	0	0	0	0	0	.000
Totals	5	171	26	48	5	0	6	26	.281

Chicago Cubs

Player-Position	G.	AB.	R.	H.	2B.	3B.	HR.	RBI.	BA.
Blake, p	2	1	0	1	0	0	0	0	1.000
Wilson, cf	5	17	2	8	0	1	0	0	.471
Grimm, 1b	5	18	2	7	0	0	1	4	.389
Stephenson, lf	5	19	3	6	1	0	0	3	.316
Cuyler, rf	5	20	4	6	1	0	0	4	.300
Malone, p	3	4	0	1	1	0	0	0	.250
Hornsby, 2b	5	21	4	5	1	1	0	1	.238
English, ss	5	21	1	4	2	0	0	0	.190
Taylor, c	5	17	0	3	0	0	0	3	.176
McMillan, 3b	5	20	0	2	0	0	0	0	.100
Heathcote, ph	1	1	0	0	0	0	0	0	.000
Gonzalez, c-ph	2	1	0	0	0	0	0	0	.000
Blair, ph	1	1	0	0	0	0	0	0	.000
Root, p	2	5	0	0	0	0	0	0	.000
Hartnett, ph	3	3	0	0	0	0	0	0	.000
Bush, p	2	3	1	0	0	0	0	0	.000
Tolson, ph	1	1	0	0	0	0	0	0	.000
Carlson, p	2	0	0	0	0	0	0	0	.000
Nehf, p	2	0	0	0	0	0	0	0	.000
Totals	5	173	17	43	6	2	1	15	.249

COMPOSITE PITCHING AVERAGES

Philadelphia Athletics

Pitcher	G.	IP.	H.	R.	ER.	BB.	SO.	W.	L.	ERA.
Grove	2	6⅓	3	0	0	1	10	0	0	0.00
Walberg	2	6⅓	3	1	0	0	8	1	0	0.00
Ehmke	2	12⅔	14	3	2	3	13	1	0	1.42
Earnshaw	2	13⅔	14	6	4	6	17	1	1	2.63
Quinn	1	5	7	6	5	2	2	0	0	9.00
Rommel	1	1	2	1	1	1	0	1	0	9.00
Totals	5	45	43	17	12	13	50	4	1	2.40

Chicago Cubs

Pitcher	G.	IP.	H.	R.	ER.	BB.	SO.	W.	L.	ERA.
Bush	2	11	12	3	1	2	4	1	0	0.82
Malone	3	13	12	9	6	7	11	0	2	4.15
Root	2	13⅓	12	7	7	2	8	0	1	4.73
Carlson	2	4	7	3	3	1	3	0	0	6.75
Blake	2	1⅓	4	2	2	0	1	0	1	13.50
Nehf	2	1	1	2	2	1	0	0	0	18.00
Totals	5	43⅔	48	26	21	13	27	1	4	4.33

1930
PHILADELPHIA ATHLETICS
VS.
ST. LOUIS CARDINALS

It had taken Connie Mack 15 years to rebuild his Philadelphia Athletics into winners, and now he was enjoying the fruits of his labor. And how.

Labor it had been. After a drastic reshaping of his club following its stunning four-game loss to the Boston Braves in the 1914 World Series, Mack suffered the ignominy of seven consecutive last-place finishes. His 1916 A's team finished 40 games out. Out of *seventh* place, that is.

It wasn't until 1925, in fact, that the Athletics reappeared in the American League's first divison.

Rube Walberg had arrived in 1923, and Al Simmons came along in 1924 to bolster the Athletics. Mickey Cochrane, Lefty Grove and Jimmie Foxx (as a 17-year-old) joined the A's in '25. And Mule Haas and George Earnshaw made their Philadelphia debuts in 1928. While it took longer to get back to the top than Mack ever imagined, the Athletics made the most of their re-entry into baseball's elite (the team's poorest record from 1927 through 1932 was 91-63). Mack's team nearly upset the heavily favored New York Yankees in the 1928 A.L. pennant race, then breezed to the flag in 1929 and won comfortably in 1930.

The '30 World Series provided Mack with an opportunity to win his fifth fall classic and second in a row. But the opposition would be a St. Louis Cardinals team that batted a composite .314 and featured an all-.300-hitting lineup.

That the Cardinals could make contact was obvious. However, everyone was making contact in 1930, baseball's Year of the Hitter if ever such a designation applied. The Cards' lofty team average placed only third in the National League, which set a modern

Philadelphia slugger Al Simmons was his usual devastating self in the 1930 fall classic, hitting .364 with a pair of homers and four RBIs.

major league record with its .303 membership-wide batting mark. Indeed, six N.L. clubs had above-.300 composite averages, with the New York Giants setting a modern team record with a .319 figure and the Philadelphia Phillies hitting at a .315 clip. (The Phillies' pitching staff rendered the offense meaningless by compiling a 6.70 earned-run average, an all-time high in the majors. As might be expected, the Phils finished last.)

Balls were flying around the American League, too, as evidenced by the junior league's .288 batting mark. And in Simmons,

Foxx, Cochrane and Bing Miller, the Athletics had more than their share of mashers.

In the Series opener, the Cardinals collected nine base hits and the A's only five—but all of Philadelphia's hits went for extra bases and each figured in the American Leaguers' scoring, which came on single runs in the second, fourth, sixth, seventh and eighth innings. Two of the A's hits were homers by Simmons and Cochrane, and they helped Grove beat veteran Burleigh Grimes, 5-2.

Unable to gather more than one hit in an inning in Game 1,

Righthander George Earnshaw was spectacular in the 1930 World Series, throttling the St. Louis Cardinals over 25 innings while winning twice and carving a 0.72 earned-run average.

Philadelphia made amends quickly in Game 2. After Cardinals pitcher Flint Rhem retired the first two A's batters in the first inning, Cochrane homered, Simmons singled and Foxx slugged a run-scoring double. The two runs would be all Earnshaw needed, but the A's added four more in the contest and went on to a 6-1 triumph.

With the scene now shifting from Philadelphia to St. Louis, the Cardinals found themselves trailing in the Series, two games to none. But coming from arrears was nothing new to the Cards, who on the morning of August 1 were tied for fourth place and trailed National League-leading Brooklyn by 11 games.

And rebound the Cardinals did. Wild Bill Hallahan shut out the A's, 5-0, in Game 3, which had been a scoreless battle until the fourth when Cardinals center fielder Taylor Douthit stroked a home run off Walberg (who had retired all nine batters he had

faced to that point). The next day, St. Louis' 37-year-old Jesse Haines, pitching in his third Series for the Redbirds, was a 3-1 winner in a duel with Grove.

Then, with the Series lead on the line in Game 5, Grimes and Earnshaw hooked up in a masterpiece. Through seven innings, each had allowed only two hits in a scoreless game. Grimes, acquired in June from the Boston Braves and also 37, ran into trouble in the eighth when he loaded the bases with one out, but the famed spitball practitioner worked out of the jam by inducing Max Bishop and Jimmie Dykes to hit into forceouts. In mounting the threat, the Athletics had used a pinch-hitter for Earnshaw — but Mack had just the man ready in the bullpen: Grove. Despite working eight innings the day before, the lefthander came through with a scoreless eighth and the tension-filled game moved into the ninth.

Cochrane opened the inning by

drawing a walk off Grimes, but Simmons popped out. Foxx, who had hit 37 home runs and driven in 156 runs in the regular season, was up next. He measured a Grimes delivery and slammed the ball into the left-field stands. Athletics 2, Cardinals 0. And that's the way the game ended as Grove nailed down the triumph.

While Earnshaw wasn't Philadelphia's pitcher of record in the dramatic fifth contest, he clearly was throwing with consummate skill. So, with one day of rest, the 30-year-old righthander was Mack's choice to start Game 6. Gabby Street, the third man to manage the Cardinals to a pennant in the last five years, opted for Hallahan.

The A's pounced quickly. And before day's end, they had parlayed their first-game offensive "strategy" into a Series-deciding victory. Cochrane and Miller rapped run-scoring doubles in the first inning, and Simmons rifled a home run in the third off Cardinals reliever Syl Johnson. Dykes solved Johnson for a two-run homer in the fourth and, for all intents and purposes, it was over.

Remarkably, the A's again made each of their hits an extra-base blow, collecting five doubles in addition to the two homers. And Earnshaw didn't allow a run until there were two out in the ninth, and he wound up with a five-hit, 7-1 victory.

In the World Series capping the Year of the Hitter, the A's reigned as champions despite batting only .197 in the classic (compared with St. Louis' .200 mark). Mack's players got the big hits, though, with 18 of their 35 hits going for extra bases. And the A's received splendid pitching from Earnshaw, who was 2-0 with a 0.72 earned-run average in 25 innings, and Grove, who followed up a 28-5 regular season by winning two of three decisions and fashioning a 1.42 ERA in 19 innings.

Their mastery of the Cardinals made the Athletics the first team in history to win two World Series in a row *twice*. The A's previously had won consecutive Series titles in 1910 and 1911.

Mack was back. And how.

Game 1

Wednesday, October 1, At Philadelphia

St. Louis	AB.	R.	H.	RBI.	PO.	A.
Douthit, cf	4	0	0	1	0	0
Adams, 3b	3	0	1	1	1	2
Frisch, 2b	4	0	2	0	1	2
Bottomley, 1b	4	0	0	0	12	0
Hafey, lf	4	0	1	0	2	0
Blades, rf	3	0	0	0	2	0
Mancuso, c	4	1	1	0	6	1
Gelbert, ss	4	1	2	0	0	4
Grimes, p	3	0	2	0	0	3
aPuccinelli	1	0	0	0	0	0
Totals	34	2	9	2	24	12

Philadelphia	AB.	R.	H.	RBI.	PO.	A.
Bishop, 2b	3	1	0	0	2	3
Dykes, 3b	4	0	1	1	1	1
Cochrane, c	3	1	1	1	7	0
Simmons, lf	3	1	1	1	2	0
Foxx, 1b	3	1	1	0	8	0
Miller, rf	2	0	0	1	2	0
Haas, cf	3	1	1	0	3	0
Boley, ss	2	0	0	1	2	3
Grove, p	3	0	0	0	0	0
Totals	26	5	5	5	27	7

St. Louis 0 0 2 0 0 0 0 0 0—2
Philadelphia 0 1 0 1 0 1 1 1 x—5

St. Louis	IP.	H.	R.	ER.	BB.	SO.
Grimes (L)	8	5	5	5	3	6

Philadelphia	IP.	H.	R.	ER.	BB.	SO.
Grove (W)	9	9	2	2	1	5

aFouled out for Grimes in ninth. LOB—St. Louis 8, Philadelphia 2. 2B—Dykes, Frisch, Hafey. 3B—Foxx, Haas. HR—Cochrane, Simmons. SH—Miller, Boley, Douthit, Adams. U—Moriarty (A.L.), Rigler (N.L.), Geisel (A.L.) and Reardon (N.L.). T—1:48. A—32,295.

Game 2

Thursday, October 2, At Philadelphia

St. Louis	AB.	R.	H.	RBI.	PO.	A.
Douthit, cf	4	0	0	0	4	0
Adams, 3b	4	0	1	0	0	1
Frisch, 2b	4	0	1	0	1	1
Bottomley, 1b	4	0	0	0	7	0
Hafey, lf	4	0	0	0	2	0
Watkins, rf	4	1	1	1	0	0
Mancuso, c	3	0	1	0	7	0
Gelbert, ss	3	0	1	0	3	1
Rhem, p	1	0	0	0	0	0
Lindsey, p	1	0	1	0	0	0
aFisher	1	0	0	0	0	0
Johnson, p	0	0	0	0	0	0
Totals	33	1	6	1	24	3

Philadelphia	AB.	R.	H.	RBI.	PO.	A.
Bishop, 2b	2	1	0	0	3	0
Dykes, 3b	3	0	1	2	4	2
Cochrane, c	3	2	1	1	9	0
Simmons, lf	4	2	2	1	3	0
Foxx, 1b	3	0	1	1	3	2
Miller, rf	4	0	1	1	1	0
Haas, cf	4	0	0	0	2	0
Boley, ss	4	1	1	0	1	1
Earnshaw, p	3	0	0	0	1	0
Totals	30	6	7	6	27	5

St. Louis 0 1 0 0 0 0 0 0 0—1
Philadelphia 2 0 2 2 0 0 0 0 x—6

St. Louis	IP.	H.	R.	ER.	BB.	SO.
Rhem (L)	3⅓	7	6	4	2	3
Lindsey	2⅔	0	0	0	0	2
Johnson	2	0	0	0	2	2

Philadelphia	IP.	H.	R.	ER.	BB.	SO.
Earnshaw (W)	9	6	1	1	1	8

aStruck out for Lindsey in seventh. E—Frisch, Rhem, Cochrane, Boley. DP—St. Louis 1, Philadelphia 1. LOB—St. Louis 6, Philadelphia 5. 2B—Dykes, Simmons, Foxx, Frisch. HR—Cochrane, Watkins. SB—Frisch. SH—Dykes. U—Rigler (N.L.), Geisel (A.L.), Reardon (N.L.) and Moriarty (A.L.). T—1:47. A—32,295.

Game 3

Saturday, October 4, At St. Louis

Philadelphia	AB.	R.	H.	RBI.	PO.	A.
Bishop, 2b	4	0	3	0	0	2
Dykes, 3b	4	0	0	0	1	1
Cochrane, c	2	0	0	0	6	0
Simmons, lf	4	0	2	0	1	1
Foxx, 1b	4	0	1	0	11	1
Miller, rf	4	0	0	0	1	0
Haas, cf	3	0	0	0	1	0
aMoore	1	0	1	0	0	0
Boley, ss	4	0	0	0	3	5
Walberg, p	2	0	0	0	0	0
Shores, p	0	0	0	0	0	0
Quinn, p	0	0	0	0	0	1
bMcNair	1	0	0	0	0	0
Totals	33	0	7	0	24	11

St. Louis	AB.	R.	H.	RBI.	PO.	A.
Douthit, cf	4	1	2	1	3	0
Adams, 3b	4	0	0	0	0	0
Frisch, 2b	4	0	0	0	2	5
Bottomley, 1b	4	1	1	0	14	0
Hafey, lf	4	1	2	1	0	0
Blades, rf	2	1	1	0	1	0
Watkins, rf	2	1	1	0	1	0
Wilson, c	4	0	2	2	6	0
Gelbert, ss	3	0	1	1	0	4
Hallahan, p	2	0	0	0	0	1
Totals	33	5	10	5	27	10

Philadelphia 0 0 0 0 0 0 0 0 0—0
St. Louis 0 0 0 1 1 0 2 1 x—5

Philadelphia	IP.	H.	R.	ER.	BB.	SO.
Walberg (L)	4⅔	4	2	2	1	3
Shores	1⅓*	3	2	2	0	0
Quinn	2	3	1	1	0	1

St. Louis	IP.	H.	R.	ER.	BB.	SO.
Hallahan (W)	9	7	0	0	5	6

*Pitched to three batters in seventh.

aSingled for Haas in ninth. bFlied out for Quinn in ninth. DP—St. Louis 1. LOB—Philadelphia 11, St. Louis 5. 2B—Bottomley, Hafey, Simmons. HR—Douthit. U—Geisel (A.L.), Reardon (N.L.), Moriarty (A.L.) and Rigler (N.L.). T—1:55. A—36,944.

Game 4

Sunday, October 5, At St. Louis

Philadelphia	AB.	R.	H.	RBI.	PO.	A.
Bishop, 2b	3	1	1	0	2	2
Dykes, 3b	2	0	0	0	1	0
Cochrane, c	4	0	0	0	3	0
Simmons, lf	3	0	2	1	0	0
Foxx, 1b	4	0	1	0	6	0
Miller, rf	4	0	0	0	7	0
Haas, cf	3	0	0	0	4	0
Boley, ss	4	0	0	0	1	1
Grove, p	3	0	0	0	0	0
Totals	30	1	4	1	24	3

St. Louis	AB.	R.	H.	RBI.	PO.	A.
Douthit, cf	4	0	0	0	0	0
Adams, 3b	4	0	0	0	2	2
Frisch, 2b	4	0	0	0	3	2
Bottomley, 1b	4	0	0	0	9	0
Hafey, lf	3	1	1	0	3	0
Blades, rf	3	1	0	0	7	0
Wilson, c	3	0	1	0	3	0
Gelbert, ss	2	1	2	1	0	4
Haines, p	2	0	1	1	0	1
Totals	29	3	5	2	27	9

Philadelphia 1 0 0 0 0 0 0 0 0—1
St. Louis 0 0 1 2 0 0 0 0 x—3

Philadelphia	IP.	H.	R.	ER.	BB.	SO.
Grove (L)	8	5	3	1	1	3

St. Louis	IP.	H.	R.	ER.	BB.	SO.
Haines (W)	9	4	1	1	4	2

E—Dykes, Frisch. DP—St. Louis 1. LOB—Philadelphia 7, St. Louis 4. 2B—Hafey. 3B—Gelbert. SH—Dykes, Haines. WP—Haines. U—Reardon (N.L.), Moriarty (A.L.), Rigler (N.L.) and Geisel (A.L.). T—1:41. A—39,946.

Game 5

Monday, October 6, At St. Louis

Philadelphia	AB.	R.	H.	RBI.	PO.	A.
Bishop, 2b	4	0	0	0	1	0
Dykes, 3b	3	0	0	0	0	1
Cochrane, c	3	1	1	0	7	1
Simmons, lf	4	0	0	0	3	0
Foxx, 1b	4	1	2	2	12	0
Miller, rf	4	0	0	0	0	0
Haas, cf	4	0	1	0	2	0
Boley, ss	3	0	1	0	2	1
Earnshaw, p	2	0	0	0	0	4
aMoore	0	0	0	0	0	0
Grove, p	0	0	0	0	0	1
Totals	31	2	5	2	27	8

St. Louis	AB.	R.	H.	RBI.	PO.	A.
Douthit, cf	4	0	0	0	2	0
Adams, 3b	4	0	1	0	0	1
Frisch, 2b	4	0	1	0	3	3
Bottomley, 1b	4	0	0	0	9	1
Hafey, lf	3	0	0	0	1	0
Watkins, rf	3	0	0	0	1	0
bBlades	0	0	0	0	0	0
Wilson, c	4	0	1	0	9	1
Gelbert, ss	2	0	0	0	2	8
Grimes, p	2	0	0	0	0	0
Totals	30	0	3	0	27	14

Philadelphia 0 0 0 0 0 0 0 0 2—2
St. Louis 0 0 0 0 0 0 0 0 0—0

Philadelphia	IP.	H.	R.	ER.	BB.	SO.
Earnshaw	7	2	0	0	3	5
Grove (W)	2	1	0	0	1	2

St. Louis	IP.	H.	R.	ER.	BB.	SO.
Grimes (L)	9	5	2	2	3	7

aWalked for Earnshaw in eighth. bWalked for Watkins in ninth. E—Frisch. 2B—St. Louis 1. LOB—Philadelphia 5, St. Louis 8. 2B—Wilson. HR—Foxx. SH—Grimes. U—Moriarty (A.L.), Rigler (N.L.), Geisel (A.L.) and Reardon (N.L.). T—1:58. A—38,844.

Game 6

Wednesday, October 8, At Philadelphia

St. Louis	AB.	R.	H.	RBI.	PO.	A.
Douthit, cf	4	0	0	0	5	0
Adams, 3b	2	0	0	0	1	1
cHigh, 3b	2	1	1	0	0	0
Watkins, rf	3	0	0	0	3	0
Frisch, 2b	4	0	1	0	3	1
Hafey, lf	4	0	2	1	1	0
Bottomley, 1b	2	0	0	0	6	1
Wilson, c	4	0	0	0	5	0
Gelbert, ss	3	0	0	0	0	2
Hallahan, p	0	0	0	0	0	0
aFisher	1	0	1	0	0	0
Johnson, p	0	0	0	0	0	0
bBlades	1	0	0	0	0	0
Lindsey, p	0	0	0	0	0	1
dOrsatti	1	0	0	0	0	0
Bell, p	0	0	0	0	0	1
Totals	31	1	5	1	24	7

Philadelphia	AB.	R.	H.	RBI.	PO.	A.
Bishop, 2b	2	2	0	0	0	2
Dykes, 3b	2	2	2	2	1	1
Cochrane, c	3	1	1	2	8	0
Simmons, cf-lf	4	1	1	1	3	0
Foxx, 1b	3	1	1	0	12	0
Miller, rf	3	0	2	1	1	0
Moore, lf	2	0	0	0	0	0
Haas, cf	1	0	0	1	2	0
Boley, ss	4	0	0	0	0	2
Earnshaw, p	4	0	0	0	0	2
Totals	28	7	7	7	27	7

St. Louis 0 0 0 0 0 0 0 0 1—1
Philadelphia 2 0 1 2 1 1 0 0 x—7

St. Louis	IP.	H.	R.	ER.	BB.	SO.
Hallahan (L)	2	2	2	2	3	2
Johnson	3	4	4	4	1	2
Lindsey	2	1	1	1	1	0
Bell	1	0	0	0	0	0

Philadelphia	IP.	H.	R.	ER.	BB.	SO.
Earnshaw (W)	9	5	1	1	3	6

aDoubled for Hallahan in third. bStruck out for Johnson in sixth. cGrounded out for Adams in sixth. dGrounded out for Lindsey in eighth. E—Watkins. DP—Philadelphia 1. LOB—St. Louis 6, Philadelphia 6. 2B—Dykes, Cochrane, Foxx, Miller 2, Hafey 2, Fisher. HR—Dykes, Simmons. SH—Cochrane, Miller, Haas. HBP—By Hallahan (Bishop). PB—Wilson. U—Rigler (N.L.), Geisel (A.L.), Reardon (N.L.) and Moriarty (A.L.). T—1:46. A—32,295.

COMPOSITE BATTING AVERAGES

Philadelphia Athletics

Player-Position	G.	AB.	R.	H.	2B.	3B.	HR.	RBI.	BA.
Simmons, lf-cf	6	22	4	8	2	0	2	4	.364
Foxx, 1b	6	21	3	7	2	1	1	3	.333
Moore, ph-lf	3	3	0	1	0	0	0	0	.333
Bishop, 2b	6	18	5	4	0	0	0	0	.222
Dykes, 3b	6	18	2	4	3	0	1	5	.222
Cochrane, c	6	18	5	4	1	0	2	4	.222
Miller, rf	6	21	0	3	2	0	0	3	.143
Haas, cf	6	18	1	2	0	1	0	1	.111
Boley, ss	6	21	1	2	0	0	0	1	.095
Grove, p	3	6	0	0	0	0	0	0	.000
Earnshaw, p	3	9	0	0	0	0	0	0	.000
Walberg, p	1	2	0	0	0	0	0	0	.000
Shores, p	1	0	0	0	0	0	0	0	.000
Quinn, p	1	0	0	0	0	0	0	0	.000
McNair, ph	1	1	0	0	0	0	0	0	.000
Totals	6	178	21	35	10	2	6	21	.197

St. Louis Cardinals

Player-Position	G.	AB.	R.	H.	2B.	3B.	HR.	RBI.	BA.
Lindsey, p	2	1	0	1	0	0	0	0	1.000
Haines, p	1	2	0	1	0	0	0	1	.500
High, ph-3b	1	2	1	1	0	0	0	0	.500
Fisher, ph	2	2	0	1	1	0	0	0	.500
Grimes, p	2	5	0	2	0	0	0	0	.400
Gelbert, ss	6	17	2	6	0	1	0	2	.353
Mancuso, c	2	7	1	2	0	0	0	0	.286
Hafey, lf	6	22	2	6	5	0	0	2	.273
Wilson, c	4	15	0	4	1	0	0	2	.267
Frisch, 2b	6	24	0	5	2	0	0	0	.208
Watkins, rf	4	12	2	2	0	0	1	1	.167
Adams, 3b	6	21	0	3	0	0	0	1	.143
Blades, rf-ph	5	9	2	1	0	0	0	0	.111
Douthit, cf	6	24	1	2	0	0	1	2	.083
Bottomley, 1b	6	22	1	1	1	0	0	0	.045
Johnson, p	2	0	0	0	0	0	0	0	.000
Hallahan, p	2	2	0	0	0	0	0	0	.000
Puccinelli, ph	1	1	0	0	0	0	0	0	.000
Rhem, p	1	1	0	0	0	0	0	0	.000
Orsatti, ph	1	1	0	0	0	0	0	0	.000
Bell, p	1	0	0	0	0	0	0	0	.000
Totals	6	190	12	38	10	1	2	11	.200

COMPOSITE PITCHING AVERAGES

Philadelphia Athletics

Pitcher	G.	IP.	H.	R.	ER.	BB.	SO.	W.	L.	ERA.
Earnshaw	3	25	13	2	2	7	19	2	0	0.72
Grove	3	19	15	5	3	3	10	2	1	1.42
Walberg	1	4⅔	4	2	2	1	3	0	1	3.86
Quinn	1	2	3	1	1	0	1	0	0	4.50
Shores	1	1⅓	3	2	2	0	0	0	0	13.50
Totals	6	52	38	12	10	11	33	4	2	1.73

St. Louis Cardinals

Pitcher	G.	IP.	H.	R.	ER.	BB.	SO.	W.	L.	ERA.
Bell	1	1	0	0	0	0	0	0	0	0.00
Haines	1	9	4	1	1	4	2	1	0	1.00
Hallahan	2	11	9	2	2	8	8	1	1	1.63
Lindsey	2	4⅔	1	1	1	1	2	0	0	1.93
Grimes	2	17	10	7	7	6	13	0	2	3.71
Johnson	2	5	4	4	4	3	4	0	0	7.20
Rhem	1	3⅓	7	6	4	2	3	0	1	10.80
Totals	6	51	35	21	19	24	32	2	4	3.35

1931
ST. LOUIS CARDINALS
VS.
PHILADELPHIA ATHLETICS

Those Philadelphia Athletics were at it again in 1931. They captured their third straight American League championship—winning 107 games along the way—and pushed their three-year victory total to 313.

Al Simmons and Lefty Grove symbolized the cut-above nature of the Athletics. Simmons won his second consecutive A.L. batting title with an eye-popping figure of .390, nine points higher than his previous year's average, and embellished his statistical sheet with 22 home runs and 128 runs batted in. Grove won 16 consecutive decisions beginning in early June and finished the season with 31 victories and only four losses. In Philadelphia's pennant run from 1929 through '31, the lefthander had contributed a 79-15 record. Some contribution.

Simmons and Grove did business as usual in Game 1 of the 1931 World Series, which again matched Connie Mack's Athletics against Gabby Street's St. Louis Cardinals. Grove permitted two first-inning runs, then shut out the Cards the rest of the way. Simmons rocketed a two-run home run in the seventh, and Philadelphia was off and running with a 6-2 triumph in its quest to become the first club to win three straight Series titles. Grove wasn't his usual stingy self, to be sure. He allowed 12 hits, including three by Cardinals center fielder Pepper Martin.

Among everyday players, Martin was the lone change from the Cardinals' cast of 1930. Martin, a "gamer" in every sense of the word, had exhibited his all-out style of play in seven minor league seasons and two brief stints with the Cards before cracking the St. Louis lineup in '31. A full-time major leaguer for the first time at age 27, Martin responded by batting .300.

In Game 2 of the Series, Martin and Wild Bill Hallahan thwarted the Athletics. Martin doubled in the second inning, stole third and scored on a fly ball. Then, in the seventh, he singled, stole second, advanced to third on a groundout and scored on a squeeze bunt. That was the extent of the Cardinals' offense, but it was enough. Despite living up to his nickname and issuing seven walks, Hallahan was miserly in the hit department. In fact, the Athletics were hitless until the fifth inning and wound up with only three hits overall. The Cards won, 2-0.

Burleigh Grimes, a 17-game winner for St. Louis at age 38, pitched brilliantly in the next

Burleigh Grimes, the Cardinals' 38-year-old spitballer, recorded two victories in St. Louis' 1931 Series triumph.

contest. While Grimes' specialty, the spitball, had been outlawed in 1920, those using the wet pitch on the major league level at the time of the rules change were given permission to throw the spitter for the remainder of their careers. Eleven years later, Grimes still was pitching. And he still was "loading up." And he still was winning, as the A's discovered in Game 3 of the 1931 Series. Grimes threw no-hit ball through seven innings, finished with a two-hitter and even came through with a two-run single of his own in a 5-2 Cards victory. Batterymate Jimmie Wilson had three hits, and Martin chipped in with two.

The excellent pitching in this Series continued when Philadelphia's George Earnshaw, a 20-game winner for the third consecutive season, spun a two-hitter in the fourth game. The Cardinal hits were a fifth-inning single and an eighth-inning double—both by the redoubtable Mr. Martin. Jimmie Foxx hit a bases-empty homer for the A's, who were 3-0 winners.

For Game 5, Mack turned to a 32-year-old righthander with vast Series experience, Waite Hoyt, who had been obtained on waivers from the Detroit Tigers in June. Hoyt had pitched in six Series for the New York Yankees and compiled a 6-3 record for the Yanks in the fall classic. Street nominated Hallahan. The victory went to Hallahan but, once again, the headlines went to Martin. Pepper hit a run-scoring fly ball in the first inning, a two-run homer in the sixth and a run-scoring single in the eighth. He also beat out a bunt for a base hit in the fourth. Martin's four-RBI performance backed Hallahan's solid pitching and the Cardinals prevailed, 5-1.

After five games, St. Louis had three victories. And Martin had a .667 batting average (12 hits in 18 at-bats), five runs scored, four doubles, one home run, five RBIs and four stolen bases. The Wild Horse of the Osage was feeling his oats.

That Martin could continue—or even approximate—his pace was, of course, doubtful. And he

The 1931 World Series belonged to St. Louis center fielder Pepper Martin, who helped the Cardinals defeat the powerful Philadelphia A's.

did not. No matter. The Cardinals survived, even after St. Louis rookie pitcher Paul Derringer absorbed his second Series defeat in Game 6, a contest in which the A's broke loose for two four-run innings and rolled to an 8-1 victory. Grove tossed a five-hitter in the Series-squaring game.

In the decisive seventh game, St.

Louis' Andy High and George Watkins—terribly unproductive in the Series to that point (a combined 3 for 22 at the plate)—came alive offensively. They scored all four of the Cardinals' runs and collected all five of their hits. After a wild pitch and an error helped St. Louis to two first-inning runs, third baseman High singled in the third and right fielder Watkins followed with a home run that staked Grimes to a 4-0 lead. Grimes pitched shutout ball through the eighth inning, but he faltered in the ninth and needed last-out relief help from Hallahan. That final out in the Cardinals' 4-2 triumph came on a fly ball to Martin, who earlier had made things happen for the Cards and now, fittingly, put an end to the proceedings. St. Louis was the World Series titlist for the second time.

Martin, hitless in Games 6 and 7, nevertheless wound up with a .500 average. And he stole his fifth base of the Series in the first inning of the finale.

Come to think of it, Pepper Martin stole the show in the 1931 World Series. Period.

Game 1

Thursday, October 1, At St. Louis

Philadelphia	AB.	R.	H.	RBI.	PO.	A.
Bishop, 2b	5	1	1	0	0	3
Haas, cf	5	1	1	1	2	0
Cochrane, c	4	2	2	0	7	0
Simmons, lf	4	1	1	1	3	0
Foxx, 1b	4	0	2	2	9	0
Miller, rf	4	0	0	0	3	0
Dykes, 3b	3	0	2	0	1	1
Williams, ss	4	1	2	0	2	5
Grove, p	4	0	0	0	0	0
Totals	37	6	11	6	27	9

St. Louis	AB.	R.	H.	RBI.	PO.	A.
High, 3b	4	0	1	0	0	1
cMancuso	1	0	0	0	0	0
Roettger, rf	5	1	2	0	1	0
Frisch, 2b	4	1	2	0	5	1
Bottomley, 1b	4	0	1	1	6	1
Hafey, lf	4	0	1	0	0	0
Martin, cf	4	0	3	1	2	0
Wilson, c	4	0	0	0	12	2
Gelbert, ss	4	0	2	0	1	5
Derringer, p	2	0	0	0	0	0
aFlowers	1	0	0	0	0	0
Johnson, p	0	0	0	0	0	0
bBlades	1	0	0	0	0	0
Totals	38	2	12	2	27	10

Philadelphia...................0 0 4   0 0 0   2 0 0—6
St. Louis.........................2 0 0   0 0 0   0 0 0—2

Philadelphia	IP.	H.	R.	ER.	BB.	SO.
Grove (W)	9	12	2	2	0	7

St. Louis	IP.	H.	R.	ER.	BB.	SO.
Derringer (L)	7	11	6	6	3	9
Johnson	2	0	0	0	0	0

aGrounded out for Derringer in seventh. bStruck out for Johnson in ninth. cFouled out for High in ninth. DP—Philadelphia 1, St. Louis 1. LOB—Philadelphia 7, St. Louis 9. 2B—Haas, Martin, Gelbert. HR—Simmons. SB—Hafey, Martin. U—Klem (N.L.), Nallin (A.L.), Stark (N.L.) and McGowan (A.L.). T—1:55. A—38,529.

Game 2

Friday, October 2, At St. Louis

Philadelphia	AB.	R.	H.	RBI.	PO.	A.
Bishop, 2b	5	0	0	0	1	5
Haas, cf	4	0	1	0	5	0
Cochrane, c	2	0	0	0	5	0

Philadelphia	AB.	R.	H.	RBI.	PO.	A.
Simmons, lf	4	0	1	0	1	0
Foxx, 1b	2	0	1	0	11	1
Miller, rf	4	0	1	0	0	0
Dykes, 3b	2	0	0	0	0	2
Williams, ss	2	0	0	0	1	2
Earnshaw, p	3	0	0	0	0	2
aMoore	1	0	0	0	0	0
Totals	29	0	3	0	24	12

St. Louis	AB.	R.	H.	RBI.	PO.	A.
Flowers, 3b	4	0	0	0	2	1
Watkins, rf	4	0	2	0	1	0
Frisch, 2b	4	0	1	0	4	4
Bottomley, 1b	3	0	0	0	7	0
Hafey, lf	4	0	0	0	4	0
Martin, cf	3	2	2	0	0	0
Wilson, c	3	0	0	1	7	0
Gelbert, ss	2	0	1	1	2	3
Hallahan, p	2	0	0	0	0	0
Totals	29	2	6	2	27	8

Philadelphia 0 0 0 0 0 0 0 0 0—0
St. Louis 0 1 0 0 0 0 1 0 x—2

Philadelphia	IP.	H.	R.	ER.	BB.	SO.
Earnshaw (L)	8	6	2	2	1	5

St. Louis	IP.	H.	R.	ER.	BB.	SO.
Hallahan (W)	9	3	0	0	7	8

aStruck out and reached first base on error for Earnshaw in ninth. E—Wilson. DP—St. Louis 1. LOB—Philadelphia 10, St. Louis 6. 2B—Watkins, Frisch, Martin. SB—Martin 2. SH—Gelbert, Hallahan, Dykes. WP—Hallahan. U—Nallin (A.L.), Stark (N.L.), McGowan (A.L.) and Klem (N.L.). T—1:49. A—35,947.

Game 3

Monday, October 5, At Philadelphia

St. Louis	AB.	R.	H.	RBI.	PO.	A.
Adams, 3b	3	0	0	0	0	1
Flowers, 3b	1	0	0	0	1	0
Roettger, rf	5	0	1	0	1	0
bWatkins, rf	0	1	0	0	0	0
Frisch, 2b	5	0	1	0	4	3
Bottomley, 1b	4	1	1	1	11	0
Hafey, lf	5	1	1	0	2	0
Martin, cf	4	2	2	0	2	0
Wilson, c	4	0	3	1	5	0
Gelbert, ss	4	0	1	1	1	6
Grimes, p	4	0	2	2	0	2
Totals	39	5	12	5	27	12

Philadelphia	AB.	R.	H.	RBI.	PO.	A.
Bishop, 2b	3	0	0	0	2	3
Haas, cf	4	0	0	0	0	0
Cochrane, c	3	0	0	0	2	0
cMcNair	0	1	0	0	0	0
Simmons, lf	4	1	1	2	3	0
Foxx, 1b	2	0	0	0	16	0
Miller, rf	3	0	1	0	2	0
Dykes, 3b	3	0	0	0	1	4
Williams, ss	3	0	0	0	1	6
Grove, p	2	0	0	0	0	0
aCramer	1	0	0	0	0	0
Mahaffey, p	0	0	0	0	0	1
Totals	28	2	2	2	27	14

St. Louis 0 2 0 2 0 0 0 0 1—5
Philadelphia 0 0 0 0 0 0 0 0 2—2

St. Louis	IP.	H.	R.	ER.	BB.	SO.
Grimes (W)	9	2	2	2	4	5

Philadelphia	IP.	H.	R.	ER.	BB.	SO.
Grove (L)	8	11	4	4	1	2
Mahaffey	1	1	1	1	1	0

aPopped out for Grove in eighth. bRan for Roettger in ninth. cRan for Cochrane in ninth. DP—St. Louis 1. LOB—St. Louis 9, Philadelphia 3. 2B—Roettger, Bottomley, Martin. HR—Simmons. U—Stark (N.L.), McGowan (A.L.), Klem (N.L.) and Nallin (A.L.). T—2:10. A—32,295.

Game 4

Tuesday, October 6, At Philadelphia

St. Louis	AB.	R.	H.	RBI.	PO.	A.
Flowers, 3b	1	0	0	0	0	1
High, 3b	3	0	0	0	0	1
Watkins, rf	4	0	0	0	2	0
Frisch, 2b	3	0	0	0	1	2
Bottomley, 1b	3	0	0	0	7	0
Hafey, lf	3	0	0	0	0	0
Martin, cf	3	0	2	0	4	0
Wilson, c	3	0	0	0	6	0
Gelbert, ss	3	0	0	0	4	4
Johnson, p	2	0	0	0	0	1
Lindsey, p	0	0	0	0	0	0
aCollins	1	0	0	0	0	0
Derringer, p	0	0	0	0	0	1
Totals	29	0	2	0	24	10

Philadelphia	AB.	R.	H.	RBI.	PO.	A.
Bishop, 2b	4	1	2	0	0	0
Haas, cf	3	0	1	0	1	0
Cochrane, c	3	0	0	0	9	0
Simmons, lf	4	0	2	1	5	0
Foxx, 1b	3	1	1	1	7	0
Miller, rf	4	1	1	0	4	0
Dykes, 3b	4	0	2	1	0	1
Williams, ss	4	0	1	0	0	1
Earnshaw, p	3	0	0	0	1	3
Totals	32	3	10	3	27	5

St. Louis 0 0 0 0 0 0 0 0 0—0
Philadelphia 1 0 0 0 0 2 0 0 x—3

St. Louis	IP.	H.	R.	ER.	BB.	SO.
Johnson (L)	5⅔	9	3	3	1	2
Lindsey	1⅓	1	0	0	1	2
Derringer	1	0	0	0	0	1

Philadelphia	IP.	H.	R.	ER.	BB.	SO.
Earnshaw (W)	9	2	0	0	1	8

aStruck out for Lindsey in eighth. E—Bottomley. DP—St. Louis 1. LOB—St. Louis 3, Philadelphia 8. 2B—Simmons, Miller, Martin. HR—Foxx. SB—Frisch, Martin. SH—Haas. U—McGowan (A.L.), Klem (N.L.), Nallin (A.L.) and Stark (N.L.). T—1:58. A—32,295.

Game 5

Wednesday, October 7, At Philadelphia

St. Louis	AB.	R.	H.	RBI.	PO.	A.
Adams, 3b	1	0	1	0	0	0
aHigh, 3b	4	1	0	0	2	3
Watkins, rf	3	1	0	0	3	0
Frisch, 2b	4	1	2	0	6	1
Martin, cf	4	1	3	4	0	0
Hafey, lf	4	0	1	0	1	0
Bottomley, 1b	4	1	2	0	7	1
Wilson, c	4	0	2	0	7	0
Gelbert, ss	4	0	1	1	1	2
Hallahan, p	4	0	0	0	0	0
Totals	36	5	12	5	27	7

Philadelphia	AB.	R.	H.	RBI.	PO.	A.
Bishop, 2b	2	0	0	0	3	2
bMcNair, 2b	2	0	0	0	1	1
Haas, cf	2	0	0	0	2	0
cMoore, lf	2	0	1	0	1	0
Cochrane, c	4	0	1	0	3	2
Simmons, lf-cf	4	1	3	0	5	0
Foxx, 1b	3	0	2	0	8	1
Miller, rf	4	0	0	1	2	0
Dykes, 3b	4	0	1	0	0	1
Williams, ss	4	0	1	0	2	5
Hoyt, p	2	0	0	0	0	0
Walberg, p	0	0	0	0	0	0
dHeving	1	0	0	0	0	0
Rommel, p	0	0	0	0	0	0
eBoley	1	0	0	0	0	0
Totals	35	1	9	1	27	12

St. Louis 1 0 0 0 0 2 0 1 1—5
Philadelphia 0 0 0 0 0 0 1 0 0—1

St. Louis	IP.	H.	R.	ER.	BB.	SO.
Hallahan (W)	9	9	1	1	1	4

Philadelphia	IP.	H.	R.	ER.	BB.	SO.
Hoyt (L)	6	7	3	3	0	1
Walberg	2	2	1	1	1	2
Rommel	1	3	1	1	0	0

aRan for Adams in first. bFouled out for Bishop in sixth. cFlied out for Haas in sixth. dFlied out for Walberg in eighth. eStruck out for Rommel in ninth. DP—St. Louis 1, Philadelphia 1. LOB—St. Louis 5, Philadelphia 8. 2B—Frisch, Simmons. HR—Martin. SB—Watkins. U—Klem (N.L.), Nallin (A.L.), Stark (N.L.) and McGowan (A.L.). T—1:56. A—32,295.

Game 6

Friday, October 9, At St. Louis

Philadelphia	AB.	R.	H.	RBI.	PO.	A.
Bishop, 2b	4	2	1	0	4	4
Haas, cf	2	0	0	1	5	0
Cochrane, c	5	0	1	1	6	0
Simmons, lf	4	1	1	2	2	0
Foxx, 1b	5	2	2	0	7	0
Miller, rf	3	1	1	0	1	0
Dykes, 3b	3	1	0	1	1	0
Williams, ss	4	1	2	1	1	3
Grove, p	4	0	0	0	0	0
Totals	34	8	8	6	27	7

St. Louis	AB.	R.	H.	RBI.	PO.	A.
Flowers, 3b	4	1	1	0	0	2
Roettger, rf	4	0	1	0	2	0
Frisch, 2b	4	0	1	1	1	4
Martin, cf	3	0	0	0	1	0
Hafey, lf	4	0	1	0	1	0
Bottomley, 1b	4	0	0	0	11	0
Wilson, c	3	0	0	0	6	0
Mancuso, c	0	0	0	0	2	0
Gelbert, ss	3	0	1	0	3	5
Derringer, p	0	0	0	0	0	1
Johnson, p	0	0	0	0	0	0
aBlades	1	0	0	0	0	0
Lindsey, p	0	0	0	0	0	0
bCollins	1	0	0	0	0	0
Rhem, p	0	0	0	0	0	0
Totals	31	1	5	1	27	12

Philadelphia 0 0 0 0 4 0 4 0 0—8
St. Louis 0 0 0 0 0 1 0 0 0—1

Philadelphia	IP.	H.	R.	ER.	BB.	SO.
Grove (W)	9	5	1	1	1	7

St. Louis	IP.	H.	R.	ER.	BB.	SO.
Derringer (L)	4⅔	3	4	0	4	4
Johnson	1⅓	1	0	0	0	2
Lindsey	2	3	4	2	2	0
Rhem	1	1	0	0	0	1

aStruck out for Johnson in sixth. bGrounded out for Lindsey in eighth. E—Cochrane, Flowers, Hafey. DP—Philadelphia 1, St. Louis 1. LOB—Philadelphia 8, St. Louis 5. 2B—Flowers, Williams. SH—Haas, Miller, Derringer. HBP—By Lindsey (Miller). WP—Derringer. U—Nallin (A.L.), Stark (N.L.), McGowan (A.L.) and Klem (N.L.). T—1:57. A—39,401.

Game 7

Saturday, October 10, At St. Louis

Philadelphia	AB.	R.	H.	RBI.	PO.	A.
Bishop, 2b	4	0	0	0	0	1
Haas, cf	3	0	0	0	2	0
Cochrane, c	4	0	0	0	8	2
Simmons, lf	3	0	1	0	0	0
Foxx, 1b	4	0	0	0	11	0
Miller, rf	4	1	3	0	0	0
Dykes, 3b	3	1	0	0	1	3
Williams, ss	4	0	2	0	0	2
Earnshaw, p	2	0	0	0	0	2
aTodt	0	0	0	0	0	0
Walberg, p	0	0	0	0	0	0
bCramer	1	0	1	2	0	0
Totals	32	2	7	2	24	10

St. Louis	AB.	R.	H.	RBI.	PO.	A.
High, 3b	4	2	3	0	1	4
Watkins, rf	3	2	2	2	2	0
Frisch, 2b	3	0	0	0	2	4
Martin, cf	3	0	0	0	1	0
Orsatti, lf	3	0	0	0	1	0
Bottomley, 1b	3	0	0	0	12	0
Wilson, c	2	0	0	0	7	1
Gelbert, ss	3	0	0	0	1	4
Grimes, p	3	0	0	0	0	1
Hallahan, p	0	0	0	0	0	0
Totals	27	4	5	2	27	14

Philadelphia 0 0 0 0 0 0 0 0 2—2
St. Louis 2 0 2 0 0 0 0 0 x—4

Philadelphia	IP.	H.	R.	ER.	BB.	SO.
Earnshaw (L)	7	4	4	3	2	7
Walberg	1	1	0	0	1	2

St. Louis	IP.	H.	R.	ER.	BB.	SO.
Grimes (W)	8⅔	7	2	2	5	6
Hallahan	⅓	0	0	0	0	0

aWalked for Earnshaw in eighth. bSingled for Walberg in ninth. E—Foxx. DP—Philadelphia 1, St. Louis 1. LOB—Philadelphia 8, St. Louis 3. HR—Watkins. SB—Martin. SH—Frisch. WP—Earnshaw. U—Stark (N.L.), McGowan (A.L.), Klem (N.L.) and Nallin (A.L.). T—1:57. A—20,805.

COMPOSITE BATTING AVERAGES

St. Louis Cardinals

Player-Position	G.	AB.	R.	H.	2B.	3B.	HR.	RBI.	BA.
Martin, cf	7	24	5	12	4	0	1	5	.500
Watkins, rf-pr	5	14	4	4	1	0	1	2	.286
Grimes, p	2	7	0	2	0	0	0	2	.286
Roettger, rf	3	14	1	4	1	0	0	0	.286
High, 3b-pr	4	15	3	4	0	0	0	0	.267
Gelbert, ss	7	23	0	6	1	0	0	3	.261
Frisch, 2b	7	27	2	7	2	0	0	1	.259
Adams, 3b	2	4	0	1	0	0	0	0	.250
Wilson, c	7	23	0	5	0	0	0	2	.217
Hafey, lf	6	24	1	4	0	0	0	0	.167
Bottomley, 1b	7	25	2	4	1	0	0	2	.160
Flowers, ph-3b	5	11	1	1	1	0	0	0	.091
Mancuso, ph-c	2	1	0	0	0	0	0	0	.000
Derringer, p	3	2	0	0	0	0	0	0	.000
Johnson, p	3	2	0	0	0	0	0	0	.000
Blades, ph	2	2	0	0	0	0	0	0	.000
Hallahan, p	3	6	0	0	0	0	0	0	.000
Lindsey, p	2	0	0	0	0	0	0	0	.000
Collins, ph	2	2	0	0	0	0	0	0	.000
Rhem, p	1	0	0	0	0	0	0	0	.000
Orsatti, lf	1	3	0	0	0	0	0	0	.000
Totals	7	229	19	54	11	0	2	17	.236

Philadelphia Athletics

Player-Position	G.	AB.	R.	H.	2B.	3B.	HR.	RBI.	BA.
Cramer, ph	2	2	0	1	0	0	0	2	.500
Foxx, 1b	7	23	3	8	0	0	1	3	.348
Simmons, lf-cf	7	27	4	9	2	0	2	8	.333
Moore, ph-lf	2	3	0	1	0	0	0	0	.333
Williams, ss	7	25	2	8	1	0	0	1	.320
Miller, rf	7	26	3	7	1	0	0	1	.269
Dykes, 3b	7	22	2	5	0	0	0	2	.227
Cochrane, c	7	25	2	4	0	0	0	1	.160
Bishop, 2b	7	27	4	4	0	0	0	0	.148
Haas, cf	7	23	1	3	1	0	0	2	.130
Grove, p	3	10	0	0	0	0	0	0	.000
Earnshaw, p	3	8	0	0	0	0	0	0	.000
McNair, pr-ph-2b	2	2	1	0	0	0	0	0	.000
Walberg, p	2	0	0	0	0	0	0	0	.000
Mahaffey, p	1	0	0	0	0	0	0	0	.000
Hoyt, p	1	2	0	0	0	0	0	0	.000
Heving, ph	1	1	0	0	0	0	0	0	.000
Rommel, p	1	0	0	0	0	0	0	0	.000
Boley, ph	1	1	0	0	0	0	0	0	.000
Todt, ph	1	0	0	0	0	0	0	0	.000
Totals	7	227	22	50	5	0	3	20	.220

COMPOSITE PITCHING AVERAGES

St. Louis Cardinals

Pitcher	G.	IP.	H.	R.	ER.	BB.	SO.	W.	L.	ERA.
Rhem	1	1	1	0	0	0	1	0	0	0.00
Hallahan	3	18⅓	12	1	1	8	12	2	0	0.49
Grimes	2	17⅔	9	4	4	9	11	2	0	2.04
Johnson	3	9	10	3	3	1	6	0	1	3.00
Derringer	3	12⅔	14	10	6	7	14	0	2	4.26
Lindsey	2	3⅓	4	4	2	3	2	0	0	5.40
Totals	7	62	50	22	16	28	46	4	3	2.32

Philadelphia Athletics

Pitcher	G.	IP.	H.	R.	ER.	BB.	SO.	W.	L.	ERA.
Earnshaw	3	24	12	6	5	4	20	1	2	1.88
Grove	3	26	28	7	7	2	16	2	1	2.42
Walberg	2	3	3	1	1	2	4	0	0	3.00
Hoyt	1	6	7	3	3	0	1	0	1	4.50
Mahaffey	1	1	1	1	1	1	0	0	0	9.00
Rommel	1	1	3	1	1	0	0	0	0	9.00
Totals	7	61	54	19	18	9	41	3	4	2.66

1932
NEW YORK YANKEES
VS.
CHICAGO CUBS

The fans at Wrigley Field were hurling verbal abuse at Babe Ruth when the New York Yankees' slugger approached the plate in the fifth inning of Game 3 of the 1932 World Series.

Invectives weren't the only things tossed Ruth's way. A lemon, among other things, sailed near the Babe.

You see, George Herman Ruth, while a national hero for his long-ball exploits, was a villain as far as the Chicago populace was concerned. Not only did he represent the power and the glory of the mighty Yankees, but Ruth also had spoken unkindly toward the Cubs' organization. He wasn't alone in the latter regard.

Remembering the contributions of shortstop Mark Koenig to the Yanks' great teams of 1926, 1927 and 1928, members of the '32 New York club lambasted the Cubs for giving Koenig, a critical late-season acquisition by the Chicago club, only a half-share of their Series pot. Koenig had batted .353 in 33 games after being obtained from the Pacific Coast League.

Besides the Koenig angle, there also was the Joe McCarthy factor in the Yankees/Cubs animosity. McCarthy had been bounced as the Cubs' manager at the tail-end of the 1930 season—the Cubs finished in second place—after having guided Chicago to the National League pennant the year before. Now, McCarthy was back at Wrigley Field—as manager of the hated Yankees. Emotions were running high.

The Yankees had won the first two games of the Series in New York, and this contest was deadlocked, 4-4, with one out in the fifth as Ruth positioned himself in the batter's box and awaited the first delivery from Cubs pitcher

Charlie Root. The Bambino, who had smashed a three-run homer off Root in the first inning, took a called strike. Then Root missed with two pitches. Another called strike followed, and Ruth acknowledged it—just as he had strike one—with a raised hand.

By now, Cubs players and fans alike were taunting the big guy; they had fresh ammunition, too, since the Babe had missed on a shoestring-catch attempt in the previous inning. The noise level was increasing dramatically.

Ruth then seemingly gestured toward center field, as if to indicate that's where he planned to deposit Root's next pitch. Or was he merely pointing at Root? Or addressing the Cubs' bench with an exaggerated sweeping motion? Or showing one and all that he still had one strike left?

Whatever the message, Ruth delivered on Root's next offering. He swung viciously and the ball arced toward center field and went over the wall near the base of the flagpole. The blast put the Yankees ahead, 5-4.

"What do you think of the nerve of that big monkey calling his shot and getting away with it?" teammate Lou Gehrig said the next day. While the Yankees' first baseman, the on-deck hitter at the time, obviously thought the Babe had indeed called his shot, Root, for one, wasn't buying it.

"If he had (pointed to an anticipated home run landing spot), I would have knocked him down with the next pitch," Root said. Ruth himself was content to go along with the called-shot scenario, although he never really expounded upon the matter.

Gehrig matched Ruth's two-homer day by following with a drive into the right-field bleachers. Lou's earlier home run had

come in the third inning. The back-to-back shots in the fifth stood up as the margin of victory as the Yankees, after trading runs with the Cubs in the ninth, prevailed, 7-5.

Trying to close out the Cubs in Game 4, the Yankees fell behind, 4-1, in the first inning as Chicago's Frank Demaree smacked a three-run homer. New York stormed back, however, as Tony Lazzeri unloaded a pair of two-run homers and Earle Combs hit a bases-empty shot. A game that was a 5-5 tie after six innings wound up 13-6, Yankees.

The Yanks had made it three sweeps in their last three World Series appearances.

A team that despite its contender status had undergone a stunning switch in managers in early August (from Rogers Hornsby, who couldn't get along with the front office, to first baseman Charley Grimm), the Cubs never gave any real indication they could compete with the Yankees. Oh, Chicago did jump to a 2-0 first-inning lead in the Series opener. And the National Leaguers maintained that edge until the fourth, when Gehrig capped a three-run Yankee outburst with a two-run homer. New York scored five more times in the sixth and Red Ruffing, in his first Series appearance, weathered his way to a 12-6 victory.

Lefty Gomez, a 24-game winner in his second full season in the majors, pitched shutout ball in the last six innings of Game 2 and New York rolled to a 5-2 victory. Catcher Bill Dickey and outfielder Ben Chapman, also Series newcomers, each knocked in two runs for the Yankees and Gehrig contributed three hits and one RBI.

While Ruth's name will forever be synonymous with the 1932

World Series, it was the less-ostentatious performance of Gehrig that really dazzled. Gehrig assaulted Cubs pitching for nine hits in 17 at-bats (.529 average), slugged three homers, scored nine runs and collected eight RBIs. Dickey batted .438 for the Yankees, Combs hit .375 and Joe Sewell and Ruth each finished at .333. For Ruth, the "called shot" was his last homer in Series play.

New York, a club that finished 13 games ahead of runner-up Philadelphia in the '32 American League pennant race, simply manhandled Grimm's club, totaling 37 runs and 45 hits in the four games. Of the eight Cubs pitchers employed in the Series, five had ERAs of 9.00 or higher against the Yankees.

Outfielder Riggs Stephenson led the Cubs with a .444 batting mark. Billy Jurges, who wound up supplanting Koenig at shortstop after Game 1, was next at .364.

When this chippiest of all World Series ended, McCarthy had his revenge against the club that had dismissed him. Ruth had his called-shot story ready for retelling on baseball book shelves, be it in the fiction or non-fiction section. And Koenig had his half share.

Game 1

Wednesday, September 28, At New York

Chicago	AB.	R.	H.	RBI.	PO.	A.
Herman, 2b	5	2	2	1	1	2
English, 3b	4	1	1	0	2	1
Cuyler, rf	5	1	1	0	2	0
Stephenson, lf	5	0	3	3	2	0
Moore, cf	4	0	0	0	1	0
Grimm, 1b	3	0	0	0	8	1
Hartnett, c	5	1	2	0	4	2
Koenig, ss	4	1	1	1	4	3
Bush, p	1	0	0	0	0	2
Grimes, p	1	0	0	0	0	0
aGudat	1	0	0	0	0	0
Smith, p	0	0	0	0	0	0
Totals	38	6	10	5	24	11

New York	AB.	R.	H.	RBI.	PO.	A.
Combs, cf	4	2	2	2	3	0
Sewell, 3b	4	1	1	1	2	1
Ruth, rf	3	3	1	1	1	0
Gehrig, 1b	4	3	2	2	7	1
Lazzeri, 2b	4	1	1	1	1	2
Dickey, c	3	0	1	2	11	0
Chapman, lf	4	1	0	2	1	0
Crosetti, ss	2	1	0	0	0	0
Ruffing, p	4	0	0	0	1	3
Totals	32	12	8	11	27	7

Chicago	2 0 0 0 0 0 2 2 0— 6
New York	0 0 0 3 0 5 3 1 x—12

Chicago	IP.	H.	R.	ER.	BB.	SO.
Bush (L)	5⅓	3	8	8	5	2
Grimes	1⅔	3	3	3	1	0
Smith	1	2	1	1	0	1

New York	IP.	H.	R.	ER.	BB.	SO.
Ruffing (W)	9	10	6	4	6	10

a Struck out for Grimes in eighth. E—English, Ruth, Crosetti. DP—Chicago 1. LOB—Chicago 11, New York 4. 2B—Combs, Hartnett 2. 3B—Koenig. HR—Gehrig. SB—Cuyler. SH—Crosetti. HBP—By Grimes (Dickey). WP—Grimes. U—Dinneen (A.L.), Klem (N.L.), Van Graflan (A.L.) and Magerkurth (N.L.). T—2:31. A—41,459.

Game 2

Thursday, September 29, At New York

Chicago	AB.	R.	H.	RBI.	PO.	A.
Herman, 2b	4	1	1	0	1	6
English, 3b	4	0	1	0	0	0
Cuyler, rf	4	0	1	0	1	0
Stephenson, lf	4	1	2	1	0	0
Demaree, cf	4	0	1	1	1	0
Grimm, 1b	4	0	2	0	8	0
Hartnett, c	3	0	1	0	9	2
Jurges, ss	3	0	0	0	4	3
Warneke, p	3	0	0	0	0	2
aHemsley	1	0	0	0	0	0
Totals	34	2	9	2	24	13

New York	AB.	R.	H.	RBI.	PO.	A.
Combs, cf	3	1	1	0	4	0
Sewell, 3b	3	1	1	0	0	1
Ruth, rf	3	1	1	0	3	0
Gehrig, 1b	4	2	3	1	5	0
Lazzeri, 2b	4	0	1	0	3	1
Dickey, c	3	0	2	2	8	0
Chapman, lf	4	0	1	2	1	1
Crosetti, ss	3	0	0	0	3	3
Gomez, p	3	0	0	0	0	3
Totals	30	5	10	5	27	9

Chicago	1 0 1 0 0 0 0 0 0—2
New York	2 0 2 0 1 0 0 0 x—5

Chicago	IP.	H.	R.	ER.	BB.	SO.
Warneke (L)	8	10	5	5	4	7

New York	IP.	H.	R.	ER.	BB.	SO.
Gomez (W)	9	9	2	1	1	8

aStruck out for Warneke in ninth. E—Crosetti. DP—Chicago 4. LOB—Chicago 7, New York 5. 2B—Herman, Stephenson. 3B—Cuyler. SH—Jurges. U—Klem (N.L.), Van Graflan (A.L.), Magerkurth (N.L.) and Dinneen (A.L.). T—1:46. A—50,709.

Game 3

Saturday, October 1, At Chicago

New York	AB.	R.	H.	RBI.	PO.	A.
Combs, cf	5	1	0	0	1	0
Sewell, 3b	2	1	0	0	2	2
Ruth, lf	4	2	2	4	2	0
Gehrig, 1b	5	2	2	2	13	1
Lazzeri, 2b	4	1	0	0	3	4
Dickey, c	4	0	1	0	2	1
Chapman, rf	4	0	2	1	0	0
Crosetti, ss	4	0	1	0	4	4
Pipgras, p	5	0	0	0	0	0
Pennock, p	0	0	0	0	0	1
Totals	37	7	8	7	27	13

Chicago	AB.	R.	H.	RBI.	PO.	A.
Herman, 2b	4	1	0	0	1	2
English, 3b	4	0	0	0	0	3
Cuyler, rf	4	1	3	2	1	0
Stephenson, lf	4	0	1	0	1	0
Moore, cf	3	1	0	0	3	0
Grimm, 1b	4	0	1	1	8	0
Hartnett, c	4	1	1	1	10	1
Jurges, ss	4	1	3	0	3	3
Root, p	2	0	0	0	0	0
Malone, p	0	0	0	0	0	0
aGudat	1	0	0	0	0	0
May, p	0	0	0	0	0	0
Tinning, p	0	0	0	0	0	0
bKoenig	0	0	0	0	0	0
cHemsley	1	0	0	0	0	0
Totals	35	5	9	4	27	9

New York	3 0 1 0 2 0 0 0 1—7
Chicago	1 0 2 1 0 0 0 0 1—5

New York	IP.	H.	R.	ER.	BB.	SO.
Pipgras (W)	8*	9	5	4	3	1
Pennock	1	0	0	0	0	1

Chicago	IP.	H.	R.	ER.	BB.	SO.
Root (L)	4⅓	6	6	5	3	4
Malone	2⅔	1	0	0	1	4
May	1⅓	1	1	0	0	1
Tinning	⅔	0	0	0	0	1

*Pitched to two batters in ninth.

aPopped out for Malone in seventh. bAnnounced for Tinning in ninth. cStruck out for Koenig in ninth. E—Lazzeri, Herman, Hartnett, Jurges 2. DP—New York 1, Chicago 1. LOB—New York 11, Chicago 6. 2B—Chapman, Cuyler, Jurges, Grimm. HR—Ruth 2, Gehrig 2, Cuyler, Hartnett. SB—Jurges. HBP—By May (Sewell). U—Van Graflan (A.L.), Magerkurth (N.L.), Dinneen (A.L.) and Klem (N.L.). T—2:11. A—49,986.

Game 4

Sunday, October 2, At Chicago

New York	AB.	R.	H.	RBI.	PO.	A.
Combs, cf	4	4	3	2	2	0
Sewell, 3b	6	1	3	2	0	2
Ruth, lf	5	0	1	1	2	0
Byrd, lf	0	0	0	0	0	0
Gehrig, 1b	4	2	2	3	12	0
Lazzeri, 2b	5	2	3	4	1	4
Dickey, c	6	2	3	0	4	0
Chapman, rf	5	0	2	1	4	0
Crosetti, ss	6	1	1	0	2	5
Allen, p	0	0	0	0	0	0
W. Moore, p	3	0	1	0	0	1
aRuffing	0	0	0	0	0	0
bHoag	0	1	0	0	0	0
Pennock, p	1	0	0	0	0	0
Totals	45	13	19	13	27	12

Chicago	AB.	R.	H.	RBI.	PO.	A.
Herman, 2b	5	1	1	0	2	2
English, 3b	5	1	1	1	1	0
Cuyler, rf	5	0	0	0	1	0
Stephenson, lf	5	1	2	0	1	0
Demaree, cf	3	1	1	3	3	0
Grimm, lb	4	2	2	0	4	2
Hartnett, c	4	0	1	0	8	0
cHack	0	0	0	0	0	0
Grimes, p	0	0	0	0	0	0
Jurges, ss	4	0	1	1	5	2
Bush, p	0	0	0	0	0	0
Warneke, p	1	0	0	0	1	0
May, p	2	0	0	0	1	0
Tinning, p	0	0	0	0	0	1
dHemsley, c	1	0	0	0	0	0
Totals	39	6	9	5	27	7

New York	1 0 2 0 0 2 4 0 4—13
Chicago	4 0 0 0 0 1 0 0 1— 6

New York	IP.	H.	R.	ER.	BB.	SO.
Allen	⅔	5	4	3	0	0
W. Moore (W)	5⅓	2	1	0	0	1
Pennock	3	2	1	4	1	3

Chicago	IP.	H.	R.	ER.	BB.	SO.
Bush	⅓	2	1	1	1	0
Warneke	2⅔*	5	2	2	1	1
May (L)	3⅓	8	6	6	3	3
Tinning	1⅔	0	0	0	0	2
Grimes	1	4	4	4	1	0

*Pitched to two batters in fourth.

aWalked for W. Moore in seventh. bRan for Ruffing in seventh. cRan for Hartnett in eighth. dStruck out for Tinning in eighth. E—Sewell, Gehrig, Crosetti 2, Demaree. DP—Chicago 1. LOB—New York 13, Chicago 7. 2B—Gehrig, Sewell, Crosetti, Chapman, Grimm. HR—Demaree, Lazzeri 2, Combs. HBP—By Bush (Ruth), by May (Gehrig). U—Magerkurth (N.L.), Dinneen (A.L.), Klem (N.L.) and Van Graflan (A.L.). T—2:27. A—49,844.

COMPOSITE BATTING AVERAGES

New York Yankees

Player-Position	G.	AB.	R.	H.	2B.	3B.	HR.	RBI.	BA.
Gehrig, 1b	4	17	9	9	1	0	3	8	.529
Dickey, c	4	16	2	7	0	0	0	4	.438
Combs, cf	4	16	8	6	1	0	1	4	.375
Sewell, 3b	4	15	4	5	1	0	0	3	.333
Ruth, rf-lf	4	15	6	5	0	0	2	6	.333
Moore, p	1	3	0	1	0	0	0	0	.333
Lazzeri, 2b	4	17	4	5	0	0	2	5	.294
Chapman, lf-rf	4	17	1	5	2	0	0	6	.294
Crosetti, ss	4	15	2	2	1	0	0	0	.133
Ruffing, p-ph	2	4	0	0	0	0	0	0	.000
Gomez, p	1	3	0	0	0	0	0	0	.000
Pipgras, p	1	5	0	0	0	0	0	0	.000
Pennock, p	2	1	0	0	0	0	0	0	.000
Byrd, lf	1	0	0	0	0	0	0	0	.000
Allen, p	1	0	0	0	0	0	0	0	.000
Hoag, pr	1	0	1	0	0	0	0	0	.000
Totals	4	144	37	45	6	0	8	36	.313

Chicago Cubs

Player-Position	G.	AB.	R.	H.	2B.	3B.	HR.	RBI.	BA.
Stephenson, lf	4	18	2	8	1	0	0	4	.444
Jurges, ss	3	11	1	4	1	0	0	1	.364
Grimm, 1b	4	15	2	5	2	0	0	1	.333
Hartnett, c	4	16	2	5	2	0	1	1	.313
Demaree, cf	2	7	1	2	0	0	1	4	.286
Cuyler, rf	4	18	2	5	1	1	1	2	.278
Koenig, ss-ph	2	4	1	1	0	1	0	1	.250
Herman, 2b	4	18	5	4	1	0	0	1	.222
English, 3b	4	17	2	3	0	0	0	1	.176
Moore, cf	2	7	1	0	0	0	0	0	.000
Bush, p	2	1	0	0	0	0	0	0	.000
Grimes, p	2	1	0	0	0	0	0	0	.000
Gudat, ph	2	2	0	0	0	0	0	0	.000
Smith, p	1	0	0	0	0	0	0	0	.000
Warneke, p	2	4	0	0	0	0	0	0	.000
Hemsley, ph-c	3	3	0	0	0	0	0	0	.000
Root, p	1	2	0	0	0	0	0	0	.000
Malone, p	1	0	0	0	0	0	0	0	.000
May, p	2	2	0	0	0	0	0	0	.000
Tinning, p	2	0	0	0	0	0	0	0	.000
Hack, pr	1	0	0	0	0	0	0	0	.000
Totals	4	146	19	37	8	2	3	16	.253

COMPOSITE PITCHING AVERAGES

New York Yankees

Pitcher	G.	IP.	H.	R.	ER.	BB.	SO.	W.	L.	ERA.
W. Moore	1	5⅓	2	1	0	0	1	1	0	0.00
Gomez	1	9	9	2	1	1	8	1	0	1.00
Pennock	2	4	2	1	1	1	4	0	0	2.25
Ruffing	1	9	10	6	4	6	10	1	0	4.00
Pipgras	1	8	9	5	4	3	1	1	0	4.50
Allen	1	⅔	5	4	3	0	0	0	0	40.50
Totals	4	36	37	19	13	11	24	4	0	3.25

Chicago Cubs

Pitcher	G.	IP.	H.	R.	ER.	BB.	SO.	W.	L.	ERA.
Malone	1	2⅔	1	0	0	4	4	0	0	0.00
Tinning	2	2⅓	0	0	0	0	3	0	0	0.00
Warneke	2	10⅔	15	7	7	5	8	0	1	5.91
Smith	1	1	2	1	1	0	1	0	0	9.00
Root	1	4⅓	6	6	5	3	4	0	1	10.38
May	2	4⅔	9	7	6	3	4	0	1	11.57
Bush	2	5⅔	5	9	9	6	2	0	1	14.29
Grimes	2	2⅔	7	7	7	2	0	0	0	23.63
Totals	4	34	45	37	35	23	26	0	4	9.26

Good pitching stops good hitting. That baseball adage doesn't always hold up, but it certainly did in the 1933 World Series when youthful Manager Joe Cronin and his hard-hitting band of Washington Senators took on the pitching-rich New York Giants.

The 26-year-old Cronin, in a bold move reminiscent of the Senators' selection of 27-year-old Bucky Harris as manager nine years earlier, succeeded Walter Johnson as Washington's pilot in '33 and led the club by example in his rookie season at the helm. Shortstop Cronin batted .309 and exceeded the 100-runs-batted-in figure for the fourth consecutive year.

Cronin had plenty of help offensively. Outfielder Heinie Manush hit .336 and knocked in 95 runs, first baseman Joe Kuhel finished at .322 and drove in 107 runs and second baseman Buddy Myer contributed a .302 mark. And outfielders Goose Goslin and Fred Schulte, obtained after the 1932 season from the St. Louis Browns, were .297 and .295 hitters, respectively. The pitching wasn't exactly shabby, either, with Alvin Crowder winning 24 games and Earl Whitehill 22. And Lefty Stewart, also acquired in the Browns trade, went 15-6.

Having outdistanced the New York Yankees by seven games in the American League pennant race, Washington appeared too strong for the Giants. Having won the National League flag in their first full season under Bill Terry, who had succeeded John McGraw as manager in June 1932, the Giants had only one .300 hitter, first baseman Terry himself, and one 100-RBI man, outfielder Mel Ott. But in Carl Hubbell, Hal Schumacher, Freddie Fitzsim-

mons, Roy Parmelee and Dolf Luque, New York was loaded with strong arms.

Hubbell and Schumacher, who had combined for 17 shutouts during the regular season, started the first two games of the Series for the Giants and were opposed by Stewart and Crowder, respectively. And while neither Giants pitcher was able to hold the Senators scoreless, each pitched extremely well. Hubbell, in fact, did not permit an earned run while allowing only five hits and striking out 10 batters in a 4-2 victory. Ott was the hitting star of the Series opener, stroking a two-run home run and a run-scoring single. Schumacher yielded only one run in Game 2, that coming on a Goslin homer, and wound up a 6-1 winner as the Giants erupted for six runs in the sixth inning. The key hit in the outburst was a bases-loaded pinch single by Lefty O'Doul, whose trip to the plate marked his only career at-bat in World Series competition.

Good pitching was indeed stopping good hitting. And what marvelous pitching the Giants possessed. Hubbell had led the National League in victories with 23, shutouts with 10 and earned-run average with a minuscule 1.66 figure. Schumacher, Hubbell and Parmelee had ranked 1-2-3 in the league in fewest hits allowed per nine innings. Schumacher had won 19 games, and his 2.16 ERA ranked third in the N.L. Fitzsimmons had won 16 times. And reliever Luque, at age 43, had prevailed in eight of 10 decisions and boasted a 2.70 ERA.

The standout hurling in this World Series continued in Game 3, only this time the stellar performance came from a member of Cronin's staff. Whitehill, another prize off-season acquisition of the

Senators (the lefthander had spent nearly a decade with the Detroit Tigers), doled out five hits and notched a 4-0 victory. Myer had three hits and two RBIs for Washington.

Cronin and company faced a major obstacle as they tried to square the Series in Game 4. That obstacle was named Hubbell. The 30-year-old screwball pitcher again did not allow an earned run, but found himself in a 1-1 tie after nine innings. Terry had accounted for the Giants' run with a fourth-inning home run off Monte Weaver, while Washington countered with a seventh-inning run on Hubbell's error, a sacrifice and Luke Sewell's single. Neither club could score in the 10th, but New York edged ahead in the 11th on Travis Jackson's bunt single, a sacrifice and Blondy Ryan's single. In the bottom of the inning, Hubbell escaped a one-out, bases-loaded situation by getting pinch-hitter Cliff Bolton to ground into a double play. The Giants' 2-1 conquest moved the New Yorkers within one victory of their first Series championship since 1922.

Schumacher was Terry's pitching choice for Game 5, and Prince Hal presented himself with a 2-0 lead by singling home Jackson and Gus Mancuso in the second inning. And by the middle of the sixth, it was 3-0. Schumacher retired the first two batters in the last of the sixth, but Manush and Cronin lashed singles and Schulte brought the Washington crowd alive with a game-tying home run to left. Before the inning was over, Prince Hal was in exile. The game was now a battle of relievers —the Giants' Luque against the Senators' Jack Russell.

The 3-3 stalemate continued until the top of the 10th when,

with two out, Ott drilled a Russell pitch into the center-field bleachers. Luque then went about the business of nailing down the Series title for the Giants. After getting two quick outs, the Cuban allowed a single to Cronin and a walk to Schulte. But the man who had first appeared in the majors in 1914 struck out Kuhel on three pitches to end the game—and the 30th World Series.

New York batted .267 in the Series, only slightly above its season figure of .263. Washington, meanwhile, was held to a .214 average after leading the majors in 1933 with a team mark of .287.

What had unfolded in the '33 Series was no mystery to anyone. Clearly, good pitching had stopped good hitting.

Game 1

Tuesday, October 3, At New York

Washington	AB.	R.	H.	RBI.	PO.	A.
Myer, 2b	4	1	1	0	2	2
Goslin, rf	4	0	0	0	1	0
Manush, lf	4	1	0	0	2	0
Cronin, ss	4	0	2	1	0	2
Schulte, cf	4	0	2	0	4	0
Kuhel, 1b	4	0	0	1	8	1
Bluege, 3b	4	0	0	0	0	2
Sewell, c	3	0	0	0	6	1
Stewart, p	1	0	0	0	0	0
Russell, p	1	0	0	0	1	3
aHarris	0	0	0	0	0	0
Thomas, p	0	0	0	0	0	0
Totals	33	2	5	2	24	11

New York	AB.	R.	H.	RBI.	PO.	A.
Moore, lf	4	1	0	0	1	0
Critz, 2b	4	1	1	0	2	2
Terry, 1b	4	1	1	0	9	0
Ott, rf	4	1	4	3	0	0
Davis, cf	4	0	2	0	0	0
Jackson, 3b	4	0	0	1	0	4
Mancuso, c	4	0	0	0	12	1
Ryan, ss	4	0	1	0	3	3
Hubbell, p	3	0	1	0	0	1
Totals	35	4	10	4	27	11

Washington	0 0 0	1 0 0	0 0 1	—2
New York	2 0 2	0 0 0	0 0 x	—4

Washington	IP.	H.	R.	ER.	BB.	SO.
Stewart (L)	2*	6	4	2	0	0
Russell	5	4	0	0	0	3
Thomas	1	0	0	0	0	2

New York	IP.	H.	R.	ER.	BB.	SO.
Hubbell (W)	9	5	2	0	2	10

*Pitched to three batters in third.

aWalked for Russell in eighth. E—Myer 3, Critz, Ryan. DP—New York 1. LOB—Washington 6, New York 7. HR—Ott. U—Moran (N.L.), Moriarty (A.L.), Pfirman (N.L.) and Ormsby (A.L.). T—2:07. A—46,672.

Game 2

Wednesday, October 4, At New York

Washington	AB.	R.	H.	RBI.	PO.	A.
Myer, 2b	3	0	0	0	1	3
Goslin, rf	4	1	2	1	0	0
Manush, lf	3	0	1	0	1	0
Cronin, ss	4	0	0	0	3	4
Schulte, cf	4	0	0	0	1	0
Kuhel, 1b	3	0	0	0	15	1
Bluege, 3b	2	0	0	0	0	3
cHarris	1	0	0	0	0	0
Sewell, c	3	0	0	0	3	0
dBolton	1	0	0	0	0	0
Crowder, p	2	0	1	0	0	1
Thomas, p	0	0	0	0	0	0
bRice	1	0	1	0	0	0
McColl, p	0	0	0	0	0	1
Totals	31	1	5	1	24	13

New York	AB.	R.	H.	RBI.	PO.	A.
Moore, lf	4	0	2	1	4	0
Critz, 2b	3	1	1	0	1	3
Terry, 1b	4	1	1	0	10	0
Ott, rf	2	1	0	0	4	0
Davis, cf	2	0	1	0	1	0
aO'Doul	1	1	1	2	0	0
Peel, cf	1	0	0	0	0	0
Jackson, 3b	3	1	1	1	1	5
Mancuso, c	4	1	1	1	4	1
Ryan, ss	4	0	1	0	2	3
Schumacher, p	4	0	1	1	0	2
Totals	32	6	10	6	27	14

Washington	0 0 1	0 0 0	0 0 0	—1
New York	0 0 0	0 0 6	0 0 x	—6

Washington	IP.	H.	R.	ER.	BB.	SO.
Crowder (L)	5⅔	9	6	6	3	3
Thomas	⅓	1	0	0	0	0
McColl	2	0	0	0	0	0

New York	IP.	H.	R.	ER.	BB.	SO.
Schumacher (W)	9	5	1	1	4	2

aSingled for Davis in sixth. bSingled for Thomas in seventh. cGrounded out for Bluege in ninth. dGrounded out for Sewell in ninth. DP—Washington 1, New York 1. LOB—Washington 7, New York 6. 2B—Terry. HR—Goslin. SH—Jackson. WP—Schumacher. U—Moriarty (A.L.), Pfirman (N.L.), Ormsby (A.L.) and Moran (N.L.). T—2:09. A—35,461.

Game 3

Thursday, October 5, At Washington

New York	AB.	R.	H.	RBI.	PO.	A.
Moore, lf	4	0	0	0	2	1
Critz, 2b	4	0	1	0	2	4
Terry, 1b	4	0	0	0	9	0
Ott, rf	3	0	0	0	1	0
Davis, cf	4	0	1	0	3	0
Jackson, 3b	3	0	1	0	0	2
Mancuso, c	4	0	0	0	4	1
Ryan, ss	3	0	0	0	3	3
Fitzsimmons, p	2	0	1	0	0	1
aPeel	1	0	1	0	0	0
Bell, p	0	0	0	0	0	0
Totals	32	0	5	0	24	12

Washington	AB.	R.	H.	RBI.	PO.	A.
Myer, 2b	4	1	3	2	3	3
Goslin, rf	4	1	1	0	2	0
Manush, lf	4	0	0	0	3	0
Cronin, ss	4	0	1	1	0	2
Schulte, cf	4	0	2	1	1	0
Kuhel, 1b	3	0	0	0	15	0
Bluege, 3b	3	1	1	0	0	6
Sewell, c	3	1	1	0	3	0
Whitehill, p	3	0	0	0	0	4
Totals	32	4	9	4	27	15

New York	0 0 0	0 0 0	0 0 0	—0
Washington	2 1 0	0 0 0	1 0 x	—4

New York	IP.	H.	R.	ER.	BB.	SO.
Fitzsimmons (W)	7	9	4	4	0	2
Bell	1	0	0	0	0	0

Washington	IP.	H.	R.	ER.	BB.	SO.
Whitehill (L)	9	5	0	0	2	2

aSingled for Fitzsimmons in eighth. E—Cronin. DP—New York 1, Washington 1. LOB—New York 7, Washington 4. 2B—Goslin, Bluege, Schulte, Myer, Jackson. SB—Sewell. WP—Whitehill. U—Pfirman (N.L.), Ormsby (A.L.), Moran (N.L.) and Moriarty (A.L.). T—1:55. A—25,727.

Game 4

Friday, October 6, At Washington

New York	AB.	R.	H.	RBI.	PO.	A.
Moore, lf	5	0	2	0	3	0
Critz, 2b	6	0	0	0	9	5
Terry, 1b	5	1	2	1	9	0
Ott, rf	4	0	2	0	4	0
Davis, cf	4	0	1	0	1	0
Jackson, 3b	5	1	1	0	0	2
Mancuso, c	2	0	0	0	5	0
Ryan, ss	5	0	2	1	1	5
Hubbell, p	4	0	1	0	1	3
Totals	40	2	11	2	33	15

Washington	AB.	R.	H.	RBI.	PO.	A.
Myer, 2b	4	0	2	0	6	4
Goslin, rf-lf	4	0	1	0	1	0
Manush, lf	2	0	0	0	1	0
Harris, rf	1	0	0	0	2	0
Cronin, ss	5	0	1	0	1	4
Schulte, cf	5	0	1	0	2	0
Kuhel, 1b	5	1	1	0	14	1
Bluege, 3b	3	0	0	0	2	1
Sewell, c	4	0	2	1	4	1
Weaver, p	4	0	0	0	0	6
Russell, p	0	0	0	0	0	0
aBolton	1	0	0	0	0	0
Totals	38	1	8	1	33	17

New York	000	100	000	01	—2
Washington	000	000	100	00	—1

New York	IP.	H.	R.	ER.	BB.	SO.
Hubbell (W)	11	8	1	0	4	5

Washington	IP.	H.	R.	ER.	BB.	SO.
Weaver (L)	10⅓	11	2	2	4	3
Russell	⅔	0	0	0	0	1

aHit into double play for Russell in eleventh. E—Hubbell. DP—New York 1, Washington 1. LOB—New York 12, Washington 11. 2B—Moore. HR—Terry. SH—Goslin, Bluege 2, Davis, Hubbell, Mancuso. U—Ormsby (A.L.), Moran (N.L.), Moriarty (A.L.) and Pfirman (N.L.). T—2:59. A—26,762.

Game 5

Saturday, October 7, At Washington

New York	AB.	R.	H.	RBI.	PO.	A.
Moore, lf	5	0	1	0	3	0
Critz, 2b	5	0	0	0	2	4
Terry, 1b	5	0	2	0	13	1
Ott, rf	5	1	1	1	1	0
Davis, cf	5	1	2	0	1	0
Jackson, 3b	3	1	1	0	2	4
Mancuso, c	3	1	1	1	7	1
Ryan, ss	2	0	1	0	0	5
Schumacher, p	3	0	1	2	0	0
Luque, p	1	0	1	0	1	0
Totals	37	4	11	4	30	15

Washington	AB.	R.	H.	RBI.	PO.	A.
Myer, 2b	5	0	0	0	3	1
Goslin, rf	4	0	1	0	4	1
Manush, lf	5	1	1	0	3	0
Cronin, ss	5	1	3	0	3	3
Schulte, cf	4	1	2	3	1	0
aKerr	0	0	0	0	0	0
Kuhel, 1b	5	0	2	0	7	0
Bluege, 3b	4	0	1	0	1	1
Sewell, c	4	0	0	0	7	0
Crowder, p	2	0	0	0	0	2
Russell, p	1	0	0	0	1	1
Totals	39	3	10	3	30	9

New York	0 2 0	0 0 1	0 0 0	1	—4
Washington	0 0 0	0 0 3	0 0 0	0	—3

New York	IP.	H.	R.	ER.	BB.	SO.
Schumacher	5⅔	8	3	3	1	1
Luque (W)	4⅓	2	0	0	2	5

Washington	IP.	H.	R.	ER.	BB.	SO.
Crowder	5⅓	7	3	3	2	4
Russell (L)	4⅔	4	1	1	0	3

aRan for Schulte in tenth. E—Jackson. DP—New York 1, Washington 1. LOB—New York 7, Washington 9. 2B—Davis, Mancuso. HR—Schulte, Ott. SH—Ryan, Jackson. WP—Crowder, Schumacher. U—Moran (N.L.), Moriarty (A.L.), Pfirman (N.L.) and Ormsby (A.L.). T—2:38. A—28,454.

COMPOSITE BATTING AVERAGES

New York Giants

Player-Position	G.	AB.	R.	H.	2B.	3B.	HR.	RBI.	BA.
O'Doul, ph	1	1	1	1	0	0	0	2	1.000
Luque, p	1	1	0	1	0	0	0	0	1.000
Fitzsimmons, p	1	2	0	1	0	0	0	0	.500
Peel, cf-ph	2	2	0	1	0	0	0	0	.500
Ott, rf	5	18	3	7	0	0	2	4	.389
Davis, cf	5	19	1	7	1	0	0	0	.368
Hubbell, p	2	7	0	2	0	0	0	0	.286
Schumacher, p	2	7	0	2	0	0	0	3	.286
Ryan, ss	5	18	0	5	0	0	0	1	.278
Terry, 1b	5	22	3	6	1	0	1	1	.273
Moore, lf	5	22	1	5	1	0	0	1	.227
Jackson, 3b	5	18	3	4	1	0	0	2	.222
Critz, 2b	5	22	2	3	0	0	0	0	.136
Mancuso, c	5	17	2	2	1	0	0	2	.118
Bell, p	1	0	0	0	0	0	0	0	.000
Totals	5	176	16	47	5	0	3	16	.267

Washington Senators

Player-Position	G.	AB.	R.	H.	2B.	3B.	HR.	RBI.	BA.
Rice, ph	1	1	0	1	0	0	0	0	1.000
Schulte, cf	5	21	1	7	1	0	1	4	.333
Cronin, ss	5	22	1	7	0	0	0	2	.318
Myer, 2b	5	20	2	6	1	0	0	2	.300
Crowder, p	2	4	0	1	0	0	0	0	.250
Goslin, rf	5	20	2	5	1	0	1	1	.250
Sewell, c	5	17	1	3	0	0	0	1	.176
Kuhel, 1b	5	20	1	3	0	0	0	1	.150
Bluege, 3b	5	16	1	2	1	0	0	0	.125
Manush, lf	5	18	2	2	0	0	0	0	.111
Stewart, p	1	1	0	0	0	0	0	0	.000
Russell, p	3	2	0	0	0	0	0	0	.000
Harris, ph-rf	3	2	0	0	0	0	0	0	.000
Thomas, p	2	0	0	0	0	0	0	0	.000
Bolton, ph	2	2	0	0	0	0	0	0	.000
McColl, p	1	0	0	0	0	0	0	0	.000
Whitehill, p	1	3	0	0	0	0	0	0	.000
Weaver, p	1	4	0	0	0	0	0	0	.000
Kerr, pr	1	0	0	0	0	0	0	0	.000
Totals	5	173	11	37	4	0	2	11	.214

COMPOSITE PITCHING AVERAGES

New York Giants

Pitcher	G.	IP.	H.	R.	ER.	BB.	SO.	W.	L.	ERA.
Hubbell	2	20	13	3	0	6	15	2	0	0.00
Luque	1	4⅓	2	0	0	2	5	1	0	0.00
Bell	1	1	0	0	0	0	0	0	0	0.00
Schumacher	2	14⅔	13	4	4	5	3	1	0	2.45
Fitzsimmons	1	7	9	4	4	0	2	0	1	5.14
Totals	5	47	37	11	8	13	25	4	1	1.53

Washington Senators

Pitcher	G.	IP.	H.	R.	ER.	BB.	SO.	W.	L.	ERA.
Whitehill	1	9	5	0	0	2	2	1	0	0.00
McColl	1	2	0	0	0	0	0	0	0	0.00
Thomas	2	1⅓	1	0	0	0	2	0	0	0.00
Russell	3	10⅓	8	1	1	0	7	0	1	0.87
Weaver	1	10⅓	11	2	2	4	3	0	1	1.74
Crowder	2	11	16	9	9	5	7	0	1	7.36
Stewart	1	2	6	4	2	0	0	0	1	9.00
Totals	5	46	47	16	14	11	21	1	4	2.74

1934
ST. LOUIS CARDINALS
VS.
DETROIT TIGERS

The 1934 St. Louis Cardinals, featuring a cast of characters as colorful as any ever assembled on one big-league club, could talk a good game. And, with the likes of Dizzy Dean, Leo Durocher, Joe Medwick and Pepper Martin on hand, they did so unabashedly.

More than talk, though, these Cardinals could *play* a good game.

The New York Giants, National League leaders most of the year and seven games ahead of Manager Frankie Frisch's roisterous group of Cardinals on the morning of September 5, found out only too well how effectively the fun-loving Cards could kick, scratch, claw and, most important, hustle their way to victory. By season's end 3½ weeks later, the Cardinals were N.L. pennant winners by a two-game margin.

The American League champion Detroit Tigers then led St. Louis, three games to two, in the World Series and felt relatively comfortable as they headed home for the conclusion of the fall classic, but Manager Mickey Cochrane's club also was bowled over by the hellbent-for-leather Redbirds. You just couldn't feel too comfortable around this gang. This *Gas House Gang*.

Sure, Detroit had the home-field advantage for the final two games of the 1934 Series. And, needing only one victory to clinch their first-ever Series championship, the Tigers were sending Schoolboy Rowe to the mound for Game 6. A second-year major leaguer, Rowe had won 16 consecutive games in a June-to-August stretch of the regular season and pitched masterfully in Game 2 against the Cardinals. St. Louis was banking on a rookie pitcher to keep it alive. But this was no typical first-year man. This was Paul Dean, who in the heat of the

When St. Louis' Joe Medwick slid hard into Detroit third baseman Marv Owen in Game 7 of the '34 Series, irate Tiger fans pelted the left fielder with garbage (above) and eventually forced Commissioner Kenesaw Mountain Landis (above) to remove Medwick from the game.

pennant race had thrown a no-hitter against Brooklyn.

Paul Dean prevailed over Rowe with his arm and bat. He held the Tigers to seven hits and, with the score tied at 3-3 in the seventh inning, delivered a game-winning single. Now, after the Cards' 4-3 victory, it was up to brother Dizzy Dean, who had given credence to his "it-ain't-bragging-if-you-can-do-it" claim by winning 30 games for the National League champions. Diz was matched against Eldon Auker in the Series finale.

As matchups go, this one was found wanting.

The Cardinals struck for seven runs in the third inning, an outburst touched off by Diz's double. The big blow in the Cardinals' rally, which was waged against four Detroit pitchers, was Frisch's three-run double. In the sixth, Medwick knocked in a run with a triple—he slid hard into Tigers third baseman Marv Owen on the play—and then scored on first baseman Rip Collins' fourth hit

of the day. It was now 9-0.

The mood among Detroit fans, festive at the start of Game 7, was a-changing with every new entry to the Cardinals' half of the scoreboard. In fact, when Medwick returned to his left-field station during the middle of the sixth inning, Tiger boosters couldn't contain themselves. Nor their containers. Bottles started flying in Medwick's direction. Plus fruit, vegetables and other debris. A 9-0 deficit and a hard slide had added up to trouble, which Commissioner Kenesaw Mountain Landis soon quelled by ordering Medwick from the game. The commissioner apparently thought the Cards hardly needed Joe's services at this point. Landis was right. Out came Medwick and in went Chick Fullis. And on St. Louis went to a Series-clinching 11-0 victory, with Diz permitting only six hits and the Cardinals collecting 17 overall.

The 22-year-old Medwick had been a pain to the Tigers and their fans right from the start. In the

St. Louis teammates carry Dizzy Dean off the field in Game 4 after the Cardinal pitcher, serving as a pinch-runner, was hit in the head by a thrown ball.

Series opener, he collected four hits—including a home run—as the Cardinals, behind Dizzy Dean's steady pitching, rolled to an 8-3 triumph. To say the Tigers had early-Series jitters may be understating the point; with one out in the St. Louis third, Detroit already had been charged with five errors.

Rowe put on an amazing pitching demonstration in the 12-inning second game, limiting the Cardinals to one hit over the final nine innings of a contest that Detroit won, 3-2. To pull out the victory, Cochrane's Tigers needed a game-tying pinch single in the ninth by Gee Walker and two 12th-inning walks and a single by Goose Goslin, who had played for Washington in the previous year's Series.

Martin, the center fielder-turned-third baseman and star of the Cardinals' Series triumph over the Philadelphia Athletics in 1931, was up to his old tricks in Game 3. He doubled, tripled and scored two runs in support of Paul Dean, who shut out Detroit for 8⅔ innings and wound up a 4-1 winner.

Detroit then seized the Series lead with 10-4 and 3-1 victories, with Billy Rogell and Hank Greenberg combining for seven RBIs and Auker going the distance in Game 4 and Tommy Bridges spinning a seven-hitter in Game 5.

But then came the Deans. Again.

After winning a total of 49 games in the regular season, Dizzy and Paul combined for all four St. Louis victories in the 1934 Series. Diz even overcame being struck in the head with a thrown ball while serving as a pinch-runner in Game 4. A day later, he yielded only two earned runs in eight innings while losing to Bridges. Then, in Game 7, he fired a shutout and collected two hits of his own.

Medwick batted .379 against Detroit pitching and drove in five runs, while Collins hit .367 and Martin finished at .355. Center fielder Ernie Orsatti proved a pesky Cardinal with a .318 mark, and right fielder Jack Rothrock—while batting only .233—had a St. Louis-high six RBIs.

Second baseman Charlie Gehringer paced Detroit with a .379 mark and Greenberg hit .321 with a Series-leading seven RBIs. Cochrane, named the Tigers' manager after being acquired in December 1933 from the Athletics, struggled in the Series with a .214 average and one RBI after helping the upstart Detroit club to the pennant with his field leadership and .320 batting mark.

That the Cardinals' all-out style of play would result in the ever-descriptive nickname of Gas House Gang—a label that really wasn't bandied about until the 1935 season—was hardly surprising. That Ol' Diz and company had the talent to back up their bombast proved, in the end, even less surprising.

Game 1

Wednesday, October 3, At Detroit

St. Louis	AB.	R.	H.	RBI.	PO.	A.
Martin, 3b	5	1	1	1	1	1
Rothrock, rf	4	0	2	2	0	0
Frisch, 2b	4	0	0	0	2	4
Medwick, lf	5	2	4	2	2	0
Collins, 1b	4	2	1	0	13	1
DeLancey, c	5	0	1	2	7	1
Orsatti, cf	4	1	2	0	1	0
Fullis, cf	1	0	1	0	0	0
Durocher, ss	5	0	0	0	0	4
J. Dean, p	5	2	1	0	1	2
Totals	42	8	13	7	27	13

Detroit	AB.	R.	H.	RBI.	PO.	A.
White, cf	2	1	0	0	6	0
Cochrane, c	4	0	1	0	2	0
Gehringer, 2b	4	0	2	1	2	3
Greenberg, 1b	4	2	2	1	8	1
Goslin, lf	4	0	2	1	3	0
Rogell, ss	4	0	1	0	1	4
Owen, 3b	4	0	0	0	2	1
Fox, rf	4	0	0	0	3	0
Crowder, p	1	0	0	0	0	0
aDoljack	1	0	0	0	0	0
Marberry, p	0	0	0	0	0	1
Hogsett, p	1	0	0	0	0	1
bG. Walker	1	0	0	0	0	0
Totals	34	3	8	3	27	11

St. Louis..............0 2 1 0 1 4 0 0 0—8
Detroit................0 0 1 0 0 1 0 1 0—3

St. Louis	IP.	H.	R.	ER.	BB.	SO.
J. Dean (W)	9	8	3	3	2	6

Detroit	IP.	H.	R.	ER.	BB.	SO.
Crowder (L)	5	6	4	1	1	1
Marberry	⅔	4	4	4	0	0
Hogsett	3⅓	3	0	0	0	1

aFlied out for Crowder in fifth. bStruck out for Hogsett in ninth. E—Orsatti 2, Gehringer, Greenberg, Rogell, Owen 2. DP—St. Louis 1. LOB—St. Louis 10, Detroit 6. 2B—DeLancey, J. Dean. HR—Medwick, Greenberg. SH—Rothrock, Frisch. U—Owens (A.L.), Klem (N.L.), Geisel (A.L.) and Reardon (N.L.). T—2:13. A—42,505.

Game 2

Thursday, October 4, At Detroit

St. Louis	AB.	R.	H.	RBI.	PO.	A.
Martin, 3b	5	1	2	0	1	1
Rothrock, rf	4	0	0	0	4	0
Frisch, 2b	5	0	1	0	3	6
Medwick, lf	5	0	1	1	0	0
Collins, 1b	5	0	1	0	12	2
DeLancey, c	5	1	1	0	10	0
Orsatti, cf	4	0	1	1	2	0
Durocher, ss	4	0	0	0	1	3
Hallahan, p	3	0	0	0	1	3
W. Walker, p	1	0	0	0	0	1
Totals	41	2	7	2	34	16

Detroit	AB.	R.	H.	RBI.	PO.	A.
White, cf	4	0	0	0	4	0
aG. Walker	1	0	1	1	0	0
Doljack, cf	1	0	0	0	1	0
Cochrane, c	4	0	0	0	8	0
Gehringer, 2b	4	1	1	0	3	6

	AB.	R.	H.	RBI.	PO.	A.
Greenberg, 1b	4	0	0	0	13	1
Goslin, lf	6	0	2	1	3	1
Rogell, ss	4	1	1	0	1	2
Owen, 3b	5	0	0	0	0	1
Fox, rf	5	1	2	1	2	0
Rowe, p	4	0	0	0	1	1
Totals	42	3	7	3	36	12

St. Louis	0 1 1 000 000 000—2
Detroit	0 0 0 100 001 001—3

One out when winning run scored.

St. Louis	IP.	H.	R.	ER.	BB.	SO.
Hallahan	8⅓	6	2	2	4	6
W. Walker (L)	3	1	1	1	3	2

Detroit	IP.	H.	R.	ER.	BB.	SO.
Rowe (W)	12	7	2	2	0	7

aSingled for White in ninth. E—Martin, Frisch, Hallahan. LOB—St. Louis 4, Detroit 13. 2B—Rogell, Fox, Martin. 3B—Orsatti. SB—Gehringer. SH—Rowe, Rothrock. U—Klem (N.L.), Geisel (A.L.), Reardon (N.L.) and Owens (A.L.). T—2:49. A—43,451.

Game 3

Friday, October 5, At St. Louis

Detroit	AB.	R.	H.	RBI.	PO.	A.
White, cf	5	1	2	0	4	0
Cochrane, c	3	0	0	0	6	3
Gehringer, 2b	5	0	2	0	3	3
Greenberg, 1b	4	0	1	1	6	0
Goslin, lf	4	0	1	0	2	0
Rogell, ss	4	0	1	0	1	2
Owen, 3b	3	0	0	0	1	0
Fox, rf	4	0	1	0	1	0
Bridges, p	1	0	0	0	0	0
Hogsett, p	2	0	0	0	0	1
Totals	35	1	8	1	24	9

St. Louis	AB.	R.	H.	RBI.	PO.	A.
Martin, 3b	3	2	2	0	2	1
Rothrock, rf	4	1	1	2	5	0
Frisch, 2b	4	0	2	1	2	1
Medwick, lf	4	0	1	0	3	0
Collins, 1b	4	1	2	0	3	0
DeLancey, c	4	0	1	0	9	0
Orsatti, cf	2	0	0	0	1	0
Durocher, ss	3	0	0	0	2	1
P. Dean, p	3	0	0	1	0	0
Totals	31	4	9	4	27	3

Detroit	0 0 0 000 001—1
St. Louis	1 1 0 020 00x—4

Detroit	IP.	H.	R.	ER.	BB.	SO.
Bridges (L)	4*	8	4	4	1	3
Hogsett	4	1	0	0	1	2

St. Louis	IP.	H.	R.	ER.	BB.	SO.
P. Dean (W)	9	8	1	1	5	7

*Pitched to three batters in fifth.

E—Rogell 2, Rothrock. DP—Detroit 2. LOB—Detroit 13, St. Louis 6. 2B—Martin, DeLancey, Gehringer. 3B—Martin, Rothrock, Greenberg. HBP—By P. Dean (Owen), by Bridges (Orsatti). U—Geisel (A.L.), Reardon (N.L.), Owens (A.L.) and Klem (N.L.). T—2:07. A—34,073.

Game 4

Saturday, October 6, At St. Louis

Detroit	AB.	R.	H.	RBI.	PO.	A.
White, cf	4	2	1	0	2	0
Cochrane, c	5	2	1	0	1	0
Gehringer, 2b	4	2	2	0	4	4
Goslin, lf	3	2	0	0	3	0
Rogell, ss	5	1	2	4	4	3
Greenberg, 1b	5	1	4	3	10	2
Owen, 3b	5	0	2	1	1	2
Fox, rf	4	0	1	0	2	0
Auker, p	4	0	0	0	0	2
Totals	39	10	13	8	27	13

St. Louis	AB.	R.	H.	RBI.	PO.	A.
Martin, 3b	4	0	1	1	1	2
Rothrock, rf	5	0	0	0	3	0
Frisch, 2b	5	1	1	0	2	4
Medwick, lf	3	1	2	0	0	0
Collins, 1b	4	0	2	1	9	1
DeLancey, c	2	0	0	0	8	1
Orsatti, cf	4	1	2	1	2	1
Durocher, ss	4	1	1	0	2	1
Carleton, p	1	0	0	0	0	0
Vance, p	0	0	0	0	0	0
aV. Davis	1	0	1	1	0	0
bJ. Dean	0	0	0	0	0	0
W. Walker, p	1	0	0	0	0	0
Haines, p	0	0	0	0	0	0
cCrawford	1	0	0	0	0	0
Mooney, p	0	0	0	0	0	1
Totals	35	4	10	4	27	11

Detroit	0 0 3 100 150—10
St. Louis	0 1 1 200 000— 4

Detroit	IP.	H.	R.	ER.	BB.	SO.
Auker (W)	9	10	4	3	4	1

St. Louis	IP.	H.	R.	ER.	BB.	SO.
Carlton	2⅔	4	3	3	2	2
Vance	1⅓	2	1	0	1	3
W. Walker (L)	3⅓	5	6	4	3	0
Haines	⅔	1	0	0	0	2
Mooney	1	1	0	0	0	0

aSingled for Vance in fourth. bRan for V. Davis in fourth. cGrounded out for Haines in eighth. E—Gehringer, Martin 3, DeLancey 1, W. Walker. DP—Detroit 3. LOB—Detroit 12, St. Louis 8. 2B—Cochrane, Greenberg 2, Fox, Collins. SB—White, Greenberg, Owen. SH—Cochrane, Gehringer, Goslin, Auker. WP—Vance. U—Reardon (N.L.), Owens (A.L.), Klem (N.L.) and Geisel (A.L.). T—2:43. A—37,492.

Game 5

Sunday, October 7, At St. Louis

Detroit	AB.	R.	H.	RBI.	PO.	A.
White, cf	2	0	0	0	2	0
Cochrane, c	4	0	1	0	10	0
Gehringer, 2b	4	1	1	1	4	1
Goslin, lf	4	0	1	0	1	0
Rogell, ss	4	1	2	0	0	2
Greenberg, 1b	3	1	0	1	6	0
Owen, 3b	4	0	0	0	1	0
Fox, rf	4	0	1	1	3	0
Bridges, p	4	0	1	0	0	2
Totals	33	3	7	3	27	5

St. Louis	AB.	R.	H.	RBI.	PO.	A.
Martin, 3b	4	0	2	0	0	1
Rothrock, rf	4	0	0	0	2	0
Frisch, 2b	4	0	1	0	2	3
Medwick, lf	4	0	0	0	3	0
Collins, 1b	4	0	1	0	5	1
DeLancey, c	4	1	1	1	6	0
Fullis, cf	3	0	0	0	5	0
dOrsatti	1	0	0	0	0	0
Durocher, ss	2	0	1	0	3	2
aV. Davis	1	0	1	0	0	0
bWhitehead, ss	0	0	0	0	1	0
J. Dean, p	2	0	0	0	0	0
cCrawford	1	0	0	0	0	0
Carleton, p	0	0	0	0	0	0
Totals	34	1	7	1	27	7

Detroit	0 1 0 002 000—3
St. Louis	0 0 0 000 100—1

Detroit	IP.	H.	R.	ER.	BB.	SO.
Bridges (W)	9	7	1	1	0	7

St. Louis	IP.	H.	R.	ER.	BB.	SO.
J. Dean (L)	8	6	3	2	3	6
Carleton	1	1	0	0	0	0

aSingled for Durocher in eighth. bRan for V. Davis in eighth. cFlied out for J. Dean in eighth. dForced runner for Fullis in ninth. E—Fullis. DP—St. Louis 1. LOB—Detroit 7, St. Louis 6. 2B—Goslin, Fox, Martin. HR—Gehringer, DeLancey. HBP—By J. Dean (White). WP—Bridges. U—Owens (A.L.), Klem (N.L.), Geisel (A.L.) and Reardon (N.L.). T—1:58. A—38,536.

Game 6

Monday, October 8, At Detroit

St. Louis	AB.	R.	H.	RBI.	PO.	A.
Martin, 3b	5	1	1	1	1	2
Rothrock, rf	4	1	2	1	1	0
Frisch, 2b	4	0	0	0	2	3
Medwick, lf	4	0	2	1	0	0
Collins, 1b	4	0	0	0	8	0
DeLancey, c	4	0	0	0	6	4
Orsatti, cf	4	0	1	0	7	0
Durocher, ss	4	2	3	0	2	2
P. Dean, p	3	0	1	1	0	0
Totals	36	4	10	4	27	11

Detroit	AB.	R.	H.	RBI.	PO.	A.
White, cf	2	2	0	0	0	0
Cochrane, c	4	0	3	1	7	0
Gehringer, 2b	4	1	1	0	0	4
Goslin, lf	4	0	1	0	4	0
Rogell, ss	4	0	0	0	1	2
Greenberg, 1b	4	0	1	1	10	0
Owen, 3b	4	0	0	0	3	3
Fox, rf	4	0	1	0	2	0
Rowe, p	3	0	0	0	0	0
Totals	33	3	7	2	27	9

St. Louis	1 0 0 020 100—4
Detroit	0 0 1 002 000—3

St. Louis	IP.	H.	R.	ER.	BB.	SO.
P. Dean (W)	9	7	3	1	2	4

Detroit	IP.	H.	R.	ER.	BB.	SO.
Rowe (L)	9	10	4	3	0	5

E—Frisch, P. Dean, Goslin. LOB—St. Louis 6, Detroit 6. 2B—Rothrock, Durocher, Fox. SH—P. Dean, Rowe. U—Klem (N.L.), Geisel (A.L.), Reardon (N.L.) and Owens (A.L.). T—1:58. A—44,551.

Game 7

Tuesday, October 9, At Detroit

St. Louis	AB.	R.	H.	RBI.	PO.	A.
Martin, 3b	5	3	2	1	0	1
Rothrock, rf	5	1	2	1	4	0
Frisch, 2b	5	1	1	3	3	5
Medwick, lf	4	1	1	1	1	0
Fullis, lf	1	0	1	0	1	0
Collins, 1b	5	1	4	2	7	2
DeLancey, c	5	1	1	1	5	0
Orsatti, cf	3	1	1	0	2	0
Durocher, ss	5	1	2	0	3	4
J. Dean, p	5	1	2	1	1	0
Totals	43	11	17	10	27	12

Detroit	AB.	R.	H.	RBI.	PO.	A.
White, cf	4	0	0	0	3	0
Cochrane, c	4	0	0	0	2	2
Hayworth, c	0	0	0	0	1	0
Gehringer, 2b	4	0	2	0	3	5
Goslin, lf	4	0	0	0	4	0
Rogell, ss	4	0	1	0	3	2
Greenberg, 1b	4	0	1	0	7	0
Owen, 3b	4	0	0	0	1	2
Fox, rf	3	0	2	0	3	0
Auker, p	0	0	0	0	0	0
Rowe, p	0	0	0	0	0	0
Hogsett, p	0	0	0	0	0	0
Bridges, p	2	0	0	0	0	0
Marberry, p	0	0	0	0	0	0
aG. Walker	1	0	0	0	0	0
Crowder, p	0	0	0	0	0	0
Totals	34	0	6	0	27	11

St. Louis	0 0 7 002 200—11
Detroit	0 0 0 000 000— 0

St. Louis	IP.	H.	R.	ER.	BB.	SO.
J. Dean (W)	9	6	0	0	0	5

Detroit	IP.	H.	R.	ER.	BB.	SO.
Auker (L)	2⅓	6	4	4	1	1
Rowe	⅓	2	2	2	0	0
Hogsett	0*	2	1	1	2	0
Bridges	4⅓	6	4	2	0	2
Marberry	1	1	0	0	1	0
Crowder	1	0	0	0	0	1

*Pitched to four batters in third.

aFlied out for Marberry in eighth. E—Collins, White, Gehringer, Goslin. DP—Detroit 1. LOB—St. Louis 9, Detroit 7. 2B—Rothrock 2, Frisch, DeLancey, J. Dean, Fox 2. 3B—Medwick, Durocher. SB—Martin 2. U—Geisel (A.L.), Reardon (N.L.), Owens (A.L.) and Klem (N.L.). T—2:19. A—40,902.

COMPOSITE BATTING AVERAGES

St. Louis Cardinals

Player-Position	G.	AB.	R.	H.	2B.	3B.	HR.	RBI.	BA.
V. Davis, ph	2	2	0	2	0	0	0	1	1.000
Fullis, cf	3	5	0	2	0	0	0	0	.400
Medwick, lf	7	29	4	11	0	1	1	5	.379
Collins, 1b	7	30	4	11	1	0	0	4	.367
Martin, 3b	7	31	8	11	3	1	0	3	.355
Orsatti, cf	7	22	3	7	0	1	0	2	.318
Durocher, ss	7	27	4	7	1	1	0	0	.259
J. Dean, p-pr	4	12	3	3	2	0	0	1	.250
Rothrock, rf	7	30	3	7	3	1	0	6	.233
Frisch, 2b	7	31	2	6	1	0	0	4	.194
DeLancey, c	7	29	3	5	3	0	1	4	.172
P. Dean, p	2	6	0	1	0	0	0	2	.167
Hallahan, p	1	3	0	0	0	0	0	0	.000
W. Walker, p	2	2	0	0	0	0	0	0	.000
Carleton, p	2	1	0	0	0	0	0	0	.000
Vance, p	1	0	0	0	0	0	0	0	.000
Whitehead, pr-ss	1	0	0	0	0	0	0	0	.000
Haines, p	1	0	0	0	0	0	0	0	.000
Crawford, ph	2	2	0	0	0	0	0	0	.000
Mooney, p	1	0	0	0	0	0	0	0	.000
Totals	7	262	34	73	14	5	2	32	.279

Detroit Tigers

Player-Position	G.	AB.	R.	H.	2B.	3B.	HR.	RBI.	BA.
Gehringer, 2b	7	29	5	11	1	0	1	2	.379
G. Walker, ph	3	3	0	1	0	0	0	1	.333
Greenberg, 1b	7	28	4	9	2	1	1	7	.321
Fox, rf	7	28	1	8	6	0	0	2	.286
Rogell, ss	7	29	3	8	1	0	0	4	.276
Goslin, lf	7	29	2	7	1	0	0	2	.241
Cochrane, c	7	28	2	6	1	0	0	1	.214
Bridges, p	3	7	0	1	0	0	0	0	.143
White, cf	7	23	6	3	0	0	0	0	.130
Owen, 3b	7	29	0	2	0	0	0	1	.069
Auker, p	2	4	0	0	0	0	0	0	.000
Doljack, ph-cf	2	2	0	0	0	0	0	0	.000
Crowder, p	2	1	0	0	0	0	0	0	.000
Marberry, p	2	0	0	0	0	0	0	0	.000
Rowe, p	3	7	0	0	0	0	0	0	.000
Hogsett, p	3	3	0	0	0	0	0	0	.000
Hayworth, c	1	0	0	0	0	0	0	0	.000
Totals	7	250	23	56	12	1	2	20	.224

COMPOSITE PITCHING AVERAGES

St. Louis Cardinals

Pitcher	G.	IP.	H.	R.	ER.	BB.	SO.	W.	L.	ERA.
Haines	1	⅔	1	0	0	0	2	0	0	0.00
Mooney	1	1	1	0	0	0	0	0	0	0.00
Vance	1	1⅓	2	1	0	1	3	0	0	0.00
P. Dean	2	18	15	4	2	7	11	2	0	1.00
J. Dean	3	26	20	6	5	5	17	2	1	1.73
Hallahan	1	8⅓	6	2	2	4	6	0	0	2.16
W. Walker	2	6⅓	6	7	5	6	2	0	2	7.11
Carleton	2	3⅔	5	3	3	2	2	0	0	7.36
Totals	7	65⅓	56	23	17	25	43	4	3	2.34

Detroit Tigers

Pitcher	G.	IP.	H.	R.	ER.	BB.	SO.	W.	L.	ERA.
Hogsett	3	7⅓	6	1	1	3	3	0	0	1.23
Crowder	2	6	6	4	1	1	2	0	1	1.50
Rowe	3	21⅓	19	8	7	0	12	1	1	2.95
Bridges	3	17⅓	21	9	7	1	12	1	1	3.63
Auker	2	11⅓	16	8	7	5	2	1	1	5.56
Marberry	2	1⅔	5	4	4	1	0	0	0	21.60
Totals	7	65	73	34	27	11	31	3	4	3.74

1935
DETROIT TIGERS
VS.
CHICAGO CUBS

Steeped in the tradition of World Series success these franchises were not.

The Detroit Tigers had never won a Series, losing in baseball's showcase event in 1907, 1908, 1909 and 1934. The Chicago Cubs had lost in their last four Series appearances, falling in 1910, 1918, 1929 and 1932.

The fortunes of one of these teams would change in 1935, a year in which the fall classic matched Charley Grimm's Cubs —winners of 21 consecutive games in September—against a Detroit team that had won the American League pennant for the second straight year.

By the time the late stages of Game 6 of the 1935 World Series rolled around, there was little clue as to which club would shake off its postseason funk and which would endure more agony. The Cubs were trailing in the Series, three games to two, but this contest was knotted at 3-3 in the top of the ninth and Chicago's Stan Hack was perched on third base with no one out. Hack had just tripled off Detroit curveballer Tommy Bridges, driving the ball over the head of center fielder Gee Walker.

Bridges, whose 21 victories paced the Detroit pitching staff in '35, was in an unenviable—but not hopeless—situation. While the potential Series-tying run was 90 feet down the third-base line, Bridges wasn't going against the heart of the Cubs' order. Instead, eighth-place hitter Billy Jurges, pitcher Larry French and leadoff man Augie Galan were due up.

Bridges was up to the challenge. First, he struck out Jurges. Then, he induced French to ground back to the mound, with Hack holding third. And, finally, he got Galan to fly out. Whatever the threesome the Cubs had sent to the plate, it was a textbook piece of clutch pitching.

Now, the Tigers could win it— not only the game, but their first-ever World Series—with a run in the last of the ninth. After French struck out Flea Clifton, Mickey Cochrane slapped a single off second baseman Billy Herman's glove and the Tigers' manager/catcher advanced to second on Gehringer's groundout. Goose Goslin, who had performed so admirably for the Washington Senators in World Series competition and the man who delivered the 12th-inning hit that won Game 2 of the '34 Series for Detroit, was up next. Goslin, in what would be his 129th and last career at-bat in World Series play, banged a single to right field and Cochrane raced home from second with the decisive run.

Detroit—the team and the city

Frank Demaree crosses the plate after a ninth-inning home run that capped Chicago's 3-0 Game 1 victory over Detroit.

Chicago's Chuck Klein crosses the plate (above) with the tying run in the ninth inning of Game 3, a contest eventually won by Detroit in 11 innings. The game featured umpire George Moriarty's ejection (below) of Cubs Manager Charley Grimm and two players.

—went bonkers.

The Tigers had won the hard way—without slugging first base-

man Hank Greenberg, who missed the last four games of the Series because of a wrist fracture

incurred in Game 2. Greenberg was coming off a remarkable season, one in which he slammed 36 home runs, drove in 170 runs (100 by the All-Star Game break) and batted .328. With Greenberg on the sideline, Detroit switched third baseman Marv Owen to first and inserted Clifton into Owen's usual position. Owen and Clifton went a combined 1 for 36 at the plate in the Series.

Greenberg had helped Detroit even the Series at a game apiece, capping a four-run Tiger first inning in Game 2 with a two-run home run off Charlie Root (who, in his first Series appearance since being victimized by Babe Ruth's "called shot" homer in 1932, failed to retire a batter as the Cubs' starter). Detroit went on to win, 8-3, as Bridges tossed a six-hitter. Chicago's Lon Warneke had won the Series opener, 3-0, permitting only four hits.

Jo Jo White's run-scoring single in the 11th inning of Game 3 lifted Detroit to a 6-5 triumph after Schoolboy Rowe, working in relief, had blown a 5-3 lead in the ninth. And the Tigers made it three straight victories the next day when Alvin Crowder outdueled Tex Carleton, 2-1.

The Cubs rebounded in Game 5, however, as Chuck Klein hammered a two-run homer and Warneke pitched six shutout innings before leaving because of a sore shoulder. Bill Lee finished up for Warneke as the Cubs posted a 3-1 triumph, setting the stage for the sixth-game dramatics.

Right fielder Pete Fox, who doubled home Detroit's first run in the finale, was the leading hitter in the Series with a .385 average. Gehringer batted .375 for the Tigers after hitting at a .379 clip in the previous year's fall classic. Herman, who drove in all three of the Cubs' runs in Game 6, had a Series-high six RBIs and tied Klein for Chicago's batting lead with a .333 mark. Pitching-wise, the Tigers' Bridges and the Cubs' Warneke stood out with 2-0 records.

While neither team excelled overall, the conquerors at least—and at last—claimed their first World Series championship. The

conquered, meanwhile, were still looking for their first fall-classic title since 1908.

Game 1

Wednesday, October 2, At Detroit

Chicago	AB.	R.	H.	RBI.	PO.	A.
Galan, lf	4	1	1	0	2	0
Herman, 2b	3	1	0	0	0	3
Lindstrom, cf	3	0	1	0	2	0
Hartnett, c	4	0	2	1	1	0
Demaree, rf	4	1	2	1	1	0
Cavarretta, 1b	3	0	0	0	17	0
Hack, 3b	4	0	0	0	1	3
Jurges, ss	4	0	1	0	2	2
Warneke, p	3	0	0	0	1	8
Totals	32	3	7	2	27	16

Detroit	AB.	R.	H.	RBI.	PO.	A.
White, cf	4	0	1	0	2	0
Cochrane, c	4	0	0	0	8	1
Gehringer, 2b	3	0	0	0	3	4
Greenberg, 1b	3	0	0	0	9	0
Goslin, lf	3	0	0	0	1	0
Fox, rf	4	0	2	0	1	0
Rogell, ss	4	0	0	0	3	0
Owen, 3b	3	0	0	0	0	0
Rowe, p	3	0	1	0	0	4
Totals	31	0	4	0	27	9

Chicago	2 0 0 0 0 0 0 0 1—3
Detroit	0 0 0 0 0 0 0 0 0—0

Chicago	IP.	H.	R.	ER.	BB.	SO.
Warneke (W)	9	4	0	0	4	1

Detroit	IP.	H.	R.	ER.	BB.	SO.
Rowe (L)	9	7	3	2	0	8

E—Greenberg, Goslin, Rowe. DP—Detroit 1. LOB—Chicago 5, Detroit 8. 2B—Galan, Fox, Rowe. HR—Demaree. SH—Herman, Lindstrom, Cavarretta. PB—Cochrane. U—Moriarty (A.L.), Quigley (N.L.), McGowan (A.L.) and Stark (N.L.). T—1:51. A—47,391.

Game 2

Thursday, October 3, At Detroit

Chicago	AB.	R.	H.	RBI.	PO.	A.
Galan, lf	4	0	0	0	3	1
Herman, 2b	4	0	1	2	2	6
Lindstrom, cf	3	0	0	0	1	0
Hartnett, c	4	0	1	0	4	2
Demaree, rf	4	0	1	0	0	1
Cavarretta, 1b	4	1	0	0	9	0
Hack, 3b	3	0	1	0	2	1
Jurges, ss	3	1	1	1	3	1
Root, p	0	0	0	0	0	0
Henshaw, p	1	0	0	0	0	1
Kowalik, p	2	1	1	0	0	2
aKlein	1	0	0	0	0	0
Totals	33	3	6	3	24	15

Detroit	AB.	R.	H.	RBI.	PO.	A.
White, cf	3	2	1	0	3	0
Cochrane, c	2	1	1	1	2	0
Gehringer, 2b	3	2	2	3	2	5
Greenberg, 1b	3	1	1	2	8	2
Goslin, lf	3	0	0	0	2	0
Fox, rf	4	0	1	1	4	0
Rogell, ss	4	0	2	0	3	2
Owen, 3b	2	1	0	0	2	0
Bridges, p	4	1	1	0	1	2
Totals	28	8	9	7	27	11

Chicago	0 0 0 0 1 0 2 0 0—3
Detroit	4 0 0 3 0 0 1 0 x—8

Chicago	IP.	H.	R.	ER.	BB.	SO.
Root (L)	0*	4	4	4	0	0
Henshaw	3⅔	2	3	3	5	2
Kowalik	4⅓	3	1	1	1	1

Detroit	IP.	H.	R.	ER.	BB.	SO.
Bridges (W)	9	6	3	2	4	2

*Pitched to four batters in first.

aFlied out for Kowalik in ninth. E—Kowalik, Greenberg 2. DP—Chicago 2, Detroit 2. LOB—Chicago 7, Detroit 5. 2B—Cochrane, Rogell, Demaree. HR—Greenberg. SH—Owen. HBP—By Henshaw (Owen), by Kowalik (Greenberg). WP—Henshaw. U—Quigley (N.L.), McGowan (A.L.), Stark (N.L.) and Moriarty (A.L.). T—1:59. A—46,742.

Game 3

Friday, October 4, At Chicago

Detroit	AB.	R.	H.	RBI.	PO.	A.
White, cf	5	1	2	1	5	0
Cochrane, c	5	0	0	0	4	2
Gehringer, 2b	5	1	2	0	4	7
Goslin, lf	5	2	3	2	2	0
Fox, rf	5	1	2	1	0	0
Rogell, ss	5	0	3	1	2	4
Owen, 1b	5	1	0	0	15	0
Clifton, 3b	4	0	0	0	0	5
Auker, p	2	0	0	0	0	2
aWalker	1	0	0	0	0	0
Hogsett, p	0	0	0	0	1	0
Rowe, p	2	0	0	0	0	0
Totals	44	6	12	5	33	20

Chicago	AB.	R.	H.	RBI.	PO.	A.
Galan, lf	4	0	2	2	1	0
Herman, 2b	5	0	1	0	3	2
Lindstrom, cf-3b	5	0	2	0	2	1
Hartnett, c	4	0	0	0	8	3
Demaree, rf-cf	4	1	1	1	2	0
Cavarretta, 1b	5	0	0	0	10	1
Hack, 3b-ss	5	2	2	0	3	2
Jurges, ss	1	1	0	0	3	4
bKlein, rf	2	1	1	0	1	0
Lee, p	1	0	0	1	0	1
Warneke, p	0	0	0	0	0	0
cO'Dea	1	0	1	1	0	0
French, p	0	0	0	0	0	0
dStephenson	1	0	0	0	0	0
Totals	38	5	10	5	33	14

Detroit	0 0 0 0 0 1 0 4 0 0 1—6
Chicago	0 2 0 0 1 0 0 0 2 0 0—5

Detroit	IP.	H.	R.	ER.	BB.	SO.
Auker	6	6	3	2	2	1
Hogsett	1	0	0	0	1	0
Rowe (W)	4	4	2	2	0	3

Chicago	IP.	H.	R.	ER.	BB.	SO.
Lee	7⅓	7	4	4	3	3
Warneke	1⅔	2	1	1	0	2
French (L)	2	3	1	0	0	1

aHit into double play for Auker in seventh. bSingled for Jurges in ninth. cSingled for Warneke in ninth. dStruck out for French in eleventh. E—Cochrane, Clifton, Herman, Lindstrom, Cavarretta. DP—Detroit 2, Chicago 1. LOB—Detroit 8, Chicago 7. 2B—Lindstrom, Gehringer, Goslin. 3B—Fox. HR—Demaree. SB—Hack. SH—Lee 2, Hartnett. HBP—By Hogsett (Jurges). U—McGowan (A.L.), Stark (N.L.), Moriarty (A.L.) and Quigley (N.L.). T—2:27. A—45,532.

Game 4

Saturday, October 5, At Chicago

Detroit	AB.	R.	H.	RBI.	PO.	A.
White, cf	3	0	1	0	0	0
Cochrane, c	4	0	1	0	6	0
Gehringer, 2b	4	0	2	1	3	3
Goslin, lf	3	0	1	0	1	0
Fox, rf	5	0	1	0	0	0
Rogell, ss	3	0	0	0	2	2
Owen, 1b	4	0	0	0	13	1
Clifton, 3b	4	1	0	0	0	4
Crowder, p	3	1	1	0	2	2
Totals	33	2	7	1	27	12

Chicago	AB.	R.	H.	RBI.	PO.	A.
Galan, lf	4	0	0	0	2	0
Herman, 2b	4	0	1	0	4	1
Lindstrom, cf	4	0	0	0	3	0
Hartnett, c	4	1	1	1	7	0
Demaree, rf	4	0	1	0	4	0
Cavarretta, 1b	4	0	2	0	3	1
Hack, 3b	4	0	0	0	0	0
Jurges, ss	1	0	0	0	4	2
Carleton, p	1	0	0	0	0	2
aKlein	1	0	0	0	0	0
Root, p	0	0	0	0	0	1
Totals	31	1	5	1	27	7

Detroit	0 0 1 0 0 1 0 0 0—2
Chicago	0 1 0 0 0 0 0 0 0—1

Detroit	IP.	H.	R.	ER.	BB.	SO.
Crowder (W)	9	5	1	1	3	5

Chicago	IP.	H.	R.	ER.	BB.	SO.
Carleton (L)	7	6	2	1	7	4
Root	2	1	0	0	1	2

aGrounded out for Carleton in seventh. E—Galan, Jurges. DP—Detroit 1, Chicago 1. LOB—Detroit 13, Chicago 6. 2B—Fox, Gehringer, Herman. HR—Hartnett. SB—Gehringer. SH—Gehringer. Balk—Carleton. U—Stark (N.L.), Moriarty (A.L.), Quigley (N.L.) and McGowan (A.L.). T—2:28. A—49,350.

Game 5

Sunday, October 6, At Chicago

Detroit	AB.	R.	H.	RBI.	PO.	A.
White, cf	4	0	0	0	4	0
Cochrane, c	4	0	2	0	5	0
Gehringer, 2b	4	1	1	0	2	2
Goslin, lf	3	0	1	0	4	0
Fox, rf	4	0	2	1	0	1
Rogell, ss	4	0	0	0	1	1
Owen, 1b	3	0	0	0	5	4
aWalker	1	0	0	0	0	0
Clifton, 3b	3	0	0	0	0	0
Rowe, p	3	0	1	0	3	1
Totals	33	1	7	1	24	9

Chicago	AB.	R.	H.	RBI.	PO.	A.
Galan, lf	4	1	0	0	2	0
Herman, 2b	4	1	2	1	3	3
Klein, rf	4	1	2	2	3	0
Hartnett, c	4	0	1	0	4	0
Demaree, cf	4	0	1	0	1	0
Cavarretta, 1b	4	0	0	0	11	1
Hack, 3b	2	0	0	0	0	0
Jurges, ss	3	0	1	0	1	4
Warneke, p	2	0	1	0	1	1
Lee, p	0	0	0	0	1	0
Totals	31	3	8	3	27	9

Detroit	0 0 0 0 0 0 0 0 1—1
Chicago	0 0 2 0 0 0 1 0 x—3

Detroit	IP.	H.	R.	ER.	BB.	SO.
Rowe (L)	8	8	3	2	1	3

Chicago	IP.	H.	R.	ER.	BB.	SO.
Warneke (W)	6	3	0	0	0	2
Lee	3	4	1	1	2	2

aGrounded out for Owen in ninth. E—Owen. DP—Chicago 1. LOB—Detroit 7, Chicago 6. 2B—Herman. 3B—Herman. HR—Klein. SH—Lee. U—Moriarty (A.L.), Quigley (N.L.), McGowan (A.L.) and Stark (N.L.). T—1:49. A—49,237.

Game 6

Monday, October 7, At Detroit

Chicago	AB.	R.	H.	RBI.	PO.	A.
Galan, lf	5	0	1	0	2	0
Herman, 2b	4	1	3	3	3	4
Klein, rf	4	0	1	0	0	0
Hartnett, c	4	0	2	0	9	1
Demaree, cf	4	0	0	0	0	0
Cavarretta, 1b	4	0	1	0	8	0
Hack, 3b	4	0	2	0	0	4
Jurges, ss	4	1	1	0	3	2
French, p	4	1	1	0	1	2
Totals	37	3	12	3	26	13

Detroit	AB.	R.	H.	RBI.	PO.	A.
Clifton, 3b	5	0	0	0	2	0
Cochrane, c	5	2	3	0	7	0
Gehringer, 2b	5	0	2	0	0	4
Goslin, lf	5	0	1	1	2	0
Fox, rf	4	0	2	1	3	1
Walker, cf	2	1	1	0	0	0
Rogell, ss	4	1	2	0	2	3
Owen, 1b	3	0	1	1	11	0
Bridges, p	4	0	0	1	0	3
Totals	37	4	12	4	27	11

Chicago	0 0 1 0 2 0 0 0 0—3
Detroit	1 0 0 1 0 1 0 0 1—4

Two out when winning run scored.

Chicago	IP.	H.	R.	ER.	BB.	SO.
French (L)	8⅔	12	4	4	2	7

Detroit	IP.	H.	R.	ER.	BB.	SO.
Bridges (W)	9	12	3	3	0	7

E—Fox. DP—Detroit 1. LOB—Chicago 7, Detroit 10. 2B—Fox, Gehringer, Rogell, Hack. 3B—Hack. HR—Herman. SH—Walker. U—Quigley (N.L.), McGowan (A.L.), Stark (N.L.) and Moriarty (A.L.). T—1:57. A—48,420.

COMPOSITE BATTING AVERAGES

Detroit Tigers

Player-Position	G.	AB.	R.	H.	2B.	3B.	HR.	RBI.	BA.
Fox, rf	6	26	1	10	3	1	0	4	.385
Gehringer, 2b	6	24	4	9	3	0	0	4	.375
Crowder, p	1	3	1	1	0	0	0	0	.333
Cochrane, c	6	24	3	7	1	0	0	1	.292
Rogell, ss	6	24	1	7	2	0	0	1	.292
Goslin, lf	6	22	2	6	1	0	0	3	.273
White, cf	5	19	3	5	0	0	0	1	.263
Rowe, p	3	8	0	2	1	0	0	0	.250
Walker, ph-cf	3	4	1	1	0	0	0	0	.250
Greenberg, 1b	2	6	1	1	0	0	1	2	.167
Bridges, p	2	8	1	1	0	0	0	1	.125
Owen, 3b-1b	6	20	2	1	0	0	0	1	.050
Clifton, 3b	4	16	1	0	0	0	0	0	.000
Auker, p	1	2	0	0	0	0	0	0	.000
Hogsett, p	1	0	0	0	0	0	0	0	.000
Totals	6	206	21	51	11	1	1	18	.248

Chicago Cubs

Player-Position	G.	AB.	R.	H.	2B.	3B.	HR.	RBI.	BA.
O'Dea, ph	1	1	0	1	0	0	0	1	1.000
Kowalik, p	1	2	1	1	0	0	0	0	.500
Herman, 2b	6	24	3	8	2	1	1	6	.333
Klein, ph-rf	5	12	2	4	0	0	1	2	.333
Hartnett, c	6	24	1	7	0	0	1	2	.292
Demaree, rf-cf	6	24	2	6	1	0	2	2	.250
French, p	2	4	1	1	0	0	0	0	.250
Jurges, ss	6	16	3	4	0	0	0	1	.250
Hack, 3b-ss	6	22	2	5	1	1	0	0	.227
Lindstrom, cf-3b	4	15	0	3	1	0	0	0	.200
Warneke, p	3	5	0	1	0	0	0	0	.200
Galan, lf	6	25	2	4	1	0	0	2	.160
Cavarretta, 1b	6	24	1	3	0	0	0	0	.125
Root, p	2	0	0	0	0	0	0	0	.000
Henshaw, p	1	1	0	0	0	0	0	0	.000
Lee, p	2	1	0	0	0	0	0	1	.000
Stephenson, ph	1	1	0	0	0	0	0	0	.000
Carleton, p	1	1	0	0	0	0	0	0	.000
Totals	6	202	18	48	6	2	5	17	.238

COMPOSITE PITCHING AVERAGES

Detroit Tigers

Pitcher	G.	IP.	H.	R.	ER.	BB.	SO.	W.	L.	ERA.
Hogsett	1	1	0	0	0	1	0	0	0	0.00
Crowder	1	9	5	1	1	3	5	1	0	1.00
Bridges	2	18	18	6	5	4	9	2	0	2.50
Rowe	3	21	19	8	6	1	14	1	2	2.57
Auker	1	6	6	3	2	2	1	0	0	3.00
Totals	6	55	48	18	14	11	29	4	2	2.29

Chicago Cubs

Pitcher	G.	IP.	H.	R.	ER.	BB.	SO.	W.	L.	ERA.
Warneke	3	16⅔	9	1	1	4	5	2	0	0.54
Carleton	1	7	6	2	1	7	4	0	1	1.29
Kowalik	1	4⅓	3	1	1	1	1	0	0	2.08
French	2	10⅔	15	5	4	2	8	0	2	3.38
Lee	2	10⅓	11	5	4	5	5	0	0	3.48
Henshaw	1	3⅔	2	3	3	5	2	0	0	7.36
Root	2	2	5	4	4	1	2	0	1	18.00
Totals	6	54⅔	51	21	18	25	27	2	4	2.96

1936
NEW YORK YANKEES
VS.
NEW YORK GIANTS

The 1936 World Series was the first fall classic involving the New York Yankees in which the Yanks did not have outfielder George Herman Ruth on their roster.

A promising development for the opposition, eh? On the surface, perhaps. It should be quickly noted, however, that the '36 Series also was the first in which the Yanks *did* have outfielder Joseph Paul DiMaggio on their roster.

Accordingly, 1936 was notable as a period of transition. But before long, the year also would prove notable because it marked the beginning of unprecedented World Series dominance. To the surprise of few, it would be the Yankees who would do the dominating.

Babe Ruth had played the last of his 15 seasons with the Yankees in 1934, two years after the Yanks' most recent appearance in the Series. Joe DiMaggio had joined the Yankees in 1936, and as a rookie he helped New York to a 19½-game victory margin in the American League pennant race by slamming 29 home runs, driving in 125 runs and batting .323.

The Yankees' return to the World Series coincided with the New York Giants' re-emergence as National League champions. And while the Giants did not have the joy ride to the pennant that the Yankees experienced — Bill Terry's team finished on top by five games — they did have a meal ticket. His name was Carl Hubbell.

At age 33, Hubbell put together an amazing season. The lefthanded pitcher won his last 16 decisions, boosting his final record to 26-6. His earned-run average was 2.31.

Hubbell, naturally, was Terry's nominee to start Game 1 of the Series. Yankees Manager Joe Mc-

A pair of aces, Giants star Carl Hubbell (left) and Yankee star Lefty Gomez, pose for photographers during the 1936 Series.

Carthy chose 20-game winner Red Ruffing.

Yanks left fielder Jake Powell, obtained from Washington in a mid-June trade, solved Hubbell for base hits in his first three trips to the plate. George Selkirk, who had replaced Ruth in right field for the American Leaguers,

clubbed a third-inning home run off the screwball-throwing veteran. Beyond that, however, little more need be said. Hubbell allowed only seven hits overall and struck out eight batters. Incredibly, not one of King Carl's outfielders was called upon to catch a fly ball. The Giants, getting a

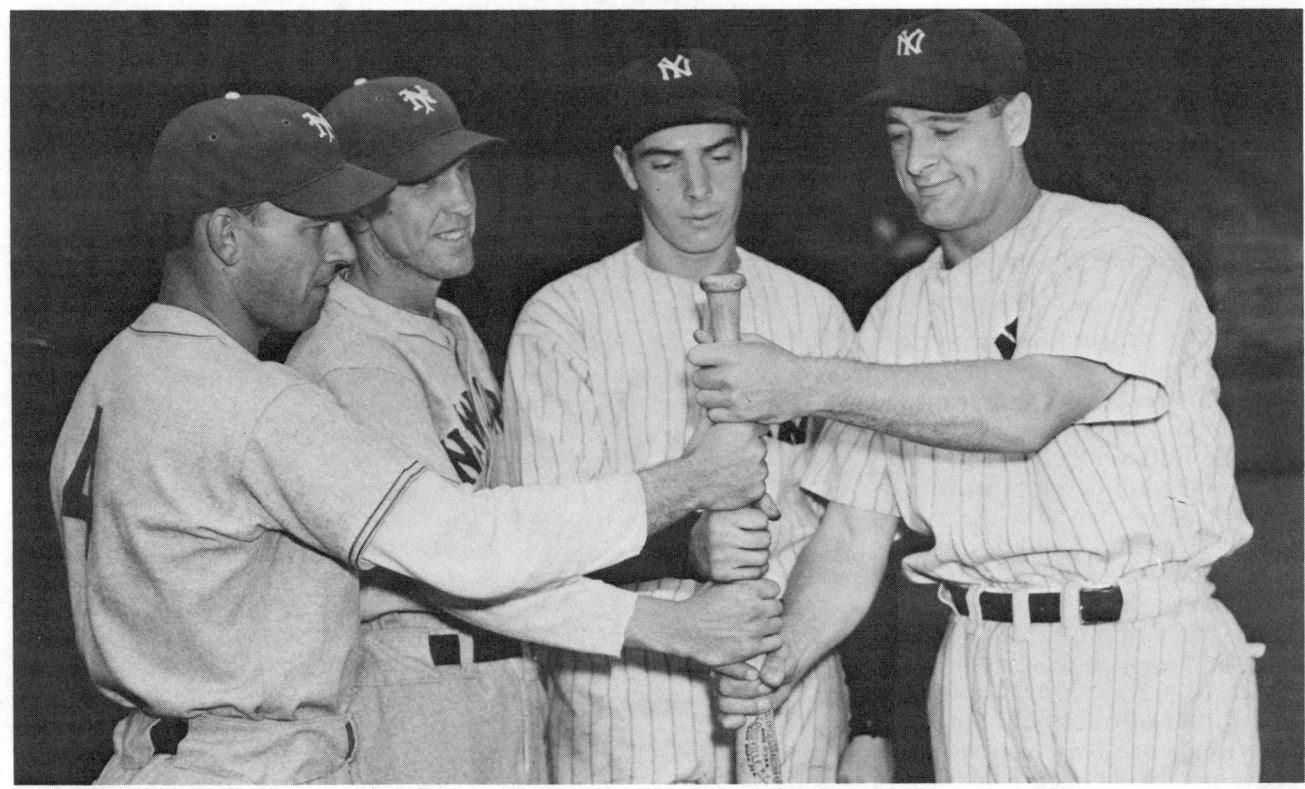

New York Giant stars Mel Ott (left) and Joe Moore enjoy a light moment with 1936 World Series oppo- **nents Joe DiMaggio and Lou Gehrig (right) of the New York Yankees.**

game-tying homer from shortstop Dick Bartell in the fifth, another run in the sixth and four more in the eighth, notched a 6-1 victory.

The Yankees proceeded to win four of the next five games, starting and ending the run with furious assaults on the Giants' pitching staff. In Game 2, the Yanks cuffed Hal Schumacher and four relievers for a total of 17 hits—including a bases-loaded home run by Tony Lazzeri, only the second grand slam in Series history. All nine Yankees had at least one hit and scored at least one run in the 18-4 laugher, with Lazzeri and Bill Dickey each driving in five runs. The next day, McCarthy's men did it with finesse. Trade acquisition Bump Hadley, with ninth-inning relief from Pat Malone, was a 2-1 winner as shortstop Frankie Crosetti delivered the tie-breaking hit in the eighth.

Hubbell, unaccustomed to defeat, received a taste of same in Game 4. He allowed four Yankee runs—two coming on Lou Gehrig's second homer in two days—in the first three innings and suffered a 5-2 setback at the hands of Monte Pearson and the

Yanks. Pearson, obtained from Cleveland after the 1935 season, had won 19 regular-season games for McCarthy's club.

On the brink of elimination, the Giants stayed alive with a 5-4, 10-inning victory in Game 5. The winning run scored on a fly ball hit by Giants Manager Terry, who was appearing in what turned out to be the next-to-last game of his major league playing career.

Elimination did come to the Giants the next afternoon. Powell homered and knocked in four runs, and he, Lazzeri, DiMaggio and Red Rolfe all collected three hits as the Yankees wrapped up matters with a 13-5 romp. Lefty Gomez, the beneficiary of a 17-hit Yankee offensive for the second time in the Series (he went the distance in Game 2), did not coast in Game 6 despite the final score. He left the contest in the seventh inning in favor of Johnny Murphy and held only a 5-4 lead at the time. But he remained the pitcher of record as the Yankees traded runs with the Giants in the eighth and then went on a seven-run onslaught in the ninth.

The Yankees pounded out 65

hits overall, with Powell and Rolfe—.455 and .400 hitters, respectively—collecting 10 each. DiMaggio batted .346. Gehrig was his usual productive self, knocking in seven runs and boosting his career RBI total in Series play to 31 in 25 games.

The Giants had their moments, the biggest of which came in the first game when Hubbell's wizardry enabled them to halt the Yankees' Series winning streak at 12 games. But as evidenced in Games 2 and 6 in particular and in the other contests in general, Terry's men were up against an irresistible force. And this was a force that was just beginning to assert itself in the World Series.

Game 1

Wednesday, September 30, At Polo Grounds

Yankees	AB.	R.	H.	RBI.	PO.	A.
Crosetti, ss	4	0	1	0	1	3
Rolfe, 3b	3	0	1	0	2	1
DiMaggio, cf	4	0	1	0	3	0
Gehrig, 1b	3	0	0	0	7	0
Dickey, c	4	0	0	0	8	0
Powell, lf	4	0	3	0	2	0
Lazzeri, 2b	3	0	0	0	1	2
Selkirk, rf	4	1	1	1	0	0
Ruffing, p	3	0	0	0	0	1
Totals	32	1	7	1	24	7
Giants	AB.	R.	H.	RBI.	PO.	A.
Moore, lf	5	0	0	0	0	0
Bartell, ss	4	1	2	1	1	2
Terry, 1b	4	1	2	0	12	2
Ott, rf	2	2	2	0	0	0
Ripple, cf	2	0	0	0	0	0
Mancuso, c	3	1	1	1	9	1

	AB.	R.	H.	RBI.	PO.	A.
Whitehead, 2b	3	1	0	1	3	4
Jackson, 3b	4	0	0	1	1	1
Hubbell, p	4	0	2	1	1	2
Totals	31	6	9	5	27	12

Yankees	0 0 1 0 0 0 0 0 0—1
Giants	0 0 0 0 1 1 0 4 x—6

Yankees	IP.	H.	R.	ER.	BB.	SO.
Ruffing (L)	8	9	6	4	4	5

Giants	IP.	H.	R.	ER.	BB.	SO.
Hubbell (W)	9	7	1	1	1	8

E—Crosetti, Dickey, Hubbell. DP—Giants 1. LOB—Yankees 7, Giants 7. 2B—Ott, Crosetti, Powell. HR—Bartell, Selkirk. SH—Ripple 2, Rolfe. HBP—By Hubbell (Gehrig). U—Pfirman (N.L.), Geisel (A.L.), Magerkurth (N.L.) and Summers (A.L.). T—2:40. A—39,419.

Game 2

Friday, October 2, At Polo Grounds

Yankees	AB.	R.	H.	RBI.	PO.	A.
Crosetti, ss	5	4	3	0	0	1
Rolfe, 3b	4	3	2	1	2	0
DiMaggio, cf	5	2	3	2	6	0
Gehrig, 1b	5	1	2	3	6	0
Dickey, c	5	3	2	5	8	0
Selkirk, rf	5	1	1	0	2	0
Powell, lf	3	2	2	0	2	0
Lazzeri, 2b	4	1	1	5	1	3
Gomez, p	5	1	1	2	0	0
Totals	41	18	17	18	27	4

Giants	AB.	R.	H.	RBI.	PO.	A.
Moore, lf	5	0	0	0	2	0
Bartell, ss	3	0	1	1	2	2
Terry, 1b	5	0	2	2	6	1
Leiber, cf	4	0	0	0	7	1
Ott, rf	4	0	0	0	4	0
Mancuso, c	2	2	1	0	3	2
Whitehead, 2b	4	0	0	0	2	1
Jackson, 3b	4	1	1	0	0	2
Schumacher, p	0	0	0	0	0	0
Smith, p	0	0	0	0	0	0
Coffman, p	0	0	0	0	0	1
aDavis	1	1	1	0	0	0
Gabler, p	0	0	0	0	1	0
bDanning	1	0	0	0	0	0
Gumbert, p	0	0	0	0	0	0
Totals	33	4	6	3	27	10

Yankees	2 0 7 0 0 1 2 0 6—18
Giants	0 1 0 3 0 0 0 0 0— 4

Yankees	IP.	H.	R.	ER.	BB.	SO.
Gomez (W)	9	6	4	4	7	8

Giants	IP.	H.	R.	ER.	BB.	SO.
Schumacher (L)	2*	3	5	4	4	1
Smith	⅓	2	3	3	1	0
Coffman	1⅔	2	1	1	0	1
Gabler	4	5	3	3	3	0
Gumbert	1	5	6	6	1	1

*Pitched to three batters in third.

aSingled for Coffman in fourth. bStruck out for Gabler in eighth. E—Jackson. DP—Giants 1. LOB—Yankees 6, Giants 9. 2B—Bartell, Mancuso, DiMaggio. HR—Dickey, Lazzeri. SB—Powell. SH—DiMaggio. WP—Schumacher, Gomez. U—Geisel (A.L.), Magerkurth (N.L.), Summers (A.L.) and Pfirman (N.L.). T—2:49. A—43,543.

Game 3

Saturday, October 3, At Yankee Stadium

Giants	AB.	R.	H.	RBI.	PO.	A.
Moore, lf	5	0	1	0	2	0
Bartell, ss	3	0	1	0	0	1
Terry, 1b	4	0	1	0	5	1
Ott, rf	4	0	2	0	4	0
Ripple, cf	4	1	1	1	2	0
Mancuso, c	4	0	1	0	7	0
Whitehead, 2b	4	0	0	0	3	4
Jackson, 3b	2	0	1	0	0	1
cKoenig	1	0	0	0	0	0
Fitzsimmons, p	3	0	2	0	1	1
dLeslie	1	0	1	0	0	0
eDavis	0	0	0	0	0	0
Totals	35	1	11	1	24	8

Yankees	AB.	R.	H.	RBI.	PO.	A.
Crosetti, ss	4	0	1	1	4	5
Rolfe, 3b	4	0	0	0	3	1
DiMaggio, cf	3	0	1	0	2	0
Gehrig, 1b	3	1	1	1	10	1
Dickey, c	2	0	0	0	3	2
Selkirk, rf	3	0	1	0	2	0
Powell, lf	2	1	0	0	1	0
Lazzeri, 2b	2	0	0	0	2	2
Hadley, p	2	0	0	0	0	3
aRuffing	1	0	0	0	0	0
bJohnson	0	0	0	0	0	0
Malone, p	0	0	0	0	0	0
Totals	26	2	4	2	27	14

Giants	0 0 0 0 1 0 0 0 0—1
Yankees	0 1 0 0 0 0 0 1 x—2

Giants	IP.	H.	R.	ER.	BB.	SO.
Fitzsimmons (L)	8	4	2	2	2	5

Yankees	IP.	H.	R.	ER.	BB.	SO.
Hadley (W)	8	10	1	1	1	2
Malone	1	1	0	0	0	1

aForced runner for Hadley in eighth. bRan for Ruffing in eighth. cGrounded out for Jackson in ninth. dSingled for Fitzsimmons in ninth. eRan for Leslie in ninth. DP—Giants 1, Yankees 1. LOB—Giants 9, Yankees 3. 2B—DiMaggio. HR—Gehrig, Ripple. SH—Lazzeri, Bartell. U—Magerkurth (N.L.), Summers (A.L.), Pfirman (N.L.) and Geisel (A.L.). T—2:01. A—64,842.

Game 4

Sunday, October 4, At Yankee Stadium

Giants	AB.	R.	H.	RBI.	PO.	A.
Moore, lf	3	0	1	0	2	0
Bartell, ss	4	1	1	0	3	4
Terry, 1b	3	0	0	1	10	1
Ott, rf	4	0	0	0	0	0
Ripple, cf	4	0	2	1	3	0
Mancuso, c	4	0	0	0	3	0
Whitehead, 2b	3	0	0	0	2	5
cKoenig	1	0	1	0	0	0
Jackson, 3b	4	0	1	0	0	3
Hubbell, p	2	0	0	0	1	0
aLeslie	1	0	1	0	0	0
bDavis	0	1	0	0	0	0
Gabler, p	0	0	0	0	0	0
Totals	33	2	7	2	24	13

Yankees	AB.	R.	H.	RBI.	PO.	A.
Crosetti, ss	4	1	2	0	4	1
Rolfe, 3b	3	1	2	1	1	2
DiMaggio, cf	4	0	0	0	1	0
Gehrig, 1b	4	2	2	2	7	0
Dickey, c	4	0	0	0	8	2
Powell, lf	4	1	1	1	2	0
Lazzeri, 2b	4	0	0	0	3	4
Selkirk, rf	3	0	1	1	0	0
Pearson, p	4	0	2	0	1	2
Totals	34	5	10	5	27	11

Giants	0 0 0 1 0 0 0 1 0—2
Yankees	0 1 3 0 0 0 0 1 x—5

Giants	IP.	H.	R.	ER.	BB.	SO.
Hubbell (L)	7	8	4	3	1	2
Gabler	1	2	1	1	1	0

Yankees	IP.	H.	R.	ER.	BB.	SO.
Pearson (W)	9	7	2	2	2	7

aSingled for Hubbell in eighth. bRan for Leslie in eighth. cSingled for Whitehead in ninth. E—Jackson, Selkirk. DP—Giants 1. LOB—Giants 6, Yankees 7. 2B—Crosetti, Gehrig, Pearson. HR—Gehrig. WP—Hubbell. U—Summers (A.L.), Pfirman (N.L.), Geisel (A.L.) and Magerkurth (N.L.). T—2:12. A—66,669.

Game 5

Monday, October 5, At Yankee Stadium

Giants	AB.	R.	H.	RBI.	PO.	A.
Moore, lf	5	2	2	0	1	0
Bartell, ss	4	1	1	1	2	2
Terry, 1b	5	0	0	1	6	2
Ott, rf	5	1	1	0	1	0
Ripple, cf	2	1	1	1	2	0
Mancuso, c	3	0	2	0	14	2
Whitehead, 2b	4	0	1	1	3	4
Jackson, 3b	4	0	0	0	1	1
Schumacher, p	4	0	0	0	0	2
Totals	36	5	8	4	30	13

Yankees	AB.	R.	H.	RBI.	PO.	A.
Crosetti, ss	5	0	0	1	2	3
Rolfe, 3b	5	0	2	0	3	1
DiMaggio, cf	4	0	1	0	4	0
Gehrig, 1b	4	0	1	0	5	1
Dickey, c	5	0	1	0	8	0
bSeeds	0	0	0	0	0	0
Selkirk, rf	4	2	2	1	2	0
Powell, lf	4	1	1	0	2	0
Lazzeri, 2b	3	1	1	1	3	1
Ruffing, p	1	0	0	0	1	2
aJohnson	1	0	0	0	0	0
Malone, p	1	0	1	0	0	2
Totals	37	4	10	3	30	10

Giants	3 0 0 0 0 1 0 0 0 1—5
Yankees	0 1 1 0 0 2 0 0 0 0—4

Giants	IP.	H.	R.	ER.	BB.	SO.
Schumacher (W)	10	10	4	3	6	10

Yankees	IP.	H.	R.	ER.	BB.	SO.
Ruffing	6	7	4	3	1	7
Malone (L)	4	1	1	1	1	1

aStruck out for Ruffing in sixth. bRan for Dickey in tenth. E—Bartell, Ott, Jackson, Crosetti. DP—Giants 3, Yankees 1. LOB—Giants 5, Yankees 9. 2B—Moore 2, Bartell, Mancuso, DiMaggio. HR—Selkirk. SH—Bartell, Mancuso. WP—Schumacher. U—Pfirman (N.L.), Geisel (A.L.), Magerkurth (N.L.) and Summers (A.L.). T—2:45. A—50,024.

Game 6

Tuesday, October 6, At Polo Grounds

Yankees	AB.	R.	H.	RBI.	PO.	A.
Crosetti, ss	4	0	0	1	0	1
Rolfe, 3b	6	1	3	2	3	2
DiMaggio, cf	6	1	3	1	2	0
Gehrig, 1b	5	1	1	1	10	0
Dickey, c	5	2	0	0	3	0
Selkirk, rf	5	2	2	0	3	0
Powell, lf	5	3	3	4	3	0
Lazzeri, 2b	4	2	3	1	3	5
Gomez, p	3	0	1	1	0	3
Murphy, p	2	1	1	1	0	0
Totals	45	13	17	12	27	11

Giants	AB.	R.	H.	RBI.	PO.	A.
Moore, lf	5	2	2	1	2	0
Bartell, ss	3	2	2	0	0	2
Terry, 1b	4	0	1	1	6	0
Leiber, cf	2	0	0	0	6	0
Mayo, 3b	1	0	0	0	0	0
Ott, rf	4	1	2	3	3	0
Mancuso, c	3	0	0	0	4	0
aLeslie	1	0	0	0	0	0
Danning, c	1	0	0	0	3	0
Whitehead, 2b	3	0	0	0	1	2
bRipple, cf	0	0	0	0	1	0
Jackson, 3b	3	0	1	0	0	0
cKoenig, 2b	1	0	0	0	1	0
Fitzsimmons, p	1	0	0	0	0	1
Castleman, p	2	0	1	0	0	0
dDavis	1	0	0	0	0	0
Coffman, p	0	0	0	0	0	0
Gumbert, p	0	0	0	0	0	0
Totals	35	5	9	5	27	5

Yankees	0 2 1 2 0 0 0 1 7—13
Giants	2 0 0 0 1 0 1 1 0— 5

Yankees	IP.	H.	R.	ER.	BB.	SO.
Gomez (W)	6⅓	8	4	4	4	1
Murphy	2⅔	1	1	1	1	1

Giants	IP.	H.	R.	ER.	BB.	SO.
Fitzsimmons (L)	3⅔	9	5	5	0	1
Castleman	4⅓	3	1	1	2	5
Coffman	0*	3	5	5	1	0
Gumbert	1	2	2	2	3	1

*Pitched to five batters in ninth.

aFouled out for Mancuso in seventh. bWalked for Whitehead in seventh. cStruck out for Jackson in seventh. dFlied out for Castleman in eighth. E—Rolfe, DiMaggio, Danning. LOB—Yankees 11, Giants 10. 2B—Bartell, Ott, Powell. 3B—Selkirk. HR—Moore, Ott, Powell. SH—Terry, Leiber. U—Geisel (A.L.), Magerkurth (N.L.), Summers (A.L.) and Pfirman (N.L.). T—2:50. A—38,427.

COMPOSITE BATTING AVERAGES

New York Yankees

Player-Position	G.	AB.	R.	H.	2B.	3B.	HR.	RBI.	BA.
Malone, p	2	1	0	1	0	0	0	0	1.000
Pearson, p	1	4	0	2	1	0	0	0	.500
Murphy, p	1	2	1	1	0	0	0	1	.500
Powell, lf	6	22	8	10	1	0	1	5	.455
Rolfe, 3b	6	25	5	10	0	0	0	4	.400
DiMaggio, cf	6	26	3	9	3	0	0	3	.346
Selkirk, rf	6	24	6	8	0	1	2	3	.333
Gehrig, 1b	6	24	5	7	1	0	2	7	.292
Crosetti, ss	6	26	5	7	2	0	0	3	.269
Lazzeri, 2b	6	20	4	5	0	0	1	7	.250
Gomez, p	2	8	1	2	0	0	0	3	.250
Dickey, c	6	25	5	3	0	0	1	5	.120
Ruffing, p-ph	3	5	0	0	0	0	0	0	.000
Johnson, pr-ph	2	1	0	0	0	0	0	0	.000
Hadley, p	1	2	0	0	0	0	0	0	.000
Seeds, pr	1	0	0	0	0	0	0	0	.000
Totals	6	215	43	65	8	1	7	41	.302

New York Giants

Player-Position	G.	AB.	R.	H.	2B.	3B.	HR.	RBI.	BA.
Leslie, ph	3	3	0	2	0	0	0	0	.667
Castleman, p	1	2	0	1	0	0	0	0	.500
Fitzsimmons, p	2	4	0	2	0	0	0	0	.500
Davis, ph-pr	4	2	2	1	0	0	0	0	.500
Bartell, ss	6	21	5	8	3	0	1	3	.381
Hubbell, p	2	6	0	2	0	0	0	1	.333
Koenig, ph-2b	3	3	0	1	0	0	0	0	.333
Ripple, cf-ph	5	12	2	4	0	0	1	3	.333
Ott, rf	6	23	4	7	2	0	1	3	.304
Mancuso, c	6	19	3	5	2	0	0	1	.263
Terry, 1b	6	25	1	6	0	0	0	5	.240
Moore, lf	6	28	4	6	2	0	1	1	.214
Jackson, 3b	6	21	1	4	0	0	0	1	.190
Whitehead, 2b	6	21	1	1	0	0	0	2	.048
Leiber, cf	2	6	0	0	0	0	0	0	.000
Schumacher, p	2	4	0	0	0	0	0	0	.000
Smith, p	1	0	0	0	0	0	0	0	.000
Coffman, p	2	0	0	0	0	0	0	0	.000
Gabler, p	2	0	0	0	0	0	0	0	.000
Danning, ph-c	2	2	0	0	0	0	0	0	.000
Gumbert, p	2	0	0	0	0	0	0	0	.000
Mayo, 3b	1	1	0	0	0	0	0	0	.000
Totals	6	203	23	50	9	0	4	20	.246

COMPOSITE PITCHING AVERAGES

New York Yankees

Pitcher	G.	IP.	H.	R.	ER.	BB.	SO.	W.	L.	ERA.
Hadley	1	8	10	1	1	1	2	1	0	1.12
Malone	2	5	2	1	1	1	2	0	1	1.80
Pearson	1	9	7	2	2	2	7	1	0	2.00
Murphy	1	2⅔	1	1	1	1	1	0	0	3.38
Ruffing	2	14	16	10	7	5	12	0	1	4.50
Gomez	2	15⅓	14	8	8	11	9	2	0	4.70
Totals	6	54	50	23	20	21	33	4	2	3.33

New York Giants

Pitcher	G.	IP.	H.	R.	ER.	BB.	SO.	W.	L.	ERA.
Castleman	1	4⅓	3	1	1	2	5	0	0	2.08
Hubbell	2	16	15	5	4	2	10	1	1	2.25
Schum'er	2	12	13	9	7	10	11	1	1	5.25
Fitzsimmons	2	11⅔	13	7	7	2	6	0	2	5.40
Gabler	2	5	7	4	4	4	0	0	0	7.20
Coffman	2	1⅔	5	6	6	1	1	0	0	32.40
Gumbert	2	2	7	8	8	4	2	0	0	36.00
Smith	1	⅓	2	3	3	1	0	0	0	81.00
Totals	6	53	65	43	40	26	35	2	4	6.79

Just how good were these New York Yankees, anyway?

Good enough to win 102 games for the second straight season. Good enough to run away with the American League pennant for the second year in a row. And good enough to make even shorter work of the crosstown-rival New York Giants in the World Series.

Oh, Joe McCarthy's 1937 Yankees fell short of the 1936 club's exploits in a couple areas. A.L. champions by 19½ games in '36, the Yanks had to settle for a mere 13-game margin in '37. And whereas the Yanks boasted five—count 'em, five—100-RBI men in '36 in Lou Gehrig, Joe DiMaggio, Tony Lazzeri, Bill Dickey and George Selkirk, they had only three in '37. But what numbers those three players put up. The incomparable DiMaggio drove in 167 runs, Gehrig totaled 159 RBIs and Dickey finished with 133—an amazing total of 459.

The Yankees had the horses, all right. And you could start with the Iron Horse, Gehrig, who enjoyed his last magnificent season in the major leagues before an insidious disease began to take its toll on his career and, soon, his life. Gehrig batted .351 and walloped 37 home runs. DiMaggio hit .346 with 46 homers, while Dickey finished at .332 and smacked 29 homers. Selkirk produced at a frantic pace that would have placed him in the DiMaggio-Gehrig-Dickey stratosphere—18 homers and 68 RBIs in just 78 games—but missed half the season because of injuries.

Beyond their big boppers, the Yankees also had the American League's only two 20-game winners in Lefty Gomez (21-11) and Red Ruffing (20-7) and a standout relief pitcher in Johnny Murphy,

who recorded 12 victories while coming out of the bullpen and 13 overall.

Bill Terry's National League-winning Giants boasted two 20-game winners of their own, but Terry's club lacked the thump of the Yankees. Carl Hubbell reached the 20-victory mark for the fifth consecutive season, fashioning a 22-8 record, and rookie Cliff Melton burst upon the scene with a 20-9 ledger. But only Mel Ott provided Yankee-type power, belting 31 homers and knocking in 95 runs.

Hubbell and the Giants were coasting along with a 1-0 lead over the vaunted Yanks entering the bottom of the sixth of Game 1 of the '37 Series. Before the inning was over, though, the Yankees had flexed their muscle and struck for seven runs. DiMaggio and Selkirk each poked bases-loaded singles in the uprising, during which notoriously poor hitter Gomez drew two walks. The Yanks, who got a bases-empty home run from Lazzeri in the eighth and six-hit pitching from Gomez, were 8-1 winners.

The next day, Melton and the Giants carried a 1-0 edge into the last of the fifth inning. This time, the Yankees struck for two runs —the second scoring on pitcher Ruffing's single. Ruffing then drilled a two-run double in the American Leaguers' four-run sixth, and the Yankees were on their way to a second consecutive 8-1 triumph. Ruffing yielded seven hits and, besides benefiting from his own batting prowess, received three-RBI offensive support from Selkirk.

The Yankees continued on their merry way in Game 3 as Monte Pearson, getting last-out relief help from Murphy in the ninth inning after the Giants had

loaded the bases, emerged as a 5-1 victor.

The big inning, so much a trademark of the Yankees, came into play again in Game 4 as the Yanks went for their fourth sweep in their last five World Series appearances. In a turnabout-is-fair-play scenario, though, it was Terry's team that set off the offensive fireworks that resulted in six second-inning runs. Center fielder Hank Leiber got things going with a base hit and then capped the outburst with a two-run single. With Hubbell capably handling the Giants' pitching chores that afternoon, the N.L. champions were in good shape. At least for one day. The Giants went on to record a 7-3 victory, as Hubbell threw a six-hitter. In the ninth, the last inning he ever pitched in World Series competition, Hubbell allowed a home run to Gehrig. The one-out drive proved to be Gehrig's last homer in Series play.

In Game 5, Myril Hoag whacked a second-inning homer for the Yanks and DiMaggio connected in the top of the third, but Ott got the runs back for the Giants with a two-run shot in the last of the third. Then, in the fifth, Lazzeri hit a leadoff triple and scored on Gomez's single off the glove of Giants second baseman Burgess Whitehead. Two outs later, Gehrig doubled home Gomez. It was now 4-2, Yankees, and that's the way the game and World Series would end as Gomez pushed his career Series record to 5-0.

The powerful New York Yankees were World Series titlists for a record sixth time, breaking the championship mark they had shared with the Philadelphia Athletics.

That the Yankees were hardly

pressed in this Series despite batting only .249 wasn't exactly reassuring news to the National League, whose member teams must have wondered what fate might possibly await them if the Yanks were playing at peak efficiency. The senior league's worst fears soon were realized: Its next two World Series representatives found the going even more difficult against McCarthy's athletes. Yes, even tougher than the four games-to-one humiliation that the New York Giants were forced to endure in 1937.

Game 1

Wednesday, October 6, At Yankee Stadium

Giants	AB.	R.	H.	RBI.	PO.	A.
Moore, lf	4	0	2	0	4	0
Bartell, ss	4	0	1	0	1	2
Ott, 3b	4	0	0	0	1	2
Leiber, cf	4	0	0	0	3	0
Ripple, rf	3	1	1	0	2	0
McCarthy, 1b	4	0	1	0	8	0
Mancuso, c	3	0	0	1	4	1
Whitehead, 2b	3	0	1	0	1	4
Hubbell, p	2	0	0	0	0	1
Gumbert, p	0	0	0	0	0	0
Coffman, p	0	0	0	0	0	0
aBerger	1	0	0	0	0	0
Smith, p	0	0	0	0	0	0
Totals	32	1	6	1	24	10

Yankees	AB.	R.	H.	RBI.	PO.	A.
Crosetti, ss	4	1	1	0	0	2
Rolfe, 3b	4	1	1	1	0	0
DiMaggio, cf	4	0	2	2	4	0
Gehrig, 1b	2	1	0	0	9	0
Dickey, c	3	1	1	1	3	0
Hoag, lf	4	1	0	0	5	0
Selkirk, rf	4	1	1	2	3	0
Lazzeri, 2b	4	1	1	1	3	2
Gomez, p	2	1	0	0	0	2
Totals	31	8	7	7	27	6

Giants ....0 0 0 0 1 0 0 0 0—1
Yankees ....0 0 0 0 0 7 0 1 x—8

Giants	IP.	H.	R.	ER.	BB.	SO.
Hubbell (L)	5⅓	6	7	4	3	3
Gumbert	0*	0	0	0	0	0
Coffman	1⅔	0	0	0	4	0
Smith	1	1	1	1	0	0

Yankees	IP.	H.	R.	ER.	BB.	SO.
Gomez (W)	9	6	1	1	1	2

*Pitched to one batter in sixth.

aFlied out for Coffman in eighth. E—Bartell, Whitehead. DP—Giants 1, Yankees 1. LOB—Giants 5, Yankees 6. 2B—Whitehead. HR—Lazzeri. U—Ormsby (A.L.), Barr (N.L.), Basil (A.L.) and Stewart (N.L.). T—2:20. A—60,573.

Game 2

Thursday, October 7, At Yankee Stadium

Giants	AB.	R.	H.	RBI.	PO.	A.
Moore, lf	5	0	2	0	2	0
Bartell, ss	4	1	2	0	3	5
Ott, 3b	4	0	1	1	2	1
Ripple, rf	4	0	0	0	0	0
McCarthy, 1b	4	0	0	0	8	1
Chiozza, cf	4	0	1	0	3	0
Mancuso, c	4	0	0	0	4	0
Whitehead, 2b	3	0	1	0	2	3
Melton, p	1	0	0	0	0	0
Gumbert, p	0	0	0	0	0	0
Coffman, p	1	0	0	0	0	1
aLeslie	0	0	0	0	0	0
Totals	34	1	7	1	24	11

Yankees	AB.	R.	H.	RBI.	PO.	A.
Crosetti, ss	5	0	0	0	1	4
Rolfe, 3b	5	0	0	0	0	3
DiMaggio, cf	4	1	2	0	4	0
Gehrig, 1b	2	1	1	0	11	0
Dickey, c	4	1	2	1	8	0
Hoag, lf	4	2	1	1	2	0
Selkirk, rf	4	2	2	3	1	0
Lazzeri, 2b	3	1	2	0	0	2
Ruffing, p	4	0	2	3	0	2
Totals	35	8	12	8	27	11

Giants ....1 0 0 0 0 0 0 0 0—1
Yankees ....0 0 0 0 2 4 2 0 x—8

Giants	IP.	H.	R.	ER.	BB.	SO.
Melton (L)	4*	6	2	2	1	2
Gumbert	1⅓	4	4	4	1	1
Coffman	2⅔	2	2	2	1	1

Yankees	IP.	H.	R.	ER.	BB.	SO.
Ruffing (W)	9	7	1	1	3	8

*Pitched to four batters in fifth.

aWalked for Coffman in ninth. DP—Giants 1. LOB—Giants 9, Yankees 6. 2B—Hoag, Selkirk, Ruffing, Moore, Bartell. U—Barr (N.L.), Basil (A.L.), Stewart (N.L.) and Ormsby (A.L.). T—2:11. A—57,675.

Game 3

Friday, October 8, At Polo Grounds

Yankees	AB.	R.	H.	RBI.	PO.	A.
Crosetti, ss	4	0	0	0	1	7
Rolfe, 3b	4	1	2	0	1	1
DiMaggio, cf	5	0	1	0	5	0
Gehrig, 1b	5	1	1	1	12	0
Dickey, c	5	1	1	1	5	0
Selkirk, rf	4	2	1	1	0	0
Hoag, lf	4	0	2	0	0	0
Lazzeri, 2b	2	0	1	1	3	3
Pearson, p	3	0	0	0	0	0
Murphy, p	0	0	0	0	0	0
Totals	36	5	9	4	27	11

Giants	AB.	R.	H.	RBI.	PO.	A.
Moore, lf	4	0	1	0	2	0
Bartell, ss	4	0	0	0	3	2
Ott, 3b	4	0	1	0	1	3
Ripple, rf	4	1	1	0	5	0
McCarthy, 1b	3	0	1	1	7	0
Chiozza, cf	3	0	1	0	3	0
Danning, c	4	0	0	0	5	0
Whitehead, 2b	3	0	0	0	1	4
Schumacher, p	1	0	0	0	0	1
aBerger	1	0	0	0	0	0
Melton, p	0	0	0	0	0	0
bLeslie	1	0	0	0	0	0
Brennan, p	0	0	0	0	0	0
Totals	32	1	5	1	27	10

Yankees ....0 1 2 1 1 0 0 0 0—5
Giants ....0 0 0 0 0 0 1 0 0—1

Yankees	IP.	H.	R.	ER.	BB.	SO.
Pearson (W)	8⅔	5	1	1	2	4
Murphy	⅓	0	0	0	0	0

Giants	IP.	H.	R.	ER.	BB.	SO.
Schumacher (L)	6	9	5	4	4	3
Melton	2	0	0	0	2	0
Brennan	1	0	0	0	0	0

aStruck out for Schumacher in sixth. bFouled out for Melton in eighth. E—McCarthy 2, Chiozza, Melton. DP—Giants 1. LOB—Yankees 11, Giants 6. 2B—Rolfe 2, McCarthy. 3B—Dickey. SH—Hoag. WP—Schumacher. U—Basil (A.L.), Stewart (N.L.), Ormsby (A.L.) and Barr (N.L.). T—2:07. A—37,385.

Game 4

Saturday, October 9, At Polo Grounds

Yankees	AB.	R.	H.	RBI.	PO.	A.
Crosetti, ss	4	1	0	0	2	3
Rolfe, 3b	4	1	2	0	0	2
DiMaggio, cf	4	0	0	1	2	0
Gehrig, 1b	4	1	1	1	10	0
Dickey, c	4	0	0	0	3	1
Hoag, lf	4	0	2	0	3	0
Selkirk, rf	3	0	0	0	0	0
Lazzeri, 2b	3	0	1	0	4	4
Hadley, p	0	0	0	0	0	0
Andrews, p	2	0	0	0	0	1
aPowell	1	0	0	0	0	0
Wicker, p	0	0	0	0	0	0
Totals	33	3	6	2	24	11

Giants	AB.	R.	H.	RBI.	PO.	A.
Moore, lf	5	1	1	1	1	0
Bartell, ss	5	1	1	1	3	2
Ott, 3b	5	0	1	0	1	0
Ripple, rf	2	0	1	0	3	0
Leiber, cf	3	2	2	2	3	0
McCarthy, 1b	4	1	2	0	9	0
Danning, c	4	0	3	2	4	0
Whitehead, 2b	3	1	1	0	3	5
Hubbell, p	4	1	0	1	0	2
Totals	35	7	12	7	27	9

Yankees ....1 0 1 0 0 0 0 0 1—3
Giants ....0 6 0 0 0 0 1 0 x—7

Yankees	IP.	H.	R.	ER.	BB.	SO.
Hadley (L)	1⅓	6	5	5	0	0
Andrews	5⅔	6	2	2	4	1
Wicker	1	0	0	0	0	0

Giants	IP.	H.	R.	ER.	BB.	SO.
Hubbell (W)	9	6	3	2	1	4

aStruck out for Andrews in eighth. E—Bartell 2, Ott. DP—Giants 2. LOB—Yankees 4, Giants 8. 2B—Danning. 3B—Rolfe. HR—Gehrig. SB—Whitehead. U—Stewart (N.L.), Ormsby (A.L.), Barr (N.L.) and Basil (A.L.). T—1:57. A—44,293.

Game 5

Sunday, October 10, At Polo Grounds

Yankees	AB.	R.	H.	RBI.	PO.	A.
Crosetti, ss	4	0	0	0	2	1
Rolfe, 3b	3	0	1	0	1	0
DiMaggio, cf	5	1	1	1	3	0
Gehrig, 1b	4	0	2	1	8	1
Dickey, c	3	0	0	0	7	0
Hoag, lf	4	1	1	1	1	0
Selkirk, rf	4	0	1	0	3	0
Lazzeri, 2b	3	1	1	0	1	5
Gomez, p	4	1	1	1	1	1
Totals	34	4	8	4	27	8

Giants	AB.	R.	H.	RBI.	PO.	A.
Moore, lf	5	0	3	0	4	0
Bartell, ss	4	1	1	0	3	0
Ott, 3b	3	1	1	2	0	3
Ripple, rf	4	0	2	0	1	0
Leiber, cf	4	0	2	0	1	0
McCarthy, 1b	4	0	0	0	6	0
Danning, c	4	0	0	0	11	1
Whitehead, 2b	4	0	1	0	1	1
Melton, p	1	0	0	0	0	0
aRyan	1	0	0	0	0	0
Smith, p	0	0	0	0	0	1
bMancuso	1	0	0	0	0	0
Brennan, p	0	0	0	0	0	0
cBerger	1	0	0	0	0	0
Totals	36	2	10	2	27	6

Yankees ....0 1 1 0 2 0 0 0 0—4
Giants ....0 0 2 0 0 0 0 0 0—2

Yankees	IP.	H.	R.	ER.	BB.	SO.
Gomez (W)	9	10	2	2	1	6

Giants	IP.	H.	R.	ER.	BB.	SO.
Melton (L)	5	6	4	4	3	5
Smith	2	1	0	0	0	1
Brennan	2	1	0	0	1	1

aStruck out for Melton in fifth. bFlied out for Smith in seventh. cGrounded out for Brennan in ninth. DP—Yankees 1. LOB—Yankees 9, Giants 8. 2B—Whitehead, Gehrig. 3B—Gehrig, Lazzeri. HR—DiMaggio, Hoag, Ott. SH—Rolfe. HBP—Smith (Lazzeri). WP—Melton. U—Ormsby (A.L.), Barr (N.L.), Basil (A.L.) and Stewart (N.L.). T—2:06. A—38,216.

COMPOSITE BATTING AVERAGES

New York Yankees

Player-Position	G.	AB.	R.	H.	2B.	3B.	HR.	RBI.	BA.
Ruffing, p	1	4	0	2	1	0	0	3	.500
Lazzeri, 2b	5	15	3	6	0	1	1	2	.400
Hoag, lf	5	20	4	6	1	0	1	2	.300
Rolfe, 3b	5	20	3	6	2	1	0	1	.300
Gehrig, 1b	5	17	4	5	1	1	1	3	.294
DiMaggio, cf	5	22	2	6	0	0	1	4	.273
Selkirk, rf	5	19	5	5	1	0	0	6	.263
Dickey, c	5	19	3	4	0	1	0	3	.211
Gomez, p	2	6	2	1	0	0	0	1	.167
Crosetti, ss	5	21	2	1	0	0	0	0	.048
Pearson, p	1	3	0	0	0	0	0	0	.000
Murphy, p	1	0	0	0	0	0	0	0	.000
Hadley, p	1	0	0	0	0	0	0	0	.000
Andrews, p	1	2	0	0	0	0	0	0	.000
Powell, ph	1	1	0	0	0	0	0	0	.000
Wicker, p	1	0	0	0	0	0	0	0	.000
Totals	5	169	28	42	6	4	4	25	.249

New York Giants

Player-Position	G.	AB.	R.	H.	2B.	3B.	HR.	RBI.	BA.
Moore, lf	5	23	1	9	1	0	0	1	.391
Leiber, cf	3	11	2	4	0	0	0	2	.364
Ripple, rf	5	17	2	5	0	0	0	0	.294
Chiozza, cf	2	7	0	2	0	0	0	0	.286
Whitehead, 2b	5	16	1	4	2	0	0	0	.250
Danning, c	3	12	0	3	1	0	0	2	.250
Bartell, ss	5	21	3	5	1	0	0	1	.238
McCarthy, 1b	5	19	1	4	1	0	0	1	.211
Ott, 3b	5	20	1	4	0	0	1	3	.200
Mancuso, c-ph	3	8	0	0	0	0	0	1	.000
Hubbell, p	2	6	1	0	0	0	0	1	.000
Gumbert, p	2	0	0	0	0	0	0	0	.000
Coffman, p	2	1	0	0	0	0	0	0	.000
Berger, ph	3	3	0	0	0	0	0	0	.000
Smith, p	2	0	0	0	0	0	0	0	.000
Melton, p	3	2	0	0	0	0	0	0	.000
Leslie, ph	2	1	0	0	0	0	0	0	.000
Schumacher, p	1	1	0	0	0	0	0	0	.000
Brennan, p	2	0	0	0	0	0	0	0	.000
Ryan, ph	1	1	0	0	0	0	0	0	.000
Totals	5	169	12	40	6	0	1	12	.237

COMPOSITE PITCHING AVERAGES

New York Yankees

Pitcher	G.	IP.	H.	R.	ER.	BB.	SO.	W.	L.	ERA.
Murphy	1	⅓	0	0	0	0	0	0	0	0.00
Wicker	1	1	0	0	0	0	0	0	0	0.00
Ruffing	1	9	7	1	1	3	8	1	0	1.00
Pearson	1	8⅔	5	1	1	2	4	1	0	1.04
Gomez	2	18	16	3	3	2	8	2	0	1.50
Andrews	1	5⅔	6	2	2	4	1	0	0	3.18
Hadley	1	1⅓	6	5	5	0	0	0	1	33.75
Totals	5	44	40	12	12	11	21	4	1	2.45

New York Giants

Pitcher	G.	IP.	H.	R.	ER.	BB.	SO.	W.	L.	ERA.
Brennan	2	3	1	0	0	1	1	0	0	0.00
Smith	2	3	2	1	1	0	1	0	0	3.00
Hubbell	2	14⅓	12	10	6	4	7	1	1	3.77
Coffman	2	4⅓	2	2	2	5	1	0	0	4.15
Melton	3	11	12	6	6	6	7	0	2	4.91
Schum'er	1	6	9	5	4	4	3	0	1	6.00
Gumbert	2	1⅓	4	4	4	1	1	0	0	27.00
Totals	5	43	42	28	23	21	21	1	4	4.81

The calendar said 1938, but it seemed an awfully lot like 1932.

After all, the Chicago Cubs had just won the National League pennant. And they had done so after changing managers during the season. The New York Yankees, under the steady leadership of Joe McCarthy, had just captured the American League flag in comfortable fashion.

Six years earlier, the Cubs copped the N.L. championship after dismissing Rogers Hornsby as manager in early August and replacing him with Charley Grimm. The Yanks, with McCarthy in command in '32, cruised to a 13-game pennant victory.

Fortunately for the Yankees and unfortunately for the Cubs, the similarities didn't end there. As in 1932, the New Yorkers were invincible in the World Series.

The Yankees had reached the 1938 World Series in typical crunching fashion. Five New York regulars compiled runs-batted-in totals exceeding 90, and those five—Joe DiMaggio, Bill Dickey, Lou Gehrig, rookie Joe Gordon and Tommy Henrich—had home run figures ranging from 32 down to 22. Red Ruffing paced the American League in victories with 21. And Lefty Gomez, Monte Pearson and Spud Chandler won 18, 16 and 14 games, respectively. The end result was a 9½-game cushion over the Boston Red Sox in the A.L. pennant chase.

The Cubs made it to the Series on a late charge that featured one particularly dramatic moment. On September 28, as darkness was descending upon Wrigley Field, Chicago Manager Gabby Hartnett walloped a two-out, ninth-inning home run that lifted the Cubs to a 6-5 victory over Pittsburgh and enabled the North Siders to slip

Chicago shortstop Billy Jurges' Game 3 relay is too late to complete a double play against the Yankees and Lou Gehrig.

past the Pirates into first place. Until Hartnett's homer—which gave Chicago a half-game lead in the standings—the Pirates had been atop the National League for 2½ months. The Cubs held on to first place, winning the pennant by two games.

Hartnett, the Cubs' 37-year-old catcher, had been thrust into the managerial role three weeks into July as successor to the deposed Grimm. As in 1932, the Cubs had dipped into their player ranks upon naming a new pilot (Grimm, strictly a dugout manager beginning in 1937, was the Cubs' first baseman when he took over the team in '32).

While Hartnett obviously lit a fire under these Cubs—the club was in a virtual tie for third place when he became manager—a powerhouse he did not have. First baseman Rip Collins led the team in homers with 13 and outfielder Augie Galan topped the Cubs in RBIs with 69. While the thunder

was missing, third baseman Stan Hack and outfielder Carl Reynolds at least provided some lightning. Hack batted .320 and led the National League with 16 stolen bases, and Reynolds hit .302. Bill Lee and Clay Bryant were the staff pitching aces with 22 and 19 victories, respectively. Dizzy Dean, who tried to come back too soon after his All-Star Game toe injury of 1937 and hurt his arm, had been obtained from the St. Louis Cardinals in April and won seven of eight decisions.

It was Lee who got the call for the Cubs in the Series opener. And while the big righthander pitched relatively well, he did not pitch well enough to win. Dickey went 4 for 4 against him, scoring a run and driving home another, and the Yankees jumped on top in the fall classic with a 3-1 triumph.

Game 2 was emotion-packed as the brash Dean, pitching mostly on guile, contained the Yankees for seven innings at Wrigley Field. Ol' Diz, changing speeds and using his experience to good advantage, had given up only three hits and led by a 3-2 score. George Selkirk collected the Yankees' fourth hit as the leadoff batter in the eighth, but two forceout grounders left Dean in a position to escape unharmed. Frankie Crosetti, the low man on the Yankee regulars' home run list in 1938 with nine homers, was up next with Myril Hoag inching off first base. Crosetti promptly sent shudders through the crowd, laying into a Dean pitch and driving it into the left-field stands. Yankees 4, Sentimentality 3.

While Ol' Diz struck out Red Rolfe to end the eighth, the 27-year-old righthander couldn't get through the ninth. Henrich began the inning with a single and Di-

Maggio dashed Dean's and the Cubs' hopes by following with a home run. Gomez was credited with the 6-3 victory, his sixth and last in Series competition against no defeats.

Ahead two games to none with the Series now shifting to Yankee Stadium, the New Yorkers seemed to be a lock. And they were.

Gordon rapped a bases-empty homer and a two-run single in Game 3, leading the Yankees to a 5-2 victory. Crosetti then flexed his muscles again in Game 4, driving in four runs with a double and a triple as New York completed its fourth sweep in its last six World Series appearances. The stinging 8-3 defeat in the finale meant the Cubs had now finished on the short end in their last six Series.

While the Yanks' dispatching of the Cubs in four games was yet another similarity to 1932, one aspect of the '38 Series bore absolutely no resemblance to what had transpired six years earlier. Gehrig, who slugged three homers and drove in eight runs in the '32 fall classic, neither hit a homer nor collected an RBI this time around. He managed four hits, all singles, in 14 at-bats in this Series, which would be his last.

Gehrig's legacy would be many-faceted, and it would include the fact he had just become a member of the first team to win the World Series in three consecutive years.

Game 1

Wednesday, October 5, At Chicago

New York	AB.	R.	H.	RBI.	PO.	A.
Crosetti, ss	4	0	1	0	4	6
Rolfe, 3b	5	0	1	0	0	1
Henrich, rf	4	1	2	0	0	0
DiMaggio, cf	4	0	0	0	2	0
Gehrig, 1b	3	1	1	0	10	0
Dickey, c	4	1	4	1	6	3
Selkirk, lf	4	0	1	1	1	0
Gordon, 2b	4	0	2	1	4	2
Ruffing, p	3	0	0	0	0	1
Totals	35	3	12	3	27	13

Chicago	AB.	R.	H.	RBI.	PO.	A.
Hack, 3b	4	0	3	1	1	1
Herman, 2b	4	0	1	0	2	5
Demaree, lf	4	0	0	0	2	0
Cavarretta, rf	4	0	2	0	1	1
Reynolds, cf	4	0	0	0	3	0
Hartnett, c	3	0	1	0	6	2
Collins, 1b	3	1	1	0	10	1
Jurges, ss	3	0	1	0	1	3
Lee, p	2	0	0	0	1	0
aO'Dea	1	0	0	0	0	0
Russell, p	0	0	0	0	0	0
Totals	32	1	9	1	27	13

New York	0 2 0 0 0 0 1 0 0—3
Chicago	0 0 1 0 0 0 0 0 0—1

New York	IP.	H.	R.	ER.	BB.	SO.
Ruffing (W)	9	9	1	1	0	5

Chicago	IP.	H.	R.	ER.	BB.	SO.
Lee (L)	8	11	3	3	1	6
Russell	1	1	0	0	0	0

aForced runner for Lee in eighth. E—Henrich, Herman. DP—New York 2, Chicago 2. LOB—New York 8, Chicago 4. 2B—Crosetti, Henrich, Gordon. 3B—Hartnett. SB—Dickey. SH—Ruffing. HBP—By Lee (Crosetti). U—Moran (N.L.), Kolls (A.L.), Sears (N.L.) and Hubbard (A.L.). T—1:53. A—43,642.

Game 2

Thursday, October 6, At Chicago

New York	AB.	R.	H.	RBI.	PO.	A.
Crosetti, ss	4	1	1	2	5	3
Rolfe, 3b	4	0	0	0	0	2
Henrich, rf	4	1	1	0	2	0
DiMaggio, cf	4	2	2	2	4	0
Gehrig, 1b	3	1	1	0	6	0
Dickey, c	4	0	0	0	6	2
Selkirk, lf	3	0	1	0	0	0
Powell, lf	0	0	0	0	0	0
Gordon, 2b	4	0	1	2	4	3
Gomez, p	2	0	0	0	0	1
aHoag	1	1	0	0	0	0
Murphy, p	0	0	0	0	0	0
Totals	33	6	7	6	27	11

Chicago	AB.	R.	H.	RBI.	PO.	A.
Hack, 3b	5	2	2	0	0	3
Herman, 2b	4	1	1	0	1	5
Demaree, rf	3	0	1	0	1	0
Marty, cf	4	0	3	3	2	0
Reynolds, lf	3	0	0	0	4	0
Hartnett, c	4	0	0	0	5	0
Collins, 1b	4	0	1	0	10	0
Jurges, ss	3	0	0	0	4	1
Dean, p	3	0	2	0	0	2
French, p	0	0	0	0	0	0
bCavarretta	1	0	1	0	0	0
Totals	34	3	11	3	27	11

New York	0 2 0 0 0 0 0 2 2—6
Chicago	1 0 2 0 0 0 0 0 0—3

New York	IP.	H.	R.	ER.	BB.	SO.
Gomez (W)	7	9	3	3	1	5
Murphy	2	2	0	0	1	1

Chicago	IP.	H.	R.	ER.	BB.	SO.
Dean (L)	8*	7	6	6	1	2
French	1	0	0	0	1	2

*Pitched to two batters in ninth.

aForced runner for Gomez in eighth. bSingled for French in ninth. E—Rolfe 2. DP—New York 2, Chicago 1. LOB—New York 2, Chicago 7. 2B—Marty, Gordon. HR—Crosetti, DiMaggio. SH—Demaree. U—Kolls (A.L.), Sears (N.L.), Hubbard (A.L.) and Moran (N.L.). T—1:53. A—42,108.

Game 3

Saturday, October 8, At New York

Chicago	AB.	R.	H.	RBI.	PO.	A.
Hack, 3b	3	1	1	0	2	0
Herman, 2b	3	0	0	0	1	1
Cavarretta, rf	4	0	1	0	2	0
Marty, cf	4	1	3	2	3	0
Reynolds, lf	4	0	0	0	0	0
Hartnett, c	4	0	0	0	3	1
Collins, 1b	4	0	0	0	8	0
Jurges, ss	3	0	0	0	5	3
bLazzeri	1	0	0	0	0	0
Bryant, p	2	0	0	0	0	0
Russell, p	0	0	0	0	0	0
aGalan	1	0	0	0	0	0
French, p	0	0	0	0	0	2
cO'Dea	1	0	0	0	0	0
Totals	34	2	5	2	24	7

New York	AB.	R.	H.	RBI.	PO.	A.
Crosetti, ss	3	0	0	0	1	0
Rolfe, 3b	4	0	1	1	0	1
Henrich, rf	4	0	0	0	3	0
DiMaggio, cf	3	1	1	0	1	0
Gehrig, 1b	4	1	1	0	4	1
Dickey, c	3	1	1	1	12	0
Selkirk, lf	3	0	0	0	2	0
Gordon, 2b	4	1	2	3	2	3
Pearson, p	3	1	1	0	2	0
Totals	31	5	7	5	27	5

Chicago	0 0 0 0 1 0 0 1 0—2
New York	0 0 0 0 2 2 0 1 x—5

Chicago	IP.	H.	R.	ER.	BB.	SO.
Bryant (L)	5⅓	6	4	4	5	3
Russell	⅔	0	0	0	1	0
French	2	1	1	1	0	0

New York	IP.	H.	R.	ER.	BB.	SO.
Pearson (W)	9	5	2	1	2	9

aPopped out for Russell in seventh. bGrounded out for Jurges in ninth. cFlied out for French in ninth. E—Herman, Crosetti, Gordon. LOB—Chicago 7, New York 8. 2B—Hack. HR—Dickey, Gordon, Marty. U—Sears (N.L.), Hubbard (A.L.), Moran (N.L.) and Kolls (A.L.). T—1:57. A—55,236.

Game 4

Sunday, October 9, At New York

Chicago	AB.	R.	H.	RBI.	PO.	A.
Hack, 3b	5	0	2	0	1	0
Herman, 2b	5	0	1	0	1	3
Cavarretta, rf	4	1	2	0	1	0
Marty, cf	4	0	0	0	2	0
Demaree, lf	3	1	0	0	3	0
O'Dea, c	3	1	1	2	5	0
Collins, 1b	4	0	0	0	10	0
Jurges, ss	4	0	2	0	1	0
Lee, p	1	0	0	0	0	0
aGalan	1	0	0	0	0	0
Root, p	0	0	0	0	0	0
bLazzeri	1	0	0	0	0	0
Page, p	0	0	0	0	0	1
French, p	0	0	0	0	0	0
Carleton, p	0	0	0	0	0	0
Dean, p	0	0	0	0	0	0
cReynolds	1	0	0	0	0	0
Totals	36	3	8	2	24	4

New York	AB.	R.	H.	RBI.	PO.	A.
Crosetti, ss	5	0	2	4	6	1
Rolfe, 3b	5	0	1	0	0	0
Henrich, rf	4	1	1	1	1	0
DiMaggio, cf	4	1	1	0	3	0
Gehrig, 1b	4	1	1	0	5	2
Dickey, c	4	0	1	0	7	0
Hoag, lf	4	2	2	1	1	0
Gordon, 2b	3	2	1	0	2	4
Ruffing, p	3	1	1	1	2	3
Totals	36	8	11	7	27	10

Chicago	0 0 0 1 0 0 0 2 0—3
New York	0 3 0 0 0 1 0 4 x—8

Chicago	IP.	H.	R.	ER.	BB.	SO.
Lee (L)	3	4	3	0	0	2
Roof	3	3	1	1	0	1
Page	1⅓	2	2	2	0	0
French	⅓	0	0	0	0	0
Carleton	0*	1	2	2	2	0
Dean	⅓	1	0	0	0	0

New York	IP.	H.	R.	ER.	BB.	SO.
Ruffing (W)	9	8	3	2	2	6

aStruck out for Lee in fourth. bStruck out for Root in seventh. cFlied out for Dean in ninth. E—Jurges, Gordon. LOB—Chicago 8, New York 6. 2B—Crosetti, Hoag, Cavarretta, Jurges. 3B—Crosetti. HR—Henrich, O'Dea. SB—Rolfe, Gordon. WP—Carleton 2. U—Hubbard (A.L.), Moran (N.L.), Kolls (A.L.) and Sears (N.L.). T—2:11. A—59,847.

COMPOSITE BATTING AVERAGES

New York Yankees

Player-Position	G.	AB.	R.	H.	2B.	3B.	HR.	RBI.	BA.
Dickey, c	4	15	2	6	0	0	1	2	.400
Gordon, 2b	4	15	3	6	2	0	1	6	.400
Hoag, ph-lf	2	5	3	2	1	0	0	1	.400
Pearson, p	1	3	1	1	0	0	0	0	.333
Gehrig, 1b	4	14	4	4	0	0	0	0	.286
DiMaggio, cf	4	15	4	4	0	0	1	2	.267
Crosetti, ss	4	16	1	4	2	1	1	6	.250
Henrich, rf	4	16	3	4	1	0	1	1	.250
Selkirk, lf	3	10	0	2	0	0	0	1	.200
Rolfe, 3b	4	18	0	3	0	0	0	1	.167
Ruffing, p	2	6	1	1	0	0	0	1	.167
Powell, lf	1	0	0	0	0	0	0	0	.000
Gomez, p	1	2	0	0	0	0	0	0	.000
Murphy, p	1	0	0	0	0	0	0	0	.000
Totals	4	135	22	37	6	1	5	21	.274

Chicago Cubs

Player-Position	G.	AB.	R.	H.	2B.	3B.	HR.	RBI.	BA.
Dean, p	2	3	0	2	0	0	0	0	.666
Marty, cf	3	12	1	6	1	0	1	5	.500
Hack, 3b	4	17	3	8	1	0	0	1	.471
Cavarretta, rf-ph	4	13	1	6	1	0	0	0	.462
Jurges, ss	4	13	0	3	1	0	0	0	.231
O'Dea, ph-c	3	5	1	1	0	0	1	2	.200
Herman, 2b	4	16	1	3	0	0	0	0	.188
Collins, 1b	4	15	1	2	0	0	0	0	.133
Demaree, lf	3	10	1	1	0	0	0	0	.100
Hartnett, c	3	11	0	1	0	1	0	0	.091
Reynolds, cf-lf-ph	4	12	0	0	0	0	0	0	.000
Lee, p	2	3	0	0	0	0	0	0	.000
Russell, p	2	0	0	0	0	0	0	0	.000
French, p	3	0	0	0	0	0	0	0	.000
Lazzeri, ph	2	2	0	0	0	0	0	0	.000
Bryant, p	1	2	0	0	0	0	0	0	.000
Galan, ph	2	2	0	0	0	0	0	0	.000
Root, p	1	0	0	0	0	0	0	0	.000
Page, p	1	0	0	0	0	0	0	0	.000
Carleton, p	1	0	0	0	0	0	0	0	.000
Totals	4	136	9	33	4	1	2	8	.243

COMPOSITE PITCHING AVERAGES

New York Yankees

Pitcher	G.	IP.	H.	R.	ER.	BB.	SO.	W.	L.	ERA.
Murphy	1	2	2	0	0	1	1	0	0	0.00
Pearson	1	9	5	2	1	2	9	1	0	1.00
Ruffing	2	18	17	4	3	2	11	2	0	1.50
Gomez	1	7	9	3	3	1	5	1	0	3.86
Totals	4	36	33	9	7	6	26	4	0	1.75

Chicago Cubs

Pitcher	G.	IP.	H.	R.	ER.	BB.	SO.	W.	L.	ERA.
Russell	2	1⅔	1	0	0	1	0	0	0	0.00
Lee	2	11	15	6	3	1	8	0	2	2.45
French	3	3⅓	1	1	1	1	2	0	0	2.70
Root	1	3	3	1	1	0	1	0	0	3.00
Dean	2	8⅓	8	6	6	1	2	0	1	6.48
Bryant	1	5⅓	6	4	4	5	3	0	1	6.75
Page	1	1⅓	2	2	2	0	0	0	0	13.50
Carleton	1	0	1	2	2	2	0	0	0	.....
Totals	4	34	37	22	19	11	16	0	4	5.03

NEW YORK YANKEES
VS.
CINCINNATI REDS

The New York Yankees managed only five hits in Game 3 of the 1939 World Series. Would you believe four of those hits were home runs?

For the fourth straight year, the National League's representative in the fall classic became a believer in the wondrous deeds performed by Joe McCarthy's Yankees. And those deeds never seemed more awe-inspiring than on October 7, 1939, when the Yanks bludgeoned the National League champion Cincinnati Reds with a five-hit attack.

Manager Bill McKechnie's Reds actually out-hit the Yankees in Game 3 by a 2-1 ratio. But all 10 of Cincinnati's hits were singles. New York, meanwhile, got two-run homers from rookie Charlie Keller in the first and fifth innings, a two-run blast from Joe DiMaggio (who batted a career-high .381 in the regular season) in the third and a bases-empty shot from Bill Dickey in the fifth. Enough said.

Before their homer-happy 7-3 triumph in Cincinnati, the Yankees had ridden the strong pitching of Red Ruffing and Monte Pearson to victories in Games 1 and 2—contests in which the major leagues' winningest pitchers of 1939 went down to defeat. In the Series opener, Ruffing's four-hitter beat 25-game winner Paul Derringer, 2-1. With the score tied at 1-1 in the ninth, Keller hit a one-out triple and, after an intentional walk to DiMaggio, trotted home on Dickey's single. Matched against 27-game winner Bucky Walters in Game 2, Pearson tossed no-hit ball until Reds catcher Ernie Lombardi singled with one out in the eighth. Babe Dahlgren doubled and homered in support of Pearson, who wound up with a two-hit, 4-0 tri-

New York's Joe DiMaggio slides past Cincinnati catcher Ernie Lombardi, who lay stunned after a Game 4 collision with Yankee Charlie Keller.

umph.

Dahlgren had supplanted Lou Gehrig at first base for the Yankees, taking over on May 2 when failing health and an accompanying decline in skills had forced Gehrig out of the New York line-up after the Iron Horse had played in 2,130 consecutive games. Not since 1923 had the Yankees engaged in postseason play without Gehrig.

Game 4 was a 0-0 battle until the seventh when Keller and Dickey slugged bases-empty home runs off Derringer. But the Reds came back in their half of the inning for three unearned runs off reliever Steve Sundra, who had replaced ailing starter Oral Hildebrand in the fifth, and tacked on an insurance run in the eighth off Johnny Murphy.

The Reds soon discovered they weren't carrying enough insur-

ance. And what they really would need, as it turned out, was *collision* insurance.

Shortstop Billy Myers' error on Dickey's potential double-play ball in the ninth—the run-scoring grounder enabled the Yankees to move within 4-3—helped turn a possibly harmless inning into a game-tying rally. New York scored again later in the inning when DiMaggio, who would have been a forceout victim at second if not for Myers' misplay, beat a throw to the plate on Gordon's grounder to third baseman Bill Werber (with Gordon being credited with a hit on the play).

With runners on the corners and one out in the Yankees' 10th, DiMaggio drove a single to right, snapping the 4-4 tie. That would have been trouble enough for Cincinnati, but right fielder Ival Goodman misplayed the ball and

another run—in the person of Keller—headed home. That, too, would have been trouble enough for Cincinnati, but catcher Lombardi not only failed to hold Goodman's throw to the plate, but he also was was knocked down by the onrushing Keller and the ball rolled away. As a result, DiMaggio was able to circle the bases as the Reds' receiver lay stunned. "Schnozz's snooze" the play was called, and it won a special place in baseball lore despite its seemingly minimal impact overall.

Murphy protected the Yankees' 7-4 lead in the last of the 10th, working out of a jam in which the Reds sent the potential tying run to the plate three times. On the third such occasion, Wally Berger lined out to shortstop Frankie Crosetti. The New York Yankees, pulling off their second straight sweep, were World Series champions for the fourth consecutive year.

That the Reds had made it into their first Series since 1919, the year of the Black Sox scandal, was an amazing advance, considering that Cincinnati had finished in the National League basement in 1937. For the Yankees, it was business as usual. Actually, a little better than usual: 106 victories and 45 defeats. They won the pennant by 17 games.

The 23-year-old Keller was the Series star, leading all regulars in runs scored (eight), hits (seven), home runs (three), RBIs (six) and batting average (.438).

Fittingly, such dominant play as that exhibited by Keller came from a member of the Yankees, who now had won 13 of their last 14 Series games and 28 of their last 31 contests in baseball's premier event.

Game 1

Wednesday, October 4, At New York

Cincinnati	AB.	R.	H.	RBI.	PO.	A.
Werber, 3b	4	0	0	0	0	1
Frey, 2b	4	0	0	0	1	2
Goodman, rf	2	1	0	0	4	0
McCormick, 1b	3	0	2	1	9	0
Lombardi, c	3	0	0	0	7	0
Craft, cf	3	0	1	0	2	0
Berger, lf	3	0	0	0	1	0
Myers, ss	3	0	1	0	1	1
Derringer, p	3	0	0	0	0	1
Totals	28	1	4	1	25	5

New York	AB.	R.	H.	RBI.	PO.	A.
Crosetti, ss	4	0	0	0	1	7
Rolfe, 3b	4	0	0	0	1	2
Keller, rf	4	1	1	0	2	0
DiMaggio, cf	3	0	1	0	2	0
Dickey, c	4	0	1	1	4	0
Selkirk, lf	3	0	0	0	2	0
Gordon, 2b	3	1	1	0	2	4
Dahlgren, 1b	3	0	1	0	13	0
Ruffing, p	3	0	1	0	0	3
Totals	31	2	6	2	27	16

Cincinnati .... 0 0 0 1 0 0 0 0 0—1
New York .... 0 0 0 0 1 0 0 0 1—2
One out when winning run scored.

Cincinnati	IP.	H.	R.	ER.	BB.	SO.
Derringer (L)	8⅓	6	2	2	1	7

New York	IP.	H.	R.	ER.	BB.	SO.
Ruffing (W)	9	4	1	1	4	4

DP—New York 3. LOB—Cincinnati 1, New York 5. 2B—Dahlgren. 3B—Keller. SB—Goodman. U—McGowan (A.L.), Reardon (N.L.), Summers (A.L.) and Pinelli (N.L.). T—1:33. A—58,541.

Game 2

Thursday, October 5, At New York

Cincinnati	AB.	R.	H.	RBI.	PO.	A.
Werber, 3b	3	0	1	0	0	1
Frey, 2b	4	0	0	0	2	2
Goodman, rf	3	0	0	0	1	0
McCormick, 1b	3	0	0	0	7	0
Lombardi, c	3	0	1	0	5	1
aBordagaray	0	0	0	0	0	0
Hershberger, c	0	0	0	0	0	0
Craft, cf	3	0	0	0	3	1
Berger, lf	3	0	0	0	1	0
Myers, ss	3	0	0	0	5	3
Walters, p	2	0	0	0	0	3
bGamble	1	0	0	0	0	0
Totals	28	0	2	0	24	11

New York	AB.	R.	H.	RBI.	PO.	A.
Crosetti, ss	4	0	1	1	1	2
Rolfe, 3b	4	1	1	0	1	1
Keller, rf	4	1	2	1	0	0
DiMaggio, cf	4	0	1	0	4	0
Dickey, c	3	0	1	1	8	1
Selkirk, lf	3	0	1	0	3	0
Gordon, 2b	3	0	0	0	2	0
Dahlgren, 1b	3	2	2	1	8	0
Pearson, p	2	0	0	0	0	5
Totals	30	4	9	4	27	9

Cincinnati .... 0 0 0 0 0 0 0 0 0—0
New York .... 0 0 3 1 0 0 0 0 x—4

Cincinnati	IP.	H.	R.	ER.	BB.	SO.
Walters (L)	8	9	4	4	0	5

New York	IP.	H.	R.	ER.	BB.	SO.
Pearson (W)	9	2	0	0	1	8

aRan for Lombardi in eighth. bStruck out for Walters in ninth. DP—Cincinnati 1, New York 1. LOB—Cincinnati 2, New York 3. 2B—Keller, Dahlgren. HR—Dahlgren. SH—Pearson. U—Reardon (N.L.), Summers (A.L.), Pinelli (N.L.) and McGowan (A.L.). T—1:27. A—59,791.

Game 3

Saturday, October 7, At Cincinnati

New York	AB.	R.	H.	RBI.	PO.	A.
Crosetti, ss	4	1	0	0	2	2
Rolfe, 3b	4	1	1	0	0	2
Keller, rf	3	3	2	4	2	0
DiMaggio, cf	4	1	1	2	2	0
Dickey, c	3	1	1	1	5	1
Selkirk, lf	2	0	0	0	3	0
Gordon, 2b	4	0	0	0	3	5
Dahlgren, 1b	4	0	0	0	9	2
Gomez, p	1	0	0	0	0	0
Hadley, p	3	0	0	0	1	1
Totals	32	7	5	7	27	13

Cincinnati	AB.	R.	H.	RBI.	PO.	A.
Werber, 3b	4	1	1	1	3	2
Frey, 2b	4	0	0	0	3	2
Goodman, rf	5	1	3	1	2	0
McCormick, 1b	5	0	2	0	9	0
Lombardi, c	3	0	1	1	5	0
bBordagaray	1	0	0	0	0	0
Hershberger, c	0	0	0	0	0	0
Craft, cf	4	0	0	0	2	0
Berger, lf	4	0	0	0	1	0
Myers, ss	3	1	2	0	1	4
Thompson, p	1	0	1	0	0	0
Grissom, p	0	0	0	0	0	0
aBongiovanni	1	0	0	0	0	0
Moore, p	1	0	0	0	0	2
Totals	36	3	10	3	27	10

New York .... 2 0 2 0 3 0 0 0 0—7
Cincinnati .... 1 2 0 0 0 0 0 0 0—3

New York	IP.	H.	R.	ER.	BB.	SO.
Gomez	1	3	1	1	2	1
Hadley (W)	8	7	2	2	3	2

Cincinnati	IP.	H.	R.	ER.	BB.	SO.
Thompson (L)	4⅔	5	7	7	4	3
Grissom	1⅓	0	0	0	1	0
Moore	3	0	0	0	2	0

aGrounded out for Grissom in sixth. bRan for Lombardi in seventh. E—Hadley. DP—New York 1. LOB—New York 3, Cincinnati 11. HR—Keller 2, DiMaggio. SH—Thompson. HBP—By Hadley (Lombardi). WP—Thompson. U—Summers (A.L.), Pinelli (N.L.), McGowan (A.L.) and Reardon (N.L.). T—2:01. A—32,723.

Game 4

Sunday, October 8, At Cincinnati

New York	AB.	R.	H.	RBI.	PO.	A.
Crosetti, ss	4	1	0	0	2	3
Rolfe, 3b	4	0	0	0	1	3
Keller, rf	5	3	2	1	2	0
DiMaggio, cf	5	2	2	1	3	0
Dickey, c	5	1	1	2	10	0
Selkirk, lf	4	0	1	0	1	0
Gordon, 2b	4	0	1	1	0	3
Dahlgren, 1b	4	0	0	0	11	0
Hildebrand, p	1	0	0	0	0	0
Sundra, p	0	0	0	0	0	0
Murphy, p	2	0	0	0	0	3
Totals	38	7	7	5	30	12

Cincinnati	AB.	R.	H.	RBI.	PO.	A.
Werber, 3b	5	0	2	1	0	1
Frey, 2b	5	0	0	0	3	4
Goodman, rf	5	1	2	0	3	1
McCormick, 1b	4	1	2	0	7	1
Lombardi, c	5	0	1	1	4	0
Craft, cf	1	0	0	0	0	0
Simmons, lf	4	1	1	0	0	0
Berger, lf-cf	5	0	0	1	4	0
Myers, ss	3	1	1	0	5	1
Derringer, p	2	0	1	0	1	0
aHershberger	1	0	1	1	0	0
Walters, p	1	0	0	0	0	0
Totals	41	4	11	4	30	8

New York .... 0 0 0 0 0 0 2 0 2 3—7
Cincinnati .... 0 0 0 0 0 3 1 0 0—4

New York	IP.	H.	R.	ER.	BB.	SO.
Hildebrand	4	2	0	0	0	3
Sundra	2⅔	4	3	0	1	0
Murphy (W)	3⅓	5	1	1	0	2

Cincinnati	IP.	H.	R.	ER.	BB.	SO.
Derringer	7	3	2	2	2	2
Walters (L)	3	4	5	2	1	1

aSingled for Derringer in seventh. E—Rolfe, Goodman, Lombardi, Meyers 2. LOB—New York 5, Cincinnati 9. 2B—Selkirk, Goodman, McCormick, Simmons. 3B—Myers. HR—Keller, Dickey. SH—Rolfe, McCormick. U—Pinelli (N.L.), McGowan (A.L.), Reardon (N.L.) and Summers (A.L.). T—2:04. A—32,794.

COMPOSITE BATTING AVERAGES

New York Yankees

Player-Position	G.	AB.	R.	H.	2B.	3B.	HR.	RBI.	BA.
Keller, rf	4	16	8	7	1	1	3	6	.438
Ruffing, p	1	3	0	1	0	0	0	0	.333
DiMaggio, cf	4	16	3	5	0	0	1	3	.313
Dickey, c	4	15	2	4	0	0	2	5	.267
Dahlgren, 1b	4	14	2	3	2	0	1	2	.214
Selkirk, lf	4	12	0	2	1	0	0	0	.167
Gordon, 2b	4	14	1	2	0	0	0	1	.143
Rolfe, 3b	4	16	2	2	0	0	0	0	.125
Crosetti, ss	4	16	2	1	0	0	0	1	.063
Pearson, p	1	2	0	0	0	0	0	0	.000
Gomez, p	1	1	0	0	0	0	0	0	.000
Hadley, p	1	3	0	0	0	0	0	0	.000
Hildebrand, p	1	1	0	0	0	0	0	0	.000
Sundra, p	1	0	0	0	0	0	0	0	.000
Murphy, p	1	2	0	0	0	0	0	0	.000
Totals	4	131	20	27	4	1	7	18	.206

Cincinnati Reds

Player-Position	G.	AB.	R.	H.	2B.	3B.	HR.	RBI.	BA.
Thompson, p	1	1	0	1	0	0	0	0	1.000
Hershberger, c-ph	3	2	0	1	0	0	0	1	.500
McCormick, 1b	4	15	1	6	1	0	0	1	.400
Goodman, rf	4	15	3	5	1	0	0	1	.333
Myers, ss	4	12	2	4	0	1	0	0	.333
Werber, 3b	4	16	1	4	0	0	0	2	.250
Simmons, lf	1	4	1	1	1	0	0	0	.250
Lombardi, c	4	14	0	3	0	0	0	2	.214
Derringer, p	2	5	0	1	0	0	0	0	.200
Craft, cf	4	11	0	1	0	0	0	0	.091
Frey, 2b	4	17	0	0	0	0	0	0	.000
Berger, lf-cf	4	15	0	0	0	0	0	1	.000
Bordagaray, pr	2	0	0	0	0	0	0	0	.000
Walters, p	2	3	0	0	0	0	0	0	.000
Gamble, ph	1	1	0	0	0	0	0	0	.000
Grissom, p	1	0	0	0	0	0	0	0	.000
Bongiovanni, ph.	1	1	0	0	0	0	0	0	.000
Moore, p	1	1	0	0	0	0	0	0	.000
Totals	4	133	8	27	3	1	0	8	.203

COMPOSITE PITCHING AVERAGES

New York Yankees

Pitcher	G.	IP.	H.	R.	ER.	BB.	SO.	W.	L.	ERA.
Pearson	1	9	2	0	0	1	8	1	0	0.00
Hildebrand	1	4	2	0	0	0	3	0	0	0.00
Sundra	1	2⅔	4	3	0	1	0	0	0	0.00
Ruffing	1	9	4	1	1	4	4	1	0	1.00
Hadley	1	8	7	2	2	3	2	1	0	2.25
Murphy	1	3⅓	5	1	1	0	2	1	0	2.70
Gomez	1	1	3	1	1	2	1	0	0	9.00
Totals	4	37	27	8	5	6	22	4	0	1.22

Cincinnati Reds

Pitcher	G.	IP.	H.	R.	ER.	BB.	SO.	W.	L.	ERA.
Moore	1	3	0	0	0	2	0	0	0	0.00
Grissom	1	1⅓	0	0	0	1	0	0	0	0.00
Derringer	2	15⅓	9	4	4	3	9	0	1	2.35
Walters	2	11	13	9	6	1	6	0	2	4.91
Thompson	1	4⅔	5	7	7	4	3	0	1	13.50
Totals	4	35⅓	27	20	17	9	20	0	4	4.33

1940 CINCINNATI REDS VS. DETROIT TIGERS

Entering the 1940 major league season, the defending National League champion Cincinnati Reds had one World Series championship to their credit. A tainted one.

The Reds had won their only Series crown in 1919, beating the Chicago White Sox. Late in the following season, eight members of the Chicago club were implicated in a fixing scandal revolving around the White Sox-Reds fall classic. While there were those who contended that the Reds had the wherewithal to beat Chicago —regardless of their underdog status—the lingering feeling was that without a little help from its enemies, Cincinnati would still be

looking for its first Series title.

Cincinnati, of course, had a chance to win an unsoiled Series in 1939. Instead, the Reds hung out their own dirty linen as the powerful New York Yankees zapped them in four games.

Plainly, this World Series competition evoked few pleasant memories for the Reds and their followers.

Hopes that 1940 might be different rose when Bill McKechnie's club raced to 100 victories and a 12-game margin in the N.L. pennant race. And the hopes rose even higher when it was determined that the noted N.L.-exterminating team from the Bronx

wouldn't qualify for this season's fall classic.

While the 1940 A.L. champions were *not* the Yankees, they looked like the Yankees. The pennant-winning Detroit Tigers, who finished one game ahead of Cleveland and two in front of New York, had a 1-2 punch that combined for 74 home runs and 284 runs batted in. Plus, four Tiger regulars batted .313 or higher.

The Tigers exhibited some of their offensive prowess in the opening game of the World Series, knocking Paul Derringer from the mound in a five-run second and coasting to a 7-2 victory. Pinky Higgins, Dick Bartell and Bruce Campbell all knocked in two runs for the Tigers, who got eight-hit pitching from Bobo Newsom. Newsom's joy over his performance ended abruptly, though, with the news the following morning of the death of his father, who had come from South Carolina to see him pitch.

Jimmy Ripple's two-run home run and Bucky Walters' three-hit pitching enabled Cincinnati to win, 5-3, the next day and even the Series. But the Tigers regained the upper hand in Game 3 as Rudy York and Higgins belted two-run homers in the seventh— the score was tied 1-1 entering the inning—and pushed the A.L. titlists toward a 7-4 decision. York had walloped 33 homers and totaled 134 RBIs in the regular season.

The Reds' Derringer rebounded from his pasting in the Series opener and spun a five-hitter in Game 4. His 5-2 victory left the combatants deadlocked at two victories apiece.

The seesaw nature of the 1940 World Series continued in Game 5, with Detroit resting on the high end of the plank after winning

The strategy for the 1940 World Series was in the hands of Cincinnati Manager Bill McKechnie (left) and Detroit Manager Del Baker.

Reds sluggers Frank McCormick (left) and Ernie Lombardi pose with Tiger offensive stars Hank Greenberg and Barney McCosky (right).

convincingly. Newsom, obviously emotion-racked, threw a three-hitter and prevailed, 8-0, as Hank Greenberg unloaded a three-run homer and drove in four runs. Greenberg was coming off a monstrous year, having mauled A.L. pitching for 41 homers, 150 RBIs and a .340 batting average.

Games 6 and 7 (if necessary) would be played in Cincinnati, but any edge the home field was providing in this Series was being offset by the pattern of alternating victories. It was Cincinnati's turn to win in the sixth game and, sure enough, the Reds delivered. Walters not only fired a five-hit shutout, but he also homered in a 4-0 conquest.

Tigers Manager Del Baker called on his best pitcher for Game 7, even if that pitcher was coming off only one day of rest. Newsom was his man. McKechnie opted for Derringer, who had two days of rest.

Newsom, a 20-game winner in the American League for the third consecutive season, was the beneficiary of an unearned run in the third inning and made that run stand up through six innings. However, Frank McCormick, easily the Reds' top power threat (19 homers and 127 RBIs in '40), and Ripple hit consecutive doubles to open the Reds' seventh. With the

game now in a 1-1 stalemate, Jimmie Wilson bunted Ripple to third. After pinch-hitter Ernie Lombardi was given an intentional walk, Billy Myers drove home Ripple with a fly ball to deep center.

Derringer, now holding a 2-1 lead, went to work in his bid to nail down the Series crown. He allowed an inning-opening single to Charlie Gehringer in the eighth, but then retired the Tigers' next six batters.

The alternating-victory sequence had ended. And so had Cincinnati's long wait for Series triumph No. 2.

Derringer and Walters, 20-game winners again in 1940 (Derringer for the third straight season and Walters for the second), atoned for their winless efforts in the '39 Series by posting two victories apiece this time. The Reds' Bill Werber batted a Series-high .370, Wilson hit .353 and Ripple finished at .333. Ripple and Ival Goodman had six and five RBIs, respectively, for the winners.

Wilson, a 40-year-old Reds coach, was pressed into late-season catching duty when Lombardi suffered an ankle injury and wound up starting six World Series games after appearing in just 16 regular-season contests.

The season, while ending on a

joyous note for Cincinnati, had sadness, too. In early August, Reds reserve catcher Willard Hershberger committed suicide in his Boston hotel room.

Detroit's standout in the Series was the gutty Newsom, who won two of three decisions and recorded a 1.38 earned-run average in 26 innings. Campbell, Greenberg and Higgins posted .360, .357 and .333 batting figures, respectively, and Barney McCosky—like Greenberg a .340 batsman in the regular season—had a .304 Series mark.

None of which was enough to prevent the Cincinnati Reds from winning their first World Series of the *non-tainted* variety.

Game 1

Wednesday, October 2, At Cincinnati

Detroit	AB.	R.	H.	RBI.	PO.	A.
Bartell, ss	4	0	2	2	2	0
McCosky, cf	5	0	2	1	2	0
Gehringer, 2b	4	0	0	0	4	3
Greenberg, lf	5	1	1	0	4	0
York, 1b	4	2	2	0	6	1
Campbell, rf	3	1	2	2	3	0
Higgins, 3b	4	1	1	2	0	5
Sullivan, c	3	1	0	0	5	1
Newsom, p	4	1	0	0	1	0
Totals	36	7	10	7	27	11

Cincinnati	AB.	R.	H.	RBI.	PO.	A.
Werber, 3b	4	1	1	0	1	2
M. McCormick, cf	4	0	1	0	2	0
Goodman, rf	4	1	2	1	1	0
F. McCormick, 1b	3	0	0	0	7	1
Ripple, lf	4	0	1	1	2	0
Wilson, c	2	0	0	0	9	1
aRiggs	1	0	0	0	0	0
Baker, c	1	0	1	0	3	0
Joost, 2b	4	0	2	0	2	1
Myers, ss	4	0	0	0	0	1
Derringer, p	0	0	0	0	0	1
Moore, p	2	0	0	0	0	1
bCraft	1	0	0	0	0	0
Riddle, p	0	0	0	0	0	0
Totals	34	2	8	2	27	8

Detroit ....0 5 0   0 2 0   0 0 0—7
Cincinnati ....0 0 0   0 0 1   0 1 0—2

Detroit	IP.	H.	R.	ER.	BB.	SO.
Newsom (W)	9	8	2	2	1	4

Cincinnati	IP.	H.	R.	ER.	BB.	SO.
Derringer (L)	1⅓	5	5	4	1	1
Moore	6⅔	5	2	2	4	7
Riddle	1	0	0	0	0	2

aStruck out for Wilson in seventh. bFlied out for Moore in eighth. E—Bartell, Werber, Baker, Myers. DP—Detroit 1, Cincinnati 1. LOB—Detroit 8, Cincinnati 6. 2B—Werber, M. McCormick, Goodman. 3B—York. HR—Campbell. SH—Campbell. U—Klem (N.L.), Ormsby (A.L.), Ballanfant (N.L.) and Basil (A.L.). T—2:09. A—31,793.

Game 2

Thursday, October 3, At Cincinnati

Detroit	AB.	R.	H.	RBI.	PO.	A.
Bartell, ss	3	1	0	0	3	2
McCosky, cf	2	1	0	0	4	0
Gehringer, 2b	4	1	1	1	3	3
Greenberg, lf	3	0	1	1	1	0
York, 1b	4	0	0	0	10	0
Campbell, rf	4	0	0	0	3	0
Higgins, 3b	3	0	1	0	1	4
Tebbetts, c	3	0	0	0	2	0
Rowe, p	0	0	0	0	0	0
Gorsica, p	2	0	0	0	0	1
Totals	29	3	3	2	24	10

Cincinnati	AB.	R.	H.	RBI.	PO.	A.
Werber, 3b	3	0	1	1	2	4
M. McCormick, cf	4	0	0	0	3	0
Goodman, rf	4	1	1	0	0	0
F. McCormick, 1b	4	1	1	0	9	0
Ripple, lf	4	1	1	2	3	0
Wilson, c	4	1	2	0	4	0
Joost, 2b	4	0	1	1	2	2
Myers, ss	3	0	1	1	3	3
Walters, p	3	1	1	0	0	2
Totals	33	5	9	5	27	11

Detroit .... 2 0 0 0 0 1 0 0 0—3
Cincinnati .... 0 2 2 1 0 0 0 0 x—5

Detroit	IP.	H.	R.	ER.	BB.	SO.
Rowe (L)	3⅓	8	5	5	1	1
Gorsica	4⅔	1	0	0	0	1

Cincinnati	IP.	H.	R.	ER.	BB.	SO.
Walters (W)	9	3	3	3	4	4

E—Tebbetts. DP—Cincinnati 1. LOB—Detroit 3, Cincinnati 5. 2B—Werber, Walters, Greenberg, Higgins. HR—Ripple. U—Ormsby (A.L.), Ballanfant (N.L.), Basil (A.L.) and Klem (N.L.). T—1:54. A—30,640.

Game 3

Friday, October 4, At Detroit

Cincinnati	AB.	R.	H.	RBI.	PO.	A.
Werber, 3b	4	1	3	1	2	3
M. McCormick, cf	5	0	2	1	3	0
Goodman, rf	4	0	1	1	1	0
F. McCormick, 1b	4	0	0	0	9	1
Ripple, lf	4	1	1	0	2	0
Lombardi, c	3	0	1	0	4	0
Baker, c	1	1	0	0	2	0
Joost, 2b	4	0	1	1	1	2
Myers, ss	4	0	1	0	0	3
Turner, p	2	0	0	0	0	1
Moore, p	0	0	0	0	0	0
aRiggs	1	1	0	0	0	0
Beggs, p	0	0	0	0	0	0
bFrey	1	0	0	0	0	0
Totals	37	4	10	4	24	10

Detroit	AB.	R.	H.	RBI.	PO.	A.
Bartell, ss	4	0	1	0	3	3
McCosky, cf	4	1	2	0	4	0
Gehringer, 2b	4	0	1	0	2	4
Greenberg, lf	4	2	2	0	1	0
York, 1b	4	1	2	2	8	0
Campbell, rf	4	2	3	1	4	0
Higgins, 3b	4	1	2	3	0	3
Tebbetts, c	4	0	0	0	5	1
Bridges, p	3	0	0	0	0	1
Totals	35	7	13	6	27	12

Cincinnati .... 1 0 0 0 0 0 0 1 2—4
Detroit .... 0 0 0 1 0 0 4 2 x—7

Cincinnati	IP.	H.	R.	ER.	BB.	SO.
Turner (L)	6*	8	5	5	0	4
Moore	1	2	0	0	0	0
Beggs	1	3	2	1	0	1

Detroit	IP.	H.	R.	ER.	BB.	SO.
Bridges (W)	9	10	4	3	1	5

*Pitched to four batters in seventh.

aForced runner for Moore in eighth. bFlied out for Beggs in ninth. E—M. McCormick, Higgins. DP—Cincinnati 2. LOB—Cincinnati 7, Detroit 4. 2B—McCosky, Campbell, Higgins, Werber, Lombardi. 3B—Greenberg. HR—York, Higgins. U—Ballanfant (N.L.), Basil (A.L.), Klem (N.L.) and Ormsby (A.L.). T—2:08. A—52,877.

Game 4

Saturday, October 5, At Detroit

Cincinnati	AB.	R.	H.	RBI.	PO.	A.
Werber, 3b	3	2	2	0	2	1
M. McCormick, cf	5	1	2	1	3	0
Goodman, rf	5	2	2	2	1	0
F. McCormick, 1b	5	0	2	0	13	0
Ripple, lf	2	0	1	1	0	0
bArnovich, lf	1	0	0	0	2	0
Wilson, c	5	0	1	0	4	0
Joost, 2b	5	0	1	0	0	1
Myers, ss	3	0	0	0	2	6
Derringer, p	4	0	0	0	0	3
Totals	38	5	11	4	27	11

Detroit	AB.	R.	H.	RBI.	PO.	A.
Bartell, ss	4	0	0	0	1	0
dFox	1	0	0	0	0	0
McCosky, cf	2	1	1	0	2	0
Gehringer, 2b	4	0	0	0	5	3
Greenberg, lf	4	0	1	1	2	0
York, 1b	2	0	0	0	13	1
Campbell, rf	4	1	1	0	1	0
Higgins, 3b	4	0	2	1	1	9
Sullivan, c	2	0	0	0	2	0
Trout, p	1	0	0	0	0	1
Smith, p	1	0	0	0	0	1
aAverill	1	0	0	0	0	0
McKain, p	0	0	0	0	0	1
cTebbetts	1	0	0	0	0	0
Totals	31	2	5	2	27	16

Cincinnati .... 2 0 1 1 0 0 0 1 0—5
Detroit .... 0 0 1 0 0 1 0 0 0—2

Cincinnati	IP.	H.	R.	ER.	BB.	SO.
Derringer (W)	9	5	2	2	6	4

Detroit	IP.	H.	R.	ER.	BB.	SO.
Trout (L)	2*	6	3	2	1	1
Smith	4	1	1	1	3	1
McKain	3	4	1	1	0	0

*Pitched to three batters in third.

aFlied out for Smith in sixth. bFlied out for Ripple in seventh. cGrounded out for McKain in ninth. dFlied out for Bartell in ninth. E—F. McCormick, Higgins. DP—Cincinnati 2. LOB—Cincinnati 11, Detroit 8. 2B—M. McCormick, Goodman, Ripple, Greenberg. 3B—Higgins. SH—Arnovich. WP—McKain. U—Basil (A.L.), Klem (N.L.), Ormsby (A.L.) and Ballanfant (N.L.). T—2:06. A—54,093.

Game 5

Sunday, October 6, At Detroit

Cincinnati	AB.	R.	H.	RBI.	PO.	A.
Werber, 3b	4	0	1	0	0	0
M. McCormick, cf	4	0	1	0	5	1
Goodman, rf	4	0	0	0	1	0
F. McCormick, 1b	4	0	1	0	5	0
Ripple, lf	2	0	0	0	4	0
Wilson, c	1	0	0	0	3	1
aBaker, c	2	0	0	0	2	0
Joost, 2b	3	0	0	0	2	1
Myers, ss	2	0	0	0	2	0
Thompson, p	1	0	0	0	0	1
Moore, p	0	0	0	0	0	0
bFrey	1	0	0	0	0	0
Vander Meer, p	0	0	0	0	0	0
cRiggs	1	0	0	0	0	0
Hutchings, p	0	0	0	0	0	1
Totals	29	0	3	0	24	5

Detroit	AB.	R.	H.	RBI.	PO.	A.
Bartell, ss	4	1	2	1	0	1
McCosky, cf	3	2	2	0	3	0
Gehringer, 2b	4	2	2	0	2	4
Greenberg, lf	5	2	3	4	1	0
York, 1b	4	0	0	0	7	0
Campbell, rf	4	0	3	2	2	0
Higgins, 3b	2	0	0	0	1	3
Sullivan, c	4	1	1	0	11	0
Newsom, p	4	0	0	0	0	0
Totals	34	8	13	7	27	8

Cincinnati .... 0 0 0 0 0 0 0 0 0—0
Detroit .... 0 0 3 4 0 0 0 1 x—8

Cincinnati	IP.	H.	R.	ER.	BB.	SO.
Thompson (L)	3⅓	8	6	6	4	2
Moore	⅔	1	1	1	2	0
Vander Meer	3	2	1	1	1	0
Hutchings	1	2	1	1	1	0

Detroit	IP.	H.	R.	ER.	BB.	SO.
Newsom (W)	9	3	0	0	2	7

aStruck out for Wilson in fifth. bGrounded out for Moore in fifth. cStruck out for Vander Meer in eighth. DP—Detroit 1. LOB—Cincinnati 4, Detroit 13. 2B—Bartell. HR—Greenberg. SH—Newsom. WP—Hutchings. PB—Wilson. U—Klem (N.L.), Ormsby (A.L.), Ballanfant (N.L.) and Basil (A.L.). T—2:26. A—55,189.

Game 6

Monday, October 7, At Cincinnati

Detroit	AB.	R.	H.	RBI.	PO.	A.
Bartell, ss	3	0	2	0	0	4
bSullivan	1	0	0	0	0	0
Croucher, ss	0	0	0	0	0	0
McCosky, cf	4	0	0	0	1	0
Gehringer, 2b	4	0	0	0	2	1
Greenberg, lf	3	0	0	0	2	0
York, 1b	4	0	2	0	10	0
Campbell, rf	3	0	0	0	2	0
Higgins, 3b	3	0	1	0	1	2
Tebbetts, c	3	0	0	0	6	2
Rowe, p	0	0	0	0	0	1
Gorsica, p	2	0	0	0	0	5
aAverill	1	0	0	0	0	0
Hutchinson, p	0	0	0	0	0	0
Totals	31	0	5	0	24	15

Cincinnati	AB.	R.	H.	RBI.	PO.	A.
Werber, 3b	5	1	2	0	1	3
M. McCormick, cf	3	0	1	0	4	0
Goodman, rf	4	1	2	1	2	0
F. McCormick, 1b	4	0	1	0	10	1
Ripple, lf	2	0	2	1	2	0
Wilson, c	3	1	1	0	4	0
Joost, 2b	3	0	0	0	2	4
Myers, ss	4	0	0	0	2	4
Walters, p	4	1	1	2	0	2
Totals	32	4	10	4	27	14

Detroit .... 0 0 0 0 0 0 0 0 0—0
Cincinnati .... 2 0 0 0 0 1 0 1 x—4

Detroit	IP.	H.	R.	ER.	BB.	SO.
Rowe (L)	⅓	4	2	2	0	0
Gorsica	6⅔	5	1	1	4	3
Hutchinson	1	1	1	1	1	1

Cincinnati	IP.	H.	R.	ER.	BB.	SO.
Walters (W)	9	5	0	0	2	2

aReached first on error for Gorsica in eighth. bFlied out for Bartell in eighth. E—F. McCormick, Myers. DP—Detroit 1, Cincinnati 3. LOB—Detroit 6, Cincinnati 11. 2B—Werber, Bartell. HR—Walters. SH—M. McCormick, Goodman. U—Ormsby (A.L.), Ballanfant (N.L.), Basil (A.L.) and Klem (N.L.). T—2:01. A—30,481.

Game 7

Tuesday, October 8, At Cincinnati

Detroit	AB.	R.	H.	RBI.	PO.	A.
Bartell, ss	4	0	0	0	3	2
McCosky, cf	3	0	0	0	3	0
Gehringer, 2b	4	0	2	0	3	2
Greenberg, lf	4	0	2	0	1	0
York, 1b	4	0	0	0	5	0
Campbell, rf	3	0	0	0	2	0
Higgins, 3b	4	0	1	0	0	4
Sullivan, c	3	1	1	0	6	0
Newsom, p	2	0	1	0	1	0
cAverill	1	0	0	0	0	0
Totals	32	1	7	0	24	8

Cincinnati	AB.	R.	H.	RBI.	PO.	A.
Werber, 3b	4	0	0	0	1	3
M. McCormick, cf	4	0	2	0	4	0
Goodman, rf	4	0	0	0	3	0
F. McCormick, lb	4	1	1	0	6	1
Ripple, lf	3	1	1	1	1	0
Wilson, c	2	0	2	0	2	0
Joost, 2b	2	0	0	0	5	1
aLombardi	0	0	0	0	0	0
bFrey, 2b	0	0	0	0	0	1
Myers, ss	3	0	1	1	5	1
Derringer, p	3	0	0	0	0	1
Totals	29	2	7	2	27	8

Detroit .... 0 0 1 0 0 0 0 0 0—1
Cincinnati .... 0 0 0 0 0 0 2 0 x—2

Detroit	IP.	H.	R.	ER.	BB.	SO.
Newsom (L)	8	7	2	2	1	6

Cincinnati	IP.	H.	R.	ER.	BB.	SO.
Derringer (W)	9	7	1	0	3	1

aWalked for Joost in seventh. bRan for Lombardi in seventh. cGrounded out for Newsom in ninth. E—Werber. DP—Detroit 1. LOB—Detroit 8, Cincinnati 5. 2B—M. McCormick, F. McCormick, Ripple, Higgins. SB—Wilson. SH—Wilson, Newsom. U—Ballanfant (N.L.), Basil (A.L.), Klem (N.L.) and Ormsby (A.L.). T—1:47. A—26,854.

COMPOSITE BATTING AVERAGES

Cincinnati Reds

Player-Position	G.	AB.	R.	H.	2B.	3B.	HR.	RBI.	BA.
Werber, 3b	7	27	5	10	4	0	0	2	.370
Wilson, c	6	17	2	6	0	0	0	0	.353
Ripple, lf	7	21	3	7	2	0	1	6	.333
Lombardi, c-ph	2	3	0	1	1	0	0	0	.333
M. McCormick, cf	7	29	1	9	3	0	0	2	.310
Walters, p	2	7	2	2	1	0	1	2	.286
Goodman, rf	7	29	5	8	2	0	0	5	.276
Baker, c	3	4	1	1	0	0	0	0	.250
F. McCormick, 1b	7	28	2	6	1	0	0	0	.214
Joost, 2b	7	25	0	5	0	0	0	2	.200
Myers, ss	7	23	0	3	0	0	0	2	.130
Aronvich, ph-lf	1	1	0	0	0	0	0	0	.000
Riggs, ph	3	3	1	0	0	0	0	0	.000
Derringer, p	3	7	0	0	0	0	0	0	.000
Moore, p	3	2	0	0	0	0	0	0	.000
Riddle, p	1	0	0	0	0	0	0	0	.000
Turner, p	1	2	0	0	0	0	0	0	.000
Beggs, p	1	0	0	0	0	0	0	0	.000
Thompson, p	1	1	0	0	0	0	0	0	.000
Vander Meer, p	1	0	0	0	0	0	0	0	.000
Hutchings, p	1	0	0	0	0	0	0	0	.000
Frey, ph-pr-2b	3	2	0	0	0	0	0	0	.000
Craft, ph	1	1	0	0	0	0	0	0	.000
Totals	7	232	22	58	14	0	2	21	.250

Detroit Tigers

Player-Position	G.	AB.	R.	H.	2B.	3B.	HR.	RBI.	BA.
Campbell, rf	7	25	4	9	1	0	1	5	.360
Greenberg, lf	7	28	5	10	2	1	1	6	.357
Higgins, 3b	7	24	2	8	3	1	1	6	.333
McCosky, cf	7	23	5	7	1	0	0	1	.304
Bartell, ss	7	26	2	7	2	0	0	3	.269
York, 1b	7	26	3	6	0	1	1	2	.231
Gehringer, 2b	7	28	3	6	0	0	0	1	.214
Sullivan, c-ph	5	13	3	2	0	0	0	0	.154
Newsom, p	3	10	1	1	0	0	0	0	.100
Croucher, ss	1	0	0	0	0	0	0	0	.000
Tebbetts, c-ph	4	11	0	0	0	0	0	0	.000
Rowe, p	2	1	0	0	0	0	0	0	.000
Gorsica, p	2	4	0	0	0	0	0	0	.000
Bridges, p	1	3	0	0	0	0	0	0	.000
Trout, p	1	1	0	0	0	0	0	0	.000
Smith, p	1	1	0	0	0	0	0	0	.000
McKain, p	1	0	0	0	0	0	0	0	.000
Hutchinson, p	1	0	0	0	0	0	0	0	.000
Averill, ph	3	3	0	0	0	0	0	0	.000
Fox, ph	1	1	0	0	0	0	0	0	.000
Totals	7	228	28	56	9	3	4	24	.246

COMPOSITE PITCHING AVERAGES

Cincinnati Reds

Pitcher	G.	IP.	H.	R.	ER.	BB.	SO.	W.	L.	ERA.
Vander Meer	1	3	2	0	0	3	2	0	0	0.00
Riddle	1	1	0	0	0	0	2	0	0	0.00
Walters	2	18	8	3	3	6	6	2	0	1.50
Derringer	3	19⅓	17	8	6	10	6	2	1	2.79
Moore	3	8⅓	8	3	3	6	7	0	0	3.24
Turner	1	6	8	5	5	0	4	0	1	7.50
Hutchings	1	1	2	1	1	1	0	0	0	9.00
Beggs	1	1	3	2	1	0	1	0	0	9.00
Thompson	1	3⅓	8	6	6	4	2	0	1	16.20
Totals	7	61	56	28	25	30	30	4	3	3.69

Detroit Tigers

Pitcher	G.	IP.	H.	R.	ER.	BB.	SO.	W.	L.	ERA.
Gorsica	2	11⅓	6	1	1	4	4	0	0	0.79
Newsom	3	26	18	4	4	4	17	2	1	1.38
Smith	1	4	1	1	1	3	1	0	0	2.25
McKain	1	3	4	1	1	0	0	0	0	3.00
Bridges	1	9	10	4	3	1	5	1	0	3.00
Hutchinson	1	1	1	1	1	1	1	0	0	9.00
Trout	1	2	6	3	2	1	1	0	1	9.00
Rowe	2	3⅔	12	7	7	1	1	0	2	17.18
Totals	7	60	58	22	20	15	30	3	4	3.00

NEW YORK YANKEES
VS.
BROOKLYN DODGERS

"That was a tough break for poor Mickey to get. I bet he feels like a nickel's worth of dog meat."

Mickey Owen surely felt a little worse than that. And even if Tommy Henrich's quaintly un-profane sizeup of the situation didn't quite capture the gravity of the misdeed, it at least conveyed some of the torment.

Owen, you see, had erred grievously in the ninth inning of Game 4 of the 1941 World Series.

With two out, no New York Yankees on base and Brooklyn leading by a 4-3 score, a third strike on the Yanks' Henrich got past Dodgers catcher Owen. And instead of salting away a victory that would have tied the Series at two victories apiece, Brooklyn saw the Yankees break loose for four runs in the inning and steal off with a 7-4 victory. New York wrapped up the Series championship the next afternoon.

"Sure, it was my fault," said Owen, nearly in tears after the game. "The ball was a low curve that broke down. It hit the edge of my glove and glanced off, but I should have had him out anyway.

"But who ever said those Yanks were such great sluggers? They're the real bums in this Series, with that great reputation of theirs."

The facts said Joe McCarthy's Yankees were great sluggers. Joe DiMaggio, Charlie Keller and Henrich all had reached the 30-homer mark in 1941, and Joe Gordon slammed 24 home runs. But Owen had a point in terms of the New Yorkers' Series production. Through the first four games of the fall classic, the Yankees had struck one home run. And in their 34 innings of Series at-bats preceding the fateful ninth of Game 4, the Yanks had scored only 10 runs.

The key play of the '41 Series occurred in Game 4 when Dodger catcher Mickey Owen gave the Yankees new life by letting Tommy Henrich's ninth-inning third strike and a potential Series-tying victory get away.

As usual, though, the Yankees were getting the job done. Gordon had homered and knocked in two runs in the Series opener, which went to New York, 3-2, on Red Ruffing's six-hitter. After losing to Brooklyn's Whitlow Wyatt, 3-2, in Game 2, the Yankees got a break and reclaimed the Series lead.

Brooklyn's Freddie Fitzsimmons was locked in a scoreless duel with Marius Russo in Game 3 when, with two out in the seventh, the Yanks' pitcher hit a line drive that caught Fitzsimmons flush on the knee. While shortstop Pee Wee Reese caught the deflected ball on the fly to end the inning, Fitzsimmons was through for the day. Dodgers reliever Hugh Casey then was cuffed for four hits and two runs in the eighth, and Brooklyn, able to get only four hits off Russo, went down to a 2-1 defeat.

Pinch-hitter Jimmy Wasdell's two-run double in the fourth inning and Pete Reiser's two-run homer in the fifth enabled Leo Durocher's Dodgers to overcome a 3-0 deficit in the fourth game. Casey, who had come on to quell New York's bases-loaded threat in the top of the fifth, then blanked the Yankees through the eighth inning. In the ninth, he got Johnny Sturm and Red Rolfe on ground balls to open the inning. Henrich was up next, and the Ebbets Field crowd—sensing victory—was poised to let out a roar.

That roar was in the here-it-comes stage when Casey struck out Henrich, but was muffled when the ball got away from Owen and Henrich raced to first base. DiMaggio followed with a single, and Keller shot the Yankees ahead with a two-run double. After a walk to Bill Dickey, Gordon further quieted the Dodger faithful with another two-run double.

The Yankees' Johnny Murphy then turned in his second straight inning of 1-2-3 relief, and New York had handed Brooklyn a

devastating defeat.

Ernie (Tiny) Bonham then put the Dodgers out of their misery, tossing a four-hitter in Game 5. Henrich homered in the Yankees' Series-clinching 3-1 triumph.

The power-laden Yanks, who had scored another of their patented pennant runaways in 1941 (winning by 17 games), hit just two home runs and batted only .247 in the World Series. Still, they managed to blot out the Dodgers, who got even less offensive production (one homer and a .182 average) and a couple of tough breaks to boot.

Game 1

Wednesday, October 1, At New York

Brooklyn	AB.	R.	H.	RBI.	PO.	A.
Walker, rf	3	0	0	0	3	0
Herman, 2b	3	0	0	0	0	6
Reiser, cf	3	0	0	0	4	0
Camilli, 1b	4	0	0	0	7	2
Medwick, lf	4	0	1	0	4	0
Lavagetto, 3b	4	1	0	0	0	0
Reese, ss	4	1	3	0	4	2
Owen, c	2	0	1	1	1	0
aRiggs	1	0	1	1	0	0
Franks, c	1	0	0	0	0	1
Davis, p	2	0	0	0	1	0
Casey, p	0	0	0	0	0	0
bWasdell	1	0	0	0	0	0
Allen, p	0	0	0	0	0	0
Totals	32	2	6	2	24	11

New York	AB.	R.	H.	RBI.	PO.	A.
Sturm, 1b	3	0	1	0	7	0
Rolfe, 3b	3	0	1	0	2	2
Henrich, rf	4	0	0	0	0	0
DiMaggio, cf	4	0	0	0	5	0
Keller, lf	2	2	0	0	4	0
Dickey, c	4	0	2	1	6	0
Gordon, 2b	2	1	2	2	0	2
Rizzuto, ss	4	0	0	0	3	5
Ruffing, p	3	0	0	0	0	0
Totals	29	3	6	3	27	9

Brooklyn	0 0 0	0 1 0	1 0 0—2
New York	0 1 0	1 0 1	0 0 x—3

Brooklyn	IP.	H.	R.	ER.	BB.	SO.
Davis (L)	5⅓	6	3	3	3	1
Casey	⅔	0	0	0	0	0
Allen	2	0	0	0	2	0

New York	IP.	H.	R.	ER.	BB.	SO.
Ruffing (W)	9	6	2	1	3	5

aSingled for Owen in seventh. bFouled out for Casey in seventh. E—Rizzuto. DP—New York 2. LOB—Brooklyn 6, New York 8. 2B—Dickey. 3B—Owen. HR—Gordon. HBP—By Allen (Sturm). U—McGowan (A.L.), Pinelli (N.L.), Grieve (A.L.) and Goetz (N.L.). T—2:08. A—68,540.

Game 2

Thursday, October 2, At New York

Brooklyn	AB.	R.	H.	RBI.	PO.	A.
Walker, rf	4	1	0	0	4	0
Herman, 2b	4	0	1	0	4	4
Reiser, cf	4	0	0	0	2	1
Camilli, 1b	3	1	1	1	8	1
Medwick, lf	4	1	2	0	0	0
Lavagetto, 3b	3	0	1	0	1	1
Reese, ss	4	0	0	1	2	4
Owen, c	2	0	1	1	6	1
Wyatt, p	3	0	0	0	0	1
Totals	31	3	6	3	27	13

New York	AB.	R.	H.	RBI.	PO.	A.
Sturm, 1b	5	0	1	0	11	0
Rolfe, 3b	5	0	1	0	1	2
Henrich, rf	4	1	1	0	0	0
DiMaggio, cf	3	0	0	0	4	0
Keller, lf	4	1	2	1	1	0
Dickey, c	4	0	0	0	5	1
aBordagaray	0	0	0	0	0	0
Rosar, c	0	0	0	0	0	0
Gordon, 2b	1	0	1	0	2	7
Rizzuto, ss	4	0	1	0	3	5
Chandler, p	2	0	1	1	0	0
Murphy, p	1	0	0	0	0	0
bSelkirk	1	0	1	0	0	0
Totals	34	2	9	2	27	15

Brooklyn	0 0 0	0 2 1	0 0 0—3
New York	0 1 1	0 0 0	0 0 0—2

Brooklyn	IP.	H.	R.	ER.	BB.	SO.
Wyatt (W)	9	9	2	2	5	5

New York	IP.	H.	R.	ER.	BB.	SO.
Chandler (L)	5*	4	3	2	2	2
Murphy	4	2	0	0	1	2

*Pitched to two batters in sixth.

aRan for Dickey in eighth. bSingled for Murphy in ninth. E—Reese 2, Gordon. DP—Brooklyn 1, New York 3. LOB—Brooklyn 4, New York 10. 2B—Henrich, Medwick. U—Pinelli (N.L.), Grieve (A.L.), Goetz (N.L.) and McGowan (A.L.). T—2:31. A—66,248.

Game 3

Saturday, October 4, At Brooklyn

New York	AB.	R.	H.	RBI.	PO.	A.
Sturm, 1b	4	0	1	0	12	0
Rolfe, 3b	4	1	2	0	1	2
Henrich, rf	3	1	1	0	2	0
DiMaggio, cf	4	0	2	1	2	0
Keller, lf	4	0	1	1	2	0
Dickey, c	4	0	0	0	4	1
Gordon, 2b	3	0	1	0	2	4
Rizzuto, ss	3	0	0	0	2	3
Russo, p	4	0	0	0	0	4
Totals	33	2	8	2	27	14

Brooklyn	AB.	R.	H.	RBI.	PO.	A.
Reese, ss	4	0	1	1	3	1
Herman, 2b	1	0	0	0	0	1
Coscarart, 2b	2	0	0	0	0	3
Reiser, cf	4	0	1	0	5	0
Medwick, lf	4	0	1	0	3	0
Lavagetto, 3b	3	0	0	0	1	0
Camilli, 1b	3	0	0	0	11	0
Walker, rf	3	1	1	0	2	0
Owen, c	3	0	0	0	2	1
Fitzsimmons, p	2	0	0	0	0	2
Casey, p	0	0	0	0	0	0
French, p	0	0	0	0	0	0
aGalan	1	0	0	0	0	0
Allen, p	0	0	0	0	0	0
Totals	30	1	4	1	27	8

New York	0 0 0	0 0 0	0 2 0—2
Brooklyn	0 0 0	0 0 0	0 1 0—1

New York	IP.	H.	R.	ER.	BB.	SO.
Russo (W)	9	4	1	1	2	5

Brooklyn	IP.	H.	R.	ER.	BB.	SO.
Fitzsimmons	7	4	0	0	3	1
Casey (L)	⅓	4	2	2	0	0
French	⅔	0	0	0	0	0
Allen	1	0	0	0	0	0

aStruck out for French in eighth. DP—New York 1, Brooklyn 1. LOB—New York 7, Brooklyn 4. 2B—Reiser, Walker. 3B—Gordon. SB—Rizzuto, Sturm. U—Grieve (A.L.), Goetz (N.L.), McGowan (A.L.) and Pinelli (N.L.). T—2:22. A—33,100.

Game 4

Sunday, October 5, At Brooklyn

New York	AB.	R.	H.	RBI.	PO.	A.
Sturm, 1b	5	0	2	2	9	1
Rolfe, 3b	5	1	2	0	0	2
Henrich, rf	4	1	0	0	3	0
DiMaggio, cf	4	1	2	0	2	0
Keller, lf	5	1	4	3	1	0
Dickey, c	2	2	0	0	7	0
Gordon, 2b	5	1	2	2	2	3
Rizzuto, ss	4	0	0	0	2	3
Donald, p	2	0	0	0	0	1
Breuer, p	1	0	0	0	0	1
bSelkirk	1	0	0	0	0	0
Murphy, p	1	0	0	0	1	0
Totals	39	7	12	7	27	11

Brooklyn	AB.	R.	H.	RBI.	PO.	A.
Reese, ss	5	0	0	0	2	4
Walker, rf	5	1	2	0	5	0
Reiser, cf	5	1	2	2	1	0
Camilli, 1b	4	0	2	0	10	1
Riggs, 3b	3	0	0	0	0	2
Medwick, lf	2	0	0	0	1	0
Allen, p	0	0	0	0	0	0
Casey, p	2	0	1	0	0	3
Owen, c	2	1	0	0	2	1
Coscarart, 2b	3	1	0	0	4	2
Higbe, p	1	0	1	0	0	1
French, p	0	0	0	0	0	0
aWasdell, lf	3	0	1	2	2	0
Totals	35	4	9	4	27	14

New York	1 0 0	2 0 0	0 0 4—7
Brooklyn	0 0 0	2 2 0	0 0 0—4

New York	IP.	H.	R.	ER.	BB.	SO.
Donald	4*	6	4	4	3	2
Breuer	3	3	0	0	1	2
Murphy (W)	2	0	0	0	0	1

Brooklyn	IP.	H.	R.	ER.	BB.	SO.
Higbe	3⅔	6	3	3	2	1
French	⅓	0	0	0	0	0
Allen	⅔	1	0	0	1	0
Casey (L)	4⅓	5	4	0	2	1

*Pitched to two batters in fifth.

aDoubled for French in fourth. bGrounded out for Breuer in eighth. E—Owen. DP—New York 1. LOB—New York 11, Brooklyn 8. 2B—Keller 2, Walker, Camilli, Wasdell, Gordon. HR—Reiser. HBP—By Allen (Henrich). U—Goetz (N.L.), McGowan (A.L.), Pinelli (N.L.) and Grieve (A.L.). T—2:54. A—33,813.

Game 5

Monday, October 6, At Brooklyn

New York	AB.	R.	H.	RBI.	PO.	A.
Sturm, 1b	4	0	1	0	9	0
Rolfe, 3b	3	0	0	0	3	0
Henrich, rf	3	1	1	1	1	0
DiMaggio, cf	4	0	1	0	6	0
Keller, lf	3	1	0	0	4	0
Dickey, c	4	1	1	0	2	0
Gordon, 2b	3	0	1	1	0	3
Rizzuto, ss	3	0	1	0	2	2
Bonham, p	4	0	0	0	0	1
Totals	31	3	6	2	27	6

Brooklyn	AB.	R.	H.	RBI.	PO.	A.
Walker, rf	3	0	1	0	0	0
Riggs, 3b	4	0	1	0	1	3
Reiser, cf	4	0	1	1	2	0
Camilli, 1b	4	0	0	0	9	1
Medwick, lf	3	0	0	0	0	0
Reese, ss	3	0	0	0	2	3
bWasdell	1	0	0	0	0	0
Owen, c	3	0	0	0	9	1
Coscarart, 2b	2	0	0	0	3	3
aGalan	1	0	0	0	0	0
Herman, 2b	0	0	0	0	0	2
Wyatt, p	3	1	1	0	1	1
Totals	31	1	4	1	27	14

New York	0 2 0	0 1 0	0 0 0—3
Brooklyn	0 0 1	0 0 0	0 0 0—1

New York	IP.	H.	R.	ER.	BB.	SO.
Bonham (W)	9	4	1	1	2	2

Brooklyn	IP.	H.	R.	ER.	BB.	SO.
Wyatt (L)	9	6	3	3	5	9

aFouled out for Coscarart in seventh. bFlied out for Reese in ninth. E—Reese. DP—Brooklyn 3. LOB—New York 6, Brooklyn 5. 2B—Wyatt. 3B—Reiser. HR—Henrich. WP—Wyatt. U—McGowan (A.L.), Pinelli (N.L.), Grieve (A.L.) and Goetz (N.L.). T—2:13. A—34,072.

COMPOSITE BATTING AVERAGES

New York Yankees

Player-Position	G.	AB.	R.	H.	2B.	3B.	HR.	RBI.	BA.
Gordon, 2b	5	14	2	7	1	1	1	5	.500
Chandler, p	1	2	0	1	0	0	0	1	.500
Selkirk, ph	2	2	0	1	0	0	0	0	.500
Keller, lf	5	18	5	7	2	0	0	5	.389
Rolfe, 3b	5	20	2	6	0	0	0	0	.300
Sturm, 1b	5	21	0	6	0	0	0	2	.286
DiMaggio, cf	5	19	1	5	0	0	0	1	.263
Henrich, rf	5	18	4	3	1	0	1	1	.167
Dickey, c	5	18	3	3	1	0	0	1	.167
Rizzuto, ss	5	18	0	2	0	0	0	0	.111
Rosar, c	1	0	0	0	0	0	0	0	.000
Ruffing, p	1	3	0	0	0	0	0	0	.000
Murphy, p	2	2	0	0	0	0	0	0	.000
Russo, p	1	4	0	0	0	0	0	0	.000
Donald, p	1	2	0	0	0	0	0	0	.000
Breuer, p	1	1	0	0	0	0	0	0	.000
Bonham, p	1	4	0	0	0	0	0	0	.000
Bordagaray, pr	1	0	0	0	0	0	0	0	.000
Totals	5	166	17	41	5	1	2	16	.247

Brooklyn Dodgers

Player-Position	G.	AB.	R.	H.	2B.	3B.	HR.	RBI.	BA.
Higbe, p	1	1	0	1	0	0	0	0	1.000
Casey, p	3	2	0	1	0	0	0	0	.500
Riggs, ph-3b	3	8	0	2	0	0	0	1	.250
Medwick, lf	5	17	1	4	1	0	0	0	.235
Walker, rf	5	18	3	4	2	0	0	0	.222
Reiser, cf	5	20	1	4	1	1	1	3	.200
Reese, ss	5	20	1	4	0	0	0	2	.200
Wasdell, ph-lf	3	5	0	1	1	0	0	2	.200
Camilli, 1b	5	18	1	3	1	0	0	1	.167
Owen, c	5	12	1	2	0	1	0	2	.167
Wyatt, p	2	6	1	1	1	0	0	0	.167
Herman, 2b	4	8	0	1	0	0	0	0	.125
Lavagetto, 3b	3	10	1	1	0	0	0	0	.100
Coscarart, 2b	3	7	1	0	0	0	0	0	.000
Franks, c	1	1	0	0	0	0	0	0	.000
Davis, p	1	2	0	0	0	0	0	0	.000
Allen, p	3	0	0	0	0	0	0	0	.000
Fitzsimmons, p	1	2	0	0	0	0	0	0	.000
French, p	2	0	0	0	0	0	0	0	.000
Galan, ph	2	2	0	0	0	0	0	0	.000
Totals	5	159	11	29	7	2	1	11	.182

COMPOSITE PITCHING AVERAGES

New York Yankees

Pitcher	G.	IP.	H.	R.	ER.	BB.	SO.	W.	L.	ERA.
Murphy	2	6	2	0	0	1	3	1	0	0.00
Breuer	1	3	3	0	0	1	2	0	0	0.00
Ruffing	1	9	6	2	1	3	5	1	0	1.00
Bonham	1	9	4	1	1	2	2	1	0	1.00
Russo	1	9	4	1	1	2	5	1	0	1.00
Chandler	1	5	4	3	2	2	2	0	1	3.60
Donald	1	4	6	4	4	3	2	0	0	9.00
Totals	5	45	29	11	9	14	21	4	1	1.80

Brooklyn Dodgers

Pitcher	G.	IP.	H.	R.	ER.	BB.	SO.	W.	L.	ERA.
Fitzsimmons	1	7	4	0	0	3	1	0	0	0.00
Allen	3	3⅔	1	0	0	3	0	0	0	0.00
French	2	1	0	0	0	0	0	0	0	0.00
Wyatt	2	18	15	5	5	10	14	1	1	2.50
Casey	3	5⅓	9	6	2	2	1	0	2	3.38
Davis	1	5⅓	6	3	3	3	1	0	1	5.06
Higbe	1	3⅔	6	3	3	2	1	0	0	7.36
Totals	5	44	41	17	13	23	18	1	4	2.66

1942
ST. LOUIS CARDINALS
VS.
NEW YORK YANKEES

Sure, it was early. Game 1 of the 1942 World Series hadn't even been concluded yet. Decided, yes; concluded, no. But, clearly, the "experts" already had this one tabbed: The talent-heavy and experience-rich New York Yankees were just too strong for the skilled-but-youthful band of St. Louis Cardinals.

The Yanks, featuring the likes of Joe DiMaggio, Charlie Keller, Joe Gordon, Bill Dickey and Red Ruffing, were appearing in the Series for the sixth time in the last seven years; the Cards, getting a stupendous season from right-hander Mort Cooper and outstanding efforts from fifth-year major leaguer Enos Slaughter, 21-year-old Stan Musial and rookie pitcher Johnny Beazley, were competing in the fall classic for the first time since 1934.

And, entering the last of the ninth inning of the Series opener, Ruffing and the Yankees held a 7-0 lead. The Cardinals had managed one base hit off the 37-year-old Ruffing, and it took them until the eighth inning—until there were two out in the eighth, in fact—to get that measly hit, a single by center fielder Terry Moore. St. Louis had four errors, New York none. If ever there was a case of savvy over jitters, this appeared to be it.

Musial, the Cardinals' left fielder, fouled out to open the ninth. Catcher Walker Cooper followed with a single, but first baseman Johnny Hopp flied out. The next batter, pinch-hitter Ray Sanders, walked. Then, the Cardinals lashed five consecutive hits that produced four runs. That brought Musial to the plate again. With the bases loaded. Spud Chandler was now pitching for New York, and he got Musial to hit a game-ending grounder to

first base.

No, the Cardinals had not made a miraculous, game-winning comeback. But they clearly had given the Yankees—and the experts—something to think about.

That Manager Billy Southworth's Redbirds could battle back was proved conclusively during the 1942 National League season. They had trailed league-leading Brooklyn by 10 games on the morning of August 5 and charged to a two-game margin of victory over the Dodgers. That Southworth's team was more than capable of winning four of six games—what it now would take to overcome the Yankees in the '42 Series—also was demonstrated in clear-cut fashion during the pennant race. Indeed, a four-of-six pace was a day at the beach for these Cardinals; in overhauling Brooklyn, St. Louis had won 43 of its last 51 games.

The Cardinals did not go out and beat the Yankees in four of six games. The fact is, it didn't take the Cards nearly that long to upend the New Yorkers.

Newcomer Beazley, who posted a 2.13 earned-run average while winning 21 games for St. Louis in 1942, carried a 3-0 lead into the eighth inning of Game 2 but surrendered a run-scoring single to DiMaggio and a two-run homer to Keller. But the Cards wound up winning, 4-3, thanks to Slaughter's double and Musial's single in the bottom of the eighth and Slaughter's ninth-inning throw from right field that nailed Yankee pinch-runner Tuck Stainback at third base (and thereby short-circuited a New York rally).

Cardinals lefthander Ernie White stole the show in Game 3, shutting off the Yankees on six hits and winning, 2-0. White got marvelous outfield support, with

Moore making a great catch in the sixth and Musial and Slaughter making homer-saving catches in the seventh.

Suddenly, St. Louis was exhibiting the skills it had honed while winning 106 regular-season games.

First-game loser Mort Cooper, who in the regular season had won 22 games, fired 10 shutouts and posted an ERA of 1.78, went against Hank Borowy the next day. Cooper lasted only 5⅓ innings and was victimized by Keller's three-run homer in New York's five-run sixth; Borowy lasted into the fourth, an inning in which St. Louis got two-run singles from third baseman Whitey Kurowski and pitcher Cooper (older brother of the Cards' catcher) and scored six times overall.

In the seventh, Walker Cooper's RBI single snapped a 6-6 tie and shortstop Marty Marion delivered a run-scoring fly ball. St. Louis reliever Max Lanier not only proceeded to pitch shutout ball the rest of the way, but he also singled home an insurance run in the ninth. The Cardinals had held on in a wild one, 9-6.

Game 5 matched oldster Ruffing aganst youngster Beazley. And the Yankees jumped on top when Phil Rizzuto, who had hit a total of seven home runs in his first two big-league seasons, hammered a Beazley pitch into the left-field stands in the first inning. St. Louis tied it in the fourth when Slaughter countered with a homer to right, but New York slipped back in front in the bottom of the inning on DiMaggio's run-scoring single. But the resilient Redbirds forged another deadlock in the sixth—Walker Cooper's fly ball drove in the run —and the teams went to the ninth in a 2-2 stalemate.

Walker Cooper touched Ruffing for a single and was sacrificed to second by Hopp. That brought up the 24-year-old Kurowski, who was 3 for 14 at the plate thus far in the Series after batting .254 with nine homers during the regular season in his first extended big-league duty. Kurowski whacked a Ruffing delivery into the left-field stands, just inside the foul pole. Cardinals 4, Yankees 2.

The World Series setback was the first since 1926 for the Yankees, who had won in all eight of their appearances in the fall classic in the interim.

Game 1

Wednesday, September 30, At St. Louis

New York	AB.	R.	H.	RBI.	PO.	A.
Rizzuto, ss	4	0	0	0	2	2
Rolfe, 3b	5	2	2	0	0	1
Cullenbine, rf	3	1	1	0	1	0
DiMaggio, cf	5	2	3	1	3	0
Keller, lf	4	0	0	0	4	0
Gordon, 2b	5	0	0	0	2	1
Dickey, c	4	1	2	0	9	0
Hassett, 1b	4	1	2	2	5	1
Ruffing, p	4	0	1	0	0	0
Chandler, p	0	0	0	0	1	0
Totals	38	7	11	3	27	5

St. Louis	AB.	R.	H.	RBI.	PO.	A.
Brown, 2b	4	0	1	0	1	2
T. Moore, cf	4	0	2	1	1	0
Slaughter, rf	3	0	1	0	1	0
Musial, lf	4	0	0	0	1	0
W. Cooper, c	4	1	1	0	8	1
Hopp, 1b	4	0	0	0	11	1
Kurowski, 3b	3	0	0	0	1	0
bSanders	0	1	0	0	0	0
Marion, ss	4	1	1	2	3	2
M. Cooper, p	2	0	0	0	0	1
Gumbert, p	0	0	0	0	0	0
aWalker	1	0	0	0	0	0
Lanier, p	0	0	0	0	0	1
cO'Dea	1	0	1	1	0	0
dCrespi	0	1	0	0	0	0
Totals	34	4	7	4	27	8

New York	0 0 0	1 1 0	0 3 2	—7
St. Louis	0 0 0	0 0 0	0 0 4	—4

New York	IP.	H.	R.	ER.	BB.	SO.
Ruffing (W)	8⅔	5	4	4	6	8
Chandler	⅓	2	0	0	0	0

St. Louis	IP.	H.	R.	ER.	BB.	SO.
M. Cooper (L)	7⅔	10	5	3	3	7
Gumbert	⅓	0	0	0	0	0
Lanier	1	1	2	0	1	1

aStruck out for Gumbert in eighth. bWalked for Kurowski in ninth. cSingled for Lanier in ninth. dRan for O'Dea in ninth. E—Brown, Slaughter, Lanier 2. LOB—New York 9, St. Louis 9. 2B—Hassett, Cullenbine. 3B—Marion. SH—Cullenbine. U—Magerkurth (N.L.), Summers (A.L.), Barr (N.L.) and Hubbard (A.L.). T—2:35. A—34,769.

Game 2

Thursday, October 1, At St. Louis

New York	AB.	R.	H.	RBI.	PO.	A.
Rizzuto, ss	4	0	1	0	0	3
Rolfe, 3b	4	0	1	0	0	2
Cullenbine, rf	4	1	1	0	2	0
DiMaggio, cf	4	1	1	1	7	0
Keller, lf	4	1	2	2	1	0
Gordon, 2b	4	0	1	0	0	3
Dickey, c	4	0	2	0	5	0
aStainback	0	0	0	0	0	0
Hassett, 1b	4	0	1	0	9	0
Bonham, p	2	0	0	0	0	0
bRuffing	1	0	0	0	0	0
Totals	35	3	10	3	24	8

St. Louis	AB.	R.	H.	RBI.	PO.	A.
Brown, 2b	3	1	0	0	0	3
Moore, cf	3	1	0	0	2	0
Slaughter, rf	4	1	1	0	2	1
Musial, lf	4	0	1	1	5	0
W. Cooper, c	4	0	1	2	4	0
Hopp, 1b	3	1	2	0	11	0
Kurowski, 3b	3	0	1	1	2	1
Marion, ss	3	0	0	0	1	4
Beazley, p	3	0	0	0	0	0
Totals	30	4	6	4	27	9

New York	0 0 0	0 0 0	0 3 0	—3
St. Louis	2 0 0	0 0 0	1 1 x	—4

New York	IP.	H.	R.	ER.	BB.	SO.
Bonham (L)	8	6	4	4	1	3

St. Louis	IP.	H.	R.	ER.	BB.	SO.
Beazley (W)	9	10	3	3	2	4

aRan for Dickey in ninth. bFlied out for Bonham in ninth. E—Rizzuto, Hassett. DP—St. Louis 1. LOB—New York 7, St. Louis 4. 2B—Slaughter, W. Cooper, Rolfe, Gordon. 3B—Kurowski. HR—Keller. SB—Rizzuto, Cullenbine. SH—T. Moore. U—Summers (A.L.), Barr (N.L.), Hubbard (A.L.) and Magerkurth (N.L.). T—1:57. A—34,255.

Game 3

Saturday, October 3, At New York

St. Louis	AB.	R.	H.	RBI.	PO.	A.
Brown, 2b	4	1	1	1	1	2
T. Moore, cf	4	0	0	0	3	0
Slaughter, rf	4	0	1	1	3	0
Musial, lf	3	0	1	0	2	0
W. Cooper, c	4	0	0	0	8	0
Hopp, 1b	4	0	0	0	8	0
Kurowski, 3b	2	1	1	0	2	2
Marion, ss	3	0	1	0	0	1
White, p	2	0	0	0	0	0
Totals	30	2	5	2	27	5

New York	AB.	R.	H.	RBI.	PO.	A.
Rizzuto, ss	4	0	2	0	2	6
Hassett, 1b	1	0	0	0	1	0
Crosetti, 3b	3	0	0	0	1	1
Cullenbine, rf	4	0	1	0	0	0
DiMaggio, cf	4	0	2	0	2	0
Gordon, 2b	4	0	0	0	3	3
Keller, lf	4	0	0	0	2	1
Dickey, c	3	0	1	0	5	1
Priddy, 3b-1b	3	0	0	0	10	1
Chandler, p	2	0	0	0	1	2
aRuffing	1	0	0	0	0	0
Breuer, p	0	0	0	0	0	0
Turner, p	0	0	0	0	0	0
Totals	33	0	6	0	27	15

St. Louis	0 0 1	0 0 0	0 0 1	—2
New York	0 0 0	0 0 0	0 0 0	—0

St. Louis	IP.	H.	R.	ER.	BB.	SO.
White (W)	9	6	0	0	0	6

New York	IP.	H.	R.	ER.	BB.	SO.
Chandler (L)	8	3	1	1	1	3
Breuer	0*	2	1	0	0	0
Turner	1	0	0	0	1	0

*Pitched to three batters in ninth.

aStruck out for Chandler in eighth. E—W. Cooper, Breuer. DP—New York 1. LOB—St. Louis 4, New York 6. SB—Rizzuto. SH—White. U—Barr (N.L.), Hubbard (A.L.), Magerkurth (N.L.) and Summers (A.L.). T—2:30. A—69,123.

Game 4

Sunday, October 4, At New York

St. Louis	AB.	R.	H.	RBI.	PO.	A.
Brown, 2b	6	0	2	0	1	5
T. Moore, cf	3	0	2	1	6	0
Slaughter, rf	4	1	0	0	1	0
Musial, lf	3	2	2	1	3	0
W. Cooper, c	5	1	2	1	2	0
Hopp, 1b	3	2	1	0	7	0
Kurowski, 3b	3	1	1	2	1	0
Marion, ss	4	1	0	1	6	4
M. Cooper, p	3	1	1	2	0	0
Gumbert, p	0	0	0	0	0	0
Pollet, p	0	0	0	0	0	0
aSanders	1	0	0	0	0	0
Lanier, p	1	0	1	1	0	0
Totals	36	9	12	9	27	9

New York	AB.	R.	H.	RBI.	PO.	A.
Rizzuto, ss	5	1	3	0	4	2
Rolfe, 3b	4	2	2	0	2	2
Cullenbine, rf	4	1	2	2	0	0
DiMaggio, cf	4	0	0	0	5	0
Keller, lf	4	1	1	3	4	0
Gordon, 2b	4	1	0	0	3	2
Dickey, c	4	0	0	0	2	0
Priddy, 1b	4	0	1	1	7	2
Borowy, p	1	0	0	0	0	1
Donald, p	2	0	0	0	0	0
Bonham, p	0	0	0	0	0	2
bRosar	1	0	1	0	0	0
Totals	37	6	10	6	27	11

St. Louis	0 0 0	6 0 0	2 0 1	—9
New York	1 0 0	0 0 5	0 0 0	—6

St. Louis	IP.	H.	R.	ER.	BB.	SO.
M. Cooper	5⅓	7	5	5	1	2
Gumbert	⅓	1	1	0	0	0
Pollet	⅓	0	0	0	0	0
Lanier (W)	3	2	0	0	0	0

New York	IP.	H.	R.	ER.	BB.	SO.
Borowy	3*	6	6	6	3	1
Donald (L)	3†	3	2	2	2	1
Bonham	3	3	1	1	2	0

*Pitched to six batters in fourth.
†Pitched to three batters in seventh.

aPopped out for Pollet in seventh. bSingled for Bonham in ninth. E—Kurowski, Dickey. DP—St. Louis 1. LOB—St. Louis 10, New York 5. 2B—T. Moore, Musial, Rolfe, Priddy. HR—Keller. SH—Hopp, T. Moore, Kurowski. U—Hubbard (A.L.), Magerkurth (N.L.), Summers (A.L.) and Barr (N.L.). T—2:28. A—69,902.

Game 5

Monday, October 5, At New York

St. Louis	AB.	R.	H.	RBI.	PO.	A.
Brown, 2b	3	0	2	0	3	4
T. Moore, cf	3	1	1	0	3	0
Slaughter, rf	4	1	2	1	2	0
Musial, lf	4	0	0	0	2	0
W. Cooper, c	4	1	2	1	2	1
Hopp, 1b	3	0	0	0	9	2
Kurowski, 3b	4	1	1	2	1	1
Marion, ss	4	0	0	0	3	5
Beazley, p	4	0	1	0	2	0
Totals	33	4	9	4	27	13

New York	AB.	R.	H.	RBI.	PO.	A.
Rizzuto, ss	4	1	2	1	7	1
Rolfe, 3b	4	1	1	0	1	0
Cullenbine, rf	4	0	0	0	3	0
DiMaggio, cf	4	0	1	1	3	0
Keller, lf	4	0	1	0	1	0
Gordon, 2b	4	0	1	0	3	3
Dickey, c	4	0	0	0	4	0
aStainback	0	0	0	0	0	0
Priddy, 1b	3	0	0	0	5	1
Ruffing, p	3	0	1	0	0	1
bSelkirk	1	0	0	0	0	0
Totals	35	2	7	2	27	6

St. Louis	0 0 0	1 0 1	0 0 2	—4
New York	1 0 0	1 0 0	0 0 0	—2

St. Louis	IP.	H.	R.	ER.	BB.	SO.
Beazley (W)	9	7	2	2	1	2

New York	IP.	H.	R.	ER.	BB.	SO.
Ruffing (L)	9	9	4	4	1	3

aRan for Dickey in ninth. bGrounded out for Ruffing in ninth. E—Brown 2, Hopp, Beazley, Priddy. DP—St. Louis 1, New York 1. LOB—St. Louis 5, New York 7. HR—Rizzuto, Slaughter, Kurowski. SH—T. Moore, Hopp. U—Magerkurth (N.L.), Summers (A.L.), Barr (N.L.) and Hubbard (A.L.). T—1:58. A—69,052.

COMPOSITE BATTING AVERAGES

St. Louis Cardinals

Player-Position	G.	AB.	R.	H.	2B.	3B.	HR.	RBI.	BA.
Lanier, p	2	1	0	1	0	0	0	1	1.000
O'Dea, ph	1	1	0	1	0	0	0	1	1.000
Brown, 2b	5	20	2	6	0	0	0	1	.300
T. Moore, cf	5	17	2	5	1	0	0	2	.294
W. Cooper, c	5	21	3	6	1	0	0	4	.286
Kurowski, 3b	5	15	3	4	0	1	1	5	.267
Slaughter, rf	5	19	3	5	1	0	1	2	.263
Musial, lf	5	18	2	4	1	0	0	2	.222
M. Cooper, p	2	5	1	1	0	0	0	2	.200
Hopp, 1b	5	17	3	3	0	0	0	0	.176
Beazley, p	2	7	0	1	0	0	0	0	.143
Marion, ss	5	18	2	2	0	1	0	3	.111
Gumbert, p	2	0	0	0	0	0	0	0	.000
White, p	1	2	0	0	0	0	0	0	.000
Pollet, p	1	0	0	0	0	0	0	0	.000
Crespi, pr	1	0	1	0	0	0	0	0	.000
Sanders, ph	2	1	1	0	0	0	0	0	.000
Walker, ph	1	1	0	0	0	0	0	0	.000
Totals	5	163	23	39	4	2	2	23	.239

New York Yankees

Player-Position	G.	AB.	R.	H.	2B.	3B.	HR.	RBI.	BA.
Rosar, ph	1	1	0	1	0	0	0	0	1.000
Rizzuto, ss	5	21	2	8	0	0	1	1	.381
Rolfe, 3b	4	17	5	6	2	0	0	0	.353
DiMaggio, cf	5	21	3	7	0	0	0	3	.333
Hassett, 1b	3	9	1	3	1	0	0	2	.333
Cullenbine, rf	5	19	3	5	1	0	0	2	.263
Dickey, c	5	19	1	5	0	0	0	0	.263
Ruffing, p-ph	4	9	0	2	0	0	0	0	.222
Keller, lf	5	20	2	4	0	0	2	5	.200
Priddy, 3b-1b	3	10	0	1	1	0	0	1	.100
Gordon, 2b	5	21	1	2	1	0	0	0	.095
Crosetti, 3b	1	3	0	0	0	0	0	0	.000
Chandler, p	2	2	0	0	0	0	0	0	.000
Bonham, p	2	2	0	0	0	0	0	0	.000
Breuer, p	1	0	0	0	0	0	0	0	.000
Turner, p	1	0	0	0	0	0	0	0	.000
Borowy, p	1	1	0	0	0	0	0	0	.000
Donald, p	1	2	0	0	0	0	0	0	.000
Selkirk, ph	1	1	0	0	0	0	0	0	.000
Stainback, pr	2	0	0	0	0	0	0	0	.000
Totals	5	178	18	44	6	0	3	14	.247

COMPOSITE PITCHING AVERAGES

St. Louis Cardinals

Pitcher	G.	IP.	H.	R.	ER.	BB.	SO.	W.	L.	ERA.
White	1	9	6	0	0	0	6	1	0	0.00
Lanier	2	4	3	2	0	1	1	1	0	0.00
Gumbert	2	⅔	1	1	0	0	0	0	0	0.00
Pollet	1	⅓	0	0	0	0	0	0	0	0.00
Beazley	2	18	17	5	5	3	6	2	0	2.50
M. Cooper	2	13	17	10	8	4	9	0	1	5.54
Totals	5	45	44	18	13	8	22	4	1	2.60

New York Yankees

Pitcher	G.	IP.	H.	R.	ER.	BB.	SO.	W.	L.	ERA.
Turner	1	1	0	0	0	1	0	0	0	0.00
Breuer	1	0	2	1	0	0	0	0	0	0.00
Chandler	2	8⅓	5	1	1	1	3	0	1	1.08
Ruffing	2	17⅔	14	8	8	7	11	1	1	4.08
Bonham	2	11	9	5	5	3	3	0	1	4.09
Donald	1	3	3	2	2	2	1	0	1	6.00
Borowy	1	3	6	6	6	3	1	0	0	18.00
Totals	5	44	39	23	22	17	19	1	4	4.50

Having gathered up a full head of steam after their remarkable pennant-race and World Series charges of the previous season, the St. Louis Cardinals blew past their National League rivals in 1943 on the way to a second successive postseason date with the New York Yankees.

Pennant-winners by two games in 1942, the Cardinals finished on top by 18 games in 1943. And while the military call-up surely weakened the opposition, it hurt the Cards as badly as any team. Outfielders Terry Moore and Enos Slaughter, second baseman Jimmy Brown and pitchers Johnny Beazley and Howie Pollet were key St. Louis players summoned by Uncle Sam for World War II duty. St. Louis got some sizable contributions from its farm system, though, with Lou Klein taking over for Brown at second base and Al Brazle and Harry Brecheen providing pitching help. Most of all, the Cards got tremendous seasons from fast-emerging outfielder Stan Musial, who in his second season as a big-league regular won his first N.L. batting title by hitting a robust .357, and pitchers Pollet (who entered the service in August), Max Lanier and Mort Cooper, who ranked 1-2-3 in the league in earned-run average with gaudy figures of 1.75, 1.90 and 2.30, respectively.

The Yankees lost Joe DiMaggio, Phil Rizzuto and Red Ruffing because of military service, but persevered. Charlie Keller and Joe Gordon were still on hand, and they provided power with 31 and 17 homers, respectively. First baseman Nick Etten, an off-season acquisition from the Philadelphia Phillies, proved a significant addition. He drove in a team-high 107 runs. Spud Chandler paced the pitching staff with 20 vic-

By the 1943 World Series, young Cardinal Stan Musial was emerging as one of the top talents in the major leagues.

tories. The cumulative result—in Joe McCarthy's 13th season at the Yankees' helm—was a 13½-game bulge over runner-up Washington in the American League race.

As in the 1942 Series, the Cardinals fell in Game 1 of the 1943 fall classic. Chandler pitched seven-hit ball in a 4-2 triumph, with McCarthy's Yanks breaking a 2-2 tie in the sixth on singles by Frankie Crosetti and rookie third baseman Billy Johnson, a wild pitch by Lanier and another single by Bill Dickey.

The Cooper brothers, playing despite the death of their father earlier in the day, formed the St. Louis battery in Game 2. Mort pitched one-run ball for eight innings—the Yankees rallied for two runs in the bottom of the ninth—and wound up a 4-3 winner. Walker singled in three at-bats and laid down a sacrifice bunt. The hitting stars for the Cards were Marty Marion, who belted a third-inning homer with

the bases empty, and Ray Sanders, who powered a two-run shot in the fourth.

Could the Cardinals possibly match their 1942 feat of wiping out the Yanks in four straight after losing the opener?

Brazle, a 29-year-old rookie who won eight of 10 decisions in the regular season and boasted a sparkling 1.53 ERA, kept the Cards' hopes alive for a repeat of '42—or at least of seizing the lead in this Series—by pitching masterfully through seven innings of Game 3. But the roof caved in on the lefthander in the eighth, when the Yankees scored five times.

Johnny Lindell, a converted pitcher who was manning center field in the absence of DiMaggio, began the inning with a single and took second when center fielder Harry Walker misplayed the ball. Pinch-hitter George Stirnweiss then bunted, and first baseman Sanders threw to third baseman Whitey Kurowski in an effort to cut down Lindell. The throw was in time, but Lindell crashed into Kurowski and jarred the ball loose. After a fly ball moved Stirnweiss to second, Crosetti was walked intentionally to load the bases. Johnson, a .280 hitter in his first season with the Yankees, proceeded to foil the strategy by clearing the bases with a triple. Gordon and Etten added run-scoring singles later in the inning, pushing the score to 6-2. Johnny Murphy worked a 1-2-3 ninth in relief of winning pitcher Hank Borowy, and the Yanks no longer had to fret about a rerun of the 1942 World Series.

Any fretting, in fact, soon went the Cardinals' way. Marius Russo, a 5-10 pitcher for the Yankees in '43, limited St. Louis to seven hits in Game 4 and doubled and scored the winning run in the

eighth as New York prevailed, 2-1.

Now, the Cardinals were thinking survival. The Yankees, ever mindful of their previous year's fate, were thinking revenge. It would be Mort Cooper against Chandler the next afternoon.

By the end of Game 5, St. Louis was thinking about next year. The Cardinals collected 10 hits off Chandler, but couldn't score off the 36-year-old righthander. The Yankees, meanwhile, got a two-run homer from Dickey in the sixth. And that was it, 2-0, New York.

And that was it for McCarthy, who in turning the five-game tables on the Cardinals had managed his seventh and last World Series champion.

Game 1

Tuesday, October 5, At New York

St. Louis	AB.	R.	H.	RBI.	PO.	A.
Klein, 2b	4	0	1	0	0	2
Walker, cf	4	0	0	0	2	0
Musial, rf	4	0	1	0	1	0
W. Cooper, c	4	1	1	0	7	1
Kurowski, 3b	3	0	0	0	1	1
Sanders, 1b	4	1	2	0	8	0
Litwhiler, lf	3	0	0	0	3	0
Marion, ss	3	0	1	1	2	3
Lanier, p	2	0	1	1	0	1
aGarms	1	0	0	0	0	0
Brecheen, p	0	0	0	0	0	1
Totals	32	2	7	2	24	9

New York	AB.	R.	H.	RBI.	PO.	A.
Stainback, rf	4	0	1	0	2	1
Crosetti, ss	4	2	1	0	3	3
Johnson, 3b	4	1	2	0	0	3
Keller, lf	4	0	1	0	0	0
Gordon, 2b	3	1	1	1	4	8
Dickey, c	4	0	1	1	4	0
Etten, 1b	4	0	0	0	11	0
Lindell, cf	3	0	0	0	3	0
Chandler, p	3	0	1	0	0	2
Totals	33	4	8	2	27	17

St. Louis .... 0 1 0 0 1 0 0 0 0—2
New York .... 0 0 0 2 0 2 0 0 x—4

St. Louis	IP.	H.	R.	ER.	BB.	SO.
Lanier (L)	7	7	4	2	0	7
Brecheen	1	1	0	0	1	1

New York	IP.	H.	R.	ER.	BB.	SO.
Chandler (W)	9	7	2	1	1	3

aStruck out for Lanier in eighth. E—Klein, Lanier, Crosetti, Etten. DP—St. Louis 1, New York 1. LOB—St. Louis 5, New York 6. 2B—Marion. HR—Gordon. SB—Crosetti. SH—Kurowski. WP—Lanier. U—Rommel (A.L.), Reardon (N.L.), Rue (A.L.) and Stewart (N.L.). T—2:07. A—68,676.

Game 2

Wednesday, October 6, At New York

St. Louis	AB.	R.	H.	RBI.	PO.	A.
Klein, 2b	4	0	1	0	4	4
Walker, cf	5	0	1	0	5	0
Musial, rf	4	1	1	0	2	0
W. Cooper, c	3	0	1	0	5	0
Kurowski, 3b	4	1	1	1	0	1
Sanders, 1b	3	1	1	2	8	0
Litwhiler, lf	3	0	0	0	3	0
Marion, ss	3	1	1	1	0	3
M. Cooper, p	3	0	0	0	0	0
Totals	32	4	7	4	27	8

New York	AB.	R.	H.	RBI.	PO.	A.
Crosetti, ss	4	1	2	0	2	2
xMetheny, rf	3	0	0	0	2	0
Johnson, 3b	4	1	2	0	0	1
Keller, lf	4	1	1	2	3	0
Dickey, c	3	0	0	0	9	2
Etten, 1b	4	0	0	1	4	0
Gordon, 2b	4	0	1	0	4	0
Stainback, cf	3	0	0	0	3	0
Bonham, p	2	0	0	0	0	0
aWeatherly	1	0	0	0	0	0
Murphy, p	0	0	0	0	0	1
Totals	32	3	6	3	27	6

St. Louis .... 0 0 1 3 0 0 0 0 0—4
New York .... 0 0 0 1 0 0 0 0 2—3

St. Louis	IP.	H.	R.	ER.	BB.	SO.
M. Cooper (W)	9	6	3	3	1	4

New York	IP.	H.	R.	ER.	BB.	SO.
Bonham (L)	8	6	4	4	3	9
Murphy	1	1	0	0	1	0

xAwarded first base on catcher's interference. aFouled out for Bonham in eighth. E—Walker, W. Cooper. DP—St. Louis 1. LOB—St. Louis 7, New York 4. 2B—Johnson. 3B—Keller. HR—Marion, Sanders. SB—Marion. SH—W. Cooper, M. Cooper. U—Reardon (N.L.), Rue (A.L.), Stewart (N.L.) and Rommel (A.L.). T—2:08. A—68,578.

Game 3

Thursday, October 7, At New York

St. Louis	AB.	R.	H.	RBI.	PO.	A.
Klein, 2b	4	0	0	0	2	2
Walker, cf	4	0	1	0	1	0
Musial, rf	3	1	1	0	1	1
W. Cooper, c	4	0	1	0	3	2
Kurowski, 3b	3	1	1	0	2	2
bO'Dea	1	0	0	0	0	0
Sanders, 1b	3	0	0	0	9	2
Litwhiler, lf	4	0	2	2	3	0
Marion, ss	2	0	0	0	2	4
Brazle, p	3	0	0	0	1	2
Krist, p	0	0	0	0	0	0
Brecheen, p	0	0	0	0	0	0
Totals	31	2	6	2	24	15

New York	AB.	R.	H.	RBI.	PO.	A.
Stainback, cf	4	0	1	0	1	0
Crosetti, ss	2	1	0	0	2	4
Johnson, 3b	4	1	1	3	0	1
Keller, lf	3	1	0	0	2	0
Gordon, 2b	4	0	1	1	3	2
Dickey, c	4	0	2	0	6	1
Etten, 1b	4	0	1	1	9	1
Lindell, rf	3	1	1	0	2	0
Borowy, p	2	1	1	0	2	0
aStirnweiss	1	1	1	0	0	0
Murphy, p	0	0	0	0	0	0
Totals	31	6	8	5	27	9

St. Louis .... 0 0 0 2 0 0 0 0 0—2
New York .... 0 0 0 0 0 1 0 5 x—6

St. Louis	IP.	H.	R.	ER.	BB.	SO.
Brazle (L)	7⅓	5	6	3	2	4
Krist	0*	1	0	0	0	0
Brecheen	⅔	2	0	0	0	0

New York	IP.	H.	R.	ER.	BB.	SO.
Borowy (W)	8	6	2	2	3	4
Murphy	1	0	0	0	0	1

*Pitched to one batter in eighth.

aReached first on error on fielder's choice for Borowy in eighth. bPopped out for Kurowski in ninth. E—Walker, Kurowski 2, Marion. DP—St. Louis 1, New York 1. LOB—St. Louis 5, New York 4. 2B—Walker, Kurowski, Borowy. 3B—Johnson. SH—Crosetti. U—Rue (A.L.), Stewart (N.L.), Rommell (A.L.) and Reardon (N.L.). T—2:10. A—69,990.

Game 4

Sunday, October 10, At St. Louis

New York	AB.	R.	H.	RBI.	PO.	A.
Stainback, cf	3	0	0	0	1	0
Crosetti, ss	4	0	1	1	2	2
Johnson, 3b	4	0	0	0	1	2
Keller, lf	4	0	1	0	4	0
Gordon, 2b	4	1	1	0	3	7
Dickey, c	3	0	1	1	2	0
Etten, 1b	4	0	0	0	11	0
Lindell, rf	3	0	0	0	3	0
Russo, p	3	1	2	0	0	2
Totals	32	2	6	2	27	13

St. Louis	AB.	R.	H.	RBI.	PO.	A.
Klein, 2b	5	0	0	0	1	4
Walker, cf	4	0	0	0	2	0
Musial, rf	4	0	2	0	2	1
W. Cooper, c	4	0	1	0	7	0
Kurowski, 3b	4	0	0	0	2	1
Sanders, 1b	4	1	1	0	9	1
Litwhiler, lf	4	0	1	0	2	0
Marion, ss	3	0	2	0	2	1
Lanier, p	2	0	0	0	0	1
aDemaree	1	0	0	0	0	0
bWhite	0	0	0	0	0	0
Brecheen, p	0	0	0	0	0	1
cNarron	1	0	0	0	0	0
Totals	36	1	7	0	27	10

New York .... 0 0 0 1 0 0 0 1 0—2
St. Louis .... 0 0 0 0 0 0 1 0 0—1

New York	IP.	H.	R.	ER.	BB.	SO.
Russo (W)	9	7	1	0	1	2

St. Louis	IP.	H.	R.	ER.	BB.	SO.
Lanier	7	4	1	1	1	5
Brecheen (L)	2	2	1	1	2	2

aReached first on error for Lanier in seventh. bRan for Demaree in seventh. cGrounded out for Brecheen in ninth. E—Crosetti, Johnson, Klein. LOB—New York 7, St. Louis 9. 2B—Russo 2, Litwhiler, Marion, Gordon. SB—Keller. SH—Stainback. U—Stewart (N.L.), Rommel (A.L.), Reardon (N.L.) and Rue (A.L.). T—2:06. A—36,196.

Game 5

Monday, October 11, At St. Louis

New York	AB.	R.	H.	RBI.	PO.	A.
Crosetti, ss	4	0	1	0	0	5
Metheny, rf	5	0	1	0	1	0
Lindell, rf	0	0	0	0	0	0
Johnson, 3b	4	0	1	0	1	2
Keller, lf	3	1	1	0	1	1
Dickey, c	4	1	1	2	7	0
Etten, 1b	3	0	1	0	11	1
Gordon, 2b	2	0	0	0	6	6
Stainback, cf	3	0	1	0	0	0
Chandler, p	3	0	0	0	0	2
Totals	31	2	7	2	27	17

St. Louis	AB.	R.	H.	RBI.	PO.	A.
Klein, 2b	5	0	1	0	3	1
Garms, lf	4	0	0	0	1	0
Musial, rf	3	0	0	0	1	0
W. Cooper, c	2	0	1	0	6	0
O'Dea, c	2	0	2	0	2	0
Kurowski, 3b	4	0	2	0	3	3
Sanders, 1b	3	0	1	0	7	2
Hopp, cf	4	0	0	0	1	0
Marion, ss	3	0	1	0	2	3
M. Cooper, p	2	0	0	0	0	1
aWalker	1	0	1	0	0	0
Lanier, p	0	0	0	0	0	1
Dickson, p	0	0	0	0	1	0
bLitwhiler	1	0	1	0	0	0
Totals	34	0	10	0	27	11

New York .... 0 0 0 0 0 2 0 0 0—2
St. Louis .... 0 0 0 0 0 0 0 0 0—0

New York	IP.	H.	R.	ER.	BB.	SO.
Chandler (W)	9	10	0	0	2	7

St. Louis	IP.	H.	R.	ER.	BB.	SO.
M. Cooper (L)	7	5	2	2	2	6
Lanier	1⅓	2	0	0	2	1
Dickson	⅔	0	0	0	1	0

aSingled for M. Cooper in seventh. bSingled for Dickson in ninth. E—Crosetti, W. Cooper. DP—New York 1, St. Louis 1. LOB—New York 9, St. Louis 11. HR—Dickey. SH—Marion, Garms, Stainback, Chandler. WP—M. Cooper. U—Rommel (A.L.), Reardon (N.L.), Rue (A.L.) and Stewart (N.L.). T—2:24. A—33,872.

COMPOSITE BATTING AVERAGES

New York Yankees

Player-Position	G.	AB.	R.	H.	2B.	3B.	HR.	RBI.	BA.
Russo, p	1	3	1	2	2	0	0	0	.667
Borowy, p	1	2	1	1	1	0	0	0	.500
Johnson, 3b	5	20	3	6	1	1	0	3	.300
Dickey, c	5	18	1	5	0	0	1	4	.278
Crosetti, ss	5	18	4	5	0	0	0	1	.278
Gordon, 2b	5	17	2	4	1	0	1	2	.235
Keller, lf	5	18	3	4	0	1	0	2	.222
Stainback, rf	5	17	0	3	0	0	0	0	.176
Chandler, p	2	6	0	1	0	0	0	0	.167
Metheny, rf	2	8	0	1	0	0	0	0	.125
Lindell, cf	4	9	1	1	0	0	0	0	.111
Etten, 1b	5	19	0	2	0	0	0	2	.105
Bonham, p	1	2	0	0	0	0	0	0	.000
Murphy, p	2	0	0	0	0	0	0	0	.000
Stirnweiss, ph	1	1	1	0	0	0	0	0	.000
Weatherly, ph	1	1	0	0	0	0	0	0	.000
Totals	5	159	17	35	5	2	2	14	.220

St. Louis Cardinals

Player-Position	G.	AB.	R.	H.	2B.	3B.	HR.	RBI.	BA.
O'Dea, ph-c	2	3	0	2	0	0	0	0	.667
Marion, ss	5	14	1	5	2	0	1	2	.357
W. Cooper, c	5	17	1	5	0	0	0	0	.294
Sanders, 1b	5	17	3	5	0	0	1	2	.294
Musial, rf	5	18	2	5	0	0	0	0	.278
Litwhiler, lf-ph	5	15	0	4	1	0	0	2	.267
Lanier, p	3	4	0	1	0	0	0	1	.250
Kurowski, 3b	5	18	2	4	1	0	0	1	.222
Walker, cf-ph	5	18	0	3	1	0	0	0	.167
Klein, 2b	5	22	0	3	0	0	0	0	.136
Garms, ph-lf	2	5	0	0	0	0	0	0	.000
Hopp, cf	1	4	0	0	0	0	0	0	.000
Brecheen, p	3	0	0	0	0	0	0	0	.000
M. Cooper, p	2	5	0	0	0	0	0	0	.000
Brazle, p	1	3	0	0	0	0	0	0	.000
Krist, p	1	0	0	0	0	0	0	0	.000
Dickson, p	1	0	0	0	0	0	0	0	.000
Demaree, ph	1	1	0	0	0	0	0	0	.000
Narron, ph	1	1	0	0	0	0	0	0	.000
White, pr	1	0	0	0	0	0	0	0	.000
Totals	5	165	9	37	5	0	2	8	.224

COMPOSITE PITCHING AVERAGES

New York Yankees

Pitcher	G.	IP.	H.	R.	ER.	BB.	SO.	W.	L.	ERA.
Russo	1	9	7	1	0	1	2	1	0	0.00
Murphy	2	2	1	0	0	1	1	0	0	0.00
Chandler	2	18	17	2	1	3	10	2	0	0.50
Borowy	1	8	6	2	2	3	4	1	0	2.25
Bonham	1	8	6	4	4	3	9	0	1	4.50
Totals	5	45	37	9	7	11	26	4	1	1.40

St. Louis Cardinals

Pitcher	G.	IP.	H.	R.	ER.	BB.	SO.	W.	L.	ERA.
Krist	1	0	1	0	0	0	0	0	0	0.00
Dickson	1	⅔	0	0	0	1	0	0	0	0.00
Lanier	3	15⅓	13	5	3	3	13	0	1	1.76
Brecheen	3	3⅔	5	1	1	3	3	0	1	2.45
M. Cooper	2	16	11	5	5	3	10	1	1	2.81
Brazle	1	7⅓	5	6	3	2	4	0	1	3.68
Totals	5	43	35	17	12	12	30	1	4	2.51

1944
ST. LOUIS CARDINALS
VS.
ST. LOUIS BROWNS

The American League franchise that competed under the banner of the St. Louis Browns from 1902 through 1953 won exactly one pennant in its obviously checkered history.

If one were trying to deduce which Browns team was able to reach the World Series, a simple check of rosters and seasonal individual production over the years would point, unequivocally it would seem, to the 1922 aggregation. You know, the team of George Sisler, Ken Williams, Baby Doll Jacobson, Marty McManus, Urban Shocker and Elam Vangilder. Sisler batted .420 that year, hit safely in 41 consecutive games and drove in 105 runs. Williams batted .332, slammed 39 home runs and had 155 runs batted in. Jacobson hit .317 and compiled 102 RBIs, and McManus finished with a .312 average and totaled 109 RBIs. And Shocker and Vangilder combined for 43 victories. Some team, this.

In 1944, the Browns fielded a team that batted .252, a mere *61* points under the .313 figure posted by the '22 club. The '44 Browns had one .300 hitter, outfielder Mike Kreevich, who barely made it at .301; one man with 20 homers, shortstop Vern Stephens, who hit exactly 20; and one player over the 85-RBI mark, Stephens, who knocked in 109 runs. Nelson Potter and Jack Kramer combined for 36 victories.

Fate, of course, isn't always kind. Or fair, for that matter. And, sure enough, it was the 1944 team that won the St. Louis Browns' only pennant. With outfielder Chet Laabs drilling two final-day homers, each with a man on base, the Browns beat the New York Yankees. The victory, combined with Detroit's loss to Washington, enabled St. Louis to

Cardinals shortstop Marty Marion scores his team's only run on Ken O'Dea's fly ball in the ninth inning of Game 1.

finish one game ahead of the Tigers in the A.L. race. On the other hand, the 1922 Browns wound up one game out of first place.

To say there were extenuating circumstances in the 1922 and 1944 A.L. pennant scenarios would be understating the case, however. The '22 Browns, as good as they were, lost out to a team that was headed for unrivaled baseball glory: The Yankees of the Babe Ruth era. The '44 Browns, as ordinary as they were, won out over an A.L. field decimated by manpower cutbacks forced by World War II.

To their credit, though, the Browns put the American League's best team on the field in 1944—regardless of the wartime backdrop. That the other major league team in St. Louis, the National League Cardinals, fielded the best club in either league in

'44 was another twist of fate, one that eventually would put a damper on the Browns' long-awaited success.

In making off with their third straight N.L. pennant in '44, Manager Billy Southworth's Cardinals won 105 games and thereby ran their three-year victory total to 316. Their lead over second-place Pittsburgh was 14½ games.

The all-Sportsman's Park World Series—the eight-time N.L. champion Cardinals were, in fact, tenants of the long-downtrodden Browns franchise—began on a high note for Manager Luke Sewell's A.L. titlists as Denny Galehouse outpitched Mort Cooper in a 2-1 game decided by George McQuinn's fourth-inning home run with Gene Moore on base. The blast by first baseman McQuinn would prove the Browns' only homer in World Series history.

Happy St. Louis Browns players mill around their dugout shortly after recording a 2-1 victory over the Cardinals in Game 1 of 1944's all-St. Louis World Series.

After Blix Donnelly's stellar relief pitching—no runs, two hits and seven strikeouts in four innings—and Ken O'Dea's run-scoring pinch single in the 11th inning won Game 2 for the Cardinals, 3-2, the Browns came back for a 6-2 triumph in Game 3 as Kramer pitched a seven-hitter and struck out 10 batters and McQuinn went 3 for 3 with two RBIs.

The Browns, ahead two games to one, appeared in good shape. But the Cardinals would proceed to bend them out of shape.

Sig Jakucki, the 35-year-old retread who won 13 games for the '44 Brownies after being away from Organized Baseball for five years (in his only previous experience in the majors, he was 0-3 for the '36 Browns), lasted only three innings in Game 4, a contest in which Cards lefthander Harry Brecheen, 16-5 in the regular season, kept the American Leaguers off stride, and Stan Musial belted a two-run homer. The Cardinals prevailed, 5-1.

The next day, Cooper fired a seven-hit shutout and beat Galehouse, 2-0. Ray Sanders socked a home run for the Cards in the sixth and Danny Litwhiler connected in the eighth. Cooper was coming off another outstanding year, having thrown seven shutouts while posting 22 victories. In the Cardinals' 1942-1943-1944 stranglehold on the N.L. championship, Cooper had won 65 games and hurled 23 shutouts.

Max Lanier and Ted Wilks, pitchers who posted identical victory totals and earned-run averages (17 triumphs, 2.65 ERA) for the Cardinals in '44, combined to bring the Browns' memorable season to a halt in Game 6. Lanier worked 5⅓ innings of three-hit ball, while 28-year-old rookie Wilks—who lost only four times in the regular season—pitched to 11 Browns batters and recorded 11 outs. The Cardinals, benefiting from Stephens' throwing error in the fourth (one of 10 Brownie errors in the Series) and getting run-scoring singles from Emil Verban and Lanier in that three-run inning, notched a 3-1 victory that wrapped up their second Series title in three years.

The World Series was becoming old hat for the St. Louis Cardinals, who had just appeared in the event for the eighth time in 19 seasons. For the St. Louis Browns, the fall classic was an experience to be enjoyed only rarely. Like once in their 52-season history.

Game 1

Wednesday, October 4, At St. Louis

Browns	AB.	R.	H.	RBI.	PO.	A.
Gutteridge, 2b	4	0	0	0	1	2
Kreevich, cf	4	0	0	0	6	0
Laabs, lf	4	0	0	0	2	0
Stephens, ss	3	0	0	0	1	3
Moore, rf	3	1	1	0	1	0
McQuinn, 1b	3	1	1	2	10	0
Christman, 3b	3	0	0	0	1	1
Hayworth, c	3	0	0	0	5	0
Galehouse, p	2	0	0	0	0	2
Totals	29	2	2	2	27	8

Cardinals	AB.	R.	H.	RBI.	PO.	A.
Hopp, cf	5	0	1	0	1	0
Sanders, 1b	3	0	1	0	12	0
Musial, rf	3	0	1	0	2	0
W. Cooper, c	3	0	0	0	8	0
Kurowski, 3b	4	0	1	0	0	3
Litwhiler, lf	2	0	0	0	1	0
Fallon, 2b	1	0	0	0	0	0
Marion, ss	4	1	2	0	1	4
Verban, 2b	2	0	1	0	1	1
aBergamo, lf	1	0	0	0	1	0
M. Cooper, p	2	0	0	0	0	3
bGarms	1	0	0	0	0	0
Donnelly, p	0	0	0	0	0	1
cO'Dea	1	0	0	1	0	0
Totals	32	1	7	1	27	12

Browns	0 0 0	2 0 0	0 0 0—2			
Cardinals	0 0 0	0 0 0	0 0 1—1			

Browns	IP.	H.	R.	ER.	BB.	SO.
Galehouse (W)	9	7	1	1	4	5
Cardinals	**IP.**	**H.**	**R.**	**ER.**	**BB.**	**SO.**
M. Cooper (L)	7	2	2	2	3	4
Donnelly	2	0	0	0	0	2

aWalked for Verban in seventh. bGrounded out for M. Cooper in seventh. cFlied out for Donnelly in ninth, scoring Marion. DP—Browns 1. LOB—Browns 3, Cardinals 9. 2B—Marion 2. HR—McQuinn. SH—Musial. U—Sears (N.L.), McGowan (A.L.), Dunn (N.L.) and Pipgras (A.L.). T—2:05. A—33,242.

Game 2

Thursday, October 5, At St. Louis

Browns	AB.	R.	H.	RBI.	PO.	A.
Gutteridge, 2b	4	0	0	0	5	4
Kreevich, cf	5	0	2	0	1	0
Laabs, lf	4	0	0	0	1	0
cZarilla, lf	1	0	0	0	0	0
Stephens, ss	5	0	0	0	2	5
McQuinn, 1b	2	0	1	0	13	1
Christman, 3b	5	0	0	0	0	5
Moore, rf	5	1	2	0	1	0
Hayworth, c	5	1	1	1	7	1
Potter, p	2	0	0	0	1	1
aMancuso	1	0	1	1	0	0
bShirley	0	0	0	0	0	0
Muncrief, p	1	0	0	0	0	0
Totals	40	2	7	2	31	17

Cardinals	AB.	R.	H.	RBI.	PO.	A.
Bergamo, lf	5	0	0	1	0	0
Hopp, cf	5	0	0	0	2	0
Musial, rf	5	0	1	0	2	0
W. Cooper, c	4	0	1	0	15	0
Sanders, 1b	3	2	1	0	8	1
Kurowski, 3b	4	0	2	0	1	4
Marion, ss	3	0	0	0	2	6
Verban, 2b	3	1	1	1	3	0
dO'Dea	1	0	1	1	0	0
Lanier, p	2	0	0	0	0	0
Donnelly, p	1	0	0	0	0	1
Totals	36	3	7	3	33	12

Browns	0 0 0	0 0 0	2 0 0	0 0	—2
Cardinals	0 0 1	1 0 0	0 0 0	0 1	—3

One out when winning run scored.

Browns	IP.	H.	R.	ER.	BB.	SO.
Potter	6	4	2	0	2	3
Muncrief (L)	4⅓	3	1	1	3	4
Cardinals	**IP.**	**H.**	**R.**	**ER.**	**BB.**	**SO.**
Lanier	7*	5	2	2	3	6
Donnelly (W)	4	2	0	0	1	7

*Pitched to one batter in eighth.

aSingled for Potter in seventh. bRan for Mancuso in seventh. cReached first on fielder's choice for Laabs in tenth. dSingled for Verban in eleventh. E—Gutteridge, Christman, Potter 2. DP—Browns 2. LOB—Browns 9, Cardinals 10. 2B—W. Cooper, Kurowski, Hayworth, Kreevich, McQuinn. SH—Lanier, W. Cooper, Kurowski. U—McGowan (A.L.), Dunn (N.L.), Pipgras (A.L.) and Sears (N.L.). T—2:32. A—35,076.

Game 3

Friday, October 6, At St. Louis

Cardinals	AB.	R.	H.	RBI.	PO.	A.
Litwhiler, lf	5	0	0	0	0	0
Hopp, cf	4	1	1	0	1	0
Musial, rf	4	0	1	0	2	0
W. Cooper, c	4	0	2	1	5	0
Sanders, 1b	3	0	1	0	11	0
Kurowski, 3b	4	1	0	0	0	4
Marion, ss	4	0	2	1	2	5
Verban, 2b	2	0	0	0	3	1
aGarms	1	0	0	0	0	0
Fallon, 2b	1	0	0	0	0	0
Wilks, p	1	0	0	0	0	0
Schmidt, p	1	0	0	0	0	0
bBergamo	0	0	0	0	0	0
Jurisich, p	0	0	0	0	0	0
Byerly, p	0	0	0	0	0	0
cO'Dea	1	0	0	0	0	0
Totals	35	2	7	2	24	10

Browns	AB.	R.	H.	RBI.	PO.	A.
Gutteridge, 2b	4	1	1	0	2	1
Kreevich, cf	4	0	0	0	1	0
Moore, rf	4	1	1	0	3	0
Stephens, ss	2	2	1	0	1	1
McQuinn, 1b	3	1	3	2	6	0
Zarilla, lf	4	1	1	1	2	0
Christman, 3b	4	0	1	1	1	0
Hayworth, c	2	0	0	0	11	0
Kramer, p	4	0	0	0	0	2
Totals	31	6	8	4	27	4

Cardinals	1 0 0	0 0 0	1 0 0	—2
Browns	0 0 4	0 0 0	2 0 x	—6

Cardinals	IP.	H.	R.	ER.	BB.	SO.
Wilks (L)	2⅔	5	4	4	3	3
Schmidt	3⅓	1	0	0	1	1
Jurisich	⅔	2	2	2	1	0
Byerly	1⅓	0	0	0	0	1
Browns	**IP.**	**H.**	**R.**	**ER.**	**BB.**	**SO.**
Kramer (W)	9	7	2	0	2	10

aFlied out for Verban in seventh. bWalked for Schmidt in seventh. cGrounded out for Byerly in ninth. E—Gutteridge, Stephens. DP—Cardinals 1. LOB—Cardinals 8, Browns 6. 2B—Gutteridge, McQuinn, W. Cooper. WP—Schmidt. PB—W. Cooper. U—Dunn (N.L.), Pipgras (A.L.), Sears (N.L.) and McGowan (A.L.). T—2:19. A—34,737.

Game 4

Saturday, October 7, At St. Louis

Cardinals	AB.	R.	H.	RBI.	PO.	A.
Litwhiler, lf	4	1	2	0	2	0
Hopp, cf	5	1	2	0	4	0
Musial, rf	4	2	3	2	2	0
W. Cooper, c	4	0	2	1	4	0
Sanders, 1b	5	1	1	0	9	0
Kurowski, 3b	4	0	0	0	0	3
Marion, ss	4	0	1	1	1	3
Verban, 2b	4	0	1	0	4	3
Brecheen, p	4	0	0	0	1	3
Totals	38	5	12	4	27	12

Browns	AB.	R.	H.	RBI.	PO.	A.
Gutteridge, 2b	4	0	2	0	3	2
Kreevich, cf	5	0	1	0	4	2
Moore, rf	3	1	0	0	1	0
Stephens, ss	4	0	1	0	1	6
Laabs, lf	4	0	2	0	1	0
McQuinn, 1b	3	0	1	0	9	0
Christman, 3b	4	0	1	0	0	1
Hayworth, c	2	0	0	0	5	0
Mancuso, c	2	0	1	0	3	0
Jakucki, p	0	0	0	0	0	1
aClary	1	0	0	0	0	0
Hollingsworth, p	1	0	0	0	0	1
bByrnes	0	0	0	0	0	0
Shirley, p	0	0	0	0	0	1
cTurner	1	0	0	0	0	0
Totals	34	1	9	0	27	14

Cardinals	2 0 2	0 0 1	0 0 0	—5
Browns	0 0 0	0 0 0	0 1 0	—1

Cardinals	IP.	H.	R.	ER.	BB.	SO.
Brecheen (W)	9	9	1	1	4	4
Browns	**IP.**	**H.**	**R.**	**ER.**	**BB.**	**SO.**
Jakucki (L)	3	5	4	3	0	4
Hollingsworth	4	5	1	1	2	1
Shirley	2	2	0	0	1	1

aFlied out for Jakucki in third. bWalked for Hollingsworth in seventh. cFlied out for Shirley in ninth. E—Gutteridge. DP—Cardinals 2. LOB—Cardinals 9, Browns 10. 2B—Marion, Laabs, Musial. 3B—W. Cooper. HR—Musial. U—Pipgras (A.L.), Sears (N.L.), McGowan (A.L.) and Dunn (N.L.). T—2:22. A—35,455.

Game 5

Sunday, October 8, At St. Louis

Cardinals	AB.	R.	H.	RBI.	PO.	A.
Litwhiler, lf	4	1	2	1	0	0
Hopp, cf	4	0	0	0	3	0
Musial, rf	3	0	1	0	1	0
W. Cooper, c	4	0	0	0	13	0
Sanders, 1b	4	1	1	1	4	0
Kurowski, 3b	4	0	1	0	3	0
Marion, ss	4	0	0	0	1	2
Verban, 2b	3	0	1	0	2	0
M. Cooper, p	2	0	0	0	0	3
Totals	32	2	6	2	27	5

Browns	AB.	R.	H.	RBI.	PO.	A.
Gutteridge, 2b	2	0	0	0	1	0
aBaker, 2b	1	0	0	0	0	0
Kreevich, cf	4	0	2	0	5	0
Moore, rf	4	0	0	0	2	0
Stephens, ss	4	0	3	0	1	1
McQuinn, 1b	3	0	0	0	6	0
Zarilla, lf	4	0	0	0	0	0
Christman, 3b	3	0	0	0	0	1
bByrnes	1	0	0	0	0	0
Hayworth, c	3	0	1	0	12	1
cLaabs	1	0	0	0	0	0
Galehouse, p	3	0	1	0	0	3
dChartak	1	0	0	0	0	0
Totals	34	0	7	0	27	6

Cardinals	0 0 0	0 0 1	0 1 0	—2
Browns	0 0 0	0 0 0	0 0 0	—0

Cardinals	IP.	H.	R.	ER.	BB.	SO.
M. Cooper (W)	9	7	0	0	2	12
Browns	**IP.**	**H.**	**R.**	**ER.**	**BB.**	**SO.**
Galehouse (L)	9	6	2	2	1	10

aStruck out for Gutteridge in seventh. bStruck out for Christman in ninth. cStruck out for Hayworth in ninth. dStruck out for Galehouse in ninth. E—Musial, Stephens. DP—Browns 1. LOB—Cardinals 5, Browns 9. 2B—Litwhiler, Musial, Kreevich, Stephens. HR—Sanders, Litwhiler. SH—M. Cooper. U—Sears (N.L.), Pipgras (A.L.), Dunn (N.L.) and McGowan (A.L.). T—2:04. A—36,568.

Game 6

Monday, October 9, At St. Louis

Browns	AB.	R.	H.	RBI.	PO.	A.
Gutteridge, 2b	3	0	0	0	3	2
bBaker, 2b	1	0	0	0	1	0
Kreevich, cf	4	0	1	0	3	0
Moore, rf	3	0	0	0	0	0
Stephens, ss	4	0	0	0	3	3
Laabs, lf	2	1	1	0	1	1
McQuinn, 1b	2	0	1	1	6	1
Christman, 3b	3	0	0	0	1	1
cByrnes	1	0	0	0	0	0
Hayworth, c	2	0	0	0	5	0
dChartak	1	0	0	0	0	0
Potter, p	2	0	0	0	1	1
Muncrief, p	0	0	0	0	0	1
aZarilla	1	0	0	0	0	0
Kramer, p	0	0	0	0	0	1
Totals	29	1	3	1	24	11

Cardinals	AB.	R.	H.	RBI.	PO.	A.
Litwhiler, lf	5	0	0	0	2	0
Hopp, cf	4	0	1	0	3	0
Musial, rf	4	0	0	0	2	0
W. Cooper, c	3	1	2	0	10	0
Sanders, 1b	3	1	1	0	7	1
Kurowski, 3b	3	1	1	1	0	1
Marion, ss	3	0	0	0	0	2
Verban, 2b	3	0	3	1	2	2
Lanier, p	2	0	2	1	1	1
Wilks, p	1	0	0	0	0	1
Totals	31	3	10	3	27	8

Browns	0 1 0	0 0 0	0 0 0	—1
Cardinals	0 0 0	3 0 0	0 0 x	—3

Browns	IP.	H.	R.	ER.	BB.	SO.
Potter (L)	3⅔	6	3	1	1	3
Muncrief	2⅓	2	0	0	1	0
Kramer	2	2	0	0	2	2
Cardinals	**IP.**	**H.**	**R.**	**ER.**	**BB.**	**SO.**
Lanier (W)	5⅓	3	1	1	5	5
Wilks	3⅔	0	0	0	0	4

aStruck out for Muncrief in seventh. bStruck out for Gutteridge in seventh. cStruck out for Christman in ninth. dStruck out for Hayworth in ninth. E—Stephens, Hayworth. LOB—Browns 7, Cardinals 10. 2B—Kreevich. 3B—Laabs. SH—McQuinn, Wilks, Marion. WP—Lanier. U—McGowan (A.L.), Dunn (N.L.), Pipgras (A.L.) and Sears (N.L.). T—2:06. A—31,630.

COMPOSITE BATTING AVERAGES

St. Louis Cardinals

Player-Position	G.	AB.	R.	H.	2B.	3B.	HR.	RBI.	BA.
Lanier, p	2	4	0	2	0	0	0	1	.500
Verban, 2b	6	17	1	7	0	0	0	2	.412
O'Dea, ph	3	3	0	1	0	0	0	2	.333
W. Cooper, c	6	22	1	7	2	1	0	2	.318
Musial, rf	6	23	2	7	2	0	1	2	.304
Sanders, 1b	6	21	5	6	0	0	1	1	.286
Marion, ss	6	22	1	5	3	0	0	2	.227
Kurowski, 3b	6	23	2	5	1	0	0	1	.217
Litwhiler, lf	5	20	2	4	1	0	1	1	.200
Hopp, cf	6	27	2	5	0	0	0	0	.185
Fallon, 2b	2	2	0	0	0	0	0	0	.000
Bergamo, ph-lf	3	6	0	0	0	0	0	1	.000
M. Cooper, p	2	4	0	0	0	0	0	0	.000
Donnelly, p	2	1	0	0	0	0	0	0	.000
Wilks, p	2	2	0	0	0	0	0	0	.000
Schmidt, p	1	1	0	0	0	0	0	0	.000
Jurisich, p	1	0	0	0	0	0	0	0	.000
Byerly, p	1	0	0	0	0	0	0	0	.000
Brecheen, p	1	4	0	0	0	0	0	0	.000
Garms, ph	2	2	0	0	0	0	0	0	.000
Totals	6	204	16	49	9	1	3	15	.240

St. Louis Browns

Player-Position	G.	AB.	R.	H.	2B.	3B.	HR.	RBI.	BA.
Mancuso, ph-c	2	3	0	2	0	0	0	1	.667
McQuinn, 1b	6	16	2	7	2	0	1	5	.438
Kreevich, cf	6	26	0	6	3	0	0	0	.231
Stephens, ss	6	22	2	5	1	0	0	0	.227
Laabs, lf-ph	5	15	1	3	1	1	0	0	.200
Galehouse, p	2	5	0	1	0	0	0	0	.200
Moore, rf	6	22	4	4	0	0	0	0	.182
Gutteridge, 2b	6	21	1	3	1	0	0	0	.143
Hayworth, c	6	17	1	2	1	0	0	1	.118
Zarilla, ph-lf	4	10	1	1	0	0	0	1	.100
Christman, 3b	6	22	0	2	0	0	0	1	.091
Baker, ph-2b	2	2	0	0	0	0	0	0	.000
Potter, p	2	4	0	0	0	0	0	0	.000
Muncrief, p	2	1	0	0	0	0	0	0	.000
Kramer, p	2	4	0	0	0	0	0	0	.000
Jakucki, p	1	0	0	0	0	0	0	0	.000
Clary, ph	1	1	0	0	0	0	0	0	.000
Hollingsworth, p	1	1	0	0	0	0	0	0	.000
Shirley, pr-p	2	0	0	0	0	0	0	0	.000
Byrnes, ph	3	2	0	0	0	0	0	0	.000
Turner, ph	1	1	0	0	0	0	0	0	.000
Chartak, ph	2	2	0	0	0	0	0	0	.000
Totals	6	197	12	36	9	1	1	9	.183

COMPOSITE PITCHING AVERAGES

St. Louis Cardinals

Pitcher	G.	IP.	H.	R.	ER.	BB.	SO.	W.	L.	ERA.
Donnelly	2	6	2	0	0	1	9	1	0	0.00
Schmidt	1	3⅓	1	0	0	1	1	0	0	0.00
Byerly	1	1⅓	0	0	1	0	1	0	0	0.00
Brecheen	1	9	9	1	1	4	4	1	0	1.00
M. Cooper	2	16	9	2	2	5	16	1	1	1.13
Lanier	2	12⅓	8	3	3	8	11	1	0	2.19
Wilks	2	6⅓	5	4	4	3	7	0	1	5.68
Jurisich	1	⅔	2	2	2	1	0	0	0	27.00
Totals	6	55	36	12	12	23	49	4	2	1.96

St. Louis Browns

Pitcher	G.	IP.	H.	R.	ER.	BB.	SO.	W.	L.	ERA.
Kramer	2	11	9	2	0	4	12	1	0	0.00
Shirley	1	2	2	0	0	1	1	0	0	0.00
Potter	2	9⅔	10	5	1	3	6	0	1	0.93
Muncrief	2	6⅔	5	1	1	4	4	0	1	1.35
Galehouse	2	18	13	3	3	5	15	1	1	1.50
H'lingsworth	1	4	5	1	1	2	1	0	0	2.25
Jakucki	1	3	5	4	3	0	4	0	1	9.00
Totals	6	54⅓	49	16	9	19	43	2	4	1.49

Hank Borowy battled gamely as he tried to help the Chicago Cubs defeat the Detroit Tigers in the not-so-classic 1945 fall classic. This was the last of the wartime World Series, one that a Chicago sportswriter—after surveying the talent on hand—doubted *either* team could win.

Try as he might, the 29-year-old Borowy couldn't win it for the Cubs. Whatever the caliber of the competition.

Acquired on waivers in late July after he had compiled a 10-5 record for the New York Yankees, Borowy proceeded to win 11 of 13 decisions for the Cubs and helped Chicago fight off the St. Louis Cardinals in the National League pennant race. Then, in Game 1 of the World Series, he held the Tigers to six singles and was a 9-0 victor as the Cubs bombed 25-game winner Hal Newhouser. Bill Nicholson singled and tripled and drove in three runs for Chicago, which got two RBIs apiece from Phil Cavarretta (who rapped two singles and a home run) and Mickey Livingston.

Standout pitching performances continued through Game 4, at which point the Cubs and Tigers were tied at two victories each. Virgil Trucks, a 16-game winner for Detroit in 1943 and only recently discharged from the Navy, pitched a seven-hitter in Game 2 and won, 4-1, as midseason service returnee Hank Greenberg unloaded a three-run homer in the fifth. Four days earlier, on the final day of the A.L. schedule and in a game that marked Trucks' only appearance of the regular season, Greenberg had smashed a pennant-clinching, bases-loaded home run in the ninth inning against the St. Louis Browns.

In Game 3, Chicago's Claude Passeau tossed a one-hitter—Rudy York singled to left field with two out in the second—and led the National Leaguers to a 3-0 triumph. Following his teammate's cue, Ray Prim set down the first 10 Detroit batters he faced in Game 4. But after yielding a walk, two singles and a double in what became a four-run fourth for the Tigers, Prim was removed in favor of Paul Derringer. While Derringer and fellow relievers Hy Vandenberg and Paul Erickson pitched shutout ball the rest of the way, it was to no avail. Detroit's 4-1 triumph, fashioned on Dizzy Trout's five-hit pitching, had knotted matters in the '45 Series.

Now, Charley Grimm went to Borowy. Not once, not twice, but three times. Grimm, in his second tour of duty as the Cubs' manager, was obviously impressed with Borowy's combined regular-season record of 21-7, his second-half heroics for the Cubs (which netted him the N.L.'s earned-run-average title with a figure of 2.14) and his 56-30 career mark with the Yankees. The man could pitch, and Grimm was going to extract every bit of talent from Borowy's right arm.

That talent had the Cubs in a 1-1 tie through five innings of Game 5, which matched Borowy against Newhouser. Talk about skill. The 24-year-old Newhouser had just led the American League in victories (he had 29 an 1944) and strikeouts for the second successive season and topped the league with a 1.81 ERA. Newhouser wound up going the distance on this day, while Borowy departed after allowing four straight hits at the outset of the sixth. Detroit scored four runs in the inning and swept to an 8-4

victory. Greenberg slugged three doubles for the Tigers.

The Trucks-Passeau pitching pairing in Game 6 hinted at a low-scoring contest, but Trucks was routed in the Cubs' four-run fifth—which featured Stan Hack's bases-loaded single—and Passeau left in the seventh, an inning in which Detroit scored twice. After the Cubs rebounded with two runs in their half of the inning, it was 7-3, Chicago. But not for long. Detroit struck for four runs in the eighth, the game-tying run coming on a Greenberg homer, and suddenly Manager Steve O'Neill's Tigers were in a position to close out the Cubs in six games.

Trout came on in relief for Detroit in the last of the eighth. And when the 7-7 game moved into the ninth, Grimm decided to make another pitching change. Having followed Passeau with Hank Wyse (the Cubs' top winner of '45 with 22 victories) and Prim, Grimm now wanted Henry Ludwig Borowy. And Borowy delivered, holding Detroit at bay with four scoreless innings. Then, in the bottom of the 12th, with two out and Billy Schuster at first base as a pinch-runner (for Frank Secory, who had come through with a pinch single), Hack hit a drive to left field that took a weird bounce and bounded over Greenberg. The hit, ruled a double, scored Schuster and gave Borowy and the Cubs a stirring 8-7 victory.

This World Series, the one that neither team supposedly could win, had gone unclaimed through six games.

Now, it would have to end. The Tigers were shooting for their second World Series crown; their only previous Series title had been won in 1935, against the Cubs. The Cubs were eyeing their third Series championship; their two

Detroit slugger Hank Greenberg (right) hit a three-run homer to help Virgil Trucks (left) record a 4-1 Game 2 victory over the Cubs.

earlier titles had been captured in 1907 and 1908, both at the Tigers' expense. It would be Newhouser, working on two days of rest, going against—no big surprise here—Borowy, who was going on one day of rest after pitching the final four innings of Game 6. Of course, Borowy also had pitched into the sixth inning in Game 5.

Try as he might, Borowy couldn't win the World Series for the Cubs. He yielded singles to the Tigers' first three batters of the game, Skeeter Webb, Eddie Mayo and Doc Cramer. And Grimm, knowing Borowy had done all he could for the 1945 Cubs, told his weary pitcher to call it a day. And a Series.

Derringer took over for Chicago, and by the end of the inning Detroit had scored five runs—

three coming around on Paul Richards' bases-loaded double. Newhouser went on to a 9-3 victory, allowing 10 hits but also striking out 10 Cubs. The Tigers were World Series kingpins.

The Cubs, on the other hand, had now finished No. 2 in their last seven Series appearances. Not even one of the more noted mid-season acquisitions of all time could do anything about that.

Game 1

Wednesday, October 3, At Detroit

Chicago	AB.	R.	H.	RBI.	PO.	A.
Hack, 3b	5	0	1	0	3	0
Johnson, 2b	5	2	2	0	3	4
Lowrey, lf	4	0	0	1	1	0
Cavarretta, 1b	4	3	3	2	8	1
Pafko, cf	4	3	3	1	4	1
Nicholson, rf	4	1	2	3	0	0
Livingston, c	4	0	2	2	5	0
Hughes, ss	3	0	0	0	2	4
Borowy, p	3	0	0	0	1	1
Totals	36	9	13	8	27	11

Detroit	AB.	R.	H.	RBI.	PO.	A.
Webb, ss	4	0	1	0	1	2
dMcHale	1	0	0	0	0	0
Mayo, 2b	4	0	2	0	4	1
Cramer, cf	3	0	0	0	6	0
Greenberg, lf	2	0	1	0	0	0
Cullenbine, rf	3	0	0	0	0	0
York, 1b	3	0	1	0	8	0
Outlaw, 3b	4	0	1	0	1	4
Richards, c	2	0	0	0	7	2
bHostetler	1	0	0	0	0	1
Newhouser, p	1	0	0	0	0	0
Benton, p	0	0	0	0	0	0
aEaton	1	0	0	0	0	0
Tobin, p	1	0	0	0	0	1
Mueller, p	0	0	0	0	0	0
cBorom	1	0	0	0	0	0
Totals	31	0	6	0	27	11

Chicago .... 4 0 3 0 0 0 2 0 0—9
Detroit .... 0 0 0 0 0 0 0 0 0—0

Chicago	IP.	H.	R.	ER.	BB.	SO.
Borowy (W)	9	6	0	0	5	4

Detroit	IP.	H.	R.	ER.	BB.	SO.
Newhouser (L)	2⅔	8	7	7	1	3
Benton	1⅓	1	0	0	0	1
Tobin	3	4	2	2	1	0
Mueller	2	0	0	0	1	1

aStruck out for Benton in fourth. bGrounded out for Richards in ninth. cGrounded out for Mueller in ninth. dFlied out for Webb in ninth. DP—Chicago 2. LOB—Chicago 5, Detroit 10. 2B—Johnson, Pafko. 3B—Nicholson. HR—Cavarretta. SB—Johnson, Pafko. SH—Lowrey, Borowy. HBP—By Borowy (Greenberg). PB—Richards 2. U—Summers (A.L.), Jorda (N.L.), Passarella (A.L.) and Conlan (N.L.). T—2:10. A—54,637.

Game 2

Thursday, October 4, At Detroit

Chicago	AB.	R.	H.	RBI.	PO.	A.
Hack, 3b	3	0	3	0	0	2
Johnson, 2b	3	0	0	0	2	4
Lowrey, lf	4	0	2	0	3	0
Cavarretta, 1b	4	1	1	0	8	0
Pafko, cf	4	0	0	0	4	0
Nicholson, rf	3	0	1	1	2	0
Gillespie, c	4	0	0	0	3	0
Hughes, ss	3	0	0	0	2	2
Wyse, p	2	0	0	0	0	0
aSecory	1	0	0	0	0	0
Erickson, p	0	0	0	0	0	0
bBecker	1	0	0	0	0	0
Totals	32	1	7	1	24	8

Detroit	AB.	R.	H.	RBI.	PO.	A.
Webb, ss	4	1	2	0	0	4
Mayo, 2b	3	1	0	0	3	3
Cramer, cf	4	1	3	1	2	0
Greenberg, lf	3	1	1	3	2	1
Cullenbine, rf	2	0	0	0	2	0
York, 1b	4	0	0	0	11	1
Outlaw, 3b	4	0	1	0	1	0
Richards, c	4	0	0	0	5	0
Trucks, p	3	0	0	0	1	1
Totals	31	4	7	4	27	10

Chicago .... 0 0 0 1 0 0 0 0 0—1
Detroit .... 0 0 0 0 4 0 0 0 x—4

Chicago	IP.	H.	R.	ER.	BB.	SO.
Wyse (L)	6	5	4	4	2	1
Erickson	2	2	0	0	1	1

Detroit	IP.	H.	R.	ER.	BB.	SO.
Trucks (W)	9	7	1	1	3	4

aFlied out for Wyse in seventh. bStruck out for Erickson in ninth. LOB—Chicago 8, Detroit 7. 2B—Cavarretta, Hack. HR—Greenberg. SH—Johnson. U—Jorda (N.L.), Passarella (A.L.), Conlan (N.L.) and Summers (A.L.). T—1:48. A—53,636.

Game 3

Friday, October 5, At Detroit

Chicago	AB.	R.	H.	RBI.	PO.	A.
Hack, 3b	5	0	2	0	1	1
Johnson, 2b	5	0	0	1	1	1
Lowrey, lf	4	1	2	0	4	0
Cavarretta, 1b	2	0	1	0	10	1
Pafko, cf	2	1	0	0	3	0
Nicholson, rf	4	0	1	1	3	0
Livingston, c	4	1	1	0	3	0
Hughes, ss	3	0	1	1	1	4
Passeau, p	4	0	0	1	1	2
Totals	33	3	8	3	27	9

Detroit	AB.	R.	H.	RBI.	PO.	A.
Webb, ss	3	0	0	0	2	3
dMcHale	1	0	0	0	0	0
Mayo, 2b	3	0	0	0	2	1
Cramer, cf	3	0	0	0	4	0
Greenberg, lf	3	0	0	0	1	0
Cullenbine, rf	3	0	0	0	1	0
York, 1b	3	0	1	0	12	0
Outlaw, 3b	3	0	0	0	0	3
Swift, c	1	0	0	0	2	0
aBorom	0	0	0	0	0	0
Richards, c	1	0	0	0	3	1
Overmire, p	1	0	0	0	0	1
bWalker	1	0	0	0	0	0
Benton, p	0	0	0	0	0	0
cHostetler	1	0	0	0	0	0
Totals	27	0	1	0	27	12

Chicago .... 0 0 0 2 0 0 1 0 0—3
Detroit .... 0 0 0 0 0 0 0 0 0—0

Chicago	IP.	H.	R.	ER.	BB.	SO.
Passeau (W)	9	1	0	0	1	1
Detroit	**IP.**	**H.**	**R.**	**ER.**	**BB.**	**SO.**
Overmire (L)	6	4	2	2	2	2
Benton	3	4	1	1	0	3

aRan for Swift in sixth. bGrounded into double play for Overmire in sixth. cGrounded out for Benton in ninth. dFouled out for Webb in ninth. E—Webb, Mayo. DP—Chicago 1. LOB—Chicago 8, Detroit 1. 2B—Lowrey, Livingston, Hack. SH—Cavarretta, Hughes, Pafko. U—Passarella (A.L.), Conlan (N.L.), Summers (A.L.) and Jorda (N.L.). T—1:55. A—55,500.

Game 4

Saturday, October 6, At Chicago

Detroit	AB.	R.	H.	RBI.	PO.	A.
Webb, ss	5	0	0	0	1	3
Mayo, 2b	3	1	0	0	1	1
Cramer, cf	4	1	2	0	4	0
Greenberg, lf	3	1	1	1	1	0
Cullenbine, rf	3	1	1	1	1	0
York, 1b	3	0	0	0	10	3
Outlaw, 3b	4	0	1	1	0	3
Richards, c	4	0	1	1	7	0
Trout, p	4	0	1	0	2	2
Totals	33	4	7	4	27	12

Chicago	AB.	R.	H.	RBI.	PO.	A.
Hack, 3b	4	0	0	0	2	2
Johnson, 2b	4	1	2	0	1	3
Lowrey, lf	4	0	1	0	3	0
Cavarretta, 1b	4	0	0	0	10	1
Pafko, cf	4	0	0	0	1	0
Nicholson, rf	4	0	0	0	1	0
Livingston, c	3	0	1	0	4	1
Hughes, ss	1	0	0	0	3	3
bBecker	1	0	1	0	0	0
cMerullo, ss	0	0	0	0	1	0
Prim, p	0	0	0	0	0	1
Derringer, p	0	0	0	0	0	0
aSecory	1	0	0	0	0	0
Vandenberg, p	0	0	0	0	1	0
dGillespie	1	0	0	0	0	0
Erickson, p	0	0	0	0	0	0
Totals	31	1	5	0	27	11

Detroit	0 0 0	4 0 0	0 0 0	—4
Chicago	0 0 0	0 0 1	0 0 0	—1

Detroit	IP.	H.	R.	ER.	BB.	SO.
Trout (W)	9	5	1	0	1	6
Chicago	**IP.**	**H.**	**R.**	**ER.**	**BB.**	**SO.**
Prim (L)	3⅓	3	4	4	1	1
Derringer	1⅔	2	0	0	2	1
Vandenberg	2	0	0	0	0	0
Erickson	2	2	0	0	1	2

aStruck out for Derringer in fifth. bSingled for Hughes in seventh. cRan for Becker in seventh. dGrounded out for Vandenberg in seventh. E—York, Nicholson. LOB—Detroit 6, Chicago 5. 2B—Cullenbine. 3B—Johnson. SH—Prim. PB—Livingston. U—Conlan (N.L.), Summers (A.L.), Jorda (N.L.) and Passarella (A.L.). T—2:00. A—42,923.

Game 5

Sunday, October 7, At Chicago

Detroit	AB.	R.	H.	RBI.	PO.	A.
Webb, ss	4	1	1	1	2	4
Mayo, 2b	4	0	2	0	2	1
Cramer, cf	4	2	1	1	1	0
Greenberg, lf	5	3	3	1	0	0
Cullenbine, rf	4	1	2	2	1	0
York, 1b	5	1	1	1	9	2
Outlaw, 3b	4	0	0	1	0	3
Richards, c	4	0	1	0	11	1
Newhouser, p	3	0	0	1	1	3
Totals	37	8	11	8	27	14

Chicago	AB.	R.	H.	RBI.	PO.	A.
Hack, 3b	3	0	1	1	2	2
Johnson, 2b	3	0	0	0	1	3
Lowrey, lf	4	1	1	0	1	0
Cavarretta, 1b	3	1	1	0	10	0
Pafko, cf	4	1	0	0	5	0
Nicholson, rf	4	0	1	2	1	0
Livingston, c	4	0	1	1	4	0
Merullo, ss	2	0	0	0	2	1
bWilliams	1	0	0	0	0	0
Schuster, ss	1	0	0	0	1	2
Borowy, p	1	1	1	0	0	1
Vandenberg, p	0	0	0	0	0	1
Chipman, p	0	0	0	0	0	0
aSauer	1	0	0	0	0	0
Derringer, p	0	0	0	0	0	0
cSecory	1	0	1	0	0	0
Erickson, p	0	0	0	0	0	1
Totals	32	4	7	4	27	11

Detroit	0 0 1	0 0 4	1 0 2	—8
Chicago	0 0 1	0 0 0	2 0 1	—4

Detroit	IP.	H.	R.	ER.	BB.	SO.
Newhouser (W)	9	7	4	4	2	9
Chicago	**IP.**	**H.**	**R.**	**ER.**	**BB.**	**SO.**
Borowy (L)	5*	8	5	5	1	4
Vandenberg	⅔	0	0	0	2	0
Chipman	⅓	0	0	0	1	0
Derringer	2	1	1	1	0	0
Erickson	1	2	2	2	0	0

*Pitched to four batters in sixth.

aStruck out for Chipman in sixth. bStruck out for Merullo in seventh. cSingled for Derringer in eighth. E—Hack, Pafko. DP—Detroit 1, Chicago 1. LOB—Detroit 9, Chicago 4. 2B—Borowy, Greenberg 3, Livingston, Cullenbine, Cavarretta. SH—Outlaw, Cullenbine, Johnson. HBP—Erickson (Cramer). U—Summers (A.L.), Jorda (N.L.), Passarella (A.L.) and Conlan (N.L.). T—2:18. A—43,463.

Game 6

Monday, October 8, At Chicago

Detroit	AB.	R.	H.	RBI.	PO.	A.
Webb, ss	3	0	0	0	3	3
cHostetler	1	0	0	0	0	0
Hoover, ss	3	1	1	1	1	1
Mayo, 2b	6	0	1	1	4	5
Cramer, cf	6	1	2	1	2	0
Greenberg, lf	5	2	1	1	4	0
Cullenbine, rf	5	1	2	1	1	0
York, 1b	6	0	2	1	9	1
Outlaw, 3b	5	0	1	0	2	0
Richards, c	0	0	0	1	4	1
aMaier	1	0	1	0	0	0
Swift, c	2	1	1	0	5	1
Trucks, p	1	0	0	0	0	0
Caster, p	0	0	0	0	0	0
bMcHale	1	0	0	0	0	0
Bridges, p	0	0	0	0	0	0
Benton, p	0	0	0	0	0	0
dWalker	1	1	1	0	0	0
Trout, p	2	0	0	0	0	3
Totals	48	7	13	7	35	15

Chicago	AB.	R.	H.	RBI.	PO.	A.
Hack, 3b	5	1	4	3	3	3
Johnson, 2b	4	0	0	0	2	6
Lowrey, lf	5	1	1	0	6	1
Cavarretta, 1b	5	1	2	2	15	0
Pafko, cf	6	0	2	0	1	1
Nicholson, rf	5	0	0	0	1	0
Livingston, c	3	2	2	0	2	2
eGillespie	1	0	0	0	0	0
Williams, c	1	0	0	0	1	1
Hughes, ss	4	1	3	2	4	3
fBecker	0	0	0	0	0	0
gBlock	0	0	0	0	0	0
Merullo, ss	0	0	0	0	1	1
hSecory	1	0	1	0	0	0
iSchuster	0	1	0	0	0	0
Passeau, p	3	1	0	0	0	1
Wyse, p	1	0	0	0	0	0
Prim, p	0	0	0	0	0	0
Borowy, p	2	0	0	0	0	0
Totals	46	8	15	7	36	19

Detroit	0 1 0	0 0 0	2 4 0	0 0 0	—7
Chicago	0 0 0	0 4 1	2 0 0	0 0 1	—8

Two out when winning run scored.

Detroit	IP.	H.	R.	ER.	BB.	SO.
Trucks	4⅓	7	4	4	2	3
Caster	⅔	0	0	0	0	1
Bridges	1⅔	3	3	3	3	1
Benton	⅓	1	0	0	0	1
Trout (L)	4⅔	4	1	1	2	3
Chicago	**IP.**	**H.**	**R.**	**ER.**	**BB.**	**SO.**
Passeau	6⅔	5	3	3	6	2
Wyse	⅔	3	3	2	1	0
Prim	⅔	1	1	0	0	0
Borowy (W)	4	4	0	0	0	0

aSingled for Richards in sixth. bStruck out for Caster in sixth. cReached first base on error for Webb in seventh. dDoubled for Benton in eighth. eGrounded out for Livingston in ninth. fWalked for Hughes in ninth. gRan for Becker in ninth. hSingled for Merullo in twelfth. iRan for Secory in twelfth. E—Richards, Hack 2, Johnson. DP—Detroit 2, Chicago 1. LOB—Detroit 12, Chicago 12. 2B—York, Livingston, Hughes, Walker, Pafko, Hack. HR—Greenberg. SB—Cullenbine. SH—Johnson 2. U—Jorda (N.L.), Passarella (A.L.), Conlan (N.L.) and Summers (A.L.). T—3:28. A—41,708.

Game 7

Wednesday, October 10, At Chicago

Detroit	AB.	R.	H.	RBI.	PO.	A.
Webb, ss	4	2	1	0	0	5
Mayo, 2b	5	2	2	1	2	1
Cramer, cf	5	2	3	1	2	0
Greenberg, lf	2	0	0	1	0	0
Mierkowicz, lf	0	0	0	0	0	0
Cullenbine, rf	2	2	0	0	2	0
York, 1b	4	0	0	1	8	1
Outlaw, 3b	4	1	1	1	1	2
Richards, c	4	0	2	4	9	0
Swift, c	1	0	0	0	2	0
Newhouser, p	4	0	0	0	1	2
Totals	35	9	9	9	27	11

Chicago	AB.	R.	H.	RBI.	PO.	A.
Hack, 3b	5	0	0	0	1	3
Johnson, 2b	5	1	1	0	1	3
Lowrey, lf	4	0	2	0	3	0
Cavarretta, 1b	4	1	3	1	10	0
Pafko, cf	4	0	1	1	6	0
Nicholson, rf	4	0	1	1	1	0
Livingston, c	4	0	1	0	4	1
Hughes, ss	3	0	1	0	1	1
Borowy, p	0	0	0	0	0	0
Derringer, p	0	0	0	0	0	0
Vandenberg, p	1	0	0	0	0	1
aSauer	1	0	0	0	0	0
Erickson, p	0	0	0	0	0	0
bSecory	1	0	0	0	0	0
Passeau, p	0	0	0	0	0	0
Wyse, p	0	0	0	0	0	0
cMcCullough	1	0	0	0	0	0
Totals	37	3	10	3	27	9

Detroit	5 1 0	0 0 0	1 2 0	—9
Chicago	1 0 0	1 0 0	0 1 0	—3

Detroit	IP.	H.	R.	ER.	BB.	SO.
Newhouser (W)	9	10	3	3	1	10
Chicago	**IP.**	**H.**	**R.**	**ER.**	**BB.**	**SO.**
Borowy (L)	0*	3	3	3	0	0
Derringer	1⅔	2	3	3	5	0
Vandenberg	3⅓	1	0	0	1	3
Erickson	2	2	1	1	1	2
Passeau	1	1	2	2	1	0
Wyse	1	0	0	0	0	0

*Pitched to three batters in first.

aStruck out for Vandenberg in fifth. bStruck out for Erickson in seventh. cStruck out for Wyse in ninth. E—Newhouser. DP—Detroit 1. LOB—Detroit 8, Chicago 8. 2B—Richards 2, Mayo, Nicholson, Johnson. 3B—Pafko. SB—Outlaw, Cramer. SH—Greenberg. WP—Newhouser. U—Passarella (A.L.), Conlan (N.L.), Summers (A.L.) and Jorda (N.L.). T—2:31. A—41,590.

COMPOSITE BATTING AVERAGES

Detroit Tigers

Player-Position	G.	AB.	R.	H.	2B.	3B.	HR.	RBI.	BA.
Maier, ph	1	1	0	1	0	0	0	0	1.000
Walker, ph	2	2	1	1	1	0	0	0	.500
Cramer, cf	7	29	7	11	0	0	0	4	.379
Hoover, ss	1	3	1	1	0	0	0	1	.333
Greenberg, lf	7	23	7	7	3	0	2	7	.304
Mayo, 2b	7	28	4	7	1	0	0	2	.250
Swift, c	3	4	1	1	0	0	0	0	.250
Cullenbine, rf	7	22	5	5	2	0	0	4	.227
Richards, c	7	19	0	4	2	0	0	6	.211
Webb, ss	7	27	4	5	0	0	0	1	.185
York, 1b	7	28	1	5	1	0	0	3	.179
Outlaw, 3b	7	28	1	5	0	0	0	3	.179
Trout, p	2	6	0	1	0	0	0	0	.167
Mierkowicz, lf	1	0	0	0	0	0	0	0	.000
Newhouser, p	3	8	0	0	0	0	0	1	.000
Benton, p	3	0	0	0	0	0	0	0	.000
Tobin, p	1	1	0	0	0	0	0	0	.000
Mueller, p	1	0	0	0	0	0	0	0	.000
Trucks, p	2	4	0	0	0	0	0	0	.000
Overmire, p	1	1	0	0	0	0	0	0	.000
Caster, p	1	0	0	0	0	0	0	0	.000
Bridges, p	1	0	0	0	0	0	0	0	.000
McHale, ph	3	3	0	0	0	0	0	0	.000
Borom, ph-pr	2	1	0	0	0	0	0	0	.000
Eaton, ph	1	1	0	0	0	0	0	0	.000
Hostetler, ph	3	3	0	0	0	0	0	0	.000
Totals	7	242	32	54	10	0	2	32	.223

Chicago Cubs

Player-Position	G.	AB.	R.	H.	2B.	3B.	HR.	RBI.	BA.
Becker, ph	3	2	0	1	0	0	0	0	.500
Cavarretta, 1b	7	26	7	11	2	0	1	5	.423
Secory, ph	5	5	0	2	0	0	0	0	.400
Hack, 3b	7	30	1	11	3	0	0	4	.367
Livingston, c	6	22	3	8	3	0	0	4	.364
Lowrey, lf	7	29	4	9	1	0	0	0	.310
Hughes, ss	6	17	1	5	1	0	0	3	.294
Pafko, cf	7	28	5	6	2	1	0	2	.214
Nicholson, rf	7	28	1	6	1	1	0	8	.214
Johnson, 2b	7	29	4	5	2	1	0	0	.172
Borowy, p	4	6	1	1	1	0	0	0	.167
Gillespie, c-ph	3	6	0	0	0	0	0	0	.000
Merullo, pr-ss	3	2	0	0	0	0	0	0	.000
Schuster, ss-pr	2	1	1	0	0	0	0	0	.000
Williams, ph-c	2	2	0	0	0	0	0	0	.000
Wyse, p	3	3	0	0	0	0	0	0	.000
Erickson, p	4	0	0	0	0	0	0	0	.000
Passeau, p	3	7	1	0	0	0	0	1	.000
Prim, p	2	0	0	0	0	0	0	0	.000
Vandenberg, p	3	1	0	0	0	0	0	0	.000
Chipman, p	1	0	0	0	0	0	0	0	.000
Derringer, p	2	0	0	0	0	0	0	0	.000
Block, pr	1	0	0	0	0	0	0	0	.000
McCullough, ph	1	1	0	0	0	0	0	0	.000
Sauer, ph	2	2	0	0	0	0	0	0	.000
Totals	7	247	29	65	16	3	1	27	.263

COMPOSITE PITCHING AVERAGES

Detroit Tigers

Pitcher	G.	IP.	H.	R.	ER.	BB.	SO.	W.	L.	ERA.
Mueller	1	2	0	0	0	1	1	0	0	0.00
Caster	1	⅔	0	0	0	0	1	0	0	0.00
Trout	2	13⅔	9	2	1	3	9	1	1	0.66
Benton	3	4⅔	6	1	1	0	5	0	0	1.93
Overmire	1	6	4	2	2	2	2	0	1	3.00
Trucks	2	13⅓	14	5	5	5	7	1	0	3.38
Tobin	1	3	4	2	2	1	0	0	0	6.00
Newhouser	3	20⅔	25	14	14	4	22	2	1	6.10
Bridges	1	1⅔	3	3	3	3	1	0	0	16.20
Totals	7	65⅔	65	29	28	19	48	4	3	3.84

Chicago Cubs

Pitcher	G.	IP.	H.	R.	ER.	BB.	SO.	W.	L.	ERA.
Vandenberg	3	6	1	0	0	3	3	0	0	0.00
Chipman	1	⅓	0	0	0	1	0	0	0	0.00
Passeau	3	16⅔	7	5	5	8	3	1	0	2.70
Erickson	4	7	8	3	3	3	5	0	0	3.86
Borowy	4	18	21	8	8	6	8	2	2	4.00
Derringer	3	5⅓	5	4	4	7	1	0	0	6.75
Wyse	3	7⅔	8	7	6	4	1	0	1	7.04
Prim	2	4	4	5	4	1	1	0	1	9.00
Totals	7	65	54	32	30	33	22	3	4	4.15

1946
ST. LOUIS CARDINALS
VS.
BOSTON RED SOX

When it comes to drama-filled conclusions to World Series-deciding contests, Game 7 of the 1946 fall classic has most of 'em beat by a Country mile.

For that you can thank, above all, one Enos Bradsher Slaughter. But the fact is, the marvelous theater that unfolded in the late stages of the climactic game of the '46 Series began a half inning ahead of Slaughter's dash into the spotlight and ended a half inning later. It just *seemed* like a one-man show.

After seven innings at Sportsman's Park, the St. Louis Cardinals held a 3-1 lead over the Boston Red Sox. Cardinals righthander Murry Dickson, after giving up singles to the game's first two batters, Wally Moses and Johnny Pesky, had allowed only one hit since the first inning. And in the fifth, Dickson had broken a 1-1 tie with a double that scored Harry Walker and then trotted home himself when Red Schoendienst followed with a single.

Now, in the top of the eighth, Dickson would face Boston's eighth-, ninth- and first-place hitters. The first scheduled batter was Hal Wagner, but Manager Joe Cronin sent up Glen (Rip) Russell to hit for the Red Sox's catcher. Russell singled to center. Joe Dobson, who had relieved starting pitcher Dave (Boo) Ferriss in the fifth, was due up next and this time Cronin opted for George Metkovich. The result was a double to left, and Boston had the potential tying runs in scoring position with no one out.

Eddie Dyer, St. Louis' rookie manager, responded to the taut situation with a call to the bullpen. He wanted lefthander Harry (The Cat) Brecheen, and for good reason. Brecheen had been the pitching standout of this Series,

tossing a four-hit shutout in Game 2 and yielding only one run in a complete-game triumph in Game 6. Furthermore, his insertion was a matter of playing the percentages: Moses and Pesky, Boston's next two batters, were lefthanded hitters. And Moses had collected five hits in his 11 Series at-bats thus far.

Brecheen, who compiled a 30-9 record overall in 1944 and 1945, had fallen off to 15-15 in 1946. But his 2.49 earned-run average and five-shutout performance of '46 stamped his .500 season as misleading. So did his Series pitching success.

Brecheen struck out Moses. He then got Pesky to line out to Slaughter, whose prompt throw to the infield kept the runners glued to their bases. Now, righthanded-hitting Dom DiMaggio was the batter. DiMaggio, who had driven in Boston's run with a first-inning fly ball, came through with a nifty piece of clutch hitting by ripping a Brecheen pitch off the wall in right-center field. The blow scored Russell and Metkovich, tying the game at 3-3. Brecheen got out of the inning by retiring Ted Williams on a popup.

When the Red Sox took the field for the bottom of the eighth, Bob Klinger was on to pitch, Roy Partee had replaced Wagner behind the plate and Leon Culberson was stationed in center field. Culberson had pinch-run in the top of the inning for DiMaggio, who twisted his ankle rounding first while running out his crucial two-base hit. Klinger, Partee and Culberson would soon be where the action was.

Slaughter, the man they called Country, promptly singled off Klinger. Whitey Kurowski popped out to the Boston pitcher while attempting to sacrifice, and

Del Rice flied out. It was now up to Walker, who already had collected six hits and five RBIs in the Series. Walker hit a shot over Pesky's head into left-center, and Slaughter was off to the races. By the time Culberson could get the ball back to the infield, Country surely would be standing on third.

Wrong. Country wasn't *standing* anywhere.

Slaughter sped around second base. And then he tore around third.

And when shortstop Pesky hesitated in making his relay throw to the plate—a throw that drew Partee up the third-base line—Slaughter was home free. The daring baserunning had thrust St. Louis into a 4-3 lead. Walker, meanwhile, had motored into second on his big hit and was credited with a double (not a single, as often reported).

Brecheen, after making the final out in the eighth, continued the suspense in the ninth by allowing singles to Rudy York and Bobby Doerr to open the inning. As the Sportsman's Park throng inched forward, Pinky Higgins hit into a forceout that moved pinch-runner Paul Campbell to third. One out. The tying run 90 feet away.

Partee then fouled out to first baseman Stan Musial. That left it all up to pinch-hitter Tom McBride, who was batting for reliever Earl Johnson. Brecheen induced the reserve outfielder to ground to second baseman Schoendienst, who flipped the ball to shortstop Marty Marion for a Series-ending forceout. The wrung-out crowd let go. The Cardinals had won their sixth World Series title.

Brecheen, of course, was a big factor in the Cards' latest cham-

Seventh-game hero Enos Slaughter (above left) clowns with teammates (left to right) George Munger, Whitey Kurowski and catcher Joe Garagiola after the Cardinals' 1946 Series victory over the Boston Red Sox. The streets of downtown St. Louis were covered by confetti in the wake of the Cardinals' victory celebration.

pionship. He won three games in the Series and fashioned a 0.45 ERA in 20 innings. After the Red Sox had opened the Series with a 3-2, 10-inning victory that was decided on a York homer, Brecheen came back the next day and hurled St. Louis to a 3-0 triumph. And following Dobson's four-hit, 6-3 decision in Game 5 that sent Boston ahead three games to two, Brecheen squared the Series by stopping the Red Sox, 4-1.

Two of the game's greatest offensive stars, St. Louis' Musial and Boston's Williams, struggled in this Series with .222 and .200 averages, respectively. While neither team hit particularly well overall, the Cardinals did have one slam-bang afternoon. One day after being shut out by Ferriss, 4-0, in Game 3, St. Louis went on a 20-hit spree at Fenway Park and buried the Red Sox, 12-3. Slaughter, Kurowski and rookie catcher Joe Garagiola all had four hits for the Cards in that contest.

Runaways weren't the Cardinals' style, though. That was evi-

dent during the just-concluded National League season, when the Cards and Brooklyn Dodgers tied for the top spot and met in the major leagues' first-ever pennant playoff. Beating the Dodgers two straight in the best-of-three match, St. Louis captured its fourth N.L. flag in five seasons and took its theatrics to the fall classic.

And while Games 1 through 6 of the 1946 World Series received favorable reviews, it is Game 7 that lives on as one of baseball's all-time show-stoppers.

Game 1

Sunday, October 6, At St. Louis

Boston	AB.	R.	H.	RBI.	PO.	A.
McBride, rf	5	0	1	1	1	0
Moses, rf	0	0	0	0	1	0
Pesky, ss	5	0	0	0	0	3
DiMaggio, cf	5	0	2	0	1	1
Williams, lf	3	0	1	0	4	0
York, 1b	4	2	1	1	10	0
Doerr, 2b	4	0	1	0	4	4
Higgins, 3b	4	0	2	1	2	0
aGutteridge	0	1	0	0	0	0
Johnson, p	1	0	0	0	0	2
H. Wagner, c	3	0	0	0	6	1
bRussell, 3b	1	0	1	0	0	0
Hughson, p	2	0	0	0	0	1
cPartee, c	1	0	0	0	1	0
Totals	38	3	9	3	30	12
St. Louis	AB.	R.	H.	RBI.	PO.	A.
Schoendienst, 2b	5	1	2	0	2	5
Moore, cf	4	0	0	0	3	1
Musial, 1b	5	0	1	1	13	0
Slaughter, rf	4	0	1	0	3	0
Kurowski, 3b	3	1	1	0	1	4
Garagiola, c	4	0	1	1	4	0
Walker, lf	2	0	1	0	3	0
dDusak, lf	1	0	0	0	0	0
Marion, ss	3	0	0	0	1	3
Pollet, p	4	0	0	0	0	0
Totals	35	2	7	2	30	13

Boston.................................0 1 0 0 0 0 0 0 1 1—3
St. Louis.............................0 0 0 0 0 1 0 1 0 0—2

Boston	IP.	H.	R.	ER.	BB.	SO.
Hughson	8	7	2	2	2	5
Johnson (W)	2	0	0	0	0	1
St. Louis	IP.	H.	R.	ER.	BB.	SO.
Pollet (L)	10	9	3	3	4	3

aRan for Higgins in ninth. bSingled for H. Wagner in ninth. cStruck out for Hughson in ninth. dFlied out for Walker in ninth. E—McBride, Pesky. LOB—Boston 10, St. Louis 8. 2B—Musial, Garagiola. 3B—Slaughter. HR—York. SB—Schoendienst. SH—Marion, Moore. HBP—By Pollet (York), by Hughson (Kurowski). U—Ballanfant (N.L.), Hubbard (A.L.), Barlick (N.L.) and Berry (A.L.). T—2:39. A—36,218.

Game 2

Monday, October 7, At St. Louis

Boston	AB.	R.	H.	RBI.	PO.	A.
McBride, rf	4	0	1	0	3	0
Pesky, ss	4	0	0	0	3	2
DiMaggio, cf	4	0	1	0	3	0
Williams, lf	4	0	0	0	1	0
York, 1b	2	0	0	0	6	2
Doerr, 2b	4	0	1	0	4	5
Higgins, 3b	2	0	0	0	0	2
Partee, c	2	0	0	0	1	0
H. Wagner, c	1	0	0	0	2	0
Harris, p	2	0	1	0	0	0
aCulberson	1	0	0	0	0	0
Dobson, p	0	0	0	0	0	0
Totals	30	0	4	0	24	11
St. Louis	AB.	R.	H.	RBI.	PO.	A.
Schoendienst, 2b	3	0	0	0	2	3
Moore, cf	3	0	1	1	3	0
Musial, 1b	4	0	0	1	11	0
Kurowski, 3b	4	0	1	0	1	1
Slaughter, rf	4	0	0	0	2	0
Dusak, lf	2	0	1	0	1	0
bSisler	1	0	0	0	0	0
Walker, lf	0	0	0	0	1	0
Marion, ss	4	0	0	0	2	6
Rice, c	2	2	2	0	4	0
Brecheen, p	3	1	1	1	0	0
Totals	30	3	6	3	27	10

Boston...............................0 0 0 0 0 0 0 0 0—0
St. Louis............................0 0 1 0 2 0 0 0 x—3

Boston	IP.	H.	R.	ER.	BB.	SO.
Harris (L)	7	6	3	2	3	3
Dobson	1	0	0	0	0	0
St. Louis	**IP.**	**H.**	**R.**	**ER.**	**BB.**	**SO.**
Brecheen (W)	9	4	0	0	3	4

aFlied out for Harris in eighth. bGrounded out for Dusak in eighth. E—Higgins. DP—St. Louis 1. LOB—Boston 6, St. Louis 7. 2B—Rice, Dusak. SH—Schoendienst. U—Hubbard (A.L.), Barlick (N.L.), Berry (A.L.) and Ballanfant (N.L.). T—1:56. A—35,815.

Game 3

Wednesday, October 9, At Boston

St. Louis	AB.	R.	H.	RBI.	PO.	A.
Schoendienst, 2b	4	0	0	0	3	2
Moore, cf	4	0	0	0	1	0
Musial, 1b	3	0	1	0	8	1
Slaughter, rf	4	0	1	0	4	0
Kurowski, 3b	3	0	0	0	1	0
Garagiola, c	3	0	1	0	3	1
Walker, lf	3	0	1	0	2	0
Marion, ss	3	0	1	0	2	3
Dickson, p	2	0	1	0	0	2
aSisler	1	0	0	0	0	0
Wilks, p	0	0	0	0	0	1
Totals	30	0	6	0	24	10

Boston	AB.	R.	H.	RBI.	PO.	A.
Moses, rf	3	0	0	0	2	0
Pesky, ss	4	1	2	0	1	3
DiMaggio, cf	4	0	1	0	4	1
Williams, lf	3	1	1	0	2	0
York, 1b	4	2	2	3	12	0
Doerr, 2b	4	0	2	0	2	8
Higgins, 3b	3	0	0	0	1	0
H. Wagner, c	3	0	0	0	3	0
Ferriss, p	4	0	0	0	0	3
Totals	32	4	8	3	27	15

St. Louis	0 0 0	0 0 0	0 0 0	—0
Boston	3 0 0	0 0 0	0 1 x	—4

St. Louis	IP.	H.	R.	ER.	BB.	SO.
Dickson (L)	7	6	3	3	3	4
Wilks	1	2	1	0	0	0
Boston	**IP.**	**H.**	**R.**	**ER.**	**BB.**	**SO.**
Ferriss (W)	9	6	0	0	1	2

aHit into force play for Dickson in eighth. E—Schoendienst. DP—Boston 2. LOB—St. Louis 4, Boston 8. 2B—DiMaggio, Dickson, Doerr. 3B—Musial. HR—York. SB—Musial. SH—H. Wagner. PB—Garagiola. U—Barlick (N.L.), Berry (A.L.), Ballanfant (N.L.) and Hubbard (A.L.). T—1:54. A—34,500.

Game 4

Thursday, October 10, At Boston

St. Louis	AB.	R.	H.	RBI.	PO.	A.
Schoendienst, 2b	6	1	1	0	1	4
Moore, cf	4	1	1	0	3	0
Musial, 1b	5	1	1	2	6	1
Slaughter, rf	6	4	4	1	5	1
Kurowski, 3b	5	2	4	1	2	0
Garagiola, c	5	1	4	3	4	0
Walker, lf	2	1	1	1	3	0
Marion, ss	4	1	3	3	2	1
Munger, p	4	0	1	0	1	0
Totals	41	12	20	11	27	7

Boston	AB.	R.	H.	RBI.	PO.	A.
Moses, rf	5	0	4	0	1	0
Pesky, ss	5	0	0	0	3	2
DiMaggio, cf	4	1	0	0	3	1
Williams, lf	3	1	1	0	0	1
York, 1b	3	0	1	1	9	1
Doerr, 2b	3	1	2	2	4	6
Gutteridge, 2b	0	0	0	0	0	0
Higgins, 3b	4	0	1	0	2	1
H. Wagner, c	4	0	0	0	5	1
Hughson, p	0	0	0	0	0	0
Bagby, p	1	0	0	0	0	1
aMetkovich	1	0	0	0	0	0
Zuber, p	0	0	0	0	0	0
bMcBride	1	0	0	0	0	0
Brown, p	0	0	0	0	0	0
Ryba, p	0	0	0	0	0	0
Dreisewerd, p	0	0	0	0	0	0
cCulberson	1	0	0	0	0	0
Totals	35	3	9	3	27	14

St. Louis	0 3 3	0 1 0	1 0 4	—12
Boston	0 0 0	1 0 0	0 2 0	— 3

St. Louis	IP.	H.	R.	ER.	BB.	SO.
Munger (W)	9	9	3	1	3	2
Boston	**IP.**	**H.**	**R.**	**ER.**	**BB.**	**SO.**
Hughson (L)	2*	5	6	3	0	1
Bagby	3	6	1	1	1	1
Zuber	2	3	1	1	1	1
Brown	1†	4	3	3	1	0
Ryba	⅔	2	1	0	1	0
Driesewerd	⅓	0	0	0	0	0

*Pitched to three batters in third.
†Pitched to three batters in ninth.

aFlied out for Bagby in fifth. bBounced out for Zuber in seventh. cLined out for Dreisewerd in ninth. E—Marion, Pesky, Higgins, Hughson, Ryba. DP—St. Louis 2, Boston 2. LOB—St. Louis 10, Boston 8. 2B—Kurowski 2, Musial, York, Slaughter, Garagiola, Marion. HR—Slaughter, Doerr. SH—Marion, Moore, Munger, Walker. U—Berry (A.L.), Ballanfant (N.L.), Hubbard (A.L.) and Barlick (N.L.). T—2:31. A—35,645.

Game 5

Friday, October 11, At Boston

St. Louis	AB.	R.	H.	RBI.	PO.	A.
Schoendienst, 2b	4	0	1	0	3	1
Moore, cf	4	0	0	0	2	0
Musial, 1b	3	1	1	0	7	0
Slaughter, rf	2	0	0	0	0	0
Dusak, lf	1	0	0	0	0	0
Kurowski, 3b	4	1	0	0	3	1
Garagiola, c	4	1	0	0	7	1
Walker, lf-rf	4	0	2	3	1	0
Marion, ss	4	0	0	0	1	7
Pollet, p	0	0	0	0	0	0
Brazle, p	2	0	0	0	0	1
aJones	1	0	0	0	0	0
Beazley, p	0	0	0	0	0	1
Totals	33	3	4	3	24	12

Boston	AB.	R.	H.	RBI.	PO.	A.
Gutteridge, 2b	5	0	2	1	0	2
Pesky, ss	5	1	3	0	2	2
DiMaggio, cf	3	1	1	0	3	0
Williams, lf	5	0	1	1	4	0
York, 1b	2	1	0	0	8	0
Higgins, 3b	4	1	1	1	0	1
Culberson, rf	3	1	2	1	2	0
Partee, c	3	1	1	1	8	1
Dobson, p	3	0	0	0	0	1
Totals	33	6	11	5	27	7

St. Louis	0 1 0	0 0 0	0 0 2	—3
Boston	1 1 0	0 0 1	3 0 x	—6

St. Louis	IP.	H.	R.	ER.	BB.	SO.
Pollet	⅓	3	1	1	0	0
Brazle (L)	6⅔	7	5	4	6	4
Beazley	1	1	0	0	0	1
Boston	**IP.**	**H.**	**R.**	**ER.**	**BB.**	**SO.**
Dobson (W)	9	4	3	0	1	8

aStruck out for Brazle in eighth. E—Marion, Pesky 2, York. DP—St. Louis 1, Boston 1. LOB—St. Louis 5, Boston 11. 2B—Walker, Musial, DiMaggio, Higgins. HR—Culberson. SB—Slaughter, Culberson, Pesky. SH—Dobson, DiMaggio. HBP—By Dobson (Slaughter). WP—Beazley. U—Ballanfant (N.L.), Hubbard (A.L.), Barlick (N.L.) and Berry (A.L.). T—2:23. A—35,982.

Game 6

Sunday, October 13, At St. Louis

Boston	AB.	R.	H.	RBI.	PO.	A.
Culberson, rf	4	0	0	0	5	0
Pesky, ss	3	0	1	0	2	3
DiMaggio, cf	4	0	1	0	5	0
Williams, lf	3	0	1	0	2	0
York, 1b	4	1	1	0	4	0
Doerr, 2b	3	0	1	1	1	1
Higgins, 3b	3	0	1	0	1	1
Partee, c	3	0	0	0	4	0
Harris, p	1	0	0	0	0	0
Hughson, p	1	0	1	0	0	0
bMcBride	1	0	0	0	0	0
Johnson, p	0	0	0	0	0	0
Totals	30	1	7	1	24	5

St. Louis	AB.	R.	H.	RBI.	PO.	A.
Schoendienst, 2b	4	1	1	0	4	3
Moore, cf	4	0	1	1	2	0
Musial, 1b	4	1	1	0	9	0
Kurowski, 3b	4	0	1	1	2	2
Slaughter, rf	2	0	1	1	2	0
Dusak, lf	0	0	0	0	0	1
aWalker, lf	3	1	0	0	1	0
Marion, ss	4	0	2	1	2	1
Rice, c	3	0	1	0	5	1
Brecheen, p	4	1	0	0	0	2
Totals	32	4	8	4	27	10

Boston	0 0 0	0 0 0	1 0 0	—1
St. Louis	0 0 3	0 0 0	0 1 x	—4

Boston	IP.	H.	R.	ER.	BB.	SO.
Harris (L)	2⅔	5	3	3	1	2
Hughson	4⅓	2	0	0	1	2
Johnson	1	1	1	1	2	0
St. Louis	**IP.**	**H.**	**R.**	**ER.**	**BB.**	**SO.**
Brecheen (W)	9	7	1	1	2	6

aLined out for Dusak in third. bFouled out for Hughson in eighth. DP—St. Louis 3. LOB—Boston 4, St. Louis 8. 2B—Schoendienst, Marion. 3B—York. U—Hubbard (A.L.), Barlick (N.L.), Berry (A.L.) and Ballanfant (N.L). T—1:56. A—35,768.

Game 7

Tuesday, October 15, At St. Louis

Boston	AB.	R.	H.	RBI.	PO.	A.
Moses, rf	4	1	1	0	1	0
Pesky, ss	4	0	1	0	2	1
DiMaggio, cf	3	0	1	3	0	0
cCulberson, cf	0	0	0	0	0	0
Williams, lf	4	0	0	0	3	1
York, 1b	4	0	1	0	10	1
dCampbell	0	0	0	0	0	0
Doerr, 2b	4	0	2	0	3	7
Higgins, 3b	4	0	0	0	0	1
H. Wagner, c	2	0	0	0	4	0
aRussell	1	1	1	0	0	0
Partee, c	1	0	0	0	0	0
Ferriss, p	2	0	0	0	0	0
Dobson, p	0	0	0	0	0	1
bMetkovich	1	1	1	0	0	0
Klinger, p	0	0	0	0	1	0
Johnson, p	0	0	0	0	0	0
eMcBride	1	0	0	0	0	0
Totals	35	3	8	3	24	12

St. Louis	AB.	R.	H.	RBI.	PO.	A.
Schoendienst, 2b	4	0	2	1	2	3
Moore, cf	4	0	1	0	3	0
Musial, 1b	3	0	1	0	6	0
Slaughter, rf	3	1	1	0	4	0
Kurowski, 3b	4	1	1	0	3	1
Garagiola, c	3	0	0	0	4	0
Rice, c	1	0	0	0	0	0
Walker, lf	3	1	2	2	3	0
Marion, ss	2	0	0	0	2	1
Dickson, p	3	1	1	1	0	1
Brecheen, p	1	0	0	0	0	0
Totals	31	4	9	4	27	6

Boston	1 0 0	0 0 0	0 2 0	—3
St. Louis	0 1 0	0 2 0	0 1 x	—4

Boston	IP.	H.	R.	ER.	BB.	SO.
Ferriss	4⅓	7	3	3	1	2
Dobson	2⅔	0	0	0	2	2
Klinger (L)	⅔	2	1	1	1	0
Johnson	⅓	0	0	0	0	0
St. Louis	**IP.**	**H.**	**R.**	**ER.**	**BB.**	**SO.**
Dickson	7*	5	3	3	1	3
Brecheen (W)	2	3	0	0	0	1

*Pitched to two batters in eighth.

aSingled for H. Wagner in eighth. bDoubled for Dobson in eighth. cRan for DiMaggio in eighth. dRan for York in ninth. eGrounded out for Johnson in ninth. E—Kurowski. LOB—Boston 6, St. Louis 8. 2B—Musial, Kurowski, Dickson, DiMaggio, Metkovich, Walker. SH—Marion. U—Barlick (N.L.), Berry (A.L.), Ballanfant (N.L.) and Hubbard (A.L.). T—2:17. A—36,143.

COMPOSITE BATTING AVERAGES

St. Louis Cardinals

Player-Position	G.	AB.	R.	H.	2B.	3B.	HR.	RBI.	BA.
Rice, c	3	6	2	3	1	0	0	0	.500
Walker, lf-rf-ph	7	17	3	7	2	0	0	6	.412
Dickson, p	2	5	1	2	2	0	0	1	.400
Slaughter, rf	7	25	5	8	1	1	1	2	.320
Garagiola, c	5	19	2	6	2	0	0	4	.316
Kurowski, 3b	7	27	5	8	3	0	0	2	.296
Dusak, ph-lf	4	4	0	1	1	0	0	0	.250
Marion, ss	7	24	1	6	2	0	0	4	.250
Munger, p	1	4	0	1	0	0	0	0	.250
Schoendienst, 2b	7	30	3	7	1	0	0	1	.233
Musial, 1b	7	27	3	6	4	1	0	4	.222
Moore, cf	7	27	1	4	0	0	0	2	.148
Brecheen, p	3	8	2	1	0	0	0	1	.125
Pollet, p	2	4	0	0	0	0	0	0	.000
Wilks, p	1	0	0	0	0	0	0	0	.000
Brazle, p	1	2	0	0	0	0	0	0	.000
Beazley, p	1	0	0	0	0	0	0	0	.000
Jones, ph	1	1	0	0	0	0	0	0	.000
Sisler, ph	2	2	0	0	0	0	0	0	.000
Totals	7	232	28	60	19	2	1	27	.259

Boston Red Sox

Player-Position	G.	AB.	R.	H.	2B.	3B.	HR.	RBI.	BA.
Russell, ph-3b	2	2	1	2	0	0	0	0	1.000
Metkovich, ph	2	2	1	1	1	0	0	0	.500
Moses, rf	4	12	1	5	0	0	0	0	.417
Doerr, 2b	6	22	1	9	1	0	1	3	.409
Gutteridge, pr-2b	3	5	1	2	0	0	0	1	.400
Harris, p	3	3	0	1	0	0	0	0	.333
Hughson, p	3	3	0	1	0	0	0	0	.333
York, 1b	7	23	6	6	1	1	2	5	.261
DiMaggio, cf	7	27	2	7	3	0	0	3	.259
Pesky, ss	7	30	2	7	0	0	0	0	.233
C'son, ph-rf-cf-pr	5	9	1	2	0	0	1	1	.222
Higgins, 3b	7	24	1	5	1	0	0	2	.208
Williams, lf	7	25	2	5	0	0	0	1	.200
McBride, rf-ph	5	12	0	2	0	0	0	1	.167
Partee, ph-c	5	10	1	1	0	0	0	1	.100
H. Wagner, c	5	13	0	0	0	0	0	0	.000
Johnson, p	3	1	0	0	0	0	0	0	.000
Dobson, p	3	3	0	0	0	0	0	0	.000
Ferriss, p	2	6	0	0	0	0	0	0	.000
Bagby, p	1	1	0	0	0	0	0	0	.000
Zuber, p	1	0	0	0	0	0	0	0	.000
Brown, p	1	0	0	0	0	0	0	0	.000
Ryba, p	1	0	0	0	0	0	0	0	.000
Dreisewerd, p	1	0	0	0	0	0	0	0	.000
Klinger, p	1	0	0	0	0	0	0	0	.000
Campbell, pr	1	0	0	0	0	0	0	0	.000
Totals	7	233	20	56	7	1	4	18	.240

COMPOSITE PITCHING AVERAGES

St. Louis Cardinals

Pitcher	G.	IP.	H.	R.	ER.	BB.	SO.	W.	L.	ERA.
Wilks	1	1	2	1	0	0	0	0	0	0.00
Beazley	1	1	1	0	0	0	1	0	0	0.00
Brecheen	3	20	14	1	1	5	11	3	0	0.45
Munger	1	9	9	3	1	3	2	1	0	1.00
Pollet	2	10⅓	12	4	4	4	3	0	1	3.48
Dickson	2	14	11	6	6	4	7	0	1	3.86
Brazle	1	6⅔	7	5	4	6	4	0	1	5.40
Totals	7	62	56	20	16	22	28	4	3	2.32

Boston Red Sox

Pitcher	G.	IP.	H.	R.	ER.	BB.	SO.	W.	L.	ERA.
Dobson	3	12⅔	4	3	0	3	10	1	0	0.00
Ryba	1	⅔	2	1	0	1	0	0	0	0.00
Dreisewerd	1	⅓	0	0	0	0	0	0	0	0.00
Ferriss	2	13⅓	13	3	3	2	4	1	0	2.03
Johnson	3	3⅓	1	1	1	2	1	1	0	2.75
Bagby	1	3	6	1	1	1	1	0	0	3.00
Hughson	3	14⅓	14	8	5	3	8	0	1	3.14
Zuber	1	2	3	1	1	1	1	0	0	4.50
Harris	2	9⅔	11	6	5	4	5	0	2	4.66
Klinger	1	⅔	2	1	1	1	0	0	1	13.50
Brown	1	1	4	3	3	1	0	0	0	27.00
Totals	7	61	60	28	20	19	30	3	4	2.95

The Brooklyn Dodgers won Game 4 of the 1947 World Series, the storied contest in which New York Yankees pitcher Floyd (Bill) Bevens lost a no-hitter—and the game—with two out in the last of the ninth inning.

Two days later in that no-holds-barred Series, the Dodgers prevailed in Game 6, which outfielder Al Gionfriddo saved for Brooklyn by robbing Joe DiMaggio of a game-tying home run with one of the greatest catches in baseball history.

Although hardly on the scale of Games 4 and 6 in terms of significance, Game 3 of the '47 fall classic also went into the Dodgers' victory column. In that game, a young Yankee catcher named Yogi Berra belted the first pinch-hit homer in Series annals. But when the page closed on this Series—more to the point, when relief ace Joe Page closed this Series—the Brooklyn Dodgers found themselves just where they had been in 1916, 1920 and 1941: in the loss column.

While the Dodgers failed to step to the front in October 1947, they clearly had been in the forefront in April. And on a much more meaningful area than the winning and losing of ball games. They introduced Jackie Robinson to big-league baseball. Robinson, the first black player to perform in the modern-day majors, made quite a first impression with a .297 batting average and a league-leading 29 stolen bases. He got opponents' attention, to say the least.

Among those opponents, the St. Louis Cardinals gave the Dodgers the best run in the National League pennant race. But the defending National League champions wound up five games behind Brooklyn, which got solid

Dodger left fielder Al Gionfriddo makes his game-saving catch in Game 6 against Joe DiMaggio and the Yankees.

production from its outfield of Pete Reiser (.309 average in 110 games), Carl Furillo (.295 mark and 88 runs batted in) and Dixie Walker (.306 and 94 RBIs), catcher Bruce Edwards (.295) and pitchers Ralph Branca (21-12 record), Joe Hatten (17-8) and Hugh Casey (10 victories in relief). These Dodgers were not the long-ball crew they soon would become, however. Shortstop Pee Wee Reese, the glue that held the Dodgers together, tied Robinson for the club homer lead with 12.

The '47 Yankees, catapulted by a 19-game winning streak that began in late June, won the American League pennant by a 12-game margin. But this club lacked the usual Yankee power,

with no player attaining the 100-RBI class and only one, Joe DiMaggio, reaching the 20-homer level. But New York got great pitching from Allie Reynolds (who won 19 games in his first season with the club after being obtained from Cleveland), Spud Chandler (the league's earned-run-average leader with a 2.46 figure despite missing most of the second half of the season because of injury), rookie Spec Shea (a 14-game winner) and ace reliever Page (also 14 victories, all out of the bullpen). Veteran Bobo Newsom, a July acquisition from Washington, and Vic Raschi, summoned from the minor leagues, each won seven games.

Shea and Reynolds got the Yankees off to a fast start in the Series, winning by 5-3 and 10-3 scores in Games 1 and 2. In the opener, the Dodgers' Branca pitched perfect ball through the fourth, then couldn't get anyone out in a five-run fifth; Shea, meanwhile, was on his way to a six-hitter. Reynolds allowed nine hits in the second game, but coasted to victory as New York banged out 15 hits of its own. Yankees left fielder Johnny Lindell had two RBIs in each contest.

Back in the friendly confines of Ebbets Field, the Dodgers responded with a 9-8 triumph in Game 3. A six-run second inning—in which Brooklyn got two-run doubles from Eddie Stanky and pinch-hitter Furillo—put New York on the ropes early, and things didn't look much better for the Yanks after four innings, with the Dodgers owning a 9-4 lead. But DiMaggio stroked a two-run homer in the fifth and Tommy Henrich doubled home a Yankee run in the sixth, cutting the deficit to 9-7. Then, with one out in the seventh, Berra was sent

up to bat for catcher Sherman Lollar and he whacked a tremendous homer to right off Branca. While the blow proved dramatic, it was the Yanks' last hurrah of the day.

Bevens, winner of only seven of 20 decisions for New York in '47, was selected to start Game 4 at Ebbets Field by Bucky Harris, who was in his first season as the Yankees' manager. And while Bevens permitted a fifth-inning run (on two walks, a sacrifice and a ground ball), he entered the ninth with a no-hitter and a 2-1 lead. Edwards began the Dodgers' half of the inning by flying out, and Furillo drew a walk. Spider Jorgensen then fouled out, bringing Bevens within one out of the first no-hit game in World Series history.

Speedy reserve outfielder Gionfriddo was sent in to run for Furillo and, with Reiser at the plate as a pinch-hitter for reliever Hugh Casey, Gionfriddo stole second. Reiser, despite the fact he represented the potential winning run, was walked intentionally (it was Bevens' 10th base on balls of the day). Eddie Miksis then was inserted into the game as a runner for Reiser, who was bothered by a leg injury. Stanky was the next scheduled hitter, but Burt Shotton, who had stepped into the Dodgers' managerial breach when Leo Durocher was suspended just before the beginning of the season, replaced him with veteran Cookie Lavagetto. And on Bevens' second pitch, Lavagetto walloped a double off the right-field wall and Gionfriddo and Miksis sped home. Incredibly, with two out in the ninth, Bevens had lost his no-hit bid and the game. Now, the Series was tied.

The American Leaguers responded to their misfortune in typical Yankee fashion, shaking it off the next day and winning, 2-1, as Shea pitched a four-hitter and singled home a run and DiMaggio homered.

Brooklyn jumped to a 4-0 lead in Game 6 at Yankee Stadium, fell behind 5-4 and then regained the lead with a four-run sixth capped by Reese's two-run single. Then, with two on and two out in the

last of the sixth and his Yankees down 8-5, DiMaggio made a valiant effort to tie the game. He slammed a Hatten pitch toward the left-field bullpen and, just as it appeared the ball might drop over the fence, Gionfriddo—inserted into the game as the Yankees came to bat in the inning—made a twisting, glove-hand catch near the 415-foot mark. DiMaggio, in a rare show of emotion, kicked at the dirt over his disappointment. Brooklyn held on for a Series-evening 8-6 victory.

Dodger hopes zoomed in Game 7 when Shotton's troops drove Shea from the mound in the second, an inning in which Brooklyn seized a 2-0 lead. But the Yankees scored a run in their half of the second, two more in the fourth and, getting tremendous relief pitching from Page, went on to a 5-2 triumph. Page threw five innings of scoreless relief, allowing only one hit.

The disappointed Brooklyn club would have other chances to succeed in the World Series, and the champion Yankee teams would have additional opportunities to excel in the fall classic. But for '47 Series principals Lavagetto, Gionfriddo and Bevens, this was the end of the line. Not only had these men played in their last Series, downward careers would mean they had participated in their last major league games.

Game 1

Tuesday, September 30, At New York

Brooklyn	AB.	R.	H.	RBI.	PO.	A.
Stanky, 2b	4	0	1	0	0	4
Robinson, 1b	2	0	0	0	8	1
Reiser, cf-lf	4	1	1	0	3	0
Walker, rf	4	0	2	1	1	0
Hermanski, lf	2	0	0	0	2	0
bFurillo, cf	1	0	1	1	2	0
Edwards, c	4	0	0	0	8	0
Jorgensen, 3b	2	0	0	0	0	1
cLavagetto, 3b	1	0	0	0	0	0
Reese, ss	4	1	1	0	0	2
Branca, p	2	0	0	0	0	0
Behrman, p	0	0	0	0	0	1
dMiksis	1	0	0	0	0	0
Casey, p	0	0	0	0	0	0
Totals	32	3	6	2	24	9

New York	AB.	R.	H.	RBI.	PO.	A.
Stirnweiss, 2b	4	0	0	0	3	1
Henrich, rf	4	0	1	2	3	0
Berra, c	4	0	0	0	5	0
DiMaggio, cf	4	1	1	0	2	0
McQuinn, 1b	3	1	0	0	7	2
Johnson, 3b	2	1	0	1	2	0
Lindell, lf	3	0	1	2	3	0
Rizzuto, ss	2	1	1	0	1	3
Shea, p	1	0	0	0	1	2
aBrown	0	1	0	1	0	0
Page, p	1	0	0	0	1	2
Totals	28	5	4	5	27	12

| Brooklyn | | | | | | 1 0 0   0 0 1   1 0 0—3 |
| New York | | | | | | 0 0 0   0 5 0   0 0 x—5 |

Brooklyn	IP.	H.	R.	ER.	BB.	SO.
Branca (L)	4*	2	5	5	3	5
Behrman	2	1	0	0	0	0
Casey	2	1	0	0	0	4

New York	IP.	H.	R.	ER.	BB.	SO.
Shea (W)	5	2	1	1	2	3
Page	4	4	2	2	1	2

*Pitched to six batters in fifth.

aWalked for Shea in fifth. bSingled for Hermanski in sixth. cPopped out for Jorgensen in seventh. dStruck out for Behrman in seventh. DP—Yankees 1. LOB—Brooklyn 5, New York 3. 2B—Lindell. SB—Robinson, Reese. HBP—By Branca (Johnson). WP—Page. Balk—Shea. U—McGowan (A.L.), Pinelli (N.L.), Rommel (A.L.), Goetz (N.L.), Magerkurth (N.L.) and Boyer (A.L.). T—2:36. A—73,365.

Game 2

Wednesday, October 1, At New York

Brooklyn	AB.	R.	H.	RBI.	PO.	A.
Stanky, 2b	4	0	1	0	3	2
Robinson, 1b	4	0	2	1	5	0
Reiser, cf	4	0	1	0	4	0
Walker, rf	4	1	1	1	1	0
Hermanski, lf	3	1	0	0	3	0
Edwards, c	4	0	1	0	5	1
Reese, ss	3	1	2	0	0	0
Jorgensen, 3b	4	0	1	1	3	5
Lombardi, p	2	0	0	0	0	0
Gregg, p	0	0	0	0	0	2
aVaughan	1	0	0	0	0	0
Behrman, p	0	0	0	0	0	0
Barney, p	0	0	0	0	0	0
bGionfriddo	1	0	0	0	0	0
Totals	34	3	9	3	24	10

New York	AB.	R.	H.	RBI.	PO.	A.
Stirnweiss, 2b	4	2	3	1	1	2
Henrich, rf	4	1	2	1	3	0
Lindell, lf	4	1	2	2	2	0
DiMaggio, cf	4	0	1	0	4	0
McQuinn, 1b	5	1	2	1	6	1
Johnson, 3b	5	2	2	1	1	2
Rizzuto, ss	5	0	1	1	3	4
Berra, c	3	1	0	0	6	1
Reynolds, p	4	2	2	1	1	0
Totals	38	10	15	8	27	10

| Brooklyn | | | | | | 0 0 1   1 0 0   0 0 1—3 |
| New York | | | | | | 1 0 1   1 2 1   4 0 x—10 |

Brooklyn	IP.	H.	R.	ER.	BB.	SO.
Lombardi (L)	4*	9	5	5	1	3
Gregg	2	2	1	1	1	2
Behrman	1/3	3	4	4	1	0
Barney	1 2/3	1	0	0	1	0

New York	IP.	H.	R.	ER.	BB.	SO.
Reynolds (W)	9	9	3	3	2	6

*Pitched to two batters in fifth.

aFlied out for Gregg in seventh. bHit into force play for Barney in ninth. E—Stanky, Reiser, Berra. DP—Brooklyn 1, New York 1. LOB—Brooklyn 6, New York 9. 2B—Rizzuto, Lindell, Robinson. 3B—Stirnweiss, Lindell, Johnson. HR—Walker, Henrich. SB—Reese. SH—Henrich. WP—Behrman, Barney. U—Pinelli (N.L.), Rommel (A.L.), Goetz (N.L.), McGowan (A.L.), Boyer (A.L.) and Magerkurth (N.L.). T—2:36. A—69,865.

Game 3

Thursday, October 2, At Brooklyn

New York	AB.	R.	H.	RBI.	PO.	A.
Stirnweiss, 2b	5	0	1	0	2	3
Henrich, rf	4	0	1	1	0	0
Lindell, lf	4	1	2	1	0	0
DiMaggio, cf	4	1	2	3	3	0
McQuinn, 1b	4	0	0	0	8	1
Johnson, 3b	4	1	1	0	2	1
Rizzuto, ss	5	0	1	0	5	2
Lollar, c	3	2	2	1	2	1
eBerra, c	2	1	1	1	2	0
Newsom, p	0	0	0	0	0	1
Raschi, p	0	0	0	0	0	0
bClark	1	0	0	0	0	0
Drews, p	0	0	0	0	0	0
cPhillips	1	0	0	0	0	0
Chandler, p	0	0	0	0	0	0
dBrown	1	1	1	0	0	0
Page, p	1	0	0	0	0	0
Totals	38	8	13	8	24	11

Brooklyn	AB.	R.	H.	RBI.	PO.	A.
Stanky, 2b	4	2	1	2	4	5
Robinson, 1b	4	1	2	0	10	1
Reiser, cf	0	0	0	0	0	0
aFurillo, cf	3	1	2	0	2	0
Walker, rf	5	0	2	1	1	0
Hermanski, lf	3	1	1	1	4	0
Edwards, c	4	1	1	1	5	0
Reese, ss	3	1	1	1	1	3
Jorgensen, 3b	4	0	2	0	1	3
Hatten, p	2	1	1	0	0	0
Branca, p	1	0	0	0	0	0
Casey, p	1	0	0	0	1	1
Totals	34	9	13	9	27	13

| New York | | | | | | 0 0 2   2 2 1   1 0 0—8 |
| Brooklyn | | | | | | 0 6 1   2 0 0   0 0 x—9 |

New York	IP.	H.	R.	ER.	BB.	SO.
Newsom (L)	1 2/3	5	5	5	2	0
Raschi	1/3	2	1	1	0	0
Drews	1	1	1	1	1	0
Chandler	2	2	2	2	3	1
Page	3	3	0	0	1	3

Brooklyn	IP.	H.	R.	ER.	BB.	SO.
Hatten	4 1/3	8	6	6	3	3
Branca	2	4	2	2	1	1
Casey (W)	2 2/3	1	0	0	1	1

aDoubled for Reiser in second. bWalked for Raschi in third. cFlied out for Drews in fourth. dDoubled for Chandler in sixth. eHomered for Lollar in seventh. E—Furillo. DP—Brooklyn 2. LOB—New York 9, Brooklyn 9. 2B—Edwards, Stanky, Furillo, Lollar, Brown, Henrich, Jorgensen. HR—DiMaggio, Berra. SB—Robinson, Walker. SH—Robinson. HBP—By Drews (Hermanski). WP—Drews, Page. PB—Lollar. U—Rommel (A.L.), Goetz (N.L.), McGowan (A.L.), Pinelli (N.L.), Magerkurth (N.L.) and Boyer (A.L.). T—3:05. A—33,098.

Game 4

Friday, October 3, At Brooklyn

New York	AB.	R.	H.	RBI.	PO.	A.
Stirnweiss, 2b	4	1	2	0	2	1
Henrich, rf	5	0	1	0	2	0
Berra, c	4	0	0	0	6	1
DiMaggio, cf	2	0	0	1	2	0
McQuinn, 1b	4	0	1	0	7	0
Johnson, 3b	4	1	1	0	3	2
Lindell, lf	3	0	2	1	3	0
Rizzuto, ss	4	0	1	0	1	2
Bevens, p	3	0	0	0	0	1
Totals	33	2	8	2	26	7

Brooklyn	AB.	R.	H.	RBI.	PO.	A.
Stanky, 2b	1	0	0	0	2	3
eLavagetto	1	0	1	2	0	0
Reese, ss	4	0	0	1	3	5
Robinson, 1b	4	0	0	0	11	1
Walker, rf	2	0	0	0	0	1
Hermanski, lf	4	0	0	0	2	0
Edwards, c	4	0	0	0	7	1
Furillo, cf	3	0	0	0	2	0
bGionfriddo	0	1	0	0	0	0
Jorgensen, 3b	2	1	0	0	0	1
Taylor, p	0	0	0	0	0	0
Gregg, p	1	0	0	0	0	1
aVaughan	0	0	0	0	0	0
Behrman, p	0	0	0	0	0	1
Casey, p	0	0	0	0	0	1
cReiser	0	0	0	0	0	0
dMiksis	0	1	0	0	0	0
Totals	26	3	1	3	27	15

New York ... 1 0 0 1 0 0 0 0 0—2
Brooklyn ... 0 0 0 0 1 0 0 0 2—3
Two out when winning run scored.

New York	IP.	H.	R.	ER.	BB.	SO.
Bevens (L)	8⅔	1	3	3	10	5

Brooklyn	IP.	H.	R.	ER.	BB.	SO.
Taylor	0*	2	1	0	1	0
Gregg	7	4	1	1	3	5
Behrman	1⅓	2	0	0	0	0
Casey (W)	⅔	0	0	0	0	0

*Pitched to four batters in first.

aWalked for Gregg in seventh. bRan for Furillo in ninth. cWalked for Casey in ninth. dRan for Reiser in ninth. eDoubled for Stanky in ninth. E—Berra, Reese, Edwards, Jorgensen. DP—Brooklyn 3. LOB—New York 9, Brooklyn 8. 2B—Lindell, Lavagetto. 3B—Johnson. SB—Rizzuto, Reese, Gionfriddo. SH—Stanky, Bevens. WP—Bevens. U—Goetz (N.L.), McGowan (A.L.), Pinelli (N.L.), Rommel (A.L.), Boyer (A.L.) and Magerkurth (N.L.). T—2:20. A—33,443.

Game 5

Saturday, October 4, At Brooklyn

New York	AB.	R.	H.	RBI.	PO.	A.
Stirnweiss, 2b	3	0	0	0	3	4
Henrich, rf	4	0	2	0	1	0
Lindell, lf	2	0	0	0	3	0
DiMaggio, cf	4	1	1	1	3	0
McQuinn, 1b	4	0	0	0	7	0
Johnson, 3b	3	0	0	0	2	1
A. Robinson, c	3	1	0	0	7	0
Rizzuto, ss	2	0	0	0	1	1
Shea, p	4	0	2	1	0	1
Totals	29	2	5	2	27	7

Brooklyn	AB.	R.	H.	RBI.	PO.	A.
Stanky, 2b	3	0	0	0	2	2
cReiser	0	0	0	0	0	0
dMiksis, 2b	0	0	0	0	1	1
Reese, ss	2	0	0	0	2	3
J. Robinson, 1b	4	0	1	1	5	0
Walker, rf	4	0	0	0	0	0
Hermanski, lf	4	0	1	0	2	0
Edwards, c	3	0	1	0	9	2
eLombardi	0	0	0	0	0	0
Furillo, cf	3	0	0	0	2	0
Jorgensen, 3b	4	0	0	0	3	0
Barney, p	1	0	0	0	0	1
Hatten, p	0	0	0	0	0	0
aGionfriddo	0	1	0	0	0	0
Behrman, p	0	0	0	0	0	1
bVaughan	1	0	1	0	0	0
Casey, p	0	0	0	0	1	0
fLavagetto	1	0	0	0	0	0
Totals	30	1	4	1	27	10

New York ... 0 0 0 1 1 0 0 0 0—2
Brooklyn ... 0 0 0 0 0 1 0 0 0—1

New York	IP.	H.	R.	ER.	BB.	SO.
Shea (W)	9	4	1	1	5	7

Brooklyn	IP.	H.	R.	ER.	BB.	SO.
Barney (L)	4⅔	3	2	2	9	3
Hatten	1⅓	0	0	0	0	1
Behrman	1	1	0	0	1	2
Casey	2	1	0	0	0	1

aWalked for Hatten in sixth. bDoubled for Behrman in seventh. cWalked for Stanky in seventh. dRan for Reiser in seventh. eRan for Edwards in ninth. fStruck out for Casey in ninth. E—Miksis. DP—Brooklyn 2. LOB—New York 11, Brooklyn 8. 2B—Henrich, Vaughan, Shea. HR—DiMaggio. SH—Furillo. HBP—By Casey (Lindell). WP—Barney. PB—Edwards 2. U—McGowan (A.L.), Pinelli (N.L.), Rommel (A.L.), Goetz (N.L.), Magerkurth (N.L.) and Boyer (A.L.). T—2:46. A—34,379.

Game 6

Sunday, October 5, At New York

Brooklyn	AB.	R.	H.	RBI.	PO.	A.
Stanky, 2b	5	2	2	0	4	2
Reese, ss	4	2	3	2	2	1
J. Robinson, 1b	5	1	2	1	7	1
Walker, rf	5	0	1	1	3	0
Hermanski, lf	1	0	0	0	0	0
bMiksis, lf	1	0	0	0	0	0
Gionfriddo, lf	2	0	0	0	1	0
Edwards, c	4	1	1	0	5	0
Furillo, cf	4	1	2	0	4	1
Jorgensen, 3b	2	0	0	0	1	1
cLavagetto, 3b	2	0	0	1	0	1
Lombardi, p	1	0	0	0	0	0
Branca, p	1	0	0	0	0	1
dBragan	1	0	1	1	0	0
eBankhead	0	1	0	0	0	0
Hatten, p	1	0	0	0	0	0
Casey, p	0	0	0	0	0	1
Totals	39	8	12	6	27	9

New York	AB.	R.	H.	RBI.	PO.	A.
Stirnweiss, 2b	5	0	0	1	1	6
Henrich, rf-lf	5	1	2	0	1	0
Lindell, lf	2	1	2	1	0	0
Berra, rf	3	0	2	1	1	0
DiMaggio, cf	5	1	1	0	5	0
Johnson, 3b	5	1	2	1	1	5
Phillips, 1b	1	0	0	0	4	0
aBrown	1	0	1	1	0	0
McQuinn, 1b	1	0	0	0	6	0
Rizzuto, ss	4	0	1	0	6	1
Lollar, c	1	1	1	0	0	0
A. Robinson, c	4	1	2	0	2	0
Reynolds, p	0	0	0	0	0	0
Drews, p	2	0	0	0	0	1
Page, p	0	0	0	0	0	0
Newsom, p	0	0	0	0	0	0
fClark	1	0	0	0	0	0
Raschi, p	0	0	0	0	0	0
gHouk	1	0	1	0	0	0
Wensloff, p	0	0	0	0	0	1
hFrey	1	0	0	1	0	0
Totals	42	6	15	6	27	14

Brooklyn ... 2 0 2 0 0 4 0 0 0—8
New York ... 0 0 4 1 0 0 0 0 1—6

Brooklyn	IP.	H.	R.	ER.	BB.	SO.
Lombardi	2⅔	5	4	4	0	2
Branca (W)	2⅓	6	1	1	0	2
Hatten	3*	3	1	1	4	0
Casey	1	1	0	0	0	0

New York	IP.	H.	R.	ER.	BB.	SO.
Reynolds	2⅓	6	4	3	1	0
Drews	2	1	0	0	1	0
Page (L)	1	4	4	4	0	1
Newsom	⅔	1	0	0	0	0
Raschi	1	0	0	0	0	1
Wensloff	2	0	0	0	0	0

*Pitched to two batters in ninth.

aSingled for Phillips in third. bPopped out for Hermanski in fifth. cFlied out for Jorgensen in sixth. dDoubled for Branca in sixth. eRan for Bragan in sixth. fLined out for Newsom in sixth. gSingled for Raschi in seventh. hHit into force play for Wensloff in ninth. E—Jorgensen, McQuinn, A. Robinson. DP—New York 1. LOB—Brooklyn 6, New York 13. 2B—Reese, J. Robinson, Walker, Lollar, Furillo, Bragan. WP—Lombardi. PB—Lollar. U—Pinelli (N.L.), Rommel (A.L.), Goetz (N.L.), McGowan (A.L.), Boyer (A.L.) and Magerkurth (N.L.). T—3:19. A—74,065.

Game 7

Monday, October 6, At New York

Brooklyn	AB.	R.	H.	RBI.	PO.	A.
Stanky, 2b	4	0	1	0	3	1
Reese, ss	3	0	0	0	0	1
J. Robinson, 1b	4	0	0	0	3	2
Walker, rf	3	0	0	0	3	0
Hermanski, lf	2	1	1	0	2	0
bMiksis, lf	2	0	1	0	2	0
Edwards, c	4	1	2	1	5	0
Furillo, cf	3	0	1	0	4	0
Jorgensen, 3b	2	0	1	1	0	1
dLavagetto, 3b	1	0	0	0	0	0
Gregg, p	2	0	0	0	1	0
Behrman, p	0	0	0	0	1	0
Hatten, p	0	0	0	0	0	0
Barney, p	0	0	0	0	0	0
eHodges	1	0	0	0	0	0
Casey, p	0	0	0	0	0	0
Totals	31	2	7	2	24	5

New York	AB.	R.	H.	RBI.	PO.	A.
Stirnweiss, 2b	2	0	0	0	5	4
Henrich, lf	5	0	1	1	2	0
Berra, rf	3	0	0	0	1	0
cClark, rf	1	0	1	1	2	0
DiMaggio, cf	3	0	0	0	3	0
McQuinn, 1b	2	1	0	0	7	0
Johnson, 3b	3	2	1	0	1	1
A. Robinson, c	3	0	0	1	4	2
Rizzuto, ss	4	2	3	1	2	2
Shea, p	0	0	0	0	0	0
Bevens, p	1	0	0	0	0	0
aBrown	1	0	1	1	0	0
Page, p	2	0	0	0	0	0
Totals	30	5	7	5	27	9

Brooklyn ... 0 2 0 0 0 0 0 0 0—2
New York ... 0 1 0 2 0 1 1 0 x—5

Brooklyn	IP.	H.	R.	ER.	BB.	SO.
Gregg (L)	3⅔	3	3	3	4	3
Behrman	1⅔	2	1	1	3	1
Hatten	⅓	1	0	0	0	1
Barney	⅓	0	0	0	0	0
Casey	2	1	1	1	0	0

New York	IP.	H.	R.	ER.	BB.	SO.
Shea	1⅓	4	2	2	1	0
Bevens	2⅔	2	0	0	1	2
Page (W)	5	1	0	0	0	1

aDoubled for Bevens in fourth. bGrounded out for Hermanski in sixth. cSingled for Berra in sixth. dPopped out for Jorgensen in seventh. eStruck out for Barney in seventh. DP—New York 1. LOB—Brooklyn 4, New York 9. 2B—Jorgensen, Brown. 3B—Hermanski, Johnson. SB—Rizzuto. SH—McQuinn. U—Rommel (A.L.), Goetz (N.L.), McGowan (A.L.), Pinelli (N.L.), Magerkurth (N.L.) and Boyer (A.L.). T—2:19. A—71,548.

COMPOSITE BATTING AVERAGES

New York Yankees

Player-Position	G.	AB.	R.	H.	2B.	3B.	HR.	RBI.	BA.
Brown, ph	4	3	2	3	2	0	0	3	1.000
Houk, ph	1	1	0	1	0	0	0	0	1.000
Lollar, c	2	4	3	3	2	0	0	1	.750
Reynolds, p	2	4	2	2	0	0	0	1	.500
Lindell, lf	6	18	3	9	3	1	0	7	.500
Clark, ph-rf	3	2	1	1	0	0	0	1	.500
Shea, p	3	5	0	2	1	0	0	1	.400
Henrich, rf-lf	7	31	2	10	2	0	1	5	.323
Rizzuto, ss	7	26	3	8	1	0	0	2	.308
Johnson, 3b	7	26	8	7	0	3	0	2	.269
Stirnweiss, 2b	7	27	3	7	0	1	0	3	.259
DiMaggio, cf	7	26	4	6	0	0	2	5	.231
A. Robinson, c	3	10	2	2	0	0	0	1	.200
Berra, c-ph-rf	6	19	2	3	0	0	1	2	.158
McQuinn, 1b	7	23	3	3	0	0	0	1	.130
Page, p	4	4	0	0	0	0	0	0	.000
Newsom, p	2	0	0	0	0	0	0	0	.000
Raschi, p	2	0	0	0	0	0	0	0	.000
Drews, p	2	2	0	0	0	0	0	0	.000
Phillips, ph-1b	2	2	0	0	0	0	0	0	.000
Chandler, p	1	0	0	0	0	0	0	0	.000
Bevens, p	2	4	0	0	0	0	0	0	.000
Wensloff, p	1	0	0	0	0	0	0	0	.000
Frey, ph	1	1	0	0	0	0	0	1	.000
Totals	7	238	38	67	11	5	4	36	.282

Brooklyn Dodgers

Player-Position	G.	AB.	R.	H.	2B.	3B.	HR.	RBI.	BA.
Bragan, ph	1	1	0	1	1	0	0	1	1.000
Vaughan, ph	3	2	0	1	1	0	0	0	.500
Furillo, ph-cf	6	17	2	6	2	0	0	3	.353
Hatten, p	4	3	1	1	0	0	0	0	.333
Reese, ss	7	23	5	7	1	0	0	4	.304
Robinson, 1b	7	27	3	7	2	0	0	3	.259
Miksis, ph-2b-lf	5	4	1	1	0	0	0	0	.255
Reiser, cf-lf-ph	5	8	1	2	0	0	0	0	.250
Stanky, 2b	7	25	4	6	1	0	0	2	.240
Walker, rf	7	27	1	6	1	0	1	4	.222
Edwards, c	7	27	3	6	1	0	0	2	.222
Jorgensen, 3b	7	20	1	4	2	0	0	3	.200
Hermanski, lf	7	19	4	3	0	1	0	1	.158
Lavagetto, ph-3b	5	7	0	1	1	0	0	3	.143
G'friddo, ph-pr-lf	4	3	2	0	0	0	0	0	.000
Branca, p	3	4	0	0	0	0	0	0	.000
Casey, p	6	1	0	0	0	0	0	0	.000
Gregg, p	3	3	0	0	0	0	0	0	.000
Barney, p	3	1	0	0	0	0	0	0	.000
Taylor, p	1	0	0	0	0	0	0	0	.000
Lombardi, p-pr	3	3	0	0	0	0	0	0	.000
Bankhead, pr	1	0	1	0	0	0	0	0	.000
Hodges, ph	1	1	0	0	0	0	0	0	.000
Totals	7	226	29	52	13	1	1	26	.230

COMPOSITE PITCHING AVERAGES

New York Yankees

Pitcher	G.	IP.	H.	R.	ER.	BB.	SO.	W.	L.	ERA.
Wensloff	1	2	0	0	0	0	0	0	0	0.00
Shea	3	15⅓	10	4	4	8	10	2	0	2.35
Bevens	2	11⅓	3	3	3	11	7	0	1	2.38
Drews	2	3	2	1	1	1	0	0	0	3.00
Page	4	13	12	6	6	2	7	1	1	4.15
Reynolds	2	11⅓	15	7	6	3	6	1	0	4.76
Raschi	2	1⅓	2	1	1	0	1	0	0	6.75
Chandler	1	2	2	2	2	3	1	0	0	9.00
Newsom	2	2⅓	6	5	5	2	0	0	1	19.29
Totals	7	61⅔	52	29	28	30	32	4	3	4.09

Brooklyn Dodgers

Pitcher	G.	IP.	H.	R.	ER.	BB.	SO.	W.	L.	ERA.
Taylor	1	0	2	1	0	1	0	0	0	0.00
Casey	6	10⅓	5	1	1	1	3	2	0	0.87
Barney	3	6⅔	4	2	2	10	3	0	1	2.70
Gregg	3	12⅔	9	5	5	8	10	0	1	3.55
Hatten	4	9	12	7	7	7	5	0	0	7.00
Behrman	5	6⅓	9	5	5	5	3	0	0	7.11
Branca	3	8⅓	12	8	8	5	8	1	1	8.64
Lombardi	2	6⅔	14	9	9	1	5	0	1	12.15
Totals	7	60	67	38	37	38	37	3	4	5.55

1948
CLEVELAND INDIANS
VS.
BOSTON BRAVES

If a manager leads by example, Lou Boudreau set some example for the 1948 Cleveland Indians.

After the regular-season schedule had been completed in the 1948 American League pennant race, Boudreau's Indians were 96-58 and tied for first place with the Boston Red Sox. And Boudreau himself, Cleveland's manager/shortstop, had contributed mightily to his club's rise from its fourth-place status of 1947 by compiling pre-playoff statistics featuring a .351 batting average, 16 home runs and 104 runs batted in.

Then, in the pressure-packed situation of a one-game playoff for the '48 A.L. championship, Boudreau lashed two bases-empty home runs and two singles as the Indians routed the Red Sox, 8-3, and won only the second pennant in club history. Boudreau's 4-for-4 performance at Fenway Park backed the five-hit pitching of rookie lefthander Gene Bearden, whose victory in the extra game was his 20th of the year.

Cleveland's other big winners in '48, Bob Feller and Bob Lemon, were Boudreau's pitching choices for the first two games of the World Series against Boston's other big-time representative, the Braves, who under Manager Billy Southworth had captured the National League pennant by 6½ games. While the Braves had a good-hitting ball club, much of the National Leaguers' hopes rested on the arms of Johnny Sain and Warren Spahn. In fact, the formula of "Spahn and Sain and two days of rain" seemed to capture not only the depth of the team's starting pitching, but also the essence of the Braves' strength.

Feller, who had won 25 or more games three times in the

First-game Boston heroes Tommy Holmes (left) and Johnny Sain celebrate the Braves' 1-0 victory over Cleveland in the 1948 Series.

majors (and 24 on another occasion), was a 19-game winner in '48. Since Feller had broken into the majors in 1936, the World Series wait had been a long one for the 29-year-old Iowan—and the hard-throwing righthander pitched superbly in his fall-classic debut.

Entering the last of the eighth inning of Game 1, Feller and Sain were locked in a scoreless duel. Boston catcher Bill Salkeld drew a leadoff walk and gave way to pinch-runner Phil Masi, who was sacrificed to second by Mike McCormick. Eddie Stanky then was issued an intentional walk, and Sibby Sisti ran for Boston's pepperpot second baseman. Feller and Boudreau proceeded to work a pickoff play, with Feller whirling and throwing to his manager,

who cut in behind Masi at second. Umpire Bill Stewart made a safe call on the sliding Masi, and Boudreau argued strenuously that he had made the tag before the baserunner got back to the bag. Sain then lined out to right field, but Tommy Holmes singled home Masi and it was 1-0, Braves.

Sain, a 24-game winner in '48, overcome third baseman Bob Elliott's two-base throwing error in the ninth and protected the one-run lead. His four-hitter had defeated Feller's two-hitter.

In Game 2, Lemon pitched shutout ball over the final eight innings as Cleveland squared the Series with a 4-1 triumph. Boudreau and Larry Doby, who had become the American League's first black player in July 1947, each singled, doubled and drove

in a run for the Indians.

Bearden continued his marvelous season by tossing a five-hit shutout against Boston in Game 3, a game in which the 28-year-old pitcher singled and doubled and scored the first run (on a throwing error) of a 2-0 contest. Steve Gromek then put the Braves on the edge of elimination by hurling Cleveland to a 2-1 triumph in a contest featuring home runs by Doby and the Braves' Marv Rickert. An end-of-the-season replacement for outfielder Jeff Heath, who had batted .319 for Boston with 20 homers before suffering an ankle fracture, Rickert wound up starting five World Series games for the Braves after appearing in only three regular-season games for Southworth's club.

Boston wasn't through. At least not yet. Before a record major league crowd of 86,288 at Cleveland Stadium, the Braves hammered out an 11-5 victory in Game 5. Elliott belted a three-run homer in the first inning for the Braves and a bases-empty shot in the third, but the Indians rallied from a 4-1 deficit with a four-run outburst—capped by Jim Hegan's three-run homer—in the fourth. Salkeld tied the game with a homer off Feller in the sixth and Boston then tore into Feller and Cleveland's relief corps for six seventh-inning runs. Spahn, who hurled one-hit, scoreless ball in 5⅔ innings of relief, was the winning pitcher. Among the five pitchers used by the losers was 42-year-old Satchel Paige, the Negro leagues legend who had been signed to his first big-league contract by Indians President Bill Veeck in July. The appearance by Paige, who compiled a 6-1 regular-season record for the Tribe, made Satch the first black pitcher to take the mound in a World Series.

Lemon, with 1⅔ innings of relief help from the steady Bearden, was a 4-3 winner in decisive Game 6. Bearden yielded a run-scoring fly ball and an RBI double in the eighth, drawing Boston within a run, but worked out of trouble and nailed down the World Series crown for Boudreau's Indians.

Lemon, who had broken into

Cleveland pitcher Gene Bearden (left) gets a handshake from Manager Lou Boudreau after pitching the Indians to a 2-0 Game 3 victory.

the majors as a third baseman and played center field for Cleveland in Feller's no-hitter against the New York Yankees in 1946, showed everyone in 1948 that his conversion into a pitcher had been a wise move. He won 20 games for the A.L. champions, a plateau he would reach six more times in the majors, and added two victories in the Series.

Cleveland prevailed against the Braves despite the Series slumps of Joe Gordon and Ken Keltner and the failure of Feller to beat the National Leaguers. Gordon, who hit 32 homers and totaled 124 RBIs while batting .280 in the regular season, had one homer, two RBIs and a .182 hitting mark in the fall classic; Keltner, coming off a .297 season in which he slugged 31 homers and knocked in 119 runs, collected two singles in 21 Series at-bats (.095) and did

not drive in a run. Feller was 0-2 with a 5.02 ERA against the Braves.

But Cleveland had Lemon, Bearden, Gromek and timely hitting. Plus, the Indians had the ever-present leadership of Lou Boudreau, who played errorless ball at shortstop during the Series and contributed a .273 batting average for a team that hit .199 overall against the Braves.

Game 1

Wednesday, October 6, At Boston

Cleveland	AB.	R.	H.	RBI.	PO.	A.
Mitchell, lf	4	0	0	0	2	0
Doby, cf	4	0	1	0	3	0
Boudreau, ss	4	0	0	0	2	1
Gordon, 2b	4	0	1	0	1	1
Keltner, 3b	4	0	1	0	1	1
Judnich, rf	4	0	0	0	2	0
Robinson, 1b	3	0	0	0	10	1
Hegan, c	3	0	1	0	2	1
Feller, p	2	0	0	0	1	4
Totals	32	0	4	0	24	9

Boston	AB.	R.	H.	RBI.	PO.	A.
Holmes, rf	4	0	1	1	5	0
Dark, ss	4	0	0	0	1	1
Torgeson, 1b	2	0	0	0	4	0
Elliott, 3b	3	0	0	0	1	0
Rickert, lf	3	0	1	0	5	0

	AB.	R.	H.	RBI.	PO.	A.
Salkeld, c	1	0	0	0	5	1
aMasi, c	0	1	0	0	1	0
M. McCormick, cf	2	0	0	0	5	0
Stanky, 2b	2	0	0	0	0	1
bSisti, 2b	0	0	0	0	0	0
Sain, p	3	0	0	0	0	0
Totals	24	1	2	1	27	3

Cleveland	0 0 0 0 0 0 0 0 0—0
Boston	0 0 0 0 0 0 0 1 x—1

Cleveland	IP.	H.	R.	ER.	BB.	SO.
Feller (L)	8	2	1	1	3	2
Boston	**IP.**	**H.**	**R.**	**ER.**	**BB.**	**SO.**
Sain (W)	9	4	0	0	0	6

aRan for Salkeld in eighth. bRan for Stanky in eighth. E—Elliott 2. LOB—Cleveland 6, Boston 4. SB—Hegan, Gordon, Torgeson. SH—Feller, Salkeld, M. McCormick. U—Barr (N.L.), Summers (A.L.), Stewart (N.L.), Grieve (A.L.), Paparella (A.L.) and Pinelli (N.L.). T—1:42. A—40,135.

Game 2

Thursday, October 7, At Boston

Cleveland	AB.	R.	H.	RBI.	PO.	A.
Mitchell, lf	5	1	1	0	1	0
Clark, rf	3	0	0	0	2	0
Kennedy, rf	1	0	1	1	0	0
Boudreau, ss	5	1	2	1	4	2
Gordon, 2b	4	1	1	1	2	3
Keltner, 3b	4	0	0	0	0	0
Doby, cf	4	0	2	1	0	0
Robinson, 1b	3	0	1	0	8	3
Hegan, c	3	1	0	0	7	0
Lemon, p	4	0	0	0	3	6
Totals	36	4	8	4	27	14

Boston	AB.	R.	H.	RBI.	PO.	A.
Holmes, rf	4	0	0	0	2	1
Dark, ss	4	1	1	0	0	2
Torgeson, 1b	4	0	2	0	14	1
Elliott, 3b	4	0	1	1	1	5
Rickert, lf	4	0	0	0	5	0
Salkeld, c	1	0	1	0	2	0
aMasi, c	1	0	0	0	1	0
M. McCormick, cf	4	0	2	0	1	0
Stanky, 2b	2	0	1	0	1	3
Spahn, p	2	0	0	0	0	1
Barrett, p	0	0	0	0	0	0
bF. McCormick	1	0	0	0	0	0
Potter, p	0	0	0	0	0	0
cSanders	1	0	0	0	0	0
Totals	32	1	8	1	27	13

Cleveland	0 0 0 2 1 0 0 0 1—4
Boston	1 0 0 0 0 0 0 0 0—1

Cleveland	IP.	H.	R.	ER.	BB.	SO.
Lemon (W)	9	8	1	0	3	5
Boston	**IP.**	**H.**	**R.**	**ER.**	**BB.**	**SO.**
Spahn (L)	4⅓	6	3	3	2	1
Barrett	2⅔	1	0	0	0	1
Potter	2	1	1	0	0	1

aRan for Salkeld in sixth. bStruck out for Barrett in seventh. cGrounded out for Potter in ninth. E—Gordon, Dark 2, Elliott. DP—Cleveland 2, Boston 1. LOB—Cleveland 8, Boston 8. 2B—Boudreau, Doby, Stanky. SH—Stanky, Clark. U—Summers (A.L.), Stewart (N.L.), Grieve (A.L.), Barr (N.L.), Pinelli (N.L.) and Paparella (A.L.). T—2:14. A—39,633.

Game 3

Friday, October 8, At Cleveland

Boston	AB.	R.	H.	RBI.	PO.	A.
Holmes, rf	4	0	0	0	2	0
Dark, ss	4	0	1	0	3	2
M. McCormick, lf	4	0	1	0	6	0
Elliott, 3b	3	0	1	0	2	1
F. McCormick, 1b	3	0	1	0	5	1
Conatser, cf	3	0	0	0	1	0
Masi, c	3	0	0	0	2	0
Stanky, 2b	3	0	1	0	2	3
Bickford, p	0	0	0	0	0	0
Voiselle, p	1	0	0	0	1	0
aRyan	1	0	0	0	0	0
Barrett, p	0	0	0	0	0	0
Totals	29	0	5	0	24	7

Cleveland	AB.	R.	H.	RBI.	PO.	A.
Mitchell, lf	3	0	0	0	2	0
Doby, cf	3	0	1	0	1	0
Boudreau, ss	3	0	0	0	1	2
Gordon, 2b	4	0	0	0	3	4
Keltner, 3b	3	1	0	0	0	4
Judnich, rf	3	0	0	0	1	0
Robinson, 1b	3	0	1	0	14	0
Hegan, c	3	0	1	1	5	0
Bearden, p	3	1	2	0	0	6
Totals	28	2	5	1	27	16

Boston	0 0 0 0 0 0 0 0 0—0
Cleveland	0 0 1 1 0 0 0 0 x—2

Boston	IP.	H.	R.	ER.	BB.	SO.
Bickford (L)	3⅓	4	2	1	5	1
Voiselle	3⅔	1	0	0	0	0
Barrett	1	0	0	0	0	0
Cleveland	**IP.**	**H.**	**R.**	**ER.**	**BB.**	**SO.**
Bearden (W)	9	5	0	0	0	4

aStruck out for Voiselle in eighth. E—Dark. DP—Boston 1, Cleveland 2. LOB—Boston 3, Cleveland 7. 2B—Bearden, Dark. SH—Bickford. U—Stewart (N.L.), Grieve (A.L.), Barr (N.L.), Summers (A.L.), Paparella (A.L.) and Pinelli (N.L.). T—1:36. A—70,306.

Game 4

Saturday, October 9, At Cleveland

Boston	AB.	R.	H.	RBI.	PO.	A.
Holmes, rf	4	0	0	0	0	1
Dark, ss	4	0	0	0	2	5
Torgeson, 1b	3	0	2	0	11	2
Elliott, 3b	4	0	0	0	2	2
Rickert, lf	4	1	2	1	2	0
M. McCormick, cf	4	0	1	0	1	0
Masi, c	3	0	0	0	3	1
aSalkeld	1	0	0	0	0	0
Stanky, 2b	3	0	1	0	1	1
Sain, p	2	0	1	0	2	2
Totals	32	1	7	1	24	14

Cleveland	AB.	R.	H.	RBI.	PO.	A.
Mitchell, lf	4	1	1	0	2	0
Doby, cf	3	1	1	1	2	0
Boudreau, ss	3	0	1	1	2	4
Gordon, 2b	3	0	0	0	4	1
Keltner, 3b	3	0	0	0	1	2
Judnich, rf	3	0	0	0	1	0
Kennedy, rf	0	0	0	0	1	0
Robinson, 1b	3	0	2	0	8	1
Hegan, c	2	0	0	0	5	1
Gromek, p	3	0	0	0	1	1
Totals	27	2	5	2	27	10

Boston	0 0 0 0 0 0 1 0 0—1
Cleveland	1 0 1 0 0 0 0 0 x—2

Boston	IP.	H.	R.	ER.	BB.	SO.
Sain (L)	8	5	2	2	0	3
Cleveland	**IP.**	**H.**	**R.**	**ER.**	**BB.**	**SO.**
Gromek (W)	9	7	1	1	1	2

aFlied out for Masi in ninth. DP—Cleveland 1. LOB—Boston 6, Cleveland 2. 2B—Torgeson 2, Boudreau. HR—Doby, Rickert. SH—Sain, Hegan. U—Grieve (A.L.), Barr (N.L.), Summers (A.L.), Stewart (N.L.), Pinelli (N.L.) and Paparella (A.L.). T—1:31. A—81,897.

Game 5

Sunday, October 10, At Cleveland

Boston	AB.	R.	H.	RBI.	PO.	A.
Holmes, rf	5	2	2	0	0	0
Dark, ss	4	1	1	0	1	1
Torgeson, 1b	5	1	2	1	10	1
Elliott, 3b	4	3	2	4	1	3
Rickert, lf	5	1	1	1	3	0
Salkeld, c	4	2	1	1	8	0
M. McCormick, cf	5	1	1	1	2	0
Stanky, 2b	3	0	1	1	1	2
Potter, p	2	0	1	0	1	0
Spahn, p	2	0	0	1	0	1
Totals	39	11	12	10	27	8

Cleveland	AB.	R.	H.	RBI.	PO.	A.
Mitchell, lf	3	1	1	1	3	0
Doby, cf	4	0	0	0	4	0
Boudreau, ss	4	0	2	0	0	3
Gordon, 2b	3	1	1	0	2	1
Keltner, 3b	3	1	0	0	1	1
Judnich, rf	3	1	1	1	3	0
bBoone	1	0	0	0	0	0
Peck, rf	0	0	0	0	0	0
Robinson, 1b	4	0	0	0	8	2
Hegan, c	4	1	1	3	4	1
Feller, p	2	0	0	0	1	0
Klieman, p	0	0	0	0	0	0
Christopher, p	0	0	0	0	0	0
Paige, p	0	0	0	0	0	0
aRosen	1	0	0	0	0	0
Muncrief, p	0	0	0	0	1	0
cTipton	1	0	0	0	0	0
Totals	33	5	6	5	27	8

Boston	3 0 1 0 0 1 6 0 0—11
Cleveland	1 0 0 4 0 0 0 0 0— 5

aPopped out for Paige in seventh. bStruck out for Judnich in eighth. cStruck out for Muncrief in ninth. E—Doby, Keltner. LOB—Boston 6, Cleveland 4. 2B—Boudreau. HR—Elliott 2, Mitchell, Hegan, Salkeld. SH—Dark. Balk—Paige. U—Barr (N.L.), Summers (A.L.), Stewart (N.L.), Grieve (A.L.), Paparella (A.L.) and Pinelli (N.L.). T—2:39. A—86,288.

Game 6

Monday, October 11, At Boston

Cleveland	AB.	R.	H.	RBI.	PO.	A.
Mitchell, lf	4	1	1	0	3	0
Kennedy, lf	1	0	0	0	1	0
Doby, rf	4	0	2	0	1	0
Boudreau, ss	3	0	1	1	2	2
Gordon, 2b	4	1	1	1	3	3
Keltner, 3b	4	1	1	0	0	3
Tucker, cf	3	1	1	0	3	1
Robinson, 1b	4	0	2	1	12	0
Hegan, c	4	0	1	1	2	2
Lemon, p	3	0	0	0	0	3
Bearden, p	1	0	0	0	0	1
Totals	35	4	10	4	27	15

Boston	AB.	R.	H.	RBI.	PO.	A.
Holmes, rf	5	1	2	0	1	0
Dark, ss	4	0	1	0	0	1
Torgeson, 1b	4	1	1	0	5	1
Elliott, 3b	3	1	3	0	4	3
Rickert, lf	3	0	0	0	5	0
bConatser, cf	1	0	0	1	0	0
Salkeld, c	2	0	0	0	4	1
cMasi, c	1	0	1	1	3	0
M. McCormick, cf-lf	4	0	1	1	2	0
Stanky, 2b	1	0	0	0	3	2
dRyan	0	0	0	0	0	0
Voiselle, p	1	0	0	0	0	0
aF. McCormick	1	0	0	0	0	0
Spahn, p	0	0	0	0	0	1
eSisti	1	0	0	0	0	0
Totals	31	3	9	3	27	9

Cleveland	0 0 1 0 0 2 0 1 0—4
Boston	0 0 0 1 0 0 0 2 0—3

Cleveland	IP.	H.	R.	ER.	BB.	SO.
Lemon (W)	7⅓	8	3	3	4	1
Bearden	1⅔	1	0	0	1	0
Boston	**IP.**	**H.**	**R.**	**ER.**	**BB.**	**SO.**
Voiselle (L)	7	7	3	3	2	2
Spahn	2	3	1	1	0	4

aGrounded out for Voiselle in seventh. bFlied out for Rickert in eighth, scoring Holmes. cDoubled for Salkeld in eighth. dRan for Stanky in ninth. eBunted into double play for Spahn in ninth. DP—Cleveland 4, Boston 1. LOB—Cleveland 7, Boston 7. 2B—Mitchell, Boudreau, Torgeson, Masi. HR—Gordon. SH—Voiselle. HBP—By Voiselle (Boudreau). Balk—Lemon. U—Summers (A.L.), Stewart (N.L.), Grieve (A.L.), Barr (N.L.), Pinelli (N.L.) and Paparella (A.L.). T—2:17. A—40,103.

COMPOSITE BATTING AVERAGES

Cleveland Indians

Player-Position	G.	AB.	R.	H.	2B.	3B.	HR.	RBI.	BA.
Bearden, p	2	4	1	2	1	0	0	0	.500
Kennedy, rf	3	2	0	1	0	0	0	1	.500
Tucker, cf	1	3	1	1	0	0	0	0	.333
Doby, cf	6	22	1	7	1	0	1	2	.318
Robinson, 1b	6	20	0	6	0	0	0	1	.300
Boudreau, ss	6	22	1	6	4	0	0	3	.273
Hegan, c	6	19	2	4	0	0	1	5	.211
Gordon, 2b	6	22	3	4	0	0	1	2	.182
Mitchell, lf	6	23	4	4	1	0	1	1	.174
Keltner, 3b	6	21	3	2	0	0	0	0	.095
Judnich, rf	4	13	1	1	0	0	0	1	.077
Clark, rf	1	3	0	0	0	0	0	0	.000
Peck, rf	1	0	0	0	0	0	0	0	.000
Feller, p	2	4	0	0	0	0	0	0	.000
Lemon, p	2	7	0	0	0	0	0	0	.000
Gromek, p	1	3	0	0	0	0	0	0	.000
Boone, ph	1	1	0	0	0	0	0	0	.000
Klieman, p	1	0	0	0	0	0	0	0	.000
Christopher, p	1	0	0	0	0	0	0	0	.000
Paige, p	1	0	0	0	0	0	0	0	.000
Muncrief, p	1	0	0	0	0	0	0	0	.000
Tipton, ph	1	1	0	0	0	0	0	0	.000
Rosen, ph	1	1	0	0	0	0	0	0	.000
Totals	6	191	17	38	7	0	4	16	.199

Boston Braves

Player-Position	G.	AB.	R.	H.	2B.	3B.	HR.	RBI.	BA.
Potter, p	2	2	0	1	0	0	0	0	.500
Torgeson, 1b	5	18	2	7	3	0	0	1	.389
Elliott, 3b	6	21	4	7	0	0	2	5	.333
Stanky, 2b	6	14	0	4	1	0	0	1	.286
M. McCor'k, cf-lf	6	23	1	6	0	0	0	2	.261
Salkeld, c-ph	5	9	2	2	0	0	1	1	.222
Rickert, lf	5	19	2	4	0	0	1	2	.211
F. McCo'k, ph-1b	3	5	0	1	0	0	0	0	.200
Sain, p	2	5	0	1	0	0	0	0	.200
Holmes, rf	6	26	3	5	0	0	0	1	.192
Dark, ss	6	24	2	4	1	0	0	0	.167
Masi, pr-c	5	8	1	1	1	0	0	1	.125
Conatser, cf-ph	2	4	0	0	0	0	0	1	.000
Sisti, pr-2b	2	1	0	0	0	0	0	0	.000
Spahn, p	3	4	0	0	0	0	0	1	.000
Barrett, p	2	0	0	0	0	0	0	0	.000
Bickford, p	1	0	0	0	0	0	0	0	.000
Voiselle, p	2	2	0	0	0	0	0	0	.000
Ryan, ph-pr	2	1	0	0	0	0	0	0	.000
Sanders, ph	1	1	0	0	0	0	0	0	.000
Totals	6	187	17	43	6	0	4	16	.230

COMPOSITE PITCHING AVERAGES

Cleveland Indians

Pitcher	G.	IP.	H.	R.	ER.	BB.	SO.	W.	L.	ERA.
Bearden	2	10⅔	6	0	0	1	4	1	0	0.00
Muncrief	1	2	1	0	0	0	0	0	0	0.00
Paige	1	⅔	0	0	0	0	0	0	0	0.00
Gromek	1	9	7	1	1	1	2	1	0	1.00
Lemon	2	16⅓	16	4	3	7	6	2	0	1.65
Feller	2	14⅓	10	8	8	5	7	0	2	5.02
Klieman	1	0	1	3	3	2	0	0	0	......
Christopher	1	0	2	1	1	0	0	0	0	......
Totals	6	53	43	17	16	16	19	4	2	2.72

Boston Braves

Pitcher	G.	IP.	H.	R.	ER.	BB.	SO.	W.	L.	ERA.
Barrett	2	3⅔	1	0	0	0	1	0	0	0.00
Sain	2	17	9	2	2	0	9	1	1	1.06
Voiselle	2	10⅔	8	3	3	2	2	0	1	2.53
Bickford	1	3⅓	4	2	1	5	1	0	1	2.70
Spahn	3	12	10	4	4	3	12	1	1	3.00
Potter	2	5⅓	6	6	5	2	1	0	0	8.44
Totals	6	52	38	17	15	12	26	2	4	2.60

1949
NEW YORK YANKEES
VS.
BROOKLYN DODGERS

The man had proved he could play in this postseason classic. And now he was about to prove he could manage in it.

The fellow's name was Charles Dillon (Casey) Stengel. In a total of 12 World Series games with the 1916 Brooklyn club and the 1922 and 1923 New York Giants, the fun-loving outfielder had batted .393. Now, 60 years old, Stengel had just completed his first season as manager of the New York Yankees and was ready to guide the Yanks against the Dodgers in the 1949 Series.

Never able to finish higher than fifth in nine seasons as a National League manager with Brooklyn and Boston in the 1930s and 1940s, Stengel subsequently fought off his "clown" reputation and enjoyed managerial success in the minor leagues. After leading Oakland to the Pacific Coast League pennant in 1948, he was named to replace Bucky Harris as the Yankees' pilot.

New York, which under Harris had tumbled from first to third place in 1948 (falling all of 2½ games behind playoff-winning Cleveland), responded to Stengel's appointment by winning its 16th American League pennant and doing so in dramatic fashion. Stengel's team trailed Boston by one game as Manager Joe McCarthy's Red Sox arrived at Yankee Stadium for a season-closing two-game set, but the Yankees proceeded to sweep the Beantowners.

Don Newcombe, who had posted a 17-8 record as a Dodger rookie in 1949 while helping Brooklyn to a one-game victory over the St. Louis Cardinals in the N.L. pennant race, did all he could to spoil Stengel's Series managerial debut. Through eight innings of Game 1 of the '49 fall classic, Newcombe had struck out 11 Yankees,

walked no one, yielded only four hits and had not permitted a run. Pitching rival Allie Reynolds wasn't doing too badly, either: nine strikeouts, four walks, two hits, no runs.

Reynolds retired Brooklyn in order in the ninth on a grounder, popup and fly ball. Newcombe wasn't so fortunate. Leading off the bottom of the inning, the Yankees' Tommy Henrich, always tough in the clutch, whacked a Newcombe pitch into the right-field stands. Old Reliable indeed.

The Dodgers countered the Yankees' triumph with a 1-0 victory of their own in Game 2, with Preacher Roe outpitching Vic Raschi and Gil Hodges singling home Jackie Robinson (who had doubled) in the second inning.

The third game, a 1-1 deadlock through the eighth, had action galore in the final inning. Former National League slugger Johnny Mize, purchased in August from the New York Giants, rapped a bases-loaded single off Dodgers starter Ralph Branca in the top of the ninth to boost the Yankees into a 3-1 lead and Jerry Coleman followed with a run-scoring single off reliever Jack Banta.

New York's Joe Page, having pitched 4⅔ innings of scoreless relief since taking over for Tommy Byrne in the fourth, shouldered that lead into the Dodgers' half of the inning. Page was rocked for two home runs, the first a one-out shot by Luis Olmo (who hit one homer for Brooklyn in the regular season) and the second a two-out smash by Roy Campanella. But no one was on base either time, and Page and the Yankees hung on dearly for a 4-3 victory.

While only four runs had been scored in the first 26 innings of the 1949 Series, the pace was being stepped up—as evidenced by the

windup to Game 3. In the fourth game, the Yankees drove Newcombe from the mound with a three-run fourth—Cliff Mapes supplied the key hit with a two-run double—and then got three more in the fifth when Bobby Brown drilled a bases-loaded triple off Joe Hatten. Brooklyn had a big inning of its own, collecting four runs in the sixth off Eddie Lopat. But Reynolds came to the rescue by retiring Brooklyn's final 10 batters of the game and New York, a 6-4 winner, was now one victory from the World Series championship.

In Game 5, the Yankees scored in five of the first six innings and built a 10-2 lead. Hodges' three-run homer in the Dodgers' four-run seventh cut into the deficit, but Page's relief work in place of Raschi shut down the Brooklyn offense. The Yankees prevailed, 10-6, with Coleman driving in three runs and Brown and Joe DiMaggio collecting two RBIs each. DiMaggio, who missed half of the season because of a heel injury, hit a bases-empty homer in the fourth.

The Yanks romped in this Series despite a poor showing by DiMaggio, who had batted .346 with 67 RBIs in 76 regular-season games. Besides his homer, DiMaggio collected only one other hit against Brooklyn.

Brown and outfielder Gene Woodling gave the Yanks a lift, however, by combining for 10 hits in 22 at-bats.

Postseason success was nothing new for the New York Yankees, who now had won 12 World Series. But a Series managerial crown was a first for Casey Stengel, erstwhile clown who would wind up having the last laugh on just about everyone come October for years to come.

Game 1

Wednesday, October 5, At New York

Brooklyn	AB.	R.	H.	RBI.	PO.	A.
Reese, ss	4	0	1	0	2	2
Jorgensen, 3b	3	0	1	0	0	2
Snider, cf	4	0	0	0	3	0
Robinson, 2b	4	0	0	0	4	0
Hermanski, lf	3	0	0	0	0	0
Furillo, rf	3	0	0	0	0	0
Hodges, 1b	2	0	0	0	4	0
Campanella, c	2	0	0	0	11	0
Newcombe, p	3	0	0	0	0	0
Totals	28	0	2	0	24	4

New York	AB.	R.	H.	RBI.	PO.	A.
Rizzuto, ss	4	0	0	0	1	2
Henrich, 1b	4	1	1	1	9	0
Berra, c	3	0	0	0	9	0
DiMaggio, cf	3	0	0	0	1	0
Lindell, lf	3	0	1	0	0	0
Johnson, 3b	3	0	0	0	2	3
Mapes, rf	3	0	0	0	4	0
Coleman, 2b	3	0	1	0	1	2
Reynolds, p	3	0	2	0	0	1
Totals	29	1	5	1	27	8

Brooklyn ... 0 0 0 0 0 0 0 0 0—0
New York ... 0 0 0 0 0 0 0 0 1—1
*None out when winning run scored.

Brooklyn	IP.	H.	R.	ER.	BB.	SO.
Newcombe (L)	8	5	1	1	0	11

New York	IP.	H.	R.	ER.	BB.	SO.
Reynolds (W)	9	2	0	0	4	9

E—Coleman. DP—New York 1. LOB—Brooklyn 6, New York 4. 2B—Jorgensen, Reynolds, Coleman. HR—Henrich. SB—Reese. SH—Hodges. U—Hubbard (A.L.), Reardon (N.L.), Passarella (A.L.), Jorda (N.L.), Hurley (A.L.) and Barr (N.L.). T—2:24. A—66,230.

Game 2

Thursday, October 6, At New York

Brooklyn	AB.	R.	H.	RBI.	PO.	A.
Reese, ss	4	0	0	0	1	3
Jorgensen, 3b	4	0	1	0	1	4
Snider, cf	4	0	1	0	3	1
Robinson, 2b	3	1	1	0	3	1
Hermanski, rf	3	0	1	0	2	0
dFurillo	1	0	0	0	0	0
McCormick, rf	0	0	0	0	1	0
Rackley, lf	2	0	0	0	0	0
Olmo, lf	2	0	1	0	2	0
Hodges, 1b	3	0	1	1	9	1
Campanella, c	2	0	1	0	4	0
Roe, p	3	0	0	0	1	1
Totals	31	1	7	1	27	11

New York	AB.	R.	H.	RBI.	PO.	A.
Rizzuto, ss	3	0	1	0	0	6
Henrich, 1b	4	0	0	0	11	1
Bauer, rf	4	0	1	0	1	0
DiMaggio, cf	4	0	1	0	1	0
Lindell, lf	4	0	0	0	2	1
Johnson, 3b	4	0	1	0	0	2
Coleman, 2b	4	0	1	0	6	3
Silvera, c	2	0	0	0	6	0
aMize	1	0	1	0	0	0
bStirnweiss	0	0	0	0	0	0
Niarhos, c	0	0	0	0	0	0
Raschi, p	2	0	0	0	0	0
cBrown	1	0	0	0	0	0
Page, p	0	0	0	0	0	0
Totals	33	0	6	0	27	13

Brooklyn ... 0 1 0 0 0 0 0 0 0—1
New York ... 0 0 0 0 0 0 0 0 0—0

Brooklyn	IP.	H.	R.	ER.	BB.	SO.
Roe (W)	9	6	0	0	0	3

New York	IP.	H.	R.	ER.	BB.	SO.
Raschi (L)	8	6	1	1	1	4
Page	1	1	0	0	0	0

aSingled for Silvera in eighth. bRan for Mize in eighth. cStruck out for Raschi in eighth. dPopped out for Hermanski in ninth. E—Reese, Roe, Lindell. DP—New York 1. LOB—Brooklyn 5, New York 7. 2B—Robinson, Coleman, Jorgensen. 3B—Hermanski. SB—Rizzuto, Johnson. SH—Rizzuto, Robinson. U—Reardon (N.L.), Passarella (A.L.), Jorda (N.L.), Hubbard (A.L.), Hurley (A.L.) and Barr (N.L.). T—2:30. A—70,053.

Game 3

Friday, October 7, At Brooklyn

New York	AB.	R.	H.	RBI.	PO.	A.
Rizzuto, ss	4	0	0	1	0	0
Henrich, 1b	3	0	0	0	10	0
Berra, c	3	1	0	0	7	2
DiMaggio, cf	4	0	0	0	4	0
Brown, 3b	4	1	1	0	0	2
Woodling, lf	3	1	1	0	2	0
Mapes, rf	2	1	0	0	2	0
aMize	1	0	1	2	0	0
bBauer, rf	0	0	0	0	0	0
Coleman, 2b	4	0	1	1	2	4
Byrne, p	1	0	1	0	0	0
Page, p	3	0	0	0	0	1
Totals	32	4	5	4	27	9

Brooklyn	AB.	R.	H.	RBI.	PO.	A.
Reese, ss	2	1	1	1	1	2
Miksis, 3b	4	0	1	0	3	1
Furillo, rf	4	0	1	0	2	0
Robinson, 2b	2	0	0	0	2	3
Hodges, 1b	3	0	0	0	8	0
Olmo, lf	4	1	1	1	0	0
Snider, cf	4	0	0	0	3	0
Campanella, c	4	1	1	1	7	0
Branca, p	3	0	0	0	1	0
Banta, p	0	0	0	0	0	0
cEdwards	1	0	0	0	0	0
Totals	31	3	5	3	27	6

New York ... 0 0 1 0 0 0 0 0 3—4
Brooklyn ... 0 0 0 1 0 0 0 0 2—3

New York	IP.	H.	R.	ER.	BB.	SO.
Byrne	3⅓	2	1	1	2	1
Page (W)	5⅔	3	2	2	2	4

Brooklyn	IP.	H.	R.	ER.	BB.	SO.
Branca (L)	8⅔	4	4	4	4	6
Banta	⅓	1	0	0	0	1

aSingled for Mapes in ninth. bRan for Mize in ninth. cStruck out for Banta in ninth. DP—New York 1. LOB—New York 5, Brooklyn 6. 2B—Woodling HR—Reese, Olmo, Campanella. HBP—By Byrne (Reese). U—Passarella (A.L.), Jorda (N.L.), Hubbard (A.L.), Reardon (N.L.), Barr (N.L.) and Hurley (A.L.). T—2:30. A—32,788.

Game 4

Saturday, October 8, At Brooklyn

New York	AB.	R.	H.	RBI.	PO.	A.
Rizzuto, ss	4	0	2	0	1	4
Henrich, 1b	4	1	3	0	10	0
Berra, c	5	1	1	0	10	1
DiMaggio, cf	3	1	0	0	1	0
R. Brown, 3b	3	1	2	3	0	3
Woodling, lf	3	1	0	0	2	0
Mapes, rf	2	1	1	2	1	0
aBauer, rf	2	0	0	0	2	0
Coleman, 2b	4	0	0	0	0	0
Lopat, p	3	0	1	1	0	1
Reynolds, p	1	0	0	0	0	0
Totals	34	6	10	6	27	9

Brooklyn	AB.	R.	H.	RBI.	PO.	A.
Reese, ss	4	1	2	0	0	2
Miksis, 3b	2	0	0	0	0	2
cCox, 3b	2	0	1	0	1	0
Snider, cf	4	0	0	0	4	0
Robinson, 2b	3	1	1	1	2	3
Hodges, 1b	4	1	1	0	8	1
Olmo, lf	4	1	1	1	2	1
Campanella, c	4	0	1	1	5	2
Hermanski, rf	4	0	2	1	4	0
Newcombe, p	1	0	0	0	1	1
Hatten, p	0	0	0	0	0	0
bT. Brown	1	0	0	0	0	0
Erskine, p	0	0	0	0	0	0
dJorgensen	1	0	0	0	0	0
Banta, p	0	0	0	0	0	0
eWhitman	1	0	0	0	0	0
Totals	35	4	9	4	27	12

New York ... 0 0 0 3 3 0 0 0 0—6
Brooklyn ... 0 0 0 0 0 4 0 0 0—4

New York	IP.	H.	R.	ER.	BB.	SO.
Lopat (W)	5⅔	9	4	4	1	4
Reynolds	3⅓	0	0	0	0	5

Brooklyn	IP.	H.	R.	ER.	BB.	SO.
Newcombe (L)	3⅔	5	3	3	3	0
Hatten	1⅓	3	3	3	2	0
Erskine	1	1	0	0	0	0
Banta	3	1	0	0	1	1

aFlied out for Mapes in fifth. bFlied out for Hatten in fifth. cSingled for Miksis in sixth. dStruck out for Erskine in sixth. eStruck out for Banta in ninth. E—Miksis. DP—New York 1, Brooklyn 1. LOB—New York 7, Brooklyn 5. 2B—Reese, R. Brown, Mapes, Lopat. 3B—R. Brown. U—Jorda (N.L.), Hubbard (A.L.), Reardon (N.L.), Passarella (A.L.), Hurley (A.L.) and Barr (N.L.). T—2:42. A—33,934.

Game 5

Sunday, October 9, At Brooklyn

New York	AB.	R.	H.	RBI.	PO.	A.
Rizzuto, ss	3	2	0	0	3	3
Henrich, 1b	4	2	1	0	8	0
Berra, c	5	0	0	1	11	0
DiMaggio, cf	4	1	1	2	0	0
R. Brown, 3b	4	2	3	2	0	1
Woodling, lf	4	2	3	0	3	0
Mapes, rf	3	1	0	0	1	0
Coleman, 2b	5	0	2	3	1	0
Raschi, p	3	0	1	1	0	0
Page, p	1	0	0	0	0	1
Totals	36	10	11	9	27	5

Brooklyn	AB.	R.	H.	RBI.	PO.	A.
Reese, ss	5	0	2	1	1	0
Jorgensen, 3b	3	1	0	0	0	0
eMiksis	1	0	1	0	0	0
Snider, cf	5	2	2	0	5	0
Robinson, 2b	4	0	1	1	1	2
Hermanski, rf	3	1	1	1	1	0
Hodges, 1b	5	1	2	3	9	1
Rackley, lf	3	0	0	0	2	0
cOlmo, lf	1	0	0	0	2	0
Campanella, c	3	1	1	0	5	0
Barney, p	0	0	0	0	1	1
Banta, p	1	0	0	0	0	1
aT. Brown	1	0	0	0	0	0
Erskine, p	0	0	0	0	0	0
Hatten, p	0	0	0	0	0	0
bCox	1	0	0	0	0	0
Palica, p	0	0	0	0	0	1
dEdwards	1	0	1	0	0	0
Minner, p	0	0	0	0	0	1
Totals	37	6	11	6	27	7

New York ... 2 0 3 1 1 3 0 0 0—10
Brooklyn ... 0 0 1 0 0 1 4 0 0— 6

New York	IP.	H.	R.	ER.	BB.	SO.
Raschi (W)	6⅔	9	6	6	4	7
Page	2⅓	2	0	0	1	4

Brooklyn	IP.	H.	R.	ER.	BB.	SO.
Barney (L)	2⅔	3	5	5	6	2
Banta	2⅓	3	2	2	0	2
Erskine	⅔	2	3	3	1	0
Hatten	⅓	1	0	0	0	0
Palica	2	1	0	0	1	1
Minner	1	1	0	0	0	0

aStruck out for Banta in fifth. bStruck out for Hatten in sixth. cStruck out for Rackley in seventh. dSingled for Palica in eighth. eDoubled for Jorgensen in ninth. E—Mapes, Robinson, Barney. DP—New York 1. LOB—New York 9, Brooklyn 9. 2B—Campanella, Woodling 2, Snider, Coleman, Miksis. 3B—R. Brown. HR—DiMaggio, Hodges. SH—Rizzuto, Mapes. U—Hubbard (A.L.), Reardon (N.L.), Passarella (A.L.), Jorda (N.L.), Barr (N.L.) and Hurley (A.L.). T—3:04. A—33,711.

COMPOSITE BATTING AVERAGES

New York Yankees

Player-Position	G.	AB.	R.	H.	2B.	3B.	HR.	RBI.	BA.
Byrne, p	1	1	0	1	0	0	0	0	1.000
Mize, ph	2	2	0	2	0	0	0	2	1.000
R. Brown, ph-3b	4	12	4	6	1	2	0	5	.500
Reynolds, p	2	4	0	2	1	0	0	0	.500
Woodling, lf	3	10	4	4	3	0	0	0	.400
Lopat, p	1	3	0	1	1	0	0	1	.333
Henrich, 1b	5	19	4	5	0	0	1	1	.263
Coleman, 2b	5	20	0	5	3	0	0	4	.250
Raschi, p	2	5	0	1	0	0	0	1	.200
Rizzuto, ss	5	18	2	3	0	0	0	1	.167
Bauer, rf-pr-ph	3	6	0	1	0	0	0	0	.167
Lindell, lf	2	7	0	1	0	0	0	0	.143
Johnson, 3b	2	7	0	1	0	0	0	0	.143
DiMaggio, cf	5	18	2	2	0	0	1	2	.111
Mapes, rf	4	10	3	1	1	0	0	2	.100
Berra, c	4	16	2	1	0	0	0	1	.063
Niarhos, c	1	0	0	0	0	0	0	0	.000
Silvera, c	1	2	0	0	0	0	0	0	.000
Page, p	3	4	0	0	0	0	0	0	.000
Stirnweiss, pr	1	0	0	0	0	0	0	0	.000
Totals	5	164	21	37	10	2	2	20	.226

Brooklyn Dodgers

Player-Position	G.	AB.	R.	H.	2B.	3B.	HR.	RBI.	BA.
Edwards, ph	2	2	0	1	0	0	0	0	.500
Cox, ph-3b	2	3	0	1	0	0	0	0	.333
Reese, ss	5	19	2	6	1	0	1	2	.316
Hermanski, lf-rf	4	13	1	4	0	1	0	2	.308
Miksis, 3b-ph	3	7	0	2	1	0	0	0	.286
Olmo, lf	4	11	2	3	0	0	1	2	.273
Campanella, c	5	15	2	4	1	0	1	2	.267
Hodges, 1b	5	17	2	4	0	0	1	4	.235
Robinson, 2b	5	16	2	3	1	0	0	2	.188
Jorgensen, 3b-ph	4	11	1	2	2	0	0	0	.182
Snider, cf	5	21	2	3	1	0	0	0	.143
Furillo, rf-ph	3	8	0	1	0	0	0	0	.125
Newcombe, p	2	4	0	0	0	0	0	0	.000
McCormick, rf	1	0	0	0	0	0	0	0	.000
Rackley, lf	2	5	0	0	0	0	0	0	.000
Roe, p	1	3	0	0	0	0	0	0	.000
Branca, p	1	3	0	0	0	0	0	0	.000
Banta, p	3	1	0	0	0	0	0	0	.000
Hatten, p	2	0	0	0	0	0	0	0	.000
Erskine, p	2	0	0	0	0	0	0	0	.000
Barney, p	1	0	0	0	0	0	0	0	.000
Palica, p	1	0	0	0	0	0	0	0	.000
Minner, p	1	0	0	0	0	0	0	0	.000
Whitman, ph	1	1	0	0	0	0	0	0	.000
T. Brown, ph	2	2	0	0	0	0	0	0	.000
Totals	5	162	14	34	7	1	4	14	.210

COMPOSITE PITCHING AVERAGES

New York Yankees

Pitcher	G.	IP.	H.	R.	ER.	BB.	SO.	W.	L.	ERA.
Reynolds	2	12⅓	2	0	0	4	14	1	0	0.00
Page	3	9	6	2	2	3	8	1	0	2.00
Byrne	1	3⅓	2	1	1	2	1	0	0	2.70
Raschi	2	14⅔	15	7	7	5	11	1	1	4.30
Lopat	1	5⅔	9	4	4	1	4	1	0	6.35
Totals	5	45	34	14	14	15	38	4	1	2.80

Brooklyn Dodgers

Pitcher	G.	IP.	H.	R.	ER.	BB.	SO.	W.	L.	ERA.
Roe	1	9	6	0	0	0	3	1	0	0.00
Palica	1	2	1	0	0	1	1	0	0	0.00
Minner	1	1	1	0	0	0	0	0	0	0.00
Newcombe	2	11⅔	10	4	4	3	11	0	2	3.09
Banta	3	5⅔	5	2	2	1	4	0	0	3.18
Branca	1	8⅔	4	4	4	4	6	0	1	4.15
Hatten	2	1⅔	4	3	3	2	0	0	0	16.20
Erskine	2	1⅔	3	3	3	1	0	0	0	16.20
Barney	1	2⅔	3	5	5	6	2	0	1	16.88
Totals	5	44	37	21	21	18	27	1	4	4.29

NEW YORK YANKEES
VS.
PHILADELPHIA PHILLIES

After four games of the 1950 World Series, the Whiz Kids had been turned into Fizz Kids.

Such a reversal of form for the Philadelphia Phillies was a major disappointment, to be sure, for the City of Brotherly Love. After all, Manager Eddie Sawyer's '50 Phils had just given the city its first National League pennant since 1915 and had done so with a nucleus of exuberant young talent. Now, six days after the Phils had attained the heights on Dick Sisler's 10th-inning, pennant-winning homer against the Brooklyn Dodgers, they had plunged to the depths of being on the short end of a Series sweep inflicted by the New York Yankees.

Losing four straight World Series games to the Yankees—while distressing—could hardly qualify as an embarrassment. Others had taken the plunge against the wrecking crew from the Bronx: The Pirates. The Cardinals. The Cubs. The Cubs again. The Reds. In fact, with their four-in-a-row dismissal of the Phillies, the Yankees had now swept six World Series in the last 24 years (in one 13-year stretch, the Yankee broom had been wielded five times) and captured 13 Series championships overall.

The truth is, the Phillies did anything but embarrass themselves in the 1950 Series.

With 20-game winner Robin Roberts having pitched three times in the last five days of the regular season in the Phils' frantic bid to nail down the pennant, Sawyer was hard-pressed to find a starting pitcher for Game 1 of the fall classic. Compounding the problem was the late-season loss of Curt Simmons (17 victories) to the Army. Plus, rookie pitchers Bob Miller and Bubba Church had nagging injuries. Sawyer

New York Yankee left fielder Gene Woodling mishandles a ninth-inning, Game 4 fly ball as members of the Phillies bullpen look on. The error on what would have been the final out of the game allowed two runs to score and ruined Whitey Ford's shutout bid.

found his man, nominating a 33-year-old righthander who had not made one start in 1950. The choice: Jim Konstanty.

While Konstanty had not started a game in the just-ended season, he had appeared in *74* games. The Phillies' standout relief pitcher had posted a 16-7 record and boasted a 2.66 earned-run average. And, clearly, he was up to the Series challenge. In eight innings of work, he allowed the Yankees only one run and four hits. Unfortunately for the Phillies, New York's Vic Raschi spun a two-hit, 1-0 shutout.

Roberts was ready for battle in Game 2. So, too, was Yankee righthander Allie Reynolds. Battle they did, to a 1-1 standoff

through nine innings. Then, Joe DiMaggio cracked a leadoff homer in the 10th and the Yanks were 2-1 winners.

Lefthander Ken Heintzelman, a 17-game winner for the Phillies in 1949 but a 3-9 pitcher for the pennant-winning team, was pressed into duty as the third-game starter and responded beautifully. Matched against Eddie Lopat, Heintzelman carried a 2-1 lead into the eighth but, after retiring the first two Yankees, walked three consecutive batters in the inning. Sawyer called for Konstanty, who seemingly extricated the Phils from the mess by inducing Bobby Brown to ground to shortstop Granny Hamner. But Hamner fumbled the ball, and the

tying run scored. The New Yorkers pushed over another run in the ninth—Jerry Coleman produced the game-winning hit—and stole away with a 3-2 victory.

Three straight one-run decisions. Embarrassing? Hardly.

Ed (Whitey) Ford, who went 9-1 as a rookie after being called up from Kansas City of the American Association, went to the mound for Casey Stengel's club in Game 4. And with batterymate Yogi Berra heading the Yankees' attack with a run-scoring single and a bases-empty home run, Ford breezed into the ninth inning with a 5-0 lead. With two out and two on, Ford apparently nailed down a shutout finish to this Series when he got Andy Seminick to hit a fly ball to left field. However, Gene Woodling dropped the ball and both Phillies runners scored. Reynolds then came in to get the last out, making the New York Yankees 5-2 victors and repeat champions of the World Series.

Woodling, who tied Hamner for the World Series batting lead with a .429 average, was distraught over his failure to protect Ford's shutout. As upset as Woodling was, consider how the Philadelphia Phillies must have felt after becoming yet another Series-sweep casualty of the New York Yankees.

Game 1

Wednesday, October 4, At Philadelphia

New York	AB.	R.	H.	RBI.	PO.	A.
Woodling, lf	3	0	1	0	1	0
Rizzuto, ss	3	0	1	0	0	2
Berra, c	4	0	0	0	7	0
DiMaggio, cf	2	0	0	0	3	0
Mize, 1b	4	0	0	0	7	0
Hopp, 1b	0	0	0	0	3	0
Brown, 3b	4	1	1	0	0	0
Johnson, 3b	0	0	0	0	0	0
Bauer, rf	4	0	1	0	5	0
Coleman, 2b	4	0	0	1	1	2
Raschi, p	3	0	1	0	0	3
Totals	31	1	5	1	27	7

Philadelphia	AB.	R.	H.	RBI.	PO.	A.
Waitkus, 1b	3	0	0	0	9	2
Ashburn, cf	4	0	0	0	2	0
Sisler, lf	4	0	0	0	3	0
Ennis, rf	3	0	0	0	4	0
Jones, 3b	3	0	1	0	4	3
Hamner, ss	3	0	0	0	0	1
Seminick, c	3	0	1	0	1	1
Goliat, 2b	3	0	0	0	3	2
Konstanty, p	2	0	0	0	1	0
aWhitman	1	0	0	0	0	0
Meyer, p	0	0	0	0	0	1
Totals	29	0	2	0	27	10

New York	0 0 0 1 0 0 0 0 0—1
Philadelphia	0 0 0 0 0 0 0 0 0—0

New York	IP.	H.	R.	ER.	BB.	SO.
Raschi (W)	9	2	0	0	1	5

Philadelphia	IP.	H.	R.	ER.	BB.	SO.
Konstanty (L)	8	4	1	1	4	0
Meyer	1	1	0	0	0	0

aFlied out for Konstanty in eighth. E—Jones. LOB—New York 9, Philadelphia 3. 2B—Brown. SH—Rizzuto, Raschi. U—Conlan (N.L.), McGowan (A.L.), Boggess (N.L.), Berry (A.L.), Barlick (N.L.) and McKinley (A.L.). T—2:17. A—30,746.

Game 2

Thursday, October 5, At Philadelphia

New York	AB.	R.	H.	RBI.	PO.	A.
Woodling, lf	5	0	2	1	2	0
Rizzuto, ss	4	0	0	0	2	1
Berra, c	5	0	1	0	7	0
DiMaggio, cf	5	1	1	1	3	0
Mize, 1b	4	0	1	0	6	0
Johnson, 3b	1	0	0	0	0	2
Brown, 3b	4	0	2	0	0	0
bHopp, 1b	1	0	0	0	3	0
Bauer, rf	5	0	1	0	1	0
Coleman, 2b	3	1	1	0	5	6
Reynolds, p	3	0	1	0	1	2
Totals	40	2	10	2	30	11

Philadelphia	AB.	R.	H.	RBI.	PO.	A.
Waitkus, 1b	4	0	2	0	8	0
Ashburn, cf	5	0	2	1	4	0
Sisler, lf	5	0	0	0	3	0
Ennis, rf	4	0	0	0	1	0
Jones, 3b	4	0	0	0	3	0
Hamner, ss	3	0	2	0	2	2
Seminick, c	2	0	0	0	5	0
aCaballero	0	0	0	0	0	0
Silvestri, c	0	0	0	0	1	0
cWhitman	0	0	0	0	0	0
Lopata, c	0	0	0	0	1	0
Goliat, 2b	4	1	1	0	2	2
Roberts, p	2	0	0	0	0	0
dMayo	0	0	0	0	0	0
Totals	33	1	7	1	30	4

New York	0 1 0 0 0 0 0 0 0 1—2
Philadelphia	0 0 0 0 1 0 0 0 0 0—1

New York	IP.	H.	R.	ER.	BB.	SO.
Reynolds (W)	10	7	1	1	4	6

Philadelphia	IP.	H.	R.	ER.	BB.	SO.
Roberts (L)	10	10	2	2	3	5

aRan for Seminick in seventh. bRan for Brown in eighth. cIntentionally walked for Silvestri in ninth. dWalked for Roberts in tenth. DP—New York 2. LOB—New York 11, Philadelphia 8. 2B—Ashburn, Waitkus, Coleman, Hamner. 3B—Hamner. HR—DiMaggio. SB—Hamner. SH—Roberts, Waitkus. U—McGowan (A.L.), Boggess (N.L.), Berry (A.L.), Conlan (N.L.), McKinley (A.L.) and Barlick (N.L.). T—3:06. A—32,660.

Game 3

Friday, October 6, At New York

Philadelphia	AB.	R.	H.	RBI.	PO.	A.
Waitkus, 1b	5	0	1	0	8	0
Ashburn, cf	4	0	1	0	0	0
Jones, 3b	3	0	1	0	1	2
Ennis, rf	4	1	1	0	3	0
Sisler, lf	4	0	1	1	2	1
Mayo, lf	0	0	0	0	1	0
Hamner, ss	4	1	3	0	2	2
Seminick, c	2	0	1	0	5	0
Goliat, 2b	3	0	1	1	4	1
dCaballero	0	0	0	0	0	0
Bloodworth, 2b	0	0	0	0	0	0
Heintzelman, p	2	0	0	0	0	2
Konstanty, p	0	0	0	0	0	0
eWhitman	1	0	0	0	0	0
Meyer, p	0	0	0	0	0	0
Totals	32	2	10	2	26	8

New York	AB.	R.	H.	RBI.	PO.	A.
Rizzuto, ss	3	1	1	0	1	1
Coleman, 2b	4	1	3	2	3	1
Berra, c	2	0	0	0	6	1
DiMaggio, cf	3	0	1	0	1	0
Bauer, lf	3	0	0	0	1	0
bBrown	1	0	0	0	0	0
cJensen	0	0	0	0	0	0
Ferrick, p	0	0	0	0	0	0
Mize, 1b	4	0	0	0	9	2
Collins, 1b	0	0	0	0	1	1
Johnson, 3b	4	0	0	0	1	3
Mapes, rf	4	0	0	0	3	0
Lopat, p	2	0	1	0	1	4
aWoodling, lf	2	1	1	0	0	0
Totals	32	3	7	2	27	13

Philadelphia	0 0 0 0 0 1 1 0 0—2
New York	0 0 1 0 0 0 0 1 1—3

Two out when winning run scored.

Philadelphia	IP.	H.	R.	ER.	BB.	SO.
Heintzelman	7⅔	4	2	1	6	3
Konstanty	⅓	0	0	0	0	0
Meyer (L)	⅔	3	1	1	0	1

New York	IP.	H.	R.	ER.	BB.	SO.
Lopat	8	9	2	2	0	5
Ferrick (W)	1	1	0	0	1	0

aPopped out for Lopat in eighth. bReached first on error for Bauer in eighth. cRan for Brown in eighth. dRan for Goliat in ninth. eReached on fielder's choice for Konstanty in ninth. E—Hamner, Seminick. DP—Philadelphia 1. LOB—Philadelphia 8, New York 9. 2B—Ennis, Hamner. SB—Rizzuto. SH—Seminick 2, Heintzelman, Jones. U—Boggess (N.L.), Berry (A.L.), Conlan (N.L.), McGowan (A.L.), Barlick (N.L.) and McKinley (A.L.). T—2:35. A—64,505.

Game 4

Saturday, October 7, At New York

Philadelphia	AB.	R.	H.	RBI.	PO.	A.
Waitkus, 1b	3	0	1	0	9	1
Ashburn, cf	4	0	0	0	3	0
Jones, 3b	4	1	2	0	0	4
Ennis, rf	3	0	1	0	1	0
Sisler, lf	4	0	0	0	2	0
bK. Johnson	0	1	0	0	0	0
Hamner, ss	4	0	1	0	2	2
Seminick, c	4	0	0	0	3	1
cMayo	0	0	0	0	0	0
Goliat, 2b	4	0	1	0	4	4
Miller, p	0	0	0	0	0	0
Konstanty, p	2	0	1	0	0	1
aCaballero	1	0	0	0	0	0
Roberts, p	0	0	0	0	0	0
dLopata	1	0	0	0	0	0
Totals	34	2	7	0	24	13

New York	AB.	R.	H.	RBI.	PO.	A.
Woodling, lf	4	1	2	0	4	0
Rizzuto, ss	4	0	0	0	2	4
Berra, c	4	2	2	2	10	0
DiMaggio, cf	3	1	2	1	1	0
Mize, 1b	3	0	1	0	5	1
Hopp, 1b	1	0	0	0	1	1
Brown, 3b	3	1	1	1	0	1
W. Johnson, 3b	1	0	0	0	0	0
Bauer, rf	3	0	0	1	1	0
Coleman, 2b	3	0	0	0	2	3
Ford, p	3	0	0	0	1	0
Reynolds, p	0	0	0	0	0	0
Totals	32	5	8	5	27	10

Philadelphia	0 0 0 0 0 0 0 0 2—2
New York	2 0 0 0 0 3 0 0 x—5

Philadelphia	IP.	H.	R.	ER.	BB.	SO.
Miller (L)	⅓	2	2	1	0	0
Konstanty	6⅔	5	3	3	0	3
Roberts	1	1	0	0	0	0

New York	IP.	H.	R.	ER.	BB.	SO.
Ford (W)	8⅔	7	2	0	1	7
Reynolds	⅓	0	0	0	0	1

aStruck out for Konstanty in eighth. bRan for Sisler in ninth. cRan for Seminick in ninth. dStruck out for Roberts in ninth. E—Goliat, Woodling, Brown. DP—New York 2. LOB—Philadelphia 7, New York 4. 2B—Jones, DiMaggio. 3B—Brown. HR—Berra. HBP—By Konstanty (DiMaggio), by Ford (Ennis). WP—Miller. U—Berry (A.L.), Conlan (N.L.), McGowan (A.L.), Boggess (N.L.), McKinley (A.L.) and Barlick (N.L.). T—2:05. A—68,098.

COMPOSITE BATTING AVERAGES

New York Yankees

Player-Position	G.	AB.	R.	H.	2B.	3B.	HR.	RBI.	BA.
Lopat, p	1	2	0	1	0	0	0	0	.500
Woodling, lf-ph	4	14	2	6	0	0	0	1	.429
Brown, 3b-ph	4	12	2	4	1	1	0	1	.333
Raschi, p	1	3	0	1	0	0	0	0	.333
Reynolds, p	2	3	0	1	0	0	0	0	.333
DiMaggio, cf	4	13	2	4	1	0	1	2	.308
Coleman, 2b	4	14	2	4	1	0	0	3	.286
Berra, c	4	15	2	3	0	0	1	2	.200
Rizzuto, ss	4	14	1	2	0	0	0	0	.143
Mize, 1b	4	15	0	2	0	0	0	0	.133
Bauer, rf-lf	4	15	0	2	0	0	0	1	.133
Collins, 1b	1	0	0	0	0	0	0	0	.000
Mapes, rf	1	4	0	0	0	0	0	0	.000
Hopp, 1b-pr	3	2	0	0	0	0	0	0	.000
W. Johnson, 3b	4	6	0	0	0	0	0	0	.000
Ferrick, p	1	0	0	0	0	0	0	0	.000
Ford, p	1	3	0	0	0	0	0	0	.000
Jensen, pr	1	0	0	0	0	0	0	0	.000
Totals	4	135	11	30	3	1	2	10	.222

Philadelphia Phillies

Player-Position	G.	AB.	R.	H.	2B.	3B.	HR.	RBI.	BA.
Hamner, ss	4	14	1	6	2	1	0	0	.429
Jones, 3b	4	14	1	4	1	0	0	0	.286
Waitkus, 1b	4	15	0	4	1	0	0	0	.267
Konstanty, p	3	4	0	1	0	0	0	0	.250
Goliat, 2b	4	14	1	3	0	0	0	1	.214
Seminick, c	4	11	0	2	0	0	0	0	.182
Ashburn, cf	4	17	0	3	1	0	0	1	.176
Ennis, rf	4	14	1	2	1	0	0	0	.143
Sisler, lf	4	17	0	1	0	0	0	1	.059
Silvestri, c	1	0	0	0	0	0	0	0	.000
Lopata, c-ph	2	1	0	0	0	0	0	0	.000
Bloodworth, 2b	1	0	0	0	0	0	0	0	.000
Mayo, ph-lf-pr	3	0	0	0	0	0	0	0	.000
Meyer, p	2	0	0	0	0	0	0	0	.000
Roberts, p	2	2	0	0	0	0	0	0	.000
Heintzelman, p	1	2	0	0	0	0	0	0	.000
Miller, p	1	0	0	0	0	0	0	0	.000
Whitman, ph	3	2	0	0	0	0	0	0	.000
K. Johnson, pr	1	0	1	0	0	0	0	0	.000
Caballero, pr-ph	3	1	0	0	0	0	0	0	.000
Totals	4	128	5	26	6	1	0	3	.203

COMPOSITE PITCHING AVERAGES

New York Yankees

Pitcher	G.	IP.	H.	R.	ER.	BB.	SO.	W.	L.	ERA.
Raschi	1	9	2	0	0	1	5	1	0	0.00
Ford	1	8⅔	7	2	0	1	7	1	0	0.00
Ferrick	1	1	1	0	0	1	0	1	0	0.00
Reynolds	2	10⅓	7	1	1	4	7	1	0	0.87
Lopat	1	8	9	2	2	0	5	0	0	2.25
Totals	4	37	26	5	3	7	24	4	0	0.73

Philadelphia Phillies

Pitcher	G.	IP.	H.	R.	ER.	BB.	SO.	W.	L.	ERA.
Heintzelman	1	7⅔	4	2	1	6	3	0	0	1.17
Roberts	2	11	11	2	2	3	5	0	1	1.64
Konstanty	3	15	9	4	4	4	3	0	1	2.40
Meyer	2	1⅔	4	1	1	0	1	0	1	5.40
Miller	1	⅓	2	2	1	0	0	0	1	27.00
Totals	4	35⅔	30	11	9	13	12	0	4	2.27

1951
NEW YORK YANKEES
VS.
NEW YORK GIANTS

For many baseball fans, the World Series was anticlimactic to the 1951 major league season. After all, arguably the best and most exciting baseball game ever played had unfolded the day before the '51 Series opener.

But if Bobby Thomson's Shot Heard 'Round the World—the ninth-inning home run that lifted the New York Giants to a National League pennant-playoff victory —so overshadowed what was to follow as to render it obscure, much of note has been overlooked amid the fuss.

Like Monte Irvin's dazzling play in the World Series, both at bat and on the bases; the entry of future superstars Mickey Mantle and Willie Mays upon the Series scene and the passing of all-time-great Joe DiMaggio from the fall classic (and the majors as well); the foreboding injury to Mantle in Game 2; Eddie Stanky's gung-ho approach to the game, as exemplified by his ball-kicking act in Game 3; a rookie infielder's magic moment at the plate with the bases loaded in the fifth game, and an outfielder atoning for past Series sins with final-game heroics at bat and afield.

The Giants, of course, had entered the Series against the New York Yankees on an emotional high. To say the least. Manager Leo Durocher's gang had rallied to win the N.L. pennant after trailing the Brooklyn Dodgers by 13½ games on the afternoon of August 11 (after the Giants had lost to the Philadelphia Phillies that day and the Dodgers had defeated the Boston Braves in the first game of a doubleheader).

Beginning August 12, the Giants won 16 straight games and 37 of their last 44 regular-season contests to forge a tie with Brooklyn. New York then beat the Dodgers in a best-of-three playoff, with Thomson's three-run homer off Ralph Branca giving the Giants a 5-4 victory in the decisive third game at the Polo Grounds.

The day after Thomson broke Dodger hearts, the Giants took aim on sending misery the Bronx's way. And for starters, Dave Koslo shackled the Yankees on seven hits and Alvin Dark slugged a three-run homer. But the big story in the Giants' 5-1 Series-opening triumph was Irvin's performance. Irvin rapped three singles and a triple and recorded the first Series steal of home plate since the Yankees' Bob Meusel turned the trick in 1928. The Giant outfielder's theft came in the first inning and seemingly indicated that momentum from the stretch-run tear and playoff success was still with the Giants.

Eddie Lopat cooled off the Giants in Game 2, pitching a five-hitter and contributing a run-scoring single in a 3-1 Yankee victory. Irvin, who would bat .458 in this Series, had three of the losers' hits. Because of a fifth-inning play involving past and future stars, the game had repercussions far beyond 1951. The 20-year-old Mays, who had slugged 20 homers for the Giants after being brought up in late May from Minneapolis (where he was batting .477), led off the Giants' fifth by flying out to DiMaggio in right-center. On the play, right fielder Mantle also went after the ball, only to catch his foot on the wooden cover of a Yankee Stadium drainage outlet. Mantle's knee buckled, forcing the 19-year-old speedster out of the game and the Series. More than that, the injury signaled the start of leg problems that would hound Mantle during his 18-season big-league career (which had begun in '51 with two stints with

the Yankees totaling 96 games, in which the Oklahoman had hit 13 homers).

Holding a 1-0 edge after 4½ innings of Game 3, the Giants capitalized on a big—and inventive— play from Stanky to expand their lead. With one out in the fifth, Stanky coaxed a walk off Vic Raschi. The Yankees, thinking the Giants were about to put on a play (a hit-and-run, run-and-hit or straight steal), called for a pitchout and catcher Yogi Berra rifled a throw to shortstop Phil Rizzuto in plenty of time to nail Stanky. But Eddie would have none of it. The feisty veteran kicked the ball out of Rizzuto's hand, scrambled to his feet and dashed to third. Instead of two out and nobody on, Stanky was resting on third with one out. Dark then delivered a run-scoring single. And the Giants scored four more times in the inning—Whitey Lockman delivered the big blow, a three-run homer—en route to a 6-2 victory at the Polo Grounds.

With a two games-to-one lead in the Series and Games 4 and 5 also scheduled on their home grounds, the Giants were in a favorable position. But storm clouds loomed. Literally. Rain caused a one-day postponement in Game 4, making possible the availability of first-game loser Allie Reynolds to the Yankees for that contest. And the Bronx Bombers' standout bested Sal Maglie and the Giants, 6-2, as DiMaggio cracked his eighth and last Series home run.

The lift provided by Reynolds seemed to inspire the Yankees, who went out the next day and bashed the Giants, 13-1. Yankees rookie Gil McDougald, who alternated between second and third base for Casey Stengel's club, belt-

Yankee center fielder Joe DiMaggio prepares to catch Willie Mays' Game 2 fly ball (above) as right fielder Mickey Mantle tumbles to the ground after tripping over a drainage outlet and suffering the type of knee injury that would haunt his career. Yankee shortstop Phil Rizzuto is welcomed back to the dugout (below) after a Game 5 homer.

this time, rifling a bases-clearing triple. Then, in the ninth inning, after the Giants closed within 4-3 and had the potential tying run in scoring position, a racing Bauer made a sensational game-ending catch on a low liner hit by pinch-hitter Sal Yvars.

The 1951 World Series was the 10th and last fall classic for DiMaggio. In fact, Game 6 marked the final major league game for the Yankee Clipper, who was headed for retirement at age 36. Mantle would appear in 11 more Series, and Mays would compete in the big event on three more occasions.

And while there were no Series histrionics to equal the playoff drama provided by Thomson (a .238 hitter against the Yankees), the '51 fall classic will forever conjure up visions of Irvin taking off for home, Willie and Mickey taking off for stardom and Joltin' Joe taking off for retirement. Of Mantle exhibiting pain and the brash Stanky exhibiting fancy footwork. Of youngster McDougald showing fearlessness in a key spot in a key game and Bauer showing toughness in the face of adversity. And of Mother Nature demonstrating her power to influence the course of events.

ed a bases-loaded home run in third inning off Larry Jansen, who like fellow 23-game winner Maglie was unable to win in this Series. McDougald's jackpot wallop—which broke a 1-1 tie—was only the third grand slam in Series history, the others being struck by Cleveland's Elmer Smith in 1920 and the Yankees' Tony Lazzeri in 1936.

The Yanks then put an inglorious end to the Giants' glorious season, beating the National Leaguers for the third straight time since the rain fell after Game 3. With the bases loaded and two out in the sixth inning of Game 6, Yankee outfielder Hank Bauer was batting against Koslo in a 1-1 game. For Bauer, it was a golden opportunity to shake off the Series blues. In 38 previous at-bats in the fall classic, Bauer had collected five hits—all singles. And, along with that .132 career Series batting average, the former Marine had exactly one RBI in postseason play. Bauer came through

Game 1

Thursday, October 4, At Yankee Stadium

Giants	AB.	R.	H.	RBI.	PO.	A.
Stanky, 2b	4	1	0	0	4	2
Dark, ss	5	1	2	3	1	2
Thompson, rf	3	0	0	0	3	0
Irvin, lf	5	1	4	0	4	0
Lockman, 1b	4	0	1	1	4	1
Thomson, 3b	3	0	1	0	2	2
Mays, cf	5	0	0	0	2	0
Westrum, c	3	1	2	0	5	0
Koslo, p	3	0	0	0	2	0
Totals	35	5	10	4	27	7

Yankees	AB.	R.	H.	RBI.	PO.	A.
Mantle, rf	3	0	0	0	4	0
Rizzuto, ss	4	0	2	0	1	2
Bauer, lf	4	0	0	0	0	0
DiMaggio, cf	4	0	0	0	3	0
Berra, c	4	0	1	0	5	1
McDougald, 3b	4	1	1	0	0	2
Coleman, 2b	3	0	1	0	3	3
Collins, 1b	3	0	1	0	11	0
bMize	1	0	0	0	0	0
Reynolds, p	2	0	1	0	0	3
Hogue, p	0	0	0	0	0	1
aBrown	1	0	0	0	0	0
Morgan, p	0	0	0	0	0	1
cWoodling	1	0	0	0	0	0
Totals	34	1	7	0	27	13

Giants .... 2 0 0   0 0 3   0 0 0—5
Yankees .... 0 1 0   0 0 0   0 0 0—1

Giants	IP.	H.	R.	ER.	BB.	SO.
Koslo (W)	9	7	1	1	3	3

Yankees	IP.	H.	R.	ER.	BB.	SO.
Reynolds (L)	6	8	5	5	7	1
Hogue	1	0	0	0	0	0
Morgan	2	2	0	0	1	3

aStruck out for Hogue in eighth. bPopped out for Collins in ninth. cStruck out for Morgan in ninth. E—Thompson, McDougald. DP—Yankees 1. LOB—Giants 13, Yankees 9. 2B—Lockman, McDougald. 3B—Irvin. HR—Dark. SB—Irvin. SH—Koslo 2. U—Summers (A.L.), Ballanfant (N.L.), Paparella (A.L.), Barlick (N.L.), Stevens (A.L.) and Gore (N.L.). T—2:58. A—65,673.

Game 2

Friday, October 5, At Yankee Stadium

Giants	AB.	R.	H.	RBI.	PO.	A.
Stanky, 2b	3	0	0	0	1	4
Dark, ss	4	0	1	0	0	4
Thomson, 3b	4	0	0	0	2	3
Irvin, lf	4	1	3	0	3	0
Lockman, 1b	4	0	1	0	11	0
Mays, cf	4	0	0	0	2	0
Westrum, c	2	0	0	0	5	0
bSchenz	0	0	0	0	0	0
Hartung, rf	1	0	0	0	0	0
Thompson, rf	2	0	0	0	0	0
aRigney	1	0	0	1	0	0
Spencer, p	0	0	0	0	0	0
Jansen, p	2	0	0	0	0	0
cNoble, c	1	0	0	0	0	0
Totals	32	1	5	1	24	11

Yankees	AB.	R.	H.	RBI.	PO.	A.
Mantle, rf	2	1	1	0	0	0
Bauer, rf	2	0	0	0	1	0
Rizzuto, ss	4	0	1	0	2	2
McDougald, 2b-3b	3	0	1	1	2	3
DiMaggio, cf	3	0	0	0	4	0
Berra, c	3	0	0	0	2	0
Woodling, lf	3	0	0	0	4	0
Brown, 3b	3	0	1	0	0	4
dMartin	0	1	0	0	0	0
Coleman, 2b	0	0	0	0	1	0
Collins, 1b	3	1	1	1	9	2
Lopat, p	3	0	1	1	2	2
Totals	29	3	6	3	27	13

Giants	0 0 0 0 0 0 1 0 0—1
Yankees	1 1 0 0 0 0 0 1 x—3

Giants	IP.	H.	R.	ER.	BB.	SO.
Jansen (L)	6	4	2	2	0	5
Spencer	2	2	1	1	0	0

Yankees	IP.	H.	R.	ER.	BB.	SO.
Lopat (W)	9	5	1	1	2	1

aFlied out for Thompson in seventh. bRan for Westrum in seventh. cFouled out for Jansen in seventh. dRan for Brown in eighth. E—Lockman. DP—Giants 1. LOB—Giants 6, Yankees 2. HR—Collins. SB—Irvin. U—Ballanfant (N.L.), Paparella (A.L.), Barlick (N.L.), Summers (A.L.), Gore (N.L.) and Stevens (A.L.). T—2:05. A—66,018.

Game 3

Saturday, October 6, At Polo Grounds

Yankees	AB.	R.	H.	RBI.	PO.	A.
Woodling, lf	4	1	1	1	3	0
Rizzuto, ss	4	1	1	0	2	4
McDougald, 2b	3	0	2	0	2	2
DiMaggio, cf	4	0	0	0	4	0
Berra, c	3	0	1	0	5	1
Brown, 3b	3	0	0	0	0	1
Collins, 1b	3	0	0	1	6	0
Bauer, rf	4	0	0	0	2	0
Raschi, p	1	0	0	0	0	0
Hogue, p	0	0	0	0	0	0
aHopp	0	0	0	0	0	0
Ostrowski, p	0	0	0	0	0	0
bMize	1	0	0	0	0	0
Totals	30	2	5	2	24	8

Giants	AB.	R.	H.	RBI.	PO.	A.
Stanky, 2b	2	1	1	0	2	2
Dark, ss	4	1	1	1	4	4
Thompson, rf	3	1	1	0	1	0
Irvin, lf	3	1	0	0	2	0
Lockman, 1b	4	1	1	3	10	1
Thomson, 3b	4	1	1	0	3	4
Mays, cf	4	0	2	1	3	0
Westrum, c	4	0	0	0	2	1
Hearn, p	3	0	0	0	0	2
Jones, p	0	0	0	0	0	1
Totals	31	6	7	5	27	15

Yankees	0 0 0 0 0 0 0 1 1—2
Giants	0 1 0 0 5 0 0 0 x—6

Yankees	IP.	H.	R.	ER.	BB.	SO.
Raschi (L)	4⅓	5	6	1	3	3
Hogue	2⅔	1	0	0	0	0
Ostrowski	2	1	0	0	0	1

Giants	IP.	H.	R.	ER.	BB.	SO.
Hearn (W)	7⅔	4	1	1	8	1
Jones	1⅓	1	1	1	0	0

aWalked for Hogue in seventh. bFlied out for Ostrowski in ninth. E—Rizzuto, Berra, Lockman, Westrum. DP—Yankees 1, Giants 2. LOB—Yankees 10, Giants 5. 2B—Thomson. HR—Lockman, Woodling. HBP—By Raschi (Stanky), by Hearn (Rizzuto). U—Paparella (A.L.), Barlick (N.L.), Summers (A.L.), Ballanfant (N.L.), Stevens (A.L.) and Gore (N.L.). T—2:42. A—52,035.

Game 4

Monday, October 8, At Polo Grounds

Yankees	AB.	R.	H.	RBI.	PO.	A.
Bauer, rf	4	0	2	0	0	0
Rizzuto, ss	5	1	1	0	5	5
Berra, c	5	1	1	0	8	1
DiMaggio, cf	5	1	2	2	2	0
Woodling, lf	4	2	1	0	1	0
McDougald, 2b-3b	4	0	1	1	3	2
Brown, 3b	4	1	2	0	0	0
Coleman, 2b	0	0	0	0	1	1
Collins, 1b	3	0	1	1	7	0
Reynolds, p	4	0	1	1	0	2
Totals	38	6	12	5	27	11

Giants	AB.	R.	H.	RBI.	PO.	A.
Stanky, 2b	4	0	1	0	3	0
Dark, ss	4	1	3	0	2	1
Thompson, rf	3	1	0	0	1	0
Irvin, lf	4	0	2	1	3	0
Lockman, 1b	4	0	0	0	4	0
Thomson, 3b	2	0	2	1	2	3
Mays, cf	4	0	0	0	5	1
Westrum, c	2	0	0	0	7	1
Maglie, p	1	0	0	0	0	0
aLohrke	1	0	0	0	0	0
Jones, p	0	0	0	0	0	0
bRigney	1	0	0	0	0	0
Kennedy, p	0	0	0	0	0	0
Totals	30	2	8	2	27	6

Yankees	0 1 0 1 2 0 2 0 0—6
Giants	1 0 0 0 0 0 0 0 1—2

Yankees	IP.	H.	R.	ER.	BB.	SO.
Reynolds (W)	9	8	2	2	4	7

Giants	IP.	H.	R.	ER.	BB.	SO.
Maglie (L)	5	8	4	4	2	3
Jones	3	4	2	0	1	2
Kennedy	1	0	0	0	0	2

aPopped out for Maglie in fifth. bStruck out for Jones in eighth. E—Stanky, Thomson. DP—Yankees 4. LOB—Yankees 8, Giants 5. 2B—Dark 3, Woodling, Brown. HR—DiMaggio. U—Barlick (N.L.), Summers (A.L.), Ballanfant (N.L.), Paparella (A.L.), Gore (N.L.) and Stevens (A.L.). T—2:57. A—49,010.

Game 5

Tuesday, October 9, At Polo Grounds

Yankees	AB.	R.	H.	RBI.	PO.	A.
Woodling, lf	3	3	1	0	5	0
Rizzuto, ss	4	3	2	3	0	6
Berra, c	4	2	1	0	3	0
DiMaggio, cf	5	1	3	3	3	0
Mize, 1b	3	1	1	1	6	0
Bauer, rf	1	0	0	0	0	0
McDougald, 2b-3b	5	1	1	4	2	2
Brown, 3b	3	0	2	0	1	3
cColeman, 2b	1	1	0	0	0	1
Collins, rf-1b	5	1	1	0	7	0
Lopat, p	5	0	0	0	0	2
Totals	39	13	12	11	27	14

Giants	AB.	R.	H.	RBI.	PO.	A.
Stanky, 2b	4	0	0	0	1	4
Dark, ss	4	1	2	0	2	3
Thomson, 3b	4	0	0	0	1	3
Irvin, lf	4	0	2	0	2	0
Lockman, 1b	4	0	0	0	9	3
Mays, cf	2	0	0	0	2	0
Hartung, rf	3	0	0	0	1	1
Westrum, c	3	0	1	0	7	0
Jansen, p	0	0	0	0	1	1
aLohrke	1	0	0	0	0	0
Kennedy, p	0	0	0	0	0	1
bRigney	1	0	0	0	0	0
Spencer, p	0	0	0	0	0	1
Corwin, p	0	0	0	0	1	0
dWilliams	1	0	0	0	0	0
Konikowski, p	0	0	0	0	0	0
Totals	31	1	5	0	27	17

Yankees	0 0 5 2 0 2 4 0 0—13
Giants	1 0 0 0 0 0 0 0 0— 1

Yankees	IP.	H.	R.	ER.	BB.	SO.
Lopat (W)	9	5	1	0	1	3

Giants	IP.	H.	R.	ER.	BB.	SO.
Jansen (L)	3	3	5	5	4	1
Kennedy	2	3	2	2	1	2
Spencer	1⅓	4	6	6	3	0
Corwin	1⅔	1	0	0	0	1
Konikowski	1	1	0	0	0	0

aStruck out for Jansen in third. bFlied out for Kennedy in fifth. cRan for Brown in seventh. dGrounded out for Corwin in eighth. E—Woodling, Thomson, Irvin, Hartung. DP—Yankees 1. LOB—Yankees 7, Giants 4. 2B—Westrum, Mize, DiMaggio. 3B—Woodling. HR—McDougald, Rizzuto. WP—Corwin. U—Summers (A.L.), Ballanfant (N.L.), Paparella (A.L.), Barlick (N.L.), Stevens (A.L.) and Gore (N.L.). T—2:31. A—47,530.

Game 6

Wednesday, October 10, At Yankee Stadium

Giants	AB.	R.	H.	RBI.	PO.	A.
Stanky, 2b	5	1	1	1	3	4
Dark, ss	3	1	1	0	1	2
Lockman, 1b	5	0	3	0	10	0
Irvin, lf	4	0	0	1	3	0
Thomson, 3b	4	0	1	1	2	0
Thompson, rf	3	0	1	0	0	0
dYvars	1	0	0	0	0	0
Westrum, c	3	0	1	0	3	0
bWilliams	0	0	0	0	0	0
Jansen, p	0	0	0	0	0	1
Mays, cf	3	1	2	0	2	0
Koslo, p	2	0	0	0	0	1
aRigney	1	0	1	0	0	0
Hearn, p	0	0	0	0	0	0
cNoble, c	1	0	0	0	0	1
Totals	35	3	11	3	24	9

Yankees	AB.	R.	H.	RBI.	PO.	A.
Rizzuto, ss	4	0	1	0	4	4
Coleman, 2b	4	1	1	0	2	1
Berra, c	4	1	2	0	4	0
DiMaggio, cf	2	1	1	0	1	0
McDougald, 3b	4	0	0	1	1	3
Mize, 1b	2	1	1	0	6	0
Collins, 1b	1	0	0	0	0	0
Bauer, rf	3	0	1	3	4	0
Woodling, lf	3	0	0	0	5	0
Raschi, p	1	0	0	0	0	0
Sain, p	1	0	0	0	0	0
Kuzava, p	0	0	0	0	0	0
Totals	29	4	7	4	27	8

Giants	0 0 0 0 1 0 0 0 2—3
Yankees	1 0 0 0 0 3 0 0 x—4

Giants	IP.	H.	R.	ER.	BB.	SO.
Koslo (L)	6	5	4	4	4	3
Hearn	1	1	0	0	0	0
Jansen	1	1	0	0	0	0

Yankees	IP.	H.	R.	ER.	BB.	SO.
Raschi (W)	6*	7	1	0	5	1
Sain	2†	4	2	2	2	2
Kuzava	1	0	0	0	0	0

*Pitched to two batters in seventh.
†Pitched to three batters in ninth.

aSingled for Koslo in seventh. bRan for Westrum in eighth. cStruck out for Hearn in eighth. dLined out for Thompson in ninth. E—Thompson. DP—Giants 1, Yankees 3. LOB—Giants 12, Yankees 5. 2B—Lockman, Berra, DiMaggio. 3B—Bauer. WP—Koslo. PB—Berra. U—Ballanfant (N.L.), Paparella (A.L.), Barlick (N.L.), Summers (A.L.), Gore (N.L.) and Stevens (A.L.). T—2:59. A—61,711.

COMPOSITE BATTING AVERAGES

New York Yankees

Player-Position	G.	AB.	R.	H.	2B.	3B.	HR.	RBI.	BA.
Brown, ph-3b	5	14	1	5	1	0	0	0	.357
Reynolds, p	2	6	0	2	0	0	0	1	.333
Rizzuto, ss	6	25	5	8	0	0	1	3	.320
Mize, ph-1b	4	7	2	2	1	0	0	1	.286
DiMaggio, cf	6	23	3	6	2	0	1	5	.261
Berra, c	6	23	4	6	1	0	0	0	.261
McDougald, 3b-2b	6	23	2	6	1	0	1	7	.261
Coleman, 2b-pr	5	8	2	2	0	0	0	0	.250
Collins, 1b-rf	6	18	2	4	0	0	1	3	.222
Mantle, rf	2	5	1	1	0	0	0	0	.200
Bauer, lf-rf	6	18	0	3	0	1	0	3	.167
Woodling, ph-lf	6	18	6	3	1	1	1	1	.167
Lopat, p	2	8	0	1	0	0	0	1	.125
Hogue, p	2	0	0	0	0	0	0	0	.000
Morgan, p	1	0	0	0	0	0	0	0	.000
Raschi, p	2	2	0	0	0	0	0	0	.000
Ostrowski, p	1	0	0	0	0	0	0	0	.000
Sain, p	1	1	0	0	0	0	0	0	.000
Kuzava, p	1	0	0	0	0	0	0	0	.000
Hopp, ph	1	0	0	0	0	0	0	0	.000
Martin, pr	1	0	1	0	0	0	0	0	.000
Totals	6	199	29	49	7	2	5	25	.246

New York Giants

Player-Position	G.	AB.	R.	H.	2B.	3B.	HR.	RBI.	BA.
Irvin, lf	6	24	3	11	0	1	0	2	.458
Dark, ss	6	24	5	10	3	0	1	4	.417
Rigney, ph	4	4	0	1	0	0	0	1	.250
Lockman, 1b	6	25	1	6	2	0	1	4	.240
Thomson, 3b	6	21	1	5	1	0	0	2	.238
Westrum, c	6	17	1	4	1	0	0	0	.235
Mays, cf	6	22	1	4	0	0	0	1	.182
Thompson, rf	5	14	3	2	0	0	0	0	.143
Stanky, 2b	6	22	3	3	0	0	0	1	.136
Noble, ph-c	2	2	0	0	0	0	0	0	.000
Hartung, rf	2	4	0	0	0	0	0	0	.000
Koslo, p	2	5	0	0	0	0	0	0	.000
Spencer, p	2	0	0	0	0	0	0	0	.000
Jansen, p	3	2	0	0	0	0	0	0	.000
Hearn, p	2	3	0	0	0	0	0	0	.000
Jones, p	2	0	0	0	0	0	0	0	.000
Maglie, p	1	1	0	0	0	0	0	0	.000
Kennedy, p	2	0	0	0	0	0	0	0	.000
Corwin, p	1	0	0	0	0	0	0	0	.000
Konikowski, p	1	0	0	0	0	0	0	0	.000
Yvars, ph	1	1	0	0	0	0	0	0	.000
Lohrke, ph	2	2	0	0	0	0	0	0	.000
Williams, ph-pr	2	1	0	0	0	0	0	0	.000
Schenz, pr	1	0	0	0	0	0	0	0	.000
Totals	6	194	18	46	7	1	2	15	.237

COMPOSITE PITCHING AVERAGES

New York Yankees

Pitcher	G.	IP.	H.	R.	ER.	BB.	SO.	W.	L.	ERA.
Hogue	2	2⅔	1	0	0	0	0	0	0	0.00
Morgan	1	2	2	0	0	1	3	0	0	0.00
Ostrowski	1	2	1	0	0	0	1	0	0	0.00
Kuzava	1	1	0	0	0	0	0	0	0	0.00
Lopat	2	18	10	2	1	3	4	2	0	0.50
Raschi	2	10⅓	12	7	1	8	4	1	1	0.87
Reynolds	2	15	16	7	7	11	8	1	1	4.20
Sain	1	2	4	2	2	2	2	0	0	9.00
Totals	6	53	46	18	11	25	22	4	2	1.87

New York Giants

Pitcher	G.	IP.	H.	R.	ER.	BB.	SO.	W.	L.	ERA.
Corwin	1	1⅔	1	0	0	0	1	0	0	0.00
Konikowski	1	1	1	0	0	0	0	0	0	0.00
Hearn	2	8⅔	5	1	1	8	1	1	0	1.04
Jones	2	4⅓	5	3	1	1	2	0	0	2.08
Koslo	2	15	12	5	5	7	6	1	1	3.00
Kennedy	2	3	3	2	2	1	4	0	0	6.00
Jansen	3	10	8	7	7	4	6	0	2	6.30
Maglie	1	5	8	4	4	2	3	0	1	7.20
Spencer	2	3⅓	6	7	7	3	0	0	0	18.90
Totals	6	52	49	29	27	26	23	2	4	4.67

The Brooklyn Dodgers had the New York Yankees exactly where they wanted 'em—at Ebbets Field, and down three games to two.

Needing to win twice within the delightfully daffy confines of the Brooklyn ball park would be an intimidating situation for most visiting teams. But, of course, the Yankees weren't just any ball club. Under Casey Stengel, the Yanks had won three consecutive World Series championships and had a shot—albeit a dwindling one—of making it four straight.

New York's Vic Raschi and Brooklyn's Billy Loes were the starting pitchers in Game 6, and for 5½ innings neither team could score. But Duke Snider ripped a Raschi pitch over the right-field screen to lead off the Dodgers' sixth, and the ever-raucous Brooklyn faithful whooped it up.

Not for long, however. Hopes that Loes could protect the 1-0 lead vanished immediately in the top of the seventh when Yogi Berra led off the inning with a drive over the same barrier. And before the Yankees were done batting, it was 2-1, New York, with Raschi knocking in the second run by singling off Loes' knee. Then, in the eighth, Yankee phenom Mickey Mantle crashed the first Series homer of his career.

Raschi, now working on a 3-1 lead, retired the first Dodger batsman in the bottom of the inning, but the irrepressible Snider followed with another home run. After George Shuba doubled with two out, Allie Reynolds relieved Raschi. Reynolds, the Yankees' big winner in 1952 with 20 victories, struck out Roy Campanella to end the inning and, outside of allowing a walk to Carl Furillo, handled the Dodgers in the ninth.

With the Series-tying 3-2 tri-

Brooklyn right fielder Andy Pafko goes high to snare Gene Woodling's home run bid in Game 5 of the 1952 Yankee-Dodger Series.

umph under their belts, the Yankees started Eddie Lopat against Joe Black in Game 7. Lopat, bothered by shoulder problems, had won only 10 games for the Yankees in '52 after going 21-9 the previous season. Black, a rookie, was coming off a 15-4 season in which he made 56 pitching appearances, the first 54 coming in relief. After getting two starting assignments in the final eight days of the regular season, Black drew starts in Games 1 and 4 of this Se-

ries (he was 1-1 in those contests).

With Mantle belting a bases-empty home run and a run-scoring single and Gene Woodling also homering with no one on, the Yankees had a 4-2 lead in the bottom of the seventh. By now, Lopat and Black had been dismissed. In fact, Lopat's successor, Reynolds, had left the game for a pinch-hitter in the top of the seventh and now Raschi was on to start Brooklyn's half of the inning. Raschi promptly gave up a walk to Furillo before getting pinch-hitter Rocky Nelson on a popup. Billy Cox then singled and Pee Wee Reese walked, loading the bases. Bob Kuzava was summoned from the bullpen, and the lefthander got Snider to pop out to third baseman Gil McDougald. Now, it was Kuzava against Jackie Robinson. The Series quite possibly was on the line.

The count went to 3-2 on Robinson, who then lifted a popup near the mound. A sure rally-killer. Under most circumstances, anyway. But this ball appeared to be going unattended. Kuzava stood transfixed. First baseman Joe Collins, the man in position to make the play, lost sight of the ball. All the while, Dodger baserunners were in full flight, with two having crossed the plate and another rounding third base. Billy Martin, New York's second baseman, quickly sized up the situation and bolted in. And the 24-year-old Martin proceeded to make a miraculous grab of the ball about knee-high.

Kuzava was in control the rest of the way, and the Yankees put a 4-2 victory in the bank. Along with their World Series checks. Winners' shares, of course.

Accepting the losers' shares was particularly difficult for Manager Charlie Dressen's Dodgers, who

Brooklyn's Jackie Robinson watches as Yankee second baseman Billy Martin streaks in to make a dramatic catch of his Game 7 pop fly.

enabled Stengel to match Joe Mc-Carthy's mark of managing a club to four straight fall-classic crowns. McCarthy had accomplished the feat with the Yanks from 1936 through 1939, Joe Di-Maggio's first four years with the New Yorkers. Now, in the first season following DiMaggio's retirement, Stengel had entered the record books alongside Marse Joe.

While Ol' Case must have had some doubts about where he and the Yankees stood after the first five games of the 1952 World Series, there was no doubting their vantage point after seven games. The Yanks had the Dodgers exactly where they wanted 'em—on the outside, looking in.

Game 1

Wednesday, October 1, At Brooklyn

New York	AB.	R.	H.	RBI.	PO.	A.
Bauer, rf	4	0	0	1	2	0
Rizzuto, ss	4	0	1	0	2	1
Mantle, cf	4	0	2	0	2	0
Berra, c	4	0	0	0	7	2
Collins, 1b	4	0	0	0	8	0
Noren, lf	3	0	0	0	1	0
McDougald, 3b	2	1	1	1	0	4
Martin, 2b	3	0	1	0	2	1
Reynolds, p	2	0	0	0	0	1
aWoodling	1	1	1	0	0	0
Scarborough, p	0	0	0	0	0	1
Totals	31	2	6	2	24	10
Brooklyn	AB.	R.	H.	RBI.	PO.	A.
Cox, 3b	3	0	0	0	1	2
Reese, ss	4	2	2	1	4	1
Snider, cf	4	1	2	2	2	0
Robinson, 2b	2	1	1	1	1	4
Campanella, c	3	0	1	0	6	0
Pafko, lf	3	0	0	0	3	1
Hodges, 1b	3	0	0	0	6	3
Furillo, rf	3	0	0	0	3	0
Black, p	3	0	0	0	1	0
Totals	28	4	6	4	27	11

| New York | ...001 000 010—2 |
| Brooklyn | ...010 002 01x—4 |

New York	IP.	H.	R.	ER.	BB.	SO.
Reynolds (L)	7	1	3	3	2	4
Scarborough	1	1	1	1	0	1
Brooklyn	IP.	H.	R.	ER.	BB.	SO.
Black (W)	9	6	2	2	2	6

aTripled for Reynolds in eighth. E—McDougald, Reynolds. DP—New York 1, Brooklyn 1. LOB—New York 4, Brooklyn 2. 2B—Snider. 3B—Woodling. HR—Robinson, McDougald, Snider, Reese. WP—Reynolds. U—Pinelli (N.L.), Passarella (A.L.), Goetz (N.L.), McKinley (A.L.), Boggess (N.L.) and Honochick (A.L.). T—2:21. A—34,861.

Game 2

Thursday, October 2, At Brooklyn

New York	AB.	R.	H.	RBI.	PO.	A.
Bauer, rf	4	0	1	0	3	0
Rizzuto, ss	4	0	0	0	2	2
Mantle, cf	5	2	3	0	2	0
Woodling, lf	4	1	1	0	2	0
Berra, c	3	0	2	1	10	2
Collins, 1b	3	1	0	0	8	1
McDougald, 3b	3	2	1	1	0	1
Martin, 2b	4	1	2	4	0	1
Raschi, p	3	0	0	0	0	0
Totals	33	7	10	6	27	7
Brooklyn	AB.	R.	H.	RBI.	PO.	A.
Cox, 3b	4	0	0	0	1	0
Reese, ss	3	1	1	0	2	5
Snider, cf	4	0	1	0	1	0
Robinson, 2b	3	0	0	0	3	3
Campanella, c	4	0	1	1	7	3
Pafko, lf	4	0	0	0	2	0
Hodges, 1b	3	0	0	0	9	0
Furillo, rf	3	0	0	0	2	0
Erskine, p	2	0	0	0	0	1
Loes, p	0	0	0	0	0	0
aNelson	0	0	0	0	0	0
Lehman, p	0	0	0	0	0	1
Totals	30	1	3	1	27	13

| New York | ...000 115 000—7 |
| Brooklyn | ...001 000 000—1 |

New York	IP.	H.	R.	ER.	BB.	SO.
Raschi (W)	9	3	1	1	5	9

had built that three games-to-two edge by winning Games 1, 3 and 5. In the Series opener, Black threw a six-hitter and Robinson, Snider and Reese slugged homers in a 4-2 victory. Preacher Roe was a 5-3 winner in the third game, while Carl Erskine prevailed, 6-5, in 11 innings in Game 5. Erskine allowed four hits and all five runs in the fifth inning, but permitted only one other hit—a bunt single by Mantle in the fourth—and retired the final 19 New York batters of the game. Snider, who wound up with four home runs and eight RBIs in this Series, hit a two-run homer in the fifth in support of Erskine, who yielded a three-run blast to Johnny Mize in the Yankees' half of the inning.

Besides his final-game clutch play, Martin contributed mightily for New York in Game 2 with a three-run homer and an RBI single in Raschi's 7-1 victory. In Game 4, Reynolds tossed a four-hitter and Mize socked a home run in the Yanks' 2-0 triumph.

The Yankees' 1952 Series title

Brooklyn	IP.	H.	R.	ER.	BB.	SO.
Erskine (L)	5*	6	4	4	6	4
Loes	2	2	3	2	0	3
Lehman	2	2	0	0	1	0

*Pitched to three batters in sixth.

aWalked for Loes in seventh. E—Hodges. DP—Brooklyn 1. LOB—New York 6, Brooklyn 7. 2B—Mantle. HR—Martin. SB—McDougald. WP—Erskine. U—Passarella (A.L.), Goetz (N.L.), McKinley (A.L.), Pinelli (N.L.), Honochick (A.L.) and Boggess (N.L.). T—2:47. A—33,792.

Game 3

Friday, October 3, At New York

Brooklyn	AB.	R.	H.	RBI.	PO.	A.
Furillo, rf	5	1	1	0	0	0
Reese, ss	5	1	3	1	1	4
Robinson, 2b	4	2	2	1	2	3
Campanella, c	5	0	1	0	9	1
Pafko, lf	5	0	2	1	2	0
Snider, cf	5	0	1	0	3	0
Hodges, 1b	3	0	0	0	9	2
Cox, 3b	2	1	1	0	0	2
Roe, p	2	0	0	0	1	0
Totals	36	5	11	3	27	12

New York	AB.	R.	H.	RBI.	PO.	A.
Rizzuto, ss	4	0	0	0	4	4
Collins, 1b	4	0	0	0	7	0
bSain	1	0	0	0	0	0
Mantle, cf	4	0	0	0	6	0
Woodling, lf	4	0	1	0	2	0
Berra, c	4	1	3	1	1	1
Bauer, rf	2	1	0	0	3	0
McDougald, 3b	4	0	0	0	1	2
Martin, 2b	1	0	0	0	3	3
Lopat, p	2	0	1	1	0	0
Gorman, p	0	0	0	0	0	0
aMize	1	1	1	1	0	0
Totals	31	3	6	3	27	10

Brooklyn	0 0 1 0 1 0 0 1 2—5
New York	0 1 0 0 0 0 0 1 1—3

Brooklyn	IP.	H.	R.	ER.	BB.	SO.
Roe (W)	9	6	3	3	5	5

New York	IP.	H.	R.	ER.	BB.	SO.
Lopat (L)	8⅓	10	5	5	4	0
Gorman	⅔	1	0	0	0	0

aHomered for Gorman in ninth. bFlied out for Collins in ninth. E—Berra, McDougald. DP—New York 2. LOB—Brooklyn 10, New York 8. 2B—Furillo, Berra. HR—Berra, Mize. SB—Snider, Reese, Robinson. SH—Bauer, Roe 2. HBP—By Roe (Martin). PB—Berra. U—Goetz (N.L.), McKinley (A.L.), Pinelli (N.L.), Passarella (A.L.), Boggess (N.L.) and Honochick (A.L.). T—2:56. A—66,698.

Game 4

Saturday, October 4, At New York

Brooklyn	AB.	R.	H.	RBI.	PO.	A.
Cox, 3b	3	0	0	0	2	2
bNelson	1	0	0	0	0	0
Morgan, 3b	0	0	0	0	0	1
Reese, ss	4	0	2	0	0	3
Snider, cf	4	0	0	0	5	0
Robinson, 2b	4	0	0	0	0	2
Campanella, c	3	0	0	0	4	0
Pafko, lf	3	0	1	0	2	0
Hodges, 1b	2	0	0	0	10	0
Furillo, rf	2	0	1	0	1	0
Black, p	1	0	0	0	0	2
aShuba	1	0	0	0	0	0
Rutherford, p	0	0	0	0	0	0
Totals	28	0	4	0	24	10

New York	AB.	R.	H.	RBI.	PO.	A.
McDougald, 3b	3	0	0	0	0	1
Rizzuto, ss	2	0	0	0	1	3
Mantle, cf	3	1	1	0	4	0
Mize, 1b	3	1	2	1	4	2
cCollins, 1b	0	0	0	0	1	0
Berra, c	4	0	0	0	12	1
Woodling, lf	3	0	1	0	1	0
Bauer, rf	4	0	0	0	1	0
Martin, 2b	3	0	0	0	2	1
Reynolds, p	3	0	0	0	1	0
Totals	28	2	4	1	27	8

Brooklyn	0 0 0 0 0 0 0 0 0—0
New York	0 0 0 1 0 0 0 1 x—2

Brooklyn	IP.	H.	R.	ER.	BB.	SO.
Black (L)	7	3	1	1	5	2
Rutherford	1	1	1	1	1	1

New York	IP.	H.	R.	ER.	BB.	SO.
Reynolds (W)	9	4	0	0	3	10

aFlied out for Black in eighth. bStruck out for Cox in eighth. cRan for Mize in eighth. E—Reese, Martin. DP—New York 1. LOB—Brooklyn 5, New York 8. 2B—Woodling, Mize. 3B—Mantle. HR—Mize. SH—Furillo. U—McKinley (A.L.), Pinelli (N.L.), Passarella (A.L.), Goetz (N.L.), Honochick (A.L.) and Boggess (N.L.). T—2:33. A—71,787.

Game 5

Sunday, October 5, At New York

Brooklyn	AB.	R.	H.	RBI.	PO.	A.
Cox, 3b	5	2	3	0	2	2
Reese, ss	5	0	1	1	1	1
Snider, cf	5	1	3	4	4	0
Robinson, 2b	2	1	0	0	2	1
Shuba, lf	2	0	1	0	4	0
Furillo, rf	4	0	1	0	3	0
Campanella, c	5	0	0	0	6	1
Pafko, rf-lf	4	0	1	1	3	0
Holmes, lf	1	0	0	0	2	0
Hodges, 1b	3	1	0	0	6	0
Erskine, p	4	1	0	0	0	1
Totals	40	6	10	6	33	6

New York	AB.	R.	H.	RBI.	PO.	A.
McDougald, 3b	4	1	0	1	0	2
Rizzuto, ss	5	1	1	0	1	4
Mantle, cf	5	0	1	0	1	0
Mize, 1b	5	1	1	3	9	1
Berra, c	4	0	0	0	10	1
Woodling, lf	4	0	0	0	5	0
Bauer, rf	3	1	0	0	1	0
Martin, 2b	4	1	1	0	6	3
Blackwell, p	1	0	0	0	0	1
aNoren	1	0	1	1	0	0
Sain, p	2	0	0	0	0	2
Totals	38	5	5	5	33	14

Brooklyn	0 1 0 0 3 0 1 0 0 0 1—6
New York	0 0 0 0 5 0 0 0 0 0 0—5

Brooklyn	IP.	H.	R.	ER.	BB.	SO.
Erskine (W)	11	5	5	5	3	6

New York	IP.	H.	R.	ER.	BB.	SO.
Blackwell	5	4	4	4	3	4
Sain (L)	6	6	2	2	3	3

aSingled for Blackwell in fifth. E—Rizzuto. DP—New York 2. LOB—Brooklyn 11, New York 3. 2B—Furillo, Snider. HR—Snider, Mize. SB—Robinson. SH—Erskine, Cox, Reese. HBP—By Sain (Snider). U—Pinelli (N.L.), Passarella (A.L.), Goetz (N.L.), McKinley (A.L.), Boggess (N.L.) and Honochick (A.L.). T—3:00. A—70,536.

Game 6

Monday, October 6, At Brooklyn

New York	AB.	R.	H.	RBI.	PO.	A.
McDougald, 3b	4	0	1	0	1	2
Rizzuto, ss	4	0	1	0	2	2
Mantle, cf	3	1	1	1	0	0
Mize, 1b	3	0	0	0	7	0
Collins, 1b	1	0	0	0	2	0
Berra, c	5	1	1	1	12	0
Woodling, lf	3	1	2	0	3	0
Noren, rf	4	0	2	0	0	0
Bauer, rf	0	0	0	0	0	0
Martin, 2b	4	0	0	0	0	3
Raschi, p	3	0	1	1	0	1
Reynolds, p	1	0	0	0	0	0
Totals	35	3	9	3	27	8

Brooklyn	AB.	R.	H.	RBI.	PO.	A.
Cox, 3b	5	0	2	0	1	3
Reese, ss	4	0	0	0	5	2
Snider, cf	3	2	2	2	4	0
Robinson, 2b	4	0	0	0	2	2
Shuba, lf	4	0	1	0	2	0
aAmoros	0	0	0	0	0	0
Holmes, lf	0	0	0	0	0	0
Campanella, c	4	0	1	0	5	0
Hodges, 1b	3	0	0	0	7	1
bNelson	1	0	0	0	0	0
Furillo, rf	3	0	1	0	1	0
Loes, p	3	0	1	0	0	2
Roe, p	0	0	0	0	0	0
cPafko	1	0	0	0	0	0
Totals	35	2	8	2	27	10

New York	0 0 0 0 0 0 2 1 0—3
Brooklyn	0 0 0 0 0 1 0 1 0—2

New York	IP.	H.	R.	ER.	BB.	SO.
Raschi (W)	7⅔	8	2	2	1	9
Reynolds	1⅓	0	0	0	1	2

Brooklyn	IP.	H.	R.	ER.	BB.	SO.
Loes (L)	8⅓	9	3	3	5	3
Roe	⅔	0	0	0	1	1

aRan for Shuba in eighth. bStruck out for Hodges in ninth. cPopped out for Roe in ninth. E—Reese. DP—Brooklyn 1. LOB—New York 11, Brooklyn 8. 2B—Cox, Shuba. HR—Snider 2, Berra, Mantle. SB—Loes. Balk—Loes. U—Passarella (A.L.), Goetz (N.L.), McKinley (A.L.), Pinelli (N.L.), Honochick (A.L.) and Boggess (N.L.). T—2:56. A—30,037.

Game 7

Tuesday, October 7, At Brooklyn

New York	AB.	R.	H.	RBI.	PO.	A.
McDougald, 3b	5	1	2	0	2	3
Rizzuto, ss	4	1	1	0	1	1
Mantle, cf	5	1	2	2	1	0
Mize, 1b	3	0	2	1	6	0
Collins, 1b	0	0	0	0	1	0
Berra, c	4	0	0	0	7	0
Woodling, lf	4	1	2	1	5	0
Noren, rf	2	0	0	0	0	0
aBauer, rf	1	0	0	0	0	0
Martin, 2b	4	0	1	0	2	4
Lopat, p	1	0	0	0	0	1
Reynolds, p	1	0	0	0	1	0
bHouk	1	0	0	0	0	0
Raschi, p	0	0	0	0	0	0
Kuzava, p	1	0	0	0	0	0
Totals	36	4	10	4	27	9

Brooklyn	AB.	R.	H.	RBI.	PO.	A.
Cox, 3b	5	1	2	0	2	3
Reese, ss	4	0	1	1	2	2
Snider, cf	4	1	1	0	4	0
Robinson, 2b	4	0	1	0	0	4
Campanella, c	4	0	2	0	2	0
Hodges, 1b	4	0	0	1	13	0
Shuba, lf	3	0	1	0	1	0
dPafko	1	0	0	0	0	0
Holmes, lf	0	0	0	0	0	0
Furillo, lf	3	0	0	0	3	0
Black, p	2	0	0	0	0	0
Roe, p	0	0	0	0	0	0
cNelson	1	0	0	0	0	0
Erskine, p	0	0	0	0	0	0
eMorgan	1	0	0	0	0	0
Totals	36	2	8	2	27	9

New York	0 0 0 1 1 1 1 0 0—4
Brooklyn	0 0 0 1 1 0 0 0 0—2

New York	IP.	H.	R.	ER.	BB.	SO.
Lopat	3*	4	1	1	0	3
Reynolds (W)	3	3	1	1	0	2
Raschi	⅓	1	0	0	2	0
Kuzava	2⅔	0	0	0	0	2

Brooklyn	IP.	H.	R.	ER.	BB.	SO.
Black (L)	5⅓	6	3	3	1	1
Roe	1⅔	3	1	1	0	1
Erskine	2	1	0	0	1	0

*Pitched to three batters in fourth.

aReached first on error for Noren in sixth. bGrounded out for Reynolds in seventh. cPopped out for Roe in seventh. dStruck out for Shuba in eighth. eFlied out for Erskine in ninth. E—McDougald 2, Woodling, Reynolds, Cox. DP—New York 1, Brooklyn 1. LOB—New York 8, Brooklyn 9. 2B—Rizzuto, Cox. HR—Woodling, Mantle. SH—Rizzuto. U—Goetz (N.L.), McKinley (A.L.), Pinelli (N.L.), Passarella (A.L.), Boggess (N.L.) and Honochick (A.L.). T—2:54. A—33,195.

COMPOSITE BATTING AVERAGES

New York Yankees

Player-Position	G.	AB.	R.	H.	2B.	3B.	HR.	RBI.	BA.
Mize, ph-1b	5	15	3	6	1	0	3	6	.400
Woodling, ph-lf	7	23	4	8	1	1	1	1	.348
Mantle, cf	7	29	5	10	1	1	2	3	.345
Lopat, p	2	3	0	1	0	0	0	1	.333
Noren, lf-ph-rf	4	10	0	3	0	0	0	1	.300
Martin, 2b	7	23	2	5	0	0	1	4	.217
Berra, c	7	28	2	6	1	0	2	3	.214
McDougald, 3b	7	25	5	5	0	0	1	3	.200
Raschi, p	3	6	0	1	0	0	0	1	.167
Rizzuto, ss	7	27	2	4	1	0	0	0	.148
Bauer, rf-ph	7	18	2	1	0	0	0	1	.056
Collins, 1b-pr	6	12	1	0	0	0	0	0	.000
Reynolds, p	4	7	0	0	0	0	0	0	.000
Scarborough, p	1	0	0	0	0	0	0	0	.000
Gorman, p	1	0	0	0	0	0	0	0	.000
Blackwell, p	1	1	0	0	0	0	0	0	.000
Kuzava, p	1	1	0	0	0	0	0	0	.000
Sain, ph-p	2	3	0	0	0	0	0	0	.000
Houk, ph	1	1	0	0	0	0	0	0	.000
Totals	7	232	26	50	5	2	10	24	.216

Brooklyn Dodgers

Player-Position	G.	AB.	R.	H.	2B.	3B.	HR.	RBI.	BA.
Snider, cf	7	29	5	10	2	0	4	8	.345
Reese, ss	7	29	4	10	0	0	1	4	.345
Loes, p	2	3	0	1	0	0	0	0	.333
Shuba, ph-lf	4	10	0	3	1	0	0	0	.300
Cox, 3b	7	27	4	8	2	0	0	0	.296
Campanella, c	7	28	0	6	0	0	0	1	.214
Pafko, lf-rf-ph	7	21	0	4	0	0	0	2	.190
Robinson, 2b	7	23	4	4	0	0	1	2	.174
Furillo, rf	7	23	1	4	2	0	0	0	.174
Holmes, lf	3	1	0	0	0	0	0	0	.000
Morgan, 3b-ph	2	1	0	0	0	0	0	0	.000
Hodges, 1b	7	21	1	0	0	0	0	1	.000
Black, p	3	6	0	0	0	0	0	0	.000
Erskine, p	3	6	1	0	0	0	0	0	.000
Lehman, p	1	0	0	0	0	0	0	0	.000
Roe, p	3	2	0	0	0	0	0	0	.000
Rutherford, p	1	0	0	0	0	0	0	0	.000
Amoros, pr	1	0	0	0	0	0	0	0	.000
Nelson, ph	4	3	0	0	0	0	0	0	.000
Totals	7	233	20	50	7	0	6	18	.215

COMPOSITE PITCHING AVERAGES

New York Yankees

Pitcher	G.	IP.	H.	R.	ER.	BB.	SO.	W.	L.	ERA.
Kuzava	1	2⅔	0	0	0	0	2	0	0	0.00
Gorman	1	⅔	1	0	0	0	0	0	0	0.00
Raschi	3	17	12	3	3	8	18	2	0	1.59
Reynolds	4	20⅓	12	4	4	6	18	2	1	1.77
Sain	1	6	6	2	2	3	3	0	1	3.00
Lopat	2	11⅓	14	6	6	4	3	0	1	4.76
Blackwell	1	5	4	4	4	3	4	0	0	7.20
Scarborough	1	1	1	1	1	0	1	0	0	9.00
Totals	7	64	50	20	20	24	49	4	3	2.81

Brooklyn Dodgers

Pitcher	G.	IP.	H.	R.	ER.	BB.	SO.	W.	L.	ERA.
Lehman	1	2	2	0	0	1	0	0	0	0.00
Black	3	21⅓	15	6	6	8	9	1	2	2.53
Roe	3	11⅓	9	4	4	6	7	1	0	3.18
Loes	2	10⅓	11	6	5	5	5	0	1	4.35
Erskine	3	18	12	9	9	10	10	1	1	4.50
Rutherford	1	1	1	1	1	1	1	0	0	9.00
Totals	7	64	50	26	25	31	32	3	4	3.52

The 1953 Brooklyn Dodgers undoubtedly ranked as one of the greatest baseball teams of all time.

The Dodgers boasted the National League's Most Valuable Player in catcher Roy Campanella, who belted 41 home runs and drove in 142 runs. They had the league's Rookie of the Year in second baseman Jim Gilliam. Center fielder Duke Snider blasted 42 homers and had 126 RBIs, and first baseman Gil Hodges drilled 31 homers and knocked in 122 runs. Right fielder Carl Furillo won the N.L. batting championship with a .344 average (Snider was fourth at .336), and outfielder/infielder Jackie Robinson hit .329. Club leader Pee Wee Reese had a fine year at shortstop and rapped 13 homers. And glove wizard Billy Cox was the main man at third base for Charlie Dressen's team, which won an impressive 105 games.

Carl Erskine paced the pitching staff with 20 victories, Russ Meyer went 15-5 and Billy Loes was 14-8. Preacher Roe posted an 11-3 record, boosting his mark to a staggering 44-8 over the last three years. Clem Labine won 10 games in relief and 11 overall. And rookie pitchers Johnny Podres and Bob Milliken combined for a 17-8 mark.

So what was Brooklyn's victory margin in the 1953 N.L. pennant race? A tidy 13 games over the Braves, who had just moved to Milwaukee.

OK, by how many games did one of baseball's finest teams win the 1953 World Series? Was it a sweep? A five-game Series? Six? Were the Dodgers extended to seven games?

The Series, in fact, went six games.

Erskine strutted his stuff in Game 3, setting a Series record with 14 strikeouts. The 26-year-old righthander fanned Mickey Mantle four times. Campanella displayed his MVP wares in that contest, stroking a tie-breaking home run in the eighth inning that lifted the Dodgers to a 3-2 victory. In Game 4, Snider smashed two doubles and a home run and drove in four runs and Gilliam whacked three doubles. Loes was a 7-3 winner.

For one of baseball's top teams of all time, that was it. Two victories in the World Series.

The New York Yankees had done it again. And so, too, had the Brooklyn Dodgers. Casey Stengel's Bronx Bombers had won the World Series for a record fifth consecutive time. The Dodgers had lost in the Series for the seventh time in seven chances.

Billy Martin, who foiled the Dodgers with his glove in the '52 Series, killed them with his bat this time around with a .500 average and eight RBIs. He collected 12 hits, a record for a six-game fall classic, and No. 12—coming in the bottom of the ninth of Game 6—brought home the Series-winning run in a 4-3 Yankee triumph. Furillo had tied the game with a dramatic two-run homer in the top half of the inning.

Martin not only capped matters for the Yankees, he got them rolling as well in the 50th World Series (which now stood 33-17 in the American League's favor). The combative second baseman hit a three-run triple in the first inning of the Series opener and collected three hits overall in a 9-5 New York conquest. Yogi Berra and Joe Collins hit homers for the Yankees, while Gilliam, Hodges

Game 3 heroes Roy Campanella (left) and Carl Erskine (center) celebrate with Brooklyn Manager Charlie Dressen after the Dodgers' 3-2 victory.

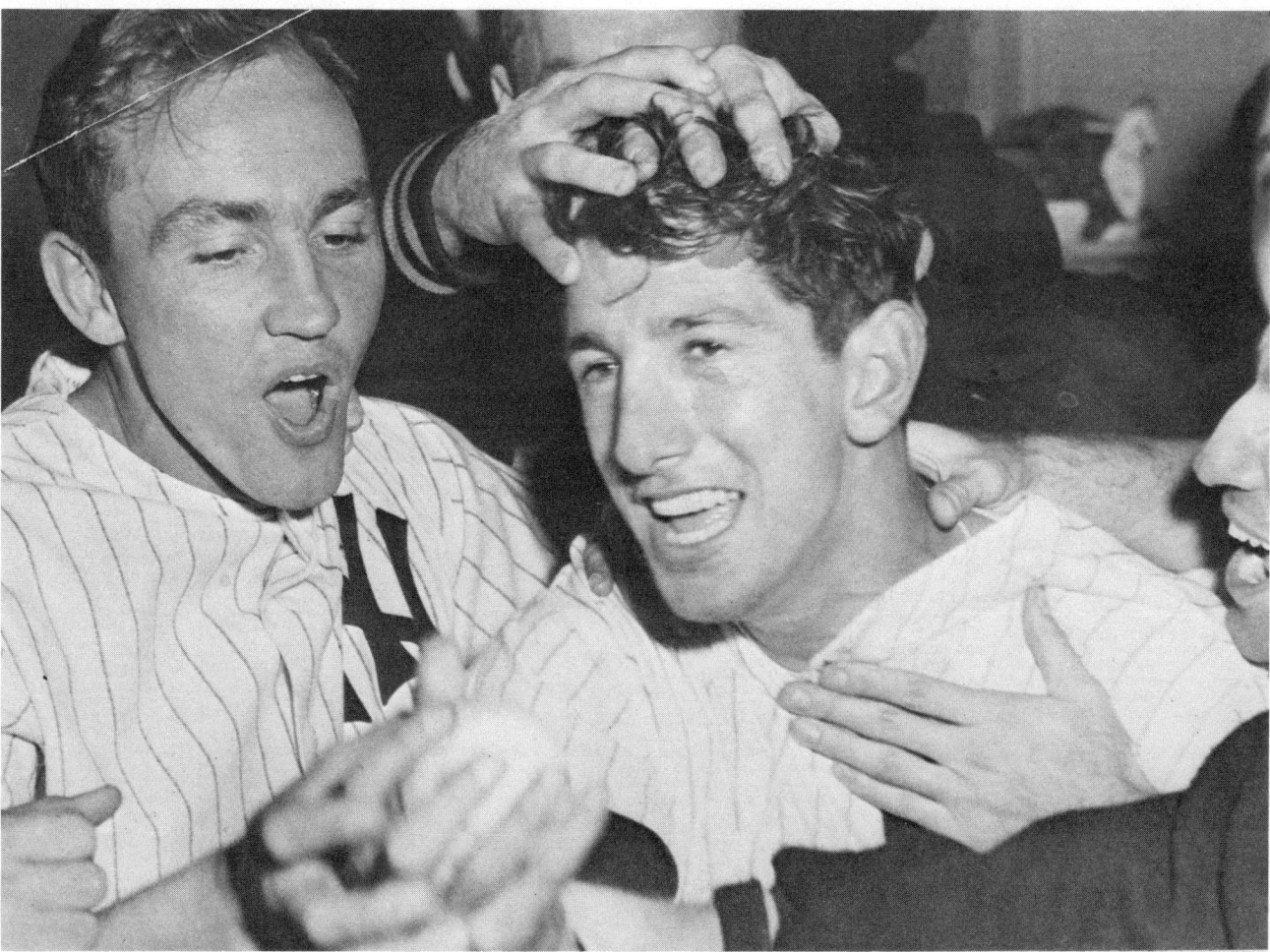

Billy Martin is the center of attention as the Yankees celebrate their sixth-game victory over Brooklyn in the 1953 World Series. To the left of Martin is reserve outfielder Irv Noren.

and George Shuba connected for the Dodgers. Shuba's shot was the first pinch homer by a National Leaguer in Series history.

In Game 2, Martin walloped a game-tying, bases-empty homer in the seventh inning and Mantle followed with a two-run drive an inning later as Eddie Lopat out-pitched Roe, 4-2. And in the fifth game, Martin homered with a man aboard as the Yankees prevailed, 11-7. The biggest blast in that game, however, came from Mantle, who belted a bases-loaded home run off Meyer in the third inning. Gene Woodling and Gil McDougald also homered for New York in the 18-run, 25-hit game.

Incredibly, the World Series title was the Yanks' 15th in their last 16 appearances in the fall classic. And, in light of the Yankees' success against Brooklyn in 1947 and Cleveland's victory over the Boston Braves in 1948, the Se-

ries championship was the seventh straight by an American League team.

The '53 A.L. representative was a typical Yankee team—well-balanced and deep. New York had power in Berra and Mantle, who combined for exactly 200 RBIs. It had solid contact hitters in Woodling (.306) and Bauer (.304). Plus, Berra batted .296, Mantle hit .295 and McDougald finished at .285. And the Yanks' top five pitchers combined for a 74-30 record, with young service returnee Whitey Ford heading the staff with 18 victories and veteran Lopat topping the league in earned-run average with a 2.43 figure. And, of course, there was the wily Stengel at the helm.

Those Yankees must have been something in their own right. After all, they won the World Series against one of the greatest baseball teams of all time. And they did it in six games.

Game 1

Wednesday, September 30, At New York

Brooklyn	AB.	R.	H.	RBI.	PO.	A.
Gilliam, 2b	5	1	2	1	3	3
Reese, ss	3	0	0	0	3	3
Snider, cf	5	0	2	0	3	0
Robinson, lf	4	0	0	0	0	0
Campanella, c	4	1	1	0	6	3
Hodges, 1b	5	1	3	1	7	0
Furillo, rf	4	0	1	1	2	0
Cox, 3b	5	1	2	0	0	1
Erskine, p	0	0	0	0	0	0
aBelardi	1	0	0	0	0	0
Hughes, p	1	0	0	0	0	0
bShuba	1	1	1	1	0	0
Labine, p	1	0	0	0	0	1
Wade, p	0	0	0	0	0	0
Totals	39	5	12	5	24	11

New York	AB.	R.	H.	RBI.	PO.	A.
McDougald, 3b	5	0	0	0	3	2
Collins, 1b	4	2	2	2	6	0
Bauer, rf	5	1	2	1	4	0
Berra, c	4	1	2	1	8	2
Mantle, cf	3	1	1	0	0	0
Woodling, lf	3	1	1	0	4	0
Martin, 2b	4	1	3	3	1	2
Rizzuto, ss	3	1	0	0	1	1
Reynolds, p	1	0	0	0	0	0
Sain, p	2	1	1	2	0	0
Totals	34	9	12	9	27	7

Brooklyn	0 0 0	0 1 3	1 0 0—5
New York	4 0 0	0 1 0	1 3 x—9

Brooklyn	IP.	H.	R.	ER.	BB.	SO.
Erskine	1	2	4	4	3	1
Hughes	4	3	1	1	1	3
Labine (L)	1⅔	4	1	1	0	1
Wade	1⅓	3	3	3	1	2

New York	IP.	H.	R.	ER.	BB.	SO.
Reynolds	5⅓	7	4	4	3	6
Sain (W)	3⅔	5	1	1	1	0

aStruck out for Erskine in second. bHomered for Hughes in sixth. E—Furillo, Hughes. LOB—Brooklyn 12, New York 6. 2B—Cox, Snider, Sain. 3B—Bauer, Martin. HR—Gilliam, Berra, Hodges, Shuba, Collins. SB—Martin.

HBP—By Reynolds (Campanella). U—Grieve (A.L.), Stewart (N.L.), Hurley (A.L.), Gore (N.L.), Soar (A.L.) and Dascoli (N.L.). T—3:10. A—69,374.

Game 2

Thursday, October 1, At New York

Brooklyn	AB.	R.	H.	RBI.	PO.	A.
Gilliam, 2b	5	0	0	0	1	2
Reese, ss	3	0	2	0	0	1
Snider, cf	5	0	0	0	2	0
Robinson, lf	4	0	1	0	3	0
Campanella, c	4	0	0	0	5	3
Hodges, 1b	3	1	2	0	9	1
Furillo, rf	4	1	2	0	3	0
Cox, 3b	3	0	1	2	0	2
Roe, p	3	0	0	0	1	1
aWilliams	1	0	1	0	0	0
Totals	35	2	9	2	24	10

New York	AB.	R.	H.	RBI.	PO.	A.
Woodling, lf	3	1	0	0	1	0
Collins, 1b	3	0	0	0	15	0
Bauer, rf	4	1	1	0	1	0
Berra, c	3	0	0	1	4	0
Mantle, cf	3	1	1	2	4	0
McDougald, 3b	3	0	0	0	0	3
Martin, 2b	3	1	2	1	1	5
Rizzuto, ss	2	0	1	0	1	5
Lopat, p	3	0	0	0	0	2
Totals	27	4	5	4	27	15

Brooklyn	0 0 0 2 0 0 0 0—2
New York	1 0 0 0 0 0 1 2 x—4

Brooklyn	IP.	H.	R.	ER.	BB.	SO.
Roe (L)	8	5	4	4	4	4

New York	IP.	H.	R.	ER.	BB.	SO.
Lopat (W)	9	9	2	2	4	3

aSingled for Roe in ninth. E—Furillo. DP—New York 1. LOB—Brooklyn 10, New York 5. 2B—Rizzuto, Cox, Furillo. 3B—Reese. HR—Martin, Mantle. SB—Hodges. SH—Rizzuto. HBP—By Roe (McDougald). U—Stewart (N.L.), Hurley (A.L.), Gore (N.L.), Grieve (A.L.), Dascoli (N.L.) and Soar (A.L.). T—2:42. A—66,786.

Game 3

Friday, October 2, At Brooklyn

New York	AB.	R.	H.	RBI.	PO.	A.
McDougald, 3b	4	0	1	1	2	3
cNoren	0	0	0	0	0	0
Collins, 1b	5	0	0	0	8	0
Bauer, rf	4	1	1	0	1	0
Berra, c	1	0	1	0	4	1
Mantle, cf	4	0	0	0	2	0
Woodling, lf	4	0	1	1	0	0
Martin, 2b	3	1	1	0	3	4
Rizzuto, ss	3	0	1	0	3	3
aBollweg	1	0	0	0	0	0
Raschi, p	2	0	0	0	1	1
bMize	1	0	0	0	0	0
Totals	32	2	6	2	24	12

Brooklyn	AB.	R.	H.	RBI.	PO.	A.
Gilliam, 2b	4	0	1	0	1	2
Reese, ss	4	0	1	0	1	4
Snider, cf	3	1	1	0	0	0
Hodges, 1b	2	0	1	0	8	1
Campanella, c	4	1	1	1	14	0
Furillo, rf	4	0	0	0	1	0
Robinson, lf	4	1	3	1	1	0
Thompson, lf	0	0	0	0	0	0
Cox, 3b	3	0	0	1	0	1
Erskine, p	3	0	1	0	1	2
Totals	31	3	9	3	27	10

New York	0 0 0 0 1 0 0 1 0—2
Brooklyn	0 0 0 0 1 1 0 1 x—3

New York	IP.	H.	R.	ER.	BB.	SO.
Raschi (L)	8	9	3	3	3	4

Brooklyn	IP.	H.	R.	ER.	BB.	SO.
Erskine (W)	9	6	2	2	3	14

aStruck out for Rizzuto in ninth. bStruck out for Raschi in ninth. cWalked for McDougald in ninth. DP—New York 1. LOB—New York 9, Brooklyn 8. 2B—Robinson. HR—Campanella. SH—Raschi, Cox. HBP—By Erskine (Berra 2). WP—Erskine. Balk—Raschi. U—Hurley (A.L.), Gore (N.L.), Grieve (A.L.), Stewart (N.L.), Soar (A.L.) and Dascoli (N.L.). T—3:00. A—35,270.

Game 4

Saturday, October 3, At Brooklyn

New York	AB.	R.	H.	RBI.	PO.	A.
Mantle, cf	5	0	1	1	1	0
Collins, 1b	4	0	0	0	9	1
Bauer, rf	4	0	1	0	4	0
Berra, c	4	0	2	0	4	0
Woodling, lf	3	1	1	0	1	0
Martin, 2b	4	1	2	0	4	2
McDougald, 3b	3	1	1	2	0	5
Rizzuto, ss	4	0	1	0	0	2
Ford, p	0	0	0	0	0	0
Gorman, p	1	0	0	0	1	0
aBollweg	1	0	0	0	0	0
Sain, p	0	0	0	0	0	0
bNoren	1	0	0	0	0	0
Schallock, p	0	0	0	0	0	1
cMize	1	0	0	0	0	0
Totals	35	3	9	3	24	11

Brooklyn	AB.	R.	H.	RBI.	PO.	A.
Gilliam, 2b	5	1	3	2	2	2
Reese, ss	5	0	0	0	2	1
Robinson, lf	4	0	1	1	1	0
Thompson, lf	0	0	0	0	0	1
Hodges, 1b	4	1	0	0	5	1
Campanella, c	2	2	0	0	10	0
Snider, cf	4	1	3	4	5	0
Furillo, rf	4	1	1	0	2	0
Cox, 3b	4	1	2	0	0	1
Loes, p	3	0	2	0	0	0
Labine, p	0	0	0	0	0	0
Totals	35	7	12	7	27	6

New York	0 0 0 0 2 0 0 0 1—3
Brooklyn	3 0 0 1 0 2 1 0 x—7

New York	IP.	H.	R.	ER.	BB.	SO.
Ford (L)	1	3	3	3	1	0
Gorman	3	4	1	1	0	1
Sain	2	3	2	2	0	1
Schallock	2	2	1	1	1	1

Brooklyn	IP.	H.	R.	ER.	BB.	SO.
Loes (W)	8*	8	3	3	2	8
Labine	1	1	0	0	0	1

*Pitched to three batters in ninth.

aStruck out for Gorman in fifth. bPopped out for Sain in seventh. cFlied out for Schallock in ninth. LOB—New York 7, Brooklyn 7. 2B—Gilliam 3, Snider 2, Cox. 3B—Martin. HR—McDougald, Snider. SH—Loes. WP—Ford. U—Gore (N.L.), Grieve (A.L.), Stewart (N.L.), Hurley (A.L.), Dascoli (N.L.) and Soar (A.L.). T—2:46. A—36,775.

Game 5

Sunday, October 4, At Brooklyn

New York	AB.	R.	H.	RBI.	PO.	A.
Woodling, lf	3	1	1	1	2	1
Collins, 1b	5	2	1	0	6	2
Bauer, rf	3	1	0	0	1	0
Berra, c	4	2	2	1	6	0
Mantle, cf	5	1	1	4	2	0
Martin, 2b	5	1	2	2	3	2
McDougald, 3b	5	1	2	1	0	1
Rizzuto, ss	3	2	1	0	4	6
McDonald, p	2	0	1	1	3	0
Kuzava, p	1	0	0	0	0	0
Reynolds, p	0	0	0	0	0	0
Totals	36	11	11	10	27	12

Brooklyn	AB.	R.	H.	RBI.	PO.	A.
Gilliam, 2b	4	2	2	1	4	3
Reese, ss	5	0	1	0	0	1
Snider, cf	5	0	2	1	3	0
Robinson, lf	5	1	1	0	0	0
Campanella, c	4	2	3	0	8	3
Hodges, 1b	4	0	2	0	11	1
Furillo, rf	4	1	1	1	0	0
Cox, 3b	4	1	1	3	1	4
Podres, p	1	0	1	0	0	1
Meyer, p	1	0	0	0	0	1
aBelardi	1	0	0	0	0	0
Wade, p	0	0	0	0	0	0
bShuba	0	0	0	0	0	0
cWilliams	1	0	0	0	0	0
Black, p	0	0	0	0	0	0
Totals	39	7	14	6	27	14

New York	1 0 5 0 0 0 3 1 1—11
Brooklyn	0 1 0 0 1 0 0 4 1— 7

New York	IP.	H.	R.	ER.	BB.	SO.
McDonald (W)	7⅔	12	6	5	0	3
Kuzava	⅔	2	1	1	0	1
Reynolds	⅔	0	0	0	0	0

Brooklyn	IP.	H.	R.	ER.	BB.	SO.
Podres (L)	2⅔	1	5	1	2	0
Meyer	4⅓	8	4	3	4	5
Wade	1	1	1	1	0	0
Black	1	1	1	1	0	2

aGrounded out for Meyer in seventh. bAnnounced for Wade in eighth. cStruck out for Shuba in eighth. E—Rizzuto, Hodges. DP—New York 3. LOB—New York 7, Brooklyn 6. 2B—McDougald, Collins. 3B—McDougald. HR—Woodling, Mantle, Martin, Cox, McDougald, Gilliam. SB—Rizzuto. SH—McDonald, Bauer. HBP—By Podres (Bauer), by McDonald (Gilliam). U—Grieve (A.L.), Stewart (N.L.), Hurley (A.L.), Gore (N.L.), Soar (A.L.) and Dascoli (N.L.). T—3:02. A—36,775.

Game 6

Monday, October 5, At New York

Brooklyn	AB.	R.	H.	RBI.	PO.	A.
Gilliam, 2b	4	0	0	0	4	4
Reese, ss	4	0	1	0	1	4
Robinson, lf	4	1	2	0	3	0
Campanella, c	4	0	1	1	4	0
Hodges, 1b	4	0	0	0	7	0
Snider, cf	3	1	0	0	4	1
Furillo, rf	4	1	3	2	2	0
Cox, 3b	4	0	1	0	0	1
Erskine, p	1	0	0	0	0	0
aWilliams	0	0	0	0	0	0
Milliken, p	0	0	0	0	0	0
bMorgan	1	0	0	0	0	0
Labine, p	1	0	0	0	0	1
Totals	34	3	8	3	25	11

New York	AB.	R.	H.	RBI.	PO.	A.
Woodling, lf	4	1	2	1	1	0
Collins, 1b	3	0	1	0	5	1
cMize	1	0	0	0	0	0
Bollweg, 1b	0	0	0	0	0	0
Bauer, rf	3	2	1	0	3	0
Berra, c	5	0	2	1	10	0
Mantle, cf	4	0	1	0	5	0
Martin, 2b	5	0	2	2	1	0
McDougald, 3b	4	0	0	0	0	0
Rizzuto, ss	4	1	2	0	2	2
Ford, p	3	0	1	0	0	1
Reynolds, p	1	0	1	0	0	0
Totals	37	4	13	4	27	4

Brooklyn	0 0 0 0 0 1 0 0 2—3
New York	2 1 0 0 0 0 0 0 1—4

One out when winning run scored.

Brooklyn	IP.	H.	R.	ER.	BB.	SO.
Erskine	4	6	3	3	3	1
Milliken	2	2	0	0	1	0
Labine (L)	2⅓	5	1	1	1	1

New York	IP.	H.	R.	ER.	BB.	SO.
Ford	7	6	1	1	1	7
Reynolds (W)	2	2	2	2	1	3

aWalked for Erskine in fifth. bLined out for Milliken in seventh. cGrounded out for Collins in eighth. E—Gilliam, Cox, Erskine. DP—Brooklyn 3. LOB—Brooklyn 6, New York 13. 2B—Berra, Furillo, Martin, Robinson. HR—Furillo. SB—Robinson. U—Stewart (N.L.), Hurley (A.L.), Gore (N.L.), Grieve (A.L.), Dascoli (N.L.) and Soar (A.L.). T—2:55. A—62,370.

COMPOSITE BATTING AVERAGES

New York Yankees

Player-Position	G.	AB.	R.	H.	2B.	3B.	HR.	RBI.	BA.
Martin, 2b	6	24	5	12	1	2	2	8	.500
McDonald, p	1	2	0	1	1	0	0	1	.500
Reynolds, p	3	2	0	1	0	0	0	0	.500
Sain, p	2	2	1	1	1	0	0	2	.500
Berra, c	6	21	3	9	1	0	1	4	.429
Ford, p	2	3	0	1	0	0	0	0	.333
Rizzuto, ss	6	19	4	6	1	0	0	0	.316
Woodling, lf	6	20	5	6	0	0	1	3	.300
Bauer, rf	6	23	6	6	0	1	0	1	.261
Mantle, cf	6	24	3	5	0	0	2	7	.208
McDougald, 3b	6	24	2	4	0	1	2	4	.167
Collins, 1b	6	24	4	4	1	0	1	2	.167
Bollweg, ph-1b	3	2	0	0	0	0	0	0	.000
Lopat, p	1	3	0	0	0	0	0	0	.000
Raschi, p	1	2	0	0	0	0	0	0	.000
Gorman, p	1	1	0	0	0	0	0	0	.000
Schallock, p	1	0	0	0	0	0	0	0	.000
Kuzava, p	1	1	0	0	0	0	0	0	.000
Mize, ph	3	3	0	0	0	0	0	0	.000
Noren, ph	2	1	0	0	0	0	0	0	.000
Totals	6	201	33	56	6	4	9	32	.279

Brooklyn Dodgers

Player-Position	G.	AB.	R.	H.	2B.	3B.	HR.	RBI.	BA.
Shuba, ph	2	1	1	1	0	0	1	2	1.000
Podres, p	1	1	0	1	0	0	0	0	1.000
Loes, p	1	3	0	2	0	0	0	0	.667
Williams, ph	3	2	0	1	0	0	0	0	.500
Hodges, 1b	6	22	3	8	0	0	1	1	.364
Furillo, rf	6	24	4	8	2	0	1	4	.333
Snider, cf	6	25	3	8	3	0	1	5	.320
Robinson, lf	6	25	3	8	2	0	0	2	.320
Cox, 3b	6	23	3	7	3	0	1	6	.304
Gilliam, 2b	6	27	4	8	3	0	2	4	.296
Campanella, c	6	22	6	6	0	0	1	2	.273
Erskine, p	3	4	0	1	0	0	0	0	.250
Reese, ss	6	24	0	5	0	1	0	0	.208
Thompson, lf	2	0	0	0	0	0	0	0	.000
Hughes, p	1	1	0	0	0	0	0	0	.000
Labine, p	3	2	0	0	0	0	0	0	.000
Wade, p	2	0	0	0	0	0	0	0	.000
Roe, p	1	3	0	0	0	0	0	0	.000
Meyer, p	1	1	0	0	0	0	0	0	.000
Black, p	1	0	0	0	0	0	0	0	.000
Milliken, p	1	0	0	0	0	0	0	0	.000
Belardi, ph	2	2	0	0	0	0	0	0	.000
Morgan, ph	1	1	0	0	0	0	0	0	.000
Totals	6	213	27	64	13	1	8	26	.300

COMPOSITE PITCHING AVERAGES

New York Yankees

Pitcher	G.	IP.	H.	R.	ER.	BB.	SO.	W.	L.	ERA.
Lopat	1	9	9	2	2	4	3	1	0	2.00
Gorman	1	3	4	1	1	0	1	0	0	3.00
Raschi	1	8	9	3	3	3	4	0	1	3.38
Ford	2	8	9	4	4	2	7	0	1	4.50
Schallock	1	2	2	1	1	1	1	0	0	4.50
Sain	2	5⅔	8	3	3	1	1	1	0	4.76
McDonald	1	7⅔	12	6	5	0	3	1	0	5.87
Reynolds	3	8	9	6	6	4	9	1	0	6.75
Kuzava	1	⅔	2	1	1	0	1	0	0	13.50
Totals	6	52	64	27	26	15	30	4	2	4.50

Brooklyn Dodgers

Pitcher	G.	IP.	H.	R.	ER.	BB.	SO.	W.	L.	ERA.
Milliken	1	2	2	0	0	1	0	0	0	0.00
Hughes	1	4	3	1	1	1	3	0	0	2.25
Loes	1	8	8	3	3	2	8	1	0	3.38
Podres	1	2⅔	1	5	1	2	0	0	1	3.38
Labine	3	5	10	2	2	1	3	0	2	3.60
Roe	1	8	5	4	4	4	4	0	1	4.50
Erskine	3	14	14	9	9	9	16	1	0	5.79
Meyer	1	4⅓	8	4	3	4	5	0	0	6.23
Black	1	1	1	1	1	0	2	0	0	9.00
Wade	2	2⅔	4	4	4	1	2	0	0	15.43
Totals	6	51⅓	56	33	28	25	43	2	4	4.91

1954
NEW YORK GIANTS
VS.
CLEVELAND INDIANS

The pairing in the 1954 World Series was a good news/bad news situation for the National League.

The good news was that the senior league, in the throes of a seven-year losing streak in the fall classic, would not have to challenge the New York Yankees, who had won five consecutive Series crowns. The bad news was that the National League's representative would, instead, have to confront a Cleveland Indians team that had established an American League record with 111 victories.

This October business simply wasn't getting any easier for the National League, which this time would send out the New York Giants in an attempt to stem the tide. Fifth-place finishers in 1953, the Giants rode the superlative play of Army returnee Willie Mays and off-season acquisition Johnny Antonelli to a five-game triumph over Brooklyn in the '54 N.L. pennant race.

That the World Series might end quickly was an opinion shared by many baseball "experts." After all, the mighty Yankees had won more games in the '54 season, 103, than in any year of their 1949-1953 domination—and the Yanks still couldn't compete with a pitching-rich Cleveland team boasting a starting rotation that included Bob Lemon, Early Wynn and Mike Garcia.

And end quickly the Series did, although the scenario was astonishingly different than envisioned in most quarters.

In Game 1 at New York's Polo Grounds, Mays made perhaps the greatest defensive play in Series history. With the Giants and Indians tied, 2-2, in the eighth inning and two Cleveland runners on base, Mays raced to deep center field and, with his back to the

The New York Giants' 1954 World Series heroes were young center fielder Willie Mays (left) and Dusty Rhodes.

plate, made an over-the-shoulder catch of a 460-foot smash off the bat of the Indians' Vic Wertz. The Giants went on to win, 5-2, when pinch-hitter Dusty Rhodes hit a three-run, 10th-inning home run off Indians starter and loser Lemon, the drive traveling all of 260 feet.

Rhodes, a .341 hitter in part-time duty for the Giants in '54 and a pinch-hitter deluxe (as evidenced by his .333 off-the-bench batting mark that season), was up to his old tricks in Game 2. He delivered a game-tying pinch single in the fifth inning and, staying in the game, rifled a homer in the seventh. New York won, 3-1, with Cleveland notching its only run on a first-pitch-of-the-game homer by Al Smith. After yielding Smith's smash, Antonelli pitched effectively the rest of the way for Manager Leo Durocher's team.

When the scene shifted to

Cleveland, Manager Al Lopez's Indians were hopeful of a turn-around. Those hopes were quickly dashed. The Giants struck for a first-inning run in Game 3, then got three in the third as that man, Rhodes, came through with a two-run pinch single with the bases loaded. New York's Ruben Gomez and Hoyt Wilhelm combined on a four-hitter, and the stunned Indians went down to a 6-2 defeat.

Cleveland, in no way resembling the club that laid waste to A.L. opponents with a .721 winning percentage, was mercifully put out of its misery in Game 4. After 4½ innings, the Giants had built a 7-0 lead. Hank Majeski gave the Cleveland throng of 78,000-plus something to cheer about in the fifth, slamming a three-run pinch homer off New York's Don Liddle. But New York wound up a 7-4 winner and World Series champion, with 1⅔

innings of hitless relief by Antonelli closing out the Tribe. Adding insult to injury, the Giants had no need to call on Rhodes in the clinching victory.

Mays, who had missed most of the 1952 season and all of the 1953 campaign because of military service, was the Giants' catalyst in '54. He batted an N.L.-leading .345, hit 41 home runs and knocked in 110 runs. Antonelli, acquired in the trade that sent 1951 Giants hero Bobby Thomson to Milwaukee, won 21 games for the Giants.

Combined with Rhodes, New York's Mays and Antonelli were the key figures in a World Series that produced a not-wholly-unexpected sweep. Only thing is, the other guys were supposed to wield the broom.

Game 1

Wednesday, September 29, At New York

Cleveland	AB.	R.	H.	RBI.	PO.	A.
Smith, lf	4	1	1	0	1	0
Avila, 2b	5	1	1	0	2	3
Doby, cf	3	0	1	0	3	0
Rosen, 3b	5	0	1	0	1	3
Wertz, 1b	5	0	4	2	11	1
dRegalado	0	0	0	0	0	0
Grasso, c	0	0	0	0	1	0
Philley, rf	3	0	0	0	0	0
aMajeski	0	0	0	0	0	0
bMitchell	0	0	0	0	0	0
Dente, ss	0	0	0	0	0	0
Strickland, ss	3	0	0	0	2	3
cPope, rf	1	0	0	0	0	0
Hegan, c	4	0	0	0	6	1
eGlynn, 1b	1	0	0	0	0	0
Lemon, p	4	0	0	0	0	1
Totals	38	2	8	2	28	12

New York	AB.	R.	H.	RBI.	PO.	A.
Lockman, 1b	5	1	1	0	9	0
Dark, ss	4	0	2	0	3	2
Mueller, rf	5	1	2	1	2	0
Mays, cf	3	1	0	0	2	0
Thompson, 3b	3	1	1	1	3	3
Irvin, lf	3	0	0	0	5	0
fRhodes	1	1	1	3	0	0
Williams, 2b	4	0	0	0	1	1
Westrum, c	4	0	2	0	5	0
Maglie, p	3	0	0	0	0	2
Liddle, p	0	0	0	0	0	0
Grissom, p	1	0	0	0	0	0
Totals	36	5	9	5	30	8

Cleveland....2 0 0 0 0 0 0 0 0 0—2
New York....0 0 2 0 0 0 0 0 0 3—5
One out when winning run scored.

Cleveland	IP.	H.	R.	ER.	BB.	SO.
Lemon (L)	9	9	5	5	5	6

New York	IP.	H.	R.	ER.	BB.	SO.
Maglie	7*	7	2	2	2	2
Liddle	⅓	0	0	0	0	0
Grissom (W)	2⅔	1	0	0	3	2

*Pitched to two batters in eighth.

aAnnounced as pinch-hitter for Philley in eighth. bWalked for Majeski in eighth. cStruck out for Strickland in eighth. dRan for Wertz in tenth. eStruck out for Hegan in tenth. fHit home run for Irvin in tenth. E—Mueller 2, Irvin. LOB—Cleveland 13, New York 9. 2B—Wertz. 3B—Wertz. HR—Rhodes. SB—Mays. SH—Irvin, Dente. HBP—By Maglie (Smith). WP—Lemon. U—Barlick (N.L.), Berry (A.L.), Conlan (N.L.), Stevens (A.L.), Warneke (N.L.) and Napp (A.L.). T—3:11. A—52,751.

Game 2

Thursday, September 30, At New York

Cleveland	AB.	R.	H.	RBI.	PO.	A.
Smith, lf	4	1	2	1	3	0
Avila, 2b	4	0	1	0	2	2
Doby, cf	5	0	0	0	2	0
Rosen, 3b	3	0	1	0	0	0
bRegalado, 3b	1	0	0	0	0	0
Wertz, 1b	3	0	1	0	5	1
Westlake, rf	3	0	1	0	3	0
Strickland, ss	3	0	0	0	1	1
cPhilley	1	0	0	0	0	0
Dente, ss	0	0	0	0	0	0
Hegan, c	4	0	1	0	7	0
Wynn, p	2	0	1	0	1	1
dMajeski	1	0	0	0	0	0
Mossi, p	0	0	0	0	0	1
Totals	34	1	8	1	24	6

New York	AB.	R.	H.	RBI.	PO.	A.
Lockman, 1b	4	0	0	0	8	0
Dark, ss	4	0	1	0	0	6
Mueller, rf	4	0	0	0	1	0
Mays, cf	2	1	0	0	1	0
Thompson, 3b	3	1	1	0	1	3
Irvin, lf	1	0	0	0	2	0
aRhodes, lf	2	1	2	2	1	0
Williams, 2b	3	0	0	0	4	0
Westrum, c	2	0	0	0	9	0
Antonelli, p	3	0	0	1	0	1
Totals	28	3	4	3	27	10

Cleveland....1 0 0 0 0 0 0 0 0—1
New York....0 0 0 0 2 0 1 0 x—3

Cleveland	IP.	H.	R.	ER.	BB.	SO.
Wynn (L)	7	4	3	3	2	5
Mossi	1	0	0	0	0	0

New York	IP.	H.	R.	ER.	BB.	SO.
Antonelli (W)	9	8	1	1	6	9

aSingled for Irvin in fifth. bRan for Rosen in seventh. cStruck out for Strickland in eighth. dGrounded out for Wynn in eighth. LOB—Cleveland 13, New York 3. 2B—Hegan, Wynn. HR—Smith, Rhodes. SF—Wynn. WP—Wynn. U—Berry (A.L.), Conlan (N.L.), Stevens (A.L.), Barlick (N.L.), Warneke (N.L.) and Napp (A.L.). T—2:50. A—49,099.

Game 3

Friday, October 1, At Cleveland

New York	AB.	R.	H.	RBI.	PO.	A.
Lockman, 1b	4	1	1	0	13	0
Dark, ss	4	0	1	0	2	2
Mueller, rf	5	2	2	0	0	0
Mays, cf	5	1	3	2	2	0
Thompson, 3b	3	2	1	0	0	3
Irvin, lf	1	0	0	0	0	0
aRhodes, lf	3	0	1	2	3	0
Williams, 2b	2	0	0	1	2	5
Westrum, c	4	0	1	1	4	0
Gomez, p	4	0	0	0	1	2
Wilhelm, p	0	0	0	0	0	0
Totals	35	6	10	6	27	12

Cleveland	AB.	R.	H.	RBI.	PO.	A.
Smith, lf	3	0	0	1	0	0
Avila, 2b	2	0	0	0	4	1
Doby, cf	4	0	1	0	2	0
Wertz, 1b	4	1	1	1	6	1
Majeski, 3b	4	0	0	0	2	1
Philley, rf	3	0	1	0	1	0
Strickland, ss	3	0	0	0	3	4
fPope	1	0	0	0	0	0
Hegan, c	2	0	0	0	8	1
dGlynn	1	1	1	0	0	0
Naragon, c	0	0	0	0	1	0
Garcia, p	0	0	0	0	0	1
bLemon	1	0	0	0	0	0
Houtteman, p	0	0	0	0	0	0
cRegalado	1	0	0	0	0	0
Narleski, p	0	0	0	0	0	1
eMitchell	1	0	0	0	0	0
Mossi, p	0	0	0	0	0	0
Totals	30	2	4	2	27	10

New York....1 0 3 0 1 1 0 0 0—6
Cleveland....0 0 0 0 0 0 1 1 0—2

New York	IP.	H.	R.	ER.	BB.	SO.
Gomez (W)	7⅓	4	2	2	3	2
Wilhelm	1⅔	0	0	0	0	2

Cleveland	IP.	H.	R.	ER.	BB.	SO.
Garcia (L)	3	5	4	3	3	3
Houtteman	2	2	1	1	1	1
Narleski	3	1	1	1	1	2
Mossi	1	2	0	0	0	1

aSingled for Irvin in third. bStruck out for Garcia in third. cGrounded out for Houtteman in fifth. dDoubled for Hegan in eighth. eGrounded out for Narleski in eighth. fGrounded out for Strickland in ninth. E—Dark, Strickland, Garcia. DP—New York 1, Cleveland 1. LOB—New York 9, Cleveland 5. 2B—Thompson, Glynn. HR—Wertz. SH—Avila, Williams, Dark. WP—Garcia. U—Conlan (N.L.), Stevens (A.L.), Barlick (N.L.), Berry (A.L.), Napp (A.L.) and Warneke (N.L.). T—2:28. A—71,555.

Game 4

Saturday, October 2, At Cleveland

New York	AB.	R.	H.	RBI.	PO.	A.
Lockman, 1b	5	0	0	0	10	1
Dark, ss	5	2	3	0	2	2
Mueller, rf	4	1	3	0	0	0
Mays, cf	4	1	1	1	5	0
Thompson, 3b	2	2	1	1	1	2
Irvin, lf	4	1	2	2	1	0
Williams, 2b	2	0	0	0	3	3
Westrum, c	1	0	0	2	5	0
Liddle, p	3	0	0	0	0	1
Wilhelm, p	1	0	0	0	0	1
Antonelli, p	0	0	0	0	0	0
Totals	31	7	10	6	27	10

Cleveland	AB.	R.	H.	RBI.	PO.	A.
Smith, lf	3	0	0	0	0	0
cPope, lf	1	0	0	0	0	0
eMitchell	1	0	0	0	0	0
Avila, 2b	4	0	0	0	4	4
Doby, cf	4	0	0	0	0	0
Rosen, 3b	4	0	1	0	1	0
Wertz, 1b	4	1	2	0	11	3
Westlake, rf	4	0	0	0	3	0
Dente, ss	3	1	0	0	1	1
Hegan, c	3	1	1	0	6	1
Lemon, p	1	0	0	0	1	1
Newhouser, p	0	0	0	0	0	0
Narleski, p	0	0	0	0	0	0
aMajeski	1	1	1	3	0	0
Mossi, p	0	0	0	0	0	1
bRegalado	1	0	1	1	0	0
Garcia, p	0	0	0	0	0	1
dPhilley	1	0	0	0	0	0
Totals	35	4	6	4	27	12

New York....0 2 1 0 4 0 0 0 0—7
Cleveland....0 0 0 0 3 0 1 0 0—4

New York	IP.	H.	R.	ER.	BB.	SO.
Liddle (W)	6⅔	5	4	1	1	2
Wilhelm	⅔	1	0	0	0	1
Antonelli	1⅔	0	0	0	0	3

Cleveland	IP.	H.	R.	ER.	BB.	SO.
Lemon (L)	4*	7	6	5	3	5
Newhouser	0†	1	1	1	1	0
Narleski	1	0	0	0	0	0
Mossi	2	1	0	0	0	0
Garcia	2	1	0	0	1	1

*Pitched to three batters in fifth.
†Pitched to two batters in fifth.

aHit home run for Narleski in fifth. bSingled for Mossi in seventh. cGrounded out for Smith in seventh. dStruck out for Garcia in ninth. eFouled out for Pope in ninth. E—Williams, Liddle, Wilhelm, Wertz, Westlake. DP—New York 1, Cleveland 1. LOB—New York 7, Cleveland 6. 2B—Irvin, Wertz, Mays. HR—Majeski. SH—Williams, Westrum, Mueller. SF—Westrum 2. WP—Liddle. U—Stevens (A.L.), Barlick (N.L.), Berry (A.L.), Conlan (N.L.), Warneke (N.L.) and Napp (A.L.). T—2:52. A—78,102.

COMPOSITE BATTING AVERAGES

New York Giants

Player-Position	G.	AB.	R.	H.	2B.	3B.	HR.	RBI.	BA.
Rhodes, ph-lf	3	6	2	4	0	0	2	7	.667
Dark, ss	4	17	2	7	0	0	0	0	.412
Mueller, rf	4	18	4	7	0	0	0	1	.389
Thompson, 3b	4	11	6	4	1	0	0	2	.364
Mays, cf	4	14	4	4	1	0	0	3	.286
Westrum, c	4	11	0	3	0	0	0	3	.273
Irvin, lf	4	9	1	2	1	0	0	2	.222
Lockman, 1b	4	18	2	2	0	0	0	0	.111
Williams, 2b	4	11	0	0	0	0	0	1	.000
Maglie, p	1	3	0	0	0	0	0	0	.000
Liddle, p	2	3	0	0	0	0	0	0	.000
Grissom, p	1	1	0	0	0	0	0	0	.000
Antonelli, p	2	3	0	0	0	0	0	1	.000
Gomez, p	1	4	0	0	0	0	0	0	.000
Wilhelm, p	2	1	0	0	0	0	0	0	.000
Totals	4	130	21	33	3	0	2	20	.254

Cleveland Indians

Player-Position	G.	AB.	R.	H.	2B.	3B.	HR.	RBI.	BA.
Wynn, p	1	2	0	1	1	0	0	0	.500
Wertz, 1b	4	16	2	8	2	1	1	3	.500
Glynn, ph-1b	2	2	1	1	1	0	0	0	.500
Rega'do, pr-3b-ph	4	3	0	1	0	0	0	1	.333
Rosen, 3b	3	12	0	3	0	0	0	0	.250
Smith, lf	4	14	2	3	0	0	1	2	.214
Majeski, ph-3b	4	6	1	1	0	0	1	3	.167
Hegan, c	4	13	1	2	1	0	0	0	.154
Westlake, rf	2	7	0	1	0	0	0	0	.143
Avila, 2b	4	15	1	2	0	0	0	0	.133
Doby, cf	4	16	0	2	0	0	0	0	.125
Philley, rf-ph	4	8	0	1	0	0	0	0	.125
Naragon, c	1	0	0	0	0	0	0	0	.000
Grasso, c	1	0	0	0	0	0	0	0	.000
Dente, ss	3	3	1	0	0	0	0	0	.000
Strickland, ss	3	9	0	0	0	0	0	0	.000
Pope, ph-rf	3	3	0	0	0	0	0	0	.000
Mossi, p	3	0	0	0	0	0	0	0	.000
Garcia, p	2	0	0	0	0	0	0	0	.000
Houtteman, p	1	0	0	0	0	0	0	0	.000
Narleski, p	2	0	0	0	0	0	0	0	.000
Newhouser, p	1	0	0	0	0	0	0	0	.000
Lemon, p-ph	3	6	0	0	0	0	0	0	.000
Totals	4	137	9	26	5	1	3	9	.190

COMPOSITE PITCHING AVERAGES

New York Giants

Pitcher	G.	IP.	H.	R.	ER.	BB.	SO.	W.	L.	ERA.
Grissom	1	2⅔	1	0	0	3	2	1	0	0.00
Wilhelm	2	2⅓	1	0	0	0	3	0	0	0.00
Antonelli	2	10⅔	8	1	1	7	12	1	0	0.84
Liddle	2	7	5	4	1	1	2	1	0	1.29
Gomez	1	7⅓	4	2	2	3	2	1	0	2.35
Maglie	1	7	7	2	2	2	2	0	0	2.57
Totals	4	37	26	9	6	16	23	4	0	1.46

Cleveland Indians

Pitcher	G.	IP.	H.	R.	ER.	BB.	SO.	W.	L.	ERA.
Mossi	3	4	3	0	0	0	1	0	0	0.00
Narleski	2	4	1	1	1	1	2	0	0	2.25
Wynn	1	7	4	3	3	2	5	0	1	3.86
Houtteman	1	2	2	1	1	1	1	0	0	4.50
Garcia	2	5	6	4	3	4	4	0	1	5.40
Lemon	2	13⅓	16	11	10	8	11	0	2	6.75
Newhouser	1	0	1	1	1	1	0	0	0	....
Totals	4	35⅓	33	21	19	17	24	0	4	4.84

1955
BROOKLYN DODGERS
VS.
NEW YORK YANKEES

Brooklyn, the Borough of Churches, had long kept the faith. Whenever a World Series title had been denied the residents' beloved Dodgers, fans and players alike would grudgingly but optimistically "wait until next year."

"Next year," though, was a long time coming. Dem Bums had won National League pennants in 1916, 1920, 1941, 1947, 1949, 1952 and 1953—but never had gone on to rule as Series champions. And while no one quite realized it when the '55 fall classic opened at Yankee Stadium, time was running out on Brooklyn's quest to hoist a Series championship banner.

Surely 1955 would be the year, Brooklyn partisans reasoned. The Dodgers won 10 consecutive games to start the season, built a 22-2 record in the first four weeks and cruised to the National League pennant with a 13½-game spread over the second-place Milwaukee Braves.

But despite the domination of their N.L. brethren, the Dodgers were, once again, up against a team that had made a habit of dominating *them*. The dreaded Yankees, after a one-year lapse, were returning to the Series as American League champions. And of the Dodgers' seven World Series setbacks, the last five had come at the hands of the Yanks.

Dodgers ace Don Newcombe, a 20-game winner in 1955, was called upon in Game 1. But big Newk, never a winner in Series play, yielded two home runs to Joe Collins and a third to Yankee rookie Elston Howard and Brooklyn went down to a 6-5 defeat. In Game 2, 35-year-old lefthander Tommy Byrne, a Yankee standout of yesteryear who had made it back to New York after winning 20 games in the minor

Catcher Roy Campanella grabs Johnny Podres, the jubilant Game 7 winning pitcher, as Don Hoak joins the celebration for the first-ever championship in Dodger history.

leagues in 1954, stopped the Dodgers on five hits and posted a 4-2 triumph.

At this juncture, one could commiserate with Brooklyn fans whose thoughts undoubtedly were turning toward 1956.

Down two games to none, the Dodgers hardly could be heartened by the pitching matchup for

Game 3: Johnny Podres, who had struggled to a 9-10 season record for Brooklyn, against 17-game winner Bob Turley of the Yankees.

Podres, working on his 23rd birthday, brought Brooklyn back to life by holding the Yankees to seven hits in an 8-3 triumph at Ebbets Field. One of those hits

was a second-inning home run by Mickey Mantle, whose leg injury allowed him to play in only two other Series games (and one of those was as a pinch-hitter).

With Roy Campanella, Gil Hodges and Duke Snider slamming homers, the Dodgers then tied the Series at 2-2 with an 8-5 victory. Snider, who also had homered in Game 1, drilled two more home runs in Game 5 in support of rookie pitcher Roger Craig, who worked six-plus innings in a 5-3 decision that produced his first Series triumph. Brooklyn had forged ahead, three games to two, but now the classic would return to the Bronx.

Buoyed by Craig's performance, Dodgers Manager Walter Alston turned to another youngster, Karl Spooner, who had burst upon the major league scene with 27 strikeouts in two games at the tail-end of the 1954 season. Spooner retired only one Yankee, however, and was pounded for five runs—three coming on Bill Skowron's homer. While relievers Russ Meyer and Ed Roebuck held the Yankees at bay, the damage had been done. New York prevailed, 5-1, as Whitey Ford tossed a four-hitter. The Series was deadlocked.

Alston, having started six different pitchers in six games, came back with Podres for Game 7. Yankees Manager Casey Stengel opted for Byrne.

The game was scoreless until the fourth inning when Campanella doubled and scored on a single by Hodges. In the sixth, Pee Wee Reese singled and Snider, attempting to sacrifice, reached base safely when he brushed the ball from Skowron's glove while sprinting down the line. Campanella bunted the runners to second and third, and Furillo was walked intentionally. Bob Grim relieved Byrne at this point, and Hodges lofted a sacrifice fly. A walk to Don Hoak reloaded the bases, but Grim and the Yankees escaped when George Shuba, batting for Don Zimmer, grounded out. Nevertheless, Podres' lead had grown to 2-0.

The departure of second baseman Zimmer from the game re-

sulted in defensive changes that paid immediate—and crucial—dividends for the Dodgers. In the bottom of the sixth, Jim Gilliam moved from left field to second base, and reserve Sandy Amoros was inserted as Gilliam's replacement in left. The Yankees' Billy Martin drew a leadoff walk in the sixth, and Gil McDougald followed with a bunt single. Yogi Berra then sliced a fly ball just inside the left-field foul line at Yankee Stadium and Amoros, shaded toward center with a lefthanded power hitter at the plate, seemed to have little chance of getting to the ball. The fleet Amoros raced toward the line, however, and made a glove-handed grab. A relay from Amoros to Reese to Hodges doubled McDougald at first. Had Berra's drive dropped safely, the game would have been tied (both runners were off with the crack of the bat) and Berra would have been in scoring position with no one out. For once, though, a "what if " situation had gone the Dodgers' way.

Podres battled out of another jam—two on, one out—in the eighth, and entered the ninth clinging to the two-run lead. Having surrendered eight hits and two walks, the lefthander had kept Brooklyn fans on the edge of their seats all day. He also had kept them on the edge of their first-ever Series championship.

Skowron started the Yankees' ninth by bouncing back to Podres. Bob Cerv then flied to Amoros. Howard loomed as the final obstacle. Podres induced him to ground to shortstop Reese, whose throw to Hodges marked the end of the game—the Dodgers had held on, 2-0—and the beginning of bedlam in the Borough of Churches.

Brooklyn's Series championship came none too soon. The Dodgers would play only two more seasons in the borough before relocating in Southern California. Dem Bums would win another pennant, in 1956, but the '55 World Series title would stand not only as Brooklyn's first Series crown, but as the borough's only such achievement.

Game 1

Wednesday, September 28, At New York

Brooklyn	AB.	R.	H.	RBI.	PO.	A.
Gilliam, lf	3	0	0	0	2	0
Reese, ss	5	0	1	0	2	5
Snider, cf	5	1	2	1	1	0
Campanella, c	5	0	0	0	5	1
Furillo, rf	4	2	3	1	1	0
Hodges, 1b	4	0	1	0	12	1
J. Robinson, 3b	4	2	1	0	0	2
Zimmer, 2b	2	0	1	2	1	3
Newcombe, p	3	0	0	0	0	1
Bessent, p	0	0	0	0	0	1
bKellert	1	0	1	0	0	0
cHoak	0	0	0	0	0	0
Labine, p	0	0	0	0	0	0
Totals	36	5	10	4	24	14

New York	AB.	R.	H.	RBI.	PO.	A.
Bauer, rf	4	0	2	0	3	0
McDougald, 3b	4	0	1	0	2	1
Noren, cf	4	0	0	1	4	0
Berra, c	3	1	1	0	5	0
Collins, 1b	3	3	2	3	6	1
Howard, lf	3	1	1	2	1	0
Martin, 2b	3	0	2	0	2	3
Rizzuto, ss	2	0	0	0	3	2
aE. Robinson	0	0	0	0	0	0
J. Coleman, ss	1	0	0	0	0	0
Ford, p	2	1	0	0	1	3
Grim, p	0	0	0	0	0	0
Totals	29	6	9	6	27	10

Brooklyn .... 0 2 1 0 0 0 0 2 0—5
New York .... 0 2 1 1 0 2 0 0 x—6

Brooklyn	IP.	H.	R.	ER.	BB.	SO.
Newcombe (L)	5⅔	8	6	6	2	4
Bessent	1⅓	0	0	0	0	0
Labine	1	1	0	0	1	0

New York	IP.	H.	R.	ER.	BB.	SO.
Ford (W)	8	9	5	3	4	2
Grim	1	1	0	0	0	2

aBatted for Rizzuto in sixth when Martin was out attempting to steal home. bSingled for Bessent in eighth. cRan for Kellert in eighth. E—McDougald. DP—Brooklyn 2, New York 1. LOB—Brooklyn 9, New York 2. 3B—J. Robinson, Martin. HR—Furillo, Howard, Snider, Collins 2. SB—J. Robinson. SF—Zimmer. U—Summers (A.L.), Ballanfant (N.L.), Honochick (A.L.), Dascoli (N.L.), Flaherty (A.L.) and Donatelli (N.L.). T—2:31. A—63,869.

Game 2

Thursday, September 29, At New York

Brooklyn	AB.	R.	H.	RBI.	PO.	A.
Gilliam, lf	4	0	1	1	0	1
Reese, ss	4	1	2	0	2	3
Snider, cf	4	0	1	1	2	0
Campanella, c	3	0	0	0	11	2
Furillo, rf	3	0	0	0	0	0
Hodges, 1b	3	0	0	0	6	1
J. Robinson, 3b	2	1	0	0	1	1
Zimmer, 2b	3	0	1	0	2	2
Loes, p	1	0	0	0	0	0
Bessent, p	0	0	0	0	0	0
cKellert	1	0	0	0	0	0
Spooner, p	0	0	0	0	0	1
dHoak	0	0	0	0	0	0
Labine, p	0	0	0	0	0	0
Totals	28	2	5	2	24	11

New York	AB.	R.	H.	RBI.	PO.	A.
Bauer, rf	1	0	1	0	3	0
Cerv, cf	3	0	0	0	0	0
McDougald, 3b	4	0	1	0	1	0
Noren, cf-lf	3	0	0	0	4	0
Berra, c	3	1	2	0	6	1
Collins, 1b	3	1	0	0	5	0
Howard, lf-rf	4	1	1	1	2	1
Martin, 2b	3	1	1	1	2	3
Rizzuto, ss	1	0	1	0	2	1
aE. Robinson	0	0	0	0	0	0
bJ. Coleman, ss	1	0	0	0	2	2
Byrne, p	3	0	1	2	0	0
Totals	29	4	8	4	27	8

Brooklyn .... 0 0 0 1 1 0 0 0 0—2
New York .... 0 0 0 4 0 0 x—4

Brooklyn	IP.	H.	R.	ER.	BB.	SO.
Loes (L)	3⅔	7	4	4	1	5
Bessent	⅓	0	0	0	0	0
Spooner	3	1	0	0	1	5
Labine	1	0	0	0	0	1

New York	IP.	H.	R.	ER.	BB.	SO.
Byrne (W)	9	5	2	2	5	6

aHit by pitch for Rizzuto in fourth. bRan for E. Robinson in fourth. cHit into double play for Bessent in fifth. dWalked for Spooner in eighth. E—Zimmer 2. DP—Brooklyn 3, New York 3. LOB—Brooklyn 4, New York 5. 2B—Reese. HBP—By Loes (Berra, E. Robinson). U—Ballanfant (N.L.), Honochick (A.L.), Dascoli (N.L.), Summers (A.L.), Flaherty (A.L.) and Donatelli (N.L.). T—2:28. A—64,707.

Game 3

Friday, September 30, At Brooklyn

New York	AB.	R.	H.	RBI.	PO.	A.
Cerv, lf-cf	4	0	0	0	3	0
McDougald, 3b	4	0	1	0	0	3
Berra, c	4	0	1	0	4	0

	AB.	R.	H.	RBI.	PO.	A.
Mantle, cf-rf	4	1	1	1	2	0
Skowron, 1b	4	1	2	0	5	2
Howard, rf-lf	4	0	0	0	5	0
Martin, 2b	4	0	0	0	3	0
Rizzuto, ss	2	1	1	0	2	1
Turley, p	1	0	0	0	0	0
Morgan, p	0	0	0	0	0	0
aBauer	1	0	0	0	0	0
Kucks, p	0	0	0	0	0	0
bCarey	1	0	1	1	0	0
Sturdivant, p	0	0	0	0	0	1
Totals	33	3	7	2	24	7

Brooklyn	AB.	R.	H.	RBI.	PO.	A.
Gilliam, 2b	3	1	1	1	2	3
Reese, ss	3	1	1	2	1	2
Snider, cf	4	1	1	0	1	0
Campanella, c	5	1	3	3	6	0
Furillo, rf	5	0	1	1	1	0
Hodges, 1b	5	0	0	0	14	0
Robinson, 3b	5	2	2	0	0	7
Amoros, lf	1	1	1	1	2	1
Podres, p	3	1	1	0	0	1
Totals	34	8	11	8	27	14

New York ......0 2 0 0 0 0 1 0 0—3
Brooklyn ......2 2 0 2 0 0 2 0 x—8

New York	IP.	H.	R.	ER.	BB.	SO.
Turley (L)	1⅓	3	4	4	2	1
Morgan	2⅔	3	2	2	3	1
Kucks	2	1	0	0	1	0
Sturdivant	2	4	2	2	1	0

Brooklyn	IP.	H.	R.	ER.	BB.	SO.
Podres (W)	9	7	3	2	2	6

aFlied out for Morgan in fifth. bTripled for Kucks in seventh. E—Campanella. DP—Brooklyn 1. LOB—New York 5, Brooklyn 11. 2B—Skowron, Furillo, Robinson, Campanella. 3B—Carey. HR—Campanella, Mantle. SH—Podres. HBP—By Turley (Amoros). U—Honochick (A.L.), Dascoli (N.L.), Summers (A.L.), Ballanfant (N.L.), Donatelli (N.L.) and Flaherty (A.L.). T—2:20. A—34,209.

Game 4

Saturday, October 1, At Brooklyn

New York	AB.	R.	H.	RBI.	PO.	A.
Noren, cf	5	0	1	0	3	0
McDougald, 3b	5	1	1	1	1	1
Mantle, rf	5	0	1	0	2	0
Berra, c	3	0	1	0	4	1
Collins, 1b	2	2	0	0	11	1
Howard, lf	3	1	1	0	0	0
Martin, 2b	4	1	2	2	1	3
Rizzuto, ss	3	0	1	1	2	2
Larsen, p	2	0	0	0	0	1
Kucks, p	0	0	0	0	0	1
aE. Robinson	1	0	1	1	0	0
bCarroll	0	0	0	0	0	0
R. Coleman, p	0	0	0	0	0	0
Morgan, p	0	0	0	0	0	0
cSkowron	1	0	0	0	0	0
Sturdivant, p	0	0	0	0	0	0
Totals	34	5	9	5	24	10

Brooklyn	AB.	R.	H.	RBI.	PO.	A.
Gilliam, 2b	4	1	2	1	1	4
Reese, ss	4	1	2	0	1	2
Snider, cf	4	1	1	3	6	0
Campanella, c	5	2	3	1	4	0
Furillo, rf	5	1	2	0	1	0
Hodges, 1b	4	1	3	3	11	0
J. Robinson, 3b	4	0	0	0	1	2
Amoros, lf	3	1	1	0	2	0
Erskine, p	1	0	0	0	0	1
Bessent, p	1	0	0	0	0	1
Labine, p	2	0	0	0	0	2
Totals	37	8	14	8	27	12

New York ......1 1 0 1 0 2 0 0 0—5
Brooklyn ......0 0 1 3 3 0 1 0 x—8

New York	IP.	H.	R.	ER.	BB.	SO.
Larsen (L)	4†	5	5	5	2	2
Kucks	1	3	2	2	0	1
R. Coleman	1‡	5	1	1	0	1
Morgan	1	0	0	0	0	0
Sturdivant	1	1	0	0	1	0

Brooklyn	IP.	H.	R.	ER.	BB.	SO.
Erskine	3*	3	3	3	2	3
Bessent	1⅔	3	0	0	1	1
Labine (W)	4⅓	3	2	2	1	0

*Pitched to two batters in fourth.
†Pitched to one batter in fifth.
‡Pitched to three batters in seventh.

aSingled for Kucks in sixth. bRan for E. Robinson in sixth. cFlied out for Morgan in eighth. DP—Brooklyn 1. LOB—New York 7, Brooklyn 9. 2B—Gilliam, Campanella, Martin. HR—McDougald, Campanella, Hodges, Snider. SB—Rizzuto, Collins, Gilliam. SH—Howard, Reese. U—Dascoli (N.L.), Summers (A.L.), Ballanfant (N.L.), Honochick (A.L.), Donatelli (N.L.) and Flaherty (A.L.). T—2:57. A—36,242.

Game 5

Sunday, October 2, At Brooklyn

New York	AB.	R.	H.	RBI.	PO.	A.
Howard, lf	4	0	1	0	0	0
Noren, cf	4	0	0	0	2	0
McDougald, 3b	3	0	0	0	1	2
Berra, c	4	2	2	1	9	1
Collins, rf-1b	3	0	0	0	0	0
E. Robinson, 1b	2	0	1	0	6	0
cCarroll	0	0	0	0	0	0
Bauer, rf	0	0	0	0	0	0
Martin, 2b	4	0	1	1	4	3
Rizzuto, ss	1	0	0	0	2	0
aSkowron	1	0	0	0	0	0
J. Coleman, ss	1	0	0	0	0	1
dCarey	1	0	0	0	0	0
Grim, p	2	0	0	0	0	1
bCerv	1	1	1	1	0	0
Turley, p	0	0	0	0	0	1
eByrne	1	0	0	0	0	0
Totals	32	3	6	3	24	9

Brooklyn	AB.	R.	H.	RBI.	PO.	A.
Gilliam, 2b	3	0	1	0	1	5
Reese, ss	3	0	0	0	4	3
Snider, cf	4	2	3	2	0	0
Campanella, c	3	0	0	0	6	0
Furillo, rf	4	1	1	0	1	0
Hodges, 1b	3	1	2	0	14	1
J. Robinson, 3b	3	0	1	1	0	3
Amoros, lf	4	1	1	2	1	0
Craig, p	0	0	0	0	0	1
Labine, p	2	0	0	0	0	1
Totals	29	5	9	5	27	14

New York ......0 0 0 1 0 0 1 1 0—3
Brooklyn ......0 2 1 0 1 0 0 1 x—5

New York	IP.	H.	R.	ER.	BB.	SO.
Grim (L)	6	6	4	4	4	5
Turley	2	3	1	1	1	5

Brooklyn	IP.	H.	R.	ER.	BB.	SO.
Craig (W)	6*	4	2	2	5	4
Labine	3	2	1	1	0	1

*Pitched to two batters in seventh.

aFouled out for Rizzuto in fourth. bHomered for Grim in seventh. cRan for E. Robinson in eighth. dGrounded out for J. Coleman in ninth. eGrounded out for Turley in ninth. E—Reese, J. Robinson. DP—New York 2, Brooklyn 3. LOB—New York 7, Brooklyn 7. 2B—Snider. HR—Amoros, Snider 2, Cerv, Berra. SH—Craig, Hodges. U—Summers (A.L.), Ballanfant (N.L.), Honochick (A.L.), Dascoli (N.L.), Donatelli (N.L.) and Flaherty (A.L.). T—2:40. A—36,796.

Game 6

Monday, October 3, At New York

Brooklyn	AB.	R.	H.	RBI.	PO.	A.
Gilliam, 2b-lf	3	0	1	0	0	0
Reese, ss	4	1	1	0	3	2
Snider, cf	1	0	0	0	1	0
aZimmer, 2b	2	0	0	0	1	1
Campanella, c	3	0	0	0	5	0
Furillo, rf	3	0	1	1	1	0
Hodges, 1b	3	0	0	0	7	1
J. Robinson, 3b	4	0	0	0	2	3
Amoros, lf-cf	4	0	1	0	2	0
Spooner, p	0	0	0	0	0	0
Meyer, p	2	0	0	0	0	1
cKellert	1	0	0	0	0	0
Roebuck, p	0	0	0	0	2	0
Totals	30	1	4	1	24	8

New York	AB.	R.	H.	RBI.	PO.	A.
Rizzuto, ss	3	1	0	0	1	5
Martin, 2b	4	0	1	0	4	2
McDougald, 3b	3	1	0	0	0	5
Berra, c	3	1	2	1	8	0
Bauer, rf	4	1	3	1	0	0
Skowron, 1b	2	1	1	3	6	0
bCollins, 1b	1	0	0	0	5	1
Cerv, cf	4	0	1	0	2	0
Howard, lf	4	0	0	0	1	0
Noren, lf	0	0	0	0	0	0
Ford, p	4	0	0	0	0	1
Totals	32	5	8	5	27	14

Brooklyn ......0 0 0 1 0 0 0 0 0—1
New York ......5 0 0 0 0 0 0 0 x—5

Brooklyn	IP.	H.	R.	ER.	BB.	SO.
Spooner (L)	⅓	3	5	5	2	1
Meyer	5⅔	4	0	0	2	4
Roebuck	2	1	0	0	0	0

New York	IP.	H.	R.	ER.	BB.	SO.
Ford (W)	9	4	1	1	4	8

aStruck out for Snider in fourth. bWalked for Skowron in fifth. cPopped out for Meyer in seventh. E—J. Robinson. DP—Brooklyn 1, New York 1. LOB—Brooklyn 7, New York 7. HR—Skowron. SB—Rizzuto. HBP—By Ford (Furillo). WP—Ford. U—Ballanfant (N.L.), Honochick (A.L.), Dascoli (N.L.), Summers (A.L.), Flaherty (A.L.) and Donatelli (N.L.). T—2:34. A—64,022.

Game 7

Tuesday, October 4, At New York

Brooklyn	AB.	R.	H.	RBI.	PO.	A.
Gilliam, lf-2b	4	0	1	0	2	0
Reese, ss	4	1	1	0	2	6
Snider, cf	3	0	0	0	2	0
Campanella, c	3	1	1	0	5	0
Furillo, rf	3	0	0	0	3	0
Hodges, 1b	2	0	1	2	10	0
Hoak, 3b	3	0	1	0	1	1
Zimmer, 2b	2	0	0	0	0	2
aShuba	1	0	0	0	0	0
Amoros, lf	0	0	0	0	2	1
Podres, p	4	0	0	0	0	1
Totals	29	2	5	2	27	11

New York	AB.	R.	H.	RBI.	PO.	A.
Rizzuto, ss	3	0	1	0	1	3
Martin, 2b	3	0	1	0	1	6
McDougald, 3b	4	0	3	0	1	1
Berra, c	4	0	1	0	4	1
Bauer, rf	4	0	0	0	1	0
Skowron, 1b	4	0	1	0	11	1
Cerv, cf	4	0	0	0	5	0
Howard, lf	4	0	1	0	2	0
Byrne, p	2	0	0	0	0	2
Grim, p	0	0	0	0	1	0
bMantle	1	0	0	0	0	0
Turley, p	0	0	0	0	0	0
Totals	33	0	8	0	27	14

Brooklyn ......0 0 0 1 0 1 0 0 0—2
New York ......0 0 0 0 0 0 0 0 0—0

Brooklyn	IP.	H.	R.	ER.	BB.	SO.
Podres (W)	9	8	0	0	2	4

New York	IP.	H.	R.	ER.	BB.	SO.
Byrne (L)	5⅓	3	2	1	3	2
Grim	1⅔	1	0	0	1	1
Turley	2	1	0	0	1	1

aGrounded out for Zimmer in sixth. bPopped out for Grim in seventh. E—Skowron. DP—Brooklyn 1. LOB—Brooklyn 8, New York 8. 2B—Skowron, Campanella, Berra. SH—Snider, Campanella. SF—Hodges. WP—Grim. U—Honochick (A.L.), Dascoli (N.L.), Summers (A.L.), Ballanfant (N.L.), Flaherty (A.L.) and Donatelli (N.L.). T—2:44. A—62,465.

COMPOSITE BATTING AVERAGES

Brooklyn Dodgers

Player-Position	G.	AB.	R.	H.	2B.	3B.	HR.	RBI.	BA.
Amoros, lf-cf	5	12	3	4	0	0	1	3	.333
Kellert, ph	3	3	0	1	0	0	0	0	.333
Hoak, pr-ph-3b	3	3	0	1	0	0	0	0	.333
Snider, cf	7	25	5	8	1	0	4	7	.320
Reese, ss	7	27	5	8	1	0	0	2	.296
Furillo, rf	7	27	4	8	1	0	1	3	.296
Gilliam, lf-2b	7	24	2	7	1	0	0	3	.292
Hodges, 1b	7	24	2	7	0	0	1	5	.292
Campanella, c	7	27	4	7	3	0	2	4	.259
Zimmer, 2b-ph	4	9	0	2	0	0	0	2	.222
J. Robinson, 3b	6	22	5	4	1	1	0	1	.182
Podres, p	2	7	1	1	0	0	0	0	.143
Newcombe, p	1	3	0	0	0	0	0	0	.000
Bessent, p	3	1	0	0	0	0	0	0	.000
Labine, p	4	4	0	0	0	0	0	0	.000
Loes, p	1	1	0	0	0	0	0	0	.000
Spooner, p	2	0	0	0	0	0	0	0	.000
Erskine, p	1	1	0	0	0	0	0	0	.000
Craig, p	1	0	0	0	0	0	0	0	.000
Meyer, p	1	2	0	0	0	0	0	0	.000
Roebuck, p	1	0	0	0	0	0	0	0	.000
Shuba, ph	1	1	0	0	0	0	0	0	.000
Totals	7	223	31	58	8	1	9	30	.260

New York Yankees

Player-Position	G.	AB.	R.	H.	2B.	3B.	HR.	RBI.	BA.
E. Rob'son, ph-1b	4	3	0	2	0	0	0	1	.667
Carey, ph	2	2	0	1	0	1	0	1	.500
Bauer, rf-ph	6	14	1	6	0	0	0	1	.429
Berra, c	7	24	5	10	1	0	1	2	.417
Skowron, 1b-ph	5	12	2	4	2	0	1	3	.333
Martin, 2b	7	25	2	8	1	1	0	4	.320
Rizzuto, ss	7	15	2	4	0	0	0	1	.267
McDougald, 3b	7	27	2	7	0	0	1	1	.259
Mantle, cf-rf-ph	3	10	1	2	0	0	1	1	.200
Howard, lf-rf	7	26	3	5	0	0	1	3	.192
Collins, 1b-rf-ph	5	12	6	2	0	0	2	3	.167
Byrne, p-ph	3	6	0	1	0	0	0	2	.167
Cerv, cf-lf-ph	5	16	1	2	0	0	1	1	.125
Noren, cf-lf	5	16	0	1	0	0	0	1	.063
J. Coleman, ss-pr	3	3	0	0	0	0	0	0	.000
Ford, p	2	6	1	0	0	0	0	0	.000
Grim, p	3	2	0	0	0	0	0	0	.000
Turley, p	3	1	0	0	0	0	0	0	.000
Morgan, p	2	0	0	0	0	0	0	0	.000
Kucks, p	2	0	0	0	0	0	0	0	.000
Sturdivant, p	2	0	0	0	0	0	0	0	.000
Larsen, p	1	2	0	0	0	0	0	0	.000
R. Coleman, p	1	0	0	0	0	0	0	0	.000
Carroll, pr	2	0	0	0	0	0	0	0	.000
Totals	7	222	26	55	4	2	8	25	.248

COMPOSITE PITCHING AVERAGES

Brooklyn Dodgers

Pitcher	G.	IP.	H.	R.	ER.	BB.	SO.	W.	L.	ERA.
Meyer	1	5⅔	4	0	0	2	4	0	0	0.00
Bessent	3	3⅓	3	0	0	1	1	0	0	0.00
Roebuck	1	2	1	0	0	0	0	0	0	0.00
Podres	2	18	15	3	2	4	10	2	0	1.00
Labine	4	9⅓	6	3	3	2	2	1	0	2.89
Craig	1	6	4	2	2	5	4	1	0	3.00
Erskine	1	3	3	3	3	2	3	0	0	9.00
Newcombe	1	5⅔	8	6	6	2	4	0	1	9.53
Loes	1	3⅔	7	4	4	1	5	0	1	9.82
Spooner	2	3⅓	4	5	5	3	6	0	1	13.50
Totals	7	60	55	26	25	22	39	4	3	3.75

New York Yankees

Pitcher	G.	IP.	H.	R.	ER.	BB.	SO.	W.	L.	ERA.
Byrne	2	14⅓	8	4	3	8	8	1	1	1.88
Ford	2	17	13	6	4	8	10	2	0	2.12
Grim	3	8⅔	8	4	4	5	8	0	1	4.15
Morgan	2	3⅔	3	2	2	3	1	0	0	4.91
Kucks	2	3	4	2	2	1	1	0	0	6.00
Sturdivant	2	3	5	2	2	2	0	0	0	6.00
Turley	3	5⅓	7	5	5	4	7	0	1	8.44
R. Coleman	1	1	5	1	1	0	1	0	0	9.00
Larsen	1	4	5	5	5	2	2	0	1	11.25
Totals	7	60	58	31	28	33	38	3	4	4.20

1956
NEW YORK YANKEES
VS.
BROOKLYN DODGERS

The last half of the sixth inning of Game 2 of the 1956 World Series was about to start, and the New York Yankees were sending their seventh pitcher of the day into action. Already, the Brooklyn Dodgers had scored 11 runs.

In the Series opener, a game in which New York had used four pitchers, Brooklyn cuffed Yankee hurlers for six runs in the first four innings.

While the Yanks had reason to wonder if their pitching would turn around, the Dodgers had reason to wonder how quickly they might be able to wrap up *another* Series championship. This from a team that only 12 months earlier had finally won its first fall-classic title. My, how things change.

And how quickly things can turn around. A pitching staff included.

After trotting out 11 pitchers in the first two games of the 1956 Series, contests they lost by 6-3 and 13-8 scores, the Yankees proceeded to get five consecutive complete-game performances. They received those efforts from five different pitchers, who combined to allow the Dodgers a meager six runs and 21 hits in 45⅔ innings.

The mound work that New York got in Game 5 shot the Yanks into the Series lead for the first time. And it shot the pitcher into the headlines for all time.

Don Larsen, a 27-year-old right-hander who couldn't get through the second inning in Game 2, was New York Manager Casey Stengel's fifth-game pitching selection following 5-3 and 6-2 Yankee victories that deadlocked the Series. While Larsen had compiled a 3-21 record for Baltimore in 1954, he was 20-7 in two seasons with the Yankees after being obtained from the Orioles in the biggest trade (17 players overall) in major league history.

Larsen's pitching opponent was 39-year-old Sal (The Barber) Maglie, the former New York Giants star who didn't look quite right in Dodger blue. But Maglie, obtained on waivers from the Cleveland Indians in May, looked just like his old intimidating self once he took the mound for Brooklyn. He won 13 of 18 regular-season decisions for Manager Walter Alston's team, including a heat-of-the-pennant-race no-hitter against the Philadelphia Phillies.

Maglie got off to a great start in Game 5 of the '56 Series at Yankee Stadium. In fact, with two out in the Yankees' fourth, he was pitching perfect baseball. Eleven Yankees up, 11 Yankees down. Surely this couldn't continue. No one had ever thrown a Series no-hitter, let alone a perfect game (and the majors hadn't seen a regular-season perfect game in 34 years). The 12th man to bat for the Yankees was Mickey Mantle, who was coming off a Triple Crown season (.353 batting average, 52 home runs and 130 runs batted in). And Mantle drilled a homer into the right-field stands, near the foul pole.

No, this perfect-game pitching couldn't and didn't continue. For Maglie, that is. Incredibly, Larsen was matching the veteran right-hander pitch for pitch—and then some. Through four innings, only one man had reached base on either side and that batter, Mantle, had touched all four of them.

While Larsen (employing a no-windup style) continued to set down the Dodgers 1-2-3, helped by a great one-handed catch by Mantle of Gil Hodges' long drive in the fifth, Maglie yielded a walk in the fifth and another run in the sixth on Andy Carey's single, Lar-

sen's sacrifice and Hank Bauer's base hit. After six innings, the Yankees had two runs and four hits (Joe Collins followed Bauer's blow with another single) and the Dodgers had no runs, no hits and no baserunners.

Larsen rolled right along, getting Jim Gilliam on a ground ball and Pee Wee Reese and Duke Snider on fly balls in the seventh and Jackie Robinson on a grounder, Hodges on an infield liner and Sandy Amoros on a fly ball in the eighth. Twenty-four consecutive batters retired.

Maglie permitted a single to Billy Martin and a walk to Gil McDougald in the seventh, but squirmed out of trouble. And, finishing with a flourish, he struck out the side in the Yankees' eighth.

Now, it was the ninth and 64,519 fans at Yankee Stadium watched intently as Larsen prepared to face Carl Furillo, Roy Campanella and a pinch-hitter for Maglie. With the count at 1-and-2, Furillo fouled off two pitches and then flied to Bauer in right. Campanella fouled off one pitch before grounding out to second baseman Martin. And now it was Dale Mitchell, a .312 career hitter, batting for Maglie. Mitchell, purchased from Cleveland in late July, took a ball outside and then a called strike. The lefthanded hitter swung and missed at the third pitch and fouled the fourth into the stands. Then came Larsen's 97th pitch of the game: strike three, called.

While Mitchell questioned the call of retirement-bound Babe Pinelli, umpiring for the last time behind the plate in his career, the pitch on the outside edge of the plate sent catcher Yogi Berra leaping into Larsen's arms and Larsen leaping into the record books.

The triumphant New York Yankees mob pitcher Johnny Kucks after the righthander's three-hit, Game 7 victory in 1956.

The first no-hitter—and perfect game—in World Series history had just been thrown.

Larsen's seven-strikeout, 2-0 history-maker kept New York on a winning course. In Game 3, a three-run homer by late-August acquisition Enos Slaughter and eight-hit pitching by Whitey Ford had sparked the Yankees to victory, while Tom Sturdivant's six-hitter and homers by Bauer and Mantle highlighted the American Leaguers' triumph in Game 4.

The Yanks were halted in Game 6, however, when Dodgers relief ace Clem Labine was pressed into starting duty and responded with a 10-inning shutout. Brooklyn prevailed, 1-0, against Bob Turley when Yankee left fielder Slaughter misplayed Robinson's bottom-of-the-10th drive into a game-win-ning single.

Don Newcombe, the ace of the Dodgers' staff but never a success in postseason play, and second-year major leaguer Johnny Kucks were matched in the decisive Game 7. And Newcombe, winner of baseball's first Cy Young Award after his 27-victory season in '56, again took his lumps. He was rocked for a pair of two-run homers by Berra, who had blast-ed a bases-full shot off Newk in Game 2, and also yielded a bases-empty home run to Elston Howard. With Bill Skowron club-bing a seventh-inning grand slam off Brooklyn's Roger Craig, Kucks was able to coast to a three-hit, 9-0 triumph that com-pleted the revival of the New Yorkers' pitching staff and re-turned the Yankees to the top of the baseball world.

The Dodgers had their mo-ments, all right, starting with a complete-game victory by Maglie in Game 1, continuing with a memorable comeback from a 6-0 deficit in Game 2 and concluding with Labine's superlative effort in Game 6.

But one of the special moments in baseball history, as supplied by Larsen, belonged to the New York Yankees. And so did an-other World Series champion-ship.

Game 1

Wednesday, October 3, At Brooklyn

New York	AB.	R.	H.	RBI.	PO.	A.
Bauer, rf	5	0	2	0	3	0
Slaughter, lf	5	1	3	0	3	0
Mantle, cf	3	1	1	2	4	1
Berra, c	3	0	0	0	4	0
Skowron, 1b	4	0	0	0	5	3
McDougald, ss	4	0	0	0	2	6
Martin, 2b-3b	3	1	1	1	2	1
Carey, 3b	3	0	1	0	0	1
cCollins	1	0	0	0	0	0
Turley, p	0	0	0	0	0	0
Ford, p	1	0	0	0	1	0
aWilson	1	0	0	0	0	0
Kucks, p	0	0	0	0	0	0
bCerv	1	0	1	0	0	0
Morgan, p	0	0	0	0	0	0
dByrne	1	0	0	0	0	0
G. Coleman, 2b	0	0	0	0	0	0
Totals	35	3	9	3	24	12

Brooklyn	AB.	R.	H.	RBI.	PO.	A.
Gilliam, 2b	3	0	1	0	3	1
Reese, ss	4	1	2	0	1	1
Snider, cf	3	1	1	0	1	0
Robinson, 3b	4	1	1	1	2	2
Hodges, 1b	4	2	2	3	4	0
Furillo, rf	4	0	1	1	2	0
Campanella, c	4	1	1	0	11	1
Amoros, lf	3	0	1	1	3	0
Maglie, p	3	0	0	0	0	0
Totals	32	6	9	6	27	5

New York...............2 0 0 1 0 0 0 0 0—3
Brooklyn...............0 2 3 1 0 0 0 0 x—6

New York	IP.	H.	R.	ER.	BB.	SO.
Ford (L)	3	6	5	5	0	1
Kucks	2	2	1	1	0	1
Morgan	2	1	0	0	2	0
Turley	1	0	0	0	0	2

Brooklyn	IP.	H.	R.	ER.	BB.	SO.
Maglie (W)	9	9	3	3	4	10

aStruck out for Ford in fourth. bSingled for Kucks in sixth. cStruck out for Carey in eighth. dFouled out for Morgan in eighth. E—Skowron. DP—New York 1, Brooklyn 1. LOB—New York 9, Brooklyn 4. 2B—Furillo, Campanella. HR—Mantle, Robinson, Hodges, Martin. SB—Gilliam. U—Pinelli (N.L.), Soar (A.L.), Boggess (N.L.), Napp (A.L.), Gorman (N.L.) and Runge (A.L.). T—2:32. A—34,479.

Game 2

Friday, October 5, At Brooklyn

New York	AB.	R.	H.	RBI.	PO.	A.
McDougald, ss	3	0	1	0	1	0
Slaughter, lf	4	3	2	1	1	0
Mantle, cf	4	1	1	0	2	0
Berra, c	4	1	2	4	10	0
Collins, 1b	4	0	1	2	3	0
Bauer, rf	5	0	1	0	2	0
Martin, 3b-2b	4	1	1	0	3	2
G. Coleman, 2b	2	0	0	0	2	2
dSkowron	1	0	0	0	0	0
Carey, 3b	0	0	0	0	0	1
Larsen, p	1	1	1	1	0	0
Kucks, p	0	0	0	0	0	0
Byrne, p	0	0	0	0	0	0
Sturdivant, p	0	0	0	0	0	0
Morgan, p	1	1	1	0	0	0
Turley, p	0	0	0	0	0	0
bSiebern	1	0	0	0	0	0
McDermott, p	1	0	1	0	0	0
Totals	35	8	12	8	24	5

Brooklyn	AB.	R.	H.	RBI.	PO.	A.
Gilliam, 2b	3	1	1	2	5	3
Reese, ss	6	1	1	2	2	5
Snider, cf	4	3	2	3	6	0
Robinson, 3b	4	2	2	0	0	2
Hodges, 1b	3	2	3	4	6	0
Amoros, lf	4	1	0	0	0	0

	AB.	R.	H.	RBI.	PO.	A.
cJackson	1	0	0	0	0	0
Cimoli, lf	0	0	0	0	1	0
Furillo, rf	4	2	2	0	2	0
Campanella, c	3	1	0	1	5	0
Newcombe, p	0	0	0	0	0	1
Roebuck, p	0	0	0	0	0	0
aMitchell	1	0	0	0	0	0
Bessent, p	2	0	1	1	0	0
Totals	35	13	12	13	27	11

New York	1 5 0	1 0 0	0 0 1	— 8
Brooklyn	0 6 1	2 2 0	0 2 x	—13

New York	IP.	H.	R.	ER.	BB.	SO.
Larsen	1⅔	1	4	0	4	0
Kucks	0*	1	1	0	0	0
Byrne	⅓	1	1	0	0	1
Sturdivant	⅔	2	1	1	2	2
Morgan (L)	2	5	4	4	2	3
Turley	⅓	0	0	0	0	1
McDermott	3	2	2	1	3	3

Brooklyn	IP.	H.	R.	ER.	BB.	SO.
Newcombe	1⅔	6	6	6	2	0
Roebuck	⅓	0	0	0	0	0
Bessent (W)	7	6	2	2	2	4

*Pitched to one batter in second.

aFouled out for Roebuck in second. bFlied out for Turley in sixth. cStruck out for Amoros in seventh. dStruck out for G. Coleman in eighth. E—Collins, Bauer. DP—New York 1, Brooklyn 1. LOB—New York 7, Brooklyn 11. 2B—Hodges 2. HR—Berra, Snider. SH—G.Coleman, McDougald, Bessent. SF—Campanella, Slaughter. WP—Bessent. U—Soar (A.L.), Boggess (N.L.), Napp (A.L.), Pinelli (N.L.), Runge (A.L.) and Gorman (N.L.). T—3:26. A—36,217.

Game 3

Saturday, October 6, At New York

Brooklyn	AB.	R.	H.	RBI.	PO.	A.
Gilliam, lf	4	0	0	0	2	0
Reese, ss	4	1	2	0	2	3
Snider, cf	3	0	0	1	4	0
Robinson, 3b	3	1	1	0	0	0
Hodges, 1b	3	1	1	0	5	1
Furillo, rf	4	0	2	0	1	0
Campanella, c	3	0	1	1	7	0
Neal, 2b	4	0	0	0	2	2
Craig, p	2	0	1	0	1	1
aJackson	1	0	0	0	0	0
Labine, p	0	0	0	0	0	0
Totals	31	3	8	2	24	7

New York	AB.	R.	H.	RBI.	PO.	A.
Bauer, rf	4	1	1	0	2	1
Collins, 1b	4	1	0	0	8	0
Mantle, cf	4	0	1	0	2	0
Berra, c	4	1	2	1	8	1
Slaughter, lf	3	1	2	3	1	0
Martin, 2b	4	1	1	1	1	3
McDougald, ss	2	0	1	0	4	2
Carey, 3b	3	0	0	0	1	5
Ford, p	3	0	0	0	0	0
Totals	31	5	8	5	27	12

Brooklyn	0 1 0	0 0 1	1 0 0	—3
New York	0 1 0	0 0 3	0 1 x	—5

Brooklyn	IP.	H.	R.	ER.	BB.	SO.
Craig (L)	6	7	4	4	1	4
Labine	2	1	1	0	1	2

New York	IP.	H.	R.	ER.	BB.	SO.
Ford (W)	9	8	3	2	2	7

aFlied out for Craig in seventh. E—Neal, Carey. DP—Brooklyn 2, New York 1. LOB—Brooklyn 5, New York 4. 2B—Berra, Furillo. 3B—Reese. HR—Martin, Slaughter. SF—Campanella, Snider. U—Boggess (N.L.), Napp (A.L.), Pinelli (N.L.), Soar (A.L.), Gorman (N.L.) and Runge (A.L.). T—2:17. A—73,977.

Game 4

Sunday, October 7, At New York

Brooklyn	AB.	R.	H.	RBI.	PO.	A.
Gilliam, 2b	4	0	0	0	1	4
Reese, ss	4	0	1	0	1	2
Snider, cf	4	1	1	0	3	0
Robinson, 3b	3	1	1	0	0	2
Hodges, 1b	4	0	1	1	10	1
Amoros, lf	3	0	0	0	2	0
Furillo, rf	3	0	0	0	0	0
Campanella, c	2	0	2	1	6	0
Erskine, p	1	0	0	0	1	2
aWalker	1	0	0	0	0	0
Roebuck, p	0	0	0	0	0	0
bMitchell	1	0	0	0	0	0
Drysdale, p	0	0	0	0	0	0
cJackson	1	0	0	0	0	0
Totals	31	2	6	2	24	11

New York	AB.	R.	H.	RBI.	PO.	A.
Bauer, rf	4	1	1	2	1	0
Collins, 1b	3	1	1	0	8	2
Mantle, cf	3	2	1	1	4	0
Berra, c	4	0	1	1	8	1
Slaughter, lf	3	1	0	0	1	0
Martin, 2b	4	0	1	1	0	3
McDougald, ss	2	0	0	1	3	3
Carey, 3b	3	1	1	0	0	0
Sturdivant, p	3	0	1	0	2	0
Totals	29	6	7	6	27	9

Brooklyn	0 0 0	1 0 0	0 0 1	—2
New York	1 0 0	2 0 1	2 0 x	—6

Brooklyn	IP.	H.	R.	ER.	BB.	SO.
Erskine (L)	4	4	3	3	2	2
Roebuck	2	1	1	1	0	2
Drysdale	2	2	2	2	1	1

New York	IP.	H.	R.	ER.	BB.	SO.
Sturdivant (W)	9	6	2	2	6	7

aHit into double play for Erskine in fifth. bFlied out for Roebuck in seventh. cStruck out for Drysdale in ninth. E—Collins, Carey. DP—Brooklyn 1, New York 2. LOB—Brooklyn 8, New York 3. 2B—Collins, Snider, Robinson. HR—Mantle, Bauer. SB—Mantle. SF—McDougald. U—Napp (A.L.), Pinelli (N.L.), Soar (A.L.), Boggess (N.L.), Runge (A.L.) and Gorman (N.L.). T—2:43. A—69,705.

Game 5

Monday, October 8, At New York

Brooklyn	AB.	R.	H.	RBI.	PO.	A.
Gilliam, 2b	3	0	0	0	2	0
Reese, ss	3	0	0	0	4	2
Snider, cf	3	0	0	0	1	0
Robinson, 3b	3	0	0	0	2	4
Hodges, 1b	3	0	0	0	5	1
Amoros, lf	3	0	0	0	3	0
Furillo, rf	3	0	0	0	0	0
Campanella, c	3	0	0	0	7	2
Maglie, p	2	0	0	0	0	1
aMitchell	1	0	0	0	0	0
Totals	27	0	0	0	24	10

New York	AB.	R.	H.	RBI.	PO.	A.
Bauer, rf	4	0	1	1	4	0
Collins, 1b	4	0	1	0	7	0
Mantle, cf	3	1	1	1	4	0
Berra, c	3	0	0	0	7	0
Slaughter, lf	2	0	0	0	1	0
Martin, 2b	3	0	1	0	3	4
McDougald, ss	2	0	0	0	0	2
Carey, 3b	3	1	1	0	1	1
Larsen, p	2	0	0	0	0	1
Totals	26	2	5	2	27	8

Brooklyn	0 0 0	0 0 0	0 0 0	—0
New York	0 0 0	1 0 1	0 0 x	—2

Brooklyn	IP.	H.	R.	ER.	BB.	SO.
Maglie (L)	8	5	2	2	2	5

New York	IP.	H.	R.	ER.	BB.	SO.
Larsen (W)	9	0	0	0	0	7

aStruck out for Maglie in ninth. DP—Brooklyn 2. LOB—Brooklyn 0, New York 3. HR—Mantle. SH—Larsen. U—Pinelli (N.L.), Soar (A.L.), Boggess (N.L.), Napp (A.L.), Gorman (N.L.) and Runge (A.L.). T—2:06. A—64,519.

Game 6

Tuesday, October 9, At Brooklyn

New York	AB.	R.	H.	RBI.	PO.	A.
Bauer, rf	5	0	2	0	2	0
Collins, 1b	5	0	2	0	4	1
Mantle, cf	3	0	0	0	2	0
Berra, c	4	0	2	0	12	0
Slaughter, lf	3	0	0	0	1	1
Martin, 2b	4	0	1	0	3	1
McDougald, ss	4	0	0	0	3	0
Carey, 3b	4	0	0	0	2	0
Turley, p	4	0	0	0	0	2
Totals	36	0	7	0	29	5

Brooklyn	AB.	R.	H.	RBI.	PO.	A.
Gilliam, 2b	3	1	1	0	0	7
Reese, ss	4	0	0	0	2	3
Snider, cf	2	0	1	0	4	0
Robinson, 3b	4	0	1	1	1	1
Hodges, 1b	3	0	0	0	14	0
Amoros, lf	3	0	0	0	2	0
Furillo, rf	4	0	0	0	2	0
Campanella, c	4	0	0	0	5	0
Labine, p	4	0	1	0	0	3
Totals	31	1	4	1	30	14

New York	0 0 0	0 0 0	0 0 0	0	—0
Brooklyn	0 0 0	0 0 0	0 0 0	1	—1

aTwo out when winning run scored.

New York	IP.	H.	R.	ER.	BB.	SO.
Turley (L)	9⅔	4	1	1	8	11

Brooklyn	IP.	H.	R.	ER.	BB.	SO.
Labine (W)	10	7	0	0	2	5

DP—Brooklyn 1. LOB—New York 8, Brooklyn 10. 2B—Berra, Collins, Labine. SH—Reese. U—Soar (A.L.), Boggess (N.L.), Napp (A.L.), Pinelli (N.L.), Runge (A.L.) and Gorman (N.L.). T—2:37. A—33,224.

Game 7

Wednesday, October 10, At Brooklyn

New York	AB.	R.	H.	RBI.	PO.	A.
Bauer, rf	5	1	1	0	0	0
Martin, 2b	5	2	2	0	2	6
Mantle, cf	4	1	1	0	0	0
Berra, c	3	3	2	4	1	1
Skowron, 1b	5	1	1	4	16	1
Howard, lf	5	1	2	1	2	0
McDougald, ss	4	0	1	0	3	3
Carey, 3b	3	0	0	0	2	2
Kucks, p	3	0	0	0	1	2
Totals	37	9	10	9	27	15

Brooklyn	AB.	R.	H.	RBI.	PO.	A.
Gilliam, 2b	4	0	0	0	6	2
Reese, ss	2	0	0	0	2	5
Snider, cf	4	0	2	0	1	0
Robinson, 3b	3	0	0	0	0	1
Hodges, 1b	3	0	0	0	10	2
Amoros, lf	3	0	0	0	0	0
Furillo, rf	3	0	1	0	0	0
Campanella, c	3	0	0	0	8	0
Newcombe, p	1	0	0	0	0	1
Bessent, p	0	0	0	0	0	0
aMitchell	1	0	0	0	0	0
Craig, p	0	0	0	0	0	0
Roebuck, p	0	0	0	0	0	0
bWalker	1	0	0	0	0	0
Erskine, p	0	0	0	0	0	0
Totals	28	0	3	0	27	11

New York	2 0 2	1 0 0	4 0 0	—9
Brooklyn	0 0 0	0 0 0	0 0 0	—0

New York	IP.	H.	R.	ER.	BB.	SO.
Kucks (W)	9	3	0	0	3	1

Brooklyn	IP.	H.	R.	ER.	BB.	SO.
Newcombe (L)	3*	5	5	5	1	4
Bessent	3	2	0	0	1	1
Craig	0†	3	4	4	2	0
Roebuck	2	0	0	0	0	3
Erskine	1	0	0	0	0	0

*Pitched to one batter in fourth.
†Pitched to five batters in seventh.

aGrounded out for Bessent in sixth. bGrounded out for Roebuck in eighth. E—Reese. DP—New York 2. LOB—New York 6, Brooklyn 4. 2B—Mantle, Howard. HR—Berra 2, Howard, Skowron. SB—Bauer. SH—Kucks. WP—Craig. U—Boggess (N.L.), Napp (A.L.), Pinelli (N.L.), Soar (A.L.), Gorman (N.L.) and Runge (A.L.). T—2:19. A—33,782.

COMPOSITE BATTING AVERAGES

New York Yankees

Player-Position	G.	AB.	R.	H.	2B.	3B.	HR.	RBI.	BA.
McDermott, p	1	1	0	1	0	0	0	0	1.000
Cerv, ph	1	1	0	1	0	0	0	0	1.000
Morgan, p	2	1	1	1	0	0	0	0	1.000
Howard, lf	1	5	1	2	1	0	1	1	.400
Berra, c	7	25	5	9	2	0	3	10	.360
Slaughter, lf	6	20	6	7	0	0	1	4	.350
Larsen, p	2	3	1	1	0	0	0	1	.333
Sturdivant, p	2	3	0	1	0	0	0	0	.333
Martin, 2b-3b	7	27	5	8	0	0	2	3	.296
Bauer, rf	7	32	3	9	0	0	1	3	.281
Mantle, cf	7	24	6	6	1	0	3	4	.250
Collins, ph-1b	6	21	2	5	2	0	0	2	.238
Carey, 3b	7	19	2	3	0	0	0	0	.158
McDougald, ss	7	21	0	3	0	0	0	1	.143
Skowron, 1b-ph	3	10	1	1	0	0	1	4	.100
G. Coleman, 2b	2	2	0	0	0	0	0	0	.000
Turley, p	3	4	0	0	0	0	0	0	.000
Ford, p	2	4	0	0	0	0	0	0	.000
Kucks, p	3	3	0	0	0	0	0	0	.000
Byrne, ph-p	2	1	0	0	0	0	0	0	.000
Siebern, ph	1	1	0	0	0	0	0	0	.000
Wilson, ph	1	1	0	0	0	0	0	0	.000
Totals	7	229	33	58	6	0	12	33	.253

Brooklyn Dodgers

Player-Position	G.	AB.	R.	H.	2B.	3B.	HR.	RBI.	BA.
Bessent, p	2	2	0	1	0	0	0	1	.500
Craig, p	2	2	0	1	0	0	0	0	.500
Snider, cf	7	23	5	7	1	0	1	4	.304
Hodges, 1b	7	23	5	7	2	0	1	8	.304
Robinson, 3b	7	24	5	6	1	0	1	2	.250
Labine, p	2	4	0	1	1	0	0	0	.250
Furillo, rf	7	25	2	6	2	0	0	1	.240
Reese, ss	7	27	3	6	0	1	0	2	.222
Campanella, c	7	22	2	4	1	0	0	3	.182
Gilliam, 2b-lf	7	24	2	2	0	0	0	2	.083
Amoros, lf	6	19	1	1	0	0	0	1	.053
Cimoli, lf	1	0	0	0	0	0	0	0	.000
Maglie, p	2	5	0	0	0	0	0	0	.000
Newcombe, p	2	1	0	0	0	0	0	0	.000
Roebuck, p	3	0	0	0	0	0	0	0	.000
Neal, 2b	1	4	0	0	0	0	0	0	.000
Erskine, p	2	1	0	0	0	0	0	0	.000
Drysdale, p	1	0	0	0	0	0	0	0	.000
Walker, ph	2	2	0	0	0	0	0	0	.000
Mitchell, ph	4	4	0	0	0	0	0	0	.000
Jackson, ph	3	3	0	0	0	0	0	0	.000
Totals	7	215	25	42	8	1	3	24	.195

COMPOSITE PITCHING AVERAGES

New York Yankees

Pitcher	G.	IP.	H.	R.	ER.	BB.	SO.	W.	L.	ERA.
Larsen	2	10⅔	1	4	0	4	7	1	0	0.00
Byrne	1	⅓	1	1	0	0	1	0	0	0.00
Turley	3	11	4	1	1	8	14	0	1	0.82
Kucks	3	11	6	2	1	3	2	1	0	0.82
Sturdivant	2	9⅔	8	3	3	8	9	1	0	2.79
McDermott	1	3	2	2	1	3	3	0	0	3.00
Ford	2	12	14	8	7	2	8	1	1	5.25
Morgan	2	4	6	4	4	4	3	0	1	9.00
Totals	7	61⅔	42	25	17	32	47	4	3	2.48

Brooklyn Dodgers

Pitcher	G.	IP.	H.	R.	ER.	BB.	SO.	W.	L.	ERA.
Labine	2	12	8	1	0	3	7	1	0	0.00
Bessent	2	10	8	2	2	3	5	1	0	1.80
Roebuck	3	4⅓	1	1	1	0	5	0	0	2.08
Maglie	2	17	14	5	5	6	15	1	1	2.65
Erskine	2	5	4	3	3	2	2	0	1	5.40
Drysdale	1	2	2	2	2	1	1	0	0	9.00
Craig	2	6	10	8	8	3	4	0	1	12.00
Newcombe	2	4⅔	11	11	11	3	4	0	1	21.21
Totals	7	61	58	33	32	21	43	3	4	4.72

1957
MILWAUKEE BRAVES
VS.
NEW YORK YANKEES

The 1957 Milwaukee Braves went off to the baseball wars with some pretty heavy artillery. And when all was said and done, a little spit and polish didn't hurt, either.

Milwaukee, a spectacular success at the box office since its re-entry into major league baseball in 1953 with the acquisition of the Braves franchise from Boston, put a spectacular team on the field in '57. Drawing a National League-record 2,215,404 fans, the Braves thundered to a 95-59 record and an eight-game margin of victory in the senior league's pennant race.

Manager Fred Haney's big gun was outfielder Hank Aaron, who in his fourth big-league season pounded 44 home runs, knocked in 132 runs and batted .322. Third baseman Eddie Mathews bashed 32 homers, and outfielder Wes Covington popped 21 in 96 games. (Milwaukee clubbed 199 homers overall.) The Braves were strong up the middle with Del Crandall behind the plate, Johnny Logan and Red Schoendienst serving as the keystone combination and Billy Bruton in center field. And after the swift Bruton went down with a season-ending knee injury, Milwaukee summoned Bob Hazle from its Wichita farm team. All Hazle did in 41 games was bat a cool .403.

Warren Spahn, Bob Buhl and Lew Burdette combined for 56 pitching victories, with Spahn reaching the 20-victory class for the eighth time in his major league career.

Milwaukee fans, understandably giddy over their club's ascension to World Series participant, had to wait until Game 3 to cheer their troops at County Stadium. And there wasn't much cheering that day.

Milwaukee third baseman Eddie Mathews rushes to join catcher Del Crandall and pitcher Lew Burdette in celebrating the Braves' Game 7 victory over the Yankees in the 1957 Series.

The teams arrived in Milwaukee in a 1-1 deadlock, New York having won the Series opener at Yankee Stadium by a 3-1 score behind Whitey Ford's five-hitter and the Braves having prevailed in the second game, 4-2, thanks to Burdette's strong pitching and left fielder Covington's rally-killing catch in the second inning.

Tony Kubek, 20-year-old rookie outfielder/infielder for the Yankees, made a triumphant return to his hometown of Milwaukee by lashing two home runs in Game 3—one with two teammates aboard, the other with the bases empty—as New York blitzed the Braves, 12-3. Things were looking up for Wisconsinites the next day when Spahn carried a 4-1 lead into the ninth. The crafty left-hander retired the first two batters, only to yield subsequent singles to Yogi Berra and Gil McDougald. Then, on a 3-2 pitch, Elston Howard walloped a long, game-tying home run into the left-field stands.

Stung by this last-gasp charge of a Series-tested team, Milwaukee fans and players alike probably

thought the other shoe would drop at any moment.

Kerplunk.

In the top of the 10th, Hank Bauer tripled home Kubek and the Yankees, one strike from defeat the inning before, had slipped into a 5-4 lead.

As it turned out, though, *another* shoe would drop (in a manner of speaking). This one was on the foot of Braves pinch-hitter Nippy Jones.

Jones led off Milwaukee's half of the 10th, batting for Spahn. Umpire Augie Donatelli called Tommy Byrne's first pitch to the 32-year-old reserve first baseman a ball, but Jones insisted he had been struck on the foot—and he set out to prove his point. Jones retrieved the baseball, showed Donatelli a smudge of shoe polish on the ball and was awarded first base. The hit-batsman ruling proved crucial as Felix Mantilla, running for Jones, came around to score on a sacrifice and Johnny Logan's double off Bob Grim. With the game now in a 5-5 tie, Mathews put an electrifying end to the proceedings by belting a home run to right. Winding up 7-5 winners in a game they had seemingly frittered away, the Braves no doubt went into Game 5 on an upbeat note.

Burdette, the fidgety righthander whose increasing success in the majors seemed to parallel mounting charges that he was throwing a spitball, got the call in that fifth game and beat Ford, 1-0. The game was scoreless in the fourth when the Yankees' McDougald smashed a leadoff drive to deep left field. Crashing into the fence, Covington made a homer-saving grab by reaching up and spearing the ball. Milwaukee then scored the game's only run in the sixth. After two were out, Mathews, Aaron and Joe Adcock rapped singles. For Adcock, it was a particularly rewarding blow after a personally frustrating year. After slugging 38 home runs in a banner 1956 season, Adcock suffered a leg fracture during the '57 campaign and got into only 65 games (he finished with 12 homers).

Whether he threw the spitter or not, Burdette no doubt used the specter of the pitch to great psychological advantage. Winner of 114 games for Milwaukee from 1956 through 1961, he was in excellent form in Game 5 of the '57 Series. He allowed seven hits (all singles), walked no one and struck out five Yankees.

Game 6 was a low-scoring but power-packed struggle, with Casey Stengel's Yankees coming out on top, 3-2, at Yankee Stadium on the strength of Bauer's seventh-inning home run off Braves reliever Ernie Johnson, who otherwise pitched brilliantly in a 4⅓-inning stint. Milwaukee had forged a 2-2 tie in the top of the inning on a bases-empty homer by Aaron. Earlier, Berra had belted a two-run shot for the Yanks and Frank Torre had connected for the Braves. Besides the two homers, Yankees righthander Bob Turley allowed only two other hits.

One year and two days after his Series perfect game against Brooklyn, Don Larsen had another chance to be a hero in the fall classic. But as the Yankees' starting pitcher in Game 7, Larsen couldn't get through the third, an inning in which Mathews stroked a two-run double and the Braves scored four times overall. In the eighth, Crandall tacked on another run with a homer and Milwaukee, behind Burdette's second straight shutout, befuddled the Yankees, 5-0.

Without major league baseball until 1953 following the shift of its American League team to St. Louis after the 1901 season, Milwaukee now ruled the majors.

Aaron provided the heavy firepower for the Braves in the World Series, batting .393, hitting three home runs and knocking in seven runs. Burdette pitched three complete-game victories and made the most of a real or imagined weapon—the spitter. And then there was the polish, as pointed out so ingeniously by Nippy Jones in a momentum-shifting turn of events in Game 4.

Game 1
Wednesday, October 2, At New York

Milwaukee	AB.	R.	H.	RBI.	PO.	A.
Schoendienst, 2b	4	0	1	1	1	2
Logan, ss	3	0	0	0	2	3
Mathews, 3b	2	0	0	0	3	1
Aaron, cf	4	0	1	0	2	0

	AB.	R.	H.	RBI.	PO.	A.
Adcock, 1b	4	0	0	0	7	0
Torre, 1b	0	0	0	0	1	0
Pafko, rf	4	0	0	0	3	0
Covington, lf	4	1	2	0	4	0
Crandall, c	4	0	1	0	4	1
Spahn, p	1	0	0	0	0	1
Johnson, p	0	0	0	0	0	0
aJones	1	0	0	0	0	0
McMahon, p	0	0	0	0	0	0
Totals	31	1	5	1	24	9

New York	AB.	R.	H.	RBI.	PO.	A.
Bauer, rf	4	0	1	1	1	0
McDougald, ss	4	0	1	0	2	6
Mantle, cf	4	0	2	0	2	0
Skowron, 1b	1	0	0	0	2	0
Howard, 1b	2	1	1	0	3	1
Collins, 1b	1	0	0	0	5	0
Berra, c	3	1	1	0	5	0
Carey, 3b	3	0	1	1	2	2
Coleman, 2b	3	1	2	1	3	4
Kubek, lf	3	0	0	0	2	0
Ford, p	3	0	0	0	1	1
Totals	31	3	9	3	27	14

Milwaukee	000	000	100—1
New York	000	012	00x—3

Milwaukee	IP.	H.	R.	ER.	BB.	SO.
Spahn (L)	5⅓	7	3	3	1	0
Johnson	⅔	0	0	0	0	1
McMahon	2	2	0	0	1	3

New York	IP.	H.	R.	ER.	BB.	SO.
Ford (W)	9	5	1	1	4	5

aGrounded out for Johnson in seventh. E—Howard. DP—Milwaukee 1, New York 1. LOB—Milwaukee 7, New York 7. 2B—Coleman, Bauer, Covington. SH—Coleman. U—Paparella (A.L.), Conlan (N.L.), McKinley (A.L.), Donatelli (N.L.), Secory (N.L.) and Chylak (A.L.). T—2:10. A—69,476.

Game 2
Thursday, October 3, At New York

Milwaukee	AB.	R.	H.	RBI.	PO.	A.
Schoendienst, 2b	4	0	0	1	0	3
Logan, ss	3	1	1	1	3	3
Mathews, 3b	4	0	0	0	1	2
Aaron, cf	4	1	1	0	2	0
Adcock, 1b	4	1	2	1	8	1
Torre, 1b	0	0	0	0	2	0
Pafko, rf	4	1	1	0	2	0
Covington, lf	4	0	2	1	3	0
Crandall, c	3	0	1	0	5	0
Burdette, p	3	0	0	0	0	4
Totals	33	4	8	3	27	13

New York	AB.	R.	H.	RBI.	PO.	A.
Bauer, rf	5	1	1	1	3	0
McDougald, ss	4	0	0	0	2	3
Mantle, cf	3	0	0	0	2	0
Berra, c	4	0	0	0	6	0
Slaughter, lf	3	1	1	0	2	0
Simpson, 1b	4	0	0	0	10	1
Kubek, 3b	4	0	2	0	1	1
Coleman, 2b	2	0	1	1	1	1
bCollins	1	0	0	0	0	0
Shantz, p	1	0	0	0	0	0
Ditmar, p	1	0	0	0	0	0
aLumpe	1	0	0	0	0	0
Grim, p	0	0	0	0	0	0
cHoward	1	0	1	0	0	0
dRichardson	0	0	0	0	0	0
Totals	34	2	7	2	27	7

Milwaukee	011	200	000—4
New York	011	000	000—2

Milwaukee	IP.	H.	R.	ER.	BB.	SO.
Burdette (W)	9	7	2	2	3	5

New York	IP.	H.	R.	ER.	BB.	SO.
Shantz (L)	3*	6	4	3	1	3
Ditmar	4	1	0	0	0	1
Grim	2	1	0	0	0	2

*Pitched to three batters in fourth.

aSingled for Ditmar in seventh. bPopped out for Coleman in ninth. cSingled for Grim in ninth. dRan for Howard in ninth. E—Mantle, Kubek. DP—New York 1. LOB—Milwaukee 5, New York 8. 2B—Slaughter. 3B—Aaron. HR—Logan, Bauer. SH—Burdette. HBP—By Ditmar (Logan). U—Conlan (N.L.), McKinley (A.L.), Donatelli (N.L.), Paparella (A.L.), Secory (N.L.) and Chylak (A.L.). T—2:26. A—65,202.

Game 3
Saturday, October 5, At Milwaukee

New York	AB.	R.	H.	RBI.	PO.	A.
Bauer, rf	5	1	1	2	3	0
Kubek, lf	5	3	3	4	4	0
Mantle, cf	3	2	2	2	1	0
Berra, c	4	2	1	0	7	0
McDougald, ss	1	2	0	1	3	3
Simpson, 1b	1	0	1	1	0	0
aHoward, 1b	2	0	0	0	6	0
Collins, 1b	1	0	0	0	1	0
Lumpe, 3b	5	0	1	2	2	3
Coleman, 2b	4	1	0	0	0	3
Turley, p	1	0	0	0	0	0
Larsen, p	2	1	0	0	0	1
Totals	34	12	9	12	27	7

Milwaukee	AB.	R.	H.	RBI.	PO.	A.
Schoendienst, 2b	5	0	3	1	0	2
Logan, ss	4	1	2	0	0	1
Mathews, 3b	2	0	0	0	3	6
Aaron, cf	5	1	2	2	2	0
Covington, lf	3	0	0	0	2	0
Adcock, 1b	3	0	0	0	9	1
Trowbridge, p	0	0	0	0	0	0
dJones	1	0	0	0	0	0
McMahon, p	0	0	0	0	0	1
fPafko	0	0	0	0	0	0
Hazle, rf	4	1	0	0	1	0
Rice, c	3	0	1	0	5	1
eDeMerit	0	0	0	0	0	0
Crandall, c	1	0	0	0	1	0
Buhl, p	0	0	0	0	0	1
Pizarro, p	1	0	0	0	0	0
Conley, p	0	0	0	0	1	0
bSawatski	1	0	0	0	0	0
Johnson, p	0	0	0	0	0	1
cTorre, 1b	2	0	0	0	3	0
Totals	35	3	8	3	27	14

New York	3 0 2 2 0 0 5 0 0—12
Milwaukee	0 1 0 0 2 0 0 0 0— 3

New York	IP.	H.	R.	ER.	BB.	SO.
Turley	1⅔	3	1	1	4	2
Larsen (W)	7⅓	5	2	2	4	4

Milwaukee	IP.	H.	R.	ER.	BB.	SO.
Buhl (L)	⅔	2	3	2	2	0
Pizarro	1⅔	3	2	2	2	1
Conley	1⅔	2	2	2	1	0
Johnson	2	0	0	0	1	2
Trowbridge	1	2	5	5	3	1
McMahon	2	0	0	0	2	2

aWalked for Simpson in third. bStruck out for Conley in fourth. cGrounded out for Johnson in sixth. dGrounded out for Trowbridge in seventh. eRan for Rice in eighth. fHit by pitched ball for McMahon in ninth. E—Buhl. DP—Milwaukee 1. LOB—Milwaukee 14, New York 7. HR—Kubek 2, Mantle, Aaron. SB—McDougald. SF—McDougald. HBP—By Larsen (Pafko). WP—Turley. PB—Rice. U—McKinley (A.L.), Donatelli (N.L.), Paparella (A.L.), Conlan (N.L.), Chylak (A.L.) and Secory (N.L.). T—3:18. A—45,804.

Game 4

Sunday, October 6, At Milwaukee

New York	AB.	R.	H.	RBI.	PO.	A.
Kubek, lf-cf	5	1	2	0	1	0
Bauer, rf	5	0	1	1	0	0
Mantle, cf	5	1	0	0	1	0
Slaughter, lf	0	0	0	0	0	0
Berra, c	3	1	2	0	8	0
McDougald, ss	4	1	2	1	1	2
Howard, 1b	4	1	1	3	13	0
Collins, 1b	0	0	0	0	0	1
Carey, 3b	4	0	1	0	1	4
Coleman, 2b	4	0	1	0	3	4
Sturdivant, p	1	0	0	0	0	1
aSimpson	1	0	0	0	0	0
Shantz, p	0	0	0	0	0	0
bLumpe	1	0	1	0	0	0
Kucks, p	0	0	0	0	0	0
Byrne, p	1	0	0	0	0	0
Grim, p	0	0	0	0	0	0
Totals	38	5	11	5	28	12

Milwaukee	AB.	R.	H.	RBI.	PO.	A.
Schoendienst, 2b	4	0	1	0	3	3
Logan, ss	4	2	1	1	1	10
Mathews, 3b	4	2	2	2	1	4
Aaron, cf	3	1	2	3	1	0
Covington, lf	4	0	0	0	0	0
Torre, 1b	3	1	1	1	15	1
cAdcock, 1b	1	0	0	0	1	0
Hazle, rf	2	0	0	0	2	0
Pafko, rf	2	0	0	0	3	0
Crandall, c	4	0	0	0	2	0
Spahn, p	3	0	0	0	1	2
dJones	0	0	0	0	0	0
eMantilla	0	1	0	0	0	0
Totals	34	7	7	7	30	20

New York	1 0 0 0 0 0 0 0 3 1—5
Milwaukee	0 0 0 4 0 0 0 0 0 3—7

One out when winning run scored.

New York	IP.	H.	R.	ER.	BB.	SO.
Sturdivant	4	4	4	4	1	1
Shantz	3	0	0	0	1	4
Kucks	⅔	1	0	0	1	1
Byrne	1⅓*	0	1	1	0	1
Grim (L)	⅓	2	2	2	0	0

Milwaukee	IP.	H.	R.	ER.	BB.	SO.
Spahn (W)	10	11	5	5	1	2

*Pitched to one batter in tenth.

aHit into double play for Sturdivant in fifth. bSingled for Shantz in eighth. cGrounded out for Torre in ninth. dHit by pitch for Spahn in tenth. eRan for Jones in tenth. DP—Milwaukee 3. LOB—New York 4, Milwaukee 4. 2B—Mathews, Carey, Schoendienst, Logan. 3B—Bauer. HR—Aaron, Torre, Howard, Mathews. SB—Covington. SH—Schoendienst. HBP—By Byrne (Jones). U—Donatelli (N.L.), Paparella (A.L.), Conlan (N.L.), McKinley (A.L.), Chylak (A.L.) and Secory (N.L.). T—2:31. A—45,804.

Game 5

Monday, October 7, At Milwaukee

New York	AB.	R.	H.	RBI.	PO.	A.
Bauer, rf	4	0	2	0	0	0
Kubek, cf	3	0	0	0	4	0
McDougald, ss	4	0	1	0	1	7
Berra, c	4	0	1	0	4	1
Slaughter, lf	3	0	2	0	3	0
Simpson, 1b	3	0	0	0	8	0
Lumpe, 3b	3	0	0	0	0	2
Coleman, 2b	3	0	1	0	4	1
aMantle	0	0	0	0	0	0
Turley, p	0	0	0	0	0	0
Ford, p	2	0	0	0	0	0
bHoward	1	0	0	0	0	0
Richardson, 2b	0	0	0	0	0	0
Totals	30	0	7	0	24	11

Milwaukee	AB.	R.	H.	RBI.	PO.	A.
Schoendienst, 2b	1	0	0	0	0	0
Mantilla, 2b	3	0	0	0	2	7
Logan, ss	4	0	0	0	3	3
Mathews, 3b	3	1	1	0	1	2
Aaron, cf	3	0	2	0	0	0
Adcock, 1b	3	0	1	1	13	0
Torre, 1b	0	0	0	0	1	0
Pafko, rf	3	0	2	0	1	0
Covington, lf	2	0	0	0	1	0
Crandall, c	3	0	0	0	5	3
Burdette, p	3	0	0	0	0	2
Totals	28	1	6	1	27	17

New York	0 0 0 0 0 0 0 0 0—0
Milwaukee	0 0 0 0 0 1 0 0 x—1

New York	IP.	H.	R.	ER.	BB.	SO.
Ford (L)	7	6	1	1	1	2
Turley	1	0	0	0	0	2

Milwaukee	IP.	H.	R.	ER.	BB.	SO.
Burdette (W)	9	7	0	0	0	5

aRan for Coleman in eighth. bStruck out for Ford in eighth. E—Adcock. DP—New York 1, Milwaukee 3. LOB—New York 4, Milwaukee 5. SH—Kubek, Covington. U—Paparella (A.L.), Conlan (N.L.), McKinley (A.L.), Donatelli (N.L.), Chylak (A.L.) and Secory (N.L.). T—2:00. A—45,811.

Game 6

Wednesday, October 9, At New York

Milwaukee	AB.	R.	H.	RBI.	PO.	A.
Mantilla, 2b	3	0	0	0	2	1
Logan, ss	4	0	0	0	2	1
Mathews, 3b	3	0	1	0	0	0
Aaron, cf	4	1	1	1	1	0
Covington, lf	4	0	0	0	1	1
Torre, 1b	3	1	2	1	7	1
Hazle, rf	3	0	0	0	0	0
Rice, c	3	0	0	0	10	1
Buhl, p	1	0	0	0	0	1
Johnson, p	1	0	0	0	1	2
aSawatski	1	0	0	0	0	0
McMahon, p	0	0	0	0	0	1
Totals	30	2	4	2	24	9

New York	AB.	R.	H.	RBI.	PO.	A.
Bauer, rf	4	1	1	1	1	0
Kubek, cf	4	0	0	0	3	0
Slaughter, lf	2	1	0	0	0	0
Berra, c	4	1	3	2	10	0
McDougald, ss	3	0	1	0	2	2
Lumpe, 3b	3	0	1	0	1	1
Simpson, 1b	3	0	0	0	6	0
Collins, 1b	0	0	0	0	1	1
Coleman, 2b	2	0	1	0	1	3
Turley, p	3	0	0	0	2	2
Totals	28	3	7	3	27	9

Milwaukee	0 0 0 0 1 0 1 0 0—2
New York	0 0 2 0 0 0 1 0 x—3

Milwaukee	IP.	H.	R.	ER.	BB.	SO.
Buhl	2⅔	4	2	2	4	4
Johnson (L)	4⅓	2	1	1	0	5
McMahon	1	1	0	0	0	0

New York	IP.	H.	R.	ER.	BB.	SO.
Turley (W)	9	4	2	2	2	8

aStruck out for Johnson in eighth. DP—Milwaukee 2, New York 1. LOB—Milwaukee 3, New York 6. 2B—Mathews, Coleman, Berra. HR—Berra, Torre, Aaron, Bauer. SH—McDougald. WP—Buhl. U—Conlan (N.L.), McKinley (A.L.), Donatelli (N.L.), Paparella (A.L.), Secory (N.L.) and Chylak (A.L.). T—2:09. A—61,408.

Game 7

Thursday, October 10, At New York

Milwaukee	AB.	R.	H.	RBI.	PO.	A.
Hazle, rf	4	1	2	0	3	0
dPafko, rf	1	0	0	0	0	0
Logan, ss	5	1	1	0	2	4
Mathews, 3b	4	1	1	2	3	4
Aaron, cf	5	1	2	1	3	0
Covington, lf	3	0	1	0	2	0
Torre, 1b	2	0	0	1	8	0
Mantilla, 2b	4	0	0	0	2	0
Crandall, c	4	1	2	1	4	0
Burdette, p	2	0	0	0	0	3
Totals	34	5	9	5	27	11

New York	AB.	R.	H.	RBI.	PO.	A.
Bauer, rf	4	0	1	0	2	0
Slaughter, lf	4	0	0	0	2	0
Mantle, cf	4	0	1	0	2	0
Berra, c	3	0	0	0	4	1
McDougald, ss	4	0	1	0	2	1
Kubek, 3b	4	0	1	0	3	4
Coleman, 2b	4	0	2	0	4	3
Collins, 1b	2	0	0	0	5	0
Sturdivant, p	0	0	0	0	0	0
cHoward	1	0	0	0	0	0
Byrne, p	1	0	1	0	0	0
Larsen, p	0	0	0	0	0	1
Shantz, p	0	0	0	0	0	0
aLumpe	1	0	0	0	0	0
Ditmar, p	0	0	0	0	0	0
bSkowron, 1b	3	0	0	0	3	2
Totals	35	0	7	0	27	12

Milwaukee	0 0 4 0 0 0 0 1 0—5
New York	0 0 0 0 0 0 0 0 0—0

Milwaukee	IP.	H.	R.	ER.	BB.	SO.
Burdette (W)	9	7	0	0	1	3

New York	IP.	H.	R.	ER.	BB.	SO.
Larsen (L)	2⅓	3	3	2	1	2
Shantz	⅔	2	1	0	0	0
Ditmar	2	1	0	0	0	1
Sturdivant	2	2	0	0	0	1
Byrne	2	1	1	1	2	0

aStruck out for Shantz in third. bHit into forceout for Ditmar in fifth. cStruck out for Sturdivant in seventh. dFouled out for Hazle in eighth. E—Mathews, Berra, McDougald, Kubek. DP—New York 1. LOB—Milwaukee 8, New York 9. 2B—Bauer, Mathews. HR—Crandall. SH—Burdette, Mathews, Covington. U—McKinley (A.L.), Donatelli (N.L.), Paparella (A.L.), Conlan (N.L.), Chylak (A.L.) and Secory (N.L.). T—2:34. A—61,207.

COMPOSITE BATTING AVERAGES

Milwaukee Braves

Player-Position	G.	AB.	R.	H.	2B.	3B.	HR.	RBI.	BA.
Aaron, cf	7	28	5	11	0	1	3	7	.393
Torre, 1b-ph	7	10	2	3	0	0	2	3	.300
Schoendienst, 2b	5	18	0	5	1	0	0	2	.278
Mathews, 3b	7	22	4	5	3	0	1	4	.227
Pafko, rf-ph	6	14	1	3	0	0	0	0	.214
Crandall, c	6	19	1	4	0	0	1	1	.211
Covington, lf	7	24	1	5	1	0	0	1	.208
Adcock, 1b-ph	5	15	1	3	0	0	0	2	.200
Logan, ss	7	27	5	5	1	0	1	2	.185
Rice, c	2	6	0	1	0	0	0	0	.167
Hazle, rf	4	13	2	2	0	0	0	0	.154
Mantilla, pr-2b	4	10	1	0	0	0	0	0	.000
Spahn, p	2	4	0	0	0	0	0	0	.000
Johnson, p	3	1	0	0	0	0	0	0	.000
McMahon, p	3	0	0	0	0	0	0	0	.000
Trowbridge, p	1	0	0	0	0	0	0	0	.000
Buhl, p	2	1	0	0	0	0	0	0	.000
Pizarro, p	1	1	0	0	0	0	0	0	.000
Conley, p	1	0	0	0	0	0	0	0	.000
Burdette, p	3	8	0	0	0	0	0	0	.000
Jones, ph	3	2	0	0	0	0	0	0	.000
DeMerit, pr	1	0	0	0	0	0	0	0	.000
Sawatski, ph	2	2	0	0	0	0	0	0	.000
Totals	7	225	23	47	6	1	8	22	.209

New York Yankees

Player-Position	G.	AB.	R.	H.	2B.	3B.	HR.	RBI.	BA.
Byrne, p	2	2	0	1	0	0	0	0	.500
Coleman, 2b	7	22	2	8	2	0	0	2	.364
Berra, c	7	25	5	8	1	0	1	2	.320
Carey, 3b	2	7	0	2	1	0	0	1	.286
Kubek, lf-3b-cf	7	28	4	8	0	0	2	4	.286
Lumpe, ph-3b	6	14	0	4	0	0	0	2	.286
Howard, 1b-ph	6	11	2	3	0	0	1	3	.273
Mantle, cf-pr	6	19	3	5	0	0	1	2	.263
Bauer, rf	7	31	3	8	2	1	2	6	.258
McDougald, ss	7	24	3	6	0	0	0	2	.250
Slaughter, lf	5	12	2	3	1	0	0	0	.250
Simpson, 1b-ph	5	12	0	1	0	0	0	1	.083
Richardson, pr-2b	2	0	0	0	0	0	0	0	.000
Skowron, 1b-ph	2	4	0	0	0	0	0	0	.000
Collins, 1b-ph	6	5	0	0	0	0	0	0	.000
Ford, p	2	5	0	0	0	0	0	0	.000
Shantz, p	3	1	0	0	0	0	0	0	.000
Ditmar, p	2	1	0	0	0	0	0	0	.000
Grim, p	2	0	0	0	0	0	0	0	.000
Turley, p	3	4	0	0	0	0	0	0	.000
Larsen, p	2	2	1	0	0	0	0	0	.000
Sturdivant, p	2	1	0	0	0	0	0	0	.000
Kucks, p	1	0	0	0	0	0	0	0	.000
Totals	7	230	25	57	7	1	7	25	.248

COMPOSITE PITCHING AVERAGES

Milwaukee Braves

Pitcher	G.	IP.	H.	R.	ER.	BB.	SO.	W.	L.	ERA.
McMahon	3	5	3	0	0	3	5	0	0	0.00
Burdette	3	27	21	2	2	4	13	3	0	0.67
Johnson	3	7	2	1	1	1	8	0	1	1.29
Spahn	2	15⅓	18	8	8	2	2	1	1	4.70
Buhl	2	3⅓	6	5	4	6	4	0	1	10.80
Pizarro	1	1⅔	3	2	2	2	1	0	0	10.80
Conley	1	1⅔	2	2	2	1	0	0	0	10.80
Trowbridge	1	1	2	5	5	3	1	0	0	45.00
Totals	7	62	57	25	24	22	34	4	3	3.48

New York Yankees

Pitcher	G.	IP.	H.	R.	ER.	BB.	SO.	W.	L.	ERA.
Ditmar	2	6	2	0	0	0	2	0	0	0.00
Kucks	1	⅔	1	0	0	1	1	0	0	0.00
Ford	2	16	11	2	2	5	7	1	1	1.13
Turley	3	11⅔	7	3	3	6	12	1	0	2.31
Larsen	2	9⅔	8	5	4	5	6	1	1	3.72
Shantz	3	6⅔	8	5	3	2	7	0	1	4.05
Byrne	2	3⅓	1	2	2	2	1	0	0	5.40
Sturdivant	2	6	6	4	4	1	2	0	0	6.00
Grim	2	2⅓	3	2	2	0	2	0	1	7.71
Totals	7	62⅓	47	23	20	22	40	3	4	2.89

1958
NEW YORK YANKEES
VS.
MILWAUKEE BRAVES

Writing in a national magazine in February 1958, Milwaukee Braves pitcher Lew Burdette looked back at his three-victory performance over the New York Yankees in the 1957 World Series and also took note of Warren Spahn's fourth-game triumph against the American Leaguers. Then, winding up the article, Burdette announced that he and Spahn "expect to share another four victories over the Yankees (in '58)—if they make the Series again!"

Well, Casey Stengel's Yankees were in the fall classic once more, and so were Fred Haney's Braves. And after Spahn had pitched a masterful two-hitter in Game 4 of the '58 World Series, Burdette's victory projection for the aces of the Milwaukee staff was right on course. Allowing only a fourth-inning triple by Mickey Mantle and a seventh-inning single by Bill Skowron in a 3-0 triumph, Spahn won for the second time in this Series. In the opening game, he was a 4-3 winner in 10 innings as Milwaukee netted its decisive run on singles by Joe Adcock, Del Crandall and Billy Bruton.

Burdette had taken Game 2, a wild affair in which the Braves' pitcher capped the National League club's seven-run first inning with a three-run homer of his own. But while Burdette cruised until the ninth, allowing only two runs and three hits to that point, he was shelled for three runs and four hits in the final inning (during which Hank Bauer belted a home run and Mantle slugged his second homer of the day). By then, Milwaukee had added to its early lead and the Braves wound up winning easily, 13-5.

The only bright spot for the Yankees in the first four games

Milwaukee catcher Del Crandall crosses the plate after hitting a game-tying sixth-inning home run in Game 7 of the 1958 fall classic.

had been the combined shutout pitching of Don Larsen and Ryne Duren in the third contest, a 4-0 New York triumph in which Bauer drove in all of the Yankees' runs with a bases-loaded single and a two-run homer and extended his Series hitting streak to 17 games (a string that Spahn snapped the next day).

Game 5 of the '58 Series would provide Burdette with the opportunity not only to follow through on his late-winter forecast of another four postseason victories for the Burdette-Spahn duo, but also with the chance to clinch a second consecutive Series championship for the powerful Braves. Staring at a three games-to-one deficit and facing old nemesis Burdette, the Yankees appeared to be in deep trouble. But Bob Turley, New York's 21-game winner who managed to retire only one batter in his second-game start, was about to get his act together. And that would spell big trouble for the Braves.

Backed by Gil McDougald's bases-empty home run in the third inning, left fielder Elston Howard's rally-snuffing catch of Red Schoendienst's sixth-inning liner (which was turned into a double play) and the Yanks' six-run explosion against Burdette and Juan Pizarro in the bottom of the sixth, Turley was a 7-0 victor. He gave up only five hits and struck out 10 Braves.

The Yankees then squared the Series with a 4-3, 10-inning victory in Game 6. New York snapped a 2-2 tie in the top of the 10th on McDougald's leadoff home run against Spahn and Skowron added a run-scoring single off reliever Don McMahon. But Turley's services were required in the last half of the inning when the Braves rallied for one run and had the potential tying run on third. Bullet Bob, the Yanks' fourth pitcher of the day, responded by nailing down the final out of the game.

For the second straight year, Larsen would be the Yankees' starting pitcher in Game 7. And for the second straight year, big Don would last exactly 2⅓ innings in the climactic game. However, the ever-present and ever-tough Turley was on call again and, after escaping a bases-loaded situation in the third, he held a 2-1 lead over Burdette and the Braves entering the Milwaukee

Milwaukee lefthander Warren Spahn (left) hugs catcher Del Crandall after stopping the Yankees on two hits in Game 4.

sixth. With two out, though, Crandall belted a game-tying home run.

After both clubs were held scoreless in the seventh, Burdette retired the first two Yankees in the eighth. Then, the roof came crashing down on Burdette and his prediction. Berra ripped a double. Howard followed with a go-ahead single. Andy Carey singled off third baseman Eddie Mathews' glove. And Skowron crashed a home run to left-center. The Yankees were ahead, 6-2, and the score would not change. With Turley yielding only one run and two hits in 6⅔ innings of relief work, the New York Yankees clinched their 18th World Series crown.

Masters of making it look easy in Series competition with a record six sweeps to their credit, the Yankees proved in 1958 that they could do it the hard way, too. By

roaring back against the Milwaukee Braves, they had become only the second team in history (the 1925 Pittsburgh Pirates were the other) to rally from a 3-1 deficit and win a seven-game World Series.

Bauer, playing in his ninth Series, led all participants in runs scored (six), hits (10), home runs (four) and RBIs (eight) and topped the Yankees with a .323 batting mark. His two-year totals against the Braves were nine runs scored, 18 hits, six homers, 14 RBIs and a .290 average, quite a reversal for a man who in his first four Series had gone 7 for 57 (.123) at the plate with two runs scored, no homers and five RBIs. Bauer's record consecutive-game Series hitting streak further indicated the extent of his turnaround.

Turley's heroics in Games 5, 6 and 7—one rescue job sand-

wiched between two victories—made him the standout of the Yankees' pitching staff.

Bruton, sidelined during the 1957 Series because of injury, made up for lost time by batting .412 for Milwaukee in 17 at-bats. And Spahn and Burdette combined for three victories. *Three*, not four. And therein is the story of the 1958 World Series.

Game 1

Wednesday, October 1, At Milwaukee

New York	AB.	R.	H.	RBI.	PO.	A.
Bauer, rf	5	1	2	2	0	0
McDougald, 2b	4	0	2	0	1	2
Mantle, cf	3	0	0	0	3	0
Howard, lf	5	0	0	0	4	0
Berra, c	4	0	2	0	13	2
Skowron, 1b	4	1	2	1	7	0
Carey, 3b	4	0	0	0	0	2
Kubek, ss	4	0	0	0	1	1
Ford, p	2	1	0	0	0	0
Duren, p	1	0	0	0	0	0
Totals	36	3	8	3	29	7

Milwaukee	AB.	R.	H.	RBI.	PO.	A.
Schoendienst, 2b	4	0	0	0	2	2
Logan, ss	4	0	1	0	2	3
bTorre	1	0	0	0	0	0
Mantilla, ss	0	0	0	0	0	0
Mathews, 3b	3	1	0	0	1	3
Aaron, rf	4	1	1	0	3	0
Adcock, 1b	5	1	2	0	8	2
Covington, lf	4	0	0	1	2	1
Crandall, c	5	1	2	1	7	0
Pafko, cf	3	0	1	0	4	0
aBruton, cf	2	0	1	1	0	0
Spahn, p	4	0	2	1	1	2
Totals	39	4	10	4	30	13

New York .... 0 0 0 1 2 0 0 0 0 0—3
Milwaukee .... 0 0 0 2 0 0 0 1 0 1—4

New York	IP.	H.	R.	ER.	BB.	SO.
Ford	7*	6	3	3	3	8
Duren (L)	2	4	1	1	1	5

Milwaukee	IP.	H.	R.	ER.	BB.	SO.
Spahn (W)	10	8	3	3	4	6

*Pitched to two batters in eighth.

aStruck out for Pafko in ninth. bPopped out for Logan in ninth. E—Kubek. LOB—New York 7, Milwaukee 11. 2B—Logan, Berra, Aaron. HR—Skowron, Bauer. SF—Covington. WP—Spahn, Ford. PB—Berra. U—Barlick (N.L.), Berry (A.L.), Gorman (N.L.), Flaherty (A.L.), Jackowski (N.L.) and Umont (A.L.). T—3:09. A—46,367.

Game 2

Thursday, October 2, At Milwaukee

New York	AB.	R.	H.	RBI.	PO.	A.
Bauer, rf	4	2	2	1	1	0
McDougald, 2b	4	1	1	0	0	6
Mantle, cf	3	2	2	3	3	0
Howard, lf	1	0	0	1	1	0
Siebern, lf	3	0	1	0	2	0
Berra, c	4	0	0	0	3	0
Skowron, 1b	4	0	0	0	11	0
Carey, 3b	2	0	0	0	1	2
cSlaughter	1	0	0	0	0	0
Richardson, 3b	1	0	0	0	0	0
Kubek, ss	3	0	0	0	2	2
Turley, p	0	0	0	0	0	0
Maas, p	0	0	0	0	0	0
Kucks, p	1	0	1	0	0	0
aLumpe	1	0	0	0	0	0
Dickson, p	0	0	0	0	0	0
dThroneberry	1	0	0	0	0	0
Monroe, p	0	0	0	0	0	0
Totals	33	5	7	5	24	10

Milwaukee	AB.	R.	H.	RBI.	PO.	A.
Bruton, cf	4	2	3	1	3	0
Schoendienst, 2b	5	2	2	0	2	6
Mathews, 3b	5	2	2	2	0	0
Aaron, rf	4	2	2	0	1	0
Covington, lf	4	1	3	2	1	0
bMantilla	0	0	0	0	0	0
Pafko, lf	0	0	0	0	1	0
Torre, 1b	5	0	1	1	10	0
Crandall, c	2	1	0	1	5	1
Logan, ss	4	1	1	2	3	5
Burdette, p	4	1	1	3	1	1
Totals	37	13	15	12	27	13

New York .... 1 0 0 1 0 0 0 0 3— 5
Milwaukee .... 7 1 0 0 0 4 1 x—13

New York	IP.	H.	R.	ER.	BB.	SO.
Turley (L)	⅓	3	4	4	1	1
Maas	⅓	3	3	3	0	0
Kucks	3⅓	3	1	1	0	0
Dickson	3	4	2	2	0	1
Monroe	1	3	3	3	0	1

Milwaukee	IP.	H.	R.	ER.	BB.	SO.
Burdette (W)	9	7	5	4	1	5

aFlied out for Kucks in fifth. bRan for Covington in seventh. cGrounded out for Carey in eighth. dStruck out for Dickson in eighth. E—Mathews. DP—Milwaukee 2. LOB—New York 2, Milwaukee 5. 2B—Schoendienst 2, Mathews. HR—Bruton, Burdette, Mantle 2, Bauer. SB—Mathews. SF—Crandall, Pafko. U—Berry (A.L.), Gorman (N.L.), Flaherty (A.L.), Barlick (N.L.), Umont (A.L.) and Jackowski (N.L.). T—2:43. A—46,367.

Game 3

Saturday, October 4, At New York

Milwaukee	AB.	R.	H.	RBI.	PO.	A.
Bruton, cf	3	0	0	0	2	0
Schoendienst, 2b	4	0	2	0	1	3
Mathews, 3b	3	0	0	0	0	1
Aaron, rf	3	0	0	0	1	0
Covington, lf	3	0	1	0	4	0
Torre, 1b	4	0	2	0	9	0
Crandall, c	4	0	1	0	4	1
Logan, ss	3	0	0	0	2	0
Rush, p	2	0	0	0	0	3
aHanebrink	1	0	0	0	0	0
McMahon, p	0	0	0	0	1	0
cWise	1	0	0	0	0	0
Totals	31	0	6	0	24	8

New York	AB.	R.	H.	RBI.	PO.	A.
Bauer, rf	4	1	3	4	2	0
Kubek, ss	4	0	0	0	2	2
Mantle, cf	2	0	0	0	4	0
Berra, c	4	0	0	0	9	2
Siebern, lf	2	1	0	0	2	0
Lumpe, 3b	3	0	1	0	2	1
Richardson, 3b	1	0	0	0	0	0
Skowron, 1b	4	0	0	0	4	1
McDougald, 2b	2	1	0	0	1	0
Larsen, p	1	0	0	0	1	0
bSlaughter	0	1	0	0	0	0
Duren, p	0	0	0	0	0	1
Totals	27	4	4	4	27	7

Milwaukee .... 0 0 0 0 0 0 0 0 0—0
New York .... 0 0 0 0 2 0 2 0 x—4

Milwaukee	IP.	H.	R.	ER.	BB.	SO.
Rush (L)	6	3	2	2	5	2
McMahon	2	1	2	2	2	2

New York	IP.	H.	R.	ER.	BB.	SO.
Larsen (W)	7	6	0	0	3	8
Duren	2	0	0	0	3	1

aPopped out for Rush in seventh. bWalked for Larsen in seventh. cStruck out for McMahon in ninth. DP—Milwaukee 1, New York 1. LOB—Milwaukee 10, New York 6. HR—Bauer. WP—Duren. U—Gorman (N.L.), Flaherty (A.L.), Barlick (N.L.), Berry (A.L.), Jackowski (N.L.) and Umont (A.L.). T—2:42. A—71,599.

Game 4

Sunday, October 5, At New York

Milwaukee	AB.	R.	H.	RBI.	PO.	A.
Schoendienst, 2b	5	1	1	0	2	2
Logan, ss	5	1	1	0	1	5
Mathews, 3b	4	0	1	1	1	1
Aaron, cf-rf	4	0	2	0	2	0
Adcock, 1b	3	0	0	0	9	0
bTorre, 1b	1	0	0	0	2	0
Crandall, c	3	1	2	0	8	0
Covington, lf	3	0	0	0	1	0
cBruton, cf	0	0	0	0	1	0
Pafko, rf-lf	4	0	1	0	0	0
Spahn, p	4	0	1	1	0	2
Totals	36	3	9	2	27	10

New York	AB.	R.	H.	RBI.	PO.	A.
Siebern, lf	3	0	0	0	1	0
McDougald, 2b	4	0	0	0	4	4
Bauer, rf	4	0	0	0	0	0
Mantle, cf	4	0	1	0	2	0
Skowron, 1b	3	0	1	0	10	0
Berra, c	3	0	0	0	7	0
Richardson, 3b	2	0	0	0	0	0
aHoward	1	0	0	0	0	0
Carey, 3b	0	0	0	0	0	1
Kubek, ss	2	0	0	0	2	6
dSlaughter	1	0	0	0	0	0
Dickson, p	0	0	0	0	0	0
Ford, p	1	0	0	0	1	1
Kucks, p	0	0	0	0	0	0
eLumpe, ss	1	0	0	0	0	0
Totals	29	0	2	0	27	12

Milwaukee .... 0 0 0 0 0 1 1 1 0—3
New York .... 0 0 0 0 0 0 0 0 0—0

Milwaukee	IP.	H.	R.	ER.	BB.	SO.
Spahn (W)	9	2	0	0	2	7

New York	IP.	H.	R.	ER.	BB.	SO.
Ford (L)	7*	8	3	2	1	6
Kucks	1	1	0	0	1	0
Dickson	1	0	0	0	0	0

*Pitched to two batters in eighth.

aStruck out for Richardson in seventh. bPopped out for Adcock in eighth. cRan for Covington in eighth. dStruck out for Kubek in eighth. ePopped out for Kucks in eighth. E—Kubek. DP—New York 1. LOB—Milwaukee 8, New York 4. 2B—Aaron, Pafko, Logan, Mathews. 3B—Mantle, Schoendienst. WP—Ford. U—Flaherty (A.L.), Barlick (N.L.), Berry (A.L.), Gorman (N.L.), Umont (A.L.) and Jackowski (N.L.). T—2:17. A—71,563.

Game 5

Monday, October 6, At New York

Milwaukee	AB.	R.	H.	RBI.	PO.	A.
Bruton, cf	3	0	2	0	2	0
Schoendienst, 2b	3	0	1	0	0	1
Mathews, 3b	4	0	1	0	1	3
Aaron, rf	4	0	0	0	1	0
Covington, lf	4	0	1	0	2	0
bWise	0	0	0	0	0	0
Torre, 1b	3	0	0	0	9	1
Crandall, c	3	0	0	0	8	1
Logan, ss	3	0	0	0	0	3
Burdette, p	2	0	0	0	1	0
Pizarro, p	0	0	0	0	0	1
aHanebrink	1	0	0	0	0	0
Willey, p	0	0	0	0	0	0
Totals	30	0	5	0	24	10

New York	AB.	R.	H.	RBI.	PO.	A.
Bauer, rf	4	1	1	0	2	0
Lumpe, 3b	3	0	1	0	0	1
Richardson, 3b	1	0	0	0	0	1
Mantle, cf	3	1	2	0	2	0
Berra, c	4	1	1	1	11	0
Howard, lf	3	1	0	0	3	1
Skowron, 1b	4	1	1	1	5	1
McDougald, 2b	4	2	2	3	3	1
Kubek, ss	4	0	1	0	1	1
Turley, p	3	0	1	2	0	0
Totals	33	7	10	7	27	6

Milwaukee .... 0 0 0 0 0 0 0 0 0—0
New York .... 0 0 1 0 0 6 0 0 x—7

Milwaukee	IP.	H.	R.	ER.	BB.	SO.
Burdette (L)	5⅓	8	6	6	1	4
Pizarro	1⅔	2	1	1	1	3
Willey	1	0	0	0	0	2

New York	IP.	H.	R.	ER.	BB.	SO.
Turley (W)	9	5	0	0	3	10

aFouled out for Pizarro in eighth. bRan for Covington in ninth. DP—Milwaukee 1, New York 1. LOB—Milwaukee 7, New York 4. 2B—Berra, McDougald. HR—McDougald. SH—Schoendienst. WP—Pizarro. U—Barlick (N.L.), Berry (A.L.), Gorman (N.L.), Flaherty (A.L.), Jackowski (N.L.) and Umont (A.L.). T—2:19. A—65,279.

Game 6

Wednesday, October 8, At Milwaukee

New York	AB.	R.	H.	RBI.	PO.	A.
Carey, 3b	5	0	0	0	0	1
McDougald, 2b	5	1	2	1	6	4
Bauer, rf	5	1	2	1	0	0
Mantle, cf	5	1	1	0	0	0
Howard, lf	5	1	2	0	3	1
Berra, c	4	0	2	1	14	1
Skowron, 1b	4	0	1	1	6	2
Kubek, ss	2	0	0	0	0	1
aSlaughter	1	0	0	0	0	0
Duren, p	2	0	0	0	0	0
Turley, p	0	0	0	0	0	0
Ford, p	1	0	0	0	0	0
Ditmar, p	1	0	0	0	1	0
bLumpe, ss	1	0	0	0	0	1
Totals	41	4	10	4	30	11

Milwaukee	AB.	R.	H.	RBI.	PO.	A.
Schoendienst, 2b	4	1	2	0	6	2
Logan, ss	2	1	0	0	1	3
Mathews, 3b	5	0	0	0	1	3
Aaron, rf	5	0	3	2	2	0
Adcock, 1b	4	0	1	0	6	0
cMantilla	0	0	0	0	0	0
Crandall, c	4	0	0	0	7	1
dTorre	1	0	0	0	0	0
Covington, lf	4	1	2	0	0	0
Pafko, cf	2	0	1	0	3	0
Bruton, cf	2	0	0	0	3	0
Spahn, p	4	0	1	1	1	2
McMahon, p	0	0	0	0	0	0
Totals	37	3	10	3	30	11

New York .... 1 0 0 0 0 1 0 0 0 2—4
Milwaukee .... 1 1 0 0 0 0 0 0 0 1—3

New York	IP.	H.	R.	ER.	BB.	SO.
Ford	1⅓	5	2	2	1	2
Ditmar	3⅔	2	0	0	0	2
Duren (W)	4⅔	3	1	1	2	8
Turley	⅓	0	0	0	0	0

Milwaukee	IP.	H.	R.	ER.	BB.	SO.
Spahn (L)	9⅔	9	4	4	2	5
McMahon	⅓	1	0	0	0	1

aGrounded out for Kubek in sixth. bStruck out for Ditmar in sixth. cRan for Adcock in tenth. dPopped out for Crandall in tenth. E—Ditmar, Schoendienst, Logan 2, Bruton. DP—New York 1, Milwaukee 1. LOB—New York 10, Milwaukee 9. 2B—Schoendienst. HR—Bauer, McDougald. SH—Logan 2. SF—Berra. U—Berry (A.L.), Gorman (N.L.), Flaherty (A.L.), Barlick (N.L.), Umont (A.L.) and Jackowski (N.L.). T—3:07. A—46,367.

Game 7

Thursday, October 9, At Milwaukee

New York	AB.	R.	H.	RBI.	PO.	A.
Bauer, rf	5	0	0	0	2	0
McDougald, 2b	5	0	2	0	3	6
Mantle, cf	4	0	0	0	2	0
Berra, c	4	2	1	0	3	1
Howard, lf	3	2	2	1	3	0
Lumpe, 3b	3	0	0	0	0	2
Carey, 3b	1	1	1	0	1	0
Skowron, 1b	4	1	2	4	12	0
Kubek, ss	2	0	0	1	1	2
Larsen, p	1	0	0	0	0	0
Turley, p	2	0	0	0	0	1
Totals	34	6	8	6	27	12

Milwaukee	AB.	R.	H.	RBI.	PO.	A.
Schoendienst, 2b	5	1	1	0	5	3
Bruton, cf	3	0	1	0	1	0
Torre, 1b	2	0	0	0	10	0
Aaron, rf	3	0	1	0	4	0
Covington, lf	4	0	0	1	1	0
Mathews, 3b	1	0	0	0	1	2
Crandall, c	4	1	1	1	4	1
Logan, ss	4	0	0	0	1	5
Burdette, p	3	0	0	0	0	2
McMahon, p	0	0	0	0	0	0
aAdcock	1	0	1	0	0	0
bMantilla	0	0	0	0	0	0
Totals	30	2	5	2	27	13

New York .... 0 2 0 0 0 0 4 0—6
Milwaukee .... 1 0 0 0 0 1 0 0 0—2

New York	IP.	H.	R.	ER.	BB.	SO.
Larsen	2	3	1	1	3	1
Turley (W)	6	2	1	1	3	2

Milwaukee	IP.	H.	R.	ER.	BB.	SO.
Burdette (L)	8	7	6	4	2	3
McMahon	1	1	0	0	1	2

aSingled for McMahon in ninth. bRan for Adcock in ninth. E—Torre 2. DP—New York 1. LOB—New York 7, Milwaukee 8. 2B—McDougald, Berra. HR—Crandall, Skowron. SB—Howard. SH—Torre, Howard, Turley. SF—Kubek. U—Gorman (N.L.), Flaherty (A.L.), Barlick (N.L.), Berry (A.L.), Jackowski (N.L.) and Umont (A.L.). T—2:31. A—46,367.

COMPOSITE BATTING AVERAGES

New York Yankees

Player-Position	G.	AB.	R.	H.	2B.	3B.	HR.	RBI.	BA.
Kucks, p	2	1	0	1	0	0	0	0	1.000
Bauer, rf	7	31	6	10	0	0	4	8	.323
McDougald, 2b	7	28	5	9	2	0	2	4	.321
Skowron, 1b	7	27	3	7	0	0	2	7	.259
Mantle, cf	7	24	4	6	0	1	2	3	.250
Howard, lf-ph	6	18	4	4	0	0	0	2	.222
Berra, c	7	27	3	6	3	0	0	2	.222
Turley, p	4	5	0	1	0	0	0	2	.200
Lumpe, ph-3b-ss	6	12	0	2	0	0	0	0	.167
Siebern, lf	3	8	1	1	0	0	0	0	.125
Carey, 3b	5	12	1	1	0	0	0	0	.083
Kubek, ss	7	21	0	1	0	0	0	1	.048
Richardson, 3b	4	5	0	0	0	0	0	0	.000
Ford, p	3	4	1	0	0	0	0	0	.000
Duren, p	3	3	0	0	0	0	0	0	.000
Maas, p	1	0	0	0	0	0	0	0	.000
Dickson, p	2	0	0	0	0	0	0	0	.000
Monroe, p	1	0	0	0	0	0	0	0	.000
Larsen, p	2	2	0	0	0	0	0	0	.000
Ditmar, p	1	1	0	0	0	0	0	0	.000
Slaughter, ph	4	3	1	0	0	0	0	0	.000
Throneberry, ph	1	1	0	0	0	0	0	0	.000
Totals	7	233	29	49	5	1	10	29	.210

Milwaukee Braves

Player-Position	G.	AB.	R.	H.	2B.	3B.	HR.	RBI.	BA.
Bruton, ph-cf-pr	7	17	2	7	0	0	1	2	.412
Spahn, p	3	12	0	4	0	0	0	3	.333
Pafko, cf-lf-rf	4	9	0	3	1	0	0	1	.333
Aaron, rf-cf	7	27	3	9	2	0	0	2	.333
Adcock, 1b-ph	4	13	1	4	0	0	0	0	.308
Schoendienst, 2b	7	30	5	9	3	1	0	0	.300
Covington, lf	7	26	2	7	0	0	0	4	.269
Crandall, c	7	25	4	6	0	0	1	3	.240
Torre, ph-1b	7	17	0	3	0	0	0	1	.176
Mathews, 3b	7	25	3	4	2	0	0	3	.160
Logan, ss	7	25	3	3	2	0	0	2	.120
Burdette, p	3	9	1	1	0	0	1	3	.111
Mantilla, ss-pr	4	0	1	0	0	0	0	0	.000
Rush, p	1	2	0	0	0	0	0	0	.000
McMahon, p	3	0	0	0	0	0	0	0	.000
Willey, p	1	0	0	0	0	0	0	0	.000
Pizarro, p	1	0	0	0	0	0	0	0	.000
Wise, ph-pr	2	1	0	0	0	0	0	0	.000
Hanebrink, ph	2	2	0	0	0	0	0	0	.000
Totals	7	240	25	60	10	1	3	24	.250

COMPOSITE PITCHING AVERAGES

New York Yankees

Pitcher	G.	IP.	H.	R.	ER.	BB.	SO.	W.	L.	ERA.
Ditmar	1	3⅔	2	0	0	0	2	0	0	0.00
Larsen	2	9⅓	9	1	1	6	9	1	0	0.96
Duren	3	9⅓	7	2	2	6	14	1	1	1.93
Kucks	2	4⅓	4	1	1	1	0	0	0	2.08
Turley	4	16⅓	10	5	5	7	13	2	1	2.76
Ford	3	15⅓	19	8	7	5	16	0	1	4.11
Dickson	2	4	4	2	2	0	1	0	0	4.50
Monroe	1	1	3	3	3	1	1	0	0	27.00
Maas	1	⅓	2	3	3	1	0	0	0	81.00
Totals	7	63⅔	60	25	24	27	56	4	3	3.39

Milwaukee Braves

Pitcher	G.	IP.	H.	R.	ER.	BB.	SO.	W.	L.	ERA.
Willey	1	1	0	0	0	0	2	0	0	0.00
Spahn	3	28⅔	19	7	7	8	18	2	1	2.20
Rush	1	6	3	2	2	5	2	0	1	3.00
McMahon	3	3⅓	3	2	2	3	5	0	0	5.40
Pizarro	1	1⅔	2	1	1	1	3	0	0	5.40
Burdette	3	22⅓	22	17	14	4	12	1	2	5.64
Totals	7	63	49	29	26	21	42	3	4	3.71

1959
LOS ANGELES DODGERS
VS.
CHICAGO WHITE SOX

The Dodgers had come a long way since 1958. From seventh place to the National League pennant.

The Dodgers also had come a long way since 1957. About 3,000 miles.

Times they were a-changing. Major league baseball, which had undergone its first alignment switch in 50 years in 1953 with the transfer of the Boston Braves to Milwaukee and then saw the St. Louis Browns move to Baltimore in 1954 and the Philadelphia Athletics shift to Kansas City in 1955, underwent a blockbuster makeover in 1958 when the New York Giants took up residence in San Francisco and the Brooklyn Dodgers settled into Los Angeles.

Los Angeles fans, expectations high for a club that had won four N.L. pennants in its last six seasons in Brooklyn, received a jolt in '58 when the Dodgers made their West Coast debut by finishing two games from the basement. But after a year of adjustment and the infusion of some new faces into a cast that had grown old in Brooklyn, the Dodgers rebounded dramatically in 1959 and captured the franchise's seventh flag in the last 13 seasons.

The Dodgers, losers of two pennant playoffs in Brooklyn, won the '59 N.L. championship by beating the Milwaukee Braves in two straight games in a best-of-three playoff after the clubs had finished in a first-place tie with 86-68 records. With one old postseason jinx disposed of, the Dodgers took aim on another, the World Series. Unable to win the fall classic as a Brooklyn-based team until the club's eighth goround in the event, the Dodgers went on to win the Series in their first appearance as a representative of Los Angeles. End of jinx

One of the key plays of the 1959 Series occurred in the eighth inning of Game 2 when Chicago catcher Sherman Lollar was tagged out by John Roseboro when he tried to score from first on Al Smith's double.

No. 2.

The 1959 World Series between the Dodgers and the American League champion Chicago White Sox began at Comiskey Park, which hadn't played host to a Series contest since the concluding game of the scandal-ridden 1919 affair. The "Go-Go" Sox, featuring a Luis Aparicio-led running attack, excellent defense and topline pitching, hauled out the lumber in Game 1.

Ted Kluszewski, a late-August acquisition from the National League and a man who three times had hit 40 or more homers in an N.L. season, drove in five runs with a pair of two-run homers and a run-scoring single as Chicago pummeled Los Angeles, 11-0. Early Wynn (sevenplus innings) and Gerry Staley combined to blank the Dodgers, who suffered yet another tough day in the fall classic. In their last Series game three years earlier,

the Dodgers had lost, 9-0, and they now had scored one run in their last four Series contests.

In Game 2, Chicago righthander Bob Shaw was guarding a 2-1 lead with two out in the seventh inning when Dodgers Manager Walter Alston sent up Chuck Essegian to bat for Johnny Podres, who had pitched creditably in his first World Series outing since hurling Brooklyn to its only Series championship in '55 (Podres had missed the '56 season because of military service). Essegian boomed a game-tying home run to left. Jim Gilliam then walked and Charlie Neal, who had smashed a bases-empty homer in the fifth, followed with a two-run homer to center.

Larry Sherry, a 24-year-old righthander who had been called up from St. Paul in early July, pitched the final three innings for the Dodgers, allowing one run and three hits. He slipped out of a

jam in the eighth when Sherman Lollar was tagged out at the plate by John Roseboro when the White Sox's catcher tried to score from first base on Al Smith's double (which already had driven in one run).

Buoyed by the 4-3 triumph, the Dodgers looked ahead to the first West Coast game in Series history.

When the Dodgers last played at home in a World Series—the date was October 10, 1956—cramped Ebbets Field in Brooklyn was the site. The attendance was 33,782. Jackie Robinson was at third base, Roy Campanella was the catcher, Duke Snider was in center field, Carl Furillo was in right, Gil Hodges was at first base, Pee Wee Reese was at shortstop and Don Newcombe was the pitcher.

Now, on October 4, 1959, massive Memorial Coliseum in Los Angeles was the site. The attendance was 92,394. Robinson was in retirement, having played his last big-league game in that '56 Series finale; Campanella was in a wheelchair, having been paralyzed in a January 1958 automobile crash; Snider, a starter in the first two games of the '59 Series, was supplanted in this game by young Don Demeter; Furillo was on the bench, having appeared in only 50 regular-season games in '59; Hodges still held down first base; Reese had become a Dodger coach, and the shortstop's job was now in the hands of speedster Maury Wills, who had been called up from Spokane seven weeks into the season; and Newcombe now was a member of the Cincinnati Reds.

While Furillo was nearing the end of his career, he had one last big hit left in him. With Game 3 in a 0-0 tie, Furillo delivered a two-run pinch single in the seventh and Los Angeles went on to a 3-1 triumph. Sherry got the final six outs for the Dodgers in relief of Don Drysdale.

Hodges' eighth-inning home run decided Game 4 as the Dodgers prevailed, 5-4. Lollar had deadlocked the contest with a three-run homer in the seventh, but Sherry came on again in the eighth and kept Manager Al Lopez's White Sox at bay.

Hoping to end the Series at home, the Dodgers sent 23-year-old lefthander Sandy Koufax to the mound against Shaw, who had enjoyed an 18-6 season for the White Sox. Koufax, still trying to get a grip on his control, had only a 28-27 record at this juncture of his major league career.

Shaw, getting 1⅓ innings of crucial help from reliever Dick Donovan, wound up a 1-0 winner in a game in which the only run was scored on a double-play grounder (by Lollar, in the fourth). The Sox got a great defensive play from Jim Rivera in the seventh. Inserted into the game moments earlier, right fielder Rivera made an outstanding running catch of Neal's two-out smash—there were Dodger baserunners at second and third—that carried near the fence in right-center. For the third straight day, a big-league-record crowd was on hand as 92,706 fans witnessed the action.

The Dodgers then clipped Wynn and reliever Donovan for eight runs in the first four innings of Game 6 at Comiskey Park, with Snider starting the onslaught with a two-run homer in the third and Wally Moon adding a two-run shot in the fourth. The lefthanded-hitting Moon had been a major cog in the Dodgers' pennant machine, perfecting an "inside-out" swing after his acquisition from the St. Louis Cardinals and becoming a master at driving balls off and over the Memorial Coliseum's left-field screen (which was a mere 251 feet from the plate).

While starter Podres failed to be the pitcher of record this time around in the Dodgers' Series-clinching victory—he lasted only 3⅓ innings and yielded a three-run homer to Kluszewski—Sherry came through once more. Pitching 5⅔ innings of four-hit, scoreless relief, he notched his second victory of the Series to go with his rescue efforts in Los Angeles' other two victories. The Dodgers won, 9-3, with Essegian putting a topper on things in the ninth with an unprecedented second pinch homer of the Series.

The White Sox got 10 RBIs—a record for a six-game Series—and a .391 batting average from Kluszewski and a .375 mark from Nellie Fox, whose bat work as the No. 2 hitter behind leadoff man Aparicio had been critical to the success of the "Go-Go" Sox. But with Sherry closing the door in one key situation after another and batterymate Roseboro making a big contribution despite a .095 batting mark (he helped limit Chicago to two stolen bases over the six games), the "Go-Go" team was gone-gone.

Game 1

Thursday, October 1, At Chicago

Los Angeles	AB.	R.	H.	RBI.	PO.	A.
Gilliam, 3b	4	0	1	0	0	1
Neal, 2b	4	0	2	0	3	3
Moon, lf	4	0	1	0	2	0
Snider, cf	2	0	0	0	2	0
Demeter, cf	1	0	0	0	0	0
Larker, rf	4	0	1	0	4	0
Hodges, 1b	4	0	2	0	10	0
Roseboro, c	4	0	0	0	5	0
Wills, ss	3	0	1	0	1	2
cFurillo	1	0	0	0	0	0
Craig, p	1	0	0	0	0	1
Churn, p	0	0	0	0	0	1
Labine, p	0	0	0	0	0	0
aEssegian	1	0	0	0	0	0
Koufax, p	0	0	0	0	0	0
bFairly	1	0	0	0	0	0
Klippstein, p	0	0	0	0	0	1
Totals	34	0	8	0	24	9

Chicago	AB.	R.	H.	RBI.	PO.	A.
Aparicio, ss	5	0	0	0	3	3
Fox, 2b	4	2	1	0	2	2
Landis, cf	4	3	3	1	1	0
Kluszewski, 1b	4	2	3	5	8	2
Lollar, c	3	1	0	1	7	0
Goodman, 3b	2	1	1	1	0	0
Esposito, 3b	2	0	0	0	1	0
Smith, lf	4	1	2	0	2	0
Rivera, rf	4	1	0	0	2	0
Wynn, p	3	0	1	1	1	1
Staley, p	1	0	0	0	0	1
Totals	36	11	11	9	27	9

Los Angeles		0 0 0	0 0 0	0 0 0—0		
Chicago		2 0 7	2 0 0	0 0 x—11		

Los Angeles	IP.	H.	R.	ER.	BB.	SO.
Craig (L)	2⅓	5	5	5	1	1
Churn	⅔*	5	6	2	0	0
Labine	1	0	0	0	0	0
Koufax	2	0	0	0	0	1
Klippstein	2	1	0	0	0	2

Chicago	IP.	H.	R.	ER.	BB.	SO.
Wynn (W)	7†	6	0	0	1	6
Staley	2	2	0	0	0	1

*Pitched to two batters in fourth.
†Pitched to one batter in eighth.

aStruck out for Labine in fifth. bGrounded out for Koufax in seventh. cFlied out for Wills in ninth. E—Neal, Snider 2. DP—Chicago 1. LOB—Los Angeles 8, Chicago 3. 2B—Fox, Smith 2, Wynn. HR—Kluszewski 2. SB—Neal. SF—Lollar. U—Summers (A.L.), Dascoli (N.L.), Hurley (A.L.), Secory (N.L.), Rice (A.L.) and Dixon (N.L.). T—2:35. A—48,013.

Game 2

Friday, October 2, At Chicago

Los Angeles	AB.	R.	H.	RBI.	PO.	A.
Gilliam, 3b	4	1	1	0	1	1
Neal, 2b	5	2	3	2	4	4
Moon, lf	3	0	1	0	1	1
Snider, cf	4	0	1	0	1	0
Demeter, cf	0	0	0	0	0	0
Larker, rf	3	0	0	0	4	0
Sherry, p	1	0	0	0	0	1
Hodges, 1b	4	0	0	0	10	1
Roseboro, c	4	0	1	0	6	0
Wills, ss	4	0	1	0	1	6
Podres, p	2	0	1	0	0	0
aEssegian	1	1	1	1	0	0
Fairly, rf	1	0	0	0	0	0
Totals	36	4	9	4	27	14

Chicago	AB.	R.	H.	RBI.	PO.	A.
Aparicio, ss	5	1	2	0	3	1
Fox, 2b	4	0	0	0	0	5
Landis, cf	3	1	0	0	2	0
Kluszewski, 1b	4	0	1	1	9	0
bTorgeson, 1b	0	0	0	0	0	0

	AB.	R.	H.	RBI.	PO.	A.
Lollar, c	4	0	2	1	4	0
Smith, lf	3	0	1	1	2	0
Phillips, 3b	3	0	1	0	2	0
cGoodman, 3b	1	0	0	0	0	0
McAnany, rf	3	0	0	0	3	0
Rivera, rf	1	0	0	0	2	0
Shaw, p	3	0	1	0	0	1
Lown, p	0	0	0	0	0	0
dCash	1	0	0	0	0	0
Totals	35	3	8	3	27	7

Los Angeles	0 0 0	0 1 0	3 0 0—4
Chicago	2 0 0	0 0 0	0 1 0—3

Los Angeles	IP.	H.	R.	ER.	BB.	SO.
Podres (W)	6	5	2	2	3	3
Sherry	3	3	1	1	0	1

Chicago	IP.	H.	R.	ER.	BB.	SO.
Shaw (L)	6⅔	8	4	4	1	1
Lown	2⅓	1	0	0	1	3

aHit home run for Podres in seventh. bRan for Kluszewski in eighth. cStruck out for Phillips in eighth. dGrounded out for Lown in ninth. E—Wills. LOB—Los Angeles 7, Chicago 8. 2B—Aparicio, Phillips, Smith. HR—Neal 2, Essegian. SB—Moon, Gilliam. U—Dascoli (N.L.), Hurley (A.L.), Secory (N.L.), Summers (A.L.), Rice (A.L.) and Dixon (N.L.). T—2:21. A—47,368.

Game 3

Sunday, October 4, At Los Angeles

Chicago	AB.	R.	H.	RBI.	PO.	A.
Aparicio, ss	4	0	2	0	0	3
Fox, 2b	4	0	3	0	3	6
Landis, cf	5	0	1	0	2	0
Kluszewski, 1b	3	1	1	0	11	1
Lollar, c	4	0	2	0	5	1
Goodman, 3b	3	0	2	0	1	1
cEsposito, 3b	0	0	0	0	0	0
Smith, lf	4	0	0	0	0	0
Rivera, rf	3	0	0	0	1	0
Donovan, p	3	0	1	0	1	1
Staley, p	0	0	0	0	0	0
dCash	1	0	0	0	0	0
Totals	34	1	12	0	24	13

Los Angeles	AB.	R.	H.	RBI.	PO.	A.
Gilliam, 3b	4	0	0	0	3	2
Neal, 2b	4	1	2	1	3	2
Moon, rf	4	0	0	0	1	0
Larker, lf	2	1	0	0	1	0
Hodges, 1b	2	0	1	0	6	1
Demeter, cf	2	0	0	0	0	0
aFurillo	1	0	1	2	0	0
bFairly, cf	0	0	0	0	0	0
Roseboro, c	3	0	0	0	9	3
Wills, ss	3	1	1	0	3	2
Drysdale, p	2	0	0	0	1	1
Sherry, p	0	0	0	0	0	0
Totals	27	3	5	3	27	11

Chicago	0 0 0	0 0 0	0 1 0—1
Los Angeles	0 0 0	0 0 0	2 1 x—3

Chicago	IP.	H.	R.	ER.	BB.	SO.
Donovan (L)	6⅔	2	2	2	2	5
Staley	1⅓	3	1	1	0	0

Los Angeles	IP.	H.	R.	ER.	BB.	SO.
Drysdale (W)	7*	11	1	1	4	5
Sherry	2	1	0	0	0	3

*Pitched to two batters in eighth.

aSingled for Demeter in seventh. bRan for Furillo in seventh. cRan for Goodman in eighth. dStruck out for Staley in ninth. DP—Chicago 1, Los Angeles 3. LOB—Chicago 11, Los Angeles 3. 2B—Neal. SB—Landis. SH—Sherry. HBP—By Sherry (Goodman). U—Hurley (A.L.), Secory (N.L.), Summers (A.L.), Dascoli (N.L.), Dixon (N.L.) and Rice (A.L.). T—2:33. A—92,394.

Game 4

Monday, October 5, At Los Angeles

Chicago	AB.	R.	H.	RBI.	PO.	A.
Landis, cf	5	1	1	0	0	0
Aparicio, ss	3	0	1	0	0	2
Fox, 2b	5	1	3	0	3	4
Kluszewski, 1b	4	1	2	1	9	0
Lollar, c	4	1	1	3	6	2
Goodman, 3b	4	0	0	0	0	0
Smith, lf	3	0	2	0	3	0
Rivera, rf	3	0	0	0	3	1
Wynn, p	1	0	0	0	0	1
Lown, p	0	0	0	0	0	0
aCash	1	0	0	0	0	0
Pierce, p	0	0	0	0	0	0
cTorgeson	1	0	0	0	0	0
Staley, p	0	0	0	0	0	0
Totals	34	4	10	4	24	10

Los Angeles	AB.	R.	H.	RBI.	PO.	A.
Gilliam, 3b	4	0	0	0	0	1
Neal, 2b	4	0	0	0	4	4
Moon, rf-lf	4	1	2	0	3	0
Larker, lf	2	1	1	0	0	0
bFurillo, rf	1	0	0	0	0	0
Fairly, rf	1	0	0	0	0	0
Hodges, 1b	4	2	2	2	10	0
Demeter, cf	3	1	2	0	1	0
Roseboro, c	3	0	1	1	7	0
Wills, ss	4	0	1	0	2	6
Craig, p	2	0	0	0	0	1
Sherry, p	0	0	0	0	0	0
Totals	32	5	9	3	27	12

Chicago	0 0 0	0 0 0	4 0 0—4
Los Angeles	0 0 4	0 0 0	0 1 x—5

Chicago	IP.	H.	R.	ER.	BB.	SO.
Wynn	2⅔	8	4	3	0	2
Lown	⅓	0	0	0	0	0
Pierce	3	0	0	0	1	2
Staley (L)	2	1	1	1	0	2

Los Angeles	IP.	H.	R.	ER.	BB.	SO.
Craig	7	10	4	4	4	7
Sherry (W)	2	0	0	0	1	0

aStruck out for Lown in fourth. bStruck out for Larker in fifth. cGrounded out for Pierce in seventh. E—Landis, Aparicio, Pierce. DP—Chicago 2. LOB—Chicago 9, Los Angeles 6. 2B—Fox. HR—Lollar, Hodges. SB—Aparicio, Wills. SH—Roseboro, Craig, Aparicio. PB—Lollar. U—Secory (N.L.), Summers (A.L.), Dascoli (N.L.), Hurley (A.L.), Dixon (N.L.) and Rice (A.L.). T—2:30. A—92,650.

Game 5

Tuesday, October 6, At Los Angeles

Chicago	AB.	R.	H.	RBI.	PO.	A.
Aparicio, ss	4	0	2	0	3	5
Fox, 2b	3	1	1	0	4	4
Landis, cf	4	0	1	0	2	0
Lollar, c	4	0	0	0	1	0
Kluszewski, 1b	4	0	0	0	12	0
Smith, rf-lf	4	0	0	0	1	0
Phillips, 3b	3	0	1	0	1	2
McAnany, lf	1	0	0	0	1	0
Rivera, rf	0	0	0	0	2	0
Shaw, p	1	0	0	0	0	3
Pierce, p	0	0	0	0	0	0
Donovan, p	0	0	0	0	0	0
Totals	28	1	5	0	27	14

Los Angeles	AB.	R.	H.	RBI.	PO.	A.
Gilliam, 3b	5	0	4	0	0	3
Neal, 2b	5	0	1	0	5	2
Moon, rf-cf	4	0	1	0	0	0
Larker, lf	4	0	0	0	3	1
Hodges, 1b	4	0	3	0	7	1
Demeter, cf	3	0	0	0	4	0
eFairly	0	0	0	0	0	0
fRepulski, rf	0	0	0	0	0	0
Roseboro, c	3	0	0	0	6	1
gFurillo	1	0	0	0	0	0
Pignatano, c	0	0	0	0	1	0
Wills, ss	2	0	0	0	1	2
aEssegian	0	0	0	0	0	0
bZimmer, ss	1	0	0	0	0	1
Koufax, p	2	0	0	0	0	0
cSnider	1	0	0	0	0	0
dPodres	0	0	0	0	0	0
Williams, p	0	0	0	0	0	0
hSherry	1	0	0	0	0	0
Totals	36	0	9	0	27	11

Chicago	0 0 0	1 0 0	0 0 0—1
Los Angeles	0 0 0	0 0 0	0 0 0—0

Chicago	IP.	H.	R.	ER.	BB.	SO.
Shaw (W)	7⅓	9	0	0	1	1
Pierce	0*	0	0	0	1	0
Donovan	1⅔	0	0	0	0	0

Los Angeles	IP.	H.	R.	ER.	BB.	SO.
Koufax (L)	7	5	1	1	1	6
Williams	2	0	0	0	2	1

*Pitched to one batter in eighth.

aWalked for Wills in seventh. bRan for Essegian in seventh. cHit into force play for Koufax in seventh. dRan for Snider in seventh. eAnnounced as batter for Demeter in eighth. fWalked intentionally for Fairly in eighth. gPopped out for Roseboro in eighth. hGrounded out for Williams in ninth. DP—Los Angeles 1. LOB—Chicago 5, Los Angeles 11. 3B—Hodges. SB—Gilliam. SH—Shaw 2. WP—Shaw. U—Summers (A.L.), Dascoli (N.L.), Hurley (A.L.), Secory (N.L.), Dixon (N.L.) and Rice (A.L.). T—2:28. A—92,706.

Game 6

Thursday, October 8, At Chicago

Los Angeles	AB.	R.	H.	RBI.	PO.	A.
Gilliam, 3b	4	1	0	0	0	2
Neal, 2b	5	1	3	2	4	4
Moon, lf	4	2	1	2	3	0
Snider, cf-rf	3	1	1	2	2	0
eEssegian	1	1	1	1	0	0
Fairly, rf	0	0	0	0	0	0
Hodges, 1b	5	0	1	0	10	0
Larker, rf	1	0	1	0	0	0
aDemeter, cf	3	1	1	0	4	0
Roseboro, c	4	0	0	0	2	0
Wills, ss	4	1	1	1	2	3
Podres, p	2	1	1	1	0	1
Sherry, p	2	0	2	0	0	2
Totals	38	9	13	9	27	12

Chicago	AB.	R.	H.	RBI.	PO.	A.
Aparicio, ss	5	0	1	0	1	2
Fox, 2b	4	0	1	0	2	2
Landis, cf	3	1	1	0	2	0
Lollar, c	3	1	0	0	5	2
Kluszewski, 1b	4	1	2	3	10	0
Smith, lf	2	0	0	0	2	0
Phillips, 3b-rf	4	0	1	0	3	1
McAnany, rf	1	0	0	0	1	0
bGoodman, 3b	3	0	0	0	0	1
Wynn, p	1	0	0	0	0	1
Donovan, p	0	0	0	0	0	0
Lown, p	0	0	0	0	0	0
cTorgeson	0	0	0	0	0	0
Staley, p	0	0	0	0	1	0
dRomano	1	0	0	0	0	0
Pierce, p	0	0	0	0	0	0
Moore, p	0	0	0	0	0	0
fCash	1	0	0	0	0	0
Totals	32	3	6	3	27	9

Los Angeles	0 0 2	6 0 0	0 0 1—9
Chicago	0 0 0	3 0 0	0 0 0—3

Los Angeles	IP.	H.	R.	ER.	BB.	SO.
Podres	3⅓	2	3	3	3	1
Sherry (W)	5⅔	4	0	0	1	1

Chicago	IP.	H.	R.	ER.	BB.	SO.
Wynn (L)	3⅓	5	5	5	3	2
Donovan	0*	2	3	3	1	0
Lown	⅔	1	0	0	0	0
Staley	3	2	0	0	0	0
Pierce	1	2	0	0	0	1
Moore	1	1	1	1	0	1

*Pitched to three batters in fourth.

aRan for Larker in fourth. bStruck out for McAnany in fourth. cWalked for Lown in fourth. dGrounded out for Staley in seventh. eHomered for Snider in ninth. fFlied out for Moore in ninth. E—Aparicio. DP—Los Angeles 1. LOB—Los Angeles 7, Chicago 7. 2B—Podres, Neal, Fox, Kluszewski. HR—Snider, Moon, Kluszewski, Essegian. SH—Roseboro. HBP—By Podres (Landis). U—Dascoli (N.L.), Hurley (A.L.), Secory (N.L.), Summers (A.L.), Rice (A.L.) and Dixon (N.L.). T—2:33. A—47,653.

COMPOSITE BATTING AVERAGES

Los Angeles Dodgers

Player-Position	G.	AB.	R.	H.	2B.	3B.	HR.	RBI.	BA.
Essegian, ph	4	3	2	2	0	0	2	2	.667
Sherry, p-ph	5	4	0	2	0	0	0	0	.500
Podres, p-pr	3	4	1	2	1	0	0	1	.500
Hodges, 1b	6	23	2	9	0	1	1	2	.391
Neal, 2b	6	27	4	10	2	0	2	6	.370
Moon, lf-rf-cf	6	23	3	6	0	0	1	2	.261
Demeter, cf-pr	6	12	2	3	0	0	0	0	.250
Wills, ss	6	20	2	5	0	0	0	1	.250
Furillo, ph-rf	4	4	0	1	0	0	0	2	.250
Gilliam, 3b	6	25	2	6	0	0	0	0	.240
Snider, cf-ph-rf	4	10	1	2	0	0	1	2	.200
Larker, rf-lf	6	16	2	3	0	0	0	0	.188
Roseboro, c	6	21	0	2	0	0	0	1	.095
Zimmer, pr-ss	1	1	0	0	0	0	0	0	.000
Pignatano, c	1	0	0	0	0	0	0	0	.000
Fairly, ph-rf-cf-pr	6	3	0	0	0	0	0	0	.000
Craig, p	2	3	0	0	0	0	0	0	.000
Churn, p	1	0	0	0	0	0	0	0	.000
Labine, p	1	0	0	0	0	0	0	0	.000
Koufax, p	2	2	0	0	0	0	0	0	.000
Klippstein, p	1	0	0	0	0	0	0	0	.000
Drysdale, p	1	2	0	0	0	0	0	0	.000
Williams, p	1	0	0	0	0	0	0	0	.000
Repulski, ph-rf	1	0	0	0	0	0	0	0	.000
Totals	6	203	21	53	3	1	7	19	.261

Chicago White Sox

Player-Position	G.	AB.	R.	H.	2B.	3B.	HR.	RBI.	BA.
Kluszewski, 1b	6	23	5	9	1	0	3	10	.391
Fox, 2b	6	24	4	9	3	0	0	0	.375
Donovan, p	3	3	0	1	0	0	0	0	.333
Aparicio, ss	6	26	1	8	1	0	0	0	.308
Phillips, 3b-rf	3	10	0	3	1	0	0	0	.300
Landis, cf	6	24	6	7	0	0	0	1	.292
Smith, lf-rf	6	20	1	5	3	0	0	1	.250
Shaw, p	2	4	0	1	0	0	0	0	.250
Goodman, 3b-ph	5	13	1	3	0	0	0	1	.231
Lollar, c	6	22	3	5	0	0	1	5	.227
Wynn, p	3	5	0	1	1	0	0	1	.200
Esposito, 3b-pr	2	2	0	0	0	0	0	0	.000
Rivera, rf	5	11	1	0	0	0	0	0	.000
Tor'son, pr-1b-ph	3	1	1	0	0	0	0	0	.000
McAnany, lf-rf	3	5	0	0	0	0	0	0	.000
Staley, p	4	1	0	0	0	0	0	0	.000
Lown, p	3	0	0	0	0	0	0	0	.000
Pierce, p	3	0	0	0	0	0	0	0	.000
Moore, p	1	0	0	0	0	0	0	0	.000
Cash, ph	4	4	0	0	0	0	0	0	.000
Romano, ph	2	1	0	0	0	0	0	0	.000
Totals	6	199	23	52	10	0	4	19	.261

COMPOSITE PITCHING AVERAGES

Los Angeles Dodgers

Pitcher	G.	IP.	H.	R.	ER.	BB.	SO.	W.	L.	ERA.
Williams	1	2	0	0	0	2	1	0	0	0.00
Klippstein	1	2	1	0	0	0	2	0	0	0.00
Labine	1	1	0	0	0	0	1	0	0	0.00
Sherry	4	12⅔	8	1	1	2	5	2	0	0.71
Koufax	2	9	5	1	1	1	7	0	1	1.00
Drysdale	1	7	11	1	1	4	5	1	0	1.29
Podres	2	9⅓	7	5	5	6	4	1	0	4.82
Craig	2	9⅓	15	9	9	5	8	0	1	8.68
Churn	1	⅔	5	6	2	0	0	0	0	27.00
Totals	6	53	52	23	19	20	33	4	2	3.23

Chicago White Sox

Pitcher	G.	IP.	H.	R.	ER.	BB.	SO.	W.	L.	ERA.
Lown	3	3⅓	2	0	0	1	3	0	0	0.00
Pierce	3	4	2	0	0	2	3	0	0	0.00
Staley	4	8⅓	8	2	2	0	3	0	1	2.16
Shaw	2	14	17	4	4	2	2	1	1	2.57
Donovan	3	8⅓	4	5	5	3	5	0	1	5.40
Wynn	3	13	19	9	8	4	10	1	1	5.54
Moore	1	1	1	1	1	0	1	0	0	9.00
Totals	6	52	53	21	20	12	27	2	4	3.46

PITTSBURGH PIRATES
VS.
NEW YORK YANKEES

After four games of the 1960 World Series, the New York Yankees had scored 32 runs and the Pittsburgh Pirates had managed only 12. A Yankee sweep, eh? Wrong. At that juncture, the Series was tied at two victories apiece.

With six games completed in the '60 fall classic, the run totals were: New York 46, Pittsburgh 17. Surely a Yankee triumph, to the tune of four games to two, had gone into the record books, correct? Guess again. Once more, the Series was deadlocked.

That the Series rivals had used vastly different methods while fashioning a 3-3 standoff would be understating the case. The Yankees wielded a bludgeon; the Pirates relied on finesse.

After the Pirates won the opener, 6-4, at Forbes Field, the Yankees unloaded in Games 2 and 3. New York, led by Mickey Mantle's two home runs and five runs batted in, clubbed six Pirate pitchers for 19 hits and rolled to a 16-3 victory in the second game. Then, as the Series shifted to Yankee Stadium, the Yankees' Bobby Richardson flexed his muscles. Having driven in only seven runs in the last 75 games of the American League season and just 26 overall in '60, the little second baseman connected for a bases-loaded home run off reliever Clem Labine in the first inning of Game 3. Richardson later contributed a two-run single, giving him a Series-record six RBIs, and Mantle stung the Pirates with a two-run homer and three other hits. New York was a 10-0 winner, with Whitey Ford pitching a four-hitter.

Battered and bruised from the successive drubbings, the Pirates gave the ball to first-game winner Vern Law in Game 4. Law, a 20-

An ecstatic Bill Mazeroski makes his triumphant trot home amid the Forbes Field delirium that he touched off with his 1960 seventh-game home run that beat the New York Yankees.

game winner in '60 and the N.L.'s Cy Young Award recipient, combined with relief ace Roy Face to beat back the Yankees, 3-2. Bill Virdon's looping single to center field in the fifth knocked in two of Pittsburgh's runs.

Art Ditmar, who lasted only one-third inning as the Game 1 starter for the Yankees, received another chance in Game 5 and lasted 1⅓ innings this time. Bill Mazeroski's double was the key hit in the Pirates' three-run second inning, the smash scoring two runs and driving Ditmar from the mound. Face, turning in 2⅔ innings of hitless relief after replacing starter and winner Harvey Haddix, nailed down the 5-2 triumph, which thrust the Pirates ahead in the Series.

The Yankees, though, called on a proven combination in Game 6 —their big bats and the pitching

guile of Ford. Richardson's two triples and Johnny Blanchard's two doubles highlighted a 17-hit Yankee spree—Roger Maris, Yogi Berra and Blanchard each collected three hits—and Ford again shut out the Pirates, this time silencing the N.L. champions on seven hits. Hoping to clinch their first Series championship in 35 years, the Pirates instead wound up 12-0 losers at Forbes Field.

While the first six games of the '60 Series had been notable because of their general wackiness (the Yankees' victories, for instance, coming by the combined score of 38-3), Game 7 proved memorable because it unfolded along classic lines.

Law, drawing his third start of the Series, was staked to a 4-0 lead when Rocky Nelson cracked a two-run homer in the first inning off Turley and Virdon stroked a

two-run single in the second against reliever Bill Stafford. But the Yankees nicked Law for a run in the fifth when Skowron powered a homer into the lower right-field stands and drove the righthander from the game during a go-ahead rally in the sixth. Richardson began the inning with a single and Tony Kubek drew a base on balls. Law gave way to Face, who got Maris to foul out. Mantle, though, singled home a run and Berra followed with a three-run homer that shot New York into a 5-4 lead.

Clinging to its one-run lead with two out in the eighth, New York went to work against Face. A walk to Berra, singles by Skowron and Blanchard and a double by Clete Boyer netted two runs and, with Yankee reliever Bobby Shantz at the top of his game as evidenced by his five scoreless innings of pitching since taking over in the third, New York appeared in good shape. Appearances were deceiving, however.

Gino Cimoli led off the Pittsburgh eighth with a pinch single and Virdon then hit a sharp grounder toward Kubek, the Yankees' shortstop. The ball took a bad hop, striking Kubek in the throat and forcing him out of the game. Virdon was alive at first with an infield single, Cimoli was stationed at second and Joe DeMaestri was summoned to replace the injured Kubek. Dick Groat's single cut the lead to 7-5, and Roberto Clemente's infield hit scored Virdon and advanced Groat to third. Now trailing 7-6, Pittsburgh had two runners on base and Hal Smith at the plate.

Smith, who had entered the game in the top of the eighth after Pirates catcher Smoky Burgess had left for a pinch-runner in the previous inning, sent shock waves through the Pittsburgh crowd by blasting a home run over the left-field wall.

The Yankees were down, but not out. Bob Friend, an 18-game winner for the Pirates and the Bucs' starting pitcher in Games 2 and 6, came on in the ninth to try to protect the 9-7 lead. Richardson and pinch-hitter Dale Long greeted Friend with singles, and

Pirates Manager Danny Murtaugh lifted the veteran pitcher in favor of Haddix. Maris fouled out, but Mantle delivered a single that scored Richardson and moved Long to third. Berra followed with a sharp grounder to first, with Nelson stepping on the base for the second out. In what at the time stood as a monumental play, Mantle, seeing he had no chance to beat a play at second, scurried back to first and avoided Nelson's tag—which would have been the third out—as McDougald raced home to score, tying the game at 9-9. Skowron's grounder forced Berra, ending the Yankees' inning.

Ralph Terry, who had gotten the final out in the Pirates' eighth, returned to the mound for New York in the bottom of the ninth and the first man he faced was Mazeroski. With a count of one ball and no strikes, the Pirates' second baseman smashed a drive over the wall in left that made the N.L. champions—outscored, 55-27, and outhit, 91-60, in the seven games—10-9 winners and improbable World Series titlists.

Game 1
Wednesday, October 5, At Pittsburgh

New York	AB.	R.	H.	RBI.	PO.	A.
Kubek, ss	5	0	3	0	2	4
Lopez, lf	5	0	1	0	0	1
Maris, rf	4	2	3	1	3	0
Mantle, cf	3	0	0	0	3	0
Berra, c	4	0	1	0	4	1
Skowron, 1b	4	0	2	1	9	0
Boyer, 3b	0	0	0	0	0	0
aLong	1	0	0	0	0	0
McDougald, 3b	3	0	1	0	1	1
Richardson, 2b	4	1	0	0	2	2
Ditmar, p	0	0	0	0	0	0
Coates, p	1	0	0	0	0	0
bBlanchard	1	0	0	0	0	0
Maas, p	0	0	0	0	0	0
cCerv	1	0	1	0	0	0
Duren, p	0	0	0	0	0	1
dHoward	1	1	1	2	0	0
Totals	37	4	13	4	24	10

Pittsburgh	AB.	R.	H.	RBI.	PO.	A.
Virdon, cf	3	1	1	1	3	0
Groat, ss	4	1	2	1	2	3
Skinner, lf	3	1	1	1	3	1
Cimoli, lf	0	0	0	0	0	0
Stuart, 1b	4	0	1	0	9	0
Clemente, rf	4	0	1	1	2	0
Burgess, c	4	0	0	0	5	0
Hoak, 3b	2	1	0	0	1	0
Mazeroski, 2b	4	2	2	2	3	2
Law, p	1	0	0	0	0	2
Face, p	1	0	0	0	0	0
Totals	30	6	8	6	27	9

New York ....1 0 0 1 0 0 0 0 2—4
Pittsburgh ....3 0 0 2 0 1 0 0 x—6

New York	IP.	H.	R.	ER.	BB.	SO.
Ditmar (L)	1/3	3	3	3	1	0
Coates	3 2/3	3	2	2	1	2
Maas	2	2	1	1	0	1
Duren	2	0	0	0	1	1

Pittsburgh	IP.	H.	R.	ER.	BB.	SO.
Law (W)	7*	10	2	2	1	3
Face	2	3	2	2	0	2

*Pitched to two batters in eighth.

aFlied out for Boyer in second. bGrounded out for Coates in fifth. cSingled for Maas in seventh. dHomered for Duren in ninth. E—Kubek, Richardson. DP—Pittsburgh 3. LOB—New York 7, Pittsburgh 6. 2B—Groat, Vir-

don. HR—Maris, Mazeroski, Howard. SB—Virdon. Skinner. SH—Law. HBP—By Coates (Law), by Duren (Skinner). WP—Law. U—Boggess (N.L.), Stevens (A.L.), Jackowski (N.L.), Chylak (A.L.), Landes (N.L.) and Honochick (A.L.). T—2:29. A—36,676.

Game 2
Thursday, October 6, At Pittsburgh

New York	AB.	R.	H.	RBI.	PO.	A.
Kubek, ss-lf	6	3	3	1	2	3
McDougald, 3b	3	1	2	2	1	0
DeMaestri, ss	2	1	1	0	0	0
Maris, rf	5	2	1	0	3	0
Mantle, cf	4	3	2	5	4	0
Berra, lf	4	1	1	2	1	0
Boyer, 3b	2	0	1	0	0	0
Skowron, 1b	6	1	2	1	11	0
Howard, c	5	1	2	1	1	0
Richardson, 2b	4	3	3	2	4	6
Turley, p	4	0	1	0	0	2
Shantz, p	0	0	0	0	0	1
Totals	45	16	19	15	27	12

Pittsburgh	AB.	R.	H.	RBI.	PO.	A.
Virdon, cf	5	0	0	0	2	0
Groat, ss	4	0	1	0	1	0
Gibbon, p	0	0	0	0	1	0
Cheney, p	0	0	0	0	0	1
cChristopher	0	1	0	0	0	0
Clemente, rf	5	0	2	0	1	0
Nelson, 1b	5	1	2	0	4	3
Cimoli, lf	4	1	2	1	2	0
Burgess, c	4	0	2	0	11	1
Hoak, 3b	5	0	2	1	0	0
Mazeroski, 2b	4	0	1	0	2	2
Friend, p	1	0	0	0	1	1
aBaker	1	0	0	0	0	0
Green, p	0	0	0	0	0	0
Labine, p	0	0	0	0	0	1
Witt, p	0	0	0	0	0	0
bSchofield, ss	1	0	1	0	2	0
Totals	39	3	13	2	27	9

New York ......0 0 2 1 2 7 3 0 1—16
Pittsburgh ....0 0 0 1 0 0 0 0 2— 3

New York	IP.	H.	R.	ER.	BB.	SO.
Turley (W)	8 1/3	13	3	2	3	0
Shantz	2/3	0	0	0	0	0

Pittsburgh	IP.	H.	R.	ER.	BB.	SO.
Friend (L)	4	6	3	2	2	6
Green	1*	3	4	4	1	0
Labine	2/3	3	5	0	1	1
Witt	1/3	2	1	1	0	1
Gibbon	2	4	3	3	0	2
Cheney	1	1	1	1	1	2

*Pitched to two batters in sixth.

aPopped out for Friend in fourth. bSingled for Witt in sixth. cHit by pitch for Cheney in ninth. E—Richardson, Groat. DP—New York 2. LOB—New York 8, Pittsburgh 13. 2B—Mazeroski, McDougald, Hoak 2, Richardson, Boyer. 3B—Howard. HR—Mantle 2. SH—Turley. HBP—By Turley (Christopher). WP—Cheney. PB—Burgess 2. U—Stevens (A.L.), Jackowski (N.L.), Chylak (A.L.), Boggess (N.L.), Landes (N.L.) and Honochick (A.L.). T—3:14. A—37,308.

Game 3
Saturday, October 8, At New York

Pittsburgh	AB.	R.	H.	RBI.	PO.	A.
Virdon, cf	4	0	1	0	3	0
Groat, ss	4	0	0	0	1	1
Clemente, rf	4	0	1	0	1	0
Stuart, 1b	4	0	0	0	6	0
Cimoli, lf	3	0	0	0	2	0
Smith, c	3	0	0	0	9	1
Hoak, 3b	3	0	0	0	1	3
Mazeroski, 2b	3	0	1	0	1	3
Mizell, p	0	0	0	0	0	0
Labine, p	0	0	0	0	0	1
Green, p	1	0	0	0	0	0
Witt, p	0	0	0	0	0	0
aBaker	1	0	0	0	0	0
Cheney, p	0	0	0	0	0	0
bSchofield	1	0	0	0	0	0
Gibbon, p	0	0	0	0	0	0
Totals	31	0	4	0	24	9

New York	AB.	R.	H.	RBI.	PO.	A.
Cerv, lf	5	1	2	0	3	0
Maris, rf	3	0	0	0	1	0
Berra, rf	1	0	1	0	1	0
Mantle, cf	5	2	4	2	2	0
Skowron, 1b	5	2	2	1	11	3
McDougald, 3b	4	2	1	0	0	3
Howard, c	4	1	2	1	3	0
Richardson, 2b	5	1	2	6	1	4
Kubek, ss	3	0	1	0	2	1
Ford, p	4	1	1	0	3	4
Totals	39	10	16	10	27	15

Pittsburgh ....0 0 0 0 0 0 0 0 0— 0
New York ....6 0 0 4 0 0 0 0 x—10

Pittsburgh	IP.	H.	R.	ER.	BB.	SO.
Mizell (L)	1/3	3	4	4	1	0
Labine	1/3	4	2	2	0	0
Green	3	5	4	4	0	3
Witt	1 1/3	3	0	0	2	1
Cheney	2	1	0	0	0	3
Gibbon	1	0	0	0	1	0

New York	IP.	H.	R.	ER.	BB.	SO.
Ford (W)	9	4	0	0	1	3

aGrounded out for Witt in sixth. bLined out for Cheney in eighth. E—Kubek. DP—New York 1. LOB—Pittsburgh 5, New York 9. 2B—Virdon, Mantle. HR—Richardson, Mantle. WP—Green, Witt. U—Jackowski (N.L.), Chylak (A.L.), Boggess (N.L.), Stevens (A.L.), Honochick (A.L.) and Landes (N.L.). T—2:41. A—70,001.

Game 4

Sunday, October 9, At New York

Pittsburgh	AB.	R.	H.	RBI.	PO.	A.
Virdon, cf	4	0	1	2	2	0
Groat, ss	4	0	0	0	1	1
Clemente, rf	4	0	1	0	4	0
Stuart, 1b	4	0	0	0	12	0
Cimoli, lf	4	1	1	0	0	0
Burgess, c	3	1	0	0	5	1
Oldis, c	0	0	0	0	0	0
Hoak, 3b	4	0	1	0	1	3
Mazeroski, 2b	3	0	1	0	2	3
Law, p	3	1	2	1	0	3
Face, p	1	0	0	0	0	1
Totals	34	3	7	3	27	12

New York	AB.	R.	H.	RBI.	PO.	A.
Cerv, lf	4	0	1	0	1	0
Kubek, ss	4	0	1	0	0	2
Maris, rf	4	0	0	0	0	0
Mantle, cf	3	0	0	0	3	0
Berra, c	4	0	0	0	7	0
Skowron, 1b	4	2	2	1	8	1
McDougald, 3b	4	0	1	0	1	1
Richardson, 2b	3	0	2	1	6	3
cLong	1	0	0	0	0	0
Terry, p	2	0	0	0	0	3
Shantz, p	0	0	0	0	0	0
aBlanchard	1	0	1	0	0	0
bDeMaestri	0	0	0	0	0	0
Coates, p	0	0	0	0	1	1
Totals	34	2	8	2	27	11

Pittsburgh	0 0 0	0 3 0	0 0 0	—3
New York	0 0 0	1 0 0	1 0 0	—2

Pittsburgh	IP.	H.	R.	ER.	BB.	SO.
Law (W)	6⅓	8	2	2	1	5
Face	2⅔	0	0	0	0	1

New York	IP.	H.	R.	ER.	BB.	SO.
Terry (L)	6⅓	6	3	3	1	5
Shantz	⅔	0	0	0	0	1
Coates	2	1	0	0	0	1

aSingled for Shantz in seventh. bRan for Blanchard in seventh. cFlied out for Richardson in ninth. DP—Pittsburgh 1. LOB—Pittsburgh 6, New York 6. 2B—Kubek, Richardson, Skowron, Law. HR—Skowron. SH—Mazeroski. U—Chylak (A.L.), Boggess (N.L.), Stevens (A.L.), Jackowski (N.L.), Landes (N.L.) and Honochick (A.L.). T—2:29. A—67,812.

Game 5

Monday, October 10, At New York

Pittsburgh	AB.	R.	H.	RBI.	PO.	A.
Virdon, cf	5	0	1	0	1	0
Groat, ss	4	1	1	0	3	4
Clemente, rf	4	0	1	1	3	0
Stuart, 1b	4	0	1	0	8	0
Nelson, 1b	0	0	0	0	2	0
Cimoli, lf	4	1	0	0	0	0
Burgess, c	4	1	2	0	6	0
cChristopher	0	1	0	0	0	0
Oldis, c	0	0	0	0	0	0
Hoak, 3b	4	1	2	2	1	1
Mazeroski, 2b	4	0	1	2	2	5
Haddix, p	3	0	1	0	1	1
Face, p	1	0	0	0	0	0
Totals	37	5	10	5	27	11

New York	AB.	R.	H.	RBI.	PO.	A.
McDougald, 3b	4	0	0	0	2	2
Maris, rf	4	1	1	1	1	0
Cerv, lf	4	0	1	0	4	0
Mantle, cf	1	0	0	0	1	0
Skowron, 1b	4	0	0	0	8	0
Howard, c	3	1	1	0	6	0
bBerra, c	1	0	0	0	2	0
Richardson, 2b	4	0	0	0	2	2
Kubek, ss	4	0	1	1	1	5
Ditmar, p	0	0	0	0	0	0
Arroyo, p	1	0	0	0	0	0
Stafford, p	1	0	0	0	0	1
aLopez	1	0	1	0	0	0
Duren, p	0	0	0	0	0	1
dBlanchard	1	0	0	0	0	0
Totals	33	2	5	2	27	11

Pittsburgh	0 3 1	0 0 0	0 0 1	—5
New York	0 1 1	0 0 0	0 0 0	—2

Pittsburgh	IP.	H.	R.	ER.	BB.	SO.
Haddix (W)	6⅓	5	2	2	2	6
Face	2⅔	0	0	0	1	1

New York	IP.	H.	R.	ER.	BB.	SO.
Ditmar (L)	7⅓	3	3	1	0	0
Arroyo	⅔*	2	1	1	0	1
Stafford	5	3	0	0	0	2
Duren	2	2	1	1	0	4

*Pitched to two batters in third.

aSingled for Stafford in seventh. bGrounded out for Howard in eighth. cRan for Burgess in ninth. dFlied out for Duren in ninth. E—Groat, Hoak, McDougald, Cerv. DP—Pittsburgh 1, New York 1. LOB—Pittsburgh 5, New York 7. 2B—Burgess, Mazeroski, Howard, Groat, Virdon. HR—Maris. WP—Duren. PB—Burgess. U—Boggess (N.L.), Stevens (A.L.), Jackowski (N.L.), Chylak (A.L.), Landes (N.L.) and Honochick (A.L.). T—2:32. A—62,753.

Game 6

Wednesday, October 12, At Pittsburgh

New York	AB.	R.	H.	RBI.	PO.	A.
Boyer, 3b	6	1	1	0	0	5
Kubek, ss-lf	5	2	1	1	2	4
Maris, rf	5	1	3	0	1	0
Mantle, cf	4	2	1	2	2	0
Berra, lf	4	3	3	2	0	0
DeMaestri, ss	0	0	0	0	0	2
Skowron, 1b	4	0	2	1	13	0
Howard, c	0	0	0	0	1	0
aGrba	0	0	0	0	0	0
Blanchard, c	4	2	3	1	4	1
Richardson, 2b	5	1	2	3	4	6
Ford, p	4	0	1	2	0	1
Totals	41	12	17	12	27	19

Pittsburgh	AB.	R.	H.	RBI.	PO.	A.
Virdon, cf	4	0	1	0	4	0
Groat, ss	4	0	1	0	1	1
Witt, p	0	0	0	0	0	0
Clemente, rf	4	0	2	0	4	0
Stuart, 1b	4	0	0	0	10	0
Cimoli, lf	4	0	1	0	1	0
Smith, c	4	0	2	0	4	0
Hoak, 3b	2	0	0	0	1	1
Mazeroski, 2b	3	0	0	0	2	7
Friend, p	0	0	0	0	0	2
Cheney, p	0	0	0	0	0	0
bBaker	1	0	0	0	0	0
Mizell, p	0	0	0	0	0	0
cNelson	1	0	0	0	0	0
Green, p	0	0	0	0	0	0
Labine, p	0	0	0	0	0	0
dSchofield, ss	1	0	0	0	0	0
Totals	32	0	7	0	27	11

New York	0 1 5	0 0 2	2 2 0	—12
Pittsburgh	0 0 0	0 0 0	0 0 0	— 0

New York	IP.	H.	R.	ER.	BB.	SO.
Ford (W)	9	7	0	0	1	5

Pittsburgh	IP.	H.	R.	ER.	BB.	SO.
Friend (L)	2*	5	5	5	1	1
Cheney	1	2	1	1	0	1
Mizell	2	1	0	0	1	1
Green	0†	3	2	2	0	0
Labine	3	6	4	4	0	1
Witt	1	0	0	0	0	0

*Pitched to four batters in third.
†Pitched to three batters in sixth.

aRan for Howard in second. bStruck out for Cheney in third. cStruck out for Mizell in fifth. dGrounded out for Labine in eighth. E—Kubek, Virdon. DP—New York 3, Pittsburgh 2. LOB—New York 8, Pittsburgh 6. 2B—Maris, Skowron, Blanchard 2. 3B—Richardson 2, Boyer. SH—Ford. SF—Skowron. HBP—By Friend (Howard, Kubek). WP—Labine. U—Stevens (A.L.), Jackowski (N.L.), Chylak (A.L.), Boggess (N.L.), Landes (N.L.) and Honochick (A.L.). T—2:38. A—38,580.

Game 7

Thursday, October 13, At Pittsburgh

New York	AB.	R.	H.	RBI.	PO.	A.
Richardson, 2b	5	2	2	0	2	5
Kubek, ss	3	1	0	0	3	2
DeMaestri, ss	0	0	0	0	0	0
dLong	1	0	1	0	0	0
eMcDougald, 3b	0	1	0	0	0	0
Maris, rf	5	0	0	0	2	0
Mantle, cf	5	1	3	2	0	0
Berra, lf	4	2	1	4	3	0
Skowron, 1b	5	2	2	1	10	2
Blanchard, c	4	0	1	1	1	1
Boyer, 3b-ss	4	0	1	1	0	3
Turley, p	0	0	0	0	0	0
Stafford, p	0	0	0	0	0	1
aLopez	1	0	1	0	0	0
Shantz, p	3	0	1	0	3	1
Coates, p	0	0	0	0	0	0
Terry, p	0	0	0	0	0	0
Totals	40	9	13	9	24	15

Pittsburgh	AB.	R.	H.	RBI.	PO.	A.
Virdon, cf	4	1	2	2	3	0
Groat, ss	4	1	1	1	3	2
Skinner, lf	2	1	0	0	1	0
Nelson, 1b	3	1	1	2	7	0
Clemente, rf	4	1	1	1	4	0
Burgess, c	3	0	2	0	0	0
bChristopher	0	0	0	0	0	0
Smith, c	1	1	1	3	1	0
Hoak, 3b	3	1	0	0	3	2
Mazeroski, 2b	4	2	2	1	5	0
Law, p	2	0	0	0	0	1
Face, p	0	0	0	0	0	1
cCimoli	1	1	1	0	0	0
Friend, p	0	0	0	0	0	0
Haddix, p	0	0	0	0	0	0
Totals	31	10	11	10	27	6

New York	0 0 0	0 1 4	0 2 2	— 9
Pittsburgh	2 2 0	0 0 0	0 5 1	—10

None out when winning run scored.

New York	IP.	H.	R.	ER.	BB.	SO.
Turley	1*	2	3	3	1	0
Stafford	1	2	1	1	1	0
Shantz	5‡	4	3	3	1	0
Coates	⅔	2	2	2	0	0
Terry (L)	⅓	1	1	1	0	0

Pittsburgh	IP.	H.	R.	ER.	BB.	SO.
Law	5†	4	3	3	1	0
Face	3	6	4	4	1	0
Friend	0y	2	2	2	0	0
Haddix (W)	1	1	0	0	0	0

*Pitched to one batter in second.
†Pitched to two batters in sixth.
‡Pitched to three batters in eighth.
yPitched to two batters in ninth.

aSingled for Stafford in third. bRan for Burgess in seventh. cSingled for Face in eighth. dSingled for DeMaestri in ninth. eRan for Long in ninth. E—Maris. DP—New York 3. LOB—New York 6, Pittsburgh 1. 2B—Boyer. HR—Nelson, Skowron, Berra, Smith, Mazeroski. SH—Skinner. U—Jackowski (N.L.), Chylak (A.L.), Boggess (N.L.), Stevens (A.L.), Landes (N.L.) and Honochick (A.L.). T—2:36. A—36,683.

COMPOSITE BATTING AVERAGES

Pittsburgh Pirates

Player-Position	G.	AB.	R.	H.	2B.	3B.	HR.	RBI.	BA.
Smith, c	3	8	1	3	0	0	1	3	.375
Schofield, ph-ss	3	3	0	1	0	0	0	0	.333
Nelson, 1b-ph	4	9	2	3	0	0	1	2	.333
Law, p	3	6	1	2	1	0	0	1	.333
Haddix, p	2	3	0	1	0	0	0	0	.333
Burgess, c	5	18	2	6	1	0	0	0	.333
Mazeroski, 2b	7	25	4	8	2	0	2	5	.320
Clemente, rf	7	29	1	9	0	0	0	3	.310
Cimoli, lf-ph	7	20	4	5	0	0	0	1	.250
Virdon, cf	7	29	2	7	3	0	0	5	.241
Hoak, 3b	7	23	3	5	2	0	0	3	.217
Groat, ss	7	28	3	6	2	0	0	2	.214
Skinner, lf	2	5	2	1	0	0	0	1	.200
Stuart, 1b	5	20	0	3	0	0	0	0	.150
Oldis, c	2	0	0	0	0	0	0	0	.000
Face, p	4	3	0	0	0	0	0	0	.000
Gibbon, p	2	0	0	0	0	0	0	0	.000
Cheney, p	3	0	0	0	0	0	0	0	.000
Friend, p	3	1	0	0	0	0	0	0	.000
Green, p	3	1	0	0	0	0	0	0	.000
Labine, p	3	0	0	0	0	0	0	0	.000
Witt, p	3	0	0	0	0	0	0	0	.000
Mizell, p	2	0	0	0	0	0	0	0	.000
Chris'pher, ph-pr	3	0	2	0	0	0	0	0	.000
Baker, ph	3	3	0	0	0	0	0	0	.000
Totals	7	234	27	60	11	0	4	26	.256

New York Yankees

Player-Position	G.	AB.	R.	H.	2B.	3B.	HR.	RBI.	BA.
DeMaestri, pr-ss	4	2	1	1	0	0	0	0	.500
Howard, ph-c	5	13	4	6	1	1	1	4	.462
Blanchard, ph-c	5	11	2	5	2	0	0	2	.455
Lopez, lf-ph	3	7	0	3	0	0	0	0	.429
Mantle, cf	7	25	8	10	1	0	3	11	.400
Skowron, 1b	7	32	7	12	2	0	2	6	.375
Richardson, 2b	7	30	8	11	2	2	1	12	.367
Cerv, ph-lf	4	14	1	5	0	0	0	0	.357
Shantz, p	3	3	0	1	0	0	0	0	.333
Long, ph	3	3	0	1	0	0	0	0	.333
Kubek, ss-lf	7	30	6	10	1	0	0	3	.333
Berra, c-lf-rf-ph	7	22	6	7	0	0	1	8	.318
McDougald, 3b-pr	6	18	4	5	1	0	0	2	.278
Maris, rf	7	30	6	8	1	0	2	2	.267
Turley, p	2	4	0	1	0	0	0	1	.250
Ford, p	2	8	1	2	0	0	0	2	.250
Boyer, 3b-ss	4	12	1	3	2	1	0	1	.250
Ditmar, p	2	0	0	0	0	0	0	0	.000
Coates, p	3	1	0	0	0	0	0	0	.000
Maas, p	1	0	0	0	0	0	0	0	.000
Duren, p	2	0	0	0	0	0	0	0	.000
Terry, p	2	2	0	0	0	0	0	0	.000
Arroyo, p	1	1	0	0	0	0	0	0	.000
Stafford, p	2	1	0	0	0	0	0	0	.000
Grba, pr	1	0	0	0	0	0	0	0	.000
Totals	7	269	55	91	13	4	10	54	.338

COMPOSITE PITCHING AVERAGES

Pittsburgh Pirates

Pitcher	G.	IP.	H.	R.	ER.	BB.	SO.	W.	L.	ERA.
Witt	3	2⅔	5	0	0	2	1	0	0	0.00
Haddix	2	7⅓	2	6	2	2	6	2	0	2.45
Law	3	18⅓	22	7	7	3	8	2	0	3.44
Cheney	3	4	4	2	2	1	6	0	0	4.50
Face	4	10⅓	9	6	6	2	4	0	0	5.23
Gibbon	2	3	4	3	3	1	2	0	0	9.00
Labine	3	4	13	11	6	1	2	0	0	13.50
Friend	3	6	13	10	9	3	7	0	2	13.50
Mizell	2	2⅓	4	4	4	2	1	0	1	15.43
Green	3	4	11	10	10	1	3	0	0	22.50
Totals	7	62	91	55	49	18	40	4	3	7.11

New York Yankees

Pitcher	G.	IP.	H.	R.	ER.	BB.	SO.	W.	L.	ERA.
Ford	2	18	11	0	0	2	8	2	0	0.00
Stafford	2	6	5	1	1	1	2	0	0	1.50
Duren	2	4	2	1	1	1	5	0	0	2.25
Shantz	3	6⅓	4	3	3	1	1	0	0	4.26
Maas	1	2	2	1	1	0	1	0	0	4.50
Turley	1	9⅓	15	6	5	4	0	1	0	4.82
Terry	2	6⅔	7	4	4	1	5	0	2	5.40
Coates	3	6⅓	6	4	4	1	3	0	0	5.68
Arroyo	1	⅔	2	1	1	0	1	0	0	13.50
Ditmar	2	1⅔	6	6	4	1	0	0	2	21.60
Totals	7	61	60	27	24	12	26	3	4	3.54

The Cincinnati Reds, surprise National League pennant winners in 1961 after finishing 20 games below .500 the previous season, were hoping to pull off another major surprise in the World Series.

The Reds' timing could not have been worse.

The American League champion New York Yankees were still smarting from their stunning Series loss to the Pittsburgh Pirates in 1960. Furthermore, the Yankees were coming off a 109-victory season that featured the home run pyrotechnics of Roger Maris and Mickey Mantle and the pitching wizardry of Whitey Ford.

The Reds clearly were overmatched. And, before long, they were overwhelmed.

New York, which had dismissed Casey Stengel after the '60 Series, was now under the guidance of Ralph Houk, former reserve catcher and coach for the Yankees. Houk inherited a wealth of talent, exemplified by veteran pitcher Ford.

The 32-year-old Ford, who had crafted a 25-4 record in '61, was in classic form in the Series opener. He stymied the Reds on two hits, both singles, as New York won, 2-0, at Yankee Stadium. Jim O'Toole pitched effectively for Cincinnati, but fell victim to the Yankees' specialty, the home run. New York, which had crushed 240 homers (a major league record) in the '61 A.L. season, broke a scoreless tie in the fourth inning when Elston Howard slammed an O'Toole delivery into the right-field stands. Two innings later, Bill Skowron homered to left.

Joey Jay, a .500 career pitcher for the Milwaukee Braves but a 21-game winner for the Reds in '61 after being obtained in a trade

Among the 1961 Yankee World Series heroes were (left to right) John Blanchard, pitcher Bud Daley and outfield replacement Hector Lopez.

the previous December, shut down the Yankees, 6-2, on four hits in Game 2 to give Cincinnati some short-lived hope. Gordy Coleman staked Jay to a 2-0 lead in the top of the fourth inning when he homered with Frank Robinson on base. The Yankees got the runs back in their half of the inning when Maris walked and Yogi Berra homered. Cincinnati went ahead in the next inning on catcher Howard's passed ball, which followed singles by Elio Chacon and Eddie Kasko. A run-scoring single by Johnny Edwards in the sixth inning extended the Reds' lead to 4-2, and a throwing error by Yankees reliever Luis Arroyo and an RBI dou-

ble by Edwards netted Jay and the Reds their final two runs in the eighth inning.

Game 3 was a thriller—and, for the Reds, a killer. In the first World Series game played in Cincinnati since 1940, the Reds guarded a 2-1 lead into the eighth inning. Skowron started the Yankees' eighth by tapping back to pitcher Bob Purkey, who was working on a four-hitter. Clete Boyer then fouled out, bringing Cincinnati within four outs of the Series lead. The next scheduled batter was New York reliever Bud Daley. John Blanchard, a catcher/outfielder who had contributed mightily to the Yankees' long-ball onslaught in '61 by

Roger Maris gets a warm reception from the New York Yankee dugout after hitting a ninth-inning **home run in Game 3 of the 1961 Series. It was Maris' first postseason hit and 62nd homer of the season.**

smashing 21 home runs in only 243 at-bats, pinch-hit for Daley and hammered the ball into the right-field bleachers.

Maris, hitless in 10 Series at-bats after walloping a record 61 home runs during the season (Mantle added 54), led off the ninth against Purkey with a homer into the same sector and, suddenly, Houk's Yankees were ahead.

Reds pinch-hitter Leo Cardenas added to the drama by hitting a one-out double off Yankee relief ace Arroyo in Cincinnati's half of the inning. But Arroyo, who had a masterful season (15-5 record, 2.19 earned-run average), induced pinch-hitters Dick Gernert and Gus Bell to ground out, ending the game. The Yankees were 3-2 winners and Maris' homer, in Reds Manager Fred Hutchinson's estimation, was "the most damaging blow of the Series."

Ford, working on a Series scoreless-inning streak of 27, had his sights set on Babe Ruth's pitching record of 29 consecutive shutout innings in the fall classic when he took the mound for Game 4. No problem. The left-hander worked five shutout innings before departing in the sixth with an ankle injury. By then the Yankees had built a four-run lead, with Boyer's two-run double in the sixth proving the key hit. Hector Lopez, who had replaced an ailing Mantle earlier in the game (a hip injury limited Mantle to six Series at-bats), stroked a two-run single in the seventh inning and the Yanks rolled to a 7-0 triumph. Jim Coates pitched four innings of one-hit relief for New York.

Game 5 was a laugher. The Yankees struck for five first-inning runs, with Blanchard launching the scoring with a two-run homer. In the fourth, the Yanks scored five more times as Skowron rapped a two-run single and Lopez drilled a three-run homer. By day's end, it was 13-5. The Yankees were World Series champions again.

New York second baseman Bobby Richardson didn't drive in 12 runs in this Series; in fact, he failed to collect an RBI. Richardson was pesky as usual, though, tying the record for a five-game Series with nine hits. And while Maris and the injured Mantle managed only three hits and two RBIs in 25 at-bats, Blanchard and Lopez stepped in and went 7 for 19 with 10 runs driven in. Lopez had a staggering seven RBIs despite making only nine official trips to the plate.

And for all their power, the Yankees exhibited some dazzling pitching in the World Series. For example, Ford and relievers Daley and Coates worked 25 innings overall and did not allow an earned run.

The Yankees were back.

Game 1

Wednesday, October 4, At New York

Cincinnati	AB.	R.	H.	RBI.	PO.	A.
Blasingame, 2b	3	0	0	0	3	2
dLynch	1	0	0	0	0	0
Kasko, ss	4	0	1	0	3	3
Pinson, cf	4	0	0	0	4	0

	AB.	R.	H.	RBI.	PO.	A.
Robinson, lf	2	0	0	0	0	0
Post, rf	3	0	1	0	2	0
Freese, 3b	3	0	0	0	1	0
Coleman, 1b	3	0	0	0	7	0
D. Johnson, c	2	0	0	0	3	1
aCardenas	1	0	0	0	0	0
Zimmerman, c	0	0	0	0	1	0
O'Toole, p	2	0	0	0	0	0
bGernert	1	0	0	0	0	0
Brosnan, p	0	0	0	0	0	0
Totals	29	0	2	0	24	6

New York	AB.	R.	H.	RBI.	PO.	A.
Richardson, 2b	4	0	3	0	1	4
Kubek, ss	3	0	0	0	2	3
Maris, cf-rf	4	0	0	0	2	0
Howard, c	4	1	1	1	6	0
Skowron, 1b	3	1	1	1	13	0
Berra, lf	2	0	0	0	1	0
Lopez, rf	2	0	0	0	0	0
cBlanchard	1	0	0	0	0	0
Reed, cf	0	0	0	0	0	0
Boyer, 3b	3	0	1	0	2	5
Ford, p	3	0	0	0	0	1
Totals	29	2	6	2	27	13

Cincinnati	0 0 0	0 0 0	0 0 0	—0
New York	0 0 0	1 0 1	0 0 x	—2

Cincinnati	IP.	H.	R.	ER.	BB.	SO.
O'Toole (L)	7	6	2	2	4	2
Brosnan	1	0	0	0	1	1

New York	IP.	H.	R.	ER.	BB.	SO.
Ford (W)	9	2	0	0	1	6

aStruck out for D. Johnson in eighth. bGrounded out for O'Toole in eighth. cPopped out for Lopez in eighth. dPopped out for Blasingame in ninth. DP—Cincinnati 1. LOB—Cincinnati 3, New York 8. HR—Howard, Skowron. U—Runge (A.L.), Conlan (N.L.), Umont (A.L.), Donatelli (N.L.), Crawford (N.L.) and Stewart (A.L.). T—2:11. A—62,397.

Game 2

Thursday, October 5, At New York

Cincinnati	AB.	R.	H.	RBI.	PO.	A.
Chacon, 2b	4	1	1	0	6	4
Kasko, ss	5	0	1	0	6	4
Pinson, cf	5	0	1	0	2	0
Robinson, lf	4	2	0	0	0	0
Coleman, 1b	5	1	2	2	5	1
Post, rf	4	2	2	0	0	0
Freese, 3b	2	0	0	0	1	1
Edwards, c	4	0	2	2	6	1
Jay, p	4	0	0	0	1	0
Totals	37	6	9	4	27	11

New York	AB.	R.	H.	RBI.	PO.	A.
Richardson, 2b	4	0	1	0	2	3
Kubek, ss	4	0	1	0	1	2
Maris, cf	3	1	0	0	1	0
Berra, lf	4	1	2	2	4	0
Blanchard, rf	4	0	0	0	0	1
Howard, c	3	0	0	0	8	0
Skowron, 1b	3	0	0	0	8	1
Boyer, 3b	2	0	0	0	2	1
Terry, p	2	0	0	0	0	1
aLopez	0	0	0	0	0	0
Arroyo, p	0	0	0	0	1	0
bGardner	1	0	0	0	0	0
Totals	30	2	4	2	27	9

Cincinnati	0 0 0	2 1 1	0 2 0	—6
New York	0 0 0	2 0 0	0 0 0	—2

Cincinnati	IP.	H.	R.	ER.	BB.	SO.
Jay (W)	9	4	2	2	6	6

New York	IP.	H.	R.	ER.	BB.	SO.
Terry (L)	7	6	4	2	2	7
Arroyo	2	3	2	1	2	1

aWalked for Terry in seventh. bLined out for Arroyo in ninth. E—Berra, Boyer, Arroyo. DP—Cincinnati 2. LOB—Cincinnati 8, New York 7. 2B—Post, Edwards, Pinson. HR—Coleman, Berra. PB—Howard. U—Conlan (N.L.), Umont (A.L.), Donatelli (N.L.), Runge (A.L.), Crawford (N.L.) and Stewart (A.L.). T—2:43. A—63,083.

Game 3

Saturday, October 7, At Cincinnati

New York	AB.	R.	H.	RBI.	PO.	A.
Richardson, 2b	4	0	1	0	2	2
Kubek, ss	4	1	1	0	0	1
Maris, rf	4	1	1	1	2	0
Mantle, cf	4	0	0	0	1	0
Reed, cf	0	0	0	0	0	0
Berra, lf	3	0	1	1	2	0
Howard, c	4	0	1	0	10	0
Skowron, 1b	3	0	0	0	9	1
Boyer, 3b	3	0	0	0	0	3
Stafford, p	2	0	0	0	1	0
Daley, p	0	0	0	0	0	0
cBlanchard	1	1	1	1	0	0
Arroyo, p	0	0	0	0	0	1
Totals	32	3	6	3	27	8

Cincinnati	AB.	R.	H.	RBI.	PO.	A.
Chacon, 2b	3	1	1	0	2	1
aLynch	0	0	0	0	0	0
bBlasingame, 2b	0	0	0	0	0	0
fBell	1	0	0	0	0	0
Kasko, ss	4	0	2	1	3	1
Pinson, cf	4	0	0	0	4	0
Robinson, rf	4	0	1	1	1	0
Coleman, 1b	4	0	2	0	6	3
Post, lf	4	0	0	0	2	0
Freese, 3b	3	0	0	0	2	0
Edwards, c	3	1	1	0	3	0
dCardenas	1	0	1	0	0	0
Purkey, p	3	0	0	0	4	2
eGernert	1	0	0	0	0	0
Totals	35	2	8	2	27	7

New York	0 0 0	0 0 0	1 1 1	—3
Cincinnati	0 0 1	0 0 0	1 0 0	—2

New York	IP.	H.	R.	ER.	BB.	SO.
Stafford	6⅔	7	2	2	2	5
Daley	⅓	0	0	0	0	0
Arroyo (W)	2	1	0	0	0	2

Cincinnati	IP.	H.	R.	ER.	BB.	SO.
Purkey (L)	9	6	3	2	1	3

aIntentionally walked for Chacon in seventh. bRan for Lynch in seventh. cHomered for Daley in eighth. dDoubled for Edwards in ninth. eGrounded out for Purkey in ninth. fGrounded out for Blasingame in ninth. E—Stafford. DP—Cincinnati 1. LOB—New York 3, Cincinnati 8. 2B—Robinson, Howard, Edwards, Cardenas. HR—Blanchard, Maris. SB—Richardson. PB—Edwards. U—Umont (A.L.), Donatelli (N.L.), Runge (A.L.), Conlan (N.L.), Crawford (N.L.) and Stewart (A.L.). T—2:15. A—32,589.

Game 4

Sunday, October 8, At Cincinnati

New York	AB.	R.	H.	RBI.	PO.	A.
Richardson, 2b	5	1	3	0	4	4
Kubek, ss	5	0	1	1	0	4
Maris, rf-cf	3	2	0	0	3	0
Mantle, cf	2	0	1	0	1	0
aLopez, rf	3	1	1	2	3	0
Howard, c	4	1	1	0	3	0
Berra, lf	2	1	0	0	4	0
Skowron, 1b	3	0	3	1	9	0
Boyer, 3b	4	0	1	2	0	2
Ford, p	2	1	0	0	0	0
Coates, p	1	0	0	0	0	0
Totals	34	7	11	6	27	10

Cincinnati	AB.	R.	H.	RBI.	PO.	A.
Chacon, 2b	4	0	1	0	4	4
Kasko, ss	4	0	1	0	1	2
Pinson, cf	4	0	0	0	4	1
Robinson, rf	1	0	0	0	2	0
Post, lf	4	0	1	0	1	0
Freese, 3b	4	0	0	0	1	2
Coleman, 1b	4	0	0	0	5	0
D. Johnson, c	2	0	2	0	5	0
cBell	1	0	0	0	0	0
Zimmerman, c	0	0	0	0	3	0
O'Toole, p	1	0	0	0	1	0
bGernert	1	0	0	0	0	0
Brosnan, p	0	0	0	0	0	0
dLynch	1	0	0	0	0	0
Henry, p	0	0	0	0	0	0
Totals	31	0	5	0	27	9

New York	0 0 0	1 1 2	3 0 0	—7
Cincinnati	0 0 0	0 0 0	0 0 0	—0

New York	IP.	H.	R.	ER.	BB.	SO.
Ford (W)	5*	4	0	0	0	1
Coates	4	1	0	0	1	2

Cincinnati	IP.	H.	R.	ER.	BB.	SO.
O'Toole (L)	5	5	2	2	3	2
Brosnan	3	6	5	5	3	3
Henry	1	0	0	0	0	2

*Pitched to one batter in sixth.

aRan for Mantle in fourth. bHit into force play for O'Toole in fifth. cGrounded out for D. Johnson in seventh. dStruck out for Brosnan in eighth. E—Pinson. DP—New York 1, Cincinnati 3. LOB—New York 6, Cincinnati 7. 2B—Richardson, Howard, Boyer. HBP—By Ford (Robinson), by Coates (Robinson). WP—Brosnan. U—Donatelli (N.L.), Runge (A.L.), Conlan (N.L.), Umont (A.L.), Crawford (N.L.) and Stewart (A.L.). T—2:27. A—32,589.

Game 5

Monday, October 9, At Cincinnati

New York	AB.	R.	H.	RBI.	PO.	A.
Richardson, 2b	6	1	1	0	1	3
Kubek, ss	6	2	2	0	2	1
Maris, cf-rf	5	0	1	1	3	1
Blanchard, rf	4	3	3	2	2	0
Reed, cf	0	0	0	0	0	0
Howard, c	5	3	2	0	4	0
Skowron, 1b	5	2	2	3	7	3
Lopez, lf	4	2	2	5	5	0
Boyer, 3b	3	0	2	1	2	1
Terry, p	1	0	0	0	1	1
Daley, p	1	0	0	1	0	0
Totals	40	13	15	13	27	10

Cincinnati	AB.	R.	H.	RBI.	PO.	A.
Blasingame, 2b	4	1	1	0	2	2
eChacon	1	0	0	0	0	0
Kasko, ss	5	1	2	0	0	3
Pinson, cf	5	0	1	0	4	0
Robinson, rf	4	1	2	3	2	0
Coleman, 1b	4	1	1	0	7	0
Post, lf	3	1	2	2	3	0
Freese, 3b	4	0	1	0	1	1
Edwards, c	4	0	1	0	8	0
Jay, p	0	0	0	0	0	0
Maloney, p	0	0	0	0	0	0
K. Johnson, p	0	0	0	0	0	0
aBell	1	0	0	0	0	0
Henry, p	0	0	0	0	0	1
Jones, p	0	0	0	0	0	0
bGernert	1	0	0	0	0	0
Purkey, p	0	0	0	0	0	1
cCardenas	1	0	0	0	0	0
Brosnan, p	0	0	0	0	0	0
dLynch	1	0	0	0	0	0
Hunt, p	0	0	0	0	0	1
Totals	38	5	11	5	27	9

New York	5 1 0	5 0 2	0 0 0	—13
Cincinnati	0 0 3	0 2 0	0 0 0	— 5

New York	IP.	H.	R.	ER.	BB.	SO.
Terry	2⅓	6	3	3	0	0
Daley (W)	6⅔	5	2	0	0	3

Cincinnati	IP.	H.	R.	ER.	BB.	SO.
Jay (L)	⅔	4	4	4	0	0
Maloney	⅔	4	2	2	1	1
K. Johnson	⅔	0	0	0	0	0
Henry	1⅓	4	5	5	2	1
Jones	⅔	0	0	0	0	0
Purkey	2	0	2	0	2	2
Brosnan	2	3	0	0	0	1
Hunt	1	0	0	0	1	1

aFouled out for K. Johnson in second. bStruck out for Jones in fourth. cFlied out for Purkey in sixth. dGrounded out for Brosnan in eighth. eGrounded out for Blasingame in ninth. E—Daley, Kasko, Coleman, Purkey. LOB—New York 10, Cincinnati 7. 2B—Howard, Boyer, Maris, Freese, Blanchard, Robinson. 3B—Lopez. HR—Blanchard, Robinson, Lopez, Post. SH—Terry, Lopez, Daley. SF—Daley. HBP—By Daley (Post). WP—Brosnan. U—Runge (A.L.), Conlan (N.L.), Umont (A.L.), Donatelli (N.L.), Crawford (N.L.) and Stewart (A.L.). T—3:05. A—32,589.

COMPOSITE BATTING AVERAGES

New York Yankees

Player-Position	G.	AB.	R.	H.	2B.	3B.	HR.	RBI.	BA.
Blanchard, ph-rf	4	10	4	4	1	0	2	3	.400
Richardson, 2b	5	23	2	9	1	0	0	0	.391
Skowron, 1b	5	17	3	6	0	0	1	5	.353
Lopez, rf-ph-pr-lf	4	9	3	3	0	1	1	7	.333
Berra, lf	4	11	2	3	0	0	1	3	.273
Boyer, 3b	5	15	0	4	2	0	0	3	.267
Howard, c	5	20	5	5	3	0	1	1	.250
Kubek, ss	5	22	3	5	0	0	0	1	.227
Mantle, cf	2	6	0	1	0	0	0	0	.167
Maris, cf-rf	5	19	4	2	1	0	1	2	.105
Reed, cf	3	0	0	0	0	0	0	0	.000
Ford, p	2	5	1	0	0	0	0	0	.000
Terry, p	2	3	0	0	0	0	0	0	.000
Arroyo, p	2	0	0	0	0	0	0	0	.000
Stafford, p	1	2	0	0	0	0	0	0	.000
Daley, p	2	1	0	0	0	0	0	1	.000
Coates, p	1	1	0	0	0	0	0	0	.000
Gardner, ph	1	1	0	0	0	0	0	0	.000
Totals	5	165	27	42	8	1	7	26	.255

Cincinnati Reds

Player-Position	G.	AB.	R.	H.	2B.	3B.	HR.	RBI.	BA.
D. Johnson, c	2	4	0	2	0	0	0	0	.500
Edwards, c	3	11	1	4	2	0	0	2	.364
Cardenas, ph	3	3	0	1	1	0	0	0	.333
Post, rf-lf	5	18	3	6	1	0	1	2	.333
Kasko, ss	5	22	1	7	0	0	0	1	.318
Chacon, 2b-ph	4	12	2	3	0	0	0	0	.250
Coleman, 1b	5	20	2	5	0	0	1	2	.250
Robinson, lf-rf	5	15	3	3	2	0	1	4	.200
Blasingame, 2b-pr	3	7	1	1	0	0	0	0	.143
Pinson, cf	5	22	0	2	1	0	0	0	.091
Freese, 3b	5	16	0	1	1	0	0	0	.063
Zimmerman, c	2	0	0	0	0	0	0	0	.000
O'Toole, p	2	3	0	0	0	0	0	0	.000
Brosnan, p	3	0	0	0	0	0	0	0	.000
Jay, p	2	4	0	0	0	0	0	0	.000
Purkey, p	2	3	0	0	0	0	0	0	.000
Henry, p	2	0	0	0	0	0	0	0	.000
Maloney, p	1	0	0	0	0	0	0	0	.000
K. Johnson,p	1	0	0	0	0	0	0	0	.000
Jones, p	1	0	0	0	0	0	0	0	.000
Hunt, p	1	0	0	0	0	0	0	0	.000
Lynch, ph	4	3	0	0	0	0	0	0	.000
Gernert, ph	4	4	0	0	0	0	0	0	.000
Bell, ph	3	3	0	0	0	0	0	0	.000
Totals	5	170	13	35	8	0	3	11	.206

COMPOSITE PITCHING AVERAGES

New York Yankees

Pitcher	G.	IP.	H.	R.	ER.	BB.	SO.	W.	L.	ERA.
Ford	2	14	6	0	0	1	7	2	0	0.00
Daley	2	7	5	2	0	0	3	1	0	0.00
Coates	1	4	1	0	0	1	2	0	0	0.00
Arroyo	2	4	4	2	1	2	3	1	0	2.25
Stafford	1	6⅔	7	2	2	2	5	0	0	2.70
Terry	2	9⅓	12	7	5	2	7	0	1	4.82
Totals	5	45	35	13	8	8	27	4	1	1.60

Cincinnati Reds

Pitcher	G.	IP.	H.	R.	ER.	BB.	SO.	W.	L.	ERA.
Hunt	1	1	0	0	0	1	1	0	0	0.00
K. Johnson	1	⅔	0	0	0	0	0	0	0	0.00
Jones	1	⅔	0	0	0	0	0	0	0	0.00
Purkey	2	11	6	5	2	3	5	0	1	1.64
O'Toole	2	12	11	4	4	7	4	0	2	3.00
Jay	2	9⅔	8	6	6	6	6	1	1	5.59
Brosnan	3	6	9	5	5	4	5	0	0	7.50
Henry	2	2⅓	4	5	5	2	3	0	0	19.29
Maloney	1	⅔	4	2	2	1	1	0	0	27.00
Totals	5	44	42	27	24	24	25	1	4	4.91

Two years earlier, New York Yankees pitcher Ralph Terry had worn the goat horns in the World Series. Now, with the potential tying and winning runs in scoring position for the San Francisco Giants in the bottom of the ninth inning of Game 7 of the 1962 fall classic, Terry had another date with destiny.

The fine line between athletic success and failure was never more clearly defined than on October 16, 1962, at Candlestick Park. Terry was one out away from a Series-clinching, shutout victory that would thrust him into the "hero" category; conversely, one bad pitch and Terry again would be consigned to "bum" status.

Entering the ninth, Terry had allowed only two hits to the Giants—the first coming with two out in the sixth—and held a 1-0 lead. After pinch-hitter Matty Alou led off the inning for San Francisco by bunting for a base hit, Terry struck out Felipe Alou and Chuck Hiller. Willie Mays, who had just completed a 49-homer, 141-RBI season, then lashed a double to right, a smash on which Roger Maris made a running grab of the bounding ball and a prompt throw to cutoff man Bobby Richardson. Maris' defensive work forced Matty Alou to hold up at third base.

With first base open, Giants cleanup hitter Willie McCovey strolled to the plate and Orlando Cepeda moved into the on-deck circle. Yankees Manager Ralph Houk decided to let righthander Terry pitch to the lefthanded-hitting McCovey, who had tripled in his previous at-bat (but was coming off a 20-homer, 54-RBI season, compared with righthanded-hitter Cepeda's 35-homer, 114-RBI year).

Terry, who in the seventh game of the 1960 Series yielded Bill Mazeroski's decisive, last-of-the-ninth home run and then in Game 2 of the 1961 Series suffered New York's only defeat of that fall classic, had won 23 games for the Yankees in 1962 and was a complete-game winner in Game 5 of this Series. Getting McCovey in this incredibly tight spot would mean postseason redemption for the 26-year-old Terry, whose overall big-league career hardly needed redeeming (as evidenced by the hurler's 39-15 regular-season record over the last two years).

With a one-ball, one-strike count on McCovey, Terry let fly with another pitch. And McCovey nailed it. The ball shot toward right field, but second baseman Richardson moved slightly to his left and threw up his glove. The ball nestled in, and the New York Yankees had won their second straight World Series.

While no one could dispute that luck had played a major role in the Yankees' Series supremacy this time—an ever-so-slight variation in the path of McCovey's liner would have made the Giants champions—there was no disputing the gaudy numbers that the American Leaguers had put up in this October showcase. By beating Manager Alvin Dark's Giants, the Yankees now had won exactly half of *all* World Series played dating to 1923 (when the Yanks won the fall classic for the first time). Twenty Series crowns in 40 years! And those 20 Yankee titles had come in 25 Series appearances by the Bronx Bombers over that 1923-1962 span.

Winning in '62 not only took talent and luck, but it also required endurance. Rain caused a one-day delay in Game 5 at Yankee Stadium and wet weather forced three consecutive postponements of Game 6 at Candlestick. With two open dates thrown in for coast-to-coast travel, it meant the Yanks and Giants waged their struggle over a 13-day period and thereby equaled the record calendar time needed to complete the rain-marred 1911 Series.

The Yankees prevailed despite failing to win consecutive games at any point in the Series and getting .174 and .120 batting marks from Maris and Mickey Mantle, who had combined for 63 home runs during the regular season after poling a total of 115 in the previous year. While Mantle failed to hit a homer or even drive in a run against the Giants, Maris did lead the New Yorkers with five RBIs and he got two of those with a first-inning double in Game 1. Whitey Ford was a 6-2 winner in the opener, posting a record 10th Series triumph and stretching his consecutive-innings scoreless streak in the fall classic to 33 before San Francisco got on the scoreboard in the second inning. The Giants' Billy O'Dell battled Ford on even terms through six innings, but Clete Boyer's homer in the seventh broke a 2-2 tie and the Yanks followed with two more runs in the eighth and one in the ninth.

San Francisco's Jack Sanford fired a three-hit shutout in Game 2 and McCovey rapped a bases-empty homer as Terry and the Yankees fell, 2-0. Billy Pierce then blanked New York through six innings of Game 3, but Maris broke a scoreless deadlock with a two-run single in the seventh and eventually scored on a forceout grounder. Yankees pitcher Bill Stafford gave up a two-run homer to Ed Bailey in the ninth but held

Pitcher Ralph Terry gets a victory ride from his jubilant Yankee teammates after throwing a four-hit shutout against the San Francisco Giants
in the seventh game of the 1962 World Series.

on for a 3-2 triumph.

Giants second baseman Hiller, who would hit only 20 homers in his eight-year major league career, took center stage in Game 4 when he walloped a bases-full homer off Yankees reliever Marshall Bridges in the seventh inning. The grand slam, the first in Series history by a National League player, snapped a 2-2 tie at Yankee Stadium and made a winner out of a 33-year-old San Francisco reliever who had retired only one batter in the game. That well-traveled pitcher was one Don Larsen, who six years before—to the very day —had pitched a Series perfect game for the Yankees against Brooklyn in the same ball park.

Terry, whose second-game loss was his fourth in Series competi- tion without a victory, scored a breakthrough in Game 5—thanks to rookie Tom Tresh, who broke

yet another 2-2 deadlock in this fall classic when he hammered a three-run, eighth-inning homer off Sanford. New York and Terry came out on top, 5-3, despite San- ford's 10-strikeout effort in 7⅓ in- nings.

Pierce's three-hitter and Cepe- da's three hits and two RBIs fea- tured San Francisco's 5-2 triumph in Game 6, which marked the first Series action in five days follow- ing a travel day and three rain- outs. The rains, in fact, had creat- ed a dry spell: The Giants' victory was their first in exactly a week. Nevertheless, this World Series was now a 3-3 standoff.

Terry's mound opponent in Game 7 was Sanford, who worked seven-plus innings and gave up the day's only run in the fifth when Bill Skowron and Boyer rapped singles, Terry walked and Tony Kubek ground-

ed into a double play. Sanford, a 24-game winner for the Giants in '62, left the game with the bases loaded and no one out in the Yankees' eighth, but reliever O'Dell got Maris to hit a grounder that forced a runner at the plate and Elston Howard to ground into a double play.

Terry wound up with a four- hitter and did not walk a batter in the 1-0 clincher. He struck out four Giants, including two in the drama-packed ninth.

The Giants took solace in hav- ing won their first N.L. pennant since moving to the West Coast after the 1957 season. And they captured the flag in particularly satisfying fashion, rallying late in the season to tie Los Angeles for first place and then beating the archrival Dodgers, two games to one, in a playoff.

Still, San Francisco came up short in the end. As McCovey, his teammates and Giants fans every- where could tell you, *inches* short.

Game 1

Thursday, October 4, At San Francisco

New York	AB.	R.	H.	RBI.	PO.	A.
Kubek, ss	5	0	2	0	3	4
Richardson, 2b	5	1	1	0	4	2
Tresh, lf	5	2	2	0	0	0
Mantle, cf	4	0	0	0	1	0
Maris, rf	4	1	2	2	2	0
Howard, c	3	1	2	1	6	0
Skowron, 1b	2	0	0	0	7	0
Long, 1b	2	0	1	1	3	0
Boyer, 3b	3	1	1	2	1	2
Ford, p	3	0	0	0	0	4
Totals	36	6	11	6	27	12

San Francisco	AB.	R.	H.	RBI.	PO.	A.
Kuenn, lf	5	0	0	0	6	0
Hiller, 2b	4	1	1	0	4	4
F. Alou, rf	4	0	1	0	1	0
Mays, cf	4	1	3	1	1	0
Cepeda, 1b	4	0	0	0	6	0
Davenport, 3b	2	0	1	0	0	2
Bailey, c	4	0	0	0	8	0
Miller, p	0	0	0	0	0	1
Pagan, ss	4	0	3	1	1	2
O'Dell, p	3	0	1	0	0	0
Larsen, p	0	0	0	0	0	0
Orsino, c	1	0	0	0	0	0
Totals	35	2	10	2	27	9

New York .... 2 0 0   0 0 0   1 2 1—6
San Francisco .... 0 1 1   0 0 0   0 0 0—2

New York	IP.	H.	R.	ER.	BB.	SO.
Ford (W)	9	10	2	2	2	6

San Francisco	IP.	H.	R.	ER.	BB.	SO.
O'Dell (L)	7⅓	9	5	5	3	8
Larsen	1	1	1	1	1	0
Miller	⅔	1	0	0	1	0

DP—New York 2, San Francisco 1. LOB—New York 10, San Francisco 8. 2B—Maris, Hiller. HR—Boyer. SB— Mantle, Tresh. SF—Boyer. HBP—By O'Dell (Howard). U —Barlick (N.L.), Berry (A.L.), Landes (N.L.), Honochick (A.L.), Burkhart (N.L.) and Soar (A.L.). T—2:43. A— 43,852.

Game 2

Friday, October 5, At San Francisco

New York	AB.	R.	H.	RBI.	PO.	A.
Kubek, ss	4	0	0	0	1	1
Richardson, 2b	4	0	0	0	3	3
Tresh, lf	3	0	1	0	0	0
Mantle, cf	4	0	1	0	3	0
Maris, rf	3	0	0	0	1	0
Berra, c	2	0	0	0	6	1
Long, 1b	3	0	0	0	6	0
Boyer, 3b	3	0	1	0	3	2
Terry, p	2	0	0	0	2	0
aBlanchard	1	0	0	0	0	0
Daley, p	0	0	0	0	0	0
Totals	29	0	3	0	24	11

San Francisco	AB.	R.	H.	RBI.	PO.	A.
Hiller, 2b	3	1	1	0	0	6
F. Alou, rf	2	0	1	0	0	0
M. Alou, lf	4	0	1	1	1	0
Mays, cf	4	0	0	0	3	0
McCovey, 1b	4	1	1	1	11	1
Haller, c	3	0	1	0	8	1
Davenport, 3b	3	0	0	0	1	0
Pagan, ss	1	0	0	0	2	4
Sanford, p	3	0	1	0	1	1
Totals	27	2	6	2	27	13

New York	0 0 0 0 0 0 0 0 0—0
San Francisco	1 0 0 0 0 0 1 0 x—2

New York	IP.	H.	R.	ER.	BB.	SO.
Terry (L)	7	5	2	2	1	5
Daley	1	1	0	0	1	0

San Francisco	IP.	H.	R.	ER.	BB.	SO.
Sanford (W)	9	3	0	0	3	6

aStruck out for Terry in eighth. E—Kubek. DP—San Francisco 1. LOB—New York 5, San Francisco 6. 2B—Hiller, Mantle. HR—McCovey. SB—Tresh. SH—F. Alou, Pagan. HBP—By Terry (Pagan). U—Berry (A.L.), Landes (N.L.), Honochick (A.L.), Barlick (N.L.), Burkhart (N.L.) and Soar (A.L.). T—2:11. A—43,910.

Game 3

Sunday, October 7, At New York

San Francisco	AB.	R.	H.	RBI.	PO.	A.
F. Alou, lf	4	0	0	0	3	0
Hiller, 2b	3	0	0	0	3	0
Mays, cf	4	1	1	0	6	0
McCovey, rf	3	0	0	0	2	0
Cepeda, 1b	4	0	0	0	4	0
Bailey, c	4	1	1	2	4	0
Davenport, 3b	4	0	1	0	1	1
Pagan, ss	3	0	1	0	1	2
Pierce, p	2	0	0	0	0	0
Larsen, p	0	0	0	0	0	0
aM. Alou	1	0	0	0	0	0
Bolin, p	0	0	0	0	0	0
Totals	32	2	4	2	24	3

New York	AB.	R.	H.	RBI.	PO.	A.
Kubek, ss	4	0	1	0	1	2
Richardson, 2b	4	0	0	0	2	4
Tresh, lf	4	1	1	0	4	0
Mantle, cf	3	1	1	0	2	0
Maris, rf	3	1	1	2	3	0
Howard, c	3	0	1	0	7	0
Skowron, 1b	2	0	0	0	7	0
Boyer, 3b	3	0	0	1	1	2
Stafford, p	3	0	0	0	0	1
Totals	29	3	5	3	27	9

San Francisco	0 0 0 0 0 0 0 2—2
New York	0 0 0 0 0 0 3 0 x—3

San Francisco	IP.	H.	R.	ER.	BB.	SO.
Pierce (L)	6*	5	3	2	0	3
Larsen	1	0	0	0	0	0
Bolin	1	0	0	0	0	1

New York	IP.	H.	R.	ER.	BB.	SO.
Stafford (W)	9	4	2	2	2	5

*Pitched to three batters in seventh.

aHit into force play for Larsen in eighth. E—F. Alou, McCovey, Davenport, Boyer. DP—San Francisco 1. LOB—San Francisco 5, New York 3. 2B—Davenport, Kubek, Howard, Mays. HR—Bailey. HBP—By Larsen (Skowron). U—Landes (N.L.), Honochick (A.L.), Barlick (N.L.), Berry (A.L.), Soar (A.L.) and Burkhart (N.L.). T—2:06. A—71,434.

Game 4

Monday, October 8, At New York

San Francisco	AB.	R.	H.	RBI.	PO.	A.
Kuenn, rf	3	0	0	0	3	0
O'Dell, p	0	0	0	0	0	0
Hiller, 2b	5	1	2	4	3	2
Mays, cf	5	0	1	0	2	0
F. Alou, lf	4	1	1	0	1	0
Cepeda, 1b	4	0	0	0	8	3
Davenport, 3b	2	1	0	0	1	1
Haller, c	4	1	2	2	6	1
Pagan, ss	2	0	1	0	0	1
bM. Alou, rf	2	2	2	0	1	0
Marichal, p	2	0	0	0	1	0
Bolin, p	0	0	0	0	0	0
Larsen, p	0	0	0	0	1	0
cBailey	0	0	0	0	0	0
dNieman	0	0	0	0	0	0
eBowman, ss	1	1	0	0	0	4
Totals	34	7	9	6	27	12

New York	AB.	R.	H.	RBI.	PO.	A.
Kubek, ss	4	1	1	0	1	4
Richardson, 2b	4	0	1	0	2	3
Tresh, lf	5	0	2	1	1	0
Mantle, cf	4	1	0	0	0	0
Maris, rf	3	1	0	0	3	0
Howard, c	4	0	0	0	7	0
Skowron, 1b	4	0	3	1	12	0
Boyer, 3b	4	0	2	1	1	4
Ford, p	2	0	0	0	0	0
aBerra	0	0	0	0	0	0
Coates, p	0	0	0	0	0	0
Bridges, p	0	0	0	0	0	1
fLopez	1	0	0	0	0	0
Totals	35	3	9	3	27	12

San Francisco	0 2 0 0 0 0 4 0 1—7
New York	0 0 0 0 0 2 0 0 1—3

San Francisco	IP.	H.	R.	ER.	BB.	SO.
Marichal	4	2	0	0	2	4
Bolin	1⅔	4	2	2	2	1
Larsen (W)	⅓	0	0	0	1	0
O'Dell	3	3	1	1	0	0

New York	IP.	H.	R.	ER.	BB.	SO.
Ford	6	5	2	2	1	3
Coates (L)	⅓	1	2	2	1	1
Bridges	2⅔	3	3	2	2	3

aWalked for Ford in sixth. bDoubled for Pagan in seventh. cAnnounced for Larsen in seventh. dWalked intentionally for Bailey in seventh. eRan for Nieman in seventh. fGrounded out for Bridges in ninth. E—Davenport, Richardson. DP—San Francisco 2, New York 1. LOB—San Francisco 5, New York 10. 2B—F. Alou, M. Alou. 3B—Skowron. HR—Haller, Hiller. SH—O'Dell. U—Honochick (A.L.), Barlick (N.L.), Berry (A.L.), Landes (N.L.), Soar (A.L.) and Burkhart (N.L.). T—2:55. A—66,607.

Game 5

Wednesday, October 10, At New York

San Francisco	AB.	R.	H.	RBI.	PO.	A.
Hiller, 2b	3	0	1	1	1	3
Davenport, 3b	4	0	0	0	0	0
M. Alou, rf	4	0	0	0	0	0
Mays, cf	4	0	0	0	1	0
McCovey, 1b	4	1	1	0	7	3
F. Alou, lf	4	0	2	0	1	0
Haller, c	4	0	1	1	10	0
Pagan, ss	4	2	2	1	2	2
Sanford, p	2	0	1	0	2	1
Miller, p	0	0	0	0	0	0
aBailey	1	0	0	0	0	0
Totals	34	3	8	3	24	9

New York	AB.	R.	H.	RBI.	PO.	A.
Kubek, ss	4	1	2	0	1	2
Richardson, 2b	4	2	2	0	2	2
Tresh, lf	3	2	2	3	2	0
Mantle, cf	3	0	0	0	2	0
Maris, rf	3	0	0	0	3	0
Howard, c	4	0	0	0	7	0
Skowron, 1b	3	0	0	0	9	1
Boyer, 3b	3	0	0	0	1	2
Terry, p	3	0	0	0	0	1
Totals	30	5	6	3	27	8

San Francisco	0 0 1 0 1 0 0 0 1—3
New York	0 0 0 1 0 1 0 3 x—5

San Francisco	IP.	H.	R.	ER.	BB.	SO.
Sanford (L)	7⅓	6	5	4	1	10
Miller	⅔	0	0	0	1	0

New York	IP.	H.	R.	ER.	BB.	SO.
Terry (W)	9	8	3	3	1	7

aFlied out for Miller in ninth. E—Hiller, McCovey. DP—San Francisco 1. LOB—San Francisco 6, New York 4. 2B—Hiller, Tresh, Haller. 3B—F. Alou. HR—Pagan, Tresh. SB—Mantle. SH—Sanford, Tresh. WP—Sanford. PB—Haller. U—Barlick (N.L.), Berry (A.L.), Landes (N.L.), Honochick (A.L.), Soar (A.L.) and Burkhart (N.L.). T—2:42. A—63,165.

Game 6

Monday, October 15, At San Francisco

New York	AB.	R.	H.	RBI.	PO.	A.
Kubek, ss	4	0	1	1	4	4
Richardson, 2b	4	0	0	0	3	5
Tresh, lf	4	0	0	0	1	0
Mantle, cf	4	0	0	0	0	0
Maris, rf	3	1	1	1	0	0
Howard, c	3	0	0	0	5	1
Skowron, 1b	3	0	0	0	11	0
Boyer, 3b	2	1	1	0	0	2
Ford, p	2	0	0	0	0	1
Coates, p	0	0	0	0	0	0
aLopez	1	0	0	0	0	0
Bridges, p	0	0	0	0	0	0
Totals	30	2	3	2	24	12

San Francisco	AB.	R.	H.	RBI.	PO.	A.
Kuenn, lf	4	1	1	0	2	0
M. Alou, lf	0	0	0	0	1	0
Hiller, 2b	4	1	2	0	4	4
F. Alou, rf	4	1	2	1	1	0
Mays, cf	3	1	1	0	5	0
Cepeda, 1b	4	1	3	2	9	1
Davenport, 3b	4	0	1	1	0	4
Bailey, c	4	0	0	0	3	0
Pagan, ss	3	0	0	0	1	1
Pierce, p	3	0	0	0	1	0
Totals	33	5	10	4	27	10

New York	0 0 0 0 1 0 0 1 0—2
San Francisco	0 0 0 3 2 0 0 0 x—5

New York	IP.	H.	R.	ER.	BB.	SO.
Ford (L)	4⅔	9	5	5	1	3
Coates	2⅓	0	0	0	0	2
Bridges	1	1	0	0	0	0

San Francisco	IP.	H.	R.	ER.	BB.	SO.
Pierce (W)	9	3	2	2	2	2

aFlied out for Coates in eighth. E—Boyer, Ford, Davenport. DP—New York 2, San Francisco 1. LOB—New York 3, San Francisco 5. 2B—Cepeda, Boyer. HR—Maris. SB—Mays. U—Berry (A.L.), Landes (N.L.), Honochick (A.L.), Barlick (N.L.), Burkhart (N.L.) and Soar (A.L.). T—2:00. A—43,948.

Game 7

Tuesday, October 16, At San Francisco

New York	AB.	R.	H.	RBI.	PO.	A.
Kubek, ss	4	0	1	0	1	0
Richardson, 2b	2	0	0	0	3	0
Tresh, lf	4	0	1	0	6	0
Mantle, cf	3	0	1	0	3	0
Maris, rf	4	0	0	0	0	0
Howard, c	4	0	0	0	5	0
Skowron, 1b	4	1	1	0	6	0
Boyer, 3b	4	0	2	0	2	2
Terry, p	3	0	1	0	1	1
Totals	32	1	7	0	27	3

San Francisco	AB.	R.	H.	RBI.	PO.	A.
F. Alou, rf	4	0	0	0	1	0
Hiller, 2b	4	0	0	0	1	3
Mays, cf	4	0	1	0	1	0
McCovey, lf	4	0	1	0	3	0
Cepeda, 1b	3	0	0	0	12	0
Haller, c	3	0	0	0	5	0
Davenport, 3b	3	0	0	0	3	4
Pagan, ss	2	0	0	0	1	2
aBailey	1	0	0	0	0	0
Bowman, ss	0	0	0	0	0	1
Sanford, p	2	0	1	0	0	1
O'Dell, p	0	0	0	0	0	0
bM. Alou	1	0	1	0	0	0
Totals	31	0	4	0	27	11

New York	0 0 0 0 1 0 0 0 0—1
San Francisco	0 0 0 0 0 0 0 0 0—0

New York	IP.	H.	R.	ER.	BB.	SO.
Terry (W)	9	4	0	0	0	4

San Francisco	IP.	H.	R.	ER.	BB.	SO.
Sanford (L)	7*	7	1	1	4	3
O'Dell	2	0	0	0	0	1

*Pitched to three batters in eighth.

aFouled out for Pagan in eighth. bBunted safely for O'Dell in ninth. E—Pagan. DP—San Francisco 2. LOB—New York 8, San Francisco 4. 2B—Mays. 3B—McCovey. U—Landes (N.L.), Honochick (A.L.), Barlick (N.L.), Berry (A.L.), Burkhart (N.L.) and Soar (A.L.). T—2:29. A—43,948.

COMPOSITE BATTING AVERAGES

New York Yankees

Player-Position	G.	AB.	R.	H.	2B.	3B.	HR.	RBI.	BA.
Tresh, lf	7	28	5	9	1	0	1	4	.321
Boyer, 3b	7	22	2	7	1	0	1	4	.318
Kubek, ss	7	29	2	8	1	0	0	1	.276
Skowron, 1b	6	18	1	4	0	1	0	1	.222
Long, 1b	2	5	0	1	0	0	0	1	.200
Maris, rf	7	23	4	4	1	0	1	5	.174
Richardson, 2b	7	27	3	4	0	0	0	0	.148
Howard, c	6	21	1	3	1	0	0	1	.143
Terry, p	3	8	0	1	0	0	0	0	.125
Mantle, cf	7	25	2	3	1	0	0	0	.120
Berra, c-ph	2	2	0	0	0	0	0	0	.000
Ford, p	3	7	0	0	0	0	0	0	.000
Daley, p	1	0	0	0	0	0	0	0	.000
Stafford, p	1	3	0	0	0	0	0	0	.000
Coates, p	2	0	0	0	0	0	0	0	.000
Bridges, p	2	0	0	0	0	0	0	0	.000
Lopez, ph	2	2	0	0	0	0	0	0	.000
Blanchard, ph	1	1	0	0	0	0	0	0	.000
Totals	7	221	20	44	6	1	3	17	.199

San Francisco Giants

Player-Position	G.	AB.	R.	H.	2B.	3B.	HR.	RBI.	BA.
Sanford, p	3	7	0	3	0	0	0	0	.429
Pagan, ss	7	19	2	7	0	0	1	2	.368
O'Dell, p	3	3	0	1	0	0	0	0	.333
M. Alou, lf-ph-rf	6	12	2	4	1	0	0	1	.333
Haller, c	4	14	1	4	1	0	1	3	.286
Hiller, 2b	7	26	4	7	3	0	1	5	.269
F. Alou, rf-lf	7	26	2	7	1	1	0	1	.269
Mays, cf	7	28	3	7	2	0	0	1	.250
McCovey, 1b-rf-lf	4	15	2	3	0	1	1	1	.200
Cepeda, 1b	5	19	1	3	1	0	0	2	.158
Davenport, 3b	7	22	1	3	1	0	0	1	.136
Kuenn, lf-rf	3	12	1	1	0	0	0	0	.083
Bailey, c-ph	6	14	1	1	0	0	1	2	.071
Orsino, c	1	1	0	0	0	0	0	0	.000
Bowman, pr-ss	2	1	1	0	0	0	0	0	.000
Miller, p	2	0	0	0	0	0	0	0	.000
Larsen, p	3	0	0	0	0	0	0	0	.000
Pierce, p	2	5	0	0	0	0	0	0	.000
Bolin, p	2	0	0	0	0	0	0	0	.000
Marichal, p	1	2	0	0	0	0	0	0	.000
Nieman, ph	1	0	0	0	0	0	0	0	.000
Totals	7	226	21	51	10	2	5	19	.226

COMPOSITE PITCHING AVERAGES

New York Yankees

Pitcher	G.	IP.	H.	R.	ER.	BB.	SO.	W.	L.	ERA.
Daley	1	1	1	0	0	1	0	0	0	0.00
Terry	3	25	17	5	5	2	16	2	1	1.80
Stafford	1	9	4	2	2	2	5	1	0	2.00
Ford	3	19⅔	24	9	9	4	12	1	1	4.12
Bridges	2	3⅔	4	3	2	2	3	0	0	4.91
Coates	2	2⅔	1	2	2	1	3	0	1	6.75
Totals	7	61	51	21	20	12	39	4	3	2.95

San Francisco Giants

Pitcher	G.	IP.	H.	R.	ER.	BB.	SO.	W.	L.	ERA.
Marichal	1	4	2	0	0	2	4	0	0	0.00
Miller	2	1⅓	1	0	0	2	0	0	0	0.00
Sanford	3	23⅓	16	6	5	8	19	1	2	1.93
Pierce	2	15	8	5	4	2	5	1	1	2.40
Larsen	3	2⅓	1	1	1	2	0	1	0	3.86
O'Dell	2	12⅓	12	6	6	3	9	0	1	4.38
Bolin	2	2⅔	4	2	2	2	2	0	0	6.75
Totals	7	61	44	20	18	21	39	3	4	2.66

LOS ANGELES DODGERS
VS.
NEW YORK YANKEES

In baseball parlance, these Dodger pitchers could bring it. And in the 1963 World Series, they brought the New York Yankees to their knees.

Foremost among the standout Los Angeles pitchers was 27-year-old lefthander Sandy Koufax, who had harnessed his blazing fastball and sharp-breaking curve with devastating results. The last time the Dodgers took part in the Series, Koufax was coming off an 8-6 season punctuated by a 4.06 earned-run average and an average yield of 5.4 bases on balls per nine innings. That was 1959. This was 1963. And in the '63 National League season, Koufax posted a 25-5 record and a 1.88 ERA—and gave up 1.7 walks per game. In baseball parlance, this is called putting it all together.

Koufax, who struck out 306 batters in 311 innings in '63 and threw 11 shutouts (he had one shutout in '59), had plenty of company in the super-pitcher class. Side-wheeling righthander Don Drysdale, himself a 25-game winner in 1962, was victorious 19 times this season and fashioned a 2.63 ERA. Crafty veteran Johnny Podres won 14 games and fired five shutouts. And relief ace Ron Perranoski made 69 appearances and went 16-3 with a 1.67 ERA.

Walter Alston's Dodgers, rebounding from a late-season collapse in 1962, fought off St. Louis in 1963 and finished six games in front of the Cardinals. Los Angeles' World Series opponent would be an old Dodger nemesis, the New York Yankees. In seven Series between the Yankees and the Brooklyn Dodgers, the American Leaguers had won six times.

The Yanks had muscle, as usual, with four players hitting more than 20 homers. They had

good pitching, too, in Whitey Ford (24 victories), Jim Bouton, Ralph Terry and Al Downing. And, incredibly, they overcame injuries that would decimate most teams. Roger Maris and Mickey Mantle played in a total of only 155 games, but the Yanks persevered and even prospered. Manager Ralph Houk's team captured the American League pennant by 10½ games.

It was Koufax against Ford in the '63 Series opener at Yankee Stadium. And Koufax quickly demonstrated just how far his star had risen. The first five Yankee batters—Tony Kubek, Bobby Richardson, Tom Tresh, Mantle and Maris—all went down on strikes.

By the time the Yankees made contact against Koufax, Los Angeles already owned a 4-0 lead. Bill Skowron, obtained from the Yankees after the 1962 season, singled home a Dodger run in the top of the second and John Roseboro cracked a three-run homer later in the inning.

Skowron singled home another run in the third, and Koufax continued to cruise. Through four innings, the Yankees did not have a baserunner.

After Mantle struck out and Maris fouled out as New York's first two batters in the fifth, the Yankees loaded the bases on consecutive singles by Elston Howard, Joe Pepitone and Clete Boyer. But the threat passed when Hector Lopez, batting for Ford, became Koufax's 11th strikeout victim of the afternoon.

Koufax struck out pinch-hitter Phil Linz to open the eighth, thereby moving within one of Carl Erskine's Series strikeout record of 14 in one game. After Kubek beat out a slow roller, Koufax fanned Richardson for

the third time and was record book-bound. But Tresh tempered any immediate elation by pounding a homer into the left-field stands.

With Koufax on the mound, though, a three-run lead was money in the bank. Outside of a walk to Mantle following Tresh's clout and a ninth-inning single by Pepitone, the Yankees went quietly the rest of the way. The first three of New York's final four outs in Koufax's 5-2 triumph came on a grounder, a liner and a fly ball. The last out of the game was record-breaking strikeout No. 15, with pinch-hitter Harry Bright being victimized.

Koufax's World Series strikeout mark, like Erskine's, had come in a Dodger uniform against the Yankees in a game played on October 2 (10 years apart). The only common strikeout victim for the Dodger pitchers was Mantle, who fanned four times against righthander Erskine and twice against Koufax.

Podres, with two-out relief help from Perranoski, beat the Yankees, 4-1, in Game 2. Willie Davis' two-run double in the first inning got Los Angeles rolling, and Skowron provided Podres with another run with a homer in the fourth. Maris, who had a chance to catch Davis' drive but slipped on the Yankee Stadium grass, injured his knee and elbow in the third when he ran into a railing while pursuing Tommy Davis' triple and left the game. New York's slugging right fielder never played another inning in the Series.

Los Angeles took its two games-to-none lead to Dodger Stadium, the palatial estate that had supplanted the Memorial Coliseum as the Dodgers' home grounds the previous year. And Drysdale made the first Series game at the

glittering park one to remember, foiling the Yankees on three hits and striking out nine batters in a 1-0 triumph. Tough-luck loser Bouton yielded the game's only run in the first inning on Jim Gilliam's walk, a wild pitch and a single by Tommy Davis, who had just captured his second straight N.L. batting championship.

Ford and Koufax went at it again in Game 4, which was a scoreless contest until the fifth when Frank Howard, the Dodgers' 6-foot-7, 250-pound right fielder, blasted a mammoth homer to left. Mantle got the run back in the seventh. Having managed only one hit in 13 Series at-bats as he dug in against Koufax, Mantle rocketed a homer to left-center.

Los Angeles, a speed-oriented team offensively (Maury Wills, the man of 104 steals in '62, was the catalyst) and quite content to scrounge for runs, regained the lead in the bottom of the seventh. Gilliam led off the inning with a high bouncer that was speared by third baseman Boyer, but first baseman Pepitone lost Boyer's on-target throw amid the white-shirted crowd and Gilliam scooted all the way to third base. Willie Davis then stroked a sacrifice fly to deep center field.

A one-run lead is hardly money in the bank under any circumstances, but Koufax—despite the fact his club collected only two hits all day—made it stand up in a six-hit, 2-1 triumph. He struck out eight Yankees and walked none.

The Dodgers had done to New York what the Yankees, in all their dominant years, had never been able to do to them. In baseball parlance, they had *swept* 'em.

Game 1

Wednesday, October 2, At New York

Los Angeles	AB.	R.	H.	RBI.	PO.	A.
Wills, ss	5	0	0	0	2	0
Gilliam, 3b	4	0	1	0	1	1
W. Davis, cf	3	1	0	0	1	0
T. Davis, lf	4	0	3	0	0	0
F. Howard, rf	4	1	1	0	0	0
Fairly, rf	0	0	0	0	0	0
Skowron, 1b	3	1	2	2	3	0
Tracewski, 2b	4	1	1	0	2	2
Roseboro, c	4	1	1	3	18	0
Koufax, p	4	0	0	0	0	1
Totals	35	5	9	5	27	4

New York	AB.	R.	H.	RBI.	PO.	A.
Kubek, ss	4	1	1	0	1	5
Richardson, 2b	3	0	0	0	2	2
Tresh, lf	3	1	1	2	0	0
Mantle, cf	3	0	0	0	1	0
Maris, rf	4	0	0	0	2	0
E. Howard, c	4	0	1	0	11	0
Pepitone, 1b	4	0	2	0	8	0
Boyer, 3b	4	0	1	0	1	2
Ford, p	1	0	0	0	1	2
aLopez	1	0	0	0	0	0
Williams, p	0	0	0	0	0	0
bLinz	1	0	0	0	0	0
Hamilton, p	0	0	0	0	0	0
cBright	1	0	0	0	0	0
Totals	33	2	6	2	27	11

Los Angeles	0 4 1	0 0 0	0 0 0	—5
New York	0 0 0	0 0 0	0 2 0	—2

Los Angeles	IP.	H.	R.	ER.	BB.	SO.
Koufax (W)	9	6	2	2	3	15

New York	IP.	H.	R.	ER.	BB.	SO.
Ford (L)	5	8	5	5	2	4
Williams	3	1	0	0	0	5
Hamilton	1	0	0	0	0	1

aStruck out for Ford in fifth. bStruck out for Williams in eighth. cStruck out for Hamilton in ninth. LOB—Los Angeles 6, New York 7. 2B—F. Howard. HR—Roseboro, Tresh. SB—T. Davis. SH—W. Davis. U—Paparella (A.L.), Gorman (N.L.), Napp (A.L.), Crawford (N.L.), Venzon (N.L.) and Rice (A.L.). T—2:09. A—69,000.

Game 2

Thursday, October 3, At New York

Los Angeles	AB.	R.	H.	RBI.	PO.	A.
Wills, ss	4	1	2	0	2	3
Gilliam, 3b	4	1	1	0	1	1
W. Davis, cf	4	1	2	2	3	0
T. Davis, lf	4	0	2	1	6	0
F. Howard, rf	3	0	0	0	2	0
bFairly, rf	0	0	0	0	0	0
Skowron, 1b	4	1	2	1	8	1
Tracewski, 2b	3	0	0	0	0	1
Roseboro, c	4	0	0	0	5	0
Podres, p	4	0	1	0	0	2
Perranoski, p	0	0	0	0	0	0
Totals	34	4	10	4	27	8

New York	AB.	R.	H.	RBI.	PO.	A.
Kubek, ss	4	0	0	0	2	4
Richardson, 2b	4	0	1	0	3	5
Tresh, lf	4	0	2	0	0	0
Mantle, cf	4	0	0	0	0	0
Maris, rf	1	0	0	0	1	0
Lopez, rf	3	1	2	0	1	0
E. Howard, c	4	0	2	1	6	0
Pepitone, 1b	3	0	0	0	13	1
Boyer, 3b	4	0	0	0	0	3
Downing, p	1	0	0	0	0	1
aBright	1	0	0	0	0	0
Terry, p	0	0	0	0	1	1
cLinz	1	0	0	0	0	0
Reniff, p	0	0	0	0	0	0
Totals	34	1	7	1	27	15

Los Angeles	2 0 0	1 0 0	0 1 0	—4
New York	0 0 0	0 0 0	0 0 1	—1

Los Angeles	IP.	H.	R.	ER.	BB.	SO.
Podres (W)	8⅓	6	1	1	1	4
Perranoski	⅔	1	0	0	0	1

New York	IP.	H.	R.	ER.	BB.	SO.
Downing (L)	5	7	3	3	1	6
Terry	3	3	1	1	1	0
Reniff	1	0	0	0	0	0

aStruck out for Downing in fifth. bWalked intentionally for F. Howard in eighth. cLined out for Terry in eighth. E—Podres. DP—New York 3. LOB—Los Angeles 5, New York 7. 2B—W. Davis 2, Lopez 2. 3B—T. Davis 2. HR—Skowron. SB—Wills. U—Gorman (N.L.), Napp (A.L.), Crawford (N.L.), Paparella (A.L.), Venzon (N.L.) and Rice (A.L.). T—2:13. A—66,455.

Game 3

Saturday, October 5, At Los Angeles

New York	AB.	R.	H.	RBI.	PO.	A.
Kubek, ss	4	0	2	0	2	2
Richardson, 2b	3	0	0	0	1	3
Tresh, lf	4	0	0	0	2	0
Mantle, cf	4	0	1	0	1	0
Pepitone, 1b	3	0	0	0	8	2
E. Howard, c	3	0	0	0	7	1
Blanchard, rf	3	0	0	0	1	0
Boyer, 3b	2	0	0	0	1	1
Bouton, p	2	0	0	0	1	2
aBerra	1	0	0	0	0	0
Reniff, p	0	0	0	0	0	0
Totals	29	0	3	0	24	11

Los Angeles	AB.	R.	H.	RBI.	PO.	A.
Wills, ss	4	0	0	0	1	2
Gilliam, 3b	2	1	0	0	0	0
W. Davis, cf	3	0	0	0	0	0
T. Davis, lf	4	0	1	1	0	0
Fairly, rf	1	0	0	0	3	0
Skowron, 1b	3	0	1	0	10	2
Roseboro, c	3	0	1	0	9	0
Tracewski, 2b	3	0	1	0	3	3
Drysdale, p	1	0	0	0	1	3
Totals	24	1	4	1	27	10

New York	0 0 0	0 0 0	0 0 0	—0
Los Angeles	1 0 0	0 0 0	0 0 x	—1

New York	IP.	H.	R.	ER.	BB.	SO.
Bouton (L)	7	4	1	1	5	4
Reniff	1	0	0	0	1	1

Los Angeles	IP.	H.	R.	ER.	BB.	SO.
Drysdale (W)	9	3	0	0	1	9

aLined out for Bouton in eighth. E—Wills. DP—New York 2. LOB—New York 5, Los Angeles 6. SH—Richardson, W. Davis. HBP—By Drysdale (Pepitone). WP—Bouton 2. U—Napp (A.L.), Crawford (N.L.), Paparella (A.L.), Gorman (N.L.), Rice (A.L.) and Venzon (N.L.). T—2:05. A—55,912.

Game 4

Sunday, October 6, At Los Angeles

New York	AB.	R.	H.	RBI.	PO.	A.
Kubek, ss	4	0	0	0	0	2
Richardson, 2b	4	0	2	0	1	4
Tresh, lf	4	0	0	0	1	0
Mantle, cf	4	1	1	1	4	0
E. Howard, c	4	0	2	0	6	1
Lopez, rf	4	0	0	0	1	0
Pepitone, 1b	3	0	0	0	8	3
Boyer, 3b	3	0	0	0	0	2
Ford, p	2	0	0	0	2	0
aLinz	1	0	1	0	0	0
Reniff, p	0	0	0	0	1	0
Totals	33	1	6	1	24	12

Los Angeles	AB.	R.	H.	RBI.	PO.	A.
Wills, ss	2	0	0	0	0	5
Gilliam, 3b	3	1	0	0	0	0
W. Davis, cf	2	0	0	1	2	0
T. Davis, lf	3	0	0	0	0	0
F. Howard, rf	3	1	2	1	2	0
Fairly, rf	0	0	0	0	0	0
Skowron, 1b	3	0	0	0	9	1
Roseboro, c	3	0	0	0	11	0
Tracewski, 2b	3	0	0	0	2	1
Koufax, p	2	0	0	0	1	2
Totals	24	2	2	2	27	9

New York	0 0 0	0 0 0	1 0 0	—1
Los Angeles	0 0 0	0 1 0	1 0 x	—2

New York	IP.	H.	R.	ER.	BB.	SO.
Ford (L)	7	2	2	1	1	4
Reniff	1	0	0	0	0	0

Los Angeles	IP.	H.	R.	ER.	BB.	SO.
Koufax (W)	9	6	1	1	0	8

aSingled for Ford in eighth. E—Pepitone, Tracewski. DP—New York 2, Los Angeles 1. LOB—New York 5, Los Angeles 0. 2B—Richardson. HR—F. Howard, Mantle. SF—W. Davis. U—Crawford (N.L.), Paparella (A.L.), Gorman (N.L.), Napp (A.L.), Rice (A.L.) and Venzon (N.L.). T—1:50. A—55,912.

COMPOSITE BATTING AVERAGES

Los Angeles Dodgers

Player-Position	G.	AB.	R.	H.	2B.	3B.	HR.	RBI.	BA.
T. Davis, lf	4	15	0	6	0	2	0	2	.400
Skowron, 1b	4	13	2	5	0	0	1	3	.385
F. Howard, rf	3	10	2	3	1	0	1	1	.300
Podres, p	1	4	0	1	0	0	0	0	.250
W. Davis, cf	4	12	2	2	2	0	0	3	.167
Gilliam, 3b	4	13	3	2	0	0	0	0	.154
Tracewski, 2b	4	13	1	2	0	0	0	0	.154
Roseboro, c	4	14	1	2	0	0	1	3	.143
Wills, ss	4	15	1	2	0	0	0	0	.133
Koufax, p	2	6	0	0	0	0	0	0	.000
Perranoski, p	1	0	0	0	0	0	0	0	.000
Drysdale, p	1	1	0	0	0	0	0	0	.000
Fairly, rf-pr	4	1	0	0	0	0	0	0	.000
Totals	4	117	12	25	3	2	3	12	.214

New York Yankees

Player-Position	G.	AB.	R.	H.	2B.	3B.	HR.	RBI.	BA.
Linz, ph	3	3	0	1	0	0	0	0	.333
E. Howard, c	4	15	0	5	0	0	0	1	.333
Lopez, ph-rf	3	8	1	2	2	0	0	0	.250
Richardson, 2b	4	14	0	3	1	0	0	0	.214
Tresh, lf	4	15	1	3	0	0	1	2	.200
Kubek, ss	4	16	1	3	0	0	0	0	.188
Pepitone, 1b	4	13	0	2	0	0	0	0	.154
Mantle, cf	4	15	1	2	0	0	1	1	.133
Boyer, 3b	4	13	0	1	0	0	0	0	.077
Maris, rf	2	5	0	0	0	0	0	0	.000
Ford, p	2	3	0	0	0	0	0	0	.000
Williams, p	1	0	0	0	0	0	0	0	.000
Hamilton, p	1	0	0	0	0	0	0	0	.000
Bright, ph	2	2	0	0	0	0	0	0	.000
Downing, p	1	1	0	0	0	0	0	0	.000
Terry, p	1	0	0	0	0	0	0	0	.000
Reniff, p	3	0	0	0	0	0	0	0	.000
Blanchard, rf	1	3	0	0	0	0	0	0	.000
Bouton, p	1	2	0	0	0	0	0	0	.000
Berra, ph	1	1	0	0	0	0	0	0	.000
Totals	4	129	4	22	3	0	2	4	.171

COMPOSITE PITCHING AVERAGES

Los Angeles Dodgers

Pitcher	G.	IP.	H.	R.	ER.	BB.	SO.	W.	L.	ERA.
Perranoski	1	⅔	1	0	0	0	1	0	0	0.00
Drysdale	1	9	3	0	0	1	9	1	0	0.00
Podres	1	8⅓	6	1	1	1	4	1	0	1.08
Koufax	2	18	12	3	3	3	23	2	0	1.50
Totals	4	36	22	4	4	5	37	4	0	1.00

New York Yankees

Pitcher	G.	IP.	H.	R.	ER.	BB.	SO.	W.	L.	ERA.
Williams	1	3	1	0	0	0	5	0	0	0.00
Reniff	3	3	0	0	0	1	1	0	0	0.00
Hamilton	1	1	0	0	0	0	1	0	0	0.00
Bouton	1	7	4	1	1	5	4	0	1	1.29
Terry	1	3	3	1	1	1	0	0	0	3.00
Ford	2	12	10	7	6	3	8	0	2	4.50
Downing	1	5	7	3	3	1	6	0	1	5.40
Totals	4	34	25	12	11	11	25	0	4	2.91

1964
ST. LOUIS CARDINALS
VS.
NEW YORK YANKEES

Since playing in their first World Series in 1921, the New York Yankees had never gone longer than three years without appearing in the fall classic.

Those three-year spans—which must have seemed interminably long for Yankee lovers and ridiculously short for Yankee haters—ran from 1929 through 1931, 1933 through 1935 and 1944 through 1946.

The Yankees were in a particularly good groove at the end of the 1964 regular season, having earned their 14th Series berth in the last 16 years. Under first-year Manager Yogi Berra, the Yankees had won the pennant by one game over the Chicago White Sox.

The '64 World Series—matching New York against the St. Louis Cardinals—would be the 15th fall classic in Yankee pinstripes for Berra, who first appeared in the Series in 1947, last performed in it in 1963 and along the way established the record for most Series games played, 75.

Mickey Mantle was about to play in his 12th Series for the Yankees, Whitey Ford in his 11th and Elston Howard in his ninth. Bobby Richardson at age 29, was gearing up for his seventh fall classic in a New York uniform, while Tony Kubek, not yet 28 when the action got under way at Busch Stadium, also would have made a seventh appearance if not for a disabling wrist injury. And Roger Maris, in his fifth season as a Yankee, would be competing in his fifth fall classic.

Being a Yankee meant playing in the World Series, and the Yankees were doing business as usual in October 1964. Little did anyone realize, though, that business was about to turn bad for this storied franchise. Very bad.

New York's four-game loss to

St. Louis' Tim McCarver is greeted at the plate after hitting a three-run, game-winning homer in the 10th inning of Game 5 of the 1964 Series.

the Los Angeles Dodgers in the 1963 Series perhaps gave hint of impending trouble for the Yankees, as did a monumental struggle to win the '64 American League pennant.

Then came a first-game pounding by the Cardinals, a team that had overcome the mid-August turmoil surrounding the ouster of General Manager Bing Devine and roared from fifth place to first (with considerable help from the Philadelphia Phillies, who blew a 6½-game league lead with 12 games to play). Ford took a 4-2 lead into the sixth inning of the Series opener, but St. Louis right fielder Mike Shannon walloped a long two-run homer off the veteran lefthander. Catcher Tim McCarver followed with a double,

and the 35-year-old Ford was through for the day. And, because of arm problems, he was through for the Series.

St. Louis scored two more runs in that inning, with pinch-hitter Carl Warwick singling home the go-ahead run and center fielder Curt Flood following with a triple. The Cards won 9-5.

Now saddled with a five-game losing streak in Series play, the Yankees suddenly revived. Rookie Mel Stottlemyre, a key contributor to the Yanks' pennant cause after his call-up from Richmond in August, beat Bob Gibson in Game 2, a contest in which New York erupted for four ninth-inning runs (after Gibson had left the game) and made off with an 8-3 victory. In Game 3 at Yankee

Stadium, Cardinals veteran Curt Simmons and the Yankees' Jim Bouton were locked in a 1-1 tie through eight innings. Manager Johnny Keane then used a pinch-hitter for Simmons in the ninth as the Cards threatened—but failed—to score. Barney Schultz, a stellar reliever down the stretch for St. Louis, entered the game in the last of the ninth and threw one pitch. Mantle deposited it into the right-field stands.

After its dramatic 2-1 triumph, New York nailed Ray Sadecki for three first-inning runs in Game 4 and lefthander Al Downing protected the lead through the fifth. Ahead two games to one in the Series and on top by a 3-0 score midway through the fourth contest, the Yankees had things going their way. Until, that is, St. Louis third baseman Ken Boyer rifled a bases-loaded home run off Downing in the sixth. With relievers Roger Craig and Ron Taylor combining for 8⅔ innings of two-hit, scoreless relief, St. Louis evened the Series with a 4-3 victory.

The next day, Gibson was one out away from a 2-0 victory when the Yanks' Tom Tresh ripped a two-run homer, but the hard-throwing righthander prevailed, 5-2, in 10 innings when battery-mate McCarver launched a three-run homer off Yanks reliever Pete Mikkelsen.

Game 6 was a 1-1 tie entering the sixth inning, but Simmons yielded consecutive-pitch homers to Maris and Mantle. New York's Joe Pepitone then erased any doubt as to the game's outcome when he socked a bases-full homer off reliever Gordon Richardson in the eighth. New York won, 8-3.

The climactic game of the 1964 World Series, featuring a Stottlemyre-Gibson pitching matchup, was scoreless through three innings, but the Cardinals broke loose for three runs in the fourth and three more in the fifth. The latter outburst was touched off by a homer by Lou Brock, the mid-June acquisition from the Chicago Cubs who proved a catalyst in the Cardinals' offense (he batted .348 and stole 33 bases for St. Louis in 103 games).

While Mantle cracked a three-run homer in the sixth and the Yanks' Clete Boyer and Phil Linz connected in the ninth, Gibson pitched doggedly and went all the way in a 7-5 Cardinals triumph. Since St. Louis' Ken Boyer already had hit two homers in this Series—the second coming in the seventh inning of Game 7—Clete's blow meant that the Boyers had become the first brothers to hit home runs in the same Series (and, of course, they even accomplished the feat in the same game).

The Series championship ended a long drought for the Cardinals, who hadn't even appeared in a fall classic since 1946. Having regained the pennant-winning knack, St. Louis would find its way into two more Series before the end of the 1960s.

It was a different story for the aging and injury-racked Yankees, who within two years would tumble all the way to last place. There would be no more World Series for Mantle, Ford, Richardson, Kubek and Boyer, among others. Howard would appear in the classic once more, with the Boston Red Sox; Maris was destined to play in two more Series, both with the Cardinals.

Mantle bid the competition a fitting adieu, breaking the Series homer record he shared with Babe Ruth when he belted No. 16 off Schultz to end Game 3 and then slamming two more homers. Richardson also went out in style, setting a one-Series mark with 13 hits against St. Louis.

In a strange twist, both Series managers were out of work the day after Game 7. Yankee management, unhappy with the way the team was handled, fired Berra. Keane, on the other hand, quit the Cardinals as an outgrowth of the Devine dismissal. While Keane soon surfaced as the Yanks' new manager, the fact that neither pennant-winning pilot would be back with his old club was a stunning development.

Not quite as stunning, perhaps, as the fact the mighty New York Yankees would not be back in the World Series for considerably longer than three years. Would you believe 12 years?

Game 1

Wednesday, October 7, At St. Louis

New York	AB.	R.	H.	RBI.	PO.	A.
Linz, ss	4	0	0	0	1	1
Richardson, 2b	5	0	2	1	2	3
Maris, cf	4	0	1	0	0	0
Mantle, rf	5	1	2	0	1	0
Howard, c	4	1	2	0	5	0
Tresh, lf	4	1	2	3	1	0
Pepitone, 1b	5	0	0	0	11	0
C. Boyer, 3b	4	1	1	0	2	4
Ford, p	1	0	1	1	0	1
Downing, p	0	0	0	0	0	0
dBlanchard	1	0	1	0	0	0
eHegan	0	1	0	0	0	0
Sheldon, p	0	0	0	0	1	1
Mikkelsen, p	0	0	0	0	0	0
Totals	37	5	12	5	24	10

St. Louis	AB.	R.	H.	RBI.	PO.	A.
Flood, cf	5	1	2	2	5	0
Brock, lf	5	1	2	1	1	1
Groat, ss	4	0	1	0	1	4
K. Boyer, 3b	3	1	1	1	1	4
White, 1b	4	0	0	0	11	0
Shannon, rf	4	3	2	2	2	0
McCarver, c	3	1	2	0	4	0
Maxvill, 2b	2	0	0	0	2	2
aJames	1	0	0	0	0	0
Schultz, p	1	0	0	0	0	0
Sadecki, p	2	0	1	1	0	1
bWarwick	1	0	1	1	0	0
cJavier, 2b	0	1	0	0	0	1
fSkinner	0	1	0	0	0	0
gBuchek, 2b	0	0	0	0	0	0
Totals	35	9	12	9	27	13

New York......0 3 0 0 1 0 0 1 0—5
St. Louis.......1 1 0 0 0 4 0 3 x—9

New York	IP.	H.	R.	ER.	BB.	SO.
Ford (L)	5⅓	8	5	5	1	4
Downing	1⅔	2	1	1	0	1
Sheldon	⅔	0	2	0	2	0
Mikkelsen	⅓	2	1	0	1	0

St. Louis	IP.	H.	R.	ER.	BB.	SO.
Sadecki (W)	6	8	4	4	5	2
Schultz	3	4	1	1	1	1

aPopped out for Maxvill in sixth. bSingled for Sadecki in sixth. cRan for Warwick in sixth. dDoubled for Downing in eighth. eRan for Blanchard in eighth. fWalked intentionally for Javier in eighth. gRan for Skinner in eighth. E—Mantle, C. Boyer. DP—New York 1, St. Louis 1. LOB—New York 11, St. Louis 7. 2B—Tresh, McCarver, Blanchard, Brock. 3B—McCarver, Flood. HR—Tresh, Shannon. SB—C. Boyer. SF—K. Boyer. PB—Howard 2. U—Secory (N.L.), McKinley (A.L.), Burkhart (N.L.), Soar (A.L.), V. Smith (N.L.) and A. Smith (A.L.). T—2:42. A—30,805.

Game 2

Thursday, October 8, At St. Louis

New York	AB.	R.	H.	RBI.	PO.	A.
Linz, ss	4	2	3	1	1	8
B. Richardson, 2b	5	1	2	1	4	2
Maris, cf	5	1	2	0	2	0
Mantle, rf	4	2	1	2	0	0
Lopez, rf	0	0	0	0	0	0
Howard, c	4	2	1	0	4	1
Pepitone, 1b	4	0	2	1	14	0
Tresh, lf	3	0	1	2	1	0
C. Boyer, 3b	3	0	0	1	0	3
Stottlemyre, p	5	0	0	0	1	3
Totals	37	8	12	8	27	18

St. Louis	AB.	R.	H.	RBI.	PO.	A.
Flood, cf	4	0	0	1	2	0
Brock, lf	4	0	0	1	1	0
White, 1b	3	0	0	0	7	0
K. Boyer, 3b	4	0	0	0	2	1
Groat, ss	3	1	1	0	2	3
McCarver, c	4	0	1	1	10	0
Shannon, rf	4	1	1	0	2	0
Maxvill, 2b	2	0	1	0	1	3
aWarwick	1	1	1	0	0	0
Schultz, p	0	0	0	0	0	0
G. Richardson, p	0	0	0	0	0	0
Craig, p	0	0	0	0	0	0
dJames	1	0	0	0	0	0
Gibson, p	1	0	0	0	0	0
bSkinner	1	0	1	0	0	0
cBuchek, 2b	0	0	0	0	0	0
Totals	32	3	7	3	27	7

New York......0 0 0 1 0 1 2 0 4—8
St. Louis.......0 0 1 0 0 0 1 1—3

New York	IP.	H.	R.	ER.	BB.	SO.
Stottlemyre (W)	9	7	3	3	2	4

St. Louis	IP.	H.	R.	ER.	BB.	SO.
Gibson (L)	8	8	4	4	3	9
Schultz	⅓	2	2	2	0	0
G. Richardson	⅓	2	2	2	0	0
Craig	⅓	0	0	0	0	1

aSingled for Maxvill in eighth. bDoubled for Gibson in eighth. cRan for Skinner in eighth. dStruck out for Craig in ninth. DP—New York 1. LOB—New York 10, St. Louis 5. 2B—B. Richardson, Howard, Pepitone, Skinner, Mantle. 3B—Groat. HR—Linz. SH—Gibson. SF—C. Boyer, Tresh. HBP—By Gibson (Pepitone). WP—Gibson. PB—Howard. U—McKinley (A.L.), Burkhart (N.L.), Soar (A.L.), V. Smith (N.L.), A. Smith (A.L.) and Secory (A.L.). T—2:29. A—30,805.

Game 3

Saturday, October 10, At New York

St. Louis	AB.	R.	H.	RBI.	PO.	A.
Flood, cf	5	0	0	0	1	0
Brock, lf	4	0	0	0	2	0
White, 1b	4	0	1	0	12	2
K. Boyer, 3b	4	0	0	0	1	3
Groat, ss	4	0	1	0	1	4
McCarver, c	2	1	1	0	3	0
Shannon, rf	3	0	1	0	1	0
Maxvill, 2b	3	0	1	0	1	2
aWarwick	0	0	0	0	0	0
Buchek, 2b	0	0	0	0	0	0
Simmons, p	2	0	1	1	2	1
bSkinner	1	0	0	0	0	0
Schultz, p	0	0	0	0	0	0
Totals	32	1	6	1	24	12

New York	AB.	R.	H.	RBI.	PO.	A.
Linz, ss	4	0	0	0	0	3
Richardson, 2b	4	0	1	0	4	3
Maris, cf	4	0	0	0	4	0
Mantle, rf	3	1	2	1	3	0
Howard, c	2	1	1	0	2	0
Tresh, lf	3	0	0	0	4	0
Pepitone, 1b	2	0	0	0	8	0
C. Boyer, 3b	3	0	1	1	1	3
Bouton, p	3	0	0	0	1	0
Totals	28	2	5	2	27	9

St. Louis 0 0 0 0 1 0 0 0 0—1
New York 0 1 0 0 0 0 0 0 1—2

None out when winning run scored.

St. Louis	IP.	H.	R.	ER.	BB.	SO.
Simmons	8	4	1	1	3	2
Schultz (L)	0*	1	1	1	0	0

New York	IP.	H.	R.	ER.	BB.	SO.
Bouton (W)	9	6	1	0	3	2

*Pitched to one batter in ninth.

aWalked for Maxvill in ninth. bFlied out for Simmons in ninth. E—Linz, Mantle. DP—St. Louis 1. LOB—St. Louis 9, New York 5. 2B—C. Boyer, Groat, Mantle, Maxvill. HR—Mantle. SH—Simmons, Shannon. U—Burkhart (N.L.), Soar (A.L.), V. Smith (N.L.), A. Smith (A.L.), Secory (N.L.) and McKinley (A.L.). T—2:16. A—67,101.

Game 4

Sunday, October 11, At New York

St. Louis	AB.	R.	H.	RBI.	PO.	A.
Flood, cf	4	1	2	0	1	0
Brock, lf	4	0	0	0	1	0
Groat, ss	4	1	1	0	1	2
K. Boyer, 3b	4	1	1	4	1	2
White, 1b	4	0	0	0	11	0
Shannon, rf	4	0	0	0	1	1
McCarver, c	3	0	1	0	10	1
Maxvill, 2b	3	0	0	0	1	1
Sadecki, p	0	0	0	0	0	0
Craig, p	1	0	0	0	0	2
aWarwick	1	1	1	0	0	0
Taylor, p	1	0	0	0	0	2
Totals	33	4	6	4	27	11

New York	AB.	R.	H.	RBI.	PO.	A.
Linz, ss	4	1	1	0	0	3
B. Richardson, 2b	4	1	1	1	1	2
Maris, cf	4	1	1	0	6	0
Mantle, rf	2	0	1	1	2	0
Howard, c	3	0	1	1	9	0
Tresh, lf	4	0	0	0	1	0
Pepitone, 1b	3	0	0	0	8	0
C. Boyer, 3b	4	0	1	0	0	3
Downing, p	2	0	0	0	0	1
Mikkelsen, p	0	0	0	0	0	0
bBlanchard	1	0	0	0	0	0
Terry, p	0	0	0	0	0	0
Totals	31	3	6	3	27	9

St. Louis 0 0 0 0 0 4 0 0 0—4
New York 3 0 0 0 0 0 0 0 0—3

St. Louis	IP.	H.	R.	ER.	BB.	SO.
Sadecki	⅓	4	3	2	0	0
Craig (W)	4⅔	2	0	0	3	8
Taylor	4	0	0	0	1	2

New York	IP.	H.	R.	ER.	BB.	SO.
Downing (L)	6*	4	4	3	2	4
Mikkelsen	1	0	0	0	0	1
Terry	2	2	0	0	0	3

*Pitched to one batter in seventh.

aSingled for Craig in sixth. bFlied out for Mikkelsen in seventh. E—K. Boyer, B. Richardson. DP—New York 1. LOB—St. Louis 4, New York 5. 2B—Linz, B. Richardson. HR—K. Boyer. U—Soar (A.L.), V. Smith (N.L.), A. Smith (A.L.), Secory (N.L.), McKinley (A.L.) and Burkhart (N.L.). T—2:18. A—66,312.

Game 5

Monday, October 12, At New York

St. Louis	AB.	R.	H.	RBI.	PO.	A.
Flood, cf	4	1	1	0	1	0
Brock, lf	5	0	2	1	1	0
White, 1b	4	1	0	1	7	0
xK. Boyer, 3b	4	0	1	0	3	1
Groat, ss	4	1	1	0	2	2
McCarver, c	5	1	3	3	13	0
Shannon, rf	5	0	0	0	1	0
Maxvill, 2b	5	0	1	0	1	1
Gibson, p	4	1	1	0	1	1
Totals	40	5	10	5	30	5

New York	AB.	R.	H.	RBI.	PO.	A.
Linz, ss	5	0	0	0	1	3
B. Richardson, 2b	5	0	3	0	5	3
Maris, cf	5	0	0	0	3	0
Mantle, rf	3	1	0	0	1	0
Howard, c	3	0	0	0	9	0
Pepitone, 1b	4	0	1	0	8	1
Tresh, lf	3	1	1	2	1	0
C. Boyer, 3b	2	0	0	0	0	3
aBlanchard	1	0	0	0	0	0
Gonzalez, 3b	1	0	0	0	1	3
Stottlemyre, p	2	0	1	0	0	1
bLopez	1	0	0	0	0	0
Reniff, p	0	0	0	0	0	0
Mikkelsen, p	0	0	0	0	1	0
cHegan	1	0	0	0	0	0
Totals	36	2	6	2	30	14

St. Louis 0 0 0 0 2 0 0 0 0 3—5
New York 0 0 0 0 0 0 0 0 2 0—2

St. Louis	IP.	H.	R.	ER.	BB.	SO.
Gibson (W)	10	6	2	0	2	13

New York	IP.	H.	R.	ER.	BB.	SO.
Stottlemyre	7	6	2	1	2	6
Reniff	⅓	2	0	0	0	0
Mikkelsen (L)	2⅔	2	3	3	1	3

xAwarded first base on catcher's interference. aPopped out for C. Boyer in seventh. bStruck out for Stottlemyre in seventh. cStruck out for Mikkelsen in tenth. E—Groat, B. Richardson, Howard. DP—St. Louis 1, New York 1. LOB—St. Louis 9, New York 7. HR—Tresh, McCarver. SB—White. HBP—By Gibson (Howard). U—V. Smith (N.L.), A. Smith (A.L.), Secory (N.L.), McKinley (A.L.), Burkhart (N.L.) and Soar (A.L.). T—2:37. A—65,633.

Game 6

Wednesday, October 14, At St. Louis

New York	AB.	R.	H.	RBI.	PO.	A.
Linz, ss	5	1	1	0	2	3
B. Richardson, 2b	4	0	2	0	2	3
Maris, cf	4	1	1	1	4	0
Mantle, rf	3	2	1	1	3	0
Howard, c	4	1	1	1	5	0
Tresh, lf	3	2	1	0	1	0
Pepitone, 1b	4	1	1	4	6	2
C. Boyer, 3b	4	0	1	0	1	1
Bouton, p	4	0	1	1	3	0
Hamilton, p	0	0	0	0	0	0
Totals	35	8	10	8	27	9

St. Louis	AB.	R.	H.	RBI.	PO.	A.
Flood, cf	3	2	1	0	1	0
Brock, lf	4	0	3	0	2	0
White, 1b	4	0	0	1	8	1
K. Boyer, 3b	4	0	0	0	0	3
Groat, ss	4	0	0	0	3	0
McCarver, c	4	0	2	0	8	0
Shannon, rf	4	1	1	0	3	0
Maxvill, 2b	2	0	0	0	2	3
aWarwick	1	0	0	0	0	0
Buchek, 2b	1	0	1	0	0	1
Simmons, p	2	0	1	0	0	0
Taylor, p	0	0	0	0	0	0
bJames	1	0	0	0	0	0
Schultz, p	0	0	0	0	0	0
G. Richardson, p	0	0	0	0	0	0
Humphreys, p	0	0	0	0	0	0
cSkinner	1	0	1	1	0	0
Totals	35	3	10	2	27	8

New York 0 0 0 0 1 2 0 5 0—8
St. Louis 1 0 0 0 0 0 0 1 1—3

New York	IP.	H.	R.	ER.	BB.	SO.
Bouton (W)	8⅓	9	3	3	2	5
Hamilton	⅔	1	0	0	0	0

St. Louis	IP.	H.	R.	ER.	BB.	SO.
Simmons (L)	6⅓	7	3	3	0	6
Taylor	⅔	0	0	0	0	0
Schultz	⅔	2	4	4	2	0
G. Richardson	⅓	1	1	1	0	0
Humphreys	1	0	0	0	0	1

aFouled out for Maxvill in seventh. bGrounded out for Taylor in seventh. cSingled for Humphreys in ninth. E—Brock. DP—New York 2, St. Louis 1. LOB—New York 3, St. Louis 7. 2B—Tresh, Brock. HR—Maris, Mantle, Pepitone. SB—B. Richardson. SH—B. Richardson. U—A. Smith (A.L.), Secory (N.L.), McKinley (A.L.), Burkhart (N.L.), Soar (A.L.) and V. Smith (N.L.). T—2:37. A—30,805.

Game 7

Thursday, October 15, At St. Louis

New York	AB.	R.	H.	RBI.	PO.	A.
Linz, ss	5	1	2	1	2	0
B. Richardson, 2b	5	1	2	0	1	3
Maris, cf	4	1	1	0	1	0
Mantle, rf	4	1	1	3	2	0
Howard, c	4	0	1	0	6	1
Pepitone, 1b	4	0	0	0	8	2
Tresh, lf	2	0	1	0	2	0
C. Boyer, 3b	4	1	1	1	1	5
Stottlemyre, p	1	0	0	0	1	1
aHegan	0	0	0	0	0	0
Downing, p	0	0	0	0	0	0
Sheldon, p	0	0	0	0	0	0
bLopez	1	0	0	0	0	0
Hamilton, p	0	0	0	0	0	0
Mikkelsen, p	0	0	0	0	0	1
cBlanchard	1	0	0	0	0	0
Totals	35	5	9	5	24	13

St. Louis	AB.	R.	H.	RBI.	PO.	A.
Flood, cf	5	0	0	0	2	0
Brock, lf	4	1	2	1	0	0
White, 1b	4	1	2	0	6	0
K. Boyer, 3b	4	3	3	1	1	2
Groat, ss	3	0	0	1	1	1
McCarver, c	2	1	1	1	9	0
Shannon, rf	4	1	1	0	3	1
Maxvill, 2b	3	0	1	1	5	3
Gibson, p	4	0	0	0	0	1
Totals	33	7	10	5	27	8

New York 0 0 0 0 0 3 0 0 2—5
St. Louis 0 0 0 3 3 0 1 0 x—7

New York	IP.	H.	R.	ER.	BB.	SO.
Stottlemyre (L)	4	5	3	3	2	2
Downing	0*	3	3	3	0	0
Sheldon	2	0	0	0	0	2
Hamilton	1⅓	2	1	1	0	2
Mikkelsen	⅔	0	0	0	0	0

St. Louis	IP.	H.	R.	ER.	BB.	SO.
Gibson (W)	9	9	5	5	3	9

*Pitched to three batters in fifth.

aWalked for Stottlemyre in fifth. bStruck out for Sheldon in seventh. cStruck out for Mikkelsen in ninth. E—Linz, C. Boyer, Groat. DP—St. Louis 2. LOB—New York 6, St. Louis 6. 2B—White, K. Boyer. HR—Brock, Mantle, K. Boyer, C. Boyer, Linz. SB—McCarver, Shannon. SH—Maxvill. SF—McCarver. U—Secory (N.L.), McKinley (A.L.), Burkhart (N.L.), Soar (A.L.), V. Smith (N.L.) and A. Smith (A.L.). T—2:40. A—30,346.

COMPOSITE BATTING AVERAGES

St. Louis Cardinals

Player-Position	G.	AB.	R.	H.	2B.	3B.	HR.	RBI.	BA.
Buchek, pr-2b	4	1	1	1	0	0	0	0	1.000
Warwick, ph	5	4	2	3	0	0	0	1	.750
Skinner, ph	4	3	0	2	1	0	0	1	.667
Sadecki, p	2	2	0	1	0	0	0	1	.500
Simmons, p	2	4	0	2	0	0	0	1	.500
McCarver, c	7	23	4	11	1	1	1	5	.478
Brock, lf	7	30	2	9	2	0	1	5	.300
Gibson, p	3	9	1	2	0	0	0	0	.222
K. Boyer, 3b	7	27	5	6	1	0	2	6	.222
Shannon, rf	7	28	6	6	0	0	1	2	.214
Flood, cf	7	30	5	6	0	1	0	3	.200
Maxvill, 2b	7	20	0	4	1	0	0	1	.200
Groat, ss	7	26	3	5	1	1	0	1	.192
White, 1b	7	27	2	3	1	0	0	2	.111
Javier, pr-2b	1	0	1	0	0	0	0	0	.000
Schultz, p	4	1	0	0	0	0	0	0	.000
G. Richardson, p	2	0	0	0	0	0	0	0	.000
Craig, p	2	1	0	0	0	0	0	0	.000
Taylor, p	2	1	0	0	0	0	0	0	.000
Humphreys, p	1	0	0	0	0	0	0	0	.000
James, ph	3	3	0	0	0	0	0	0	.000
Totals	7	240	32	61	8	3	5	29	.254

New York Yankees

Player-Position	G.	AB.	R.	H.	2B.	3B.	HR.	RBI.	BA.
Ford, p	1	1	0	1	0	0	0	1	1.000
B. Richardson, 2b	7	32	3	13	2	0	0	3	.406
Mantle, rf	7	24	8	8	2	0	3	8	.333
Howard, c	7	24	5	7	1	0	0	2	.292
Tresh, lf	7	22	4	6	2	0	2	7	.273
Blanchard, ph	4	4	0	1	1	0	0	0	.250
Linz, ss	7	31	5	7	1	0	2	2	.226
C. Boyer, 3b	7	24	2	5	1	0	1	3	.208
Maris, cf	7	30	4	6	0	0	1	1	.200
Pepitone, 1b	7	26	1	4	1	0	1	5	.154
Bouton, p	2	7	0	1	0	0	0	1	.143
Stottlemyre, p	3	8	0	1	0	0	0	0	.125
Gonzalez, 3b	1	1	0	0	0	0	0	0	.000
Lopez, rf-ph	3	2	0	0	0	0	0	0	.000
Downing, p	3	2	0	0	0	0	0	0	.000
Sheldon, p	2	0	0	0	0	0	0	0	.000
Mikkelsen, p	4	0	0	0	0	0	0	0	.000
Terry, p	1	0	0	0	0	0	0	0	.000
Reniff, p	1	0	0	0	0	0	0	0	.000
Hamilton, p	2	0	0	0	0	0	0	0	.000
Hegan, pr-ph	3	1	1	0	0	0	0	0	.000
Totals	7	239	33	60	11	0	10	33	.251

COMPOSITE PITCHING AVERAGES

St. Louis Cardinals

Pitcher	G.	IP.	H.	R.	ER.	BB.	SO.	W.	L.	ERA.
Craig	2	5	2	0	0	3	9	1	0	0.00
Taylor	2	4⅔	0	0	0	1	2	0	0	0.00
Humphreys	1	1	0	0	0	0	1	0	0	0.00
Simmons	2	14⅓	11	4	4	3	8	0	1	2.51
Gibson	3	27	23	11	9	8	31	2	1	3.00
Sadecki	2	6⅓	12	7	6	5	2	1	0	8.53
Schultz	4	4	9	8	8	3	1	0	1	18.00
G. Richardson	2	⅔	3	3	3	2	0	0	0	40.50
Totals	7	63	60	33	30	25	54	4	3	4.29

New York Yankees

Pitcher	G.	IP.	H.	R.	ER.	BB.	SO.	W.	L.	ERA.
Sheldon	2	2⅔	0	2	0	2	2	0	0	0.00
Terry	1	2	2	0	0	0	3	0	0	0.00
Reniff	1	⅓	2	0	0	0	0	0	0	0.00
Bouton	2	17⅓	15	4	3	5	7	2	0	1.56
Stottlemyre	3	20	18	8	7	6	12	1	1	3.15
Hamilton	2	2	3	1	1	0	2	0	0	4.50
Mikkelsen	4	4⅔	4	4	3	2	4	0	1	5.79
Downing	3	7⅔	9	8	7	2	5	0	1	8.22
Ford	1	5⅓	8	5	5	1	4	0	1	8.44
Totals	7	62	61	32	26	18	39	3	4	3.77

1965
LOS ANGELES DODGERS
VS.
MINNESOTA TWINS

Sandy Koufax and Don Drysdale weren't invincible. They just seemed that way. And the Minnesota Twins wanted to demonstrate quickly and unmistakably that Los Angeles' sensational pitching combination was vulnerable to their high-powered offense.

The Dodgers had relied on lightning and the Koufax-Drysdale duo to win their way into the 1965 World Series. Maury Wills stole 94 bases in the regular season to lead Los Angeles' speed-oriented offense, while Koufax and Drysdale combined for 49 victories and 15 shutouts. The Twins had emphasized thunder—four of their players hit 20 or more home runs and another belted 19—and the steady pitching of Jim (Mudcat) Grant and Jim Kaat.

While Koufax, coming off a 26-8 season in which he boasted a 2.04 earned-run average and

tossed a perfect game (his fourth no-hitter in four seasons), obviously had Series-opener credentials, he didn't start Game 1 because it fell on the Jewish holiday of Yom Kippur. Drysdale got the call, and the 6-foot-6 right-hander lasted 2⅔ innings at Metropolitan Stadium in Bloomington, Minn. Don Mincher solved Drysdale for a bases-empty homer in the second inning and Zoilo Versalles blasted a three-run homer in Minnesota's six-run third, an inning in which Frank Quilici singled and doubled for the American League champions. Minnesota went on to win, 8-2, behind Grant.

Koufax was on the mound the next day, and he and Kaat matched ciphers through the fifth inning. But the Twins, helped by an inning-opening error by Dodgers third baseman Jim Gilliam, burst into a 2-0 lead in the sixth on Tony Oliva's run-scoring

double and Harmon Killebrew's RBI single. Minnesota then roughed up reliever Ron Perranoski for three runs in the next two innings, and Kaat sailed to a 5-1 triumph. Left fielder Bob Allison's lunging, one-handed catch on rain-soaked turf of Jim Lefebvre's curving liner in the fifth —the Dodgers had one on and nobody out—proved crucial for Kaat in what was still a 0-0 game.

Having shown emphatically that they could beat the best the Dodgers had to offer, the Twins took their two games-to-none Series lead to Dodger Stadium and showed they couldn't beat the third-best pitcher that Los Angeles had to offer. At least not on this day. While lacking the statistics and reputation of Koufax and Drysdale, lefthander Claude Osteen was a gifted pitcher in his own right. Acquired after the 1964 season from Washington at considerable expense (the multi-player trade sent slugger Frank Howard to the Senators), Osteen had won 15 games and posted a 2.79 ERA for the '65 Dodgers. In Game 3 of the Series, he got Los Angeles back on the right track with a five-hit, 4-0 triumph. Batterymate John Roseboro supplied Osteen with all the offense he needed with a two-run single in the fourth off Twins starter Camilo Pascual.

While the loss surely was disappointing to the 31-year-old Pascual, the Series start undoubtedly was a gratifying experience to the native of Havana, Cuba. Pascual had labored non-stop for this Washington Senators-turned-Minnesota Twins franchise since 1954 and had pitched for some pretty down-and-out clubs in Washington, for whom he compiled such records as 2-12, 6-18 and 8-17 preceding the team's re-

Winning pitcher Mudcat Grant is flanked by home run hitters Zoilo Versalles (left) and Don Mincher (right) after the Minnesota Twins' 8-2 Game 1 victory over the Dodgers in the 1965 World Series.

Game 7 heroes, pitcher Sandy Koufax (left) and Lou Johnson, celebrate the Dodgers' 1965 Series triumph over Minnesota.

location to Minnesota in 1961.

Drysdale rebounded from his rough first-game treatment and struck out 11 Twins in Game 4. Getting three RBIs from Ron Fairly and home runs from Wes Parker and Lou Johnson, Drysdale and the Dodgers notched a Series-evening 7-2 conquest. Homers by Killebrew and Oliva accounted for Minnesota's runs.

Koufax then matched—even surpassed—Drysdale's turnaround, yielding only four hits (all singles) and striking out 10 batters in Game 5. The contest was Dodger-style baseball at its best: Los Angeles mounted an 11-single attack (and threw in three doubles for good measure), stole four bases, executed three double plays, played errorless ball and got great pitching. It all added up to a 7-0 victory—in which Wills rapped four hits and Willie Davis stole three bases—and a Series lead of three games to two.

Hoping that a return to Metropolitan Stadium would be just the tonic that Minnesota needed, Twins Manager Sam Mele sent 21-game winner Grant back to the mound after only two days of rest. Allison, who would bat only .125 in this Series, gave the veter-

an pitcher a 2-0 lead in the fourth when he homered off Osteen following an error by Dodgers second baseman Dick Tracewski. Then, in the sixth, Grant himself powered a three-run homer off Howie Reed (working in relief of Osteen, who again had pitched effectively) and the Twins were en route to a 5-1 victory.

Minnesota, having deadlocked the Series, now was confronted with the necessity of beating one of the Dodgers' two pitching greats for a second time. Despite the fact he would be working with only two days of rest, Koufax was selected as the seventh-game starter over Drysdale by Manager Walter Alston. For the third time, his opponent would be Kaat, who had won 18 games for Minnesota in '65. Kaat, like Koufax, had pitched in Game 5.

Koufax won out. He tossed a three-hit shutout and fanned 10 Twins. Kaat left the game three batters into the fourth, an inning in which he surrendered a leadoff home run to Johnson, a double to Fairly and a run-scoring single to Parker. The homer capped a notable season for the 32-year-old Johnson, a minor league veteran who proved a Dodger leader after

being summoned from Spokane in May following a disabling ankle injury to outfielder Tommy Davis.

While relievers Al Worthington, Johnny Klippstein, Jim Merritt and Jim Perry shut down Los Angeles the rest of the way, the Twins could not break through against Koufax and went down to a 2-0 defeat. The Dodgers were World Series champions for the second time in three years.

No, Koufax and Drysdale weren't invincible. Not until the chips were down, anyway.

Game 1

Wednesday, October 6, At Minnesota

Los Angeles	AB.	R.	H.	RBI.	PO.	A.
Wills, ss	5	0	2	1	3	2
Gilliam, 3b	5	0	1	0	0	1
W. Davis, cf	4	0	1	0	2	0
Fairly, rf	4	1	1	1	2	0
Johnson, lf	4	0	1	0	4	0
Lefebvre, 2b	4	1	1	0	0	4
Parker, 1b	3	0	1	0	7	0
Roseboro, c	4	0	0	0	6	0
Drysdale, p	1	0	0	0	0	1
Reed, p	0	0	0	0	0	0
aCrawford	1	0	1	0	0	0
Brewer, p	0	0	0	0	0	0
bMoon	1	0	0	0	0	0
Perranoski, p	0	0	0	0	0	1
cLeJohn	1	0	0	0	0	0
Totals	37	2	10	2	24	9

Minnesota	AB.	R.	H.	RBI.	PO.	A.
Versalles, ss	5	1	2	4	3	2
Valdespino, lf	4	1	1	0	4	0
Oliva, rf	4	0	0	0	7	0
Killebrew, 3b	3	1	1	0	3	0
Hall, cf	3	0	1	0	1	0
Mincher, 1b	3	2	1	1	3	0
Battey, c	4	0	1	2	5	0
Quilici, 2b	4	1	2	1	1	1
Grant, p	3	2	1	0	0	0
Totals	33	8	10	8	27	3

Los Angeles ....0 1 0   0 0 0   0 0 1—2
Minnesota ....0 1 6   0 0 1   0 0 x—8

Los Angeles	IP.	H.	R.	ER.	BB.	SO.
Drysdale (L)	2⅔	7	7	3	1	4
Reed	1⅓	0	0	0	0	1
Brewer	2	3	1	1	0	1
Perranoski	2	0	0	0	2	0

Minnesota	IP.	H.	R.	ER.	BB.	SO.
Grant (W)	9	10	2	2	1	5

aSingled for Reed in fifth. bFouled out for Brewer in seventh. cStruck out for Perranoski in ninth. E—Lefebvre. DP—Los Angeles 1. LOB—Los Angeles 9, Minnesota 5. 2B—Quilici, Valdespino, Grant. HR—Fairly, Mincher, Versalles. SB—Versalles. SH—Grant. WP—Brewer. U—Hurley (A.L.), Venzon (N.L.), Flaherty (A.L.), Sudol (N.L.), Stewart (A.L.) and Vargo (N.L.). T—2:29. A—47,797.

Game 2

Thursday, October 7, At Minnesota

Los Angeles	AB.	R.	H.	RBI.	PO.	A.
Wills, ss	4	0	1	0	1	2
Gilliam, 3b	4	0	0	0	1	0
W. Davis, cf	4	0	0	0	1	0
Johnson, lf	4	0	0	0	3	0
Fairly, rf	4	1	2	0	1	0
Lefebvre, 2b	4	0	2	0	2	0
Parker, 1b	1	0	1	0	3	1
Roseboro, c	4	0	1	1	12	1
Koufax, p	2	0	0	0	1	2
aDrysdale	1	0	0	0	0	0
Perranoski, p	0	0	0	0	0	0
Miller, p	0	0	0	0	0	0
bTracewski	1	0	0	0	0	0
Totals	33	1	7	1	24	6

Minnesota	AB.	R.	H.	RBI.	PO.	A.
Versalles, ss	5	2	1	0	4	0
Nossek, cf	3	0	1	0	4	0
Oliva, rf	4	1	1	1	3	0
Killebrew, 3b	3	0	2	1	2	1
Battey, c	4	0	1	0	3	1
Allison, lf	4	1	1	0	2	0
Mincher, 1b	4	1	1	0	7	4
Quilici, 2b	4	0	1	0	1	3
Kaat, p	4	0	1	2	5	0
Totals	33	5	9	4	27	9

Los Angeles ....0 0 0   0 0 0   1 0 0—1
Minnesota ....0 0 0   0 0 2   1 2 x—5

Los Angeles	IP.	H.	R.	ER.	BB.	SO.
Koufax (L)	6	6	2	1	1	9
Perranoski	1⅔	3	3	3	2	1
Miller	⅓	0	0	0	0	0

Minnesota	IP.	H.	R.	ER.	BB.	SO.
Kaat (W)	9	7	1	1	1	3

aStruck out for Koufax in seventh. bLined out for Miller in ninth. E—Gilliam 2, Johnson. LOB—Los Angeles 8, Minnesota 8. 2B—Oliva, Allison. 3B—Versalles. SH—Parker, Nossek. HBP—By Kaat (Parker). WP—Perranoski. Balk—Perranoski. U—Venzon (N.L.), Flaherty (A.L.), Sudol (N.L.), Stewart (A.L.), Vargo (N.L.) and Hurley (A.L.). T—2:13. A—48,700.

Game 3

Saturday, October 9, At Los Angeles

Minnesota	AB.	R.	H.	RBI.	PO.	A.
Versalles, ss	3	0	2	0	3	3
Nossek, cf	4	0	1	0	3	0
Oliva, rf	4	0	1	0	2	0
Killebrew, 3b	3	0	0	0	1	1
Battey, c	3	0	0	0	0	0
Zimmerman, c	1	0	0	0	1	1
Allison, lf	3	0	0	0	3	0
Mincher, 1b	3	0	1	0	7	0
Quilici, 2b	3	0	0	0	4	2
Pascual, p	1	0	0	0	0	1
aRollins	1	0	0	0	0	0
Merritt, p	0	0	0	0	0	2
bValdespino	1	0	0	0	0	0
Klippstein, p	0	0	0	0	0	0
Totals	30	0	5	0	24	10

Los Angeles	AB.	R.	H.	RBI.	PO.	A.
Wills, ss	4	0	1	1	2	5
Gilliam, 3b	4	0	1	0	1	1
Kennedy, 3b	0	0	0	0	0	0
W. Davis, cf	4	1	1	0	2	0
Fairly, rf	4	1	1	0	1	0
Johnson, lf	2	0	2	1	0	0
Lefebvre, 2b	2	1	1	0	1	3
Tracewski, 2b	2	0	0	0	2	3
Parker, 1b	3	1	1	0	14	2
Roseboro, c	3	0	1	2	2	2
Osteen, p	2	0	1	0	2	2
Totals	30	4	10	4	27	18

Minnesota	0 0 0 0 0 0 0 0 0—0
Los Angeles	0 0 0 2 1 1 0 0 x—4

Minnesota	IP.	H.	R.	ER.	BB.	SO.
Pascual (L)	5	8	3	3	1	0
Merritt	2	2	1	1	0	0
Klippstein	1	0	0	0	1	1

Los Angeles	IP.	H.	R.	ER.	BB.	SO.
Osteen (W)	9	5	0	0	2	2

aGrounded out for Pascual in sixth. bPopped out for Merritt in eighth. E—Kennedy. DP—Minnesota 1, Los Angeles 2. LOB—Minnesota 5, Los Angeles 6. 2B—Versalles, Gilliam, Johnson 2, Fairly, Wills. SB—Wills, Parker, Roseboro. SH—Johnson, Osteen. U—Flaherty (A.L.), Sudol (N.L.), Stewart (A.L.), Vargo (N.L.), Hurley (A.L.) and Venzon (N.L.). T—2:06. A—55,934.

Game 4

Sunday, October 10, At Los Angeles

Minnesota	AB.	R.	H.	RBI.	PO.	A.
Versalles, ss	4	0	1	0	3	2
Valdespino, lf	4	0	1	0	2	0
Oliva, rf	4	1	1	1	2	0
Killebrew, 3b	2	1	1	1	1	0
Hall, cf	4	0	0	0	1	0
Mincher, 1b	4	0	0	0	8	0
Battey, c	3	0	0	0	3	2
Zimmerman, c	0	0	0	0	1	0
Quilici, 2b	3	0	0	0	3	3
Grant, p	2	0	0	0	0	0
Worthington, p	0	0	0	0	0	0
bNossek	1	0	1	0	0	0
Pleis, p	0	0	0	0	0	1
Totals	31	2	5	2	24	8

Los Angeles	AB.	R.	H.	RBI.	PO.	A.
Wills, ss	4	1	2	0	1	2
Gilliam, 3b	2	1	0	0	1	1
aKennedy, 3b	0	0	0	0	0	1
W. Davis, cf	4	1	2	0	3	0
Fairly, rf	4	1	1	3	1	0
Johnson, lf	4	1	2	1	1	1
Parker, 1b	4	2	2	1	8	0
Roseboro, c	3	0	1	0	10	1
Tracewski, 2b	4	0	0	0	2	3
Drysdale, p	3	0	0	0	0	1
Totals	32	7	10	5	27	10

Minnesota	0 0 0 1 0 1 0 0 0—2
Los Angeles	1 1 0 1 0 3 0 1 x—7

Minnesota	IP.	H.	R.	ER.	BB.	SO.
Grant (L)	5*	6	5	4	1	2
Worthington	2	2	1	0	1	2
Pleis	1	2	1	1	0	0

Los Angeles	IP.	H.	R.	ER.	BB.	SO.
Drysdale (W)	9	5	2	2	2	11

*Pitched to two batters in sixth.

aRan for Gilliam in seventh. bSingled for Worthington in eighth. E—Quilici, Worthington. DP—Minnesota 1. LOB—MInnesota 4, Los Angeles 4. HR—Killebrew, Parker, Oliva, Johnson. SB—Wills, Parker. HBP—By Worthington (Gilliam). WP—Grant. U—Sudol (N.L.), Stewart (A.L.), Vargo (N.L.), Hurley (A.L.), Venzon (N.L.) and Flaherty (A.L.). T—2:15. A—55,920.

Game 5

Monday, October 11, At Los Angeles

Minnesota	AB.	R.	H.	RBI.	PO.	A.
Versalles, ss	4	0	0	0	2	0
Nossek, cf	4	0	1	0	2	0
Oliva, rf	3	0	0	0	2	0
Killebrew, 3b	3	0	1	0	1	2
Battey, c	3	0	0	0	7	1
Allison, lf	2	0	0	0	3	0
Mincher, 1b	3	0	0	0	5	0
Quilici, 2b	3	0	1	0	2	3
Kaat, p	1	0	0	0	0	1
Boswell, p	0	0	0	0	0	0
aRollins	1	0	0	0	0	0
Perry, p	0	0	0	0	0	1
bValdespino	1	0	1	0	0	0
Totals	28	0	4	0	24	8

Los Angeles	AB.	R.	H.	RBI.	PO.	A.
Wills, ss	5	2	4	1	1	7
Gilliam, 3b	4	1	2	2	0	0
Kennedy, 3b	1	0	0	0	0	0
W. Davis, cf	4	1	2	0	1	0
Johnson, lf	5	1	1	1	2	0
Fairly, rf	5	1	3	1	2	0
Parker, 1b	4	0	0	0	7	0
Tracewski, 2b	3	0	1	0	4	2
Roseboro, c	2	1	0	0	10	0
Koufax, p	4	0	1	1	0	1
Totals	37	7	14	6	27	10

Minnesota	0 0 0 0 0 0 0 0 0—0
Los Angeles	2 0 2 1 0 0 2 0 x—7

Minnesota	IP.	H.	R.	ER.	BB.	SO.
Kaat (L)	2⅓	6	4	3	0	1
Boswell	2⅔	3	1	1	2	3
Perry	3	5	2	2	1	3

Los Angeles	IP.	H.	R.	ER.	BB.	SO.
Koufax (W)	9	4	0	0	1	10

aFlied out for Boswell in sixth. bSingled for Perry in ninth. E—Quilici. DP—Los Angeles 3. LOB—Minnesota 2, Los Angeles 11. 2B—Wills 2, Fairly. SB—W. Davis 3, Wills. SH—W. Davis, Parker. U—Stewart (A.L.), Vargo (N.L.), Hurley (A.L.), Venzon (N.L.), Flaherty (A.L.) and Sudol (N.L.). T—2:34. A—55,801.

Game 6

Wednesday, October 13, At Minnesota

Los Angeles	AB.	R.	H.	RBI.	PO.	A.
Wills, ss	4	0	1	0	4	4
Gilliam, 3b	4	0	0	0	0	3
W. Davis, cf	4	0	0	0	1	0
Fairly, rf	4	1	2	1	1	0
Johnson, lf	4	0	1	0	0	0
Parker, 1b	4	0	0	0	10	1
Roseboro, c	3	0	1	0	5	0
Tracewski, 2b	3	0	1	0	2	3
Osteen, p	1	0	0	0	0	1
aCrawford	1	0	0	0	0	0
Reed, p	0	0	0	0	1	0
bMoon	1	0	0	0	0	0
Miller, p	0	0	0	0	0	0
Totals	33	1	6	1	24	12

Minnesota	AB.	R.	H.	RBI.	PO.	A.
Versalles, ss	3	0	1	0	2	3
Nossek, cf	4	0	0	0	4	0
Oliva, rf	4	0	2	0	0	0
Killebrew, 3b	4	0	0	0	1	1
Battey, c	4	1	1	0	5	1
Allison, lf	3	2	1	2	2	0
Mincher, 1b	3	0	0	0	11	0
Quilici, 2b	2	1	0	0	2	4
Grant, p	3	1	1	3	0	1
Totals	30	5	6	5	27	10

Los Angeles	0 0 0 0 0 0 1 0 0—1
Minnesota	0 0 0 2 0 3 0 0 x—5

Los Angeles	IP.	H.	R.	ER.	BB.	SO.
Osteen (L)	5	4	2	1	3	2
Reed	2	2	3	3	2	3
Miller	1	0	0	0	0	0

Minnesota	IP.	H.	R.	ER.	BB.	SO.
Grant (W)	9	6	1	1	0	5

aStruck out for Osteen in sixth. bGrounded out for Reed in eighth. E—Tracewski, Killebrew. DP—Los Angeles 1, Minnesota 1. LOB—Los Angeles 5, Minnesota 6. 3B—Battey. HR—Fairly, Allison, Grant. SB—Allison. U—Vargo (N.L.), Hurley (A.L.), Venzon (N.L.), Flaherty (A.L.), Sudol (N.L.) and Stewart (A.L.). T—2:16. A—49,578.

Game 7

Thursday, October 14, At Minnesota

Los Angeles	AB.	R.	H.	RBI.	PO.	A.
Wills, ss	4	0	0	0	2	4
Gilliam, 3b	5	0	2	0	2	1
Kennedy, 3b	0	0	0	0	0	1
W. Davis, cf	2	0	0	0	1	0
Johnson, lf	4	1	1	1	3	0
Fairly, rf	4	1	1	0	0	0
Parker, 1b	4	0	2	1	6	0
Tracewski, 2b	4	0	0	0	1	0
Roseboro, c	2	0	1	0	12	0
Koufax, p	3	0	0	0	0	1
Totals	32	2	7	2	27	7

Minnesota	AB.	R.	H.	RBI.	PO.	A.
Versalles, ss	4	0	1	0	0	2
Nossek, cf	4	0	0	0	0	0
Oliva, rf	3	0	0	0	4	0
Killebrew, 3b	3	0	1	0	2	2
Battey, c	4	0	0	0	8	1
Allison, lf	4	0	0	0	1	0
Mincher, 1b	3	0	0	0	10	0
Quilici, 2b	3	0	1	0	1	3
Kaat, p	1	0	0	0	0	1
Worthington, p	0	0	0	0	1	1
aRollins	0	0	0	0	0	0
Klippstein, p	0	0	0	0	0	0
Merritt, p	0	0	0	0	0	0
bValdespino	1	0	0	0	0	0
Perry, p	0	0	0	0	0	0
Totals	30	0	3	0	27	10

Los Angeles	0 0 0 2 0 0 0 0 0—2
Minnesota	0 0 0 0 0 0 0 0 0—0

Los Angeles	IP.	H.	R.	ER.	BB.	SO.
Koufax (W)	9	3	0	0	3	10

Minnesota	IP.	H.	R.	ER.	BB.	SO.
Kaat (L)	3*	5	2	2	1	2
Worthington	2	0	0	0	1	0
Klippstein	1⅔	2	0	0	1	2
Merritt	1⅓	0	0	0	0	1
Perry	1	0	0	0	1	1

*Pitched to three batters in fourth.

aWalked for Worthington in fifth. bFlied out for Merritt in eighth. E—Oliva. LOB—Los Angeles 9, Minnesota 6. 2B—Roseboro, Fairly, Quilici. 3B—Parker. HR—Johnson. SH—W. Davis. HBP—By Klippstein (W. Davis). U—Hurley (A.L.), Venzon (N.L.), Flaherty (A.L.), Sudol (N.L.), Stewart (A.L.) and Vargo (N.L.). T—2:27. A—50,596.

COMPOSITE BATTING AVERAGES

Los Angeles Dodgers

Player-Position	G.	AB.	R.	H.	2B.	3B.	HR.	RBI.	BA.
Crawford, ph	2	2	0	1	0	0	0	0	.500
Lefebvre, 2b	3	10	2	4	0	0	0	0	.400
Fairly, rf	7	29	7	11	3	0	2	6	.379
Wills, ss	7	30	3	11	3	0	0	3	.367
Osteen, p	3	3	0	1	0	0	0	0	.333
Parker, 1b	7	23	3	7	0	1	1	2	.304
Johnson, lf	7	27	3	8	2	0	2	4	.296
Roseboro, c	7	21	1	6	1	0	0	3	.286
W. Davis, cf	7	26	3	6	0	0	0	0	.231
Gilliam, 3b	7	28	2	6	1	0	0	2	.214
Tracewski, ph-2b	6	17	0	2	0	0	0	0	.118
Koufax, p	3	9	0	1	0	0	0	1	.111
Kennedy, 3b-pr	4	1	0	0	0	0	0	0	.000
Reed, p	2	0	0	0	0	0	0	0	.000
Brewer, p	1	0	0	0	0	0	0	0	.000
Perranoski, p	2	0	0	0	0	0	0	0	.000
Miller, p	2	0	0	0	0	0	0	0	.000
Drysdale, p-ph	3	5	0	0	0	0	0	0	.000
Moon, ph	2	2	0	0	0	0	0	0	.000
LeJohn, ph	1	1	0	0	0	0	0	0	.000
Totals	7	234	24	64	10	1	5	21	.274

Minnesota Twins

Player-Position	G.	AB.	R.	H.	2B.	3B.	HR.	RBI.	BA.
Killebrew, 3b	7	21	2	6	0	0	1	2	.286
Versalles, ss	7	28	3	8	1	1	1	4	.286
Valdespino, lf-ph	5	11	1	3	1	0	0	0	.273
Grant, p	3	8	3	2	1	0	1	3	.250
Nossek, cf-ph	6	20	0	4	0	0	0	0	.200
Quilici, 2b	7	20	2	4	2	0	0	1	.200
Oliva, rf	7	26	2	5	1	0	1	2	.192
Kaat, p	3	6	0	1	0	0	0	2	.167
Hall, cf	2	7	0	1	0	0	0	0	.143
Mincher, 1b	7	23	3	3	0	0	1	1	.130
Allison, lf	5	16	3	2	1	0	1	2	.125
Battey, c	7	25	1	3	0	1	0	2	.120
Zimmerman, c	2	1	0	0	0	0	0	0	.000
Pascual, p	1	1	0	0	0	0	0	0	.000
Merritt, p	2	0	0	0	0	0	0	0	.000
Klippstein, p	2	0	0	0	0	0	0	0	.000
Worthington, p	2	0	0	0	0	0	0	0	.000
Pleis, p	1	0	0	0	0	0	0	0	.000
Boswell, p	1	0	0	0	0	0	0	0	.000
Perry, p	2	0	0	0	0	0	0	0	.000
Rollins, ph	3	2	0	0	0	0	0	0	.000
Totals	7	215	20	42	7	2	6	19	.195

COMPOSITE PITCHING AVERAGES

Los Angeles Dodgers

Pitcher	G.	IP.	H.	R.	ER.	BB.	SO.	W.	L.	ERA.
Miller	2	1⅓	0	0	0	0	0	0	0	0.00
Koufax	3	24	13	2	1	5	29	2	1	0.38
Osteen	2	14	9	2	1	5	4	1	1	0.64
Drysdale	2	11⅔	12	9	5	3	15	1	1	3.86
Brewer	1	2	3	1	1	0	1	0	0	4.50
Perranoski	2	3⅔	3	3	3	4	1	0	0	7.36
Reed	2	3⅓	2	3	3	2	4	0	0	8.10
Totals	7	60	42	20	14	19	54	4	3	2.10

Minnesota Twins

Pitcher	G.	IP.	H.	R.	ER.	BB.	SO.	W.	L.	ERA.
Worthington	2	4	2	1	0	2	2	0	0	0.00
Klippstein	2	2⅔	2	0	0	2	3	0	0	0.00
Merritt	2	3⅓	2	1	1	0	1	0	0	2.70
Grant	3	23	22	8	7	2	12	2	1	2.74
Boswell	1	2⅔	3	1	1	2	3	0	0	3.38
Kaat	3	14⅓	18	7	6	2	6	1	2	3.77
Perry	2	4	5	2	2	2	4	0	0	4.50
Pascual	1	5	8	3	3	1	0	0	1	5.40
Pleis	1	1	2	1	1	0	0	0	0	9.00
Totals	7	60	64	24	21	13	31	3	4	3.15

1966
BALTIMORE ORIOLES
VS.
LOS ANGELES DODGERS

When Los Angeles' Lou Johnson crossed home plate following a bases-loaded walk in the third inning of Game 1 of the 1966 World Series, he scored what proved to be an unforgettable run for the National League champion Dodgers.

You see, it was the Dodgers' *last* run of the '66 fall classic.

The ability to get great pitching certainly was no problem for the Dodgers, who themselves had held the powerful New York Yankees to four runs in the four-game 1963 Series and then limited the hard-hitting Minnesota Twins to seven runs over the last five games of the 1965 Series. Now, though, the Dodgers proved helpless in their ability to hit great pitching.

It was the Baltimore Orioles' pitching staff that quieted the Dodgers in what turned out to be record fashion. Oddly, though, the Orioles' first-game starter, left-hander Dave McNally, failed to survive the third inning as the '66 Series got under way at Dodger Stadium.

Staked to a 4-1 lead, thanks in large measure to consecutive first-inning home runs by Frank Robinson (who hit a two-run shot) and Brooks Robinson, McNally retired the first Dodger batter in the third but then allowed three consecutive bases on balls. Orioles Manager Hank Bauer exhibited a semi-quick hook, replacing the 23-year-old McNally with Moe Drabowsky. The veteran reliever struck out Wes Parker, but then yielded the walk—to Jim Gilliam —that sent Johnson skipping across the plate. Drabowsky subsequently induced John Roseboro to foul out, and the Dodgers did not score again. Period.

While Drabowsky had gotten Baltimore out of the inning in

An ecstatic Brooks Robinson leaps toward pitcher Dave McNally and catcher Andy Etchebarren after Baltimore had shut out the Los Angeles Dodgers, 1-0, in the fourth and deciding game of the 1966 Series.

good shape, the 31-year-old right-hander was just getting warmed up. He struck out the side in the fourth and fifth innings, tying the Series record of six straight strike-outs, and finished with 11 strike-outs in 6⅔ innings of scoreless pitching. He allowed one hit. The Baltimore Orioles, formerly the downtrodden St. Louis Browns (the Brownies moved to Maryland after the 1953 season), were 5-2 winners in their first Series game.

Jim Palmer, who at age 20 had led Baltimore pitchers with 15 victories, was given the sizable task of matching pitches with Sandy Koufax in Game 2. Koufax, arthritic elbow and all, had won 27 games and achieved a 1.73 earned-run average for the Dodgers in '66. The game was scoreless until the fifth, when the

Orioles scored three unearned runs in a nightmarish inning for the Dodgers' Willie Davis. Center fielder Davis dropped consecutive fly balls after losing both in the sun, and he threw wildly past third base after the second misplay. The only RBI of the inning came on Luis Aparicio's double.

After being victimized by Davis' three-error inning, Koufax yielded an earned run in the sixth when Frank Robinson tripled and Boog Powell singled him home. Sandy wriggled out of a bases-loaded jam to end the inning, getting Andy Etchebarren to ground into a double play. Koufax was done for the day. And as fate would have it, he was done for his career. Fearing permanent injury to his elbow, he would announce his retirement at age 30 in mid-November.

ner wound up allowing only four hits in the second game and winning, 6-0. Walter Alston's Dodgers wound up committing six errors in the contest.

In the first Series game ever played in Baltimore, the Orioles' 21-year-old Wally Bunker spun a six-hitter and beat Los Angeles, 1-0. Bauer's crew managed only three hits, but one of them was Paul Blair's 430-foot homer off Claude Osteen in the fifth inning.

Now, McNally would get a chance to atone for his first-game shakiness. And atone he did. The Dodgers managed only four singles in Game 4 and suffered another 1-0 setback. Los Angeles' Don Drysdale also allowed only four hits, but like Osteen made one big mistake. And Frank Robinson whacked that fourth-inning blunder deep into the left-field stands.

Supplying the winning blow in the decisive game of the World Series was a fitting accomplishment for Frank Robinson, who won the Triple Crown (49 home runs, 122 RBIs and a .316 batting average) for the Orioles in 1966 after being acquired from the Cincinnati Reds following the 1965 season.

The Orioles didn't exactly tear the cover off the ball in this Series, managing only 10 earned runs and 24 hits. But the Dodgers hardly scuffed up the baseball, setting World Series records (in the all-time-low category) with only two runs, 17 hits, a .142 batting average and 33 consecutive scoreless innings.

Game 1

Wednesday, October 5, At Los Angeles

Baltimore	AB.	R.	H.	RBI.	PO.	A.
Aparicio, ss	5	0	0	1	4	1
Snyder, cf-lf	3	1	1	1	2	0
F. Robinson, rf	5	1	2	2	1	0
B. Robinson, 3b	5	1	1	1	2	1
Powell, 1b	5	0	1	0	3	0
Blefary, lf	3	0	1	0	2	0
Blair, cf	0	0	0	0	0	0
D. Johnson, 2b	4	1	2	0	0	2
Etchebarren, c	3	1	1	0	13	0
McNally, p	0	0	0	0	0	0
Drabowsky, p	2	0	0	0	0	0
Totals	35	5	9	5	27	4

Los Angeles	AB.	R.	H.	RBI.	PO.	A.
Wills, ss	3	0	0	0	6	5
W. Davis, cf	4	0	1	0	1	0
L. Johnson, rf	3	1	0	0	3	0
T. Davis, lf	3	0	0	0	1	0
Lefebvre, 2b	3	1	1	1	3	5
Parker, 1b	4	0	1	0	9	0
Gilliam, 3b	2	0	0	1	1	1
Roseboro, c	4	0	0	0	3	0
Drysdale, p	0	0	0	0	0	1
aStuart	1	0	0	0	0	0
Moeller, p	0	0	0	0	0	0
bBarbieri	1	0	0	0	0	0
R. Miller, p	0	0	0	0	0	1
cCovington	1	0	0	0	0	0
Perranoski, p	0	0	0	0	0	1
dFairly	1	0	0	0	0	0
Totals	30	2	3	2	27	14

Baltimore .... 3 1 0 1 0 0 0 0 0—5
Los Angeles .... 0 1 1 0 0 0 0 0 0—2

Baltimore	IP.	H.	R.	ER.	BB.	SO.
McNally	2⅓	2	2	2	5	1
Drabowsky (W)	6⅔	1	0	0	2	11

Los Angeles	IP.	H.	R.	ER.	BB.	SO.
Drysdale (L)	2	4	4	4	2	1
Moeller	2	1	1	1	1	0
R. Miller	3	2	0	0	2	1
Perranoski	2	2	0	0	0	1

aFlied out for Drysdale in second. bStruck out for Moeller in fourth. cStruck out for R. Miller in seventh. dStruck out for Perranoski in ninth. LOB—Baltimore 9, Los Angeles 8. 2B—Parker, D. Johnson, Powell. HR—F. Robinson, B. Robinson, Lefebvre. SB—Wills. SH—McNally. U—Jackowski (N.L.), Chylak (A.L.), Pelekoudas (N.L.), Rice (A.L.), Steiner (N.L.) and Drummond (A.L.). T—2:56. A—55,941.

Game 2

Thursday, October 6, At Los Angeles

Baltimore	AB.	R.	H.	RBI.	PO.	A.
Aparicio, ss	5	0	2	1	4	1
Blefary, lf	5	0	0	0	1	0
F. Robinson, rf	3	2	1	0	1	0
B. Robinson, 3b	4	1	1	0	1	1
Powell, 1b	3	1	2	1	8	0
D. Johnson, 2b	4	0	2	1	2	4
Blair, cf	3	1	0	0	4	0
Etchebarren, c	3	1	0	0	6	0
Palmer, p	4	0	0	0	0	2
Totals	34	6	8	3	27	8

Los Angeles	AB.	R.	H.	RBI.	PO.	A.
Wills, ss	4	0	0	0	3	1
Gilliam, 3b	4	0	0	0	2	3
W. Davis, cf	4	0	0	0	2	0
Fairly, rf	3	0	0	0	3	0
Lefebvre, 2b	3	0	0	0	3	0
L. Johnson, lf	4	0	1	0	1	0
Roseboro, c	4	0	1	0	8	1
Parker, 1b	2	0	1	0	5	1
Koufax, p	2	0	0	0	0	1
Perranoski, p	0	0	0	0	0	1
Regan, p	0	0	0	0	0	0
aT. Davis	1	0	1	0	0	0
Brewer, p	0	0	0	0	0	0
Totals	31	0	4	0	27	8

Baltimore .... 0 0 0 0 3 1 0 2 0—6
Los Angeles .... 0 0 0 0 0 0 0 0 0—0

Baltimore	IP.	H.	R.	ER.	BB.	SO.
Palmer (W)	9	4	0	0	3	6

Los Angeles	IP.	H.	R.	ER.	BB.	SO.
Koufax (L)	6	6	4	1	2	2
Perranoski	1⅓	2	2	2	1	1
Regan	⅔	0	0	0	1	1
Brewer	1	0	0	0	0	1

aSingled for Regan in eighth. E—Gilliam, W. Davis 3, Fairly, Perranoski. DP—Los Angeles 1. LOB—Baltimore 6, Los Angeles 7. 2B—L. Johnson, Aparicio. 3B—F. Robinson. SH—Powell. WP—Regan, Palmer. U—Chylak (A.L.), Pelekoudas (N.L.), Rice (A.L.), Steiner (N.L.), Drummond (A.L.) and Jackowski (N.L.). T—2:26. A—55,947.

Game 3

Saturday, October 8, At Baltimore

Los Angeles	AB.	R.	H.	RBI.	PO.	A.
Wills, ss	3	0	1	0	1	6
Parker, 1b	4	0	1	0	10	1
Regan, p	0	0	0	0	0	1
W. Davis, cf	4	0	0	0	2	0
Fairly, rf-1b	3	0	1	0	2	0
Lefebvre, 2b	4	0	0	0	3	4
L. Johnson, lf-rf	4	0	2	0	1	0
Roseboro, c	3	0	0	0	4	0
Kennedy, 3b	3	0	0	0	0	2
Osteen, p	2	0	0	0	1	0
aT. Davis, lf	1	0	1	0	0	0
Totals	31	0	6	0	24	14

Baltimore	AB.	R.	H.	RBI.	PO.	A.
Aparicio, ss	3	0	1	0	1	3
Blefary, lf	3	0	0	0	3	0
Snyder, lf	0	0	0	0	0	0
F. Robinson, rf	3	0	0	0	1	0
B. Robinson, 3b	2	0	0	0	1	1
Powell, 1b	3	0	1	0	9	1
D. Johnson, 2b	3	0	0	0	3	3
Blair, cf	3	1	1	1	3	0
Etchebarren, c	3	0	0	0	6	0
Bunker, p	2	0	0	0	0	3
Totals	25	1	3	1	27	11

Los Angeles .... 0 0 0 0 0 0 0 0 0—0
Baltimore .... 0 0 0 0 1 0 0 0 x—1

Los Angeles	IP.	H.	R.	ER.	BB.	SO.
Osteen (L)	7	3	1	1	1	3
Regan	1	0	0	0	0	1

Baltimore	IP.	H.	R.	ER.	BB.	SO.
Bunker (W)	9	6	0	0	1	6

aSingled for Osteen in eighth. DP—Los Angeles 2, Baltimore 1. LOB—Los Angeles 6, Baltimore 1. 2B—Parker. HR—Blair. SH—Wills. U—Pelekoudas (N.L.), Rice (A.L.), Steiner (N.L.), Drummond (A.L.), Jackowski (N.L.) and Chylak (A.L.). T—1:55. A—54,445.

Game 4

Sunday, October 9, At Baltimore

Los Angeles	AB.	R.	H.	RBI.	PO.	A.
Wills, ss	3	0	0	0	2	3
W. Davis, cf	4	0	0	0	1	0
L. Johnson, rf	4	0	1	0	4	0
T. Davis, lf	3	0	0	0	2	0
Lefebvre, 2b	2	0	1	0	1	1
Parker, 1b	3	0	0	0	7	0
Roseboro, c	3	0	0	0	7	1
Kennedy, 3b	2	0	1	0	0	1
aStuart	1	0	0	0	0	0
Drysdale, p	2	0	0	0	0	2
bFerrara	1	0	1	0	0	0
cOliver	0	0	0	0	0	0
Totals	28	0	4	0	24	8

Baltimore	AB.	R.	H.	RBI.	PO.	A.
Aparicio, ss	3	0	1	0	0	3
Snyder, cf-lf	3	0	0	0	0	0
F. Robinson, rf	3	1	1	1	3	0
B. Robinson, 3b	3	0	1	0	0	3
Powell, 1b	3	0	1	0	7	0
Blefary, lf	2	0	0	0	1	0
Blair, cf	0	0	0	0	2	0
D. Johnson, 2b	3	0	0	0	7	3
Etchebarren, c	3	0	0	0	7	1
McNally, p	3	0	0	0	0	0
Totals	26	1	4	1	27	10

Los Angeles .... 0 0 0 0 0 0 0 0 0—0
Baltimore .... 0 0 0 1 0 0 0 0 x—1

Los Angeles	IP.	H.	R.	ER.	BB.	SO.
Drysdale (L)	8	4	1	1	1	5

Baltimore	IP.	H.	R.	ER.	BB.	SO.
McNally (W)	9	4	0	0	2	4

aStruck out for Kennedy in ninth. bSingled for Drysdale in ninth. cRan for Ferrara in ninth. DP—Los Angeles 1, Baltimore 3. LOB—Los Angeles 3, Baltimore 2. HR—F. Robinson. U—Rice (A.L.), Steiner (N.L.), Drummond (A.L.), Jackowski (N.L.), Chylak (A.L.) and Pelekoudas (N.L.). T—1:45. A—54,458.

COMPOSITE BATTING AVERAGES

Baltimore Orioles

Player-Position	G.	AB.	R.	H.	2B.	3B.	HR.	RBI.	BA.
Powell, 1b	4	14	1	5	1	0	0	1	.357
F. Robinson, rf	4	14	4	4	0	1	2	3	.286
D. Johnson, 2b	4	14	1	4	1	0	0	1	.286
Aparicio, ss	4	16	0	4	1	0	0	2	.250
B. Robinson, 3b	4	14	2	3	0	0	1	1	.214
Snyder, cf-lf	3	6	1	1	0	0	0	1	.167
Blair, cf	4	6	2	1	0	0	1	1	.167
Etchebarren, c	4	12	2	1	0	0	0	0	.083
Blefary, lf	4	13	0	1	0	0	0	0	.077
McNally, p	2	3	0	0	0	0	0	0	.000
Drabowsky, p	1	2	0	0	0	0	0	0	.000
Palmer, p	1	4	0	0	0	0	0	0	.000
Bunker, p	1	2	0	0	0	0	0	0	.000
Totals	4	120	13	24	3	1	4	10	.200

Los Angeles Dodgers

Player-Position	G.	AB.	R.	H.	2B.	3B.	HR.	RBI.	BA.
Ferrara, ph	1	1	0	1	0	0	0	0	1.000
L. Johnson, rf-lf	4	15	1	4	1	0	0	0	.267
T. Davis, lf-ph	4	8	0	2	0	0	0	0	.250
Parker, 1b	4	13	0	3	2	0	0	0	.231
Kennedy, 3b	2	5	0	1	0	0	0	0	.200
Lefebvre, 2b	4	12	1	2	0	0	1	1	.167
Fairly, ph-rf-1b	3	7	0	1	0	0	0	0	.143
Wills, ss	4	13	0	1	0	0	0	0	.077
Roseboro, c	4	14	0	1	0	0	0	0	.071
W. Davis, cf	4	16	0	1	0	0	0	0	.063
Gilliam, 3b	2	6	0	0	0	0	0	1	.000
Drysdale, p	2	2	0	0	0	0	0	0	.000
Moeller, p	1	0	0	0	0	0	0	0	.000
R. Miller, p	1	0	0	0	0	0	0	0	.000
Perranoski, p	2	0	0	0	0	0	0	0	.000
Koufax, p	1	2	0	0	0	0	0	0	.000
Regan, p	2	0	0	0	0	0	0	0	.000
Brewer, p	1	0	0	0	0	0	0	0	.000
Osteen, p	1	2	0	0	0	0	0	0	.000
Covington, ph	1	1	0	0	0	0	0	0	.000
Barbieri, ph	1	1	0	0	0	0	0	0	.000
Stuart, ph	2	2	0	0	0	0	0	0	.000
Oliver, pr	1	0	0	0	0	0	0	0	.000
Totals	4	120	2	17	3	0	1	2	.142

COMPOSITE PITCHING AVERAGES

Baltimore Orioles

Pitcher	G.	IP.	H.	R.	ER.	BB.	SO.	W.	L.	ERA.
Palmer	1	9	4	0	0	3	6	1	0	0.00
Bunker	1	9	6	0	0	1	6	1	0	0.00
Drabowsky	1	6⅔	1	0	0	2	11	1	0	0.00
McNally	2	11⅓	6	2	2	7	5	1	0	1.59
Totals	4	36	17	2	2	13	28	4	0	0.50

Los Angeles Dodgers

Pitcher	G.	IP.	H.	R.	ER.	BB.	SO.	W.	L.	ERA.
R. Miller	1	3	2	0	0	2	1	0	0	0.00
Regan	2	1⅔	0	0	0	1	2	0	0	0.00
Brewer	1	1	0	0	0	0	1	0	0	0.00
Osteen	1	7	3	1	1	1	3	0	1	1.29
Koufax	1	6	6	4	1	2	2	0	1	1.50
Drysdale	2	10	8	5	5	3	6	0	2	4.50
Moeller	1	2	1	1	1	1	0	0	0	4.50
Perranoski	2	3⅓	4	2	2	1	2	0	0	5.40
Totals	4	34	24	13	10	11	17	0	4	2.65

1967
ST. LOUIS CARDINALS
VS.
BOSTON RED SOX

Suffering a leg fracture in mid-July would be enough to put a damper on almost anyone's season. In fact, it likely would be just cause for calling it a summer.

Bob Gibson of the St. Louis Cardinals wasn't like anyone else, however. He was, above all else, a competitor. Oh, sure, the line drive off the bat of Roberto Clemente that felled Gibson sent the Cardinals' righthander to the sidelines. For all of eight weeks. Then, 11 days after Gibson's return to action, there he was pitching St. Louis' pennant-clinching game against the Philadelphia Phillies.

While Gibson had won 19, 20 and 21 games in the previous three years and was bound for even greater success in the next three seasons, 1967 was in many ways most representative of the man's will to win and his ability to turn that determination into success.

Forced to settle for 13 regular-season victories for the surprising Cardinals, who raced to a 10½-game victory margin in the National League race, Gibson was ready to shoulder the load in the World Series against an even more upstart aggregation: The Boston Red Sox.

Under rookie Manager Dick Williams, the Red Sox were the victors in a torrid four-team American League pennant chase —they finished one game ahead of the Detroit Tigers and Minnesota Twins and three games in front of the Chicago White Sox— after ending up ninth in 1966. The Triple Crown season of Carl Yastrzemski and the pitching wizardry of Jim Lonborg were principal factors in Boston's realization of its "impossible dream" rise to the pennant; Yastrzemski bashed 44 home runs, drove in 121 runs and batted .326;

Lonborg won 22 games, 10 more than anyone else on the Red Sox's staff.

The Cardinals, sparked by slugging Orlando Cepeda (25 homers, 111 RBIs and a .325 batting mark) and known as "El Birdos" largely in tribute to the first baseman's leadership, gave Red Schoendienst a pennant in his third year as St. Louis manager. Other key contributors besides Cepeda, a May 1966 acquisition from the San Francisco Giants, included outfielders Curt Flood (a .335 hitter), Lou Brock (52 stolen bases), 29-year-old rookie righthander Dick Hughes (16 victories) and young pitchers Nelson Briles and Steve Carlton. The 24-year-old Briles, converted into a starter after the loss of Gibson, won his last nine decisions of the season and, like the 22-year-old Carlton, won 14 times overall.

Then there was Gibson, who had won 10 games by the time of his injury and lost only once (by a 2-1 score) after his return. And when the '67 Series opened in Fenway Park, Gibson got the ball.

Matched against Jose Santiago (Lonborg had pitched on the final day of the regular season), Gibson emerged a 2-1 winner as he allowed only six hits—one of them a homer by Santiago—and struck out 10 batters. Roger Maris, a valuable addition to the Cardinals' roster after being obtained from the New York Yankees in December 1966, knocked in St. Louis' runs with third- and seventh-inning ground balls.

In Game 2, Yastrzemski and Lonborg continued where they left off in the regular season. Yastrzemski clubbed two homers good for four runs and Lonborg pitched no-hit ball for 7⅔ innings before winding up with a one-hit (Julian Javier's double), 5-0 tri-

umph.

Then, with the action shifting to St. Louis' Busch Memorial Stadium, which had opened in 1966, the Cardinals rolled to 5-2 and 6-0 victories. Briles' seven-hitter and Mike Shannon's two-run homer proved decisive in Game 3, while Gibson's five-hit hurling and two RBIs apiece by Maris and Tim McCarver foiled Boston in the fourth game.

Lonborg was in sensational form again in Game 5, thereby keeping the Red Sox in the Series and sending the teams back to Boston. The 25-year-old righthander tossed two-hit, shutout ball over 8⅔ innings, then settled for a 3-1 decision when Maris rammed a last-gasp homer to right.

Going for the clincher in enemy territory, the Cards took a 2-1 lead into the fourth inning of Game 6 when Hughes proceeded to write his name into the record books. Negatively speaking, that is. The N.L. leader in winning percentage (.727) in 1967 after spending nine years in the minor leagues, Hughes was bombed for a Series-record three homers in one inning. Yastrzemski led off the fourth with a drive over the wall in left-center and, two outs later, rookie Reggie Smith and Rico Petrocelli belted consecutive shots, Petrocelli's smash being his second of the game.

While Brock tied the game at 4-4 with a two-run homer in the seventh, Boston retaliated with four runs in the last half of the inning—Joe Foy's double broke the deadlock—and scored a Series-squaring 8-4 triumph.

The pitching matchup for Game 7 was what many observers had waited for all along: Gibson vs. Lonborg. Gibson was 2-0 thus far in the Series, having allowed

Dejected Boston pitcher Jim Lonborg, so brilliant in his earlier 1967 Series performances, looks down as St. Louis second baseman Julian Javier rounds the bases after hitting a three-run, Game 7 homer.

only one run and 11 hits in 18 innings; Lonborg also was 2-0, having given up one run and a mere four hits in 18 innings. Gibson would enter this head-to-head meeting of aces with three days of rest, Lonborg with two.

Gibson was far superior, permitting only three hits and striking out 10 batters. Plus, he nailed Lonborg for a home run in the fifth. Javier then belted a three-run shot off Lonborg in the sixth, and Schoendienst's club was on easy street. It was a path down which Gibson—the great competitor—was clearly qualified to lead his team. For the second time in four years, he pitched a complete-game victory in the Series-deciding game. This time, the score was 7-2.

Gibson now boasted a 5-1 record and a 2.00 ERA in World Series competition, with 57 strikeouts in 54 innings and only 37 hits allowed. You hardly could expect anyone to pitch much better than this in the fall classic. Unless, of course, that certain someone happened to be Bob Gibson himself.

Game 1

Wednesday, October 4, At Boston

St. Louis	AB.	R.	H.	RBI.	PO.	A.
Brock, lf	4	2	4	0	2	0
Flood, cf	5	0	1	0	2	0
Maris, rf	4	0	1	2	3	0
Cepeda, 1b	4	0	0	0	6	0
McCarver, c	3	0	0	0	11	2
Shannon, 3b	4	0	2	0	0	1
Javier, 2b	4	0	2	0	1	1
Maxvill, ss	2	0	0	0	2	2
Ro. Gibson, p	4	0	0	0	0	0
Totals	34	2	10	2	27	6

Boston	AB.	R.	H.	RBI.	PO.	A.
Adair, 2b	4	0	0	0	2	3
Jones, 3b	4	0	1	0	2	4
Yastrzemski, lf	4	0	0	0	4	1
Harrelson, rf	3	0	0	0	1	0
Wyatt, p	0	0	0	0	0	0
cFoy	1	0	0	0	0	0
Scott, 1b	3	0	2	0	8	0
Petrocelli, ss	3	0	0	0	0	0
dAndrews	1	0	0	0	0	0
Smith, cf	3	0	1	0	1	0
Ru. Gibson, c	2	0	0	0	8	0
aSiebern, rf	1	0	1	0	0	0
bTartabull, rf	0	0	0	0	1	0
Santiago, p	2	1	1	1	0	0
Howard, c	0	0	0	0	1	0
Totals	31	1	6	1	27	6

St. Louis .... 0 0 1 0 0 0 1 0 0—2
Boston .... 0 0 1 0 0 0 0 0 0—1

St. Louis	IP.	H.	R.	ER.	BB.	SO.
Ro. Gibson (W)	9	6	1	1	1	10

Boston	IP.	H.	R.	ER.	BB.	SO.
Santiago (L)	7	10	2	2	3	5
Wyatt	2	0	0	0	2	1

aAt bat for Ru. Gibson when side was retired in seventh. bRan for Siebern in eighth. cGrounded out for Wyatt in ninth. dFlied out for Petrocelli in ninth. DP—Boston 2. LOB—St. Louis 10, Boston 5. 2B—Flood, Scott. HR—Santiago. SB—Brock 2. SH—Howard. PB—Ru. Gibson. Balk—Wyatt. U—Stevens (A.L.), Barlick (N.L.), Umont (A.L.), Donatelli (N.L.), Runge (A.L.) and Pryor (N.L.). T—2:22. A—34,796.

Game 2

Thursday, October 5, At Boston

St. Louis	AB.	R.	H.	RBI.	PO.	A.
Brock, lf	4	0	0	0	4	0
Flood, cf	3	0	0	0	3	0
Maris, rf	3	0	0	0	4	0
Cepeda, 1b	3	0	0	0	1	1
McCarver, c	3	0	0	0	9	0
Shannon, 3b	3	0	0	0	1	1
Javier, 2b	3	0	1	0	0	1
Maxvill, ss	2	0	0	0	1	0
aTolan	1	0	0	0	0	0
Bressoud, ss	0	0	0	0	0	0
Hughes, p	2	0	0	0	1	0
Willis, p	0	0	0	0	0	0
Hoerner, p	0	0	0	0	0	0
Lamabe, p	0	0	0	0	0	0
bRicketts	1	0	0	0	0	0
Totals	28	0	1	0	24	3

Boston	AB.	R.	H.	RBI.	PO.	A.
Tartabull, rf	4	1	0	0	2	0
Jones, 3b	5	1	2	0	0	3
Yastrzemski, lf	4	2	3	4	3	0
Scott, 1b	4	1	1	0	12	1
Smith, cf	3	0	0	0	1	0
Adair, 2b	4	0	2	0	1	4
Petrocelli, ss	2	0	1	1	3	5
Howard, c	3	0	0	0	4	0
Lonborg, p	4	0	0	0	1	0
Totals	33	5	9	5	27	13

St. Louis .... 0 0 0 0 0 0 0 0 0—0
Boston .... 0 0 0 1 0 1 3 0 x—5

St. Louis	IP.	H.	R.	ER.	BB.	SO.
Hughes (L)	5⅓	4	2	1	3	5
Willis	⅔*	1	2	2	1	0
Hoerner	⅔	2	1	1	1	0
Lamabe	1⅓	2	0	0	0	2

Boston	IP.	H.	R.	ER.	BB.	SO.
Lonborg (W)	9	1	0	0	1	4

*Pitched to two batters in seventh.

aGrounded out for Maxvill in eighth. bPopped out for Lamabe in ninth. E—Shannon. LOB—St. Louis 2, Boston 11. 2B—Javier. HR—Yastrzemski 2. SB—Adair. SF—Petrocelli. U—Barlick (N.L.), Umont (A.L.), Donatelli (N.L.), Runge (A.L.), Pryor (N.L.) and Stevens (A.L.). T—2:24. A—35,188.

Game 3

Saturday, October 7, At St. Louis

Boston	AB.	R.	H.	RBI.	PO.	A.
Tartabull, rf	4	0	0	0	3	0
Jones, 3b	4	0	3	1	2	1
Yastrzemski, lf	3	0	0	0	2	0
Scott, 1b	4	0	0	0	8	1
Smith, cf	4	1	2	1	2	0
Adair, 2b	4	0	0	0	2	2
Petrocelli, ss	3	0	0	0	1	5
Howard, c	3	0	1	0	5	0
Bell, p	0	0	0	0	0	1
aThomas	1	0	0	0	0	0
Waslewski, p	0	0	0	0	1	0
bAndrews	1	1	1	0	0	0
Stange, p	0	0	0	0	0	0
cFoy	1	0	0	0	0	0
Osinski, p	0	0	0	0	0	0
Totals	32	2	7	2	24	11

St. Louis	AB.	R.	H.	RBI.	PO.	A.
Brock, lf	4	2	2	0	2	0
Flood, cf	4	0	1	1	3	0
Maris, rf	4	1	2	1	0	0
Cepeda, 1b	4	0	1	1	13	0
McCarver, c	4	1	1	0	5	1
Shannon, 3b	3	1	2	2	2	2
Javier, 2b	3	0	1	0	0	6
Maxvill, ss	3	0	0	0	2	4
Briles, p	3	0	0	0	0	2
Totals	32	5	10	5	27	15

Boston	0 0 0	0 0 1	1 0 0—2	
St. Louis	1 2 0	0 0 1	0 1 x—5	

Boston	IP.	H.	R.	ER.	BB.	SO.
Bell (L)	2	5	3	3	0	1
Waslewski	3	0	0	0	0	3
Stange	2	3	1	0	0	0
Osinski	1	2	1	1	0	0

St. Louis	IP.	H.	R.	ER.	BB.	SO.
Briles (W)	9	7	2	2	0	4

aStruck out for Bell in third. bSingled for Waslewski in sixth. cGrounded out for Stange in eighth. E—Strange. DP—Boston 1, St. Louis 1. LOB—Boston 4, St. Louis 3. 2B—Cepeda. 3B—Brock. HR—Shannon, Smith. HBP—By Briles (Yastrzemski). U—Umont (A.L.), Donatelli (N.L.), Runge (A.L.), Pryor (N.L.), Stevens (A.L.) and Barlick (N.L.). T—2:15. A—54,575.

Game 4

Sunday, October 8, At St. Louis

Boston	AB.	R.	H.	RBI.	PO.	A.
Tartabull, rf	4	0	2	0	1	0
Jones, 3b	4	0	0	0	0	2
Yastrzemski, lf	4	0	2	0	3	0
Scott, 1b	4	0	1	0	9	0
Smith, cf	3	0	0	0	3	0
Adair, 2b	4	0	0	0	2	2
Petrocelli, ss	3	0	0	0	2	4
Howard, c	2	0	0	0	0	0
Morehead, p	0	0	0	0	0	0
bSiebern	1	0	0	0	0	0
Brett, p	0	0	0	0	0	0
Santiago, p	0	0	0	0	0	0
Bell, p	0	0	0	0	0	0
aFoy	1	0	0	0	0	0
Stephenson, p	0	0	0	0	0	0
Ryan, c	2	0	0	0	4	0
Totals	32	0	5	0	24	8

St. Louis	AB.	R.	H.	RBI.	PO.	A.
Brock, lf	4	1	2	0	2	0
Flood, cf	4	1	1	0	3	0
Maris, rf	4	1	1	2	2	0
Cepeda, 1b	4	1	1	0	11	1
McCarver, c	3	1	1	2	7	0
Shannon, 3b	3	1	0	0	0	2
Javier, 2b	4	0	2	1	0	2
Maxvill, ss	3	0	1	1	0	2
Gibson, p	3	0	0	0	2	2
Totals	32	6	9	6	27	9

Boston	0 0 0	0 0 0	0 0 0—0
St. Louis	4 0 2	0 0 0	0 0 x—6

Boston	IP.	H.	R.	ER.	BB.	SO.
Santiago (L)	⅔	6	4	4	0	0
Bell	1⅓	0	0	0	0	0
Stephenson	2	3	2	2	1	0
Morehead	3	0	0	0	1	2
Brett	1	0	0	0	1	1

St. Louis	IP.	H.	R.	ER.	BB.	SO.
Ro. Gibson (W)	9	5	0	0	1	6

aStruck out for Bell in third. bFlied out for Morehead in eighth. LOB—Boston 6, St. Louis 6. 2B—Maris, Cepeda, Brock, Javier, Yastrzemski. SB—Brock. SF—McCarver. WP—Stephenson. U—Donatelli (N.L.). Runge (A.L.), Pryor (N.L.), Stevens (A.L.), Barlick (N.L.) and Umont (A.L.). T—2:05. A—54,575.

Game 5

Monday, October 9, At St. Louis

Boston	AB.	R.	H.	RBI.	PO.	A.
Foy, 3b	5	1	1	0	2	4
Andrews, 2b	3	0	1	0	1	2
Yastrzemski, lf	3	0	1	0	2	0
Harrelson, rf	3	0	1	1	1	0
Tartabull, rf	0	0	0	0	0	0
Scott, 1b	3	1	0	0	14	0
Smith, cf	4	1	1	0	1	0
Petrocelli, ss	3	0	0	0	1	2
Howard, c	4	0	1	1	5	0
Lonborg, p	4	0	0	0	0	2
Totals	32	3	6	2	27	10

St. Louis	AB.	R.	H.	RBI.	PO.	A.
Brock, lf	4	0	0	0	0	0
Flood, cf	4	0	0	0	2	0
Maris, rf	4	1	2	1	3	0
Cepeda, 1b	4	0	0	0	5	0
McCarver, c	3	0	0	0	9	1
Shannon, 3b	3	0	0	0	1	3
Javier, 2b	3	0	0	0	4	3
Maxvill, ss	2	0	1	0	3	4
bRicketts	1	0	0	0	0	0
Willis, p	0	0	0	0	0	0
Lamabe, p	0	0	0	0	0	1
Carlton, p	1	0	0	0	0	0
aTolan	1	0	0	0	0	0
Washburn, p	0	0	0	0	0	1
cGagliano	1	0	0	0	0	0
Bressoud, ss	0	0	0	0	0	0
Totals	31	1	3	1	27	13

Boston	0 0 1	0 0 0	0 0 2—3
St. Louis	0 0 0	0 0 0	0 0 1—1

Boston	IP.	H.	R.	ER.	BB.	SO.
Lonborg (W)	9	3	1	1	0	4

St. Louis	IP.	H.	R.	ER.	BB.	SO.
Carlton (L)	6	3	1	0	2	5
Washburn	2	1	0	0	0	2
Willis	0*	1	2	1	2	0
Lamabe	1	1	0	0	0	2

*Pitched to three batters in ninth.

aStruck out for Carlton in sixth. bGrounded out for Maxvill in eighth. cPopped out for Washburn in eighth. E—Petrocelli, Maris, Shannon. DP—St. Louis 2. LOB—Boston 7, St. Louis 3. 2B—Yastrzemski, Smith. HR—Maris. SH—Andrews. WP—Carlton. U—Runge (A.L.), Pryor (N.L.), Stevens (A.L.), Barlick (N.L.), Umont (A.L.) and Donatelli (N.L.). T—2:20. A—54,575.

Game 6

Wednesday, October 11, At Boston

St. Louis	AB.	R.	H.	RBI.	PO.	A.
Brock, lf	5	2	2	3	2	0
Flood, cf	5	0	1	1	2	0
Maris, rf	4	0	2	0	2	0
Cepeda, 1b	5	0	1	0	10	0
McCarver, c	3	0	0	0	2	0
Shannon, 3b	4	0	1	0	1	4
Javier, 2b	4	1	1	0	3	3
Maxvill, ss	3	0	0	0	2	2
Hughes, p	1	0	0	0	0	0
Willis, p	0	0	0	0	0	0
aSpiezio	1	0	0	0	0	0
Briles, p	0	0	0	0	0	2
bTolan	0	1	0	0	0	0
Lamabe, p	0	0	0	0	0	0
Hoerner, p	0	0	0	0	0	0
Jaster, p	0	0	0	0	0	0
Washburn, p	0	0	0	0	0	0
eRicketts	1	0	0	0	0	0
Woodeshick, p	0	0	0	0	0	1
Totals	36	4	8	4	24	12

Boston	AB.	R.	H.	RBI.	PO.	A.
Foy, 3b	4	1	1	1	3	3
Andrews, 2b	5	1	2	1	0	2
Yastrzemski, lf	4	2	3	1	2	0
Harrelson, rf	3	0	0	0	1	0
Tartabull, rf	0	0	0	0	0	0
dAdair	0	0	0	1	0	0
Bell, p	0	0	0	0	0	1
Scott, 1b	4	0	1	0	10	1
Smith, cf	4	1	2	2	4	0
Petrocelli, ss	3	2	2	2	1	3
Howard, c	4	0	0	0	4	0
Waslewski, p	1	0	0	0	1	0
Wyatt, p	0	0	0	0	0	0
cJones	1	1	1	0	0	0
Thomas, rf	1	0	0	0	1	0
Totals	34	8	12	8	27	10

St. Louis	0 0 2	0 0 0	2 0 0—4
Boston	0 1 0	3 0 0	4 0 x—8

St. Louis	IP.	H.	R.	ER.	BB.	SO.
Hughes	3⅔	5	4	4	0	2
Willis	⅓	0	0	0	0	0
Briles	2	0	0	0	1	0
Lamabe (L)	⅓	2	2	2	0	0
Hoerner	0*	2	2	2	0	0
Jaster	⅓	2	0	0	0	0
Washburn	⅓	0	0	0	1	0
Woodeshick	1	1	0	0	0	0

Boston	IP.	H.	R.	ER.	BB.	SO.
Waslewski	5⅓	4	2	2	2	4
Wyatt (W)	1⅔	1	2	2	1	0
Bell	2	3	0	0	1	0

*Pitched to two batters in seventh.

aGrounded out for Willis in fifth. bWalked for Briles in seventh. cSingled for Wyatt in seventh. dHit sacrifice fly for Tartabull in seventh. eFlied out for Washburn in eighth. E—Petrocelli. LOB—St. Louis 9, Boston 7. 2B—Javier, Foy, Shannon. HR—Petrocelli 2, Yastrzemski, Smith, Brock. SB—Brock. SH—Foy. SF—Adair. HBP—By Briles (Waslewski). U—Pryor (N.L.), Stevens (A.L.), Barlick (N.L.), Umont (A.L.), Donatelli (N.L.) and Runge (A.L.). T—2:48. A—35,188.

Game 7

Thursday, October 12, At Boston

St. Louis	AB.	R.	H.	RBI.	PO.	A.
Brock, lf	4	1	2	0	1	0
Flood, cf	3	1	1	1	0	0
Maris, rf	3	0	2	1	1	0
Cepeda, 1b	5	0	0	0	6	2
McCarver, c	5	1	1	0	12	0
Shannon, 3b	4	1	0	0	0	0
Javier, 2b	4	1	2	3	4	4
Maxvill, ss	4	1	1	0	3	3
Ro. Gibson, p	4	1	1	1	0	1
Totals	36	7	10	6	27	10

Boston	AB.	R.	H.	RBI.	PO.	A.
Foy, 3b	3	0	0	0	2	3
Morehead, p	0	0	0	0	0	0
Osinski, p	0	0	0	0	0	0
Brett, p	0	0	0	0	0	0
Andrews, 2b	3	0	0	0	1	2
Yastrzemski, lf	3	0	1	0	2	0
Harrelson, rf	4	0	0	0	3	0
Scott, 1b	4	1	1	0	9	0
Smith, cf	3	0	0	0	2	0
Petrocelli, ss	3	1	1	0	3	2
Howard, c	2	0	0	0	4	1
bJones, 3b	0	0	0	0	0	0
Lonborg, p	1	0	0	0	0	0
aTartabull	1	0	0	0	0	0
Santiago, p	0	0	0	0	0	0
cSiebern	1	0	0	1	0	0
Ru. Gibson, c	0	0	0	0	1	0
Totals	28	2	3	1	27	8

St. Louis	0 0 2	0 2 3	0 0 0—7
Boston	0 0 0	0 1 0	0 1 0—2

St. Louis	IP.	H.	R.	ER.	BB.	SO.
Ro. Gibson (W)	9	3	2	2	3	10

Boston	IP.	H.	R.	ER.	BB.	SO.
Lonborg (L)	6	10	7	6	1	3
Santiago	2	0	0	0	0	1
Morehead	⅓	0	0	0	3	1
Osinski	⅓	0	0	0	0	0
Brett	⅓	0	0	0	0	0

aStruck out for Lonborg in sixth. bWalked for Howard in eighth. cHit into force play for Santiago in eighth. E—Javier, Foy. DP—St. Louis 1. LOB—St. Louis 7, Boston 3. 2B—McCarver, Brock, Petrocelli. 3B—Maxvill, Scott. HR—Ro. Gibson, Javier. SB—Brock 3. SH—Andrews. SF—Maris. WP—Lonborg, Ro. Gibson. U—Stevens (A.L.), Barlick (N.L.), Umont (A.L.), Donatelli (N.L.), Runge (A.L.) and Pryor (N.L.). T—2:23. A—35,188.

COMPOSITE BATTING AVERAGES

St. Louis Cardinals

Player-Position	G.	AB.	R.	H.	2B.	3B.	HR.	RBI.	BA.
Brock, lf	7	29	8	12	2	1	1	3	.414
Maris, rf	7	26	3	10	1	0	1	7	.385
Javier, 2b	7	25	2	9	3	0	1	4	.360
Shannon, 3b	7	24	3	5	1	0	1	2	.208
Flood, cf	7	28	2	5	1	0	0	3	.179
Maxvill, ss	7	19	1	3	0	1	0	1	.158
McCarver, c	7	24	3	3	1	0	0	2	.125
Cepeda, 1b	7	29	1	3	2	0	0	1	.103
Ro. Gibson, p	3	11	1	1	0	0	1	1	.091
Jaster, p	1	0	0	0	0	0	0	0	.000
Woodeshick, p	1	0	0	0	0	0	0	0	.000
Bressoud, ss	2	0	0	0	0	0	0	0	.000
Hoerner, p	2	0	0	0	0	0	0	0	.000
Washburn, p	2	0	0	0	0	0	0	0	.000
Lamabe, p	3	0	0	0	0	0	0	0	.000
Willis, p	3	0	0	0	0	0	0	0	.000
Carlton, p	1	1	0	0	0	0	0	0	.000
Gagliano, ph	1	1	0	0	0	0	0	0	.000
Spiezio, ph	1	1	0	0	0	0	0	0	.000
Tolan, ph	3	2	1	0	0	0	0	0	.000
Briles, p	2	3	0	0	0	0	0	0	.000
Hughes, p	2	3	0	0	0	0	0	0	.000
Ricketts, ph	3	3	0	0	0	0	0	0	.000
Totals	7	229	25	51	11	2	5	24	.223

Boston Red Sox

Player-Position	G.	AB.	R.	H.	2B.	3B.	HR.	RBI.	BA.
Santiago, p	3	2	1	1	0	0	1	1	.500
Yastrzemski, lf	7	25	4	10	2	0	3	5	.400
Jones, 3b-ph	6	18	2	7	0	0	0	1	.389
Siebern, ph-rf	3	3	0	1	0	0	0	1	.333
Andrews, ph-2b	5	13	2	4	0	0	0	1	.308
Smith, cf	7	24	3	6	1	0	2	3	.250
Scott, 1b	7	26	3	6	1	1	0	1	.231
Petrocelli, ss	7	20	3	4	1	0	2	3	.200
Tartab'l, pr-rf-ph	7	13	1	2	0	0	0	0	.154
Foy, ph-3b	6	15	2	2	1	0	0	1	.133
Adair, 2b-ph	5	16	0	2	0	0	0	1	.125
Howard, c	7	18	0	2	0	0	0	1	.111
Harrelson, rf	4	13	0	1	0	0	0	1	.077
Stange, p	1	0	0	0	0	0	0	0	.000
Stephenson, p	1	0	0	0	0	0	0	0	.000
Brett, p	2	0	0	0	0	0	0	0	.000
Morehead, p	2	0	0	0	0	0	0	0	.000
Wyatt, p	2	0	0	0	0	0	0	0	.000
Bell, p	3	0	0	0	0	0	0	0	.000
Osinski, p	2	0	0	0	0	0	0	0	.000
Ryan, c	1	2	0	0	0	0	0	0	.000
Thomas, ph-rf	2	2	0	0	0	0	0	0	.000
Waslewski, p	2	1	0	0	0	0	0	0	.000
Ru. Gibson, c	2	2	0	0	0	0	0	0	.000
Lonborg, p	3	9	0	0	0	0	0	0	.000
Totals	7	222	21	48	6	1	8	19	.216

COMPOSITE PITCHING AVERAGES

St. Louis Cardinals

Pitcher	G.	IP.	H.	R.	ER.	BB.	SO.	W.	L.	ERA.
Carlton	1	6	3	1	0	2	5	0	1	0.00
Washburn	2	2⅓	1	0	0	1	2	0	0	0.00
Woodeshick	1	1	1	0	0	0	0	0	0	0.00
Jaster	1	⅓	2	0	0	0	0	0	0	0.00
Ro. Gibson	3	27	14	3	3	5	26	3	0	1.00
Briles	2	11	7	2	2	1	4	1	0	1.64
Hughes	2	9	9	6	5	3	7	0	1	5.00
Lamabe	3	2⅔	5	2	2	0	4	0	1	6.75
Willis	3	1	2	4	3	4	1	0	0	27.00
Hoerner	2	⅔	4	3	3	1	0	0	0	40.50
Totals	7	61	48	21	18	17	49	4	3	2.66

Boston Red Sox

Pitcher	G.	IP.	H.	R.	ER.	BB.	SO.	W.	L.	ERA.
Morehead	2	3⅓	0	0	0	4	3	0	0	0.00
Stange	1	2	3	1	0	0	0	0	0	0.00
Brett	2	1⅓	0	0	0	1	1	0	0	0.00
Waslewski	2	8⅓	4	2	2	2	7	0	0	2.16
Lonborg	3	24	14	8	7	2	11	2	1	2.63
Wyatt	2	3⅔	1	2	2	3	1	1	0	4.91
Bell	3	5⅓	8	3	3	1	1	0	1	5.06
Santiago	3	9⅔	16	6	6	3	6	0	2	5.59
Osinski	2	1⅓	2	1	1	0	0	0	0	6.75
Stephenson	1	2	3	2	2	1	0	0	0	9.00
Totals	7	61	51	25	23	17	30	3	4	3.39

1968
DETROIT TIGERS
VS.
ST. LOUIS CARDINALS

It was the Year of the Pitcher, a season in which Detroit Tigers righthander Denny McLain became the major leagues' first 30-game winner since 1934 and St. Louis Cardinals standout Bob Gibson established a big-league record for the lowest earned-run average in 300 or more innings.

And, fittingly, when the 1968 World Series between the Tigers and Cardinals began in St. Louis, 31-game winner McLain was on the mound for the visitors and the 1.12 ERA man, Gibson, was toiling for the home forces.

Decision, Gibson. And it was unanimous.

McLain was nicked for three fourth-inning runs by the Cardinals, who got a run-scoring single from Mike Shannon and a two-run single from Julian Javier in an uprising helped along by left fielder Willie Horton's misplay on Shannon's base hit. In the seventh, reliever Pat Dobson, working his second inning, yielded a bases-empty home run to Lou Brock.

Gibson, meanwhile, was making an inexorable march toward the Series record book. Through seven innings, the Cardinals' strong-armed righthander had struck out 13 batters, two shy of the fall-classic mark established by Los Angeles' Sandy Koufax in 1963. He had permitted four hits and no runs. With Gibson in total command and the Cards ahead, 4-0, all attention was riveted on the 32-year-old pitcher's quest to shatter Koufax's strikeout standard.

Gibson didn't disappoint. He struck out pinch-hitter Eddie Mathews to open the eighth. Then, after yielding a leadoff single to Mickey Stanley in the ninth, Gibson made Al Kaline his record-equaling 15th strikeout victim, Norm Cash record-break-

ing No. 16 and Horton one-more-for-good-measure No. 17.

The Tigers, obviously awed by what they saw (or perhaps didn't see) of Gibson's fastball, bounced back from the 4-0 defeat in impressive style. Seventeen-game winner Mickey Lolich not only held the Cardinals to six singles in Game 2, but also hit the only home run of his major league career as Detroit won, 8-1. Horton and Cash also homered for the winners.

In Game 3, Tim McCarver shot the Cardinals into a 4-2 lead with a three-run homer in the fifth, Orlando Cepeda belted a two-on shot in the seventh and Brock stole three bases as St. Louis regained the Series lead with a 7-3 conquest. Kaline, playing in his first Series after 16 seasons with Detroit and installed as the starting right fielder by Manager Mayo Smith in a Series stratagem that sent center fielder Stanley to shortstop and regular right fielder Jim Northrup to center, walloped a two-run homer for the losers, who also got a bases-empty blast from Dick McAuliffe.

Gibson then posted a record seventh consecutive triumph in the fall classic, breezing to victory in a 10-1 laugher in which he aided his own cause with his second career homer in Series play (a record for a pitcher). Brock doubled, tripled and homered and knocked in four runs for St. Louis and the swift outfielder also recorded his seventh stolen base of this Series (tying a classic mark he had established in 1967). The free-spirited McLain, losing for the second straight time to Gibson, was lifted after 2⅔ innings. The Tigers were on the ropes.

While Brock's running game unquestionably was a big plus for St. Louis, his baserunning in

Game 5 proved costly. After doubling with one out in the fifth, Brock tried to score standing up on Javier's single to left, but Horton threw him out with a great throw (which probably wouldn't have gotten a sliding Brock). Detroit, trailing by a 3-2 score at the time, seemingly received a boost from the reprieve and broke loose for three runs in the seventh as the 33-year-old Kaline, supplying the savvy that Smith had sought from the longtime superstar-turned-reserve, delivered a bases-loaded single. Lolich, rocked for a two-run homer by Cepeda in a three-run Detroit first, pitched scoreless ball over the final eight innings and Detroit stayed alive with a 5-3 triumph.

Detroit's man of panache, McLain, went against Ray Washburn and not Gibson in Game 6 and came out a 13-1 winner as Northrup slammed a bases-loaded home run in Detroit's 10-run outburst in the third. The Tigers' spree matched the one-inning Series scoring record set by the Philadelphia Athletics against the Chicago Cubs in Game 4 of the 1929 fall classic.

Game 7 matched Detroit's man of paunch, Lolich, against Gibson, and the fact it was a 0-0 game after six innings surprised absolutely no one. The Cardinals got two runners on in the sixth—Brock via his record-tying 13th hit of the Series and Flood with a single—but Lolich picked off each Redbird.

Then, with two out in the Detroit seventh, Cash and Horton singled. Northrup then hit a drive to center field that the normally reliable—if not usually sensational—Flood misjudged. The Cardinal outfielder broke in on the ball, realized he had been fooled by the carry of the smash and ran

St. Louis stars Lou Brock (above left) and Bob Gibson were shining bright after the Cardinals' impressive Game 1 victory. But the ultimate moment was enjoyed by Detroit pitcher Mickey Lolich and catcher Bill Freehan (below) after the Tigers' Game 7 victory.

back. The ball sailed past Flood, and Cash and Horton scored on the play (which was ruled a triple). Bill Freehan then doubled home Northrup, and Detroit was in control.

The Tigers and Cardinals traded runs in the ninth—Shannon accounted for the Cardinals' score with a two-out homer—and the crafty-if-unathletic-looking Lolich wound up with a five-hit, 4-1 victory. The triumph brought Detroit its first Series title since 1945 and made the Tigers only the third team in history to rally from a 3-1 deficit to win a seven-game fall classic.

It was the Year of the Pitcher, all right. And while McLain and Gibson (22 victories and 13 shutouts to go along with that gaudy ERA) stole the show in the regular season and Gibby was phenomenal in Game 1 of the Series and dominant in Game 4, it was three-time winner Lolich who surfaced as the Pitcher of the World Series.

Game 1
Wednesday, October 2, At St. Louis

Detroit	AB.	R.	H.	RBI.	PO.	A.
McAuliffe, 2b	4	0	1	0	4	0
Stanley, ss	4	0	2	0	3	2
Kaline, rf	4	0	1	0	2	0
Cash, 1b	4	0	0	0	6	1
Horton, lf	4	0	0	0	2	0
Northrup, cf	3	0	0	0	2	0
Freehan, c	2	0	0	0	4	1
Wert, 3b	2	0	1	0	0	1
bMathews	1	0	0	0	0	0
Tracewski, 3b	0	0	0	0	0	0
McLain, p	1	0	0	0	0	2
aMatchick	1	0	0	0	0	0
Dobson, p	0	0	0	0	0	0
cBrown	1	0	0	0	0	0
McMahon, p	0	0	0	0	1	0
Totals	31	0	5	0	24	7

St. Louis	AB.	R.	H.	RBI.	PO.	A.
Brock, lf	4	1	1	1	2	0
Flood, cf	4	0	1	0	1	0
Maris, rf	3	1	0	0	1	0
Cepeda, 1b	4	0	0	0	1	1
McCarver, c	3	1	1	0	17	1
Shannon, 3b	4	1	2	1	0	0
Javier, 2b	3	0	1	2	2	0
Maxvill, ss	2	0	0	0	2	0
Gibson, p	2	0	0	0	1	0
Totals	29	4	6	4	27	2

Detroit .... 0 0 0   0 0 0   0 0 0—0
St. Louis .... 0 0 0   3 0 0   1 0 x—4

Detroit	IP.	H.	R.	ER.	BB.	SO.
McLain (L)	5	3	3	2	3	3
Dobson	2	2	1	1	1	0
McMahon	1	1	0	0	0	0

St. Louis	IP.	H.	R.	ER.	BB.	SO.
Gibson (W)	9	5	0	0	1	17

aGrounded out for McLain in sixth. bStruck out for Wert in eighth. cFlied out for Dobson in eighth. E—Cash, Horton, Freehan. LOB—Detroit 5, St. Louis 6. 2B—Kaline. 3B—McCarver. HR—Brock. SB—Brock, Javier, Flood. SH—Gibson. U—Gorman (N.L.), Honochick (A.L.), Landes (N.L.), Kinnamon (A.L.), Harvey (N.L.) and Haller (A.L.). T—2:29. A—54,692.

Game 2
Thursday, October 3, At St. Louis

Detroit	AB.	R.	H.	RBI.	PO.	A.
McAuliffe, 2b	5	0	2	2	1	5
Stanley, ss-cf	5	0	1	0	0	3
Kaline, rf	5	2	2	0	2	0
Cash, 1b	5	2	3	1	11	0
Horton, lf	3	2	2	1	0	0
Oyler, ss	0	0	0	0	0	0
Northrup, cf-lf	5	1	1	0	4	0
Freehan, c	4	0	0	0	9	1
Wert, 3b	2	0	0	1	0	2
Lolich, p	4	1	2	2	0	0
Totals	38	8	13	7	27	11

St. Louis	AB.	R.	H.	RBI.	PO.	A.
Brock, lf	3	1	1	0	0	0
Javier, 2b	4	0	2	0	3	2
Flood, cf	3	0	1	0	2	0
Cepeda, 1b	4	0	2	1	6	0
Shannon, 3b	4	0	0	0	1	3
McCarver, c	4	0	0	0	7	0
Davis, rf	4	0	0	0	4	0
Maxvill, ss	3	0	0	0	4	3
Briles, p	2	0	0	0	0	0
Carlton, p	0	0	0	0	0	0
Willis, p	0	0	0	0	0	0
aGagliano	1	0	0	0	0	0
Hoerner, p	0	0	0	0	0	0
Totals	32	1	6	1	27	8

Detroit .... 0 1 1   0 0 3   1 0 2—8
St. Louis .... 0 0 0   0 0 1   0 0 0—1

Detroit	IP.	H.	R.	ER.	BB.	SO.
Lolich (W)	9	6	1	1	2	9

St. Louis	IP.	H.	R.	ER.	BB.	SO.
Briles (L)	5*	7	4	4	1	2
Carlton	1†	4	2	2	1	1
Willis	2	1	0	0	2	2
Hoerner	1	1	2	2	3	1

*Pitched to two batters in sixth.
†Pitched to two batters in seventh.

aGrounded out for Willis in eighth. E—Stanley, Shannon. DP—Detroit 1, St. Louis 2. LOB—Detroit 11, St. Louis 6. HR—Horton, Lolich, Cash. SB—Brock 2. SH—Oyler. U—Honochick (A.L.), Landes (N.L.), Kinnamon (A.L.), Harvey (N.L.), Haller (A.L.) and Gorman (N.L.). T—2:41. A—54,692.

Game 3
Saturday, October 5, At Detroit

St. Louis	AB.	R.	H.	RBI.	PO.	A.
Brock, lf	4	1	3	0	5	0
Flood, cf	4	2	2	1	1	0
Maris, rf	3	2	1	0	2	0
Cepeda, 1b	5	1	1	3	10	0
McCarver, c	5	1	2	3	5	0
Shannon, 3b	4	0	2	0	0	1
Javier, 2b	4	0	1	0	2	5
Maxvill, ss	4	0	0	0	2	2
Washburn, p	3	0	0	0	0	1
Hoerner, p	2	0	1	0	0	0
Totals	38	7	13	7	27	9

Detroit	AB.	R.	H.	RBI.	PO.	A.
McAuliffe, 2b	4	2	2	1	0	1
Stanley, ss	3	0	0	0	0	2
Kaline, rf	4	1	1	2	1	0
Cash, 1b	3	0	0	0	8	1
Horton, lf	2	0	0	0	1	0
Northrup, cf	4	0	0	0	7	0
Freehan, c	3	0	0	0	6	2
Wert, 3b	4	0	0	0	3	2
Wilson, p	1	0	0	0	0	2
Dobson, p	0	0	0	0	0	0
aMatchick	1	0	0	0	0	0
McMahon, p	0	0	0	0	0	0
Patterson, p	0	0	0	0	0	0
bComer	1	0	1	0	0	0
Hiller, p	0	0	0	0	1	0
cPrice	1	0	0	0	0	0
Totals	31	3	4	3	27	10

St. Louis	0 0 0 0 4 0 3 0 0—7
Detroit	0 0 2 0 1 0 0 0 0—3

St. Louis	IP.	H.	R.	ER.	BB.	SO.
Washburn (W)	5⅓	3	3	3	4	3
Hoerner	3⅔	1	0	0	1	2

Detroit	IP.	H.	R.	ER.	BB.	SO.
Wilson (L)	4⅓	4	3	3	6	3
Dobson	⅔	2	1	1	0	0
McMahon	1*	3	3	3	0	1
Patterson	1	0	0	0	0	0
Hiller	2	4	0	0	1	1

*Pitched to three batters in seventh.

aStruck out for Dobson in fifth. bSingled for Patterson in seventh. cFlied out for Hiller in ninth. DP—Detroit 1. LOB—St. Louis 11, Detroit 6. 2B—Flood, Maris. HR—Kaline, McCarver, McAuliffe, Cepeda. SB—Brock 3. U—Landes (N.L.), Kinnamon (A.L.), Harvey (N.L.), Haller (A.L.), Gorman (N.L.) and Honochick (A.L.). T—3:17. A—53,634.

Game 4

Sunday, October 6, At Detroit

St. Louis	AB.	R.	H.	RBI.	PO.	A.
Brock, lf	5	2	3	4	2	0
Flood, cf	5	1	1	0	3	0
Maris, rf	5	1	0	1	0	0
Cepeda, 1b	4	0	1	0	9	1
McCarver, c	5	1	3	1	10	0
Shannon, 3b	5	1	2	2	1	0
Javier, 2b	4	1	2	0	0	2
Maxvill, ss	4	1	0	0	2	1
Gibson, p	3	2	1	2	0	0
Totals	40	10	13	10	27	4

Detroit	AB.	R.	H.	RBI.	PO.	A.
McAuliffe, 2b	4	0	0	0	2	4
Stanley, ss	4	0	0	0	3	3
Kaline, rf	4	0	2	0	1	0
Cash, 1b	4	0	1	0	10	2
Horton, lf	3	0	0	0	1	0
Northrup, cf	4	1	1	1	5	0
Mathews, 3b	2	0	1	0	0	1
Freehan, c	3	0	0	0	4	1
McLain, p	1	0	0	0	0	0
Sparma, p	0	0	0	0	0	0
Patterson, p	0	0	0	0	0	1
aPrice	1	0	0	0	0	0
Lasher, p	0	0	0	0	0	1
bMatchick	1	0	0	0	0	0
Hiller, p	0	0	0	0	0	0
Dobson, p	0	0	0	0	1	0
Totals	31	1	5	1	27	13

St. Louis	2 0 2 2 0 0 0 4 0—10
Detroit	0 0 0 1 0 0 0 0 0— 1

St. Louis	IP.	H.	R.	ER.	BB.	SO.
Gibson (W)	9	5	1	1	2	10

Detroit	IP.	H.	R.	ER.	BB.	SO.
McLain (L)	2⅔	6	4	3	1	3
Sparma	⅓*	2	2	1	0	0
Patterson	2	1	0	0	1	0
Lasher	2	1	0	0	0	1
Hiller	0†	2	4	3	2	0
Dobson	2	1	0	0	0	0

*Pitched to two batters in fourth.
†Pitched to five batters in eighth.

aStruck out for Patterson in fifth. bFlied out for Lasher in seventh. E—Northrup, Mathews, Freehan, McLain. DP—St. Louis 1. LOB—St. Louis 7, Detroit 5. 2B—Kaline, Shannon, Javier, Brock. 3B—McCarver, Brock. HR—Brock, Gibson, Northrup. SB—Brock. U—Kinnamon (A.L.), Harvey (N.L.), Haller (A.L.), Gorman (N.L.), Honochick (A.L.) and Landes (N.L.). T—2:34. A—53,634.

Game 5

Monday, October 7, At Detroit

St. Louis	AB.	R.	H.	RBI.	PO.	A.
Brock, lf	5	1	3	0	2	0
Javier, 2b	4	0	2	0	2	1
Flood, cf	4	1	1	1	3	0
Cepeda, 1b	4	1	1	2	7	0
Shannon, 3b	4	0	0	0	1	2
McCarver, c	3	0	1	0	6	0
Davis, rf	3	0	0	0	1	0
aGagliano	1	0	0	0	0	0
Maxvill, ss	3	0	0	0	1	2
bSpiezio	1	0	1	0	0	0
cSchofield	0	0	0	0	0	0
Briles, p	2	0	0	0	0	2
Hoerner, p	0	0	0	0	0	0
Willis, p	0	0	0	0	1	0
dMaris	1	0	0	0	0	0
Totals	35	3	9	3	24	7

Detroit	AB.	R.	H.	RBI.	PO.	A.
McAuliffe, 2b	4	1	1	0	1	2
Stanley, ss-cf	3	2	1	0	2	3
Kaline, rf	4	0	2	2	3	0
Cash, 1b	2	0	2	2	7	1
Horton, lf	4	1	1	0	1	1
Oyler, ss	0	0	0	0	1	0
Northrup, cf-lf	3	0	1	1	2	0
Freehan, c	4	0	0	0	9	0
Wert, 3b	3	0	0	0	0	1
Lolich, p	4	1	1	0	1	2
Totals	31	5	9	5	27	11

St. Louis	3 0 0 0 0 0 0 0 0—3
Detroit	0 0 0 2 0 0 3 0 x—5

St. Louis	IP.	H.	R.	ER.	BB.	SO.
Briles	6⅓	6	3	3	3	5
Hoerner (L)	0*	3	2	2	1	0
Willis	1⅔	0	0	0	0	1

Detroit	IP.	H.	R.	ER.	BB.	SO.
Lolich (W)	9	9	3	3	1	8

*Pitched to four batters in seventh.

aFlied out for Davis in ninth. bSingled for Maxvill in ninth. cRan for Spiezio in ninth. dStruck out for Willis in ninth. E—Cash. DP—St. Louis 1. LOB—St. Louis 7, Detroit 7. 2B—Brock 2. 3B—Stanley, Horton. HR—Cepeda. SB—Flood. SF—Cash. HBP—By Lolich (Briles). U—Harvey (N.L.), Haller (A.L.), Gorman (N.L.), Honochick (A.L.), Landes (N.L.) and Kinnamon (A.L.). T—2:43. A—53,634.

Game 6

Wednesday, October 9, At St. Louis

Detroit	AB.	R.	H.	RBI.	PO.	A.
McAuliffe, 2b	2	2	0	0	3	1
Stanley, ss-cf	5	2	1	0	2	1
Kaline, rf	4	3	3	4	7	0
Cash, 1b	4	2	3	2	5	0
Horton, lf	3	2	2	2	0	0
Oyler, ss	0	0	0	0	0	0
Northrup, cf-lf	5	1	2	4	1	0
Freehan, c	4	0	1	1	7	0
Wert, 3b	3	1	0	0	2	2
McLain, p	4	0	0	0	0	1
Totals	34	13	12	13	27	5

St. Louis	AB.	R.	H.	RBI.	PO.	A.
Brock, lf	4	0	1	0	1	0
Flood, cf	4	0	0	0	0	0
Maris, rf	4	1	2	0	2	0
Cepeda, 1b	4	0	2	0	7	2
McCarver, c	4	0	1	0	8	0
Shannon, 3b	4	0	1	0	1	1
Javier, 2b	4	0	1	1	3	2
Maxvill, ss	4	0	0	0	4	6
Washburn, p	0	0	0	0	0	0
Jaster, p	0	0	0	0	0	0
Willis, p	0	0	0	0	0	0
Hughes, p	0	0	0	0	0	0
aRicketts	1	0	1	0	0	0
Carlton, p	0	0	0	0	1	1
bTolan	1	0	0	0	0	0
Granger, p	0	0	0	0	0	1
cEdwards	1	0	0	0	0	0
Nelson, p	0	0	0	0	0	0
Totals	35	1	9	1	27	13

Detroit	0 2 10 0 1 0 0 0 0—13
St. Louis	0 0 0 0 0 0 0 0 1— 1

Detroit	IP.	H.	R.	ER.	BB.	SO.
McLain (W)	9	9	1	1	0	7

St. Louis	IP.	H.	R.	ER.	BB.	SO.
Washburn (L)	2*	4	5	5	3	3
Jaster	0*	2	3	3	1	0
Willis	⅔	1	4	4	2	0
Hughes	⅓	2	0	0	0	0
Carlton	3	3	1	1	0	2
Granger	2	0	0	0	1	1
Nelson	1	0	0	0	0	1

*Pitched to three batters in third.

aSingled for Hughes in third. bStruck out for Carlton in sixth. cStruck out for Granger in eighth. E—Stanley, Brock. DP—Detroit 1, St. Louis 3. LOB—Detroit 5, St. Louis 7. 2B—Horton. HR—Northrup, Kaline. SH—McLain. HBP—By Willis (Wert), by Granger (Kaline, Horton). U—Haller (A.L.), Gorman (N.L.), Honochick (A.L.), Landes (N.L.), Kinnamon (A.L.) and Harvey (N.L.). T—2:26. A—54,692.

Game 7

Thursday, October 10, At St. Louis

Detroit	AB.	R.	H.	RBI.	PO.	A.
McAuliffe, 2b	4	0	0	0	1	3
Stanley, ss-cf	4	0	1	0	5	2
Kaline, rf	4	0	0	0	2	0
Cash, 1b	4	1	1	0	11	2
Horton, lf	4	1	2	0	0	0
bTracewski	0	1	0	0	0	0
Oyler, ss	0	0	0	0	1	0
Northrup, cf-lf	4	1	2	2	1	0
Freehan, c	4	0	1	1	6	0
Wert, 3b	3	0	1	1	0	6
Lolich, p	4	0	0	0	0	2
Totals	35	4	8	4	27	15

St. Louis	AB.	R.	H.	RBI.	PO.	A.
Brock, lf	3	0	1	0	1	0
Javier, 2b	4	0	0	0	3	2
Flood, cf	4	0	2	0	3	0
Cepeda, 1b	3	0	0	0	7	0
Shannon, 3b	4	1	1	1	1	2
McCarver, c	3	0	1	0	8	0
Maris, rf	3	0	0	0	3	0
Maxvill, ss	2	0	0	0	0	1
aGagliano	1	0	0	0	0	0
Schofield, ss	0	0	0	0	0	0
Gibson, p	3	0	0	0	1	0
Totals	30	1	5	1	27	5

Detroit	0 0 0 0 0 0 3 0 1—4
St. Louis	0 0 0 0 0 0 0 0 1—1

Detroit	IP.	H.	R.	ER.	BB.	SO.
Lolich (W)	9	5	1	1	3	4

St. Louis	IP.	H.	R.	ER.	BB.	SO.
Gibson (L)	9	8	4	4	1	8

aGrounded out for Maxvill in eighth. bRan for Horton in ninth. E—Northrup. DP—Detroit 1. LOB—Detroit 5, St. Louis 5. 2B—Freehan. 3B—Northrup. HR—Shannon. SB—Flood. U—Gorman (N.L.), Honochick (A.L.), Landes (N.L.), Kinnamon (A.L.), Harvey (N.L.) and Haller (A.L.). T—2:07. A—54,692.

COMPOSITE BATTING AVERAGES

Detroit Tigers

Player-Position	G.	AB.	R.	H.	2B.	3B.	HR.	RBI.	BA.
Comer, ph	1	1	0	1	0	0	0	0	1.000
Cash, 1b	7	26	5	10	0	0	1	5	.385
Kaline, rf	7	29	6	11	2	0	2	8	.379
Mathews, ph-3b	2	3	0	1	0	0	0	0	.333
Horton, lf	7	23	6	7	1	1	1	3	.304
Northrup, cf-lf	7	28	4	7	0	1	2	8	.250
Lolich, p	3	12	2	3	0	0	1	2	.250
McAuliffe, 2b	7	27	5	6	0	0	1	3	.222
Stanley, ss-cf	7	28	4	6	0	1	0	0	.214
Wert, 3b	6	17	1	2	0	0	0	2	.118
Freehan, c	7	24	0	2	1	0	0	2	.083
Brown, ph	1	1	0	0	0	0	0	0	.000
Wilson, p	1	1	0	0	0	0	0	0	.000
Price, ph	2	2	0	0	0	0	0	0	.000
Matchick, ph	3	3	0	0	0	0	0	0	.000
McLain, p	3	6	0	0	0	0	0	0	.000
Oyler, ss	4	0	0	0	0	0	0	0	.000
Dobson, p	3	0	0	0	0	0	0	0	.000
Hiller, p	2	0	0	0	0	0	0	0	.000
McMahon, p	2	0	0	0	0	0	0	0	.000
Patterson, p	2	0	0	0	0	0	0	0	.000
Tracewski, 3b-pr	2	0	1	0	0	0	0	0	.000
Lasher, p	1	0	0	0	0	0	0	0	.000
Sparma, p	1	0	0	0	0	0	0	0	.000
Totals	7	231	34	56	4	3	8	33	.242

St. Louis Cardinals

Player-Position	G.	AB.	R.	H.	2B.	3B.	HR.	RBI.	BA.
Ricketts, ph	1	1	0	1	0	0	0	0	1.000
Spiezio, ph	1	1	0	1	0	0	0	0	1.000
Hoerner, p	3	2	0	1	0	0	0	0	.500
Brock, lf	7	28	6	13	3	1	2	5	.464
McCarver, c	7	27	3	9	0	2	1	4	.333
Javier, 2b	7	27	1	9	1	0	0	3	.333
Flood, cf	7	28	4	8	1	0	0	2	.286
Shannon, 3b	7	29	3	8	1	0	1	4	.276
Cepeda, 1b	7	28	2	7	0	0	2	6	.250
Maris, rf-ph	6	19	5	3	1	0	0	1	.158
Gibson, p	3	8	2	1	0	0	1	2	.125
Edwards, ph	1	1	0	0	0	0	0	0	.000
Tolan, ph	1	1	0	0	0	0	0	0	.000
Gagliano, ph	3	3	0	0	0	0	0	0	.000
Washburn, p	2	3	0	0	0	0	0	0	.000
Briles, p	2	4	0	0	0	0	0	0	.000
Davis, rf	2	7	0	0	0	0	0	0	.000
Maxvill, ss	7	22	1	0	0	0	0	0	.000
Willis, p	3	0	0	0	0	0	0	0	.000
Carlton, p	2	0	0	0	0	0	0	0	.000
Schofield, pr-ss	2	0	0	0	0	0	0	0	.000
Granger, p	1	0	0	0	0	0	0	0	.000
Hughes, p	1	0	0	0	0	0	0	0	.000
Jaster, p	1	0	0	0	0	0	0	0	.000
Nelson, p	1	0	0	0	0	0	0	0	.000
Totals	7	239	27	61	7	3	7	27	.255

COMPOSITE PITCHING AVERAGES

Detroit Tigers

Pitcher	G.	IP.	H.	R.	ER.	BB.	SO.	W.	L.	ERA.
Patterson	2	3	1	0	0	1	0	0	0	0.00
Lasher	1	2	1	0	0	0	1	0	0	0.00
Lolich	3	27	20	5	5	6	21	3	0	1.67
McLain	3	16⅔	18	8	6	4	13	1	2	3.24
Dobson	3	4⅔	5	2	2	1	0	0	0	3.86
Wilson	1	4⅓	4	3	3	6	3	0	1	6.23
Hiller	2	2	6	4	3	3	1	0	0	13.50
McMahon	2	2	4	3	3	0	1	0	0	13.50
Sparma	1	⅓	2	2	1	0	0	0	0	27.00
Totals	7	62	61	27	23	21	40	4	3	3.34

St. Louis Cardinals

Pitcher	G.	IP.	H.	R.	ER.	BB.	SO.	W.	L.	ERA.
Granger	1	2	0	0	0	1	1	0	0	0.00
Nelson	1	1	0	0	0	0	1	0	0	0.00
Hughes	1	⅓	2	0	0	0	0	0	0	0.00
Gibson	3	27	18	5	5	4	35	2	1	1.67
Hoerner	3	4⅔	5	4	2	5	3	0	1	3.86
Briles	2	11⅓	13	7	7	4	7	0	1	5.56
Carlton	2	4	7	3	3	1	3	0	0	6.75
Willis	3	4⅓	2	4	4	4	3	0	0	8.31
Washburn	2	7⅓	7	8	8	7	6	1	1	9.82
Jaster	1	0*	2	3	3	1	0	0	0	......
Totals	7	62	56	34	32	27	59	3	4	4.65

*Pitched to three batters in third inning of sixth game.

The Baltimore Orioles were loaded. In the first season of major league baseball's four-division alignment, the Orioles had swept to 109 victories and a 19-game bulge in the American League East race and then disposed of the West Division champion Minnesota Twins in three games in the best-of-five A.L. Championship Series.

The New York Mets were, well, hard to figure. They had won 100 games while capturing the National League East crown by eight games over the fast-unraveling Chicago Cubs and then beat the Atlanta Braves in three straight N.L. Championship Series contests. But the Mets had made such an amazing turnaround—before '69 they had finished no higher than ninth place since entering the N.L. as an expansion team in 1962—that it was hard to get a good read on the club's talent. Were the Mets merely coming of age? Playing over their heads? While the New Yorkers had some skilled young pitchers in Tom Seaver, Jerry Koosman, Gary Gentry and Tug McGraw, they fielded a lineup that hardly struck fear into the hearts of the enemy.

So, when Don Buford of the talented and deep Baltimore club slammed Seaver's second pitch of Game 1 of the 1969 World Series over the fence, and Baltimore tacked on three more runs in the fourth inning, you could hear mutterings of "I told you so" at Baltimore's Memorial Stadium.

By afternoon's end, lefthander Mike Cuellar had yielded only six hits and struck out eight. Baltimore was an easy 4-1 winner in a game in which its four big boppers—Boog Powell (37 home runs, 121 runs batted in during the regular season), Frank Robinson (32 homers, 100 RBIs),

Brooks Robinson (23 homers, 84 RBIs) and Paul Blair (26 homers, 76 RBIs)—managed one single in 15 at-bats.

Koosman kept Baltimore's big guns quiet again in Game 2. In fact, the 26-year-old lefthander kept the entire Oriole lineup still through six innings. While he was pitching no-hit baseball, Donn Clendenon had lifted the Mets into a 1-0 lead with a fourth-inning home run off Dave McNally.

The Orioles tied the score in the seventh when Blair led off with Baltimore's first hit, stole second and scored on Brooks Robinson's two-out single. New York put together just enough offense in the ninth, though, to beat McNally as Ed Charles, Jerry Grote and Al Weis came through with two-out singles. Koosman then got last-out relief help from Ron Taylor and was a 2-1 victor. Baltimore's Powell, the Robinson duo and Blair went 2 for 14 against Mets pitching in this one.

Game 3 at the Mets' Shea Stadium featured another bad day at the office (3 for 15) for Baltimore's fearsome foursome. More than that, it featured one of the greatest individual performances in the 66-year history of the World Series, courtesy of the Mets' Tommie Agee. Center fielder Agee gave his club all the run production it would need with a first-inning homer off Jim Palmer. Then with two out and Oriole runners on first and third in the fourth, Agee raced to the 396-foot sign in left-center and made a backhanded, fingertip catch of Elrod Hendricks' smash. In the seventh, with the bases loaded and two out, Agee made a headlong, diving grab of Blair's liner that appeared headed up the alley in right-center. The Mets, also getting a home run from Ed Krane-

pool, came out on top, 5-0, as Gentry and reliever Nolan Ryan combined on a four-hitter.

Seaver, a 25-game winner for the Mets in '69 (his third big-league season), took a 1-0 edge into the ninth inning of Game 4, thanks to Clendenon's homer in the second. But with one out in the ninth, Frank Robinson and Powell rapped singles and Brooks Robinson followed with a line drive to right-center. Mets right fielder Ron Swoboda, not known for his defensive prowess, made a diving, one-handed catch of the liner. While Frank Robinson tagged up and scored from third, Swoboda had short-circuited a potential big inning.

The game remained 1-1 until the last of the 10th when the Mets pushed across the winning run on Grote's double and Oriole reliever Pete Richert's errant throw on pinch-hitter J.C. Martin's bunt. Richert's peg struck Martin on the wrist, with the ball rolling toward the outfield and Rod Gaspar—pinch-running for Grote—rolling toward home. Gaspar scored and the Mets won, 2-1.

Manager Earl Weaver's stunned Orioles, now down three games to one, seemed headed for a recovery of sorts in Game 5 as pitcher McNally, thanks to his own two-run homer and a solo shot by Frank Robinson, held a 3-0 lead after five innings. But the resilient Mets struck again. Cleon Jones led off the New York sixth and was struck on the foot by a McNally pitch. Clendenon—the Mets' valuable June acquisition from the Montreal Expos—followed with a home run.

Weis, who would see duty in 10 seasons in the big leagues and hit only seven home runs, then tied the contest with a leadoff homer in the seventh against McNally.

And, with Eddie Watt working in relief for Baltimore in the eighth, Jones and Swoboda hit doubles that sent New York ahead, 4-3, and another Mets run scored on an error.

Besides yielding a single and Baltimore's two homers in the third, Koosman permitted the Orioles only two other hits. And those big-four Oriole hitters, who had gone 3 for 15 in Game 4, were 2 for 15 against Koosman in what proved to be the Series finale.

Game 1

Saturday, October 11, At Baltimore

New York	AB.	R.	H.	RBI.	PO.	A.
Agee, cf	4	0	0	0	4	0
Harrelson, ss	3	0	1	0	0	1
Jones, lf	4	0	1	0	1	0
Clendenon, 1b	4	1	2	0	9	1
Swoboda, rf	3	0	1	0	0	0
Charles, 3b	4	0	0	0	1	4
Grote, c	4	0	1	0	6	0
Weis, 2b	1	0	0	1	3	1
Seaver, p	1	0	0	0	0	0
aDyer	1	0	0	0	0	0
Cardwell, p	0	0	0	0	0	0
bGaspar	1	0	0	0	0	0
Taylor, p	0	0	0	0	0	1
cShamsky	1	0	0	0	0	0
Totals	31	1	6	1	24	8

Baltimore	AB.	R.	H.	RBI.	PO.	A.
Buford, lf	4	1	2	2	2	0
Blair, cf	3	0	0	0	2	0
F. Robinson, rf	4	0	0	0	2	0
Powell, 1b	4	0	1	0	11	0
B. Robinson, 3b	4	0	0	0	0	6
Hendricks, c	3	1	1	0	8	0
Johnson, 2b	2	1	0	0	1	3
Belanger, ss	3	1	1	1	1	3
Cuellar, p	3	0	1	1	0	0
Totals	30	4	6	4	27	12

New York	0 0 0 0 0 0 1 0 0—1
Baltimore	1 0 0 3 0 0 0 0 x—4

New York	IP.	H.	R.	ER.	BB.	SO.
Seaver (L)	5	6	4	4	1	3
Cardwell	1	0	0	0	0	0
Taylor	2	0	0	0	1	3

Baltimore	IP.	H.	R.	ER.	BB.	SO.
Cuellar (W)	9	6	1	1	4	8

aGrounded out for Seaver in sixth. bGrounded out for Cardwell in seventh. cGrounded out for Taylor in ninth. E—Weis. DP—Baltimore 1. LOB—New York 8, Baltimore 4. 2B—Clendenon, Buford. HR—Buford. SF—Weis. U—Soar (A.L.), Secory (N.L.), Napp (A.L.), Crawford (N.L.), DiMuro (A.L.) and Weyer (N.L.). T—2:13. A—50,429.

Game 2

Sunday, October 12, At Baltimore

New York	AB.	R.	H.	RBI.	PO.	A.
Agee, cf	4	0	0	0	3	0
Harrelson, ss	3	0	0	0	3	3
Jones, lf	4	0	0	0	2	0
Clendenon, 1b	3	1	1	1	7	0
Swoboda, rf	4	0	0	0	5	0
Charles, 3b	4	1	2	0	0	3
Grote, c	4	0	1	0	4	0
Weis, 2b	3	0	2	1	3	1
Koosman, p	4	0	0	0	0	1
Taylor, p	0	0	0	0	0	0
Totals	33	2	6	2	27	8

Baltimore	AB.	R.	H.	RBI.	PO.	A.
Buford, lf	4	0	0	0	1	0
Blair, cf	4	1	1	0	2	0
F. Robinson, rf	3	0	0	0	2	0
aRettenmund	0	0	0	0	0	0
Powell, 1b	3	0	0	0	10	1
B. Robinson, 3b	4	0	1	1	0	2
Johnson, 2b	2	0	0	0	1	3
Etchebarren, c	3	0	0	0	8	0
Belanger, ss	3	0	0	0	2	4
McNally, p	3	0	0	0	1	1
Totals	29	1	2	1	27	11

New York	0 0 0 1 0 0 0 0 1—2
Baltimore	0 0 0 0 0 0 1 0 0—1

New York	IP.	H.	R.	ER.	BB.	SO.
Koosman (W)	8⅔	2	1	1	3	4
Taylor (S)	⅓	0	0	0	0	0

Baltimore	IP.	H.	R.	ER.	BB.	SO.
McNally (L)	9	6	2	2	3	7

aRan for F. Robinson in ninth. LOB—New York 7, Baltimore 4. 2B—Charles. HR—Clendenon. SB—Blair. WP—McNally. U—Secory (N.L.), Napp (A.L.), Crawford (N.L.), DiMuro (A.L.), Weyer (N.L.) and Soar (A.L.). T—2:20. A—50,850.

Game 3

Tuesday, October 14, At New York

Baltimore	AB.	R.	H.	RBI.	PO.	A.
Buford, lf	3	0	0	0	2	0
Blair, cf	5	0	0	0	0	0
F. Robinson, rf	2	0	1	0	7	0
Powell, 1b	4	0	2	0	5	1
B. Robinson, 3b	4	0	0	0	0	1
Hendricks, c	4	0	0	0	6	0
Johnson, 2b	4	0	0	0	1	3
Belanger, ss	2	0	0	0	2	0
Palmer, p	2	0	0	0	1	0
aMay	0	0	0	0	0	0
Leonhard, p	0	0	0	0	0	1
bDalrymple	1	0	1	0	0	0
cSalmon	0	0	0	0	0	0
Totals	31	0	4	0	24	6

New York	AB.	R.	H.	RBI.	PO.	A.
Agee, cf	3	1	1	1	6	0
Garrett, 3b	1	0	0	0	1	0
Jones, lf	4	0	0	0	0	0
Shamsky, rf	4	0	0	0	1	0
Weis, 2b	0	0	0	0	0	0
Boswell, 2b	3	1	1	0	0	1
Gaspar, rf	1	0	0	0	2	0
Kranepool, 1b	4	1	1	1	7	0
Grote, c	3	1	1	1	7	0
Harrelson, ss	3	1	1	0	3	5
Gentry, p	3	0	1	2	0	0
Ryan, p	0	0	0	0	0	0
Totals	29	5	6	5	27	6

Baltimore	0 0 0 0 0 0 0 0 0—0
New York	1 2 0 0 0 1 0 1 x—5

Baltimore	IP.	H.	R.	ER.	BB.	SO.
Palmer (L)	6	5	4	4	4	5
Leonhard	2	1	1	1	1	1

New York	IP.	H.	R.	ER.	BB.	SO.
Gentry (W)	6⅔	3	0	0	5	4
Ryan (S)	2⅓	1	0	0	2	3

aWalked for Palmer in seventh. bSingled for Leonhard in ninth. cRan for Dalrymple in ninth. E—Palmer. LOB—Baltimore 11, New York 6. 2B—Gentry, Grote. HR—Agee, Kranepool. SH—Garrett. U—Napp (A.L.), Crawford (N.L.), DiMuro (A.L.), Weyer (N.L.), Soar (A.L.) and Secory (N.L.). T—2:23. A—56,335.

Game 4

Wednesday, October 15, At New York

Baltimore	AB.	R.	H.	RBI.	PO.	A.
Buford, lf	5	0	0	0	2	0
Blair, cf	4	0	1	0	0	0
F. Robinson, rf	4	1	1	0	0	0
Powell, 1b	4	0	1	0	14	0
B. Robinson, 3b	3	0	0	1	0	3
Hendricks, c	3	0	0	0	7	1
Johnson, 2b	4	0	0	0	4	6
Belanger, ss	4	0	1	0	0	6
Cuellar, p	2	0	1	0	0	1
aMay	1	0	0	0	0	0
Watt, p	0	0	0	0	0	0
cDalrymple	1	0	1	0	0	0
Hall, p	0	0	0	0	0	0
Richert, p	0	0	0	0	0	0
Totals	35	1	6	1	27	17

New York	AB.	R.	H.	RBI.	PO.	A.
Agee, cf	4	0	1	0	2	0
Harrelson, ss	4	0	1	0	5	2
Jones, lf	4	0	1	0	1	0
Clendenon, 1b	4	1	1	1	6	3
Swoboda, rf	4	0	3	0	4	0
Charles, 3b	3	0	0	0	2	1
bShamsky	1	0	0	0	0	0
Garrett, 3b	0	0	0	0	0	0
Grote, c	4	0	1	0	7	2
dGaspar	0	1	0	0	0	0
Weis, 2b	3	0	2	0	1	1
Seaver, p	3	0	0	0	2	1
eMartin	0	0	0	0	0	0
Totals	34	2	10	1	30	10

Baltimore	0 0 0 0 0 0 0 0 1 0—1
New York	0 1 0 0 0 0 0 0 0 1—2

None out when winning run scored.

Baltimore	IP.	H.	R.	ER.	BB.	SO.
Cuellar	7	7	1	1	0	5
Watt	2	2	0	0	0	2
Hall (L)	0*	1	1	0	1	0
Richert	0†	0	0	0	0	0

New York	IP.	H.	R.	ER.	BB.	SO.
Seaver (W)	10	6	1	1	2	6

*Pitched to two batters in tenth.
†Pitched to one batter in tenth.

aStruck out for Cuellar in eighth. bGrounded out for Charles in ninth. cSingled for Watt in tenth. dRan for Grote in tenth. eSacrificed and was safe on error for Seaver in tenth. E—Richert, Garrett. DP—Baltimore 3. LOB—Baltimore 7, New York 7. 2B—Grote. HR—Clendenon. SH—Martin. SF—B. Robinson. U—Crawford (N.L.), DiMuro (A.L.), Weyer (N.L.), Soar (A.L.), Secory (N.L.) and Napp (A.L.). T—2:33. A—57,367.

Game 5

Thursday, October 16, At New York

Baltimore	AB.	R.	H.	RBI.	PO.	A.
Buford, lf	4	0	0	0	1	0
Blair, cf	4	0	0	0	3	0
F. Robinson, rf	3	1	1	1	2	0
Powell, 1b	4	0	1	0	6	0
bSalmon	0	0	0	0	0	0
B. Robinson, 3b	4	0	0	0	1	4
Johnson, 2b	4	0	1	0	1	0
Etchebarren, c	3	0	0	0	8	0
Belanger, ss	3	1	1	0	2	1
McNally, p	2	1	1	2	0	0
aMotton	1	0	0	0	0	0
Watt, p	0	0	0	0	0	0
Totals	32	3	5	3	24	5

New York	AB.	R.	H.	RBI.	PO.	A.
Agee, cf	3	0	1	0	4	0
Harrelson, ss	4	0	0	0	1	6
Jones, lf	3	2	1	0	3	0
Clendenon, 1b	3	1	1	2	8	0
Swoboda, rf	4	1	2	1	5	0
Charles, 3b	4	0	0	0	0	1
Grote, c	4	0	0	0	5	0
Weis, 2b	4	1	1	1	1	2
Koosman, p	3	0	1	0	0	1
Totals	32	5	7	4	27	10

Baltimore	0 0 3 0 0 0 0 0 0—3
New York	0 0 0 0 0 2 1 2 x—5

Baltimore	IP.	H.	R.	ER.	BB.	SO.
McNally	7	5	3	3	2	6
Watt (L)	1	2	2	1	0	1

New York	IP.	H.	R.	ER.	BB.	SO.
Koosman (W)	9	5	3	3	1	5

aGrounded out for McNally in eighth. bRan for Powell in ninth. E—Powell, Watt. LOB—Baltimore 3, New York 6. 2B—Koosman, Jones, Swoboda. HR—McNally, F. Robinson, Clendenon, Weis. SB—Agee. HBP—By McNally (Jones). U—DiMuro (A.L.), Weyer (N.L.), Soar (A.L.), Secory (N.L.), Napp (A.L.) and Crawford (N.L.). T—2:14. A—57,397.

COMPOSITE BATTING AVERAGES

New York Mets

Player-Position	G.	AB.	R.	H.	2B.	3B.	HR.	RBI.	BA.
Weis, 2b	5	11	1	5	0	0	1	3	.455
Swoboda, rf	4	15	1	6	1	0	0	1	.400
Clendenon, 1b	4	14	4	5	1	0	3	4	.357
Boswell, 2b	1	3	1	1	0	0	0	0	.333
Gentry, p	1	3	0	1	1	0	0	2	.333
Kranepool, 1b	1	4	1	1	0	0	1	1	.250
Grote, c	5	19	1	4	2	0	0	1	.211
Harrelson, ss	5	17	1	3	0	0	0	0	.176
Agee, cf	5	18	1	3	0	0	1	1	.167
Jones, lf	5	19	2	3	1	0	0	0	.158
Koosman, p	2	7	0	1	1	0	0	0	.143
Charles, 3b	4	15	1	2	1	0	0	0	.133
Shamsky, ph-rf	3	6	0	0	0	0	0	0	.000
Seaver, p	2	4	0	0	0	0	0	0	.000
Gaspar, ph-rf-pr	3	2	1	0	0	0	0	0	.000
Garrett, 3b	2	1	0	0	0	0	0	0	.000
Dyer, ph	1	1	0	0	0	0	0	0	.000
Taylor, p	2	0	0	0	0	0	0	0	.000
Cardwell, p	1	0	0	0	0	0	0	0	.000
Martin, ph	1	0	0	0	0	0	0	0	.000
Ryan, p	1	0	0	0	0	0	0	0	.000
Totals	5	159	15	35	8	0	6	13	.220

Baltimore Orioles

Player-Position	G.	AB.	R.	H.	2B.	3B.	HR.	RBI.	BA.
Dalrymple, ph	2	2	0	2	0	0	0	0	1.000
Cuellar, p	2	5	0	2	0	0	0	1	.400
Powell, 1b	5	19	0	5	0	0	0	0	.263
Belanger, ss	5	15	2	3	0	0	0	1	.200
McNally, p	2	5	1	1	0	0	1	2	.200
F. Robinson, rf	5	16	2	3	0	0	1	1	.188
Blair, cf	5	20	1	2	0	0	0	0	.100
Buford, lf	5	20	1	2	1	0	1	2	.100
Hendricks, c	3	10	1	1	0	0	0	0	.100
Johnson, 2b	5	16	1	1	0	0	0	0	.063
B. Robinson, 3b	5	19	0	1	0	0	0	2	.053
Etchebarren, c	2	6	0	0	0	0	0	0	.000
Palmer, p	1	2	0	0	0	0	0	0	.000
May, ph	2	1	0	0	0	0	0	0	.000
Motton, ph	1	1	0	0	0	0	0	0	.000
Salmon, pr	2	0	0	0	0	0	0	0	.000
Watt, p	2	0	0	0	0	0	0	0	.000
Hall, p	1	0	0	0	0	0	0	0	.000
Leonhard, p	1	0	0	0	0	0	0	0	.000
Rettenmund, pr	1	0	0	0	0	0	0	0	.000
Richert, p	1	0	0	0	0	0	0	0	.000
Totals	5	157	9	23	1	0	3	9	.146

COMPOSITE PITCHING AVERAGES

New York Mets

Pitcher	G.	IP.	H.	R.	ER.	BB.	SO.	W.	L.	ERA.
Gentry	1	6⅔	3	0	0	5	4	1	0	0.00
Taylor	2	2⅓	0	0	0	1	3	0	0	0.00
Ryan	1	2⅓	1	0	0	2	3	0	0	0.00
Cardwell	1	1	0	0	0	0	0	0	0	0.00
Koosman	2	17⅔	7	4	4	4	9	2	0	2.04
Seaver	2	15	12	5	5	3	9	1	1	3.00
Totals	5	45	23	9	9	15	28	4	1	1.80

Baltimore Orioles

Pitcher	G.	IP.	H.	R.	ER.	BB.	SO.	W.	L.	ERA.
Cuellar	2	16	13	2	2	4	13	1	0	1.13
McNally	2	16	11	5	5	5	13	0	1	2.81
Watt	2	3	4	2	1	0	3	0	1	3.00
Leonhard	1	2	1	1	1	1	1	0	0	4.50
Palmer	1	6	5	4	4	4	5	0	1	6.00
Hall	1	0*	1	1	0	1	0	0	1	0.00
Richert	1	0†	0	0	0	0	0	0	0	0.00
Totals	5	43	35	15	13	15	35	1	4	2.72

*Pitched to two batters in tenth inning of fourth game.
†Pitched to one batter in tenth inning of fourth game.

1970
BALTIMORE ORIOLES
VS.
CINCINNATI REDS

The Baltimore Orioles weren't quite the club in 1970 that they were in 1969. After winning 109 games in '69, Manager Earl Weaver's Orioles slumped off to a 108-victory season in '70.

That the Baltimore club was a particularly gifted unit went without saying. And that these Orioles were intent on avenging their World Series setback of a year earlier also didn't need articulating. They whetted their appetite by sweeping Minnesota in the A.L. Championship Series.

Avenge, the Orioles did. Only it wasn't against their 1969 conquerors, the New York Mets, but instead against the Cincinnati Reds. Playing under rookie Manager Sparky Anderson, the Reds ran away with the N.L. West championship and swept Pittsburgh in the Championship Series.

In the first World Series game ever contested at Riverfront Stadium, which supplanted Crosley Field as the Reds' home in late June of the just-completed season, Cincinnati jumped to a 3-0 lead—Lee May's two-run home run was the big blow—before the Orioles rebounded for a 4-3 triumph on homers by Boog Powell (a two-run shot), Elrod Hendricks and Brooks Robinson. Baltimore was helped along by a controversial sixth-inning call at the plate by umpire Ken Burkhart.

With one out and Bernie Carbo on third base and Tommy Helms stationed at first, Reds pinch-hitter Ty Cline bounced a high chopper in front of the plate. Burkhart straddled the third-base line and signaled a fair ball. Catcher Hendricks fielded the ball and, after apparently planning to throw to first base, whirled around at pitcher Jim Palmer's urging and attempted to tag out Carbo, who was trying to score. Hendricks

plowed into Burkhart and lunged for Carbo, and the umpire signaled "out" from the tangle of bodies. Replays showed that Hendricks, holding the ball in his right hand, tagged Carbo with his empty glove.

The Reds' sixth-inning at-bat also was notable in that it marked the beginning of the Brooks Robinson Show afield. Always known as a fielding wizard, third baseman Brooks outdid himself in the 1970 Series—the first fall classic to be played on artificial surface—and the eye-popping exhibition began when May led off the sixth by smoking the ball between Robinson and the bag. Robinson took a few quick steps, backhanded the ball when it was past him and, while moving toward foul territory, turned and threw out May.

Cincinnati seized a 3-0 lead again the next day, but Powell hit a fourth-inning homer and Hendricks then capped a five-run Baltimore fifth with a two-run double. Baltimore won, 6-5.

Anderson's Reds seemed poised to grab yet another quick advantage in Game 3—but Brooks Robinson would have none of it. After Pete Rose and Bobby Tolan began the game at Baltimore's Memorial Stadium with consecutive hits, Robinson made a sensational, leaping grab of Tony Perez's hopper, stepped on third and fired to first for a double play. Orioles lefthander Dave McNally ended the inning by retiring Johnny Bench on a liner.

Robinson then jolted the Reds with his bat, staking McNally to a 2-0 lead with a first-inning double that scored Don Buford and Frank Robinson. In the second inning, Brooks raced in for Helms' slow roller and threw out the Reds' second baseman. And in the sixth, he made a diving stab of

Bench's liner.

McNally, like Mike Cuellar a 24-game winner for the '70 Orioles, obviously was grateful for Brooks' handy work. But McNally left little to chance, hammering a bases-loaded homer in the sixth off Wayne Granger and thereby equaling Bob Gibson's career mark of two Series homers by a pitcher. Buford and Frank Robinson also homered, giving the Orioles a 9-3 triumph.

No doubt hurting with 14-3 pitcher Wayne Simpson unavailable for Series duty because of a shoulder injury and 20-game winner Jim Merritt yet to appear because of a tender elbow, Cincinnati trotted out first-game starter Gary Nolan again in Game 4. And while Nolan, 18-7 for the Reds in '70, couldn't rescue his club (he lasted only 2⅔ innings), May did. With the N.L. champions trailing 5-3 in the eighth, May blasted a three-run homer and the Reds held on for a 6-5 victory.

The ailing Merritt gave it a try in Game 5, but couldn't make it through the second inning. Orioles starter Cuellar had problems initially, too, as Cincinnati—up to its old quick-strike tricks—cuffed him for three runs and four hits in the top of the first. But Cuellar pitched shutout ball the rest of the way, allowing only two additional hits, and Baltimore romped to a Series-clinching 9-3 decision.

Game 1

Saturday, October 10, At Cincinnati

Baltimore	AB.	R.	H.	RBI.	PO.	A.
Buford, lf	4	0	1	0	1	0
Blair, cf	4	1	1	0	7	0
Powell, 1b	3	1	1	2	6	0
F. Robinson, rf	4	0	0	0	2	0
B. Robinson, 3b	4	1	1	1	3	3
Hendricks, c	4	1	1	1	4	1
Johnson, 2b	3	0	1	0	2	0
Belanger, ss	3	0	1	0	2	3
Palmer, p	4	0	0	0	0	0
Richert, p	0	0	0	0	0	0
Totals	33	4	7	4	27	7

Cincinnati	AB.	R.	H.	RBI.	PO.	A.
xRose, rf	3	0	0	0	3	0
Tolan, cf	4	2	1	0	0	0
Perez, 3b	3	0	0	0	0	3
Bench, c	4	0	1	1	12	0

	AB.	R.	H.	RBI.	PO.	A.
May, 1b	4	1	2	2	7	1
Carbo, lf	2	0	0	0	2	0
Helms, 2b	4	0	1	0	1	1
Woodward, ss	2	0	0	0	2	1
aCline	1	0	0	0	0	0
Chaney, ss	0	0	0	0	0	0
bStewart	1	0	0	0	0	0
Nolan, p	2	0	0	0	0	0
Carroll, p	0	0	0	0	0	0
cBravo	1	0	0	0	0	0
Totals	31	3	5	3	27	6

Baltimore	0 0 0 2 1 0 1 0 0—4
Cincinnati	1 0 2 0 0 0 0 0 0—3

Baltimore	IP.	H.	R.	ER.	BB.	SO.
Palmer (W)	8⅔	5	3	3	5	2
Richert (S)	⅓	0	0	0	0	0

Cincinnati	IP.	H.	R.	ER.	BB.	SO.
Nolan (L)	6⅔	5	4	4	1	7
Carroll	2⅓	2	0	0	2	4

xAwarded first base on catcher's interference. aGrounded into fielder's choice for Woodward in sixth. bStruck out for Chaney in ninth. cStruck out for Carroll in ninth. E—B. Robinson, Hendricks. DP—Cincinnati 1. LOB—Baltimore 5, Cincinnati 8. 2B—Tolan, Johnson. HR—May, Powell, Hendricks, B. Robinson. SB—Tolan. SH—Nolan. WP—Palmer. U—Burkhart (N.L.), Flaherty (A.L.), Venzon (N.L.), Stewart (A.L.), Williams (N.L.) and Ashford (A.L.). T—2:24. A—51,531.

Game 2

Sunday, October 11, At Cincinnati

Baltimore	AB.	R.	H.	RBI.	PO.	A.
Buford, lf	4	1	2	0	1	1
Blair, cf	5	1	2	1	6	0
Powell, 1b	3	2	2	2	9	2
F. Robinson, rf	5	0	0	0	1	0
B. Robinson, 3b	4	1	1	1	1	6
Hendricks, c	3	0	1	2	3	0
Johnson, 2b	3	0	1	0	5	3
Belanger, ss	4	0	0	0	0	3
Cuellar, p	1	0	0	0	0	0
Phoebus, p	0	0	0	0	0	0
aSalmon	1	1	1	0	0	0
Drabowsky, p	1	0	0	0	1	0
Lopez, p	0	0	0	0	0	0
Hall, p	1	0	0	0	0	0
Totals	35	6	10	6	27	15

Cincinnati	AB.	R.	H.	RBI.	PO.	A.
Rose, rf	3	0	0	0	3	0
Tolan, cf	4	2	1	1	0	0
Perez, 3b	4	1	1	0	0	3
Bench, c	3	1	1	1	5	0
May, 1b	4	1	1	2	13	1
McRae, lf	4	0	2	1	0	0
Helms, 2b	4	0	0	0	4	4
Woodward, ss	2	0	0	0	2	4
bCline	1	0	1	0	0	0
Chaney, ss	0	0	0	0	0	1
dCarbo	1	0	0	0	0	0
McGlothlin, p	2	0	0	0	0	0
Wilcox, p	0	0	0	0	0	0
Carroll, p	0	0	0	0	0	0
cBravo	0	0	0	0	0	0
Gullett, p	0	0	0	0	0	0
eStewart	1	0	0	0	0	0
Totals	33	5	7	5	27	13

Baltimore	0 0 0 1 5 0 0 0 0—6
Cincinnati	3 0 1 0 0 1 0 0 0—5

Baltimore	IP.	H.	R.	ER.	BB.	SO.
Cuellar	2⅓	4	4	1	1	1
Phoebus (W)	1⅔	1	0	0	0	0
Drabowsky	2⅓	2	1	1	1	1
Lopez	⅓	0	0	0	0	0
Hall (S)	2⅓	0	0	0	0	0

Cincinnati	IP.	H.	R.	ER.	BB.	SO.
McGlothlin	4⅓	6	4	4	2	2
Wilcox (L)	⅓	3	2	2	0	0
Carroll	2⅓	1	0	0	0	1
Gullett	2	0	0	0	3	2

aSingled for Phoebus in fifth. bSingled for Woodward in seventh. cSacrificed for Carroll in seventh. dGrounded out for Chaney in ninth. eFlied out for Gullett in ninth. E—Blair, Belanger. DP—Baltimore 1, Cincinnati 2. LOB—Baltimore 7, Cincinnati 4. 2B—May, McRae, Hendricks. HR—Tolan, Powell, Bench. SH—Bravo. U—Flaherty (A.L.), Venzon (N.L.), Stewart (A.L.), Williams (N.L.), Ashford (A.L.) and Burkhart (N.L.). T—2:26. A—51,531.

Game 3

Tuesday, October 13, At Baltimore

Cincinnati	AB.	R.	H.	RBI.	PO.	A.
Rose, rf	5	0	2	1	4	0
Tolan, cf	4	0	1	0	2	0
Perez, 3b	3	0	0	0	0	2
Bench, c	4	0	0	0	5	2
May, 1b	3	1	1	0	9	0
McRae, lf	4	1	2	0	1	1
Helms, 2b	4	1	1	0	3	1
Concepcion, ss	3	0	1	2	0	2
Cloninger, p	2	0	0	0	0	0
Granger, p	0	0	0	0	0	1
aWoodward	1	0	1	0	0	0
Gullett, p	0	0	0	0	0	0
bCline	1	0	0	0	0	0
Totals	34	3	9	3	24	9

Baltimore	AB.	R.	H.	RBI.	PO.	A.
Buford, lf	3	2	1	1	3	0
Belanger, ss	4	0	0	0	2	3
Powell, 1b	3	1	0	0	8	0
F. Robinson, rf	4	2	3	1	2	0
Blair, cf	3	1	3	1	0	0
B. Robinson, 3b	4	1	2	2	3	3
Johnson, 2b	2	1	0	0	4	2
Etchebarren, c	4	0	0	0	5	0
McNally, p	4	1	1	4	0	1
Totals	31	9	10	9	27	9

Cincinnati	0 1 0 0 0 0 2 0 0—3
Baltimore	2 0 1 0 1 4 1 0 x—9

Cincinnati	IP.	H.	R.	ER.	BB.	SO.
Cloninger (L)	5⅓	6	5	5	3	3
Granger	⅔	2	3	3	1	1
Gullett	2	2	1	1	1	0

Baltimore	IP.	H.	R.	ER.	BB.	SO.
McNally (W)	9	9	3	3	2	5

aSingled for Granger in seventh. bGrounded into force play for Gullett in ninth. E—Etchebarren. DP—Cincinnati 1, Baltimore 1. LOB—Cincinnati 7, Baltimore 3. 2B—B. Robinson 2, Blair. HR—F. Robinson, Buford, McNally. SF—Concepcion. U—Venzon (N.L.), Stewart (A.L.), Wiliams (N.L.), Ashford (A.L.), Burkhart (N.L.) and Flaherty (A.L.). T—2:09. A—51,773.

Game 4

Wednesday, October 14, At Baltimore

Cincinnati	AB.	R.	H.	RBI.	PO.	A.
Tolan, cf	3	1	1	0	1	0
Rose, rf	5	1	2	1	1	1
Perez, 3b	4	1	0	0	0	3
Bench, c	4	1	1	0	8	1
May, 1b	3	2	2	4	13	0
Carbo, lf	4	0	0	0	2	0
Helms, 2b	3	0	1	0	1	3
Concepcion, ss	3	0	1	1	0	0
Carroll, p	1	0	0	0	0	0
Nolan, p	1	0	0	0	0	1
Gullett, p	1	0	0	0	0	0
Woodward, ss	0	0	0	0	0	0
aBravo	1	0	0	0	0	0
Chaney, ss	1	0	0	0	1	1
Totals	34	6	8	6	27	10

Baltimore	AB.	R.	H.	RBI.	PO.	A.
Buford, lf	4	0	0	0	1	0
Blair, cf	3	0	0	0	3	0
Powell, 1b	3	1	0	0	6	0
F. Robinson, rf	4	1	1	2	1	0
B. Robinson, 3b	4	2	4	0	1	0
Hendricks, c	4	0	2	1	10	1
Johnson, 2b	4	0	0	0	2	3
Belanger, ss	3	0	0	0	3	1
bCrowley	1	0	0	0	0	0
Palmer, p	3	1	1	0	0	0
Watt, p	0	0	0	0	0	0
Drabowsky, p	0	0	0	0	0	0
cRettenmund	1	0	0	0	0	0
Totals	34	5	8	3	27	5

Cincinnati	0 1 1 0 1 0 0 3 0—6
Baltimore	0 1 3 0 0 1 0 0 0—5

Cincinnati	IP.	H.	R.	ER.	BB.	SO.
Nolan	2⅔	4	4	4	2	2
Gullett	2⅔	3	1	0	0	2
Carroll (W)	3⅔	1	0	0	0	4

Baltimore	IP.	H.	R.	ER.	BB.	SO.
Palmer	7*	6	5	5	4	7
Watt (L)	1†	2	1	1	1	3
Drabowsky	1	0	0	0	0	0

*Pitched to two batters in eighth.
†Pitched to one batter in ninth.

aPopped out for Woodward in seventh. bGrounded out for Belanger in ninth. cReached first on error for Drabowsky in ninth. E—Tolan, Rose, Perez. LOB—Cincinnati 6, Baltimore 5. 3B—Concepcion. HR—B. Robinson, Rose, May. SH—Blair. U—Stewart (A.L.), Williams (N.L.), Ashford (A.L.), Burkhart (N.L.), Flaherty (A.L.) and Venzon (N.L.). T—2:26. A—53,007.

Game 5

Thursday, October 15, At Baltimore

Cincinnati	AB.	R.	H.	RBI.	PO.	A.
Tolan, cf	4	0	0	0	1	0
Rose, rf	4	1	1	0	3	0
Perez, 3b	4	0	0	0	3	2
Bench, c	4	1	1	1	6	0
May, 1b	4	1	1	0	6	1
McRae, lf	3	0	1	2	1	0
cCorrales	1	0	0	0	0	0
Helms, 2b	3	0	1	0	1	4
Concepcion, ss	3	0	1	0	2	0
Merritt, p	1	0	0	0	0	0
Granger, p	0	0	0	0	0	0
Wilcox, p	0	0	0	0	0	1
aBravo	1	0	0	0	0	0
Cloninger, p	0	0	0	0	0	1
bCarbo	1	0	0	0	0	0
Washburn, p	0	0	0	0	1	3
Carroll, p	0	0	0	0	0	0
Totals	32	3	6	3	24	12

Baltimore	AB.	R.	H.	RBI.	PO.	A.
Belanger, ss	5	0	1	1	4	4
Blair, cf	4	2	3	1	2	0
F. Robinson, rf	5	2	2	2	1	0
Powell, 1b	5	1	2	1	9	0
Rettenmund, lf	4	2	2	2	3	0
B. Robinson, 3b	5	0	1	0	1	2
Johnson, 2b	4	1	3	2	2	1
Etchebarren, c	3	1	1	0	5	0
Cuellar, p	3	0	0	0	0	1
Totals	38	9	15	9	27	8

Cincinnati	3 0 0 0 0 0 0 0 0—3
Baltimore	2 2 2 0 1 0 0 2 x—9

Cincinnati	IP.	H.	R.	ER.	BB.	SO.
Merritt (L)	1⅔	3	4	4	1	0
Granger	⅔	5	2	2	0	0
Wilcox	1⅔	0	0	0	0	2
Cloninger	2	4	1	1	2	1
Washburn	1⅓	2	2	2	2	0
Carroll	⅔	1	0	0	0	2

Baltimore	IP.	H.	R.	ER.	BB.	SO.
Cuellar (W)	9	6	3	3	1	4

aWalked for Wilcox in fifth. bGrounded into double play for Cloninger in seventh. cGrounded out for McRae in ninth. DP—Baltimore 1. LOB—Cincinnati 3, Baltimore 11. 2B—Rose, May, McRae, Powell, Johnson. HR—F. Robinson, Rettenmund. SH—Cuellar. U—Williams (N.L.), Ashford (A.L.), Burkhart (N.L.), Flaherty (A.L.), Venzon (N.L.) and Stewart (A.L.). T—2:35. A—45,341.

COMPOSITE BATTING AVERAGES

Baltimore Orioles

Player-Position	G.	AB.	R.	H.	2B.	3B.	HR.	RBI.	BA.
Salmon, ph	1	1	1	1	0	0	0	0	1.000
Blair, cf	5	19	5	9	1	0	0	3	.474
B. Robinson, 3b	5	21	5	9	2	0	2	6	.429
R'tenmund, ph-lf	2	5	2	2	0	0	1	2	.400
Hendricks, c	3	11	1	4	1	0	1	4	.364
Johnson, 2b	5	16	2	5	2	0	0	2	.313
Powell, 1b	5	17	6	5	1	0	2	5	.294
F. Robinson, rf	5	22	5	6	0	0	2	4	.273
Buford, lf	4	15	3	4	0	0	1	1	.267
McNally, p	1	4	1	1	0	0	1	4	.250
Etchebarren, c	2	7	1	1	0	0	0	0	.143
Palmer, p	2	7	1	1	0	0	0	0	.143
Belanger, ss	5	19	0	2	0	0	0	1	.105
Drabowsky, p	2	1	0	0	0	0	0	0	.000
Crowley, ph	1	1	0	0	0	0	0	0	.000
Hall, p	1	1	0	0	0	0	0	0	.000
Cuellar, p	2	4	0	0	0	0	0	0	.000
Lopez, p	1	0	0	0	0	0	0	0	.000
Phoebus, p	1	0	0	0	0	0	0	0	.000
Richert, p	1	0	0	0	0	0	0	0	.000
Watt, p	1	0	0	0	0	0	0	0	.000
Totals	5	171	33	50	7	0	10	32	.292

Cincinnati Reds

Player-Position	G.	AB.	R.	H.	2B.	3B.	HR.	RBI.	BA.
McRae, lf	3	11	1	5	2	0	0	3	.455
May, 1b	5	18	6	7	2	0	2	8	.389
Concepcion, ss	3	9	0	3	0	1	0	3	.333
Cline, ph	3	3	0	1	0	0	0	0	.333
Rose, rf	5	20	2	5	1	0	1	2	.250
Helms, 2b	5	18	1	4	0	0	0	0	.222
Bench, c	5	19	3	4	0	0	1	3	.211
Tolan, cf	5	19	5	4	1	0	1	1	.211
Woodward, ss-ph	4	5	0	1	0	0	0	0	.200
Perez, 3b	5	18	2	1	0	0	0	0	.056
Carroll, p	4	1	0	0	0	0	0	0	.000
Chaney, ss	3	1	0	0	0	0	0	0	.000
Gullett, p	3	1	0	0	0	0	0	0	.000
Corrales, ph	1	1	0	0	0	0	0	0	.000
Merritt, p	1	1	0	0	0	0	0	0	.000
Bravo, ph	4	2	0	0	0	0	0	0	.000
Cloninger, p	2	2	0	0	0	0	0	0	.000
Stewart, ph	2	2	0	0	0	0	0	0	.000
McGlothlin, p	1	2	0	0	0	0	0	0	.000
Nolan, p	2	3	0	0	0	0	0	0	.000
Carbo, lf-ph	4	8	0	0	0	0	0	0	.000
Granger, p	2	0	0	0	0	0	0	0	.000
Wilcox, p	2	0	0	0	0	0	0	0	.000
Washburn, p	1	0	0	0	0	0	0	0	.000
Totals	5	164	20	35	6	1	5	20	.213

COMPOSITE PITCHING AVERAGES

Baltimore Orioles

Pitcher	G.	IP.	H.	R.	ER.	BB.	SO.	W.	L.	ERA.
Hall	1	2⅓	0	0	0	0	0	0	0	0.00
Phoebus	1	1⅔	1	0	0	0	0	1	0	0.00
Lopez	1	⅓	0	0	0	0	0	0	0	0.00
Richert	1	⅓	0	0	0	0	0	0	0	0.00
Drabowsky	2	3⅓	2	1	1	1	1	0	0	2.70
McNally	1	9	9	3	3	2	5	1	0	3.00
Cuellar	2	11⅓	10	7	4	2	5	1	0	3.18
Palmer	2	15⅔	11	8	8	9	9	1	0	4.60
Watt	1	1	2	1	1	1	3	0	1	9.00
Totals	5	45	35	20	17	15	23	4	1	3.40

Cincinnati Reds

Pitcher	G.	IP.	H.	R.	ER.	BB.	SO.	W.	L.	ERA.
Carroll	4	9	5	0	0	2	11	1	0	0.00
Gullett	3	6⅔	5	2	1	4	4	0	0	1.35
Cloninger	2	7⅓	10	6	6	5	4	0	1	7.36
Nolan	2	9⅓	9	8	8	3	9	0	1	7.71
McGlothlin	1	4⅓	6	4	4	2	2	0	0	8.31
Wilcox	2	2	3	2	2	0	2	0	1	9.00
Washburn	1	1⅓	2	2	2	2	0	0	0	13.50
Merritt	1	1⅔	3	4	4	1	0	0	1	21.60
Granger	2	1⅓	7	5	5	1	1	0	0	33.75
Totals	5	43	50	33	32	20	33	1	4	6.70

1971 PITTSBURGH PIRATES VS. BALTIMORE ORIOLES

Roberto Clemente had won four National League batting titles, captured one Most Valuable Player award, hit .323 in 14 All-Star Games, received 11 Gold Gloves and played for one World Series championship team.

But by the end of the 1971 regular season, the 37-year-old Pittsburgh outfielder somehow had failed to achieve the acclaim he thought he deserved. Forever feeling unappreciated, Clemente found it difficult—if not impossible—to escape the shadows of Willie Mays, Hank Aaron and other superstar contemporaries. To say Clemente never complained and simply went about his work would be a misrepresentation of the facts. He did speak out against what he perceived as unfair treatment from those who passed judgment on the relative skills of baseball's best players.

More than talk, though, Clemente went out and fiercely displayed his vast array of skills. Maybe someday his critics would wake up to the fact that he could run, hit, field and throw as well as anyone and better than most. And just maybe by the end of the 1971 World Series, Roberto Clemente would attain some measure of the respect he had been seeking.

Clemente and the Pirates had earned their way into the '71 Series by winning the N.L. East crown by seven games and then beating the San Francisco Giants, three games to one, in the Championship Series. Amazingly, the Baltimore Orioles had pulled off their third successive Championship Series sweep—this time the up-and-coming Oakland A's were the victims—after topping the 100-victory mark for the third straight year.

The '71 Orioles had become the

One of the spotlights for the 1971 Series belonged to Roberto Clemente, who responded with two homers and a .414 average.

second club in modern major league history (the 1920 Chicago White Sox were the other) to boast four 20-game winners, with Dave McNally, Jim Palmer, Mike Cuellar and Pat Dobson reaching the coveted figure. And Baltimore Manager Earl Weaver would start those four hurlers against Dock Ellis, Bob Johnson, Steve Blass and Luke Walker in the first four games of the Series. Ellis had been the Pirates' big winner with 19 victories and Blass won 15 times. Walker had won only 10 games, while Johnson compiled a losing record (9-10). Advantage, Baltimore. Clearly.

At least that's the way it looked on paper. But after four games, the 1971 Series was deadlocked.

In the Series opener at Baltimore, McNally was roughed up for three second-inning runs, but the lefthander settled down and didn't allow a hit after the third

inning. Baltimore, getting a three-run homer from Merv Rettenmund and solo blasts from Frank Robinson and Don Buford, posted a 5-3 victory. Clemente collected two of the three hits off McNally.

Palmer followed with an 11-3 triumph in Game 2, a contest in which Baltimore prospered from a popgun attack. The Orioles banged out 14 hits, all singles, with Frank Robinson and Brooks Robinson each notching three hits and Brooks reaching base five consecutive times (he walked twice). Richie Hebner accounted for all of the Pirates' scoring when he clubbed a two-on homer in the eighth. Besides Hebner's blast, the only other extra-base hit of the day was a double by Clemente, who for the second straight game was the only Pittsburgh player with two hits.

The Series then shifted to Pittsburgh, and the Pirates shifted into high gear. Blass tossed a three-hitter in Game 3 and Bob Robertson whacked a three-run homer as Danny Murtaugh's team beat Cuellar and company, 5-1. In Game 4, the first night contest in Series history, Baltimore drove Walker from the mound in a three-run first, but a pair of 21-year-olds rallied the Pirates. Bruce Kison relieved Walker two outs into the first inning and threw 6⅓ innings of one-hit, scoreless ball and Milt May stroked a tie-breaking pinch single in the seventh as Pittsburgh tied the Series with a 4-3 triumph. Clemente went 3 for 4.

Nelson Briles, who made only 14 starts for the Pirates in '71 and recorded just four complete games, went out and fired a two-hitter in Game 5 as Baltimore fell, 4-0. Briles helped his own cause with a run-scoring single.

An emotional Steve Blass hugs Pirate teammate Bob Robertson after shutting down the Orioles in the seventh game of the '71 Series.

Having rebounded in this Series by sweeping the Orioles in Pittsburgh, the Pirates would need to win once in Baltimore to rule as fall-classic champions. Clemente helped steer the Bucs in that direction with a bases-empty home run in Game 6, but that contest evolved into a 2-2 standoff after nine innings. Then, in the 10th, Baltimore's Frank Robinson—playing the game in the all-out manner that was his specialty—walked, dared to take third on Rettenmund's dribbler up the middle and scored the game-winning run on Brooks Robinson's shallow fly to center field.

Game 7 pitted Blass against Cuellar, and the climactic contest was 0-0 with two out in the Pittsburgh fourth. Clemente then drilled a Cuellar pitch over the wall in left-center. In the eighth, the Pirates made it 2-0 as Willie Stargell singled and Jose Pagan doubled him home. The Orioles then put runners on second and third with one out in the last half of the inning, but managed only an RBI grounder by Buford. Blass went on to record a 1-2-3 ninth, and the Pittsburgh Pirates were 2-1 winners and World Series champions.

Blass had pitched two complete games, allowing only one run in each, and was deserving of all the accolades tossed his way. Kison and Briles had made major mound contributions, catcher Manny Sanguillen had hit .379 and first baseman Robertson had belted two homers and knocked in five runs.

The spotlight, though, shone brightly on Roberto Clemente. No shadows here. He basked in the glow of a .414 batting performance (12 hits in 29 at-bats) while playing on his second Series title team. As in the 1960 classic, Clemente had hit safely in *each* game. That's right, with the conclusion of the 1971 World Series, Roberto Walker Clemente had appeared in 14 Series games and hit safely in every single one of them.

There wasn't much more Clemente could do on the diamond; he had shown 'em, once and for all. Nor was there much time left for the ever-striving player to accomplish more (although he did collect big-league career hit No. 3,000 late in the 1972 season). Fourteen and a half months after the 1971 World Series, he would die in a plane crash off the coast of his native Puerto Rico as he attempted to take food, clothing and medical supplies to earthquake victims in Nicaragua.

Game 1

Saturday, October 9, At Baltimore

Pittsburgh	AB.	R.	H.	RBI.	PO.	A.
Cash, 2b	4	0	1	1	1	3
Clines, cf	4	0	0	0	1	0
Clemente, rf	4	0	2	0	2	0
Stargell, lf	3	0	0	0	2	0
Robertson, 1b	3	1	0	0	8	1
Sanguillen, c	4	1	0	0	6	0
Pagan, 3b	4	0	0	0	2	0
Hernandez, ss	2	1	0	1	0	4
bOliver	1	0	0	0	0	0
Ellis, p	1	0	0	0	1	0
Moose, p	1	0	0	0	0	1
aMazeroski	1	0	0	0	0	0
Miller, p	0	0	0	0	1	1
Totals	32	3	3	2	24	10

Baltimore	AB.	R.	H.	RBI.	PO.	A.
Buford, lf	4	2	2	1	4	0
Blair, cf	0	0	0	0	0	0
Rettenmund, cf-lf	4	1	1	3	4	0
Powell, 1b	3	0	0	0	6	0
F. Robinson, 1b	4	1	2	1	3	0
Hendricks, c	4	0	1	0	9	0
B. Robinson, 3b	4	0	1	0	0	3
Johnson, 2b	4	0	1	0	1	1
Belanger, ss	4	1	2	0	0	2
McNally, p	3	0	0	0	0	1
Totals	34	5	10	5	27	7

Pittsburgh....................0 3 0 0 0 0 0 0 0—3
Baltimore.....................0 1 3 0 1 0 0 0 x—5

Pittsburgh	IP.	H.	R.	ER.	BB.	SO.
Ellis (L)	2⅓	4	4	4	1	1
Moose	3⅔	3	1	1	0	4
Miller	2	3	0	0	0	1

Baltimore	IP.	H.	R.	ER.	BB.	SO.
McNally (W)	9	3	3	0	2	9

aFlied out for Moose in seventh. bStruck out for Hernandez in ninth. E—Hendricks, Belanger 2. LOB—Pittsburgh 5, Baltimore 6. 2B—Clemente. 3B—Belanger. HR—F. Robinson, Rettenmund, Buford. SH—Hernandez. WP—McNally, Moose. U—Chylak (A.L.), Sudol (N.L.), Rice (A.L.), Vargo (N.L.), Odom (A.L.) and Kibler (N.L.). T—2:06. A—53,229.

Game 2

Monday, October 11, At Baltimore

Pittsburgh	AB.	R.	H.	RBI.	PO.	A.
Cash, 2b	5	0	0	0	2	6
Hebner, 3b	3	1	1	3	0	0
Clemente, rf	5	0	2	0	2	0
Stargell, lf	3	0	1	0	2	1
Giusti, p	0	0	0	0	0	0
Oliver, cf	5	0	1	0	1	0
Robertson, 1b	3	0	0	0	8	1
Sanguillen, c	5	0	1	0	4	0
Hernandez, ss	2	1	1	0	2	1
dMay	1	0	0	0	0	0
R. Johnson, p	2	0	0	0	2	0
Kison, p	0	0	0	0	0	0
Moose, p	0	0	0	0	0	0
Veale, p	0	0	0	0	0	1
aSands	1	0	0	0	0	0
Miller, p	0	0	0	0	0	0
cDavalillo, lf	1	1	1	0	1	0
Totals	36	3	8	3	24	10

Baltimore	AB.	R.	H.	RBI.	PO.	A.
Buford, lf	5	0	0	1	2	0
Rettenmund, cf-rf	5	1	2	1	3	0
Powell, 1b	5	1	1	0	4	3
F. Robinson, rf	4	2	3	0	1	0
bBlair, pr-cf	1	1	1	0	1	0
Hendricks, c	3	2	2	1	10	0
B. Robinson, 3b	3	2	3	3	0	1
D. Johnson, 2b	5	1	2	2	1	3
Belanger, ss	3	1	0	0	2	1
Palmer, p	2	0	0	2	2	0
Hall, p	0	0	0	0	1	0
Totals	36	11	14	10	27	8

Pittsburgh.....................0 0 0 0 0 0 0 3 0—3
Baltimore......................0 1 0 3 6 1 0 0 x—11

Pittsburgh	IP.	H.	R.	ER.	BB.	SO.
R. Johnson (L)	3⅓	4	4	4	2	1
Kison	0*	2	0	0	0	0
Moose	1	5	5	5	0	0
Veale	⅔	1	1	2	0
Miller	2	3	1	1	0	1
Giusti	1	1	0	0	1	0

Baltimore	IP.	H.	R.	ER.	BB.	SO.
Palmer (W)	8	7	3	3	8	10
Hall	1	1	0	0	0	0

*Pitched to two batters in fourth.

aStruck out for Veale in sixth. bRan for F. Robinson in sixth. cSingled for Miller in eighth. dGrounded out for Hernandez in ninth. E—Oliver, Belanger. DP—Pittsburgh 2. LOB—Pittsburgh 14, Baltimore 9. 2B—Clemente. HR—Hebner. HBP—By R. Johnson (Hendricks). U—Sudol (N.L.), Rice (A.L.), Vargo (N.L.), Odom (A.L.), Kibler (N.L.) and Chylak (A.L.). T—2:55. A—53,239.

Game 3

Tuesday, October 12, At Pittsburgh

Baltimore	AB.	R.	H.	RBI.	PO.	A.
Buford, lf	4	0	0	0	3	0
Rettenmund, cf	4	0	0	0	3	0
Powell, 1b	4	0	0	0	7	0
F. Robinson, rf	4	1	2	1	2	0
Hendricks, c	3	0	0	0	4	1
B. Robinson, 3b	3	0	1	0	1	5
Johnson, 2b	3	0	0	0	3	2
Belanger, ss	3	0	0	0	1	2
Cuellar, p	1	0	0	0	0	0
Dukes, p	0	0	0	0	0	0
aShopay	1	0	0	0	0	0
Watt, p	0	0	0	0	0	0
Totals	30	1	3	1	24	10

Pittsburgh	AB.	R.	H.	RBI.	PO.	A.
Cash, 2b	4	1	1	0	2	2
Oliver, cf	4	0	0	0	2	0
Clemente, rf	4	1	1	1	3	0
Stargell, lf	1	1	0	0	2	0
Robertson, 1b	4	1	1	3	8	1
Sanguillen, c	4	1	2	0	8	0
Pagan, 3b	4	0	2	1	0	0
Alley, ss	2	0	0	0	1	2
Hernandez, ss	1	0	0	0	0	1
Blass, p	4	0	0	0	1	2
Totals	32	5	7	5	27	8

Baltimore..........0 0 0 0 0 0 1 0 0—1
Pittsburgh..........1 0 0 0 0 1 3 0 x—5

Baltimore	IP.	H.	R.	ER.	BB.	SO.
Cuellar (L)	6*	7	5	4	6	4
Dukes	1	0	0	0	0	0
Watt	1	0	0	0	0	1

Pittsburgh	IP.	H.	R.	ER.	BB.	SO.
Blass (W)	9	3	1	1	2	8

*Pitched to three batters in seventh.

aGrounded out for Dukes in eighth. E—Powell, B. Robinson, Cuellar. DP—Baltimore 1. LOB—Baltimore 4, Pittsburgh 9. 2B—Cash, Pagan, Sanguillen. HR—F. Robinson, Robertson. U—Rice (A.L.), Vargo (N.L.), Odom (A.L.), Kibler (N.L.), Chylak (A.L.) and Sudol (N.L.). T—2:20. A—50,403.

Game 4

Wednesday, October 13, At Pittsburgh

Baltimore	AB.	R.	H.	RBI.	PO.	A.
Blair, cf	4	1	2	0	2	1
Belanger, ss	4	1	1	0	3	4
Rettenmund, lf	4	1	1	0	1	0
F. Robinson, rf	2	0	0	0	2	0
B. Robinson, 3b	3	0	0	1	1	1
Powell, 1b	3	0	0	1	6	0
Johnson, 2b	3	0	0	0	3	2
Etchebarren, c	2	0	0	0	6	0
Dobson, p	2	0	0	0	0	3
Jackson, p	0	0	0	0	0	0
aShopay	1	0	0	0	0	0
Watt, p	0	0	0	0	0	0
Richert, p	0	0	0	0	0	0
Totals	28	3	4	2	24	11

Pittsburgh	AB.	R.	H.	RBI.	PO.	A.
Cash, 2b	4	1	1	0	3	3
Hebner, 3b	5	1	1	0	1	1
Clemente, rf	4	0	3	0	0	0
Stargell, lf	5	1	2	1	1	0
Oliver, cf	4	0	2	2	6	0
Robertson, 1b	4	1	1	0	11	0
Sanguillen, c	4	0	2	0	4	0
Hernandez, ss	3	0	1	0	1	2
bDavalillo	1	0	0	0	0	0
Giusti, p	0	0	0	0	0	0
Walker, p	0	0	0	0	0	0
Kison, p	2	0	0	0	0	1
cMay	1	0	1	1	0	0
dAlley, ss	0	0	0	0	0	2
Totals	37	4	14	4	27	9

Baltimore..........3 0 0 0 0 0 0 0 0—3
Pittsburgh..........2 0 1 0 0 0 1 0 x—4

Baltimore	IP.	H.	R.	ER.	BB.	SO.
Dobson	5⅓	10	3	3	3	4
Jackson	⅔	0	0	0	1	0
Watt (L)	1⅓	4	1	1	0	1
Richert	⅔	0	0	0	0	1

Pittsburgh	IP.	H.	R.	ER.	BB.	SO.
Walker	⅔	3	3	3	1	0
Kison (W)	6⅓	1	0	0	0	3
Giusti (S)	2	0	0	0	0	1

aGrounded into fielder's choice for Jackson in seventh. bReached first on error for Hernandez in seventh. cSingled for Kison in seventh. dRan for May in seventh. E—Blair. DP—Baltimore 1, Pittsburgh 1. LOB—Baltimore 4, Pittsburgh 13. 2B—Stargell, Oliver, Blair. SB—Sanguillen, Hernandez. SF—B. Robinson, Powell. HBP—By Kison (Johnson, F. Robinson, Etchebarren). PB—Sanguillen. U—Vargo (N.L.), Odom (A.L.), Kibler (N.L.), Chylak (A.L.), Sudol (N.L.) and Rice (A.L.). T—2:48. A—51,378.

Game 5

Thursday, October 14, At Pittsburgh

Baltimore	AB.	R.	H.	RBI.	PO.	A.
Buford, lf	3	0	0	0	1	0
Blair, cf	4	0	0	0	3	1
Powell, 1b	3	0	1	0	8	0
F. Robinson, rf	3	0	0	0	1	0
Hendricks, c	2	0	0	0	4	3
B. Robinson, 3b	3	0	1	0	2	2
Johnson, 2b	3	0	0	0	3	1
Belanger, ss	3	0	0	0	2	3
McNally, p	1	0	0	0	0	1
Leonhard, p	0	0	0	0	0	0
aShopay	1	0	0	0	0	0
Dukes, p	0	0	0	0	0	0
bRettenmund	1	0	0	0	0	0
Totals	27	0	2	0	24	11

Pittsburgh	AB.	R.	H.	RBI.	PO.	A.
Cash, 2b	4	0	0	0	5	2
Clines, cf	3	2	1	0	3	0
Clemente, rf	4	0	1	1	4	0
Stargell, lf	4	0	1	0	2	0
Robertson, 1b	3	1	1	1	9	0
Sanguillen, c	4	1	1	0	2	0
Pagan, 3b	4	0	1	0	0	6
Hernandez, ss	3	0	2	0	2	1
Briles, p	2	0	1	1	0	1
Totals	31	4	9	3	27	10

Baltimore..........0 0 0 0 0 0 0 0 0—0
Pittsburgh..........0 2 1 0 1 0 0 0 x—4

Baltimore	IP.	H.	R.	ER.	BB.	SO.
McNally (L)	4*	7	4	3	2	3
Leonhard	1	0	0	0	1	0
Dukes	3	2	0	0	0	1

Pittsburgh	IP.	H.	R.	ER.	BB.	SO.
Briles (W)	9	2	0	0	2	2

*Pitched to two batters in fifth.

aFlied out for Leonhard in sixth. bGrounded out for Dukes in ninth. E—B. Robinson. DP—Pittsburgh 2. LOB—Baltimore 2, Pittsburgh 9. 3B—Clines. HR—Robertson. SB—Clines, Sanguillen. SH—Briles 2. HBP—By Dukes (Hernandez). WP—McNally. U—Odom (A.L.), Kibler (N.L.), Chylak (A.L.), Sudol (N.L.), Rice (A.L.) and Vargo (N.L.). T—2:16. A—51,377

Game 6

Saturday, October 16, At Baltimore

Pittsburgh	AB.	R.	H.	RBI.	PO.	A.
Cash, 2b	5	0	1	0	3	4
Hebner, 3b	4	0	0	0	0	2
Clemente, rf	4	1	2	1	2	0
Stargell, lf	4	0	0	0	2	0
Oliver, cf	5	1	1	0	2	0
Miller, p	0	0	0	0	0	0
Robertson, 1b	4	0	2	1	9	0
Sanguillen, c	4	0	3	0	8	0
Hernandez, ss	4	0	0	0	2	2
Moose, p	1	0	0	0	0	2
R. Johnson, p	1	0	0	0	0	0
Giusti, p	0	0	0	0	0	0
bDavalillo, cf	1	0	0	0	1	0
Totals	37	2	9	2	29	10

Baltimore	AB.	R.	H.	RBI.	PO.	A.
Buford, lf	4	1	3	1	3	1
D. Johnson, 2b	5	0	1	1	5	1
Powell, 1b	5	0	1	0	9	1
F. Robinson, rf	4	1	0	0	0	0
Rettenmund, cf	5	0	1	0	4	0
B. Robinson, 3b	4	0	1	1	1	0
Hendricks, c	4	0	0	0	6	0
Belanger, ss	1	1	1	0	2	5
Palmer, p	2	0	0	0	0	1
aShopay	1	0	0	0	0	0
Dobson, p	0	0	0	0	0	0
McNally, p	0	0	0	0	0	0
Totals	35	3	8	3	30	9

Pittsburgh..........0 1 1 0 0 0 0 0 0 0—2
Baltimore..........0 0 0 0 0 1 1 0 0 1—3

Two out when winning run scored.

Pittsburgh	IP.	H.	R.	ER.	BB.	SO.
Moose	5*	4	1	1	2	3
R. Johnson	1⅔	1	1	1	1	2
Giusti	2⅓	2	0	0	1	3
Miller (L)	⅔	1	1	1	1	0

Baltimore	IP.	H.	R.	ER.	BB.	SO.
Palmer	9	8	2	2	1	5
Dobson	⅔	1	0	0	1	1
McNally (W)	⅓	0	0	0	1	0

*Pitched to three batters in sixth.

aFlied out for Palmer in ninth. bLined out for Giusti in tenth. E—Hebner. DP—Pittsburgh 1. LOB—Pittsburgh 9, Baltimore 10. 2B—Oliver, Buford. 3B—Clemente. HR—Clemente, Buford. SB—Belanger, Cash. SH—Moose, Palmer. SF—B. Robinson. U—Kibler (N.L.), Chylak (A.L.), Sudol (N.L.), Rice (A.L.), Vargo (N.L.) and Odom (A.L.). T—2:59. A—44,174.

Game 7

Sunday, October 17, At Baltimore

Pittsburgh	AB.	R.	H.	RBI.	PO.	A.
Cash, 2b	4	0	0	0	4	3
Clines, cf	4	0	0	0	2	0
Clemente, rf	4	1	1	1	2	0
Robertson, 1b	4	0	1	0	11	1
Sanguillen, c	4	0	2	0	5	0
Stargell, lf	4	1	1	0	0	0
Pagan, 3b	3	0	1	1	0	2
Hernandez, ss	3	0	0	0	2	5
Blass, p	3	0	0	0	1	2
Totals	33	2	6	2	27	13

Baltimore	AB.	R.	H.	RBI.	PO.	A.
Buford, lf	3	0	1	1	0	0
Johnson, 2b	4	0	0	0	2	2
Powell, 1b	4	0	0	0	12	0
F. Robinson, rf	4	0	0	0	3	0
Rettenmund, cf	4	0	0	0	2	0
B. Robinson, 3b	2	0	0	0	1	5
Hendricks, c	3	1	2	0	7	0
Belanger, ss	3	0	1	0	0	3
Cuellar, p	2	0	0	0	0	3
aShopay	0	0	0	0	0	0
Dobson, p	0	0	0	0	0	0
McNally, p	0	0	0	0	0	0
Totals	29	1	4	1	27	13

Pittsburgh..........0 0 0 1 0 0 0 1 0—2
Baltimore..........0 0 0 0 0 0 0 1 0—1

Pittsburgh	IP.	H.	R.	ER.	BB.	SO.
Blass (W)	9	4	1	1	2	5

Baltimore	IP.	H.	R.	ER.	BB.	SO.
Cuellar (L)	8	4	2	2	0	6
Dobson	⅔	2	0	0	0	1
McNally	⅓	0	0	0	0	0

aSacrificed for Cuellar in eighth. E—Robertson. DP—Pittsburgh 1. LOB—Pittsburgh 4, Baltimore 4. 2B—Hendricks, Pagan. HR—Clemente. SH—Shopay. U—Chylak (A.L.), Sudol (N.L.), Rice (A.L.), Vargo (N.L.), Odom (A.L.) and Kibler (N.L.). T—2:10. A—47,291.

COMPOSITE BATTING AVERAGES

Pittsburgh Pirates

Player-Position	G.	AB.	R.	H.	2B.	3B.	HR.	RBI.	BA.
May, ph	2	2	0	1	0	0	0	1	.500
Briles, p	1	2	0	1	0	0	0	1	.500
Clemente, rf	7	29	3	12	2	1	2	4	.414
Sanguillen, c	7	29	3	11	1	0	0	0	.379
Dav'illo, ph-lf-cf	3	3	1	1	0	0	0	0	.333
Pagan, 3b	4	15	0	4	2	0	0	2	.267
Robertson, 1b	7	25	4	6	0	0	2	5	.240
Hernandez, ss	7	18	2	4	0	0	0	1	.222
Oliver, ph-cf	5	19	1	4	2	0	0	2	.211
Stargell, lf	7	24	3	5	1	0	0	1	.208
Hebner, 3b	3	12	2	2	0	0	1	3	.167
Cash, 2b	7	30	2	4	1	0	0	1	.133
Clines, cf	3	11	2	1	0	1	0	0	.091
Ellis, p	1	1	0	0	0	0	0	0	.000
Mazeroski, ph	1	1	0	0	0	0	0	0	.000
Sands, ph	1	1	0	0	0	0	0	0	.000
Alley, ss-pr	2	2	0	0	0	0	0	0	.000
Kison, p	2	2	0	0	0	0	0	0	.000
Moose, p	3	2	0	0	0	0	0	0	.000
R. Johnson, p	2	3	0	0	0	0	0	0	.000
Blass, p	2	7	0	0	0	0	0	0	.000
Giusti, p	3	0	0	0	0	0	0	0	.000
Miller, p	3	0	0	0	0	0	0	0	.000
Veale, p	1	0	0	0	0	0	0	0	.000
Walker, p	1	0	0	0	0	0	0	0	.000
Totals	7	238	23	56	9	2	5	21	.235

Baltimore Orioles

Player-Position	G.	AB.	R.	H.	2B.	3B.	HR.	RBI.	BA.
Blair, cf-pr	4	9	2	3	1	0	0	0	.333
B. Robinson, 3b	7	22	2	7	0	0	0	5	.318
F. Robinson, rf	7	25	5	7	0	0	2	2	.280
Hendricks, c	6	19	3	5	1	0	0	1	.263
Buford, lf	6	23	3	6	1	0	2	4	.261
Belanger, ss	7	21	4	5	0	1	0	0	.238
Ret'nd, cf-rf-lf-ph	7	27	3	5	0	0	1	4	.185
D. Johnson, 2b	7	27	1	4	0	0	0	3	.148
Powell, 1b	7	27	1	3	0	0	0	1	.111
Dobson, p	3	2	0	0	0	0	0	0	.000
Etchebarren, c	1	2	0	0	0	0	0	0	.000
Cuellar, p	2	3	0	0	0	0	0	0	.000
McNally, p	4	4	0	0	0	0	0	0	.000
Palmer, p	2	4	0	0	0	0	0	2	.000
Shopay, ph	5	4	0	0	0	0	0	0	.000
Dukes, p	2	0	0	0	0	0	0	0	.000
Watt, p	2	0	0	0	0	0	0	0	.000
Hall, p	1	0	0	0	0	0	0	0	.000
Jackson, p	1	0	0	0	0	0	0	0	.000
Leonhard, p	1	0	0	0	0	0	0	0	.000
Richert, p	1	0	0	0	0	0	0	0	.000
Totals	7	219	24	45	3	1	5	22	.205

COMPOSITE PITCHING AVERAGES

Pittsburgh Pirates

Pitcher	G.	IP.	H.	R.	ER.	BB.	SO.	W.	L.	ERA.
Briles	1	9	2	0	0	2	2	1	0	0.00
Kison	2	6⅓	1	0	0	2	3	1	0	0.00
Giusti	3	5⅓	3	0	0	2	4	0	0	0.00
Blass	2	18	7	2	2	4	13	2	0	1.00
Miller	3	4⅔	7	2	2	1	2	0	1	3.86
Moose	3	9⅔	12	7	7	2	7	0	0	6.52
R. Johnson	2	5	5	5	5	3	3	0	1	9.00
Veale	1	⅔	1	1	1	2	0	0	0	13.50
Ellis	1	2⅓	4	4	4	1	1	0	1	15.43
Walker	1	⅔	3	3	3	1	0	0	0	40.50
Totals	7	61⅔	45	24	24	20	35	4	3	3.50

Baltimore Orioles

Pitcher	G.	IP.	H.	R.	ER.	BB.	SO.	W.	L.	ERA.
Dukes	2	4	2	0	0	0	1	0	0	0.00
Hall	1	1	1	0	0	0	0	0	0	0.00
Leonhard	1	1	0	0	0	1	0	0	0	0.00
Jackson	1	⅔	0	0	0	1	0	0	0	0.00
Richert	1	⅔	0	0	0	0	1	0	0	0.00
McNally	4	13⅔	10	7	3	5	12	2	1	1.98
Palmer	2	17	15	5	5	9	15	1	0	2.65
Cuellar	2	14	11	7	6	6	10	0	2	3.86
Watt	2	2⅓	4	1	1	0	2	0	1	3.86
Dobson	3	6⅔	13	3	3	4	6	0	0	4.05
Totals	7	61	56	23	18	26	47	3	4	2.66

1972
OAKLAND A's
VS.
CINCINNATI REDS

Good things had been happening to the A's franchise since the American League's longtime Eastern-based team arrived on the West Coast by way of the Midwest. And now they were getting better and better.

The Philadelphia A's, charter members of the American League, won three of the first 10 World Series ever played and captured five Series championships overall before leaving the City of Brotherly Love after a 54-season stay and moving to Kansas City following the 1954 season. As the Kansas City A's, the club never finished higher than sixth—such a lofty standing was achieved once, in the team's first of 13 seasons in the Missouri city—and wound up 10th in three of its last four years before the franchise again pulled up stakes.

The last edition of the Kansas City A's, the 1967 team, was a typically overmatched aggregation and finished with 99 losses. But a check of that club's roster shows not a ragtag collection of over-the-hill athletes, but a valuable collection of promising Athletics. Jim (Catfish) Hunter was 21 years old and a 13-game winner for the A's in '67. John (Blue Moon) Odom was 22 and a promising righthander. Bert Campaneris, 25, led the A.L. in stolen bases for the third straight season. Joe Rudi was a player of exciting potential, having won the starting left-field job in spring training at age 20 (although he wound up back in the minors later in '67). Third-base prospect Sal Bando, 23, got into 47 games for Kansas City. And then there was that wet-behind-the-ears slugger who spent most of the season at Birmingham. The kid hit only one homer and batted just .178 for the A's in 35 games, but you had to like the

Oakland left fielder Joe Rudi pulls Denis Menke's long, ninth-inning drive off the wall (left) and then turns (right) to show that he held on. Rudi's spectacular catch short-circuited a Cincinnati rally.

way he swung at the ball. Name: Reggie Jackson. Age: 21.

Potential doesn't always translate into success, of course, so no one really knew what would become of the young hotshots A's Owner Charlie Finley had assembled. But, sure enough, this talent did come of age *after* the A's left Kansas City for Oakland.

In their maiden season in California, the A's achieved their first winning record since the Philadelphia days of 1952. By the next year, 1969, they were second-place finishers in the A.L. West and Jackson had emerged as a 47-homer man. And come 1971, the A's were West Division cham-

pions and winners of 101 regular-season games.

Now, in 1972, the A's were American League titlists after edging the Detroit Tigers, three games to two, in the Championship Series, and were ready to take on the Cincinnati Reds in the World Series.

Ready indeed.

Manager Dick Williams' A's, never known as an uptight bunch, blew into Cincinnati for the first two games of the Series and exhibited few of the jitters usually associated with a sudden thrust into the spotlight. Gene Tenace, a utility player who hit only five home runs in the regu-

lar season, was the least flustered of all. He blasted homers in his first two Series at-bats (a record accomplishment), driving in all of Oakland's runs, as the A's copped the Series opener by a 3-2 score. Having lost Jackson in the final game of the A.L. playoffs because of a hamstring injury, the A's were looking for muscle and got it from an unexpected source.

Rudi foiled the Reds in Game 2, belting a bases-empty home run in the third inning and making a spectacular catch in the ninth. With one Cincinnati player on base and Oakland ahead, 2-0, in the final inning, Rudi raced to the left-field fence and made a leaping, backhanded catch of Denis Menke's smash. Hunter, getting last-out relief from Rollie Fingers after pinch-hitter Hal McRae singled home a Reds run, was a 2-1 winner.

After Jack Billingham (eight innings-plus) and Clay Carroll combined to shut out Oakland, 1-0, in Game 3 at the Oakland-Alameda County Coliseum, the A's dealt Cincinnati a stinging loss in the fourth contest. Down 2-1 with one out in the last of the ninth, Williams' crew laced four consecutive singles good for two runs and a 3-2 victory. Pinch-hitter Gonzalo Marquez got the first hit, catcher Tenace the second and pinch batter Don Mincher delivered the third, which tied the score. Then Angel Mangual, yet another pinch-hitter, ended the game by getting the ball through the right side of a drawn-in infield.

Pete Rose sparked Cincinnati in Game 5, leading off the contest with a home run and then breaking a 4-4 tie in the ninth with a single. Menke also homered for the Reds in their must-win 5-4 triumph, while Tenace cracked a three-run shot for Oakland. The game concluded on a dramatic note in the last of the ninth when, with pinch-runner Odom on third base and Dave Duncan on first, Campaneris lifted a foul pop behind first base. Joe Morgan, ranging over from his second-base position, made the catch and, after stumbling, threw out a gambling Odom at the plate as Blue

Moon tried to score after tagging up.

After five consecutive one-run games, the Series was due for a blowout. And the Reds, getting two-run singles from Bobby Tolan and Cesar Geronimo in a five-run seventh, did the honors with an 8-1 romp in Game 6.

Tenace, who had started this Series with such a bang at Riverfront Stadium, wound it up in fine style at the same site. He rapped a run-scoring single in the first inning and an RBI double in the sixth, sparking Oakland to a 3-2 triumph in which Williams—doing whatever was necessary to nail down the World Series crown—used 21-game winner Hunter, 19-victory lefthander Ken Holtzman and Fingers in relief of Odom.

The victory gave the A's their first Series championship since 1930, when the team represented Philadelphia. The '72 title, then, was pretty heady stuff for a club that just five years earlier didn't quite know where it was headed. Other than for Oakland, that is.

Game 1

Saturday, October 14, At Cincinnati

Oakland	AB.	R.	H.	RBI.	PO.	A.
Campaneris, ss	3	0	0	0	2	3
Rudi, lf	4	0	0	0	3	0
Alou, rf	3	0	0	0	1	0
Epstein, 1b	3	0	0	0	6	1
cLewis	0	0	0	0	0	0
Hegan, 1b	0	0	0	0	2	0
Bando, 3b	4	0	0	0	0	3
Hendrick, cf	2	1	0	0	2	0
Tenace, c	3	2	2	3	7	2
Green, 2b	2	0	0	0	3	1
bMarquez	1	0	0	0	0	0
Kubiak, 2b	0	0	0	0	1	2
Holtzman, p	2	0	0	0	0	1
Fingers, p	0	0	0	0	0	0
Blue, p	0	0	0	0	0	0
Totals	27	3	4	3	27	13

Cincinnati	AB.	R.	H.	RBI.	PO.	A.
Rose, lf	4	0	0	0	3	0
Morgan, 2b	3	0	0	0	5	5
Tolan, cf	4	0	1	0	2	0
Bench, c	3	2	2	0	1	2
Perez, 1b	4	0	2	0	10	0
Menke, 3b	3	0	0	1	2	2
Geronimo, rf	3	0	0	0	3	0
dMcRae	1	0	1	0	0	0
eFoster	0	0	0	0	0	0
Concepcion, ss	2	0	1	1	1	1
Nolan, p	2	0	0	0	0	1
Borbon, p	0	0	0	0	0	1
aUhlaender	1	0	0	0	0	0
Carroll, p	0	0	0	0	0	1
fJavier	1	0	0	0	0	0
Totals	31	2	7	2	27	13

Oakland .... 0 2 0 0 1 0 0 0 0—3
Cincinnati .... 0 1 0 1 0 0 0 0 0—2

Oakland	IP.	H.	R.	ER.	BB.	SO.
Holtzman (W)	5*	5	2	2	3	3
Fingers	1⅔	1	0	0	1	3
Blue (S)	2⅓	1	0	0	1	1

Cincinnati	IP.	H.	R.	ER.	BB.	SO.
Nolan (L)	6	4	3	3	2	0
Borbon	1	0	0	0	0	0
Carroll	2	0	0	0	2	1

*Pitched to one batter in sixth.

aStruck out for Borbon in seventh. bPopped out for Green in eighth. cRan for Epstein in ninth. dSingled for Geronimo in ninth. eRan for McRae in ninth. fGrounded out for Carroll in ninth. DP—Cincinnati 1. LOB—Oakland 2, Cincinnati 8. 2B—Bench. HR—Tenace 2. SH—Campan-

eris, Concepcion. WP—Blue. U—Pelekoudas (N.L.), Honochick (A.L.), Steiner (N.L.), Umont (A.L.), Engel (N.L.) and Haller (A.L.). T—2:18. A—52,918.

Game 2

Sunday, October 15, At Cincinnati

Oakland	AB.	R.	H.	RBI.	PO.	A.
Campaneris, ss	5	0	1	0	2	1
Alou, rf	4	0	1	0	4	0
Rudi, lf	3	1	2	1	4	0
Epstein, 1b	2	0	0	0	2	0
bLewis	0	0	0	0	0	0
Hegan, 1b	1	0	0	0	3	0
Bando, 3b	4	0	1	0	0	1
Hendrick, cf	4	1	1	0	3	0
Tenace, c	4	0	0	0	7	0
Green, 2b	4	0	2	0	2	1
Hunter, p	3	0	1	1	0	1
Fingers, p	0	0	0	0	0	0
Totals	34	2	9	2	27	4

Cincinnati	AB.	R.	H.	RBI.	PO.	A.
Rose, lf	4	0	1	0	2	1
Morgan, 2b	4	0	0	0	0	3
Tolan, cf	4	0	0	0	1	0
Bench, c	3	0	1	0	8	1
Perez, 1b	3	1	2	0	11	0
Menke, 3b	4	0	0	0	0	2
Geronimo, rf	4	0	0	0	3	0
Chaney, ss	2	0	0	0	2	4
dMcRae	1	0	1	1	0	0
eConcepcion	0	0	0	0	0	0
Grimsley, p	1	0	0	0	0	2
aUhlaender	1	0	1	0	0	0
Borbon, p	0	0	0	0	0	0
cHague	1	0	0	0	0	0
Hall, p	0	0	0	0	0	0
fJavier	1	0	0	0	0	0
Totals	33	1	6	1	27	13

Oakland .... 0 1 1 0 0 0 0 0 0—2
Cincinnati .... 0 0 0 0 0 0 0 0 1—1

Oakland	IP.	H.	R.	ER.	BB.	SO.
Hunter (W)	8⅔	6	1	1	3	6
Fingers (S)	⅓	0	0	0	0	0

Cincinnati	IP.	H.	R.	ER.	BB.	SO.
Grimsley (L)	5	6	2	2	0	1
Borbon	2	0	0	0	1	4
Hall	2	3	0	0	2	2

aDoubled for Grimsley in fifth. bRan for Epstein in sixth. cFlied out for Borbon in seventh. dSingled for Chaney in ninth. eRan for McRae in ninth. fFouled out for Hall in ninth. E—Epstein, Hunter. DP—Oakland 1, Cincinnati 1. LOB—Oakland 8, Cincinnati 8. 2B—Uhlaender. HR—Rudi. SB—Morgan, Alou. U—Honochick (A.L.), Steiner (N.L.), Umont (A.L.), Engel (N.L.), Haller (A.L.) and Pelekoudas (N.L.). T—2:26. A—53,224.

Game 3

Wednesday, October 18, At Oakland

Cincinnati	AB.	R.	H.	RBI.	PO.	A.
Rose, lf	3	0	0	0	0	0
Morgan, 2b	3	0	0	0	3	3
Tolan, cf	4	0	1	0	3	0
Bench, c	4	0	0	0	7	1
Perez, 1b	3	1	1	0	11	0
Menke, 3b	2	0	1	0	0	3
Geronimo, rf	4	0	1	1	0	0
Chaney, ss	4	0	0	0	3	6
Billingham, p	4	0	0	0	0	1
Carroll, p	0	0	0	0	0	1
Totals	31	1	4	1	27	15

Oakland	AB.	R.	H.	RBI.	PO.	A.
Campaneris, ss	3	0	0	0	0	0
Alou, rf	3	0	0	0	0	0
Rudi, lf	4	0	1	0	1	0
Epstein, 1b	2	0	0	0	8	0
Bando, 3b	4	0	0	0	1	1
Hendrick, cf	4	0	0	0	1	0
Tenace, c	3	0	0	0	14	0
Green, 2b	2	0	1	0	0	3
aMarquez	1	0	1	0	0	0
bLewis	0	0	0	0	0	0
Kubiak, 2b	0	0	0	0	2	0
Odom, p	2	0	0	0	0	3
cHegan	1	0	0	0	0	0
Blue, p	0	0	0	0	0	0
Fingers, p	0	0	0	0	0	0
Totals	29	0	3	0	27	7

Cincinnati .... 0 0 0 0 0 0 1 0 0—1
Oakland .... 0 0 0 0 0 0 0 0 0—0

Cincinnati	IP.	H.	R.	ER.	BB.	SO.
Billingham (W)	8*	3	0	0	3	7
Carroll (S)	1	0	0	0	0	0

Oakland	IP.	H.	R.	ER.	BB.	SO.
Odom (L)	7	3	1	1	2	11
Blue	⅓	1	0	0	1	0
Fingers	1⅔	0	0	0	1	3

*Replaced with three balls and no strikes on first batter in ninth.

aSingled for Green in seventh. bRan for Marquez in seventh. cLined out for Odom in seventh. E—Morgan, Bench, Epstein, Tenace. DP—Cincinnati 1. LOB—Cincinnati 8, Oakland 6. SB—Rose, Geronimo, Tolan. SH—Alou, Menke. U—Steiner (N.L.), Umont (A.L.), Engel (N.L.), Haller (A.L.), Pelekoudas (N.L.) and Honochick (A.L.). T—2:24. A—49,410.

Game 4

Thursday, October 19, At Oakland

Cincinnati	AB.	R.	H.	RBI.	PO.	A.
Rose, lf	4	0	0	0	3	0
Morgan, 2b	3	1	0	0	2	1
Tolan, cf	4	0	1	2	0	0
Bench, c	4	0	2	0	4	0
Perez, 1b	4	0	2	0	11	0
McRae, rf	4	0	1	0	2	0
Geronimo, rf	0	0	0	0	0	0
Menke, 3b	4	0	0	0	1	4
Concepcion, ss	3	1	1	0	2	5
Gullett, p	2	0	0	0	0	1
aJavier	0	0	0	0	0	0
Borbon, p	0	0	0	0	0	0
Carroll, p	0	0	0	0	0	0
Totals	32	2	7	2	25	11

Oakland	AB.	R.	H.	RBI.	PO.	A.
Campaneris, ss	4	0	0	0	3	3
Alou, rf	3	0	0	0	2	0
Rudi, lf	4	0	2	0	2	0
Bando, 3b	3	0	2	0	1	4
Epstein, 1b	3	0	0	0	7	0
Hegan, 1b	1	0	0	0	3	1
Hendrick, cf	3	0	0	0	3	0
bMarquez	1	0	1	0	0	0
cLewis	0	1	0	0	0	0
Tenace, c	4	2	2	1	2	1
Green, 2b	3	0	1	0	4	6
dMincher	1	0	1	1	0	0
eOdom	0	0	0	0	0	0
Holtzman, p	3	0	0	0	0	2
Blue, p	0	0	0	0	0	0
Fingers, p	0	0	0	0	0	1
fMangual	1	0	1	1	0	0
Totals	34	3	10	3	27	18

Cincinnati	0 0 0	0 0 0	0 2 0	—2
Oakland	0 0 0	0 1 0	0 0 2	—3

One out when winning run scored.

Cincinnati	IP.	H.	R.	ER.	BB.	SO.
Gullett	7	5	1	1	2	4
Borbon	1⅓	2	1	1	0	0
Carroll (L)	0†	3	1	1	0	0

Oakland	IP.	H.	R.	ER.	BB.	SO.
Holtzman	7⅔	5	1	1	0	1
Blue	⅓*	2	1	1	1	0
Fingers (W)	1	0	0	0	0	1

*Pitched to one batter in ninth.

†Pitched to three batters in ninth.

aSacrificed for Gullett in eighth. bSingled for Hendrick in ninth. cRan for Marquez in ninth. dSingled for Green in ninth. eRan for Mincher in ninth. fSingled for Fingers in ninth. E—Perez, Holtzman. DP—Cincinnati 1, Oakland 1. LOB—Cincinnati 5, Oakland 8. 2B—Green, Tolan. HR—Tenace. SB—Bench. SH—Javier. U—Umont (A.L.), Engel (N.L.), Haller (A.L.), Pelekoudas (N.L.), Honochick (A.L.), Steiner (N.L.). T—2:06. A—49,410.

Game 5

Friday, October 20, At Oakland

Cincinnati	AB.	R.	H.	RBI.	PO.	A.
Rose, lf	5	1	3	2	2	0
Morgan, 2b	3	2	0	0	3	2
Tolan, cf	4	0	2	2	2	0
Bench, c	4	0	0	0	6	2
Perez, 1b	4	0	1	0	10	2
Menke, 3b	3	1	1	1	2	3
Geronimo, rf	4	1	1	0	1	0
Chaney, ss	1	0	0	0	0	1
dHague	1	0	0	0	0	0
Carroll, p	0	0	0	0	1	0
Grimsley, p	0	0	0	0	0	0
Billingham, p	0	0	0	0	0	0
McGlothlin, p	1	0	0	0	0	1
Borbon, p	0	0	0	0	0	1
cUhlaender	1	0	0	0	0	0
Hall, p	0	0	0	0	0	1
eConcepcion, ss	2	0	0	0	0	0
Totals	33	5	8	5	27	13

Oakland	AB.	R.	H.	RBI.	PO.	A.
Campaneris, ss	5	0	0	0	2	3
Alou, rf	4	0	0	0	1	1
Rudi, lf	3	0	0	0	4	0
Epstein, 1b	2	1	0	0	6	0
Hegan, 1b	1	0	1	0	2	0
Bando, 3b	3	1	1	0	0	1
Hendrick, cf	2	1	1	0	3	0
fMincher	0	0	0	0	0	0
gMangual, cf	1	0	0	0	0	0
Tenace, c	2	1	1	3	7	0
iOdom	0	0	0	0	0	0
Green, 2b	1	0	0	0	1	0
aMarquez	1	0	1	1	0	0
bLewis	0	0	0	0	0	0
Kubiak, 2b	2	0	1	0	1	1
Hunter, p	2	0	0	0	0	2
Fingers, p	0	0	0	0	0	1
Hamilton, p	0	0	0	0	0	0
hDuncan	1	0	1	0	0	0
Totals	30	4	7	4	27	9

Cincinnati	1 0 0	1 1 0	0 1 1	—5
Oakland	0 3 0	1 0 0	0 0 0	—4

Cincinnati	IP.	H.	R.	ER.	BB.	SO.
McGlothlin	3*	2	4	4	2	3
Borbon	1	1	0	0	1	0
Hall	2	0	0	0	0	0
Carroll	1⅔	3	0	0	0	1
Grimsley (W)	⅔	0	0	0	1	0
Billingham (S)	⅔	1	0	0	0	0

Oakland	IP.	H.	R.	ER.	BB.	SO.
Hunter	4⅔	5	3	3	2	2
Fingers (L)	3⅔	3	2	2	1	4
Hamilton	⅔	0	0	0	0	0

*Pitched to two batters in fourth.

aSingled for Green in fourth. bRan for Marquez in fourth. cGrounded out for Borbon in fifth. dGrounded out for Chaney in seventh. eFlied out for Hall in seventh. fAnnounced to bat for Hendrick in eighth. gGrounded out for Mincher in eighth. hSingled for Hamilton in ninth. iRan for Tenace in ninth. E—Alou, Bando. DP—Cincinnati 1, Oakland 1. LOB—Cincinnati 6, Oakland 6. 2B—Perez. HR—Rose, Tenace, Menke. SB—Tolan 2, Morgan. SH—Menke, Hendrick, Fingers, Grimsley. HBP—By McGlothlin (Rudi). WP—Fingers. U—Engel (N.L.), Haller (A.L.), Pelekoudas (N.L.), Honochick (A.L.), Steiner (N.L.) and Umont (A.L.). T—2:26. A—49,410.

Game 6

Saturday, October 21, At Cincinnati

Oakland	AB.	R.	H.	RBI.	PO.	A.
Campaneris, ss	4	0	0	0	2	4
Alou, rf	4	0	0	0	1	0
Rudi, lf	4	0	1	0	1	0
Epstein, 1b	4	0	0	0	6	1
Bando, 3b	4	1	2	0	0	1
Mangual, cf	4	0	2	0	3	0
Tenace, c	4	0	1	0	8	1
Green, 2b	2	0	1	1	2	1
aMarquez	1	0	0	0	0	0
Kubiak, 2b	1	0	0	0	0	0
Blue, p	1	0	0	0	0	1
Locker, p	0	0	0	0	0	0
bMincher	0	0	0	0	0	0
cDuncan	1	0	0	0	0	0
Hamilton, p	0	0	0	0	0	0
Horlen, p	0	0	0	0	1	0
Totals	34	1	7	1	24	9

Cincinnati	AB.	R.	H.	RBI.	PO.	A.
Rose, lf	3	1	0	0	3	0
Morgan, 2b	5	1	2	1	2	1
Tolan, cf	4	2	2	2	3	0
Bench, c	2	2	1	1	5	0
Perez, 1b	3	0	1	1	10	0
McRae, rf	3	1	1	0	2	0
Geronimo, rf	1	0	1	2	0	0
Menke, 3b	4	0	0	0	1	2
Concepcion, ss	3	1	2	1	1	3
Nolan, p	1	0	0	0	0	1
Grimsley, p	1	0	0	0	0	0
Borbon, p	0	0	0	0	0	1
Hall, p	2	0	0	0	0	0
Totals	32	8	10	8	27	8

Oakland	0 0 0	0 1 0	0 0 0	—1
Cincinnati	0 0 0	1 1 1	5 0 x	—8

Oakland	IP.	H.	R.	ER.	BB.	SO.
Blue (L)	5⅔	4	3	3	2	4
Locker	⅓	1	0	0	0	0
Hamilton	⅔	3	4	4	1	1
Horlen	1⅓	2	1	1	2	1

Cincinnati	IP.	H.	R.	ER.	BB.	SO.
Nolan	4⅔	3	1	1	0	3
Grimsley (W)	1	1	0	0	1	0
Borbon	1	1	0	0	0	0
Hall (S)	2⅓	2	0	0	0	1

aGrounded into forceout for Green in seventh. bAnnounced to bat for Locker in seventh. cStruck out for Mincher in seventh. E—Mangual. LOB—Oakland 7, Cincinnati 6. 2B—Morgan, Green, McRae. 3B—Concepcion. HR—Bench. SB—Tolan 2, Concepcion. SF—Concepcion. WP—Horlen. U—Haller (A.L.), Pelekoudas (N.L.), Honochick (A.L.), Steiner (N.L.), Umont (A.L.) and Engel (N.L.). T—2:21. A—52,737.

Game 7

Sunday, October 22, At Cincinnati

Oakland	AB.	R.	H.	RBI.	PO.	A.
Campaneris, ss	4	1	2	0	6	1
Mangual, cf	4	1	0	0	3	0
Rudi, lf	3	0	0	0	5	0
Tenace, 1b	3	0	2	2	3	1
bLewis	0	1	0	0	0	0
Hegan, 1b	1	0	0	0	1	0
Bando, 3b	4	0	1	1	1	1
Alou, rf	3	0	0	0	2	0
Duncan, c	3	0	0	0	5	1
Green, 2b	4	0	1	0	0	1
Odom, p	2	0	0	0	1	0
Hunter, p	0	0	0	0	0	0
Holtzman, p	0	0	0	0	0	0
Fingers, p	1	0	0	0	0	0
Totals	32	3	6	3	27	5

Cincinnati	AB.	R.	H.	RBI.	PO.	A.
Rose, lf	5	1	2	0	1	0
Morgan, 2b	3	0	1	0	3	3
Tolan, cf	2	0	0	0	0	0
Foster, rf	0	0	0	0	0	0
dJavier	0	0	0	0	0	0
eHague, rf	1	0	0	0	0	0
Bench, c	3	0	0	0	10	1
Perez, 1b	2	1	1	1	10	1
Menke, 3b	4	0	0	0	0	7
Geronimo, rf-cf	3	0	0	0	2	0
Concepcion, ss	3	0	0	0	0	2
Billingham, p	1	0	0	0	1	0
aMcRae	0	0	0	1	0	0
Borbon, p	0	0	0	0	0	0
Carroll, p	0	0	0	0	0	1
Grimsley, p	0	0	0	0	0	0
cUhlaender	1	0	0	0	0	0
Hall, p	0	0	0	0	0	1
fChaney	0	0	0	0	0	0
Totals	28	2	4	2	27	16

Oakland	1 0 0	0 0 2	0 0 0	—3
Cincinnati	0 0 0	0 1 0	0 1 0	—2

Oakland	IP.	H.	R.	ER.	BB.	SO.
Odom	4⅓	2	1	1	4	2
Hunter (W)	2⅔*	1	1	1	1	3
Holtzman	0*	1	0	0	0	0
Fingers (S)	2	0	0	0	1	0

Cincinnati	IP.	H.	R.	ER.	BB.	SO.
Billingham	5	2	1	0	1	4
Borbon (L)	⅔	3	2	2	0	0
Carroll	1	0	0	0	2	1
Grimsley	⅓	0	0	0	1	1
Hall	2	1	0	0	0	3

*Pitched to one batter in eighth.

aHit sacrifice fly for Billingham in fifth. bRan for Tenace in sixth. cFlied out for Grimsley in seventh. dAnnounced to bat for Foster in eighth. ePopped out for Javier in eighth. fHit by pitch for Hall in ninth. E—Campaneris, Tolan, Concepcion. DP—Oakland 1. LOB—Oakland 8, Cincinnati 8. 2B—Perez, Tenace, Bando, Morgan. SB—Bench. SH—Mangual, Campaneris. SF—McRae, Perez. HBP—By Fingers (Chaney). WP—Hunter. U—Pelekoudas (N.L.), Honochick (A.L.), Steiner (N.L.), Umont (A.L.), Engel (N.L.) and Haller (A.L.). T—2:50. A—56,040.

COMPOSITE BATTING AVERAGES

Oakland Athletics

Player-Position	G.	AB.	R.	H.	2B.	3B.	HR.	RBI.	BA.
Mincher, ph	3	1	0	1	0	0	0	1	1.000
Marquez, ph	5	5	0	3	0	0	0	1	.600
Tenace, c-1b	7	23	5	8	1	0	4	9	.348
Green, 2b	7	18	0	6	2	0	0	1	.333
Kubiak, 2b	4	3	0	1	0	0	0	0	.333
Mangual, ph-cf	4	10	1	3	0	0	0	1	.300
Bando, 3b	7	26	2	7	1	0	0	1	.269
Rudi, lf	7	25	1	6	0	0	1	1	.240
Hegan, 1b-ph	6	5	0	1	0	0	0	0	.200
Duncan, ph-c	3	5	0	1	0	0	0	0	.200
Hunter, p	3	5	0	1	0	0	0	1	.200
Campaneris, ss	7	28	1	5	0	0	0	0	.179
Hendrick, cf	5	15	3	2	0	0	0	0	.133
Alou, rf	7	24	0	1	0	0	0	0	.042
Fingers, p	6	1	0	0	0	0	0	0	.000
Blue, p	4	1	0	0	0	0	0	0	.000
Odom, p-pr	4	4	0	0	0	0	0	0	.000
Holtzman, p	3	5	0	0	0	0	0	0	.000
Epstein, 1b	6	16	1	0	0	0	0	0	.000
Lewis, pr	6	0	2	0	0	0	0	0	.000
Hamilton, p	2	0	0	0	0	0	0	0	.000
Horlen, p	1	0	0	0	0	0	0	0	.000
Locker, p	1	0	0	0	0	0	0	0	.000
Totals	7	220	16	46	4	0	5	16	.209

Cincinnati Reds

Player-Position	G.	AB.	R.	H.	2B.	3B.	HR.	RBI.	BA.
McRae, ph-rf	5	9	1	4	1	0	0	2	.444
Perez, 1b	7	23	3	10	2	0	0	2	.435
Co'pcion, ss-pr-ph	6	13	2	4	0	1	0	2	.308
Tolan, cf	7	26	2	7	1	0	0	6	.269
Bench, c	7	23	4	6	1	0	1	1	.261
Uhlaender, ph	4	4	0	1	1	0	0	0	.250
Rose, lf	7	28	3	6	0	0	1	2	.214
Geronimo, rf-cf	7	19	1	3	0	0	0	3	.158
Morgan, 2b	7	24	4	3	2	0	0	1	.125
Menke, 3b	7	24	1	2	0	0	1	2	.083
McGlothlin, p	1	1	0	0	0	0	0	0	.000
Gullett, p	1	2	0	0	0	0	0	0	.000
Grimsley, p	4	2	0	0	0	0	0	0	.000
Hall, p	4	2	0	0	0	0	0	0	.000
Javier, ph	4	2	0	0	0	0	0	0	.000
Nolan, p	2	3	0	0	0	0	0	0	.000
Hague, ph-rf	3	3	0	0	0	0	0	0	.000
Billingham, p	3	5	0	0	0	0	0	0	.000
Chaney, ss-ph	4	7	0	0	0	0	0	0	.000
Foster, pr-rf	2	0	0	0	0	0	0	0	.000
Carroll, p	5	0	0	0	0	0	0	0	.000
Borbon, p	6	0	0	0	0	0	0	0	.000
Totals	7	220	21	46	8	1	3	21	.209

COMPOSITE PITCHING AVERAGES

Oakland Athletics

Pitcher	G.	IP.	H.	R.	ER.	BB.	SO.	W.	L.	ERA.
Locker	1	⅓	1	0	0	0	0	0	0	0.00
Odom	2	11⅓	5	2	2	6	13	0	1	1.59
Fingers	6	10⅓	4	2	2	4	11	1	1	1.74
Holtzman	3	12⅔	11	3	3	3	4	1	0	2.13
Hunter	3	16	12	5	5	6	11	2	0	2.81
Blue	4	8⅔	8	4	4	5	5	0	1	4.15
Horlen	1	1⅓	2	1	1	2	1	0	0	6.75
Hamilton	2	1⅓	3	4	4	1	1	0	0	27.00
Totals	7	62	46	21	21	27	46	4	3	3.05

Cincinnati Reds

Pitcher	G.	IP.	H.	R.	ER.	BB.	SO.	W.	L.	ERA.
Billingham	3	13⅔	6	1	0	4	11	1	0	0.00
Hall	4	8⅓	6	0	0	2	7	0	0	0.00
Gullett	1	7	5	1	1	2	4	0	0	1.29
Carroll	5	5⅔	6	1	1	4	3	0	1	1.59
Grimsley	4	7	7	2	2	3	2	2	1	2.57
Nolan	2	10⅔	7	4	4	2	3	0	1	3.38
Borbon	6	7	7	3	3	2	4	0	1	3.86
McGlothlin	1	3	2	4	4	2	3	0	0	12.00
Totals	7	62⅓	46	16	15	21	37	3	4	2.17

1973 OAKLAND A's VS. NEW YORK METS

For the New York Mets to stay with the Oakland A's in the 1973 World Series, it surely would require an amazing effort by the National League champions.

The '73 Mets, it turned out, were downright amazin'.

Manager Yogi Berra's Mets had won the National League pennant in a fiercely contested five-game Championship Series against a seemingly superior Cincinnati Reds team. While that triumph boosted the Mets' stock, the fact remained that Berra's club had qualified for the N.L. playoffs despite barely finishing over the .500 mark. In a wacky does-anybody-really-want-to-win-this-thing race, the Mets had won the East Division crown with an 82-79 record. A juggernaut this was not.

The A's, meanwhile, had captured their third straight American League West championship and second consecutive A.L. pennant. They boasted big hitters in Reggie Jackson, Sal Bando, Gene Tenace and Deron Johnson and 20-game winners in Jim (Catfish) Hunter, Ken Holtzman and Vida Blue.

New York's Jon Matlack (14-16), one of only four pitchers in big-league history to start a World Series opener despite compiling a losing record in the regular season, pitched masterfully against the A's in Game 1—he allowed two unearned runs and three hits in six innings—but wound up a 2-1 loser. Matlack's mound rival, Holtzman, worked five innings and got the victory and even helped his own cause with a third-inning double.

Considering that A.L. pitchers didn't bat during the '73 regular season because of the introduction of the designated-hitter rule, Holtzman's extra-base blow in the first Series at-bat by an A's hurler

A dejected Mike Andrews contemplates the error of his ways during a 1973 Series Game 2 performance that resulted in his eventual 'firing' by Oakland Owner Charlie Finley.

was something of a stunner for the Mets, whose second baseman, Felix Millan, allowed Holtzman to score from second when Bert Campaneris' ensuing grounder got through his legs. After Campaneris stole second, Joe Rudi rifled a run-scoring single.

Game 2 was the longest contest in World Series history in terms of the clock, lasting four hours and 13 minutes. And the day must have been one of the longest in Mike Andrews' life.

After Oakland rallied from a 6-4 deficit to tie the second game on two-out, ninth-inning singles by Jackson and Tenace, New York slipped ahead, 7-6, in the 12th on former Giants star Willie Mays'

single (which proved the last hit of Mays' 22-year major league career, which was winding up where it started, in New York). Then, with the bases loaded later in the inning, A's second baseman Andrews let John Milner's grounder skip through his legs for a two-run error. Jerry Grote followed with another grounder to Andrews, whose poor throw pulled Tenace off the bag and enabled another run to score.

While the A's battled back in the last of the 12th—they scored once and had the bases loaded with only one out—the Mets hung on for a 10-7 victory.

The day after Game 2, A's Owner Charlie Finley in effect

"fired" Andrews with the announcement that he was deactivating the 30-year-old infielder. Finley tried to place Andrews on the disabled list, citing a shoulder injury, but Commissioner Bowie Kuhn—much to the delight of the Oakland squad—stepped in and ordered the A's boss to reinstate Andrews.

Amid the Andrews drama, the fall-classic scene shifted from Oakland to New York and Dick Williams' A's regained the Series lead on Campaneris' 11th-inning single in Game 3. The hit lifted the A's to a 3-2 triumph in a game featuring terrific pitching by New York's Tom Seaver, who struck out 12 batters in eight innings.

Mets right fielder Rusty Staub and Oakland's Andrews got everyone's attention in Game 4— Staub by putting on a hitting clinic in the National Leaguers' Series-squaring 6-1 victory and Andrews by merely being announced as a pinch-hitter. Staub belted a three-run homer in the first inning, drove in five runs overall and went 4 for 4 in support of Matlack's three-hit pitching over eight innings. Andrews, back in uniform after the post-Game 2 brouhaha, received a rousing greeting from sympathetic New York fans before grounding out in an eighth-inning at-bat that proved to be his last trip to the plate in the majors.

The upstart Mets then went out and snatched the Series lead, getting a combined fifth-game shutout from Jerry Koosman (6⅓ innings) and Tug McGraw and key extra-base hits from Cleon Jones and Don Hahn. Jones doubled in the second and scored on Milner's single, while Hahn tripled home a run in the sixth. Blue and the A's fell, 2-0.

Needing one victory in Oakland to cap an unbelievable season, the Mets started Seaver against Hunter in Game 6. Seaver allowed only six hits in seven innings, but two of the blows were run-scoring doubles by Jackson that staked Hunter to a 2-0 lead. Reggie, making up for lost time (an injury kept him out of the '72 fall classic), singled and scored Oakland's final run in the eighth

as the A's prevailed, 3-1.

New York's hopes of springing a monumental upset were jolted early in Game 7 as Oakland rediscovered the long-ball aspect of its offense. Without a home run in the first six games against the Mets, the A's got two-run shots from Campaneris and Jackson in the third inning—both homers were off Matlack—and rolled to a 5-2 victory. Holtzman notched the victory, although he needed help from Rollie Fingers, who appeared in six games of the '73 Series, and Darold Knowles, who pitched in all seven contests.

Despite a second straight World Series championship, Williams walked away as the A's manager. While he reportedly had tired of Finley's interference long before the Andrews turmoil and may have intended to quit anyway, Williams seemingly was pushed over the brink by the Andrews "firing."

The A's themselves had been pushed to the brink by a New York team that was amazin' almost to the very end.

Game 1

Saturday, October 13, At Oakland

New York	AB.	R.	H.	RBI.	PO.	A.
Garrett, 3b	5	0	0	0	0	0
Millan, 2b	4	0	1	0	1	2
Mays, cf	4	0	1	0	0	0
Jones, lf	4	1	2	0	3	0
Milner, 1b	4	0	2	1	11	0
Grote, c	4	0	0	0	5	2
Hahn, rf	2	0	0	0	0	0
cKranepool	1	0	0	0	0	0
Harrelson, ss	2	0	0	0	4	6
dHodges	0	0	0	0	0	0
eMartinez	0	0	0	0	0	0
Matlack, p	0	0	0	0	0	0
bBoswell	1	0	1	0	0	0
McGraw, p	0	0	0	0	0	0
fStaub	0	0	0	0	0	0
gBeauchamp	1	0	0	0	0	0
Totals	32	1	7	1	24	10

Oakland	AB.	R.	H.	RBI.	PO.	A.
Campaneris, ss	4	1	1	0	3	1
Rudi, lf	3	0	1	1	0	0
Bando, 3b	3	0	1	0	1	3
Jackson, cf-rf	3	0	0	0	4	0
Tenace, 1b	3	0	0	0	11	0
Alou, rf	3	0	0	0	1	0
Davalillo, cf	0	0	0	0	0	0
Fosse, c	3	0	0	0	4	1
Green, 2b	2	0	0	0	2	3
Holtzman, p	1	1	1	0	1	3
aMangual	1	0	0	0	0	0
Fingers, p	1	0	0	0	0	0
Knowles, p	0	0	0	0	0	0
Totals	27	2	4	1	27	11

New York..................000 100 000—1
Oakland....................002 000 00x—2

New York	IP.	H.	R.	ER.	BB.	SO.
Matlack (L)	6	3	2	0	2	3
McGraw	2	1	0	0	1	1

Oakland	IP.	H.	R.	ER.	BB.	SO.
Holtzman (W)	5	4	1	1	3	2
Fingers	3⅓	3	0	0	1	3
Knowles (S)	⅔	0	0	0	0	0

aLined out for Holtzman in fifth. bSingled for Matlack in seventh. cLined out for Hahn in ninth. dWalked for Harrelson in ninth. eRan for Hodges in ninth. fAnnounced to bat for McGraw in ninth. gPopped out for Staub in ninth. E—Millan, Mays. DP—Oakland 2. LOB—New York 9, Oakland 5. 2B—Holtzman, Jones. 3B—Millan. SB—Campaneris. SH—Matlack, Rudi. PB—Fosse. U—Springstead (A.L.), Donatelli (N.L.), Neudecker (A.L.), Pryor (N.L.), Goetz (A.L.) and Wendelstedt (N.L.). T—2:26. A—46,021.

Game 2

Sunday October 14, At Oakland

New York	AB.	R.	H.	RBI.	PO.	A.
Garrett, 3b	6	1	1	1	1	5
Millan, 2b	6	0	0	0	4	5
Staub, rf	5	0	1	0	0	0
gMays, cf	2	1	1	1	1	0
Jones, lf	5	3	3	1	0	0
Milner, 1b	6	1	2	0	15	0
Grote, c	6	1	2	0	15	2
Hahn, cf-rf	7	1	1	1	0	0
Harrelson, ss	6	1	3	1	0	4
Koosman, p	1	0	0	0	0	0
Sadecki, p	0	0	0	0	0	1
aTheodore	1	0	0	0	0	0
Parker, p	0	0	0	0	0	0
bKranepool	0	0	0	0	0	0
cBeauchamp	1	0	0	0	0	0
McGraw, p	2	1	1	0	0	2
Stone, p	0	0	0	0	0	0
Totals	54	10	15	5	36	19

Oakland	AB.	R.	H.	RBI.	PO.	A.
Campaneris, ss	6	2	1	0	0	6
Rudi, lf	5	1	2	1	3	1
Bando, 3b	5	2	1	1	1	4
Jackson, cf	6	1	4	2	3	0
Tenace, 1b	3	0	1	1	13	0
Alou, rf	6	0	3	2	2	0
Fosse, c	5	0	0	0	11	0
Green, 2b	2	0	0	0	0	1
dMangual	1	0	0	0	0	0
Kubiak, 2b	0	0	0	0	1	0
fAndrews, 2b	2	0	0	0	1	0
Blue, p	2	0	0	0	0	0
Pina, p	0	0	0	0	0	0
Knowles, p	0	0	0	0	0	1
eConigliaro	1	0	0	0	0	0
Odom, p	0	0	0	0	0	0
hJohnson	1	0	1	0	0	0
iLewis	0	1	0	0	0	0
Fingers, p	1	0	0	0	0	1
Lindblad, p	0	0	0	0	1	0
jDavalillo	1	0	0	0	0	0
Totals	47	7	13	7	36	13

New York..............011 004 000 004—10
Oakland..................210 000 102 001— 7

New York	IP.	H.	R.	ER.	BB.	SO.
Koosman	2⅓	6	3	3	3	4
Sadecki	1⅔	0	0	0	0	3
Parker	1	1	0	0	0	0
McGraw (W)	6†	5	4	4	3	8
Stone	1	1	0	0	1	0

Oakland	IP.	H.	R.	ER.	BB.	SO.
Blue	5⅓	4	4	4	2	4
Pina	0*	2	2	0	0	0
Knowles	1⅔	1	0	0	2	2
Odom	2	2	0	0	2	0
Fingers (L)	2⅓	6	4	1	0	2
Lindblad	⅓	0	0	0	0	0

*Pitched to three batters in sixth.
†Pitched to two batters in twelfth.

aGrounded out for Sadecki in fifth. bAnnounced to bat for Parker in sixth. cSafe on error for Kranepool in sixth. dStruck out for Green in sixth. eGrounded out for Knowles in seventh. fGrounded out for Kubiak in eighth. gRan for Staub in ninth. hDoubled for Odom in ninth. iRan for Johnson in ninth. jPopped out for Lindblad in twelfth. E—Koosman, Bando, Tenace, Andrews 2, Knowles. DP—New York 1, Oakland 1. LOB—New York 15, Oakland 12. 2B—Rudi, Alou, Jackson, Johnson, Harrelson. 3B—Bando, Campaneris, Jackson. HR—Jones, Garrett. SB—Campaneris. SH—McGraw. HBP—By Pina (Grote), by McGraw (Campaneris), by Fingers (Jones). U—Donatelli (N.L.), Neudecker (A.L.), Pryor (N.L.), Goetz (A.L.), Wendelstedt (N.L.) and Springstead (A.L.). T—4:13. A—49,151.

Game 3

Tuesday, October 16, At New York

Oakland	AB.	R.	H.	RBI.	PO.	A.
Campaneris, ss	6	1	3	1	2	7
Rudi, lf	5	0	2	1	7	0
Bando, 3b	4	1	2	0	0	1
Jackson, rf	5	0	0	0	2	0
Tenace, 1b-c	3	0	1	1	4	0
Davalillo, cf-1b	5	0	1	0	7	0
Fosse, c	2	0	0	0	5	0
aBourque, 1b	2	0	1	0	2	0
eLewis	0	0	0	0	0	0
Lindblad, p	1	0	0	0	0	0
Fingers, p	0	0	0	0	0	0
Green, 2b	2	0	0	0	1	0
bAlou	1	0	0	0	0	0
Kubiak, 2b	1	0	0	0	2	2
Hunter, p	2	0	0	0	0	2
cJohnson	1	0	0	0	0	0
Knowles, p	0	0	0	0	0	0
fMangual, cf	2	0	0	0	0	0
Totals	42	3	10	3	33	12

New York	AB.	R.	H.	RBI.	PO.	A.
Garrett, 3b	4	1	2	1	1	2
Millan, 2b	5	1	2	0	3	2
Staub, rf	6	0	2	0	2	0
Jones, lf	5	0	0	0	2	0
Milner, 1b	5	0	1	0	5	1
Grote, c	5	0	0	0	15	0
Hahn, cf	4	0	1	0	4	1
Harrelson, ss	5	0	2	0	1	3
Seaver, p	3	0	0	0	0	0

	AB.	R.	H.	RBI.	PO.	A.
dBeauchamp	1	0	0	0	0	0
Sadecki	0	0	0	0	0	0
McGraw, p	0	0	0	0	0	1
gMays	1	0	0	0	0	0
Parker, p	0	0	0	0	0	0
Totals	43	2	10	1	33	11

```
Oakland .......... 0 0 0  0 0 1  0 1 0  0 1—3
New York ......... 2 0 0  0 0 0  0 0 0  0 0—2
```

Oakland	IP.	H.	R.	ER.	BB.	SO.
Hunter	6	7	2	2	3	5
Knowles	2	0	0	0	1	0
Lindblad (W)	2†	3	0	0	1	0
Fingers (S)	1	0	0	0	0	0

New York	IP.	H.	R.	ER.	BB.	SO.
Seaver	8	7	2	2	1	12
Sadecki	0*	1	0	0	0	0
McGraw	2	1	0	0	1	1
Parker (L)	1	1	1	1	0	1

*Pitched to two batters in ninth.
†Pitched to one batter in eleventh.

aFlied out for Fosse in seventh. bGrounded out for Green in seventh. cStruck out for Hunter in seventh. dFlied out for Seaver in eighth. eRan for Bourque in ninth. fStruck out for Knowles in ninth. gGrounded into force out for McGraw in tenth. E—Hunter, Millan 2. LOB—Oakland 14, New York 14. 2B—Rudi, Hahn, Bando, Tenace, Staub. HR—Garrett. SB—Campaneris. SH—Bando, Millan. PB—Grote. WP—Hunter. U—Neudecker (A.L.), Pryor (N.L.), Goetz (A.L.), Wendelstedt (N.L.), Springstead (A.L.) and Donatelli (N.L.). T—3:15. A—54,817.

Game 4
Wednesday, October 17, At New York

Oakland	AB.	R.	H.	RBI.	PO.	A.
Campaneris, ss	4	0	0	0	1	2
Rudi, lf	4	0	1	0	1	1
Bando, 3b	3	1	0	0	3	4
Jackson, cf	4	0	1	0	0	0
Tenace, 1b	3	0	1	1	12	0
Alou, rf	4	0	0	0	1	0
Fosse, c	4	0	0	0	4	2
Green, 2b	1	0	0	0	1	3
aMangual	1	0	0	0	0	0
Kubiak, 2b	1	0	0	0	1	3
dJohnson	1	0	1	0	0	0
Holtzman, p	0	0	0	0	0	1
Odom, p	1	0	0	0	0	1
Knowles, p	0	0	0	0	0	0
bConigliaro	1	0	0	0	0	0
Pina, p	0	0	0	0	0	0
cAndrews	1	0	0	0	0	0
Lindblad, p	0	0	0	0	0	0
eDavalillo	0	0	0	0	0	0
Totals	33	1	5	1	24	17

New York	AB.	R.	H.	RBI.	PO.	A.
Garrett, 3b	4	1	1	0	1	4
Millan, 2b	5	1	1	0	4	1
Staub, rf	4	1	4	5	1	0
Jones, lf	3	0	1	0	2	0
Theodore, lf	1	0	0	0	1	0
Milner, 1b	3	0	0	0	9	0
Grote, c	4	0	3	0	7	0
Hahn, cf	4	1	1	0	2	0
Harrelson, ss	2	1	1	0	1	3
Matlack, p	3	0	1	0	0	1
Sadecki, p	0	0	0	0	0	0
Totals	33	6	13	5	27	9

```
Oakland .......... 0 0 0  1 0 0  0 0 0—1
New York ......... 3 0 0  3 0 0  0 0 x—6
```

Oakland	IP.	H.	R.	ER.	BB.	SO.
Holtzman (L)	1/3	4	3	3	1	0
Odom	2 2/3*	3	2	2	2	0
Knowles	1	1	0	0	1	1
Pina	3	4	0	0	0	1
Lindblad	1	1	0	0	0	1

New York	IP.	H.	R.	ER.	BB.	SO.
Matlack (W)	8	3	1	0	2	5
Sadecki (S)	1	2	0	0	1	2

*Pitched to two batters in fourth.

aPopped out for Green in fifth. bFlied out for Knowles in fifth. cGrounded out for Pina in eighth. dSingled for Kubiak in ninth. eWalked for Lindblad in ninth. E—Green, Garrett. DP—Oakland 3. LOB—Oakland 9, New York 10. HR—Staub. HBP—By Knowles (Garrett), by Matlack (Campaneris). WP—Odom. U—Pryor (N.L.), Goetz (A.L.), Wendelstedt (N.L.), Springstead (A.L.) and Donatelli (N.L.). T—2:41. A—54,817.

Game 5
Thursday, October 18, At New York

Oakland	AB.	R.	H.	RBI.	PO.	A.
Campaneris, ss	3	0	1	0	0	4
Rudi, lf	4	0	0	0	3	0
Bando, 3b	3	0	1	0	1	1
Jackson, cf	3	0	0	0	1	0
Tenace, 1b	1	0	0	0	7	2
dOdom	0	0	0	0	0	0
Bourque, 1b	0	0	0	0	2	0
Alou, rf	4	0	0	0	1	0
Fosse, c	4	0	1	0	6	0
Green, 2b	2	0	0	0	1	1
aJohnson	0	0	0	0	0	0
bLewis	0	0	0	0	0	0
Kubiak, 2b	1	0	0	0	2	2
Blue, p	2	0	0	0	0	1

	AB.	R.	H.	RBI.	PO.	A.
Knowles, p	0	0	0	0	0	0
cMangual	1	0	0	0	0	0
Fingers, p	0	0	0	0	0	0
eConigliaro	1	0	0	0	0	0
Totals	29	0	3	0	24	11

New York	AB.	R.	H.	RBI.	PO.	A.
Garrett, 3b	3	0	0	0	1	2
Millan, 2b	4	0	0	0	2	1
Staub, rf	3	0	1	0	0	0
Jones, lf	4	1	2	0	2	0
Milner, 1b	4	0	2	1	7	0
Grote, c	3	1	1	0	10	0
Hahn, cf	4	0	1	1	2	0
Harrelson, ss	2	0	0	0	3	4
Koosman, p	3	0	0	0	0	1
McGraw, p	1	0	0	0	0	0
Totals	31	2	7	2	27	8

```
Oakland .......... 0 0 0  0 0 0  0 0 0—0
New York ......... 0 1 0  0 0 1  0 0 x—2
```

Oakland	IP.	H.	R.	ER.	BB.	SO.
Blue (L)	5 2/3	6	2	2	1	4
Knowles	1/3	0	0	0	1	1
Fingers	2	1	0	0	2	1

New York	IP.	H.	R.	ER.	BB.	SO.
Koosman (W)	6 1/3	3	0	0	4	4
McGraw (S)	2 2/3	0	0	0	3	3

aWalked for Green in seventh. bRan for Johnson in seventh. cPopped out for Knowles in seventh. dRan for Tenace in eighth. eStruck out for Fingers in ninth. E—Campaneris, Garrett. DP—New York 1. LOB—Oakland 9, New York 10. 2B—Jones, Fosse. 3B—Hahn. SH—Grote. WP—Blue. U—Goetz (A.L.), Wendelstedt (N.L.), Springstead (A.L.), Donatelli (N.L.), Neudecker (A.L.) and Pryor (N.L.). T—2:39. A—54,817.

Game 6
Saturday, October 20, At Oakland

New York	AB.	R.	H.	RBI.	PO.	A.
Garrett, 3b	3	0	1	0	0	2
Millan, 2b	4	0	1	1	2	1
Staub, rf	4	0	1	0	0	0
Jones, lf	4	0	0	0	0	0
Milner, 1b	4	0	1	0	10	0
Grote, c	4	0	1	0	7	1
Hahn, cf	3	0	0	0	4	0
cKranepool	1	0	0	0	0	0
Harrelson, ss	3	0	0	0	0	2
Seaver, p	2	0	0	0	0	1
aBoswell	1	1	1	0	0	0
McGraw, p	0	0	0	0	0	0
Totals	33	1	6	1	24	8

Oakland	AB.	R.	H.	RBI.	PO.	A.
Campaneris, ss	4	0	0	0	2	4
Rudi, lf	3	1	1	0	3	0
Bando, 3b	4	1	1	0	0	0
Jackson, rf-cf	4	1	3	2	2	0
Tenace, c-1b	3	0	0	0	3	0
Davalillo, cf	2	0	0	0	6	0
bAlou, rf	0	0	0	0	1	0
Johnson, 1b	4	0	1	0	5	1
Fosse, c	0	0	0	0	0	0
Green, 2b	3	0	1	0	4	2
Hunter, p	3	0	0	0	0	0
Knowles, p	0	0	0	0	0	0
Fingers, p	0	0	0	0	0	0
Totals	30	3	7	3	27	7

```
New York ......... 0 0 0  0 0 0  0 1 0—1
Oakland .......... 1 0 1  0 0 0  0 1 x—3
```

New York	IP.	H.	R.	ER.	BB.	SO.
Seaver (L)	7	6	2	2	2	6
McGraw	1	1	1	0	1	1

Oakland	IP.	H.	R.	ER.	BB.	SO.
Hunter (W)	7 1/3	4	1	1	1	1
Knowles	1/3	0	0	0	0	0
Fingers (S)	1 1/3	0	0	0	0	0

aSingled for Seaver in eighth. bHit sacrifice fly for Davalillo in eighth. cPopped out for Hahn in eighth. E—Garrett, Hahn. DP—New York 1. LOB—New York 6, Oakland 7. 2B—Jackson 2. SF—Alou. WP—Seaver. U—Wendelstedt (N.L.), Springstead (A.L.), Donatelli (N.L.), Neudecker (A.L.), Pryor (N.L.) and Goetz (A.L.). T—2:07. A—49,333.

Game 7
Sunday, October 21, At Oakland

New York	AB.	R.	H.	RBI.	PO.	A.
Garrett, 3b	5	0	0	0	1	4
Millan, 2b	4	1	1	0	2	1
Staub, rf	4	0	2	1	2	0
Jones, lf	3	0	0	0	1	0
Milner, 1b	3	1	0	0	9	0
Grote, c	4	0	1	0	8	0
Hahn, cf	4	0	3	0	1	0
Harrelson, ss	4	0	0	0	2	2
Matlack, p	2	0	0	0	0	1
Parker, p	0	0	0	0	0	0
bBeauchamp	1	0	0	0	0	0
Sadecki, p	0	0	0	0	0	0
cBoswell	1	0	0	0	0	0
Stone, p	0	0	0	0	0	0
dKranepool	1	0	0	0	0	0
eMartinez	0	0	0	0	0	0
Totals	35	2	8	1	24	7

Oakland	AB.	R.	H.	RBI.	PO.	A.
Campaneris, ss	4	2	3	2	2	4
Rudi, lf	3	1	2	1	3	0
Bando, 3b	4	0	0	0	0	1
Jackson, cf-rf	4	1	1	2	5	0
Tenace, c-1b	3	0	0	0	7	0
Alou, rf	1	0	0	0	0	0
aDavalillo	3	0	0	0	2	0
Johnson, 1b	3	0	0	0	3	0
Fosse, c	1	0	1	0	2	0
Green, 2b	4	0	1	0	3	2
Holtzman, p	2	1	1	0	0	0
Fingers, p	1	0	0	0	0	1
Knowles, p	0	0	0	0	0	0
Totals	33	5	9	5	27	8

```
New York ......... 0 0 0  0 0 1  0 0 1—2
Oakland .......... 0 0 4  0 1 0  0 0 x—5
```

New York	IP.	H.	R.	ER.	BB.	SO.
Matlack (L)	2 2/3	4	4	4	1	3
Parker	1 1/3	0	0	0	1	1
Sadecki	2	2	1	1	0	1
Stone	2	3	0	0	0	3

Oakland	IP.	H.	R.	ER.	BB.	SO.
Holtzman (W)	5 1/3	5	1	1	4	4
Fingers	3 1/3	3	1	0	1	2
Knowles (S)	1/3	0	0	0	0	0

aFlied out for Alou in third. bStruck out for Parker in fifth. cSingled for Sadecki in seventh. dSafe on error for Stone in ninth. eRan for Kranepool in ninth. E—Jones, Tenace. DP—Oakland 1. LOB—New York 8, Oakland 6. 2B—Holtzman, Millan, Staub. HR—Campaneris, Jackson. U—Springstead (A.L.), Donatelli (N.L.), Neudecker (A.L.), Pryor (N.L.), Goetz (A.L.) and Wendelstedt (N.L.). T—2:37. A—49,333.

COMPOSITE BATTING AVERAGES
Oakland Athletics

Player-Position	G.	AB.	R.	H.	2B.	3B.	HR.	RBI.	BA.
Holtzman, p	3	3	2	2	2	0	0	0	.667
Bourque, ph-1b	2	2	0	1	0	0	0	0	.500
Rudi, lf	7	27	9	9	2	0	0	4	.333
Fingers, p	6	3	0	1	0	0	0	0	.333
Jackson, cf-rf	7	29	3	9	3	1	1	6	.310
Johnson, ph-1b	6	10	0	3	1	0	0	0	.300
Campaneris, ss	7	31	6	9	0	1	1	3	.290
Bando, 3b	7	26	5	6	1	1	0	1	.231
Alou, rf-ph	7	19	0	3	1	0	0	3	.158
Fosse, c	7	19	0	3	0	0	0	0	.158
Tenace, 1b-c	7	19	3	3	0	0	0	0	.158
Da.lillo, cf-ph-1b	6	11	0	1	0	0	0	0	.091
Green, 2b	7	16	0	1	0	0	0	0	.063
Knowles, p	7	0	0	0	0	0	0	0	.000
Lewis, pr	3	0	1	0	0	0	0	0	.000
Pina, p	2	0	0	0	0	0	0	0	.000
Lindblad, p	3	0	0	0	0	0	0	0	.000
Odom, p-pr	3	0	0	0	0	0	0	0	.000
Conigliaro, ph	3	3	0	0	0	0	0	0	.000
Andrews, ph-2b	2	3	0	0	0	0	0	0	.000
Kubiak, 2b	4	3	0	0	0	0	0	0	.000
Blue, p	2	4	0	0	0	0	0	0	.000
Hunter, p	2	5	0	0	0	0	0	0	.000
Mangual, ph-cf	5	6	0	0	0	0	0	0	.000
Totals	7	241	21	51	12	3	2	20	.212

New York Mets

Player-Position	G.	AB.	R.	H.	2B.	3B.	HR.	RBI.	BA.
Boswell, ph	3	3	1	3	0	0	0	0	1.000
Staub, ph-rf	7	26	1	11	2	0	1	6	.423
McGraw, p	5	3	1	1	0	0	0	0	.333
Milner, 1b	7	27	2	8	0	0	0	0	.296
Jones, lf	7	28	5	8	2	0	1	1	.286
Mays, cf-pr-ph	3	7	1	2	0	0	0	1	.286
Grote, c	7	30	2	8	0	0	0	0	.267
Harrelson, ss	7	24	2	6	1	0	0	1	.250
Matlack, p	3	4	1	0	0	0	0	0	.250
Hahn, rf-cf	7	29	2	7	1	1	0	2	.241
Millan, 2b	7	32	3	6	1	1	0	1	.188
Garrett, 3b	7	30	4	5	0	0	2	2	.167
Martinez, pr	2	0	0	0	0	0	0	0	.000
Hodges, ph	1	0	0	0	0	0	0	0	.000
Stone, p	2	0	0	0	0	0	0	0	.000
Parker, p	3	0	0	0	0	0	0	0	.000
Sadecki, p	4	0	0	0	0	0	0	0	.000
Theodore, ph-lf	2	1	0	0	0	0	0	0	.000
Kranepool, ph	4	3	0	0	0	0	0	0	.000
Beauchamp, ph	4	4	0	0	0	0	0	0	.000
Koosman, p	2	4	0	0	0	0	0	0	.000
Seaver, p	2	5	0	0	0	0	0	0	.000
Totals	7	261	24	66	7	2	4	16	.253

COMPOSITE PITCHING AVERAGES
Oakland Athletics

Pitcher	G.	IP.	H.	R.	ER.	BB.	SO.	W.	L.	ERA.
Knowles	7	6 1/3	4	1	0	5	5	0	0	0.00
Lindblad	3	3 1/3	4	0	0	1	2	1	0	0.00
Pina	2	3	4	0	0	0	2	0	0	0.00
Fingers	6	13 2/3	13	5	1	4	8	0	1	0.66
Hunter	2	13 1/3	11	3	3	4	6	1	0	2.03
Odom	2	4 2/3	5	2	2	2	0	0	0	3.86
Holtzman	3	10 2/3	13	5	5	6	2	1	0	4.22
Blue	2	11	10	6	6	3	8	0	1	4.91
Totals	7	66	66	24	17	26	36	4	3	2.32

New York Mets

Pitcher	G.	IP.	H.	R.	ER.	BB.	SO.	W.	L.	ERA.
Parker	3	3 1/3	2	0	0	4	2	0	1	0.00
Stone	2	3	4	0	0	1	3	0	0	0.00
Sadecki	4	4 2/3	5	2	1	2	4	0	0	1.93
Matlack	3	16 2/3	10	7	4	5	11	1	2	2.16
Seaver	2	15	13	4	4	3	16	0	1	2.40
McGraw	5	13 2/3	8	5	4	9	14	1	0	2.63
Koosman	2	8 2/3	9	3	3	7	8	1	0	3.12
Totals	7	65	51	21	16	28	62	3	4	2.22

1974 OAKLAND A's VS. LOS ANGELES DODGERS

The Oakland A's were feudin' and fightin' in 1974. And, as had become their custom, winnin'.

So, the stormy atmosphere surrounding the '74 World Series was no big surprise to anyone. Nor was the result of the 71st fall classic.

Jim (Catfish) Hunter was on record as saying he would attempt to declare himself a free agent after the Series—which would match the A's against the Los Angeles Dodgers in baseball's first all-West Coast classic—unless A's Owner Charlie Finley paid Hunter the back salary that the four-time 20-game winner contended Finley owed him. Former A's infielder Mike Andrews announced he was filing a libel-and-slander suit against Finley in the aftermath of Andrews' "firing" by Finley during the '73 Series. And Oakland teammates Rollie Fingers and John (Blue Moon) Odom engaged in pre-Series fisticuffs—against each other.

But while these A's may not have been "in sync" off the field, they were together on the diamond. And the Dodgers, like the New York Mets and the Cincinnati Reds before them, would find that out once the World Series got underway.

Reggie Jackson, showing a certain flair for excelling in October, accounted for the first run of the '74 Series by cracking a second-inning home run off Andy Messersmith in Game 1 at Dodger Stadium. Pitcher Ken Holtzman, whose double in the 1973 Series opener proved crucial, rapped a two-base hit off Messersmith in the fifth inning and eventually scored on Bert Campaneris' squeeze bunt. And Dodger third baseman Ron Cey's throwing error in the eighth gave Oakland its final run in a 3-2 A's triumph.

Pitcher-turned-slugger Ken Holtzman watches the flight of his Game 4 home run in the 1974 Series against the Dodgers.

Fingers was the winning pitcher, working 4⅓ innings in relief of Holtzman and yielding only four hits (although one was a ninth-inning homer by Jim Wynn).

Walter Alston's Dodgers came back in Game 2, riding Joe Ferguson's two-run homer in the sixth to a 3-2 victory. In a key ninth-inning play, Los Angeles reliever Mike Marshall picked off Herb Washington at a time when Oakland's "designated runner" represented his club's potential tying run. Washington, who would play in 105 regular-season games in the majors but never bat, was a former Michigan State track star who had been signed by Finley expressly for the purpose of pinch-running. But in his Series debut, Washington was caught off base after replacing Joe Rudi, who had just singled home two runs.

Hunter, with relief help from Fingers, stretched his career Series record to 4-0 in Game 3 as Oak-land got two unearned runs in the third and went on to victory in yet another 3-2 decision.

The designated-hitter rule would not be used in Series competition for two more years, so Holtzman was digging in at the plate again in the fourth game. This time, he nailed Messersmith for a bases-empty home run in the third inning before the Dodgers moved ahead, 2-1, in the fourth on Bill Russell's two-run triple. But Manager Alvin Dark's A's went on a four-run spree in the sixth—pinch-hitter Jim Holt broke a 2-2 deadlock with a two-run single—and the American Leaguers came away with a 5-2 victory.

Game 5 was deadlocked at 2-2 entering the last of the seventh when Dodgers fireman Marshall, coming off a 15-victory season in which he made *106* appearances (a major league record), served up a home run pitch to Rudi. In the next inning, Bill Buckner tried to run the Dodgers back into the game, but his hustling effort backfired. Leading off the eighth, Buckner singled to right-center off Fingers and when the ball got past center fielder Bill North, Buckner tried to make it all the way to third base. But perfect throws in a Jackson-to-Dick Green-to-Sal Bando relay nailed the daring baserunner, and for all intents and purposes the Los Angeles Dodgers were dead.

Long live the king. And Oakland, after another 3-2 outcome, was king of the baseball world. Again.

By becoming only the second franchise to win as many as three straight World Series crowns (the New York Yankees, of course, had made the record their special province), the A's demonstrated that camaraderie—while surely

desirable—was no substitute for talent.

Game 1

Saturday, October 12, At Los Angeles

Oakland	AB.	R.	H.	RBI.	PO.	A.
Campaneris, ss	2	1	1	1	0	5
North, cf	2	0	0	0	4	0
Bando, 3b	4	0	0	0	1	1
Jackson, rf	3	1	1	1	0	0
C. Washington, rf	0	0	0	0	0	0
Rudi, lf	4	0	2	0	6	0
Tenace, 1b	3	0	1	0	6	1
Fosse, c	3	0	0	0	7	0
Green, 2b	3	0	0	0	3	2
cHolt	1	0	0	0	0	0
Maxvill, 2b	0	0	0	0	0	0
Holtzman, p	1	1	1	0	0	1
Fingers, p	2	0	0	0	0	0
Hunter, p	0	0	0	0	0	0
Totals	28	3	6	2	27	10

Los Angeles	AB.	R.	H.	RBI.	PO.	A.
Lopes, 2b	5	1	0	0	5	0
Buckner, lf	5	0	2	0	2	0
Wynn, cf	4	1	1	1	1	0
Garvey, 1b	5	0	2	0	6	1
dPaciorek	0	0	0	0	0	0
Ferguson, rf-c	3	0	0	0	2	1
Cey, 3b	3	0	1	0	0	5
Russell, ss	4	0	1	0	2	0
Yeager, c	3	0	1	0	9	1
aCrawford, rf	1	0	1	0	0	0
Messersmith, p	3	0	2	0	0	4
bJoshua	1	0	0	0	0	0
Marshall, p	0	0	0	0	0	0
Totals	37	2	11	1	27	12

Oakland 0 1 0 0 1 0 0 1 0—3
Los Angeles 0 0 0 0 1 0 0 0 1—2

Oakland	IP.	H.	R.	ER.	BB.	SO.
Holtzman	4⅓	7	1	0	2	3
Fingers (W)	4⅓	4	1	1	1	3
Hunter (S)	⅓	0	0	0	0	1

Los Angeles	IP.	H.	R.	ER.	BB.	SO.
Messersmith (L)	8	5	3	2	3	8
Marshall	1	1	0	0	1	1

aSingled for Yeager in eighth. bGrounded out for Messersmith in eighth. cPopped out for Green in ninth. dRan for Garvey in ninth. E—Campaneris, Jackson, Cey. DP—Oakland 1, Los Angeles 1. LOB—Oakland 6, Los Angeles 12. 2B—Holtzman. HR—Jackson, Wynn. SH—Campaneris 2, North, Tenace. HBP—By Fingers (Ferguson). WP—Messersmith. U—Gorman (N.L.), Kunkel (A.L.), Harvey (N.L.), Denkinger (A.L.), Olsen (N.L.) and Luciano (A.L.). T—2:43. A—55,974.

Game 2

Sunday, October 13, At Los Angeles

Oakland	AB.	R.	H.	RBI.	PO.	A.
Campaneris, ss	4	0	1	0	0	1
North, cf	4	0	0	0	3	0
Haney, c	0	0	0	0	2	0
Bando, 3b	3	1	0	0	0	1
Jackson, rf	3	1	2	0	2	0
Rudi, lf	4	0	1	2	3	0
fH. Washington	0	0	0	0	0	0
Tenace, 1b	3	0	0	0	8	0
Fosse, c	2	0	0	0	5	0
aAlou	1	0	0	0	0	0
Odom, p	0	0	0	0	0	0
eMangual	1	0	0	0	0	0
Green, 2b	2	0	0	0	1	2
bHolt	1	0	1	0	0	0
cMaxvill, 2b	0	0	0	0	0	0
Blue, p	2	0	0	0	0	1
dC. Washington, cf	1	0	1	0	0	0
Totals	31	2	6	2	24	5

Los Angeles	AB.	R.	H.	RBI.	PO.	A.
Lopes, 2b	4	0	0	0	3	2
Buckner, lf	4	0	0	0	3	0
Wynn, cf	3	0	0	0	0	0
Garvey, 1b	4	1	2	0	7	0
Ferguson, rf	3	1	1	2	0	0
Cey, 3b	3	1	0	0	2	1
Russell, ss	3	0	1	0	2	3
Yeager, c	3	0	2	1	10	1
Sutton, p	2	0	0	0	0	1
Marshall, p	0	0	0	0	0	1
Totals	29	3	6	3	27	9

Oakland 0 0 0 0 0 0 0 0 2—2
Los Angeles 0 1 0 0 0 2 0 0 x—3

Oakland	IP.	H.	R.	ER.	BB.	SO.
Blue (L)	7	6	3	3	2	5
Odom	1	0	0	0	1	2

Los Angeles	IP.	H.	R.	ER.	BB.	SO.
Sutton (W)	8*	5	2	2	2	9
Marshall (S)	1	1	0	0	0	2

*Pitched to two batters in ninth.

aStruck out for Fosse in eighth. bSingled for Green in eighth. cRan for Holt in eighth. dSingled for Blue in eighth. eStruck out for Odom in ninth. fRan for Rudi in ninth. E—Russell. DP—Los Angeles 2. LOB—Oakland 5, Los Angeles 6. 2B—Campaneris, Jackson. HR—Ferguson. SB—Ferguson. SH—Sutton. HBP—By Sutton (Bando). WP—Sutton. U—Kunkel (A.L.), Harvey (N.L.), Denkinger (A.L.), Olsen (N.L.), Luciano (A.L.) and Gorman (N.L.). T—2:40. A—55,989.

Game 3

Tuesday, October 15, At Oakland

Los Angeles	AB.	R.	H.	RBI.	PO.	A.
Lopes, 2b	3	0	2	0	1	0
Buckner, lf	4	1	1	1	2	0
Wynn, cf	4	0	1	0	0	0
Garvey, 1b	4	0	1	0	10	0
Crawford, rf	4	1	1	1	1	0
Ferguson, c	3	0	0	0	9	0
dAuerbach	0	0	0	0	0	0
Cey, 3b	4	0	0	0	1	3
Russell, ss	4	0	1	0	0	3
Downing, p	1	0	0	0	0	3
Brewer, p	0	0	0	0	0	0
aLacy	1	0	0	0	0	0
Hough, p	0	0	0	0	0	0
bJoshua	1	0	0	0	0	0
Marshall, p	0	0	0	0	0	1
Totals	33	2	7	2	24	10

Oakland	AB.	R.	H.	RBI.	PO.	A.
North, cf	4	1	1	0	5	0
Campaneris, ss	4	0	2	1	3	2
Bando, 3b	3	1	0	0	0	1
Jackson, rf	3	0	0	0	2	0
C. Washington, rf	0	0	0	0	0	0
Rudi, lf	4	0	1	1	2	0
Tenace, 1b	2	0	1	0	4	0
cH. Washington	0	0	0	0	0	0
Holt, 1b	0	0	0	0	1	0
Fosse, c	4	0	0	0	5	0
Green, 2b	3	1	0	0	4	4
Hunter, p	2	0	0	0	1	1
Fingers, p	0	0	0	0	0	0
Totals	29	3	5	2	27	8

Los Angeles 0 0 0 0 0 0 0 1 1—2
Oakland 0 0 2 1 0 0 0 0 x—3

Los Angeles	IP.	H.	R.	ER.	BB.	SO.
Downing (L)	3⅔	4	3	1	4	3
Brewer	⅓	0	0	0	0	1
Hough	2	0	0	0	1	4
Marshall	2	1	0	0	0	1

Oakland	IP.	H.	R.	ER.	BB.	SO.
Hunter (W)	7⅓	5	1	1	2	4
Fingers	1⅔	2	1	0	0	1

aStruck out for Brewer in fifth. bFlied out for Hough in seventh. cRan for Tenace in eighth. dRan for Ferguson in ninth. E—Ferguson 2, Campaneris, Green. DP—Oakland 3. LOB—Los Angeles 6, Oakland 8. 2B—Campaneris. HR—Buckner, Crawford. SB—Lopes 2, Jackson. SH—Hunter. WP—Hough. U—Harvey (N.L.), Denkinger (A.L.), Olsen (N.L.), Luciano (A.L.), Gorman (N.L.) and Kunkel (A.L.). T—2:35. A—49,347.

Game 4

Wednesday, October 16, At Oakland

Los Angeles	AB.	R.	H.	RBI.	PO.	A.
Lopes, 2b	4	0	0	0	8	5
Buckner, lf	4	0	1	0	1	0
Wynn, cf	3	0	1	0	1	0
Garvey, 1b	4	1	2	0	7	2
Ferguson, rf	3	1	0	0	0	0
Cey, 3b	4	0	1	0	0	0
Russell, ss	4	0	1	2	0	4
Yeager, c	3	0	1	0	6	1
dJoshua	1	0	0	0	0	0
Messersmith, p	1	0	0	0	1	0
cPaciorek	1	0	0	0	0	0
Marshall, p	0	0	0	0	0	1
Totals	32	2	7	2	24	13

Oakland	AB.	R.	H.	RBI.	PO.	A.
Campaneris, ss	3	0	0	0	1	4
North, cf	3	1	0	0	3	0
Bando, 3b	3	1	1	1	0	4
Jackson, rf	3	1	1	0	0	0
Rudi, 1b-lf	3	0	0	0	10	0
C. Washington, lf	3	1	2	0	0	0
Tenace, 1b	0	0	0	0	1	0
Fosse, c	2	0	1	0	6	0
aHolt	1	0	1	2	0	0
bH. Washington	0	0	0	0	0	0
Haney, c	0	0	0	0	4	0
Green, 2b	2	0	0	1	2	4
Holtzman, p	3	1	1	1	0	2
Fingers, p	0	0	0	0	0	0
Totals	26	5	7	5	27	14

Los Angeles 0 0 0 2 0 0 0 0 0—2
Oakland 0 0 1 0 0 4 0 0 x—5

Los Angeles	IP.	H.	R.	ER.	BB.	SO.
Messersmith (L)	6	6	5	5	4	4
Marshall	2	1	0	0	0	2

Oakland	IP.	H.	R.	ER.	BB.	SO.
Holtzman (W)	7⅔	6	2	2	2	7
Fingers (S)	1⅓	1	0	0	0	2

aSingled for Fosse in sixth. bRan for Holt in sixth. cGrounded out for Messersmith in seventh. dGrounded into double play for Yeager in ninth. E—Messersmith. DP—Los Angeles 2, Oakland 1. LOB—Los Angeles 6, Oakland 4. 2B—Buckner, Yeager, Wynn. 3B—Russell. HR—Holtzman. SH—Messersmith, Green, Rudi. HBP—By Messersmith (Campaneris). WP—Holtzman. U—Denkinger (A.L.), Olsen (N.L.), Luciano (A.L.), Gorman (N.L.), Kunkel (A.L.) and Harvey (N.L.). T—2:17. A—49,347.

Game 5

Thursday, October 17, At Oakland

Los Angeles	AB.	R.	H.	RBI.	PO.	A.
Lopes, 2b	2	1	0	0	2	2
Buckner, lf	3	0	1	0	3	0
Wynn, cf	2	0	0	1	3	0
Garvey, 1b	4	0	1	1	4	0
Ferguson, rf	4	0	1	0	3	0
Cey, 3b	3	0	1	0	2	0
Russell, ss	3	0	0	0	0	1
bCrawford	1	0	0	0	0	0
Yeager, c	2	0	0	0	7	1
cJoshua	1	0	0	0	0	0
Sutton, p	1	0	0	0	0	1
aPaciorek	1	1	1	0	0	0
Marshall, p	0	0	0	0	0	1
Totals	27	2	5	2	24	6

Oakland	AB.	R.	H.	RBI.	PO.	A.
Campaneris, ss	4	0	2	0	2	4
North, cf	4	1	0	0	2	0
Bando, 3b	3	0	0	1	1	3
Jackson, rf	2	0	0	0	2	1
Rudi, 1b-lf	3	1	2	1	7	0
C. Washington, lf	3	0	1	0	3	0
Fingers, p	0	0	0	0	0	1
Fosse, c	3	1	1	1	4	1
Green, 2b	3	0	0	0	5	2
Blue, p	2	0	0	0	0	2
Odom, p	0	0	0	0	0	0
Tenace, 1b	1	0	0	0	1	0
Totals	28	3	6	3	27	14

Los Angeles 0 0 0 0 0 2 0 0 0—2
Oakland 1 1 0 0 0 0 1 0 x—3

Los Angeles	IP.	H.	R.	ER.	BB.	SO.
Sutton	5	4	2	2	1	3
Marshall (L)	3	2	1	1	0	4

Oakland	IP.	H.	R.	ER.	BB.	SO.
Blue	6⅔	4	2	2	5	4
Odom (W)	⅓	0	0	0	0	0
Fingers (S)	2	1	0	0	1	0

aDoubled for Sutton in sixth. bPopped out for Russell in ninth. cGrounded out for Yeager in ninth. E—Yeager, North. DP—Oakland 1. LOB—Los Angeles 6, Oakland 3. 2B—Paciorek. HR—Fosse, Rudi. SB—North, Campaneris. SH—Buckner. SF—Bando, Wynn. U—Olsen (N.L.), Luciano (A.L.), Gorman (N.L.), Kunkel (A.L.), Harvey (N.L.) and Denkinger (A.L.). T—2:23. A—49,347.

COMPOSITE BATTING AVERAGES

Oakland Athletics

Player-Position	G.	AB.	R.	H.	2B.	3B.	HR.	RBI.	BA.
Holt, ph-1b	4	3	0	2	0	0	0	2	.667
C.W'ton,rf-ph-cf-lf	5	7	1	4	0	0	0	0	.571
Holtzman, p	2	4	2	2	1	0	1	1	.500
Campaneris, ss	5	17	1	6	2	0	0	2	.353
Rudi, lf-1b	5	18	1	6	0	0	1	4	.333
Jackson, rf	5	14	3	4	1	0	1	1	.286
Tenace, 1b	5	9	0	2	0	0	0	0	.222
Fosse, c	5	14	1	2	0	0	1	1	.143
Bando, 3b	5	16	3	1	0	0	0	2	.063
North, cf	5	17	3	1	0	0	0	0	.059
Alou, ph	1	1	0	0	0	0	0	0	.000
Mangual, ph	1	1	0	0	0	0	0	0	.000
Fingers, p	4	2	0	0	0	0	0	0	.000
Hunter, p	2	2	0	0	0	0	0	0	.000
Blue, p	2	4	0	0	0	0	0	0	.000
Green, 2b	5	13	1	0	0	0	0	1	.000
H. Washington, pr	3	0	0	0	0	0	0	0	.000
Haney, c	2	0	0	0	0	0	0	0	.000
Maxvill, 2b-pr	2	0	0	0	0	0	0	0	.000
Odom, p	2	0	0	0	0	0	0	0	.000
Totals	5	142	16	30	4	0	4	14	.211

Los Angeles Dodgers

Player-Position	G.	AB.	R.	H.	2B.	3B.	HR.	RBI.	BA.
Messersmith, p	2	4	0	2	0	0	0	0	.500
Paciorek, pr-ph	3	2	1	1	1	0	0	0	.500
Garvey, 1b	5	21	2	8	0	0	0	1	.381
Yeager, c	4	11	0	4	1	0	0	1	.364
Crawford, ph-rf	3	6	1	2	0	0	1	1	.333
Buckner, lf	5	20	1	5	1	0	1	1	.250
Russell, ss	5	18	0	4	0	1	0	2	.222
Wynn, cf	5	16	1	3	1	0	1	2	.188
Cey, 3b	5	17	1	3	0	0	0	0	.176
Ferguson, rf-c	5	16	2	2	0	0	1	2	.125
Lopes, 2b	5	18	2	2	0	0	0	0	.111
Downing, p	1	1	0	0	0	0	0	0	.000
Lacy, ph	1	1	0	0	0	0	0	0	.000
Sutton, p	2	3	0	0	0	0	0	0	.000
Joshua, ph	4	4	0	0	0	0	0	0	.000
Marshall, p	5	0	0	0	0	0	0	0	.000
Auerbach, pr	1	0	0	0	0	0	0	0	.000
Brewer, p	1	0	0	0	0	0	0	0	.000
Hough, p	1	0	0	0	0	0	0	0	.000
Totals	5	158	11	36	4	1	4	10	.228

COMPOSITE PITCHING AVERAGES

Oakland Athletics

Pitcher	G.	IP.	H.	R.	ER.	BB.	SO.	W.	L.	ERA.
Odom	2	1⅓	0	0	0	1	2	1	0	0.00
Hunter	2	7⅔	5	1	1	2	5	1	0	1.17
Holtzman	2	12	13	3	2	4	10	1	0	1.50
Fingers	4	9⅓	8	2	2	2	6	1	0	1.93
Blue	2	13⅔	10	5	5	7	9	0	1	3.29
Totals	5	44	36	11	10	16	32	4	1	2.05

Los Angeles Dodgers

Pitcher	G.	IP.	H.	R.	ER.	BB.	SO.	W.	L.	ERA.
Hough	1	2	0	0	0	1	4	0	0	0.00
Brewer	1	⅓	0	0	0	1	0	0	0	0.00
Marshall	5	9	6	1	1	1	10	0	1	1.00
Downing	1	3⅔	4	3	1	4	3	0	1	2.45
Sutton	2	13	9	4	4	3	12	1	0	2.77
Messersmith	2	14	11	8	7	7	12	0	2	4.50
Totals	5	42	30	16	13	16	42	1	4	2.79

1975 CINCINNATI REDS VS. BOSTON RED SOX

Game 6 of the 1975 World Series between the Cincinnati Reds and the Boston Red Sox was scheduled for October 18 at Boston's Fenway Park. The game wasn't played, though, until the night of October 21.

It probably took the baseball gods about that long to piece together the twists and turns of the spellbinding script they had written for that Series contest.

In truth, a drenching New England rain caused the 72-hour postponement, a delay that proved frustrating for Manager Sparky Anderson's Big Red Machine. Coming off a 20-game romp in the National League West race and a sweep of the Pittsburgh Pirates in the Championship Series, the Reds were primed to wrap up their first Series crown in 35 years. Anderson's team had lost Game 1 of this fall classic to Boston standout Luis Tiant, 6-0, but proceeded to win three of the next four contests and held a three games-to-two edge.

The Red Sox, who had ended Oakland's three-year reign as major league baseball's kingpin by sweeping the A's in the American League Championship Series, were eager to send Tiant to the mound for the third time in this Series as they eyeballed a chance to square the Series. Besides firing a five-hit shutout in the opening game, Tiant had posted a route-going 5-4 triumph in the fourth contest.

Game 6 was well worth the wait—not only for one of the participating clubs, but for all of baseball. It may have been the finest World Series game ever played.

Boston bolted to a 3-0 lead in the first inning when Fred Lynn homered into the bleachers in right-center following two-out singles by Carl Yastrzemski and Carlton Fisk. Lynn and fellow Red Sox rookie outfielder Jim Rice had enjoyed sensational seasons in 1975, Lynn batting .331 with 21 home runs and 105 runs batted in and Rice hitting .309 with 22 homers and 102 RBIs before suffering a season-ending arm injury in September.

Tiant protected the three-run edge through four innings, but Ken Griffey's two-run triple and Johnny Bench's run-scoring single knotted the score in the fifth. Cincinnati's George Foster then crashed a two-run double off the center-field wall in the seventh, and Cesar Geronimo drove Tiant from the mound when he cracked a leadoff homer in the eighth.

At this juncture—the Reds were on top, 6-3, and needed only six more outs to clinch the Series title—the game had been well played but unspectacular. The spectacular was just around the corner.

Pedro Borbon, Cincinnati's fifth pitcher of the night, began his third inning of work by yielding a single to Lynn and a walk to Rico Petrocelli in the last of the eighth. With the potential tying run approaching the plate in the person of Dwight Evans, the Reds' Anderson summoned relief ace Rawly Eastwick. And Eastwick seemed up to the challenge, striking out Evans and getting Rick Burleson on a liner to short left. Up next would be reserve outfielder Bernie Carbo, pinch-hitting for reliever Roger Moret.

Carbo, who had walloped a pinch homer in Game 3, sent a charge into the Fenway Park throng by drilling an Eastwick pitch into the center-fielder bleachers. The blow drew Boston even at 6-6 and made Carbo only the second man in Series history to belt two pinch homers in one fall classic (Chuck Essegian of the Los Angeles Dodgers accomplished the feat in 1959).

After Dick Drago retired the Reds in order in the top of the ninth, the Red Sox went to work against Eastwick in the bottom of the frame. Denny Doyle coaxed an inning-opening walk and Yastrzemski followed with a single that sent Doyle scampering to third and Eastwick heading to the showers. Will McEnaney then issued an intentional walk to Fisk, loading the bases with no one out.

It would take some doing for the Reds to dodge this bullet. But duck they did. Lynn lofted a foul fly to short left, where Foster made the catch. Red Sox second baseman Doyle, exhibiting considerable derring-do but perhaps questionable judgment, tried to score on the play and was thrown out, Foster to Bench. Petrocelli then grounded out.

The Red Sox had blown a golden opportunity, the kind of misdeed that often proves haunting. And so it seemed in the 11th when, with Griffey on base and one out, Joe Morgan smashed a drive toward the right-field seats. Evans, a 23-year-old outfielder in his third full season with the Red Sox, raced to the front of the stands and made a leaping, one-handed catch. Griffey, well past second base, was doubled up at first.

Reds righthander Pat Darcy then retired Boston in order for the second consecutive inning, sending the game into the 12th. Rick Wise, the Red Sox's top winner in '75 with 19 victories, came on to pitch and quickly found himself in a two-on, one-out situation. But Wise got Dave Concepcion on a fly ball and Geronimo on a strikeout.

Darcy, Cincinnati's Series rec-

ord-tying eighth pitcher of the game, went head-to-head against Fisk to begin the bottom of the 12th. And while the Reds had dodged a bullet in the ninth, they couldn't dodge a cannon blast here. Fisk blasted a high drive to left field. The only question was: fair or foul? Fisk, applying some body English as he left the batter's box, jumped in ecstasy as the ball ricocheted off the foul pole. Home run! Boston 7, Cincinnati 6.

Players and fans alike were wrung out. There clearly was no way that Game 7—despite being the decisive contest—could match what had unfolded in Game 6.

The seventh game did take a back seat, all right. Still, the finale was up for grabs down to the last inning. Boston had seized a 3-0 lead in the third inning, but Red Sox lefthander Bill Lee yielded a two-run homer to Tony Perez in the sixth and was charged with another run in the seventh when Pete Rose tied the game with a single off reliever Moret. The teams remained in a 3-3 deadlock entering the ninth.

In the ninth, Griffey walked and reached third on a sacrifice and a groundout. After a walk to Rose, Morgan looped a single to center off lefthanded reliever Jim Burton. Cincinnati was on top, 4-3, and Reds bullpen standout McEnaney made the lead stand up with a 1-2-3 ninth. The Reds were World Series champions.

Anderson's powerhouse team had been pushed to the limit. After losing Game 1, Cincinnati was down by a 2-1 score at the end of eight innings in Game 2. However, Concepcion came through with a two-out, game-tying infield single in the ninth and, after Concepcion stole second, Griffey followed with a game-winning double as the Reds notched a 3-2 victory.

Getting homers from Bench, Concepcion and Geronimo, Cincinnati mounted a 5-1 lead in the third game, but Lynn's sacrifice fly in the sixth, Carbo's pinch homer in the seventh and Evans' two-run homer in the ninth made it a 5-5 contest. Geronimo then opened the last of the 10th with a single and pinch-hitter Ed Armbrister attempted to sacrifice. Armbrister's bunt bounced just a few feet in front of the plate and catcher Fisk sprinted out to field it. With Armbrister in his path, Fisk had trouble getting to the ball and then threw wildly to second base. The ball sailed into center field, enabling Geronimo to reach third and Armbrister to get to second.

The Red Sox screamed for an interference call from home-plate umpire Larry Barnett, but never got it. Rose was walked intentionally, filling the bases with no one out. After pinch-hitter Merv Rettenmund struck out, Morgan drove a fly ball over the head of drawn-in center fielder Lynn and the Reds were 6-5 winners.

Tiant's second victory of the Series tied the classic at two games apiece, but Cincinnati regained the edge when Perez came alive in Game 5. Hitless in the first four games and 0 for 15 against Boston after striking out in his first at-bat in the fifth game, Perez proceeded to rock Reggie Cleveland for a bases-empty home run and a three-run shot. Don Gullett, receiving last-out help from Eastwick, was a 6-2 victor.

Now, after a day of travel, the action would shift back to Boston. Of course, it turned out to be a travel day plus three days of plotting by the baseball gods.

Game 1

Saturday, October 11, At Boston

Cincinnati	AB.	R.	H.	RBI.	PO.	A.
Rose, 3b	4	0	0	0	0	0
Morgan, 2b	4	0	2	0	2	2
Bench, c	4	0	0	0	6	1
Perez, 1b	4	0	0	0	9	0
Foster, lf	4	0	2	0	1	0
Concepcion, ss	4	0	0	0	2	3
Griffey, rf	3	0	1	0	2	0
Geronimo, cf	1	0	0	0	2	1
Gullett, p	3	0	0	0	0	0
Carroll, p	0	0	0	0	0	0
McEnaney, p	0	0	0	0	0	0
Totals	31	0	5	0	24	7

Boston	AB.	R.	H.	RBI.	PO.	A.
Evans, rf	4	1	1	0	4	0
Doyle, 2b	3	1	2	0	3	3
Yastrzemski, lf	4	1	1	1	3	0
Fisk, c	3	1	0	1	4	1
Lynn, cf	4	0	2	0	3	0
Petrocelli, 3b	3	1	2	2	1	3
Burleson, ss	3	0	3	1	1	1
Cooper, 1b	3	0	0	1	8	0
Tiant, p	3	1	1	0	0	0
Totals	30	6	12	6	27	8

Cincinnati	0 0 0	0 0 0	0 0 0	—0
Boston	0 0 0	0 0 0	6 0 x	—6

Cincinnati	IP.	H.	R.	ER.	BB.	SO.
Gullett (L)	6*	10	4	4	4	3
Carroll	0†	0	1	1	1	0
McEnaney	2	2	1	1	1	1

Boston	IP.	H.	R.	ER.	BB.	SO.
Tiant (W)	9	5	0	0	2	3

*Pitched to four batters in seventh.
†Pitched to one batter in seventh.

DP—Cincinnati 2. LOB—Cincinnati 6, Boston 9. 2B—Morgan, Petrocelli, Griffey. SH—Doyle, Evans. SF—Cooper. Balk—Tiant. U—Frantz (A.L.) plate, Colosi (N.L.) first, Barnett (A.L.) second, Stello (N.L.) third, Maloney (A.L.) left and Davidson (N.L.) right. T—2:27. A—35,205.

Game 2

Sunday, October 12, At Boston

Cincinnati	AB.	R.	H.	RBI.	PO.	A.
Rose, 3b	4	0	2	0	1	1
Morgan, 2b	3	1	0	0	0	4
Bench, c	4	1	2	0	9	3
Perez, 1b	3	0	0	1	8	0
Foster, lf	4	0	1	0	2	0
Concepcion, ss	4	1	1	1	2	4
Griffey, rf	4	0	1	1	2	0
Geronimo, cf	3	0	0	0	3	0
Billingham, p	2	0	0	0	0	2
Borbon, p	0	0	0	0	0	0
McEnaney, p	0	0	0	0	0	0
aRettenmund	1	0	0	0	0	0
Eastwick, p	1	0	0	0	0	0
Totals	33	3	7	3	27	14

Boston	AB.	R.	H.	RBI.	PO.	A.
Cooper, 1b	5	0	1	0	10	1
Doyle, 2b	4	0	1	0	2	5
Yastrzemski, lf	3	2	1	0	1	0
Fisk, c	3	0	1	1	5	1
Lynn, cf	4	0	0	0	5	0
Petrocelli, 3b	4	0	2	1	0	0
Evans, rf	2	0	0	0	2	0
Burleson, ss	4	0	1	0	2	4
Lee, p	3	0	0	0	0	0
Drago, p	0	0	0	0	0	0
bCarbo	1	0	0	0	0	0
Totals	33	2	7	2	27	11

Cincinnati	0 0 0	1 0 0	0 0 2	—3
Boston	1 0 0	0 0 1	0 0 0	—2

Cincinnati	IP.	H.	R.	ER.	BB.	SO.
Billingham	5⅔	6	2	1	2	5
Borbon	⅓	0	0	0	0	0
McEnaney	1	0	0	0	0	2
Eastwick (W)	2	1	0	0	1	1

Boston	IP.	H.	R.	ER.	BB.	SO.
Lee	8*	5	2	2	2	5
Drago (L)	1	2	1	1	1	0

*Pitched to one batter in ninth.

aFouled out for McEnaney in eighth. bLined out for Drago in ninth. E—Concepcion. DP—Cincinnati 1. LOB—Cincinnati 6, Boston 8. 2B—Cooper, Bench, Griffey. SB—Concepcion. HBP—By Billingham (Evans). U—Colosi (N.L.) plate, Barnett (A.L.) first, Stello (N.L.) second, Maloney (A.L.) third, Davidson (N.L.) left and Frantz (A.L.) right. T—2:38. A—35,205.

Game 3

Tuesday, October 14, At Cincinnati

Boston	AB.	R.	H.	RBI.	PO.	A.
Cooper, 1b	5	0	0	0	14	0
Doyle, 2b	5	0	1	0	0	6
Yastrzemski, lf	4	1	0	0	1	0
Fisk, c	3	1	1	1	5	0
Lynn, cf	3	0	1	1	6	0
Petrocelli, 3b	4	1	2	0	1	5
Evans, rf	4	1	2	2	1	0
Burleson, ss	4	0	2	0	0	1
Wise, p	2	0	0	0	0	0
Burton, p	0	0	0	0	0	0
Cleveland, p	0	0	0	0	0	0
aCarbo	1	1	1	1	0	0
Willoughby, p	0	0	0	0	0	0
Moret, p	0	0	0	0	0	0
Totals	35	5	10	5	28	12

Cincinnati	AB.	R.	H.	RBI.	PO.	A.
Rose, 3b	4	1	1	0	2	1
Griffey, rf	3	0	0	0	1	1
cRettenmund	1	0	0	0	0	0
Morgan, 2b	4	0	1	2	4	5
Perez, 1b	3	1	0	0	13	1
Bench, c	4	1	1	2	2	1
Foster, lf	3	0	0	0	3	0
Concepcion, ss	4	1	1	1	2	5
Geronimo, cf	4	2	2	1	3	0
Nolan, p	1	0	0	0	0	0
Darcy, p	1	0	0	0	0	0
Carroll, p	0	0	0	0	0	0
McEnaney, p	1	0	1	0	0	0
Eastwick, p	0	0	0	0	0	0
bArmbrister	1	0	0	0	0	0
Totals	34	6	7	6	30	14

Boston	0 1 0	0 0 1	1 0 2	0	—5
Cincinnati	0 0 0	2 3 0	0 0 0	1	—6

One out when winning run scored.

Boston	IP.	H.	R.	ER.	BB.	SO.
Wise	4⅓	4	5	5	2	1
Burton	⅓	0	0	0	1	0
Cleveland	1⅓	0	0	0	0	2
Willoughby (L)	3†	2	1	0	0	1
Moret	⅓	1	0	0	1	1

Cincinnati	IP.	H.	R.	ER.	BB.	SO.
Nolan	4	3	1	1	1	0
Darcy	2*	2	1	1	2	0
Carroll	⅔	1	1	1	0	0
McEnaney	1⅔	1	1	1	0	2
Eastwick (W)	1⅔	3	1	1	0	0

*Pitched to one batter in seventh.
†Pitched to two batters in tenth.

aHomered for Cleveland in seventh. bReached first on error for Eastwick in tenth. cStruck out for Griffey in tenth. E—Fisk 2. DP—Boston 1, Cincinnati 2. LOB—Boston 5, Cincinnati 5. 3B—Rose. HR—Fisk, Bench, Concepcion, Geronimo, Carbo, Evans. SB—Foster, Perez, Griffey. SH—Willoughby. SF—Morgan, Lynn. WP—Darcy. U—Barnett (A.L.) plate, Stello (N.L.) first, Maloney (A.L.) second, Davidson (N.L.) third, Frantz (A.L.) left and Colosi (N.L.) right. T—3:03. A—55,392.

Game 4

Wednesday, October 15, At Cincinnati

Boston	AB.	R.	H.	RBI.	PO.	A.
Beniquez, lf	4	0	1	1	4	0
Miller, lf	1	0	0	0	1	0
Doyle, 2b	5	0	1	0	2	3
Yastrzemski, 1b	4	0	2	1	8	0
Fisk, c	5	1	1	0	4	0
Lynn, cf	4	1	1	0	4	1
Petrocelli, 3b	4	0	1	0	1	2
Evans, rf	4	1	2	2	3	0
Burleson, ss	4	1	1	1	0	2
Tiant, p	3	1	1	0	0	2
Totals	38	5	11	5	27	10

Cincinnati	AB.	R.	H.	RBI.	PO.	A.
Rose, 3b	3	1	1	0	1	3
Griffey, rf	5	0	1	1	0	0
Morgan, 2b	3	1	0	0	2	7
Perez, 1b	4	0	0	0	12	1
Bench, c	4	0	1	1	4	0
Foster, lf	4	1	2	0	0	0
Concepcion, ss	4	1	1	1	3	4
Geronimo, cf	4	0	3	1	4	0
Norman, p	1	0	0	0	0	0
Borbon, p	0	0	0	0	0	0
aCrowley	1	0	0	0	0	0
Carroll, p	0	0	0	0	1	0
bChaney	1	0	0	0	0	0
Eastwick, p	0	0	0	0	0	0
cArmbrister	0	0	0	0	0	0
Totals	34	4	9	4	27	15

Boston	0 0 0	5 0 0	0 0 0	—5
Cincinnati	2 0 0	2 0 0	0 0 0	—4

Boston	IP.	H.	R.	ER.	BB.	SO.
Tiant (W)	9	9	4	4	4	4

Cincinnati	IP.	H.	R.	ER.	BB.	SO.
Norman (L)	3⅓	7	4	4	1	2
Borbon	⅔	2	1	0	0	0
Carroll	2	2	0	0	0	2
Eastwick	3	0	0	0	1	0

aStruck out for Borbon in fourth. bStruck out for Carroll in sixth. cSacrificed for Eastwick in ninth. E—Doyle, Perez. DP—Cincinnati 1. LOB—Boston 8, Cincinnati 8. 2B—Griffey, Bench, Burleson, Concepcion. 3B—Evans, Geronimo. SH—Armbrister. WP—Norman. U—Stello (N.L.) plate, Maloney (A.L.) first, Davidson (N.L.) second, Frantz (A.L.) third, Colosi (N.L.) left and Barnett (A.L.) right. T—2:52. A—55,667.

Game 5

Thursday, October 16, At Cincinnati

Boston	AB.	R.	H.	RBI.	PO.	A.
Beniquez, lf	3	0	0	0	2	1
Doyle, 2b	4	1	1	0	1	1
Yastrzemski, 1b	3	1	1	1	6	0
Fisk, c	4	0	1	0	6	0
Lynn, cf	4	0	1	1	2	0
Petrocelli, 3b	4	0	0	0	2	1
Evans, rf	3	0	1	0	3	0
Burleson, ss	3	0	0	0	1	2
Cleveland, p	2	0	0	0	0	0
Willoughby, p	0	0	0	0	1	0
aGriffin	1	0	0	0	0	0
Pole, p	0	0	0	0	0	0
Segui, p	0	0	0	0	0	0
Totals	31	2	5	2	24	5

Cincinnati	AB.	R.	H.	RBI.	PO.	A.
Rose, 3b	3	0	2	1	1	0
Griffey, rf	4	0	1	0	2	0
Morgan, 2b	3	1	1	0	3	2
Bench, c	3	2	1	0	8	1
Perez, 1b	3	2	2	4	5	0
Foster, lf	4	0	0	0	2	0
Concepcion, ss	2	0	0	1	0	0
Geronimo, cf	4	0	0	0	6	0
Gullett, p	3	1	1	0	0	0
Eastwick, p	0	0	0	0	0	0
Totals	29	6	8	6	27	3

Boston	1 0 0	0 0 0	0 0 1	—2
Cincinnati	0 0 0	1 1 3	0 1 x	—6

Boston	IP.	H.	R.	ER.	BB.	SO.
Cleveland (L)	5*	7	5	5	2	3
Willoughby	2	1	0	0	0	1
Pole	0†	0	1	1	2	0
Segui	1	0	0	0	0	0

Cincinnati	IP.	H.	R.	ER.	BB.	SO.
Gullett (W)	8⅔	5	2	2	1	7
Eastwick (S)	⅓	0	0	0	0	1

*Pitched to three batters in sixth.
†Pitched to two batters in eighth.

aLined out for Willoughby in eighth. DP—Boston 2. LOB—Boston 4, Cincinnati 5. 2B—Rose, Lynn. 3B—Doyle. HR—Perez 2. SB—Morgan, Concepcion. SF—Yastrzemski, Concepcion. HBP—By Willoughby (Concepcion). U—Maloney (A.L.) plate, Davidson (N.L.) first, Frantz (A.L.) second, Colosi (N.L.) third, Barnett (A.L.) left and Stello (N.L.) right. T—2:23. A—56,393.

Game 6

Tuesday, October 21, At Boston

Cincinnati	AB.	R.	H.	RBI.	PO.	A.
Rose, 3b	5	1	2	0	0	2
Griffey, rf	5	2	2	2	0	0
Morgan, 2b	6	1	1	0	4	4
Bench, c	6	0	1	1	8	0
Perez, 1b	6	0	2	0	11	2
Foster, lf	6	0	2	2	4	1
Concepcion, ss	6	0	1	0	3	4
Geronimo, cf	6	1	2	1	2	0
Nolan, p	0	0	0	0	1	0
aChaney	1	0	0	0	0	0
Norman, p	0	0	0	0	0	0
Billingham, p	0	0	0	0	0	0
bArmbrister	0	1	0	0	0	0
Carroll, p	0	0	0	0	0	0
cCrowley	1	0	1	0	0	0
Borbon, p	1	0	0	0	0	0
Eastwick, p	0	0	0	0	0	0
McEnaney, p	0	0	0	0	0	0
eDriessen	1	0	0	0	0	0
Darcy, p	0	0	0	0	0	1
Totals	50	6	14	6	33	14

Boston	AB.	R.	H.	RBI.	PO.	A.
Cooper, 1b	5	0	0	0	8	0
Drago, p	0	0	0	0	0	0
fMiller	1	0	0	0	0	0
Wise, p	0	0	0	0	0	0
Doyle, 2b	5	0	1	0	0	2
Yastrzemski, lf-1b	6	1	3	0	7	1
Fisk, c	4	2	2	1	9	1
Lynn, cf	4	2	2	3	2	0
Petrocelli, 3b	4	1	0	0	1	1
Evans, rf	5	0	1	0	5	1
Burleson, ss	3	0	0	0	3	2
Tiant, p	2	0	0	0	0	2
Moret, p	0	0	0	0	0	1
dCarbo, lf	2	1	1	3	1	0
Totals	41	7	10	7	36	11

Cincinnati	000	030	210	000	—6
Boston	300	000	030	001	—7

None out when winning run scored.

Cincinnati	IP.	H.	R.	ER.	BB.	SO.
Nolan	2	3	3	3	0	2
Norman	⅔	1	0	0	2	0
Billingham	1⅓	1	0	0	1	1
Carroll	1	1	0	0	0	0
Borbon	2†	1	2	2	2	1
Eastwick	1‡	2	1	1	1	2
McEnaney	1	0	0	0	1	0
Darcy (L)	2§	1	1	1	0	1

Boston	IP.	H.	R.	ER.	BB.	SO.
Tiant	7*	11	6	6	2	5
Moret	1	0	0	0	0	0
Drago	3	1	0	0	0	1
Wise (W)	1	2	0	0	0	1

*Pitched to one batter in eighth.
†Pitched to two batters in eighth.
‡Pitched to two batters in ninth.
§Pitched to one batter in twelfth.

aFlied out for Nolan in third. bWalked for Billingham in fifth. cSingled for Carroll in sixth. dHomered for Moret in eighth. eFlied out for McEnaney in tenth. fFlied out for Drago in eleventh. E—Burleson. DP—Cincinnati 1, Boston 1. LOB—Cincinnati 11, Boston 9. 2B—Doyle, Evans, Foster. 3B—Griffey. HR—Lynn, Geronimo, Carbo, Fisk. SB—Concepcion. SH—Tiant. HBP—By Drago (Rose). U—Davidson (N.L.) plate, Frantz (A.L.) first, Colosi (N.L.) second, Barnett (A.L.) third, Stello (N.L.) left and Maloney (A.L.) right. T—4:01. A—35,205.

Game 7

Wednesday, October 22, At Boston

Cincinnati	AB.	R.	H.	RBI.	PO.	A.
Rose, 3b	4	0	2	1	2	2
Morgan, 2b	4	0	2	1	2	4
Bench, c	4	1	0	0	7	0
Perez, 1b	5	1	1	2	8	1
Foster, lf	4	0	1	0	1	0
Concepcion, ss	4	0	1	0	0	2
Griffey, rf	2	2	1	0	3	0
Geronimo, cf	3	0	0	0	3	0
Gullett, p	1	0	1	0	0	0
aRettenmund	1	0	0	0	0	0
Billingham, p	0	0	0	0	0	0
bArmbrister	0	0	0	0	0	0
Carroll, p	0	0	0	0	1	0
dDriessen	1	0	0	0	0	0
McEnaney, p	0	0	0	0	0	0
Totals	33	4	9	4	27	9

Boston	AB.	R.	H.	RBI.	PO.	A.
Carbo, lf	3	1	1	0	0	1
Miller, lf	0	0	0	0	0	0
eBeniquez	1	0	0	0	0	0
Doyle, 2b	4	1	1	0	5	3
fMontgomery	1	0	0	0	0	0
Yastrzemski, 1b	5	1	1	1	9	0
Fisk, c	3	0	0	0	4	0
Lynn, cf	2	0	0	0	1	0
Petrocelli, 3b	3	0	1	1	1	3
Evans, rf	2	0	0	1	5	0
Burleson, ss	3	0	0	0	2	7
Lee, p	3	0	1	0	0	1
Moret, p	0	0	0	0	0	0
Willoughby, p	0	0	0	0	0	0
cCooper	1	0	0	0	0	0
Burton, p	0	0	0	0	0	0
Cleveland, p	0	0	0	0	0	0
Totals	31	3	5	3	27	15

Cincinnati	0 0 0	0 0 2	1 0 1	—4
Boston	0 0 3	0 0 0	0 0 0	—3

Cincinnati	IP.	H.	R.	ER.	BB.	SO.
Gullett	4	4	3	3	5	5
Billingham	2	1	0	0	2	1
Carroll (W)	2	0	0	0	1	1
McEnaney (S)	1	0	0	0	0	0

Boston	IP.	H.	R.	ER.	BB.	SO.
Lee	6⅓	7	3	3	1	2
Moret	⅓	1	0	0	2	0
Willoughby	1⅓	0	0	0	0	0
Burton (L)	⅔	1	1	1	2	0
Cleveland	⅓	0	0	0	1	0

aHit into double play for Gullett in fifth. bWalked for Billingham in seventh. cFouled out for Willoughby in eighth. dGrounded out for Carroll in ninth. eFlied out for Miller in ninth. fGrounded out for Doyle in ninth. E—Doyle 2. DP—Cincinnati 1, Boston 2. LOB—Cincinnati 9, Boston 9. 2B—Carbo. HR—Perez. SB—Morgan, Griffey. SH—Geronimo. WP—Gullett. U—Frantz (A.L.) plate, Colosi (N.L.) first, Barnett (A.L.) second, Stello (N.L.) third, Maloney (A.L.) left and Davidson (N.L.) right. T—2:52. A—35,205.

COMPOSITE BATTING AVERAGES

Cincinnati Reds

Player-Position	G.	AB.	R.	H.	2B.	3B.	HR.	RBI.	BA.
McEnaney, p	5	1	0	1	0	0	0	0	1.000
Crowley, ph	2	2	0	1	0	0	0	0	.500
Rose, 3b	7	27	3	10	1	1	0	2	.370
Gullett, p	3	7	1	2	0	0	0	0	.286
Geronimo, cf	7	25	3	7	0	1	2	3	.280
Foster, lf	7	29	1	8	1	0	0	2	.276
Griffey, rf	7	26	4	7	3	1	0	4	.269
Morgan, 2b	7	27	4	7	1	0	0	3	.259
Bench, c	7	29	5	6	2	0	1	4	.207
Concepcion, ss	7	28	3	5	1	0	1	4	.179
Perez, 1b	7	28	4	5	0	0	3	7	.179
Armbrister, ph	4	1	1	0	0	0	0	0	.000
Eastwick, p	5	1	0	0	0	0	0	0	.000
Borbon, p	3	1	0	0	0	0	0	0	.000
Darcy, p	2	1	0	0	0	0	0	0	.000
Nolan, p	2	1	0	0	0	0	0	0	.000
Norman, p	2	1	0	0	0	0	0	0	.000
Billingham, p	3	2	0	0	0	0	0	0	.000
Chaney, ph	2	2	0	0	0	0	0	0	.000
Driessen, ph	2	2	0	0	0	0	0	0	.000
Rettenmund, ph	3	3	0	0	0	0	0	0	.000
Carroll, p	5	0	0	0	0	0	0	0	.000
Totals	7	244	29	59	9	3	7	29	.242

Boston Red Sox

Player-Position	G.	AB.	R.	H.	2B.	3B.	HR.	RBI.	BA.
Carbo, ph-lf	4	7	3	3	1	0	2	4	.429
Yastrzemski, lf-1b	7	29	7	9	0	0	0	4	.310
Petrocelli, 3b	7	26	3	8	1	0	0	4	.308
Burleson, ss	7	24	1	7	1	0	0	2	.292
Evans, rf	7	24	3	7	1	1	1	5	.292
Lynn, cf	7	25	3	7	1	0	1	5	.280
Doyle, 2b	7	30	3	8	1	1	0	0	.267
Tiant, p	3	8	2	2	0	0	0	0	.250
Fisk, c	7	25	5	6	0	0	2	4	.240
Lee, p	2	6	0	1	0	0	0	0	.167
Beniquez, lf-ph	3	8	0	1	0	0	0	1	.125
Cooper, 1b-ph	5	19	0	1	1	0	0	1	.053
Griffin, ph	1	1	0	0	0	0	0	0	.000
Montgomery, ph	1	1	0	0	0	0	0	0	.000
Cleveland, p	3	2	0	0	0	0	0	0	.000
Miller, lf-ph	3	2	0	0	0	0	0	0	.000
Wise, p	2	2	0	0	0	0	0	0	.000
Moret, p	3	0	0	0	0	0	0	0	.000
Willoughby, p	3	0	0	0	0	0	0	0	.000
Burton, p	2	0	0	0	0	0	0	0	.000
Drago, p	2	0	0	0	0	0	0	0	.000
Pole, p	1	0	0	0	0	0	0	0	.000
Segui, p	1	0	0	0	0	0	0	0	.000
Totals	7	239	30	60	7	2	6	30	.251

COMPOSITE PITCHING AVERAGES

Cincinnati Reds

Pitcher	G.	IP.	H.	R.	ER.	BB.	SO.	W.	L.	ERA.
Billingham	3	9	8	2	1	5	7	0	0	1.00
Eastwick	5	8	6	2	2	3	4	2	0	2.25
McEnaney	5	6⅔	3	2	2	2	5	0	0	2.70
Carroll	5	5⅔	4	2	2	2	3	1	0	3.18
Gullett	3	18⅔	19	9	9	10	15	1	1	4.34
Darcy	2	4	3	2	2	2	1	0	1	4.50
Nolan	2	6	6	4	4	1	2	0	0	6.00
Borbon	3	3	3	3	2	2	1	0	0	6.00
Norman	2	4	8	4	4	3	2	0	1	9.00
Totals	7	65	60	30	28	30	40	4	3	3.88

Boston Red Sox

Pitcher	G.	IP.	H.	R.	ER.	BB.	SO.	W.	L.	ERA.
Willoughby	3	6⅓	3	1	0	0	2	0	1	0.00
Moret	3	1⅔	2	0	0	3	1	0	0	0.00
Segui	1	1	0	0	0	0	0	0	0	0.00
Drago	2	4	3	1	1	1	1	0	1	2.25
Lee	2	14⅓	12	5	5	3	7	0	0	3.14
Tiant	3	25	25	10	10	8	12	2	0	3.60
Cleveland	3	6⅔	7	5	5	3	5	0	1	6.75
Wise	2	5⅓	6	5	5	2	2	1	0	8.44
Burton	2	1	1	1	1	3	0	0	1	9.00
Pole	1	0	0	1	1	2	0	0	0	......
Totals	7	65⅓	59	29	28	25	30	3	4	3.86

1976 CINCINNATI REDS VS. NEW YORK YANKEES

After 11 seasons on the sidelines, the New York Yankees were back in their accustomed arena of competition in 1976: the World Series. While the Yankees' 30th appearance in the fall classic stirred memories of the way it was, what really reminded everyone of the Yankees of bygone eras was the play of the team in the *other* dugout.

The Cincinnati Reds were baseball's Big Red Machine, a team with power, speed, excellent defense and a pitching staff deep enough to boast seven hurlers with 11 or more victories. Managed deftly by Sparky Anderson, the Reds won 102 games in '76 and swept the National League Championship Series for the second consecutive year.

Anderson presided over a talent-rich club that featured Johnny Bench behind the plate, George Foster, Cesar Geronimo and Ken Griffey in the outfield and Pete Rose at third base, Dave Concepcion at shortstop, Joe Morgan at second base and Tony Perez at first. On the bench, among others, were promising young hitter Dan Driessen, veteran Bob Bailey and handyman Doug Flynn. Gary Nolan headed the pitching staff with 15 victories, Pat Zachry won 14 times and Fred Norman and Jack Billingham each won 12 games. Don Gullett, Santo Alcala and relief ace Rawly Eastwick posted 11 victories apiece and combined for a 33-12 record.

While the Reds' standing as an outstanding team seemed secure —they had won 108 regular-season games in their World Series championship year of 1975 and posted 98 and 99 victories in the previous two seasons—Anderson and company knew that their greatness would be measured not by the quantity of their victories, but rather by the magnitude of their accomplishments. And a second straight Series crown would leave little doubt that these Cincinnati Reds deserved prominent mention on any list of baseball's all-time best teams.

The Yankees, in their fourth season under the ownership of George Steinbrenner and in their first full year with Billy Martin as manager, had plugged numerous holes in their third-place team of '75 with shrewd trading and also had holdover talent in Thurman Munson, Chris Chambliss, Graig Nettles, Sparky Lyle and Jim (Catfish) Hunter, the latter having joined the club on December 31, 1974, after being declared a free agent because of a breach in his Oakland A's contract.

Yes, the Yanks were back in the Series fray. But not for long.

Cincinnati won the Series opener at Riverfront Stadium, 5-1, as Morgan poled a first-inning home run, Perez banged out three hits and Gullett and reliever Pedro Borbon combined on a five-hitter. In Game 2, Perez's two-out single in the ninth scored Griffey and lifted the Reds to a 4-3 triumph over Hunter and the Yanks. Hunter had retired the Reds' first two batters in the ninth, but New York shortstop Fred Stanley's two-base throwing error on Griffey's roller put the National League champions in business.

The Series then moved to most familiar territory—Yankee Stadium. Well, not totally familiar. While 27 Series had been played there from 1923 through 1964, the House That Ruth Built had a new look in 1976. The modernized stadium, in fact, had just reopened its gates in '76 following a two-year renovation period during which the Yankees played their home games at Shea Stadium (home of the National League's New York Mets).

Whatever the site, the Reds rolled merrily along. With the A.L.'s designated-hitter rule being used in Series play for the first time (it would be implemented in alternating years), Driessen had found a spot in the Cincinnati lineup. And he cracked a homer and went 3 for 3 in the third game, helping the Reds to a 6-2 victory. Driessen wound up batting .357 as the Reds' "DH" in the '76 fall classic; New York's designated hitters—the Yanks employed three—managed only one hit in the entire Series.

One bright spot for the Yankees in Game 3 was shortstop Jim Mason, who entered the game defensively in the fifth inning and then poked a bases-empty homer in the seventh. The trip to the plate was Mason's first and last in World Series competition, making him the only man to hit a home run in his lone Series career at-bat.

The Reds' Bench then leveled the Yankees in Game 4, blasting two-run and three-run homers, and it was all over. The 7-2 triumph made Cincinnati the National League's first repeat winner of the World Series since the New York Giants of 1921 and 1922.

Seven of the Reds' nine everyday players in this Series (including the designated hitter) batted above .300, led by Bench's .533 average and Foster's .429 mark. Amazingly, Anderson did not make a single change during the entire Series among his nine regulars, forsaking the use of a pinch-hitter or a pinch-runner and never making a switch in either his batting order or defensive alignment. Reds pitchers did their

part, combining for a 2.00 earned-run average against the Yankees (who did get a marvelous performance from Munson, who followed up his .435 Championship Series batting mark against the Kansas City Royals with a .529 World Series effort against the Reds).

Cincinnati's two-year booty now consisted of 210 regular-season victories, a 6-0 record in Championship Series play and World Series triumphs over the Boston Red Sox and the New York Yankees, the latter conquest achieved via a sweep. Truly resembling the Yanks of old, these Reds proved emphatically that they were worthy of the super-team label being bestowed upon them.

Morgan, who had batted .320 for the Reds in the regular season with 27 home runs and 111 RBIs, wondered aloud: "How can you have a much better team than this one?"

Game 1

Saturday, October 16, At Cincinnati

New York	AB.	R.	H.	RBI.	PO.	A.
Rivers, cf	4	0	0	0	3	0
White, lf	4	0	1	0	4	0
Munson, c	4	0	0	0	5	1
Piniella, dh	3	1	1	0	0	0
bMay, dh	1	0	0	0	0	0
Chambliss, 1b	3	0	1	0	4	0
Nettles, 3b	3	0	0	1	3	0
Maddox, rf	2	0	1	0	0	0
cGamble	1	0	0	0	0	0
Randolph, 2b	2	0	0	0	3	2
Stanley, ss	1	0	0	0	2	3
aVelez	1	0	0	0	0	0
Mason, ss	0	0	0	0	0	1
Alexander, p	0	0	0	0	0	1
Lyle, p	0	0	0	0	0	0
Totals	29	1	5	1	24	8

Cincinnati	AB.	R.	H.	RBI.	PO.	A.
Rose, 3b	2	0	0	1	2	2
Griffey, rf	4	1	0	0	2	0
Morgan, 2b	4	1	1	1	3	4
Perez, 1b	4	0	3	1	11	0
Driessen, dh	4	0	0	0	0	0
Foster, lf	3	1	2	0	0	0
Bench, c	3	1	2	1	5	1
Geronimo, cf	3	0	1	0	2	0
Concepcion, ss	3	1	1	0	2	3
Gullett, p	0	0	0	0	0	1
Borbon, p	0	0	0	0	0	1
Totals	30	5	10	4	27	12

New York ....0 1 0 0 0 0 0 0 0—1
Cincinnati ....1 0 1 0 0 1 2 0 x—5

New York	IP.	H.	R.	ER.	BB.	SO.
Alexander (L)	6*	9	5	5	2	1
Lyle	2	1	0	0	0	3

Cincinnati	IP.	H.	R.	ER.	BB.	SO.
Gullett (W)	7⅓	5	1	1	3	4
Borbon	1⅔	0	0	0	0	0

*Pitched to two batters in seventh.

aStruck out for Stanley in seventh. bFlied out for Piniella in eighth. cFouled out for Maddox in ninth. E—Chambliss, Geronimo. DP—New York 2, Cincinnati 2. LOB—New York 6, Cincinnati 4. 2B—Piniella, Perez, Geronimo. 3B—Concepcion, Maddox, Bench. HR—Morgan. SB—Griffey. SF—Nettles, Rose. HBP—By Gullett (Chambliss). WP—Lyle. U—Weyer (N.L.) plate, DiMuro (A.L.) first, B. Williams (N.L.) second, Deegan (A.L.) third, Froemming (N.L.) left and Phillips (A.L.) right. T—2:10. A—54,826.

Game 2

Sunday, October 17, At Cincinnati

New York	AB.	R.	H.	RBI.	PO.	A.
Rivers, cf	5	0	0	0	6	0
White, lf	3	0	1	0	6	0
Munson, c	4	1	1	1	7	1
Piniella, rf	4	0	2	0	1	0
Chambliss, 1b	4	0	2	0	2	0
Nettles, 3b	4	0	1	1	2	1
Maddox, dh	3	0	0	0	0	0
aMay, dh	1	0	0	0	0	0
Randolph, 2b	4	1	1	0	2	0
Stanley, ss	3	1	1	1	0	0
Hunter, p	0	0	0	0	0	1
Totals	35	3	9	3	26	3

Cincinnati	AB.	R.	H.	RBI.	PO.	A.
Rose, 3b	4	0	0	0	0	0
Griffey, rf	4	1	0	1	1	0
Morgan, 2b	4	0	2	0	6	3
Perez, 1b	5	0	2	1	8	1
Driessen, dh	4	1	2	0	0	0
Foster, lf	4	0	1	1	2	0
Bench, c	4	1	2	0	3	0
Geronimo, cf	2	1	0	0	4	0
Concepcion, ss	4	0	1	1	2	3
Norman, p	0	0	0	0	0	1
Billingham, p	0	0	0	0	1	0
Totals	35	4	10	4	27	8

New York ....0 0 0 1 0 0 2 0 0—3
Cincinnati ....0 3 0 0 0 0 0 0 1—4

Two out when winning run scored.

New York	IP.	H.	R.	ER.	BB.	SO.
Hunter (L)	8⅔	10	4	3	4	5

Cincinnati	IP.	H.	R.	ER.	BB.	SO.
Norman	6⅓	9	3	3	2	2
Billingham (W)	2⅔	0	0	0	0	1

aGrounded out for Maddox in eighth. E—Stanley. DP—Cincinnati 1. LOB—New York 7, Cincinnati 10. 2B—Driessen, Bench, Stanley. 3B—Morgan. SB—Morgan, Concepcion. SF—Griffey. U—DiMuro (A.L.) plate, B. Williams (N.L.) first, Deegan (A.L.) second, Froemming (N.L.) third, Phillips (A.L.) left and Weyer (N.L.) right. T—2:33. A—54,816.

Game 3

Tuesday, October 19, At New York

Cincinnati	AB.	R.	H.	RBI.	PO.	A.
Rose, 3b	5	1	2	0	1	1
Griffey, rf	4	0	1	0	0	0
Morgan, 2b	4	1	1	1	2	0
Perez, 1b	4	0	0	0	7	2
Driessen, dh	3	2	3	1	0	0
Foster, lf	4	1	2	2	4	0
Bench, c	4	0	2	0	8	0
Geronimo, cf	4	1	1	1	3	0
Concepcion, ss	4	0	1	1	1	2
Zachry, p	0	0	0	0	0	2
McEnaney, p	0	0	0	0	1	0
Totals	36	6	13	6	27	7

New York	AB.	R.	H.	RBI.	PO.	A.
Rivers, cf	4	0	2	0	1	0
White, lf	3	0	0	0	1	0
Munson, c	5	0	3	0	6	2
Chambliss, 1b	5	1	1	0	11	1
May, dh	4	0	0	0	0	0
Nettles, 3b	2	0	0	0	1	4
Gamble, rf	3	0	1	1	2	0
bPiniella, rf	1	0	0	0	0	0
Randolph, 2b	4	0	0	0	4	4
Stanley, ss	1	0	0	0	1	2
aHendricks	1	0	0	0	0	0
Mason, ss	1	1	1	1	0	1
cVelez	1	0	0	0	0	0
Ellis, p	0	0	0	0	0	0
Jackson, p	0	0	0	0	0	3
Tidrow, p	0	0	0	0	0	0
Totals	35	2	8	2	27	17

Cincinnati ....0 3 0 1 0 0 0 2 0—6
New York ....0 0 0 1 0 0 1 0 0—2

Cincinnati	IP.	H.	R.	ER.	BB.	SO.
Zachry (W)	6⅔	6	2	2	5	6
McEnaney (S)	2⅓	2	0	0	0	1

New York	IP.	H.	R.	ER.	BB.	SO.
Ellis (L)	3⅓	7	4	4	0	1
Jackson	3⅔*	4	2	2	0	3
Tidrow	2	2	0	0	1	1

*Pitched to three batters in eighth.

aFlied out for Stanley in fourth. bGrounded out for Gamble in eighth. cStruck out for Mason in ninth. E—Morgan, Zachry. DP—Cincinnati 1, New York 3. LOB—Cincinnati 4, New York 11. 2B—Foster, Driessen, Morgan. HR—Driessen, Mason. SB—Driessen, Geronimo. U—B. Williams (N.L.) plate, Deegan (A.L.) first, Froemming (N.L.) second, Phillips (A.L.) third, Weyer (N.L.) left and DiMuro (A.L.) right. T—2:40. A—56,667.

Game 4

Thursday, October 21, At New York

Cincinnati	AB.	R.	H.	RBI.	PO.	A.
Rose, 3b	5	0	1	0	3	0
Griffey, rf	5	0	0	0	2	0
Morgan, 2b	3	1	1	0	2	3
Perez, 1b	3	1	0	0	6	1
Driessen, dh	3	1	0	0	0	0
Foster, lf	3	1	1	1	8	0
Bench, c	4	2	2	5	2	1
Geronimo, cf	4	1	2	0	3	0
Concepcion, ss	3	0	2	1	1	3
Nolan, p	0	0	0	0	0	1
McEnaney, p	0	0	0	0	0	0
Totals	33	7	9	7	27	9

New York	AB.	R.	H.	RBI.	PO.	A.
Rivers, cf	5	1	1	0	4	0
White, lf	5	0	0	0	2	0
Munson, c	4	1	4	1	3	3
Chambliss, 1b	4	0	1	1	9	2
May, dh	3	0	0	0	0	0
bPiniella, dh	1	0	0	0	0	0
Nettles, 3b	3	0	2	0	2	3
Gamble, rf	4	0	0	0	1	0
Randolph, 2b	4	0	0	0	4	2
Stanley, ss	1	0	0	0	1	2
aHendricks	1	0	0	0	0	0
Mason, ss	0	0	0	0	1	0
cVelez	1	0	0	0	0	0
Figueroa, p	0	0	0	0	0	1
Tidrow, p	0	0	0	0	0	0
Lyle, p	0	0	0	0	0	0
Totals	36	2	8	2	27	13

Cincinnati ....0 0 0 3 0 0 0 0 4—7
New York ....1 0 0 0 1 0 0 0 0—2

Cincinnati	IP.	H.	R.	ER.	BB.	SO.
Nolan (W)	6⅔	8	2	2	1	1
McEnaney (S)	2⅓	0	0	0	1	1

New York	IP.	H.	R.	ER.	BB.	SO.
Figueroa (L)	8*	6	5	5	5	2
Tidrow	⅓	3	2	2	0	0
Lyle	⅔	0	0	0	0	0

*Pitched to two batters in ninth.

aFouled out for Stanley in sixth. bFlied out for May in eighth. cStruck out for Mason in ninth. E—Morgan, Concepcion. DP—New York 1. LOB—Cincinnati 4, New York 9. 2B—Rose, Chambliss, Geronimo, Concepcion. HR—Bench 2. SB—Geronimo, Morgan, Rivers. WP—Figueroa. U—Deegan (A.L.) plate, Froemming (N.L.) first, Phillips (A.L.) second, Weyer (N.L.) third, DiMuro (A.L.) left and B. Williams (N.L.) right. T—2:36. A—56,700.

COMPOSITE BATTING AVERAGES

Cincinnati Reds

Player-Position	G.	AB.	R.	H.	2B.	3B.	HR.	RBI.	BA.
Bench, c	4	15	4	8	1	1	2	6	.533
Foster, lf	4	14	3	6	1	0	0	4	.429
Concepcion, ss	4	14	1	5	1	1	0	3	.357
Driessen, dh	4	14	4	5	2	0	1	1	.357
Morgan, 2b	4	15	3	5	1	1	1	2	.333
Perez, 1b	4	16	1	5	1	0	0	2	.313
Geronimo, cf	4	13	3	4	2	0	0	1	.308
Rose, 3b	4	16	1	3	1	0	0	1	.188
Griffey, rf	4	17	2	1	0	0	0	1	.059
McEnaney, p	2	0	0	0	0	0	0	0	.000
Borbon, p	1	0	0	0	0	0	0	0	.000
Billingham, p	1	0	0	0	0	0	0	0	.000
Gullett, p	1	0	0	0	0	0	0	0	.000
Nolan, p	1	0	0	0	0	0	0	0	.000
Norman, p	1	0	0	0	0	0	0	0	.000
Zachry, p	1	0	0	0	0	0	0	0	.000
Totals	4	134	22	42	10	3	4	21	.313

New York Yankees

Player-Position	G.	AB.	R.	H.	2B.	3B.	HR.	RBI.	BA.
Mason, ss	3	1	1	1	0	0	1	1	1.000
Munson, c	4	17	2	9	0	0	0	2	.529
Piniella, dh-rf-ph	4	9	1	3	1	0	0	0	.333
Chambliss, 1b	4	16	1	5	1	0	0	1	.313
Nettles, 3b	4	12	0	3	0	0	0	2	.250
Maddox, rf-dh	2	5	0	1	0	1	0	0	.200
Rivers, cf	4	18	1	3	0	0	0	0	.167
Stanley, ss	4	6	1	1	1	0	0	1	.167
White, lf	4	15	0	2	0	0	0	0	.133
Gamble, ph-rf	3	8	0	1	0	0	0	1	.125
Randolph, 2b	4	14	1	1	0	0	0	0	.071
Hendricks, ph	2	2	0	0	0	0	0	0	.000
Velez, ph	3	3	0	0	0	0	0	0	.000
May, ph-dh	4	9	0	0	0	0	0	0	.000
Tidrow, p	2	0	0	0	0	0	0	0	.000
Lyle, p	2	0	0	0	0	0	0	0	.000
Alexander, p	1	0	0	0	0	0	0	0	.000
Ellis, p	1	0	0	0	0	0	0	0	.000
Figueroa, p	1	0	0	0	0	0	0	0	.000
Hunter, p	1	0	0	0	0	0	0	0	.000
Jackson, p	1	0	0	0	0	0	0	0	.000
Totals	4	135	8	30	3	1	1	8	.222

COMPOSITE PITCHING AVERAGES

Cincinnati Reds

Pitcher	G.	IP.	H.	R.	ER.	BB.	SO.	W.	L.	ERA.
McEnaney	2	4⅔	2	0	0	1	2	0	0	0.00
Billingham	1	2⅔	0	0	0	0	1	1	0	0.00
Borbon	1	1⅔	0	0	0	0	0	0	0	0.00
Gullett	1	7⅓	5	1	1	3	4	1	0	1.23
Nolan	1	6⅔	8	2	2	1	1	1	0	2.70
Zachry	1	6⅔	6	2	2	5	6	1	0	2.70
Norman	1	6⅓	9	3	3	2	2	0	0	4.26
Totals	4	36	30	8	8	12	16	4	0	2.00

New York Yankees

Pitcher	G.	IP.	H.	R.	ER.	BB.	SO.	W.	L.	ERA.
Lyle	2	2⅔	1	0	0	0	3	0	0	0.00
Hunter	1	8⅔	10	4	3	4	5	0	1	3.12
Jackson	1	3⅔	4	2	2	0	3	0	0	4.91
Figueroa	1	8	6	5	5	5	2	0	1	5.63
Alexander	1	6	9	5	5	2	1	0	1	7.50
Tidrow	2	2⅓	5	2	2	1	1	0	0	7.71
Ellis	1	3⅓	7	4	4	0	1	0	1	10.80
Totals	4	34⅔	42	22	21	12	16	0	4	5.45

1977
NEW YORK YANKEES
VS.
LOS ANGELES DODGERS

Reginald Martinez Jackson already had put together some pretty good numbers in World Series competition. As he approached the plate in the fourth inning of Game 6 of the 1977 fall classic, the 31-year-old outfielder boasted a .317 career Series batting average in 17 games, with four home runs and 10 runs batted in.

Jackson, signed by the New York Yankees as a free agent following the 1976 season after playing out his option year with the Baltimore Orioles, had appeared in his first 12 Series games with the Oakland A's. Now, in Yankee pin stripes, he was trying to provide the New Yorkers with the same winning edge that he had lent to the rambunctious A's—and Reggie wasn't doing too badly.

The lefthanded-hitting slugger had belted 32 home runs and knocked in 110 runs in his first season with the Yankees, helping New York to its second straight American League pennant. After having a poor Championship Series against the Kansas City Royals (two hits in 16 at-bats), he was enjoying a fine World Series against the Los Angeles Dodgers. Jackson had homered in his last official at-bat, connecting in the eighth inning of Game 5, and was batting .353 in this Series. He had rapped a double and a home run in Game 4.

As Jackson dug in against Dodgers starter Burt Hooton, off whom Reggie had drawn a second-inning walk, the Yankees led Los Angeles, three games to two, in the Series but trailed in this contest by a 3-2 score. Thurman Munson was on first base for the Yanks with an inning-opening single. Hooton delivered his first pitch to Jackson and Reggie rocketed it into the right-field stands,

sending New York into a 4-3 lead. Lou Piniella added a sacrifice fly later in the inning and the Yankees suddenly had built a two-run lead.

With two out in the Yanks' fifth and Willie Randolph on first base, Jackson drilled another first-pitch homer into the right-field seats, victimizing Elias Sosa this time around.

Then, facing Charlie Hough, Jackson electrified the Yankee Stadium throng of 56,407 by leading off the eighth with a prodigious wallop into the center-field bleachers. You guessed it, he blasted Hough's first offering.

Jackson had made his 18th World Series game one of the most memorable contests in the history of the fall classic, becoming only the second player in history to smash three home runs in one Series game (Babe Ruth achieved the feat twice, in 1926 and 1928). Furthermore, Reggie's five home runs in one Series and his four consecutive homers over two Series games were unprecedented feats.

The incredible display provided an emotional turnaround for Jackson, who had been embroiled in season-long squabbles with Manager Billy Martin and who exactly four months earlier had been pulled off the field by Martin at Boston's Fenway Park for what the manager termed a lack of hustle. Jackson's removal and ensuing dugout confrontation with Martin during the Saturday afternoon game were captured by national television cameras, and Reggie's spirits plunged. The strong-willed Messrs. Jackson and Martin bruised each other's ego right and left in 1977, but they patched up their differences long enough to work together in the common quest of bringing a

World Series championship back to Yankee Stadium. And bring it they did.

New York, getting its second complete-game performance of the Series from Mike Torrez (an April acquisition from Oakland), rode Jackson's five RBIs to a clinching 8-4 triumph that earned the Yankees their first World Series crown since 1962 and 21st title overall.

The Dodgers, guided by first-year Manager Tommy Lasorda, had upset the vaunted Cincinnati Reds in the National League West race and bowled over the Philadelphia Phillies in the Championship Series. They had a talented pitching staff headed by 20-game winner Tommy John and a potent offense that featured the long-ball exploits of Steve Garvey, Reggie Smith, Ron Cey and Dusty Baker. For the first time in big-league history, four players on one club hit 30 or more homers in the same season—and Garvey (33), Smith (32), Cey (30) and Baker (30) did the honors.

The Dodgers battled gamely in the Series opener, tying the game at 3-3 in the ninth on pinch-hitter Lee Lacy's single. But the Yankees prevailed in the 12th when Randolph doubled and Paul Blair singled. In Game 2, Cey, Smith and Steve Yeager cracked early-inning homers off Jim (Catfish) Hunter and Hooton tossed a five-hitter as Los Angeles scored a 6-1 victory.

New York then leaped to a three games-to-one lead, taking Game 3 by a 5-3 count as Torrez outpitched John and then winning the fourth contest, 4-2, behind the effective pitching of blossoming lefthander Ron Guidry. But the Dodgers stayed in contention by roughing up free-agent signee Don Gullett in Game 5. Yeager blasted a three-run homer

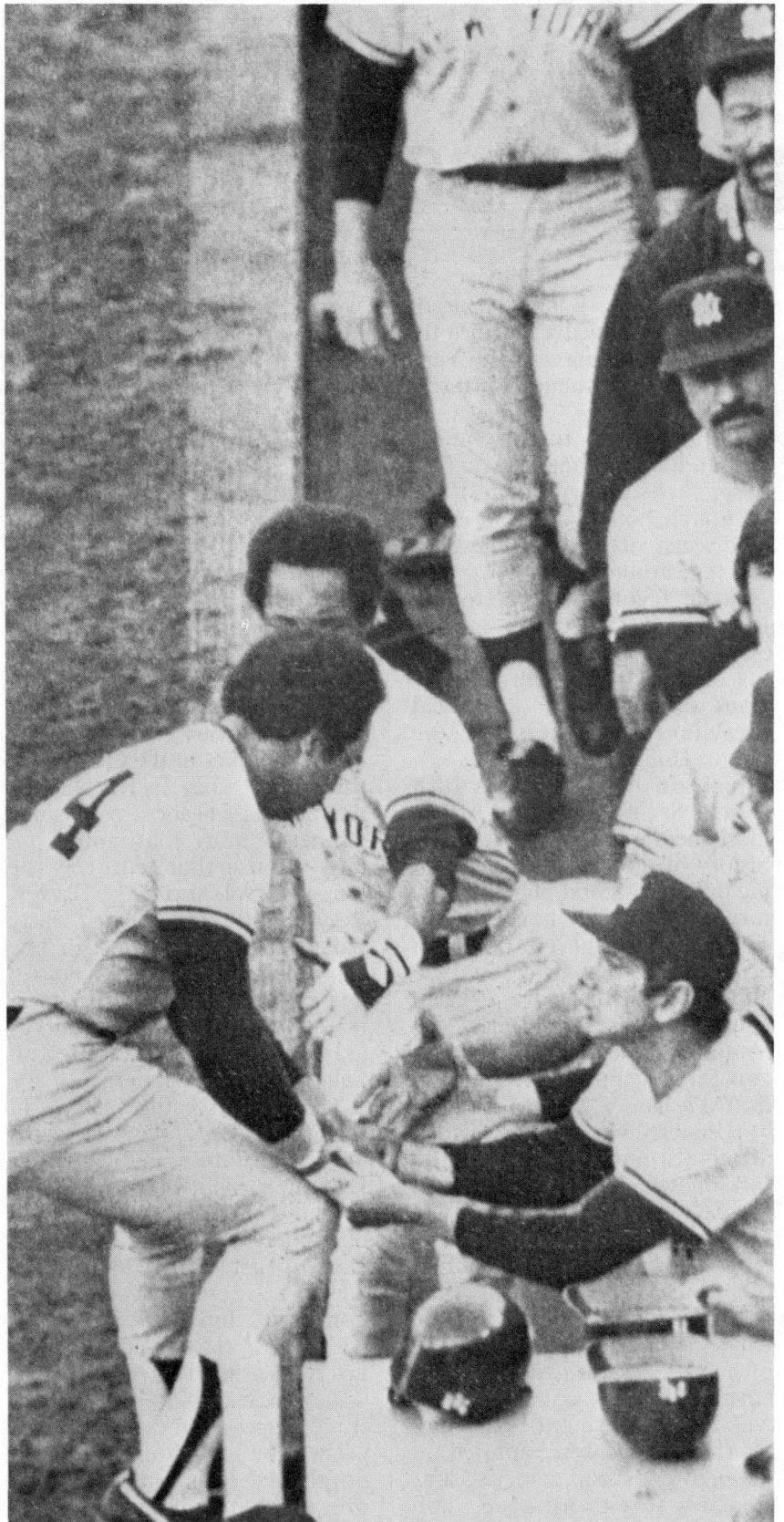

Yankee slugger Reggie Jackson gets a warm greeting from the New York dugout after one of his big 1977 World Series hits.

off the former Cincinnati Reds stalwart in the fourth inning and Los Angeles, receiving steady pitching from Don Sutton, went on to a 10-4 triumph.

That set the stage for Reggie

Jackson's heroics.

The Yankees needed every bit of Jackson's offensive production —his final numbers against the Dodgers included a .450 batting mark, five homers and eight RBIs —plus solid pitching contributions from Torrez (2-0 record, 2.50 earned-run average) and Guidry (a four-hit, seven-strikeout performance in his lone outing) to overcome some shaky performances from their big-name hurlers. Gullett and Hunter, both of whom had arm problems during the regular season, allowed 14 earned runs in their 17 innings of Series work and absorbed the Yankees' two losses.

Persevere the New Yorkers did, and once again the month of October belonged to the Yankees. It also belonged to Reggie Jackson.

Game 1

Tuesday, October 11, At New York

Los Angeles	AB.	R.	H.	RBI.	PO.	A.
Lopes, 2b	5	1	0	0	4	2
Russell, ss	6	1	1	1	4	3
Smith, rf	4	0	1	0	2	1
Cey, 3b	3	0	0	1	3	2
Garvey, 1b	4	0	1	0	8	3
Baker, lf	4	1	1	0	2	0
Burke, cf	3	0	1	0	2	0
aMota	1	0	0	0	0	0
Monday, cf	1	0	0	0	0	0
Yeager, c	3	0	0	0	4	1
cLandestoy	0	0	0	0	0	0
Grote, c	1	0	0	0	3	3
Sutton, p	2	0	0	0	1	1
Rautzhan, p	0	0	0	0	0	1
Sosa, p	0	0	0	0	0	0
bLacy	1	0	1	1	0	0
Garman, p	0	0	0	0	0	0
dDavalillo	1	0	0	0	0	0
Rhoden, p	0	0	0	0	0	0
Totals	39	3	6	3	33	17

New York	AB.	R.	H.	RBI.	PO.	A.
Rivers, cf	6	0	0	0	8	1
Randolph, 2b	5	3	2	1	2	4
Munson, c	4	1	2	1	9	1
Jackson, rf	2	0	1	0	1	0
Blair, rf	2	0	1	1	1	0
Chambliss, 1b	5	0	1	1	11	1
Nettles, 3b	4	0	0	0	0	4
Piniella, lf	5	0	2	0	3	0
Dent, ss	5	0	2	0	0	3
Gullett, p	1	0	0	0	1	1
Lyle, p	2	0	0	0	0	0
Totals	41	4	11	4	36	15

```
Los Angeles.................2 0 0  0 0 0  0 0 1  0 0 0—3
New York......................1 0 0  0 0 1  0 1 0  0 0 1—4
```
None out when winning run scored.

Los Angeles	IP.	H.	R.	ER.	BB.	SO.
Sutton	7*	8	3	3	1	4
Rautzhan	⅓	0	0	0	2	0
Sosa	⅔	0	0	0	0	1
Garman	3	1	0	0	1	3
Rhoden (L)	0†	2	1	1	1	0

New York	IP.	H.	R.	ER.	BB.	SO.
Gullett	8⅓	5	3	3	6	6
Lyle (W)	3⅔	1	0	0	0	2

*Pitched to two batters in eighth.
†Pitched to three batters in twelfth.

aFlied out for Burke in ninth. bSingled for Sosa in ninth. cRan for Yeager in ninth. dGrounded out for Garman in twelfth. LOB—Los Angeles 8, New York 12. 2B—Munson, Randolph. 3B—Russell. HR—Randolph. SH—Gullett 2. SF —Cey. HBP—By Gullett (Baker), by Sutton (Jackson). U —Chylak (A.L.) plate, Sudol (N.L.) first, McCoy (A.L.) second, Dale (N.L.) third, Evans (A.L.) left and McSherry (N.L.) right. T—3:24. A—56,668.

Game 2

Wednesday, October 12, At New York

Los Angeles	AB.	R.	H.	RBI.	PO.	A.
Lopes, 2b	4	0	0	0	2	1
Russell, ss	4	1	1	0	0	4
Smith, rf	3	2	2	2	2	0

	AB.	R.	H.	RBI.	PO.	A.
Cey, 3b	4	1	1	2	1	1
Garvey, 1b	4	1	2	1	6	1
Baker, lf	4	0	0	0	2	0
Monday, cf	3	0	1	0	0	0
Burke, cf	1	0	0	0	5	0
Yeager, c	4	1	2	1	9	0
Hooton, p	3	0	0	0	0	0
Totals	34	6	9	6	27	7

New York	AB.	R.	H.	RBI.	PO.	A.
Rivers, cf	4	0	0	0	4	0
Randolph, 2b	4	1	1	0	2	2
Munson, c	4	0	1	0	3	3
Jackson, rf	4	0	0	0	0	0
Chambliss, 1b	4	0	0	0	11	2
Nettles, 3b	2	0	1	0	0	6
Piniella, lf	3	0	1	0	4	0
Dent, ss	2	0	1	0	0	1
bJohnson	1	0	0	0	0	0
Stanley, ss	0	0	0	0	1	0
Hunter, p	0	0	0	0	1	0
Tidrow, p	1	0	0	0	0	0
aZeber	1	0	0	0	0	0
Clay, p	0	0	0	0	1	1
cWhite	1	0	0	0	0	0
Lyle, p	0	0	0	0	0	0
Totals	31	1	5	0	27	15

Los Angeles .... 2 1 2 0 0 0 0 0 1—6
New York .... 0 0 0 1 0 0 0 0 0—1

Los Angeles	IP.	H.	R.	ER.	BB.	SO.
Hooton (W)	9	5	1	1	1	8

New York	IP.	H.	R.	ER.	BB.	SO.
Hunter (L)	2⅓	5	5	5	0	0
Tidrow	2⅔	3	0	0	0	1
Clay	3	0	0	0	1	0
Lyle	1	1	1	1	0	0

aStruck out for Tidrow in fifth. bFlied out for Dent in seventh. cFlied out for Clay in eighth. DP—Los Angeles 1. LOB—Los Angeles 2, New York 4. 2B—Smith. HR—Cey, Yeager, Smith, Garvey. U—Sudol (N.L.) plate, McCoy (A.L.) first, Dale (N.L.) second, Evans (A.L.) third, McSherry (N.L.) left and Chylak (A.L.) right. T—2:27. A—56,691.

Game 3

Friday, October 14, At Los Angeles

New York	AB.	R.	H.	RBI.	PO.	A.
Rivers, cf	5	1	3	1	4	0
Randolph, 2b	4	0	0	0	1	2
Munson, c	5	1	1	1	9	0
Jackson, rf	3	2	1	1	0	0
Blair, rf	1	0	0	0	0	0
Piniella, lf	3	0	2	1	2	0
Chambliss, 1b	4	0	1	1	8	1
Nettles, 3b	4	1	1	0	1	4
Dent, ss	3	0	1	0	1	2
Torrez, p	3	0	0	0	1	1
Totals	35	5	10	5	27	10

Los Angeles	AB.	R.	H.	RBI.	PO.	A.
Lopes, 2b	4	0	0	0	1	4
Russell, ss	4	0	0	0	2	4
Smith, rf	3	1	1	0	2	0
Cey, 3b	3	0	0	0	1	1
Garvey, 1b	4	1	2	0	9	1
Baker, lf	4	1	2	3	1	0
Monday, cf	4	0	0	0	2	0
Yeager, c	4	0	2	0	9	1
John, p	2	0	0	0	0	0
aDavalillo	1	0	0	0	0	0
Hough, p	0	0	0	0	0	0
bMota	1	0	0	0	0	0
Totals	34	3	7	3	27	11

New York .... 3 0 0 1 1 0 0 0 0—5
Los Angeles .... 0 0 3 0 0 0 0 0 0—3

New York	IP.	H.	R.	ER.	BB.	SO.
Torrez (W)	9	7	3	3	3	9

Los Angeles	IP.	H.	R.	ER.	BB.	SO.
John (L)	6	9	5	4	3	7
Hough	3	1	0	0	0	2

aHit into force play for John in sixth. bStruck out for Hough in ninth. E—Baker. DP—Los Angeles 1. LOB—New York 8, Los Angeles 7. 2B—Rivers 2, Munson, Yeager. HR—Baker. SB—Lopes, Rivers. SH—Torrez. HBP—By John (Piniella). U—McCoy (A.L.) plate, Dale (N.L.) first, Evans (A.L.) second, McSherry (N.L.) third, Chylak (A.L.) left and Sudol (N.L.) right. T—2:31. A—55,992.

Game 4

Saturday, October 15, At Los Angeles

New York	AB.	R.	H.	RBI.	PO.	A.
Rivers, cf	4	0	1	0	3	0
Randolph, 2b	4	0	0	0	3	2
Munson, c	4	0	1	0	8	1
Jackson, rf	4	2	2	1	2	0
Blair, rf	0	0	0	0	0	0
Piniella, lf	4	1	1	1	2	0
Chambliss, 1b	3	1	1	0	8	0
Nettles, 3b	3	0	0	1	1	3
Dent, ss	3	0	1	1	0	2
Guidry, p	2	0	0	0	0	0
Totals	31	4	7	4	27	8

Los Angeles	AB.	R.	H.	RBI.	PO.	A.
Lopes, 2b	2	1	1	2	3	6
Russell, ss	4	0	0	0	1	5
Smith, cf	4	0	0	0	1	0
Cey, 3b	4	0	2	0	0	0
Garvey, 1b	4	0	0	0	14	1
Baker, lf	4	0	0	0	2	0
Lacy, rf	2	0	0	0	1	0
Yeager, c	3	0	0	0	4	2
Rau, p	0	0	0	0	0	0
Rhoden, p	2	1	1	0	1	1
aMota	1	0	0	0	0	0
Garman, p	0	0	0	0	0	0
Totals	30	2	4	2	27	15

New York .... 0 3 0 0 0 1 0 0 0—4
Los Angeles .... 0 0 2 0 0 0 0 0 0—2

New York	IP.	H.	R.	ER.	BB.	SO.
Guidry (W)	9	4	2	2	3	7

Los Angeles	IP.	H.	R.	ER.	BB.	SO.
Rau (L)	1*	4	3	3	0	0
Rhoden	7	2	1	1	0	5
Garman	1	1	0	0	0	0

*Pitched to three batters in second.

aFlied out for Rhoden in eighth. DP—Los Angeles 2. LOB—New York 1, Los Angeles 4. 2B—Jackson, Chambliss, Rhoden, Cey. HR—Lopes, Jackson. SB—Lopes. SH—Guidry. U—Dale (N.L.) plate, Evans (A.L.) first, McSherry (N.L.) second, Chylak (A.L.) third, Sudol (N.L.) left and McCoy (A.L.) right. T—2:07. A—55,995.

Game 5

Sunday, October 16, At Los Angeles

New York	AB.	R.	H.	RBI.	PO.	A.
Rivers, cf	4	0	0	0	4	0
Randolph, 2b	4	0	1	0	3	1
Munson, c	4	1	2	1	5	0
Johnson, c	0	0	0	0	0	0
Jackson, rf	4	2	2	1	1	0
Chambliss, 1b	4	1	2	0	8	0
Nettles, 3b	4	0	2	1	0	3
Piniella, lf	4	0	0	0	3	0
Dent, ss	4	0	0	1	0	3
Gullett, p	1	0	0	0	0	1
Clay, p	0	0	0	0	0	0
aZeber	1	0	0	0	0	0
Tidrow, p	0	0	0	0	0	1
bWhite	1	0	0	0	0	0
Hunter, p	0	0	0	0	0	0
dBlair	1	0	0	0	0	0
Totals	36	4	9	4	24	9

Los Angeles	AB.	R.	H.	RBI.	PO.	A.
Lopes, 2b	5	1	2	0	2	5
Russell, ss	5	1	2	1	1	1
Smith, cf-rf	4	2	1	2	6	0
Cey, 3b	4	0	0	0	0	2
Garvey, 1b	4	2	2	0	9	0
Baker, lf	4	2	3	2	2	0
Lacy, rf	3	1	2	1	1	0
Burke, cf	1	0	0	0	3	0
Yeager, c	2	1	1	4	2	0
cOates, c	1	0	0	0	1	0
Sutton, p	4	0	0	0	0	0
Totals	37	10	13	10	27	8

New York .... 0 0 0 0 0 0 2 2 0— 4
Los Angeles .... 1 0 0 4 3 2 0 0 x—10

New York	IP.	H.	R.	ER.	BB.	SO.
Gullett (L)	4⅓	8	7	6	1	4
Clay	⅔	2	1	1	0	0
Tidrow	1	2	2	2	0	0
Hunter	2	1	0	0	0	1

Los Angeles	IP.	H.	R.	ER.	BB.	SO.
Sutton (W)	9	9	4	4	0	2

aStruck out for Clay in sixth. bPopped out for Tidrow in seventh. cFlied out for Yeager in seventh. dFlied out for Hunter in ninth. E—Nettles, Piniella. LOB—New York 5, Los Angeles 5. 2B—Garvey, Randolph, Nettles. 3B—Lopes. HR—Yeager, Smith, Munson, Jackson. SF—Yeager. U—Evans (A.L.) plate, McSherry (N.L.) first, Chylak (A.L.) second, Sudol (N.L.) third, McCoy (A.L.) left and Dale (N.L.) right. T—2:29. A—55,955.

Game 6

Tuesday, October 18, At New York

Los Angeles	AB.	R.	H.	RBI.	PO.	A.
Lopes, 2b	4	0	1	0	0	4
Russell, ss	3	0	0	0	1	4
Smith, rf	4	2	1	1	1	0
Cey, 3b	3	1	1	0	0	1
Garvey, 1b	4	1	2	2	13	0
Baker, lf	4	0	1	0	2	0
Monday, cf	4	0	1	0	3	0
Yeager, c	3	0	1	0	4	2
bDavalillo	1	0	1	1	0	0
Hooton, p	2	0	0	0	0	0
Sosa, p	0	0	0	0	0	0
Rau, p	0	0	0	0	0	0
aGoodson	1	0	0	0	0	0
Hough, p	0	0	0	0	0	0
cLacy	1	0	0	0	0	0
Totals	34	4	9	4	24	11

New York	AB.	R.	H.	RBI.	PO.	A.
Rivers, cf	4	0	2	0	1	0
Randolph, 2b	4	1	0	0	2	3
Munson, c	4	1	1	0	6	0
Jackson, rf	3	4	3	5	5	0
Chambliss, 1b	4	2	2	2	9	1
Nettles, 3b	4	0	0	0	0	0
Piniella, lf	3	0	0	1	2	1
Dent, ss	2	0	0	0	1	4
Torrez, p	3	0	0	0	1	2
Totals	31	8	8	8	27	11

Los Angeles .... 2 0 1 0 0 0 0 0 1—4
New York .... 0 2 0 3 2 0 0 1 x—8

Los Angeles	IP.	H.	R.	ER.	BB.	SO.
Hooton (L)	3*	3	4	4	1	1
Sosa	1⅔	3	3	3	1	0
Rau	1⅓	0	0	0	0	1
Hough	2	2	1	1	0	3

New York	IP.	H.	R.	ER.	BB.	SO.
Torrez (W)	9	9	4	2	2	6

*Pitched to three batters in fourth.

aStruck out for Rau in seventh. bBunted safely for Yeager in ninth. cPopped out for Hough in ninth. E—Dent. DP—New York 2. LOB—Los Angeles 5, New York 2. 2B—Chambliss. 3B—Garvey. HR—Chambliss, Smith, Jackson 3. SF—Piniella. PB—Munson. U—McSherry (N.L.) plate, Chylak (A.L.) first, Sudol (N.L.) second, McCoy (A.L.) third, Dale (N.L.) left and Evans (A.L.) right. T—2:18. A—56,407.

COMPOSITE BATTING AVERAGES

New York Yankees

Player-Position	G.	AB.	R.	H.	2B.	3B.	HR.	RBI.	BA.
Jackson, rf	6	20	10	9	1	0	5	8	.450
Munson, c	6	25	4	8	2	0	1	3	.320
Chambliss, 1b	6	24	4	7	2	0	1	4	.292
Piniella, lf	6	22	1	6	0	0	0	3	.273
Dent, ss	6	19	0	5	0	0	0	2	.263
Blair, rf-ph	4	4	0	1	0	0	0	1	.250
Rivers, cf	6	27	1	6	2	0	0	1	.222
Nettles, 3b	6	21	1	4	1	0	0	2	.190
Randolph, 2b	6	25	5	4	2	0	1	1	.160
Johnson, ph-c	2	1	0	0	0	0	0	0	.000
Tidrow, p	2	1	0	0	0	0	0	0	.000
Guidry, p	1	2	0	0	0	0	0	0	.000
Gullett, p	2	2	0	0	0	0	0	0	.000
Lyle, p	2	2	0	0	0	0	0	0	.000
White, ph	2	2	0	0	0	0	0	0	.000
Zeber, ph	2	2	0	0	0	0	0	0	.000
Torrez, p	2	6	0	0	0	0	0	0	.000
Clay, p	2	0	0	0	0	0	0	0	.000
Hunter, p	2	0	0	0	0	0	0	0	.000
Stanley, ss	1	0	0	0	0	0	0	0	.000
Totals	6	205	26	50	10	0	8	25	.244

Los Angeles Dodgers

Player-Position	G.	AB.	R.	H.	2B.	3B.	HR.	RBI.	BA.
Rhoden, p	2	2	1	1	1	0	0	0	.500
Lacy, ph-rf	4	7	1	3	0	0	0	2	.429
Garvey, 1b	6	24	5	9	1	1	1	3	.375
Davalillo, ph	3	3	0	1	0	0	0	1	.333
Yeager, c	6	19	2	6	1	0	2	5	.316
Baker, lf	6	24	4	7	0	0	1	5	.292
Smith, rf-cf	6	22	7	6	1	0	3	5	.273
Burke, cf	3	5	0	1	0	0	0	0	.200
Cey, 3b	6	21	2	4	1	0	1	3	.190
Lopes, 2b	6	24	3	4	0	1	1	2	.167
Monday, cf	4	12	0	2	0	0	0	0	.167
Russell, ss	6	26	3	4	0	1	0	2	.154
Goodson, ph	1	1	0	0	0	0	0	0	.000
Grote, c	1	1	0	0	0	0	0	0	.000
Oates, ph-c	1	1	0	0	0	0	0	0	.000
John, p	1	2	0	0	0	0	0	0	.000
Mota, ph	3	3	0	0	0	0	0	0	.000
Hooton, p	2	5	0	0	0	0	0	0	.000
Sutton, p	2	6	0	0	0	0	0	0	.000
Garman, p	2	0	0	0	0	0	0	0	.000
Hough, p	2	0	0	0	0	0	0	0	.000
Rau, p	2	0	0	0	0	0	0	0	.000
Sosa, p	2	0	0	0	0	0	0	0	.000
Landestoy, pr	1	0	0	0	0	0	0	0	.000
Rautzhan, p	1	0	0	0	0	0	0	0	.000
Totals	6	208	28	48	5	3	9	28	.231

COMPOSITE PITCHING AVERAGES

New York Yankees

Pitcher	G.	IP.	H.	R.	ER.	BB.	SO.	W.	L.	ERA.
Lyle	2	4⅔	2	1	1	0	2	1	0	1.93
Guidry	1	9	4	2	2	3	7	1	0	2.00
Clay	2	3⅔	2	1	1	1	0	0	0	2.45
Torrez	2	18	16	7	5	5	15	2	0	2.50
Tidrow	2	3⅔	5	2	2	0	1	0	0	4.91
Gullett	2	12⅔	13	10	9	7	10	0	1	6.39
Hunter	2	4⅓	6	5	5	0	1	0	1	10.38
Totals	6	56	48	28	25	16	36	4	2	4.02

Los Angeles Dodgers

Pitcher	G.	IP.	H.	R.	ER.	BB.	SO.	W.	L.	ERA.
Garman	2	4	2	0	0	1	3	0	0	0.00
Rautzhan	1	⅓	0	0	0	2	0	0	0	0.00
Hough	2	5	3	1	1	0	5	0	0	1.80
Rhoden	2	7	4	2	2	1	5	0	1	2.57
Hooton	2	12	8	5	5	2	9	1	1	3.75
Sutton	2	16	17	7	7	1	6	1	0	3.94
John	1	6	9	5	4	3	7	0	1	6.00
Rau	2	2⅓	4	3	3	0	1	0	1	11.57
Sosa	2	2⅓	3	3	3	1	1	0	0	11.57
Totals	6	55	50	26	25	11	37	2	4	4.09

1978
NEW YORK YANKEES
VS.
LOS ANGELES DODGERS

Staring at a two games-to-none deficit in the World Series would be enough to deflate most teams. But such a predicament didn't faze the 1978 New York Yankees.

Which is clearly understandable. The Yankees, after all, had been down this road before. On the morning of July 20, New York trailed the Boston Red Sox by 14 games in the American League East race; on the afternoon of October 2, after finishing the regular season in a tie with the Red Sox, the Yanks won a one-game playoff with Boston for the East title.

A two-game deficit? No problem.

Well, that's the way it turned out. But considering the way the Los Angeles Dodgers played in Games 1 and 2 of the 1978 Series, the Yankees must have had some misgivings about their ability to come back this time.

In the Series opener at Dodger Stadium, Davey Lopes drove in five runs with a pair of homers as Los Angeles thumped the Yankees, 11-5. Dusty Baker also homered for the Dodgers, who raked 20-game winner Ed Figueroa and three relievers for 15 hits. Dodgers lefthander Tommy John pitched shutout ball for six innings in notching the first Series victory of his career. John's chief tormentor was Reggie Jackson, who picked up where he had left off last October by rapping two singles and a home run.

Roy Cey and rookie pitcher Bob Welch foiled the New Yorkers in Los Angeles' 4-3 triumph in Game 2. Cey knocked in all of the Dodgers' runs with a single in the fourth inning and a three-run homer in the sixth, while Welch came on in relief in the ninth and got his club out of a two-on, one-out jam. With New York trailing by one run and the Yanks' Bucky Dent on second base and Paul Blair on first, Welch retired Thurman Munson on a liner to right fielder Reggie Smith. Up next was Jackson. It was a classic case of the out-to-prove-himself kid against the proven veteran, the potential star against the bigger-than-life superstar. Welch, 21, had been summoned from the minor leagues in June; Jackson, 32, had just completed his 11th full season in the big leagues, a year in which he boosted his career homer total to 340.

In a fiercely contested battle of strength against strength (Welch's fastball against Jackson's ability to hit same), the count went to 3-2 as the crowd roared with every pitch. Reggie, who had fouled off three two-strike pitches en route to the full count, then swung mightily—and missed.

Game 3 at Yankee Stadium matched 15-game winner Don Sutton of the Dodgers against New York's Ron Guidry, who had turned in a dazzling 25-3 record in 1978 and embellished the mark with a 1.74 earned-run average and nine shutouts. Guidry labored in this game, allowing seven walks and eight hits. But the Yankees clipped Sutton for five runs and nine hits in 6⅓ innings, with Roy White delivering a first-inning homer and scoring two runs to spark the Yanks' offense. The big story for the New Yorkers, though, was third baseman Graig Nettles, whose sensational fielding thwarted Los Angeles time and again.

With two out and one on in the third inning, Nettles foiled the Dodgers by throwing out Smith after making a diving, backhanded stop of his hard smash down the third-base line. In the fifth, with Los Angeles baserunners on first and second and two out, he knocked down another drive by Smith over the bag and held the Dodger power hitter to an infield single. On the next play, with the bases loaded, he speared a hard-hit grounder by Steve Garvey and forced Smith at second. And in the sixth, he sank the Dodgers by making another brilliant stop on a two-out, bases-loaded shot down the line (this ball was hit by Lopes), again getting a force at second. Los Angeles couldn't cope with Nettles' wizardry afield and fell, 5-1.

New York's Jackson exhibited more of his October magic in Game 4. He did it with his bat. And his hip. His hip?

With Los Angeles' John holding a 3-0 lead on the strength of Smith's fifth-inning homer, the Yankees had one out in the sixth when White singled, Munson walked and Jackson stroked a run-scoring base hit. Lou Piniella then hit a sinking liner to the left of Dodgers shortstop Bill Russell. The ball hit off Russell's glove and fell to the ground. Munson, who had hustled back to second when it appeared the ball would be caught, took off for third. Russell ignored Munson, instead stepping on second to force Jackson and then throwing on to first in an attempt to complete an inning-ending double play. Jackson, though, froze in the basepath and, with Russell's throw in flight, turned toward first baseman Garvey and his right hip swiveled toward the ball. The ball struck Reggie and bounced into short right field, with Munson scoring the Yanks' second run. The Dodgers argued vehemently that Jackson had intentionally interfered with the ball and that Piniella should be ruled out. The umpires stood by their call.

Reggie Jackson (left) and pitcher Ron Guidry smile for photographers after the Yankees' Game 6 victory over the Los Angeles Dodgers.

New York tied the score in the eighth when Blair singled, advanced to second on White's sacrifice and scooted home on Munson's double. And after free-agent acquisition Goose Gossage (27 saves and a 2.01 ERA in his first season with the Yanks) retired Los Angeles in order in the top of the 10th, the Yankees struck for the game-winning run in the last half of the inning. With two out and White on first with a walk, Jackson gained a measure of revenge against Dodgers reliever Welch by rapping a single and Piniella then ended matters with another base hit. The 4-3 New York triumph squared the Series at two games apiece.

Bob Lemon, who had succeeded Billy Martin as Yankees manager in July, started rookie Jim Beattie in Game 5 and the righthander responded with the first complete-game performance of his big-league career. Yankee bats stole the show, however, as New York erupted for 18 hits and cruised to a 12-2 victory. Munson drove in five runs and was one of four Yankees to collect three hits (Dent, Mickey Rivers and Brian Doyle were the others).

Dent and Doyle repeated their three-hit salvos in Game 6 as New York wrapped up its 22nd World Series championship. Shortstop Dent, whose three-run homer had proved the decisive blow in the Yanks' East Division playoff game with Boston, drove in three runs and Doyle, a Series starter only because of an injury to regular second baseman Willie Randolph, knocked in two. Also delivering two RBIs was Jackson, who exacted full revenge against Welch by

belting a seventh-inning home run off the fastballer. Jim (Catfish) Hunter, with two innings of relief help from Gossage, was a 7-2 winner at Dodger Stadium.

In becoming the first team in World Series history to fall behind two games to none and then prevail in *six* games, the Yankees received another clutch performance from Reggie Jackson. Mr. October hit .391 in this fall classic, with two homers and eight RBIs. Reggie's batting average was no better than third among the Yankees, though, as eighth-place hitter Doyle (a .192 batter in 52 regular-season at-bats) finished at a gaudy .438 and ninth-place batter Dent (a .243 contributor in the regular season) wound up at .417.

Game 1

Tuesday, October 10, At Los Angeles

New York	AB.	R.	H.	RBI.	PO.	A.
Rivers, cf	4	0	0	0	4	0
Blair, cf	1	0	0	0	1	0
White, lf	4	0	1	0	2	0
Munson, c	4	1	0	0	4	1
Jackson, dh	4	1	3	1	0	0
Piniella, rf	4	2	1	1	2	0
Nettles, 3b	4	0	1	1	0	2
Chambliss, 1b	4	1	1	0	5	0
Stanley, 2b	2	0	1	0	4	1
bJohnson	1	0	0	0	0	0
Doyle, 2b	0	0	0	0	1	0
Dent, ss	4	0	1	2	1	3
Figueroa, p	0	0	0	0	0	0
Clay, p	0	0	0	0	0	0
Lindblad, p	0	0	0	0	0	0
Tidrow, p	0	0	0	0	0	0
Totals	36	5	9	5	24	7

Los Angeles	AB.	R.	H.	RBI.	PO.	A.
Lopes, 2b	5	2	2	5	2	2
Russell, ss	5	1	3	0	3	5
Smith, rf	5	0	1	1	1	0
Garvey, 1b	5	1	2	0	14	0
Cey, 3b	4	1	1	0	0	4
Baker, lf	4	2	3	1	1	0
Monday, cf	2	2	1	0	0	0
aNorth, cf	1	1	1	2	0	0
Lacy, dh	3	0	1	1	0	0
Yeager, c	4	1	0	0	7	0
John, p	0	0	0	0	0	4
Forster, p	0	0	0	0	0	0
Totals	38	11	15	10	27	15

New York .... 0 0 0 0 0 0 3 2 0— 5
Los Angeles .... 0 3 0 3 1 0 3 1 x—11

New York	IP.	H.	R.	ER.	BB.	SO.
Figueroa (L)	1⅔	5	3	3	1	0
Clay	2⅓*	4	4	3	2	2
Lindblad	2⅓	4	3	3	0	1
Tidrow	1⅔	2	1	1	0	1

Los Angeles	IP.	H.	R.	ER.	BB.	SO.
John (W)	7⅔	8	5	3	2	4
Forster	1⅓	1	0	0	0	3

*Pitched to two batters in fifth.

aDoubled for Monday in seventh. bStruck out for Stanley in eighth. E—Dent, Lopes, Russell. DP—New York 2, Los Angeles 1. LOB—New York 6, Los Angeles 6. 2B—Monday, Stanley, North, Russell. HR—Baker, Lopes 2, Jackson. WP—Clay. U—Vargo (N.L.) plate, Haller (A.L.) first, Kibler (N.L.) second, Springstead (A.L.) third, Pulli (N.L.) left and Brinkman (A.L.) right. T—2:48. A—55,997.

Game 2

Wednesday, October 11, At Los Angeles

New York	AB.	R.	H.	RBI.	PO.	A.
White, lf	5	2	2	0	1	0
Thomasson, cf	3	0	1	0	2	0
aBlair, cf	1	0	1	0	2	0
Munson, c	4	1	1	0	3	1
Jackson, dh	4	0	1	3	0	0
Nettles, 3b	4	0	0	0	3	3
Piniella, rf	4	0	2	0	2	0
Spencer, 1b	4	0	1	0	8	1
Doyle, 2b	3	0	1	0	2	1
bJohnson	1	0	0	0	0	0
Stanley, 2b	0	0	0	0	0	0

	AB.	R.	H.	RBI.	PO.	A.
Dent, ss	4	0	1	0	0	1
Hunter, p	0	0	0	0	1	0
Gossage, p	0	0	0	0	0	0
Totals	37	3	11	3	24	7

Los Angeles	AB.	R.	H.	RBI.	PO.	A.
Lopes, 2b	4	1	1	0	3	4
Russell, ss	4	0	1	0	2	1
Smith, rf	4	2	1	0	3	0
Garvey, 1b	3	0	1	0	6	1
Cey, 3b	3	1	2	4	1	1
Baker, lf	3	0	0	0	2	0
Monday, cf	3	0	0	0	1	0
North, cf	0	0	0	0	0	0
Lacy, dh	3	0	0	0	0	0
Yeager, c	3	0	1	0	8	1
Hooton, p	0	0	0	0	1	0
Forster, p	0	0	0	0	0	1
Welch, p	0	0	0	0	0	0
Totals	30	4	7	4	27	9

New York	0 0 2 0 0 0 1 0 0—3
Los Angeles	0 0 0 1 0 3 0 0 x—4

New York	IP.	H.	R.	ER.	BB.	SO.
Hunter (L)	6	7	4	4	0	2
Gossage	2	0	0	0	0	0

Los Angeles	IP.	H.	R.	ER.	BB.	SO.
Hooton (W)	6*	8	3	3	1	5
Forster	2⅓	3	0	0	1	3
Welch (S)	⅔	0	0	0	0	1

*Pitched to one batter in seventh.

aDoubled for Thomasson in seventh. bHit into double play for Doyle in eighth. DP—New York 1, Los Angeles 1. LOB—New York 10, Los Angeles 2. 2B—Munson, Jackson, Blair. HR—Cey. SB—White. HBP—By Hooton (Jackson). WP—Hooton. U—Haller (A.L.) plate, Kibler (N.L.) first, Springstead (A.L.) second, Pulli (N.L.) third, Brinkman (A.L.) left and Vargo (N.L.) right. T—2:37. A—55,982.

Game 3

Friday, October 13, At New York

Los Angeles	AB.	R.	H.	RBI.	PO.	A.
Lopes, 2b	5	0	1	0	3	2
Russell, ss	4	0	2	1	2	3
Smith, rf	4	0	1	0	2	0
Garvey, 1b	4	0	1	0	4	2
Cey, 3b	3	0	0	0	0	1
Baker, lf	3	0	2	0	5	0
Lacy, dh	4	0	1	0	0	0
North, cf	3	1	0	0	5	0
Yeager, c	1	0	0	0	2	1
aMota	0	0	0	0	0	0
Grote, c	0	0	0	0	0	0
Ferguson, c	1	0	0	0	0	0
Sutton, p	0	0	0	0	0	0
Rautzhan, p	0	0	0	0	0	0
Hough, p	0	0	0	0	1	0
Totals	32	1	8	1	24	9

New York	AB.	R.	H.	RBI.	PO.	A.
Rivers, cf	4	0	3	0	2	0
bBlair, cf	0	0	0	0	0	0
White, lf	3	2	1	1	2	0
Munson, c	4	1	1	1	4	1
Jackson, dh	3	0	1	1	0	0
Piniella, rf	4	0	1	1	1	0
Nettles, 3b	4	1	1	0	2	5
Chambliss, 1b	3	0	1	0	8	0
Doyle, 2b	4	0	0	0	7	2
Dent, ss	4	1	1	1	0	5
Guidry, p	0	0	0	0	1	1
Totals	33	5	10	5	27	14

Los Angeles	0 0 1 0 0 0 0 0 0—1
New York	1 1 0 0 0 0 3 0 x—5

Los Angeles	IP.	H.	R.	ER.	BB.	SO.
Sutton (L)	6⅓	9	5	5	3	2
Rautzhan	⅔	1	0	0	0	0
Hough	1	0	0	0	0	0

New York	IP.	H.	R.	ER.	BB.	SO.
Guidry (W)	9	8	1	1	7	4

aWalked for Yeager in sixth. bRan for Rivers in seventh. E—Dent. DP—New York 2. LOB—Los Angeles 11, New York 7. 2B—Garvey. HR—White. SB—North, Piniella. U—Kibler (N.L.) plate, Springstead (A.L.) first, Pulli (N.L.) second, Brinkman (A.L.) third, Vargo (N.L.) left and Haller (A.L.) right. T—2:27. A—56,447.

Game 4

Saturday, October 14, At New York

Los Angeles	AB.	R.	H.	RBI.	PO.	A.
Lopes, 2b	4	1	0	0	0	4
Russell, ss	5	0	2	0	3	4
Smith, rf	4	1	1	3	1	1
Garvey, 1b	4	0	0	0	15	0
Cey, 3b	4	0	1	0	0	4
Baker, lf	4	0	0	0	0	0
Monday, dh	2	0	1	0	0	0
North, cf	4	0	0	0	2	0
Yeager, c	3	1	1	0	5	0
aDavalillo	1	0	0	0	0	0
Grote, c	0	0	0	0	3	0
John, p	0	0	0	0	0	0
Forster, p	0	0	0	0	0	0
Welch, p	0	0	0	0	0	0
Totals	35	3	6	3	29	13

New York	AB.	R.	H.	RBI.	PO.	A.
Blair, cf	4	1	2	0	2	0
cRivers	1	0	0	0	0	0
White, lf	3	2	1	0	4	0
Munson, c	3	1	2	1	8	0
Jackson, dh	4	0	2	1	0	0
Piniella, rf	5	0	1	1	5	1
Nettles, 3b	4	0	0	0	2	1
Chambliss, 1b	4	0	0	0	4	1
Stanley, 2b	3	0	0	0	1	1
bSpencer	1	0	0	0	0	0
Doyle, 2b	0	0	0	0	0	0
Dent, ss	4	0	1	0	4	2
Figueroa, p	0	0	0	0	0	0
Tidrow, p	0	0	0	0	0	0
Gossage, p	0	0	0	0	0	0
Totals	36	4	9	3	30	6

Los Angeles	0 0 0 0 3 0 0 0 0 0—3
New York	0 0 0 0 0 2 0 1 0 1—4

Two out when winning run scored.

Los Angeles	IP.	H.	R.	ER.	BB.	SO.
John	7*	6	3	2	2	2
Forster	⅓	1	0	0	0	0
Welch (L)	2⅓	2	1	1	1	3

New York	IP.	H.	R.	ER.	BB.	SO.
Figueroa	5	4	3	3	4	2
Tidrow	3	2	0	0	0	4
Gossage (W)	2	0	0	0	1	2

*Pitched to one batter in eighth.

aFlied out for Yeager in ninth. bStruck out for Stanley in ninth. cFouled out for Blair in tenth. E—Russell. DP—New York 1. LOB—Los Angeles 7, New York 8. 2B—Yeager, Munson. HR—Smith. SB—Garvey, Munson. SH—White. HBP—By Forster (Jackson). U—Springstead (A.L.) plate, Pulli (N.L.) first, Brinkman (A.L.) second, Vargo (N.L.) third, Haller (A.L.) left and Kibler (N.L.) right. T—3:17. A—56,445.

Game 5

Sunday, October 15, At New York

Los Angeles	AB.	R.	H.	RBI.	PO.	A.
Lopes, 2b	4	2	2	0	3	5
Russell, ss	5	0	2	1	1	4
Smith, rf	4	0	1	1	2	0
Garvey, 1b	4	0	1	0	10	0
Cey, 3b	3	0	1	0	0	0
Baker, lf	4	0	0	0	2	0
Monday, cf	3	0	0	0	2	0
Lacy, dh	4	0	0	0	0	0
Yeager, c	2	0	1	0	1	0
aOates, c	1	0	1	0	3	1
Hooton, p	0	0	0	0	0	0
Rautzhan, p	0	0	0	0	0	0
Hough, p	0	0	0	0	0	0
Totals	34	2	9	2	24	10

New York	AB.	R.	H.	RBI.	PO.	A.
Rivers, cf	5	2	3	1	0	0
bBlair, cf	1	1	0	0	0	0
White, lf	5	2	2	3	2	0
Johnstone, rf	0	0	0	0	1	0
Munson, c	5	1	3	5	8	1
Heath, c	0	0	0	0	0	0
Jackson, dh	3	0	1	0	0	0
Piniella, rf	4	0	1	1	4	0
Thomasson, lf	1	0	0	0	0	0
Nettles, 3b	5	0	1	0	1	2
Spencer, 1b	4	2	1	0	6	0
Doyle, 2b	5	2	3	0	5	1
Dent, ss	4	2	3	1	0	2
Beattie, p	0	0	0	0	0	1
Totals	42	12	18	11	27	7

Los Angeles	1 0 1 0 0 0 0 0 0— 2
New York	0 0 4 3 0 0 4 1 x—12

Los Angeles	IP.	H.	R.	ER.	BB.	SO.
Hooton (L)	2⅓	5	4	3	2	1
Rautzhan	1⅓	3	3	3	0	0
Hough	4⅓	10	5	2	2	5

New York	IP.	H.	R.	ER.	BB.	SO.
Beattie (W)	9	9	2	2	4	8

aWalked for Yeager in seventh. bRan for Rivers in seventh. E—Russell, Smith, Garvey. DP—Los Angeles 2, New York 1. LOB—Los Angeles 9, New York 10. 2B—Russell, Munson, Dent. SB—Lopes, Rivers, White, Russell. WP—Hough. PB—Yeager, Oates. U—Pulli (N.L.) plate, Brinkman (A.L.) first, Vargo (N.L.) second, Haller (A.L.) third, Kibler (N.L.) left and Springstead (A.L.) right. T—2:56. A—56,448.

Game 6

Tuesday, October 17, At Los Angeles

New York	AB.	R.	H.	RBI.	PO.	A.
Rivers, cf	4	0	0	0	1	0
Blair, cf	1	0	0	0	0	0
White, lf	4	1	1	0	4	0
Thomasson, lf	0	0	0	0	1	0
Munson, c	5	0	1	0	6	1
Jackson, dh	5	1	1	2	0	0
Piniella, rf	4	1	1	0	0	0
Johnstone, rf	0	0	0	0	0	0
Nettles, 3b	4	1	1	0	0	5
Spencer, 1b	3	1	0	0	9	1
Doyle, 2b	4	2	3	2	2	3
Dent, ss	4	0	3	3	3	3
Hunter, p	0	0	0	0	1	0
Gossage, p	0	0	0	0	0	0
Totals	38	7	11	7	27	13

Los Angeles	AB.	R.	H.	RBI.	PO.	A.
Lopes, 2b	4	1	2	2	0	2
Russell, ss	3	0	1	0	0	3
Smith, rf	4	0	0	0	2	0
Garvey, 1b	4	0	0	0	9	0
Cey, 3b	4	0	1	0	1	2
Baker, lf	3	0	0	0	2	0
Monday, cf	3	0	0	0	2	0
Ferguson, c	3	1	2	0	11	0
Davalillo, dh	2	0	1	0	0	0
Sutton, p	0	0	0	0	0	0
Welch, p	0	0	0	0	0	0
Rau, p	0	0	0	0	0	1
Totals	30	2	7	2	27	8

New York	0 3 0 0 0 2 2 0 0—7
Los Angeles	1 0 1 0 0 0 0 0 0—2

New York	IP.	H.	R.	ER.	BB.	SO.
Hunter (W)	7*	6	2	2	1	3
Gossage	2	1	0	0	0	2

Los Angeles	IP.	H.	R.	ER.	BB.	SO.
Sutton (L)	5⅔	8	5	5	1	6
Welch	1⅓	2	2	2	1	2
Rau	2	1	0	0	0	3

*Pitched to one batter in eighth.

E—Ferguson. DP—New York 2. LOB—New York 6, Los Angeles 3. 2B—Doyle, Ferguson 2. HR—Lopes, Jackson. SB—Lopes. SH—Davalillo. WP—Sutton. U—Brinkman (A.L.) plate, Vargo (N.L.) first, Haller (A.L.) second, Kibler (N.L.) third, Springstead (A.L.) left and Pulli (N.L.) right. T—2:34. A—55,985.

COMPOSITE BATTING AVERAGES

New York Yankees

Player-Position	G.	AB.	R.	H.	2B.	3B.	HR.	RBI.	BA.
Doyle, 2b	6	16	4	7	1	0	0	2	.438
Dent, ss	6	24	3	10	1	0	0	7	.417
Jackson, dh	6	23	2	9	1	0	2	8	.391
Blair, cf-ph-pr	6	8	2	3	1	0	0	0	.375
White, lf	6	24	9	8	0	0	1	4	.333
Rivers, cf-ph	5	18	2	6	0	0	0	1	.333
Munson, c	6	25	5	8	3	0	0	7	.320
Piniella, rf	6	25	3	7	0	0	0	4	.280
Thomasson, cf-lf	3	4	0	1	0	0	0	0	.250
Stanley, 2b	3	5	0	1	1	0	0	0	.200
Chambliss, 1b	3	11	1	2	0	0	0	0	.182
Spencer, 1b-ph	4	12	3	2	0	0	0	0	.167
Nettles, 3b	6	25	2	4	0	0	0	1	.160
Johnson, ph	2	2	0	0	0	0	0	0	.000
Beattie, p	1	0	0	0	0	0	0	0	.000
Clay, p	1	0	0	0	0	0	0	0	.000
Figueroa, p	2	0	0	0	0	0	0	0	.000
Gossage, p	3	0	0	0	0	0	0	0	.000
Guidry, p	1	0	0	0	0	0	0	0	.000
Heath, c	1	0	0	0	0	0	0	0	.000
Hunter, p	2	0	0	0	0	0	0	0	.000
Johnstone, rf	2	0	0	0	0	0	0	0	.000
Lindblad, p	1	0	0	0	0	0	0	0	.000
Tidrow, p	2	0	0	0	0	0	0	0	.000
Totals	6	222	36	68	8	0	3	34	.306

Los Angeles Dodgers

Player-Position	G.	AB.	R.	H.	2B.	3B.	HR.	RBI.	BA.
Oates, ph-c	1	1	0	1	0	0	0	0	1.000
Ferguson, c	2	4	1	2	2	0	0	0	.500
Russell, ss	6	26	1	11	2	0	0	2	.423
Davalillo, ph-dh	2	3	0	1	0	0	0	0	.333
Lopes, 2b	6	26	7	8	0	0	3	7	.308
Cey, 3b	6	21	2	6	0	0	1	4	.286
Baker, lf	6	21	2	5	0	0	1	1	.238
Yeager, c	5	13	2	3	1	0	0	0	.231
Garvey, 1b	6	24	1	5	1	0	0	0	.208
Smith, rf	6	25	3	5	0	0	1	5	.200
Monday, cf-dh	5	13	2	2	1	0	0	0	.154
Lacy, dh	4	14	0	2	0	0	0	1	.143
North, ph-cf	4	8	2	1	1	0	0	2	.125
Forster, p	3	0	0	0	0	0	0	0	.000
Grote, c	2	0	0	0	0	0	0	0	.000
Hooton, p	2	0	0	0	0	0	0	0	.000
Hough, p	2	0	0	0	0	0	0	0	.000
John, p	2	0	0	0	0	0	0	0	.000
Mota, ph	1	0	0	0	0	0	0	0	.000
Rau, p	1	0	0	0	0	0	0	0	.000
Rautzhan, p	2	0	0	0	0	0	0	0	.000
Sutton, p	2	0	0	0	0	0	0	0	.000
Welch, p	3	0	0	0	0	0	0	0	.000
Totals	6	199	23	52	8	0	6	22	.261

COMPOSITE PITCHING AVERAGES

New York Yankees

Pitcher	G.	IP.	H.	R.	ER.	BB.	SO.	W.	L.	ERA.
Gossage	3	6	1	0	0	1	4	1	0	0.00
Guidry	1	9	8	1	1	7	4	1	0	1.00
Tidrow	2	4⅔	4	1	1	0	5	0	0	1.93
Beattie	1	9	9	2	2	4	8	1	0	2.00
Hunter	2	13	13	6	6	1	5	1	1	4.15
Figueroa	2	6⅔	9	6	6	5	2	0	1	8.10
Clay	1	2⅓	4	4	3	2	2	0	0	11.57
Lindblad	1	2⅓	4	3	3	0	1	0	0	11.57
Totals	6	53	52	23	22	20	31	4	2	3.74

Los Angeles Dodgers

Pitcher	G.	IP.	H.	R.	ER.	BB.	SO.	W.	L.	ERA.
Forster	3	4	5	0	0	1	6	0	0	0.00
Rau	1	2	1	0	0	0	3	0	0	0.00
John	2	14⅔	14	8	5	4	6	1	0	3.07
Welch	3	4⅓	4	3	3	2	6	0	1	6.23
Hooton	2	8⅓	13	7	6	3	6	1	1	6.48
Sutton	2	12	17	10	10	4	8	0	2	7.50
Hough	2	5⅓	10	5	5	2	5	0	0	8.44
Rautzhan	2	2	4	3	3	0	0	0	0	13.50
Totals	6	52⅔	68	36	32	16	40	2	4	5.46

The family unit was doing quite nicely in 1979, thank you. Particularly as it applied to major league baseball.

The 1979 Pittsburgh Pirates, emphasizing the team concept to the point that they thought of themselves as a family (and even adopted a popular disco record reflecting same as their theme song), parlayed their togetherness into a World Series championship. And, fittingly enough, a fellow known affectionately as "Pops" was the big man in this family.

"Pops" was veteran first baseman Wilver Dornel Stargell, whose fun-loving nature kept things loose in the clubhouse and whose powerful bat kept the opposition loose on the field. At age 38, Willie Stargell had thumped 32 home runs for Manager Chuck Tanner's Pirates, helping the Bucs to a National League East championship that wasn't nailed down until the final day of the season. Stargell then drilled two homers, drove in six runs and batted a cool .455 in three Championship Series games as Pittsburgh swept past the Cincinnati Reds.

Next up for the Pirates was a World Series date against the Baltimore Orioles. But no matter how hard team captain Stargell tried to inspire his teammates—whether it be along the lines of awarding gold stars for superior performances or supplying such notable performances himself—Willie saw the National League champions fall dangerously behind the Orioles.

Baltimore jolted the Pirates with five first-inning runs in the Series opener—Doug DeCinces capped the uprising with a two-run homer—and 23-game winner Mike Flanagan made the runs stand up. Barely. The Pirates

Willie Stargell (top center) is surrounded by his Pittsburgh 'Family' after leading the Pirates to a Game 7 World Series victory over Baltimore.

pecked away, with Phil Garner and Stargell (a two-time N.L. home run champion and possessor of 461 career homers) each collecting two RBIs and Dave Parker finishing with four hits. Stargell accounted for the game's final run with an eighth-inning homer, but Flanagan held on for a 5-4 victory at Baltimore's Memorial Stadium.

Veteran Manny Sanguillen gave Pittsburgh a lift in Game 2, delivering a ninth-inning pinch single that broke a 2-2 tie and enabled the Pirates to beat the Orioles and their ace reliever, Don Stanhouse. Despite the 3-2 triumph, the Bucs went flat when the Series shifted to Three Rivers Stadium. In Game 3, Orioles shortstop Kiko Garcia banged out two singles, a double and a triple

and totaled four RBIs and Benny Ayala cracked a two-run homer as the American League titlists prevailed, 8-4. Pinch-hitters John Lowenstein and Terry Crowley each belted two-run doubles in the eighth inning of Game 4 as Baltimore roared from a 6-3 deficit to a 9-6 conquest. The loss was extremely distressing to the Pirates. Not only did they lose a game they seemingly had won, but the defeat also left them facing a three games-to-one deficit. And Pittsburgh would be going against Orioles ace Flanagan in Game 5.

A disheartening situation. Unless, of course, you come together in tight situations. Like a *family* tends to do.

Bill Madlock and Tim Foli, key in-season acquisitions for Pitts-

burgh, kept Tanner's troops in the hunt in the fifth game. Madlock, obtained from San Francisco in late June and installed as the Pirates' regular third baseman (he had been playing out of position, at second base, for the Giants), went 4 for 4 and shortstop Foli, acquired from the New York Mets two weeks into the season, drove in three runs as the Pirates dealt Flanagan a 7-1 setback. Bert Blyleven, working four scoreless innings of relief, got the victory.

While Madlock, Foli and Blyleven got the headlines after Game 5, Jim Rooker perhaps made the biggest contribution for Pittsburgh. Winner of only four games during the regular season, the lefthander nevertheless was Tanner's choice to start the do-or-die contest. And Rooker kept the Bucs in the game—and in the Series—before turning things over to Blyleven. He permitted only one run and three hits over five innings, then departed for a pinch-hitter.

Now, the Pirates would go with their ace—if a 14-game winner qualifies for such billing. John Candelaria was, in fact, the top winner for the pennant-winning Pirates despite his modest 14-victory total (six Bucs had 10 or more triumphs). And the Candy Man combined with relief ace Kent Tekulve to stymie the Orioles on seven hits in Game 6, which went into the books as a Series-squaring, 4-0 Pirate victory.

Pittsburgh's Jim Bibby and Baltimore's Scott McGregor hooked up in Game 7, and the Orioles scored the first run of the game when Rich Dauer led off the last of the third inning with a homer to left. The game remained 1-0 until the sixth, when the Pirates broke through. McGregor retired Parker on an inning-opening groundout, but allowed a single to Bill Robinson. Stargell, with a single and a double in two at-bats thus far in the game, followed Robinson to the plate and whacked a McGregor pitch over the right-field fence. The Pirates were ahead—to stay. The Bucs got two more runs in the ninth, an inning in which Weaver trotted out five pitchers in an attempt to

keep his club in the game. It was to no avail.

While Bibby had left the contest for a pinch-hitter in the fifth inning, Pirate relievers Grant Jackson and Tekulve combined to pitch hitless ball over the final 4⅓ innings. The Orioles, having scored two runs in the final 28 innings of the Series, were dead. And the Pirates, 4-1 winners in the finale, had become the fourth team in history to come from a three games-to-one deficit and win a best-of-seven World Series.

Five Pirates collected 10 or more hits in the '79 Series, with Garner (who batted a Series-high .500) and Stargell getting 12 apiece, Omar Moreno 11 and Parker and Foli 10 each. Madlock was right behind with nine.

It was Stargell, though, who posted the best all-around numbers with a .400 batting mark, three home runs and seven RBIs. And, of course, his home run in the seventh game—a contest in which he went 4 for 5—proved the Series-deciding blow.

No doubt about it, "Pops" had made the 1979 World Series a very special family outing for the Pittsburgh Pirates.

Game 1

Wednesday, October 10, At Baltimore

Pittsburgh	AB.	R.	H.	RBI.	PO.	A.
Moreno, cf	5	0	0	0	4	0
Foli, ss	5	1	1	0	1	3
Parker, rf	5	1	4	0	3	0
B. Robinson, lf	5	1	1	0	2	0
Stargell, 1b	5	1	1	2	7	0
Madlock, 3b	3	0	0	0	0	1
Nicosia, c	4	0	0	0	4	1
Garner, 2b	4	0	3	2	3	2
Kison, p	0	0	0	0	0	1
Rooker, p	1	0	0	0	0	2
aSanguillen	1	0	0	0	0	0
Romo, p	0	0	0	0	0	0
bLacy	1	0	0	0	0	0
D. Robinson, p	0	0	0	0	0	0
cStennett	1	0	1	0	0	0
Jackson, p	0	0	0	0	0	0
Totals	40	4	11	4	24	10

Baltimore	AB.	R.	H.	RBI.	PO.	A.
Bumbry, cf	4	1	1	0	3	0
Belanger, ss	3	1	0	0	1	4
Singleton, rf	3	0	1	0	2	0
Murray, 1b	2	1	1	0	12	1
Lowenstein, lf	4	1	0	1	1	0
Roenicke, lf	0	0	0	0	0	0
DeCinces, 3b	3	1	1	2	0	4
Smith, 2b	2	0	1	0	1	3
dDauer, 2b	1	0	1	0	0	1
Dempsey, c	4	0	0	0	7	0
Flanagan, p	4	0	0	0	0	2
Totals	30	5	6	3	27	15

Pittsburgh ....0 0 0　1 0 2　0 1 0—4
Baltimore ....5 0 0　0 0 0　0 0 x—5

Pittsburgh	IP.	H.	R.	ER.	BB.	SO.
Kison (L)	⅓	3	5	4	2	0
Rooker	3⅔	2	0	0	1	2
Romo	1	0	0	0	0	0
D. Robinson	2	0	0	0	1	1
Jackson	1	1	0	0	0	0

Baltimore	IP.	H.	R.	ER.	BB.	SO.
Flanagan (W)	9	11	4	2	1	7

aGrounded out for Rooker in fifth. bReached first base on error for Romo in sixth. cSingled for D. Robinson in eighth. dSingled for Smith in eighth. E—Foli, Stargell, Garner, Belanger, DeCinces 2. DP—Pittsburgh 1. LOB—

Pittsburgh 10, Baltimore 8. 2B—Parker, Garner. HR—DeCinces, Stargell. SB—Murray. SH—Bumbry. WP—Kison. U—Neudecker (A.L.) plate, Engel (N.L.) first, Goetz (A.L.) second, Tata (N.L.) third, McKean (A.L.) left and Runge (N.L.) right. T—3:18. A—53,735.

Game 2

Thursday, October 11, At Baltimore

Pittsburgh	AB.	R.	H.	RBI.	PO.	A.
Moreno, cf	5	0	1	0	1	0
Foli, ss	4	0	1	0	0	5
Parker, rf	4	0	1	0	1	1
Stargell, 1b	4	1	1	0	12	0
Milner, lf	3	1	1	0	3	0
dB. Robinson	1	0	1	0	0	0
eAlexander, lf	0	0	0	0	0	0
Madlock, 3b	4	0	2	1	0	4
Ott, c	3	1	1	1	6	0
Garner, 2b	2	0	1	0	4	6
Blyleven, p	2	0	0	0	0	0
aEasler	1	0	0	0	0	0
D. Robinson, p	0	0	0	0	0	1
fSanguillen	1	0	1	1	0	0
Tekulve, p	0	0	0	0	0	0
Totals	33	3	11	3	27	17

Baltimore	AB.	R.	H.	RBI.	PO.	A.
Bumbry, cf	5	0	0	0	5	0
Belanger, ss	3	0	0	0	1	2
cCrowley	0	0	0	0	0	0
T. Martinez, p	0	0	0	0	0	0
Stanhouse, p	0	0	0	0	0	0
Singleton, rf	4	1	1	0	1	0
Murray, 1b	3	1	3	2	10	2
DeCinces, 3b	4	0	0	0	0	6
Lowenstein, lf	3	0	1	0	1	0
Smith, 2b	4	0	0	0	3	0
Dempsey, c	3	0	1	0	4	2
Palmer, p	2	0	0	0	1	1
bKelly	0	0	0	0	0	0
Garcia, ss	1	0	0	0	1	0
Totals	32	2	6	2	27	13

Pittsburgh ....0 2 0　0 0 0　0 0 1—3
Baltimore ....0 1 0　0 0 1　0 0 0—2

Pittsburgh	IP.	H.	R.	ER.	BB.	SO.
Blyleven	6	5	2	2	2	1
D. Rob'son (W)	2	1	0	0	3	2
Tekulve (S)	1	0	0	0	0	0

Baltimore	IP.	H.	R.	ER.	BB.	SO.
Palmer	7	8	2	2	2	3
T. Martinez	1*	1	0	0	0	1
Stanhouse (L)	1	2	1	1	1	0

*Pitched to one batter in ninth.

aWalked for Blyleven in seventh. bWalked for Palmer in seventh. cWalked for Belanger in seventh. dSingled for Milner in ninth. eRan for B. Robinson in ninth. fSingled for D. Robinson in ninth. E—Foli, Parker, DeCinces. DP—Pittsburgh 3, Baltimore 2. LOB—Pittsburgh 7, Baltimore 8. 2B—Murray. HR—Murray. SF—Ott. WP—Palmer. U—Engel (N.L.) plate, Goetz (A.L.) first, Tata (N.L.) second, McKean (A.L.) third, Runge (N.L.) left and Neudecker (A.L.) right. T—3:13. A—53,739.

Game 3

Friday, October 12, At Pittsburgh

Baltimore	AB.	R.	H.	RBI.	PO.	A.
Garcia, ss	4	2	4	4	0	4
Ayala, lf	2	1	2	2	0	0
aBumbry, cf	2	1	1	0	2	0
Singleton, rf	5	0	2	1	4	0
Murray, 1b	4	0	0	0	7	1
DeCinces, 3b	5	0	0	1	0	1
Roenicke, cf-lf	5	0	1	0	5	1
Dauer, 2b	5	1	1	0	2	3
Dempsey, c	5	2	2	0	7	0
McGregor, p	3	1	0	0	0	0
Totals	40	8	13	8	27	10

Pittsburgh	AB.	R.	H.	RBI.	PO.	A.
Moreno, cf	4	1	2	0	2	0
Foli, ss	4	0	0	0	0	6
Parker, rf	3	0	0	1	2	0
B. Robinson, lf	4	0	1	0	4	1
Stargell, 1b	4	2	2	0	8	1
Madlock, 3b	4	0	1	1	0	0
Nicosia, c	4	1	1	0	8	0
Garner, 2b	4	0	1	2	2	1
Candelaria, p	1	0	1	0	0	0
Romo, p	1	0	0	0	0	1
Jackson, p	0	0	0	0	0	0
bLacy	1	0	0	0	0	0
Tekulve, p	0	0	0	0	1	0
Totals	34	4	9	4	27	11

Baltimore ....0 0 2　5 0 0　1 0 0—8
Pittsburgh ....1 2 0　0 0 1　0 0 0—4

Baltimore	IP.	H.	R.	ER.	BB.	SO.
McGregor (W)	9	9	4	4	0	6

Pittsburgh	IP.	H.	R.	ER.	BB.	SO.
Candelaria (L)	3*	8	6	5	2	2
Romo	3⅔	5	2	2	1	4
Jackson	⅓	0	0	0	0	0
Tekulve	2	0	0	0	0	1

*Pitched to four batters in fourth.

aHit by pitcher for Ayala in fourth. bLined out for Jackson in seventh. E—Foli, Stargell. LOB—Baltimore 9, Pittsburgh 4. 2B—Garcia, Moreno 2, Garner, Dauer, Stargell, Dempsey. 3B—Garcia. HR—Ayala. SF—Parker. HBP—By Romo (Bumbry). WP—Romo. Balk—Mc-

Gregor. U—Goetz (A.L.) plate, Tata (N.L.) first, McKean (A.L.) second, Runge (N.L.) third, Neudecker (A.L.) left and Engel (N.L.) right. T—2:51. A—50,848.

Game 4

Saturday, October 13, At Pittsburgh

Baltimore	AB.	R.	H.	RBI.	PO.	A.
Bumbry, cf	5	1	1	1	1	1
Garcia, ss	5	2	2	2	6	5
Belanger, ss	0	0	0	0	0	0
Singleton, rf	5	0	3	1	0	0
Murray, 1b	5	1	0	0	8	1
DeCinces, 3b	1	1	0	0	2	0
Roenicke, lf	3	0	0	0	2	0
cLowenstein, lf	2	1	1	2	1	0
Dauer, 2b	3	0	1	0	1	2
dSmith, 2b	0	1	0	0	0	0
Skaggs, c	3	1	1	0	2	2
eCrowley	1	0	1	2	0	0
fDempsey, c	0	1	0	0	3	0
D. Martinez, p	0	0	0	0	0	1
Stewart, p	1	0	0	0	1	2
aMay	1	0	0	0	0	0
Stone, p	0	0	0	0	0	0
bKelly	1	0	1	0	0	0
Stoddard, p	1	0	1	1	0	2
Totals	37	9	12	9	27	16

Pittsburgh	AB.	R.	H.	RBI.	PO.	A.
Moreno, cf	5	0	2	1	2	0
Foli, ss	4	2	3	0	1	5
Parker, rf	5	0	2	1	1	0
Stargell, 1b	5	1	3	1	8	0
Milner, lf	3	1	2	1	2	0
D. Robinson, p	0	0	0	0	0	0
Tekulve, p	0	0	0	0	0	0
gEasler	1	0	0	0	0	0
Madlock, 3b	3	1	2	0	0	1
Ott, c	5	0	1	2	8	0
Garner, 2b	4	1	2	0	5	7
Bibby, p	3	0	0	0	0	0
Jackson, p	0	0	0	0	0	0
B. Robinson, lf	1	0	0	0	0	0
Totals	39	6	17	6	27	13

Baltimore	0 0 3	0 0 0	0 6 0	—9
Pittsburgh	0 4 0	0 1 1	0 0 0	—6

Baltimore	IP.	H.	R.	ER.	BB.	SO.
D. Martinez	1⅓	6	4	4	0	0
Stewart	2⅔	4	0	0	1	0
Stone	2	4	2	2	2	2
Stoddard (W)	3	3	0	0	1	3

Pittsburgh	IP.	H.	R.	ER.	BB.	SO.
Bibby	6⅓	7	3	2	2	7
Jackson	⅔	0	0	0	0	0
D. Robinson	⅓	2	3	3	1	0
Tekulve (L)	1⅔	3	3	3	2	1

aStruck out for Stewart in fifth. bSingled for Stone in seventh. cDoubled for Roenicke in eighth. dIntentionally walked for Dauer in eighth. eDoubled for Skaggs in eighth. fRan for Crowley in eighth. gFlied out for Tekulve in ninth. E—Madlock. DP—Baltimore 2, Pittsburgh 3. LOB—Baltimore 6, Pittsburgh 10. 2B—Madlock, Ott, Garcia, Singleton, Stargell, Milner, Parker, Lowenstein, Crowley. HR—Stargell. SB—DeCinces. U—Tata (N.L.) plate, McKean (A.L.) first, Runge (N.L.) second, Neudecker (A.L.) third, Engel (N.L.) left and Goetz (A.L.) right. T—3:48. A—50,883.

Game 5

Sunday, October 14, At Pittsburgh

Baltimore	AB.	R.	H.	RBI.	PO.	A.
Garcia, ss	4	0	0	0	2	1
Ayala, lf	1	0	0	0	2	0
bBumbry, cf	1	0	0	0	1	0
Singleton, rf	4	0	0	0	0	0
Murray, 1b	4	0	0	0	7	1
Roenicke, cf-lf	4	1	1	0	2	0
DeCinces, 3b	4	0	2	0	1	4
Dauer, 2b	3	0	0	0	2	1
dLowenstein	1	0	1	0	0	0
Dempsey, c	3	0	2	0	7	0
eCrowley	1	0	0	0	0	0
Flanagan, p	1	0	0	0	0	2
cKelly	1	0	0	0	0	0
Stoddard, p	0	0	0	0	0	1
T. Martinez, p	0	0	0	0	0	0
Stanhouse, p	0	0	0	0	0	0
Totals	32	1	6	0	24	10

Pittsburgh	AB.	R.	H.	RBI.	PO.	A.
Moreno, cf	4	1	0	0	3	0
Foli, ss	4	2	2	3	3	7
Parker, rf	4	1	2	1	1	0
B. Robinson, lf	4	0	1	0	2	0
Stargell, 1b	3	1	1	1	10	0
Madlock, 3b	4	1	4	1	0	1
Nicosia, c	4	0	0	0	5	0
Garner, 2b	4	1	2	1	2	3
Rooker, p	1	0	0	0	1	0
aLacy,	1	0	1	0	0	0
Blyleven, p	1	0	0	0	0	1
Totals	34	7	13	7	27	12

Baltimore	0 0 0	0 1 0	0 0 0	—1
Pittsburgh	0 0 0	0 0 2	2 3 x	—7

Baltimore	IP.	H.	R.	ER.	BB.	SO.
Flanagan (L)	6	6	2	2	1	6
Stoddard	⅔	2	2	2	0	0
T. Martinez	⅓†	2	1	1	0	0
Stanhouse	1	3	2	2	2	0

Pittsburgh	IP.	H.	R.	ER.	BB.	SO.
Rooker	5	3	1	1	2	2
Blyleven (W)	4	3	0	0	1	3

†Pitched to one batter in eighth.

aSingled for Rooker in fifth. bFlied out for Ayala in sixth. cStruck out for Flanagan in seventh. dSingled for Dauer in ninth. eFlied out for Dempsey in ninth. E—Stoddard, Stanhouse, Garner. DP—Pittsburgh 2. LOB—Baltimore 7, Pittsburgh 9. 2B—B. Robinson, Roenicke, Dempsey, Parker. 3B—Foli. SH—B. Robinson, Blyleven. SF—Stargell. U—McKean (A.L.) plate, Runge (N.L.) first, Neudecker (A.L.) second, Engel (N.L.) third, Goetz (A.L.) left and Tata (N.L.) right. T—2:54. A—50,920.

Game 6

Tuesday, October 16, At Baltimore

Pittsburgh	AB.	R.	H.	RBI.	PO.	A.
Moreno, cf	5	1	3	1	4	0
Foli, ss	5	1	2	0	0	5
Parker, rf	4	0	1	1	3	0
Stargell, 1b	4	0	0	1	8	0
Milner, lf	3	0	0	0	0	0
Tekulve, p	1	0	0	0	0	0
Madlock, 3b	3	0	0	0	1	2
Ott, c	4	1	2	0	6	0
Garner, 2b	3	1	2	0	4	2
Candelaria, p	2	0	0	0	0	1
aLacy	1	0	0	0	0	0
B. Robinson, lf	0	0	0	1	1	0
Totals	35	4	10	4	27	10

Baltimore	AB.	R.	H.	RBI.	PO.	A.
Garcia, ss	3	0	1	0	1	2
eKelly	1	0	0	0	0	0
Belanger, ss	0	0	0	0	0	0
Ayala, lf	3	0	0	0	2	0
fCrowley	1	0	0	0	0	0
Stoddard, p	0	0	0	0	1	0
Singleton, rf	4	0	3	0	1	0
Murray, 1b	4	0	0	0	5	1
DeCinces, 3b	4	0	0	0	1	3
Roenicke, cf	2	0	0	0	4	0
bBumbry, cf	1	0	0	0	2	0
Dauer, 2b	2	0	1	0	1	1
cSmith, 2b	1	0	1	0	0	0
Dempsey, c	3	0	1	0	7	0
Palmer, p	2	0	0	0	1	0
dLowenstein, lf	1	0	0	0	1	0
Totals	32	0	7	0	27	7

Pittsburgh	0 0 0	0 0 0	2 2 0	—4
Baltimore	0 0 0	0 0 0	0 0 0	—0

Pittsburgh	IP.	H.	R.	ER.	BB.	SO.
Candelaria (W)	6	6	0	0	0	2
Tekulve (S)	3	1	0	0	0	4

Baltimore	IP.	H.	R.	ER.	BB.	SO.
Palmer (L)	8	10	4	4	3	5
Stoddard	1	0	0	0	0	0

aStruck out for Candelaria in seventh. bFlied out for Roenicke in seventh. cSingled for Dauer in seventh. dStruck out for Palmer in eighth. eFlied out for Garcia in eighth. fGrounded out for Ayala in eighth. E—Bumbry. DP—Pittsburgh 2. LOB—Pittsburgh 10, Baltimore 5. 2B—Foli, Garner. SF—Stargell, B. Robinson. HBP—By Palmer (Garner). U—Runge (N.L.) plate, Neudecker (A.L.) first, Engel (N.L.) second, Goetz (A.L.) third, Tata (N.L.) left and McKean (A.L.) right. T—2:30. A—53,739.

Game 7

Wednesday, October 17, At Baltimore

Pittsburgh	AB.	R.	H.	RBI.	PO.	A.
Moreno, cf	5	1	3	1	4	0
Foli, ss	4	0	1	0	3	1
Parker, rf	4	0	0	0	2	0
B. Robinson, lf	4	1	1	1	2	0
Stargell, 1b	5	1	4	2	6	1
Madlock, 3b	3	0	0	0	2	1
Nicosia, c	4	0	0	0	6	1
Garner, 2b	3	1	1	0	1	2
Bibby, p	1	0	0	0	1	0
aSanguillen	1	0	0	0	0	0
D. Robinson, p	0	0	0	0	0	0
Jackson, p	1	0	0	0	0	0
Tekulve, p	1	0	0	0	0	0
Totals	36	4	10	4	27	6

Baltimore	AB.	R.	H.	RBI.	PO.	A.
Bumbry, cf	3	0	0	0	0	0
Garcia, ss	3	0	1	0	0	5
eAyala	0	0	0	0	0	0
fCrowley	1	0	0	0	0	0
Stoddard, p	0	0	0	0	0	1
Flanagan, p	0	0	0	0	0	0
Stanhouse, p	0	0	0	0	0	0
T. Martinez, p	0	0	0	0	0	0
D. Martinez, p	0	0	0	0	0	0
Singleton, rf	3	0	0	0	1	0
Murray, 1b	4	0	0	0	11	0
Lowenstein, lf	2	0	0	0	2	0
bRoenicke, lf	2	0	0	0	1	0
DeCinces, 3b	4	0	2	0	3	3
Dempsey, c	3	0	0	0	3	0
gKelly	1	0	0	0	0	0
Dauer, 2b	3	1	1	1	4	2
McGregor, p	1	0	0	0	1	2
cMay	0	0	0	0	0	0
dBelanger, ss	0	0	0	0	1	1
Totals	30	1	4	1	27	14

Pittsburgh	0 0 0	0 0 2	0 0 2	—4
Baltimore	0 0 1	0 0 0	0 0 0	—1

Pittsburgh	IP.	H.	R.	ER.	BB.	SO.
Bibby	4	3	1	1	0	3
D. Robinson	⅔	1	0	0	1	0
Jackson (W)	2⅔	0	0	0	2	1
Tekulve (S)	1⅔	0	0	0	1	2

Baltimore	IP.	H.	R.	ER.	BB.	SO.
McGregor (L)	8	7	2	2	2	2
Stoddard	⅓	1	1	1	0	0
Flanagan	0*	1	1	1	0	0
Stanhouse	0*	1	0	0	0	0
T. Martinez	0*	0	0	0	0	0
D. Martinez	⅔	0	0	0	0	0

*Pitched to one batter in ninth.

aGrounded out for Bibby in fifth. bStruck out for Lowenstein in seventh. cWalked for McGregor in eighth. dRan for May in eighth. eAnnounced as pinch-hitter for Garcia in eighth. fGrounded out for Ayala in eighth. gFlied out for Dempsey in ninth. E—Garcia, Lowenstein. DP—Baltimore 1. LOB—Pittsburgh 10, Baltimore 6. 2B—Stargell 2, Garner. HR—Dauer, Stargell. SH—Foli. HBP—By T. Martinez (Parker), by D. Martinez (B. Robinson). U—Neudecker (A.L.) plate, Engel (N.L.) first, Goetz (A.L.) second, Tata (N.L.) third, McKean (A.L.) left and Runge (N.L.) right. T—2:54. A—53,733.

COMPOSITE BATTING AVERAGES

Pittsburgh Pirates

Player-Position	G.	AB.	R.	H.	2B.	3B.	HR.	RBI.	BA.
Stennett, ph	1	1	0	1	0	0	0	0	1.000
Garner, 2b	7	24	4	12	4	0	0	5	.500
Stargell, 1b	7	30	7	12	4	0	3	7	.400
Madlock, 3b	7	24	2	9	1	0	0	3	.375
Parker, rf	7	29	2	10	3	0	0	4	.345
Moreno, cf	7	33	4	11	2	0	0	3	.333
Foli, ss	7	30	6	10	1	1	0	3	.333
Ott, c	3	12	2	4	1	0	0	3	.333
Milner, lf	3	9	2	3	1	0	0	1	.333
Candelaria, p	2	3	0	1	0	0	0	0	.333
Sanguillen, ph	3	3	0	1	0	0	0	1	.333
B. Robinson, lf-ph	7	19	2	5	1	0	0	2	.263
Lacy, ph	4	4	0	1	0	0	0	0	.250
Nicosia, c	4	16	1	1	0	0	0	0	.063
Alexander, pr-lf	1	0	0	0	0	0	0	0	.000
Kison, p	1	0	0	0	0	0	0	0	.000
D. Robinson, p	4	0	0	0	0	0	0	0	.000
Easler, ph	2	1	0	0	0	0	0	0	.000
Jackson, p	4	1	0	0	0	0	0	0	.000
Romo, p	2	1	0	0	0	0	0	0	.000
Rooker, p	2	2	0	0	0	0	0	0	.000
Tekulve, p	5	2	0	0	0	0	0	0	.000
Blyleven, p	2	3	0	0	0	0	0	0	.000
Bibby, p	2	4	0	0	0	0	0	0	.000
Totals	7	251	32	81	18	1	3	32	.323

Baltimore Orioles

Player-Position	G.	AB.	R.	H.	2B.	3B.	HR.	RBI.	BA.
Stoddard, p	4	1	0	1	0	0	0	1	1.000
Garcia, ss	6	20	4	8	2	1	0	6	.400
Singleton, rf	7	28	1	10	1	0	0	2	.357
Ayala, lf-ph	4	6	1	2	0	0	1	2	.333
Skaggs, c	1	3	1	1	0	0	0	0	.333
Dauer, ph-2b	6	17	2	5	1	0	1	1	.294
Dempsey, c-pr	7	21	3	6	2	0	0	0	.286
Smith, 2b-ph	4	7	1	2	0	0	0	0	.286
Crowley, ph	5	4	0	1	1	0	0	2	.250
Kelly, ph	5	4	0	1	0	0	0	0	.250
Lowenstein, lf-ph	6	13	2	3	1	0	0	3	.231
DeCinces, 3b	7	25	2	5	0	0	1	3	.200
Murray, 1b	7	26	3	4	1	0	1	2	.154
Bumbry, cf-ph	7	21	3	3	0	0	0	1	.143
Roenicke, lf-cf-ph	6	16	1	2	1	0	0	0	.125
D. Martinez, p	2	0	0	0	0	0	0	0	.000
T. Martinez, p	3	0	0	0	0	0	0	0	.000
Stanhouse, p	3	0	0	0	0	0	0	0	.000
Stone, p	1	0	0	0	0	0	0	0	.000
May, ph	2	1	0	0	0	0	0	0	.000
Stewart, p	1	1	0	0	0	0	0	0	.000
McGregor, p	2	4	1	0	0	0	0	0	.000
Palmer, p	2	4	0	0	0	0	0	0	.000
Flanagan, p	3	5	0	0	0	0	0	0	.000
Belanger, ss-pr	5	6	1	0	0	0	0	0	.000
Totals	7	233	26	54	10	1	4	23	.232

COMPOSITE PITCHING AVERAGES

Pittsburgh Pirates

Pitcher	G.	IP.	H.	R.	ER.	BB.	SO.	W.	L.	ERA.
Jackson	4	4⅔	1	0	0	2	2	1	0	0.00
Rooker	2	8⅔	5	1	1	3	4	0	0	1.04
Blyleven	2	10	8	2	2	3	4	1	0	1.80
Bibby	2	10⅓	10	4	3	2	10	0	0	2.61
Tekulve	5	9⅓	4	3	3	3	10	0	1	2.89
Romo	2	4⅔	5	2	2	3	4	0	0	3.86
Candelaria	2	9	14	6	5	2	4	1	1	5.00
D. Robinson	4	5	4	3	3	6	3	1	0	5.40
Kison	1	⅓	3	5	4	2	0	0	1	108.00
Totals	7	62	54	26	22	26	41	4	3	3.19

(NOTE: Pittsburgh individual earned runs do not add up to team total because of rule 10.18(i) applied in Game 3.)

Baltimore Orioles

Pitcher	G.	IP.	H.	R.	ER.	BB.	SO.	W.	L.	ERA.
Stewart	1	2⅔	4	0	0	1	0	0	0	0.00
Flanagan	3	15	18	7	5	2	13	1	1	3.00
McGregor	2	17	16	6	6	2	8	1	1	3.18
Palmer	2	15	18	6	6	5	8	0	1	3.60
Stoddard	4	5	6	3	3	1	3	1	0	5.40
T. Martinez	3	1⅓	3	1	1	0	1	0	0	6.75
Stone	1	2	4	2	2	2	2	0	0	9.00
Stanhouse	3	2	6	3	3	3	0	0	1	13.50
D. Martinez	2	2	6	4	4	0	0	0	0	18.00
Totals	7	62	81	32	30	16	35	3	4	4.35

Of the 16 teams playing major league baseball in 1903, the year of the first World Series, two still had not won a fall classic when the 1980s dawned.

One, the long-gone St. Louis Browns, never will be credited with a World Series crown. Unless, that is, historians take the liberty of crediting the Browns with the postseason success enjoyed by the club after its move to Baltimore following the 1953 season. Despite the lineage—the old Brownies became the Baltimore Orioles and proceeded to win Series titles under that banner in 1966, 1970 and 1983—no one really seems inclined to link the two clubs when it comes to such heavyweight matters as sorting out championships.

So, with the Browns out of the running, only one still-existing club from '03 was still trying to hoist its first World Series flag: the long-futile Philadelphia Phillies.

The Phillies would get another crack at a Series title in 1980. "Another" might be overstating the case. They had qualified for the big event just twice previously, having won National League pennants only in 1915 and 1950 in their first 97 seasons of N.L. play.

In their 98th season, the Phillies had vented considerable frustration even before the World Series began. So, too, had their Series opponents, the Kansas City Royals.

One step away from World Series berths in 1976, 1977 and 1978, both the Phillies and the Royals lost in Championship Series play all three years. While the Phils didn't exact revenge against their conquerors (having lost to the Cincinnati Reds once and the Los Angeles Dodgers twice), they were able to clear the N.L. Champion-

Tug McGraw, dripping champagne, looks for relief after putting the cap on the Phillies' 1980 Series triumph over Kansas City.

ship Series hurdle in 1980 and did so at the expense of the Houston Astros. The Royals, on the other hand, reveled in overcoming an opponent that had been a bane to their existence. After losing down-to-the-wire A.L. Championship Series to New York in '76 and '77 and then falling to the Yankees again in '78, Kansas City blotted out the Yanks in three straight games in the 1980 playoffs.

Long-suffering Phillies fans couldn't wait for the World Series to start. Then, in the early innings of Game 1 at Veterans Stadium, they suffered a little more. Amos Otis, a Royals outfield fixture since 1970 (the second year of the expansion team's operation), cracked a two-run homer in his first Series at-bat, which came in the second inning, and Willie Aikens followed with a one-on

blast in the third.

Staked to a 4-0 lead, 20-game winner Dennis Leonard couldn't hold it. Not even for an inning. The Phils erupted for five runs in their half of the third, the final three coming on a homer by Bake McBride. The National Leaguers got single runs in the next two innings, with Bob Boone delivering the first with his second run-scoring double of the game and Garry Maddox driving home the second with a sacrifice fly. The runs proved crucial when Aikens, celebrating his 26th birthday, rammed his second two-run homer of the night in the eighth. At this point, with the Phils clinging to a 7-6 lead, relief specialist Tug McGraw took over for starter Bob Walk. And McGraw, doing what he did best, closed out the Royals and made a winner out of rookie Walk.

In Game 2, Otis shot Kansas City into a 3-2 lead with a two-run double off Phillies standout Steve Carlton in the seventh. John Wathan followed Otis' drive with a sacrifice fly, and the Royals subsequently turned the two-run lead over to bullpen master Dan Quisenberry. Working in relief of Larry Gura, Quisenberry fashioned a 1-2-3 seventh but ran into trouble in the eighth. Big trouble. The Phils tattooed the submariner for four hits and four runs, with McBride singling home the tying run and Mike Schmidt doubling in the go-ahead run. Ron Reed pitched the final inning for the Phils, who chalked up a 6-4 victory.

A 2-0 deficit in games obviously was bad news for the Royals. But it was just part of the bad news. George Brett, Kansas City's superstar third baseman who thrilled fans nationwide during the regular season with his quest to bat

.400 (he wound up at .390), had left Game 2 in the middle of the sixth inning after going 2 for 2 at the plate. It was disclosed that Brett was suffering from hemorrhoids and was in considerable pain. Could Brett possibly be available in 48 hours for Game 3, the first Series game ever to be played in Kansas City? Could he come back at all after undergoing minor surgery?

Never fear. Hours after leaving a Kansas City hospital on the day of the third game, Brett stepped to the plate at Royals Stadium and belted a first-inning home run off the Phillies' Dick Ruthven. The two clubs then engaged in run-trading, with the Phils matching Kansas City's run with one of their own in the top of the second, the Royals scoring in the fourth and Philadelphia tying the game at 2-2 in the fifth. Rookie Manager Jim Frey's American Leaguers regained the lead on an Otis homer in the seventh only to see the N.L. champions forge another deadlock in the eighth. Kansas City then foiled the Phillies' next-inning-comeback scenario by scoring in the bottom of the 10th. With Willie Wilson on second base after a walk and a steal and Brett on first following an intentional walk, Aikens drilled a two-out single to the gap in left-center and the Royals emerged with a 4-3 victory.

Aikens continued to smoke in Game 4, walloping a two-run homer in the Royals' four-run first inning and then hitting a bases-empty shot in the second. The two drives made Aikens the first man in history to connect for a pair of two-homer games in one Series. Leonard worked into the eighth inning and took a 5-3 triumph.

What had once been a deteriorating situation for the Royals was turning brighter all the time. After trailing two games to none and not knowing the status of Brett, Kansas City had regained Brett's services and also deadlocked the Series. And soon the Royals would be on the verge of seizing the Series lead.

After Schmidt broke a scoreless tie in Game 5 by depositing a

Gura pitch over the wall for a two-run homer in the fourth inning, the Royals broke through against rookie Marty Bystrom on Brett's RBI groundout in the fifth. Otis then rapped a game-tying, leadoff homer in the sixth off Bystrom, and U.L. Washington stroked a sacrifice fly later in the sixth off reliever Reed (with the run being charged to Bystrom).

Now armed with a 3-2 edge, Kansas City's Gura quickly found himself in a two-on, one-out jam in the seventh. Quisenberry came to his rescue, though, and the game slipped through the eighth and into the ninth with the Royals still guarding the one-run lead.

Schmidt led off the final frame by singling off Brett's glove. Pinch-hitter Del Unser then whacked a Quisenberry pitch past Aikens, the Royals' hulking first baseman, and down the right-field line. The hit went for a double, scoring Schmidt and tying the game. After Keith Moreland sacrificed Unser to third, Maddox grounded out to third as Unser retreated to the bag. But Manny Trillo singled off Quisenberry's glove—Brett grabbed the ball and fired to first, but his throw was too late—and Unser dashed home with the go-ahead run.

McGraw proceeded to tug at Royals fans' heartstrings—not to mention his own—when he issued three walks in the last of the ninth. But Jose Cardenal struck out, ending the game.

Now, 24-game winner Carlton would get his second start for the Phillies. And he was in outstanding form. Through seven innings, it was 4-0, Phils, with Schmidt having supplied the big hit with a two-run single off Royals starter Rich Gale in the third.

The Royals got Carlton out of the game, though, when their first two batters reached base in the eighth. Dallas Green, in his first full season as the Phils' manager, again went to McGraw. And the lefthanded reliever got the job, even if in not-so-pretty fashion. Kansas City managed to load the bases three times in the last two innings, but cashed in only one run.

The crowning achievement—it all but crowned the Phillies as World Series champions—came with one out in the ninth, the bases full of Kansas Citians and the Phils on top, 4-1. McGraw induced Frank White to hit a foul pop near the Philadelphia dug-out, and catcher Boone camped under it. The ball popped in and out of Boone's mitt—Royals' hopes rose for a fleeting moment —but first baseman Pete Rose, also giving chase on the ball, was there to snatch it out of the air. Then the Royals' Wilson struck out for a Series-record 12th time, ending the 1980 fall classic.

At long last, the Phillies had done it.

Game 1

Tuesday, October 14, At Philadelphia

Kansas City	AB.	R.	H.	RBI.	PO.	A.
Wilson, lf	5	0	0	0	2	1
McRae, dh	3	1	1	0	0	0
G. Brett, 3b	4	1	1	0	0	2
Aikens, 1b	4	2	2	4	13	0
Porter, c	2	1	0	0	5	1
Otis, cf	4	1	3	2	1	0
Hurdle, rf	3	0	1	0	1	0
aWathan, rf	1	0	0	0	1	0
White, 2b	4	0	1	0	0	5
Washington, ss	4	0	0	0	1	6
Leonard, p	0	0	0	0	0	0
Martin, p	0	0	0	0	0	0
Quisenberry, p	0	0	0	0	0	0
Totals	34	6	9	6	24	15

Philadelphia	AB.	R.	H.	RBI.	PO.	A.
Smith, lf	4	0	2	0	3	1
Gross, lf	1	0	0	0	1	0
Rose, 1b	3	1	0	0	7	2
Schmidt, 3b	2	2	1	0	2	3
McBride, rf	4	1	3	3	3	0
Luzinski, dh	3	0	0	0	0	0
Maddox, cf	3	0	1	0	2	0
Trillo, 2b	4	1	1	0	1	2
Bowa, ss	4	1	1	0	0	3
Boone, c	4	1	3	2	6	0
Walk, p	0	0	0	0	2	0
McGraw, p	0	0	0	0	0	0
Totals	32	7	11	6	27	11

Kansas City	0	2	2	0	0	0	0	2	0	—6
Philadelphia	0	0	5	1	1	0	0	0	x	—7

Kansas City	IP.	H.	R.	ER.	BB.	SO.
Leonard (L)	3⅔	6	6	6	1	3
Martin	4	5	1	1	1	1
Quisenberry	⅓	0	0	0	0	0

Philadelphia	IP.	H.	R.	ER.	BB.	SO.
Walk (W)	7*	8	6	6	3	3
McGraw (S)	2	1	0	0	0	2

*Pitched to two batters in eighth.

Game-winning RBI—McBride.

aGrounded into double play for Hurdle in eighth. E—Leonard. DP—Philadelphia 1. LOB—Kansas City 4, Philadelphia 6. 2B—Boone 2, G. Brett. HR—Otis, Aikens 2, McBride. SB—Bowa, White. SF—Maddox. HBP—By Leonard (Rose), by Martin (Luzinski). WP—Walk. U—Wendelstedt (N.L.) plate, Kunkel (A.L.) first, Pryor (N.L.) second, Denkinger (A.L.) third, Rennert (N.L.) left and Bremigan (A.L.) right. T—3:01. A—65,791.

Game 2

Wednesday, October 15, At Philadelphia

Kansas City	AB.	R.	H.	RBI.	PO.	A.
Wilson, lf	4	1	1	0	1	0
Washington, ss	4	0	1	0	0	3
G. Brett, 3b	2	0	2	0	2	2
Chalk, 3b	0	1	0	0	0	1
cPorter	1	0	0	0	0	0
McRae, dh	4	1	3	0	0	0
Otis, cf	5	1	2	2	5	0
Wathan, c	3	0	0	1	2	0
Aikens, 1b	3	0	1	0	6	0
LaCock, 1b	0	0	0	0	2	0
Cardenal, rf	4	0	0	0	1	0
White, 2b	4	0	1	0	3	3
Gura, p	0	0	0	0	0	0
Quisenberry, p	0	0	0	0	0	0
Totals	34	4	11	3	24	9

Philadelphia	AB.	R.	H.	RBI.	PO.	A.
Smith, lf	3	0	0	0	0	0
aUnser, cf	1	1	1	1	0	0
Rose, 1b	4	0	0	0	7	1
McBride, rf	3	1	1	1	2	0
Schmidt, 3b	4	1	2	1	1	1
Moreland, dh	4	1	2	1	0	0
Maddox, cf	3	1	1	0	1	1
bGross, lf	1	0	0	0	0	0
Trillo, 2b	2	0	0	1	6	3
Bowa, ss	3	0	1	1	0	6
Boone, c	1	1	0	0	10	1
Carlton, p	0	0	0	0	0	1
Reed, p	0	0	0	0	0	0
Totals	29	6	8	6	27	14

Kansas City .... 0 0 0 0 0 1 3 0 0—4
Philadelphia .... 0 0 0 0 2 0 0 4 x—6

Kansas City	IP.	H.	R.	ER.	BB.	SO.
Gura	6	4	2	2	2	2
Quisenberry (L)	2	4	4	4	1	0

Philadelphia	IP.	H.	R.	ER.	BB.	SO.
Carlton (W)	8	10	4	3	6	10
Reed (S)	1	1	0	0	0	2

Game-winning RBI—Schmidt.

aDoubled for Smith in eighth. bGrounded into double play for Maddox in eighth. cStruck out for Chalk in ninth. E—Trillo. DP—Kansas City 2, Philadelphia 4. LOB—Kansas City 11, Philadelphia 3. 2B—Maddox, Otis, Unser, Schmidt. SB—Wilson, Chalk. SH—Washington. SF—Trillo, Wathan. WP—Carlton. U—Kunkel (A.L.) plate, Pryor (N.L.) first, Denkinger (A.L.) second, Rennert (N.L.) third, Bremigan (A.L.) left and Wendelstedt (N.L.) right. T—3:01. A—65,775.

Game 3

Friday, October 17, At Kansas City

Philadelphia	AB.	R.	H.	RBI.	PO.	A.
Smith, lf	4	0	2	1	0	0
bGross, lf	0	0	0	0	0	0
Rose, 1b	4	0	1	1	11	0
Schmidt, 3b	5	1	1	1	3	3
McBride, rf	5	0	2	0	1	0
Moreland, dh	5	0	1	0	0	0
Maddox, cf	4	0	1	0	3	0
Trillo, 2b	5	1	2	0	2	6
Bowa, ss	5	1	3	0	1	3
Boone, c	4	0	1	0	8	1
Ruthven, p	0	0	0	0	0	0
McGraw, p	0	0	0	0	0	0
Totals	41	3	14	3	29	13

Kansas City	AB.	R.	H.	RBI.	PO.	A.
Wilson, lf	4	1	0	0	3	0
White, 2b	5	0	0	0	4	2
G. Brett, 3b	4	1	2	1	0	3
Aikens, 1b	5	1	2	1	7	1
McRae, dh	4	0	2	1	0	0
Otis, cf	4	1	2	1	9	0
Hurdle, rf	4	0	2	0	1	0
aConcepcion	0	0	0	0	0	0
Cardenal, rf	0	0	0	0	0	0
Porter, c	4	0	0	0	4	0
Washington, ss	4	0	1	0	1	2
Gale, p	0	0	0	0	0	1
Martin, p	0	0	0	0	0	0
Quisenberry, p	0	0	0	0	1	1
Totals	38	4	11	4	30	10

Philadelphia .... 0 1 0 0 1 0 0 1 0 0—3
Kansas City .... 1 0 0 1 0 0 1 0 0 1—4

Two out when winning run scored.

Philadelphia	IP.	H.	R.	ER.	BB.	SO.
Ruthven	9	9	3	3	0	7
McGraw (L)	⅔	2	1	1	2	1

Kansas City	IP.	H.	R.	ER.	BB.	SO.
Gale	4⅓	7	2	2	3	3
Martin	3⅓	5	1	1	1	1
Quisenberry (W)	2⅓	2	0	0	2	0

Game-winning RBI—Aikens.

aRan for Hurdle in ninth. bSacrificed for Smith in tenth. DP—Philadelphia 1, Kansas City 2. LOB—Philadelphia 15, Kansas City 7. 2B—Trillo, G. Brett. 3B—Aikens. HR—G. Brett, Schmidt, Otis. SB—Hurdle, Bowa, Wilson. SH—Gross. U—Pryor (N.L.) plate, Denkinger (A.L.) first, Rennert (N.L.) second, Bremigan (A.L.) third, Wendelstedt (N.L.) left and Kunkel (A.L.) right. T—3:19. A—42,380.

Game 4

Saturday, October 18, At Kansas City

Philadelphia	AB.	R.	H.	RBI.	PO.	A.
Smith, dh	4	0	0	0	0	0
Rose, 1b	4	1	2	0	8	2
McBride, rf	3	0	1	0	3	0
Schmidt, 3b	3	0	1	1	2	0
Unser, lf	4	0	1	0	1	0
Maddox, cf	4	0	1	0	2	0
Trillo, 2b	4	2	1	0	0	6
Bowa, ss	4	0	2	1	1	1
Boone, c	3	0	1	1	6	0
Christenson, p	0	0	0	0	0	0
Noles, p	0	0	0	0	1	0
Saucier, p	0	0	0	0	0	0
Brusstar, p	0	0	0	0	0	0
Totals	33	3	10	3	24	9

Kansas City	AB.	R.	H.	RBI.	PO.	A.
Wilson, lf	4	1	1	0	4	0
White, 2b	5	0	0	0	2	4
G. Brett, 3b	5	1	1	1	0	7
Aikens, 1b	3	2	2	3	13	0
McRae, dh	4	1	2	0	0	0
Otis, cf	4	0	2	1	1	0
Hurdle, rf	2	0	1	0	3	0
Porter, c	3	0	0	0	2	1
Washington, ss	4	0	1	0	2	3
Leonard, p	0	0	0	0	0	0
Quisenberry, p	0	0	0	0	0	0
Totals	34	5	10	5	27	15

Philadelphia .... 0 1 0 0 0 0 1 1 0—3
Kansas City .... 4 1 0 0 0 0 0 0 x—5

Philadelphia	IP.	H.	R.	ER.	BB.	SO.
Christenson (L)	⅓	5	4	4	0	0
Noles	4⅔	5	1	1	2	6
Saucier	⅔	0	0	0	2	0
Brusstar	2⅓	0	0	0	1	0

Kansas City	IP.	H.	R.	ER.	BB.	SO.
Leonard (W)	7*	9	3	2	1	2
Quisenberry (S)	2	1	0	0	0	0

*Pitched to one batter in eighth.

Game-winning RBI—G. Brett.

E—Christenson, White, Washington. DP—Kansas City 1. LOB—Philadelphia 6, Kansas City 10. 2B—McRae 2, Otis, Hurdle, McBride, Trillo, Rose. 3B—G. Brett. HR—Aikens 2. SB—Bowa. SF—Boone, Schmidt. WP—Leonard, Saucier. U—Denkinger (A.L.) plate, Rennert (N.L.) first, Bremigan (A.L.) second, Wendelstedt (N.L.) third, Kunkel (A.L.) left and Pryor (N.L.) right. T—2:37. A—42,363.

Game 5

Sunday, October 19, At Kansas City

Philadelphia	AB.	R.	H.	RBI.	PO.	A.
Rose, 1b	4	0	0	0	7	1
McBride, rf	4	1	0	0	2	1
Schmidt, 3b	4	2	2	2	1	1
Luzinski, lf	2	0	0	0	1	0
aSmith, lf	0	0	0	0	0	0
cUnser, lf	1	1	1	1	0	0
Moreland, dh	3	0	1	0	0	0
Maddox, cf	4	0	0	0	2	0
Trillo, 2b	4	0	1	1	3	5
Bowa, ss	4	0	1	0	0	2
Boone, c	3	0	1	0	10	0
Bystrom, p	0	0	0	0	1	1
Reed, p	0	0	0	0	0	0
McGraw, p	0	0	0	0	0	1
Totals	33	4	7	4	27	12

Kansas City	AB.	R.	H.	RBI.	PO.	A.
Wilson, lf	5	0	2	0	2	0
White, 2b	3	0	0	0	2	6
G. Brett, 3b	5	0	1	1	1	2
Aikens, 1b	3	0	1	0	10	1
dConcepcion	0	0	0	0	0	0
McRae, dh	5	0	1	0	0	0
Otis, cf	3	1	2	1	3	0
Hurdle, rf	3	1	1	0	3	0
bCardenal, rf	2	0	0	0	0	0
Porter, c	4	0	2	0	2	0
Washington, ss	3	1	2	1	2	2
Gura, p	0	0	0	0	2	4
Quisenberry, p	0	0	0	0	0	0
Totals	36	3	12	3	27	15

Philadelphia .... 0 0 0 2 0 0 0 0 2—4
Kansas City .... 0 0 0 0 1 2 0 0 0—3

Philadelphia	IP.	H.	R.	ER.	BB.	SO.
Bystrom	5*	10	3	3	1	4
Reed	1	1	0	0	0	0
McGraw (W)	3	1	0	0	4	5

Kansas City	IP.	H.	R.	ER.	BB.	SO.
Gura	6⅓	4	2	1	1	2
Quisenberry (L)	2⅔	3	2	2	0	0

*Pitched to three batters in sixth.

Game-winning RBI—Trillo.

aRan for Luzinski in seventh. bFlied out for Hurdle in seventh. cDoubled for Smith in ninth. dRan for Aikens in ninth. E—G. Brett, Aikens. DP—Kansas City 2. LOB—Philadelphia 4, Kansas City 13. 2B—Wilson, McRae, Unser. HR—Schmidt, Otis. SB—G. Brett. SH—White, Moreland. SF—Washington. U—Rennert (N.L.) plate, Bremigan (A.L.) first, Wendelstedt (N.L.) second, Kunkel (A.L.) third, Pryor (N.L.) left and Denkinger (A.L.) right. T—2:51. A—42,369.

Game 6

Tuesday, October 21, At Philadelphia

Kansas City	AB.	R.	H.	RBI.	PO.	A.
Wilson, lf	4	0	0	0	3	0
Washington, ss	3	0	1	1	2	4
G. Brett, 3b	4	0	2	0	1	1
McRae, dh	4	0	0	0	0	0
Otis, cf	3	0	0	0	2	0
Aikens, 1b	2	0	0	0	6	0
aConcepcion	0	0	0	0	0	0
Wathan, c	3	1	2	0	4	1
Cardenal, rf	4	0	2	0	4	0
White, 2b	4	0	0	0	2	1
Gale, p	0	0	0	0	0	0
Martin, p	0	0	0	0	0	0
Splittorff, p	0	0	0	0	0	1
Pattin, p	0	0	0	0	0	0
Quisenberry, p	0	0	0	0	0	0
Totals	31	1	7	1	24	8

Philadelphia	AB.	R.	H.	RBI.	PO.	A.
Smith, lf	4	2	1	0	1	0
Gross, lf	0	0	0	0	0	0
Rose, 1b	4	0	3	0	9	0
Schmidt, 3b	3	0	1	2	0	0
McBride, rf	4	0	0	1	2	0
Luzinski, dh	4	0	0	0	0	0
Maddox, cf	4	0	2	0	1	0
Trillo, 2b	4	0	0	0	2	3
Bowa, ss	4	1	1	0	3	3
Boone, c	2	1	1	1	9	1
Carlton, p	0	0	0	0	0	2
McGraw, p	0	0	0	0	0	0
Totals	33	4	9	4	27	9

Kansas City .... 0 0 0 0 0 0 0 1 0—1
Philadelphia .... 0 0 2 0 1 1 0 0 x—4

Kansas City	IP.	H.	R.	ER.	BB.	SO.
Gale (L)	2†	4	2	1	1	1
Martin	2⅓	1	1	1	1	0
Splittorff	1⅔‡	4	1	1	0	0
Pattin	1	0	0	0	0	2
Quisenberry	1	0	0	0	0	0

Philadelphia	IP.	H.	R.	ER.	BB.	SO.
Carlton (W)	7§	4	1	1	3	7
McGraw (S)	2	3	0	0	2	2

†Pitched to four batter in third.
‡Pitched to one batter in seventh.
§Pitched to two batters in eighth.

Game-winning RBI—Schmidt.

aRan for Aikens in ninth. E—Aikens, White. DP—Kansas City 1, Philadelphia 2. LOB—Kansas City 9, Philadelphia 7. 2B—Maddox, Smith, Bowa. SF—Washington. U—Bremigan (A.L.) plate, Wendelstedt (N.L.) first, Kunkel (A.L.) second, Pryor (N.L.) third, Denkinger (A.L.) left and Rennert (N.L.) right. T—3:00. A—65,838.

COMPOSITE BATTING AVERAGES

Philadelphia Phillies

Player-Position	G.	AB.	R.	H.	2B.	3B.	HR.	RBI.	BA.
Unser, ph-cf-lf	3	6	2	3	2	0	0	2	.500
Boone, c	6	17	3	7	2	0	0	4	.412
Schmidt, 3b	6	21	6	8	1	0	2	7	.381
Bowa, ss	6	24	3	9	1	0	0	2	.375
Moreland, dh	3	12	1	4	0	0	0	1	.333
McBride, rf	6	23	3	7	1	0	1	5	.304
Smith, pr-lf-dh	6	19	2	5	1	0	0	1	.263
Rose, 1b	6	23	2	6	1	0	0	1	.261
Maddox, cf	6	22	1	5	2	0	0	1	.227
Trillo, 2b	6	23	4	5	2	0	0	2	.217
Brusstar, p	1	0	0	0	0	0	0	0	.000
Bystrom, p	1	0	0	0	0	0	0	0	.000
Carlton, p	2	0	0	0	0	0	0	0	.000
Christenson, p	1	0	0	0	0	0	0	0	.000
McGraw, p	4	0	0	0	0	0	0	0	.000
Noles, p	1	0	0	0	0	0	0	0	.000
Reed, p	2	0	0	0	0	0	0	0	.000
Ruthven, p	1	0	0	0	0	0	0	0	.000
Saucier, p	1	0	0	0	0	0	0	0	.000
Walk, p	1	0	0	0	0	0	0	0	.000
Gross, ph-lf	4	2	0	0	0	0	0	0	.000
Luzinski, dh-lf	3	9	0	0	0	0	0	0	.000
Totals	6	201	27	59	13	0	3	26	.294

Kansas City Royals

Player-Position	G.	AB.	R.	H.	2B.	3B.	HR.	RBI.	BA.
Otis, cf	6	23	4	11	2	0	3	7	.478
Hurdle, rf	4	12	1	5	1	0	0	0	.417
Aikens, 1b	6	20	5	8	0	1	4	8	.400
G. Brett, 3b	6	24	3	9	2	1	1	3	.375
McRae, dh	6	24	3	9	3	0	0	1	.375
Wathan, ph-rf-c	3	7	1	2	0	0	0	1	.286
Washington, ss	6	22	1	6	0	0	0	2	.273
Cardenal, ph-rf	4	10	0	2	0	0	0	0	.200
Wilson, lf	6	26	3	4	1	0	0	0	.154
Porter, ph-c	5	14	1	2	0	0	0	0	.143
White, 2b	6	25	0	2	0	0	0	0	.080
Chalk, 3b	1	0	1	0	0	0	0	0	.000
Concepcion, pr	3	0	0	0	0	0	0	0	.000
Gale, p	2	0	0	0	0	0	0	0	.000
Gura, p	2	0	0	0	0	0	0	0	.000
LaCock, 1b	1	0	0	0	0	0	0	0	.000
Leonard, p	2	0	0	0	0	0	0	0	.000
Martin, p	3	0	0	0	0	0	0	0	.000
Pattin, p	1	0	0	0	0	0	0	0	.000
Quisenberry, p	6	0	0	0	0	0	0	0	.000
Splittorff, p	1	0	0	0	0	0	0	0	.000
Totals	6	207	23	60	9	2	8	22	.290

COMPOSITE PITCHING AVERAGES

Philadelphia Phillies

Pitcher	G.	IP.	H.	R.	ER.	BB.	SO.	W.	L.	ERA.
Brusstar	1	2⅓	0	0	0	1	0	0	0	0.00
Reed	2	2	2	0	0	0	2	0	0	0.00
Saucier	1	⅔	0	0	0	2	0	0	0	0.00
McGraw	4	7⅔	7	1	1	8	10	1	1	1.17
Noles	1	4⅔	5	1	1	2	6	0	0	1.93
Carlton	2	15	14	5	4	9	17	2	0	2.40
Ruthven	1	9	9	3	3	0	7	0	0	3.00
Bystrom	1	5	10	3	3	1	4	0	0	5.40
Walk	1	7	8	6	6	3	3	1	0	7.71
Christenson	1	⅓	5	4	4	0	0	0	1	108.00
Totals	6	53⅔	60	23	22	26	49	4	2	3.69

Kansas City Royals

Pitcher	G.	IP.	H.	R.	ER.	BB.	SO.	W.	L.	ERA.
Pattin	1	1	0	0	0	0	2	0	0	0.00
Gura	2	12⅓	8	4	3	3	4	0	0	2.19
Martin	3	9⅔	11	3	3	3	2	0	0	2.79
Gale	2	6⅓	11	4	3	4	4	0	1	4.26
Quisenberry	6	10⅓	10	6	6	3	0	1	2	5.23
Splittorff	1	1⅔	4	1	1	0	0	0	0	5.40
Leonard	2	10⅔	15	9	8	2	5	1	1	6.75
Totals	6	52	59	27	24	15	17	2	4	4.15

1981 LOS ANGELES DODGERS VS. NEW YORK YANKEES

Yankees vs. Dodgers.

It must be World Series time. And, sure enough, the clubs once again were getting together to do battle in October. For the *11th* time.

This postseason rivalry dated to 1941, the year of Dodger catcher Mickey Owen's third-strike muff. The teams last had met in 1978, when the Yankees dropped the first two games of the Series and then beat the Dodgers four consecutive times. In the 10 Series meetings between the clubs, New York had prevailed as champions on eight occasions (the Yanks were 6-1 against the Brooklyn Dodgers and 2-1 against the Los Angeles Dodgers).

When the 1981 World Series finally got under way on October 20—a lengthy, two-tiered playoff system was formulated after a players strike interrupted the regular season—the Yankees' dominance over the Dodgers didn't seem in jeopardy. Fresh from a divisional-playoff triumph over the Milwaukee Brewers (three games to two) and a Championship Series sweep of the Oakland A's, the Yanks struck in a hurry against Los Angeles lefthander Jerry Reuss as Bob Watson cracked a three-run homer in the first inning of Game 1.

Collecting single runs in the third and fourth innings, New York carried a 5-1 lead into the eighth. Yankees Manager Bob Lemon then replaced starter Ron Guidry with Ron Davis, who walked the only two batters he faced.

Goose Gossage followed Davis to the mound and yielded a run-scoring single to pinch-hitter Jay Johnstone and a sacrifice fly to Dusty Baker, but the intimidating reliever got out of the inning when third baseman Graig Net-

Game 3 heroes Fernando Valenzuela (left) and Ron Cey celebrate after leading the Los Angeles Dodgers to a 5-4 win over the Yankees.

tles—flashing his '78 Series form afield—made a diving grab of Steve Garvey's line smash that ap-

peared headed for the left-field corner and Ron Cey grounded into a forceout. New York won,

5-3, at Yankee Stadium.

Former Dodger Tommy John, a free-agent signee of the Yankees after the 1978 season, teamed with Gossage to blank Los Angeles on four hits in Game 2. New York shortstop Larry Milbourne garnered the game's only extra-base hit, a fifth-inning double that drove in the first run of the game. Watson had two hits and an RBI as the Yanks won, 3-0, and extended their Series winning streak against the Dodgers to six games.

Tommy Lasorda's National League titlists needed to regroup. Having played 10 postseason games before the World Series ever started (five games against the Houston Astros in the divisional playoffs and five more against the Montreal Expos in the Championship Series), Los Angeles eagerly awaited the off day that would precede resumption of the Series on the West Coast. The Dodgers also looked ahead to using rookie sensation Fernando Valenzuela for the first time in the Series.

Lefthander Valenzuela, who had pitched shutouts in five of his first seven games of the 1981 campaign and wound up with eight shutouts in a 13-7 season, permitted nine hits—including homers by Watson and Rick Cerone—and seven walks in Game 3. But the 20-year-old pitcher came out a 5-4 winner at Dodger Stadium, thanks to Cey's three-run homer in the first inning and a two-run Dodger uprising in the fifth that featured Pedro Guerrero's RBI double and Mike Scioscia's run-producing double-play grounder.

Dodgers starter Bob Welch failed to retire a single batter in Game 4, a contest in which Los Angeles fell behind, 6-3. But Lasorda's club tied the game in the sixth when Johnstone belted a two-run pinch homer and Davey Lopes, who reached second when right fielder Reggie Jackson dropped his fly ball and then stole third, scored on Bill Russell's single. Los Angeles then went ahead, 8-6, in the seventh on Steve Yeager's sacrifice fly and Lopes' run-scoring infield hit.

Jackson, his Mr. October status tarnished just a bit because of his sixth-inning misplay, polished his image in the eighth when he homered to right-center. It was the third hit of the game for Jackson, who had missed the first three games of the Series because of a leg injury. Jackson's wallop, though, ended the scoring. Los Angeles, an 8-7 winner, had tied the Series at two victories apiece.

Guidry and Reuss engaged in a tremendous duel in Game 5, and Reuss came out on top, 2-1, when Guerrero and Yeager slugged back-to-back home runs in the seventh inning. Reuss tossed a complete-game five-hitter, one of the hits being a fifth-inning single by Yankees outfielder Dave Winfield. The hit was the first and last of the Series for former San Diego standout Winfield, who had signed a free-agent contract with the Yankees after the 1980 season for a reported $21 million over 10 years.

Game 6 at Yankee Stadium was a 1-1 tie in the bottom of the fourth when Lemon elected to use a pinch-hitter for starting pitcher John. New York failed to score in the inning, and the Dodgers then roughed up reliever George Frazier for three runs in the fifth. Cey, coming back from a scary beaning episode in the fifth game (a Gossage fastball had crashed into the left side of his batting helmet), snapped the tie with a single and Guerrero contributed a two-run triple.

Guerrero later stroked a two-run single and a bases-empty home run, and his five RBIs highlighted the Dodgers' Series-clinching 9-2 runaway. Losing pitcher Frazier had suffered his third defeat, equaling the Series record established by Claude Williams of the 1919 Black Sox.

The Dodgers had come from a 2-0 deficit in games to defeat New York in four straight. Turnabout (from 1978) was fair play and, coming against a longtime Series adversary and nemesis, it was particularly gratifying as well.

Game 1

Tuesday, October 20, At New York

Los Angeles	AB.	R.	H.	RBI.	PO.	A.
Lopes, 2b	3	1	0	0	3	1
Russell, ss	3	0	0	0	2	1
cJohnstone	1	0	1	1	0	0
Stewart, p	0	0	0	0	0	0
Baker, lf	2	0	1	1	3	0
Garvey, 1b	4	0	1	0	5	0
Cey, 3b	4	0	1	0	0	1
Guerrero, cf	3	0	0	0	3	0
Monday, rf	4	0	0	0	4	0
Yeager, c	3	1	1	1	3	0
dLandreaux	1	0	0	0	0	0
Reuss, p	1	0	0	0	0	1
Castillo, p	0	0	0	0	0	2
Goltz, p	0	0	0	0	0	0
aSax, ph	1	0	0	0	0	0
Niedenfuer, p	0	0	0	0	0	0
bThomas, ss	0	1	0	0	1	1
Totals	30	3	5	3	24	7

New York	AB.	R.	H.	RBI.	PO.	A.
Randolph, 2b	3	0	0	0	3	3
Mumphrey, cf	3	2	2	0	3	0
Winfield, lf	3	0	0	0	1	0
Piniella, rf	4	1	2	1	4	0
Watson, 1b	3	1	2	3	8	0
Nettles, 3b	3	0	0	0	1	3
Cerone, c	3	0	0	0	8	0
Milbourne, ss	4	1	0	0	0	2
Guidry, p	2	0	0	0	0	0
Davis, p	0	0	0	0	0	0
Gossage, p	0	0	0	0	0	1
Totals	28	5	6	5	27	9

Los Angeles ....0 0 0 0 1 0 0 2 0—3
New York ....3 0 1 1 0 0 0 x—5

Los Angeles	IP.	H.	R.	ER.	BB.	SO.
Reuss (L)	2⅔	5	4	4	0	2
Castillo	1	0	1	1	5	0
Goltz	⅓	0	0	0	0	0
Niedenfuer	3	1	0	0	0	1
Stewart	1	0	0	0	1	0

New York	IP.	H.	R.	ER.	BB.	SO.
Guidry (W)	7	4	1	1	2	6
Davis	0†	0	2	2	2	0
Gossage (S)	2	1	0	0	0	2

†Pitched to two batters in eighth.

Game-winning RBI—Watson.

aFlied out for Goltz in fifth. bWalked for Niedenfuer in eighth. cSingled for Russell in eighth. dGrounded out for Yeager in ninth. DP—Los Angeles 1. LOB—Los Angeles 5, New York 6. 2B—Piniella. HR—Yeager, Watson. SB—Mumphrey, Piniella. SH—Guidry. SF—Baker. PB—Cerone. U—Barnett (A.L.) plate, Colosi (N.L.) first, Cooney (A.L.) second, Harvey (N.L.) third, Garcia (A.L.) left and Stello (N.L.) right. T—2:32. A—56,470.

Game 2

Wednesday, October 21, At New York

Los Angeles	AB.	R.	H.	RBI.	PO.	A.
Lopes, 2b	3	0	0	0	7	3
eMonday	1	0	0	0	0	0
Howe, p	0	0	0	0	0	0
Stewart, p	0	0	0	0	0	0
Russell, ss	4	0	1	0	0	5
Baker, lf	4	0	0	0	0	0
Garvey, 1b	3	0	2	0	6	0
Cey, 3b	4	0	0	0	0	3
Guerrero, rf	4	0	0	0	4	0
Landreaux, cf	3	0	0	0	4	0
Yeager, c	2	0	0	0	1	0
bJohnstone	1	0	0	0	0	0
Scioscia, c	0	0	0	0	1	0
Hooton, p	2	0	0	0	0	1
Forster, p	0	0	0	0	0	1
cSmith	1	0	1	0	0	0
dSax, 2b	0	0	0	0	1	0
Totals	32	0	4	0	24	12

New York	AB.	R.	H.	RBI.	PO.	A.
Mumphrey, cf	2	0	0	0	1	0
Milbourne, ss	4	0	1	1	1	3
Winfield, lf	4	0	0	0	1	0
Gamble, rf	2	0	0	0	2	0
fPiniella	1	0	1	0	0	0
gBrown, rf	0	1	0	0	0	0
Nettles, 3b	4	1	2	0	1	5
Watson, 1b	4	0	2	1	13	0
Cerone, c	2	0	0	0	7	0
Randolph, 2b	2	1	0	1	1	3
John, p	1	0	0	0	0	2
aMurcer	0	0	0	0	0	0
Gossage, p	1	0	0	0	0	0
Totals	27	3	6	3	27	13

Los Angeles ....0 0 0 0 0 0 0 0 0—0
New York ....0 0 0 0 1 0 0 2 x—3

Los Angeles	IP.	H.	R.	ER.	BB.	SO.
Hooton (L)	6†	3	1	0	4	1
Forster	1	0	0	0	1	0
Howe	⅓	2	2	2	0	0
Stewart	⅔	1	0	0	1	1

New York	IP.	H.	R.	ER.	BB.	SO.
John (W)	7	3	0	0	0	4
Gossage (S)	2	1	0	0	1	3

†Pitched to two batters in seventh.

Game-winning RBI—Milbourne.

aSacrificed for John in seventh. bFlied out for Yeager in eighth. cSingled for Forster in eighth. dRan for Smith in eighth. eStruck out for Lopes in eighth. fSingled for Gamble in eighth. gRan for Piniella in eighth. E—Lopes, Stewart, Milbourne. DP—Los Angeles 1. LOB—Los Angeles 6, New York 9. 2B—Milbourne. SH—John, Murcer. SF—Randolph. U—Colosi (N.L.) plate, Cooney (A.L.) first,

Harvey (N.L.) second, Garcia (A.L.) third, Stello (N.L.) left and Barnett (A.L.) right. T—2:29. A—56,505.

Game 3

Friday, October 23, At Los Angeles

New York	AB.	R.	H.	RBI.	PO.	A.
Randolph, 2b	2	0	0	0	5	3
Mumphrey, cf	5	0	0	0	0	0
Winfield, lf	3	0	0	0	2	0
Piniella, rf	5	1	1	0	0	0
Watson, 1b	4	1	2	1	9	0
Cerone, c	4	2	2	1	5	1
Rodriguez, 3b	4	0	2	0	1	3
Milbourne, ss	2	0	2	1	2	4
Righetti, p	1	0	0	0	0	0
Frazier, p	1	0	0	0	0	0
May, p	0	0	0	0	0	0
cMurcer	1	0	0	0	0	0
Davis, p	0	0	0	0	0	0
Totals	32	4	9	3	24	11

Los Angeles	AB.	R.	H.	RBI.	PO.	A.
Lopes, 2b	4	1	2	0	7	3
Russell, ss	5	1	2	0	0	3
Baker, lf	4	0	0	0	2	0
Garvey, 1b	4	1	2	0	7	1
Cey, 3b	2	2	2	3	2	3
Guerrero, cf-rf	3	0	1	1	1	0
Monday, rf	2	0	1	0	2	0
bThomas, cf	1	0	0	0	0	0
Yeager, c	1	0	0	0	2	0
aScioscia, c	3	0	1	0	4	1
Valenzuela, p	3	0	0	0	0	1
Totals	32	5	11	4	27	12

New York	0 2 2 0 0 0 0 0 0—4
Los Angeles	3 0 0 0 2 0 0 0 x—5

New York	IP.	H.	R.	ER.	BB.	SO.
Righetti	2†	5	3	3	2	1
Frazier (L)	2‡	3	2	2	2	1
May	3	2	0	0	0	2
Davis	1	1	0	0	0	1

Los Angeles	IP.	H.	R.	ER.	BB.	SO.
Valenzuela (W)	9	9	4	4	7	6

†Pitched to two batters in third.
‡Pitched to four batters in fifth.

Game-winning RBI—None.

aGrounded out for Yeager in third. bHit into double play for Monday in seventh. cBunted into double play for May in eighth. E—Lopes. DP—New York 2, Los Angeles 2. LOB—New York 9, Los Angeles 9. 2B—Lopes, Cerone, Watson, Guerrero. HR—Cey, Watson, Cerone. SH—Righetti, Lopes. HBP—By Righetti (Guerrero). U—Cooney (A.L.) plate, Harvey (N.L.) first, Garcia (A.L.) second, Stello (N.L.) third, Barnett (A.L.) left and Colosi (N.L.) right. T—3:04. A—56,236.

Game 4

Saturday, October 24, At Los Angeles

New York	AB.	R.	H.	RBI.	PO.	A.
Randolph, 2b	5	3	2	1	2	0
Milbourne, ss	4	1	1	1	1	3
Winfield, cf-lf-cf	4	0	0	0	4	0
Jackson, rf	3	2	3	1	2	0
Gamble, lf	4	1	2	1	2	0
cBrown, cf	0	0	0	0	1	0
fPiniella, lf	1	0	0	0	0	0
Watson, 1b	3	0	1	2	5	0
Cerone, c	5	0	2	1	7	0
hRobertson	0	0	0	0	0	0
Rodriguez, 3b	4	0	2	0	0	3
gFoote	1	0	0	0	0	0
Reuschel, p	2	0	0	0	0	0
May, p	1	0	0	0	0	1
Davis, p	0	0	0	0	0	0
Frazier, p	1	0	0	0	0	0
John, p	0	0	0	0	0	0
iMurcer	1	0	0	0	0	0
Totals	39	7	13	7	24	7

Los Angeles	AB.	R.	H.	RBI.	PO.	A.
Lopes, 2b	5	2	2	2	5	2
Russell, ss	5	0	1	1	2	5
Garvey, 1b	5	1	3	0	5	1
Cey, 3b	5	0	2	2	1	1
Baker, lf	5	1	1	0	4	0
Monday, rf	3	1	1	0	2	0
Thomas, cf	1	0	0	0	3	0
Guerrero, cf-rf	3	0	2	0	2	1
Scioscia, c	1	1	0	0	2	0
eYeager, c	0	0	0	1	1	0
Welch, p	0	0	0	0	0	0
Goltz, p	0	0	0	0	0	0
aLandreaux	1	1	1	0	0	0
Forster, p	0	0	0	0	0	0
bSmith	1	0	0	0	0	0
Niedenfuer, p	0	0	0	0	0	0
dJohnstone	1	1	1	2	0	0
Howe, p	0	0	0	0	0	1
Totals	36	8	14	8	27	11

New York	2 1 1 0 0 2 0 1 0—7
Los Angeles	0 0 2 0 1 3 2 0 x—8

New York	IP.	H.	R.	ER.	BB.	SO.
Reuschel	3‡	6	2	2	1	2
May	1⅓	2	1	1	0	1
Davis	1	2	3	2	1	2
Frazier (L)	⅔§	2	2	2	1	0
John	2	2	0	0	0	2

Los Angeles	IP.	H.	R.	ER.	BB.	SO.
Welch	0†	3	2	2	1	0
Goltz	3	4	2	2	1	2
Forster	1	1	0	0	2	0
Niedenfuer	2	2	2	0	1	0
Howe (W)	3	3	1	1	0	1

†Pitched to four batters in first.
‡Pitched to two batters in fourth.
§Pitched to three batters in seventh.

Game-winning RBI—Yeager.

aDoubled for Goltz in third. bStruck out for Forster in fourth. cRan for Gamble in sixth. dHit home run for Niedenfuer in sixth. eHit sacrifice fly for Scioscia in seventh. fGrounded out for Brown in eighth. gStruck out for Rodriguez in ninth. hRan for Cerone in ninth. iReached first base safely on error in ninth. E—Jackson, Russell, Howe. LOB—New York 12, Los Angeles 10. 2B—Milbourne, Landreaux, Garvey, Monday. 3B—Randolph. HR—Randolph, Johnstone, Jackson. SB—Lopes 2, Winfield. SH—Milbourne, Scioscia, Howe. SF—Watson, Yeager. U—Harvey (N.L) plate, Garcia (A.L.) first, Stello (N.L.) second, Barnett (A.L.) third, Colosi (N.L.) left and Cooney (A.L.) right. T—3:32. A—56,242.

Game 5

Sunday, October 25, At Los Angeles

New York	AB.	R.	H.	RBI.	PO.	A.
Randolph, 2b	3	0	0	0	0	0
Milbourne, ss	4	0	1	0	1	1
Winfield, cf-lf	4	0	1	0	4	0
Jackson, rf	4	1	1	0	0	0
Gossage, p	0	0	0	0	0	0
Watson, 1b	3	0	0	0	6	0
Piniella, lf-rf	4	0	2	1	3	0
bBrown	0	0	0	0	0	0
Cerone, c	4	0	0	0	8	1
Rodriguez, 3b	3	0	0	0	2	3
Guidry, p	3	0	0	0	0	0
Mumphrey, cf	0	0	0	0	0	0
Totals	32	1	5	1	24	5

Los Angeles	AB.	R.	H.	RBI.	PO.	A.
Lopes, 2b	3	0	0	0	3	3
Russell, ss	4	0	0	0	0	7
Garvey, 1b	4	0	1	0	12	1
Cey, 3b	2	0	0	0	0	2
aLandreaux, cf	0	0	0	0	1	0
Baker, lf	4	0	0	0	2	0
Guerrero, rf	3	1	1	1	1	0
Yeager, c	3	1	2	1	7	0
Thomas, cf-3b	3	0	0	0	0	0
Reuss, p	2	0	0	0	1	2
Totals	28	2	4	2	27	15

New York	0 1 0 0 0 0 0 0 0—1
Los Angeles	0 0 0 0 0 0 2 0 x—2

New York	IP.	H.	R.	ER.	BB.	SO.
Guidry (L)	7	4	2	2	2	9
Gossage	1	0	0	0	1	0

Los Angeles	IP.	H.	R.	ER.	BB.	SO.
Reuss (W)	9	5	1	1	3	6

Game-winning RBI—Yeager.

aRan for Cey in eighth. bRan for Piniella in ninth. E—Lopes 3. DP—Los Angeles 2. LOB—New York 7, Los Angeles 6. 2B—Jackson, Yeager. HR—Guerrero, Yeager. SB—Lopes, Landreaux. HBP—By Gossage (Cey). U—Garcia (A.L.) plate, Stello (N.L.) first, Barnett (A.L.) second, Colosi (N.L.) third, Cooney (A.L.) left and Harvey (N.L.) right. T—2:19. A—56,115.

Game 6

Wednesday, October 28, At New York

Los Angeles	AB.	R.	H.	RBI.	PO.	A.
Lopes, 2b	4	2	1	0	1	2
Russell,ss	4	0	2	1	0	5
Garvey, 1b	4	1	1	0	9	0
Cey, 3b	3	1	2	1	1	1
bThomas, 3b	2	1	0	1	0	0
Baker, lf	5	2	2	0	2	0
Guerrero, cf-rf	5	1	3	5	6	0
Monday, rf	3	0	1	0	1	0
Landreaux, cf	1	0	0	0	1	0
Yeager, c	5	0	1	1	6	0
Hooton, p	2	1	0	0	0	0
Howe, p	2	0	0	0	0	0
Totals	40	9	13	9	27	8

New York	AB.	R.	H.	RBI.	PO.	A.
Randolph, 2b	3	1	2	1	2	2
Mumphrey, cf	5	0	1	0	2	0
Winfield, lf	4	0	0	0	2	0
Jackson, rf	5	0	0	0	3	0
Watson, 1b	5	0	0	0	10	0
Nettles, 3b	3	0	2	0	1	2
cRodriguez, 3b	1	1	1	0	0	0
Cerone, c	3	0	0	0	7	2
Milbourne, ss	2	0	0	0	0	3
John, p	1	0	0	0	0	1
aMurcer	1	0	0	0	0	0
Frazier, p	0	0	0	0	0	0
Davis, p	0	0	0	0	0	0
Reuschel, p	0	0	0	0	0	0
dGamble	0	0	0	0	0	0
ePiniella	1	0	1	1	0	0
May, p	0	0	0	0	0	0
fBrown	1	0	0	0	0	0
LaRoche, p	0	0	0	0	0	0
Totals	35	2	7	2	27	10

Los Angeles	0 0 0 1 3 4 0 1 0—9
New York	0 0 1 0 0 1 0 0 0—2

Los Angeles	IP.	H.	R.	ER.	BB.	SO.
Hooton (W)	5⅓	5	2	2	5	2
Howe (S)	3⅔	2	0	0	1	3

New York	IP.	H.	R.	ER.	BB.	SO.
John	4	6	1	1	0	2
Frazier (L)	1	4	3	3	0	1
Davis	⅓	1	3	2	2	1
Reuschel	⅔	1	1	0	2	0
May	2	1	1	1	1	2
LaRoche	1	0	0	0	0	2

Game-winning RBI—Cey.

aFlied out for John in fourth. bHit into forceout for Cey in sixth. cRan for Nettles in sixth. dAnnounced as pinch-hitter for Reuschel in sixth. eSingled for Gamble in sixth. fStruck out for May in eighth. E—Lopes, Nettles, Milbourne. LOB—Los Angeles 10, New York 12. 2B—Nettles, Randolph. 3B—Guerrero. HR—Randolph, Guerrero. SB—Randolph, Lopes, Russell. SH—Russell. U—Stello (N.L.) plate, Barnett (A.L.) first, Colosi (N.L.) second, Cooney (A.L.) third, Harvey (N.L.) left and Garcia (A.L.) right. T—3:09. A—56,513.

COMPOSITE BATTING AVERAGES

Los Angeles Dodgers

Player-Position	G.	AB.	R.	H.	2B.	3B.	HR.	RBI.	BA.
Johnstone, ph	3	3	1	2	0	0	1	3	.667
Smith, ph	2	2	0	1	0	0	0	0	.500
Garvey, 1b	6	24	3	10	1	0	0	0	.417
Cey, 3b	6	20	3	7	0	0	1	6	.350
Guerrero, cf-rf	6	21	2	7	1	1	2	7	.333
Yeager, ph-c	6	14	2	4	1	0	2	4	.286
Scioscia, c-ph	3	4	1	1	0	0	0	0	.250
Russell, ss	6	25	1	6	0	0	0	2	.240
Monday, rf-ph	5	13	1	3	1	0	0	0	.231
Lopes, 2b	6	22	6	5	1	0	0	2	.227
L'ndreaux, ph-cf-pr	5	6	1	1	1	0	0	0	.167
Baker, lf	6	24	3	4	0	0	0	1	.167
Forster, p	2	0	0	0	0	0	0	0	.000
Goltz, p	2	0	0	0	0	0	0	0	.000
Niedenfuer, p	2	0	0	0	0	0	0	0	.000
Stewart, p	2	0	0	0	0	0	0	0	.000
Castillo, p	1	0	0	0	0	0	0	0	.000
Welch, p	1	0	0	0	0	0	0	0	.000
Sax, ph-pr-2b	2	1	0	0	0	0	0	0	.000
Howe, p	3	2	0	0	0	0	0	0	.000
Reuss, p	2	3	0	0	0	0	0	0	.000
Valenzuela, p	1	3	0	0	0	0	0	0	.000
Hooton, p	2	4	1	0	0	0	0	0	.000
Th'mas, ph-ss-cf-3b	5	7	2	0	0	0	0	1	.000
Totals	6	198	27	51	6	1	6	26	.258

New York Yankees

Player-Position	G.	AB.	R.	H.	2B.	3B.	HR.	RBI.	BA.
Piniella, rf-ph-lf	6	16	2	7	1	0	0	3	.438
Rodriguez, 3b-pr	4	12	1	5	0	0	0	0	.417
Nettles, 3b	3	10	1	4	1	0	0	0	.400
Jackson, rf	3	12	3	4	1	0	1	1	.333
Gamble, rf-lf-ph	3	6	1	2	0	0	0	1	.333
Watson, 1b	6	22	2	7	1	0	2	7	.318
Milbourne, ss	6	20	2	5	2	0	0	3	.250
Randolph, 2b	6	18	5	4	1	1	2	3	.222
Mumphrey, cf	5	15	2	3	0	0	0	0	.200
Cerone, c	6	21	2	4	1	0	1	3	.190
Winfield, lf-cf	6	22	0	1	0	0	0	1	.045
Davis, p	4	0	0	0	0	0	0	0	.000
LaRoche, p	1	0	0	0	0	0	0	0	.000
Robertson, pr	1	0	0	0	0	0	0	0	.000
Brown, pr-rf-cf-ph	4	1	1	0	0	0	0	0	.000
Foote, ph	1	1	0	0	0	0	0	0	.000
Gossage, p	3	1	0	0	0	0	0	0	.000
May, p	3	1	0	0	0	0	0	0	.000
Righetti, p	1	1	0	0	0	0	0	0	.000
Frazier, p	3	2	0	0	0	0	0	0	.000
John, p	3	2	0	0	0	0	0	0	.000
Reuschel, p	2	2	0	0	0	0	0	0	.000
Murcer, ph	4	3	0	0	0	0	0	0	.000
Guidry, p	2	5	0	0	0	0	0	0	.000
Totals	6	193	22	46	8	1	6	22	.238

COMPOSITE PITCHING AVERAGES

Los Angeles Dodgers

Pitcher	G.	IP.	H.	R.	ER.	BB.	SO.	W.	L.	ERA.
Niedenfuer	2	5	3	2	0	1	0	0	0	0.00
Forster	2	2	1	0	0	3	0	0	0	0.00
Stewart	2	1⅔	1	0	0	2	1	0	0	0.00
Hooton	2	11⅓	8	3	2	9	3	1	1	1.59
Reuss	2	11⅔	10	5	5	3	8	1	1	3.86
Howe	3	7	7	3	3	1	4	1	0	3.86
Valenzuela	1	9	9	4	4	7	6	1	0	4.00
Goltz	2	3⅓	4	2	2	1	2	0	0	5.40
Castillo	1	1	0	1	1	5	0	0	0	9.00
Welch	1	0*	3	2	2	1	0	0	0	......
Totals	6	52	46	22	19	33	24	4	2	3.29

*Pitched to four batters in first inning of fourth game.

New York Yankees

Pitcher	G.	IP.	H.	R.	ER.	BB.	SO.	W.	L.	ERA.
Gossage	3	5	2	0	0	2	5	0	0	0.00
LaRoche	1	1	0	0	0	0	2	0	0	0.00
John	3	13	11	1	1	0	8	1	0	0.69
Guidry	2	14	8	3	3	4	15	1	1	1.93
May	3	6⅓	5	2	2	1	5	0	0	2.84
Reuschel	2	3⅔	7	3	2	3	2	0	0	4.91
Righetti	1	2	5	3	3	2	1	0	0	13.50
Frazier	3	3⅔	9	7	7	3	2	0	3	17.18
Davis	4	2⅓	4	8	6	5	4	0	0	23.14
Totals	6	51	51	27	24	20	44	2	4	4.24

1982
ST. LOUIS CARDINALS
VS.
MILWAUKEE BREWERS

It was the kind of first-game pounding that could affect a team's collective psyche. Just how good were those other guys, anyway?

The club victimized by the pounding was the St. Louis Cardinals. The team administering the pounding was the Milwaukee Brewers. The final score in Game 1 of the 1982 World Series was 10-0, and the game may not have been as close as the score would indicate.

The Brewers, a team that started out as the expansion Seattle Pilots in 1969 before moving to Milwaukee the next year, put on quite a show in the club's first-ever World Series game. And Manager Harvey Kuenn's heavy-hitting American League champions did it not in the friendly and relatively cozy confines of Milwaukee's County Stadium, but at expansive Busch Memorial Stadium in St. Louis.

Milwaukee cuffed four St. Louis pitchers for 17 hits. Leadoff man Paul Molitor banged out a Series-record five hits. Robin Yount drilled four hits. Former Cardinal Ted Simmons belted a home run for the team that had cracked 216 homers during the record season (and thus earned the nickname "Harvey's Wallbangers"). Lefthanded pitcher Mike Caldwell spun a three-hitter. And the Brewers' defense played flawlessly.

It was a wipeout.

It also was reminiscent of Series-opening games in 1945 and 1959. Cubs 9, Tigers 0. White Sox 11, Dodgers 0. And we all know what happened to the thoroughly overwhelmed and dispirited Tigers and Dodgers of yesteryear. They scrambled back for next-day victories and went on to become World Series champions, that's

Ecstatic St. Louis players celebrate after the Cardinals' 6-3 Game 7 victory over the Milwaukee Brewers.

what.

The Cardinals demonstrated a similar resolve. Trailing by a 4-2 score midway through Game 2, they tied matters on catcher Darrell Porter's two-out, two-run double in the sixth inning.

The blow was a satisfying one for Porter, who hadn't exactly won over St. Louis fans since his free-agent signing with the Cardinals in December 1980. In the wake of a blockbuster Milwau-

kee-St. Louis trade of the same time frame that included the dispatching of catcher Simmons to the Brewers, Porter was to fill the shoes of the sweet-swinging and popular switch-hitter. But Porter had terrible seasons in 1981 and 1982 and found himself in the fans' doghouse. His outstanding Championship Series play preceding this fall classic had assuaged the St. Louis populace, at least to some degree.

With the game still tied at 4-4 in the eighth, Cardinals pinch-hitter Steve Braun coaxed a bases-loaded walk off reliever Pete Ladd and Whitey Herzog's team had a lead for the first time in the Series. Relief ace Bruce Sutter made sure it didn't get away, and St. Louis was back in business with a 5-4 victory.

Cardinals rookie Willie McGee, who had hit only four home runs in the regular season, drilled two of Pete Vuckovich's pitches out of County Stadium in Game 3, sparking St. Louis to a 6-2 victory. Along with his power show that netted four RBIs, center fielder McGee made two sterling defensive plays. He made a leaping catch of a 400-foot Molitor drive in the first inning, then robbed Gorman Thomas of a home run in the ninth with a leaping grab above the fence in left-center.

One not-so-bright spot for St. Louis was a seventh-inning injury to starting pitcher Joaquin Andujar, who was felled by a Simmons line drive that struck him just below the kneecap. Andujar had allowed only three hits.

The Cardinals were coasting, 5-1, in the seventh inning of Game 4 when, with one out, pitcher Dave LaPoint dropped a throw from Keith Hernandez on Ben Oglivie's grounder to the St. Louis first baseman. While it wasn't much of an opening, Milwaukee made the most of it. The Brewers erupted for six runs, with Yount and Thomas connecting for two-run singles. The 7-5 score held up for Kuenn's club, which had found itself in a 4-0 hole after an inning and a half and suffered the indignity of yielding a two-run sacrifice fly in the process.

With McGee on third base and Ozzie Smith, the fielding magician obtained from San Diego in February, on second with one out in the second inning, Tom Herr hit a long drive to center field. Thomas tracked down the ball and made the catch, but slipped on the warning track. McGee tagged up after the catch and scored and Smith steamed into third, going on home when Thomas lost his footing.

Milwaukee's Caldwell followed his nifty three-hitter of Game 1 with a not-so-nifty 14-hitter in Game 5. But, with two-out relief help from Bob McClure, it was good enough to win. The Brewers beat Bob Forsch for the second time, winning by a 6-4 score and getting four hits from Yount. The Milwaukee shortstop thus became the first player to have two four-hit games in career World Series competition—and, of course, he achieved the feat within one Series.

Down three games to two as the Series moved back to St. Louis, the Cardinals frolicked in Game 6 much the way Milwaukee had in Game 1. Rookie John Stuper, despite waiting out two rain delays totaling more than 2½ hours, pitched a complete-game four-hitter in a 13-1 laugher. Hernandez and Porter belted two-run homers, and Hernandez wound up with four RBIs overall. Dane Iorg, St. Louis' designated hitter, drilled two doubles and a triple.

Third-game casualty Andujar pronounced himself fit for Game 7. The Brewers went with Vuckovich. Andujar won out, thanks to a Cardinals comeback and two innings of perfect relief from Sutter. St. Louis faced a 3-1 deficit entering the last of the sixth, but the Cardinals got a game-tying, bases-full single from Hernandez and a go-ahead base hit from George Hendrick.

Porter and Braun then provided valuable insurance with run-scoring singles in the eighth as the Milwaukee relief corps, minus Rollie Fingers (injured in September), stumbled at a critical juncture. The Cardinals won, 6-3, and thereby claimed their ninth World Series crown, tops among National League teams and second only to the New York Yankees' staggering total of 22.

So much for damaged psyches.

Game 1

Tuesday, October 12, At St. Louis

Milwaukee	AB.	R.	H.	RBI.	PO.	A.
Molitor, 3b	6	1	5	2	0	2
Yount, ss	6	1	4	2	1	1
Cooper, 1b	4	1	0	0	14	3
Simmons, c	5	1	2	1	3	0
Oglivie, lf	4	1	0	0	0	0
Thomas, cf	4	0	1	1	2	0
Howell, dh	2	0	0	0	0	0
aMoney, dh	2	1	1	1	0	0
Moore, rf	5	2	2	2	4	0
Gantner, 2b	4	2	2	0	4	7
Caldwell, p	0	0	0	0	3	1
Totals	42	10	17	9	27	14

Game 2

Wednesday, October 13, At St. Louis

Milwaukee	AB.	R.	H.	RBI.	PO.	A.
Molitor, 3b	5	1	2	0	0	1
Yount, ss	4	1	1	1	4	3
Cooper, 1b	5	0	3	1	9	2
Simmons, c	3	1	1	1	5	0
Oglivie, lf	4	0	1	0	2	0
Thomas, cf	3	0	0	0	1	0
Howell, dh	4	1	0	0	0	0
Moore, rf	4	0	2	1	3	0
Gantner, 2b	3	0	0	0	0	3
Sutton, p	0	0	0	0	0	0
McClure, p	0	0	0	0	0	0
Ladd, p	0	0	0	0	0	0
Totals	35	4	10	4	24	9

St. Louis	AB.	R.	H.	RBI.	PO.	A.
Herr, 2b	3	1	1	1	2	1
Oberkfell, 3b	3	1	2	1	0	3
bTenace	1	0	0	0	0	0
Ramsey, 3b	0	0	0	0	0	0
Hernandez, 1b	3	0	0	0	7	2
Hendrick, rf	3	2	0	0	0	0
Porter, c	4	0	2	2	8	1
L. Smith, lf	3	0	0	0	1	0
Iorg, dh	2	0	1	0	0	0
aGreen, dh	1	0	0	0	0	0
cBraun, dh	0	0	0	1	0	0
McGee, cf	4	1	0	0	4	0
O. Smith, ss	4	0	2	0	5	3
Stuper, p	0	0	0	0	0	0
Bair, p	0	0	0	0	0	0
Sutter, p	0	0	0	0	0	0
Totals	31	5	8	5	27	10

Milwaukee	0 1 2 0 1 0 0 0 0—4
St. Louis	0 0 2 0 0 2 0 1 x—5

Milwaukee	IP.	H.	R.	ER.	BB.	SO.
Sutton	6	5	4	4	1	3
McClure (L)	1⅓	2	1	1	2	2
Ladd	⅔	1	0	0	2	0

St. Louis	IP.	H.	R.	ER.	BB.	SO.
Stuper	4*	6	4	4	3	3
Kaat	⅔	0	0	0	0	0
Bair	2	1	0	0	0	3
Sutter (W)	2⅓	2	0	0	1	1

*Pitched to one batter in fifth.

Game-winning RBI—Braun.

aStruck out for Iorg in seventh. bFlied out for Oberkfell in seventh. cWalked for Green in eighth. E—Oglivie. DP —St. Louis 1. LOB—Milwaukee 8, St. Louis 7. 2B—Moore, Herr, Yount, Porter, Cooper. HR—Simmons. SB—Molitor, McGee, Oberkfell, O. Smith. WP—Stuper. U—Haller (A.L.) plate, Kibler (N.L.) first, Phillips (A.L.) second, Davidson (N.L.) third, Evans (A.L.) left and Weyer (N.L.) right. T—2:54. A—53,723.

Game 3

Friday, October 15, At Milwaukee

St. Louis	AB.	R.	H.	RBI.	PO.	A.
Herr, 2b	5	0	0	0	1	3
Oberkfell, 3b	4	0	0	1	1	1
Hernandez, 1b	4	0	0	0	8	0
xHendrick, rf	2	1	1	0	3	0
Porter, c	4	0	0	0	6	0
L. Smith, lf	4	2	2	0	1	0
Green, lf	0	0	0	0	0	0
Iorg, dh	4	1	1	0	0	0
McGee, cf	3	2	2	4	6	0
O. Smith, ss	3	0	0	1	1	3
Andujar, p	0	0	0	0	0	1
Kaat, p	0	0	0	0	0	0
Bair, p	0	0	0	0	0	0
Sutter, p	0	0	0	0	0	0
Totals	33	6	6	5	27	8

St. Louis	AB.	R.	H.	RBI.	PO.	A.
Herr, 2b	3	0	0	0	2	5
L. Smith, lf	4	0	0	0	2	0
Hernandez, 1b	4	0	0	0	14	1
Hendrick, rf	4	0	0	0	1	0
Tenace, dh	3	0	0	0	0	0
Porter, c	3	0	2	0	3	0
Green, cf	3	0	0	0	2	0
Oberkfell, 3b	3	0	1	0	0	4
O. Smith, ss	3	0	0	0	3	3
Forsch, p	0	0	0	0	0	0
Kaat, p	0	0	0	0	0	0
LaPoint, p	0	0	0	0	0	0
Lahti, p	0	0	0	0	0	0
Totals	30	0	3	0	27	13

Milwaukee	2 0 0 1 1 2 0 0 4—10
St. Louis	0 0 0 0 0 0 0 0 0— 0

Milwaukee	IP.	H.	R.	ER.	BB.	SO.
Caldwell (W)	9	3	0	0	1	3

St. Louis	IP.	H.	R.	ER.	BB.	SO.
Forsch (L)	5⅔	10	6	4	1	1
Kaat	1⅓	1	0	0	1	1
LaPoint	1⅔	3	2	1	0	1
Lahti	⅓	3	2	2	0	1

Game-winning RBI—None.

aFlied out for Howell in seventh. E—Hernandez. DP —St. Louis 1. LOB—Milwaukee 10, St. Louis 4. 2B—Moore, Yount, Porter. 3B—Gantner. HR—Simmons. SH—Gantner. HBP—By Forsch (Howell). U—Weyer (N.L.) plate, Haller (A.L.) first, Kibler (N.L.) second, Phillips (A.L.) third, Davidson (N.L.) left and Evans (A.L.) right. T—2:30. A—53,723.

Milwaukee	AB.	R.	H.	RBI.	PO.	A.
Molitor, 3b	4	0	0	0	1	0
Yount, ss	3	1	0	0	5	5
Cooper, 1b	4	1	1	2	14	0
Simmons, c	4	0	1	0	1	1
Oglivie, lf	4	0	0	0	4	0
Thomas, cf	4	0	1	0	2	0
Howell, dh	2	0	0	0	0	0
aMoney, dh	1	0	0	0	0	0
Moore, rf	3	0	0	0	0	0
Gantner, 2b	3	0	2	0	0	6
Vuckovich, p	0	0	0	0	0	2
McClure, p	0	0	0	0	0	0
Totals	32	2	5	2	27	14

St. Louis	0 0 0 0 3 0 2 0 1—6
Milwaukee	0 0 0 0 0 0 0 2 0—2

St. Louis	IP.	H.	R.	ER.	BB.	SO.
Andujar (W)	6⅓	3	0	0	1	3
Kaat	⅓	1	0	0	0	1
Bair	0*	0	0	0	1	0
Sutter (S)	2⅓	1	2	2	1	1

Milwaukee	IP.	H.	R.	ER.	BB.	SO.
Vuckovich (L)	8⅔	6	6	4	3	1
McClure	⅓	0	0	0	0	0

*Pitched to one batter in seventh.

Game-winning RBI—McGee.

xAwarded first base on catcher's interference. aWalked for Howell in seventh. E—Hernandez, Cooper, Simmons, Gantner. DP—St. Louis 1. LOB—St. Louis 4, Milwaukee 6. 2B—Gantner, L. Smith, Iorg. 3B—L. Smith. HR—McGee 2, Cooper. U—Kibler (N.L.) plate, Phillips (A.L.) first, Davidson (N.L.) second, Evans (A.L.) third, Weyer (N.L.) left and Haller (A.L.) right. T—2:53. A—56,556.

Game 4

Saturday, October 16, At Milwaukee

St. Louis	AB.	R.	H.	RBI.	PO.	A.
Herr, 2b	4	0	0	2	1	1
Oberkfell, 3b	2	2	1	0	0	2
bTenace	1	0	0	0	0	0
Hernandez, 1b	4	0	0	0	8	1
Hendrick, rf	4	0	1	1	1	0
Porter, c	3	0	1	0	5	0
L. Smith, lf	4	1	1	0	2	0
Iorg, dh	4	0	2	1	0	0
aGreen, dh	0	0	0	0	0	0
McGee, cf	4	1	1	0	4	0
O. Smith, ss	3	1	1	0	3	1
LaPoint, p	0	0	0	0	0	2
Bair, p	0	0	0	0	0	0
Kaat, p	0	0	0	0	0	0
Lahti, p	0	0	0	0	0	1
Totals	33	5	8	4	24	8

Milwaukee	AB.	R.	H.	RBI.	PO.	A.
Molitor, 3b	4	1	0	0	1	0
Yount, ss	4	1	2	2	3	3
Cooper, 1b	4	1	2	1	10	0
Simmons, c	2	0	0	0	6	0
Thomas, cf	4	0	1	2	4	0
Oglivie, lf	3	1	1	0	1	0
Money, dh	4	2	2	0	0	0
Moore, rf	4	0	1	0	0	0
Gantner, 2b	4	1	1	1	1	5
Haas, p	0	0	0	0	1	2
Slaton, p	0	0	0	0	0	0
McClure, p	0	0	0	0	0	0
Totals	33	7	10	6	27	10

St. Louis	1 3 0 0 0 1 0 0 0—5
Milwaukee	0 0 0 0 1 0 6 0 x—7

St. Louis	IP.	H.	R.	ER.	BB.	SO.
LaPoint	6⅔	7	4	1	1	3
Bair (L)	0*	1	2	2	1	0
Kaat	0*	1	1	1	1	0
Lahti	1⅓	1	0	0	1	0

Milwaukee	IP.	H.	R.	ER.	BB.	SO.
Haas	5⅓	7	5	4	2	3
Slaton (W)	2	1	0	0	2	1
McClure (S)	1⅔	0	0	0	0	2

*Pitched to two batters in seventh.

Game-winning RBI—Thomas.

aRan for Iorg in eighth. bStruck out for Oberkfell in ninth. E—LaPoint, Yount, Gantner. DP—St. Louis 2, Milwaukee 2. LOB—St. Louis 6, Milwaukee 6. 2B—Oberkfell, Money, L. Smith, Iorg, Gantner. 3B—Oglivie. SB—McGee, Oberkfell. SF—Herr. WP—Haas, Kaat. U—Phillips (A.L.) plate, Davidson (N.L.) first, Evans (A.L.) second, Weyer (N.L.) third, Haller (A.L.) left and Kibler (N.L.) right. T—3:04. A—56,560.

Game 5

Sunday, October 17, At Milwaukee

St. Louis	AB.	R.	H.	RBI.	PO.	A.
L. Smith, dh	5	0	2	0	0	0
Green, lf	5	2	2	0	2	0
Hernandez, 1b	4	1	3	2	5	1
Hendrick, rf	5	0	3	2	1	0
Porter, c	5	0	1	0	5	1
bRamsey	0	0	0	0	0	0
McGee, cf	5	0	1	0	4	0
Oberkfell, 3b	4	0	3	0	0	2
aTenace	1	0	0	0	0	0
Herr, 2b	4	0	0	0	3	2
O. Smith, ss	3	1	0	0	3	2
Forsch, p	0	0	0	0	1	0
Sutter, p	0	0	0	0	0	0
Totals	41	4	15	4	24	8

Milwaukee	AB.	R.	H.	RBI.	PO.	A.
Molitor, 3b	4	1	1	1	2	5
Yount, ss	4	2	4	1	3	3
Cooper, 1b	4	0	1	1	8	2
Simmons, c	3	0	0	1	4	1
Oglivie, lf	4	1	2	0	1	0
Thomas, cf	4	0	0	0	3	0
Money, dh	3	1	0	0	0	0
Moore, rf	4	1	2	1	1	0
Gantner, 2b	4	0	1	1	4	4
Caldwell, p	0	0	0	0	1	1
McClure, p	0	0	0	0	0	0
Totals	34	6	11	6	27	16

St. Louis	0 0 1 0 0 0 1 0 2—4
Milwaukee	1 0 1 0 1 0 1 2 x—6

St. Louis	IP.	H.	R.	ER.	BB.	SO.
Forsch (L)	7	8	4	3	2	3
Sutter	1	3	2	2	1	2

Milwaukee	IP.	H.	R.	ER.	BB.	SO.
Caldwell (W)	8⅓	14	4	4	2	3
McClure (S)	⅔	1	0	0	0	1

Game-winning RBI—Cooper.

aFlied out for Oberkfell in ninth. bRan for Porter in ninth. E—Herr, Forsch, Gantner. DP—St. Louis 2, Milwaukee 1. LOB—St. Louis 12, Milwaukee 7. 2B—Hernandez 2, Yount, Moore, Green. 3B—Green. HR—Yount. SB—L. Smith. U—Davidson (N.L.) plate, Evans (A.L.) first, Weyer (N.L.) second, Haller (A.L.) third, Kibler (N.L.) left and Phillips (A.L.) right. T—3:02. A—56,562.

Game 6

Tuesday, October 19, At St. Louis

Milwaukee	AB.	R.	H.	RBI.	PO.	A.
Molitor, 3b	4	0	1	0	0	0
Yount, ss	4	0	0	0	0	3
Cooper, 1b	4	0	0	0	8	2
Simmons, c	2	0	0	0	4	0
Yost, c	0	0	0	0	1	0
Oglivie, lf	4	0	1	0	5	0
Thomas, cf	3	0	0	0	0	0
aEdwards, cf	0	0	0	0	0	0
Money, dh	3	0	0	0	0	0
Moore, rf	3	0	1	0	2	0
Gantner, 2b	3	1	1	0	3	2
Sutton, p	0	0	0	0	1	2
Slaton, p	0	0	0	0	0	0
Medich, p	0	0	0	0	0	0
Bernard, p	0	0	0	0	0	0
Totals	30	1	4	0	24	9

St. Louis	AB.	R.	H.	RBI.	PO.	A.
L. Smith, lf	3	1	1	0	1	0
Green, lf	1	1	0	0	0	0
Oberkfell, 3b	5	1	0	0	1	4
Hernandez, 1b	5	2	2	4	8	0
Hendrick, rf	5	2	2	1	3	0
Porter, c	4	1	1	2	2	0
Brummer, c	0	0	0	0	0	0
Iorg, dh	4	3	3	0	0	0
McGee, cf	4	1	1	1	5	0
Herr, 2b	3	1	2	2	1	2
O. Smith, ss	4	0	0	0	5	3
Stuper, p	0	0	0	0	1	1
Totals	38	13	12	10	27	10

Milwaukee	0 0 0 0 0 0 0 0 1— 1
St. Louis	0 2 0 3 2 6 0 0 x—13

Milwaukee	IP.	H.	R.	ER.	BB.	SO.
Sutton (L)	4⅓	7	7	5	0	2
Slaton	⅔	0	0	0	0	0
Medich	2	5	6	4	1	0
Bernard	1	0	0	0	0	1

St. Louis	IP.	H.	R.	ER.	BB.	SO.
Stuper (W)	9	4	1	1	2	2

Game-winning RBI—None.

aRan for Thomas in eighth. E—Yount 2, Gantner 2, Oberkfell. DP—St. Louis 2. LOB—Milwaukee 4, St. Louis 3. 2B—Iorg 2, Herr, Gantner. 3B—Iorg. HR—Porter, Hernandez. SB—L. Smith. SH—Herr. WP—Medich 2, Stuper. Balk—Sutton. U—Evans (A.L.) plate, Weyer (N.L.) first, Haller (A.L.) second, Kibler (N.L.) third, Phillips (A.L.) left and Davidson (N.L.) right. T—2:21. A—53,723.

Game 7

Wednesday, October 20, At St. Louis

Milwaukee	AB.	R.	H.	RBI.	PO.	A.
Molitor, 3b	4	1	2	0	0	1
Yount, ss	4	0	1	0	4	1
Cooper, 1b	3	0	1	1	8	1
Simmons, c	4	0	0	0	5	0
Oglivie, lf	4	1	1	1	0	0
Thomas, cf	4	0	0	0	3	0
Howell, dh	3	0	0	0	0	0
Moore, rf	3	0	1	0	3	0
Gantner, 2b	3	1	1	0	1	6
Vuckovich, p	0	0	0	0	0	0
McClure, p	0	0	0	0	0	0
Haas, p	0	0	0	0	0	0
Caldwell, p	0	0	0	0	0	0
Totals	32	3	7	2	24	9

St. Louis	AB.	R.	H.	RBI.	PO.	A.
L. Smith, lf	5	2	3	1	4	0
Oberkfell, 3b	3	0	0	0	1	5
aTenace	0	0	0	0	0	0
bRamsey, 3b	1	1	0	0	0	0
Hernandez, 1b	3	1	2	2	12	2
Hendrick, rf	5	0	2	1	1	1
Porter, c	5	0	1	1	4	0
Iorg, dh	3	0	2	0	0	0
cGreen, dh	0	0	0	0	0	0
dBraun, dh	2	0	1	1	0	0
McGee, cf	5	1	1	0	1	0
Herr, 2b	3	0	1	0	1	5
O. Smith, ss	4	1	2	0	2	2
Andujar, p	0	0	0	0	1	1
Sutter, p	0	0	0	0	0	1
Totals	39	6	15	6	27	17

Milwaukee	0 0 0 0 1 2 0 0 0—3
St. Louis	0 0 0 1 0 3 0 2 x—6

Milwaukee	IP.	H.	R.	ER.	BB.	SO.
Vuckovich	5⅓	10	3	3	2	3
McClure (L)	⅓	2	1	1	1	0
Haas	2	1	2	2	1	1
Caldwell	⅓	2	0	0	0	0

St. Louis	IP.	H.	R.	ER.	BB.	SO.
Andujar (W)	7	7	3	2	0	1
Sutter (S)	2	0	0	0	0	2

Game-winning RBI—Hendrick.

aWalked for Oberkfell in sixth. bRan for Tenace in sixth. cAnnounced as pinch-hitter for Iorg in sixth. dGrounded out for Green in sixth. E—Andujar. LOB—Milwaukee 3, St. Louis 13. 2B—Gantner, L. Smith 2. HR—Oglivie. SF—Cooper. U—Weyer (N.L.) plate, Haller (A.L.) first, Kibler (N.L.) second, Phillips (A.L.) third, Davidson (N.L.) left and Evans (A.L.) right. T—2:50. A—53,723.

COMPOSITE BATTING AVERAGES

St. Louis Cardinals

Player-Position	G.	AB.	R.	H.	2B.	3B.	HR.	RBI.	BA.
Iorg, dh	5	17	4	9	4	1	0	1	.529
Braun, ph-dh	2	2	0	1	0	0	0	2	.500
Hendrick, rf	7	28	5	9	0	0	0	5	.321
L. Smith, lf-dh	7	28	6	9	4	1	0	1	.321
Oberkfell, 3b	7	24	4	7	1	0	0	1	.292
Porter, c	7	28	1	8	2	0	1	5	.286
Hernandez, 1b	7	27	4	7	2	0	1	8	.259
McGee, cf	6	25	6	6	0	0	2	5	.240
O. Smith, ss	7	24	3	5	0	0	0	1	.208
Green, cf-ph-dh-lf-pr	7	10	3	2	1	1	0	0	.200
Herr, 2b	7	25	2	4	2	0	0	5	.160
Andujar, p	2	0	0	0	0	0	0	0	.000
Bair, p	3	0	0	0	0	0	0	0	.000
Brummer, c	1	0	0	0	0	0	0	0	.000
Forsch, p	2	0	0	0	0	0	0	0	.000
Kaat, p	4	0	0	0	0	0	0	0	.000
Lahti, p	2	0	0	0	0	0	0	0	.000
LaPoint, p	2	0	0	0	0	0	0	0	.000
Ramsey, 3b-pr	3	1	1	0	0	0	0	0	.000
Stuper, p	2	0	0	0	0	0	0	0	.000
Sutter, p	4	0	0	0	0	0	0	0	.000
Tenace, dh-ph	5	6	0	0	0	0	0	0	.000
Totals	7	245	39	67	16	3	4	34	.273

Milwaukee Brewers

Player-Position	G.	AB.	R.	H.	2B.	3B.	HR.	RBI.	BA.
Yount, ss	7	29	6	12	3	0	1	6	.414
Molitor, 3b	7	31	5	11	0	0	0	3	.355
Moore, rf	7	26	3	9	3	0	0	2	.346
Gantner, 2b	7	24	5	8	4	1	0	4	.333
Cooper, 1b	7	28	3	8	1	0	1	6	.286
Money, ph-dh	5	13	4	3	1	0	0	1	.231
Oglivie, lf	7	27	4	6	0	1	1	1	.222
Simmons, c	7	23	2	4	0	0	2	3	.174
Thomas, cf	7	26	0	3	0	0	0	3	.115
Bernard, p	1	0	0	0	0	0	0	0	.000
Caldwell, p	3	0	0	0	0	0	0	0	.000
Edwards, pr-cf	1	0	0	0	0	0	0	0	.000
Haas, p	2	0	0	0	0	0	0	0	.000
Howell, dh	4	11	1	0	0	0	0	0	.000
Ladd, p	1	0	0	0	0	0	0	0	.000
McClure, p	5	0	0	0	0	0	0	0	.000
Medich, p	1	0	0	0	0	0	0	0	.000
Slaton, p	2	0	0	0	0	0	0	0	.000
Sutton, p	2	0	0	0	0	0	0	0	.000
Vuckovich, p	2	0	0	0	0	0	0	0	.000
Yost, c	1	0	0	0	0	0	0	0	.000
Totals		238	33	64	12	2	5	29	.269

COMPOSITE PITCHING AVERAGES

St. Louis Cardinals

Pitcher	G.	IP.	H.	R.	ER.	BB.	SO.	W.	L.	ERA.
Andujar	2	13⅓	10	3	2	1	4	2	0	1.35
LaPoint	2	8⅓	10	6	3	2	3	0	0	3.24
Stuper	2	13	10	5	5	5	5	1	0	3.46
Kaat	4	2⅓	4	1	1	2	2	0	0	3.86
Sutter	4	7⅔	6	4	4	3	6	1	0	4.70
Forsch	2	12⅔	18	10	7	3	4	0	2	4.97
Bair	3	2	2	2	2	2	3	0	1	9.00
Lahti	2	1⅔	4	2	2	1	1	0	0	10.80
Totals	7	61	64	33	*23	19	28	4	3	3.39

(NOTE: St. Louis' individual earned runs do not add up to team total because of rule 10.18(i) applied in Game 4.)

Milwaukee Brewers

Pitcher	G.	IP.	H.	R.	ER.	BB.	SO.	W.	L.	ERA.
Slaton	2	2⅔	1	0	0	2	1	1	0	0.00
Bernard	1	1	0	0	0	0	1	0	0	0.00
Ladd	1	⅔	1	0	0	2	0	0	0	0.00
Caldwell	3	17⅔	19	4	4	3	6	2	0	2.04
McClure	5	4⅓	5	2	2	3	5	0	2	4.15
Vuckovich	2	14	16	9	7	5	4	0	1	4.50
Haas	2	7⅓	8	7	6	3	4	0	0	7.36
Sutton	2	10⅓	12	11	9	1	5	0	1	7.84
Medich	1	2	5	6	4	1	0	0	0	18.00
Totals	7	60	67	39	32	20	26	3	4	4.80

1983
BALTIMORE ORIOLES
VS.
PHILADELPHIA PHILLIES

First came the Whiz Kids. Now the Philadelphia Phillies took pride in the Wheeze Kids.

When it came to the World Series, though, 1983 was very much like 1950 for the National League champions. The Phillies' Whiz Kids of '50 were swept by the New York Yankees; the '83 Wheeze Kids version of the Phils coughed, sputtered and then succumbed in five games to the Baltimore Orioles, and in some minds it even took intervention by the President of the United States to steer Philadelphia to its one victory.

The 1983 Phillies featured such oldsters as Pete Rose, age 42; Joe Morgan, 40; Tony Perez, 41; Steve Carlton, 38; and Ron Reed, 40. Mike Schmidt (34), Garry Maddox (34) and Gary Matthews (33) weren't fuzzy-cheeked youngsters, either. But just as youth had served the '50 team well, age was a positive factor for the '83 club.

One of Philadelphia's younger standouts, 30-year-old John Denny, was Manager Paul Owens' pitching choice for Game 1 of the World Series at Baltimore. The Orioles' Joe Altobelli opted for Scott McGregor. The Orioles jumped in front when their second batter of the game, Jim Dwyer, hit a home run. Sparkplug Morgan then tied the rainswept game with a two-out homer in the Phils' sixth.

The game was still 1-1 when McGregor went out to the mound for the top of the eighth. It was about five minutes, though, before the lefthander was able to deliver a pitch. President Ronald Reagan, on hand for the Series opener, was interviewed for approximately three minutes on television and the game was held up accordingly. After a commercial, McGregor finally got to deliver his first pitch of the inning

and Maddox hit a home run.

While there was considerable speculation about the impact of the delay on McGregor, the Baltimore pitcher merely accepted his fate, which turned out to be a 2-1 loss at the hands of Denny and reliever Al Holland.

Baltimore won the battle of rookie pitchers in Game 2, with Mike Boddicker throwing a three-hitter. Philadelphia's Charles Hudson pitched scoreless ball through the fourth, but allowed three fifth-inning runs as John Lowenstein homered, Rick Dempsey rapped a run-scoring double and Boddicker delivered a sacrifice fly. The Orioles prevailed, 4-1.

Unhappy with his offense as the Series moved to Philadelphia, Owens shook things up and shook up first baseman Rose in the process. He sat down the 3,990-hit man (for one game) and replaced him with Perez.

With the Phillies ahead, 2-1, and threatening in the sixth inning of the third game, Owens re-entered the spotlight when he went out and talked with Carlton in the on-deck circle.

Carlton indicated he was strong enough to continue pitching, so Owens—not wanting to dip into his bullpen quite yet—let him bat in a key situation. With two on and two out, Carlton struck out. The 300-game winner then went out and retired the first two Baltimore batters in the seventh, but Dempsey doubled and advanced to third on a wild pitch and Benny Ayala followed with a pinch single to tie the score.

At this point, Holland was summoned. After a single by John Shelby, Phils shortstop Ivan DeJesus booted Dan Ford's grounder and Ayala scored. The Orioles had the lead, 3-2, and they kept it.

Baltimore's Rich Dauer cracked

three hits and knocked in three runs in Game 4 as the Orioles made it three straight victories. Altobelli sent up four consecutive pinch-hitters in the sixth, an inning in which Baltimore overcame a 3-2 deficit on the way to a 5-4 triumph. Ken Singleton, the second pinch batsman, drew a game-tying, bases-loaded walk and Shelby, pinch-hitter No. 3, delivered a go-ahead sacrifice fly.

While power hitters Cal Ripken of Baltimore and Schmidt of Philadelphia never did get going in this Series—Ripken went 3 for 18 and Schmidt was 1 for 20—the third noted slugger on hand, the Orioles' Eddie Murray, broke loose in Game 5. Showing only two hits in 16 at-bats through four games with no RBIs, Murray crashed two homers good for three RBIs. And with McGregor pitching a five-hitter, the Orioles rolled to a 5-0 victory and their third World Series championship.

Game 1

Tuesday, October 11, At Baltimore

Philadelphia	AB.	R.	H.	RBI.	PO.	A.
Morgan, 2b	4	1	2	1	1	5
Rose, 1b	4	0	1	0	11	0
Schmidt, 3b	4	0	0	0	0	1
Lezcano, rf	3	0	0	0	0	0
dHayes, rf	1	0	0	0	0	0
Matthews, lf	3	0	1	0	4	0
Maddox, cf	3	1	1	1	3	0
Diaz, c	3	0	0	0	7	0
DeJesus, ss	3	0	0	0	1	5
Denny, p	3	0	0	0	0	0
Holland, p	0	0	0	0	0	0
Totals	31	2	5	2	27	11

Baltimore	AB.	R.	H.	RBI.	PO.	A.
Bumbry, cf	4	0	1	0	4	0
Stewart, p	0	0	0	0	0	0
T. Martinez, p	0	0	0	0	0	0
Dwyer, rf	3	1	1	1	2	0
cFord, rf	1	0	0	0	0	0
Ripken, ss	4	0	1	0	1	4
Murray, 1b	4	0	1	0	8	0
Lowenstein, lf	3	0	1	0	2	0
eRoenicke	1	0	0	0	0	0
Dauer, 2b	3	0	0	0	3	1
Cruz, 3b	3	0	0	0	0	3
Dempsey, c	2	0	0	0	6	1
aShelby, cf	1	0	0	0	0	0
McGregor, p	2	0	0	0	1	0
bNolan, c	1	0	0	0	1	0
Totals	32	1	5	1	27	9

Philadelphia .... 0 0 0 0 0 1 0 1 0—2
Baltimore .... 1 0 0 0 0 0 0 0 0—1

Philadelphia	IP.	H.	R.	ER.	BB.	SO.
Denny (W)	7⅔	5	1	1	0	5
Holland (S)	1⅓	0	0	0	0	1

Baltimore	IP.	H.	R.	ER.	BB.	SO.
McGregor (L)	8	4	2	2	0	6
Stewart	⅔	1	0	0	0	1
T. Martinez	⅓	0	0	0	0	0

Game-winning RBI—Maddox.

aStruck out for Dempsey in eighth. bGrounded out for McGregor in eighth. cFlied out for Dwyer in eighth. dGrounded out for Lezcano in ninth. eFlied out for Lowenstein in ninth. E—Cruz. DP—Baltimore 1. LOB—Philadelphia 2, Baltimore 4. 2B—Bumbry. HR—Dwyer, Morgan, Maddox. U—Springstead (A.L.) plate, Vargo (N.L.) first, Clark (A.L.) second, Pulli (N.L.) third, Palermo (A.L.) left and Rennert (N.L.) right. T—2:22. A—52,204.

Game 2

Wednesday, October 12, At Baltimore

Philadelphia	AB.	R.	H.	RBI.	PO.	A.
Morgan, 2b	4	1	1	0	1	1
Rose, 1b	4	0	0	0	7	1
Schmidt, 3b	4	0	0	0	0	3
Lefebvre, rf	2	0	0	1	1	0
Matthews, lf	3	0	1	0	2	0
G. Gross, cf	3	0	0	0	5	0
Diaz, c	3	0	1	0	5	1
cSamuel	0	0	0	0	0	0
Virgil, c	0	0	0	0	1	0
DeJesus, ss	3	0	0	0	1	1
Hudson, p	1	0	0	0	0	0
Hernandez, p	0	0	0	0	0	0
bHayes	1	0	0	0	0	0
Andersen, p	0	0	0	0	1	0
dPerez	1	0	0	0	0	0
Reed, p	0	0	0	0	0	0
Totals	29	1	3	1	24	7

Baltimore	AB.	R.	H.	RBI.	PO.	A.
Bumbry, cf	2	0	0	0	2	0
aShelby, cf	2	1	1	0	1	0
Ford, rf	3	0	1	0	1	0
Ripken, ss	3	0	1	1	1	6
Murray, 1b	4	0	0	0	13	1
Lowenstein, lf	4	1	3	1	0	0
eLandrum, lf	0	0	0	0	0	0
Dauer, 2b	4	1	1	0	2	2
Cruz, 3b	4	1	1	0	0	3
Dempsey, c	3	0	1	1	6	1
Boddicker, p	3	0	0	1	1	2
Totals	32	4	9	4	27	15

Philadelphia.......0 0 0 1 0 0 0 0 0—1
Baltimore.......0 0 0 0 3 0 1 0 x—4

Philadelphia	IP.	H.	R.	ER.	BB.	SO.
Hudson (L)	4⅓	5	3	3	0	3
Hernandez	⅔	0	0	0	1	1
Andersen	2	3	1	1	0	1
Reed	1	1	0	0	1	1

Baltimore	IP.	H.	R.	ER.	BB.	SO.
Boddicker (W)	9	3	1	0	0	6

Game-winning RBI—Dempsey.

aStruck out for Bumbry in fifth. bStruck out for Hernandez in sixth. cRan for Diaz in eighth. dGrounded into double play for Andersen in eighth. eRan for Lowenstein in eighth. E—Murray. DP—Baltimore 1. LOB—Philadelphia 2, Baltimore 8. 2B—Lowenstein, Dempsey. HR—Lowenstein. SB—Morgan, Landrum. SF—Lefebvre, Boddicker. HBP—By Hernandez (Ford). U—Vargo (N.L.) plate, Clark (A.L.) first, Pulli (N.L.) second, Palermo (A.L.) third, Rennert (N.L.) left and Springstead (A.L.) right. T—2:27. A—52,132.

Game 3

Friday, October 14, At Philadelphia

Baltimore	AB.	R.	H.	RBI.	PO.	A.
Shelby, cf	4	0	2	0	5	0
Ford, rf	3	1	1	1	1	1
Ripken, ss	3	0	0	0	1	3
Murray, 1b	4	0	0	0	10	0
Roenicke, lf	4	0	0	0	1	1
Dauer, 2b	4	0	0	0	4	2
Cruz, 3b	3	0	0	0	0	4
Dempsey, c	4	1	2	0	5	2
Flanagan, p	1	0	0	0	0	0
aSingleton	1	0	0	0	0	0
Palmer, p	0	0	0	0	0	0
bAyala	1	1	1	1	0	0
Stewart, p	1	0	0	0	0	0
T. Martinez, p	0	0	0	0	0	0
Totals	33	3	6	2	27	13

Philadelphia	AB.	R.	H.	RBI.	PO.	A.
Morgan, 2b	3	1	1	1	5	2
Lezcano, rf	4	0	1	0	1	0
Hayes, rf	0	0	0	0	1	0
Schmidt, 3b	4	0	0	0	0	4
Matthews, lf	3	1	1	1	0	0
Perez, 1b	4	0	1	0	8	0
Maddox, cf	4	0	0	0	1	0
Diaz, c	3	0	2	0	11	0
cLefebvre	0	0	0	0	0	0
dRose	1	0	0	0	0	0
DeJesus, ss	3	0	2	0	0	5
Carlton, p	3	0	0	0	0	0
Holland, p	0	0	0	0	0	0
eVirgil	1	0	0	0	0	0
Totals	33	2	8	2	27	11

Baltimore.......0 0 0 0 0 1 2 0 0—3
Philadelphia.......0 1 1 0 0 0 0 0 0—2

Baltimore	IP.	H.	R.	ER.	BB.	SO.
Flanagan	4	6	2	2	1	1
Palmer (W)	2	2	0	0	1	1
Stewart	2	0	0	0	1	3
T. Martinez (S)	1	0	0	0	0	0

Philadelphia	IP.	H.	R.	ER.	BB.	SO.
Carlton (L)	6⅔	5	3	2	3	7
Holland	2⅓	1	0	0	0	4

Game-winning RBI—None.

aStruck out for Flanagan in fifth. bSingled for Palmer in seventh. cAnnounced as pinch-hitter for Diaz in ninth. dGrounded out for Lefebvre in ninth. eGrounded out for Holland in ninth. E—Cruz, Schmidt, DeJesus. DP—Philadelphia 2. LOB—Baltimore 6, Philadelphia 7. 2B—Dempsey 2. HR—Matthews, Morgan, Ford. WP—Palmer, Carlton. U—Clark (A.L.) plate, Pulli (N.L.) first, Palermo (A.L.) second, Rennert (N.L.) third, Springstead (A.L.) left and Vargo (N.L.) right. T—2:35. A—65,792.

Game 4

Saturday, October 15, At Philadelphia

Baltimore	AB.	R.	H.	RBI.	PO.	A.
Bumbry, cf	3	0	0	0	3	0
eFord	1	0	0	0	0	0
Stewart, p	1	0	0	0	0	0
T. Martinez, p	0	0	0	0	0	0
Dwyer, rf	5	2	2	0	0	0
Landrum, rf	0	0	0	0	0	0
Ripken, ss	5	1	1	0	0	1
Murray, 1b	4	0	1	0	9	0
Lowenstein, lf	4	1	1	0	2	0
Dauer, 2b-3b	4	1	3	3	3	2
Cruz, 3b	2	0	1	0	0	1
aNolan, c	1	0	0	0	2	0
Dempsey, c	1	0	0	0	3	0
bSingleton	0	0	0	1	0	0
cSakata, 2b	1	0	0	0	2	2
Davis, p	2	0	0	0	0	1
dShelby, cf	1	0	1	1	3	0
Totals	35	5	10	5	27	7

Philadelphia	AB.	R.	H.	RBI.	PO.	A.
Morgan, 2b	5	0	0	0	1	1
Rose, 1b	3	1	2	1	5	3
Schmidt, 3b	4	0	1	0	0	0
Lefebvre, rf	3	0	1	1	2	0
gPerez	1	0	1	0	0	0
hSamuel	0	0	0	0	0	0
Lezcano, rf	0	0	0	0	1	0
Matthews, lf	3	0	1	0	3	0
G. Gross, cf	3	0	0	0	3	0
iMaddox	1	0	0	0	0	0
Diaz, c	4	1	2	0	7	0
jDernier	0	1	0	0	0	0
DeJesus, ss	4	0	0	0	2	1
Denny, p	2	1	1	1	3	1
Hernandez, p	0	0	0	0	0	0
Reed, p	0	0	0	0	0	0
fHayes	1	0	0	0	0	0
Andersen, p	0	0	0	0	0	1
kVirgil	1	0	1	1	0	0
Totals	35	4	10	4	27	7

Baltimore.......0 0 0 2 0 2 1 0 0—5
Philadelphia.......0 0 0 1 2 0 0 0 1—4

Baltimore	IP.	H.	R.	ER.	BB.	SO.
Davis (W)	5	6	3	3	1	3
Stewart	2⅓	1	0	0	1	2
T. Martinez (S)	1⅔	3	1	1	0	0

Philadelphia	IP.	H.	R.	ER.	BB.	SO.
Denny (L)	5⅓	7	4	4	3	4
Hernandez	⅓	0	0	0	0	0
Reed	1⅓	2	1	1	1	3
Andersen	2	1	0	0	0	0

Game-winning RBI—Shelby.

aWalked intentionally for Cruz in sixth. bWalked for Dempsey in sixth. cRan for Singleton in sixth. dHit sacrifice fly for Davis in sixth. eStruck out for Bumbry in sixth. fGrounded out for Reed in seventh. gSingled for Lefebvre in eighth. hRan for Perez in eighth. iGrounded out for G. Gross in ninth. jRan for Diaz in ninth. kSingled for Andersen in ninth. E—Lowenstein. DP—Baltimore 2, Philadelphia 1. LOB—Baltimore 8, Philadelphia 6. 2B—Lefebvre, Diaz, Rose, Dauer, Dwyer. SF—Shelby. WP—Davis. Balk—Stewart. U—Pulli (N.L.) plate, Palermo (A.L.), first, Rennert (N.L.) second, Springstead (A.L.) third, Vargo (N.L.) left and Clark (A.L.) right. T—2:50. A—66,947.

Game 5

Sunday, October 16, At Philadelphia

Baltimore	AB.	R.	H.	RBI.	PO.	A.
Bumbry, cf	2	0	0	1	3	0
cShelby, cf	1	0	0	0	1	0
Ford, rf	4	0	0	0	3	0
Landrum, rf	0	0	0	0	1	0
Ripken, ss	3	1	0	0	3	0
Murray, 1b	4	2	3	3	6	0
Lowenstein, lf	2	0	0	0	0	0
bRoenicke, lf	2	0	0	0	1	0
Dauer, 2b	4	0	0	0	2	1
Cruz, 3b	4	0	0	0	0	6
Dempsey, c	3	2	2	1	7	0
McGregor, p	3	0	0	0	0	0
Totals	32	5	5	5	27	7

Philadelphia	AB.	R.	H.	RBI.	PO.	A.
Morgan, 2b	3	0	1	0	0	1
Rose, rf	4	0	2	0	3	0
Schmidt, 3b	4	0	1	0	1	2
Matthews, lf	4	0	0	0	6	0
Perez, 1b	4	0	0	0	5	1
Maddox, cf	4	0	2	0	3	0
Diaz, c	2	0	0	0	7	0
DeJesus, ss	3	0	0	0	1	2
Hudson, p	1	0	0	0	0	0
Bystrom, p	0	0	0	0	0	0
aSamuel	1	0	0	0	0	0
Hernandez, p	0	0	0	0	1	0
dLezcano	1	0	0	0	0	0
Reed, p	0	0	0	0	0	0
Totals	31	0	5	0	27	6

Baltimore.......0 1 1 2 1 0 0 0 0—5
Philadelphia.......0 0 0 0 0 0 0 0 0—0

Baltimore	IP.	H.	R.	ER.	BB.	SO.
McGregor (W)	9	5	0	0	2	6

Philadelphia	IP.	H.	R.	ER.	BB.	SO.
Hudson (L)	4*	4	5	5	1	3
Bystrom	1	0	0	0	0	1
Hernandez	3	0	0	0	0	3
Reed	1	1	0	0	0	0

*Pitched to one batter in fifth.

Game-winning RBI—Murray.

aFlied out for Bystrom in fifth. bStruck out for Lowenstein in sixth. cFlied out for Bumbry in eighth. dGrounded out for Hernandez in eighth. E—Diaz. DP—Baltimore 1. LOB—Baltimore 2, Philadelphia 6. 2B—Dempsey, Maddox. 3B—Morgan. HR—Murray 2, Dempsey. SF—Bumbry. WP—Bystrom. U—Palermo (A.L.) plate, Rennert (N.L.) first, Springstead (A.L.) second, Vargo (N.L.) third, Clark (A.L.) left and Pulli (N.L.) right. T—2:21. A—67,064.

COMPOSITE BATTING AVERAGES

Baltimore Orioles

Player-Position	G.	AB.	R.	H.	2B.	3B.	HR.	RBI.	BA.
Ayala, ph	1	1	1	1	0	0	0	1	1.000
Shelby, ph-cf	5	9	1	4	0	0	0	1	.444
Dempsey, c	5	13	3	5	4	0	1	2	.385
Lowenstein, lf	4	13	2	5	1	0	1	1	.385
Dwyer, rf	2	8	3	3	1	0	1	1	.375
Murray, 1b	5	20	2	5	0	0	2	3	.250
Dauer, 2b-3b	5	19	2	4	1	0	0	3	.211
Ripken, ss	5	18	2	3	0	0	0	1	.167
Ford, ph-rf	5	12	1	2	0	0	1	1	.167
Cruz, 3b	5	16	1	2	0	0	0	0	.125
Bumbry, cf	4	11	0	1	1	0	0	1	.091
Landrum, pr-lf-rf	3	0	0	0	0	0	0	0	.000
T. Martinez, p	3	0	0	0	0	0	0	0	.000
Palmer, p	1	0	0	0	0	0	0	0	.000
Flanagan, p	1	1	0	0	0	0	0	0	.000
Sakata, pr-2b	1	1	0	0	0	0	0	0	.000
Singleton, ph	2	1	0	0	0	0	0	1	.000
Davis, p	1	2	0	0	0	0	0	0	.000
Nolan, ph-c	2	2	0	0	0	0	0	0	.000
Stewart, p	3	2	0	0	0	0	0	0	.000
Boddicker, p	1	3	0	0	0	0	0	1	.000
McGregor, p	2	5	0	0	0	0	0	0	.000
Roenicke, ph-lf	3	7	0	0	0	0	0	0	.000
Totals	5	164	18	35	8	0	6	17	.213

Philadelphia Phillies

Player-Position	G.	AB.	R.	H.	2B.	3B.	HR.	RBI.	BA.
Virgil, ph-c	3	2	0	1	0	0	0	1	.500
Diaz, c	5	15	1	5	1	0	0	0	.333
Rose, ph-1b-rf	5	16	1	5	1	0	0	1	.313
Morgan, 2b	5	19	3	5	0	1	2	2	.263
Matthews, lf	5	16	1	4	0	0	1	1	.250
Maddox, ph-cf	4	12	1	3	1	0	1	1	.250
Perez, ph-1b	4	10	0	2	0	0	0	0	.200
Denny, p	2	5	1	1	0	0	0	1	.200
Lefebvre, ph-rf	3	5	0	1	1	0	0	2	.200
DeJesus, ss	5	16	0	2	0	0	0	0	.125
Lezcano, ph-rf	4	8	0	1	0	0	0	0	.125
Schmidt, 3b	5	20	0	1	0	0	0	0	.050
Andersen, p	2	0	0	0	0	0	0	0	.000
Bystrom, p	1	0	0	0	0	0	0	0	.000
Dernier, pr	1	0	1	0	0	0	0	0	.000
Hernandez, p	3	0	0	0	0	0	0	0	.000
Holland, p	2	0	0	0	0	0	0	0	.000
Reed, p	3	0	0	0	0	0	0	0	.000
Samuel, pr-ph	3	1	0	0	0	0	0	0	.000
Hudson, p	2	2	0	0	0	0	0	0	.000
Carlton, p	1	3	0	0	0	0	0	0	.000
Hayes, ph-rf	4	3	0	0	0	0	0	0	.000
G. Gross, cf	2	6	0	0	0	0	0	0	.000
Totals	5	159	9	31	4	1	4	9	.195

COMPOSITE PITCHING AVERAGES

Baltimore Orioles

Pitcher	G.	IP.	H.	R.	ER.	BB.	SO.	W.	L.	ERA.
Boddicker	1	9	3	1	0	0	6	1	0	0.00
Stewart	3	5	2	0	0	2	6	0	0	0.00
Palmer	1	2	2	0	0	1	1	1	0	0.00
McGregor	2	17	9	2	2	2	12	1	1	1.06
T. Martinez	3	3	3	1	1	0	0	0	0	3.00
Flanagan	1	4	6	2	2	1	1	0	0	4.50
Davis	1	5	6	3	3	1	3	1	0	5.40
Totals	5	45	31	9	8	7	29	4	1	1.60

Philadelphia Phillies

Pitcher	G.	IP.	H.	R.	ER.	BB.	SO.	W.	L.	ERA.
Hernandez	3	4	0	0	0	1	4	0	0	0.00
Holland	2	3⅔	1	0	0	0	5	0	0	0.00
Bystrom	1	1	0	0	0	0	1	0	0	0.00
Andersen	2	4	4	1	1	0	1	0	0	2.25
Carlton	1	6⅔	5	3	2	3	7	0	1	2.70
Reed	3	3⅓	4	1	1	2	4	0	0	2.70
Denny	2	13	12	5	5	3	9	1	1	3.46
Hudson	2	8⅓	9	8	8	1	6	0	2	8.64
Totals	5	44	35	18	17	10	37	1	4	3.48

DETROIT TIGERS VS. SAN DIEGO PADRES

The National League champion San Diego Padres didn't have a prayer.

The same could be said, of course, for the American League West-winning Kansas City Royals. And for the six also-rans in the A.L. East.

The 1984 Detroit Tigers were simply too good. For everyone. They won 35 of their first 40 regular-season games, sprinted to the A.L. East championship with 104 victories and a 15-game bulge over their nearest competitor, swept the Royals in the A.L. Championship Series and then made short work of the Padres in the World Series.

And short work is what Detroit really made of San Diego's starting pitching. In the last four games of a five-game dismissal from the fall classic, the Padres saw two of their starters fail to get through the first inning, one unable to last through the second and the other not effective enough to survive the third.

Mark Thurmond was the long-distance man among the Padres' Series starters, going five innings in Game 1. Just long enough to lose. Nursing a 2-1 lead in the first Series game ever played in San Diego, Thurmond yielded a two-out, two-run homer to Larry Herndon in the fifth.

The Padres had their chances thereafter. Graig Nettles and Terry Kennedy singled to open the San Diego sixth, but Detroit's Jack Morris proceeded to strike out the side. Then, in the seventh, Kurt Bevacqua slapped a leadoff double into the right-field corner but was thrown out trying for a triple. Morris was in control the rest of the way—he finished with nine strikeouts—and Detroit broke on top in this Series with a 3-2 triumph.

Manager Sparky Anderson's Tigers knocked Ed Whitson from the box with three first-inning runs in Game 2, but Padre relievers Andy Hawkins and Craig Lefferts and designated hitter Bevacqua combined to give San Diego one bright Series moment. Hawkins, taking over with two out in the first, pitched 5⅓ innings of one-hit ball and Lefferts struck out five Tigers in three scoreless innings. And with San Diego trailing 3-2 in the fifth, Bevacqua belted a three-run homer off Dan Petry. The Padres' 5-3 edge held up as the San Diego bullpen choked off the Detroit offense.

In Game 3 at Detroit, San Diego pitchers issued 11 walks—all of which came in the first five innings—and the Tigers strolled to a 5-2 triumph. Detroit got two of its runs when Herndon drew a walk with the bases loaded in the second inning and Kirk Gibson was hit by a pitch with the bases full in the third. Padres starter Tim Lollar gave up four hits (including a two-run homer to Marty Castillo), four walks and four runs before departing with two out in the second inning. Milt Wilcox worked six innings for Detroit and got the victory.

Morris and Alan Trammell then put Dick Williams' Padres on the brink of elimination. Morris, who spun a no-hitter in the first week of the regular season and went on to post 19 victories, recorded his second complete game of the Series, hurling a five-hitter in Game 4. Trammell accounted for all of the Tigers' runs in the 4-2 decision by rocking Eric Show for two-run homers in the first and third innings.

Kirk Gibson put on a big show for the Tigers in Game 5, blasting upper-deck home runs in the first and eighth innings good for five RBIs. His first homer came off Thurmond, who retired only one batter this time around.

Gibson also stood out on the basepaths. When the game was tied 3-3 in the fifth, he raced home from third with the tie-breaking run on a shallow fly ball to right field that Padres second baseman Alan Wiggins wound up catching.

Lance Parrish also homered for the Tigers, who sailed to a Series-clinching 8-4 victory. Petry again stumbled as the Tigers' starter, but relievers Aurelio Lopez and Willie Hernandez (who combined for a 19-4 regular-season record and 46 saves) shackled the Padres.

While Petry may have stumbled in his starting roles, San Diego's rotation out and out took a pratfall. In 10⅓ innings, starters Thurmond, Whitson, Lollar and Show had a combined 13.94 earned-run average.

The triumph made Anderson, pilot of the 1975 and 1976 champion Cincinnati Reds, the first manager to guide teams from both leagues to Series crowns.

Game 1

Tuesday, October 9, At San Diego

Detroit	AB.	R.	H.	RBI.	PO.	A.
Whitaker, 2b	4	1	1	0	3	3
Trammell, ss	5	0	2	1	0	2
Gibson, rf	4	0	0	0	1	1
Parrish, c	3	1	2	0	9	1
Herndon, lf	3	1	2	2	1	0
Garbey, dh	4	0	0	0	0	0
Lemon, cf	4	0	1	0	2	0
Evans, 1b	3	0	0	0	4	1
cBergman, 1b	0	0	0	0	3	0
Castillo, 3b	2	0	0	0	1	0
bGrubb	0	0	0	0	0	0
dBrookens, 3b	1	0	0	0	0	0
Morris, p	0	0	0	0	3	0
Totals	33	3	8	3	27	10

San Diego	AB.	R.	H.	RBI.	PO.	A.
Wiggins, 2b	4	0	1	0	1	2
Gwynn, rf	2	0	1	0	3	0
Garvey, 1b	4	1	1	0	9	2
Nettles, 3b	2	1	2	0	3	1
aSalazar, 3b	1	0	0	0	0	0
Kennedy, c	4	0	2	2	3	0
Brown, cf	4	0	0	0	3	0
Martinez, lf	4	0	0	0	3	0
Templeton, ss	4	0	0	0	2	2
Bevacqua, dh	3	0	1	0	0	0
Thurmond, p	0	0	0	0	0	2
Hawkins, p	0	0	0	0	0	1
Dravecky, p	0	0	0	0	0	0
Totals	32	2	8	2	27	10

Detroit	1 0 0	0 2 0	0 0 0—3			
San Diego	2 0 0	0 0 0	0 0 0—2			

Detroit	IP.	H.	R.	ER.	BB.	SO.
Morris (W)	9	8	2	2	3	9

San Diego	IP.	H.	R.	ER.	BB.	SO.
Thurmond (L)	5	7	3	3	3	2
Hawkins	2⅔	1	0	0	3	0
Dravecky	1⅓	0	0	0	0	1

Game-winning RBI—Herndon.

aRan for Nettles in sixth. bAnnounced as pinch-hitter for Castillo in eighth. cRan for Evans in eighth. dFlied out for Grubb in eighth. E—Martinez. DP—Detroit 1, San Diego 1. LOB—Detroit 9, San Diego 6. 2B—Whitaker, Kennedy, Parrish, Bevacqua. HR—Herndon. SB—Trammell, Gwynn. U—Harvey (N.L.) plate, Barnett (A.L.) first, Froemming (N.L.) second, Garcia (A.L.) third, Runge (N.L.) left and Reilly (A.L.) right. T—3:18. A—57,908.

Game 2

Wednesday, October 10, At San Diego

Detroit	AB.	R.	H.	RBI.	PO.	A.
Whitaker, 2b	4	1	1	0	2	1
Trammell, ss	4	1	2	0	3	2
Gibson, rf	4	1	2	1	1	0
Parrish, c	3	0	0	1	3	2
Evans, 3b-1b	4	0	1	1	4	1
Jones, lf	2	0	0	0	2	0
aHerndon, lf	2	0	0	0	0	0
Grubb, dh	2	0	1	0	0	0
bKuntz	1	0	0	0	0	0
Lemon, cf	3	0	0	0	5	0
Bergman, 1b	2	0	0	0	4	1
cBrookens, 3b	1	0	0	0	0	1
Petry, p	0	0	0	0	0	1
Lopez, p	0	0	0	0	0	0
Scherrer, p	0	0	0	0	0	1
Bair, p	0	0	0	0	0	0
Hernandez, p	0	0	0	0	0	0
Totals	32	3	7	3	24	10

San Diego	AB.	R.	H.	RBI.	PO.	A.
Wiggins, 2b	5	1	3	0	2	1
Gwynn, rf	3	0	1	0	2	1
Garvey, 1b	3	0	0	0	7	0
Nettles, 3b	1	1	0	1	1	4
Kennedy, c	4	1	1	0	9	0
Bevacqua, dh	4	2	3	3	0	0
Martinez, lf	3	0	0	0	1	0
Templeton, ss	4	0	3	0	4	0
Brown, cf	3	0	0	1	0	0
Salazar, cf	1	0	0	0	1	0
Whitson, p	0	0	0	0	0	0
Hawkins, p	0	0	0	0	0	0
Lefferts, p	0	0	0	0	0	0
Totals	31	5	11	5	27	6

Detroit .... 3 0 0 0 0 0 0 0 0—3
San Diego .... 1 0 0 1 3 0 0 0 x—5

Detroit	IP.	H.	R.	ER.	BB.	SO.
Petry (L)	4⅓	8	5	5	3	2
Lopez	⅔	1	0	0	1	0
Scherrer	1⅓	2	0	0	0	0
Bair	⅔	0	0	0	0	1
Hernandez	1	0	0	0	0	0

San Diego	IP.	H.	R.	ER.	BB.	SO.
Whitson	⅔	5	3	3	0	0
Hawkins (W)	5⅓	1	0	0	0	3
Lefferts (S)	3	1	0	0	0	5

Game-winning RBI—Bevacqua.

aFlied out for Jones in seventh. bStruck out for Grubb in seventh. cStruck out for Bergman in eighth. E—Trammell, Gibson 2. DP—Detroit 1, San Diego 1. LOB—Detroit 3, San Diego 8. HR—Bevacqua. SB—Gibson. SH—Garvey. SF—Parrish, Nettles. Balk—Petry. U—Barnett (A.L.) plate, Froemming (N.L.) first, Garcia (A.L.) second, Runge (N.L.) third, Reilly (A.L.) left and Harvey (N.L.) right. T—2:44. A—57,911.

Game 3

Friday, October 12, At Detroit

San Diego	AB.	R.	H.	RBI.	PO.	A.
Wiggins, 2b	5	1	2	0	4	1
Gwynn, rf	5	1	2	0	2	0
Garvey, 1b	5	0	1	1	7	0
Nettles, 3b	2	0	0	1	0	2
Kennedy, c	3	0	0	0	5	0
Bevacqua, dh	4	0	1	0	0	0
Martinez, lf	4	0	1	0	0	0
Templeton, ss	4	0	2	0	1	3
Brown, cf	3	0	0	0	5	0
aSalazar	1	0	1	0	0	0
Lollar, p	0	0	0	0	0	0
Booker, p	0	0	0	0	0	1
Harris, p	0	0	0	0	0	0
Totals	36	2	10	2	24	7

Detroit	AB.	R.	H.	RBI.	PO.	A.
Whitaker, 2b	3	1	0	0	3	4
Trammell, ss	3	1	2	1	3	1
Gibson, rf	2	0	0	1	1	0
Parrish, c	3	0	1	0	6	0
Herndon, lf	4	0	1	1	1	0
Garbey, dh	5	0	0	0	0	0
Lemon, cf	5	1	2	0	4	0
Evans, 1b	2	1	0	0	3	1
Bergman, 1b	0	0	0	0	3	0
Castillo, 3b	4	1	1	2	2	2
Wilcox, p	0	0	0	0	1	1
Scherrer, p	0	0	0	0	0	0
Hernandez, p	0	0	0	0	0	0
Totals	31	5	7	5	27	9

San Diego .... 0 0 1 0 0 0 1 0 0—2
Detroit .... 0 4 1 0 0 0 0 0 x—5

San Diego	IP.	H.	R.	ER.	BB.	SO.
Lollar (L)	1⅔	4	4	4	4	0
Booker	1	0	1	1	4	0
Harris	5⅓	3	0	0	3	5

Detroit	IP.	H.	R.	ER.	BB.	SO.
Wilcox (W)	6	7	1	1	2	4
Scherrer	⅔	2	1	1	0	0
Hernandez (S)	2⅓	1	0	0	0	0

Game-winning RBI—Castillo.

aSingled for Brown in ninth. LOB—San Diego 10, Detroit 14. 2B—Wiggins, Trammell, Garvey. HR—Castillo. SB—Gibson. SF—Nettles. HBP—By Harris (Gibson). WP—Lollar. U—Froemming (N.L.) plate, Garcia (A.L.) first, Runge (N.L.) second, Reilly (A.L.) third, Harvey (N.L.) left and Barnett (A.L.) right. T—3:11. A—51,970.

Game 4

Saturday, October 13, At Detroit

San Diego	AB.	R.	H.	RBI.	PO.	A.
Wiggins, 2b	3	0	0	0	2	2
dSummers	1	0	0	0	0	0
Roenicke, lf	0	0	0	0	0	0
Gwynn, rf	4	0	1	0	1	0
Garvey, 1b	4	1	1	0	8	0
Nettles, 3b	4	0	0	0	1	4
Kennedy, c	4	1	1	1	8	1
Bevacqua, dh	3	0	1	0	0	0
Martinez, lf	2	0	0	0	1	0
cFlannery, 2b	1	0	1	0	1	0
Templeton, ss	3	0	0	0	0	3
Brown, cf	3	0	0	0	2	0
Show, p	0	0	0	0	0	0
Dravecky, p	0	0	0	0	0	0
Lefferts, p	0	0	0	0	0	0
Gossage, p	0	0	0	0	0	0
Totals	32	2	5	1	24	10

Detroit	AB.	R.	H.	RBI.	PO.	A.
Whitaker, 2b	4	2	2	0	3	7
Trammell, ss	4	2	3	4	2	1
Gibson, rf	4	0	1	0	1	0
Parrish, c	4	0	0	0	4	0
Evans, 3b	2	0	0	0	1	1
Brookens, 3b	1	0	0	0	0	0
Grubb, dh	1	0	0	0	0	0
aGarbey, dh	2	0	0	0	0	0
Jones, lf	1	0	0	0	1	0
bHerndon, lf	2	0	1	0	0	0
Lemon, cf	2	0	0	0	2	0
Bergman, 1b	3	0	0	0	11	2
Morris, p	0	0	0	0	2	1
Totals	30	4	7	4	27	12

San Diego .... 0 1 0 0 0 0 0 0 1—2
Detroit .... 2 0 2 0 0 0 0 0 x—4

San Diego	IP.	H.	R.	ER.	BB.	SO.
Show (L)	2⅔	4	4	3	1	2
Dravecky	3⅓	3	0	0	1	4
Lefferts	1	0	0	0	0	0
Gossage	1	0	0	0	0	0

Detroit	IP.	H.	R.	ER.	BB.	SO.
Morris (W)	9	5	2	2	0	4

Game-winning RBI—Trammell.

aHit into forceout for Grubb in third. bStruck out for Jones in fourth. cSingled for Martinez in eighth. dStruck out for Wiggins in eighth. E—Wiggins, Gwynn. DP—San Diego 2. LOB—San Diego 3, Detroit 4. 2B—Bevacqua, Whitaker, Garvey. HR—Trammell 2, Kennedy. SB—Gibson, Lemon. WP—Morris 2. U—Garcia (A.L.) plate, Runge (N.L.) first, Reilly (A.L.) second, Harvey (N.L.) third, Barnett (A.L.) left and Froemming (N.L.) right. T—2:20. A—52,130.

Game 5

Sunday, October 14, At Detroit

San Diego	AB.	R.	H.	RBI.	PO.	A.
Wiggins, 2b	5	0	2	1	4	0
Gwynn, rf	5	0	0	0	4	0
Garvey, 1b	4	0	1	1	3	1
Nettles, 3b	3	0	1	0	2	1
Kennedy, c	4	0	0	0	5	1
Bevacqua, dh	3	2	1	1	0	0
Martinez, lf	4	0	2	0	2	0
dSalazar, cf	0	0	0	0	0	0
Templeton, ss	4	1	1	0	1	3
Brown, cf-lf	2	1	1	1	3	0
eBochy	1	0	1	0	0	0
fRoenicke	0	0	0	0	0	0
Thurmond, p	0	0	0	0	0	0
Hawkins, p	0	0	0	0	0	0
Lefferts, p	0	0	0	0	0	0
Gossage, p	0	0	0	0	0	1
Totals	35	4	10	4	24	7

Detroit	AB.	R.	H.	RBI.	PO.	A.
Whitaker, 2b	3	1	1	0	4	3
Trammell, ss	4	1	0	0	0	3
Gibson, rf	4	3	3	5	1	0
Parrish, c	5	2	2	1	8	0
Herndon, lf	4	0	1	0	4	0
Lemon, cf	3	0	2	1	2	0
Garbey, dh	1	0	0	0	0	0
aGrubb	0	0	0	0	0	0
bKuntz	0	0	0	1	0	0
cJohnson	1	0	0	0	0	0
Evans, 1b	4	0	0	0	6	1
Bergman, 1b	0	0	0	0	1	1
Castillo, 3b	3	1	2	0	0	1
Petry, p	0	0	0	0	1	0
Scherrer, p	0	0	0	0	0	1
Lopez, p	0	0	0	0	0	0
Hernandez, p	0	0	0	0	0	1
Totals	32	8	11	8	27	11

San Diego .... 0 0 1 2 0 0 0 1 0—4
Detroit .... 3 0 0 0 1 0 1 3 x—8

San Diego	IP.	H.	R.	ER.	BB.	SO.
Thurmond	⅓	5	3	3	0	0
Hawkins (L)	4	2	1	1	3	1
Lefferts	2	1	0	0	1	2
Gossage	1⅔	3	4	4	1	2

Detroit	IP.	H.	R.	ER.	BB.	SO.
Petry	3⅔	6	3	3	2	2
Scherrer	1	1	0	0	0	0
Lopez (W)	2⅓	0	0	0	0	4
Hernandez (S)	2	3	1	1	0	0

Game-winning RBI—Kuntz.

aHit by pitch for Garbey in fourth. bHit sacrifice fly for Grubb in fifth. cReached first base on error for Kuntz in seventh. dRan for Martinez in eighth. eSingled for Brown in ninth. fRan for Bochy in ninth. E—Wiggins, Parrish. DP—San Diego 1. LOB—San Diego 7, Detroit 9. 2B—Templeton. HR—Gibson 2, Parrish, Bevacqua. SB—Wiggins, Parrish, Lemon. SH—Whitaker, Trammell. SF—Brown, Kuntz. HBP—By Hawkins (Grubb). WP—Hawkins. U—Runge (N.L.) plate, Reilly (A.L.) first, Harvey (N.L.) second, Barnett (A.L.) third, Froemming (N.L.) left and Garcia (A.L.) right. T—2:55. A—51,901.

COMPOSITE BATTING AVERAGES

Detroit Tigers

Player-Position	G.	AB.	R.	H.	2B.	3B.	HR.	RBI.	BA.
Trammell, ss	5	20	5	9	1	0	2	6	.450
Gibson, rf	5	18	4	6	0	0	2	7	.333
Herndon, lf-ph	5	15	1	5	0	0	1	3	.333
Castillo, 3b	3	9	2	3	0	0	1	2	.333
Grubb, ph-dh	4	3	0	1	0	0	0	0	.333
Lemon, cf	5	17	1	5	0	0	0	1	.294
Parrish, c	5	18	3	5	1	0	1	2	.278
Whitaker, 2b	5	18	6	5	2	0	0	0	.278
Evans, 1b-3b	5	15	1	1	0	0	0	1	.067
Bair, p	1	0	0	0	0	0	0	0	.000
Hernandez, p	3	0	0	0	0	0	0	0	.000
Lopez, p	2	0	0	0	0	0	0	0	.000
Morris, p	2	0	0	0	0	0	0	0	.000
Petry, p	2	0	0	0	0	0	0	0	.000
Scherrer, p	3	0	0	0	0	0	0	0	.000
Wilcox, p	1	0	0	0	0	0	0	0	.000
Johnson, ph	1	1	0	0	0	0	0	0	.000
Kuntz, ph	2	1	0	0	0	0	0	1	.000
Brookens, ph-3b	3	3	0	0	0	0	0	0	.000
Jones, lf	2	3	0	0	0	0	0	0	.000
Bergman, pr-1b	5	5	0	0	0	0	0	0	.000
Garbey, dh-ph	4	12	0	0	0	0	0	0	.000
Totals	5	158	23	40	4	0	7	23	.253

San Diego Padres

Player-Position	G.	AB.	R.	H.	2B.	3B.	HR.	RBI.	BA.
Bochy, ph	1	1	0	1	0	0	0	0	1.000
Flannery, ph-2b	1	1	0	1	0	0	0	0	1.000
Bevacqua, dh	5	17	4	7	2	0	2	4	.412
Wiggins, 2b	5	22	2	8	1	0	0	1	.364
S'zar, pr-3b-cf-ph	4	3	0	1	0	0	0	0	.333
Templeton, ss	5	19	1	6	1	0	0	0	.316
Gwynn, rf	5	19	1	5	0	0	0	0	.263
Nettles, 3b	5	12	2	3	0	0	0	2	.250
Kennedy, c	5	19	2	4	1	0	1	3	.211
Garvey, 1b	5	20	2	4	2	0	0	2	.200
Martinez, lf	5	17	0	3	0	0	0	0	.176
Brown, cf-lf	5	15	1	1	0	0	0	2	.067
Booker, p	1	0	0	0	0	0	0	0	.000
Dravecky, p	2	0	0	0	0	0	0	0	.000
Gossage, p	2	0	0	0	0	0	0	0	.000
Harris, p	1	0	0	0	0	0	0	0	.000
Hawkins, p	3	0	0	0	0	0	0	0	.000
Lefferts, p	3	0	0	0	0	0	0	0	.000
Lollar, p	1	0	0	0	0	0	0	0	.000
Roenicke, lf-pr	2	0	0	0	0	0	0	0	.000
Show, p	1	0	0	0	0	0	0	0	.000
Thurmond, p	2	0	0	0	0	0	0	0	.000
Whitson, p	1	0	0	0	0	0	0	0	.000
Summers, ph	1	1	0	0	0	0	0	0	.000
Totals	5	166	15	44	7	0	3	14	.265

COMPOSITE PITCHING AVERAGES

Detroit Tigers

Pitcher	G.	IP.	H.	R.	ER.	BB.	SO.	W.	L.	ERA.
Lopez	2	3	1	0	0	1	4	1	0	0.00
Bair	1	⅔	0	0	0	0	1	0	0	0.00
Wilcox	1	6	7	1	1	2	4	1	0	1.50
Hernandez	3	5⅓	4	1	1	0	0	0	0	1.69
Morris	2	18	13	4	4	3	13	2	0	2.00
Scherrer	3	3	5	1	1	0	0	0	0	3.00
Petry	2	8	14	8	8	5	4	0	1	9.00
Totals	5	44	44	15	15	11	26	4	1	3.07

San Diego Padres

Pitcher	G.	IP.	H.	R.	ER.	BB.	SO.	W.	L.	ERA.
Lefferts	3	6	2	0	0	1	7	0	0	0.00
Harris	1	5⅓	3	0	0	3	5	0	0	0.00
Dravecky	2	4⅔	3	0	0	1	5	0	0	0.00
Hawkins	3	12	4	1	1	6	4	1	1	0.75
Booker	1	1	0	1	1	4	0	0	0	9.00
Thurmond	2	5⅓	12	6	6	3	2	0	1	10.13
Show	1	2⅔	4	4	3	1	2	0	1	10.13
Gossage	2	2⅔	3	4	4	1	2	0	0	13.50
Lollar	1	1⅔	4	4	4	4	0	0	1	21.60
Whitson	1	⅔	5	3	3	0	0	0	0	40.50
Totals	5	42	40	23	22	24	27	1	4	4.71

1985 KANSAS CITY ROYALS VS. ST. LOUIS CARDINALS

Kansas City's Jim Sundberg slides around St. Louis catcher Darrell Porter to score the winning run in the controversial ninth inning of Game 6.

It was a tough loss for the Kansas City Royals. And in a historical context, it was a doubly tough setback.

Royals lefthander Charlie Leibrandt had entered the ninth inning of Game 2 of the 1985 World Series with a two-hit shutout against the St. Louis Cardinals. But with two out and Willie McGee on second base with a leadoff double, things unraveled for the 29-year-old pitcher as he tried to protect a 2-0 lead.

Jack Clark belted a single to left field, scoring McGee. Tito Landrum blooped a double down the right-field line, sending Clark to third. Cesar Cedeno was given an intentional walk, loading the bases. And then Terry Pendleton doubled down the line in left, sending Clark, Landrum and Cedeno across the plate.

What had been a pitching masterpiece blew up in Leibrandt's face. Unable to bounce back in the last of the ninth at Royals Stadium, Kansas City went down to a stinging 4-2 defeat. Coupled with a Series-opening 3-1 defeat in the same ball park at the hands of Cardinals lefthander John Tudor, Manager Dick Howser's Royals were in a two games-to-none hole.

The deficit was hardly insurmountable. Or was it? The record books showed that seven teams previously had rebounded to win best-of-seven Series after falling behind 2-0. But those same record books also showed that no team had ever rallied to win the Series after losing the first two games in its home park.

Howser entrusted 21-year-old righthander Bret Saberhagen with the job of righting the Royals' course when the all-Missouri fall classic resumed in St. Louis. Saberhagen, a second-year major leaguer who in '85 had emerged as one of the bright young talents in the majors as evidenced by his 20-6 record, didn't disappoint. Besides flashing television messages from the Royals' bench to his soon-to-deliver wife, Saberhagen flashed a message to the Cardinals: Kansas City was down, but far from out. The pitcher's missive came in the form of a six-hit, eight-strikeout performance. Frank White socked a two-run homer and a run-scoring double in support of Saberhagen, who was a 6-1 winner. Former Cardinal Lonnie Smith got Kansas City rolling in the fourth inning with a two-run double off Joaquin Andujar that snapped a scoreless tie.

Tudor, who was 1-7 at one juncture of the 1985 campaign and then won 20 of his last 21 regular-season decisions, baffled the Royals again in Game 4. The crafty lefthander set down the American Leaguers on five hits and got home run backing from Landrum and McGee. Landrum, in the Cardinals' lineup because of a Championship Series pregame injury suffered by rookie base-stealing sensation Vince Coleman, hit a bases-empty shot off Kansas City starter Bud Black in the second inning and McGee followed with a solo blast the next inning. Tom Nieto's squeeze bunt in the fifth netted the final run in St. Louis' 3-0 conquest. As was the case in their triumphant American League Championship Series against Toronto, the Royals found themselves down three games to one.

Looking to close out the Royals in the final Series game scheduled in St. Louis, the Cardinals sent

veteran Bob Forsch to the mound to oppose 23-year-old Danny Jackson in Game 5. Both clubs notched single runs in the first inning before Kansas City struck for three in the second—the outburst featured a two-run triple by Willie Wilson—and drove Forsch from the game. Jackson, on the other hand, was around at the finish as he completed a five-hit, 6-1 victory that sent the Series back to the western side of the state.

Leibrandt, Kansas City's tough-luck loser in Game 2, wasn't exactly blessed in Game 6. Through seven innings, he had pitched scoreless ball and permitted only two hits. But to that point his stellar effort had gotten the Royals no more than a tie against St. Louis' Danny Cox, whose shutout hurling had been punctuated with eight strikeouts.

A breakthrough in the pitchers' duel came in the eighth when Brian Harper, batting for Cox, looped a two-out single to center field that scored Pendleton. Pendleton had singled with one out and moved to second on a walk.

Lefthander Key Dayley took over for Cox, worked a scoreless eighth and was on the mound preparing to guard a 1-0 lead when the Royals came to bat in the last of the ninth. Howser sent up a righthanded-hitting pinch batter, Darryl Motley, to lead off the inning and St. Louis Manager Whitey Herzog immediately called for hard-throwing right-hander Todd Worrell, who two months earlier had been in the minor leagues. Howser then countered with Jorge Orta, a left-handed batter, to hit for Motley. Orta grounded to first baseman Clark, whose throw to Worrell covering the bag appeared to be in time. But umpire Don Denkinger called Orta safe, enraging Herzog and the Cardinals. Television replays indicated Denkinger had blown the call, but Orta remained perched on first base.

Steve Balboni then lifted a catchable popup near the first-base dugout, but Clark inexplicably failed to make the play. Balboni then singled Orta to second base. After Onix Concepcion ran

for Balboni, Jim Sundberg bunted into a forceout at third base. Hal McRae then went to the plate as a pinch-hitter for Buddy Biancalana and, after Cardinals catcher Darrell Porter committed a passed ball that advanced runners to second and third, he was given an intentional walk. Dane Iorg batted for Royals reliever Dan Quisenberry and poked a single to right field. Concepcion trotted home on the play and Sundberg made it, too, although the Royals' catcher had to slide around a tag by Porter. The Royals had pulled a victory out of the hat, 2-1, and thereby tied the Series.

Saberhagen, exhibiting poise far beyond his years, then blew the Cardinals away in Game 7 by tossing a five-hitter in a game that deteriorated into a blowout and a blowup. Motley blasted a two-run homer off Tudor in the second inning, Balboni delivered a two-run single in the Royals' three-run third and Smith bashed a two-run double in a six-run fifth during which Herzog and Cardinals pitcher Andujar—incensed by the umpiring—were ejected in a stormy and disturbing scene. George Brett went 4 for 5 for the Royals and Motley finished with three hits in the 11-0 blitz.

World Series hero Saberhagen, who became a father for the first time the day before the finale against the Cards, had much to celebrate. He wasn't alone.

In putting away the Cardinals, the Royals hadn't flinched either after losing the first two games at home or falling behind three games to one. As a result, they were World Series champions for the first time.

Game 1
Saturday, October 19, At Kansas City

St. Louis	AB.	R.	H.	RBI.	PO.	A.
McGee, cf	4	0	1	1	1	0
O. Smith, ss	3	0	0	0	1	2
Herr, 2b	4	1	0	1	3	0
Clark, 1b	4	0	1	1	6	1
Landrum, lf	4	1	2	0	3	0
Cedeno, rf	3	0	1	1	3	0
Worrell, p	1	0	0	0	0	0
Pendleton, 3b	2	1	0	0	1	4
Porter, c	3	0	1	0	7	2
Tudor, p	1	0	0	0	0	2
Van Slyke, rf	2	0	0	0	2	0
Totals	31	3	7	3	27	11

Kansas City	AB.	R.	H.	RBI.	PO.	A.
L. Smith, lf	3	0	1	0	0	1
Wilson, cf	4	0	1	0	0	1
Brett, 3b	4	0	1	0	1	3
White, 2b	3	0	0	0	0	3
Sundberg, c	3	1	1	0	11	0
Motley, rf	3	0	1	0	1	0
dSheridan	1	0	1	0	0	0
Balboni, 1b	4	0	1	1	11	0

	AB.	R.	H.	RBI.	PO.	A.
Biancalana, ss	1	0	0	0	0	1
aL. Jones	1	0	1	0	0	0
Quisenberry, p	0	0	0	0	0	0
Black, p	0	0	0	0	0	0
eOrta	1	0	0	0	0	0
Jackson, p	2	0	0	0	0	2
bMcRae	0	0	0	0	0	0
cConcepcion, ss	0	0	0	0	0	2
fIorg	1	0	0	0	0	0
Totals	32	1	8	1	27	15

St. Louis .... 0 0 1　1 0 0　0 0 1—3
Kansas City ..... 0 1 0　0 0 0　0 0 0—1

St. Louis	IP.	H.	R.	ER.	BB.	SO.
Tudor (W)	6⅔	7	1	1	2	5
Worrell (S)	2⅓	1	0	0	1	0

Kansas City	IP.	H.	R.	ER.	BB.	SO.
Jackson (L)	7	4	2	2	2	7
Quisenberry	1⅔	3	1	1	0	2
Black	⅓	0	0	0	2	1

Game-winning RBI—Cedeno.

aTripled for Biancalana in seventh. bHit by pitch for Jackson in seventh. cRan for McRae in seventh. dDoubled for Motley in ninth. eFlied out for Black in ninth. fFlied out for Concepcion in ninth. E—Pendleton. DP—St. Louis 1. LOB—St. Louis 6, Kansas City 8. 2B—Landrum, Cedeno, Sundberg, McGee, Clark, Sheridan. 3B—L. Jones. SB—O. Smith. SH—Tudor. HBP—By Tudor (McRae). PB—Sundberg. U—Denkinger (A.L.) plate, B. Williams (N.L.) first, McKean (A.L.) second, Engel (N.L.) third, Shulock (A.L.) left and Quick (N.L.) right. T—2:48. A—41,650.

Game 2
Sunday, October 20, At Kansas City

St. Louis	AB.	R.	H.	RBI.	PO.	A.
McGee, cf	4	1	1	0	2	0
O. Smith, ss	4	0	0	0	3	3
Herr, 2b	4	0	0	0	1	5
Clark, 1b	3	1	1	1	10	0
Landrum, lf	4	1	2	0	2	1
Cedeno, rf	3	1	0	0	0	0
Lahti, p	0	0	0	0	0	0
Pendleton, 3b	4	0	2	3	1	2
Porter, c	3	0	0	0	7	0
Cox, p	2	0	0	0	1	2
aHarper	1	0	0	0	0	0
Dayley, p	0	0	0	0	0	0
bVan Slyke, rf	1	0	0	0	0	0
Totals	33	4	6	4	27	13

Kansas City	AB.	R.	H.	RBI.	PO.	A.
L. Smith, lf	4	0	2	0	0	0
L. Jones, lf	0	0	0	0	2	0
Wilson, cf	4	1	2	0	3	0
Brett, 3b	4	1	1	1	1	5
White, 2b	3	0	3	1	0	0
Sheridan, rf	4	0	0	0	1	0
Quisenberry, p	0	0	0	0	0	0
Sundberg, c	4	0	0	0	7	0
Balboni, 1b	4	0	1	0	12	0
Biancalana, ss	1	0	0	0	1	4
cOrta	1	0	0	0	0	0
Leibrandt, p	2	0	0	0	0	2
Motley, rf	0	0	0	0	0	0
Totals	31	2	9	2	27	11

St. Louis .... 0 0 0　0 0 0　0 0 4—4
Kansas City ..... 0 0 0　2 0 0　0 0 0—2

St. Louis	IP.	H.	R.	ER.	BB.	SO.
Cox	7	7	2	2	3	5
Dayley (W)	1	1	0	0	0	1
Lahti (S)	1	1	0	0	0	0

Kansas City	IP.	H.	R.	ER.	BB.	SO.
Leibrandt (L)	8⅔	6	4	4	2	6
Quisenberry	⅓	0	0	0	1	0

Game-winning RBI—Pendleton.

aFlied out for Cox in eighth. bFlied out for Dayley in ninth. cGrounded into double play for Biancalana in ninth. DP—St. Louis 3. LOB—St. Louis 5, Kansas City 6. 2B—Brett, White 2, McGee, Landrum, Pendleton. SB—White, Wilson. SH—Leibrandt. U—B. Williams (N.L.) plate, McKean (A.L.) first, Engel (N.L.) second, Shulock (A.L.) third, Quick (N.L.) left and Denkinger (A.L.) right. T—2:44. A—41,656.

Game 3
Tuesday, October 22, At St. Louis

Kansas City	AB.	R.	H.	RBI.	PO.	A.
L. Smith, lf	5	0	2	2	1	0
L. Jones, lf	0	0	0	0	1	0
Wilson, cf	5	0	2	0	3	0
Brett, 3b	2	2	2	0	2	3
White, 2b	4	2	2	3	1	3
Sheridan, rf	5	0	0	0	1	0
Sundberg, c	2	1	1	0	8	2
Balboni, 1b	4	0	0	0	9	0
Biancalana, ss	5	1	2	1	1	1
Saberhagen, p	3	0	0	0	0	0
Totals	35	6	11	6	27	9

St. Louis	AB.	R.	H.	RBI.	PO.	A.
McGee, cf	4	0	1	0	1	0
O. Smith, ss	4	1	1	0	1	5
Herr, 2b	3	0	1	0	2	1
Clark, 1b	4	0	1	1	9	0
Van Slyke, rf	4	0	0	0	1	0
Pendleton, 3b	4	0	1	0	0	0

	AB.	R.	H.	RBI.	PO.	A.
Porter, c	3	0	0	0	8	1
Landrum, lf	3	0	1	0	4	0
Andujar, p	1	0	0	0	0	1
Campbell, p	0	0	0	0	0	0
aJorgensen	1	0	0	0	0	0
Horton, p	0	0	0	0	1	0
bHarper	1	0	0	0	0	0
Dayley, p	0	0	0	0	0	0
Totals	32	1	6	1	27	8

Kansas City	0 0 0 2 2 0 2 0 0—6
St. Louis	0 0 0 0 0 1 0 0 0—1

Kansas City	IP.	H.	R.	ER.	BB.	SO.
Saberhagen (W)	9	6	1	1	1	8

St. Louis	IP.	H.	R.	ER.	BB.	SO.
Andujar (L)	4*	9	4	4	3	3
Campbell	1	0	0	0	1	2
Horton	2	2	2	2	2	1
Dayley	2	0	0	0	2	2

*Pitched to two batters in fifth.

Game-winning RBI—L. Smith.

aGrounded out for Campbell in fifth. bGrounded out for Horton in seventh. DP—Kansas City 1, St. Louis 1. LOB—Kansas City 11, St. Louis 5. 2B—L. Smith, White. HR—White. SB—Wilson, McGee. SH—Saberhagen. Balk—Horton. U—McKean (A.L.) plate, Engel (N.L.) first, Shulock (A.L.) second, Quick (N.L.) third, Denkinger (A.L.) left and B. Williams (N.L.) right. T—2:59. A—53,634.

Game 4

Wednesday, October 23, At St. Louis

Kansas City	AB.	R.	H.	RBI.	PO.	A.
L. Smith, lf	4	0	0	0	1	1
Wilson, cf	4	0	1	0	1	0
Brett, 3b	4	0	1	0	0	3
White, 2b	4	0	0	0	2	3
Sundberg, c	4	0	1	0	7	1
Motley, rf	4	0	0	0	0	0
Balboni, 1b	2	0	1	0	11	1
Biancalana, ss	2	0	0	0	0	4
bMcRae	1	0	0	0	0	0
Concepcion, ss	0	0	0	0	0	0
Black, p	1	0	0	0	1	2
aWathan	1	0	0	0	0	0
Beckwith, p	0	0	0	0	0	0
cL. Jones	1	0	1	0	0	0
Quisenberry, p	0	0	0	0	1	1
Totals	32	0	5	0	24	16

St. Louis	AB.	R.	H.	RBI.	PO.	A.
McGee, cf	3	1	2	1	2	0
O. Smith, ss	2	0	0	0	0	0
Herr, 2b	3	0	1	0	0	2
Clark, 1b	3	0	1	0	10	0
Landrum, lf	4	1	1	1	1	0
Cedeno, rf	3	0	0	0	4	0
Van Slyke, rf	0	0	0	0	0	0
Pendleton, 3b	3	1	1	0	1	2
Nieto, c	1	0	0	1	9	0
Tudor, p	3	0	0	0	0	1
Totals	25	3	6	3	27	5

Kansas City	0 0 0 0 0 0 0 0 0—0
St. Louis	0 1 1 0 1 0 0 0 x—3

Kansas City	IP.	H.	R.	ER.	BB.	SO.
Black (L)	5	4	3	3	3	3
Beckwith	2	1	0	0	0	3
Quisenberry	1	1	0	0	2	0

St. Louis	IP.	H.	R.	ER.	BB.	SO.
Tudor (W)	9	5	0	0	1	8

Game-winning RBI—Landrum.

aStruck out for Black in sixth. bGrounded into forceout for Biancalana in seventh. cDoubled for Beckwith in eighth. E—Black. DP—Kansas City 1. LOB—Kansas City 6, St. Louis 5. 2B—Herr, L. Jones. 3B—Pendleton. HR—Landrum, McGee. SH—Nieto, O. Smith. WP—Quisenberry. U—Engel (N.L.) plate, Shulock (A.L.) first, Quick (N.L.) second, Denkinger (A.L.) third, B. Williams (N.L.) left and McKean (A.L.) right. T—2:19. A—53,634.

Game 5

Thursday, October 24, At St. Louis

Kansas City	AB.	R.	H.	RBI.	PO.	A.
L. Smith, lf	4	2	2	0	2	0
L. Jones, lf	0	0	0	0	0	0
Wilson, cf	5	0	2	2	2	0
Brett, 3b	4	0	1	0	1	1
Pryor, 3b	0	0	0	0	0	1
White, 2b	5	1	0	1	2	2
Sheridan, rf	5	0	2	1	2	0
Balboni, 1b	4	0	1	0	11	1
Sundberg, c	4	2	1	0	6	0
Biancalana, ss	3	1	2	1	1	5
Jackson, p	4	0	0	0	0	2
Totals	38	6	11	5	27	12

St. Louis	AB.	R.	H.	RBI.	PO.	A.
McGee, cf	4	0	2	0	0	0
O. Smith, ss	3	0	0	0	1	1
Herr, 2b	4	1	1	0	2	1
Clark, 1b	3	0	1	1	5	2
Landrum, lf	4	0	1	0	1	0
Cedeno, rf	4	0	0	0	1	0
Pendleton, 3b	3	0	0	0	1	4
Nieto, c	4	0	0	0	14	1
Forsch, p	0	0	0	0	0	0
Horton, p	1	0	0	0	1	0
Campbell, p	0	0	0	0	1	0
aDeJesus	1	0	0	0	0	0
Worrell, p	0	0	0	0	0	0
bHarper	1	0	0	0	0	0
Lahti, p	0	0	0	0	0	0
Totals	32	1	5	1	27	9

Kansas City	1 3 0 0 0 0 0 1 1—6
St. Louis	1 0 0 0 0 0 0 0 0—1

Kansas City	IP.	H.	R.	ER.	BB.	SO.
Jackson (W)	9	5	1	1	3	5

St. Louis	IP.	H.	R.	ER.	BB.	SO.
Forsch (L)	1⅔	5	4	4	1	2
Horton	2	1	0	0	3	4
Campbell	1⅓	0	0	0	0	2
Worrell	2	0	0	0	0	6
Lahti	2	5	2	1	0	1

Game-winning RBI—Biancalana.

aFlied out for Campbell in fifth. bStruck out for Worrell in seventh. E—Brett, Jackson, O. Smith. DP—St. Louis 1. LOB—Kansas City 9, St. Louis, 7. 2B—Herr, Clark, Sundberg, Sheridan. 3B—Wilson. SB—L. Smith. U—Shulock (A.L.) plate, Quick (N.L.) first, Denkinger (A.L.) second, B. Williams (N.L.) third, McKean (A.L.) left and Engel (N.L.) right. T—2:52. A—53,634.

Game 6

Saturday, October 26, At Kansas City

St. Louis	AB.	R.	H.	RBI.	PO.	A.
O. Smith, ss	3	0	0	0	2	3
McGee, cf	4	0	0	0	4	0
Herr, 2b	4	0	0	0	1	2
Clark, 1b	4	0	0	0	5	0
Landrum, lf	4	0	1	0	1	0
Pendleton, 3b	4	1	1	0	1	1
Cedeno, rf	2	0	1	0	1	0
bVan Slyke, rf	0	0	0	0	0	0
Porter, c	3	0	1	0	10	1
Cox, p	2	0	0	0	0	0
aHarper	1	0	1	1	0	0
cLawless	0	0	0	0	0	0
Dayley, p	0	0	0	0	0	0
Worrell, p	0	0	0	0	0	1
Totals	31	1	5	1	25	8

Kansas City	AB.	R.	H.	RBI.	PO.	A.
L. Smith, lf	4	0	1	0	0	0
Wilson, cf	3	0	1	0	3	0
Brett, 3b	4	0	0	0	3	4
White, 2b	4	0	1	0	2	2
Sheridan, rf	3	0	1	0	2	0
dMotley	0	0	0	0	0	0
eOrta	1	0	1	0	0	0
Balboni, 1b	3	0	2	0	9	1
fConcepcion	0	1	0	0	0	0
Sundberg, c	4	1	1	0	6	0
Biancalana, ss	3	0	1	0	1	4
gMcRae	0	0	0	0	0	0
hWathan	0	0	0	0	0	0
Leibrandt, p	2	0	0	0	1	0
Quisenberry, p	0	0	0	0	0	0
iIorg	1	0	1	2	0	0
Totals	32	2	10	2	27	11

St. Louis	0 0 0 0 0 0 0 1 0—1
Kansas City	0 0 0 0 0 0 0 0 2—2

One out when winning run scored.

St. Louis	IP.	H.	R.	ER.	BB.	SO.
Cox	7	7	0	0	1	8
Dayley	1	0	0	0	1	2
Worrell (L)	⅓	3	2	2	1	0

Kansas City	IP.	H.	R.	ER.	BB.	SO.
Leibrandt	7⅔	4	1	1	2	4
Quisenberry (W)	1⅓	1	0	0	0	1

Game-winning RBI—Iorg.

aSingled for Cox in eighth. bRan for Cedeno in eighth. cRan for Harper in eighth. dAnnounced as a pinch-hitter for Sheridan in ninth. eSingled for Motley in ninth. fRan for Balboni in ninth. gWalked intentionally for Biancalana in ninth. hRan for McRae in ninth. iSingled for Quisenberry in ninth. DP—St. Louis 1, Kansas City 1. LOB—St. Louis 5, Kansas City 9. 2B—L. Smith. SH—Leibrandt. PB—Porter. U—Quick (N.L.) plate, Denkinger (A.L.) first, B. Williams (N.L.) second, McKean (A.L.) third, Engel (N.L.) left and Shulock (A.L.) right. T—2:47. A—41,628.

Game 7

Sunday, October 27, At Kansas City

St. Louis	AB.	R.	H.	RBI.	PO.	A.
O. Smith, ss	4	0	1	0	2	2
McGee, cf	4	0	0	0	5	0
Herr, 2b	4	0	0	0	2	2
Clark, 1b	4	0	1	0	4	1
Van Slyke, rf	4	0	1	0	5	0
Pendleton, 3b	3	0	1	0	1	1
Landrum, lf	2	0	1	0	0	0
Andujar, p	0	0	0	0	0	0
Forsch, p	0	0	0	0	0	0
aBraun	1	0	0	0	0	0
Dayley, p	0	0	0	0	0	0
Porter, c	3	0	0	0	4	0
Tudor, p	1	0	0	0	0	0
Campbell, p	0	0	0	0	0	0
Lahti, p	0	0	0	0	0	0
Horton, p	0	0	0	0	0	0
Jorgensen, lf	2	0	0	0	1	0
Totals	32	0	5	0	24	6

Kansas City	AB.	R.	H.	RBI.	PO.	A.
L. Smith, lf	3	2	1	2	3	0
L. Jones, lf	1	0	0	0	1	0
Wilson, cf	5	1	2	1	7	0
Brett, 3b	5	2	4	0	2	0
White, 2b	4	1	1	1	0	5
Sundberg, c	3	1	1	1	2	0
Balboni, 1b	4	2	2	2	7	0
Motley, rf	4	1	3	3	3	0
Biancalana, ss	3	0	0	0	2	1
Saberhagen, p	4	1	0	0	0	0
Totals	36	11	14	10	27	6

St. Louis	0 0 0 0 0 0 0 0 0— 0
Kansas City	0 2 3 0 6 0 0 0 x—11

St. Louis	IP.	H.	R.	ER.	BB.	SO.
Tudor (L)	2⅓	3	5	5	4	1
Campbell	1⅔*	4	1	1	1	1
Lahti	⅔	4	4	4	0	1
Horton	0*	1	1	1	0	0
Andujar	0†	1	0	0	1	0
Forsch	1⅓	1	0	0	0	1
Dayley	2	0	0	0	0	0

Kansas City	IP.	H.	R.	ER.	BB.	SO.
Saberhagen (W)	9	5	0	0	0	2

*Pitched to one batter in fifth.
†Pitched to two batters in fifth.

Game-winning RBI—Motley.

aFlied out for Forsch in seventh. DP—St. Louis 2. LOB—St. Louis 5, Kansas City 7. 2B—L. Smith. HR—Motley. SB—L. Smith, Brett, Wilson. WP—Forsch. U—Denkinger (A.L.) plate, B. Williams (N.L.) first, McKean (A.L.) second, Engel (N.L.) third, Shulock (A.L.) left and Quick (N.L.) right. T—2:46. A—41,658.

COMPOSITE BATTING AVERAGES

Kansas City Royals

Player-Position	G.	AB.	R.	H.	2B.	3B.	HR.	RBI.	BA.
L. Jones, ph-lf	6	3	0	2	1	1	0	0	.667
Iorg, ph	2	2	0	1	0	0	0	2	.500
Brett, 3b	7	27	5	10	1	0	0	1	.370
Wilson, cf	7	30	2	11	0	1	0	3	.367
Motley, rf-ph	5	11	1	4	0	0	1	3	.364
L. Smith, lf	7	27	4	9	3	0	0	4	.333
Orta, ph	3	3	0	1	0	0	0	0	.333
Balboni, 1b	7	25	2	8	0	0	0	3	.320
Biancalana, ss	7	18	2	5	0	0	0	2	.278
White, 2b	7	28	4	7	3	0	1	6	.250
Sundberg, c	7	24	6	6	2	0	0	1	.250
Sheridan, ph-rf	5	18	0	4	2	0	0	1	.222
Beckwith, p	1	0	0	0	0	0	0	0	.000
Concepcion, pr-ss	3	0	1	0	0	0	0	0	.000
Pryor, 3b	1	0	0	0	0	0	0	0	.000
Quisenberry, p	4	0	0	0	0	0	0	0	.000
Black, p	2	1	0	0	0	0	0	0	.000
McRae, ph	3	1	0	0	0	0	0	0	.000
Wathan, ph-pr	2	1	0	0	0	0	0	0	.000
Leibrandt, p	2	4	0	0	0	0	0	0	.000
Jackson, p	2	6	0	0	0	0	0	0	.000
Saberhagen, p	2	7	1	0	0	0	0	0	.000
Totals	7	236	28	68	12	2	2	26	.288

St. Louis Cardinals

Player-Position	G.	AB.	R.	H.	2B.	3B.	HR.	RBI.	BA.
Landrum, lf	7	25	3	9	2	0	1	1	.360
Pendleton, 3b	7	23	3	6	1	1	0	3	.261
McGee, cf	7	27	2	7	2	0	1	2	.259
Harper, ph	4	4	0	1	0	0	0	1	.250
Clark, 1b	7	25	1	6	2	0	0	4	.240
Herr, 2b	7	26	2	4	2	0	0	0	.154
Cedeno, rf	5	15	1	2	1	0	0	1	.133
Porter, c	5	15	0	2	0	0	0	0	.133
Van Slyke, rf-ph-pr	6	11	0	1	0	0	0	0	.091
O. Smith, ss	7	23	1	2	0	0	0	0	.087
Campbell, p	3	0	0	0	0	0	0	0	.000
Dayley, p	4	0	0	0	0	0	0	0	.000
Forsch, p	2	0	0	0	0	0	0	0	.000
Lahti, p	3	0	0	0	0	0	0	0	.000
Lawless, pr	1	0	0	0	0	0	0	0	.000
Andujar, p	2	1	0	0	0	0	0	0	.000
Braun, ph	1	1	0	0	0	0	0	0	.000
DeJesus, ph	1	1	0	0	0	0	0	0	.000
Horton, p	3	1	0	0	0	0	0	0	.000
Worrell, p	3	1	0	0	0	0	0	0	.000
Jorgensen, ph-lf	2	3	0	0	0	0	0	0	.000
Cox, p	2	4	0	0	0	0	0	0	.000
Nieto, c	2	5	0	0	0	0	0	1	.000
Tudor, p	3	5	0	0	0	0	0	0	.000
Totals	7	216	13	40	10	1	2	13	.185

COMPOSITE PITCHING AVERAGES

Kansas City Royals

Pitcher	G.	IP.	H.	R.	ER.	BB.	SO.	W.	L.	ERA.
Beckwith	1	2	1	0	0	0	3	0	0	0.00
Saberhagen	2	18	11	1	1	1	10	2	0	0.50
Jackson	2	16	9	3	3	5	12	1	1	1.69
Quisenberry	4	4⅓	5	1	1	3	3	1	0	2.08
Leibrandt	2	16⅓	10	5	5	4	10	0	1	2.76
Black	2	5⅓	4	3	3	5	4	0	1	5.06
Totals	7	62	40	13	13	18	42	4	3	1.89

St. Louis Cardinals

Pitcher	G.	IP.	H.	R.	ER.	BB.	SO.	W.	L.	ERA.
Dayley	4	6	1	0	0	3	5	1	0	0.00
Cox	2	14	14	2	2	4	13	0	0	1.29
Campbell	3	4	4	1	1	2	5	0	0	2.25
Tudor	3	18	15	6	6	7	14	2	1	3.00
Worrell	3	4⅔	4	2	2	2	6	0	1	3.86
Horton	3	4	4	3	3	5	5	0	0	6.75
Andujar	2	4	10	4	4	4	3	0	1	9.00
Forsch	2	3	6	4	4	1	3	0	1	12.00
Lahti	3	3⅔	10	6	5	0	2	0	0	12.27
Totals	7	61⅓	68	28	27	28	56	3	4	3.96

1986
NEW YORK METS
VS.
BOSTON RED SOX

"There is a fifth dimension beyond that which is known to man. It is a dimension as vast as space and as timeless as infinity. It is the middle ground between light and shadow, between science and superstition, and it lies between the pit of man's fears and the summit of his knowledge. This is the dimension of imagination . . . ."

—Rod Serling

Television playwright Serling called this dimension "The Twilight Zone." Baseball people call it the bottom of the 10th inning of Game 6 of the 1986 World Series.

An unbelievable half inning capped by a hard-to-fathom at-bat, the last of the 10th forever will be a source of exhilaration for New York Mets fans and devastation for Boston Red Sox followers. The Red Sox, ahead three games to two in the Series after lefthander Bruce Hurst's 4-2 triumph in Game 5, had broken a 3-3 tie in the sixth game when Dave Henderson led off the top of the 10th with a home run against Rick Aguilera. Boston then increased its lead to 5-3 later in the inning as Wade Boggs doubled and Marty Barrett singled him home.

Red Sox reliever Calvin Schiraldi, who had entered the game in the eighth and promptly yielded the run that tied the contest at 3-3, retired the Mets' first two batters in the 10th, Wally Backman and Keith Hernandez, on fly balls. Boston now was within one out of its first Series crown since 1918, when Babe Ruth pitched the Beantowners to two victories over the Chicago Cubs.

Gary Carter then kept the Mets' faint hopes alive by rapping a single on a 2-1 pitch and Kevin Mitchell, batting for Aguilera, followed with a one-strike base hit.

Schiraldi proceeded to get a no-ball, two-strike count on New York's Ray Knight. Now, one more strike and the Boston Red Sox would be World Series champions. Knight managed to make contact, though, and looped a single to center field. Carter scored from second, reducing the Mets' deficit to 5-4, and Mitchell moved on to third. Bob Stanley took over for Schiraldi at this point. Then came *the at-bat*.

Stanley and Mets outfielder Mookie Wilson waged a 10-pitch battle as a frenzied Shea Stadium crowd looked on. Wilson fouled off a 2-1 pitch, bringing Boston within one strike of the Series title for the second time. Mookie then fouled off the next delivery. And the next as well. The Red Sox were oh-so-close.

Stanley's seventh pitch to Wilson was wild, with Mitchell racing home with the game-tying run and Knight advancing to second base. With the count now at 3-2, Wilson fouled a pitch back. He then hit a foul ball past third.

Wilson, having hit four fouls off Stanley when the Red Sox's big righthander was one strike away from wrapping up this Series, then slapped a full-count offering to first baseman Bill Buckner. The grounder somehow got through Buckner's legs, and Knight bolted home on the error. New York, time and again getting extended life, had won, 6-5, and deadlocked the 1986 fall classic.

No one could quite believe what had just unfolded. One thing seemed certain, though: It would be extremely difficult for Manager John McNamara's Red Sox to rebound from such a crushing setback. While they had shown their mettle in the American League Championship Series —one strike away from elimination in the fifth game, the Red Sox roared back to win the playoffs in seven games—the Sox now had to come to grips with a stunningly painful situation.

The Red Sox needed time to get themselves back together, mentally. And they received an unexpected boost in this regard when Game 7 was postponed 24 hours because of rain.

With Hurst seeking his third victory of the Series (besides winning Game 5, he was a 1-0 victor in Game 1), the Red Sox clipped Ron Darling for three second-inning runs in the climactic game when Dwight Evans and Rich Gedman belted back-to-back homers and Boggs delivered an RBI single. Hurst protected the 3-0 lead until the sixth when New York tied the game on Hernandez's bases-loaded single that scored Lee Mazzilli and Wilson and Carter's looper to right that brought Backman around.

Schiraldi then came in to pitch the seventh, and Knight greeted him with a tie-breaking homer. Before the inning was over, Rafael Santana had stroked a run-scoring single and Hernandez had hit a sacrifice fly. The Mets were on top, 6-3.

Boston, shut down in the middle innings by Sid Fernandez, threatened to tie the contest in the eighth as Evans ripped a two-run, no-out double off Roger McDowell. But Jesse Orosco came on and got Gedman to line out, Henderson to strike out and pinch-hitter Don Baylor to bounce out to shortstop Santana.

New York, winner of 108 regular-season games, expanded its lead from 6-5 to 8-5 in the last of the eighth when Darryl Strawberry cracked a long homer and

Orosco slapped a single up the middle through a drawn-in infield. Orosco then went out and disposed of the Red Sox 1-2-3 in the ninth, and the New York Mets—21½-game winners in the 1986 National League East race and heavy World Series favorites—were the Series champions everyone expected them to be.

Considering the way the Series began and New York's status with Carter approaching the plate in the 10th inning of Game 6, what everyone expected to happen took considerable time in unfolding. Hurst, with last-inning help from Schiraldi, had set down Manager Dave Johnson's club in Game 1 at New York and Boston belted Mets ace Dwight Gooden en route to a 9-3 second-game victory that featured homers by Henderson and Evans.

New York lefthander Bob Ojeda, acquired from the Red Sox after the 1985 season in an eight-player trade that sent Schiraldi from the Mets to Boston, pitched five-hit ball over seven innings in Game 3 at Fenway Park and the National Leaguers broke through with a 7-1 victory. Lenny Dykstra led off the game with a homer off Dennis Boyd, and the Mets collected three more runs in the first inning, two scoring on designated hitter Danny Heep's single. (The '86 fall classic was the first under which revised designated-hitter rules were implemented for the Series; now, instead of the designated hitter being used throughout the Series in alternating years, the "DH" would be employed yearly, but only in games played at the American League participant's park.)

Carter, who had driven home three runs in the third game, collected three more RBIs in the Mets' Series-squaring 6-2 victory in Game 4. He broke a scoreless tie with a two-run homer in the fourth off Al Nipper and then smacked a bases-empty shot in the eighth off Steve Crawford. Dykstra connected with a man aboard in the seventh, also off Crawford, as his drive to right field deflected off Evans' glove and sailed over the wall. Winning pitcher Darling walked six batters in a seven-in-

ning effort, but he allowed only four hits and no runs.

Hurst's fifth-game victory, against Gooden, thrust Boston back into the Series lead and set up a Roger Clemens-vs.-Ojeda pitching matchup in Game 6. Clemens was coming off a spectacular season, one in which he had compiled a 24-4 record and set a major league mark with 20 strikeouts in a nine-inning game. In Game 2 against the Mets, he had gone against Gooden in a much-ballyhooed duel but lasted only 4⅓ innings in a Red Sox romp that Crawford wound up winning.

The hard-throwing Clemens left with a 3-2 lead in Game 6 but, of course, did not get the decision in one of the most talked-about games in Series history. As it turned out, neither he nor fire-baller Gooden (0-2 against the Sox) won a game in this classic.

The failure of Clemens and Gooden to excel in the Series drew considerable attention. So did Barrett's record-equaling total of 13 Series hits. And then there was the fact that the Mets became only the second team in World Series history to lose the first two games at home and rally for the championship.

But when it comes to drawing attention, it would be difficult to match what transpired in the last half of the 10th inning of Game 6 of the 1986 World Series.

Indeed, Rod Serling couldn't have written a more imaginative script.

Boston										
Boston............0 0 0 0 0 0 1 0 0—1
New York.........0 0 0 0 0 0 0 0 0—0

Boston	IP.	H.	R.	ER.	BB.	SO.
Hurst (W)	8	4	0	0	4	8
Schiraldi (S)	1	0	0	0	1	1

New York	IP.	H.	R.	ER.	BB.	SO.
Darling (L)	7	3	1	0	3	8
McDowell	2	2	0	0	2	0

Game-winning RBI—None.

aRan for Teufel in seventh. bStruck out for Darling in seventh. cFlied out for Hurst in ninth. dStruck out for Santana in ninth. E—Teufel. DP—Boston 1, New York 1. LOB—Boston 8, New York 8. SB—Wilson, Strawberry. SH—Santana. WP—Darling 2. U—Kibler (N.L.) plate, Evans (A.L.) first, Wendelstedt (N.L.) second, Brinkman (A.L.) third, Montague (N.L.) left and Ford (A.L.) right. T—2:59. A—55,076.

Game 2
Sunday, October 19, At New York

Boston	AB.	R.	H.	RBI.	PO.	A.
Boggs, 3b	5	1	2	2	0	4
Barrett, 2b	5	0	2	1	0	1
Buckner, 1b	5	0	2	1	6	1
bStapleton, 1b	1	0	0	0	1	1
Rice, lf	6	2	3	0	2	0
Evans, rf	4	2	2	2	3	0
Gedman, c	5	0	1	0	8	1
Henderson, cf	5	2	3	2	4	0
Owen, ss	4	1	3	1	1	1
dRomero, ss	0	0	0	0	0	0
Clemens, p	1	1	0	0	1	1
Crawford, p	1	0	0	0	0	0
aGreenwell	1	0	0	0	0	0
Stanley, p	1	0	0	0	1	0
Totals	44	9	18	9	27	10

New York	AB.	R.	H.	RBI.	PO.	A.
Dykstra, cf	3	0	1	0	2	0
Backman, 2b	3	1	2	1	2	4
Hernandez, 1b	4	0	1	1	5	1
Carter, c	4	0	1	1	12	0
Strawberry, rf	4	0	0	0	2	0
Heep, lf	2	0	0	0	1	0
Aguilera, p	0	0	0	0	0	0
Orosco, p	0	0	0	0	0	0
cMazzilli	1	0	0	0	0	0
Fernandez, p	0	0	0	0	0	0
Sisk, p	0	0	0	0	0	0
Johnson, 3b	4	0	0	0	1	0
Santana, ss	4	1	2	0	1	3
Gooden, p	2	1	1	0	0	0
Wilson, lf	2	0	0	0	1	0
Totals	33	3	8	3	27	8

Boston...........0 0 3 1 2 0 2 0 1—9
New York........0 0 2 0 1 0 0 0 0—3

Boston	IP.	H.	R.	ER.	BB.	SO.
Clemens	4⅓	5	3	3	4	3
Crawford (W)	1⅔	1	0	0	0	2
Stanley (S)	3	2	0	0	1	3

New York	IP.	H.	R.	ER.	BB.	SO.
Gooden (L)	5	8	6	5	2	6
Aguilera	1*	5	2	2	1	1
Orosco	2	2	0	0	0	3
Fernandez	⅓	3	1	1	0	1
Sisk	⅔	0	0	0	1	1

*Pitched to five batters in seventh.

Game-winning RBI—Boggs.

aStruck out for Crawford in seventh. bRan for Buckner in eighth. cFlied out for Orosco in eighth. dRan for Owen in ninth. E—Hernandez. DP—New York 1. LOB—Boston 13, New York 9. 2B—Boggs 2. HR—Henderson, Evans. SH—Dykstra, Clemens. U—Evans (A.L.) plate, Wendelstedt (N.L.) first, Brinkman (A.L.) second, Montague (N.L.) third, Ford (A.L.) left and Kibler (N.L.) right. T—3:36. A—55,063.

Game 1
Saturday, October 18, At New York

Boston	AB.	R.	H.	RBI.	PO.	A.
Boggs, 3b	4	0	0	0	1	2
Barrett, 2b	4	0	1	0	2	3
Buckner, 1b	4	0	1	0	4	0
Stapleton, 1b	0	0	0	0	0	1
Rice, lf	2	1	1	0	2	0
Evans, rf	3	0	0	0	2	0
Gedman, c	4	0	0	0	9	0
Henderson, cf	4	0	2	0	5	0
Owen, ss	2	0	0	0	2	0
Hurst, p	3	0	0	0	0	2
cGreenwell	1	0	0	0	0	0
Schiraldi, p	0	0	0	0	0	0
Totals	31	1	5	0	27	8

New York	AB.	R.	H.	RBI.	PO.	A.
Wilson, lf	4	0	1	0	1	0
McDowell, p	0	0	0	0	1	2
Dykstra, cf	3	0	0	0	4	0
Hernandez, 1b	3	0	0	0	7	0
Carter, c	4	0	1	0	9	0
Strawberry, rf	2	0	0	0	2	0
Knight, 3b	3	0	0	0	1	2
Teufel, 2b	3	0	2	0	1	1
aBackman, 2b	1	0	0	0	0	0
Santana, ss	3	0	0	0	3	2
dHeep	1	0	0	0	0	0
Darling, p	2	0	0	0	0	1
bMitchell, lf	1	0	0	0	0	1
Totals	29	0	4	0	27	10

Game 3
Tuesday, October 21, At Boston

New York	AB.	R.	H.	RBI.	PO.	A.
Dykstra, cf	5	2	4	1	0	0
Backman, 2b	5	1	1	0	2	3
Hernandez, 1b	4	1	2	0	11	1
Carter, c	5	1	2	3	7	1
Strawberry, rf	4	1	1	0	2	0
Knight, 3b	4	0	1	1	2	2
Heep, dh	3	0	1	2	0	0
aMitchell	0	0	0	0	0	0
bMazzilli	1	0	0	0	0	0
Wilson, lf	4	0	0	0	1	0
Santana, ss	4	1	1	0	1	5
Ojeda, p	0	0	0	0	0	2
McDowell, p	0	0	0	0	1	1
Totals	39	7	13	7	27	15

Boston	AB.	R.	H.	RBI.	PO.	A.
Boggs, 3b	3	0	1	0	0	2
Barrett, 2b	4	0	2	1	4	5
Buckner, 1b	4	0	0	0	9	2
Rice, lf	3	0	0	0	1	1
Baylor, dh	4	0	1	0	0	0
Evans, rf	4	0	0	0	2	0
Gedman, c	4	0	0	0	4	1
Henderson, cf	2	1	1	0	4	0
Owen, ss	3	0	0	0	2	3
Boyd, p	0	0	0	0	1	0
Sambito, p	0	0	0	0	0	0
Stanley, p	0	0	0	0	0	1
Totals	31	1	5	1	27	15

New York	4 0 0	0 0 0	2 1 0—7
Boston	0 0 1	0 0 0	0 0 0—1

New York	IP.	H.	R.	ER.	BB.	SO.
Ojeda (W)	7	5	1	1	3	6
McDowell	2	0	0	0	0	0

Boston	IP.	H.	R.	ER.	BB.	SO.
Boyd (L)	7	9	6	6	1	3
Sambito	0*	2	1	1	0	0
Stanley	2	2	0	0	0	1

*Pitched to two batters in eighth.

Game-winning RBI—Dykstra.

aAnnounced as pinch-hitter for Heep in eighth. bGrounded out for Mitchell in eighth. DP—Boston 1, New York 1. LOB—New York 6, Boston 6. 2B—Carter, Baylor, Knight. HR—Dykstra. WP—Ojeda, Sambito. PB—Gedman. U—Wendelstedt (N.L.) plate, Brinkman (A.L.) first, Montague (N.L.) second, Ford (A.L.) third, Kibler (N.L.) left and Evans (A.L.) right. T—2:58. A—33,595.

Game 4

Wednesday, October 22, At Boston

New York	AB.	R.	H.	RBI.	PO.	A.
Dykstra, cf	5	1	1	2	3	0
Backman, 2b	4	1	2	0	4	1
Hernandez, 1b	3	0	0	0	6	0
Carter, c	4	2	3	3	5	0
Strawberry, rf	4	1	2	0	2	0
Knight, 3b	4	0	2	1	1	0
Heep, dh	4	0	0	0	0	0
Wilson, lf	4	1	2	0	3	1
Santana, ss	4	0	0	0	3	3
Darling, p	0	0	0	0	0	1
McDowell, p	0	0	0	0	0	0
Orosco, p	0	0	0	0	0	0
Totals	36	6	12	6	27	6

Boston	AB.	R.	H.	RBI.	PO.	A.
Boggs, 3b	5	0	0	0	1	1
Barrett, 2b	4	0	2	0	1	3
Buckner, 1b	5	0	0	0	11	2
Rice, lf	4	1	1	0	2	1
Baylor, dh	3	0	0	0	0	0
Evans, rf	3	1	1	1	3	0
Gedman, c	4	0	3	0	6	1
Henderson, cf	3	0	0	1	1	0
Owen, ss	1	0	0	0	1	3
aGreenwell	0	0	0	0	0	0
bRomero, ss	0	0	0	0	0	0
Nipper, p	0	0	0	0	1	2
Crawford, p	0	0	0	0	0	0
Stanley, p	0	0	0	0	0	1
Totals	32	2	7	2	27	14

New York	0 0 0	3 0 0	2 1 0—6
Boston	0 0 0	0 0 0	0 2 0—2

New York	IP.	H.	R.	ER.	BB.	SO.
Darling (W)	7	4	0	0	6	4
McDowell	⅔	3	2	2	1	0
Orosco (S)	1⅓	0	0	0	0	1

Boston	IP.	H.	R.	ER.	BB.	SO.
Nipper (L)	6	7	3	3	1	2
Crawford	2	4	3	3	0	2
Stanley	1	1	0	0	0	0

Game-winning RBI—Carter.

aWalked for Owen in eighth. bRan for Greenwell in eighth. E—Gedman. DP—Boston 3. LOB—New York 4, Boston 11. 2B—Barrett, Gedman, Strawberry, Carter, Rice. HR—Carter 2, Dykstra. SB—Backman, Wilson 2. SF—Henderson. U—Brinkman (A.L.) plate, Montague (N.L.) first, Ford (A.L.) second, Kibler (N.L.) third, Evans (A.L.) left and Wendelstedt (N.L.) right. T—3:22. A—33,920.

Game 5

Thursday, October 23, At Boston

New York	AB.	R.	H.	RBI.	PO.	A.
Dykstra, cf	5	0	1	0	1	0
Teufel, 2b	4	1	2	1	0	2
Hernandez, 1b	4	0	1	0	7	1
Carter, c	4	0	0	0	8	0
Strawberry, rf	4	0	1	0	1	0
Knight, 3b	4	0	1	0	1	0
Mitchell, dh	4	0	1	0	0	0
Wilson, lf	4	1	2	0	4	0
Santana, ss	2	0	1	1	1	1
Gooden, p	0	0	0	0	1	2
Fernandez, p	0	0	0	0	0	0
Totals	35	2	10	2	24	6

Boston	AB.	R.	H.	RBI.	PO.	A.
Boggs, 3b	5	0	2	0	1	6
Barrett, 2b	4	0	2	0	3	5
Buckner, 1b	5	1	1	0	9	1
Stapleton, 1b	0	0	0	0	2	0
Rice, lf	3	1	2	0	2	0
Baylor, dh	3	1	1	1	0	0
Evans, rf	4	0	2	1	2	0
Gedman, c	4	0	0	0	6	0
Henderson, cf	4	1	2	1	0	0
Owen, ss	3	0	0	1	1	1
Hurst, p	0	0	0	0	1	0
Totals	35	4	12	4	27	13

New York	0 0 0	0 0 0	0 1 1—2
Boston	0 1 1	0 2 0	0 0 x—4

New York	IP.	H.	R.	ER.	BB.	SO.
Gooden (L)	4*	9	4	3	2	3
Fernandez	4	3	0	0	0	5

Boston	IP.	H.	R.	ER.	BB.	SO.
Hurst (W)	9	10	2	2	1	6

*Pitched to three batters in fifth.

Game-winning RBI—Owen.

E—Santana. DP—Boston 1. LOB—New York 8, Boston 11. 2B—Teufel, Henderson, Barrett, Wilson. 3B—Henderson, Rice. HR—Teufel. SH—Santana. SF—Owen. HBP—By Gooden (Baylor). U—Montague (N.L.) plate, Ford (A.L.) first, Kibler (N.L.) second, Evans (A.L.) third, Wendelstedt (N.L.) left and Brinkman (A.L.) right. T—3:09. A—34,010.

Game 6

Saturday, October 25, At New York

Boston	AB.	R.	H.	RBI.	PO.	A.
Boggs, 3b	5	2	3	0	1	0
Barrett, 2b	4	1	3	2	1	4
Buckner, 1b	5	0	0	0	5	0
Rice, lf	5	0	0	0	5	0
Evans, rf	4	0	1	2	1	0
Gedman, c	5	0	1	0	9	0
Henderson, cf	5	1	2	1	5	0
Owen, ss	4	1	3	0	2	2
Clemens, p	3	0	0	0	0	1
bGreenwell	1	0	0	0	0	0
Schiraldi, p	1	0	0	0	0	1
Stanley, p	0	0	0	0	0	0
Totals	42	5	13	5	29	8

New York	AB.	R.	H.	RBI.	PO.	A.
Dykstra, cf	4	0	0	0	4	0
Backman, 2b	4	0	1	0	0	4
Hernandez, 1b	4	0	1	0	6	1
Carter, c	4	1	1	1	9	0
Strawberry, rf	2	1	0	0	5	0
Aguilera, p	0	0	0	0	0	0
eMitchell	1	1	1	0	0	0
Knight, 3b	4	2	2	2	0	0
Wilson, lf	5	0	1	0	2	1
Santana, ss	1	0	0	0	0	1
aHeep	1	0	0	0	0	0
Elster, ss	1	0	0	0	3	3
dJohnson, ss	1	0	0	0	0	0
Ojeda, p	2	0	0	0	0	0
McDowell, p	0	0	0	0	0	1
Orosco, p	0	0	0	0	0	0
cMazzilli, rf	2	1	1	0	1	0
Totals	36	6	8	3	30	11

Boston	1 1 0	0 0 0	1 0 0	2—5
New York	0 0 0	0 2 0	0 1 0	3—6

Two out when winning run scored.

Boston	IP.	H.	R.	ER.	BB.	SO.
Clemens	7	4	2	1	2	8
Schiraldi (L)	2⅔	4	4	3	2	1
Stanley	0*	0	0	0	0	0

New York	IP.	H.	R.	ER.	BB.	SO.
Ojeda	6	8	2	2	2	3
McDowell	1⅔	2	1	0	3	1
Orosco	⅓	0	0	0	0	0
Aguilera (W)	2	3	2	2	0	3

*Pitched to one batter in tenth.

Game-winning RBI—None.

aGrounded into double play for Santana in fifth. bStruck out for Clemens in eighth. cSingled for Orosco in eighth. dStruck out for Elster in ninth. eSingled for Aguilera in tenth. E—Buckner, Evans, Gedman, Knight, Elster. DP—Boston 1, New York 1. LOB—Boston 14, New York 8. 2B—Evans, Boggs. HR—Henderson. SB—Strawberry 2. SH—Owen, Dykstra, Backman. SF—Carter. HBP—By Aguilera (Buckner). WP—Stanley. U—Ford (A.L.) plate, Kibler (N.L.) first, Evans (A.L.) second, Wendelstedt (N.L.) third, Brinkman (A.L.) left and Montague (N.L.) right. T—4:02. A—55,078.

Game 7

Monday, October 27, At New York

Boston	AB.	R.	H.	RBI.	PO.	A.
Boggs, 3b	4	0	1	1	0	0
Barrett, 2b	5	0	1	0	2	4
Buckner, 1b	4	1	2	0	9	1
Rice, lf	4	1	2	0	2	0
Evans, rf	4	1	2	3	3	1
Gedman, c	4	1	1	1	4	0
Henderson, cf	2	1	0	0	3	0
Owen, ss	3	0	0	0	1	3
eBaylor	1	0	0	0	0	0
Nipper, p	0	0	0	0	0	0
Crawford, p	0	0	0	0	0	0
Hurst, p	0	0	0	0	0	1
cArmas	1	0	0	0	0	0
Schiraldi, p	0	0	0	0	0	0
Sambito, p	0	0	0	0	0	0
Stanley, p	0	0	0	0	0	0
Romero, ss	1	0	0	0	0	1
Totals	33	5	9	5	24	11

New York	AB.	R.	H.	RBI.	PO.	A.
Wilson, cf-lf	3	1	1	0	3	0
Teufel, 2b	2	0	0	0	0	0
bBackman, 2b	1	1	0	0	1	1
Hernandez, 1b	4	0	1	3	6	0
Carter, c	4	0	0	1	7	0
Strawberry, rf	4	1	1	1	5	0
Knight, 3b	4	2	3	1	0	2
Mitchell, lf	2	0	0	0	0	0
dDykstra, cf	2	1	1	0	0	0
Santana, ss	3	1	1	1	2	2
Darling, p	1	0	0	0	0	1
Fernandez, p	0	0	0	0	0	0
aMazzilli	1	1	1	0	0	0
McDowell, p	0	0	0	0	0	0
Orosco, p	1	0	1	1	0	0
Totals	32	8	10	8	27	7

Boston	0 3 0	0 0 0	0 2 0—5
New York	0 0 0	0 0 3	3 2 x—8

Boston	IP.	H.	R.	ER.	BB.	SO.
Hurst	6	4	3	3	1	3
Schiraldi (L)	⅓	3	3	3	0	0
Sambito	⅓	0	0	0	2	0
Stanley	⅓	0	0	0	0	0
Nipper	⅓	3	2	2	1	0
Crawford	⅔	0	0	0	0	0

New York	IP.	H.	R.	ER.	BB.	SO.
Darling	3⅔	6	3	3	1	0
Fernandez	2⅓	0	0	0	1	4
McDowell (W)	1*	3	2	2	0	1
Orosco (S)	2	0	0	0	0	2

*Pitched to three batters in eighth.

Game winning RBI—Knight.

aSingled for Fernandez in sixth. bRan for Teufel in sixth. cStruck out for Hurst in seventh. dSingled for Mitchell in seventh. eGrounded out for Owen in eighth. LOB—Boston 6, New York 7. 2B—Evans. HR—Evans, Gedman, Knight, Strawberry. SH—Hurst 2, McDowell. SF—Hernandez. HBP—By Darling (Henderson), by Crawford (Wilson). WP—Schiraldi. U—Kibler (N.L.) plate, Evans (A.L.) first, Wendelstedt (N.L.) second, Brinkman (A.L.) third, Montague (N.L.) left and Ford (A.L.) right. T—3:11. A—55,032.

COMPOSITE BATTING AVERAGES

New York Mets

Player-Position	G.	AB.	R.	H.	2B.	3B.	HR.	RBI.	BA.
Orosco, p	4	1	0	1	0	0	0	1	1.000
Gooden, p	2	2	1	1	0	0	0	0	.500
Teufel, 2b	3	9	1	4	1	0	1	1	.444
Mazzilli, ph-rf	4	5	2	2	0	0	0	0	.400
Knight, 3b	6	23	4	9	1	0	1	5	.391
Backman, pr-2b	6	18	4	6	0	0	0	1	.333
Dykstra, cf-ph	7	27	4	8	0	0	2	3	.296
Carter, c	7	29	4	8	2	0	2	9	.276
Wilson, lf-cf	7	26	3	7	1	0	0	0	.269
Santana, ss	7	20	3	5	0	0	0	2	.250
Mitchell, ph-lf-dh	5	8	1	2	0	0	0	0	.250
Hernandez, 1b	7	26	1	6	0	0	0	4	.231
Strawberry, rf	7	24	4	5	1	0	1	1	.208
Heep, ph-lf-dh	5	11	0	1	0	0	0	2	.091
Aguilera, p	2	0	0	0	0	0	0	0	.000
Fernandez, p	3	0	0	0	0	0	0	0	.000
McDowell, p	5	0	0	0	0	0	0	0	.000
Sisk, p	1	0	0	0	0	0	0	0	.000
Elster, ss	1	1	0	0	0	0	0	0	.000
Ojeda, p	2	2	0	0	0	0	0	0	.000
Darling, p	3	3	0	0	0	0	0	0	.000
Johnson, 3b-ph-ss	2	5	0	0	0	0	0	0	.000
Totals	7	240	32	65	6	0	7	29	.271

Boston Red Sox

Player-Position	G.	AB.	R.	H.	2B.	3B.	HR.	RBI.	BA.
Barrett, 2b	7	30	1	13	2	0	0	4	.433
Henderson, cf	7	25	6	10	1	1	2	5	.400
Rice, lf	7	27	6	9	1	1	0	0	.333
Evans, rf	7	26	4	8	2	0	2	9	.308
Owen, ss	7	20	2	6	0	0	0	2	.300
Boggs, 3b	7	31	3	9	3	0	0	3	.290
Gedman, c	7	30	1	6	1	0	1	1	.200
Buckner, 1b	7	32	2	6	0	0	0	1	.188
Baylor, dh-ph	4	11	1	2	1	0	0	1	.182
Boyd, p	1	0	0	0	0	0	0	0	.000
Nipper, p	2	0	0	0	0	0	0	0	.000
Sambito, p	2	0	0	0	0	0	0	0	.000
Armas, ph	1	1	0	0	0	0	0	0	.000
Crawford, p	3	1	0	0	0	0	0	0	.000
Romero, pr-ss	3	1	0	0	0	0	0	0	.000
Schiraldi, p	3	1	0	0	0	0	0	0	.000
Stanley, p	5	1	0	0	0	0	0	0	.000
Stapleton, 1b-pr	3	1	0	0	0	0	0	0	.000
Greenwell, ph	4	3	0	0	0	0	0	0	.000
Hurst, p	3	3	0	0	0	0	0	0	.000
Clemens, p	2	4	1	0	0	0	0	0	.000
Totals	7	248	27	69	11	2	5	26	.278

COMPOSITE PITCHING AVERAGES

New York Mets

Pitcher	G.	IP.	H.	R.	ER.	BB.	SO.	W.	L.	ERA.
Orosco	4	5⅔	2	0	0	0	6	0	0	0.00
Sisk	1	⅔	0	0	0	1	1	0	0	0.00
Fernandez	3	6⅔	6	1	1	1	10	0	0	1.35
Darling	3	17⅔	13	4	3	10	12	1	1	1.53
Ojeda	2	13	13	3	3	5	9	1	0	2.08
McDowell	5	7⅓	10	5	4	6	2	1	0	4.91
Gooden	2	9	17	10	8	4	9	0	2	8.00
Aguilera	2	3	8	4	4	1	4	1	0	12.00
Totals	7	63	69	27	23	28	53	4	3	3.29

Boston Red Sox

Pitcher	G.	IP.	H.	R.	ER.	BB.	SO.	W.	L.	ERA.
Stanley	5	6⅓	5	0	0	1	4	0	0	0.00
Hurst	3	23	18	5	5	6	17	2	0	1.96
Clemens	2	11⅓	9	5	4	6	11	0	0	3.18
Crawford	3	4⅓	5	3	3	0	4	1	0	6.23
Nipper	2	6⅓	10	5	5	2	2	0	1	7.11
Boyd	1	7	9	6	6	1	3	0	1	7.71
Schiraldi	3	4	7	7	6	3	2	0	2	13.50
Sambito	2	⅓	2	1	1	2	0	0	0	27.00
Totals	7	62⅔	65	32	30	21	43	3	4	4.31

1987
MINNESOTA TWINS
VS.
ST. LOUIS CARDINALS

"They'd probably finish fourth in either the National League East or the American League East," St. Louis Manager Whitey Herzog said of the 1987 Minnesota Twins, who finished atop the supposedly inferior A.L. West with a mediocre 85-77 record.

The Twins won their divisional crown despite compiling a 29-52 road mark during the '87 American League regular season. Furthermore, the Twins were victorious only nine times away from home after the All-Star Game and they played sub-.500 baseball overall (36-37) following the midsummer classic.

Herzog's Cardinals, on the other hand, went 95-67 and ruled the roost in the N.L. East. And, as fate would have it, Herzog's club and Manager Tom Kelly's Twins wound up as opponents in the 84th World Series.

While St. Louis entered the Series with manpower problems—slugger Jack Clark was disabled because of an ankle injury and a rib ailment would curtail Terry Pendleton's playing time—many so-called experts still favored the Cardinals because of their post-season experience, pitching depth, speed and year-long knack of overcoming injuries. The quality of the Cards' opposition and the presence of Herzog, acknowledged as perhaps the best manager in the game today, were additional factors.

The flip side of the Twins' road futility was the fact that Kelly's club was very good at home. Very, very good. It had posted the best home-field record in the major leagues in 1987, a sparkling 56-25 mark. And wouldn't you know it, the World Series would begin in the A.L. champion's home park and four games would be played at that site if the fall

Happy Minnesota Twins players celebrate their 1987 World Series title.

classic were to go the distance.

That site in '87 was the Hubert H. Humphrey Metrodome, a baseball purist's nightmare with its Teflon roof, lighting and acoustical problems, artifical turf and trash-can lining serving as a right-field wall. Yes, for the first time, World Series games were to be played *indoors*.

While the cozy Metrodome couldn't hold long fly balls (the homer-happy Twins "have a very good ball club—in their park," Herzog said pointedly), it was very good at holding crowd noise. And the combination of Minnesota batting power and Minnesota fans' lung power set Herzog and the Cardinals on their collective ear in a hurry.

In the Series opener, Minnesota's Dan Gladden capped a seven-run fourth inning with a bases-loaded home run off reliever Bob Forsch and Steve Lombardozzi cracked a two-run homer against Forsch in the fifth. Frank Viola pitched five-hit ball over eight innings, and the Twins were off and

running with a 10-1 victory.

The fourth inning proved the Cardinals' undoing again in Game 2. Randy Bush belted a two-run double and Tim Laudner contributed a two-run single—both blows came off starter Danny Cox —as the Twins erupted for six runs. Bert Blyleven worked seven innings and was an 8-4 winner for Minnesota, which got a bases-empty homer from Gary Gaetti in the second inning, a solo shot from Laudner in the sixth and vocal support from its fans throughout.

The speed-oriented Cardinals, confident they would prosper in their own, large ball park, made noise of their own after escaping the Metrodome din. They won Games 3, 4 and 5 in St. Louis, where baseball is played *outdoors* (one plus for the purist) but on artificial surface and in such a roomy stadium that the game being played on the floor below often resembles a track meet (a couple of minuses for the purist).

In Game 3, Twins Manager Kelly excused rookie Les Straker after six innings of shutout pitching—Straker led, 1-0—and turned things over to Juan Berenguer. The Cards hammered Berenguer for three runs and four hits in one-third inning, and St. Louis lefthander John Tudor emerged a 3-1 winner. The fourth game was a 1-1 tie in the fourth when Tom Lawless, who had only two hits all season and only one home run in a 215-game major league career, clubbed a three-run homer off Viola that sent the Cardinals winging to a 7-2 victory. And a Cox-Blyleven duel in Game 5 went St. Louis' way when Curt Ford snapped a scoreless tie with a two-run single in the sixth inning. An error by Twins shortstop Greg Gagne on the next play

added a third run, and the Cards were en route to a 4-2 triumph.

Herzog's team now was within one victory of the Series crown, but to clinch it the Cards would have to score a breakthrough at the Metrodome.

Tommy Herr hit a first-inning homer for the Cardinals in Game 6 at Minneapolis, and the Cards built a 5-2 lead after 4½ innings. Tudor, who had made a strong comeback from an early-season leg fracture, seemed just the man to close it out for St. Louis—but it wasn't to be. Kirby Puckett started the Twins' fifth with a single, Gaetti doubled him home and Don Baylor followed with a home run. The shellshocked Cards were suddenly in a 5-5 standoff. And before the inning came to an end, Lombardozzi singled in the go-ahead run off reliever Rick Horton.

Things only got worse for the visitors as both the decibel level and the Twins' run total rose dramatically. With lefthanded-hitting Kent Hrbek coming up with the bases loaded and two out in the Twins' sixth, Herzog removed righthander Forsch and brought in lefthander Ken Dayley. Hrbek walloped Dayley's first pitch over the center-field fence. The grand slam made it 10-5, Minnesota. It wound up 11-5.

First-game pitching rivals Viola and Joe Magrane (a rookie) were paired again in Game 7, which evolved into such an outstanding game that everyone forgot—if only temporarily—just where all this great baseball was being played. After Tony Pena and Steve Lake singled home Cardinal runs in the second inning at the Metrodome, St. Louis left fielder Vince Coleman threw out two runners at the plate—Baylor in the second inning and Gaetti in the fifth—to keep the National Leaguers in business.

Catcher Lake, who had held the ball despite being crashed into by Gaetti, had made another key play earlier in the fifth, nailing Puckett when the Twins' star tried to advance from second to third after a Cox pitch bounced in front of the plate. Despite the Cards' stellar defensive work,

Minnesota nevertheless had forged a 2-2 tie on Lombardozzi's second-inning RBI single and Puckett's run-scoring double three innings later.

After the Twins loaded the bases in the sixth with three walks (two of which were yielded by losing pitcher Cox), Gagne hit a two-out grounder down the third-base line that went for a tie-breaking base hit when Lawless was unable to throw him out. And Gladden rapped an eighth-inning RBI double that pushed Minnesota's lead to 4-2 in a game that had few misplays of any kind (unless you count blown calls by umpires, mistakes that occurred with unusual frequency and were caught by the television cameras).

Viola had pitched well through eight innings, allowing only six hits, walking no one and striking out seven. But Kelly went to relief ace Jeff Reardon to open the ninth, and Reardon responded with a 1-2-3 inning.

In the first Series featuring home-field victories throughout, the Minnesota Twins won out. Maybe, as Herzog suggested, Minnesota wouldn't have finished higher than fourth if forced to compete season-long in the East Division of either league.

While Herzog dealt in what if, the 1987 Twins were content to bask in what was. And they were A.L. West titlists, American League pennant-winners and World Series champions.

Game 1
Saturday, October 17, At Minnesota

St. Louis	AB.	R.	H.	RBI.	PO.	A.
Coleman, lf	4	0	0	0	0	0
Smith, ss	4	0	0	0	1	4
Herr, 2b	4	0	0	0	3	3
Lindeman, 1b	4	1	2	0	11	0
McGee, cf	3	0	2	0	2	1
Pena, c	3	0	1	1	2	0
Lake, c	0	0	0	0	1	0
Oquendo, rf	3	0	0	0	4	0
Pagnozzi, dh	3	0	1	0	0	0
Lawless, 3b	3	0	0	0	1	4
Magrane, p	0	0	0	0	0	0
Forsch, p	0	0	0	0	0	0
Horton, p	0	0	0	0	0	0
Totals	31	1	5	1	24	12

Minnesota	AB.	R.	H.	RBI.	PO.	A.
Gladden, lf	4	1	2	5	3	0
Gagne, ss	5	0	0	0	1	5
Puckett, cf	5	0	1	0	1	0
Gaetti, 3b	5	1	2	0	0	4
Baylor, dh	5	1	1	0	0	0
Brunansky, rf	3	1	1	0	1	0
Davidson, rf	0	0	0	0	0	0
Hrbek, 1b	2	2	1	2	12	0
Larkin, 1b	0	0	0	0	1	0
Lombardozzi, 2b	3	3	2	2	3	2
Laudner, c	3	1	1	1	5	0
Viola, p	0	0	0	0	0	4
Atherton, p	0	0	0	0	0	0
Totals	35	10	11	10	27	15

St. Louis .... 0 1 0 0 0 0 0 0 0— 1
Minnesota .... 0 0 0 7 2 0 1 0 x—10

St. Louis	IP.	H.	R.	ER.	BB.	SO.
Magrane (L)	3*	4	5	5	4	1
Forsch	3	4	4	4	2	0
Horton	2	3	1	1	0	1

Minnesota	IP.	H.	R.	ER.	BB.	SO.
Viola (W)	8	5	1	1	0	5
Atherton	1	0	0	0	0	0

*Pitched to five batters in fourth.

Game-winning RBI—Hrbek.

E—Lawless. DP—Minnesota 1, St. Louis 1. LOB—St. Louis 3, Minnesota 7. 2B—Lindeman, Gaetti, Gladden. HR—Gladden, Lombardozzi. SB—Gladden. U—Phillips (A.L.) plate, Weyer (N.L.) first, Kosc (A.L.) second, McSherry (N.L.) third, Kaiser (A.L.) left and Tata (N.L.) right. T—2:39. A—55,171.

Game 2
Sunday, October 18, At Minnesota

St. Louis	AB.	R.	H.	RBI.	PO.	A.
Coleman, lf	4	1	1	0	1	0
Smith, ss	4	0	1	0	1	2
Herr, 2b	4	0	0	0	1	3
Driessen, 1b	4	1	1	1	10	0
McGee, cf	4	0	1	1	4	0
Pendleton, dh	4	1	1	0	0	0
Ford, rf	3	1	2	0	2	0
Oquendo, 3b	4	0	1	0	0	3
Pena, c	4	0	1	2	5	1
Cox, p	0	0	0	0	0	0
Tunnell, p	0	0	0	0	0	1
Dayley, p	0	0	0	0	0	0
Worrell, p	0	0	0	0	0	0
Totals	35	4	9	4	24	10

Minnesota	AB.	R.	H.	RBI.	PO.	A.
Gladden, lf	5	0	1	1	3	0
Gagne, ss	4	0	1	1	0	3
Puckett, cf	4	1	1	0	2	0
Hrbek, 1b	3	1	1	0	11	0
Gaetti, 3b	3	2	2	1	1	1
Bush, dh	3	1	1	2	0	0
aLarkin	1	0	0	0	0	0
Brunansky, rf	3	1	0	0	3	0
Lombardozzi, 2b	3	0	0	0	1	4
bSmalley	1	0	1	0	0	0
cNewman, 2b	0	0	0	0	0	0
Laudner, c	3	2	2	3	8	0
Blyleven, p	0	0	0	0	0	0
Berenguer, p	0	0	0	0	0	0
Reardon, p	0	0	0	0	0	0
Totals	33	8	10	8	27	9

St. Louis .... 0 0 0 0 1 0 1 2 0—4
Minnesota .... 0 1 0 6 0 1 0 0 x—8

St. Louis	IP.	H.	R.	ER.	BB.	SO.
Cox (L)	3⅔	6	7	7	2	3
Tunnell	2⅓	3	1	1	1	1
Dayley	1⅓	0	0	0	0	1
Worrell	⅔	1	0	0	1	0

Minnesota	IP.	H.	R.	ER.	BB.	SO.
Blyleven (W)	7	6	2	2	1	8
Berenguer	1	3	2	2	0	0
Reardon	1	0	0	0	0	0

Game-winning RBI—Gaetti.

aFlied out for Bush in eighth. bDoubled for Lombardozzi in eighth. cRan for Smalley in eighth. LOB—St. Louis 5, Minnesota 5. 2B—Bush, Gagne, Driessen, Smalley. HR—Gaetti, Laudner. SB—Coleman. WP—Cox. U—Weyer (N.L.) plate, Kosc (A.L.) first, McSherry (N.L.) second, Kaiser (A.L.) third, Tata (N.L.) left and Phillips (A.L.) right. T—2:42. A—55,257.

Game 3
Tuesday, October 20, At St. Louis

Minnesota	AB.	R.	H.	RBI.	PO.	A.
Gladden, lf	4	0	1	0	1	0
Gagne, ss	3	1	0	0	1	3
Puckett, cf	3	0	1	0	4	0
Gaetti, 3b	4	0	0	0	0	2
Brunansky, rf	4	0	1	1	0	0
Hrbek, 1b	4	0	0	0	10	0
Laudner, c	3	0	2	0	5	1
cBush	1	0	0	0	0	0
Lombardozzi, 2b	3	0	0	0	3	5
Straker, p	2	0	0	0	0	0
aLarkin	1	0	0	0	0	0
Berenguer, p	0	0	0	0	0	0
Schatzeder, p	0	0	0	0	0	0
Totals	32	1	5	1	24	11

St. Louis	AB.	R.	H.	RBI.	PO.	A.
Coleman, lf	4	1	1	2	1	0
Smith, ss	4	0	2	1	1	0
Herr, 2b	4	0	1	0	3	1
Driessen, 1b	4	0	0	0	6	0
Worrell, p	0	0	0	0	0	0
McGee, cf	4	0	2	0	4	0
Ford, rf	4	0	1	0	1	0
Oquendo, 3b	3	1	1	0	1	1
Pena, c	2	1	1	0	9	0
Tudor, p	2	0	0	0	0	0
aPendleton	1	0	0	0	0	0
Lindeman, 1b	0	0	0	0	1	0
Totals	31	3	9	3	27	7

Minnesota .... 0 0 0 0 0 1 0 0 0—1
St. Louis .... 0 0 0 0 0 0 3 0 x—3

Minnesota	IP.	H.	R.	ER.	BB.	SO.
Straker	6	4	0	0	2	4
Berenguer (L)	⅓	4	3	3	0	0
Schatzeder	1⅔	1	0	0	0	1

St. Louis	IP.	H.	R.	ER.	BB.	SO.
Tudor (W)	7	4	1	1	2	7
Worrell (S)	2	1	0	0	0	1

Game-winning RBI—Coleman.

aGrounded out for Straker in seventh. bSacrificed for Tudor in seventh. cFlied out for Laudner in ninth. E—Pena, Gagne. DP—Minnesota 1. 2B—McGee, Laudner, Coleman. 3B—Puckett. SB—Coleman 2. SH—Pendleton. Balk—Straker. U—Kosc (A.L.) plate, McSherry (N.L.) first, Kaiser (A.L.) second, Tata (N.L.) third, Phillips (A.L.) left and Weyer (N.L.) right. T—2:45. A—55,347.

Game 4

Wednesday, October 21, At St. Louis

Minnesota	AB.	R.	H.	RBI.	PO.	A.
Gladden, lf	5	0	1	0	4	0
Newman, 2b	3	0	1	0	1	1
dBaylor	1	0	1	0	0	0
Puckett, cf	4	0	1	1	1	0
Gaetti, 3b	3	0	1	0	1	1
Brunansky, rf	4	0	0	0	2	0
Hrbek, 1b	4	0	1	0	7	0
Laudner, c	3	0	0	0	8	0
Butera, c	0	0	0	0	0	0
Gagne, ss	4	1	1	1	0	3
Viola, p	1	0	0	0	0	0
Schatzeder, p	0	0	0	0	0	0
aLarkin	0	1	0	0	0	0
Niekro, p	0	0	0	0	0	1
bSmalley	1	0	0	0	0	0
Frazier, p	0	0	0	0	0	1
cDavidson	1	0	0	0	0	0
Totals	34	2	7	2	24	7

St. Louis	AB.	R.	H.	RBI.	PO.	A.
Coleman, lf	4	1	1	0	3	0
Smith, ss	4	1	0	0	1	4
Herr, 2b	3	1	2	0	6	3
Lindeman, 1b	4	1	2	2	6	1
McGee, cf	4	0	2	2	1	0
Pena, c	3	1	1	0	8	0
Oquendo, rf	4	1	1	0	1	0
Lawless, 3b	4	1	1	3	0	1
Mathews, p	1	0	0	0	0	1
Forsch, p	2	0	0	0	1	0
Dayley, p	1	0	0	0	0	0
Totals	34	7	10	7	27	10

Minnesota	0 0 1 0 1 0 0 0 0—2
St. Louis	0 0 1 6 0 0 0 0 x—7

Minnesota	IP.	H.	R.	ER.	BB.	SO.
Viola (L)	3⅓	6	5	5	3	4
Schatzeder	⅔	2	2	2	1	1
Niekro	2	1	0	0	1	1
Frazier	2	1	0	0	0	2

St. Louis	IP.	H.	R.	ER.	BB.	SO.
Mathews	3⅔	2	1	1	2	3
Forsch (W)	2⅔	4	1	1	1	3
Dayley (S)	2⅔	1	0	0	0	2

Game-winning RBI—Lawless.

aWalked for Schatzeder in fifth. bReached safely on two-base error for Niekro in seventh. cFlied out for Frazier in ninth. dSingled for Newman in ninth. E—Puckett, Lindeman. DP—St. Louis 1. LOB—Minnesota 10, St. Louis 9. 2B—McGee, Coleman. HR—Gagne, Lawless. SB—Gaetti, Brunansky, Coleman. HBP—By Mathews (Gaetti), by Niekro (Lindeman), by Forsch (Puckett). WP—Mathews. U—McSherry (N.L.) plate, Kaiser (A.L.) first, Tata (N.L.) second, Phillips (A.L.) third, Weyer (N.L.) left and Kosc (A.L.) right. T—3:11. A—55,347.

Game 5

Thursday, October 22, At St. Louis

Minnesota	AB.	R.	H.	RBI.	PO.	A.
Gladden, lf	3	1	1	0	1	0
Gagne, ss	4	1	1	0	1	1
fBaylor	1	0	0	0	0	0
Puckett, cf	4	0	0	0	1	0
Hrbek, 1b	4	0	1	0	9	0
Gaetti, 3b	4	0	1	2	2	2
Brunansky, rf	4	0	1	0	1	0
Laudner, c	2	0	0	0	8	1
cNewman	1	0	0	0	0	0
Lombardozzi, 2b	2	0	1	0	1	6
dSmalley	0	0	0	0	0	0
Blyleven, p	1	0	0	0	0	1
aLarkin	1	0	0	0	0	0
Atherton, p	0	0	0	0	0	0
Reardon, p	0	0	0	0	0	0
eBush	1	0	0	0	0	0
Totals	32	2	6	2	24	11

St. Louis	AB.	R.	H.	RBI.	PO.	A.
Coleman, lf	3	2	1	0	2	0
Smith, ss	4	1	2	1	1	2
Herr, 2b	4	0	0	0	6	2
Driessen, 1b	3	1	1	0	7	1
Dayley, p	0	0	0	0	0	0
Worrell, p	0	0	0	0	0	0
McGee, cf	4	0	0	0	3	0
Ford, rf	4	0	1	2	0	0
Oquendo, 3b	4	0	2	0	0	4
Pena, c	4	0	3	0	6	0
bJohnson	0	0	0	0	0	0
Lake, c	0	0	0	0	0	0
Cox, p	2	0	0	0	1	1
Lindeman, 1b	1	0	0	0	1	0
Totals	33	4	10	3	27	10

Minnesota	0 0 0 0 0 0 0 2 0—2
St. Louis	0 0 0 0 0 3 1 0 x—4

Minnesota	IP.	H.	R.	ER.	BB.	SO.
Blyleven (L)	6	7	3	2	1	4
Atherton	⅓	0	1	1	1	0
Reardon	1⅔	3	0	0	0	3

St. Louis	IP.	H.	R.	ER.	BB.	SO.
Cox (W)	7⅓	5	2	2	3	6
Dayley	⅓	0	0	0	0	0
Worrell (S)	1⅓	1	0	0	2	0

Game-winning RBI—Ford.

aFlied out for Blyleven in seventh. bRan for Pena in eighth. cGrounded out for Laudner in ninth. dWalked for Lombardozzi in ninth. ePopped out for Reardon in ninth. fPopped out for Gagne in ninth. E—Gagne. DP—Minnesota 1. LOB—Minnesota 9, St. Louis 8. 3B—Gaetti. SB—Gladden, Coleman 2, Smith 2, Johnson. SH—Cox, Blyleven. Balk—Atherton. U—Kaiser (A.L.) plate, Tata (N.L.) first, Phillips (A.L.) second, Weyer (N.L.) third, Kosc (A.L.) left and McSherry (N.L.) right. T—3:21. A—55,347.

Game 6

Saturday, October 24, At Minnesota

St. Louis	AB.	R.	H.	RBI.	PO.	A.
Coleman, lf	5	0	0	0	1	0
Smith, ss	4	1	1	0	3	3
Herr, 2b	5	1	3	1	3	3
Driessen, 1b	2	1	1	0	4	0
bPagnozzi	1	0	0	0	0	0
Morris, rf	2	0	0	0	2	0
McGee, cf	4	1	2	1	4	0
Pendleton, dh	3	1	2	1	0	0
Ford, rf	1	0	0	0	1	0
aLindeman, rf-1b	3	0	0	0	4	0
Oquendo, 3b	3	0	1	2	0	2
Pena, c	3	0	1	0	2	0
Tudor, p	0	0	0	0	0	2
Horton, p	0	0	0	0	0	1
Forsch, p	0	0	0	0	0	0
Dayley, p	0	0	0	0	0	0
Tunnell, p	0	0	0	0	0	0
Totals	36	5	11	5	24	11

Minnesota	AB.	R.	H.	RBI.	PO.	A.
Gladden, lf	5	1	2	0	0	0
Gagne, ss	5	1	1	0	1	4
Puckett, cf	4	4	4	1	4	0
Gaetti, 3b	5	1	1	1	1	0
Baylor, dh	3	2	2	3	0	0
cBush	1	0	0	0	0	0
Brunansky, rf	4	1	1	1	5	0
Hrbek, 1b	4	1	1	4	9	1
Laudner, c	5	0	0	0	5	0
Lombardozzi, 2b	4	0	3	1	1	5
Straker, p	0	0	0	0	1	0
Schatzeder, p	0	0	0	0	0	0
Berenguer, p	0	0	0	0	0	0
Reardon, p	0	0	0	0	0	0
Totals	40	11	15	11	27	10

St. Louis	1 1 0 2 1 0 0 0 0— 5
Minnesota	2 0 0 0 4 4 0 1 x—11

St. Louis	IP.	H.	R.	ER.	BB.	SO.
Tudor (L)	4†	11	6	6	1	1
Horton	1‡	2	1	1	0	0
Forsch	⅔	0	2	2	2	0
Dayley	⅓	1	1	1	0	0
Tunnell	2	1	1	0	1	0

Minnesota	IP.	H.	R.	ER.	BB.	SO.
Straker	3*	5	4	4	1	2
Schatzeder (W)	2	1	1	1	2	1
Berenguer	3	3	0	0	0	1
Reardon	1	2	0	0	0	0

*Pitched to three batters in fourth.
†Pitched to four batters in fifth.
‡Pitched to one batter in sixth.

Game-winning RBI—Lombardozzi.

aFouled out for Ford in fourth. bFlied out for Driessen in fifth. cReached first base on error for Baylor in eighth. E—McGee, Lindeman. DP—Minnesota 1. LOB—St. Louis 8, Minnesota 9. 2B—Driessen, Lombardozzi, Gaetti. 3B—Gladden. HR—Herr, Baylor, Hrbek. SB—Puckett, Pendleton 2. SF—Oquendo. PB—Pena. U—Tata (N.L.) plate, Phillips (A.L.) first, Weyer (N.L.) second, Kosc (A.L.) third, McSherry (N.L.) left and Kaiser (A.L.) right. T—3:22. A—55,293.

Game 7

Sunday, October 25, At Minnesota

St. Louis	AB.	R.	H.	RBI.	PO.	A.
Coleman, lf	4	0	0	0	2	2
Smith, ss	4	0	0	0	0	1
Herr, 2b	4	0	1	0	1	2
Lindeman, 1b	3	1	1	0	5	1
cFord	1	0	0	0	0	0
McGee, cf	4	1	1	0	3	0
Pena, dh	3	0	2	1	0	0
Oquendo, rf	3	0	0	0	2	0
Lawless, 3b	3	0	0	0	2	1
Lake, c	3	0	1	1	8	1
Magrane, p	0	0	0	0	1	1
Cox, p	0	0	0	0	0	0
Worrell, p	0	0	0	0	0	0
Totals	32	2	6	2	24	9

Minnesota	AB.	R.	H.	RBI.	PO.	A.
Gladden, lf	5	0	1	1	0	0
Gagne, ss	5	1	2	1	2	1
Puckett, cf	4	0	2	1	4	0
Gaetti, 3b	3	0	0	0	1	5
Baylor, dh	3	0	1	0	0	0
Brunansky, rf	3	2	1	0	2	0
Hrbek, 1b	3	0	0	0	10	1
Laudner, c	3	1	2	0	7	0
Lombardozzi, 2b	2	0	1	1	0	2
aSmalley	0	0	0	0	0	0
bNewman, 2b	1	0	0	0	0	1
Viola, p	0	0	0	0	1	1
Reardon, p	0	0	0	0	0	0
Totals	32	4	10	4	27	11

St. Louis	0 2 0 0 0 0 0 0 0—2
Minnesota	0 1 0 0 1 1 0 1 x—4

St. Louis	IP.	H.	R.	ER.	BB.	SO.
Magrane	4⅓	5	2	2	1	4
Cox (L)	⅔*	2	1	1	3	0
Worrell	3	3	1	1	1	2

Minnesota	IP.	H.	R.	ER.	BB.	SO.
Viola (W)	8	6	2	2	0	7
Reardon (S)	1	0	0	0	0	0

*Pitched to two batters in sixth.

Game-winning RBI—Gagne.

aWalked for Lombardozzi in sixth. bRan for Smalley in sixth. cPopped out for Lindeman in ninth. E—Lindeman. LOB—St. Louis 3, Minnesota 10. 2B—Puckett, Pena, Gladden. SB—Gaetti, Pena. HBP—By Magrane (Baylor). U—Phillips (A.L.) plate, Weyer (N.L.) first, Kosc (A.L.) second, McSherry (N.L.) third, Kaiser (A.L.) left and Tata (N.L.) right. T—3:04. A—55,376.

COMPOSITE BATTING AVERAGES

Minnesota Twins

Player-Position	G.	AB.	R.	H.	2B.	3B.	HR.	RBI.	BA.
Smalley, ph	4	2	0	1	1	0	0	0	.500
Lombardozzi, 2b	6	17	3	7	1	0	1	4	.412
Baylor, dh-ph	5	13	3	5	0	0	1	3	.385
Puckett, cf	7	28	5	10	1	1	0	3	.357
Laudner, c	7	22	4	7	1	0	1	4	.318
Gladden, lf	7	31	3	9	2	1	1	7	.290
Gaetti, 3b	7	27	4	7	2	1	1	4	.259
Hrbek, 1b	7	24	4	5	0	0	1	6	.208
Gagne, ss	7	30	5	6	1	0	1	3	.200
Brunansky, rf	7	25	5	5	0	0	0	2	.200
Newman, pr-2b-ph	4	5	0	1	0	0	0	0	.200
Bush, dh-ph	4	6	1	1	1	0	0	2	.167
Larkin, 1b-ph	5	3	1	0	0	0	0	0	.000
Straker, p	2	2	0	0	0	0	0	0	.000
Blyleven, p	2	1	0	0	0	0	0	0	.000
Davidson, rf-ph	2	1	0	0	0	0	0	0	.000
Viola, p	3	1	0	0	0	0	0	0	.000
Atherton, p	2	0	0	0	0	0	0	0	.000
Berenguer, p	3	0	0	0	0	0	0	0	.000
Butera, c	1	0	0	0	0	0	0	0	.000
Frazier, p	1	0	0	0	0	0	0	0	.000
Niekro, p	1	0	0	0	0	0	0	0	.000
Reardon, p	4	0	0	0	0	0	0	0	.000
Schatzeder, p	3	0	0	0	0	0	0	0	.000
Totals	7	238	38	64	10	3	7	38	.269

St. Louis Cardinals

Player-Position	G.	AB.	R.	H.	2B.	3B.	HR.	RBI.	BA.
Pendleton, dh-ph	3	7	2	3	0	0	0	1	.429
Pena, c-dh	7	22	2	9	1	0	0	4	.409
McGee, cf	7	27	2	10	2	0	0	4	.370
Lindeman, 1b-ph-rf	6	15	3	5	1	0	0	2	.333
Lake, c	3	3	0	1	0	0	0	1	.333
Ford, rf-ph	5	13	1	4	0	0	0	2	.308
Herr, 2b	7	28	2	7	0	0	1	1	.250
Oquendo, rf-3b	7	24	2	6	0	0	0	2	.250
Pagnozzi, dh-ph	2	4	0	1	0	0	0	0	.250
Driessen, 1b	4	13	3	3	2	0	0	1	.231
Smith, ss	7	28	3	6	0	0	0	2	.214
Coleman, lf	7	28	5	4	2	0	0	2	.143
Lawless, 3b	3	10	1	1	0	0	1	3	.100
Cox, p	3	2	0	0	0	0	0	0	.000
Forsch, p	3	2	0	0	0	0	0	0	.000
Morris, rf	1	2	0	0	0	0	0	0	.000
Tudor, p	2	2	0	0	0	0	0	0	.000
Dayley, p	4	1	0	0	0	0	0	0	.000
Mathews, p	1	1	0	0	0	0	0	0	.000
Horton, p	2	0	0	0	0	0	0	0	.000
Johnson, pr	1	0	0	0	0	0	0	0	.000
Magrane, p	2	0	0	0	0	0	0	0	.000
Tunnell, p	2	0	0	0	0	0	0	0	.000
Worrell, p	4	0	0	0	0	0	0	0	.000
Totals	7	232	26	60	8	0	2	25	.259

COMPOSITE PITCHING AVERAGES

Minnesota Twins

Pitcher	G.	IP.	H.	R.	ER.	BB.	SO.	W.	L.	ERA.
Reardon	4	4⅔	5	0	0	0	3	0	0	0.00
Frazier	1	2	1	0	0	0	2	0	0	0.00
Niekro	1	2	1	0	0	1	1	0	0	0.00
Blyleven	2	13	13	5	4	2	12	1	1	2.77
Viola	3	19⅓	17	8	8	3	16	2	1	3.72
Straker	2	9	9	4	4	3	6	0	0	4.00
Schatzeder	3	4⅓	4	3	3	3	3	1	0	6.23
Atherton	2	1⅓	0	1	1	1	0	0	0	6.75
Berenguer	3	4⅓	10	5	5	0	1	0	1	10.38
Totals	7	60	60	26	25	13	44	4	3	3.75

St. Louis Cardinals

Pitcher	G.	IP.	H.	R.	ER.	BB.	SO.	W.	L.	ERA.
Worrell	4	7	6	1	1	4	3	0	0	1.29
Dayley	4	4⅔	2	1	1	0	3	0	0	1.93
Tunnell	2	4⅓	4	2	1	2	1	0	0	2.08
Mathews	1	3⅔	2	1	1	2	3	0	0	2.45
Tudor	2	11	15	7	7	3	8	1	1	5.73
Horton	2	3	5	2	2	0	1	0	0	6.00
Cox	3	11⅔	13	10	10	8	9	1	2	7.71
Magrane	2	7⅓	9	7	7	5	5	0	1	8.59
Forsch	3	6⅓	8	7	7	5	3	1	0	9.95
Totals	7	59	64	38	37	29	36	3	4	5.64

World Series Eligibles

Note—This list includes all players who were eligible for a World Series. When an asterisk (*) precedes a player's name, it means he never appeared in a Series game, while an asterisk (*) before a year indicates the player was eligible for that particular Series but did not play.

A

Aaron, Henry L.—Milwaukee NL 1957-58.
Abbaticchio, Edward J.—Pittsburgh NL 1909.
*Abbott, W. Glenn—Oakland AL *1974.
Abstein, William H.—Pittsburgh NL 1909.
Adair, K. Jerry—Boston AL 1967.
Adams, Charles B.—Pittsburgh NL 1909-25.
Adams, Earl J.—St. Louis NL 1930-31.
*Adams, Elvin C.—St. Louis NL *1946.
*Adams, John B.—Philadelphia NL *1915.
Adams, Spencer D.—Washington AL 1925; New York AL 1926.
Adcock, Joseph W.—Milwaukee NL 1957-58.
Agee, Tommie L.—New York NL 1969.
Agnew, Samuel—Boston AL *1916-18.
Aguilera, Richard W.—New York NL 1986.
Aikens, Willie M.—Kansas City AL 1980.
*Albosta, Edward J.—Brooklyn NL *1941.
*Alcala, Santo—Cincinnati NL *1976.
Aldridge, Victor E.—Pittsburgh NL 1925-27.
Alexander, Doyle L.—New York AL 1976.
Alexander, Grover C.—Philadelphia NL 1915; St. Louis NL 1926-28.
Alexander, Matthew—Pittsburgh NL 1979.
*Allen, Artemus W.—Cincinnati NL *1919.
Allen, John T.—New York AL 1932; Brooklyn NL 1941.
Alley, L. Eugene—Pittsburgh NL 1971.
Allison, W. Robert—Minnesota AL 1965.
*Alomar, Santos—New York AL *1976.
Alou, Felipe R.—San Francisco NL 1962.
Alou, Jesus M.—Oakland AL 1973-74.
Alou, Mateo R.—San Francisco NL 1962; Oakland AL 1972.
Altrock, Nicholas—Chicago AL 1906.
*Amalfitano, J. Joseph—New York NL *1954.
Ames, Leon—New York NL 1905-11-12.
Amoros, Edmundo—Brooklyn NL 1952-55-56.
Andersen, Larry E.—Philadelphia NL 1983.
Anderson, J. Fred—New York NL 1917.
Andrews, Ivy P.—New York AL 1937-*38.
Andrews, Michael J.—Boston AL 1967; Oakland AL 1973.
Andujar, Joaquin—St. Louis NL 1982-85.
Antonelli, John A.—New York NL 1954.
*Antonello, William J.—Brooklyn NL *1953.
Aparicio, Luis E.—Chicago AL 1959; Baltimore AL 1966.
*Appleton, Edward S.—Brooklyn NL *1916.
Archer, P. James—Detroit AL 1907; Chicago NL 1910.
*Arias, Rodolfo—Chicago AL *1959.
Armas, Antonio R.—Boston AL 1986.
Armbrister, Edison R.—Cincinnati NL 1975-*76.
Arnovich, Morris—Cincinnati NL 1940.
Arroyo, Luis E.—New York AL 1960-61-*62.
*Asbell, James M.—Chicago NL *1938.
Ashburn, Richie—Philadelphia NL 1950.
Atherton, Keith R.—Minnesota AL 1987.
*Atkins, Frank M.—Philadelphia AL *1910.
Auerbach, Frederick S.—Los Angeles NL 1974.
Auker, Elden L.—Detroit AL 1934-35.
Averill, H. Earl—Detroit AL 1940.
Avila, Roberto—Cleveland AL 1954.
*Aviles, Ramon A. A.—Philadelphia NL *1980.
Ayala, Benigno—Baltimore AL 1979-83.

B

*Babe, Loren B.—New York AL *1952.
Backman, Walter W.—New York NL 1986.
Bagby, James C., Jr.—Boston AL 1946.
Bagby, James C., Sr.—Cleveland AL 1920.
Bailey, L. Edgar—San Francisco NL 1962.
*Bailey, Robert S.—Cincinnati NL *1976.
Bair, C. Douglas—St. Louis NL 1982; Detroit AL 1984.
*Baird, Albert W.—New York NL *1917.
*Baker, Douglas L.—Detroit AL *1984.
Baker, Eugene W.—Pittsburgh NL 1960.
Baker, Floyd W.—St. Louis AL 1944.
Baker, J. Frank—Philadelphia AL 1910-11-13-14; New York AL 1921-22.
Baker, Johnnie B.—Los Angeles NL 1977-78-81.
*Baker, Thomas C.—New York NL *1937.
Baker, William P.—Cincinnati NL 1940.
Balboni, Stephen C.—Kansas City AL 1985.
Baldwin, Howard E.—New York NL 1924.
Ball, Neal—Boston AL 1912.
Ballou, N. Winford—Washington AL 1925.
Bancroft, David J.—Philadelphia NL 1915; New York NL 1921-22-23.
Bando, Salvatore L.—Oakland AL 1972-73-74.
Bankhead, Daniel R.—Brooklyn NL 1947.
Banta, John K.—Brooklyn NL 1949.
Barber, S. Turner—Chicago NL 1918.
Barbieri, James P.—Los Angeles NL 1966.
Barnes, Jesse L.—New York NL 1921-22.
Barnes, Virgil J.—New York NL *1922-23-24.
Barney, Rex—Brooklyn NL 1947-49.
Barnhart, Clyde L.—Pittsburgh NL 1925-27.
Barrett, Charles H.—St. Louis NL *1946; Boston NL 1948.
Barrett, Martin G.—Boston AL 1986.
Barry, John J.—Philadelphia AL 1910-11-13-14; Boston AL 1915-*16.
Bartell, Richard W.—New York NL 1936-37; Detroit AL 1940.
*Barton, Harry L.—Philadelphia AL *1905.
Battey, Earl J.—Chicago AL *1959; Minnesota AL 1965.
Bauer, Henry A.—New York AL 1949-50-51-52-53-55-56-57-58.
*Baumgartner, Stanwood F.—Philadelphia NL *1915.
Baylor, Donald E.—Boston AL 1986; Minnesota AL 1987.
*Beall, Walter E.—New York AL *1926.
Beauchamp, James E.—New York NL 1973.
Bearden, H. Eugene—Cleveland AL 1948.
Beattie, James L.—New York AL 1978.
Beaumont, Clarence H.—Pittsburgh NL 1903; Chicago NL 1910.
Beazley, John A.—St. Louis NL 1942-46.
*Beck, Clyde E.—Chicago NL *1929.
Becker, Beals—New York NL 1911-12; Philadelphia NL 1915.
Becker, Heinz R.—Chicago NL 1945.
*Beckendorf, Henry W.—Detroit AL *1909.
Beckwith, T. Joseph—Kansas City AL 1985.
Bedient, Hugh C.—Boston AL 1912.
Beggs, Joseph A.—Cincinnati NL 1940.
*Behney, Melvin B.—Cincinnati NL *1970.
Behrman, Henry B.—Brooklyn NL 1947.
Belanger, Mark H.—Baltimore AL 1969-70-71-79.
Belardi, Wayne—Brooklyn NL 1953.
Bell, David R.—Cincinnati NL 1961.
Bell, Gary—Boston AL 1967.
Bell, Herman S.—St. Louis NL 1926-30; New York NL 1933.
Bell, Lester R.—St. Louis NL 1926.
Bench, Johnny L.—Cincinnati NL 1970-72-75-76.
Bender, Charles A.—Philadelphia AL 1905-10-11-13-14.
Bengough, Bernard O.—New York AL *1923-*26-27-28.
Beniquez, Juan J.—Boston AL 1975.
Bentley, John N.—New York NL 1923-24.
Benton, J. Alton—Detroit AL *1940-45.
Benton, John C.—New York NL 1917.
*Benz, Joseph L.—Chicago AL *1917.
*Berardino, John—Cleveland AL *1948.
Berenguer, Juan B.—Detroit AL *1984; Minnesota AL 1987.
*Berg, Morris—Washington AL *1933.
Bergamo, August S.—St. Louis NL 1944.
Berger, Walter A.—New York NL 1937; Cincinnati NL 1939.
Bergman, David B.—Detroit AL 1984.
Bernard, Dwight V.—Milwaukee AL 1982.
Berra, Lawrence P.—New York AL 1947-49-50-51-52-53-55-56-57-58-60-61-62-63.
*Bertaina, Frank L.—Baltimore AL *1966.
Bessent, F. Donald—Brooklyn NL 1955-56.
Bevacqua, Kurt A.—San Diego NL 1984.
Bevens, Floyd C.—New York AL 1947.
Biancalana, Roland A.—Kansas City AL 1985.
Bibby, James B.—Pittsburgh NL 1979.
Bickford, Vernon E.—Boston NL 1948.
Bigbee, Carson L.—Pittsburgh NL 1925.
Billingham, John E.—Cincinnati NL 1972-75-76.
Bishop, Max F.—Philadelphia AL 1929-30-31.
*Bithorn, Hiram G.—Chicago NL *1945.
Black, Harry R.—Kansas City AL 1985.
Black, Joseph—Brooklyn NL 1952-53.
Blackwell, Ewell—New York AL 1952.
*Blackwell, Timothy P.—Boston AL *1975.
Blades, F. Raymond—St. Louis NL *1926-28-30-31.
Blair, Clarence V.—Chicago NL 1929.
Blair, Paul L.—Baltimore AL 1966-69-70-71; New York AL 1977-78.
Blake, J. Frederick—Chicago NL 1929.
Blanchard, John E.—New York AL 1960-61-62-63-64.
Blasingame, Donald L.—Cincinnati NL 1961.
Blass, Stephen R.—Pittsburgh NL 1971.
Blefary, Curtis L.—Baltimore AL 1966.
Block, Seymour—Chicago NL 1945.
Bloodworth, James H.—Philadelphia NL 1950.
Blue, Vida R.—Oakland AL 1972-73-74.
Bluege, Oswald L.—Washington AL 1924-25-33.
*Blume, Clinton W.—New York NL *1922.
Blyleven, Rikalbert—Pittsburgh NL 1979; Minnesota AL 1987.
Bochy, Bruce D.—San Diego NL 1984.
Boddicker, Michael J.—Baltimore AL 1983.
Boggs, Wade A.—Boston AL 1986.
*Boken, Robert A.—Washington AL *1933.
*Boles, Carl T.—San Francisco NL *1962.
Boley, John P.—Philadelphia AL 1929-30-31.
Bolin, Bobby D.—San Francisco NL 1962.
Bollweg, Donald R.—New York AL 1953.
Bolton, W. Clifton—Washington AL 1933.
Bongiovanni, Anthony T.—Cincinnati NL 1939.
Bonham, Ernest E.—New York AL 1941-42-43.
Booker, Gregory S.—San Diego NL 1984.
Boone, Raymond O.—Cleveland AL 1948.
Boone, Robert R.—Philadelphia NL 1980.
Borbon, Pedro R.—Cincinnati NL 1972-75-76.
Bordagaray, Stanley G.—Cincinnati NL 1939; New York AL 1941.
Borom, Edward J.—Detroit AL 1945.
Borowy, Henry L.—New York AL 1942-43; Chicago NL 1945.
Boswell, David W.—Minnesota AL 1965.
Boswell, Kenneth G.—New York NL 1969-73.
Bottomley, James L.—St. Louis NL 1926-28-30-31.
Boudreau, Louis—Cleveland AL 1948.
Bourque, Patrick D.—Oakland AL 1973.
Bouton, James A.—New York AL *1962-63-64.
Bowa, Lawrence R.—Philadelphia NL 1980.
*Bowens, Samuel E.—Baltimore AL *1966.
Bowman, Ernest F.—San Francisco NL 1962.
*Bowerman, Frank E.—New York NL *1905.
Boyd, Dennis R.—Boston AL 1986.
Boyer, Cletis L.—New York AL 1960-61-62-63-64.
Boyer, Kenton L.—St. Louis NL 1964.
*Brabender, Eugene M.—Baltimore AL *1966.
*Bradley, Hugh F.—Boston AL *1912.
Bragan, Robert R.—Brooklyn NL 1947.
Branca, Ralph T.—Brooklyn NL 1947-49-*52.

*Branch, Norman D.—New York AL *1941.
*Brandon, Chester M.—Pittsburgh NL *1909.
Bransfield, William E.—Pittsburgh NL 1903.
Braun, Stephen R.—St. Louis NL 1982-85.
Bravo, Angel A.—Cincinnati NL 1970.
*Braxton, E. Garland—New York AL *1926.
Brazle, Alpha E.—St. Louis NL 1943-46.
Brecheen, Harry D.—St. Louis NL 1943-44-46.
*Breckinridge, William R.—Philadelphia AL *1929.
*Breeding, Marvin E.—Los Angeles NL *1963.
Brennan, J. Donald—New York NL 1937.
Bresnahan, Roger P.—New York NL 1905.
*Bressler, Raymond B.—Philadelphia AL *1914; Cincinnati NL *1919.
Bressoud, Edward F.—St. Louis NL 1967.
Brett, George H.—Kansas City AL 1980-85.
Brett, Kenneth A.—Boston AL 1967; Kansas City AL *1980.
Breuer, Marvin H.—New York AL 1941-42-*43.
Brewer, James T.—Los Angeles, NL 1965-66-74.
Brickell, Frederick B.—Pittsburgh NL 1927.
*Brideweser, James E.—New York AL *1952.
*Bridges, Everett L.—Brooklyn NL *1952.
Bridges, Marshall—New York AL 1962-*63.
Bridges, Thomas J.—Detroit AL 1934-35-40-45.
Bright, Harry J.—New York AL 1963.
Briles, Nelson K.—St. Louis NL 1967-68; Pittsburgh NL 1971.
*Broaca, John J.—New York AL *1936.
Brock, Louis C.—St. Louis NL 1964-67-68.
Brookens, Thomas D.—Detroit AL 1984.
Brosnan, James P.—Cincinnati NL 1961.
*Brouhard, Mark S.—Milwaukee AL *1982.
*Brown, Carroll W.—Philadelphia AL *1913.
*Brown, Edward W.—New York NL *1921.
Brown, James R.—St. Louis NL 1942.
Brown, Mace S.—Boston AL 1946.
Brown, Mordecai P.—Chicago NL 1906-07-08-10.
Brown, Robert W.—New York AL 1947-49-50-51.
Brown, Rogers L.—New York AL 1981; San Diego NL 1984.
Brown, Thomas M.—Brooklyn NL *1947-49.
*Brown, Walter G.—New York AL *1932-*36.
Brown, W. Gates—Detroit AL 1968.
Browne, George E.—New York NL 1905.
Brummer, Glenn E.—St. Louis NL 1982.
Brunansky, Thomas A.—Minnesota AL 1987.
Brusstar, Warren S.—Philadelphia NL 1980.
Bruton, William H.—Milwaukee NL 1958.
Bryant, Claiborne H.—Chicago NL 1938.
Buchek, Gerald P.—St. Louis NL 1964.
Buckner, William J.—Los Angeles NL 1974; Boston AL 1986.
Buford, Donald A.—Baltimore AL 1969-70-71.
Buhl, Robert R.—Milwaukee NL 1957-*58.
Bumbry, Alonza B.—Baltimore AL 1979-83.
Bunker, Wallace E.—Baltimore AL 1966.
Burdette, S. Lewis—Milwaukee NL 1957-58.
Burgess, Forrest H.—Pittsburgh NL 1960.
Burke, Glenn L.—Los Angeles NL 1977.
*Burke, Robert J.—Washington AL *1933.
*Burkhart, W. Kenneth—St. Louis NL *1946.
Burleson, Richard P.—Boston AL 1975.
Burns, Edward J.—Philadelphia NL 1915.
Burns, George H.—Cleveland AL 1920; Philadelphia AL 1929.
Burns, George J.—New York NL *1912-13-17-21.
Burton, James S.—Boston AL 1975.
Bush, Guy T.—Chicago NL 1929-32.
Bush, Leslie A.—Philadelphia AL 1913-14; Boston AL 1918; New York AL 1922-23.
Bush, Owen J.—Detroit AL 1909.
Bush, R. Randall—Minnesota AL 1987.

Butera, Salvatore P.—Minnesota AL 1987.
*Buxton, Ralph X.—New York AL *1949.
Byerly, Eldred W.—St. Louis NL 1944.
Byrd, Samuel D.—New York AL 1932.
Byrne, Robert M.—Pittsburgh NL 1909; Philadelphia NL 1915; Chicago AL *1917.
Byrne, Thomas J.—New York AL *1943-49-*50-55-56-57.
Byrnes, Milton J.—St. Louis AL 1944.
Bystrom, Martin E.—Philadelphia NL 1980-83.

C

Caballero, Ralph J.—Philadelphia NL 1950.
Cadore, Leon J.—Brooklyn NL 1920.
Cady, Forrest L.—Boston AL 1912-15-16.
Caldwell, R. Michael—Milwaukee AL 1982.
Caldwell, Raymond B.—Cleveland AL 1920.
*Calmus, Richard L.—Los Angeles NL *1963.
Camilli, Adolph L.—Brooklyn NL 1941.
*Camilli, Douglas J.—Los Angeles NL *1963.
Camnitz, S. Howard—Pittsburgh NL 1909.
Campanella, Roy—Brooklyn NL 1949-52-53-55-56.
Campaneris, Dagoberto B.—Oakland AL 1972-73-74.
Campbell, Bruce D.—Detroit AL 1940.
Campbell, Paul M.—Boston AL 1946.
Campbell, William R.—St. Louis NL 1985.
Candelaria, John R.—Pittsburgh NL 1979.
*Candini, Milo C.—Philadelphia NL *1950.
*Capra, Lee W.—New York NL *1973.
Carbo, Bernardo—Cincinnati NL 1970; Boston AL 1975.
Cardenal, Jose D.—Kansas City AL 1980.
Cardenas, Leonardo A.—Cincinnati NL 1961.
Carey, Andrew A.—New York AL *1953-55-56-57-58.
Carey, Max G.—Pittsburgh NL 1925.
*Carisch, Frederick B.—Pittsburgh NL *1903.
Carleton, James O.—St. Louis NL 1934; Chicago NL 1935-38.
Carlson, Harold G.—Chicago NL 1929.
Carlton, Steven N.—St. Louis NL 1967-68; Philadelphia NL 1980-83.
*Carlyle, Roy E.—New York AL *1926.
Carrigan, William F.—Boston AL 1912-15-16.
Carroll, Clay P.—Cincinnati NL 1970-72-75.
Carroll, Thomas E.—New York AL 1955-*56.
Carter, Gary E.—New York NL 1986.
*Carter, Paul W.—Chicago NL *1918.
Casey, Hugh T.—Chicago NL *1935; Brooklyn NL 1941-47.
Cash, David—Pittsburgh NL 1971.
Cash, Norman D.—Chicago AL 1959; Detroit AL 1968.
Caster, George J.—St. Louis AL *1944; Detroit AL 1945.
Castillo, Martin H.—Detroit AL 1984.
Castillo, Robert E.—Los Angeles NL 1981.
Castleman, Clydell—New York NL 1936-*37.
*Castleman, Foster E.—New York NL *1954.
Cather, Theodore P.—Boston NL 1914.
*Causey, Cecil A.—New York NL *1921.
Cavarretta, Philip J.—Chicago NL 1935-38-45.
Cedeno, Cesar—St. Louis NL 1985.
Cepeda, Orlando M.—San Francisco NL 1962; St. Louis NL 1967-68.
Cerone, Richard A.—New York AL 1981.
Cerv, Robert H.—New York AL 1955-56-60.
Cey, Ronald C.—Los Angeles NL 1974-77-78-81.
Chacon, Elio—Cincinnati NL 1961.
Chalk, David L.—Kansas City AL 1980.
Chalmers, George W.—Philadelphia NL 1915.
Chambliss, C. Christopher—New York AL 1976-77-78.
Chance, Frank L.—Chicago NL 1906-07-08-10.
Chandler, Spurgeon F.—New York AL *1937-*38-*39-41-42-43-47.
Chaney, Darrel L.—Cincinnati NL 1970-72-75.

*Chapman, Edwin V.—Washington AL *1933.
Chapman, W. Benjamin—New York AL 1932.
Charles, Edwin D.—New York NL 1969.
Chartak, Michael G.—St. Louis AL 1944.
Cheney, Lawrence R.—Brooklyn NL 1916.
Cheney, Thomas E.—Pittsburgh NL 1960.
Chiozza, Louis P.—New York NL 1937.
Chipman, Robert H.—Chicago NL 1945.
Christenson, Larry R.—Philadelphia NL 1980.
Christman, Marquette J.—St. Louis AL 1944.
Christopher, Joseph O.—Pittsburgh NL 1960.
Christopher, Russell O.—Cleveland AL 1948.
*Church, Emory N.—Philadelphia NL *1950.
Churn, Clarence N.—Los Angeles NL 1959.
*Cicotte, Alva W.—New York AL *1957.
Cicotte, Edward V.—Chicago AL 1917-19.
Cimoli, Gino N.—Brooklyn NL 1956; Pittsburgh NL 1960.
Clark, Alfred A.—New York AL 1947; Cleveland AL 1948.
Clark, Jack A.—St. Louis NL 1985.
*Clark, Robert W.—Cleveland AL *1920.
*Clark, W. Watson—New York NL *1933.
Clarke, Frederick C.—Pittsburgh NL 1903-09.
*Clarke, Thomas A.—Chicago NL *1918.
*Clarke, William J.—New York NL *1905.
Clary, Ellis—St. Louis AL 1944.
Clay, Kenneth E.—New York AL 1977-78.
Clemens, W. Roger—Boston AL 1986.
Clemente, Roberto W.—Pittsburgh NL 1960-71.
Clendenon, Donn A.—New York NL 1969.
Cleveland, Reginald L.—Boston AL 1975.
*Clevenger, Truman E.—New York AL *1961-*62.
Clifton, Herman E.—Detroit AL *1934-35.
Cline, Tyrone A.—Cincinnati NL 1970.
Clines, Eugene—Pittsburgh NL 1971.
Cloninger, Tony L.—Cincinnati NL 1970.
*Clough, Edgar G.—St. Louis NL *1926.
Coakley, Andrew J.—Philadelphia AL 1905.
Coates, James A.—New York AL 1960-61-62.
Cobb, Tyrus R.—Detroit AL 1907-08-09.
*Cochrane, George L.—Boston AL *1918.
Cochrane, Gordon S.—Philadelphia AL 1929-30-31; Detroit AL 1934-35.
*Cocreham, Eugene—Boston NL *1914.
*Coffey, John F.—Boston AL *1918.
Coffman, S. Richard—New York NL 1936-37.
Cole, Leonard L.—Chicago NL 1910.
Coleman, Gerald F.—New York AL 1949-50-51-*53-55-56-57.
Coleman, Gordon C.—Cincinnati NL 1961.
Coleman, Vincent M.—St. Louis NL *1985-87.
Coleman, W. Gary—New York AL 1955-*56.
Collins, Edward T.—Philadelphia AL 1910-11-13-14; Chicago AL 1917-19; Philadelphia AL *1929-*30.
Collins, H. Warren—New York AL 1921.
Collins, James A.—St. Louis NL 1931-34; Chicago NL 1938.
Collins, James J.—Boston AL 1903.
Collins, John F.—Chicago AL 1917-19.
Collins, Joseph E.—New York AL 1950-51-52-53-55-56-57.
Collins, Raymond W.—Boston AL 1912-*15.
Collins, T. Patrick—New York AL 1926-27-28.
Combs, Earle B.—New York AL 1926-27-28-32.
Comer, H. Wayne—Detroit AL 1968.
Conaster, Clinton A.—Boston NL 1948.
Concepcion, David I.—Cincinnati NL 1970-72-75-76.
Concepcion, Onix—Kansas City AL 1980-85.
Conigliaro, William M.—Oakland AL 1973.
Conley, D. Eugene—Milwaukee NL 1957-*58.
Coombs, John W.—Philadelphia AL 1910-11-*13-*14; Brooklyn NL 1916.
Connolly, Joseph A.—Boston NL 1914.
Cooper, Cecil C.—Boston AL 1975; Milwaukee AL 1982.
Cooper, Claude—New York NL 1913.

*Ferrell, Wesley C.—New York AL *1938.
Ferrick, Thomas J.—New York AL 1950.
Ferris, Albert S.—Boston AL 1903.
Ferriss, David M.—Boston AL 1946.
Fewster, Wilson L.—New York AL 1921.
*Fiene, Louis H.—Chicago AL *1906.
Figueroa, Eduardo—New York AL 1976-*77-78.
Fingers, Roland G.—Oakland AL 1972-73-74; Milwaukee AL *1982.
*Fischer, Charles W.—Detroit AL *1934.
*Fisher, Eddie G.—Baltimore AL *1966.
Fisher, George A.—Washington AL *1924; St. Louis NL 1930.
Fisher, Raymond L.—Cincinnati NL 1919.
Fisk, Carlton E.—Boston AL 1975.
Fitzsimmons, Frederick L.—New York NL 1933-36; Brooklyn NL 1941—
Flack, Max O.—Chicago NL 1918.
Flanagan, Michael K.—Baltimore AL 1979-83.
Flannery, Timothy E.—San Diego NL 1984.
Fletcher, Arthur—New York NL 1911-12-13-17.
Flood, Curtis C.—St. Louis NL 1964-67-68.
Flowers, D'Arcy R.—St. Louis NL 1926-31.
*Floyd, Robert N.—Baltimore AL *1969.
*Flynn, R. Douglas—Cincinnati NL *1975-*76.
Foli, Timothy J.—Pittsburgh NL 1979.
Foote, Barry C.—New York AL 1981.
Ford, Curtis G.—St. Louis NL 1987.
Ford, Darnell G.—Baltimore AL 1983.
Ford, Edward C.—New York AL 1950-53-55-56-57-58-60-61-62-63-64.
Forsch, Robert H.—St. Louis NL 1982-85-87.
Forster, Terry J.—Los Angeles NL 1978-81.
Fosse, Raymond E.—Oakland AL 1973-74.
Foster, George—Boston AL 1915-16.
Foster, George A.—Cincinnati NL 1972-75-76.
Fox, Ervin—Detroit AL 1934-35-40.
Fox, Nelson J.—Chicago AL 1959.
*Foxen, William A.—Chicago NL *1910.
Foxx, James E.—Philadelphia AL 1929-30-31.
Foy, Joseph A.—Boston AL 1967.
*Frankhouse, Frederick M.—St. Louis NL *1928.
Franks, Herman L.—Brooklyn NL 1941.
*Fraser, Charles C.—Chicago NL *1907-*08.
Frazier, George A.—New York AL 1981; Minnesota AL 1987.
Freehan, William A.—Detroit AL 1968.
Freeman, John B.—Boston AL 1903.
Freese, Gene L.—Cincinnati NL 1961.
French, Lawrence H.—Chicago NL 1935-38; Brooklyn NL 1941.
French, Walter E.—Philadelphia AL 1929.
Frey, Linus R.—Cincinnati NL 1939-40; New York AL 1947.
Friend, Robert B.—Pittsburgh NL 1960.
Frisch, Frank F.—New York NL 1921-22-23-24; St. Louis NL 1928-30-31-34.
*Frock, Samuel W.—Pittsburgh NL *1909.
*Fromme, Arthur L.—New York NL *1913.
Fullis, Charles P.—St. Louis NL 1934.
Furillo, Carl A.—Brooklyn NL 1947-49-52-53-55-56; Los Angeles NL 1959.

G

Gabler, Frank H.—New York NL 1936.
Gaetti, Gary J.—Minnesota AL 1987.
Gagliano, Philip J.—St. Louis NL 1967-68.
Gagne, Gregory C.—Minnesota AL 1987.
Gainor, Delos E.—Boston AL 1915-16.
Galan, August J.—Chicago NL 1935-38; Brooklyn NL 1941.
Gale, Richard B.—Kansas City AL 1980.
Galehouse, Dennis W.—St. Louis AL 1944.
Gamble, Lee J.—Cincinnati NL 1939.
Gamble, Oscar C.—New York AL 1976-81.
Gandil, Charles A.—Chicago AL 1917-19.
Gantner, James E.—Milwaukee AL 1982.
Garagiola, Joseph H.—St. Louis NL 1946.
*Garbark, Robert M.—Chicago NL *1938.
Garbey, Barbaro G.—Detroit AL 1984.
Garcia, Alfonso R.—Baltimore AL 1979; Philadelphia NL *1983.
Garcia, E. Mike—Cleveland AL 1954.
Gardner, W. Lawrence—Boston AL 1912-15-16; Cleveland AL 1920.
Gardner, William F.—New York NL *1954; New York AL 1961.

*Garibaldi, Bob R.—San Francisco NL *1962.
Garman, Michael D.—Los Angeles NL 1977.
Garms, Debs—St. Louis NL 1943-44.
Garner, Philip M.—Pittsburgh NL 1979.
Garrett, R. Wayne—New York NL 1969-73.
Garvey, Steven P.—Los Angeles NL 1974-77-78-81; San Diego NL 1984.
Gaspar, Rodney E.—New York NL 1969.
*Gaston, Alexander N.—New York NL *1921-*22-*23.
Gazella, Michael—New York AL *1923-26-*27-*28.
Gearin, Dennis J.—New York NL 1923.
Gedman, Richard L.—Boston AL 1986.
Gehrig, H. Louis—New York AL 1926-27-28-32-36-37-38-*39.
Gehringer, Charles L.—Detroit AL 1934-35-40.
Gelbert, Charles M.—St. Louis NL 1930-31.
Gentry, Gary E.—New York NL 1969.
*Gerner, Edwin F.—Cincinnati NL *1919.
Gernert, Richard E.—Cincinnati NL 1961.
Geronimo, Cesar F.—Cincinnati NL 1972-75-76.
Gessler, Harry H.—Chicago NL 1906.
Getz, Gustave—Brooklyn NL 1916.
*Giard, Joseph O.—New York AL *1927.
Gibbon, Joseph C.—Pittsburgh NL 1960.
Gibson, George—Pittsburgh NL 1909; New York NL *1917.
Gibson, J. Russell—Boston AL 1967.
Gibson, Kirk H.—Detroit AL 1984.
*Gibson, Norwood R.—Boston AL *1903.
Gibson, Robert—St. Louis NL 1964-67-68.
*Giel, Paul R.—New York NL *1954.
Gilbert, Lawrence W.—Boston NL 1914.
Gilbert, William O.—New York NL 1905.
Gillespie, Paul A.—Chicago NL 1945.
Gilliam, James—Brooklyn NL 1953-55-56; Los Angeles NL 1959-63-65-66.
Gionfriddo, Albert F.—Brooklyn NL 1947.
Giusti, David J.—Pittsburgh NL 1971.
Gladden, C. Daniel—Minnesota AL 1987.
*Glenn, Joseph C.—New York AL *1936-*37-*38.
Glynn, William V.—Cleveland AL 1954.
Goliat, Mike M.—Philadelphia NL 1950.
Goltz, David A.—Los Angeles NL 1981.
Gomez, Ruben—New York NL 1954.
Gomez, Vernon L.—New York AL 1932-36-37-38-39-*41-*42.
*Gonzalez, Julio C.—St. Louis NL *1982.
Gonzalez, Miguel A.—New York NL *1921; Chicago NL 1929; St. Louis NL*1931.
Gonzalez, Pedro—New York AL 1964.
Gooch, John B.—Pittsburgh NL 1925-27.
Gooden, Dwight E.—New York NL 1986.
Goodman, Ival R.—Cincinnati NL 1939-40.
Goodman, William D.—Chicago AL 1959.
Goodson, James E.—Los Angeles NL 1977.
Gordon, Joseph L.—New York AL 1938-39-41-42-43; Cleveland AL 1948.
Gorman, Thomas A.—New York AL 1952-53.
Gorsica, John J.—Detroit AL 1940.
Goslin, Leon A.—Washington AL 1924-25-33; Detroit AL 1934-35.
Gossage, Richard M.—New York AL 1978-81; San Diego NL 1984.
Gowdy, Henry M.—Boston NL 1914; New York NL 1923-24.
*Grabowski, Albert F.—St. Louis NL *1930.
Grabowski, John P.—New York AL 1927-*28.
*Grampp, Henry E.—Chicago NL *1929.
Graney, John G.—Cleveland AL 1920.
Granger, Wayne A.—St. Louis NL 1968; Cincinnati NL 1970.
Grant, Edward L.—New York NL 1913.
Grant, James T.—Minnesota AL 1965.
Grantham, George F.—Pittsburgh NL 1925-27.
Grasso, Newton M.—Cleveland AL 1954.
Grba, Eli—New York AL 1960.
Green, David A.—St. Louis NL 1982.
Green, Fred A.—Pittsburgh NL 1960.
Green, Richard L.—Oakland AL 1972-73-74.
Greenberg, Henry B.—Detroit AL 1934-35-40-45.
Greenwell, Michael L.—Boston AL 1986.
Gregg, Harold D.—Brooklyn NL 1947.
*Gregg, Sylveanus A.—Boston AL *1915-*16.
*Grich, Robert—Baltimore AL *1970.

Griffey, G. Kenneth—Cincinnati NL 1975-76.
Griffin, Douglas L.—Boston AL 1975.
Griffith, Thomas H.—Brooklyn NL 1920.
Grim, Robert A.—New York AL 1955-*56-57.
Grimes, Burleigh A.—Brooklyn NL 1920; St. Louis NL 1930-31; Chicago NL 1932.
*Grimes, Oscar R., Jr.—New York AL *1943.
Grimm, Charles J.—Chicago NL 1929-32-*35.
Grimsley, Ross A.—Cincinnati NL 1972.
Grissom, Leo T.—Cincinnati NL 1939.
Grissom, Marvin E.—New York NL 1954.
Groat, Richard M.—Pittsburgh NL 1960; St. Louis NL 1964.
*Grodzicki, John—St. Louis NL *1946.
Groh, Henry K.—New York AL *1912; Cincinnati NL 1919; New York NL 1922-23-24; Pittsburgh NL 1927.
Gromek, Stephen J.—Cleveland AL 1948.
Gross, Gregory E.—Philadelphia NL 1980-83.
*Gross, Kevin F.—Philadelphia NL *1983.
Grote, Gerald W.—New York NL 1969-73; Los Angeles NL 1977-78.
Grove, Robert M.—Philadelphia AL 1929-30-31.
Grubb, John M.—Detroit AL 1984.
*Gubicza, Mark S.—Kansas City AL *1985.
Gudat, Marvin J.—Chicago NL 1932.
Guerrero, Pedro—Los Angeles NL 1981.
Guidry, Ronald A.—New York AL *76-77-78-81.
*Guise, Witt O.—Cincinnati NL *1940.
Gullett, Donald E.—Cincinnati NL 1970-72-75-76; New York AL 1977.
Gumbert, Harry E.—New York NL 1936-37; St. Louis NL 1942-*43.
*Gumpert, Randall P.—New York AL *1947.
Gura, Lawrence C.—Kansas City AL 1980.
Gutteridge, Donald J.—St. Louis AL 1944; Boston AL 1946.
Gwynn, Anthony K.—San Diego NL 1984.

H

Haas, Bryan—Milwaukee AL 1982.
Haas, George W.—Pittsburgh NL *1925; Philadelphia AL 1929-30-31.
Hack, Stanley C.—Chicago NL 1932-35-38-45.
Haddix, Harvey—Pittsburgh NL 1960.
Hadley, Irving D.—New York AL 1936-37-*38-39.
Hafey, Charles J.—St. Louis NL 1926-28-30-31.
Hague, Joe C.—Cincinnati NL 1972.
Hahn, Donald A.—New York NL 1973.
Hahn, Edgar—Chicago AL 1906.
*Haid, Harold A.—St. Louis NL *1928.
Haines, Henry L.—New York AL 1923.
Haines, Jesse J.—St. Louis NL 1926-28-30-*31-34.
*Hale, Robert H.—New York AL *1961.
*Hale, Samuel D.—Philadelphia AL *1929.
Hall, Charles L.—Boston AL 1912.
Hall, Jimmie R.—Minnesota AL 1965.
Hall, Richard W.—Baltimore AL *1966-69-70-71.
Hall, Tom E.—Cincinnati NL 1972.
Hallahan, William A.—St. Louis NL 1926-30-31-34.
Haller, Thomas F.—San Francisco NL 1962.
Hamilton, David E.—Oakland AL 1972-*74.
Hamilton, Steve A.—New York AL 1963-64.
*Hamlin, Luke D.—Detroit AL *1934; Brooklyn NL *1941.
Hamner, Granville W.—Philadelphia NL 1950.
Hanebrink, Harry A.—Milwaukee NL 1958.
Haney, W. Larry—Baltimore AL *1966; Oakland AL 1974.
*Hanyzewski, Edward M.—Chicago NL *1945.
*Hardin, James W.—Baltimore AL *1969-*70.
*Hargrave, William M.—Washington AL *1924.
Harper, Brian D.—St. Louis NL 1985.
*Harper, Charles W.—Chicago NL *1906.
Harper, George W.—St. Louis NL 1928.
Harper, Harry C.—New York AL 1921.

Harrelson, Derrel M.—New York NL 1969-73.
Harrelson, Kenneth S.—Boston AL 1967.
Harris, David S.—Washington AL 1933.
Harris, Greg A.—San Diego NL 1984.
Harris, Joseph—Washington AL 1925; Pittsburgh NL 1927.
Harris, Maurice C.—Boston AL 1946.
Harris, Stanley R.—Washington AL 1924-25.
*Hart, James H.—Chicago AL *1906.
*Hartley, Grover C.—New York NL *1911-*12-*13.
Hartnett, Charles L.—Chicago NL 1929-32-35-38.
Hartsel, T. Frederick—Philadelphia AL 1905-10-*11.
Hartung, Clinton C.—New York NL 1951.
*Hasbrouck, Robert L.—Chicago AL *1917.
*Haslin, Michael J.—New York NL *1937.
Hassett, John A.—New York AL 1942.
Hatten, Joseph H.—Brooklyn NL 1947-49.
Hawkins, M. Andrew—San Diego NL 1984.
*Hawks, Nelson L.—New York AL *1921.
Hayes, Von F.—Philadelphia NL 1983.
Hayworth, Myron C.—St. Louis AL 1944.
Hayworth, Raymond H.—Detroit AL 1934-*35.
Hazle, Robert S.—Milwaukee NL 1957.
*Healy, Francis X.—St. Louis NL *1934.
*Healy, Francis X.—New York AL *1976-*77.
*Hearn, Edward J.—New York NL *1986.
Hearn, James T.—New York NL 1951-*54.
Heath, Michael T.—New York AL 1978.
Heathcote, Clifton E.—Chicago NL 1929.
Hebner, Richard J.—Pittsburgh NL 1971.
Heep, Daniel W.—New York NL 1986.
*Heffner, Donald H.—New York AL *1936-*37.
Hegan, James E.—Cleveland AL 1948-54.
Hegan, J. Michael—New York AL 1964; Oakland AL 1972.
*Heimach, Fred A.—New York AL *1928.
Heintzelman, Kenneth A.—Philadelphia NL 1950.
*Heise, Robert L.—Boston AL *1975.
*Held, Woodson G.—Baltimore AL *1966.
Helms, Tommy V.—Cincinnati NL 1970.
Hemsley, Ralston B.—Chicago NL 1932; New York AL *1942-*43.
Henderson, David L.—Boston AL 1986.
Hendrick, George A.—Oakland AL 1972; St. Louis NL 1982.
Hendrick, Harvey L.—New York AL 1923.
Hendricks, Elrod J.—Baltimore AL 1969-70-71; New York AL 1976.
Hendrix, Claude R.—Chicago NL 1918.
*Henley, Weldon—Philadelphia AL *1905.
Henrich, Thomas D.—New York AL *1937-38-*39-41-47-49.
Henriksen, Olaf—Boston AL 1912-15-16.
Henry, William R.—Cincinnati NL 1961.
Henshaw, Roy J.—Chicago NL 1935.
Herman, William J.—Chicago NL 1932-35-38; Brooklyn NL 1941.
Hermanski, Eugene V.—Brooklyn NL 1947-49.
Hernandez, Guillermo—Philadelphia NL 1983; Detroit AL 1984.
Hernandez, Jacinto—Pittsburgh NL 1971.
Hernandez, Keith—St. Louis NL 1982; New York NL 1986.
Herndon, Larry D.—Detroit AL 1984.
Herr, Thomas M.—St. Louis NL 1982-85-87.
*Herrmann, LeRoy G.—Chicago NL *1932.
Hershberger, Willard M.—Cincinnati NL 1939.
Herzog, Charles L.—New York NL 1911-12-13-17.
*Hess, Otto C.—Boston NL *1914.
Heving, John A.—Philadelphia AL 1931.
Higbe, W. Kirby—Brooklyn NL 1941.
Higgins, Michael F.—Philadelphia AL *1930; Detroit AL 1940; Boston AL 1946.
High, Andrew A.—St. Louis NL 1928-30-31.
Hildebrand, Oral C.—New York AL 1939.
Hill, Carmen P.—New York NL *1922; Pittsburgh NL 1927.
Hiller, Charles J.—San Francisco NL 1962.
Hiller, John F.—Detroit AL 1968.
Hoag, Myril O.—New York AL 1932-37-38.
Hoak, Donald A.—Brooklyn NL 1955; Pittsburgh NL 1960.
Hoblitzell, Richard C.—Boston AL 1915-16.
Hodges, Gilbert R.—Brooklyn NL 1947-49-52-53-55-56; Los Angeles NL1959.
Hodges, Ronald W.—New York NL 1973.

Hoerner, Joseph W.—St. Louis NL 1967-68.
Hoffman, Daniel J.—Philadelphia AL 1905.
Hofman, Arthur F.—Chicago NL 1906-*07-08-10.
*Hofman, Robert G.—New York NL *1954.
Hofmann, Fred—New York AL *1922-23.
Hogsett, Elon C.—Detroit AL 1934-35.
Hogue, Robert C.—Boston NL *1948; New York AL 1951.
Holke, Walter H.—New York NL 1917.
Holland, Alfred W.—Philadelphia NL 1983.
Hollingsworth, Albert W.—St. Louis AL 1944.
*Hollmig, Stanley E.—Philadelphia NL *1950.
Hollocher, Charles J.—Chicago NL 1918.
Holm, Roscoe A.—St. Louis NL 1926-28.
Holmes, Thomas F.—Boston NL 1948; Brooklyn NL 1952.
Holt, James W.—Oakland AL 1974.
Holtzman, Kenneth D.—Oakland AL 1972-73-74; New York AL *1976-*77.
*Hook, James W.—Cincinnati NL *1961.
Hooper, Harry B.—Boston AL 1912-15-16-18.
*Hooper, Robert N.—Cleveland AL *1954.
Hooton, Burt C.—Los Angeles NL 1977-78-81.
Hoover, Robert J.—Detroit AL 1945.
Hopkins, Gail D.—Los Angeles NL *1974.
Hopp, John L.—St. Louis NL 1942-43-44; New York AL 1950-51.
Horlen, Joel E.—Oakland AL 1972.
Hornsby, Rogers—St. Louis NL 1926; Chicago NL 1929.
Horton, Ricky N.—St. Louis NL 1985-87.
Horton, William W.—Detroit AL 1968.
Hostetler, Charles C.—Detroit AL 1945.
*Houck, Byron W.—Philadelphia AL *1913.
Hough, Charles O.—Los Angeles NL 1974-77-78.
Houk, Ralph G.—New York AL 1947-*50-*51-52.
*Houser, Benjamin F.—Philadelphia AL *1910.
Houtteman, Arthur J.—Detroit AL *1945; Cleveland AL 1954.
Howard, Elston G.—New York AL 1955-56-57-58-60-61-62-63-64; Boston AL 1967.
Howard, Frank O.—Los Angeles NL 1963.
Howard, George E.—Chicago NL 1907-08.
Howe, Steven R.—Los Angeles NL 1981.
*Howell, Homer E.—Brooklyn NL *1955-*56.
Howell, Roy L.—Milwaukee AL 1982.
Hoyt, Waite C.—New York AL 1921-22-23-26-27-28; Philadelphia AL 1931.
Hrbek, Kent A.—Minnesota AL 1987.
Hubbell, Carl O.—New York NL 1933-36-37.
*Hudlin, G. Willis—St. Louis AL *1944.
Hudson, Charles L.—Philadelphia NL 1983.
Hughes, James R.—Brooklyn NL 1953.
Hughes, Richard H.—St. Louis NL 1967-68.
Hughes, Roy J.—Chicago NL 1945.
Hughes, Thomas J.—Boston AL 1903.
Hughson, Cecil C.—Boston AL 1946.
Humphreys, Robert W.—St. Louis NL 1964.
Hunt, Kenneth R.—Cincinnati NL 1961.
*Hunter, G. William—New York AL *1956.
Hunter, James A.—Oakland AL 1972-73-74; New York AL 1976-77-78.
*Huntzinger, Walter H.—New York NL *1924.
Hurdle, Clinton M.—Kansas City AL 1980.
Hurst, Bruce V.—Boston AL 1986.
Hutchings, John R.—Cincinnati NL 1940.
Hutchinson, Frederick C.M Detroit AL 1940.
Hyatt, R. Hamilton—Pittsburgh NL 1909.

I

Iorg, Dane C.—St. Louis NL 1982; Kansas City AL 1985.
Irvin, Monford M.—New York NL 1951-54.
Isbell, W. Frank—Chicago AL 1906.

J

*Jackson, Alvin N.—St. Louis NL *1967.
Jackson, Danny L.—Kansas City AL 1985.
Jackson, Grant D.—Baltimore AL 1971; New York AL 1976; Pittsburgh NL 1979.
Jackson, Joseph J.—Chicago AL 1917-19.
Jackson, Ransom J.—Brooklyn NL 1956.
Jackson, Reginald M.—Oakland AL 1973-74; New York AL 1977-78-81.

Jackson, Travis C.—New York NL 1923-24-33-36.
Jakucki, S. Jack—St. Louis AL 1944.
*James, R. Byrne—New York NL *1933.
James, Charles W.—St. Louis NL 1964.
James, William H.—Chicago AL 1919.
James, William L.—Boston NL 1914.
Jamieson, Charles D.—Cleveland AL 1920.
Jansen, Lawrence J.—New York NL 1951.
Janvrin, Harold C.—Boston AL 1915-16.
Jaster, Larry E.—St. Louis NL 1967-68.
Javier, M. Julian—St. Louis NL 1964-67-68; Cincinnati NL 1972.
Jay, Joseph R.—Cincinnati NL 1961.
*Jeanes, Ernest L.—Washington AL *1925.
*Jenkins, Joseph D.—Chicago AL *1917-*19.
Jensen, Jack E.—New York AL 1950.
John, Thomas, E.—Los Angeles NL 1977-78; New York AL 1981.
*Johnson, Alexander—St. Louis NL *1967.
Johnson, Clifford—New York AL 1977-78.
Johnson, Darrell D.—New York AL *1957-*58.; Cincinnati NL 1961.
Johnson, David A.—Baltimore AL 1966-69-70-71.
Johnson, Deron R.—Oakland AL 1973.
*Johnson, Donald R.—New York AL *1947.
Johnson, Donald S.—Chicago NL 1945.
Johnson, Earl D.—Boston AL 1946.
Johnson, Ernest R.—New York AL 1923.
Johnson, Ernest T.—Milwaukee NL 1957-*58.
*Johnson, Henry W.—Cincinnati NL *1939.
Johnson, Howard M.—Detroit AL 1984; New York NL 1986.
Johnson, K. Lance—St. Louis NL 1987.
Johnson, Kenneth C.—Philadelphia NL 1950.
Johnson, Kenneth T.—Cincinnati NL 1961.
Johnson, Louis B.—Los Angeles NL 1965-66.
Johnson, Robert D.—Pittsburgh NL 1971.
*Johnson, Robert W.—Baltimore AL *1966.
Johnson, Roy C.—New York AL 1936.
Johnson, Sylvester W.—St. Louis NL *1926-28-30-31.
Johnson, Walter P.—Washington AL 1924-25.
Johnson, William R.—New York AL 1943-47-49-50.
Johnston, James H.—Brooklyn NL 1916-20.
Johnston, Wheeler R.—Cleveland AL 1920.
Johnstone, John W.—New York AL 1978; Los Angeles NL 1981.
*Jolly, David—Milwaukee NL *1957.
Jones, Cleon J.—New York NL 1969-73.
Jones, David J.—Detroit AL 1907-08-09.
Jones, Fielder A.—Chicago AL 1906.
Jones, J. Dalton—Boston AL 1967.
Jones, Lynn M.—Kansas City AL 1985.
Jones, Ruppert S.—Detroit AL 1984.
Jones, Samuel P.—Boston AL *1916-18; New York AL 1922-23-26.
Jones, Sheldon L.—New York NL 1951.
Jones, Sherman J.—Cincinnati NL 1961.
Jones, Thomas—Detroit AL 1909.
Jones, Vernal L.—St. Louis NL 1946; Milwaukee NL 1957.
Jones, Willie E.—Philadelphia NL 1950.
Jonnard, Claude A.—New York NL *1922-23-24.
Joost, Edwin D.—Cincinnati NL *1939-40.
*Jorgens, Arndt, L.—New York AL *1932-*36-*37-*38-*39.
Jorgensen, John D.—Brooklyn NL 1947-49.
Jorgensen, Michael—St. Louis NL 1985.
Joshua, Von E.—Los Angeles NL 1974.
*Jourdan, Theodore C.—Chicago AL *1917.
Judge, Joseph I.—Washington AL 1924-25.
Judnich, Walter F.—Cleveland AL 1948.
Jurges, William F.—Chicago NL 1932-35-38.
Jurisich, Alvin J.—St. Louis NL 1944.

K

Kaat, James L.—Minnesota AL 1965; St. Louis NL 1982.
Kaline, Albert W.—Detroit AL 1968.
Kane, John F.—Chicago NL 1910.
Kasko, Edward M.—Cincinnati NL 1961.
*Katt, Raymond F.—New York NL *1954.
Kauff, Benjamin M.—New York NL 1917.
*Kaufmann, Anthony C.—St. Louis NL *1931.
*Keely, Robert W.—St. Louis NL *1944.
Keen, H. Victor—St. Louis NL 1926.

*Kekich, Michael D.—Los Angeles NL *1965.
Keller, Charles E.—New York AL 1939-41-42-43-*47-*49.
Kellert, Frank W.—Brooklyn NL 1955.
Kelly, George L.—New York NL 1921-22-23-24.
Kelly, H. Patrick—Baltimore AL 1979.
Keltner, Kenneth F.—Cleveland AL 1948.
Kennedy, John E.—Los Angeles NL 1965-66.
Kennedy, Montia C.—New York NL 1951.
Kennedy, Robert D.—Cleveland AL 1948.
Kennedy, Terrence E.—San Diego NL 1984.
Kennedy, William V.—Pittsburgh NL 1903.
Kerr, John F.—Washington AL 1933.
Kerr, Richard H.—Chicago AL 1919.
Kilduff, Peter J.—Brooklyn NL 1920.
Killebrew, Harmon C.—Minnesota AL 1965.
*Killefer, Wade H.—Detroit AL *1908.
Killefer, William L.—Philadelphia NL 1915; Chicago NL 1918.
Killian, Edward H.—Detroit AL 1907-08-*09.
*Kimball, Newell W.—Brooklyn NL *1941.
*Kindall, Gerald D.—Minnesota AL *1965.
*King, Clyde E.—Brooklyn NL *1947-*52.
King, Lee—New York NL 1922.
*Kinney, Walter W.—Boston AL *1918.
*Kirby, Clayton L.—Cincinnati NL *1975.
Kison, Bruce E.—Pittsburgh NL 1971-79.
Klein, Charles H.—Chicago NL 1935.
Klein, Louis F.—St. Louis NL 1943.
Klieman, Edward F.—Cleveland AL 1948.
Kling, John G.—Chicago NL 1906-07-08-10.
Klinger, Robert H.—Boston AL 1946.
Klippstein, John C.—Los Angeles NL 1959; Minnesota AL 1965.
Kluszewski, Theodore B.—Chicago AL 1959.
*Klutts, Gene E.—New York AL *1977.
*Kluttz, Clyde F.—St. Louis NL *1946.
*Knabe, F. Otto—Chicago NL *1918.
*Knickerbocker, William H.—New York AL *1938-*39.
Knight, C. Ray—New York NL 1986.
*Knight, John W.—Philadelphia AL *1905.
Knowles, Darold D.—Oakland AL 1973-*74.
Koenig, Mark A.—New York AL 1926-27-28; Chicago NL 1932; New York NL 1936.
Konetchy, Edward J.—Brooklyn NL 1920.
Konikowski, Alexander J.—New York NL 1951-*54.
Konstanty, C. James—Philadelphia NL 1950.
*Koonce, Calvin L.—New York NL *1969.
Koosman, Jerry M.—New York NL 1969-73.
*Kopf, Walter H.—New York NL *1921.
Kopf, William L.—Philaldephia AL *1914; Cincinnati NL 1919.
Koslo, George B.—New York NL 1951.
Koufax, Sanford—Brooklyn NL *1955-*56; Los Angeles NL 1959-63-65-66.
Kowalik, Fabian L.—Chicago NL 1935.
*Kraly, Steve C.—New York AL *1953.
Kramer, John H.—St. Louis AL 1944.
Kranepool Edward E.—New York NL 1969-73.
*Krause, Harry W.—Philadelphia AL *1910-*11.
*Krausse, Lewis B.—Philadelphia AL *1931.
Kreevich, Michael A.—St. Louis AL 1944.
Kremer, Remy—Pittsburgh NL 1925-27.
Krist, Howard V.—St. Louis NL 1942-43-*46.
*Kroh, Floyd H.—Chicago NL *1908.
Krueger, Ernest G.—Brooklyn NL 1920.
*Krug, Martin J.—Boston AL *1912.
*Kruger, Lloyd D.—Pittsburgh NL *1903.
Kubek, Anthony C.—New York AL 1957-58-60-61-62-63.
Kubiak, Theodore R.—Oakland AL 1972-73-*74.
Kucks, John C.—New York AL 1955-56-57-58.
Kuenn, Harvey E.—San Francisco NL 1962.
Kuhel, Joseph A.—Washington AL 1933.
*Kunkel, William G.—New York AL *1963.
Kuntz, Russell J.—Detroit AL 1984.
Kurowski, George J.—St. Louis NL 1942-43-44-46.

Kuzava, Robert L.—New York AL 1951-52-53.

L

Laabs, Chester P.—St. Louis AL 1944.
Labine, Clement W.—Brooklyn NL *1952-53-55-56; Los Angeles NL 1959; Pittsburgh NL 1960.
Lacy, Leondaus—Los Angeles NL 1974-77-78; Pittsburgh NL 1979.
LaChance, George—Boston AL 1903.
LaCock, Ralph P.—Kansas City AL 1980.
Ladd, Peter L.—Milwaukee AL 1982.
Lahti, Jeffrey A.—St. Louis NL 1982-85.
Lake, Steven M.—St. Louis NL 1987.
Lamabe, John A.—St. Louis NL 1967.
Lamar, William H.—Brooklyn NL 1920.
Landestoy, Rafael S.—Los Angeles NL 1977.
Landis, James H.—Chicago AL 1959.
Landreaux, Kenneth F.—Los Angeles NL 1981.
*Landrum, Joseph B.—Brooklyn NL *1952.
Landrum, Terry L.—Baltimore AL 1983; St. Louis NL 1985.
Lanier, H. Max—St. Louis NL 1942-43-44.
LaPoint, David J.—St. Louis NL 1982.
Lapp, John W.—Philadelphia AL 1910-11-13-14.
Larker, Norman H.—Los Angeles NL 1959.
Larkin, Eugene T.—Minnesota AL 1987.
LaRoche, David E.—New York AL 1981.
Larsen, Don J.—New York AL 1955-56-57-58; San Francisco NL 1962.
*Lary, Lynford H.—New York AL *1932.
Lasher, Frederick W.—Detroit AL 1968.
*Latman, A. Barry—Chicago AL *1959.
Laudner, Timothy J.—Minnesota AL 1987.
Lavagetto, Harry A.—Brooklyn NL 1941-47.
*Lavan, John L.—Philadelphia AL *1913.
Law, Vernon S.—Pittsburgh NL 1960.
Lawless, Thomas J.—St. Louis NL 1985-87.
*Lawson, Alfred V.—Detroit AL *1935.
*Lazor, John P.—Boston AL *1946.
Lazzeri, Anthony M.—New York AL 1926-27-28-32-36-37; Chicago NL 1938.
Leach, Thomas W.—Pittsburgh NL 1903-09.
*LeBourveau, DeWitt W.—Philadelphia AL *1929.
Lee, William C.—Chicago NL 1935-38.
Lee, William F.—Boston AL 1975.
Leever, Samuel W.—Pittsburgh NL 1903-09.
Lefebvre, James K.—Los Angeles NL 1965-66.
Lefebvre, Joseph H.—Philadelphia NL 1983.
Lefferts, Craig L.—San Diego NL 1984.
Lehman, Kenneth—Brooklyn NL 1952-*56.
Leiber, Henry E.—New York NL 1936-37.
Leibold, Harry L.—Chicago AL 1917-19; Washington AL 1924-25.
Leibrandt, Charles L.—Kansas City AL 1985.
Leifield, Albert P.—Pittsburgh NL 1909.
*Leja, Frank J.—New York AL *1955.
LeJohn, Donald E.—Los Angeles NL 1965.
Lemon, Chester E.—Detroit AL 1984.
Lemon, Robert G.—Cleveland AL 1948-54.
Leonard, Dennis P.—Kansas City AL 1980.
Leonard, Hubert B.—Boston AL 1915-16.
Leonhard, David P.—Baltimore AL 1969-*70-71.
Leslie, Samuel A.—New York NL 1936-37.
Lewis, Allan S.—Oakland AL 1972-73.
Lewis, George E.—Boston AL 1912-15-16.
Lezcano, Sixto—Philadelphia NL 1983.
Liddle, Donald E.—New York NL 1954.
Lindblad, Paul A.—Oakland AL 1973-*74; New York AL 1978.
Lindell, John H.—New York AL *1942-43-47-49.
Lindeman, James W.—St. Louis NL 1987.
Lindsey, James K.—St. Louis NL 1930-31.
Lindstrom, Frederick C.—New York NL 1924; Chicago NL 1935.
Linz, Philip F.—New York AL *1962-63-64.
Litwhiler, Daniel W.—St. Louis NL 1943-44.
*Livingston, Patrick J.—Philadelphia AL *1910-*11.
Livingston, Thompson O.—Chicago NL 1945.
*Lobert, John B.—New York NL *1917.
Locker, Robert A.—Oakland AL 1972.

Lockman, Carroll W.—New York NL 1951-54.
Loes, William—Brooklyn NL 1952-53-55.
Logan, John—Milwaukee NL 1957-58.
Lohrke, Jack W.—New York NL 1951.
Lolich, Michael S.—Detroit AL 1968.
Lollar, J. Sherman—New York AL 1947; Chicago AL 1959.
Lollar, W. Timothy—San Diego NL 1984; Boston AL *1986.
Lombardi, Ernesto N.—Cincinnati NL 1939-40.
Lombardi, Victor A.—Brooklyn NL 1947.
Lombardozzi, Stephen P.—Minnesota AL 1987.
Lonborg, James R.—Boston AL 1967.
Long, R. Dale—New York AL 1960-62.
Lopat, Edmund W.—New York AL 1949-50-51-52-53.
Lopata, Stanley E.—Philadelphia NL 1950.
Lopes, David E.—Los Angeles NL 1974-77-78-81.
Lopez, Aurelio A.—Detroit AL 1984.
Lopez, Hector H.—New York AL 1960-61-62-63-64.
Lopez, Marcelino—Baltimore AL *1969-70.
Lord, Briscoe R.—Philadelphia AL 1905-10-11.
*Lowe, Robert L.—Detroit AL *1907.
Lowdermilk, Grover C.—Chicago AL 1919.
Lowenstein, John L.—Baltimore AL 1979-83.
Lowrey, Harry L.—Chicago NL 1945.
Lown, Omar J.—Chicago AL 1959.
Luderus, Frederick W.—Philadelphia NL 1915.
*Lum, Michael K.—Cincinnati NL *1976.
Lumpe, Jerry D.—New York AL 1957-58.
*Lundgren, Carl L.—Chicago NL *1906-*07-*08.
Lunte, Harry A.—Cleveland AL 1920.
Luque, Adolfo—Cincinnati NL 1919; New York NL 1933.
Luzinski, Gregory M.—Philadelphia NL 1980.
Lyle, Albert W.—New York AL 1976-77-*78.
Lynch, Gerald T.—Cincinnati NL 1961.
Lynn, Byrd—Chicago AL 1917-19.
Lynn, Fredric M.—Boston AL 1975.
*Lyons, Albert H.—Boston NL *1948.

M

Maas, Duane F.—New York AL 1958-60.
*MacFayden, Daniel K.—New York AL *1932.
Maddox, Elliott—New York AL 1976.
Maddox, Garry L.—Philadelphia NL 1980-83.
Maddox, Nicholas—Pittsburgh NL 1909.
*Madjeski, Edward W.—New York NL *1937.
Madlock, Bill—Pittsburgh NL 1979.
Magee, Sherwood R.—Cincinnati NL 1919.
Maglie, Salvatore A.—New York NL 1951-54; Brooklyn NL 1956.
Magrane, Joseph D.—St. Louis NL 1987.
Maguire, Frederick E.—New York NL 1923.
Mahaffey, Lee Roy—Philadelphia AL *1930-31.
Maier, Robert P.—Detroit AL 1945.
Mails, J. Walter—Brooklyn NL *1916; Cleveland AL 1920.
Majeski, Henry—Cleveland AL 1954.
*Makosky, Frank—New York AL *1937.
Malone, Perce L.—Chicago NL 1929-32; New York AL 1936-*37.
Maloney, James W.—Cincinnati NL 1961.
Mamaux, Albert L.—Brooklyn NL 1920.
Mancuso, August R.—St. Louis NL 1930-31; New York NL 1933-36-37.
Mancuso, Frank O.—St. Louis AL 1944.
Mangual, Angel L.—Oakland AL 1972-73-74.
Mann, Leslie—Boston NL 1914; Chicago NL 1918.
Mantilla, Felix—Milwaukee NL 1957-58.
Mantle, Mickey C.—New York AL 1951-52-53-55-56-57-58-60-61-62-63-64.
Manush, Henry E.—Washington AL 1933.
Mapes, Clifford E.—New York AL 1949-50.
Maranville, Walter J.—Boston NL 1914; St. Louis NL 1928.
Marberry, Frederick—Washington AL 1924-25; Detroit AL 1934.
Marichal, Juan A.—San Francisco NL 1962.

Marion, Martin W.—St. Louis NL 1942-43-44-46.
Maris, Roger E.—New York AL 1960-61-62-63-64; St. Louis NL 1967-68.
Marquard, Richard—New York NL 1911-12-13; Brooklyn NL 1916-20.
Marquez, Gonzalo—Oakland AL 1972.
*Marshall, Clarence W.—New York AL *1949.
*Marshall, Joseph H.—Pittsburgh NL *1903.
Marshall, Michael G.—Los Angeles NL 1974.
*Marshall, William R.—Chicago NL *1908.
Martin, Alfred M.—New York AL *1950-51-52-53-55-56.
Martin, D. Renie—Kansas City AL 1980.
*Martin, Elwood G.—Chicago NL *1918.
*Martin, Harold W.—Philadelphia AL *1911.
Martin, John L.—St. Louis NL 1928-31-34-*44.
*Martin, John R.—St. Louis NL *1982.
Martin, Joseph C.—New York NL 1969.
*Martin, William G.—Boston NL 1914.
Martina, Joseph J.—Washington AL 1924.
Martinez, Carmelo—San Diego NL 1984.
Martinez, Felix A.—Baltimore AL 1979-83.
Martinez, J. Dennis—Baltimore AL 1979-*83.
Martinez, Teodoro N.—New York NL 1973; Los Angeles NL *1978.
Marty, Joseph A.—Chicago NL 1938.
Masi, Philip S.—Boston NL 1948.
Mason, James P.—New York AL 1976.
Matchick, J. Thomas—Detroit AL 1968.
Mathews, Edwin L.—Milwaukee NL 1957-58; Detroit AL 1968.
Mathews, Gregory I.—St. Louis NL 1987.
Mathewson, Christopher—New York NL 1905-11-12-13.
Matlack, Jonathan T.—New York NL 1973.
Matthews, Gary N.—Philadelphia NL 1983.
*Maun, Ernest G.—New York NL *1924.
Maxvill, C. Dallan—St. Louis NL 1964-67-68; Oakland AL *1972-74.
May, Carlos—New York AL 1976.
May, David L.—Baltimore AL 1969.
May, Frank S.—Chicago NL 1932.
May, Lee A.—Cincinnati NL 1970; Baltimore AL 1979.
May, Milton S.—Pittsburgh NL 1971.
May, Rudolph—New York AL 1981.
Mayer, J. Erskine—Philadelphia NL 1915; Chicago AL 1919.
*Mayer, Walter A.—Boston AL *1918.
Mayo, Edward J.—New York NL 1936; Detroit AL 1945.
Mayo, John L.—Philadelphia NL 1950.
Mays, Carl W.—Boston AL *1915-16-18; New York AL 1921-22-*23.
Mays, Willie H.—New York NL (Giants) 1951-54; San Francisco NL 1962; New York NL (Mets) 1973.
Mazeroski, William S.—Pittsburgh NL 1960-71.
Mazzilli, Lee L.—New York NL 1986.
McAnany, James—Chicago AL 1959.
*McAndrew, James C.—New York NL *1969-*73.
McAuliffe, Richard J.—Detroit AL 1968.
*McAvoy, James E.—Philadelphia AL *1914.
McBride, Arnold R.—Philadelphia NL 1980.
*McBride, Kenneth F.—Chicago AL *1959.
McBride, Thomas R.—Boston AL 1946.
McCabe, William F.—Chicago NL 1918; Brooklyn NL 1920.
*McCall, John W.—New York NL *1954.
McCarthy, John J.—New York NL 1937.
McCarty, G. Lewis—New York NL 1917.
McCarver, J. Timothy—St. Louis NL 1964-67-68.
*McClellan, Harvey M.—Chicago AL *1919.
McClure, Robert C.—Milwaukee AL 1982.
McColl, Alexander B.—Washington AL 1933.
McCormick, Frank A.—Cincinnati NL 1939-40; Boston NL 1948.
McCormick, Harry E.—New York NL 1912-13.
*McCormick, Michael—San Francisco NL *1962.
McCormick, Myron W.—Cincinnati NL 1940; Boston NL 1948; Brooklyn NL 1949.

McCosky, W. Barney—Detroit AL 1940.
McCovey, Willie L.—San Francisco NL 1962.
McCullough, Clyde E.—Chicago NL 1945.
McDermott, Maurice J.—New York AL 1956.
*McDevitt, Daniel E.—Los Angeles NL *1959.
*McDonald, Henry M.—Philadelphia AL *1931.
McDonald, James L.—New York AL *1952-53.
McDougald, Gilbert J.—New York AL 1951-52-53-55-56-57-58-60.
McDowell, Roger A.—New York NL 1986.
McEnaney, William H.—Cincinnati NL 1975-76.
McFarland, Edward W.—Chicago AL 1906.
*McGah, Edward J.—Boston AL *1946.
McGann, Dennis L.—New York NL 1905.
McGee, Willie D.—St. Louis NL 1982-85-87.
McGinnity, Joseph J.—New York NL 1905.
McGlothlin, James M.—Cincinnati NL 1970-72.
McGraw, Frank E.—New York NL *1969-73; Philadelphia NL 1980.
McGregor, Scott H.—Baltimore AL 1979-83.
McHale, John P.—Detroit AL 1945.
McInnis, John P.—Philadelphia AL *1910-11-13-14; Boston AL 1918; Pittsburgh NL 1925.
McIntire, Harry M.—Chicago NL 1910.
McIntyre, Matthew W.—Detroit AL *1907-08-09.
McKain, Archibald R.—Detroit AL 1940.
McLain, Dennis D.—Detroit AL 1968.
McLean, John B.—New York NL 1913.
McMahon, Donald J.—Milwaukee NL 1957-58; Detroit AL 1968.
McMillan, Norman A.—New York AL 1922; Chicago NL 1929.
*McMullen, Kenneth L.—Los Angeles NL *1963-*74.
McMullin, Frederick W.—Chicago AL 1917-19.
McNair, D. Eric—Philadelphia AL 1930-31.
McNally, David A.—Baltimore AL 1966-69-70-71.
McNally, Michael J.—Boston AL *1915-16; New York AL 1921-22-*23.
McNeely, G. Earl—Washington AL 1924-25.
*McQuaid, Herbert G.—New York AL *1926.
*McQuillan, George W.—Philadelphia NL *1915.
McQuillan, Hugh A.—New York NL 1922-23-24.
McQuinn, George H.—St. Louis AL 1944; New York AL 1947.
McRae, Harold A.—Cincinnati NL 1970-72; Kansas City AL 1980-85.
Meadows, H. Lee—Pittsburgh NL 1925-27.
Medich, George F.—Milwaukee AL 1982.
Medwick, Joseph M.—St. Louis NL 1934; Brooklyn NL 1941.
Melton, Clifford, G.—New York NL 1937.
Menke, Denis J.—Cincinnati NL 1972.
Merkle, Frederick C.—New York NL 1911-12-13; Brooklyn NL 1916; Chicago NL 1918.
Merritt, James J.—Minnesota AL 1965; Cincinnati NL 1970.
Mertes, Samuel B.—New York NL 1905.
Merullo, Leonard R.—Chicago NL 1945.
Messersmith, John A. (Andy)—Los Angeles NL 1974.
*Metcalf, Thomas J.—New York AL *1963.
Metheny, Arthur B.—New York AL 1943.
Metkovich, George M.—Boston AL 1946.
Meusel, Emil F.—New York NL 1921-22-23-24.
Meusel, Robert W.—New York AL 1921-22-23-26-27-28.
*Meyer, Lambert D.—Detroit AL *1940.
Meyer, Russell C.—Philadelphia NL 1950; Brooklyn NL 1953-55.
Meyers, John T.—New York NL 1911-12-13; Brooklyn NL 1916.
Mierkowicz, Edward F.—Detroit AL 1945.
Mikkelsen, Peter J.—New York AL 1964.
Miksis, Edward T.—Brooklyn NL 1947-49.
Milbourne, Lawrence W.—New York AL 1981.
Miljus, John K.—Brooklyn NL *1920; Pittsburgh NL 1927.

Millan, Felix B. M.—New York NL 1973.
Miller, Edmund J.—Philadelphia AL 1929-30-31.
Miller, Elmer—New York AL 1921.
*Miller, James E.—Detroit *1945.
Miller, John B.—Pittsburgh NL 1909.
*Miller, John E.—Baltimore AL *1966.
Miller, Lawrence H.—Boston AL 1918.
Miller, Otto L.—Brooklyn, NL 1916-20.
Miller, Ralph J.—Washington AL 1924.
Miller, Richard A.—Boston AL 1975.
Miller, Robert J.—Philadelphia NL 1950.
Miller, Robert L.—Los Angeles NL *1963-65-66; Pittsburgh NL 1971.
Miller, Stuart L.—San Francisco NL 1962; Baltimore AL *1966.
*Miller, William F.—New York AL *1952-*53.
Milliken, Robert—Brooklyn NL 1953.
Milner, John D.—New York NL 1973; Pittsburgh NL 1979.
Mincher, Donald R.—Minnesota AL 1965; Oakland AL 1972.
Minner, Paul E.—Brooklyn NL 1949.
*Miranda, Guillermo P.—New York AL *1953.
*Mitchell, A. Roy—Cincinnati *1919.
Mitchell, Clarence E.—Brooklyn NL 1920; St. Louis NL 1928.
*Mitchell, John F.—New York AL *1921.
Mitchell, Kevin D.—New York NL 1986.
Mitchell, L. Dale—Cleveland AL 1948-54; Brooklyn NL 1956.
Mize, John R.—New York AL 1949-50-51-52-53.
Mizell, Wilmer D.—Pittsburgh NL 1960.
Moeller, Joseph D.—Los Angeles NL 1966.
Mogridge, George A.—Washington AL 1924.
*Mohart, George B.—Brooklyn NL *1920.
Molitor, Paul L.—Milwaukee AL 1982.
Monday, Robert J.—Los Angeles NL 1977-78-81.
Money, Donald—Milwaukee AL 1982.
Monroe, Zackie C.—New York AL 1958.
Montgomery, Robert E.—Boston AL 1975.
Moon, Wallace W.—Los Angeles NL 1959-*63-65.
Mooney, James I.—St. Louis NL 1934.
*Moore, Archie F.—New York AL *1964.
Moore, Charles W.—Milwaukee AL 1982.
Moore, Eugene, Jr.—St. Louis AL 1944.
*Moore, Eugene, Sr.—Pittsburgh NL *1909.
Moore, G. Edward—Pittsburgh NL 1925.
Moore, James W.—Philadelphia AL 1930-31.
Moore, John F.—Chicago NL *1929-32.
Moore, Joseph G.—New York NL 1933-36-37.
Moore, Lloyd A.—Cincinnati NL 1939-40; St. Louis NL *1942.
Moore, Raymond L.—Brooklyn NL *1952; Chicago AL 1959.
Moore, Terry B.—St. Louis NL 1942-46.
Moore, W. Wilcey—New York AL 1927-32.
Moose, Robert R.—Pittsburgh NL 1971.
Moran, J. Herbert—Boston NL 1914.
Moran, Patrick J.—Chicago NL 1906-07-*08.
*Morehart, Raymond—New York AL *1927.
Morehead, David M.—Boston AL 1967.
Moreland, B. Keith—Philadelphia NL 1980.
Moreno, Omar R.—Pittsburgh NL 1979.
Moret, Rogelio—Boston AL 1975.
*Morgan, Harry R.—Philadelphia AL *1910-*11.
Morgan, Joe L.—Cincinnati NL 1972-75-76; Philadelphia NL 1983.
Morgan, Robert, M.—Brooklyn NL 1952-53.
Morgan, Thomas S.—New York AL 1951-55-56.
Moriarty, George J.—Detroit AL 1909.
Morris, John D.—St. Louis NL 1987.
Morris, John S.—Detroit AL 1984.
Morrison, John D.—Pittsburgh NL 1925.
*Morton, Guy—Cleveland AL *1920.
Moses, Wallace—Boston AL 1946.
Mossi, Donald L.—Cleveland AL 1954.
Mota, Manuel R.—Los Angeles NL *1974-77-78.
Motley, Darryl D.—Kansas City AL 1985.
Motton, Curtell H.—Baltimore AL 1969-*70-*71.
Mowrey, Harry H.—Brooklyn NL 1916.
Mueller, Donald F.—N. York NL *1951-54.

Mueller, Leslie C.—Detroit AL 1945.
Mullin, George E.—Detroit AL 1907-08-09.
*Mulliniks, S. Rance—Kansas City AL *1980.
Mumphrey, Jerry W.—New York AL 1981.
Muncrief, Robert C.—St. Louis AL 1944; Cleveland AL 1948.
Munger, George D.—St. Louis NL *1943-46.
Munson, Thurman L.—New York AL 1976-77-78.
*Mura, Stephen A.—St. Louis NL *1982.
Murcer, Bobby R.—New York AL 1981.
Murphy, Daniel F.—Philadelphia AL 1905-10-11-*13.
Murphy, J. Edward—Philadelphia AL 1913-14; Chicago AL *1917-19.
Murphy, John J.—New York AL 1936-37-38-39-41-*42-43.
Murray, Eddie C.—Baltimore AL 1979-83.
*Murray, George K.—New York AL *1922.
Murray, John J.—New York NL 1911-12-13-*17.
Musial, Stanley F.—St. Louis NL 1942-43-44-46.
Myer, Charles S.—Washington AL 1925-33.
Myers, Henry H.—Brooklyn NL 1916-20.
Myers, William H.—Cincinnati NL 1939-40.

N

Naragon, Harold—Cleveland AL 1954.
Narleski, Raymond E.—Cleveland AL 1954.
Narron, Samuel—St. Louis NL *1942-43.
Neal, Charles L.—Brooklyn NL 1956; Los Angeles NL 1959.
Neale, Alfred E.—Cincinnati NL 1919.
Needham, Thomas J.—Chicago NL 1910.
Nehf, Arthur N.—New York NL 1921-22-23-24; Chicago NL 1929.
Neis, Bernard E.—Brooklyn NL 1920.
Nelson, Glenn R.—Brooklyn NL 1952; Pittsburgh NL 1960.
Nelson, Melvin—Minnesota AL *1965; St. Louis NL 1968.
Nettles, Graig—New York AL 1976-77-78-81; San Diego NL 1984.
Newcombe, Donald—Brooklyn NL 1949-55-56.
Newhouser, Harold—Detroit AL *1940-45; Cleveland AL 1954.
Newman, Albert D.—Minnesota AL 1987.
Newsom, Louis N.—Detroit AL 1940; New York AL 1947.
Niarhos, Constantine—New York AL 1949.
Nicholson, William B.—Chicago NL 1945.
Nicosia, Steven R.—Pittsburgh NL 1979.
Niedenfuer, Thomas E.—Los Angeles NL 1981.
Niehoff, J. Albert—Philadelphia NL 1915.
Niekro, Joseph F.—Minnesota AL 1987.
Nieman, Robert C.—San Francisco NL 1962.
*Niemann, Randy H.—New York NL *1986.
Nieto, Thomas A.—St. Louis NL 1985.
*Niggeling, John A.—Cincinnati NL *1939.
Noble, Rafael—New York NL 1951.
Nolan, Gary L.—Cincinnati NL 1970-72-75-76.
Nolan, Joseph W.—Baltimore AL 1983.
Noles, Dickie R.—Philadelphia NL 1980.
Noren, Irving A.—New York AL 1952-53-55.
Norman, Fredie H.—Cincinnati NL 1975-76.
North, William A.—Oakland AL 1974; Los Angeles NL 1978.
Northrup, James T.—Detroit AL 1968.
Nossek, Joseph R.—Minnesota AL 1965.
Nunamaker, Leslie G.—Boston AL *1912; Cleveland AL 1920.
*Nunn, Howard R.—Cincinnati NL *1961.

O

Oates, Johnny L.—Los Angeles NL 1977-78.
Oberkfell, Kenneth R.—St. Louis NL 1982.
O'Brien, John J.—Boston AL 1903.
O'Brien, Thomas J.—Boston AL 1912.
O'Connell, James J.—New York NL 1923-*24.
O'Connor, Patrick F.—Pittsburgh NL 1909.
O'Dea, J. Kenneth—Chicago NL 1935-38; St. Louis NL 1942-43-44.
O'Dell, William O.—San Francisco NL 1962.

Odom, Johnny L.—Oakland AL 1972-73-74.
O'Doul, Francis J.—New York AL *1922; New York NL 1933.
O'Farrell, Robert A.—Chicago NL 1918; St. Louis NL 1926.
Ogden, Warren H.—Washington AL 1924.
Oglivie, Benjamin—Milwaukee AL 1982.
Ojeda, Robert M.—New York NL 1986.
O'Leary, Charles T.—Detroit AL 1907-08-09.
Oldham, John C.—Pittsburgh NL 1925.
Oldis, Robert C.—Pittsburgh NL 1960.
Oldring, Reuben N.—Philadelphia AL *1910-11-13-14.
Oliva, Pedro—Minnesota AL 1965.
Oliver, Albert—Pittsburgh NL 1971.
Oliver, Nathaniel—Los Angeles NL 1966.
Olmo, Luis R.—Brooklyn NL 1949.
Olson, Ivan M.—Brooklyn NL 1916-20.
O'Mara, Oliver E.—Brooklyn NL 1916.
O'Neill, Stephen F.—Cleveland AL 1920.
O'Neill, William J.—Chicago AL 1906.
*Onslow, John J.—New York AL *1917.
Oquendo, Jose M.—St. Louis NL 1987.
Orosco, Jesse—New York NL 1986.
*Orr, William J.—Philadelphia AL *1913.
Orsatti, Ernest R.—St. Louis NL 1928-30-31-34.
Orsino, John—San Francisco NL 1962.
Orta, Jorge—Kansas City AL 1985.
Osinski, Daniel—Boston AL 1967.
Osteen, Claude W.—Los Angeles NL 1965-66.
Ostrowski, Joseph P.—New York AL *1950-51-*52.
Otis, Amos J.—Kansas City AL 1980.
O'Toole, James J.—Cincinnati NL 1961.
Ott, Melvin T.—New York NL 1933-36-37.
Ott, N. Edward—Pittsburgh NL 1979.
Outlaw, James P.—Detroit AL 1945.
Overall, Orval—Chicago NL 1906-07-08-10.
Overmire, Frank—Detroit AL 1945; New York AL * 1951.
Owen, Arnold M.—Brooklyn NL 1941.
Owen, Frank M.—Chicago AL 1906.
Owen, Marvin J.—Detroit AL 1934-35.
Owen, Spike D.—Boston AL 1986.
Oyler, Raymond F.—Detroit AL 1968.

P

Paciorek, Thomas M.—Los Angeles NL 1974.
Pafko, Andrew—Chicago NL 1945; Brooklyn NL 1952; Milwaukee NL 1957-58.
Pagan, Jose A.—San Francisco NL 1962; Pittsburgh NL 1971.
Page, Joseph F.—New York AL 1947-49-*50.
Page, Vance L.—Chicago NL 1938.
Pagnozzi, Thomas A.—St. Louis NL 1987.
Paige, Leroy—Cleveland AL 1948.
Palica, Ervin M.—Brooklyn NL 1949-*53.
Palmer, James A.—Baltimore AL 1966-69-70-71-79-83.
*Palmisano, Joseph A.—Philadelphia AL *1931.
*Pape, Lawrence A.—Boston AL *1912.
Parent, Frederick A.—Boston AL 1903.
Parker, David G.—Pittsburgh NL 1979.
Parker, Harry W.—New York NL 1973.
Parker, M. Wesley—Los Angeles NL 1965-66.
*Parmelee, LeRoy E.—New York NL *1933.
Parrish, Lance M.—Detroit AL 1984.
Partee, Roy R.—Boston AL 1946.
Paschal, Benjamin E.—New York AL 1926-*27-28.
Pascual, Camilo—Minnesota, AL 1965.
Paskert, George H.—Philadelphia NL 1915; Chicago NL 1918.
Passeau, Claude W.—Chicago NL 1945.
Patterson, Daryl A.—Detroit AL 1968.
*Patterson, Roy C.—Chicago AL *1906.
Pattin, Martin W.—Kansas City AL 1980.
*Paulette, E. Eugene—New York NL *1911.
Payne, Frederick T.—Detroit AL 1907.
Pearson, Marcellus M.—New York AL 1936-37-38-39.
Peck, Harold A.—Cleveland AL 1948.
Peckinpaugh, Roger T.—New York AL 1921; Washington AL 1924-25.
*Peek, Stephen G.—New York AL *1941.
Peel, Homer H.—New York NL 1933.
*Pellagrini, Edward C.—Boston AL *1946.
*Pena, Alejandro—Los Angeles NL 1981.

Pena, Antonio F.—St. Louis NL 1987.
Pendleton, Terry L.—St. Louis NL 1985-87.
*Penner, Kenneth W.—Chicago NL *1929.
Pennock, Herbert J.—Philadelphia AL *1913-14; New York AL 1923-26-27-*28-32.
Pepitone, Joseph A.—New York AL 1963-64.
Perez, Atanasio R.—Cincinnati NL 1970-72-75-76; Philadelphia NL 1983.
*Perkins, Charles S.—Philadelphia AL *1930.
*Perkins, Ralph F.—Philadelphia AL *1929-*30.
Perranoski, Ronald P.—Los Angeles NL 1963-65-66.
Perritt, William D.—New York NL 1917.
Perry, James E.—Minnesota AL 1965.
*Pertica, William A.—Boston AL *1918.
Pesky, John M.—Boston AL 1946.
*Peterson, James N.—Philadelphia AL *1931.
Petrocelli, Americo P.—Boston AL 1967-75.
Petry, Daniel J.—Detroit AL 1984.
Pfeffer, Edward J.—Brooklyn NL 1916-20.
*Pfeffer, Francis X.—Chicago NL *1910.
Pfiester, John T.—Pittsburgh NL *1903; Chicago NL 1906-07-08-10.
Phelps, Edward J.—Pittsburgh NL 1903.
Philley, David E.—Cleveland AL 1954.
Phillippe, Charles L.—Pittsburgh NL 1903-09.
Phillips, John D.—New York AL 1947.
Phillips, John M.—Chicago AL 1959.
*Phillips, W. Taylor—Milwaukee AL *1957.
Phoebus, Thomas H.—Baltimore AL *1969-70.
*Picciolo, Robert M.—Milwaukee AL *1982.
Pick, Charles T.—Chicago NL 1918.
Pierce, W. William—Detroit AL *1945; Chicago AL 1959; San Francisco NL 1962.
Piercy, William B.—New York AL 1921.
Pignatano, Joseph B.—Los Angeles NL 1959.
*Pillette, Duane X.—New York AL *1949.
Pina, Horacio—Oakland AL 1973.
Piniella, Louis V.—New York AL 1976-77-78-81.
Pinson, Vada E.—Cincinnati NL 1961.
Pipgras, George W.—New York AL *1923-27-28-32.
Pipp, Walter C.—New York AL 1921-22-23.
Pizarro, Juan—Milwaukee NL 1957-58.
Plank, Edward S.—Philadelphia AL 1905-*10-11-13-14.
Pleis, William—Minnesota AL 1965.
*Plummer, William F.—Cincinnati *1972-*75-*76.
Podres, John J.—Brooklyn NL 1953-55; Los Angeles NL 1959-63-*65.
Pole, Richard H.—Boston AL 1975.
Pollet, Howard J.—St. Louis NL 1942-46.
Pope, David—Cleveland AL 1954.
Porter, Darrell R.—Kansas City AL 1980; St. Louis NL 1982-85.
Post, Walter C.—Cincinnati NL 1961.
Potter, Nelson T.—St. Louis AL 1944; Boston NL 1948.
Powell, A. Jacob—New York AL 1936-37-38-*39.
Powell, John W.—Baltimore AL 1966-69-70-71.
*Powell, William B.—Pittsburgh NL *1909.
Powers, Michael R.—Philadelphia AL 1905.
Price, Jimmy W.—Detroit AL 1968.
Priddy, Gerald E.—New York AL *1941-42.
Prim, Raymond L.—Chicago NL 1945.
Pryor, Gregory R.—Kansas City AL 1985.
Puccinelli, George C.—St. Louis NL 1930.
Puckett, Kirby—Minnesota AL 1987.
*Purdin, John N.—Los Angeles NL *1965.
Purkey, Robert T.—Cincinnati NL 1961.

Q

Quilici, Frank R.—Minnesota AL 1965.
Quinn, John P.—New York AL 1921; Philadelphia AL 1929-30.
*Quirk, James P.—Kansas City AL *1980-*85.
Quisenberry, Daniel R.—Kansas City AL 1980-85.

R

Rackley, Marvin E.—Brooklyn NL 1949.
*Ramirez, Mario—San Diego NL *1984.
Ramsey, Michael J.—St. Louis NL 1982.
Randolph, William L.—New York AL 1976-77-81.
Rariden, William A.—New York NL 1917; Cincinnati NL 1919.
Raschi, Victor J.—New York AL 1947-49-50-51-52-53.
Rath, Maurice C.—Cincinnati NL 1919.
Rau, Douglas J.—Los Angeles NL *1974-77-78.
Rautzhan, Clarence G.—Los Angeles NL 1977-78.
Rawlings, John W.—New York NL 1921-*22; Pittsburgh NL *1925.
Reardon, Jeffrey J.—Minnesota AL 1987.
Reed, Howard D.—Los Angeles NL 1965.
Reed, John B.—New York AL 1961-*62-*63.
Reed, Ronald L.—Philadelphia NL 1980-83.
Reese, Harold H.—Brooklyn NL 1941-47-49-52-53-55-56.
Regalado, Rudolph—Cleveland AL 1954.
Regan, Philip R.—Los Angeles NL 1966.
*Reiber, Frank B.—Detroit AL *1935.
Reinhart, Arthur C.—St. Louis NL 1926-*28.
Reiser, Harold P.—Brooklyn NL 1941-47.
Reniff, Harold E.—New York AL *1961-63-64.
*Renna, William B.—New York AL *1953.
Repulski, Eldon J.—Los Angeles NL 1959.
Rettenmund, Mervin W.—Baltimore AL 1969-70-71; Cincinnati NL 1975.
Reulbach, Edward M.—Chicago NL 1906-07-08-10.
Reuschel, Rick E.—New York AL 1981.
Reuss, Jerry—Los Angeles NL 1981.
*Revering, David A.—New York AL 1981.
Reynolds, Allie P.—New York AL 1947-49-50-51-52-53.
Reynolds, Carl N.—Chicago NL 1938.
Rhem, Charles F.—St. Louis NL 1926-28-30-31.
Rhoden, Richard A.—Los Angeles NL 1977-*78.
Rhodes, James L.—New York NL 1954.
Rhyne, Harold J.—Pittsburgh NL 1927.
Rice, Delbert W.—St. Louis NL 1946; Milwaukee NL 1957-*58.
Rice, Edgar C.—Washington AL 1924-25-33.
Rice, James E.—Boston AL 1986.
*Rice, Leonard O.—Chicago NL *1945.
Richards, Paul R.—New York NL *1933; Detroit AL 1945.
Richardson, Gordon C.—St. Louis NL 1964.
Richardson, Robert C.—New York AL 1957-58-60-61-62-63-64.
Richert, Peter G.—Los Angeles NL *1963; Baltimore AL 1969-70-71.
Richie, Lewis A.—Chicago NL 1910.
Rickert, Marvin A.—Boston NL 1948.
Ricketts, David W.—St. Louis NL 1967-68.
Riddle, Elmer R.—Cincinnati NL 1940.
Riggs, Lewis S.—Cincinnati NL *1939-40; Brooklyn NL 1941.
Righetti, David A.—New York AL 1981.
Rigney, William J.—New York NL 1951.
Ring, James J.—Cincinnati NL 1919.
Ripken, Calvin E.—Baltimore AL 1983.
Ripple, James A.—New York NL 1936-37; Cincinnati NL 1940.
Risberg, Charles A.—Chicago AL 1917-19.
Ritchey, Claude C.—Pittsburgh NL 1903.
Rivera, Manuel J.—Chicago AL 1959.
Rivers, John M.—New York AL 1976-77-78.
Rixey, Eppa—Philadelphia NL 1915.
Rizzuto, Philip F.—New York AL 1941-42-47-49-50-51-52-53-55.
*Roach, Melvin E.—Milwaukee *1957.
*Roberts, David A.—Pittsburgh NL *1979.
Roberts, Robin E.—Philadelphia NL 1950.
Robertson, Andre L.—New York AL 1981.
Robertson, Davis A.—New York NL 1917-*22.
Robertson, Eugene E.—New York AL 1928.
Robertson, Robert E.—Pittsburgh NL 1971.
Robinson, Aaron A.—New York AL 1947.
Robinson, Brooks C.—Baltimore AL 1966-69-70-71.
Robinson, Don A.—Pittsburgh NL 1979.

Robinson, Frank—Cincinnati NL 1961; Baltimore AL 1966-69-70-71.
*Robinson, Humberto V.—Milwaukee *1958.
Robinson, Jack R.—Brooklyn NL 1947-49-52-53-55-56.
Robinson, W. Edward—Cleveland AL 1948; New York AL 1955.
Robinson, William H.—Pittsburgh NL 1979.
Rodriguez, Aurelio—New York AL 1981.
Roe, Elwin C.—Brooklyn NL 1949-52-53.
Roebuck, Edward J.—Brooklyn NL 1955-56.
Roenicke, Gary S.—Baltimore NL 1979-83.
Roenicke, Ronald J.—San Diego NL 1984.
*Roettger, Oscar F. L.—New York AL *1923.
Roettger, Walter H.—St. Louis NL *1928-31.
Rogell, William G.—Detroit AL 1934-35.
Rogers, Thomas A.—New York AL 1921.
Rohe, George A.—Chicago AL 1906.
*Rojek, Stanley A.—Brooklyn NL *1947.
Rolfe, Robert A.—New York AL 1936-37-38-39-41-42.
Rollins, Richard J.—Minnesota AL 1965.
Romano, John A.—Chicago AL 1959.
Romero, Edgardo—Milwaukee AL *1982; Boston AL 1986.
Rommel, Edwin A.—Philadelphia AL 1929-*30-31.
Romo, Enrique—Pittsburgh NL 1979.
Rooker, James P.—Pittsburgh NL 1979.
Root, Charles H.—Chicago NL 1929-32-35-38.
Rosar, Warren V.—New York AL *1939-41-42.
Rose, Peter E.—Cincinnati NL 1970-72-75-76; Philadelphia NL 1980-83.
Roseboro, John—Los Angeles NL 1959-63-65-66.
Rosen, Albert L.—Cleveland AL 1948-54.
Rossman, Claude R.—Detroit AL 1907-08.
*Roth, Robert F.—New York AL *1921.
Rothrock, John H.—St. Louis NL 1934.
Roush, Edd J.—Cincinnati NL 1919.
*Rowe, Kenneth D.—Los Angeles NL *1963.
Rowe, Lynwood T.—Detroit AL 1934-35-40.
*Rozema, David S.—Detroit AL *1984.
*Roznovsky, Victor J.—Baltimore AL *1966.
Rucker, George N.—Brooklyn NL 1916.
Rudolph, Richard—Boston NL 1914.
Rudi, Joseph O.—Oakland AL 1972-73-74.
Ruel, Herold D.—Washington AL 1924-25.
Ruether, Walter H.—Cincinnati NL 1919; Washington AL 1925; New York AL 1926-*27.
Ruffing, Charles H.—New York AL 1932-36-37-38-39-41-42.
Rush, Robert R.—Milwaukee NL 1958.
Russell, Allan E.—Washington AL 1924-*25.
Russell, Ewell A.—Chicago AL 1917.
Russell, Glen D.—Boston AL 1946.
Russell, Jack E.—Washington AL 1933; Chicago NL 1938.
Russell, William E.—Los Angeles NL 1974-77-78-81.
Russo, Marius U.—New York AL *1939-41-*42-43.
Ruth, George H.—Boston AL 1915-16-18; New York AL 1921-22-23-26-27-28-32.
Rutherford, John W.—Brooklyn NL 1952.
Ruthven, Richard D.—Philadelphia NL 1980.
Ryan, Cornelius J.—Boston NL 1948.
Ryan, John C.—New York AL 1933-37.
Ryan, L. Nolan—New York NL 1969.
Ryan, Michael J.—Boston AL 1967.
Ryan, Wilfred D.—New York NL *1921-22-23-24; New York AL *1928.
Ryba, Dominic J.—Boston AL 1946.

S

Saberhagen, Bret W.—Kansas City AL 1985.
Sadecki, Raymond M.—St. Louis NL 1964; New York NL 1973.
Sain, John F.—Boston NL 1948; New York AL 1951-52-53.
Sakata, Lenn H.—Baltimore AL 1983.
Salazar, Luis E.—San Diego NL 1984.
Salkeld, William F.—Boston NL 1948.
Sallee, Harry F.—New York NL 1917; Cincinnati NL 1919; New York NL *1921.

Salmon, Ruthford E.—Baltimore AL 1969-70-*71.
*Saltzgaver, Otto H.—New York AL *1936-*37.
*Salveson, John T.—New York NL *1933.
Sambito, Joseph C.—Boston AL 1986.
Samuel, Juan M.—Philadelphia NL 1983.
Sanders, Raymond F.—St. Louis NL 1942-43-44; Boston NL 1948.
Sands, Charles D.—Pittsburgh NL 1971.
*Sanford, J. Frederick—New York AL *1949-*50.
Sanford, John S.—San Francisco NL 1962.
Sanguillen, Manuel de J.—Pittsburgh NL 1971-79.
Santana, Rafael F.—New York NL 1986.
Santiago, Jose R.—Boston AL 1967.
*Sarmiento, Manuel E.—Cincinnati NL *1976.
Saucier, Kevin A.—Philadelphia NL 1980.
Sauer, Edward—Chicago NL 1945.
Sawatski, Carl E.—Milwaukee NL 1957.
Sax, Steven L.—Los Angeles NL 1981.
Scarborough, Ray W.—New York AL 1952.
*Scarsella, Leslie G.—Cincinnati NL *1939.
Schaefer, Herman A.—Detroit AL 1907-08.
Schalk, Raymond W.—Chicago AL 1917-1919.
Schallock, Arthur L.—New York AL *1951-53.
Schang, Walter H.—Philadelphia AL 1913-14; Boston AL 1918; New York AL 1921-22-23; Philadelphia AL *1930.
Schatzeder, Daniel E.—Minnesota AL 1987.
Schenz, Henry L.—New York NL 1951.
Scherrer, William J.—Detroit AL 1984.
Schiraldi, Calvin D.—Boston AL 1986.
Schmandt, Raymond H.—Brooklyn NL 1920.
Schmidt, Charles—Detroit AL 1907-08-09.
Schmidt, Charles J.—Boston NL 1914.
Schmidt, Frederick A.—St. Louis NL 1944-*46.
Schmidt, Michael J.—Philadelphia NL 1980-83.
Schoendienst, Albert F.—St. Louis NL 1946; Milwaukee NL 1957-58.
Schofield, J. Richard—Pittsburgh NL 1960; St. Louis NL 1968.
Schreckengost, Ossee F.—Philadelphia AL 1905.
*Schreiber, Henry W.—Cincinnati NL *1919.
*Schuble, Henry G.—Detroit AL *1934-*35.
Schulte, Frank—Chicago NL 1906-07-08-10.
Schulte, Frederick W.—Washington AL 1933.
*Schulte, John C.—Chicago NL *1929.
Schultz, George W.—St. Louis NL 1964.
Schumacher, Harold H.—New York NL 1933-36-37.
Schupp, Ferdinand M.—New York NL 1917.
Schuster, William C.—Chicago NL 1945.
Scioscia, Michael L.—Los Angeles NL 1981.
Scott, George—Boston AL 1967.
*Scott, James—Chicago AL *1917.
Scott, John W.—New York NL 1922-23.
Scott, L. Everett—Boston AL 1915-16-18; New York AL 1922-23; Washington AL *1925.
*Sears, Kenneth E.—New York AL *1943.
*Seats, Thomas E.—Detroit AL *1940.
Seaver, G. Thomas—New York NL 1969-73.
Sebring, James D.—Pittsburgh NL 1903.
Secory, Frank E.—Chicago NL 1945.
*See, Charles H.—Cincinnati NL *1919.
Seeds, Robert I.—New York AL 1936.
Segui, Diego P.—Boston AL 1975.
Selkirk, George A.—New York AL 1936-37-38-39-41-42.
Seminick, Andrew W.—Philadelphia NL 1950.
*Sessi, Walter A.—St. Louis NL *1946.
*Sevcik, John J.—Minnesota AL *1965.
Severeid, Henry L.—Washington AL 1925; New York AL 1926.
Sewell, J. Luther—Washington AL 1933.
Sewell, Joseph W.—Cleveland AL 1920; New York AL 1932.
Seybold, Ralph O.—Philadelphia AL 1905.
Shafer, Arthur J.—New York NL 1912-13.
Shamsky, Arthur L.—New York NL 1969.
Shannon, T. Michael—St. Louis NL 1964-67-68.
Shantz, Robert C.—New York AL 1957-*58-60.

Shaw, Robert J.—Chicago AL 1959.
Shawkey, J. Robert—Philadelphia AL *1913-14; New York AL 1921-22-23-26-*27.
Shea, Francis J.—New York AL 1947-*51.
*Shea, Patrick H.—New York AL *1921.
Shean, David W.—Boston AL 1918.
Sheckard, S. James T.—Chicago NL 1906-07-08-10.
Sheehan, John T.—Brooklyn NL 1920.
*Sheehan, Thomas C.—Pittsburgh NL *1925.
Shelby, John T.—Baltimore AL 1983.
Sheldon, Roland F.—New York AL *1961-*62-64.
*Shelley, Hubert L.—Detroit AL *1935.
Sherdel, William H.—St. Louis NL 1926-28.
Sheridan, Patrick A.—Kansas City AL 1985.
Sherry, Lawrence—Los Angeles NL 1959-*63.
*Shinners, Ralph P.—New York NL *1923.
Shirley, A. Newman—St. Louis AL 1944.
Shirley, Ernest R.—Washington AL 1924.
Shocker, Urban J.—New York AL 1926-*27.
*Shoffner, Milburn J.—Cincinnati NL *1939-*40.
Shopay, Thomas M.—Baltimore AL 1971.
Shore, Ernest G.—Boston AL 1915-16.
Shores, William D.—Philadelphia AL *1929-30.
Shorten, Charles H.—Boston AL 1916.
*Shoun, Clyde M.—Chicago NL *1935; Boston NL *1948.
Show, Eric V.—San Diego NL 1984.
Shuba, George T.—Brooklyn NL 1952-53-55.
Siebern, Norman L.—New York AL 1956-58; Boston AL 1967.
Siever, Edward T.—Detroit AL 1907.
*Signer, Walter D.—Chicago NL *1945.
Silvera, Charles A.—New York AL 1949-*50-*51-*52-*53-*55-*56.
Silvestri, Kenneth J.—New York AL *1941; Philadelphia NL 1950.
Simmons, Aloysius H.—Philadelphia AL 1929-30-31; Cincinnati NL 1939.
Simmons, Curtis T.—St. Louis NL 1964.
Simmons, Ted L.—Milwaukee AL 1982.
*Simon, Michael E.—Pittsburgh NL *1909.
Simpson, Harry L.—New York AL 1957.
*Simpson, Wayne K.—Cincinnati NL *1972.
Singleton, Kenneth W.—Baltimore AL 1979-83.
Sisk, Douglas R.—New York NL 1986.
Sisler, Richard A.—St. Louis NL 1946; Philadelphia NL 1950.
Sisti, Sebastian D.—Boston NL 1948.
Skaggs, David L.—Baltimore AL 1979.
*Skinner, E. Camp—New York AL *1922.
Skinner, Robert R.—Pittsburgh NL 1960; St. Louis NL 1964.
Skowron, William J.—New York AL 1955-56-57-58-60-61-62; Los Angeles NL 1963.
Slagle, James J.—Chicago NL *1906-07-*08.
Slaton, James M.—Milwaukee AL 1982.
Slaughter, Enos B.—St. Louis NL 1942-46; New York AL 1956-57-58.
Smalley, Roy F.—Minnesota AL 1987.
Smith, Alfred J.—New York NL 1936-37.
Smith, Alphonse E.—Cleveland AL 1954; Chicago AL 1959.
Smith, Billy E.—Baltimore AL 1979.
Smith, C. Reginald—Boston AL 1967; Los Angeles NL 1977-78-81.
Smith, Clay J.—Detroit AL 1940.
Smith, Earl S.—New York NL 1921-22; Pittsburgh NL 1925-27; St. Louis NL 1928.
Smith, Elmer J.—Cleveland AL 1920; New York AL 1922-*23.
*Smith, Frank E.—Chicago AL *1906.
Smith, Harold W.—Pittsburgh NL 1960.
Smith, Harry T.—Pittsburgh NL 1903.
*Smith, J. Carlisle—Boston NL *1914.
Smith, James L.—New York NL *1917; Cincinnati NL 1919.
Smith, Lonnie—Philadelphia NL 1980; St. Louis NL 1982; Kansas City AL 1985.
Smith, Osborne E.—St. Louis NL 1982-85-87.
Smith, Robert E.—Chicago NL 1932.
Smith, Sherrod M.—Brooklyn NL 1916-20.
Snider, Edwin D.—Brooklyn NL 1949-52-53-55-56; Los Angeles NL 1959.

Snodgrass, Frederick C.—New York NL 1911-12-13.
Snyder, Frank J.—New York NL 1921-22-23-24.
Snyder, Russell H.—Baltimore AL 1966.
*Solomon, Eddie—Los Angeles NL *1974.
*Sorrell, Victor G.—Detroit AL *1934-*35.
Sosa, Elias—Los Angeles NL 1977.
*Sothoron, Allan S.—St. Louis NL *1926.
Southworth, Willam H.—New York NL 1924; St. Louis NL 1926.
Spahn, Warren E.—Boston NL 1948; Milwaukee NL 1957-58.
Sparma, Joseph B.—Detroit AL 1968.
Speaker, Tristram—Boston AL 1912-15; Cleveland AL 1920.
Speece, Byron F.—Washington AL 1924.
*Speer, George N.—Detroit AL *1909.
Spencer, George E.—New York NL 1951.
*Spencer, Glenn E.—New York NL *1933.
Spencer, James L.—New York AL 1978.
Spencer, Roy H.—Pittsburgh NL *1925-27; New York NL *1936.
Spiezio, Edward W.—St. Louis NL *1964-67-68.
Splittorff, Paul W.—Kansas City AL 1980.
Spooner, Karl B.—Brooklyn NL 1955.
*Sprague, Edward N.—Cincinnati NL *1972.
Stafford, William C.—New York AL 1960-61-62-*63-*64.
Stahl, Charles S.—Boston AL 1903.
Stahl, J. Garland—Boston AL *1903-12.
Stainback, George T.—Chicago NL *1935; Detroit AL *1940; New York AL 1942-43.
Staley, Gerald L.—Chicago AL 1959.
*Stanceu, Charles—New York AL *1941.
Stanage, Oscar H.—Detroit AL 1909.
Stange, A. Lee—Boston AL 1967.
Stanhouse, Donald J.—Baltimore AL 1979.
Stanky, Edward R.—Brooklyn NL 1947; Boston NL 1948; New York NL 1951.
Stanley, Frederick B.—New York AL 1976-77-78.
Stanley, Mitchell J.—Detroit AL 1968.
Stanley, Robert W.—Boston AL 1986.
Stapleton, David L.—Boston AL 1986.
Stargell, Wilver D.—Pittsburgh NL 1971-79.
*Starr, Raymond F.—Chicago NL *1945.
Staub, Daniel J.—New York NL 1973.
Steinfeldt, Harry M.—Chicago NL 1906-07-08-10.
Stengel, Charles D.—Brooklyn NL 1916; New York NL *1921-22-23.
Stennett, Renaldo A.—Pittsburgh NL 1979.
Stephens, Vernon D.—St. Louis AL 1944.
Stephenson, J. Riggs—Chicago NL 1929-32.
Stephenson, Jerry J.—Boston AL 1967.
Stephenson, Walter M.—Chicago NL 1935.
Stewart, David L.—Los Angeles NL 1981.
Stewart, James F.—Cincinnati NL 1970.
Stewart, Samuel L.—Baltimore AL 1979-83; Boston AL *1986.
Stewart, Walter C.—Washington AL 1933.
*Stigman, Richard L.—Minnesota AL *1965.
Stirnweiss, George H.—New York AL 1943-47-49.
Stock, Milton J.—Philadelphia NL 1915.
Stoddard, Timothy P.—Baltimore AL 1979-*83.
Stone, George H.—New York NL 1973.
Stone, Steven M.—Baltimore AL 1979.
Stottlemyre, Melvin L.—New York AL 1964.
*Stout, Allyn M.—St. Louis NL *1931.
Straker, Lester P.—Minnesota AL 1987.
*Strand, Paul E.—Boston NL *1914.
Strang, Samuel N.—New York NL 1905.
Strawberry, Darryl E.—New York NL 1986.
Strickland, George B.—Cleveland AL 1954.
Strunk, Amos A.—Philadelphia AL 1910-11-13-14; Boston AL 1918.
Stuart, Richard L.—Pittsburgh NL 1960; Los Angeles NL 1966.
Stuper, John A.—St. Louis NL 1982.
Sturdivant, Thomas V.—New York AL 1955-56-57-*58.
*Sturgeon, Robert H.—Boston NL *1948.
Sturm, John P.—New York AL 1941.
*Suggs, George F.—Detroit AL *1908.
*Sullivan, John J.—Chicago AL *1919.
*Sullivan, Joseph—Detroit AL *1935.
*Sullivan, Marc C.—Boston AL *1986.
Sullivan, William J., Sr.—Chicago AL 1906.
Sullivan, William J., Jr.—Detroit AL 1940.

Summa, Homer W.—Philadelphia AL 1929-*30.
Summers, John J.—Detroit AL 1984.
Summers, Oren E.—Detroit AL 1908-09.
Sundberg, James H.—Kansas City AL 1985.
Sundra, Stephen R.—New York AL *1938-39.
Sutter, H. Bruce—St. Louis NL 1982.
Sutton, Donald H.—Los Angeles NL *1966-74-77-78; Milwaukee AL 1982.
Swift, Robert V.—Detroit AL 1945.
Swoboda, Ronald A.—New York NL 1969.

T

Tannehill, Lee F.—Chicago AL 1906.
Tartabull, Jose—Boston AL 1967.
Tate, H. Bennett—Washington AL 1924-*25.
Taylor, James H.—Brooklyn NL 1947.
Taylor, James W.—Brooklyn NL *1920; Chicago NL 1929-*32.
*Taylor, John W.—Chicago NL *1906.
*Taylor, Luther H.—New York NL *1905.
Taylor, Ronald W.—St. Louis NL 1964; New York NL 1969.
Taylor, Thomas L.—Washington AL 1924.
*Taylor, William M.—New York NL *1954.
Tebbetts, George R.—Detroit AL 1940.
Tekulve, Kenton C.—Pittsburgh NL 1979.
Templeton, Garry L.—San Diego NL 1984.
Tenace, F. Gene—Oakland AL 1972-73-74; St. Louis NL 1982.
Terry, Ralph W.—New York AL 1960-61-62-63-64.
Terry, William H.—New York NL 1924-33-36.
Tesreau, Charles M.—New York NL 1912-13-17.
Teufel, Timothy S.—New York NL 1986.
Thevenow, Thomas J.—St. Louis NL 1926-28.
Theodore, George B.—New York NL 1973.
Thomas, Alphonse T.—Washington AL 1933.
Thomas, Chester D.—Boston AL *1912-15-16; Cleveland AL 1920.
Thomas, Derrel—Los Angeles NL 1981.
Thomas, Frederick H.—Boston AL 1918.
Thomas, George E.—Boston AL 1967.
Thomas, J. Gorman—Milwaukee AL 1982.
Thomas, Ira F.—Detroit AL 1908; Philadelphia AL 1910-11-*13-*14.
Thomas, Myles L.—New York AL 1926-*27-*28.
Thomasson, Gary L.—New York AL 1978.
Thompson, Donald N.—Brooklyn NL 1953.
Thompson, Eugene E.—Cincinnati NL 1939-40.
Thompson, Henry—New York NL 1951-54.
Thompson, John G.—Pittsburgh NL 1903.
*Thompson, James A.—Philadelphia AL *1914.
*Thompson, John S.—Philadelphia NL *1950.
*Thompson, L. Fresco—Pittsburgh NL *1925.
Thomson, Robert B.—New York NL 1951.
Thorpe, James F.—New York NL *1913-17.
Throneberry, Marvin E.—New York AL 1958.
Thurmond, Mark A.—San Diego NL 1984.
Tiant, Luis C.—Boston AL 1975.
Tidrow, Richard W.—New York AL 1976-77-78.
*Tincup, A. Ben—Philadelphia NL *1915.
Tinker, Joseph B.—Chicago NL 1906-07-08-10.
Tinning, Lyle F.—Chicago NL 1932.
Tipton, Joseph J.—Cleveland AL 1948.
Tobin, James A.—Detroit AL 1945.
Todt, Philip J.—Philadelphia AL 1931.
Tolan, Robert—St. Louis NL 1967-68; Cincinnati NL 1970-72.
Tolson, Charles J.—Chicago NL 1929.
Toney, Frederick A.—New York NL 1921.
Toporcer, George—St. Louis NL 1926.
*Torborg, Jeffrey A.—Los Angeles NL *1965-*1966.
Torgeson, C. Earl—Boston NL 1948; Chicago AL 1959.
Torre, Frank J.—Milwaukee NL 1957-58.
Torrez, Michael A.—New York AL 1977.
Towne, Jay K.—Chicago AL 1906.
Tracewski, Richard J.—Los Angeles NL 1963-65; Detroit AL 1968.
*Trail, Chester B.—New York AL *1964.

Trammell, Alan S.—Detroit AL 1984.
Traynor, Harold J.—Pittsburgh NL 1925-27.
Tresh, Thomas M.—New York AL 1962-63-64.
*Triandos, C. Gus—New York AL *1953.
Trillo, J. Manuel—Philadelphia NL 1980.
*Triplett, H. Coaker—St. Louis NL *1942.
Trout, Paul H.—Detroit AL 1940-45.
Trowbridge, Robert—Milwaukee NL 1957-*58.
Trucks, Virgil O.—Detroit AL 1945; New York AL *1958.
Tucker, Thurman L.—Cleveland AL 1948.
Tudor, John T.—St. Louis NL 1985-87.
Tunnell, B. Lee—St. Louis NL 1987.
Turley, Robert L.—New York AL 1955-56-57-58-60-*61-*62.
Turner, James R.—Cincinnati NL 1940; New York AL 1942-*43.
Turner, Thomas R.—St. Louis AL 1944.
*Twitty, Jeffrey D.—Kansas City AL *1980.
Tyler, George A.—Boston NL 1914; Chicago NL 1918.

U

*Uecker, Robert G.—St. Louis NL *1964.
Uhlaender, Theodore O.—Cincinnati NL 1972.
Uhle, George E.—Cleveland AL 1920.
Unser, Delbert B.—Philadelphia NL 1980.

V

Valdespino, Hilario—Minnesota AL 1965.
Valenzuela, Fernando—Los Angeles NL 1981.
Vance, Arthur C.—St. Louis NL 1934.
Vandenberg, Harold H.—Chicago NL 1945.
Vander Meer, John S.—Cincinnati NL *1939-40.
Van Slyke, Andrew J.—St. Louis NL 1985.
Vaughan, J. Floyd—Brooklyn NL 1947.
Vaughn, James L.—Chicago NL 1918.
Veach, Robert H.—Washington AL 1925.
Veale, Robert A.—Pittsburgh NL 1971.
Veil, Frederick W.—Pittsburgh NL 1903.
Velez, Otoniel—New York AL 1976.
Verban, Emil M.—St. Louis NL 1944.
*Vergez, John L.—New York NL *1933.
Versalles, Zoilo—Minnesota AL 1965.
*Vick, Henry A.—St. Louis NL *1926.
Viola, Frank J.—Minnesota AL 1987.
Virdon, William C.—Pittsburgh NL 1960.
Virgil, Osvaldo J.—Philadelphia NL 1983.
Voiselle, William S.—Boston NL 1948.
Vuckovich, Peter D.—Milwaukee AL 1982.
*Vukovich, George S.—Philadelphia NL *1980.
*Vukovich, John C.—Philadelphia NL *1980.

W

*Waddell, George E.—Philadelphia AL *1905.
Wade, Benjamin S.—Brooklyn NL *1952-53.
*Wagner, Charles T.—Boston AL *1946.
Wagner, Charles F.—Boston AL 1912-*15-*16-*18.
Wagner, Harold E.—Boston AL 1946.
Wagner, John P.—Pittsburgh NL 1903-09.
Waitkus, Edward S.—Philadelphia NL 1950.
Walberg, George E.—Philadelphia AL 1929-30-31.
Walk, Robert V.—Philadelphia NL 1980.
Walker, Albert B.—Brooklyn NL *1952-*53-*55-56.
Walker, Clarence W.—Boston AL 1916.
Walker, Fred—Brooklyn NL 1941-47.
Walker, Gerald H.—Detroit AL 1934-35.
Walker, Harry W.—St. Louis NL 1942-43-46.
Walker, Harvey W.—Detroit AL 1945.
Walker, James Luke—Pittsburgh NL 1971.
*Walker, James R.—Chicago AL *1918.
Walker, William H.—St. Louis NL 1934.
*Walls, R. Lee—Los Angeles NL *1963.
Walsh, Edward A.—Chicago AL 1906.
Walsh, James C.—Philadelphia AL *1913-14; Boston AL 1916.
*Walsh, Thomas J.—Chicago NL *1906-*07.
Walters, William H.—Cincinnati NL 1939-40.
Wambsganss, William A.—Cleveland AL 1920.
Waner, Lloyd J.—Pittsburgh NL 1927.

Waner, Paul G.—Pittsburgh NL 1927.
Ward, Aaron L.—New York AL 1921-22-23-*26.
*Ward, Charles W.—Brooklyn NL *1920.
*Warden, Jonathan E.—Detroit AL *1968.
Warneke, Lonnie—Chicago NL 1932-35-*45.
Warwick, Carl W.—St. Louis NL 1964.
Wasdell, James C.—Brooklyn NL 1941.
Washburn, Ray C.—St. Louis NL *1964-67-68; Cincinnati NL 1970.
Washington, Claudell—Oakland AL 1974.
Washington, Herbert—Oakland AL 1974.
Washington, U. L.—Kansas City AL 1980.
Wathan, John D.—Kansas City AL 1980-85.
Watkins, George A.—St. Louis NL 1930-31.
Watson, John R.—New York NL 1923-24.
Watson, Robert J.—New York AL 1981.
Watt, Edward D.—Baltimore AL *1966-69-70-71.
Weatherly, C. Roy—New York AL 1943.
*Weaver, Arthur C.—Pittsburgh NL *1903.
Weaver, George D.—Chicago AL 1917-19.
Weaver, Montgomery M.—Washington AL 1933.
*Weaver, Orville F.—Chicago NL *1910.
Webb, James L.—Detroit AL 1945.
Weis, Albert J.—New York NL 1969.
*Weiser, Harry—Philadelphia NL *1915.
Welch, Robert L.—Los Angeles NL 1978-81.
*Wells, Edwin L.—New York AL *1932.
Wensloff, Charles W.—New York AL *1943-47.
*Wera, Julian V.—New York AL *1927.
Werber, William M.—Cincinnati NL 1939-40.
Wert, Donald R.—Detroit AL 1968.
Wertz, Victor W.—Cleveland AL 1954.
Westlake, Waldon T.—Cleveland AL 1954.
Westrum, Wesley N.—New York NL 1951-54.
*Whaling, Albert—Boston NL *1914.
Wheat, Zachary D.—Brooklyn NL 1916-20.
Whitaker, Louis R.—Detroit AL 1984.
White, Ernest D.—St. Louis NL 1942-43; Boston NL *1948.
White, Frank—Kansas City AL 1980-85.
White, G. Harris—Chicago AL 1906.
White, Joyner C.—Detroit AL 1934-35.
White, Roy H.—New York AL 1976-77-78.
White, William D.—St. Louis NL 1964.
Whitehead, Burgess U.—St. Louis NL 1934; New York NL 1936-37.
Whitehill, Earl O.—Washington AL 1933.
Whiteman, George—Boston AL 1918.
Whitman, Richard C.—Brooklyn NL 1949; Philadelphia NL 1950.
Whitson, Eddie L.—San Diego NL 1984.
Whitted, George B.—Boston NL 1914; Philadelphia NL 1915.
Wicker, Kemp C.—New York AL *1936-37.
*Wiesler, Robert G.—New York AL *1955.
Wiggins, Alan A.—San Diego NL 1984.
Wilcox, Milton E.—Cincinnati NL 1970; Detroit AL 1984.
*Wilhelm, Irving K.—Pittsburgh NL *1903.
Wilhelm, J. Hoyt—New York NL 1954.
Wilhoit, Joseph W.—New York NL 1917.
Wilkinson, Roy H.—Chicago AL 1919.
Wilks, Theodore—St. Louis NL 1944-46.
Willett, Robert E.—Detroit AL *1907-*08-09.
Willey, Carlton F.—Milwaukee NL 1958.
*Willhite, J. Nicholas—Los Angeles NL *1965.
Williams, Claude P.—Chicago AL 1917-19.
Williams, David C.—New York NL 1951-54.
Williams, Dewey E.—Chicago NL 1945.
Williams, E. Dibrell—Philadelphia AL *1930-31.
Williams, Richard H.—Brooklyn NL *1952-53.
Williams, Stanley W.—Los Angeles NL 1959; New York AL 1963-*64.
Williams, Theodore S.—Boston AL 1946.
*Williamson, N. Howard—St. Louis NL *1928.
Willis, Ronald E.—St. Louis NL 1967-68.
Willis, Victor G.—Pittsburgh NL 1909.
Willoughby, James A.—Boston NL 1975.
Wills, Maurice M.—Los Angeles NL 1959-63-65-66.
Wilson, Arthur E.—New York NL 1911-12-13.

Wilson, George W.—New York AL 1956.
Wilson, James—St. Louis NL 1928-30-31; Cincinnati NL 1940.
Wilson, J. Owen—Pittsburgh NL 1909.
Wilson, Lewis R.—New York NL 1924; Chicago NL 1929.
Wilson, R. Earl—Detroit AL 1968.
*Wilson, Walter W.—Detroit AL *1945.
Wilson, William H.—New York NL 1986.
Wilson, Willie J.—Kansas City AL 1980-85.
Wiltse, George L.—New York NL *1905-11-*12-13.
Winfield, David M.—New York AL 1981.
Wingo, Ivy B.—Cincinnati NL 1919.
Winter, George L.—Boston AL *1903; Detroit AL 1908.
Wise, Kendall C.—Milwaukee NL 1958.
Wise, Richard C.—Boston AL 1975.
Witt, George A.—Pittsburgh NL 1960.
Witt, Lawton W.—New York AL 1922-23.
*Wolfgang, Meldon J.—Chicago AL *1917.
Wood, Joseph—Boston AL 1912-*15; Cleveland AL 1920.
Woodeshick, Harold J.—St. Louis NL 1967.
Woodling, Eugene R.—New York AL 1949-50-51-52-53.
Woodward, William F.—Cincinnati NL 1970.
Works, Ralph T.—Detroit AL 1909.
Worrell, Todd R.—St. Louis NL 1985-87.
Worthington, Allan F.—New York NL *1954; Minnesota AL 1965.
Wortman, William L.—Chicago NL 1918.
Wright, F. Glenn—Pittsburgh NL 1925-27.
Wyatt, John T.—Boston AL 1967.
Wyatt, J. Whitlow—Brooklyn NL 1941.
Wyckoff, J. Weldon—Philadelphia AL *1913-14; Boston AL *1916.
Wynn, Early—Cleveland AL 1954; Chicago AL 1959.
Wynn, James S.—Los Angeles NL 1974.
Wyse, Henry W.—Chicago NL 1945.

Y

Yastrzemski, Carl M.—Boston AL 1967-75.
Yde, Emil O.—Pittsburgh NL 1925-27.
Yeager, Stephen W.—Los Angeles NL 1974-77-78-81.
*Yerkes, C. Carroll—Philadelphia AL *1929.
Yerkes, Stephen D.—Boston AL 1912.
York, Rudolph P.—Detroit AL 1940-45; Boston AL 1946.
Yost, Edgar F.—Milwaukee AL 1982.
Young, Denton T.—Boston AL 1903.
*Youngblood, Joel R.—Cincinnati NL *1976.
Youngs, Ross—New York NL 1921-22-23-24.
Yount, Robin R.—Milwaukee AL 1982.
Yvars, Salvatore A.—New York NL 1951.

Z

Zachary, Jonathan T.—Washington AL 1924-25; New York AL 1928.
Zachry, Patrick P.—Cincinnati NL 1976.
*Zahn, Geoffrey C.—Los Angeles NL *1974.
*Zahniser, Paul V.—Washington AL *1924.
Zarilla, Allen L.—St. Louis AL 1944.
Zeber, George W.—New York AL 1977.
Zeider, Rolla H.—Chicago NL 1918.
Zimmer, Donald W.—Brooklyn NL 1955; Los Angeles NL 1959.
Zimmerman, Gerald R.—Cincinnati NL 1961; Minnesota AL 1965.
Zimmerman, Henry—Chicago NL 1907-*08-10; New York NL 1917.
*Zoldak, Samuel W.—St. Louis AL *1944; Cleveland AL *1948.
Zuber, William H.—New York AL *1943; Boston AL 1946.

Managers

Alston, Walter E.—Brooklyn NL 1955-56; Los Angeles NL 1959-63-65-66-74.
Altobelli, Joseph S.—Baltimore AL 1983.
Anderson, George L.—Cincinnati NL 1970-72-75-76; Detroit AL 1984.
Baker, Delmer D.—Detroit AL 1940.
Barrow, Edward G.—Boston AL 1918.
Bauer, Henry A.—Baltimore AL 1966.
Berra, Lawrence P.—New York AL 1964; New York NL 1973.
Boudreau, Louis—Cleveland AL 1948.
Bush, Owen J.—Pittsburgh NL 1927.
Carrigan, William F.—Boston AL 1915-16.

Chance, Frank L.—Chicago NL 1906-07-08-10.

Clarke, Fred C.—Pittsburgh NL 1903-09.

Cochrane, Gordon S.—Detroit AL 1934-35.

Collins, James J.—Boston AL 1903.

Cronin, Joseph E.—Washington AL 1933; Boston AL 1946.

Dark, Alvin R.—San Francisco NL 1962; Oakland AL 1974.

Dressen, Charles W.—Brooklyn NL 1952-53.

Durocher, Leo E.—Brooklyn NL 1941; New York NL 1951-54.

Dyer, Edwin H.—St. Louis NL 1946.

Frey, James G.—Kansas City AL 1980.

Frisch, Frank F.—St. Louis NL 1934.

Gleason, William—Chicago AL 1919.

Green, G. Dallas—Philadelphia NL 1980.

Grimm, Charles J.—Chicago NL 1932-35-45.

Haney, Fred G.—Milwaukee NL 1957-58.

Harris, Stanley R.—Washington AL 1924-25; New York AL 1947.

Hartnett, Charles L.—Chicago NL 1938.

Herzog, Dorrel N.—St. Louis NL 1982-85-87.

Hodges, Gilbert R.—New York NL 1969.

Hornsby, Rogers—St. Louis NL 1926.

Houk, Ralph G.—New York AL 1961-62-63.

Howser, Richard D.—Kansas City AL 1985.

Huggins, Miller J.—New York AL 1921-22-23-26-27-28.

Hutchinson, Frederick C.—Cincinnati NL 1961.

Jennings, Hugh A.—Detroit AL 1907-08-09.

Johnson, Darrell D.—Boston AL 1975.

Johnson, David A.—New York NL 1986.

Jones, Fielder A.—Chicago AL 1906.

Keane, John J.—St. Louis NL 1964.

Kelly, J. Thomas—Minnesota AL 1987.

Kuenn, Harvey E.—Milwaukee AL 1982.

Lasorda, Thomas C.—Los Angeles NL 1977-78-81.

Lemon, Robert G.—New York AL 1978-81.

Lopez, Alfonso R.—Cleveland AL 1954; Chicago AL 1959.

Mack, Connie—Philadelphia AL 1905-10-11-13-14-29-30-31.

Martin, Alfred M.—New York AL 1976-77.

McCarthy, Joseph V.—Chicago NL 1929; New York AL 1932-36-37-38-39-41-42-43.

McGraw, John J.—New York NL 1905-11-12-13-17-21-22-23-24.

McKechnie, William B.—Pittsburgh NL 1925; St. Louis NL 1928; Cincinnati NL 1939-40.

McNamara, John F.—Boston AL 1986.

Mele, Sabath A.—Minnesota AL 1965.

Mitchell, Fred F.—Chicago NL 1918.

Moran, Patrick J.—Philadelphia NL 1915; Cincinnati NL 1919.

Murtaugh, Daniel E.—Pittsburgh NL 1960-71.

O'Neill, Stephen F.—Detroit AL 1945.

Owens, Paul F.—Philadelphia NL 1983.

Robinson, Wilbert—Brooklyn NL 1916-20.

Rowland, Clarence H.—Chicago AL 1917.

Sawyer, Edwin M.—Philadelphia NL 1950.

Schoendienst, Albert F.—St. Louis NL 1967-68.

Sewell, J. Luther—St. Louis AL 1944.

Shotton, Burton E.—Brooklyn NL 1947-49.

Smith, E. Mayo—Detroit AL 1968.

Southworth, William H.—St. Louis NL 1942-43-44; Boston NL 1948.

Speaker, Tris E.—Cleveland AL 1920.

Stahl, J. Garland—Boston AL 1912.

Stallings, George T.—Boston NL 1914.

Stengel, Charles D.—New York AL 1949-50-51-52-53-55-56-57-58-60.

Street, Charles E.—St. Louis NL 1930-31.

Tanner, Charles W.—Pittsburgh NL 1979.

Terry, William H.—New York NL 1933-36-37.

Weaver, Earl S.—Baltimore AL 1969-70-71-79.

Williams, Richard H.—Boston AL 1967; Oakland AL 1972-73; San Diego NL 1984.

WORLD SERIES TOP 20
BATTING

Series (Pitchers Excluded)

Player	S.
Yogi Berra	14
Mickey Mantle	12
Joe DiMaggio	10
Elston Howard	10
Babe Ruth	10
Hank Bauer	9
Phil Rizzuto	9
Bill Dickey	8
Frankie Frisch	8
Gil McDougald	8
Bill Skowron	8
Many tied with	7

Games

Player	G.
Yogi Berra	75
Mickey Mantle	65
Elston Howard	54
Hank Bauer	53
Gil McDougald	53
Phil Rizzuto	52
Joe DiMaggio	51
Frankie Frisch	50
Pee Wee Reese	44
Roger Maris	41
Babe Ruth	41
Carl Furillo	40
Jim Gilliam	39
Gil Hodges	39
Bill Skowron	39
Bill Dickey	38
Jackie Robinson	38
Tony Kubek	37
Three tied with	36

Batting Average (75+ AB)

Player	AB.	PCT.
Lou Brock	87	.391
Home Run Baker	91	.363
Lou Gehrig	119	.361
Reggie Jackson	98	.357
Billy Martin	99	.333
Eddie Collins	128	.328
Babe Ruth	129	.326
Charlie Gehringer	81	.321
Steve Garvey	113	.319
Hank Greenberg	85	.318
Gene Woodling	85	.318
Johnny Evers	76	.316
Frank Schulte	81	.309
Bobby Richardson	131	.305
Frankie Frisch	197	.294
Harry Hooper	92	.293
Bill Skowron	133	.293
Willie McGee	79	.291
Enos Slaughter	79	.291
Two tied with	94 or 129	.287

Slugging Average (75+ AB)

Player	AB.	SLG.
Reggie Jackson	98	.755
Babe Ruth	129	.744
Lou Gehrig	119	.731
Lou Brock	87	.655
Hank Greenberg	85	.624
Duke Snider	133	.594
Billy Martin	99	.566
Frank Robinson	92	.554
Home Run Baker	91	.538
Mickey Mantle	230	.535
Gene Woodling	85	.529
Johnny Bench	86	.523
Bill Skowron	133	.519
Goose Goslin	129	.488
Enos Slaughter	79	.468
Emil Meusel	87	.460
Willie McGee	79	.456
Yogi Berra	259	.452
Tommy Henrich	84	.452
Two tied with	85 or 92	.435

At-Bats

Player	AB.
Yogi Berra	259
Mickey Mantle	230
Joe DiMaggio	199
Frankie Frisch	197
Gil McDougald	190
Hank Bauer	188
Phil Rizzuto	183
Elston Howard	171
Pee Wee Reese	169
Roger Maris	152
Jim Gilliam	147
Tony Kubek	146
Bill Dickey	145
Jackie Robinson	137
Bill Skowron	133
Duke Snider	133
Gil Hodges	131
Bobby Richardson	131
Pete Rose	130
Three tied with	129

Runs

Player	R.
Mickey Mantle	42
Yogi Berra	41
Babe Ruth	37
Lou Gehrig	30
Joe DiMaggio	27
Roger Maris	26
Elston Howard	25
Gil McDougald	23
Jackie Robinson	22
Hank Bauer	21
Reggie Jackson	21
Phil Rizzuto	21
Duke Snider	21
Gene Woodling	21
Eddie Collins	20
Pee Wee Reese	20
Bill Dickey	19
Frank Robinson	19
Bill Skowron	19
Two tied with	18

Hits

Player	H.
Yogi Berra	71
Mickey Mantle	59
Frankie Frisch	58
Joe DiMaggio	54
Hank Bauer	46
Pee Wee Reese	46
Gil McDougald	45
Phil Rizzuto	45
Lou Gehrig	43
Eddie Collins	42
Elston Howard	42
Babe Ruth	42
Bobby Richardson	40
Bill Skowron	39
Duke Snider	38
Bill Dickey	37
Goose Goslin	37
Steve Garvey	36
Four tied with	35

Total Bases

Player	TB.
Mickey Mantle	123
Yogi Berra	117
Babe Ruth	96
Lou Gehrig	87
Joe DiMaggio	84
Duke Snider	79
Hank Bauer	75
Frankie Frisch	74
Reggie Jackson	74
Gil McDougald	72
Bill Skowron	69
Elston Howard	66
Goose Goslin	63
Pee Wee Reese	59
Lou Brock	57
Roger Maris	56
Billy Martin	56
Bill Dickey	55
Gil Hodges	54
Phil Rizzuto	54

Doubles

Player	2B.
Yogi Berra	10
Frankie Frisch	10
Jack Barry	9
Pete Fox	9
Carl Furillo	9
Lou Gehrig	8
Lonnie Smith	8
Duke Snider	8
Home Run Baker	7
Lou Brock	7
Eddie Collins	7
Hank Greenberg	7
Chick Hafey	7
Elston Howard	7
Reggie Jackson	7
Marty Marion	7
Pepper Martin	7
Danny Murphy	7
Stan Musial	7
Jackie Robinson	7

Triples

Player	3B.
Bill Johnson	4
Tommy Leach	4
Tris Speaker	4
Hank Bauer	3
Bobby Brown	3
Dave Concepcion	3
Buck Freeman	3
Frankie Frisch	3
Lou Gehrig	3
Billy Martin	3
Tim McCarver	3
Bob Meusel	3
Fred Parent	3
Chick Stahl	3
Many tied with	2

Home Runs

Player	HR.
Mickey Mantle	18
Babe Ruth	15
Yogi Berra	12
Duke Snider	11
Lou Gehrig	10
Reggie Jackson	10
Joe DiMaggio	8
Frank Robinson	8
Bill Skowron	8
Hank Bauer	7
Goose Goslin	7
Gil McDougald	7
Roger Maris	6
Al Simmons	6
Reggie Smith	6
Many tied with	5

Runs Batted In

Player	RBI.
Mickey Mantle	40
Yogi Berra	39
Lou Gehrig	35
Babe Ruth	33
Joe DiMaggio	30
Bill Skowron	29
Duke Snider	26
Hank Bauer	24
Bill Dickey	24
Reggie Jackson	24
Gil McDougald	24
Hank Greenberg	22
Gil Hodges	21
Goose Goslin	19
Elston Howard	19
Tony Lazzeri	19
Billy Martin	19
Home Run Baker	18
Charlie Keller	18
Roger Maris	18

Game-Winning RBIs (1980—Present)

Player	GW.
Mike Schmidt	2
Steve Yeager	2
Many tied with	1

Bases on Balls

Player	BB.
Mickey Mantle	43
Babe Ruth	33
Yogi Berra	32
Phil Rizzuto	30
Lou Gehrig	26
Mickey Cochrane	25
Jim Gilliam	23
Jackie Robinson	21
Gil McDougald	20
Joe DiMaggio	19
Gene Woodling	19
Roger Maris	18
Pee Wee Reese	18
Gil Hodges	17
Gene Tenace	17
Ross Youngs	17
Pete Rose	16
Five tied with	15

Strikeouts

Player	SO.
Mickey Mantle	54
Elston Howard	37
Duke Snider	33
Babe Ruth	30
Gil McDougald	29
Bill Skowron	26
Hank Bauer	25
Reggie Jackson	24
Bob Meusel	24
Joe DiMaggio	23
George Kelly	23
Tony Kubek	23
Frank Robinson	23
Jim Bottomley	22
Joe Collins	22
Gil Hodges	22
Steve Garvey	21
Roger Maris	21
Tony Perez	21
Three tied with	20

Stolen Bases

Player	SB.
Lou Brock	14
Eddie Collins	14
Frank Chance	10
Dave Lopes	10
Phil Rizzuto	10
Frankie Frisch	9
Honus Wagner	9
Johnny Evers	8
Pepper Martin	7
Joe Morgan	7
Vince Coleman	6
Jackie Robinson	6
Jimmy Slagle	6
Joe Tinker	6
Bob Tolan	6
Maury Wills	6
Dave Concepcion	5
Bob Meusel	5
Pee Wee Reese	5
Willie Wilson	5

WORLD SERIES TOP 20
PITCHING

Series

Pitcher	S.
Whitey Ford	11
Waite Hoyt	7
Red Ruffing	7
Jim Hunter	6
Johnny Murphy	6
Jim Palmer	6
Vic Raschi	6
Allie Reynolds	6
Many tied with	5

Games

Pitcher	G.
Whitey Ford	22
Rollie Fingers	16
Allie Reynolds	15
Bob Turley	15
Clay Carroll	14
Clem Labine	13
Waite Hoyt	12
Jim Hunter	12
Art Nehf	12
Paul Derringer	11
Carl Erskine	11
Rube Marquard	11
Christy Mathewson	11
Vic Raschi	11
Chief Bender	10
Pedro Borbon	10
Don Gullett	10
Don Larsen	10
Herb Pennock	10
Red Ruffing	10

Innings

Pitcher	IP.
Whitey Ford	146
Christy Mathewson	101⅔
Red Ruffing	85⅔
Chief Bender	85
Waite Hoyt	83⅔
Bob Gibson	81
Art Nehf	79
Allie Reynolds	77⅓
Jim Palmer	64⅔
Jim Hunter	63
George Earnshaw	62⅔
Joe Bush	60⅔
Vic Raschi	60⅓
Rube Marquard	58⅔
George Mullin	58
Mordecai Brown	57⅔
Carl Mays	57⅓
Sandy Koufax	57
Burleigh Grimes	56⅔
Warren Spahn	56

ERA (40+ Innings)

Pitcher	IP.	ERA.
Sandy Koufax	57	0.95
Christy Mathewson	101⅔	1.15
Eddie Plank	54⅔	1.32
George Earnshaw	62⅔	1.58
Orval Overall	51⅓	1.58
Stan Coveleski	41⅓	1.74
Lefty Grove	51⅓	1.75
Carl Hubbell	50⅓	1.79
Waite Hoyt	83⅔	1.83
George Mullin	58	1.86
Bob Gibson	81	1.89
Herb Pennock	55⅓	1.95
Art Nehf	79	2.16
Walter Johnson	50	2.16
Carl Mays	57⅓	2.20
Vic Raschi	60⅓	2.24
Dave McNally	50	2.34
Ed Cicotte	44⅔	2.42
Chief Bender	85	2.44
Ed Lopat	52	2.60

Games Started

Pitcher	GS.
Whitey Ford	22
Waite Hoyt	11
Christy Mathewson	11
Chief Bender	10
Red Ruffing	10
Bob Gibson	9
Jim Hunter	9
Art Nehf	9
Allie Reynolds	9
George Earnshaw	8
Rube Marquard	8
Jim Palmer	8
Vic Raschi	8
Don Sutton	8
Bob Turley	8
Many tied with	7

Wins

Pitcher	W.
Whitey Ford	10
Bob Gibson	7
Allie Reynolds	7
Red Ruffing	7
Chief Bender	6
Lefty Gomez	6
Waite Hoyt	6
Mordecai Brown	5
Jack Coombs	5
Jim Hunter	5
Christy Mathewson	5
Herb Pennock	5
Vic Raschi	5
Many tied with	4

Losses

Pitcher	L.
Whitey Ford	8
Joe Bush	5
Rube Marquard	5
Christy Mathewson	5
Eddie Plank	5
Schoolboy Rowe	5
Chief Bender	4
Mordecai Brown	4
Paul Derringer	4
Bill Donovan	4
Burleigh Grimes	4
Waite Hoyt	4
Carl Mays	4
Art Nehf	4
Don Newcombe	4
Willie Sherdel	4
Ed Summers	4
Ralph Terry	4
Many tied with	3

Winning Pct. (3+ Dec.)

Pitcher	W-L	PCT.
Lefty Gomez	6-0	1.000
Jack Coombs	5-0	1.000
Herb Pennock	5-0	1.000
Monte Pearson	4-0	1.000
Babe Adams	3-0	1.000
Jerry Koosman	3-0	1.000
Mickey Lolich	3-0	1.000
George Pipgras	3-0	1.000
Babe Ruth	3-0	1.000
Tom Zachary	3-0	1.000
Harry Brecheen	4-1	.800
Tommy Bridges	4-1	.800
Ken Holtzman	4-1	.800
Ed Lopat	4-1	.800
Johnny Podres	4-1	.800
Bob Gibson	7-2	.778
Allie Reynolds	7-2	.778
Red Ruffing	7-2	.778
Many tied with	3-1	.750

Complete Games

Pitcher	CG.
Christy Mathewson	10
Chief Bender	9
Bob Gibson	8
Whitey Ford	7
Red Ruffing	7
Waite Hoyt	6
George Mullin	6
Art Nehf	6
Eddie Plank	6
Mordecai Brown	5
Joe Bush	5
Bill Donovan	5
George Earnshaw	5
Walter Johnson	5
Carl Mays	5
Deacon Phillippe	5
Allie Reynolds	5
Many tied with	4

Hits

Pitcher	H.
Whitey Ford	132
Waite Hoyt	81
Christy Mathewson	76
Red Ruffing	74
Chief Bender	64
Allie Reynolds	61
Jim Hunter	57
Walter Johnson	56
Bob Gibson	55
Jim Palmer	55
Don Sutton	55
Tommy Bridges	52
Rube Marquard	52
Vic Raschi	52
Lefty Gomez	51
Ed Lopat	51
Mordecai Brown	50
Art Nehf	50
Schoolboy Rowe	50
Two tied with	49

Runs

Pitcher	R.
Whitey Ford	51
Red Ruffing	32
Don Sutton	32
Chief Bender	28
Burleigh Grimes	28
Rube Marquard	28
Carl Erskine	27
Mordecai Brown	26
Paul Derringer	26
Allie Reynolds	25
Bob Shawkey	25
Jim Hunter	24
Art Nehf	23
Don Gullett	23
Jim Palmer	23
Schoolboy Rowe	23
Tommy Bridges	22
Bob Forsch	21
Don Newcombe	21
Two tied with	20

Earned Runs

Pitcher	ER.
Whitey Ford	44
Don Sutton	30
Carl Erskine	27
Burleigh Grimes	27
Red Ruffing	25
Allie Reynolds	24
Chief Bender	23
Jim Hunter	23
Jim Palmer	23
Bob Shawkey	22
Don Gullett	21
Don Newcombe	21
Paul Derringer	20
Schoolboy Rowe	20
Roger Craig	19
Rube Marquard	19
Art Nehf	19
Warren Spahn	19
Bob Turley	19
Five tied with	18

Bases on Balls

Pitcher	BB.
Whitey Ford	34
Art Nehf	32
Allie Reynolds	32
Jim Palmer	31
Bob Turley	29
Paul Derringer	27
Red Ruffing	27
Burleigh Grimes	26
Don Gullett	26
Vic Raschi	25
Carl Erskine	24
Bill Hallahan	23
Waite Hoyt	22
Chief Bender	21
Jack Coombs	21
Joe Bush	20
Don Larsen	19
Dave McNally	19
Hal Schumacher	19
Four tied with	17

Strikeouts

Pitcher	SO.
Whitey Ford	94
Bob Gibson	92
Allie Reynolds	62
Sandy Koufax	61
Red Ruffing	61
Chief Bender	59
George Earnshaw	56
Waite Hoyt	49
Christy Mathewson	48
Bob Turley	46
Jim Palmer	44
Vic Raschi	43
Don Gullett	37
Don Drysdale	36
Lefty Grove	36
Many tied with	35

Saves (1969—Present)

Pitcher	SV.
Rollie Fingers	6
Will McEnaney	3
Tug McGraw	3
Kent Tekulve	3
Todd Worrell	3
Rich Gossage	2
Dick Hall	2
Willie Hernandez	2
Darold Knowles	2
Tippy Martinez	2
Bob McClure	2
Jesse Orosco	2
Bruce Sutter	2
Many tied with	1

Shutouts

Pitcher	ShO.
Christy Mathewson	4
Mordecai Brown	3
Whitey Ford	3
Lew Burdette	2
Bill Dinneen	2
Bob Gibson	2
Bill Hallahan	2
Sandy Koufax	2
Art Nehf	2
Allie Reynolds	2
Many tied with	1

1969 TO 1987

CHAMPIONSHIP SERIES

1969 BALTIMORE ORIOLES VS. MINNESOTA TWINS

Baltimore was the belle of the American League ball in 1969. The Orioles overwhelmed the opposition in winning the East Division title by 19 games. They were equally devastating in their treatment of the West Division champion Minnesota Twins in the A.L. Championship Series.

The Orioles disposed of the Twins in three straight games, vindicating those who had crowed that Baltimore was the best team to represent the American League since the New York Yankees' halcyon days.

The Twins were stubborn foes in the first two matches, played in Baltimore. The Orioles had to go 12 innings in taking the opener, 4-3, on October 4. Next day, Baltimore prevailed in 11 innings, 1-0. That was the Twins' last gasp. When the series moved to the Twin Cities October 6, the Orioles lowered the boom in an 11-2 romp.

Mike Cuellar and Dave McNally were Baltimore's 20-game winners. Cuellar performed satisfactorily in the playoff opener, though failing to receive credit for a victory. McNally pitched brilliantly in blanking Minnesota in the second game. Jim Palmer, author of a no-hitter against Oakland during the regular season, coasted to victory behind Baltimore's 18-hit attack in the playoff finale.

Oriole bats were impressive, too. Frank Robinson, Mark Belanger and Boog Powell rapped homers in the opener. The winning hit, however, was a perfectly executed bunt by Paul Blair, who squeezed Belanger home from third in the 12th inning.

Blair, the swift center fielder who enjoyed a banner season, whacked five hits and drove in five runs in the third-game rout.

Righthander Jim Palmer pitched the Orioles to an 11-2 victory in the finale of the 1969 Championship Series.

Left fielder Don Buford contributed four hits after going 0 for 9 in the first two games.

Oriole Manager Earl Weaver employed simple strategy to deal with Minnesota's Harmon Killebrew, A. L. home run and RBI champ: Walk him in any dangerous situation. The Killer got nothing good to swing at until the third game was on ice. Baltimore pitchers walked him five times in the first two games and pitched to him only when he could not wreck them with one swing.

Rod Carew and Tony Oliva were the Twins' other top hitters during the season. Carew, A.L. batting champ, was a dud in the playoffs, going 1-for-14. Oliva hit

safely in each of the three games, including a homer in the opener, but was guilty of some shoddy fielding in the third game.

In the opener, 20-game winner Jim Perry held a 3-2 lead over the Orioles entering the ninth inning. Powell tied the score with a smash over the right-field fence. Reliever Ron Perranoski, who worked in all three games, shut off Baltimore's offense at that point.

Then, with two down in the 12th and Belanger on third, Blair stepped to the plate. Acting on his own, he bunted toward third. Neither third sacker Killebrew nor catcher John Roseboro could make a play as Belanger sped across the plate with the winning run. Dick Hall, who pitched two-thirds of an inning, was the winner. Perranoski didn't allow a ball to leave the infield in the 12th, but was the loser nevertheless.

Winner of 15 games in a row during the season, McNally was saddled with a "lucky" tag because Baltimore frequently rallied to win after McNally had left on the short end of the score. He won the second game of the playoffs on his own exceptional pitching and Curt Motton's 11th-inning pinch-single. It scored Powell from second base with the only run of the game. McNally's victim was Dave Boswell, who was a mighty tough opponent. McNally yielded only three hits, none after the fourth inning.

Twins' Manager Billy Martin, confronted with a pitching shortage, started Bob Miller, normally a reliever, in the third game. Miller lasted less than two innings, and his six successors fared no better. Every Oriole except pitcher Palmer hit safely in an assault that eliminated Minnesota and sent Baltimore into the World Series.

Game 1

Saturday, October 4, At Baltimore

Minnesota	AB.	R.	H.	RBI.	PO.	A.
Tovar, cf	4	0	0	0	3	0
Carew, 2b	5	0	1	0	3	1
Killebrew, 3b	2	1	0	0	3	2
Oliva, rf	5	2	2	2	3	0
Allison, lf	3	0	0	1	3	0
Uhlaender, lf	1	0	1	0	0	0
Reese, 1b	4	0	0	0	10	1
Cardenas, ss	5	0	0	0	5	5
Mitterwald, c	4	0	0	0	5	1
Roseboro, c	1	0	0	0	2	0
Perry, p	3	0	0	0	0	0
Perranoski, p	1	0	0	0	0	0
Totals	38	3	4	3	35	10

Baltimore	AB.	R.	H.	RBI.	PO.	A.
Buford, lf	6	0	0	0	3	0
Blair, cf	5	0	1	1	1	0
F. Robinson, rf	3	1	1	1	1	0
Powell, 1b	5	1	2	1	13	0
B. Robinson, 3b	5	0	4	0	2	4
Hendricks, c	3	0	0	0	9	0
Motton, ph	1	0	0	0	0	0
Watt, p	0	0	0	0	0	0
Salmon, ph	1	0	0	0	0	0
Lopez, p	0	0	0	0	0	0
Hall, p	0	0	0	0	0	0
Johnson, 2b	5	0	0	0	3	3
Belanger, ss	5	2	2	1	1	2
Cuellar, p	2	0	0	0	0	0
May, ph	1	0	0	0	0	0
Richert, p	0	0	0	0	0	0
Rettenmund, ph	0	0	0	0	0	0
Etchebarren, c	1	0	0	0	3	0
Totals	43	4	10	4	36	9

Minnesota .... 0 0 0   0 1 0   2 0 0   0 0 0—3
Baltimore .... 0 0 0   1 1 0   0 0 1   0 0 1—4

Two out when winning run scored.

Minnesota	IP.	H.	R.	ER.	BB.	SO.
Perry	8*	6	3	3	3	8
Perranoski (L)	3⅔	4	1	1	0	1

Baltimore	IP.	H.	R.	ER.	BB.	SO.
Cuellar	8	3	3	2	1	7
Richert	1	0	0	0	2	2
Watt	2	0	0	0	2	2
Lopez	⅓	1	0	0	2	0
Hall (W)	⅔	0	0	0	0	1

*Pitched to two batters in ninth.

E—F. Robinson, Uhlaender, Carew. DP—Baltimore 1. LOB—Minnesota 5, Baltimore 8. 2B—Oliva. HR—F. Robinson, Belanger, Oliva, Powell. SB—Tovar. SH—Etchebarren. SF—Allison. WP—Lopez. U—Chylak, Runge, Umont, Stewart, Rice and Flaherty. T—3:29. A—39,324.

Game 2

Sunday, October 5, At Baltimore

Minnesota	AB.	R.	H.	RBI.	PO.	A.
Tovar, cf	5	0	1	0	2	0
Carew, 2b	4	0	0	0	2	1
Killebrew, 3b	3	0	0	0	1	0
Oliva, rf	4	0	1	0	1	0
Allison, lf	5	0	0	0	3	0
Reese, 1b	4	0	0	0	11	3
Mitterwald, c	3	0	1	0	5	2
Cardenas, ss	4	0	0	0	6	5
Boswell, p	4	0	0	0	1	4
Perranoski, p	0	0	0	0	0	0
Totals	36	0	3	0	32	15

Baltimore	AB.	R.	H.	RBI.	PO.	A.
Buford, lf	3	0	0	0	1	0
Blair, cf	4	0	0	0	6	0
F. Robinson, rf	5	0	2	0	1	0
Powell, 1b	3	1	1	0	10	0
B. Robinson, 3b	4	0	2	0	3	3
Johnson, 2b	4	0	2	0	1	2
Belanger, ss	5	0	0	0	4	4
Etchebarren, c	3	0	0	0	8	0
Hendricks, ph-c	0	0	0	0	3	0
Motton, ph	1	0	1	1	0	0
McNally, p	4	0	0	0	0	0
Totals	36	1	8	1	33	9

Minnesota .... 0 0 0   0 0 0   0 0 0   0 0—0
Baltimore .... 0 0 0   0 0 0   0 0 0   0 1—1

Two out when winning run scored.

Minnesota	IP.	H.	R.	ER.	BB.	SO.
Boswell (L)	10⅔	7	1	1	7	4
Perranoski	0*	1	0	0	0	0

Baltimore	IP.	H.	R.	ER.	BB.	SO.
McNally (W)	11	3	0	0	5	11

*Pitched to one batter in eleventh.

E—Cardenas. DP—Minnesota 2. LOB—Minnesota 8, Baltimore 11. 2B—F. Robinson 2. SB—Oliva. SH—B. Robinson. WP—Boswell. U—Runge, Umont, Stewart, Rice, Flaherty and Chylak. T—3:17. A—41,704.

Game 3

Monday, October 6, At Minnesota

Baltimore	AB.	R.	H.	RBI.	PO.	A.
Buford, lf	5	3	4	1	4	0
Blair, cf	6	1	5	5	1	0
F. Robinson, rf	4	0	1	1	0	0
Powell, 1b	5	0	2	0	11	0
B. Robinson, 3b	5	1	1	0	1	3
Johnson, 2b	4	2	1	0	1	6
Hendricks, c	5	2	2	3	6	0
Belanger, ss	5	2	2	0	3	3
Palmer, p	5	0	0	0	0	1
Totals	44	11	18	10	27	13

Minnesota	AB.	R.	H.	RBI.	PO.	A.
Uhlaender, lf	5	0	0	0	4	0
Carew, 2b	5	0	0	0	0	0
Oliva, rf	4	1	2	0	2	1
Killebrew, 3b	3	1	1	0	0	0
Reese, 1b	4	0	2	2	5	1
Tovar, cf	4	0	0	0	5	0
Roseboro, c	4	0	1	0	6	1
Cardenas, ss	4	0	2	0	2	4
Miller, p	0	0	0	0	0	0
Woodson, p	1	0	1	0	0	0
Hall, p	0	0	0	0	0	0
Manuel, ph	0	0	0	0	0	0
Worthington, p	0	0	0	0	0	0
Grzenda, p	0	0	0	0	0	0
Renick, ph	1	0	0	0	0	0
Chance, p	0	0	0	0	0	0
Perranoski, p	0	0	0	0	0	0
Nettles, ph	1	0	1	0	0	0
Totals	36	2	10	2	27	9

Baltimore .... 0 3 0   2 0 1   0 2 3—11
Minnesota .... 1 0 0   0 1 0   0 0 0— 2

Baltimore	IP.	H.	R.	ER.	BB.	SO.
Palmer (W)	9	10	2	2	2	4

Minnesota	IP.	H.	R.	ER.	BB.	SO.
Miller (L)	1⅔	5	3	1	0	0
Woodson	1⅔	3	2	2	3	2
Hall	⅔	0	0	0	0	0
Worthington	1⅓	3	1	1	0	1
Grzenda	⅔	0	0	0	0	0
Chance	2*	4	3	3	0	2
Perranoski	1	3	2	2	0	1

*Pitched to one batter in ninth.

E—Oliva 2. DP—Baltimore 1, Minnesota 1. LOB—Baltimore 9, Minnesota 9. 2B—Oliva, B. Robinson, Hendricks 2, Blair 2, Killebrew, Buford. 3B—Belanger, Cardenas. HR—Blair. WP—Palmer. U—Umont, Stewart, Rice, Flaherty, Chylak and Runge. T—2:48. A—32,735.

COMPOSITE BATTING AVERAGES

Baltimore Orioles

Player-Position	G.	AB.	R.	H.	2B.	3B.	HR.	RBI.	BA.
B. Robinson, 3b	3	14	1	7	1	0	0	0	.500
Motton, ph	2	2	0	1	0	0	0	1	.500
Blair, cf	3	15	1	6	2	0	1	6	.400
Powell, 1b	3	13	2	5	0	0	1	1	.385
F. Robinson, rf	3	12	1	4	2	0	1	2	.333
Buford, lf	3	14	3	4	1	0	0	1	.286
Belanger, ss	3	15	4	4	0	1	1	1	.267
Hendricks, ph-c	3	8	2	2	2	0	0	3	.250
Johnson, 2b	3	13	2	3	0	0	0	0	.231
Watt, p	1	0	0	0	0	0	0	0	.000
Lopez, p	1	0	0	0	0	0	0	0	.000
R. Hall, p	1	0	0	0	0	0	0	0	.000
Richert, p	1	0	0	0	0	0	0	0	.000
Rettenmund, ph	1	0	0	0	0	0	0	0	.000
Salmon, ph	1	1	0	0	0	0	0	0	.000
May, ph	1	1	0	0	0	0	0	0	.000
Cuellar, p	1	2	0	0	0	0	0	0	.000
Etchebarren, c	2	4	0	0	0	0	0	0	.000
McNally, p	1	4	0	0	0	0	0	0	.000
Palmer, p	1	5	0	0	0	0	0	0	.000
Totals	3	123	16	36	8	1	4	15	.293

Minnesota Twins

Player-Position	G.	AB.	R.	H.	2B.	3B.	HR.	RBI.	BA.
Nettles, ph	1	1	0	1	0	0	0	0	1.000
Woodson, p	1	1	0	1	0	0	0	0	1.000
Oliva, rf	3	13	3	5	2	0	1	2	.385
Roseboro, c	2	5	0	1	0	0	0	0	.200
Reese, 1b	3	12	0	2	0	0	0	2	.167
Uhlaender, lf	2	6	0	1	0	0	0	0	.167
Cardenas, ss	3	13	0	2	0	1	0	0	.154
Mitterwald, c	2	7	0	1	0	0	0	0	.143
Killebrew, 3b	3	8	2	1	1	0	0	0	.125
Tovar, cf	3	13	0	1	0	0	0	0	.077
Carew, 2b	3	14	0	1	0	0	0	0	.071
Chance, p	1	0	0	0	0	0	0	0	.000
Miller, p	1	0	0	0	0	0	0	0	.000
T. Hall, p	1	0	0	0	0	0	0	0	.000
Manuel, ph	1	0	0	0	0	0	0	0	.000
Worthington, p	1	0	0	0	0	0	0	0	.000
Grzenda, p	1	0	0	0	0	0	0	0	.000
Renick, ph	1	1	0	0	0	0	0	0	.000
Perranoski, p	3	1	0	0	0	0	0	0	.000
Perry, p	1	3	0	0	0	0	0	0	.000
Boswell, p	1	4	0	0	0	0	0	0	.000
Allison, lf	2	8	0	0	0	0	0	1	.000
Totals	3	110	5	17	3	1	1	5	.155

COMPOSITE PITCHING AVERAGES

Baltimore Orioles

Pitcher	G.	IP.	H.	R.	ER.	BB.	SO.	W.	L.	ERA.
McNally	1	11	3	0	0	5	11	1	0	0.00
Watt	1	2	0	0	0	2	2	0	0	0.00
Richert	1	1	0	0	0	2	2	0	0	0.00
R. Hall	1	⅔	0	0	0	1	1	1	0	0.00
Lopez	1	⅓	1	0	0	2	0	0	0	0.00
Palmer	1	9	10	2	2	2	4	1	0	2.00
Cuellar	1	8	3	3	2	1	7	0	0	2.25
Totals	3	32	17	5	4	12	27	3	0	1.13

Minnesota Twins

Pitcher	G.	IP.	H.	R.	ER.	BB.	SO.	W.	L.	ERA.
Grzenda	1	⅔	0	0	0	0	0	0	0	0.00
T. Hall	1	⅔	0	0	0	0	0	0	0	0.00
Boswell	1	10⅔	7	1	1	7	4	0	1	0.84
Perry	1	8	6	3	3	3	8	0	0	3.38
Miller	1	1⅔	5	3	1	0	0	0	1	5.40
Perranoski	3	4⅔	8	3	3	0	2	0	1	5.79
Worthington	1	1⅓	3	1	1	0	1	0	0	6.75
Woodson	1	1⅔	3	2	2	3	2	0	0	10.80
Chance	1	2	4	3	3	0	2	0	0	13.50
Totals	3	31⅓	36	16	14	13	14	0	3	4.02

1969
NEW YORK METS
VS.
ATLANTA BRAVES

Thirty-to-one shots do come through occasionally. And the National League's first experience with the two-division playoff system provided one of those rare instances. Note the East Division playoff.

Adding another lustrous chapter, the New York Mets swept the Atlanta Braves into oblivion in three Championship Series games to win their first league title after five 10th-place and two ninth-place finishes.

In the first game, played before 50,122 at Atlanta October 4, Tom Seaver, the Mets' 25-game winner, hooked up with Phil Niekro, winner of 23 decisions for the Braves.

Neither righthander finished. Niekro lasted eight innings, including the five-run eighth by which the Mets sewed up the verdict. Seaver departed for a pinch-hitter in the same decisive inning.

Wayne Garrett opened the tell-tale frame with a double and tied the score at 5-5 when Cleon Jones singled. Art Shamsky's third hit sent Jones to second. When Ken Boswell missed an attempted sacrifice, Jones was trapped off second. Catcher Bob Didier committed the cardinal sin of throwing behind the runner and Jones beat the relay throw to third base.

When Boswell bounced to the mound, the Braves retired only one runner, Al Weis, who ran for Shamsky at second base. On Ed Kranepool's grounder to first base, Orlando Cepeda fired wildly to the plate, Jones scoring the go-ahead run.

After Jerry Grote was retired, Bud Harrelson was walked intentionally, loading the bases. With Seaver due to bat, Hodges went to his bench and found just what he wanted. J. C. Martin pinch-singled three runs across the plate, providing the final nail in a 9-5 vic-

Ron Taylor (left) and Tug McGraw were the aces of the Miracle Mets' bullpen in 1969.

tory.

In the second game, witnessed by 50,270 October 5, Jerry Koos-

man, New York's 17-game winner, was staked to leads of 8-0 and 9-1, yet failed to survive the fifth

inning.

The Mets tagged Ron Reed for four runs in one and two-thirds innings, added two off Paul Doyle and three off Milt Pappas before the Atlanta guns went to work.

A homer by Hank Aaron, who hit for the circuit in each of the three games, provided three runs. A single by Felix Millan, a double by Cepeda and a single by Clete Boyer accounted for two more tallies and shelled Koosman, then leading by only 9-6.

Ron Taylor and Tug McGraw shut out the Braves on two hits the rest of the way. The Mets picked up their final runs in the seventh when Jones homered with Tommie Agee on base, making the score 11-6.

With the series switched to New York, the Mets applied the clincher before 53,195 delirious devotees on October 6.

This game belonged to Nolan Ryan, who replaced Gary Gentry with none out in the third inning, runners on second and third and the Braves leading, 2-0.

Ryan fanned Rico Carty as a starter, walked Cepeda intentionally, whiffed Boyer and got Didier on a fly to left to escape damage.

The hard-throwing righthander made his only mistake in the fifth, when he grooved a two-run homer pitch to Cepeda, that gave the Braves a 4-3 margin.

Ryan quickly made amends for that boner, leading off the home portion of the inning with a single. Agee was retired, but Garrett, who had hit his last homer on May 6, exactly five months earlier, clouted Jarvis' first pitch into the upper stands in right and the Mets were in front to stay.

Ryan, who had appeared in only 89 innings during the regular season, allowed three hits in his seven innings, walked two and fanned seven, in addition to collecting a second hit in the 7-4 victory.

Game 1

Saturday, October 4, At Atlanta

New York	AB.	R.	H.	RBI.	PO.	A.
Agee, cf	5	0	0	0	2	0
Garrett, 3b	4	1	2	0	1	2
Jones, lf	5	1	1	1	5	0
Shamsky, rf	4	1	3	0	2	0
Weis, pr-2b	0	0	0	0	1	1
Boswell, 2b	3	2	0	0	0	1
Gaspar, rf	0	0	0	0	0	0
Kranepool, 1b	4	2	1	0	7	2
Grote, c	3	1	1	1	4	1

	AB.	R.	H.	RBI.	PO.	A.
Harrelson, ss	3	1	1	2	2	1
Seaver, p	3	0	0	1	0	1
Martin, ph	1	0	1	2	0	0
Taylor, p	0	0	0	1	0	0
Totals	35	9	10	6	27	9

Atlanta	AB.	R.	H.	RBI.	PO.	A.
Millan, 2b	5	1	2	0	3	2
Gonzalez, cf	5	2	2	2	0	1
H. Aaron, rf	5	1	2	2	1	0
Carty, lf	3	1	1	0	0	0
Lum, lf	1	0	1	0	0	0
Cepeda, 1b	4	0	1	0	14	0
Boyer, 3b	1	0	0	1	2	5
Didier, c	4	0	0	0	5	0
Garrido, ss	4	0	1	0	2	7
Niekro, p	3	0	0	0	0	3
Aspromonte, ph	1	0	0	0	0	0
Upshaw, p	0	0	0	0	0	1
Totals	36	5	10	5	27	19

New York .... 0 2 0   2 0 0   0 5 0—9
Atlanta .... 0 1 2   0 1 0   1 0 0—5

New York	IP.	H.	R.	ER.	BB.	SO.
Seaver (W)	7	8	5	5	3	2
Taylor (S)	2	2	0	0	2	0

Atlanta	IP.	H.	R.	ER.	BB.	SO.
Niekro (L)	8	9	9	4	4	0
Upshaw	1	1	0	0	0	1

E—Boswell, Cepeda, Gonzalez. DP—Atlanta 2. LOB—New York 3, Atlanta 9. 2B—Carty, Millan, Gonzalez, H. Aaron, Garrett, Lum. 3B—Harrelson. HR—Gonzalez, H. Aaron. SB—Cepeda, Jones. SF—Boyer. HBP—By Seaver (Cepeda). PB—Didier, Grote. U—Barlick, Donatelli, Sudol, Vargo, Pelekoudas and Steiner. T—2:37. A—50,122.

Game 2

Sunday, October 5, At Atlanta

New York	AB.	R.	H.	RBI.	PO.	A.
Agee, cf	4	3	2	2	3	0
Garrett, 3b	5	1	2	1	0	1
Jones, lf	5	2	3	3	3	0
Shamsky, rf	5	1	3	1	0	0
Gaspar, pr-rf	0	0	0	0	2	0
Boswell, 2b	5	1	1	2	2	1
McGraw, p	0	0	0	0	0	0
Kranepool, 1b	4	0	1	1	6	0
Grote, c	5	1	0	0	9	0
Harrelson, ss	5	1	1	1	2	2
Koosman, p	2	1	0	0	0	1
Taylor, p	0	0	0	0	0	0
Martin, ph	1	0	0	0	0	0
Weis, 2b	1	0	0	0	0	2
Totals	42	11	13	11	27	7

Atlanta	AB.	R.	H.	RBI.	PO.	A.
Millan, 2b	2	1	2	0	0	5
Gonzalez, cf	4	1	1	0	2	0
H. Aaron, rf	5	1	3	3	0	0
Carty, lf	4	2	1	0	1	0
Cepeda, 1b	4	1	2	1	8	0
Boyer, 3b	4	0	1	2	1	2
Didier, c	4	0	0	0	12	1
Garrido, ss	4	0	1	0	0	4
Reed, p	0	0	0	0	0	1
Doyle, p	0	0	0	0	0	0
Pappas, p	1	0	0	0	0	0
T. Aaron, ph	1	0	0	0	0	0
Britton, p	0	0	0	0	0	0
Upshaw, p	1	0	0	0	0	0
Aspromonte, ph	1	0	0	0	0	0
Neibauer, p	0	0	0	0	0	0
Totals	35	6	9	6	27	9

New York .... 1 3 2   2 1 0   2 0 0—11
Atlanta .... 0 0 0   1 5 0   0 0 0—6

New York	IP.	H.	R.	ER.	BB.	SO.
Koosman	4⅔	7	6	6	4	5
Taylor (W)	1⅓	1	0	0	0	2
McGraw (S)	3	1	0	0	1	0

Atlanta	IP.	H.	R.	ER.	BB.	SO.
Reed (L)	1⅔	5	4	4	3	3
Doyle	1	2	2	0	1	3
Pappas	2⅓	4	3	3	0	4
Britton	⅓	0	0	0	0	0
Upshaw	2⅔	2	2	2	1	1
Neibauer	1	0	0	0	0	1

E—H. Aaron, Cepeda, Harrelson, Boyer. DP—New York 2, Atlanta 1. LOB—New York 10, Atlanta 7. 2B—Jones, Harrelson, Carty, Garrett, Cepeda. HR—Agee, Boswell, H. Aaron, Jones. SB—Agee 2, Garrett, Jones. U—Donatelli, Sudol, Vargo, Pelekoudas, Steiner and Barlick. T—3:10. A—50,270.

Game 3

Monday, October 6, At New York

Atlanta	AB.	R.	H.	RBI.	PO.	A.
Millan, 2b	5	0	0	0	0	2
Gonzalez, cf	5	1	2	0	1	0
H. Aaron, rf	4	1	2	2	0	0
Carty, lf	3	1	1	0	2	0
Cepeda, 1b	3	1	2	2	7	1
Boyer, 3b	4	0	0	0	1	1
Didier, c	3	0	0	0	7	0
Lum, ph	1	0	1	0	0	0
Jackson, ss	0	0	0	0	0	0
Garrido, ss	2	0	0	0	2	1
Alou, ph	1	0	0	0	0	0
Tillman, c	0	0	0	0	0	0

	AB.	R.	H.	RBI.	PO.	A.
Jarvis, p	2	0	0	0	1	2
Stone, p	1	0	0	0	1	1
Upshaw, p	0	0	0	0	0	0
Aspromonte, ph	1	0	0	0	0	0
Totals	35	4	8	4	24	9

New York	AB.	R.	H.	RBI.	PO.	A.
Agee, cf	5	1	3	2	4	0
Garrett, 3b	4	1	1	2	0	3
Jones, lf	4	1	2	0	3	0
Shamsky, rf	4	1	1	0	1	0
Gaspar, pr-rf	0	0	0	0	0	0
Boswell, 2b	4	1	3	3	1	0
Weis, 2b	0	0	0	0	0	0
Kranepool, 1b	4	0	1	0	7	1
Grote, c	4	1	1	0	8	0
Harrelson, ss	3	0	0	0	2	3
Gentry, p	0	0	0	0	0	0
Ryan, p	4	1	2	0	1	0
Totals	36	7	14	7	27	7

Atlanta .... 2 0 0   2 0 0   0 0 0—4
New York .... 0 0 1   2 3 1   0 0 x—7

Atlanta	IP.	H.	R.	ER.	BB.	SO.
Jarvis (L)	4⅓	10	6	6	0	6
Stone	1	2	1	1	0	0
Upshaw	2⅔	2	0	0	0	2

New York	IP.	H.	R.	ER.	BB.	SO.
Gentry	2*	5	2	2	1	1
Ryan (W)	7	3	2	2	2	7

*Pitched to three batters in third.

E—Millan. DP—Atlanta 1. LOB—Atlanta 7, New York 6. 2B—Cepeda, Agee, H. Aaron, Kranepool, Jones, Grote. HR—H. Aaron, Agee, Boswell, Cepeda, Garrett. SH—Harrelson. U—Sudol, Vargo, Pelekoudas, Steiner, Barlick and Donatelli. T—2:24. A—53,195.

COMPOSITE BATTING AVERAGES

New York Mets

Player-Position	G.	AB.	R.	H.	2B.	3B.	HR.	RBI.	BA.
Shamsky, rf	3	13	3	7	0	0	0	1	.538
Ryan, p	1	4	1	2	0	0	0	0	.500
Martin, ph	2	2	0	1	0	0	0	2	.500
Jones, lf	3	14	4	6	2	0	1	4	.429
Garrett, 3b	3	13	3	5	2	0	1	3	.385
Agee, cf	3	14	5	5	1	0	2	4	.357
Boswell, 2b	3	12	4	4	0	0	2	5	.333
Kranepool, 1b	3	12	2	3	1	0	0	1	.250
Harrelson, ss	3	11	2	2	1	1	0	3	.182
Grote, c	3	12	3	2	1	0	0	1	.167
Gaspar, rf-pr	3	0	0	0	0	0	0	0	.000
McGraw, p	1	0	0	0	0	0	0	0	.000
Gentry, p	1	0	0	0	0	0	0	0	.000
Taylor, p	2	0	0	0	0	0	0	0	.000
Weis, pr-2b	3	1	0	0	0	0	0	0	.000
Koosman, p	1	2	1	0	0	0	0	0	.000
Seaver, p	1	3	0	0	0	0	0	0	.000
Totals	3	113	27	37	8	1	6	24	.327

Atlanta Braves

Player-Position	G.	AB.	R.	H.	2B.	3B.	HR.	RBI.	BA.
Lum, lf-ph	2	2	0	2	0	0	0	0	1.000
Cepeda, 1b	3	11	2	5	2	0	1	3	.455
H. Aaron, rf	3	14	3	5	1	0	3	7	.357
Gonzalez, cf	3	14	5	5	1	0	1	2	.357
Millan, 2b	3	12	2	4	1	0	0	0	.333
Carty, lf	3	10	4	3	2	0	0	0	.300
Garrido, ss	3	10	0	2	0	0	0	0	.200
Boyer, 3b	3	9	0	1	0	0	0	3	.111
Tillman, c	1	0	0	0	0	0	0	0	.000
Reed, p	1	0	0	0	0	0	0	0	.000
Jackson, ss	1	0	0	0	0	0	0	0	.000
Doyle, p	1	0	0	0	0	0	0	0	.000
Britton, p	1	0	0	0	0	0	0	0	.000
Neibauer, p	1	0	0	0	0	0	0	0	.000
Stone, p	1	1	0	0	0	0	0	0	.000
Upshaw, p	3	1	0	0	0	0	0	0	.000
T. Aaron, ph	1	1	0	0	0	0	0	0	.000
Alou, ph	1	1	0	0	0	0	0	0	.000
Pappas, p	1	1	0	0	0	0	0	0	.000
Jarvis, p	1	2	0	0	0	0	0	0	.000
Aspromonte, ph	3	3	0	0	0	0	0	0	.000
Niekro, p	1	3	0	0	0	0	0	0	.000
Didier, c	3	11	0	0	0	0	0	0	.000
Totals	3	106	15	27	9	0	5	15	.255

COMPOSITE PITCHING AVERAGES

New York Mets

Pitcher	G.	IP.	H.	R.	ER.	BB.	SO.	W.	L.	ERA.
Taylor	2	3⅓	3	0	0	4	1	0	0.00
McGraw	1	3	1	0	0	1	0	0	0	0.00
Ryan	1	7	3	2	2	7	1	0	2.57
Seaver	1	7	8	5	5	3	2	1	0	6.43
Gentry	1	2	5	2	2	1	1	0	0	9.00
Koosman	1	4⅔	7	6	6	4	5	0	0	11.57
Totals	3	27	25	15	15	11	20	3	0	5.00

Atlanta Braves

Pitcher	G.	IP.	H.	R.	ER.	BB.	SO.	W.	L.	ERA.
Neibauer	1	1	0	0	0	0	1	0	0	0.00
Doyle	1	1	2	2	0	1	3	0	0	0.00
Britton	1	⅓	0	0	0	0	0	0	0	0.00
Upshaw	3	6⅓	5	2	2	1	4	0	0	2.84
Niekro	1	8	9	9	4	4	0	0	1	4.50
Stone	1	1	2	1	1	0	0	0	0	9.00
Pappas	1	2⅓	4	3	3	0	4	0	0	11.57
Jarvis	1	4⅓	10	6	6	0	6	0	1	12.46
Reed	1	1⅔	5	4	4	3	3	0	1	21.60
Totals	3	26	37	27	20	10	25	0	3	6.92

1970
BALTIMORE ORIOLES
VS.
MINNESOTA TWINS

Sweeping success was once more the name of the game for the Baltimore Orioles in the 1970 American League Championship Series.

And for the Minnesota Twins, it was again dismal defeat in three games.

For Manager Earl Weaver's Baltimore brigade, which won a total of 217 games in two seasons, the playoff sweep was a continuation of their winning ways in the regular A. L. campaign, which finished with 11 consecutive victories.

The Twins enjoyed the lead only once, a 1-0 edge in the first inning of the opening game. Their only tie was forged one inning later. At all other points, the Baltimore behemoths dominated action.

Mike Cuellar, half of Baltimore's 24-win duo, received the Oriole opening-game assignment in the Twin Cities. Although staked to an early 9-3 lead, the Cuban lefthander was unable to attain maximum efficiency on the cool and windy afternoon and departed in the fifth inning. Dick Hall, 40-year-old relief specialist, allowed only one hit in the final 4⅔ innings to pick up the victory.

With the teams deadlocked, 2-2, the Orioles put the game beyond Minnesota's reach in the fourth inning, aided considerably by Cuellar's bat and the lusty blasts of a strong wind blowing across Metropolitan Stadium.

Two singles and Brooks Robinson's sacrifice fly produced one fourth-inning run off Jim Perry, the Twins' 24-game winner, and the Orioles then loaded the bases with one out.

The lefthanded-hitting Cuellar, with an .089 batting average and seven RBIs to show for his season's efforts, then pulled a Perry

Baltimore first baseman Boog Powell (right) congratulates pitcher Mike Cuellar, who failed to win the 1970 Championship Series opener but helped the Orioles by hitting a fourth-inning grand slam.

pitch toward foul territory in right field. As the ball passed first base it was patently foul, maybe as much as 15 feet. Cuellar himself stood transfixed at the plate, watching the pellet transcribe a high parabola in the direction of the right-field seats.

As the ball soared into the 29-mile-an-hour current, however, it started drifting toward fair territory. Cuellar started jogging from the plate. By the time he arrived at first base, the wind had worked its devilry against the home forces, depositing the ball over the fence in fair territory, and giving Cuellar a grand-slam homer.

Before the inning was completed, Don Buford cuffed Perry for a knock-out homer and Bill Zepp yielded a left-field round-tripper to southpaw-swinging Boog

Powell to complete the seven-run outburst.

Dave McNally, who registered a 10-inning, 1-0 three-hitter in the second game of the 1969 playoffs, received the second-game assignment again and once more responded with victory, although with considerably more ease.

The Birds handed McNally a four-run cushion. Powell doubled home Mark Belanger in the first inning, Frank Robinson homered with Belanger aboard in the third and McNally himself singled home Andy Etchebarren in the fourth.

The Twins nearly erased that lead with two swings of the bat in their turn, Killebrew connecting for a homer after a pass to Leo Cardenas and Tony Oliva hitting a solo smash.

Stan Williams, following Tom Hall and Bill Zepp to the mound, blanked Baltimore the next three frames and Ron Perranoski zeroed the visitors in the eighth before the East Division champs erupted for their second seven-run rally in the series.

McNally's bat ignited the conflagration with a wrong-field double and Dave Johnson concluded it with a three-run homer. All the Birds except Blair participated in the 13-hit feast, Belanger and Powell accounting for three apiece.

When the series shifted to Baltimore on October 5, Weaver called on his workhorse, Jim Palmer, to wrap it all up.

The big righthander, just 10 days short of his 25th birthday and two years removed from an arm ailment that threatened his career, was razor sharp, scattering seven hits.

In fairness, Palmer was entitled to a shutout. A brilliant sun blinded Frank Robinson while he was tracking down Cesar Tovar's fifth-inning fly that fell for a single. Cardenas' single produced a run, but that was all for the Twins.

A 20-game winner with a 2.71 ERA in regular play, Palmer set a personal career high of 12 strikeouts and issued only three walks.

He also laced a double and figured prominently in the second-inning Oriole run when his looper to short center field was misplayed for a two-base error. Palmer subsequently scored on Buford's double.

The Minnesota starting assignment went to Jim Kaat, a 14-game winner who had been handicapped by late-season arm miseries. The lefthander departed with none out in the third after yielding six hits. By that time the trend of the game had been established and three successors, while more effective, were helpless to change the outcome, the Birds cruising to an easy 6-1 victory.

Game 1

Saturday, October 3, At Minnesota

Baltimore	AB.	R.	H.	RBI.	PO.	A.
Buford, lf	3	1	1	1	0	0
Blair, cf	5	0	0	0	3	0
Powell, 1b	5	1	2	5	10	1
F. Robinson, rf	4	1	1	0	4	0
Hendricks, c	5	2	2	0	5	0
B. Robinson, 3b	3	1	3	1	2	1
Johnson, 2b	3	1	1	0	4	2
Belanger, ss	4	1	1	1	2	5
Cuellar, p	2	1	1	4	1	3
Hall, p	2	1	1	0	0	0
Totals	36	10	13	9	27	12

Minnesota	AB.	R.	H.	RBI.	PO.	A.
Tovar, cf-2b	5	1	2	1	1	0
Cardenas, ss	4	0	0	0	2	5
Killebrew, 3b	5	1	2	2	1	1
Oliva, rf	4	1	3	0	3	0
Alyea, lf	3	1	0	0	0	0
Reese, 1b	4	0	0	0	10	1
Mitterwald, c	4	2	3	2	7	1
Thompson, 2b	3	0	1	0	1	3
Williams, p	0	0	0	0	0	0
Holt, ph-cf	1	0	0	0	0	0
Perry, p	1	0	0	1	1	0
Zepp, p	0	0	0	0	0	0
Allison, ph	1	0	0	0	0	0
Woodson, p	0	0	0	0	1	1
Quilici, 2b	1	0	0	0	0	1
Carew, ph	1	0	0	0	0	0
Perranoski, p	0	0	0	0	0	0
Totals	37	6	11	6	27	12

Baltimore	0	2	0	7	0	1	0	0	0—10
Minnesota	1	1	0	1	3	0	0	0	0— 6

Baltimore	IP.	H.	R.	ER.	BB.	SO.
Cuellar	4⅓	10	6	6	1	2
Hall (W)	4⅔	1	0	0	0	3

Minnesota	IP.	H.	R.	ER.	BB.	SO.
Perry (L)	3⅓	8	8	7	1	1
Zepp	⅔	0	1	0	2	0
Woodson	1*	2	1	1	1	0
Williams	3	2	0	0	1	1
Perranoski	1	0	0	0	0	2

*Pitched to two batters in sixth.

E—Thompson, Killebrew. DP—Baltimore 1, Minnesota 3. LOB—Baltimore 4, Minnesota 6. 2B—Thompson, Oliva 2, B. Robinson. HR—Cuellar, Buford, Powell, Killebrew. SH—Cardenas. SF—B. Robinson. HBP—By Perry (Johnson). U—Stevens, Deegan, Satchell and Berry. T—2:36. A—26,847.

Game 2

Sunday, October 4, At Minnesota

Baltimore	AB.	R.	H.	RBI.	PO.	A.
Belanger, ss	4	3	3	0	1	5
Blair, cf	4	0	0	0	0	0
F. Robinson, rf	3	2	1	2	1	0
Powell, 1b	5	1	3	3	9	0
Rettenmund, lf	3	1	1	1	3	1
B. Robinson, 3b	5	1	1	0	1	4
Johnson, 2b	5	1	1	3	5	1
Etchebarren, c	5	1	1	0	6	0
McNally, p	5	1	2	1	0	0
Totals	39	11	13	10	27	11

Minnesota	AB.	R.	H.	RBI.	PO.	A.
Tovar, cf-lf	4	0	1	0	2	0
Cardenas, ss	3	1	1	0	4	3
Killebrew, 1b	3	1	1	2	7	0
Oliva, rf	4	1	1	1	4	2
Alyea, lf	3	0	0	0	0	0
Holt, pr-cf	0	0	0	0	0	0
Mitterwald, c	4	0	1	0	9	0
Renick, 3b	4	0	1	0	1	3
Thompson, 2b	4	0	0	0	0	0
Hall, p	1	0	0	0	0	0
Zepp, p	0	0	0	0	0	0
Williams, p	0	0	0	0	0	0
Allison, ph	1	0	0	0	0	0
Perranoski, p	0	0	0	0	0	1
Tiant, p	0	0	0	0	0	0
Quilici, ph	1	0	0	0	0	0
Totals	31	3	6	3	27	9

Baltimore	1	0	2	1	0	0	0	0	7—11
Minnesota	0	0	0	3	0	0	0	0	0— 3

Baltimore	IP.	H.	R.	ER.	BB.	SO.
McNally (W)	9	6	3	3	5	5

Minnesota	IP.	H.	R.	ER.	BB.	SO.
Hall (L)	3⅓	6	4	4	3	4
Zepp	⅔*	1	0	0	2	0
Williams	3	0	0	0	0	1
Perranoski	1⅓	5	5	5	1	1
Tiant	⅔	1	2	2	1	0

*Pitched to three batters in fifth.

E—Cardenas 2. DP—Baltimore 1, Minnesota 2. LOB—Baltimore 7, Minnesota 6. 2B—Powell 2, Mitterwald, McNally. HR—F. Robinson, Killebrew, Oliva, Johnson. SB—Rettenmund. U—Haller, Odom, Neudecker, Honochick, Goetz and Springstead. T—2:59. A—27,490.

Game 3

Monday, October 5, At Baltimore

Minnesota	AB.	R.	H.	RBI.	PO.	A.
Tovar, lf	4	1	2	0	3	0
Cardenas, ss	4	0	1	1	0	3
Oliva, rf	4	0	2	0	3	0
Killebrew, 3b	3	0	0	0	0	3
Holt, 1b	4	0	0	0	3	0
Ratliff, c	4	0	1	0	7	0
Reese, 1b	3	0	1	0	6	1
Tiant, pr	0	0	0	0	0	0

	AB.	R.	H.	RBI.	PO.	A.
Thompson, 2b	1	0	0	0	0	1
Allison, ph	1	0	0	0	0	0
Quilici, 2b	0	0	0	0	0	0
Alyea, ph	1	0	0	0	0	0
Kaat, p	1	0	0	0	0	0
Blyleven, p	0	0	0	0	0	1
Manuel, ph	1	0	0	0	0	0
Hall, p	0	0	0	0	0	0
Carew, ph	1	0	0	0	0	0
Perry, p	0	0	0	0	0	0
Renick, ph	1	0	0	0	0	0
Totals	33	1	7	1	24	7

Baltimore	AB.	R.	H.	RBI.	PO.	A.
Buford, lf	4	1	2	2	2	0
Blair, cf	4	0	1	0	1	0
F. Robinson, rf	3	0	0	0	1	0
Powell, 1b	4	0	1	1	5	0
B. Robinson, 3b	4	1	3	0	2	1
Johnson, 2b	3	2	2	1	2	1
Etchebarren, c	4	0	0	0	12	0
Belanger, ss	4	1	0	0	3	4
Palmer, p	4	1	1	1	1	1
Totals	34	6	10	5	27	6

Minnesota	0	0	0	0	1	0	0	0	0—1
Baltimore	1	1	3	0	0	0	1	0	x—6

Minnesota	IP.	H.	R.	ER.	BB.	SO.
Kaat (L)	2*	6	4	2	2	1
Blyleven	2	2	1	0	0	2
Hall	2	0	0	0	1	2
Perry	2	2	1	1	0	2

Baltimore	IP.	H.	R.	ER.	BB.	SO.
Palmer (W)	9	7	1	1	3	12

*Pitched to two batters in third.

E—Holt, Ratliff. DP—Baltimore 1. LOB—Minnesota 8, Baltimore 9. 2B—Buford, B. Robinson, Palmer. 3B—Tovar. HR—Johnson. SH—Blair. SF—Buford. U—Odom, Neudecker, Springstead, Honochick, Haller and Goetz. T—2:20. A—27,608.

COMPOSITE BATTING AVERAGES
Baltimore Orioles

Player-Position	G.	AB.	R.	H.	2B.	3B.	HR.	RBI.	BA.
B. Robinson, 3b	3	12	3	7	2	0	0	1	.583
Cuellar, p	1	2	1	1	0	0	1	4	.500
R. Hall, p	1	2	1	1	0	0	0	0	.500
Powell, 1b	3	14	2	6	2	0	1	6	.429
Buford, lf	2	7	2	3	1	0	1	3	.429
Hendricks, c	1	5	2	2	0	0	0	0	.400
McNally, p	1	5	1	2	1	0	0	1	.400
Johnson, 2b	3	11	4	10	0	0	2	4	.364
Belanger, ss	3	12	5	4	0	0	0	1	.333
Rettenmund, lf	1	3	1	1	0	0	0	1	.333
Palmer, p	1	4	1	1	1	0	0	1	.250
F. Robinson, rf	3	10	3	2	0	0	1	2	.200
Etchebarren, c	2	9	1	1	0	0	0	0	.111
Blair, cf	3	13	0	1	0	0	0	0	.077
Totals	3	109	27	36	7	0	6	24	.330

Minnesota Twins

Player-Position	G.	AB.	R.	H.	2B.	3B.	HR.	RBI.	BA.
Oliva, rf	3	12	2	6	2	0	1	1	.500
Mitterwald, c	2	8	2	4	1	0	0	2	.500
Tovar, cf-2b-lf	3	13	2	5	0	1	0	1	.385
Killebrew, 3b-1b	3	11	3	3	0	0	2	4	.273
Ratliff, c	1	4	0	1	0	0	0	0	.250
Renick, 3b-ph	2	5	0	1	0	0	0	0	.200
Cardenas, ss	3	11	1	2	0	0	0	1	.182
Reese, 1b	2	7	0	1	0	0	0	0	.143
Thompson, 2b	3	8	0	1	1	0	0	0	.125
Blyleven, p	1	0	0	0	0	0	0	0	.000
Perranoski, p	2	0	0	0	0	0	0	0	.000
Tiant, p-pr	2	0	0	0	0	0	0	0	.000
Williams, p	2	0	0	0	0	0	0	0	.000
Woodson, p	1	0	0	0	0	0	0	0	.000
Zepp, p	2	0	0	0	0	0	0	0	.000
T. Hall, p	2	1	0	0	0	0	0	0	.000
Kaat, p	1	1	0	0	0	0	0	0	.000
Manuel, ph	1	1	0	0	0	0	0	0	.000
Perry, p	2	1	0	0	0	0	0	1	.000
Allison, ph	3	2	0	0	0	0	0	0	.000
Carew, ph	2	2	0	0	0	0	0	0	.000
Quilici, 2b-ph	3	2	0	0	0	0	0	0	.000
Holt, ph-cf-lf	3	5	0	0	0	0	0	0	.000
Alyea, lf-ph	3	7	1	0	0	0	0	0	.000
Totals	3	101	10	24	4	1	3	10	.238

COMPOSITE PITCHING AVERAGES
Baltimore Orioles

Pitcher	G.	IP.	H.	R.	ER.	BB.	SO.	W.	L.	ERA.
R. Hall	1	4⅔	1	0	0	0	3	1	0	0.00
Palmer	1	9	7	1	1	3	12	1	0	1.00
McNally	1	9	6	3	3	5	5	1	0	3.00
Cuellar	1	4⅓	10	6	6	1	2	0	0	12.46
Totals	3	27	24	10	10	9	22	3	0	3.33

Minnesota Twins

Pitcher	G.	IP.	H.	R.	ER.	BB.	SO.	W.	L.	ERA.
Williams	2	6	2	0	0	1	2	0	0	0.00
Blyleven	1	2	2	1	0	0	2	0	0	0.00
T. Hall	2	5⅓	6	4	4	4	6	0	1	6.75
Zepp	2	1⅓	1	1	1	4	0	0	0	6.75
Kaat	1	2	6	4	2	2	1	0	1	9.00
Woodson	1	1	2	1	1	1	0	0	0	9.00
Perry	2	5⅓	10	9	8	1	3	0	1	13.50
Tiant	1	⅔	1	2	1	1	0	0	0	13.50
Perranoski	2	2⅓	5	5	5	1	3	0	0	19.29
Totals	3	26	36	27	22	12	19	0	3	7.62

1970
CINCINNATI REDS
VS.
PITTSBURGH PIRATES

A potent attack and a question-mark pitching staff. That was the consensus view of the Cincinnati Reds as the 1970 National League Championship Series began in Pittsburgh's Three Rivers Stadium October 3. Two days later, it was all over. The Reds reigned as National League champions, but not because of their menacing bats. It was that shaky pitching staff that carried the Reds to three successive victories over the Pirates.

Cincinnati sluggers had whacked 191 home runs in cruising to the West Division title by 14½ games. East Division champ Pittsburgh wasn't that easy for the Reds, despite their three-game sweep. The Reds had all they could handle in each conquest, particularly the finale, in which the Pirates repeatedly threatened but could not deliver.

Cincinnati boasted dual heroes in subduing the Pirates, 3-0, in 10 innings in the playoff opener. Gary Nolan, an 18-game winner during the regular season, pitched nine shutout innings to edge Dock Ellis. Nolan departed for pinch-hitter Ty Cline in the 10th, which turned out to be a stroke of genius by Reds Manager Sparky Anderson. Cline socked a triple to lead off the inning. He scored the decisive run on Pete Rose's single, and Lee May doubled to provide two insurance tallies, sealing Ellis' fate. Reliever Clay Carroll protected Nolan's victory by holding Pittsburgh hitless in the 10th.

Another key contributor to the Reds' opening triumph was second baseman Tommy Helms. With Pirate runners on second and third and two out in the third inning, Dave Cash rifled a shot to Helms' right. Helms' diving stop and quick throw to first prevented two Buc runs.

Cincinnati's Bobby Tolan is congratulated by teammates after hitting a big home run in the Reds' Game 2 victory.

Four minor league umpires worked the opener while the regularly assigned arbiters (and several others) picketed the Pittsburgh park. The umps were striking for higher pay in the pennant playoffs and World Series. An hour before Game 2 was scheduled to start, the striking umps reached an agreement with the major leagues and returned to work.

The Reds didn't cut it quite as close in Game 2. They led from the third inning on, but never by much, in posting a 3-1 victory. Pittsburgh's chief tormentors in this one were Bobby Tolan, the swift center fielder, and Don Gullett, 19-year-old fireballing reliever.

Tolan was a complete mystery to Buc starter Luke Walker. Bobby began his three-hit salvo with a single in the third inning. He stole second base and wound up at third on catcher Manny Sanguillen's wild peg into center field. Walker's wild pitch permitted Tolan to score. Bobby delivered his kayo punch in the fifth, belting a home run over the wall in right-center, and capped his big day with a single off reliever Dave

Giusti in the eighth.

Lefty Jim Merritt, Cincinnati's lone 20-game winner, was the second-game starter. Arm trouble had kept Merritt on the shelf in the closing weeks of the regular season, but Manager Anderson had precedent going for him in this case. Merritt had beaten the Pirates six times in six starts over a two-year period. He made it seven for seven by lasting 5⅓ innings this time. Carroll relieved Merritt in the sixth, but gave up two hits and had retired only one batter when Anderson signaled for Gullett.

That did it. Gullett shut off the Pirate threat immediately, striking out the side in the seventh and finishing with 3⅓ hitless rounds.

When the scene shifted to Cincinnati for Game 3, the Reds wrapped it up, 3-2, but not without a struggle. The Pirates scored a run in the first inning off Tony Cloninger, who averted disaster three times before Anderson finally yanked him for a pinch-hitter in the fifth with the score 2-2.

The slugging Reds uncorked their only power show of the playoffs in the first inning, Tony Perez and Bench smacking successive homers off Bob Moose. Pirate starter Moose showed more courage than stuff in the early going. But he hung on and proceeded to halt the Reds until he had two out in the eighth. Then he walked pinch-hitter Cline and gave up a single to Rose.

With Tolan coming up, Pirate Manager Danny Murtaugh brought in lefty Joe Gibbon. Tolan whacked a single to left. Cline took off from second and sped for the plate. He arrived just a hair ahead of Willie Stargell's peg, and the Reds had a 3-2 lead.

The Reds had a pitching star in this one, too, young Milt Wilcox, who worked three shutout innings in relief of Cloninger and earned the victory. Wilcox vanished for pinch-hitter Cline in the eighth. Wayne Granger tried to protect the Reds' 3-2 lead in the ninth, but was removed with two down and a runner on first. Gullett was Anderson's choice to wrap it up. The teen-ager wasn't invincible this time, yielding a single to Stargell. But with runners on first and third, Al Oliver swung at Gullett's first pitch and grounded to Helms.

Game 1

Saturday, October 3, At Pittsburgh

Cincinnati	AB.	R.	H.	RBI.	PO.	A.
Rose, rf	5	1	2	1	1	0
Tolan, cf	5	0	1	0	2	0
Perez, 3b-1b	4	0	1	0	1	1
Bench, c	3	1	0	0	8	3
May, 1b	5	0	1	2	9	0
Concepcion, pr-ss	0	0	0	0	0	0
Carbo, lf	3	0	0	0	0	0
McRae, ph	1	0	0	0	0	0
Carroll, p	0	0	0	0	0	0
Helms, 2b	4	0	2	0	5	5
Woodward, ss-3b	4	0	0	0	4	4
Nolan, p	3	0	1	0	0	2
Cline, ph-lf	1	1	1	0	0	0
Totals	38	3	9	3	30	15

Pittsburgh	AB.	R.	H.	RBI.	PO.	A.
Alou, cf	3	0	2	0	4	0
Cash, 2b	5	0	0	0	3	3
Clemente, rf	5	0	0	0	3	0
Stargell, lf	4	0	3	0	2	0
Jeter, pr-lf	1	0	0	0	2	0
Oliver, 1b	3	0	0	0	10	0
Sanguillen, c	4	0	1	0	2	0
Hebner, 3b	4	0	2	0	0	2
Alley, ss	3	0	0	0	4	3
Ellis, p	2	0	0	0	0	3
Gibbon, p	0	0	0	0	0	0
Totals	34	0	8	0	30	11

Cincinnati	0 0 0 0 0 0 0 0 0 3—3
Pittsburgh	0 0 0 0 0 0 0 0 0 0—0

Cincinnati	IP.	H.	R.	ER.	BB.	SO.
Nolan (W)	9	8	0	0	4	6
Carroll (S)	1	0	0	0	0	2

Pittsburgh	IP.	H.	R.	ER.	BB.	SO.
Ellis (L)	9⅔	9	3	3	4	1
Gibbon	⅓	0	0	0	0	1

DP—Pittsburgh 1. LOB—Cincinnati 9, Pittsburgh 10. 2B—Alou, Perez, Stargell, May. 3B—Cline. SH—Ellis 2. U—Grimsley, Blandford, Morgenweck and Grygiel. T—2:23. A—33,088.

Game 2

Sunday, October 4, At Pittsburgh

Cincinnati	AB.	R.	H.	RBI.	PO.	A.
Rose, rf	4	0	0	0	2	0
Tolan, cf	4	3	3	1	2	0
Perez, 3b	4	0	2	1	2	3
Concepcion, ss	0	0	0	0	1	1
Bench, c	3	0	0	0	5	0
May, 1b	4	0	1	0	10	0
McRae, lf	3	0	0	0	2	0
Carroll, p	0	0	0	0	0	0
Gullett, p	1	0	0	0	0	0
Helms, 2b	4	0	1	0	3	3
Woodward, ss-3b	3	0	1	0	0	2
Merritt, p	2	0	0	0	0	2
Stewart, lf	2	0	0	0	0	0
Totals	34	3	8	2	27	11

Pittsburgh	AB.	R.	H.	RBI.	PO.	A.
Alou, cf	4	0	0	0	1	0
Cash, 2b	3	1	1	0	3	5
Clemente, rf	4	0	1	1	2	0
Sanguillen, c	4	0	1	0	6	0
Robertson, 1b	4	0	1	0	11	1
Stargell, lf	4	0	0	0	1	0
Pagan, 3b	3	0	1	0	0	4
Alley, ss	4	0	0	0	2	4
Walker, p	2	0	0	0	0	0
Jeter, ph	1	0	0	0	0	0
Giusti, p	0	0	0	0	1	0
Totals	33	1	5	1	27	14

Cincinnati	0 0 1 0 1 0 0 1 0—3
Pittsburgh	0 0 0 0 0 1 0 0 0—1

Cincinnati	IP.	H.	R.	ER.	BB.	SO.
Merritt (W)	5⅓	3	1	1	0	2
Carroll	⅓	2	0	0	0	0
Gullett (S)	3⅓	0	0	0	2	3

Pittsburgh	IP.	H.	R.	ER.	BB.	SO.
Walker (L)	7	5	2	1	1	5
Giusti	2	3	1	1	1	0

E—Walker, Perez, Sanguillen. DP—Pittsburgh 2. LOB—Cincinnati 6, Pittsburgh 7. 2B—Robertson, Cash, Perez. HR—Tolan. SB—Tolan. WP—Walker. U—Landes, Pryor, Harvey, Engel, Wendelstedt and Colosi. T—2:10. A—39,317.

Game 3

Monday, October 5, At Cincinnati

Pittsburgh	AB.	R.	H.	RBI.	PO.	A.
Patek, ss	3	0	0	0	1	2
Robertson, ph	1	0	0	0	0	0
Alou, cf	5	1	1	0	1	0
Clemente, rf	5	1	2	0	2	0
Stargell, lf	4	0	3	1	1	0
Jeter, pr	0	0	0	0	0	0
Oliver, 1b	5	0	2	1	12	1
Sanguillen, c	4	0	0	0	5	1
Hebner, 3b	2	0	2	0	0	2
Mazeroski, 2b	2	0	0	0	1	4
Moose, p	4	0	0	0	1	2
Gibbon, p	0	0	0	0	0	0
Giusti, p	0	0	0	0	0	0
Totals	35	2	10	2	24	12

Cincinnati	AB.	R.	H.	RBI.	PO.	A.
Rose, rf	4	0	1	0	0	0
Tolan, cf	3	0	1	1	1	0
Perez, 3b	4	1	1	1	3	2
Granger, p	0	0	0	0	0	0
Gullett, p	0	0	0	0	0	0
Bench, c	3	1	2	1	7	0
May, 1b	3	0	0	0	12	1
Carbo, lf	3	0	0	0	0	0
Helms, 2b	3	0	0	0	3	4
Woodward, ss-3b	3	0	0	0	1	3
Cloninger, p	1	0	0	0	0	2
Bravo, ph	1	0	0	0	0	0
Wilcox, p	0	0	0	0	0	1
Cline, ph	0	1	0	0	0	0
Concepcion, ss	0	0	0	0	0	0
Totals	28	3	5	3	27	13

Pittsburgh	1 0 0 0 1 0 0 0 0—2
Cincinnati	2 0 0 0 0 0 0 1 x—3

Pittsburgh	IP.	H.	R.	ER.	BB.	SO.
Moose (L)	7⅔	4	3	3	2	4
Gibbon	0*	1	0	0	0	0
Giusti	⅓	0	0	0	0	1

Cincinnati	IP.	H.	R.	ER.	BB.	SO.
Cloninger	5	7	2	2	4	1
Wilcox (W)	3	1	0	0	2	5
Granger	⅔	1	0	0	0	0
Gullett (S)	⅓	1	0	0	0	0

*Pitched to one batter in eighth.

DP—Cincinnati 1. LOB—Pittsburgh 12, Cincinnati 3. 2B—Hebner 2. HR—Perez, Bench. WP—Cloninger. U—Pryor, Harvey, Engel, Wendelstedt, Colosi and Landes. T—2:38. A—40,538.

COMPOSITE BATTING AVERAGES

Cincinnati Reds

Player-Position	G.	AB.	R.	H.	2B.	3B.	HR.	RBI.	BA.
Cline, ph-lf	2	1	2	1	0	1	0	0	1.000
Tolan, cf	3	12	3	5	0	0	1	2	.417
Perez, 3b-1b	3	12	1	4	2	0	1	2	.333
Nolan, p	1	3	0	1	0	0	0	0	.333
Helms, 2b	3	11	0	3	0	0	0	0	.273
Rose, rf	3	13	1	3	0	0	0	1	.231
Bench, c	3	9	2	2	0	0	1	1	.222
May, 1b	3	12	0	2	1	0	0	2	.167
Woodward, ss-3b	3	10	0	1	0	0	0	0	.100
Carroll, p	2	0	0	0	0	0	0	0	.000
Concepcion, pr-ss	3	0	0	0	0	0	0	0	.000
Granger, p	1	0	0	0	0	0	0	0	.000
Wilcox, p	1	0	0	0	0	0	0	0	.000
Bravo, ph	1	1	0	0	0	0	0	0	.000
Cloninger, p	1	1	0	0	0	0	0	0	.000
Gullett, p	2	1	0	0	0	0	0	0	.000
Merritt, p	1	2	0	0	0	0	0	0	.000
Stewart, lf	1	2	0	0	0	0	0	0	.000
McRae, ph-lf	2	4	0	0	0	0	0	0	.000
Carbo, lf	2	6	0	0	0	0	0	0	.000
Totals	3	100	9	22	3	1	3	8	.220

Pittsburgh Pirates

Player-Position	G.	AB.	R.	H.	2B.	3B.	HR.	RBI.	BA.
Hebner, 3b	2	6	0	4	2	0	0	0	.667
Stargell, lf	3	12	0	6	1	0	0	1	.500
Pagan, 3b	1	3	0	1	0	0	0	0	.333
Alou, cf	3	12	1	3	1	0	0	0	.250
Oliver, 1b	2	8	0	2	0	0	0	1	.250
Clemente, rf	3	14	1	3	0	0	0	1	.214
Robertson, 1b-ph	2	5	0	1	1	0	0	0	.200
Sanguillen, c	3	12	0	2	0	0	0	0	.167
Cash, 2b	2	8	1	1	1	0	0	0	.125
Gibbon, p	2	0	0	0	0	0	0	0	.000
Giusti, p	2	0	0	0	0	0	0	0	.000
Ellis, p	1	2	0	0	0	0	0	0	.000
Jeter, pr-lf-ph	3	2	0	0	0	0	0	0	.000
Mazeroski, 2b	1	2	0	0	0	0	0	0	.000
Walker, p	1	2	0	0	0	0	0	0	.000
Patek, ss	1	3	0	0	0	0	0	0	.000
Moose, p	1	4	0	0	0	0	0	0	.000
Alley, ss	2	7	0	0	0	0	0	0	.000
Totals	3	102	3	23	6	0	0	3	.225

COMPOSITE PITCHING AVERAGES

Cincinnati Reds

Pitcher	G.	IP.	H.	R.	ER.	BB.	SO.	W.	L.	ERA.
Nolan	1	9	8	0	0	4	6	1	0	0.00
Gullett	2	3⅔	1	0	0	2	3	0	0	0.00
Wilcox	1	3	1	0	0	2	5	1	0	0.00
Carroll	2	1⅓	2	0	0	0	2	0	0	0.00
Granger	1	⅔	1	0	0	0	0	0	0	0.00
Merritt	1	5⅓	3	1	1	0	2	1	0	1.69
Cloninger	1	5	7	2	2	4	1	0	0	3.60
Totals	3	28	23	3	3	12	19	3	0	0.96

Pittsburgh Pirates

Pitcher	G.	IP.	H.	R.	ER.	BB.	SO.	W.	L.	ERA.
Gibbon	2	⅓	1	0	0	0	1	0	0	0.00
Walker	1	7	5	2	1	1	5	0	1	1.29
Ellis	1	9⅔	9	3	3	4	1	0	1	2.79
Moose	1	7⅔	4	3	3	2	4	0	1	3.52
Giusti	2	2⅓	3	1	1	1	1	0	0	3.86
Totals	3	27	22	9	8	8	12	0	3	2.67

In 1971, the Orioles' victims were the Oakland A's, who had cruised to the West Division crown as impressively as the Orioles had shattered their Eastern rivals.

Oakland never was in it after seeing ace Vida Blue clubbed for four runs in the seventh inning of the opener October 3 in Baltimore. Blue went into that frame with a 3-1 lead. He emerged a 5-3 loser, and the A's might as well have capitulated then and there. They fell before Mike Cuellar, 5-1, the next day, and the day after that Jim Palmer killed them off, 5-3, in Oakland.

That made it nine victories in nine playoff games for the Orioles, starting in 1969, when they flattened the Minnesota Twins. The Twins came back for another dose of the same in 1970.

Baltimore entered the '71 playoffs with a pitching staff bristling with aces—four 20-game winners. The Orioles were the first to boast that kind of pitching firepower since the 1920 White Sox.

Dave McNally, Cuellar, Palmer and Pat Dobson were Manager Earl Weaver's 20-win artists. McNally defeated Blue in the playoff opener, Cuellar won the second game and Palmer the third. Dobson, despite his 20-8 record, delivered not a single pitch in the playoffs.

The Orioles fired a four-homer salvo, including two by Boog Powell, off Catfish Hunter in game two. Aside from that, Baltimore's noted sluggers were not devastating. Frank Robinson, longtime kingpin of the Oriole offense, made only one hit in 12 trips off Oakland pitching.

McNally, a 20-game winner for the fourth season in a row, survived a rocky start to win the opener. He trailed, 3-0, after 3½

Baltimore lefthander Dave McNally outdueled Oakland's Vida Blue in Game 1 of the 1971 Championship Series.

innings, giving up three doubles and a triple. The A's had McNally tottering in the second. With two runs home, a runner on second and none out, second baseman Dick Green came to bat.

It was at this point that A's Manager Dick Williams made the first of several ultra-cautious moves which were to fuel criticism of his playoff strategy. He ordered Green to sacrifice, which put runner Dave Duncan on third with one out.

The next batter was Blue, whose bunting ability is well known. Vida tried to squeeze the run home, but the O's had guessed correctly on what was coming. McNally pitched out and Duncan was nailed in a rundown. Blue proceeded to strike out, and the A's splurge was over.

McNally gave up another run in the fourth, but that ended the A's scoring forays. Meanwhile, 24-game winner Blue yielded just one run and three hits the first six innings.

However, disaster overtook Vida in the very next frame. Frank Robinson led off with a walk and Powell struck out. Brooks Robinson's single sent F. Robby to second, after which Andy Etchebarren's fly to right advanced F. Robby to third.

Now there were runners on first and third with two down, and Blue appeared likely to quell the flurry without damage. After all, he'd beaten the O's twice in two tries during the season. And the next hitter was shortstop Mark Belanger, hardly a nemesis to any pitcher. But Belanger rifled a single to center to score F. Robby and ignite thunderous cheering from the crowd of 42,621.

Then Curt Motton, pinch-hitter hero of a '69 Oriole playoff victory over Minnesota, stepped up to bat for McNally. Curt slammed a double to the left-field corner, plating B. Robby and tying the score. Center fielder Paul Blair followed with the blow that

doomed Blue, a two-run double to left.

Reliever Eddie Watt blanked the A's the last two innings and Oakland was one game down. Skipper Williams was subjected to further sharpshooting for his failure to remove Blue, or even visit the mound, during the seventh-inning barrage.

Next day, the A's put it to 20-game winner Hunter to stop the crafty Cuellar, who had won 20 for the third consecutive year.

The Catfish held Baltimore to seven hits, but unfortunately for him, four of them were home runs. Powell walloped two, Brooks Robinson and Ellie Hendricks the others.

Cuellar displayed his usual pitching artistry, a baffling assortment of curves and change-ups which the A's solved for a mere six hits.

Typical of the A's super-cautious approach to their task was an incident in the sixth inning when they were trailing, 2-1. Reggie Jackson led off against Cuellar with a double. Cleanup hitter Tommy Davis was up next and to the surprise of everyone in the park, he bunted. The next two hitters were easy outs. Davis' sacrifice, it turned out, was not ordered by Williams.

Now one game from oblivion, the A's had to send Diego Segui against Palmer in Oakland October 5. Segui got the call in place of Chuck Dobson, Oakland's No. 3 starter, who had a sore elbow.

Palmer's performance was not among his most noteworthy—he permitted three home runs, two of them by the slugging Jackson and the other by Sal Bando. But all three shots were struck with the bases empty, and Palmer had more than enough to pitch Baltimore's pennant clincher for the third straight year.

Loser of his only two starts against Baltimore during the season, Segui reached the fifth inning October 5 with the score 1-1. Then he met his Waterloo. The crusher was Brooks Robinson's two-run single. It came after Williams ordered an intentional pass to Hendricks, loading the bases.

Bando's homer cut the A's defi-

cit to 3-2 in the sixth; but, in the seventh, F. Robby's double and Darold Knowles' wild pitch scored two runs and put Baltimore out of danger. The Orioles collected 12 hits off Segui and his four successors, with Don Buford's triple and two singles leading the way.

Game 1

Sunday, October 3 At Baltimore

Oakland	AB.	R.	H.	RBI.	PO.	A.
Campaneris, ss	4	0	1	0	0	0
Rudi, lf	4	0	1	0	2	0
Jackson, rf	4	0	0	0	3	0
Davis, 1b	4	1	1	0	4	0
Bando, 3b	4	1	2	0	2	1
Mangual, cf	4	1	2	2	2	0
Duncan, c	3	0	2	1	9	0
Epstein, ph	1	0	0	0	0	0
Green, 2b	1	0	0	0	2	3
Blue, p	3	0	0	0	1	0
Fingers, p	0	0	0	0	0	0
Totals	32	3	9	3	24	5

Baltimore	AB.	R.	H.	RBI.	PO.	A.
Blair, cf	4	0	1	2	2	0
Johnson, 2b	4	1	1	0	1	3
Rettenmund, lf	4	0	1	1	3	0
F. Robinson, rf	3	1	0	0	2	0
Powell, 1b	4	0	1	0	9	1
B. Robinson, 3b	3	1	1	0	0	2
Etchebarren, c	3	0	0	0	7	0
Belanger, ss	2	1	1	1	3	4
McNally, p	2	0	0	0	0	0
Motton, ph	1	0	1	1	0	0
Palmer, pr	0	1	0	0	0	0
Watt, p	0	0	0	0	0	1
Totals	30	5	7	5	27	13

Oakland .... 0 2 0 1 0 0 0—3
Baltimore .... 0 0 0 1 0 0 4 0 x—5

Oakland	IP.	H.	R.	ER.	BB.	SO.
Blue (L)	7	7	5	5	2	8
Fingers	1	0	0	0	0	1

Baltimore	IP.	H.	R.	ER.	BB.	SO.
McNally (W)	7	7	3	3	1	5
Watt (S)	2	2	0	0	0	1

E—Johnson. DP—Oakland 1, Baltimore 2. LOB—Oakland 4, Baltimore 3. 2B—Rudi, Bando, Duncan, Mangual, Johnson, Rettenmund, Motton, Blair, Campaneris. 3B—Mangual. SH—Green. U—Soar, Napp, DiMuro, O'Donnell, Luciano and Kunkel. T—2:23. A—42,621.

Game 2

Monday, October 4, At Baltimore

Oakland	AB.	R.	H.	RBI.	PO.	A.
Campaneris, ss	4	0	1	0	2	3
Rudi, lf	3	0	0	0	2	0
Jackson, rf	4	0	1	0	4	1
Davis, 1b	3	0	1	0	4	0
Bando, 3b	4	1	1	0	2	0
Mangual, cf	4	0	0	0	2	0
Duncan, c	3	0	1	1	6	0
Green, 2b	3	0	1	0	2	0
Hunter, p	3	0	0	0	0	0
Totals	31	1	6	1	24	4

Baltimore	AB.	R.	H.	RBI.	PO.	A.
Buford, lf	3	0	0	0	1	0
Blair, cf	0	0	0	0	0	0
Johnson, 2b	3	1	0	0	1	1
Powell, 1b	4	2	2	3	12	0
F. Robinson, rf	4	0	0	0	4	0
Rettenmund, cf-lf	4	0	1	0	4	0
B. Robinson, 3b	3	1	1	1	1	3
Hendricks, c	3	1	2	1	2	0
Belanger, ss	3	0	0	0	2	4
Cuellar, p	3	0	1	0	0	2
Totals	30	5	7	5	27	10

Oakland .... 0 0 0 1 0 0 0 0—1
Baltimore .... 0 1 1 0 0 0 1 2 x—5

Oakland	IP.	H.	R.	ER.	BB.	SO.
Hunter (L)	8	7	5	5	2	6

Baltimore	IP.	H.	R.	ER.	BB.	SO.
Cuellar (W)	9	6	1	1	1	2

LOB—Oakland 5, Baltimore 3. 2B—Davis, Bando, Jackson. HR—B. Robinson, Powell 2, Hendricks. SH—Davis. U—Napp, O'Donnell, Luciano, DiMuro, Kunkel and Soar. T—2:04. A—35,003.

Game 3

Tuesday, October 5, At Oakland

Baltimore	AB.	R.	H.	RBI.	PO.	A.
Buford, lf	4	1	3	0	0	0
Rettenmund, pr-lf	0	0	0	0	0	0
Blair, cf	5	1	2	0	3	0
Powell, 1b	2	2	0	0	7	1
F. Robinson, rf	5	1	1	1	1	0
Hendricks, c	1	0	0	1	4	0
Etchebarren, ph-c	2	0	0	0	4	0
B. Robinson, 3b	5	0	2	2	3	2
Johnson, 2b	3	0	2	0	3	2
Belanger, ss	3	0	1	0	1	3
Palmer, p	5	0	1	0	1	0
Totals	35	5	12	4	27	8

Oakland	AB.	R.	H.	RBI.	PO.	A.
Campaneris, ss	4	0	0	0	1	3
Monday, cf	3	0	0	0	4	0
Jackson, rf	4	2	3	2	2	0
Epstein, 1b	4	0	1	0	4	0
Bando, 3b	3	1	1	1	2	1
Mangual, lf	4	0	0	0	2	0
Tenace, c	3	0	0	0	8	0
Green, 2b	3	0	1	0	4	1
Hegan, ph	1	0	0	0	0	0
Segui, p	2	0	0	0	0	0
Fingers, p	0	0	0	0	0	0
Knowles, p	0	0	0	0	0	0
Locker, p	0	0	0	0	0	0
Davis, ph	1	0	1	0	0	0
Grant, p	0	0	0	0	0	1
Blefary, ph	1	0	0	0	0	0
Totals	33	3	7	3	27	6

Baltimore .... 1 0 0 0 2 0 2 0 0—5
Oakland .... 0 0 1 0 0 1 0 1 0—3

Baltimore	IP.	H.	R.	ER.	BB.	SO.
Palmer (W)	9	7	3	3	3	8

Oakland	IP.	H.	R.	ER.	BB.	SO.
Segui (L)	4⅔	6	3	3	6	4
Fingers	1⅓ *	2	2	2	1	1
Knowles	⅓	1	0	0	0	0
Locker	⅔	0	0	0	2	0
Grant	2	3	0	0	0	2

*Pitched to two batters in seventh.

DP—Baltimore 1, Oakland 3. LOB—Baltimore 13, Oakland 6. 2B—Johnson, F. Robinson. 3B—Buford. HR—Jackson 2, Bando. SF—Hendricks. WP—Palmer, Knowles. U—DiMuro, Luciano, Soar, Kunkel, O'Donnell and Napp. T—2:49. A—33,176.

COMPOSITE BATTING AVERAGES
Baltimore Orioles

Player-Position	G.	AB.	R.	H.	2B.	3B.	HR.	RBI.	BA.
Motton, ph	1	1	0	1	0	0	0	1	1.000
Hendricks, c	2	4	1	2	0	0	1	2	.500
Buford, lf	2	7	1	3	0	1	0	0	.429
B. Robinson, 3b	3	11	2	4	1	0	1	3	.364
Blair, cf	3	9	1	3	1	0	0	2	.333
Cuellar, p	1	3	0	1	0	0	0	0	.333
Johnson, 2b	3	10	2	3	2	0	0	0	.300
Powell, 1b	3	10	4	3	0	0	2	3	.300
Belanger, ss	3	8	1	2	0	0	0	1	.250
Rettenmund, lf-cf-pr	3	8	0	2	1	0	0	1	.250
Palmer, pr-p	2	5	1	1	0	0	0	0	.200
F. Robinson, rf	3	12	2	1	1	0	0	1	.083
Watt, p	1	0	0	0	0	0	0	0	.000
McNally, p	1	2	0	0	0	0	0	0	.000
Etchebarren, c-ph	2	5	0	0	0	0	0	0	.000
Totals	3	95	15	26	7	1	4	14	.274

Oakland Athletics

Player-Position	G.	AB.	R.	H.	2B.	3B.	HR.	RBI.	BA.
Duncan, c	2	6	0	3	1	0	0	2	.500
Davis, 1b-ph	3	8	1	3	1	0	0	0	.375
Bando, 3b	3	11	3	4	2	0	1	1	.364
Jackson, rf	3	12	2	4	1	0	2	2	.333
Green, 2b	3	7	0	2	0	0	0	0	.286
Epstein, ph-1b	2	5	0	1	0	0	0	0	.200
Campaneris, ss	3	12	0	2	1	0	0	0	.167
Mangual, cf-lf	3	12	1	2	1	1	0	2	.167
Rudi, lf	2	7	0	1	1	0	0	0	.143
Fingers, p	2	0	0	0	0	0	0	0	.000
Grant, p	1	0	0	0	0	0	0	0	.000
Knowles, p	1	0	0	0	0	0	0	0	.000
Locker, p	1	0	0	0	0	0	0	0	.000
Blefary, ph	1	1	0	0	0	0	0	0	.000
Hegan, ph	1	1	0	0	0	0	0	0	.000
Segui, p	1	2	0	0	0	0	0	0	.000
Blue, p	1	3	0	0	0	0	0	0	.000
Hunter, p	1	3	0	0	0	0	0	0	.000
Monday, cf	1	3	0	0	0	0	0	0	.000
Tenace, c	1	3	0	0	0	0	0	0	.000
Totals	3	96	7	22	8	1	3	7	.229

COMPOSITE PITCHING AVERAGES
Baltimore Orioles

Pitcher	G.	IP.	H.	R.	ER.	BB.	SO.	W.	L.	ERA.
Watt	1	2	2	0	0	0	1	0	0	0.00
Cuellar	1	9	6	1	1	1	2	1	0	1.00
Palmer	1	9	7	3	3	3	8	1	0	3.00
McNally	1	7	7	3	3	1	5	1	0	3.86
Totals	3	27	22	7	7	5	16	3	0	2.33

Oakland Athletics

Pitcher	G.	IP.	H.	R.	ER.	BB.	SO.	W.	L.	ERA.
Grant	1	2	3	0	0	0	2	0	0	0.00
Locker	1	⅔	0	0	0	2	0	0	0	0.00
Knowles	1	⅓	1	0	0	0	0	0	0	0.00
Hunter	1	8	7	5	5	2	6	0	1	5.63
Segui	1	4⅔	6	3	3	6	4	0	1	5.79
Blue	1	7	7	5	5	2	8	0	1	6.43
Fingers	2	2⅓	2	2	2	1	2	0	0	7.71
Totals	3	25	26	15	15	13	22	0	3	5.40

PITTSBURGH PIRATES
VS.
SAN FRANCISCO GIANTS

The big bat that led all major league home run hitters in 1971 was strangely silent during the National League Championship Series.

But another bat, swung by Bob Robertson, produced at a frenzied pace and the Pittsburgh Pirates defeated the San Francisco Giants, three games to one, to capture their first pennant since 1960.

While Willie Stargell drew a complete blank in the four games, going 0 for 14, Robertson collected seven hits in 16 trips to the plate, cracked four home runs and drove in six runs.

The big first baseman, who was inactivated by a kidney ailment for the entire 1968 season and by a knee condition for 31 games in 1971, enjoyed his most productive performance in the second contest, at Candlestick Park in San Francisco.

The Pirates, who lost the opening game, 5-4, although outhitting the Giants, 9 to 7, trailed, 2-1, after three innings of the second encounter. At this point, Robertson, who had doubled and scored in the second inning, hit a John Cumberland pitch into the right-field seats for a home run.

In the seventh inning, Robertson poled a three-run shot to left field off Ron Bryant and, in the ninth, he connected off Steve Hamilton, driving the ball over the left-center field fence.

The 9-4 victory, credited to Dock Ellis, first of three Pittsburgh pitchers, was the Pirates' first at Candlestick Park after six consecutive defeats.

When the series shifted to Pittsburgh, Manager Danny Murtaugh nominated Nelson Briles (8-4 for the season) as the Pirates' starting pitcher.

In warming up, however, the righthander suffered a recurrence

Pittsburgh's Bob Robertson was the toast of the Pirates' locker room after belting three Game 2 home runs against the Giants in 1971.

of a hamstring pull and Bob Johnson, who compiled a 9-10 regular-season record, was tabbed as a replacement.

The 28-year-old righthander, who was allowed extra time to warm up, dueled Juan Marichal, the Giants' 18-game winner, on equal terms for seven innings and was returned a 2-1 winner when Richie Hebner poled a right-field home run in the last of the eighth.

Marichal, with a 25-10 lifetime record against the Pirates, yielded only three hits in the first seven innings, including a no-harm single to Roberto Clemente in the first inning, Robertson's second-inning homer, his third in as many consecutive trips, and Hebner's non-productive single in the sixth.

In the eighth, Hebner drilled "a screwball out over the plate" to deep right field where Bonds missed a leaping catch by about

five inches, the ball falling into home run territory for the deciding tally.

With the Pirates just one victory away from the pennant that eluded them in 1970 via three consecutive losses to the Cincinnati Reds, Murtaugh called on Steve Blass to face his first-game opponent, Perry.

Blass, who lasted five innings in the opener, was less a mystery in his second try. In two innings, the righthander yielded eight hits and five runs, two of the blows being homers by Chris Speier and Willie McCovey.

Trailing, 5-2, the Pirates tagged Perry for three second-inning runs. Sanguillen and Bill Mazeroski singled around a fielder's choice and Hebner again reached home run territory in right field.

Perry, touched for 10 of the Pirates' 11 hits, blanked the N.L. East champions for the next three

innings.

In the sixth stanza, however, the Bucs tagged him for one run on singles by Dave Cash and Clemente, around an infield out.

After Jerry Johnson relieved Perry, a passed ball permitted Cash to score and Clemente to go to second base. An intentional walk to Stargell was followed by Al Oliver's home run, giving the Pirates a 9-5 edge.

Bruce Kison, 20-year-old right-hander who took over Pittsburgh mound duties in the third inning and allowed only two hits in 4⅔ innings, ran into trouble in the seventh inning when the Giants placed two runners on base.

Dave Giusti, who saved 30 Pittsburgh wins in the regular season and appeared in the first three championship contests, responded again and turned back the Giants without a run.

Game 1

Saturday, October 2, At San Francisco

Pittsburgh	AB.	R.	H.	RBI.	PO.	A.
Cash, 2b	5	2	2	1	3	2
Hebner, 3b	5	0	1	0	0	0
Clemente, rf	4	0	0	0	3	0
Stargell, lf	4	0	0	0	1	0
Oliver, cf	4	0	1	2	3	0
Robertson, 1b	4	0	2	0	1	1
Sanguillen, c	4	0	1	0	10	0
Hernandez, ss	2	1	1	0	1	0
Davalillo, ph	1	0	0	0	0	0
Moose, p	0	0	0	0	0	0
May, ph	1	0	0	0	0	0
Giusti, p	0	0	0	0	0	0
Blass, p	1	0	0	0	1	1
Alley, ss	2	1	1	0	1	1
Totals	37	4	9	3	24	5

San Francisco	AB.	R.	H.	RBI.	PO.	A.
Henderson, lf	4	0	2	1	2	0
Fuentes, 2b	4	1	1	2	2	3
Mays, cf	2	1	1	0	0	0
McCovey, 1b	3	1	1	2	12	0
Kingman, rf	3	0	0	0	3	0
Bonds, rf	1	0	0	0	1	0
Dietz, c	4	0	0	0	5	1
Gallagher, 3b	2	0	0	0	0	1
Lanier, 3b	1	0	0	0	1	0
Speier, ss	3	2	2	0	1	5
Perry, p	1	0	0	0	0	2
Totals	28	5	7	5	27	12

Pittsburgh	0 0 2	0 0 0	2 0 0	—4
San Francisco	0 0 1	0 4 0	0 0 x	—5

Pittsburgh	IP.	H.	R.	ER.	BB.	SO.
Blass (L)	5	6	5	5	2	9
Moose	2	0	0	0	0	0
Giusti	1	1	0	0	1	1

San Francisco	IP.	H.	R.	ER.	BB.	SO.
Perry (W)	9	9	4	3	1	5

E—McCovey, Speier. DP—Pittsburgh 1. LOB—Pittsburgh 9, San Francisco 4. 2B—Cash, Henderson, Mays. HR—Fuentes, McCovey. SH—Blass, Perry 2. HBP—By Perry (Stargell). U—Gorman, Crawford, Weyer, Olsen, Stello and Davidson. T—2:44. A—40,977.

Game 2

Sunday, October 3, At San Francisco

Pittsburgh	AB.	R.	H.	RBI.	PO.	A.
Cash, 2b	5	1	3	0	3	3
Clines, cf	3	1	1	1	1	0
Oliver, ph-cf	1	1	1	0	0	0
Clemente, rf	5	1	3	1	3	0
Stargell, lf	5	0	0	0	1	0
Robertson, 1b	5	4	4	5	9	1
Sanguillen, c	5	1	2	1	5	0
Pagan, 3b	1	0	0	0	1	2
Hebner, ph-3b	3	0	0	0	1	1
Hernandez, ss	4	0	1	1	2	2
Ellis, p	3	0	0	0	0	0
Miller, p	1	0	0	0	1	0
Giusti, p	0	0	0	0	0	0
Totals	41	9	15	9	27	9

San Francisco	AB.	R.	H.	RBI.	PO.	A.
Henderson, lf	3	0	1	1	0	0
Fuentes, 2b	5	2	2	0	4	0
Mays, cf	5	1	2	3	2	0
McCovey, 1b	3	0	1	0	4	0
Rosario, pr	0	0	0	0	0	0
Kingman, rf	4	0	1	0	2	0
Dietz, c	4	0	0	0	14	1
Gallagher, 3b	4	0	0	0	0	0
Speier, ss	3	1	2	0	1	5
Cumberland, p	0	0	0	0	0	0
Barr, p	1	0	0	0	0	0
McMahon, p	0	0	0	0	0	0
Duffy, ph	1	0	0	0	0	0
Carrithers, p	0	0	0	0	0	0
Bryant, p	0	0	0	0	0	0
Hart, ph	1	0	0	0	0	0
Hamilton, p	0	0	0	0	0	0
Totals	34	4	9	4	27	6

Pittsburgh	0 1 0	2 1 0	4 0 1	—9
San Francisco	1 1 0	0 0 0	0 0 2	—4

Pittsburgh	IP.	H.	R.	ER.	BB.	SO.
Ellis (W)	5‡	6	2	2	4	1
Miller	3x	3	2	2	3	3
Giusti (S)	1	0	0	0	0	0

San Francisco	IP.	H.	R.	ER.	BB.	SO.
Cumberland (L)	3*	7	3	3	0	4
Barr	1†	3	1	1	0	2
McMahon	2	0	0	0	0	2
Carrithers	0§	3	3	3	0	0
Bryant	2	1	1	1	1	2
Hamilton	1	1	1	1	0	3

*Pitched to two batters in fourth.
†Pitched to two batters in fifth.
‡Pitched to two batters in sixth.
§Pitched to three batters in seventh.
xPitched to three batters in ninth.

DP—Pittsburgh 1, San Francisco 1. LOB—Pittsburgh 7, San Francisco 12. 2B—Mays, Robertson, Speier, Cash, Fuentes. HR—Robertson 3, Clines, Mays. SH—Cumberland. SB—Henderson, Sanguillen. HBP—By Ellis (Gallagher), by Bryant (Hebner). PB—Sanguillen. U—Crawford, Weyer, Olsen, Stello, Davidson and Gorman. T—3:23. A—42,562.

Game 3

Tuesday, October 5, At Pittsburgh

San Francisco	AB.	R.	H.	RBI.	PO.	A.
Henderson, lf	4	1	1	0	2	0
Fuentes, 2b	3	0	0	0	1	2
Mays, cf	4	0	1	0	0	0
McCovey, 1b	3	0	1	0	11	2
Bonds, rf	3	0	1	0	1	0
Dietz, c	3	0	0	0	7	0
Gallagher, 3b	3	0	1	0	0	3
Hart, ph	1	0	0	0	0	0
Speier, ss	4	0	0	0	0	2
Marichal, p	3	0	0	0	2	4
Kingman, ph	1	0	0	0	0	0
Totals	32	1	5	0	24	13

Pittsburgh	AB.	R.	H.	RBI.	PO.	A.
Cash, 2b	4	0	0	0	2	4
Hebner, 3b	4	1	2	1	1	1
Clemente, rf	4	0	1	0	5	0
Stargell, lf	3	0	0	0	2	0
Oliver, cf	3	0	0	0	0	0
Robertson, 1b	3	1	1	1	8	0
Sanguillen, c	3	0	0	0	7	1
Hernandez, ss	3	0	0	0	2	5
Johnson, p	2	0	0	0	0	0
Davalillo, ph	1	0	0	0	0	0
Giusti, p	0	0	0	0	0	0
Totals	30	2	4	2	27	11

San Francisco	0 0 0	0 0 1	0 0 0	—1
Pittsburgh	0 1 0	0 0 0	0 1 x	—2

San Francisco	IP.	H.	R.	ER.	BB.	SO.
Marichal (L)	8	4	2	2	0	6

Pittsburgh	IP.	H.	R.	ER.	BB.	SO.
Johnson (W)	8	5	1	0	3	7
Giusti (S)	1	0	0	0	0	0

E—Bonds, Hebner, Fuentes. LOB—San Francisco 8, Pittsburgh 4. HR—Robertson, Hebner. SB—Mays. SH—Fuentes. WP—Marichal 2. U—Weyer, Olsen, Stello, Davidson, Gorman and Crawford. T—2:26. A—38,322.

Game 4

Wednesday, October 6, At Pittsburgh

San Francisco	AB.	R.	H.	RBI.	PO.	A.
Henderson, lf	5	2	1	0	0	0
Fuentes, 2b	4	1	2	0	2	0
Mays, cf	4	0	0	0	3	0
McCovey, 1b	5	1	3	4	7	1
Bonds, rf	4	0	1	0	1	0
Dietz, c	4	0	1	0	8	0
Hart, 3b	3	0	0	0	0	2
Gallagher, 3b	1	0	0	0	0	0
Speier, ss	4	1	1	1	1	2
Perry, p	3	0	1	0	1	0
Johnson, p	0	0	0	0	0	0
Kingman, ph	1	0	0	0	0	0
McMahon, p	0	0	0	0	1	1
Totals	38	5	10	5	24	6

Pittsburgh	AB.	R.	H.	RBI.	PO.	A.
Cash, 2b	5	2	3	0	3	2
Hebner, 3b	5	2	2	3	2	1
Clemente, rf	5	1	2	3	1	0
Stargell, lf	2	1	0	0	2	0
Oliver, cf	4	1	1	3	2	0
Robertson, 1b	4	0	0	0	7	0
Sanguillen, c	3	0	1	0	8	0
Hernandez, ss	4	1	1	0	2	2
Blass, p	0	0	0	0	0	0
Mazeroski, ph	1	1	1	0	0	0
Kison, p	2	0	0	0	0	1
Giusti, p	1	0	0	0	0	1
Totals	36	9	11	9	27	7

San Francisco	1 4 0	0 0 0	0 0 0	—5
Pittsburgh	2 3 0	0 0 4	0 0 x	—9

San Francisco	IP.	H.	R.	ER.	BB.	SO.
Perry (L)	5⅔	10	7	7	2	6
Johnson	1⅓	1	2	2	1	2
McMahon	1	0	0	0	0	1

Pittsburgh	IP.	H.	R.	ER.	BB.	SO.
Blass	2	8	5	4	0	2
Kison (W)	4⅔	2	0	0	2	3
Giusti (S)	2⅓	0	0	0	1	2

E—Cash, Hernandez. DP—Pittsburgh 1. LOB—San Francisco 9, Pittsburgh 6. 2B—Hebner. HR—Speier, McCovey, Hebner, Oliver. SB—Cash. WP—Perry, Kison. PB—Dietz. U—Olsen, Stello, Davidson, Gorman, Crawford and Weyer. T—3:00. A—35,487.

COMPOSITE BATTING AVERAGES

Pittsburgh Pirates

Player-Position	G.	AB.	R.	H.	2B.	3B.	HR.	RBI.	BA.
Mazeroski, ph	1	1	1	1	0	0	0	0	1.000
Alley, ss	1	2	1	1	0	0	0	0	.500
Robertson, 1b	4	16	5	7	1	0	4	6	.438
Cash, 2b	4	19	5	8	2	0	0	1	.421
Clemente, rf	4	18	2	6	0	0	0	4	.333
Clines, cf	1	3	1	1	0	0	1	1	.333
Hebner, 3b-ph	4	17	3	5	1	0	2	4	.294
Sanguillen, c	4	15	1	4	0	0	0	1	.267
Oliver, cf-ph	4	12	2	3	0	0	1	5	.250
Hernandez, ss	4	13	2	3	0	0	0	1	.231
Moose, p	1	0	0	0	0	0	0	0	.000
Blass, p	2	1	0	0	0	0	0	0	.000
Giusti, p	4	1	0	0	0	0	0	0	.000
May, ph	1	1	0	0	0	0	0	0	.000
Miller, p	1	1	0	0	0	0	0	0	.000
Pagan, 3b	1	1	0	0	0	0	0	0	.000
Davalillo, ph	2	2	0	0	0	0	0	0	.000
R. Johnson, p	1	2	0	0	0	0	0	0	.000
Kison, p	1	2	0	0	0	0	0	0	.000
Ellis, p	1	3	0	0	0	0	0	0	.000
Stargell, lf	4	14	1	0	0	0	0	0	.000
Totals	4	144	24	39	4	0	8	23	.271

San Francisco Giants

Player-Position	G.	AB.	R.	H.	2B.	3B.	HR.	RBI.	BA.
McCovey, 1b	4	14	2	6	0	0	2	6	.429
Speier, ss	4	14	4	5	1	0	1	1	.357
Fuentes, 2b	4	16	4	5	1	0	1	2	.313
Henderson, lf	4	16	3	5	1	0	0	2	.313
Mays, cf	4	15	2	4	2	0	1	3	.267
Bonds, rf	3	8	0	2	0	0	0	0	.250
Perry, p	2	4	0	1	0	0	0	0	.250
Kingman, rf-ph	4	9	0	1	0	0	0	0	.111
Gallagher, 3b	4	10	0	1	0	0	0	0	.100
Dietz, c	4	15	0	1	0	0	0	0	.067
Bryant, p	1	0	0	0	0	0	0	0	.000
Carrithers, p	1	0	0	0	0	0	0	0	.000
Cumberland, p	1	0	0	0	0	0	0	0	.000
Hamilton, p	1	0	0	0	0	0	0	0	.000
J. Johnson, p	1	0	0	0	0	0	0	0	.000
McMahon, p	2	0	0	0	0	0	0	0	.000
Rosario, pr	1	0	0	0	0	0	0	0	.000
Barr, p	1	1	0	0	0	0	0	0	.000
Duffy, ph	1	1	0	0	0	0	0	0	.000
Lanier, 3b	1	1	0	0	0	0	0	0	.000
Marichal, p	1	3	0	0	0	0	0	0	.000
Hart, ph-3b	3	5	0	0	0	0	0	0	.000
Totals	4	132	15	31	5	0	5	14	.235

COMPOSITE PITCHING AVERAGES

Pittsburgh Pirates

Pitcher	G.	IP.	H.	R.	ER.	BB.	SO.	W.	L.	ERA.
R. Johnson	1	8	5	1	0	3	7	1	0	0.00
Giusti	4	5⅓	1	0	0	2	3	0	0	0.00
Kison	1	4⅔	2	0	0	2	3	1	0	0.00
Moose	1	2	0	0	0	0	0	0	0	0.00
Ellis	1	5	6	2	2	4	1	1	0	3.60
Miller	1	3	3	2	2	3	3	0	0	6.00
Blass	2	7	14	10	9	2	11	0	1	11.57
Totals	4	35	31	15	13	16	28	3	1	3.34

San Francisco Giants

Pitcher	G.	IP.	H.	R.	ER.	BB.	SO.	W.	L.	ERA.
McMahon	2	3	0	0	0	0	3	0	0	0.00
Marichal	1	8	4	2	2	0	6	0	1	2.25
Bryant	1	2	1	1	1	1	2	0	0	4.50
Perry	2	14⅔	19	11	10	3	11	1	1	6.14
Cumberland	1	3	7	3	3	0	4	0	1	9.00
Barr	1	1	3	1	1	0	2	0	0	9.00
Hamilton	1	1	1	1	1	0	3	0	0	9.00
J. Johnson	1	1⅓	1	2	2	1	2	0	0	13.50
Carrithers	1	0*	3	3	3	0	0	0	0	......
Totals	4	34	39	24	23	5	33	1	3	6.09

*Pitched to three batters in seventh inning of second game.

1972
OAKLAND A's
VS.
DETROIT TIGERS

Back in 1931, the Philadelphia A's won their third straight American League pennant. The A's were to wait 41 years for their next. When it finally came in 1972, the A's were long gone from Philadelphia, having traipsed across the country to Oakland after a stop in Kansas City.

Retaining their West Division crown in a breeze in '72, the A's outfought the East champion Detroit Tigers in a memorable pennant playoff, three games to two. It was the first A. L. Championship Series in the four-year history of the event that did not end in a three-game sweep.

The A's scored only 13 runs and logged just 38 hits, including one homer, in five playoff games, two of which were extra-inning struggles. Their eight-man pitching staff was equal to the task, granting the Tigers a mere 10 runs and 32 hits.

Blue Moon Odom, who pitched a shutout in winning game two, 5-0, was the only Oakland pitcher to go the route in the playoffs. That was no indictment of the A's starters. Rather, it was indicative of the superb relief pitching Manager Dick Williams could and did call upon at the first hint of trouble. Reliever Rollie Fingers appeared in three playoff games and was credited with the A's 3-2 victory in the 11-inning opener October 7 in Oakland.

Vida Blue nursed a season-long grudge against Owner Charlie Finley, the aftermath of Blue's holdout well into May. Nevertheless, the griping Blue was a brilliant fireman in the playoffs, blanking the Tigers for 5⅓ innings in four appearances. He saved the best for last, rescuing Odom in the sixth inning of game five and saving Oakland's pennant-clinching 2-1 triumph with

four shutout rounds.

The playoffs dripped with drama and suspense from start to finish. Tiger ace Mickey Lolich carried a 2-1 lead into the last of the 11th in the opener. The A's thereupon scored twice to win it. The hero was Gonzalo Marquez, an obscure late addition to the A's roster. He lashed a pinch-single off Chuck Seelbach with one out and two aboard to score the tying run. On the same play, right fielder Al Kaline's throw shot past third sacker Aurelio Rodriguez, enabling Gene Tenace to cross the plate with the winning tally.

Kaline was charged with an error, which rubbed out his hero halo in a hurry. Kaline had belted a homer off Fingers in the top of the 11th to give Detroit a 2-1 edge. Catfish Hunter pitched well for the A's, leaving in the ninth with the score tied, 1-1.

Buoyed by their opening-game success, the A's came on strong the next day, handing the Tigers a 5-0 beating behind Odom's three-hitter. Shortstop Campy Campaneris, with three singles, two runs and two stolen bases, was the Tigers' No. 1 nemesis. He also precipitated a near riot in the seventh inning when he threw his bat at Lerrin LaGrow, who had plunked Campy on the ankle with a pitch. Tiger Manager Billy Martin, noted for his fistic conquests, dashed from the dugout, along with his players. Three umpires managed to keep Martin from Campaneris, a feat which nipped a budding brawl. Plate umpire Nestor Chylak banished both Campy and LaGrow. Later, A. L. President Joe Cronin fined Campaneris $500 and suspended him from the remaining playoff games. He was allowed to play in the World Series, but sat out the first seven games of the 1973 sea-

son by order of the Commissioner.

Needing one more win to kill off the Tigers, the A's proceeded to swoon, 3-0, before Joe Coleman's 14-strikeout job October 10 as the scene shifted to Detroit. Coleman's whiff total surpassed the old playoff record of 12 set by Baltimore's Jim Palmer against Minnesota in 1970.

Nobody could brand the Tigers quitters. Still one game from oblivion, they tied the series the next day in a 10-inning thriller, 4-3. It was a crushing defeat for the A's, who had taken a 3-1 lead with two runs in the top of the 10th, only to see the Tigers score three to win it.

Lolich pitched creditably for Detroit, as he had in the opener, but left for a pinch-hitter in the ninth with the score 1-1.

Next day, with a chill wind blowing and Detroit fans in one of their boisterous, destructive moods, the A's put it all together. Behind Odom and Blue, they turned back the Tigers and Woodie Fryman, 2-1, to hoist the pennant.

Game 1

Saturday, October 7, At Oakland

Detroit	AB.	R.	H.	RBI.	PO.	A.
McAuliffe, 2b	5	0	0	0	2	3
Kaline, rf	5	1	1	1	2	0
Sims, c	5	0	2	0	4	0
Cash, 1b	3	1	1	1	12	0
Horton, lf	3	0	0	0	3	0
G. Brown, ph	1	0	0	0	0	0
Stanley, cf	1	0	0	0	0	0
Northrup, cf-lf	3	0	1	0	5	0
Rodriguez, 3b	4	0	0	0	1	0
Brinkman, ss	4	0	1	0	1	2
Lolich, p	4	0	0	0	0	3
Seelbach, p	0	0	0	0	0	0
Totals	38	2	6	2	31	12

Oakland	AB.	R.	H.	RBI.	PO.	A.
Campaneris, ss	4	1	0	0	3	5
Alou, rf	5	0	1	0	0	0
Rudi, lf	4	0	0	1	4	0
Jackson, cf	5	0	2	0	4	0
Bando, 3b	4	0	2	0	2	4
Odom, pr	0	0	0	0	0	0
Epstein, 1b	3	0	2	0	14	0
Hegan, ph	0	1	0	0	0	0
Tenace, c	5	1	0	0	5	0
Green, 2b	0	0	0	0	1	0
Mangual, ph	1	0	0	0	0	0
Kubiak, 2b	2	0	1	0	0	5
Hendrick, ph	1	0	0	0	0	0
Maxvill, 2b	0	0	0	0	0	1
Marquez, ph	1	0	1	1	0	0
Hunter, p	3	0	1	0	0	0

	AB.	R.	H.	RBI.	PO.	A.
Blue, p.	0	0	0	0	0	0
Fingers, p.	1	0	0	0	0	0
Totals	39	3	10	2	33	15

Detroit........0 1 0 0 0 0 0 0 0 0 1—2
Oakland........0 0 1 0 0 0 0 0 0 0 2—3
One out when winning run scored.

Detroit	IP.	H.	R.	ER.	BB.	SO.
Lolich (L)	10†	9	3	2	3	4
Seelbach	⅓	1	0	0	0	0

Oakland	IP.	H.	R.	ER.	BB.	SO.
Hunter	8*	4	1	1	2	4
Blue	0*	0	0	0	0	0
Fingers (W)	3	2	1	1	0	1

*Pitched to one batter in ninth.
†Pitched to two batters in eleventh.

E—McAuliffe, Kubiak, Kaline. DP—Detroit 1, Oakland 1. LOB—Detroit 6, Oakland 10. 2B—Brinkman, Sims. 3B—Sims. HR—Cash, Kaline. SH—Bando, Cash. SF—Rudi. U—Flaherty, Chylak, Rice, Denkinger, Barnett and Frantz. T—3:09. A—29,536.

Game 2

Sunday, October 8, At Oakland

Detroit	AB.	R.	H.	RBI.	PO.	A.
McAuliffe, ss.	4	0	0	0	4	1
Kaline, rf.	4	0	1	0	3	0
Sims, c	3	0	0	0	9	1
Cash, 1b	3	0	1	0	2	2
Horton, lf	3	0	0	0	3	0
Northrup, cf	3	0	1	0	1	0
Taylor, 2b	3	0	0	0	1	1
Rodriguez, 3b	3	0	0	0	1	0
Fryman, p	1	0	0	0	0	1
Zachary, p	0	0	0	0	0	0
Scherman, p	0	0	0	0	0	0
Haller, ph	1	0	0	0	0	0
LaGrow, p	0	0	0	0	0	0
Hiller, p	0	0	0	0	0	0
G. Brown, ph	1	0	0	0	0	0
Totals	29	0	3	0	24	6

Oakland	AB.	R.	H.	RBI.	PO.	A.
Campaneris, ss	3	2	3	0	0	2
Maxvill, pr-ss	0	0	0	0	0	0
Alou, rf	4	1	1	1	3	0
Rudi, lf	3	1	2	1	0	0
Jackson, cf	4	0	1	2	3	0
Bando, 3b	4	0	0	0	1	6
Epstein, 1b	3	0	0	0	13	2
Hegan, 1b	0	0	0	0	1	0
Tenace, c	3	0	0	0	2	2
Green, 2b	1	0	0	0	1	2
Hendrick, ph	1	1	1	0	0	0
Kubiak, 2b	1	0	0	0	1	1
Odom, p	2	0	0	0	2	0
Totals	29	5	8	4	27	15

Detroit........0 0 0 0 0 0 0 0 0—0
Oakland........1 0 0 0 4 0 0 0 x—5

Detroit	IP.	H.	R.	ER.	BB.	SO.
Fryman (L)	4⅓	7	4	4	1	5
Zachary	0*	0	1	1	1	0
Scherman	⅔	1	0	0	0	1
LaGrow	1†	0	0	0	0	1
Hiller	2	0	0	0	0	1

Oakland	IP.	H.	R.	ER.	BB.	SO.
Odom (W)	9	3	0	0	0	2

*Pitched to one batter in fifth.
†Pitched to one batter in seventh.

E—McAuliffe. DP—Detroit 1. LOB—Detroit 2, Oakland 4. 2B—Rudi, Jackson. SB—Campaneris 2. SH—Odom. HBP—By LaGrow (Campaneris). WP—Zachary 2. U—Chylak, Rice, Frantz, Barnett, Denkinger and Flaherty. T—2:37. A—31,088.

Game 3

Tuesday, October 10, At Detroit

Oakland	AB.	R.	H.	RBI.	PO.	A.
Alou, rf	5	0	3	0	1	0
Maxvill, ss	2	0	0	0	1	2
Duncan, ph-c	1	0	0	0	1	0
Rudi, lf	4	0	3	0	2	0
Jackson, cf	4	0	0	0	4	0
Epstein, 1b	4	0	0	0	9	0
Bando, 3b	4	0	1	0	0	3
Tenace, c-2b	2	0	0	0	3	3
Green, 2b	1	0	0	0	1	0
Mincher, ph	1	0	0	0	0	0
Kubiak, 2b	0	0	0	0	2	2
Marquez, ph	1	0	0	0	0	0
Cullen, ss	1	0	0	0	0	0
Holtzman, p	1	0	0	0	0	1
Mangual, ph	1	0	0	0	0	0
Fingers, p	0	0	0	0	0	0
Blue, p	0	0	0	0	0	0
Hegan, ph	1	0	0	0	0	0
Locker, p	0	0	0	0	0	0
Hendrick, ph	1	0	0	0	0	0
Totals	34	0	7	0	24	11

Detroit	AB.	R.	H.	RBI.	PO.	A.
Taylor, 2b	4	0	0	0	2	3
Rodriguez, 3b	4	0	0	0	0	0
Kaline, rf	3	1	2	0	0	0
Freehan, c	3	2	2	1	14	1
Horton, lf	2	0	0	0	0	0
Northrup, lf	1	0	0	0	1	0
Stanley, cf	3	0	1	0	3	0
I. Brown, 1b	2	0	1	2	2	0
Cash, ph-1b	1	0	0	0	0	1
McAuliffe, ss	3	0	1	0	5	2
Coleman, p	2	0	1	0	0	0
Totals	28	3	8	3	27	7

Oakland........0 0 0 0 0 0 0 0 0—0
Detroit........0 0 0 2 0 0 0 1 x—3

Oakland	IP.	H.	R.	ER.	BB.	SO.
Holtzman (L)	4	4	2	2	2	2
Fingers	1⅔	2	0	0	1	1
Blue	⅓	0	0	0	0	0
Locker	2	2	1	1	0	1

Detroit	IP.	H.	R.	ER.	BB.	SO.
Coleman (W)	9	7	0	0	3	14

E—McAuliffe. DP—Oakland 3, Detroit 1. LOB—Oakland 10, Detroit 5. 2B—Alou 2, Freehan. HR—Freehan. SB—Alou, Maxvill. SH—Freehan. U—Rice, Denkinger, Chylak, Frantz, Flaherty and Barnett. T—2:27. A—41,156.

Game 4

Wednesday, October 11, At Detroit

Oakland	AB.	R.	H.	RBI.	PO.	A.
Alou, rf	5	1	2	1	1	0
Maxvill, ss	2	0	1	0	0	1
Hendrick, ph	1	0	0	0	0	0
Cullen, ss	0	0	0	0	0	2
Mangual, ph	1	0	0	0	0	0
Kubiak, ss	1	0	1	1	0	0
Rudi, lf	5	0	0	0	3	0
Jackson, cf	5	0	2	0	3	0
Bando, 3b	5	0	0	0	1	2
Epstein, 1b	3	1	1	1	9	0
Tenace, c-2b	4	0	0	0	5	0
Green, 2b	2	0	1	0	1	3
Duncan, ph-c	1	0	0	0	4	1
Hunter, p	3	0	0	0	0	0
Fingers, p	0	0	0	0	0	0
Blue, p	0	0	0	0	0	0
Marquez, ph	1	1	1	0	0	0
Locker, p	0	0	0	0	0	0
Horlen, p	0	0	0	0	0	0
Hamilton, p	0	0	0	0	0	0
Totals	39	3	9	3	27	9

Detroit	AB.	R.	H.	RBI.	PO.	A.
McAuliffe, ss	4	2	2	1	1	1
Kaline, rf	3	1	1	0	1	0
Sims, lf	3	0	1	0	2	0
Stanley, cf	1	0	1	0	3	0
G. Brown, ph	0	1	0	0	0	0
Freehan, c	5	0	1	1	7	0
Cash, 1b	4	0	1	1	12	0
Northrup, cf-lf	5	0	1	1	2	0
Taylor, 2b	4	0	2	0	1	2
Rodriguez, 3b	2	0	0	0	0	7
Lolich, p	3	0	0	0	1	0
Horton, ph	1	0	0	0	0	0
Seelbach, p	0	0	0	0	0	0
Hiller, p	0	0	0	0	0	0
Totals	35	4	10	4	30	10

Oakland........0 0 0 0 0 0 1 0 0 2—3
Detroit........0 0 1 0 0 0 0 0 0 3—4
None out when winning run scored.

Oakland	IP.	H.	R.	ER.	BB.	SO.
Hunter	7⅓	6	1	1	3	5
Fingers	⅔	0	0	0	0	1
Blue	1	1	0	0	1	2
Locker	0*	2	2	2	0	0
Horlen (L)	0*	0	1	1	1	0
Hamilton	0*	1	0	0	1	0

Detroit	IP.	H.	R.	ER.	BB.	SO.
Lolich	9	5	1	1	2	6
Seelbach	⅔	3	2	2	0	0
Hiller (W)	⅓	1	0	0	0	0

*Pitched to two batters in tenth.

E—Jackson, Rodriguez, Tenace. DP—Oakland 1. LOB—Oakland 8, Detroit 11. 2B—Sims, Green, Taylor 2, Alou 2. HR—McAuliffe, Epstein. SH—Kaline. WP—Horlen. U—Denkinger, Chylak, Rice, Flaherty, Barnett and Frantz. T—3:04. A—37,615.

Game 5

Thursday, October 12, At Detroit

Oakland	AB.	R.	H.	RBI.	PO.	A.
Alou, rf	2	0	1	0	3	0
Maxvill, ss	4	0	0	0	2	4
Rudi, lf	4	0	0	0	2	0
Jackson, cf	0	1	0	0	0	0
Hendrick, cf	3	1	0	0	1	0
Bando, 3b	3	0	1	0	2	1
Epstein, 1b	3	0	0	0	10	0
Tenace, c	3	0	1	1	6	0
Green, 2b	4	0	0	0	1	2
Odom, p	2	0	1	0	0	1
Blue, p	1	0	0	0	0	1
Totals	29	2	4	1	27	9

Detroit	AB.	R.	H.	RBI.	PO.	A.
McAuliffe, ss	4	1	1	0	0	3
Kaline, rf	4	0	0	0	6	0
Sims, lf	3	0	0	0	1	0
Freehan, c	4	0	0	1	3	2
Cash, 1b	4	0	1	0	13	0
Niekro, pr	0	0	0	0	0	0
Northrup, cf	2	0	2	0	3	0
Stanley, ph	1	0	0	0	0	0
Taylor, 2b	4	0	0	0	1	3
Rodriguez, 3b	3	0	0	0	0	3
Fryman, p	2	0	0	0	0	2
Horton, ph	1	0	1	0	0	0
Knox, pr	0	0	0	0	0	0
Hiller, p	0	0	0	0	0	0
Totals	32	1	5	1	27	13

Oakland........0 1 0 1 0 0 0 0 0—2
Detroit........1 0 0 0 0 0 0 0 0—1

Oakland	IP.	H.	R.	ER.	BB.	SO.
Odom (W)	5	2	1	0	2	3
Blue (S)	4	3	0	0	0	3

Detroit	IP.	H.	R.	ER.	BB.	SO.
Fryman (L)	8	4	2	1	1	3
Hiller	1	0	0	0	1	0

E—McAuliffe, Sims. DP—Detroit 1. LOB—Oakland 6, Detroit 6. 2B—Odom. SB—Jackson 2, Epstein. SH—Bando, Alou. HBP—By Fryman (Epstein, Alou). WP—Odom. Balk—Fryman. PB—Tenace. U—Chylak, Rice, Barnett, Flaherty, Frantz and Denkinger. T—2:48. A—50,276.

COMPOSITE BATTING AVERAGES

Oakland Athletics

Player-Position	G.	AB.	R.	H.	2B.	3B.	HR.	RBI.	BA.
Marquez, ph	3	3	1	2	0	0	0	1	.667
Kubiak, 2b-ss	4	4	0	2	0	0	0	1	.500
Campaneris, ss	2	7	3	3	0	0	0	0	.429
Alou, rf	5	21	2	8	4	0	0	2	.381
Jackson, cf	5	18	1	5	1	0	0	2	.278
Rudi, lf	5	20	1	5	1	0	0	2	.250
Odom, pr-p	3	4	0	1	1	0	0	0	.250
Bando, 3b	5	20	0	4	0	0	0	0	.200
Epstein, 1b	5	16	1	3	0	0	1	1	.188
Hunter, p	2	6	0	1	0	0	0	0	.167
Hendrick, ph-cf	5	7	2	1	0	0	0	0	.143
Green, 2b	5	8	0	1	1	0	0	0	.125
Maxvill, 2b-pr-ss	5	8	0	1	0	0	0	0	.125
Tenace, c-2b	5	17	1	1	0	0	0	1	.059
Hamilton, p	1	0	0	0	0	0	0	0	.000
Horlen, p	1	0	0	0	0	0	0	0	.000
Locker, p	2	0	0	0	0	0	0	0	.000
Holtzman, p	1	1	0	0	0	0	0	0	.000
Mincher, ph	1	1	0	0	0	0	0	0	.000
Cullen, ss	2	1	0	0	0	0	0	0	.000
Fingers, p	3	1	0	0	0	0	0	0	.000
Hegan, pr-1b-ph	3	1	1	0	0	0	0	0	.000
Blue, p	4	1	0	0	0	0	0	0	.000
Duncan, ph-c	2	2	0	0	0	0	0	0	.000
Mangual, ph	3	3	0	0	0	0	0	0	.000
Totals	5	170	13	38	8	0	1	10	.224

Detroit Tigers

Player-Position	G.	AB.	R.	H.	2B.	3B.	HR.	RBI.	BA.
I. Brown, 1b	1	2	0	1	0	0	0	2	.500
Coleman, p	1	2	0	1	0	0	0	0	.500
Northrup, cf-lf	5	14	0	5	0	0	0	1	.357
Stanley, cf-ph	4	6	0	2	0	0	0	0	.333
Cash, 1b-ph	5	15	1	4	0	0	1	2	.267
Kaline, rf	5	19	3	5	0	0	1	1	.263
Freehan, c	3	12	2	3	1	0	1	3	.250
Brinkman, ss	1	4	0	1	1	0	0	0	.250
Sims, c-lf	4	14	0	3	2	1	0	0	.214
McAuliffe, 2b-ss	5	20	3	4	0	0	1	1	.200
Taylor, 2b	4	15	0	2	2	0	0	0	.133
Horton, lf-ph	5	10	0	1	0	0	0	0	.100
Knox, pr	1	0	0	0	0	0	0	0	.000
LaGrow, p	1	0	0	0	0	0	0	0	.000
Niekro, pr	1	0	0	0	0	0	0	0	.000
Scherman, p	1	0	0	0	0	0	0	0	.000
Zachary, p	1	0	0	0	0	0	0	0	.000
Seelbach, p	2	0	0	0	0	0	0	0	.000
Hiller, p	3	0	0	0	0	0	0	0	.000
Haller, ph	1	1	0	0	0	0	0	0	.000
G. Brown, ph	3	2	1	0	0	0	0	0	.000
Fryman, p	2	3	0	0	0	0	0	0	.000
Lolich, p	2	7	0	0	0	0	0	0	.000
Rodriguez, 3b	5	16	0	0	0	0	0	0	.000
Totals	5	162	10	32	6	1	4	10	.198

COMPOSITE PITCHING AVERAGES

Oakland Athletics

Pitcher	G.	IP.	H.	R.	ER.	BB.	SO.	W.	L.	ERA.
Odom	2	14	5	1	0	2	5	2	0	0.00
Blue	4	5⅓	4	0	0	1	5	0	0	0.00
Hamilton	1	0*	1	0	0	1	0	0	0	0.00
Hunter	2	15⅓	10	2	2	5	9	0	0	1.17
Fingers	3	5⅓	4	1	1	1	3	1	0	1.69
Holtzman	1	4	4	2	2	2	2	0	1	4.50
Locker	2	2	4	3	3	0	1	0	0	13.50
Horlen	1	0*	0	1	1	1	0	0	1	....
Totals	5	46	32	10	9	13	25	3	2	1.76

Detroit Tigers

Pitcher	G.	IP.	H.	R.	ER.	BB.	SO.	W.	L.	ERA.
Coleman	1	9	7	0	0	3	14	1	0	0.00
Hiller	3	3⅓	1	0	0	1	1	1	0	0.00
LaGrow	1	1	0	0	0	0	1	0	0	0.00
Scherman	1	⅔	1	0	0	0	1	0	0	0.00
Lolich	2	19	14	4	3	5	10	0	1	1.42
Fryman	2	12⅓	11	6	5	2	8	0	2	3.65
Seelbach	2	1	4	2	2	0	0	0	0	18.00
Zachary	1	0†	0	1	1	1	0	0	0	....
Totals	5	46⅓	38	13	11	12	35	2	3	2.11

*Pitched to two batters in tenth inning of fourth game.
†Pitched to one batter in fifth inning of second game.

1972
CINCINNATI REDS
VS.
PITTSBURGH PIRATES

You're ahead by one run in the last of the ninth and the other team has its righthanded power hitters coming up. So whom do you want to pitch?

That was the situation facing Pittsburgh Pirate Manager Bill Virdon in the final game of the 1972 National League Championship Series.

And the Buc skipper brought in his best—righthander Dave Giusti, who had saved 22 games and won seven others during the regular season. But, unfortunately for the Pirates, Virdon went to the well and came up dry.

The first batter Giusti faced was Johnny Bench, home run king of the senior circuit during the regular season. Bench unloaded one of his specialties over the right-field fence and the score was tied at 3-3.

When Tony Perez and Denis Menke followed with singles, Virdon came to the mound and led Giusti away, replacing him with another righthander, Bob Moose.

Cesar Geronimo flied out deep to right, sending George Foster, running for Perez, to third. Darrel Chaney popped out for the second out.

With Hal McRae, batting for pitcher Clay Carroll, at bat, Moose uncorked a pitch that bounced in front of the plate and skipped past catcher Manny Sanguillen. Foster raced home with the run that gave the Reds the National League pennant.

Up to the fifth game, the two teams had staged a series which had held the interest of fans throughout the country and put to rest speculation that the Championship Series had failed to catch on.

Joe Morgan, second man up in the opener, hit a home run off Steve Blass.

But that was just a prelude to

Jubilant Cincinnati Reds celebrate after their Game 5 victory over Pittsburgh in 1972.

the Pirate outburst. Rennie Stennett singled, Al Oliver tripled, Willie Stargell doubled and Hebner singled. It all added up to three runs, more than enough, as events proved, to win the game.

The Reds returned the favor the next day with their own big first inning as starter Moose failed to retire a batter. Pete Rose and Morgan singled and Bobby Tolan, Bench and Perez hit successive doubles to plate a total of four runs.

The Pirates picked up single runs in the fourth, fifth and sixth and actually were in good position to get much more in the fifth. They had two men on with two out and a two-ball, no-strike count on Stargell when Tom Hall replaced starter Jack Billingham on the hill for the Reds. He got Stargell on a called third strike.

The scene shifted to Cincinnati's Riverfront Stadium for the third game and the Pirates won it, 3-2.

Cincinnati jumped off to a lead

with two runs in the third on singles by Chaney, Morgan and Tolan. A stolen base by Morgan had set up the second run.

Sanguillen's homer off starter Gary Nolan gave the Bucs a counter in the fifth. Nolan left the game after hurling six innings when his arm tightened.

Pedro Borbon took the mound for the Reds in the seventh and hit Hebner with a pitch. Sanguillen singled and Gene Alley's sacrifice moved the runners along. Carroll relieved Borbon and issued an intentional pass to Vic Davalillo, pinch-hitting for Nelson Briles. A run came in on a hit by Stennett which bounced over the head of Perez at first. A double play got the Reds out of the inning with the score tied.

But Pittsburgh was not to be denied in the eighth. With one out, Stargell walked, Oliver doubled and Hebner was purposely passed to load the bases. Sanguillen forced Hebner at second, Chaney to Morgan, but the Pirates' catcher beat the relay to first and the winning run scored.

Pittsburgh was in a position at that stage to clinch its second successive flag, but the Pirates never came close the next day. Lefty Ross Grimsley set them down with just two hits, both by Roberto Clemente, as his teammates battered four Pirate pitchers for 11 hits and seven runs.

That brought the teams to the climactic fifth game.

Game 1
Saturday, October 7, At Pittsburgh

Cincinnati	AB.	R.	H.	RBI.	PO.	A.
Rose, lf	5	0	2	0	1	0
Morgan, 2b	4	1	1	1	0	6
Tolan, cf	5	0	1	0	4	0
Bench, c	3	0	0	0	3	0
Perez, 1b	4	0	1	0	14	0
Menke, 3b	3	0	1	0	0	1
Geronimo, rf	4	0	0	0	0	0
Chaney, ss	4	0	0	0	0	4
Gullett, p	2	0	0	0	0	0
Uhlaender, ph	1	0	1	0	0	0
Borbon, p	0	0	0	0	0	0
Hague, ph	0	0	0	0	0	0
Totals	35	1	8	1	24	11

Pittsburgh	AB.	R.	H.	RBI.	PO.	A.
Stennett, lf	4	2	2	0	7	0
Oliver, cf	4	2	2	3	8	0
Clemente, rf	4	0	0	0	3	0
Stargell, 1b	3	1	1	1	2	0
Robertson, 1b	0	0	0	0	1	0
Sanguillen, c	3	0	0	0	2	0
Hebner, 3b	3	0	1	1	0	0
Cash, 2b	3	0	0	0	0	2
Alley, ss	3	0	0	0	3	0
Blass, p	3	0	0	0	1	0
R. Hernandez, p	0	0	0	0	0	0
Totals	30	5	6	5	27	2

Cincinnati	1 0 0 0 0 0 0 0 0—1
Pittsburgh	3 0 0 0 2 0 0 0 x—5

Cincinnati	IP.	H.	R.	ER.	BB.	SO.
Gullett (L)	6	6	5	5	0	3
Borbon	2	0	0	0	0	0
Pittsburgh	**IP.**	**H.**	**R.**	**ER.**	**BB.**	**SO.**
Blass (W)	8⅓	8	1	1	4	1
R. Hernandez (S)	⅔	0	0	0	0	1

LOB—Cincinnati 11, Pittsburgh 1. 2B—Stargell, Rose. 3B—Oliver. HR—Morgan, Oliver. PB—Bench. U—Donatelli, Burkhart, Harvey, Williams, Kibler and Wendelstedt. T—1:57. A—50,476.

Game 2

Sunday, October 8, At Pittsburgh

Cincinnati	AB.	R.	H.	RBI.	PO.	A.
Rose, lf	4	1	1	0	2	0
Morgan, 2b	4	2	2	1	3	4
Tolan, cf	4	1	2	2	1	0
Bench, c	4	1	1	0	8	0
Perez, 1b	4	0	1	2	7	2
Menke, 3b	3	0	0	0	1	2
Geronimo, rf	4	0	1	0	1	0
Chaney, ss	2	0	0	0	2	2
Concepcion, ph-ss	2	0	0	0	0	0
Billingham, p	2	0	0	0	1	0
Hall, p	1	0	0	0	1	0
Totals	34	5	8	5	27	10

Pittsburgh	AB.	R.	H.	RBI.	PO.	A.
Stennett, lf-2b	4	0	1	0	2	0
Oliver, cf	5	1	2	0	3	0
Clemente, rf	3	0	0	1	1	0
Stargell, 1b-lf	3	0	0	0	6	0
Hebner, 3b	4	0	0	0	1	3
May, c	2	0	1	1	8	1
Sanguillen, ph-c	2	1	1	0	2	0
Cash, 2b	4	0	1	1	2	1
Giusti, p	0	0	0	0	0	0
Alley, ss	3	1	0	0	1	1
Moose, p	0	0	0	0	0	0
Johnson, p	1	0	0	0	0	0
Mazeroski, ph	1	0	1	0	0	0
Ellis, pr	0	0	0	0	0	0
Kison, p	0	0	0	0	0	0
Clines, ph	1	0	0	0	0	0
R. Hernandez, p	0	0	0	0	0	2
Robertson, 1b	0	0	0	0	1	0
Totals	33	3	7	3	27	8

Cincinnati	4 0 0 0 0 0 0 1 0—5
Pittsburgh	0 0 0 1 1 1 0 0 0—3

Cincinnati	IP.	H.	R.	ER.	BB.	SO.
Billingham	4⅔	5	2	2	2	4
Hall (W)	4⅓	2	1	1	2	4
Pittsburgh	**IP.**	**H.**	**R.**	**ER.**	**BB.**	**SO.**
Moose (L)	0*	5	4	4	0	0
Johnson	5	1	0	0	1	6
Kison	1	0	0	0	0	2
R. Hernandez	2	1	1	1	0	1
Giusti	1	1	0	0	0	1

*Pitched to five batters in first.

E—Bench, Cash. DP—Cincinnati 1, Pittsburgh 2. LOB—Cincinnati 3, Pittsburgh 8. 2B—Tolan, Bench, Perez, Oliver, Sanguillen. HR—Morgan. HBP—By Billingham (Alley). WP—Johnson. U—Burkhart, Harvey, Williams, Kibler, Wendelstedt and Donatelli. T—2:43. A—50,584.

Game 3

Monday, October 9, At Cincinnati

Pittsburgh	AB.	R.	H.	RBI.	PO.	A.
Stennett, lf	5	0	2	1	4	1
Cash, 2b	5	0	1	0	1	0
Clemente, rf	3	0	1	0	2	0
Stargell, 1b	3	0	0	0	4	2
Clines, pr	0	1	0	0	0	0
Robertson, 1b	0	0	0	0	0	1
Oliver, cf	4	0	1	0	1	1
Hebner, 3b	2	1	0	0	1	1
Sanguillen, c	4	1	2	2	8	0
Alley, ss	3	0	0	0	4	1
Briles, p	2	0	0	0	1	1
Davalillo, ph	0	0	0	0	0	0
Kison, p	0	0	0	0	0	0
Giusti, p	1	0	0	0	1	0
Totals	32	3	7	3	27	8

Cincinnati	AB.	R.	H.	RBI.	PO.	A.
Rose, lf	4	0	3	0	3	0
Morgan, 2b	4	1	1	1	5	1
Tolan, cf	4	0	1	1	2	0
Bench, c	4	0	1	0	5	2
Perez, 1b	4	0	1	0	5	0
Concepcion, pr	0	0	0	0	0	0
Menke, 3b	3	0	0	0	1	3
Geronimo, rf	4	0	0	0	4	1
Chaney, ss	3	1	1	0	2	3
Nolan, p	2	0	0	0	0	0
Borbon, p	0	0	0	0	0	0
Carroll, p	0	0	0	0	0	1
Hague, ph	1	0	0	0	0	0
McGlothlin, p	0	0	0	0	0	0
Totals	33	2	8	2	27	11

Pittsburgh	0 0 0 0 1 0 1 1 0—3
Cincinnati	0 0 2 0 0 0 0 0 0—2

Pittsburgh	IP.	H.	R.	ER.	BB.	SO.
Briles	6	6	2	2	1	3
Kison (W)	1⅓	1	0	0	0	1
Giusti (S)	1⅔	1	0	0	0	2
Cincinnati	**IP.**	**H.**	**R.**	**ER.**	**BB.**	**SO.**
Nolan	6	4	1	1	1	4
Borbon	⅓	1	1	1	0	0
Carroll (L)	1⅔	2	1	1	3	0
McGlothlin	1	0	0	0	0	0

E—Chaney. DP—Pittsburgh 1, Cincinnati 1. LOB—Pittsburgh 8, Cincinnati 5. 2B—Rose 2, Clemente, Oliver. 3B—Bench. HR—Sanguillen. SB—Morgan. SH—Alley. HBP—By Borbon (Hebner). WP—Nolan. U—Harvey, Williams, Kibler, Wendelstedt, Donatelli and Burkhart. T—2:33. A—52,420.

Game 4

Tuesday, October 10, At Cincinnati

Pittsburgh	AB.	R.	H.	RBI.	PO.	A.
Stennett, lf	4	0	0	0	3	0
Oliver, cf	4	0	0	0	4	0
Clemente, rf	4	1	2	1	1	0
Stargell, 1b	3	0	0	0	7	1
Sanguillen, c	3	0	0	0	5	0
Cash, 2b	3	0	0	0	0	2
Hebner, 3b	3	0	0	0	3	5
Alley, ss	3	0	0	0	1	1
Ellis, p	1	0	0	0	0	0
Mazeroski, ph	1	0	0	0	0	0
Johnson, p	0	0	0	0	0	0
Walker, p	0	0	0	0	0	0
Clines, ph	1	0	0	0	0	0
Miller, p	0	0	0	0	0	0
Totals	30	1	2	1	24	9

Cincinnati	AB.	R.	H.	RBI.	PO.	A.
Rose, lf	4	0	2	1	1	0
Morgan, 2b	3	1	1	0	1	4
Tolan, cf	4	2	1	1	4	0
Bench, c	3	1	2	1	5	0
Perez, 1b	4	0	0	0	11	0
Menke, 3b	4	1	2	0	0	1
Geronimo, rf	4	1	0	0	2	0
Chaney, ss	3	1	1	1	3	6
Grimsley, p	4	0	2	1	0	0
Totals	33	7	11	5	27	11

Pittsburgh	0 0 0 0 0 0 1 0 0—1
Cincinnati	1 0 0 2 0 2 2 0 x—7

Pittsburgh	IP.	H.	R.	ER.	BB.	SO.
Ellis (L)	5	5	3	0	1	3
Johnson	1	3	2	2	1	1
Walker	1	3	2	2	0	0
Miller	1	0	0	0	0	1
Cincinnati	**IP.**	**H.**	**R.**	**ER.**	**BB.**	**SO.**
Grimsley (W)	9	2	1	1	0	5

E—Sanguillen, Chaney, Alley 2. LOB—Pittsburgh 2, Cincinnati 6. 2B—Grimsley, Menke. 3B—Tolan. HR—Clemente. SB—Bench 2, Chaney. SH—Morgan. SF—Bench. U—Williams, Kibler, Wendelstedt, Donatelli, Burkhart and Harvey. T—1:58. A—39,447.

Game 5

Wednesday, October 11, At Cincinnati

Pittsburgh	AB.	R.	H.	RBI.	PO.	A.
Stennett, lf	4	0	1	0	1	0
Oliver, cf	3	0	0	0	1	0
Clemente, rf	3	0	1	0	3	0
Stargell, 1b	4	0	0	0	13	0
Robertson, 1b	0	0	0	0	0	0
Sanguillen, c	4	2	2	0	5	0
Hebner, 3b	4	1	2	0	0	2
Cash, 2b	4	0	2	2	2	5
Alley, ss	4	0	0	0	1	1
Blass, p	3	0	0	0	0	3
R. Hernandez, p	0	0	0	0	0	0
Giusti, p	0	0	0	0	0	0
Moose, p	0	0	0	0	0	0
Totals	33	3	8	2	26	11

Cincinnati	AB.	R.	H.	RBI.	PO.	A.
Rose, lf	3	0	1	1	3	0
Morgan, 2b	4	0	0	0	2	3
Tolan, cf	4	0	0	0	2	0
Bench, c	4	1	2	1	7	1
Perez, 1b	4	0	1	0	8	1
Foster, pr	0	1	0	0	0	0
Menke, 3b	3	0	1	0	1	4
Geronimo, rf	4	1	1	1	2	0
Chaney, ss	4	1	1	0	1	1
Gullett, p	0	0	0	0	0	0
Borbon, p	0	0	0	0	1	0
Uhlaender, ph	1	0	0	0	0	0
Hall, p	0	0	0	0	0	0
Hague, ph	0	0	0	0	0	0
Concepcion, pr	0	0	0	0	0	0
Carroll, p	0	0	0	0	0	0
McRae, ph	0	0	0	0	0	0
Totals	31	4	7	3	27	10

Pittsburgh	0 2 0 1 0 0 0 0 0—3
Cincinnati	0 0 1 0 1 0 0 0 2—4

Two out when winning run scored.

Pittsburgh	IP.	H.	R.	ER.	BB.	SO.
Blass	7⅓	4	2	2	2	4
R. Hernandez	⅔	0	0	0	0	1
Giusti (L)	0†	3	2	2	0	0
Moose	⅔	0	0	0	0	0
Cincinnati	**IP.**	**H.**	**R.**	**ER.**	**BB.**	**SO.**
Gullett	3*	6	3	3	0	2
Borbon	2	1	0	0	0	1
Hall	3	1	0	0	1	4
Carroll (W)	1	0	0	0	0	0

*Pitched to two batters in fourth.
†Pitched to three batters in ninth.

E—Chaney. DP—Cincinnati 1. LOB—Pittsburgh 5, Cincinnati 5. 2B—Hebner, Rose. HR—Geronimo, Bench. SH—Gullett, Oliver, Rose. WP—Gullett, Moose. U—Donatelli, Kibler, Wendelstedt, Burkhart, Harvey and Williams. T—2:19. A—41,887.

COMPOSITE BATTING AVERAGES

Cincinnati Reds

Player-Position	G.	AB.	R.	H.	2B.	3B.	HR.	RBI.	BA.
Grimsley, p	1	4	0	2	1	0	0	1	.500
Gullett, p	2	2	0	1	0	0	0	0	.500
Uhlaender, ph	2	2	0	1	0	0	0	0	.500
Rose, lf	5	20	1	9	4	0	0	2	.450
Bench, c	5	18	3	6	1	1	1	2	.333
Morgan, 2b	5	19	5	5	0	0	2	3	.263
Menke, 3b	5	16	1	4	1	0	0	0	.250
Tolan, cf	5	21	3	5	1	1	0	4	.238
Perez, 1b	5	20	0	4	1	0	0	2	.200
Chaney, ss	5	16	3	3	0	0	0	1	.188
Geronimo, rf	5	20	2	2	0	0	1	1	.100
Foster, pr	1	0	1	0	0	0	0	0	.000
McGlothlin, p	1	0	0	0	0	0	0	0	.000
McRae, ph	1	0	0	0	0	0	0	0	.000
Carroll, p	2	0	0	0	0	0	0	0	.000
Borbon, p	3	0	0	0	0	0	0	0	.000
Hague, ph	3	1	0	0	0	0	0	0	.000
Hall, p	2	1	0	0	0	0	0	0	.000
Billingham, p	1	2	0	0	0	0	0	0	.000
Nolan, p	1	2	0	0	0	0	0	0	.000
Concepcion, ph-ss-pr	3	2	0	0	0	0	0	0	.000
Totals	5	166	19	42	9	2	4	16	.253

Pittsburgh Pirates

Player-Position	G.	AB.	R.	H.	2B.	3B.	HR.	RBI.	BA.
May, c	1	2	0	1	0	0	0	1	.500
Mazeroski, ph	2	2	0	1	0	0	0	0	.500
Sanguillen, c-ph	5	16	4	5	1	0	1	2	.313
Stennett, lf-2b	5	21	2	6	0	0	0	1	.286
Oliver, cf	5	20	3	5	2	1	1	3	.250
Clemente, rf	5	17	1	4	1	0	1	2	.235
Cash, 2b	5	19	0	4	0	0	0	3	.211
Hebner, 3b	5	16	2	3	1	0	0	1	.188
Stargell, 1b-lf	5	16	1	1	1	0	0	1	.063
Davalillo, ph	1	0	0	0	0	0	0	0	.000
Miller, p	1	0	0	0	0	0	0	0	.000
Walker, p	1	0	0	0	0	0	0	0	.000
Kison, p	2	0	0	0	0	0	0	0	.000
Moose, p	2	0	0	0	0	0	0	0	.000
R. Hernandez, p	3	0	0	0	0	0	0	0	.000
Robertson, 1b	4	0	0	0	0	0	0	0	.000
Ellis, pr-p	2	1	0	0	0	0	0	0	.000
Johnson, p	2	1	0	0	0	0	0	0	.000
Giusti, p	3	1	0	0	0	0	0	0	.000
Briles, p	1	2	0	0	0	0	0	0	.000
Clines, ph-pr	3	2	1	0	0	0	0	0	.000
Blass, p	2	6	0	0	0	0	0	0	.000
Alley, ss	5	16	1	0	0	0	0	0	.000
Totals	5	158	15	30	6	1	3	14	.190

COMPOSITE PITCHING AVERAGES

Cincinnati Reds

Pitcher	G.	IP.	H.	R.	ER.	BB.	SO.	W.	L.	ERA.
McGlothlin	1	1	0	0	0	0	0	0	0	0.00
Grimsley	1	9	2	1	1	0	5	1	0	1.00
Hall	2	7⅓	3	1	1	3	8	1	0	1.23
Nolan	1	6	4	1	1	1	4	0	0	1.50
Borbon	3	4⅓	2	1	1	0	1	0	0	2.08
Carroll	2	2⅔	2	1	1	3	0	1	1	3.38
Billingham	1	4⅔	5	2	2	2	4	0	0	3.86
Gullett	2	9	12	8	8	0	5	0	1	8.00
Totals	5	44	30	15	15	9	27	3	2	3.07

Pittsburgh Pirates

Pitcher	G.	IP.	H.	R.	ER.	BB.	SO.	W.	L.	ERA.
Ellis	1	5	5	3	0	1	3	0	1	0.00
Kison	2	2⅓	1	0	0	0	3	1	0	0.00
Miller	1	1	0	0	0	0	1	0	0	0.00
Blass	2	15⅔	12	3	3	6	5	1	0	1.72
R. Hernandez	3	3⅓	1	1	1	0	3	0	0	2.70
Briles	1	6	6	2	2	1	3	0	0	3.00
Johnson	2	6	4	2	2	2	7	0	0	3.00
Giusti	3	2⅔	5	2	2	0	3	0	1	6.75
Walker	1	1	3	2	2	0	0	0	0	18.00
Moose	2	⅔	5	4	4	0	0	0	1	54.00
Totals	5	43⅔	42	19	16	10	28	2	3	3.30

1973 OAKLAND A's VS. BALTIMORE ORIOLES

The Oakland A's won their second straight American League pennant when they downed the Baltimore Orioles in a five-game Championship Series.

They almost won it in four games, but a last-ditch Baltimore rally sent the series to a climactic fifth game.

The Orioles, who had been in three previous Championship Series (1969, 1970, 1971) and had never lost a game, continued their winning ways in the opening contest, played at Memorial Stadium in Baltimore.

Jim Palmer spent 16 minutes retiring the side in the top of the first inning. He walked the first two batters and struck out the next three.

The Orioles went to work against lefty Vida Blue and his successor, Horacio Pina. During that time, Merv Rettenmund singled, Paul Blair walked, Tommie Davis doubled, Don Baylor walked, Earl Williams singled, Andy Etchebarren was hit by a pitch and Mark Belanger singled. When the carnage was over, the Orioles had four runs. It was much more than they needed as Palmer proceeded to hurl a five-hit shutout, striking out 12 A's along the way. The final score was 6-0.

The Orioles' playoff winning streak was snapped at 10 the next day when Sal Bando hit two home runs off Dave McNally while Campy Campaneris and Joe Rudi hit one apiece. Catfish Hunter, who served up so many during the season that he threatened an A.L. record, didn't allow any, and the A's won the game, 6-3.

The third game, postponed a day by rain—the postponement triggered a rhubarb between A. L. President Joe Cronin and A's President Charlie Finley—was

Little Oakland shortstop Campy Campaneris muscled up and hit two home runs while helping the A's beat Baltimore in 1973.

played at the Oakland-Alameda County Coliseum and produced a brilliant pitching battle between a pair of southpaws, Mike Cuellar of Baltimore and Ken Holtzman. It was decided in favor of the A's when Campaneris, first man up in the bottom of the 11th, snapped a 1-1 tie by hitting Cuellar's second pitch over the left-field fence for a home run.

Up to that point, Cuellar had allowed only three hits. He had a one-hit shutout for the first seven innings as he carefully nursed a 1-0 lead given him by Earl Williams' homer in the second inning. But in the eighth, pinch-hitter Jesus Alou singled and pinch-runner Allan Lewis was sacrificed to second by Mike An-

drews. The play was controversial in that Cuellar appeared to have a force out at second base, but he ignored catcher Etchebarren's yells and took the safe out at first. This proved costly as, one out later, Joe Rudi singled home Lewis to tie the score.

The Oakland club appeared to have the flag safely tucked away in the fourth contest but it escaped them.

The A's knocked out Palmer with a three-run outburst in the second inning and, going into the top of the seventh, Blue was breezing along with a 4-0 bulge when he suddenly came apart at the seams. Williams drew a base on balls and Baylor followed with a single. Brooks Robinson came through with a run-producing single and Etchebarren hit the next pitch for a home run, making the score 4-4.

The tie didn't last long. The next inning Bobby Grich hit a home run off Rollie Fingers and that, coupled with Grant Jackson's stout relief pitching, gave the game to the Orioles and set up the contest for all the money the next afternoon.

A surprisingly small crowd of 24,265 showed up for the final game and they saw Hunter pitch a five-hit shutout, winning 3-0. Righthander Doyle Alexander was the Baltimore starter but he lasted only until the fourth inning. In that frame he was the victim of singles by Gene Tenace and Alou wrapped around a triple by Vic Davalillo. He was relieved by Palmer, who shut out Oakland the rest of the way, but the Orioles were helpless against Hunter's powerful pitching.

The A's first run in the game had come in the third inning on an error by Robinson, a sacrifice, and a single by Rudi.

Game 1

Saturday, October 6, At Baltimore

Oakland	AB.	R.	H.	RBI.	PO.	A.
Campaneris, ss	3	0	1	0	0	2
Rudi, lf	2	0	0	0	4	0
Bando, 3b	3	0	0	0	2	2
Jackson, rf	4	0	1	0	1	0
Johnson, dh	2	0	0	0	0	0
Bourque, dh	1	0	0	0	0	0
Tenace, 1b-c	4	0	1	0	5	0
Mangual, cf	4	0	0	0	1	0
Fosse, c	2	0	0	0	8	1
Davalillo, ph-1b	2	0	2	0	1	0
Green, 2b	2	0	0	0	2	0
Alou, ph	1	0	0	0	0	0
Kubiak, 2b	1	0	0	0	0	0
Blue, p	0	0	0	0	0	0
Pina, p	0	0	0	0	0	0
Odom, p	0	0	0	0	0	1
Fingers, p	0	0	0	0	0	0
Totals	31	0	5	0	24	6

Baltimore	AB.	R.	H.	RBI.	PO.	A.
Rettenmund, rf	4	1	1	0	0	0
Grich, 2b	5	0	0	0	3	0
Blair, cf	4	2	1	0	2	0
Davis, dh	5	1	3	1	0	0
Baylor, lf	3	2	2	1	4	0
Robinson, 3b	5	0	0	0	0	2
Williams, 1b	4	0	2	2	3	1
Etchebarren, c	3	0	2	1	12	0
Belanger, ss	3	0	1	1	2	2
Palmer, p	0	0	0	0	1	0
Totals	36	6	12	6	27	5

Oakland	0 0 0	0 0 0	0 0 0	—0
Baltimore	4 0 0	0 0 0	1 1 x	—6

Oakland	IP.	H.	R.	ER.	BB.	SO.
Blue (L)	⅔	3	4	4	2	2
Pina	2	3	0	0	1	1
Odom	5	6	2	1	2	4
Fingers	⅓	0	0	0	0	0
Baltimore	**IP.**	**H.**	**R.**	**ER.**	**BB.**	**SO.**
Palmer (W)	9	5	0	0	5	12

E—Campaneris. DP—Oakland 1, Baltimore 1. LOB—Oakland 9, Baltimore 12. 2B—Davis, Williams, Davalillo. SB—Campaneris. HBP—By Pina (Etchebarren). WP—Blue. U—Chylak, Haller, Maloney, Odom, Anthony and McCoy. T—2:51. A—41,279.

Game 2

Sunday, October 7, At Baltimore

Oakland	AB.	R.	H.	RBI.	PO.	A.
Campaneris, ss	5	2	3	2	5	3
Rudi, lf	4	1	2	1	2	0
Bando, 3b	4	2	2	3	1	1
R. Jackson, rf	5	0	0	0	3	0
Tenace, 1b	3	0	0	0	6	1
Johnson, dh	4	0	1	0	0	0
Mangual, cf	4	1	1	0	1	0
Fosse, c	3	0	0	0	7	0
Green, 2b	4	0	0	0	1	4
Hunter, p	0	0	0	0	1	0
Fingers, p	0	0	0	0	0	0
Totals	36	6	9	6	27	9

Baltimore	AB.	R.	H.	RBI.	PO.	A.
Bumbry, lf	4	1	0	0	2	0
Coggins, rf-cf	5	1	2	0	2	0
Davis, dh	5	0	2	1	0	0
Powell, 1b	4	1	0	0	7	0
Williams, c	4	0	2	1	8	0
Blair, cf	3	0	0	0	4	0
Crowley, ph-rf	1	0	0	0	1	0
Robinson, 3b	3	0	1	1	0	2
Hood, pr	0	0	0	0	0	0
Baker, ss	0	0	0	0	0	0
Grich, 2b	2	0	0	0	2	0
Belanger, ss	3	0	1	0	0	6
Baylor, ph	1	0	0	0	0	0
Brown, 3b	0	0	0	0	0	0
McNally, p	0	0	0	0	0	0
Reynolds, p	0	0	0	0	1	0
G. Jackson, p	0	0	0	0	0	0
Totals	35	3	8	3	27	8

Oakland	1 0 0	0 0 2	0 2 1	—6
Baltimore	1 0 0	0 0 1	0 1 0	—3

Oakland	IP.	H.	R.	ER.	BB.	SO.
Hunter (W)	7⅓	7	3	3	3	5
Fingers (S)	1⅔	1	0	0	1	1
Baltimore	**IP.**	**H.**	**R.**	**ER.**	**BB.**	**SO.**
McNally (L)	7⅔	7	5	5	2	7
Reynolds	1	2	1	1	1	2
G. Jackson	⅓	0	0	0	0	0

LOB—Oakland 7, Baltimore 9. 2B—Williams. HR—Campaneris, Rudi, Bando 2. SB—Campaneris 2. SH—Fosse. WP—McNally. PB—Williams. U—Haller, Chylak, Maloney, Odom, Anthony and McCoy. T—2:42. A—48,425.

Game 3

Tuesday, October 9, At Oakland

Baltimore	AB.	R.	H.	RBI.	PO.	A.
Rettenmund, rf	5	0	0	0	2	0
Grich, 2b	5	0	1	0	1	4
Blair, cf	4	0	1	0	1	0
Davis, dh	3	0	0	0	0	0
Baylor, lf	4	0	0	0	1	0
Robinson, 3b	4	0	0	0	0	4
Williams, 1b	4	1	1	1	13	0
Etchebarren, c	4	0	0	0	10	1
Belanger, ss	4	0	0	0	2	2
Cuellar, p	0	0	0	0	0	2
Totals	37	1	3	1	30	13

Oakland	AB.	R.	H.	RBI.	PO.	A.
Campaneris, ss	5	1	1	1	1	3
Rudi, lf	4	0	1	1	1	0
Bando, 3b	4	0	0	0	2	2
Jackson, rf	4	0	0	0	4	0
Tenace, 1b-c	4	0	1	0	9	1
Johnson, dh	2	0	0	0	0	0
Conigliaro, cf	4	0	0	0	5	0
Fosse, c	1	0	0	0	6	0
Alou, ph	1	0	1	0	0	0
Lewis, pr	0	1	0	0	0	0
Davalillo, 1b	1	0	0	0	2	0
Green, 2b	2	0	0	0	2	2
Andrews, ph	0	0	0	0	0	0
Kubiak, 2b	1	0	0	0	0	1
Holtzman, p	0	0	0	0	1	2
Totals	33	2	4	2	33	11

Baltimore	0 1 0	0 0 0	0 0 0	0 0	—1
Oakland	0 0 0	0 0 0	0 1 0	0 1	—2

None out when winning run scored.

Baltimore	IP.	H.	R.	ER.	BB.	SO.
Cuellar (L)	10*	4	2	2	3	11
Oakland	**IP.**	**H.**	**R.**	**ER.**	**BB.**	**SO.**
Holtzman (W)	11	3	1	1	1	7

*Pitched to one batter in eleventh.

E—Green 2, Davalillo. DP—Oakland 1. LOB—Baltimore 4, Oakland 5. HR—Williams, Campaneris. SH—Andrews. U—Maloney, Haller, Anthony, Chylak, McCoy and Odom. T—2:23. A—34,367.

Game 4

Wednesday, October 10, At Oakland

Baltimore	AB.	R.	H.	RBI.	PO.	A.
Rettenmund, rf	2	0	0	0	1	0
Grich, 2b	4	1	1	1	4	3
Blair, cf	4	0	1	0	0	0
Davis, dh	4	0	1	0	0	0
Williams, 1b	3	1	0	0	9	0
Baylor, lf	3	1	1	0	2	0
Robinson, 3b	4	1	2	1	1	3
Etchebarren, c	4	1	2	3	6	1
Belanger, ss	4	0	0	0	4	2
Palmer, p	0	0	0	0	0	0
Reynolds, p	0	0	0	0	0	0
Watt, p	0	0	0	0	0	1
G. Jackson, p	0	0	0	0	0	0
Totals	32	5	8	5	27	10

Oakland	AB.	R.	H.	RBI.	PO.	A.
Campaneris, ss	4	0	1	0	0	3
Rudi, lf	4	0	0	0	2	0
Bando, 3b	3	0	0	0	0	1
R. Jackson, rf	4	0	1	0	7	0
Tenace, 1b-c	3	2	1	0	7	1
Davalillo, cf	3	1	2	0	1	0
Mangual, ph-cf	1	0	0	0	0	0
Johnson, dh	2	0	0	0	0	0
Bourque, ph-dh	0	0	0	0	0	0
Andrews, ph-1b	1	0	0	0	1	0
Fosse, c	2	1	1	3	3	2
Lewis, pr	0	0	0	0	0	0
Kubiak, 2b	0	0	0	0	0	0
Green, 2b	3	0	1	1	5	3
Alou, ph	1	0	0	0	0	0
Fingers, p	0	0	0	0	0	0
Blue, p	0	0	0	0	1	0
Totals	31	4	7	4	27	10

Baltimore	0 0 0	0 0 0	4 1 0	—5
Oakland	0 3 0	0 0 1	0 0 0	—4

Baltimore	IP.	H.	R.	ER.	BB.	SO.
Palmer	1⅓	4	3	3	2	2
Reynolds	4⅔*	3	1	1	2	3
Watt	⅓	0	0	0	0	0
G. Jackson (W)	2⅔	0	0	0	1	0
Oakland	**IP.**	**H.**	**R.**	**ER.**	**BB.**	**SO.**
Blue	6⅓	5	4	4	3	1
Fingers (L)	2⅔	3	1	1	1	3

*Pitched to one batter in seventh.

DP—Oakland 2. LOB—Baltimore 4, Oakland 8. 2B—Tenace, Fosse, Green, Robinson. HR—Etchebarren, Grich. SH—Rudi. SF—Fosse. HBP—By Watt (Bando). U—Chylak, Haller, Maloney, Odom, Anthony and McCoy. T—2:31. A—27,497.

Game 5

Thursday, October 11, At Oakland

Baltimore	AB.	R.	H.	RBI.	PO.	A.
Bumbry, lf	3	0	0	0	2	1
Coggins, rf	4	0	2	0	2	0
Davis, dh	4	0	0	0	0	0
Williams, 1b	3	0	0	0	10	1
Blair, cf	3	0	0	0	1	0
Robinson, 3b	4	0	2	0	1	3
Grich, 2b	4	0	0	0	6	2
Etchebarren, c	3	0	1	0	2	0
Belanger, ss	2	0	0	0	0	5
Crowley, ph	1	0	0	0	0	0
Baker, ss	0	0	0	0	0	0
Alexander, p	0	0	0	0	0	2
Palmer, p	0	0	0	0	0	1
Totals	31	0	5	0	24	15

Oakland	AB.	R.	H.	RBI.	PO.	A.
Campaneris, ss	4	0	1	0	0	4
Rudi, lf	4	0	1	1	2	0
Bando, 3b	4	0	1	0	2	4
Jackson, rf	4	0	1	0	4	0
Tenace, 1b	3	1	1	0	13	0
Davalillo, cf	2	1	1	1	3	0
Alou, dh	3	0	1	1	0	0
Fosse, c	3	1	0	0	1	1
Green, 2b	2	0	0	0	2	2
Hunter, p	0	0	0	0	0	0
Totals	29	3	7	3	27	11

Baltimore	0 0 0	0 0 0	0 0 0	—0
Oakland	0 0 1	2 0 0	0 0 x	—3

Baltimore	IP.	H.	R.	ER.	BB.	SO.
Alexander (L)	3⅔	5	3	2	0	1
Palmer	4⅓	2	0	0	1	1
Oakland	**IP.**	**H.**	**R.**	**ER.**	**BB.**	**SO.**
Hunter (W)	9	5	0	0	2	1

E—Robinson, Bumbry. DP—Baltimore 1. LOB—Baltimore 7, Oakland 5. 2B—Etchebarren, Coggins, Campaneris, Robinson. 3B—Davalillo. SB—Bumbry. SH—Green. HBP—By Hunter (Blair), by Alexander (Tenace). U—Haller, Chylak, Maloney, Odom, Anthony and McCoy. T—2:11. A—24,265.

COMPOSITE BATTING AVERAGES

Oakland Athletics

Player-Position	G.	AB.	R.	H.	2B.	3B.	HR.	RBI.	BA.
Davalillo, ph-1b-cf	4	8	2	5	1	1	0	1	.625
Campaneris, ss	5	21	3	7	1	0	2	3	.333
Alou, ph-dh	4	6	0	2	0	0	0	1	.333
Tenace, 1b-c	5	17	3	4	1	0	0	0	.235
Rudi, lf	5	18	1	4	0	0	1	3	.222
Bando, 3b	5	18	2	3	0	0	2	3	.167
R. Jackson, rf	5	21	0	3	0	0	0	0	.143
Mangual, cf-ph	3	9	1	1	0	0	0	0	.111
Johnson, dh	4	10	0	1	0	0	0	0	.100
Fosse, c	5	11	2	1	1	0	0	3	.091
Green, 2b	5	13	0	1	1	0	0	1	.077
Lewis, pr	2	0	1	0	0	0	0	0	.000
Blue, p	2	0	0	0	0	0	0	0	.000
Fingers, p	3	0	0	0	0	0	0	0	.000
Holtzman, p	1	0	0	0	0	0	0	0	.000
Hunter, p	2	0	0	0	0	0	0	0	.000
Odom, p	1	0	0	0	0	0	0	0	.000
Pina, p	1	0	0	0	0	0	0	0	.000
Andrews, ph-1b	2	1	0	0	0	0	0	0	.000
Bourque, ph-dh	2	1	0	0	0	0	0	0	.000
Kubiak, 2b	3	2	0	0	0	0	0	0	.000
Conigliaro, cf	1	4	0	0	0	0	0	0	.000
Totals	5	160	15	32	5	1	5	15	.200

Baltimore Orioles

Player-Position	G.	AB.	R.	H.	2B.	3B.	HR.	RBI.	BA.
Coggins, rf-cf	2	9	1	4	1	0	0	0	.444
Etchebarren, c	4	14	1	5	1	0	1	4	.357
Davis, dh	5	21	1	6	1	0	0	2	.286
Williams, 1b-c	5	18	2	5	2	0	1	4	.278
Baylor, lf-ph	4	11	3	3	0	0	0	1	.273
Robinson, 3b	5	20	1	5	2	0	0	2	.250
Blair, cf	5	18	2	3	0	0	0	0	.167
Belanger, ss	5	16	0	2	0	0	0	1	.125
Grich, 2b	5	20	1	2	0	0	1	1	.100
Rettenmund, rf	3	11	1	1	0	0	0	0	.091
Alexander, p	1	0	0	0	0	0	0	0	.000
Baker, ss	2	0	0	0	0	0	0	0	.000
Brown, 3b	1	0	0	0	0	0	0	0	.000
Cuellar, p	1	0	0	0	0	0	0	0	.000
Hood, pr	1	0	0	0	0	0	0	0	.000
G. Jackson, p	2	0	0	0	0	0	0	0	.000
McNally, p	1	0	0	0	0	0	0	0	.000
Palmer, p	3	0	0	0	0	0	0	0	.000
Reynolds, p	2	0	0	0	0	0	0	0	.000
Watt, p	1	0	0	0	0	0	0	0	.000
Crowley, ph-rf	2	2	0	0	0	0	0	0	.000
Powell, 1b	1	4	1	0	0	0	0	0	.000
Bumbry, lf	2	7	1	0	0	0	0	0	.000
Totals	5	171	15	36	7	0	3	15	.211

COMPOSITE PITCHING AVERAGES

Oakland Athletics

Pitcher	G.	IP.	H.	R.	ER.	BB.	SO.	W.	L.	ERA.
Pina	1	2	3	0	0	1	1	0	0	0.00
Holtzman	1	11	3	1	1	1	7	1	0	0.82
Hunter	2	16⅓	12	3	3	5	6	2	0	1.65
Odom	1	5	6	2	1	2	4	0	0	1.80
Fingers	3	4⅔	4	1	1	2	4	0	1	1.93
Blue	2	7	8	8	8	5	3	0	1	10.29
Totals	5	46	36	15	14	16	25	3	2	2.74

Baltimore Orioles

Pitcher	G.	IP.	H.	R.	ER.	BB.	SO.	W.	L.	ERA.
G. Jackson	2	3	0	0	0	1	0	1	0	0.00
Watt	1	⅓	0	0	0	0	0	0	0	0.00
Cuellar	1	10	4	2	2	3	11	0	1	1.80
Palmer	3	14⅔	11	3	3	8	15	1	0	1.84
Reynolds	2	5⅔	5	2	2	3	5	0	0	3.18
Alexander	1	3⅔	5	3	2	0	1	0	1	4.91
McNally	1	7⅔	7	5	5	2	7	0	1	5.87
Totals	5	45	32	15	14	17	39	2	3	2.80

1973
NEW YORK METS
VS.
CINCINNATI REDS

The New York Mets dethroned the Cincinnati Reds in a five-game Championship Series in 1973 marked by riotous scenes unparalleled in baseball history.

The New Yorkers pinned their hopes in the Championship Series on pitching and to that end they sent their big ace, Tom Seaver, to the mound in the opening game, played at Cincinnati's Riverfront Stadium.

Seaver almost staged a personal tour de force. His double drove in his team's lone run in the second inning and the lead held up until the eighth inning when Pete Rose, later to become a storm center in the series, hit a home run. Johnny Bench hit a home run in the ninth inning and so Seaver, who had walked none and struck out 13, came out on the losing end.

While Seaver had come close to a shutout in the opener, teammate Jon Matlack did post a shutout the next afternoon. He yielded but two singles while the Mets collected five runs and seven hits off four Cincinnati pitchers.

Paced by Rusty Staub's two home runs and the steady pitching of lefty Jerry Koosman, the Mets had an easy win in the third game, played at Shea Stadium. Easy, that is, if only the box score is considered. For it was in this game that the fireworks were ignited.

In the ninth inning, Rose slid hard into Bud Harrelson in an attempt to break up a double play.

Harrelson completed the play and then he and Rose began pushing and shoving and finally fell to the ground flailing away at each other. Players from both benches and bullpens raced onto the field.

It took several minutes to restore peace, but neither Rose nor Harrelson was ejected.

When Rose returned to left

Pete Rose makes a triumphant return to the Cincinnati dugout after hitting his game-winning homer in Game 4 of the 1973 title series.

field, the fans began throwing bottles, garbage and other assorted debris at him. The barrage became so intense that Manager Sparky Anderson pulled the Reds off the field.

Finally, Yogi Berra, Willie Mays, Staub, Cleon Jones and Seaver walked out to left field and pleaded with the fans to cease and desist. The appeal was heeded and the game proceeded to its finish.

Game No. 4 could be aptly entitled "Rose's Revenge." The peppery Cincinnati outfielder hit a home run in the 12th inning to give his team a 2-1 victory and square the series at two games apiece. Earlier in the contest, while out in the field, Rose had been given a beer shower by a Mets "fan."

The New York club salted the final game away in the fifth in-

ning. With the score tied at 2-2, Wayne Garrett opened the frame with a double. Then Reds rookie third baseman Dan Driessen made a grievous mental blunder. When Felix Millan laid down a sacrifice bunt, pitcher Jack Billingham fielded the ball and threw to third, apparently in plenty of time to get the runner. But Driessen, thinking (or not thinking) he had a force play, stepped on the bag but neglected to tag the runner. Jones then doubled, and Milner walked. Mays got a pinch-hit single to score another run and still another scored on a fielder's choice before Harrelson's single plated the fourth and final tally of the inning.

Seaver, pitching for the Mets, protected his lead with the help of Tug McGraw's relief and the Mets were N.L. Champions for 1973.

Game 1

Saturday, October 6, At Cincinnati

New York	AB.	R.	H.	RBI.	PO.	A.
Garrett, 3b	4	0	1	0	2	1
Millan, 2b	3	0	0	0	1	1
Staub, rf	2	0	0	0	2	0
Milner, 1b	3	0	1	0	3	1
Jones, lf	4	0	0	0	2	0
Grote, c	4	0	0	0	13	0
Hahn, cf	3	0	0	0	0	0
Harrelson, ss	2	1	0	0	2	1
Seaver, p	3	0	1	1	0	0
Totals	28	1	3	1	25	4

Cincinnati	AB.	R.	H.	RBI.	PO.	A.
Rose, lf	4	1	1	1	2	0
Morgan, 2b	4	0	0	0	2	6
Driessen, 3b	4	0	1	0	0	0
Perez, 1b	4	0	0	0	11	1
Bench, c	4	1	3	1	6	0
Griffey, rf	2	0	0	0	1	0
Geronimo, cf	3	0	1	0	5	0
Chaney, ss	2	0	0	0	0	2
Stahl, ph	1	0	0	0	0	0
Crosby, ss	0	0	0	0	0	2
Billingham, p	1	0	0	0	0	1
King, ph	1	0	0	0	0	0
Hall, p	0	0	0	0	0	0
Borbon, p	0	0	0	0	0	0
Totals	30	2	6	2	27	12

New York .... 0 1 0 0 0 0 0 0 0—1
Cincinnati .... 0 0 0 0 0 0 0 1 1—2
One out when winning run scored.

New York	IP.	H.	R.	ER.	BB.	SO.
Seaver (L)	8⅓	6	2	2	0	13

Cincinnati	IP.	H.	R.	ER.	BB.	SO.
Billingham	8	3	1	1	3	6
Hall	0*	0	0	0	1	0
Borbon (W)	1	0	0	0	0	0

*Pitched to one batter in ninth.

DP—Cincinnati 1. LOB—New York 5, Cincinnati 5. 2B—Seaver, Bench, Driessen. HR—Rose, Bench. SH—Millan, Billingham. HBP—By Seaver (Griffey). U—Sudol, Vargo, Pelekoudas, Engel, Froemming and Dale. T—2:00. A—53,431.

Game 2

Sunday, October 7, At Cincinnati

New York	AB.	R.	H.	RBI.	PO.	A.
Garrett, 3b	5	0	0	0	0	3
Millan, 2b	4	1	1	0	1	0
Staub, rf	3	2	1	1	3	0
Jones, lf	3	1	1	1	2	0
Milner, 1b	3	1	0	0	6	2
Grote, c	4	0	1	2	9	0
Hahn, cf	3	0	2	0	3	0
Harrelson, ss	4	0	1	1	3	4
Matlack, p	2	0	0	0	0	1
Totals	31	5	7	5	27	10

Cincinnati	AB.	R.	H.	RBI.	PO.	A.
Rose, lf	4	0	0	0	2	0
Morgan, 2b	4	0	0	0	3	3
Perez, 1b	4	0	0	0	5	1
Bench, c	4	0	0	0	7	2
Kosco, rf	2	0	2	0	4	0
Driessen, 3b	3	0	0	0	1	1
Geronimo, cf	3	0	0	0	3	0
Chaney, ss	0	0	0	0	1	1
Armbrister, ph	1	0	0	0	0	0
Hall, p	0	0	0	0	1	0
Borbon, p	0	0	0	0	0	0
Gullett, p	0	0	0	0	0	0
Gagliano, ph	1	0	0	0	0	0
Carroll, p	0	0	0	0	0	1
Menke, ph-ss	1	0	0	0	0	0
Totals	27	0	2	0	27	9

New York .... 0 0 0 1 0 0 0 4—5
Cincinnati .... 0 0 0 0 0 0 0 0—0

New York	IP.	H.	R.	ER.	BB.	SO.
Matlack (W)	9	2	0	0	3	9

Cincinnati	IP.	H.	R.	ER.	BB.	SO.
Gullett (L)	5	2	1	1	2	3
Carroll	3	0	0	0	1	2
Hall	⅓	2	4	4	2	0
Borbon	⅔	3	0	0	0	1

DP—Cincinnati 1. LOB—New York 5, Cincinnati 4. HR—Staub. SH—Gullett, Matlack. U—Vargo, Pelekoudas, Engel, Froemming, Dale and Sudol. T—2:19. A—54,041.

Game 3

Monday, October 8, At New York

Cincinnati	AB.	R.	H.	RBI.	PO.	A.
Rose, lf	4	0	2	0	3	0
Morgan, 2b	4	0	1	1	0	5
Perez, 1b	4	0	0	0	8	0
Bench, c	4	0	1	0	6	0
Kosco, rf	4	0	0	0	4	0
Armbrister, cf	4	0	1	0	3	0
Menke, 3b	4	1	1	1	0	1
Chaney, ss	3	0	0	0	0	1
Gagliano, ph	1	0	0	0	0	0
Grimsley, p	0	0	0	0	0	0
Hall, p	0	0	0	0	0	0
Stahl, ph	1	1	1	0	0	0
Tomlin, p	0	0	0	0	0	0
Nelson, p	1	0	0	0	0	0
King, ph	1	0	1	0	0	0
Borbon, p	0	0	0	0	0	1
Totals	35	2	8	2	24	8

New York	AB.	R.	H.	RBI.	PO.	A.
Garrett, 3b	4	0	0	1	1	0
Millan, 2b	3	2	1	1	2	0
Staub, rf	5	2	2	4	0	0
Jones, lf	3	1	2	0	1	0
Milner, 1b	4	0	1	1	4	1
Grote, c	3	2	1	0	9	0
Hahn, cf	4	1	2	0	8	0
Harrelson, ss	4	0	0	0	2	3
Koosman, p	4	1	2	1	0	0
Totals	34	9	11	8	27	4

Cincinnati .... 0 0 2 0 0 0 0 0 0—2
New York .... 1 5 1 2 0 0 0 0 x—9

Cincinnati	IP.	H.	R.	ER.	BB.	SO.
Grimsley (L)	1⅔	5	5	5	1	2
Hall	⅓	1	1	1	1	1
Tomlin	1⅔	5	3	3	1	1
Nelson	2⅓	0	0	0	1	0
Borbon	2	0	0	0	0	2

New York	IP.	H.	R.	ER.	BB.	SO.
Koosman (W)	9	8	2	2	0	9

E—Kosco, Garrett. DP—New York 1. LOB—Cincinnati 6, New York 6. 2B—Jones, Bench. HR—Staub 2, Menke. SF—Garrett. U—Pelekoudas, Engel, Froemming, Dale, Sudol and Vargo. T—2:48. A—53,967.

Game 4

Tuesday, October 9, At New York

Cincinnati	AB.	R.	H.	RBI.	PO.	A.
Rose, lf	5	1	3	1	3	0
Morgan, 2b	4	0	0	0	4	7
Perez, 1b	6	1	1	1	13	1
Bench, c	4	0	1	0	7	0
Kosco, rf	4	0	1	0	4	0
Menke, 3b-ss	4	0	1	0	0	3
Geronimo, cf	5	0	0	0	2	0
Chaney, ss	2	0	0	0	0	3
Armbrister, ph	1	0	0	0	0	0
Crosby, ss	1	0	1	0	1	0
Driessen, pr-3b	1	0	0	0	0	0
Norman, p	1	0	0	0	1	0
Stahl, ph	1	0	0	0	0	0
Gullett, p	1	0	0	0	1	0
Gagliano, ph	1	0	0	0	0	0
Carroll, p	0	0	0	0	0	0
Griffey, ph	1	0	0	0	0	0
Borbon, p	0	0	0	0	0	1
Totals	42	2	8	2	36	15

New York	AB.	R.	H.	RBI.	PO.	A.
Garrett, 3b	5	0	0	0	1	1
Millan, 2b	5	0	2	1	4	3
Staub, rf	5	0	0	0	5	0
Jones, lf	5	0	0	0	5	0
Milner, 1b	4	0	0	0	10	1
Grote, c	4	0	1	0	7	1
Hahn, cf	3	1	0	0	0	0
Harrelson, ss	4	0	0	0	2	5
Stone, p	1	0	0	0	1	2
McGraw, p	1	0	0	0	1	0
Boswell, ph	1	0	0	0	0	0
Parker, p	0	0	0	0	0	0
Totals	38	1	3	1	36	13

Cincinnati .... 0 0 0 0 0 0 1 0 0 0 0 1—2
New York .... 0 0 1 0 0 0 0 0 0 0 0 0—1

Cincinnati	IP.	H.	R.	ER.	BB.	SO.
Norman	5	1	1	1	3	3
Gullett	4	2	0	0	0	3
Carroll (W)	2	0	0	0	0	0
Borbon (S)	1	0	0	0	0	0

New York	IP.	H.	R.	ER.	BB.	SO.
Stone	6⅔	3	1	1	2	4
McGraw	4⅓	4	0	0	3	3
Parker (L)	1	1	1	1	0	0

E—McGraw, Grote. DP—Cincinnati 1, New York 2. LOB—Cincinnati 10, New York 4. HR—Perez, Rose. SH—Morgan. WP—McGraw. U—Engel, Froemming, Dale, Sudol, Vargo and Pelekoudas. T—3:07. A—50,786.

Game 5

Wednesday, October 10, At New York

Cincinnati	AB.	R.	H.	RBI.	PO.	A.
Rose, lf	4	1	2	0	0	1
Morgan, 2b	4	1	1	0	3	6
Driessen, 3b	4	0	1	1	2	1
Perez, 1b	4	0	1	1	10	1
Bench, c	3	0	0	0	5	0
Griffey, rf	4	0	1	0	1	0
Geronimo, cf	4	0	0	0	1	1
Chaney, ss	2	0	0	0	1	3
Stahl, ph	1	0	1	0	0	0
Billingham, p	2	0	0	0	0	1
Gullett, p	0	0	0	0	0	0
Carroll, p	0	0	0	0	0	1
Crosby, ph	1	0	0	0	0	0
Grimsley, p	0	0	0	0	1	0
King, ph	0	0	0	0	0	0
Totals	33	2	7	2	24	15

New York	AB.	R.	H.	RBI.	PO.	A.
Garrett, 3b	5	1	1	0	0	1
Millan, 2b	4	2	2	0	1	7
Jones, rf-lf	5	1	3	2	0	0
Milner, 1b	3	1	1	0	14	1
Kranepool, lf	2	0	1	2	2	0
Mays, ph-cf	3	1	1	1	1	0
Grote, c	4	0	1	0	4	0
Hahn, cf-rf	4	0	0	1	1	0
Harrelson, ss	4	0	2	1	3	1
Seaver, p	3	1	1	0	0	3
McGraw, p	0	0	0	0	1	0
Totals	37	7	13	7	27	13

Cincinnati .... 0 0 1 0 1 0 0 0 0—2
New York .... 2 0 0 0 4 1 0 0 x—7

Cincinnati	IP.	H.	R.	ER.	BB.	SO.
Billingham (L)	4*	6	5	5	1	3
Gullett	0†	0	1	1	1	0
Carroll	2	5	1	1	0	0
Grimsley	2	2	0	0	1	1

New York	IP.	H.	R.	ER.	BB.	SO.
Seaver (W)	8⅓	7	2	1	5	4
McGraw (S)	⅔	0	0	0	0	0

*Pitched to three batters in fifth.
†Pitched to one batter in fifth.

E—Jones, Driessen. LOB—Cincinnati 10, New York 10. 2B—Morgan, Griffey, Rose, Garrett, Jones, Seaver. SH—Millan. SF—Driessen. WP—Seaver. U—Froemming, Dale, Sudol, Vargo, Pelekoudas and Engel. T—2:40. A—50,323.

COMPOSITE BATTING AVERAGES

New York Mets

Player-Position	G.	AB.	R.	H.	2B.	3B.	HR.	RBI.	BA.
Koosman, p	1	4	1	2	0	0	0	1	.500
Kranepool, lf	1	2	0	1	0	0	0	2	.500
Seaver, p	2	6	1	2	2	0	0	1	.333
Mays, ph-cf	1	3	1	1	0	0	0	1	.333
Millan, 2b	5	19	5	6	0	0	0	2	.316
Jones, lf-rf	5	20	3	6	2	0	0	3	.300
Hahn, cf-rf	5	17	2	4	0	0	0	1	.235
Grote, c	5	19	2	4	0	0	0	2	.211
Staub, rf	4	15	4	3	0	0	3	5	.200
Milner, 1b	5	17	2	3	0	0	0	1	.176
Harrelson, ss	5	18	1	3	0	0	0	2	.167
Garrett, 3b	5	23	1	2	1	0	0	1	.087
Parker, p	1	0	0	0	0	0	0	0	.000
Boswell, ph	1	1	0	0	0	0	0	0	.000
McGraw, p	2	1	0	0	0	0	0	0	.000
Stone, p	1	1	0	0	0	0	0	0	.000
Matlack, p	1	2	0	0	0	0	0	0	.000
Totals	5	168	23	37	5	0	3	22	.220

Cincinnati Reds

Player-Position	G.	AB.	R.	H.	2B.	3B.	HR.	RBI.	BA.
Stahl, ph	4	4	1	2	0	0	0	0	.500
Crosby, ss-ph	3	2	0	1	0	0	0	0	.500
King, ph	3	2	0	1	0	0	0	0	.500
Rose, lf	5	21	3	8	1	0	2	2	.381
Kosco, rf	3	10	0	3	0	0	0	0	.300
Bench, c	5	19	1	5	2	0	1	1	.263
Menke, ph-ss-1b	3	9	1	2	0	0	1	1	.222
Driessen, 3b-pr	4	12	0	2	1	0	0	1	.167
Armbrister, ph-cf	3	6	0	1	0	0	0	0	.167
Griffey, rf-ph	3	7	0	1	1	0	0	0	.143
Morgan, 2b	5	20	1	2	1	0	0	1	.100
Perez, 1b	5	22	1	2	0	0	1	2	.091
Geronimo, cf	4	15	0	1	0	0	0	0	.067
Borbon, p	4	0	0	0	0	0	0	0	.000
Carroll, p	3	0	0	0	0	0	0	0	.000
Grimsley, p	2	0	0	0	0	0	0	0	.000
Hall, p	3	0	0	0	0	0	0	0	.000
Tomlin, p	1	0	0	0	0	0	0	0	.000
Gullett, p	3	1	0	0	0	0	0	0	.000
Nelson, p	1	1	0	0	0	0	0	0	.000
Norman, p	1	1	0	0	0	0	0	0	.000
Billingham, p	2	3	0	0	0	0	0	0	.000
Gagliano, ph	3	3	0	0	0	0	0	0	.000
Chaney, ss	5	9	0	0	0	0	0	0	.000
Totals	5	167	8	31	6	0	5	8	.186

COMPOSITE PITCHING AVERAGES

New York Mets

Pitcher	G.	IP.	H.	R.	ER.	BB.	SO.	W.	L.	ERA.
Matlack	1	9	2	0	0	3	9	1	0	0.00
McGraw	2	5	4	0	0	3	3	0	0	0.00
Stone	1	6⅔	3	1	1	2	4	0	0	1.35
Seaver	2	16⅔	13	4	3	5	17	1	1	1.62
Koosman	1	9	8	2	2	0	9	1	0	2.00
Parker	1	1	1	1	1	0	0	0	1	9.00
Totals	5	47⅓	31	8	7	13	42	3	2	1.33

Cincinnati Reds

Pitcher	G.	IP.	H.	R.	ER.	BB.	SO.	W.	L.	ERA.
Borbon	4	4⅔	3	0	0	0	3	1	0	0.00
Nelson	1	2⅓	0	0	0	1	0	0	0	0.00
Carroll	3	7	5	1	1	1	2	1	0	1.29
Norman	1	5	1	1	1	3	3	0	0	1.80
Gullett	3	9	4	2	2	3	6	0	1	2.00
Billingham	2	12	9	6	6	4	9	0	1	4.50
Grimsley	2	3⅔	7	5	5	2	3	0	1	12.27
Tomlin	1	1⅔	5	3	3	1	1	0	0	16.20
Hall	3	⅔	3	5	5	4	1	0	0	67.50
Totals	5	46	37	23	23	19	28	2	3	4.50

1974
OAKLAND A's
VS.
BALTIMORE ORIOLES

The Oakland A's won their third consecutive American League pennant when they downed the Baltimore Orioles, three games to one, in the Championship Series.

The Orioles, who came into their fifth playoff in the last six years on the impetus of nine straight victories and 28 wins in their last 34 games of the regular season, carried their momentum into the Championship Series opener, played at Oakland.

The Birds jumped all over the ace of the Oakland staff, Jim Hunter, pounding him for six runs and eight hits, including three homers, in less than five innings. Hunter had a skein of seven straight decisions over the Birds going into the game. Southpaw Mike Cuellar pitched steady ball for the winners and got the decision with relief help in the ninth inning from Ross Grimsley.

A portent of things to happen came in the first inning when Paul Blair, second man in the batting order, hit a Hunter pitch for a home run. Bert Campaneris' single that followed a fielder's choice and a stolen base by Bill North gave the A's a temporary tie in the third inning. But a double by Bobby Grich and Tommy Davis' single put the Orioles ahead to stay in the fourth. A four-run outburst in the fifth, featuring homers by Brooks Robinson and Bobby Grich, locked up the game and sent Hunter to the showers.

When Cuellar yielded a single to Jesus Alou and a double to Claudell Washington, both pinch-hitters, to open the last of the ninth, he was pulled in favor of Grimsley, who got the last three outs without trouble.

The A's assumed command the next day when Ken Holtzman

Oakland's Gene Tenace pours champagne over teammate Sal Bando after the A's four-game victory over Baltimore in the 1974 A.L. playoffs.

permitted the Orioles only five hits en route to a 5-0 triumph. The Oakland club got an unearned run in the fourth when Bobby Grich dropped a foul pop by Sal Bando for an error. Two pitches later, Bando drove a Dave McNally pitch over the left-field fence for a homer. Joe Rudi tripled home North in the sixth for the second run. In the eighth inning, with two men on—the result of a walk and an error—Ray Fosse hit a home run off reliever Grant Jackson to put the game on ice.

The third game of the set,

played in Baltimore, produced a brilliant pitching duel between A's lefty Vida Blue and Jim Palmer. Blue hurled a two-hitter and Palmer a four-hitter. But one of the four safe blows yielded by the Oriole righthander was a home run by Bando in the fourth inning. It was the only run of the game.

The fourth game saw the A's capture a 2-1 verdict, although their batting order was able to produce only one safe hit for the afternoon. Cuellar pitched a no-hitter for four and two-thirds innings but walked four consecutive

batters to give Oakland a run. During his stint on the mound, the Oriole lefty walked no less than nine batters and was removed while yet to give up a hit.

The run that was to prove decisive came in the seventh off reliever Grimsley. Bando walked and Reggie Jackson stroked a double off the left-field wall to plate Bando.

The Orioles almost pulled the game out of the bag in their last turn at bat. With one out and Rollie Fingers pitching in relief of Hunter, Blair walked and Grich singled. A force play provided the second out of the inning but Boog Powell's single drove in one run. Fingers, however, was equal to the occasion, striking out Baylor on a fast ball to clinch the league crown for Oakland.

The triumph of the A's was notable in a couple of ways. Besides marking Oakland's third straight pennant, it placed Manager Alvin Dark in the company of only two other managers who have won pennants in both major leagues. Joe McCarthy did it with the Cubs and the Yankees and Yogi Berra did it with the Yankees and the Mets.

Game 1

Saturday, October 5, At Oakland

Baltimore	AB.	R.	H.	RBI.	PO.	A.
Coggins, rf	4	0	0	0	3	0
Blair, cf	4	2	2	2	2	0
Grich, 2b	4	2	2	2	1	2
Davis, dh	4	0	2	1	0	0
Powell, 1b	4	0	0	0	8	1
Baylor, lf	4	0	2	0	2	0
Robinson, 3b	4	1	1	1	0	5
Hendricks, c	4	1	1	0	5	0
Belanger, ss	3	0	0	0	6	2
Cuellar, p	0	0	0	0	0	3
Grimsley, p	0	0	0	0	0	0
Totals	35	6	10	6	27	13

Oakland	AB.	R.	H.	RBI.	PO.	A.
North, cf	5	2	1	0	3	0
Campaneris, ss	4	0	3	3	0	5
Jackson, rf	4	0	0	0	0	0
Bando, 2b	4	0	1	0	1	2
Rudi, lf	4	0	0	0	2	0
Tenace, 1b	3	0	0	0	12	1
Mangual, dh	4	0	1	0	0	0
Fosse, c	2	0	1	0	6	0
Alou, ph,	1	0	1	0	0	0
Trillo, pr	0	1	0	0	0	0
Green, 2b	2	0	0	0	2	3
C. Washington, ph	1	0	1	0	0	0
Hunter, p	0	0	0	0	1	1
Odom, p	0	0	0	0	0	0
Fingers, p	0	0	0	0	0	0
Totals	34	3	9	3	27	12

Baltimore	1 0 0 1 4 0 0 0 0—6
Oakland	0 0 1 0 1 0 0 0 1—3

Baltimore	IP.	H.	R.	ER.	BB.	SO.
Cuellar (W)	8*	9	3	3	4	4
Grimsley	1	0	0	0	0	0

Oakland	IP.	H.	R.	ER.	BB.	SO.
Hunter (L)	4⅔	8	6	6	0	3
Odom	3⅓	1	0	0	0	1
Fingers	1	1	0	0	0	1

*Pitched to two batters in ninth.

DP—Oakland 1. LOB—Baltimore 3, Oakland 9. 2B—Grich, North, C. Washington. HR—Blair, Robinson, Grich. SB—North, Campaneris. SH—Belanger. SF—Campaneris. PB—Fosse. U—Napp, Neudecker, Goetz, Phillips, Springstead and Deegan. T—2:29. A—41,609.

Game 2

Sunday, October 6, At Oakland

Baltimore	AB.	R.	H.	RBI.	PO.	A.
Belanger, ss	3	0	0	0	0	1
Motton, ph	1	0	0	0	0	0
Baker, ss	0	0	0	0	1	0
Blair, cf	3	0	1	0	0	0
Grich, 2b	4	0	0	0	7	5
Davis, dh	4	0	1	0	0	0
Baylor, lf	4	0	0	0	2	0
Robinson, 3b	2	0	0	0	1	3
Williams, 1b	3	0	0	0	7	1
Cabell, rf	3	0	1	0	2	0
Etchebarren, c	3	0	2	0	3	0
Bumbry, pr	0	0	0	0	0	0
Hendricks, c	0	0	0	0	1	1
McNally, p	0	0	0	0	0	0
Garland, p	0	0	0	0	0	0
Reynolds, p	0	0	0	0	0	0
G. Jackson, p	0	0	0	0	0	0
Totals	30	0	5	0	24	11

Oakland	AB.	R.	H.	RBI.	PO.	A.
Campaneris, ss	4	0	0	0	0	6
North, cf	2	1	0	0	6	0
Bando, 3b	3	1	1	1	1	4
R. Jackson, dh	3	0	0	0	0	0
H. Washington, pr	0	0	0	0	0	0
Rudi, lf	4	0	2	1	1	0
Tenace, 1b	3	1	0	0	13	0
C. Washington, rf	4	1	1	0	0	0
Fosse, c	4	1	3	3	3	1
Green, 2b	1	0	1	0	1	2
Holt, ph	0	0	0	0	0	0
Odom, pr	0	0	0	0	0	0
Maxvill, 2b	1	0	0	0	2	1
Holtzman, p	0	0	0	0	0	1
Totals	29	5	8	5	27	15

Baltimore	0 0 0 0 0 0 0 0 0—0
Oakland	0 0 0 1 0 1 0 3 x—5

Baltimore	IP.	H.	R.	ER.	BB.	SO.
McNally (L)	5⅔	6	2	1	2	2
Garland	⅔	1	0	0	1	0
Reynolds	1⅓	0	1	0	3	1
G. Jackson	⅓	1	2	0	0	1

Oakland	IP.	H.	R.	ER.	BB.	SO.
Holtzman (W)	9	5	0	0	2	3

E—Grich, Baker. DP—Baltimore 2, Oakland 2. LOB—Baltimore 5, Oakland 7. 2B—Fosse. 3B—Rudi. HR—Bando, Fosse. SB—Tenace. SH—Green. WP—McNally. U—Neudecker, Goetz, Phillips, Springstead, Deegan and Napp. T—2:23. A—42,810.

Game 3

Tuesday, October 8, At Baltimore

Oakland	AB.	R.	H.	RBI.	PO.	A.
Campaneris, ss	4	0	0	0	1	2
North, cf	4	0	0	0	2	0
Bando, 3b	4	1	1	1	0	1
Jackson, dh	4	0	1	0	0	0
Rudi, lf	4	0	0	0	2	0
Tenace, 1b	2	0	0	0	6	0
H. Washington, pr	0	0	0	0	0	0
Holt, 1b	0	0	0	0	1	0
C. Washington, rf	2	0	1	0	4	0
Fosse, c	2	0	0	0	7	1
Green, 2b	3	0	1	0	4	2
Blue, p	0	0	0	0	0	1
Totals	29	1	4	1	27	7

Baltimore	AB.	R.	H.	RBI.	PO.	A.
Coggins, rf	3	0	0	0	2	0
Cabell, ph	1	0	0	0	0	0
Blair, cf	4	0	0	0	2	0
Grich, 2b	4	0	1	0	3	2
Davis, dh	3	0	0	0	0	0
Baylor, lf	3	0	1	0	4	0
Robinson, 3b	3	0	0	0	2	3
Williams, 1b	3	0	0	0	9	0
Etchebarren, c	3	0	0	0	4	1
Belanger, ss	3	0	0	0	1	3
Palmer, p	0	0	0	0	0	2
Totals	30	0	2	0	27	11

Oakland	0 0 0 1 0 0 0 0 0—1
Baltimore	0 0 0 0 0 0 0 0 0—0

Oakland	IP.	H.	R.	ER.	BB.	SO.
Blue (W)	9	2	0	0	0	7

Baltimore	IP.	H.	R.	ER.	BB.	SO.
Palmer (L)	9	4	1	1	1	4

E—Williams, Green 2. DP—Baltimore 1. LOB—Oakland 4, Baltimore 3. HR—Bando. SH—Fosse. HBP—By Palmer (C. Washington). U—Goetz, Phillips, Springstead, Deegan, Napp and Neudecker. T—1:57. A—32,060.

Game 4

Wednesday, October 9, At Baltimore

Oakland	AB.	R.	H.	RBI.	PO.	A.
Campaneris, ss	5	0	0	0	2	4
North, cf	5	0	0	0	3	0
Bando, 3b	2	2	0	0	1	1
Jackson, dh	1	0	1	1	0	0
Odom, pr	0	0	0	0	0	0
Rudi, lf	1	0	0	0	0	0
Tenace, 1b	3	0	0	1	4	1
C. Washington, rf	4	0	0	0	7	0
Fosse, c	4	0	0	0	5	1
Green, 2b	3	0	0	0	3	1
Hunter, p	0	0	0	0	2	1
Fingers, p	0	0	0	0	0	0
Totals	28	2	1	2	27	9

Baltimore	AB.	R.	H.	RBI.	PO.	A.
Coggins, rf	4	0	0	0	1	0
Blair, cf	3	1	1	0	3	0
Grich, 2b	4	0	1	0	2	3
Davis, dh	4	0	1	0	0	0
Cabell, pr	0	0	0	0	0	0
Powell, 1b	4	0	1	1	14	0
Palmer, pr	0	0	0	0	0	0
Baylor, lf	4	0	1	0	1	0
Robinson, 3b	3	0	0	0	1	2
Hendricks, c	2	0	0	0	5	0
Belanger, ss	0	0	0	0	0	6
Bumbry, ph	1	0	0	0	0	0
Baker, ss	0	0	0	0	0	1
Cuellar, p	0	0	0	0	0	2
Grimsley, p	0	0	0	0	0	1
Totals	29	1	5	1	27	15

Oakland	0 0 0 0 1 0 1 0 0—2
Baltimore	0 0 0 0 0 0 0 0 1—1

Oakland	IP.	H.	R.	ER.	BB.	SO.
Hunter (W)	7*	3	0	0	2	3
Fingers (S)	2	2	1	1	1	2

Baltimore	IP.	H.	R.	ER.	BB.	SO.
Cuellar (L)	4⅔	0	1	1	9	2
Grimsley	4⅓	1	1	1	2	2

*Pitched to one batter in eighth.

E—Belanger. DP—Oakland 1, Baltimore 1. LOB—Oakland 10, Baltimore 5. 2B—Jackson. SH—Belanger. WP—Cuellar. U—Phillips, Springstead, Deegan, Napp, Neudecker and Goetz. T—2:46. A—28,136.

COMPOSITE BATTING AVERAGES

Oakland Athletics

Player-Position	G.	AB.	R.	H.	2B.	3B.	HR.	RBI.	BA.
Alou, ph	1	1	0	1	0	0	0	0	1.000
Fosse, c	4	12	1	4	1	0	1	3	.333
C. Washington, ph-rf	4	11	1	3	1	0	0	0	.273
Mangual, dh	1	4	0	1	0	0	0	0	.250
Bando, 3b	4	13	4	3	0	0	2	2	.231
Green, 2b	4	9	0	2	0	0	0	0	.222
Campaneris, ss	4	17	0	3	0	0	0	3	.176
R. Jackson, rf-dh	4	12	0	2	1	0	0	1	.167
Rudi, lf	4	13	0	2	0	1	0	1	.154
North, cf	4	16	3	1	1	0	0	0	.063
Blue, p	1	0	0	0	0	0	0	0	.000
Fingers, p	2	0	0	0	0	0	0	0	.000
Holt, ph-1b	2	0	0	0	0	0	0	0	.000
Holtzman, p	1	0	0	0	0	0	0	0	.000
Hunter, p	2	0	0	0	0	0	0	0	.000
Odom, p-pr	3	0	0	0	0	0	0	0	.000
Trillo, pr	1	0	1	0	0	0	0	0	.000
H. Washington, pr	2	0	0	0	0	0	0	0	.000
Maxvill, 2b	1	1	0	0	0	0	0	0	.000
Tenace, 1b	4	11	1	0	0	0	0	1	.000
Totals	4	120	11	22	4	1	3	11	.183

Baltimore Orioles

Player-Position	G.	AB.	R.	H.	2B.	3B.	HR.	RBI.	BA.
Etchebarren, c	2	6	0	2	0	0	0	0	.333
Blair, cf	4	14	3	4	0	0	1	2	.268
Baylor, lf	4	15	0	4	0	0	0	0	.267
Davis, dh	4	15	0	4	0	0	0	1	.267
Grich, 2b	4	16	2	4	1	0	1	2	.250
Cabell, rf-ph-pr	3	4	0	1	0	0	0	0	.250
Hendricks, c	3	6	1	1	0	0	0	0	.167
Powell, 1b	2	8	0	1	0	0	0	1	.125
Robinson, 3b	4	12	1	1	0	0	1	1	.083
Baker, ss	2	0	0	0	0	0	0	0	.000
Cuellar, p	2	0	0	0	0	0	0	0	.000
Garland, p	1	0	0	0	0	0	0	0	.000
Grimsley, p	2	0	0	0	0	0	0	0	.000
G. Jackson, p	1	0	0	0	0	0	0	0	.000
McNally, p	1	0	0	0	0	0	0	0	.000
Palmer, p-pr	2	0	0	0	0	0	0	0	.000
Reynolds, p	1	0	0	0	0	0	0	0	.000
Bumbry, pr-ph	2	1	0	0	0	0	0	0	.000
Motton, ph	1	1	0	0	0	0	0	0	.000
Williams, 1b	2	6	0	0	0	0	0	0	.000
Belanger, ss	4	9	0	0	0	0	0	0	.000
Coggins, rf	3	11	0	0	0	0	0	0	.000
Totals	4	124	7	22	1	0	3	7	.177

COMPOSITE PITCHING AVERAGES

Oakland Athletics

Pitcher	G.	IP.	H.	R.	ER.	BB.	SO.	W.	L.	ERA.
Blue	1	9	2	0	0	0	7	1	0	0.00
Holtzman	1	9	5	0	0	2	3	1	0	0.00
Odom	1	3⅓	1	0	0	0	1	0	0	0.00
Fingers	2	3	3	1	1	1	3	0	0	3.00
Hunter	2	11⅔	11	6	6	2	6	1	1	4.63
Totals	4	36	22	7	7	5	20	3	1	1.75

Baltimore Orioles

Pitcher	G.	IP.	H.	R.	ER.	BB.	SO.	W.	L.	ERA.
Reynolds	1	1⅓	0	1	0	3	1	0	0	0.00
Garland	1	⅔	1	0	0	1	0	0	0	0.00
G. Jackson	1	⅓	1	2	0	0	1	0	0	0.00
Palmer	1	9	4	1	1	1	4	0	1	1.00
McNally	1	5⅔	6	2	1	2	2	0	1	1.59
Grimsley	2	5⅓	1	1	1	2	2	0	0	1.69
Cuellar	2	12⅔	9	4	4	13	6	1	1	2.84
Totals	4	35	22	11	7	22	16	1	3	1.80

1974
LOS ANGELES DODGERS
VS.
PITTSBURGH PIRATES

With Don Sutton giving up only one run in 17 innings of pitching in two starting assignments, the Los Angeles Dodgers subdued the Pittsburgh Pirates in the National League Championship Series, three games to one, in 1974.

The Dodgers had been winless in six games played at Pittsburgh's Three Rivers Stadium during the regular season but they remedied that situation in postseason play. In the opening game, Sutton was opposed by Jerry Reuss. The Pirate lefty yielded just one run in seven innings, but left the game in favor of an ineffectual pinch-hitter. Dave Giusti came on in the eighth inning and gave up two insurance tallies. Meanwhile, Sutton set the Pittsburgh club down on four hits and no runs.

The Pittsburgh string of scoreless innings was extended to 15 before the Bucs finally got on the board in the seventh inning of the second game. But when they did score, there were no big base hits. One run came in on a groundout and the other on a high bouncer that escaped an infielder's glove and was scored as a single. But those two runs were enough to enable the Pirates to equalize the two runs that Los Angeles had scored earlier off starter Jim Rooker.

With the game tied going into the eighth stanza, it was a battle between ace relievers Mike Marshall, of Los Angeles, and Giusti.

Marshall retired six straight batters in the last two innings but Giusti couldn't retire even one. He was clubbed for three runs and four hits before getting the hook. An error by his catcher, Manny Sanguillen, didn't help matters. The final score was 5-2, and on

Pitcher Don Sutton, Dodger Manager Walter Alston's ace, cut Pittsburgh down to size with two 1974 Championship Series victories.

the plane trip to Los Angeles, the Pirates had time to think about getting only a dozen singles in 18 innings and failing to score in 17 innings. That's not much for a club whose strength was supposed to be power hitting.

A record crowd for Dodger Stadium—55,953—showed up for the third game, confidently expecting the local nine to apply the coup de grace. But the home partisans were sorely disappointed.

Dodger starter Doug Rau lingered on the premises for barely 10 minutes, during which time he was bombed for five runs. With Bruce Kison pitching effectively for Pittsburgh and the Dodgers contributing five errors, the game was, for all practical purposes, over early. Kison gave up only two hits in the six and two-thirds innings he worked and his reliever, Ramon Hernandez, slammed the door on the Dodgers the rest of the way. The big blows for the Bucs were home runs by Willie Stargell and Richie Hebner. At game's end the Pirates had seven

runs and the Dodgers had none.

Sutton and Reuss, as in the opener, were the opposing pitchers in the fourth game.

Sutton was just as good as he ever was, permitting but one run and three hits and striking out seven in eight innings of work before allowing the ubiquitous Marshall to mop up. Reuss simply didn't have his best stuff and was kayoed in the third inning.

His successors didn't fare much better. The unfortunate Giusti made his third appearance of the series and was just as ineffective as he had been in the first two, being charged with three runs in an inning and a third of toil.

The biggest thunder came off the bat of Dodger first baseman Steve Garvey. He had four hits, including two homers, and drove in four runs. The final score was 12-1, a decisive margin by any standard and the largest in any game previously played in a Championship Series.

Game 1

Saturday, October 5, At Pittsburgh

Los Angeles	AB.	R.	H.	RBI.	PO.	A.
Lopes, 2b	4	1	0	1	2	4
Buckner, lf	5	0	1	0	3	0
Wynn, cf	3	1	1	1	2	0
Garvey, 1b	4	0	2	0	9	1
Ferguson, rf	4	1	2	1	1	0
Cey, 3b	3	0	0	0	0	3
Russell, ss	5	0	2	0	3	2
Yeager, c	4	0	0	0	6	1
Sutton, p	3	0	1	0	1	0
Totals	35	3	9	3	27	11

Pittsburgh	AB.	R.	H.	RBI.	PO.	A.
Stennett, 2b	4	0	0	0	5	1
Hebner, 3b	3	0	0	0	1	3
Oliver, cf	4	0	0	0	5	0
Stargell, lf	4	0	2	0	5	0
Zisk, rf	4	0	0	0	0	0
Sanguillen, c	4	0	1	0	3	0
Kirkpatrick, 1b	3	0	0	0	5	0
Taveras, ss	2	0	0	0	2	1
Popovich, ph-ss	1	0	1	0	1	0
Reuss, p	2	0	0	0	0	0
Parker, ph	1	0	0	0	0	0
Giusti, p	0	0	0	0	0	2
Totals	32	0	4	0	27	7

Los Angeles .... 0 1 0 0 0 0 0 2—3
Pittsburgh .... 0 0 0 0 0 0 0 0 0—0

Los Angeles	IP.	H.	R.	ER.	BB.	SO.
Sutton (W)	9	4	0	0	1	6

Pittsburgh	IP.	H.	R.	ER.	BB.	SO.
Reuss (L)	7	5	1	1	4	3
Giusti	2	4	2	2	3	0

E—Cey 2. DP—Los Angeles 1. LOB—Los Angeles 13, Pittsburgh 7. 2B—Garvey, Buckner, Wynn. SB—Lopes. SH—Ferguson. HBP—By Sutton (Hebner). U—Colosi, Pryor, Weyer, McSherry, Crawford and Davidson. T—2:25. A—40,638.

Game 2

Sunday, October 6, At Pittsburgh

Los Angeles	AB.	R.	H.	RBI.	PO.	A.
Lopes, 2b	4	1	2	1	3	7
Buckner, lf	5	0	2	0	2	0
Wynn, cf	2	0	0	0	3	0
Garvey, 1b	5	0	1	1	13	1
Ferguson, rf-c	4	0	0	0	2	0
Cey, 3b	5	2	4	1	0	0
Russell, ss	4	1	1	0	3	3
Yeager, c	3	0	0	0	0	0
Crawford, ph-rf	2	1	1	1	0	0
Messersmith, p	3	0	0	0	1	2
Mota, ph	1	0	1	1	0	0
Lacy, pr	0	0	0	0	0	0
Marshall, p	0	0	0	0	0	0
Totals	38	5	12	5	27	13

Pittsburgh	AB.	R.	H.	RBI.	PO.	A.
Stennett, 2b	3	0	0	0	2	0
Hebner, 3b	3	0	1	1	2	1
Oliver, cf	4	0	1	1	3	0
Stargell, lf	3	0	1	0	0	0
Giusti, p	0	0	0	0	0	0
Demery, p	0	0	0	0	0	0
Hernandez, p	0	0	0	0	0	1
Parker, rf	4	0	0	0	3	0
Sanguillen, c	4	0	2	0	7	1
Kirkpatrick, 1b	4	0	0	0	9	0
Taveras, ss	0	0	0	0	0	0
Mendoza, ss	1	0	0	0	0	1
Popovich, ph-ss	2	1	1	0	1	0
Rooker, p	2	0	1	0	0	3
Zisk, ph	1	0	1	0	0	0
Clines, pr-lf	1	1	0	0	0	0
Totals	32	2	8	2	27	7

Los Angeles .... 1 0 0 1 0 0 0 3 0—5
Pittsburgh .... 0 0 0 0 0 0 2 0 0—2

Los Angeles	IP.	H.	R.	ER.	BB.	SO.
Messersmith (W)	7	8	2	2	3	0
Marshall	2	0	0	0	0	0

Pittsburgh	IP.	H.	R.	ER.	BB.	SO.
Rooker	7	6	2	2	5	4
Giusti (L)	0*	4	3	3	0	0
Demery	0†	1	0	0	0	0
Hernandez	2	1	0	0	1	1

*Pitched to four batters in eighth.
†Pitched to one batter in eighth.

E—Sanguillen 2, Rooker. DP—Los Angeles 2, Pittsburgh 1. LOB—Los Angeles 12, Pittsburgh 8. 2B—Cey 2. HR—Cey. SB—Taveras, Wynn, Lopes. SH—Stennett. HBP—By Messersmith (Taveras). WP—Demery. U—Pryor, Weyer, McSherry, Crawford, Davidson and Colosi. T—2:44. A—49,247.

Game 3

Tuesday, October 8, At Los Angeles

Pittsburgh	AB.	R.	H.	RBI.	PO.	A.
Stennett, 2b	5	1	1	0	1	4
Sanguillen, c	5	0	1	0	6	1
Oliver, cf	3	1	1	0	1	0
Stargell, lf	5	2	2	3	3	0
Zisk, rf	5	1	2	0	2	0
Clines, rf	0	0	0	0	0	0
Robertson, 1b	5	1	0	0	11	0
xHebner, 3b	3	1	2	3	1	0
Mendoza, ss	3	0	1	1	1	5
Kison, p	3	0	0	0	1	1
Hernandez, p	1	0	0	0	0	0
Totals	38	7	10	7	27	11

Los Angeles	AB.	R.	H.	RBI.	PO.	A.
Lopes, 2b	3	0	0	0	3	5
Buckner, lf	3	0	0	0	0	0
Mota, ph-lf	1	0	0	0	1	0
Wynn, cf	3	0	0	0	4	0
Garvey, 1b	4	0	0	0	9	0
Crawford, rf	2	0	0	0	0	0
Paciorek, ph-rf	1	0	1	0	0	0
Cey, 3b	4	0	0	0	1	0
Ferguson, c	3	0	0	0	3	0
Russell, ss	4	0	2	0	6	7
Rau, p	0	0	0	0	0	0
Hough, p	0	0	0	0	0	0
Joshua, ph	0	0	0	0	0	0
Downing, p	1	0	0	0	0	0
McMullen, ph	1	0	0	0	0	0
Solomon, p	0	0	0	0	0	0
Auerbach, ph	1	0	1	0	0	0
Totals	31	0	4	0	27	12

Pittsburgh .... 5 0 2 0 0 0 0 0 0—7
Los Angeles .... 0 0 0 0 0 0 0 0 0—0

Pittsburgh	IP.	H.	R.	ER.	BB.	SO.
Kison (W)	6⅔	2	0	0	6	5
Hernandez	2⅓	2	0	0	0	1

Los Angeles	IP.	H.	R.	ER.	BB.	SO.
Rau (L)	⅔	3	5	3	1	0
Hough	2⅓	4	2	2	0	2
Downing	4	1	0	0	1	0
Solomon	2	2	0	0	1	1

xAwarded first base on catcher's interference. E—Garvey, Hough, Lopes, Ferguson, Downing. DP—Los Angeles 3. LOB—Pittsburgh 8, Los Angeles 10. 2B—Sanguillen, Auerbach. HR—Stargell, Hebner. PB—Ferguson, Sanguillen. U—Weyer, McSherry, Crawford, Davidson, Colosi and Pryor. T—2:41. A—55,953.

Game 4

Wednesday, October 9, At Los Angeles

Pittsburgh	AB.	R.	H.	RBI.	PO.	A.
Stennett, 2b	4	0	0	0	2	5
Hebner, 3b	4	0	0	0	1	3
Oliver, cf	3	0	0	0	0	0
Stargell, lf	3	1	1	1	5	0
Parker, rf	3	0	1	0	1	1
Sanguillen, c	3	0	0	0	3	0
Kirkpatrick, 1b	2	0	0	0	8	0
Mendoza, ss	1	0	0	0	3	1
Popovich, ph-ss	2	0	1	0	0	0
Reuss, p	0	0	0	0	0	0
Brett, p	1	0	0	0	0	1
Demery, p	0	0	0	0	0	1
Giusti, p	0	0	0	0	1	0
Pizarro, p	0	0	0	0	0	0
Howe, ph	1	0	0	0	0	0
Totals	27	1	3	1	24	12

Los Angeles	AB.	R.	H.	RBI.	PO.	A.
Lopes, 2b	4	2	2	1	1	2
Buckner, lf	5	0	0	0	1	0
Wynn, cf	2	3	1	1	2	0
Garvey, 1b	5	4	4	4	9	0
Ferguson, rf	2	2	1	1	3	0
Cey, 3b	4	0	1	0	1	1
Russell, ss	5	0	2	3	1	4
Yeager, c	2	1	0	0	8	0
Sutton, p	4	0	1	1	1	3
Mota, ph	1	0	0	0	0	0
Marshall, p	0	0	0	0	0	0
Totals	34	12	12	11	27	10

Pittsburgh .... 0 0 0 0 0 0 1 0 0—1
Los Angeles .... 1 0 2 0 2 2 2 3 x—12

Pittsburgh	IP.	H.	R.	ER.	BB.	SO.
Reuss (L)	2⅔	2	3	3	4	0
Brett	2⅓	3	2	2	2	1
Demery	1*	2	4	4	2	0
Giusti	1⅓	5	3	3	2	1
Pizarro	⅔	0	0	0	1	0

Los Angeles	IP.	H.	R.	ER.	BB.	SO.
Sutton (W)	8	3	1	1	1	7
Marshall	1	0	0	0	0	1

*Pitched to two batters in seventh.

E—Stennett. DP—Pittsburgh 1, Los Angeles 2. LOB—Pittsburgh 1, Los Angeles 9. 2B—Wynn, Cey. 3B—Lopes. HR—Garvey 2, Stargell. SB—Lopes, Yeager. SH—Reuss. U—McSherry, Crawford, Davidson, Colosi, Pryor and Weyer. T—2:36. A—54,424.

COMPOSITE BATTING AVERAGES

Los Angeles Dodgers

Player-Position	G.	AB.	R.	H.	2B.	3B.	HR.	RBI.	BA.
Auerbach, ph	1	1	0	1	1	0	0	0	1.000
Paciorek, ph-rf	1	1	0	1	0	0	0	0	1.000
Garvey, 1b	4	18	4	7	1	0	2	5	.389
Russell, ss	4	18	1	7	0	0	0	3	.389
Mota, ph-lf	3	3	0	1	0	0	0	1	.333
Cey, 3b	4	16	2	5	3	0	1	1	.313
Sutton, p	2	7	0	2	0	0	0	1	.286
Lopes, 2b	4	15	4	4	0	1	0	3	.267
Crawford, ph-rf	2	4	1	1	0	0	0	1	.250
Ferguson, rf-c	4	13	3	3	0	0	0	2	.231
Wynn, cf	4	10	4	2	2	0	0	2	.200
Buckner, lf	4	18	0	3	1	0	0	0	.167
Hough, p	1	0	0	0	0	0	0	0	.000
Joshua, ph	1	0	0	0	0	0	0	0	.000
Lacy, pr	1	0	0	0	0	0	0	0	.000
Marshall, p	2	0	0	0	0	0	0	0	.000
Rau, p	1	0	0	0	0	0	0	0	.000
Solomon, p	1	0	0	0	0	0	0	0	.000
Downing, p	1	1	0	0	0	0	0	0	.000
McMullen, ph	1	1	0	0	0	0	0	0	.000
Messersmith, p	1	3	0	0	0	0	0	0	.000
Yeager, c	3	9	1	0	0	0	0	0	.000
Totals	4	138	20	37	8	1	3	19	.268

Pittsburgh Pirates

Player-Position	G.	AB.	R.	H.	2B.	3B.	HR.	RBI.	BA.
Popovich, ph-ss	3	5	1	3	0	0	0	0	.600
Rooker, p	1	2	0	1	0	0	0	0	.500
Stargell, lf	4	15	3	6	0	0	2	4	.400
Zisk, rf-ph	3	10	1	3	0	0	0	0	.300
Sanguillen, c	4	16	0	4	1	0	0	0	.250
Hebner, 3b	4	13	1	3	0	0	1	4	.231
Mendoza, ss	3	5	0	1	0	0	0	1	.200
Oliver, cf	4	14	1	2	0	0	0	1	.143
Parker, ph-rf	3	8	0	1	0	0	0	0	.125
Stennett, 2b	4	16	1	1	0	0	0	0	.063
Demery, p	2	0	0	0	0	0	0	0	.000
Giusti, p	3	0	0	0	0	0	0	0	.000
Pizarro, p	1	0	0	0	0	0	0	0	.000
Brett, p	1	1	0	0	0	0	0	0	.000
Clines, pr-lf-rf	2	1	1	0	0	0	0	0	.000
Hernandez, p	2	1	0	0	0	0	0	0	.000
Howe, ph	1	1	0	0	0	0	0	0	.000
Reuss, p	2	2	0	0	0	0	0	0	.000
Taveras, ss	2	2	0	0	0	0	0	0	.000
Kison, p	1	3	0	0	0	0	0	0	.000
Robertson, 1b	1	5	1	0	0	0	0	0	.000
Kirkpatrick, 1b	3	9	0	0	0	0	0	0	.000
Totals	4	129	10	25	1	0	3	10	.194

COMPOSITE PITCHING AVERAGES

Los Angeles Dodgers

Pitcher	G.	IP.	H.	R.	ER.	BB.	SO.	W.	L.	ERA.
Downing	1	4	1	0	0	1	0	0	0	0.00
Marshall	2	3	0	0	0	0	1	0	0	0.00
Solomon	1	2	2	0	0	1	1	0	0	0.00
Sutton	2	17	7	1	1	2	13	2	0	0.53
Messersmith	1	7	8	2	2	3	0	1	0	2.57
Hough	1	2⅓	4	2	2	0	2	0	0	7.71
Rau	1	⅔	3	5	3	1	0	0	1	40.50
Totals	4	36	25	10	8	8	17	3	1	2.00

Pittsburgh Pirates

Pitcher	G.	IP.	H.	R.	ER.	BB.	SO.	W.	L.	ERA.
Kison	1	6⅔	2	0	0	6	5	1	0	0.00
Hernandez	2	4⅓	3	0	0	1	2	0	0	0.00
Pizarro	1	⅔	0	0	0	1	0	0	0	0.00
Rooker	1	7	6	2	2	5	4	0	0	2.57
Reuss	2	9⅔	7	4	4	8	3	0	2	3.72
Brett	1	2⅓	3	2	2	2	1	0	0	7.71
Giusti	3	3⅓	13	8	8	5	1	0	1	21.60
Demery	2	1	3	4	4	2	0	0	0	36.00
Totals	4	35	37	20	20	30	16	1	3	5.14

1975
BOSTON RED SOX
VS.
OAKLAND A's

The Boston Red Sox captured their first pennant since 1967 and stopped the Oakland A's bid for their fourth straight American League title by sweeping the Championship Series in three straight games.

Many observers had felt before the playoffs that the A's might be at a disadvantage because the first two games of the set were slated for Boston's Fenway Park, a nightmare arena for lefthanders. But the A's were still rated favorites on the strength of their championship experience, despite their heavy reliance on southpaw starters.

In the opener, Luis Tiant pitched a three-hitter as the Bosox batted out lefty Ken Holtzman in less than seven innings. Holtzman's cause wasn't helped at all by four errors behind him, three of the miscues coming on two consecutive first-inning plays.

The tone of the series was set in the opening inning when, with two out and Carl Yastrzemski on first, Bando let Carlton Fisk's grounder go through him. A's outfielder Claudell Washington threw over the cutoff man's head, off Bando's glove. As Yastrzemski scored, Fisk moved to second, from where he immediately scored on an error by second baseman Phil Garner.

The Sox added five more tallies in the seventh frame as a dropped fly by Bill North and Washington's problems at the wall added to the A's troubles.

The A's jumped off to a three-run lead in the second game, Reggie Jackson's two-run homer in the first being the big blow. But the Sox chased lefty Vida Blue in the fourth inning on the strength of Yastrzemski's two-run homer, Fisk's double, Fred Lynn's single and a double play grounder.

Fisk's single plated Yastrzemski, who had doubled, with the go-ahead run in the sixth. Rico Petrocelli's homer in the seventh and an RBI single by Lynn in the eighth added to the margin.

The A's, going down to the wire with resolute obstinancy, tried in the third game with another left-hander. It was again Holtzman, this time with just two days' rest.

The lefty left the game in the fifth inning with four runs charged against him, enough for the Boston victory. Once more, Holtzman received less than decent support from his teammates, an error by Washington giving the Red Sox their first run of the game.

As a matter of fact, the difference in outfield play between the two clubs was startling. The Boston outfielders, especially Yastrzemski, time and again thwarted A's rallies with great catches and throws, while the A's outfielders struggled.

Boston catcher Carlton Fisk hugs pitcher Luis Tiant as other teammates close in after the Red Sox's 1975 Championship Series win in Game 1.

Oakland's Reggie Jackson upends Boston's Denny Doyle, but not before the second baseman's relay completed a Game 2 double play.

Game 1

Saturday, October 4, At Boston

Oakland	AB.	R.	H.	RBI.	PO.	A.
North, cf	3	0	0	1	2	0
Washington, lf	4	0	0	0	1	0
Bando, 3b	4	0	0	0	1	4
Jackson, rf	4	0	1	0	2	0
Tenace, c	3	0	0	0	4	0
Rudi, 1b	4	0	1	0	10	1
Williams, dh	3	0	0	0	0	0
Hopkins, pr-dh	0	0	0	0	0	0
Campaneris, ss	4	1	0	0	1	2
Garner, 2b	2	0	0	0	2	1
Holt, ph	1	0	1	0	0	0
Martinez, pr-2b	0	0	0	0	0	1
Holtzman, p	0	0	0	0	1	1
Todd, p	0	0	0	0	0	0
Lindblad, p	0	0	0	0	0	0
Bosman, p	0	0	0	0	0	0
Abbott, p	0	0	0	0	0	0
Totals	32	1	3	1	24	10

Boston	AB.	R.	H.	RBI.	PO.	A.
Beniquez, dh	4	1	2	1	0	0
Doyle, 2b	3	1	0	1	0	1
Yastrzemski, lf	4	1	1	0	3	0
Fisk, c	4	2	1	0	9	0
Lynn, cf	4	0	1	2	7	0
Petrocelli, 3b	4	0	0	0	1	0
Evans, rf	4	1	1	0	4	0
Cooper, 1b	3	0	1	0	2	0
Burleson, ss	3	1	1	1	1	0
Tiant, p	0	0	0	0	0	1
Totals	33	7	8	5	27	2

Oakland	0 0 0 0 0 0 0 1 0—1
Boston	2 0 0 0 0 0 5 0 x—7

Oakland	IP.	H.	R.	ER.	BB.	SO.
Holtzman (L)	6⅓	5	4	2	1	4
Todd	0*	1	1	1	0	0
Lindblad	⅓	2	2	0	0	0
Bosman	⅓	0	0	0	0	0
Abbott	1	0	0	0	0	0

Boston	IP.	H.	R.	ER.	BB.	SO.
Tiant (W)	9	3	1	0	3	8

*Pitched to one batter in seventh.

E—Bando, Washington, Garner, Lynn, North, Burleson, Cooper. LOB—Oakland 7, Boston 5. 2B—Evans, Burleson, Lynn, Holt. SB—Beniquez 2. SH—Cooper. SF—Doyle. U—Denkinger, DiMuro, Kunkel, Luciano, Evans and Morgenweck. T—2:40. A—35,578.

Game 2

Sunday, October 5, At Boston

Oakland	AB.	R.	H.	RBI.	PO.	A.
North, cf	4	0	0	0	0	0
Campaneris, ss	3	0	0	0	1	6
Bando, 3b	4	1	4	0	0	3
Jackson, rf	4	1	2	2	1	1
Tenace, 1b-c	4	0	0	0	11	1
Rudi, lf	4	1	2	0	1	0
Washington, dh	4	0	2	1	0	0
Garner, 2b	2	0	0	0	4	2
Harper, ph	0	0	0	0	0	0
Holt, 1b	1	0	0	0	1	2
Fosse, c	2	0	0	0	3	0
Williams, ph	1	0	0	0	0	0
Martinez, 2b	0	0	0	0	1	0
Tovar, ph	1	0	0	0	0	0
Blue, p	0	0	0	0	0	0
Todd, p	0	0	0	0	0	0
Fingers, p	0	0	0	0	1	0
Totals	34	3	10	3	24	15

Boston	AB.	R.	H.	RBI.	PO.	A.
Beniquez, dh	4	1	1	0	0	0
Doyle, 2b	3	1	1	0	2	1
Yastrzemski, lf	3	2	2	2	2	1
Fisk, c	4	1	2	1	4	0
Lynn, cf	4	0	2	1	4	1
Petrocelli, 3b	4	1	1	1	2	3
Evans, rf	3	0	0	0	1	0
Cooper, 1b	3	0	2	0	11	0
Burleson, ss	2	0	1	0	1	6
Cleveland, p	0	0	0	0	0	1
Moret, p	0	0	0	0	0	0
Drago, p	0	0	0	0	0	0
Totals	30	6	12	5	27	13

Oakland	2 0 0 1 0 0 0 0 0—3
Boston	0 0 0 3 0 1 1 1 x—6

Oakland	IP.	H.	R.	ER.	BB.	SO.
Blue	3*	6	3	3	0	2
Todd	1†	1	0	0	0	0
Fingers (L)	4	5	3	3	1	3

Boston	IP.	H.	R.	ER.	BB.	SO.
Cleveland	5‡	7	3	3	1	2
Moret (W)	1§	1	0	0	1	0
Drago (S)	3	2	0	0	0	2

*Pitched to four batters in fourth.
†Pitched to one batter in fifth.
‡Pitched to one batter in sixth.
§Pitched to one batter in seventh.

DP—Oakland 4, Boston 2. LOB—Oakland 6, Boston 3. 2B—Bando 2, Rudi 2, Washington. Fisk, Cooper 2, Yastrzemski. HR—Jackson, Yastrzemski, Petrocelli. SH—Burleson, Doyle. WP—Drago. U—DiMuro, Kunkel, Luciano, Evans, Morgenweck and Denkinger. T—2:27. A—35,578.

Game 3

Tuesday, October 7, At Oakland

Boston	AB.	R.	H.	RBI.	PO.	A.
Beniquez, dh	4	0	0	0	0	0
Doyle, 2b	5	1	2	1	3	6
Yastrzemski, lf	4	1	2	0	2	1
Fisk, c	4	1	2	1	2	0
Lynn, cf	3	1	1	0	1	0
Petrocelli, 3b	4	0	1	1	1	0
Evans, rf	3	0	0	0	2	0
Cooper, 1b	4	0	1	1	11	1
Burleson, ss	4	1	2	0	2	6
Wise, p	0	0	0	0	2	3
Drago, p	0	0	0	0	1	1
Totals	35	5	11	4	27	18

Oakland	AB.	R.	H.	RBI.	PO.	A.
Campaneris, ss	4	0	0	0	0	2
Washington, lf	4	1	1	0	0	0
Bando, 3b	4	0	2	2	2	4
Jackson, rf	4	0	2	1	2	0
Rudi, 1b	4	0	0	0	11	1
Williams, dh	4	0	0	0	0	0
Tenace, c	2	0	0	0	4	0
North, cf	3	0	0	0	4	1
Garner, 2b	1	0	0	0	1	1
Tovar, ph-2b	1	2	1	0	2	2
Martinez, 2b	0	0	0	0	0	0
Holt, ph	1	0	0	0	0	0
Holtzman, p	0	0	0	0	0	0
Todd, p	0	0	0	0	0	0
Lindblad, p	0	0	0	0	1	4
Totals	32	3	6	3	27	15

Boston	0 0 0 1 3 0 0 1 0—5
Oakland	0 0 0 0 0 1 0 2 0—3

Boston	IP.	H.	R.	ER.	BB.	SO.
Wise (W)	7⅓	6	3	2	3	2
Drago (S)	1⅔	0	0	0	1	0

Oakland	IP.	H.	R.	ER.	BB.	SO.
Holtzman (L)	4⅔	7	4	3	0	3
Todd	0*	1	0	0	0	0
Lindblad	4⅓	3	1	0	1	0

*Pitched to one batter in fifth.

E—Washington, Tovar, Doyle. DP—Boston 1. LOB—Boston 6, Oakland 6. 2B—Burleson. SB—Fisk. SH—Beniquez, Lynn. WP—Lindblad. U—Kunkel, Luciano, Evans, Morgenweck, Denkinger and DiMuro. T—2:30. A—49,358.

COMPOSITE BATTING AVERAGES

Boston Red Sox

Player-Position	G.	AB.	R.	H.	2B.	3B.	HR.	RBI.	BA.
Yastrzemski, lf	3	11	4	5	1	0	1	2	.455
Burleson, ss	3	9	2	4	2	0	0	1	.444
Fisk, c	3	12	4	5	1	0	0	2	.417
Cooper, 1b	3	10	0	4	2	0	0	1	.400
Lynn, cf	3	11	1	4	1	0	0	3	.364
Doyle, 2b	3	11	3	3	0	0	0	2	.273
Beniquez, dh	3	12	2	3	0	0	0	1	.250
Petrocelli, 3b	3	12	1	2	0	0	1	2	.167
Evans, rf	3	10	1	1	1	0	0	0	.100
Cleveland, p	1	0	0	0	0	0	0	0	.000
Drago, p	2	0	0	0	0	0	0	0	.000
Moret, p	1	0	0	0	0	0	0	0	.000
Tiant, p	1	0	0	0	0	0	0	0	.000
Wise, p	1	0	0	0	0	0	0	0	.000
Totals	3	98	18	31	8	0	2	14	.316

Oakland Athletics

Player-Position	G.	AB.	R.	H.	2B.	3B.	HR.	RBI.	BA.
Bando, 3b	3	12	1	6	2	0	0	2	.500
Tovar, ph-2b	2	2	2	1	0	0	0	0	.500
Jackson, rf	3	12	1	5	0	0	1	3	.417
Holt, ph-1b	3	3	0	1	1	0	0	0	.333
Rudi, 1b-lf	3	12	1	3	2	0	0	0	.250
Washington, lf-dh	3	12	1	3	1	0	0	1	.250
Fosse, c	1	2	0	0	0	0	0	0	.000
Garner, 2b	3	5	0	0	0	0	0	0	.000
Williams, dh-ph	3	8	0	0	0	0	0	0	.000
Tenace, c-1b	3	9	0	0	0	0	0	0	.000
North, cf	3	10	0	0	0	0	0	1	.000
Campaneris, ss	3	11	1	0	0	0	0	0	.000
Abbott, p	1	0	0	0	0	0	0	0	.000
Blue, p	1	0	0	0	0	0	0	0	.000
Bosman, p	1	0	0	0	0	0	0	0	.000
Fingers, p	1	0	0	0	0	0	0	0	.000
Harper, ph	1	0	0	0	0	0	0	0	.000
Holtzman, p	2	0	0	0	0	0	0	0	.000
Hopkins, pr-dh	1	0	0	0	0	0	0	0	.000
Lindblad, p	2	0	0	0	0	0	0	0	.000
Martinez, pr-2b	3	0	0	0	0	0	0	0	.000
Todd, p	3	0	0	0	0	0	0	0	.000
Totals	3	98	7	19	6	0	1	7	.194

COMPOSITE PITCHING AVERAGES

Boston Red Sox

Pitcher	G.	IP.	H.	R.	ER.	BB.	SO.	W.	L.	ERA.
Tiant	1	9	3	1	0	3	8	1	0	0.00
Drago	2	4⅔	2	0	0	1	2	0	0	0.00
Moret	1	1	1	0	0	1	0	1	0	0.00
Wise	1	7⅓	6	3	2	3	2	1	0	2.45
Cleveland	1	5	7	3	3	1	2	0	0	5.40
Totals	3	27	19	7	5	9	14	3	0	1.67

Oakland Athletics

Pitcher	G.	IP.	H.	R.	ER.	BB.	SO.	W.	L.	ERA.
Lindblad	2	4⅔	5	3	0	1	0	0	0	0.00
Abbott	1	1	0	0	0	0	0	0	0	0.00
Bosman	1	⅓	0	0	0	0	0	0	0	0.00
Holtzman	2	11	12	8	5	1	7	0	2	4.09
Fingers	1	4	5	3	3	1	3	0	1	6.75
Blue	1	3	6	3	3	0	2	0	0	9.00
Todd	3	1	3	1	1	0	0	0	0	9.00
Totals	3	25	31	18	12	3	12	0	3	4.32

1975 CINCINNATI REDS VS. PITTSBURGH PIRATES

The Cincinnati Reds, easy winners of the National League's West Division, were expected to have little trouble with their Championship Series rivals, the Pittsburgh Pirates. And that's just the way things turned out.

The Cincinnati club swept the three-game series and only the third game provided any of the dramatics that one might expect from two clubs contesting for baseball's oldest title, the National League pennant.

The Reds cuffed four Pirate hurlers for 11 hits in the opener, breezing to an 8-3 triumph. Even Reds pitcher Don Gullett got into the act, getting two hits, one a home run, and driving in three runs.

The Cincinnati regulars took batting practice in the second game, banging out 12 hits as four more Pirate hurlers trudged to the mound. Tony Perez was the big cannon in the Reds' artillery, getting three hits, one a homer, as he drove in three runs. The final score was 6-1.

The only drama of the series came in the third game, played at Pittsburgh's Three Rivers Stadium.

The home team sent lefthander John Candelaria to the hill to try and stem the Red tide and the 21-year-old rookie responded magnificently. He yielded a solo homer to Concepcion in the second inning, but going into the eighth had a 2-1 lead, the result of Al Oliver's two-run homer in the Pirate sixth.

Candelaria struck out the first two batters in the eighth. That gave him a total of 14 for the game, a playoff record. Concepcion's circuit clout had been the only Reds hit to that point.

But, inexplicably, he lost his control and walked the weak-hitting Merv Rettenmund, a pinch-hitter. Pete Rose then blasted a home run to put the Reds ahead, 3-2. When Joe Morgan followed Rose's homer with a double, Candelaria left the game.

The Pirates tied the game in the ninth when Reds relief pitcher Rawly Eastwick walked in the tying run with two out.

But it all served to merely delay the inevitable.

The Reds got three hits and two runs off veteran Ramon Hernandez, the third Pittsburgh hurler, in the top of the 10th and then held on to clinch their third pennant of the decade.

Much of Cincinnati's 1975 firepower was provided by (left to right) Joe Morgan, Ken Griffey, Johnny Bench and Cesar Geronimo.

	AB.	R.	H.	RBI.	PO.	A.
Parker, rf	4	0	0	0	5	0
Zisk, lf	3	0	2	0	4	0
Sanguillen, c	4	0	1	0	15	0
Taveras, ss	1	0	0	0	0	1
Kirkpatrick, ph	1	0	0	0	0	0
Reynolds, ss	1	0	0	0	0	0
Robertson, ph-1b	0	0	0	0	1	0
Candelaria, p	3	0	0	0	0	0
Giusti, p	0	0	0	0	0	0
Dyer, ph	0	0	0	1	0	0
Hernandez, p	0	0	0	0	0	0
Tekulve, p	0	0	0	0	0	0
Totals	37	3	7	3	30	2

Cincinnati .... 0 1 0   0 0 0   0 2 0   2—5
Pittsburgh .... 0 0 0   0 0 2   0 0 1   0—3

Cincinnati	IP.	H.	R.	ER.	BB.	SO.
Nolan	6	5	2	2	0	5
C. Carroll	1	0	0	0	1	1
McEnaney	1⅓	1	1	1	0	1
Eastwick (W)	⅔	1	0	0	2	0
Borbon (S)	1	0	0	0	0	1

Pittsburgh	IP.	H.	R.	ER.	BB.	SO.
Candelaria	7⅔	3	3	3	2	14
Giusti	1⅓	0	0	0	0	1
Hernandez (L)	⅔	3	2	2	0	0
Tekulve	⅓	0	0	0	0	0

E—Reynolds, Sanguillen. LOB—Cincinnati 4, Pittsburgh 7. 2B—Morgan 2. HR—Concepcion, Oliver, Rose. SB—Bench. SF—Armbrister. Balk—Hernandez. U—Pulli, W. Williams, Gorman, A. Williams, Kibler and Olsen. T—2:47. A—46,355.

COMPOSITE BATTING AVERAGES
Cincinnati Reds

Player-Position	G.	AB.	R.	H.	2B.	3B.	HR.	RBI.	BA.
Gullett, p	1	4	1	2	0	0	1	3	.500
Concepcion, ss	3	11	2	5	0	0	1	1	.455
Perez, 1b	3	12	3	5	0	0	1	4	.417
Foster, lf	3	11	3	4	0	0	0	0	.364
Rose, 3b	3	14	3	5	0	0	1	2	.357
Griffey, rf	3	12	3	4	1	0	0	4	.333
Morgan, 2b	3	11	2	3	3	0	0	1	.273
Bench, c	3	13	1	1	0	0	0	0	.077
Norman, p	1	1	0	0	0	0	0	1	.000
Rettenmund, ph	2	1	0	0	0	0	0	0	.000
Nolan, p	1	2	0	0	0	0	0	0	.000
Geronimo, cf	3	10	0	0	0	0	0	1	.000
Armbrister, ph	2	0	0	0	0	0	0	1	.000
Borbon, p	1	0	0	0	0	0	0	0	.000
Carroll, p	1	0	0	0	0	0	0	0	.000
Crowley, ph	1	0	0	0	0	0	0	0	.000
Eastwick, p	2	0	0	0	0	0	0	0	.000
McEnaney, p	1	0	0	0	0	0	0	0	.000
Totals	3	102	19	29	4	0	4	18	.284

Pittsburgh Pirates

Player-Position	G.	AB.	R.	H.	2B.	3B.	HR.	RBI.	BA.
Zisk, lf	3	10	1	5	1	0	0	0	.500
Robertson, ph-1b	3	2	0	1	0	0	0	1	.500
Hebner, 3b	3	12	4	4	1	0	0	2	.333
Stennett, 2b-ss	3	14	0	3	0	0	0	0	.214
Oliver, cf	3	11	1	2	0	0	1	2	.182
Stargell, 1b	3	11	1	2	1	0	0	0	.182
Sanguillen, c	3	12	0	2	0	0	0	0	.167
Taveras, ss	3	7	0	1	0	0	0	1	.143
Reuss, p	1	1	0	0	0	0	0	0	.000
Reynolds, pr-ss	2	1	0	0	0	0	0	0	.000
Rooker, p	1	1	0	0	0	0	0	0	.000
Kirkpatrick, ph	2	2	0	0	0	0	0	0	.000
Randolph, ph-pr-2b	2	2	1	0	0	0	0	0	.000
Robinson, ph	2	2	0	0	0	0	0	0	.000
Candelaria, p	1	3	0	0	0	0	0	0	.000
Parker, rf	3	10	2	0	0	0	0	0	.000
Brett, p	2	0	0	0	0	0	0	0	.000
Demery, p	1	0	0	0	0	0	0	0	.000
Dyer, ph	1	0	0	0	0	0	0	1	.000
Ellis, p	1	0	0	0	0	0	0	0	.000
Giusti, p	1	0	0	0	0	0	0	0	.000
Hernandez, p	1	0	0	0	0	0	0	0	.000
Kison, p	1	0	0	0	0	0	0	0	.000
Tekulve, p	2	0	0	0	0	0	0	0	.000
Totals	3	101	7	20	3	0	1	7	.198

Cincinnati Manager Sparky Anderson (left) and other Reds congratulate pitcher Don Gullett after his surprise Game 1 home run.

Game 1
Saturday, October 4, At Cincinnati

Pittsburgh	AB.	R.	H.	RBI.	PO.	A.
Stennett, 2b	5	0	1	0	1	5
Sanguillen, c	4	0	1	0	5	1
Oliver, cf	4	0	1	0	3	0
Stargell, 1b	4	0	0	0	8	0
Zisk, lf	4	0	1	0	2	0
Parker, rf	2	2	0	0	4	0
Hebner, 3b	4	1	2	1	0	1
Taveras, ss	3	0	1	1	1	2
Reuss, p	1	0	0	0	0	1
Brett, p	0	0	0	0	0	0
Robinson, ph	1	0	0	0	0	0
Demery, p	0	0	0	0	0	0
Randolph, ph	1	0	0	0	0	0
Ellis, p	0	0	0	0	0	0
Robertson, ph	1	0	1	1	0	0
Reynolds, pr	0	0	0	0	0	0
Totals	34	3	8	3	24	10

Cincinnati	AB.	R.	H.	RBI.	PO.	A.
Rose, 3b	5	0	2	0	0	0
Morgan, 2b	3	1	0	0	1	2
Bench, c	4	1	1	0	5	0
Perez, 1b	4	2	2	1	6	3
Foster, lf	4	2	2	0	2	0
Concepcion, ss	3	0	1	0	0	3
Griffey, rf	4	1	1	3	2	1
Geronimo, cf	3	0	0	1	7	0
Gullett, p	4	1	2	3	4	1
Totals	34	8	11	8	27	10

Pittsburgh .... 0 2 0   0 0 0   0 0 1—3
Cincinnati .... 0 1 3   0 4 0   0 0 x—8

Pittsburgh	IP.	H.	R.	ER.	BB.	SO.
Reuss (L)	2⅔	4	4	4	4	1
Brett	1⅓	1	0	0	0	1
Demery	2	4	4	4	1	1
Ellis	2	2	0	0	0	2

Cincinnati	IP.	H.	R.	ER.	BB.	SO.
Gullett (W)	9	8	3	3	2	5

LOB—Pittsburgh 7, Cincinnati 8. 2B—Hebner, Griffey. HR—Gullett. SB—Morgan 3. SF—Geronimo. HBP—By Gullett (Parker). WP—Gullett. PB—Sanguillen 2. U—Kibler, Olsen, Pulli, W. Williams, Gorman and A. Williams. T—3:00. A—54,633.

Game 2
Sunday, October 5, At Cincinnati

Pittsburgh	AB.	R.	H.	RBI.	PO.	A.
Stennett, 2b	4	0	2	0	4	3
Sanguillen, c	4	0	0	0	9	0
Oliver, cf	2	0	0	0	0	0
Stargell, 1b	3	1	1	0	6	0
Zisk, lf	3	0	2	0	2	0
Parker, rf	4	0	0	0	4	1
Hebner, 3b	3	0	0	1	0	1
Taveras, ss	3	0	0	0	3	3
Robertson, ph	1	0	0	0	0	0
Rooker, p	1	0	0	0	0	0
Robinson, ph	1	0	0	0	0	0
Tekulve, p	0	0	0	0	0	0
Brett, p	0	0	0	0	0	0
Kirkpatrick, ph	1	0	0	0	0	0
Kison, p	0	0	0	0	0	0
Totals	30	1	5	1	24	8

Cincinnati	AB.	R.	H.	RBI.	PO.	A.
Rose, 3b	4	1	1	0	0	1
Morgan, 2b	3	1	1	0	1	2
Bench, c	4	0	0	0	5	3
Perez, 1b	4	1	3	3	12	1
Foster, lf	4	1	2	0	2	0
Concepcion, ss	4	1	3	0	5	4
Griffey, rf	4	1	2	1	0	0
Geronimo, cf	3	0	0	0	1	0
Norman, p	1	0	0	1	0	1
Armbrister, ph	0	0	0	0	0	0
Crowley, ph	0	0	0	0	0	0
Rettenmund, ph	1	0	0	0	0	0
Eastwick, p	0	0	0	0	1	0
Totals	32	6	12	5	27	13

Pittsburgh .... 0 0 0   1 0 0   0 0 0—1
Cincinnati .... 2 0 0   2 0 1   1 0 x—6

Pittsburgh	IP.	H.	R.	ER.	BB.	SO.
Rooker (L)	4	7	4	4	0	5
Tekulve	1*	3	1	1	1	2
Brett	1	0	0	0	0	0
Kison	2	2	1	1	1	1

Cincinnati	IP.	H.	R.	ER.	BB.	SO.
Norman (W)	6	4	1	1	5	4
Eastwick (S)	3	1	0	0	0	1

*Pitched to two batters in sixth.

E—Concepcion. DP—Pittsburgh 3, Cincinnati 2. LOB—Pittsburgh 7, Cincinnati 5. 2B—Stargell, Zisk, Morgan. HR—Perez. SB—Foster, Concepcion 2, Griffey 3, Morgan. SF—Norman. WP—Norman. Balk—Brett. U—Olsen, Pulli, W. Williams, Gorman, A. Williams and Kibler. T—2:51. A—54,752.

Game 3
Tuesday, October 7, At Pittsburgh

Cincinnati	AB.	R.	H.	RBI.	PO.	A.
Rose, 3b	5	2	2	2	2	0
Morgan, 2b	5	0	2	1	0	5
Bench, c	5	0	0	0	8	1
Perez, 1b	4	0	0	0	9	0
Foster, lf	3	0	0	0	3	0
Concepcion, ss	4	1	1	1	1	1
Griffey, rf	4	1	1	0	2	0
Geronimo, cf	4	0	0	0	5	0
Nolan, p	2	0	0	0	0	0
C. Carroll, p	0	0	0	0	0	1
Rettenmund, ph	1	0	0	0	0	0
McEnaney, p	0	0	0	0	0	0
Eastwick, p	0	0	0	0	0	0
Armbrister, ph	0	0	0	1	0	0
Borbon, p	0	0	0	0	0	0
Totals	36	5	6	5	30	8

Pittsburgh	AB.	R.	H.	RBI.	PO.	A.
Stennett, 2b-ss	5	0	0	0	2	0
Hebner, 3b	5	1	2	0	0	0
Oliver, cf	5	1	1	2	2	0
Stargell, 1b	4	0	1	0	10	0
Randolph, pr-2b	1	1	0	0	0	1

LOB—Pittsburgh 7, Cincinnati 8. 2B—Hebner, Griffey. HR—Gullett. SB—Morgan 3. SF—Geronimo. HBP—By Gullett (Parker). WP—Gullett. PB—Sanguillen 2. U—Kibler, Olsen, Pulli, W. Williams, Gorman and A. Williams. T—3:00. A—54,633.

COMPOSITE PITCHING AVERAGES
Cincinnati Reds

Pitcher	G.	IP.	H.	R.	ER.	BB.	SO.	W.	L.	ERA.
Eastwick	2	3⅔	2	0	0	2	1	1	0	0.00
Borbon	1	1	0	0	0	1	0	0	0	0.00
Carroll	1	1	0	0	0	1	1	0	0	0.00
Norman	1	6	4	1	1	5	4	1	0	1.50
Gullett	1	9	8	3	3	2	5	1	0	3.00
Nolan	1	6	5	2	2	0	5	0	0	3.00
McEnaney	1	1⅓	1	1	1	0	1	0	0	6.75
Totals	3	28	20	7	7	10	18	3	0	2.25

Pittsburgh Pirates

Pitcher	G.	IP.	H.	R.	ER.	BB.	SO.	W.	L.	ERA.
Brett	2	2⅓	1	0	0	0	2	0	0	0.00
Ellis	1	2	2	0	0	0	2	0	0	0.00
Giusti	1	1⅓	0	0	0	0	1	0	0	0.00
Candelaria	1	7⅔	3	3	3	2	14	0	0	3.52
Kison	1	2	2	1	1	1	1	0	0	4.50
Tekulve	2	1⅓	3	1	1	1	2	0	0	6.75
Rooker	1	4	7	4	4	0	5	0	1	9.00
Reuss	1	2⅔	4	4	4	4	1	0	1	13.50
Demery	1	2	4	4	4	1	1	0	0	18.00
Hernandez	1	⅔	3	2	2	0	0	0	1	27.00
Totals	3	26	29	19	19	9	28	0	3	6.58

1976
NEW YORK YANKEES VS. KANSAS CITY ROYALS

With one swing of the bat, New York Yankee first baseman Chris Chambliss propelled his team to its first American League pennant since 1964 and touched off one of the wildest mob scenes in the history of American sports.

With the score tied, 6-6, in the bottom of the ninth inning in the fifth game of the Championship Series, Chambliss sent the first pitch from the Kansas City Royals' fireballing righthander, Mark Littell, over the right-field fence. Littell had yielded only one homer during the regular season.

As soon as it was clear that the 1976 American League season was over and the Yankees were winners, Yankee fans, who had been wandering in a desert of pennant-less seasons—something to which they were not accustomed—rushed onto the field.

By the time Chambliss reached first base, he was surrounded by spectators. When he reached second, the bag had already been removed by a souvenir collector and Chambliss had to reach out to touch it. He never did reach third and came nowhere near home, although his teammates brought him out later to stamp his feet in the general vicinity of home plate.

The hero of the evening was fortune to escape without serious injury, as were his teammates. The fans' victory "celebration" turned into an orgy of hoodlumism and looting and resulted in about $100,000 worth of damage being done to Yankee Stadium.

Chambliss' homer was the climax of an exciting game. After the lead seesawed back and forth in the early going, the Yankees finally managed to carry a 6-3 bulge into the eighth frame. But the Royals' third baseman, George Brett, tied the game with a

First baseman Chris Chambliss delivered the blow that returned the New York Yankees to World Series competition in 1976.

three-run home run. That set the stage for the pulsating finish.

The Yankees had been substantial favorites to win the playoff but the Royals, even after losing ace center fielder Amos Otis because of a leg injury in the first game, battled right down to the wire.

The Series opened in Kansas City and the Royals showed their nervousness by handing the Yanks two runs in the first inning with Brett committing a pair of misplays. Catfish Hunter subdued the home team easily, giving up only five hits, and the New Yorkers captured the game, 4-1.

In the second contest, the Royals found Yankee 19-game winner Ed Figueroa no puzzle and pounded out a 7-3 triumph.

The Yankees won the third engagement, 5-3, as Chambliss got two hits, including a home run,

and drove in three runs.

The Royals knocked Hunter out of the box in the fourth inning of the fourth game, and copped a 7-4 decision to deadlock the Series.

That set up the climactic game of the 1976 American League season wherein Chambliss' big blow was the hit of the year.

Game 1

Saturday, October 9, At Kansas City

New York	AB.	R.	H.	RBI.	PO.	A.
Rivers, cf	5	2	2	0	0	0
R. White, lf	4	0	1	2	4	0
Munson, c	5	1	1	0	5	2
Piniella, dh	4	0	2	0	0	0
Chambliss, 1b	4	0	2	1	7	0
Nettles, 3b	4	0	0	0	3	3
Maddox, rf	4	0	1	0	4	0
Randolph, 2b	4	0	0	0	2	2
Stanley, ss	4	1	3	0	2	1
Hunter, p	0	0	0	0	0	2
Totals	38	4	12	3	27	10

Kansas City	AB.	R.	H.	RBI.	PO.	A.
Otis, cf	1	0	0	0	0	0
Wohlford, lf	3	0	0	0	2	0
Brett, 3b	4	0	3	0	1	3
McRae, dh	4	0	0	0	0	0
Mayberry, 1b	3	0	0	0	10	0
Cowens, rf-cf	3	1	1	0	3	0
Poquette, lf-rf	3	0	0	1	4	0
F. White, 2b	2	0	0	0	2	3
Rojas, ph-2b	1	0	0	0	0	0

	AB.	R.	H.	RBI.	PO.	A.
Patek, ss	3	0	1	0	1	3
Martinez, c	2	0	0	0	4	0
Quirk, ph	0	0	0	0	0	0
Wathan, c	0	0	0	0	0	0
Stinson, ph	1	0	0	0	0	0
Gura, p	0	0	0	0	0	0
Littell, p	0	0	0	0	0	0
Totals	30	1	5	1	27	9

New York	2 0 0 0 0 0 0 0 2—4
Kansas City	0 0 0 0 0 0 0 1 0—1

New York	IP.	H.	R.	ER.	BB.	SO.
Hunter (W)	9	5	1	1	0	5

Kansas City	IP.	H.	R.	ER.	BB.	SO.
Gura (L)	8⅔	12	4	3	1	4
Littell	⅓	0	0	0	0	0

E—Brett 2. DP—Kansas City 1. LOB—New York 8, Kansas City 2. 2B—Stanley, R. White. 3B—Chambliss, Cowens. U—Brinkman, Haller, Maloney, Barnett, Franz and McCoy. T—2:06. A—41,077.

Game 2

Sunday, October 10, At Kansas City

New York	AB.	R.	H.	RBI.	PO.	A.
Rivers, cf	4	0	0	0	3	0
R. White, lf	4	1	2	0	2	0
Munson, c	5	1	2	1	2	1
Chambliss, 1b	5	0	3	1	9	1
May, dh	5	1	2	0	0	0
Nettles, 3b	3	0	1	0	2	5
Gamble, rf	4	0	1	1	3	0
Randolph, 2b	3	0	0	0	1	3
Stanley, ss	3	0	1	0	0	4
Piniella, ph	1	0	0	0	0	0
Mason, ss	0	0	0	0	1	0
Figueroa, p	0	0	0	0	0	0
Tidrow, p	0	0	0	0	1	0
Totals	37	3	12	3	24	14

Kansas City	AB.	R.	H.	RBI.	PO.	A.
Wohlford, lf	4	1	1	0	2	0
Cowens, cf	5	1	1	0	5	0
Brett, 3b	3	1	1	0	0	1
Mayberry, 1b	4	1	1	1	12	0
McRae, dh	3	0	0	0	0	0
Poquette, rf	3	1	2	2	2	0
F. White, 2b	4	1	1	0	3	5
Patek, ss	4	1	1	1	1	6
Martinez, c	4	0	1	2	2	0
Leonard, p	0	0	0	0	0	0
Splittorff, p	0	0	0	0	0	1
Mingori, p	0	0	0	0	0	0
Totals	34	7	9	7	27	13

New York	0 1 2 0 0 0 0 0 0—3
Kansas City	2 0 0 0 0 2 0 3 x—7

New York	IP.	H.	R.	ER.	BB.	SO.
Figueroa (L)	5⅓	6	4	4	2	2
Tidrow	2⅔	3	3	2	1	0

Kansas City	IP.	H.	R.	ER.	BB.	SO.
Leonard	2⅓	6	3	3	2	0
Splittorff (W)	5⅔	4	0	0	2	1
Mingori	1	2	0	0	0	1

E—Munson 2, Chambliss, Stanley, Gamble. DP—Kansas City 2. LOB—New York 11, Kansas City 7. 2B—May, R. White, Munson, Stanley, Nettles, Poquette. 3B—Brett. SB—Cowens 2, Wohlford. SF—Brett. U—Barnett, Maloney, Haller, Frantz, McCoy and Brinkman. T—2:45. A—41,091.

Game 3

Tuesday, October 12, At New York

Kansas City	AB.	R.	H.	RBI.	PO.	A.
Wohlford, lf	2	1	0	0	0	0
Cowens, cf	4	0	1	0	1	0
Brett, 3b	3	1	2	1	1	0
Mayberry, 1b	4	1	1	0	11	0
McRae, dh	2	0	0	1	0	0
Poquette, rf	3	0	1	1	2	0
Nelson, ph	1	0	0	0	0	0
F. White, 2b	2	0	0	0	1	3
Rojas, ph-2b	1	0	0	0	0	1
Patek, ss	3	0	1	0	3	5
Martinez, c	2	0	0	0	5	1
Quirk, ph	1	0	0	0	0	0
Stinson, c	0	0	0	0	0	0
Hassler, p	0	0	0	0	0	0
Pattin, p	0	0	0	0	0	0
Hall, p	0	0	0	0	0	0
Mingori, p	0	0	0	0	0	0
Littell, p	0	0	0	0	0	1
Totals	28	3	6	3	24	11

New York	AB.	R.	H.	RBI.	PO.	A.
Rivers, cf	5	0	1	0	1	0
R. White, lf	3	1	0	0	0	0
Munson, c	4	1	2	0	5	2
Piniella, dh	2	1	1	0	0	0
May, ph-dh	1	0	0	0	0	0
Chambliss, 1b	4	2	2	3	10	2
Nettles, 3b	3	0	1	1	0	3
Maddox, rf	4	0	1	1	4	0
Randolph, 2b	3	0	1	0	3	3
Stanley, ss	3	0	0	0	3	4
Ellis, p	0	0	0	0	1	0
Lyle, p	0	0	0	0	0	0
Totals	32	5	9	5	27	14

Kansas City	3 0 0 0 0 0 0 0 0—3
New York	0 0 0 2 0 3 0 0 x—5

Kansas City	IP.	H.	R.	ER.	BB.	SO.
Hassler (L)	5*	4	4	4	3	3
Pattin	0†	0	1	1	1	0
Hall	⅓	1	0	0	0	0
Mingori	0†	1	0	0	0	0
Littell	2⅔	3	0	0	1	2

New York	IP.	H.	R.	ER.	BB.	SO.
Ellis (W)	8	6	3	3	2	5
Lyle (S)	1	0	0	0	1	0

*Pitched to two batters in sixth.
†Pitched to one batter in sixth.

DP—Kansas City 1, New York 2. LOB—Kansas City 3, New York 8. 2B—Poquette, Piniella, Munson, Maddox. HR—Chambliss. SB—Wohlford, Chambliss, Randolph. SF—McRae. HBP—By Ellis (McRae). PB—Munson. U—Maloney, Haller, Frantz, McCoy, Brinkman and Barnett. T—3:00. A—56,808.

Game 4

Wednesday, October 13, At New York

Kansas City	AB.	R.	H.	RBI.	PO.	A.
Cowens, cf	5	0	0	0	4	0
Poquette, lf-rf	4	0	0	0	3	0
Brett, 3b	4	0	0	0	1	2
Mayberry, 1b	3	1	0	0	9	0
McRae, rf	4	2	2	0	2	0
Wohlford, lf	0	0	0	0	3	0
Quirk, dh	2	1	1	2	0	0
Nelson, ph-dh	1	0	0	0	0	0
Rojas, 2b	3	1	2	1	1	3
F. White, pr-2b	0	1	0	0	0	0
Patek, ss	4	1	3	3	3	3
Martinez, c	3	0	1	1	1	1
Gura, p	0	0	0	0	0	0
Bird, p	0	0	0	0	0	1
Mingori, p	0	0	0	0	0	0
Totals	33	7	9	7	27	10

New York	AB.	R.	H.	RBI.	PO.	A.
Rivers, cf	4	0	1	0	5	0
R. White, lf	4	0	1	0	7	0
Munson, c	4	0	2	0	2	1
Piniella, dh	4	0	0	0	0	0
Chambliss, 1b	4	1	1	0	9	0
Nettles, 3b	4	2	2	3	0	2
Maddox, rf	1	0	0	0	1	0
Gamble, ph-rf	2	1	1	0	1	0
Velez, ph	1	0	0	0	0	0
Randolph, 2b	4	0	1	1	1	1
Stanley, ss	2	0	1	0	1	1
Hendricks, ph	1	0	1	0	0	0
Guidry, pr	0	0	0	0	0	0
Mason, ss	0	0	0	0	0	2
Alomar, ph	1	0	0	0	0	0
Hunter, p	0	0	0	0	0	1
Tidrow, p	0	0	0	0	0	0
Jackson, p	0	0	0	0	0	1
Totals	36	4	11	4	27	9

Kansas City	0 3 0 2 0 1 0 1 0—7
New York	0 2 0 0 0 0 1 0 1—4

Kansas City	IP.	H.	R.	ER.	BB.	SO.
Gura	2*	6	2	2	0	0
Bird (W)	4⅔	4	1	1	0	1
Mingori (S)	2⅓	1	1	1	0	0

New York	IP.	H.	R.	ER.	BB.	SO.
Hunter (L)	3†	5	5	5	1	0
Tidrow	3⅔	2	1	1	2	0
Jackson	2⅓	2	1	1	1	2

*Pitched to one batter in third.
†Pitched to two batters in fourth.

E—Bird. DP—Kansas City 1. LOB—Kansas City 5, New York 5. 2B—R. White, Patek 2, McRae, Gamble. 3B—Quirk, McRae. HR—Nettles 2. SF—Rojas, Quirk. U—Haller, Frantz, McCoy, Brinkman, Barnett and Maloney. T—2:50. A—56,355.

Game 5

Thursday, October 14, At New York

Kansas City	AB.	R.	H.	RBI.	PO.	A.
Cowens, cf	4	1	1	0	2	0
Poquette, lf	3	0	0	0	2	0
Wohlford, ph-lf	2	1	1	0	0	0
Brett, 3b	4	2	2	3	0	1
Mayberry, 1b	4	1	2	2	6	1
McRae, rf	4	0	0	0	3	1
Quirk, dh	4	0	0	0	0	0
Rojas, 2b	4	1	1	0	3	2
Patek, ss	4	0	1	0	5	1
Martinez, c	4	0	3	1	3	2
Leonard, p	0	0	0	0	0	0
Splittorff, p	0	0	0	0	0	0
Pattin, p	0	0	0	0	0	0
Hassler, p	0	0	0	0	0	0
Littell, p	0	0	0	0	0	0
Totals	37	6	11	6	24	8

New York	AB.	R.	H.	RBI.	PO.	A.
Rivers, cf	5	3	4	0	2	0
R. White, lf	2	2	1	1	4	0
Munson, c	5	0	3	2	4	0
Chambliss, 1b	4	2	3	3	15	0
May, dh	4	0	0	0	0	0
Alomar, pr-dh	0	0	0	0	0	0
Nettles, 3b	3	0	0	0	0	1
Gamble, rf	2	0	0	0	0	0
Randolph, 2b	3	0	0	0	1	5
Stanley, ss	3	0	0	0	1	5
Figueroa, p	0	0	0	0	0	2
Jackson, p	0	0	0	0	0	0
Tidrow, p	0	0	0	0	0	0
Totals	31	7	11	6	27	13

Kansas City	2 1 0 0 0 0 0 3 0—6
New York	2 0 2 0 0 2 0 0 1—7

None out when winning run scored.

Kansas City	IP.	H.	R.	ER.	BB.	SO.
Leonard	0*	3	2	2	0	0
Splittorff	3⅔	3	2	2	3	1
Pattin	⅓	0	0	0	0	0
Hassler	2⅓	4	2	1	3	1
Littell (L)	1⅔‡	1	1	1	0	1

New York	IP.	H.	R.	ER.	BB.	SO.
Figueroa	7†	8	4	4	0	3
Jackson	1	2	2	2	0	1
Tidrow (W)	1	1	0	0	1	0

*Pitched to three batters in first.
†Pitched to one batter in eighth.
‡Pitched to one batter in ninth.

E—Gamble, Brett. DP—New York 1. LOB—Kansas City 5, New York 9. 2B—Brett, Chambliss. 3B—Rivers. Home runs—Mayberry, Brett, Chambliss. SB—R. White, Rojas, Chambliss. SH—R. White, Gamble. SF—Chambliss. U—Frantz, McCoy, Brinkman, Barnett, Maloney and Haller. T—3:13. A—56,821.

COMPOSITE BATTING AVERAGES

New York Yankees

Player-Position	G.	AB.	R.	H.	2B.	3B.	HR.	RBI.	BA.
Hendricks, ph	1	1	0	1	0	0	0	0	1.000
Chambliss, 1b	5	21	5	11	1	1	2	8	.524
Munson, c	5	23	3	10	2	0	0	3	.435
Rivers, cf	5	23	5	8	0	1	0	0	.348
Stanley, ss	5	15	1	5	2	0	0	0	.333
R. White, lf	5	17	4	5	3	0	0	3	.294
Piniella, dh-ph	4	11	1	3	1	0	0	0	.273
Gamble, rf-ph	3	8	1	2	1	0	0	1	.250
Nettles, 3b	5	17	2	4	1	0	2	4	.235
Maddox, rf	3	9	0	2	1	0	0	1	.222
May, dh-ph	3	10	1	2	1	0	0	0	.200
Randolph, 2b	5	17	0	2	0	0	0	1	.118
Ellis, p	1	0	0	0	0	0	0	0	.000
Guidry, pr	1	0	0	0	0	0	0	0	.000
Lyle, p	1	0	0	0	0	0	0	0	.000
Figueroa, p	2	0	0	0	0	0	0	0	.000
Hunter, p	2	0	0	0	0	0	0	0	.000
Jackson, p	2	0	0	0	0	0	0	0	.000
Mason, ss	2	0	0	0	0	0	0	0	.000
Tidrow, p	3	0	0	0	0	0	0	0	.000
Alomar, ph-pr-dh	2	1	0	0	0	0	0	0	.000
Velez, ph	1	1	0	0	0	0	0	0	.000
Totals	5	174	23	55	13	2	4	21	.316

Kansas City Royals

Player-Position	G.	AB.	R.	H.	2B.	3B.	HR.	RBI.	BA.
Brett, 3b	5	18	4	8	1	1	1	5	.444
Patek, ss	5	18	2	7	2	0	0	4	.389
Martinez, c	5	15	0	5	0	0	0	4	.333
Rojas, ph-2b	4	9	2	3	0	0	0	1	.333
Mayberry, 1b	5	18	4	4	0	0	1	3	.222
Cowens, rf-cf	5	21	3	4	0	1	0	0	.190
Poquette, lf-cf	5	16	1	3	2	0	0	4	.188
Wohlford, lf-ph	5	11	3	2	0	0	0	0	.182
Quirk, ph-dh	4	7	1	1	0	1	0	2	.143
F. White, 2b-pr	4	8	2	1	0	0	0	0	.125
McRae, dh-rf	5	17	2	2	1	1	0	1	.118
Bird, p	1	0	0	0	0	0	0	0	.000
Hall, p	1	0	0	0	0	0	0	0	.000
Wathan, c	1	0	0	0	0	0	0	0	.000
Gura, p	2	0	0	0	0	0	0	0	.000
Hassler, p	2	0	0	0	0	0	0	0	.000
Leonard, p	2	0	0	0	0	0	0	0	.000
Pattin, p	2	0	0	0	0	0	0	0	.000
Splittorff, p	2	0	0	0	0	0	0	0	.000
Littell, p	3	0	0	0	0	0	0	0	.000
Mingori, p	3	0	0	0	0	0	0	0	.000
Otis, cf	1	1	0	0	0	0	0	0	.000
Stinson, ph-c	2	1	0	0	0	0	0	0	.000
Nelson, ph-dh	2	2	0	0	0	0	0	0	.000
Totals	5	162	24	40	6	4	2	24	.247

COMPOSITE PITCHING AVERAGES

New York Yankees

Pitcher	G.	IP.	H.	R.	ER.	BB.	SO.	W.	L.	ERA.
Lyle	1	1	0	0	0	1	0	0	0	0.00
Ellis	1	8	6	3	3	2	5	1	0	3.38
Tidrow	3	7⅓	6	4	3	4	0	1	0	3.68
Hunter	2	12	10	6	6	1	5	1	1	4.50
Figueroa	2	12⅓	14	8	8	2	5	0	1	5.84
Jackson	2	3⅓	4	3	3	1	3	0	0	8.10
Totals	5	44	40	24	23	11	18	3	2	4.70

Kansas City Royals

Pitcher	G.	IP.	H.	R.	ER.	BB.	SO.	W.	L.	ERA.
Hall	1	⅓	1	0	0	0	0	0	0	0.00
Splittorff	2	9⅓	7	2	2	5	2	1	0	1.93
Bird	1	4⅔	4	1	1	0	1	1	0	1.93
Littell	3	4⅔	4	1	1	1	3	0	1	1.93
Mingori	3	3⅓	4	1	1	0	1	0	0	2.70
Gura	2	10⅔	18	6	5	1	4	0	1	4.22
Hassler	2	7⅓	8	6	5	6	4	0	1	6.14
Leonard	2	2⅓	9	5	5	2	0	0	0	19.29
Pattin	2	⅓	0	1	1	1	0	0	0	27.00
Totals	5	43	55	23	21	16	15	2	3	4.40

1976
CINCINNATI REDS
VS.
PHILADELPHIA PHILLIES

For most of the summer of 1976, baseball fans had been looking forward to what promised to be a great Championship Series between two fine teams, the Cincinnati Reds and the Philadelphia Phillies, each of whom had been impressive winners in their respective divisions.

The Series began in Philadelphia with each club sending its ace lefthander to the mound, Don Gullett for the Reds and Steve Carlton for the Phils. It was no contest. After a spate of first-inning wildness, Gullett was in command all the way, finishing an eight-inning stint with only one run and two hits against his record.

Carlton, meanwhile, was the victim of some shoddy support. A liner by Pete Rose was misplayed into a triple by right fielder Ollie Brown and that gave Cincinnati one of its runs. The Reds got another of their tallies when Phillies third sacker Mike Schmidt passed up an easy throw to first base and attempted, unsuccessfully, to tag a runner off third. Carlton was finally kayoed in the eighth frame and his successor, Tug McGraw, was rapped for a couple of hits that resulted in three runs to put the game out of reach.

After Gullett left the game with an injury to his left leg, the Phils managed to score a pair of runs off reliever Rawly Eastwick. But it was a meaningless gesture and served only to make the final score a respectable 6-3.

The largest crowd ever to see a Championship Series game—62,651—saw Phillies righthander Jim Lonborg ride a 2-0 lead and a no-hitter into the sixth inning of the second contest.

But in the sixth he walked lead-off batter Dave Concepcion, who moved to second on a groundout. Rose then got the first hit off Lonborg, a single to right that plated Concepcion. Ken Griffey followed with a single sending Rose to third and took second on the futile throw to third base. Lonborg was given the hook and replaced by Gene Garber. Joe Morgan drew an intentional walk to load the bases and Tony Perez then rammed a hot liner down the first-base line. Dick Allen was unable to handle it, two runs scored and the sun had begun to set on the Phillies' season.

Cincinnati added another run before the inning was over and again pounded McGraw in the next inning to walk away with a 6-2 victory.

The third game, played at Cincinnati's Riverfront Stadium, was the most exciting. The Phils carried a 6-4 lead into the bottom of the ninth but were hit by lightning in the form of successive home runs by the first two batters of the inning, George Foster and Johnny Bench. Both blows came off reliever Ron Reed.

After Bench's homer, Garber relieved and stayed only long enough to give up a single to Concepcion. Lefty Tom Underwood came on and loaded the bases on a walk, a sacrifice and another walk. Griffey then ended the 1976 National League season by chopping a high bounding hit off the glove of first baseman Bobby Tolan. Concepcion raced home with the run that gave the Reds a 7-6 triumph and their second straight flag.

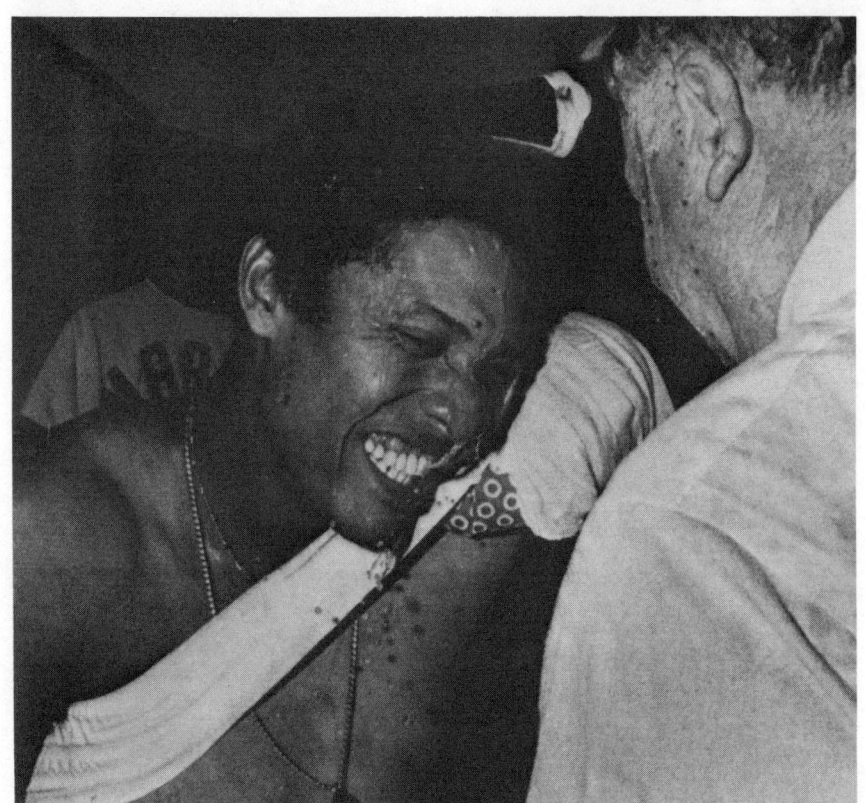

Cincinnati President Bob Howsam douses Tony Perez with champagne after the Reds' 1976 title series victory over Philadelphia.

Cincinnati's Dave Concepcion is hugged by Manager Sparky Anderson (left) and Joe Morgan (right) after scoring the pennant-clinching run.

Cincinnati	AB.	R.	H.	RBI.	PO.	A.
Rose, 3b	4	0	1	0	0	1
Griffey, rf	5	1	2	1	2	0
Morgan, 2b	3	1	0	0	3	3
Perez, 1b	4	1	2	1	9	1
Foster, lf	3	1	1	2	3	0
Bench, c	3	2	1	1	3	1
Concepcion, ss	4	1	1	0	1	5
Geronimo, cf	3	0	1	2	5	0
Nolan, p	0	0	0	0	1	0
Sarmiento, p	1	0	0	0	0	0
Borbon, p	0	0	0	0	0	0
Lum, ph	1	0	0	0	0	0
Eastwick, p	0	0	0	0	0	0
Armbrister, ph	0	0	0	0	0	0
Totals	31	7	9	7	27	11

Philadelphia .... 0 0 0 1 0 0 2 2 1—6
Cincinnati .... 0 0 0 0 0 0 4 0 3—7
One out when winning run scored.

Philadelphia	IP.	H.	R.	ER.	BB.	SO.
Kaat	6*	2	2	2	2	1
Reed	2†	5	4	4	1	1
Garber (L)	0‡	1	1	1	0	0
Underwood	1/3	1	0	0	2	0

Cincinnati	IP.	H.	R.	ER.	BB.	SO.
Nolan	5 2/3	6	1	1	2	1
Sarmiento	1	2	2	2	1	0
Borbon	1/3	0	0	0	0	0
Eastwick (W)	2	3	3	2	2	1

*Pitched to two batters in seventh.
†Pitched to two batters in ninth.
‡Pitched to one batter in ninth.

E—Rose, Perez. DP—Philadelphia 1, Cincinnati 1. LOB—Philadelphia 10, Cincinnati 6. 2B—Maddox, Schmidt 2, Luzinski, Johnstone, Bowa. 3B—Johnstone, Geronimo. HR—Foster, Bench. SH—Kaat, Armbrister. SF—Cash, Foster. WP—Eastwick. U—Stello, Vargo, Harvey, Tata, Sudol and Dale. T—2:43. A—55,047.

COMPOSITE BATTING AVERAGES
Cincinnati Reds

Player-Position	G.	AB.	R.	H.	2B.	3B.	HR.	RBI.	BA.
Gullett, p	1	4	1	2	1	0	0	3	.500
Rose, 3b	3	14	3	6	2	1	0	2	.429
Griffey, rf	3	13	2	5	0	1	0	2	.385
Bench, c	3	12	3	4	1	0	1	1	.333
Concepcion, ss	3	10	4	2	1	0	0	0	.200
Perez, 1b	3	10	1	2	0	0	0	3	.200
Geronimo, cf	3	11	0	2	0	1	0	2	.182
Foster, lf	3	12	2	2	0	0	2	4	.167
Armbrister, ph	1	0	0	0	0	0	0	0	.000
Eastwick, p	2	0	0	0	0	0	0	0	.000
Flynn, 2b	1	0	0	0	0	0	0	0	.000
Nolan, p	1	0	0	0	0	0	0	0	.000
Driessen, ph	1	1	0	0	0	0	0	0	.000
Lum, ph	1	1	0	0	0	0	0	0	.000
Sarmiento, p	1	1	0	0	0	0	0	0	.000
Zachry, p	1	1	0	0	0	0	0	0	.000
Borbon, p	2	2	0	0	0	0	0	0	.000
Morgan, 2b	3	7	2	0	0	0	0	0	.000
Totals	3	99	19	25	5	3	3	17	.253

Philadelphia Phillies

Player-Position	G.	AB.	R.	H.	2B.	3B.	HR.	RBI.	BA.
Johnstone, ph-rf	3	9	1	7	1	1	0	2	.778
Kaat, p	1	2	0	1	0	0	0	0	.500
Cash, 2b	3	13	1	4	1	0	0	1	.308
Schmidt, 3b	3	13	1	4	2	0	0	2	.308
Boone, c	3	7	0	2	0	0	0	1	.286
Luzinski, lf	3	11	3	3	2	0	1	3	.273
Maddox, cf	3	13	2	3	1	0	0	1	.231
Allen, 1b	3	9	1	2	0	0	0	0	.222
Bowa, ss	3	8	1	1	1	0	0	1	.125
Garber, p	2	0	0	0	0	0	0	0	.000
Harmon, pr	1	0	1	0	0	0	0	0	.000
McGraw, p	2	0	0	0	0	0	0	0	.000
Underwood, p	1	0	0	0	0	0	0	0	.000
Hutton, ph	1	1	0	0	0	0	0	0	.000
Lonborg, p	1	1	0	0	0	0	0	0	.000
Martin, lf	1	1	1	0	0	0	0	0	.000
Oates, c	1	1	0	0	0	0	0	0	.000
Reed, p	2	1	0	0	0	0	0	0	.000
Brown, rf	1	2	0	0	0	0	0	0	.000
Carlton, p	1	2	0	0	0	0	0	0	.000
Tolan, ph-lf-1b	3	2	0	0	0	0	0	0	.000
McCarver, c-ph	2	4	0	0	0	0	0	0	.000
Totals	3	100	11	27	8	1	1	11	.270

COMPOSITE PITCHING AVERAGES
Cincinnati Reds

Pitcher	G.	IP.	H.	R.	ER.	BB.	SO.	W.	L.	ERA.
Borbon	2	4 1/3	4	0	0	1	0	0	0	0.00
Gullett	1	8	2	1	1	3	4	1	0	1.13
Nolan	1	5 2/3	6	1	1	2	1	0	0	1.59
Zachry	1	5	6	2	2	3	3	1	0	3.60
Eastwick	2	3	7	5	4	2	1	1	0	12.00
Sarmiento	1	1	2	2	2	1	0	0	0	18.00
Totals	3	27	27	11	10	12	9	3	0	3.33

Philadelphia Phillies

Pitcher	G.	IP.	H.	R.	ER.	BB.	SO.	W.	L.	ERA.
Underwood	1	1/3	1	0	0	2	0	0	0	0.00
Lonborg	1	5 1/3	2	3	1	2	2	0	1	1.69
Kaat	1	6	2	2	2	2	1	0	0	3.00
Carlton	1	7	8	5	4	5	6	0	1	5.14
Reed	2	4 2/3	6	4	4	2	2	0	0	7.71
McGraw	2	2 1/3	4	3	3	1	5	0	0	11.57
Garber	2	2/3	2	2	1	1	0	0	1	13.50
Totals	3	26 1/3	25	19	15	15	16	0	3	5.13

Game 1

Saturday, October 9, At Philadelphia

Cincinnati	AB.	R.	H.	RBI.	PO.	A.
Rose, 3b	5	1	3	1	1	2
Griffey, rf	4	0	1	0	5	0
Morgan, 2b	2	0	0	0	1	1
Eastwick, p	0	0	0	0	0	1
Perez, 1b	3	0	0	1	8	0
Foster, lf	5	1	1	1	4	0
Bench, c	5	1	2	0	4	2
Concepcion, ss	3	2	1	0	0	2
Geronimo, cf	4	0	0	0	4	0
Gullett, p	4	1	2	3	0	0
Flynn, 2b	0	0	0	0	0	0
Totals	35	6	10	6	27	8

Philadelphia	AB.	R.	H.	RBI.	PO.	A.
Cash, 2b	4	1	1	0	2	0
Maddox, cf	4	1	2	0	2	0
Schmidt, 3b	3	0	0	1	3	3
Luzinski, lf	3	1	1	1	2	0
Allen, 1b	3	0	1	0	5	0
Brown, rf	2	0	0	0	2	0
Johnstone, ph	1	0	1	1	0	0
McCarver, c	3	0	0	0	6	0
McGraw, p	0	0	0	0	0	0
Tolan, ph	1	0	0	0	0	0
Bowa, ss	3	0	0	0	1	4
Hutton, ph	1	0	0	0	0	0
Carlton, p	2	0	0	0	0	0
Boone, c	1	0	0	0	4	0
Totals	31	3	6	3	27	7

Cincinnati ...... 0 0 1 0 0 2 0 3 0—6
Philadelphia .... 1 0 0 0 0 0 0 2—3

Cincinnati	IP.	H.	R.	ER.	BB.	SO.
Gullett (W)	8	2	1	1	3	4
Eastwick	1	4	2	2	0	0

Philadelphia	IP.	H.	R.	ER.	BB.	SO.
Carlton (L)	7*	8	5	4	5	6
McGraw	2	2	1	1	1	4

*Pitched to two batters in eighth.

E—Schmidt. DP—Philadelphia 2. LOB—Cincinnati 9, Philadelphia 5. 2B—Rose 2, Concepcion, Bench, Gullett, Cash, Luzinski. 3B—Rose, Griffey. HR—Foster. SB—Griffey, Bench, Morgan 2. SF—Schmidt, Perez. WP—McGraw, Eastwick. U—Sudol, Dale, Stello, Vargo, Harvey and Tata. T—2:39. A—62,640.

Game 2

Sunday, October 10, At Philadelphia

Cincinnati	AB.	R.	H.	RBI.	PO.	A.
Rose, 3b	5	2	2	1	1	2
Griffey, rf	4	1	2	1	4	0
Morgan, 2b	2	1	0	0	5	1
Perez, 1b	3	0	0	1	10	1
Foster, lf	4	0	0	1	0	0
Bench, c	4	0	1	0	4	1
Geronimo, cf	4	0	1	0	1	0
Concepcion, ss	3	1	0	0	1	5
Zachry, p	1	0	0	0	1	3
Driessen, ph	1	0	0	0	0	0
Borbon, p	2	1	0	0	0	0
Totals	33	6	6	4	27	13

Philadelphia	AB.	R.	H.	RBI.	PO.	A.
Cash, 2b	5	0	2	0	0	3
Maddox, cf	4	0	0	0	6	0
Schmidt, 3b	5	0	1	0	0	2
Luzinski, lf	4	1	1	1	4	0
Allen, 1b	3	1	1	0	12	0
Johnstone, rf	4	0	3	1	0	0
Boone, c	3	0	2	1	3	2
Bowa, ss	2	0	0	0	1	4
Lonborg, p	1	0	0	0	0	2
Garber, p	0	0	0	0	0	0
Tolan, ph	1	0	0	0	0	0
McGraw, p	0	0	0	0	0	1
Reed, p	0	0	0	0	0	0
McCarver, ph	1	0	0	0	0	0
Totals	33	2	10	2	27	14

Cincinnati ...... 0 0 0 0 0 4 2 0 0—6
Philadelphia .... 0 1 0 0 1 0 0 0 0—2

Cincinnati	IP.	H.	R.	ER.	BB.	SO.
Zachry (W)	5	6	2	2	3	3
Borbon (S)	4	4	0	0	1	0

Philadelphia	IP.	H.	R.	ER.	BB.	SO.
Lonborg (L)	5 1/3	2	3	1	2	2
Garber	2/3	1	1	0	1	0
McGraw	1/3	2	2	2	0	1
Reed	2 2/3	1	0	0	1	1

E—Allen. DP—Cincinnati 2. LOB—Cincinnati 5, Philadelphia 10. HR—Luzinski. SB—Griffey. SH—Boone, Lonborg. SF—Perez. WP—McGraw. U—Dale, Stello, Vargo, Harvey, Tata and Sudol. T—2:24. A—62,651.

Game 3

Tuesday, October 12, At Cincinnati

Philadelphia	AB.	R.	H.	RBI.	PO.	A.
Cash, 2b	4	0	1	1	6	5
Maddox, cf	5	1	1	1	1	0
Schmidt, 3b	5	1	3	1	1	4
Luzinski, lf	4	0	1	1	0	0
Reed, p	1	0	0	0	0	0
Garber, p	0	0	0	0	0	0
Underwood, p	0	0	0	0	0	0
Allen, 1b	3	0	0	0	11	0
Martin, lf	1	1	1	0	0	0
Johnstone, rf	4	1	3	1	2	0
Boone, c	3	0	0	0	1	0
Harmon, pr	0	1	0	0	0	0
Oates, c	1	0	0	0	1	0
Bowa, ss	3	1	1	0	3	1
Kaat, p	2	0	0	0	0	1
Tolan, lf-1b	0	0	0	0	0	1
Totals	36	6	11	6	25	13

1977 NEW YORK YANKEES VS. KANSAS CITY ROYALS

There they were, Yankee Manager Billy Martin and his boss, George Steinbrenner, shaking hands and embracing in their mutual joy after the Bronx Bombers had disposed of the Kansas City Royals in five games of the American League Championship Series.

The joy expressed in that setting was pure ecstasy. The Yankees, billed as "the best club money can buy," had to score three runs in the ninth inning to overtake the Royals in the final game, 5-3.

Pitchers Mike Torrez and Sparky Lyle were the key men in the final-game triumph. They held the Royals off the scoreboard on only four hits for the last 6⅔ innings, while the Yankees fought back from a 3-1 deficit.

The evening started in what had become typical Yankee high drama when Martin benched star outfielder Reggie Jackson, a 1-for-14 performer in the first four games.

Kansas City aggressively took a 2-0 lead in the first inning. With one out, Hal McRae got an infield single. George Brett followed with a triple to right-center. When he came up from his hard slide, Brett fired a right hand in the direction of New York third baseman Graig Nettles and the two wrestled to the ground. Both benches emptied. (In game two, McRae had set the fierce tempo in bowling over Yankee second baseman Willie Randolph on a force play in the sixth inning.)

After order was restored, Al Cowens' grounder scored Brett. A run-scoring single by Cowens in the third made the score 3-1. Enter third-game loser Torrez for a 5⅓-inning scoreless stint. Lyle, who hurled 5⅓ innings of scoreless ball to win the fourth game, followed with his second straight

Yankee Manager Billy Martin and Owner George Steinbrenner (left) get a champagne bath from Cliff Johnson after New York's 1977 title victory.

victory by setting down the Royals for the final 1⅓ innings.

The Yanks struck for one run in the eighth, with Jackson's pinch-single being a key blow. Kansas City Manager Whitey Herzog, who had already called on three pitchers—excusing starter Paul Splittorff after an impressive seven-inning performance—went to his ace starter and 20-game winner Dennis Leonard in the ninth.

Paul Blair, who started in right field in place of Jackson, opened with a single. Pinch-hitter Roy White drew a walk. Lefthander Larry Gura, who had been routed for six hits and four runs in two innings a day earlier, was summoned by Herzog to face Mickey Rivers.

Rivers, who had gone 2 for 2 against Gura's deliveries in Game 4, slapped a single to right, scoring Blair and sending White to third. Mark Littell then took the

mound and surrendered a sacrifice fly to Randolph for the go-ahead run. An insurance run followed on Brett's error.

Kansas City and New York had split their 10-game series during the 1977 season, but it was the Royals who showed no timidity, waltzing right into Yankee Stadium for a stunning 7-2 first-game victory.

The Royals flexed their muscles with three home runs and almost pulled off a triple play to end the game.

McRae's previously mentioned bodyblock of second baseman Randolph was the cause celebre in the second game.

Aroused by what they considered violent tactics by McRae, the Yankees broke a 2-2 tie with three runs in their half of the sixth. And lefty Ron Guidry held Kansas City to three hits in a 6-2 victory.

Thus, the scene shifted to Royals Stadium for Game 3 and Kansas City righthander Dennis Leonard was in complete control, limiting New York to four hits in a 6-2 triumph.

The Yankees pulled away to a 4-0 lead in three innings against Larry Gura in Game 4.

But Yankee starter Ed Figueroa couldn't stand prosperity and departed in the fourth with a 5-3 lead. Reliever Dick Tidrow yielded a run-producing double by Frank White.

Then Lyle entered with runners on first and third and two out in a one-run ball game. He quickly enticed Brett to fly out. For the next five innings, Sparky faced 16 batters, one over the minimum, while permitting only two hits.

Meanwhile, Mickey Rivers, who was 4 for 5, scored an insurance run in the ninth for the 6-4 final score.

Game 1

Wednesday, October 5, At New York

Kansas City	AB.	R.	H.	RBI.	PO.	A.
Patek, ss	4	1	2	2	6	0
McRae, dh	5	1	1	2	0	0
Brett, 3b	5	0	0	0	2	2
Cowens, rf	4	2	3	1	4	0
Otis, cf	4	0	0	0	2	0
Mayberry, 1b	3	1	1	2	3	0
Zdeb, lf	4	0	0	0	3	0
Porter, c	2	1	1	0	3	0
F. White, 2b	4	1	1	0	4	0
Splittorff, p	0	0	0	0	0	2
Bird, p	0	0	0	0	0	0
Totals	35	7	9	7	27	4

New York	AB.	R.	H.	RBI.	PO.	A.
Rivers, cf	4	1	3	0	4	0
Nettles, 3b	4	0	0	0	0	2
Munson, c	4	1	1	2	4	1
Jackson, rf	4	0	0	0	1	0
Piniella, lf	4	0	1	0	2	0
Chambliss, 1b	3	0	1	0	5	2
Johnson, dh	4	0	2	0	0	0
Randolph, 2b	4	0	1	0	4	1
Dent, ss	3	0	0	0	6	3
R. White, ph	1	0	0	0	0	0
Gullett, p	0	0	0	0	0	0
Tidrow, p	0	0	0	0	1	2
Lyle, p	0	0	0	0	0	0
Totals	35	2	9	2	27	11

Kansas City 2 2 2 0 0 0 0 1 0—7
New York 0 0 2 0 0 0 0 0 0—2

Kansas City	IP.	H.	R.	ER.	BB.	SO.
Splittorff (W)	8*	8	2	2	1	2
Bird	1	1	0	0	0	0

New York	IP.	H.	R.	ER.	BB.	SO.
Gullett (L)	2	4	4	4	2	0
Tidrow	6⅔	5	3	3	2	3
Lyle	⅓	0	0	0	0	0

*Pitched to one batter in ninth.

DP—Kansas City 1. LOB—Kansas City 5, New York 7. 2B—Patek, Randolph, Rivers. HR—McRae, Mayberry, Munson, Cowens. SB—Zdeb. U—Neudecker, Goetz, McKean, Springstead, Bremigan and Deegan. T—2:40. A—54,930.

Game 2

Thursday, October 6, At New York

Kansas City	AB.	R.	H.	RBI.	PO.	A.
Patek, ss	3	1	1	1	1	3
McRae, dh	2	0	0	0	0	0
Brett, 3b	4	0	1	0	0	3
Cowens, rf	4	0	0	0	0	0
Otis, cf	4	0	0	0	3	1
Mayberry, 1b	3	0	0	0	9	1
Zdeb, lf	3	0	0	0	1	0
Porter, c	1	1	0	0	3	0
Wathan, ph-c	1	0	0	0	2	0
White, 2b	3	0	1	0	4	3
Hassler, p	0	0	0	0	1	0
Littell, p	0	0	0	0	0	0
Mingori, p	0	0	0	0	0	0
Totals	28	2	3	1	24	11

New York	AB.	R.	H.	RBI.	PO.	A.
Rivers, cf	5	0	0	0	7	0
Nettles, 3b	4	0	0	0	0	1
Munson, c	4	1	3	0	7	2
Jackson, rf	4	1	1	0	3	0
Blair, rf	0	0	0	0	0	0
Piniella, lf	4	1	1	0	1	0
Johnson, dh	4	2	2	2	0	0
Chambliss, 1b	2	0	0	0	3	1
Randolph, 2b	4	1	2	1	3	1
Dent, ss	3	0	1	1	2	2
Guidry, p	0	0	0	0	1	0
Totals	34	6	10	4	27	7

Kansas City 0 0 1 0 0 1 0 0 0—2
New York 0 0 0 0 2 3 0 1 x—6

Kansas City	IP.	H.	R.	ER.	BB.	SO.
Hassler (L)	5⅔	5	3	3	0	3
Littell	2	5	3	1	3	1
Mingori	⅓	0	0	0	0	1

New York	IP.	H.	R.	ER.	BB.	SO.
Guidry (W)	9	3	2	2	3	7

E—Dent, Brett. LOB—Kansas City 3, New York 7. 2B—Patek, Johnson. HR—Johnson. SB—Jackson. SF—Patek. Balk—Hassler. U—Goetz, McKean, Springstead, Bremigan, Deegan and Neudecker. T—2:58. A—56,230.

Game 3

Friday, October 7, At Kansas City

New York	AB.	R.	H.	RBI.	PO.	A.
Rivers, cf	4	0	0	0	2	0
R. White, lf	4	1	2	0	2	0
Munson, c	4	0	0	0	2	0
Jackson, rf	3	0	0	0	4	1
Chambliss, 1b	4	0	0	0	9	3
Nettles, 3b	3	1	1	0	2	2
Piniella, dh	3	0	1	1	0	0
Randolph, 2b	3	0	0	0	1	3
Dent, ss	2	0	0	0	0	2
Johnson, ph	1	0	0	0	0	0
Stanley, ss	0	0	0	0	0	0
Torrez, p	0	0	0	0	2	1
Lyle, p	0	0	0	0	0	0
Totals	31	2	4	1	24	12

Kansas City	AB.	R.	H.	RBI.	PO.	A.
Poquette, rf	3	0	1	0	3	0
Otis, ph-cf	2	0	1	2	1	0
McRae, lf	4	2	2	0	2	1
Zdeb, lf	0	0	0	0	0	0
Brett, 3b	4	1	2	0	1	1
Cowens, cf-rf	4	0	0	2	2	0
Mayberry, 1b	4	0	1	1	12	0
Lahoud, dh	1	2	0	0	0	0
Wathan, ph-dh	1	0	0	0	0	0
Porter, c	4	1	3	0	6	0
Patek, ss	2	0	1	1	0	5
F. White, 2b	4	0	1	0	0	3
Leonard, p	0	0	0	0	0	0
Totals	33	6	12	6	27	10

New York 0 0 0 0 1 0 0 0 1—2
Kansas City 0 1 1 0 1 2 1 0 x—6

New York	IP.	H.	R.	ER.	BB.	SO.
Torrez (L)	5⅔	8	5	5	2	1
Lyle	2⅓	4	1	1	0	1

Kansas City	IP.	H.	R.	ER.	BB.	SO.
Leonard (W)	9	4	2	1	1	4

E—R. White, Mayberry. LOB—New York 3, Kansas City 7. 2B—R. White 2, McRae 2, Piniella, Otis, Mayberry. SF—F. White, Otis. SH—Patek 2. U—McKean, Springstead, Bremigan, Deegan, Neudecker and Goetz. T—2:19. A—41,285.

Game 4

Saturday, October 8, At Kansas City

New York	AB.	R.	H.	RBI.	PO.	A.
Rivers, cf	5	2	4	1	4	0
Nettles, 3b	5	0	2	1	0	3
Munson, c	4	1	1	2	4	0
Jackson, rf	3	0	0	0	2	0
Blair, rf	1	0	1	0	1	0
Piniella, lf	5	0	2	1	3	0
Johnson, dh	4	0	1	0	0	0
R. White, pr-dh	0	0	0	0	0	0
Chambliss, 1b	4	0	0	0	10	0
Randolph, 2b	4	2	1	0	2	2
Dent, ss	3	1	1	1	1	4
Figueroa, p	0	0	0	0	0	0
Tidrow, p	0	0	0	0	0	0
Lyle, p	0	0	0	0	0	0
Totals	38	6	13	6	27	9

Kansas City	AB.	R.	H.	RBI.	PO.	A.
Poquette, lf	3	0	0	0	0	0
Zdeb, ph-lf	2	0	0	0	0	0
McRae, dh	3	1	2	0	0	0
Brett, 3b	4	0	2	1	1	3
Cowens, rf	3	0	0	0	3	0
Mayberry, 1b	2	0	0	0	5	0
Wathan, 1b	2	0	0	0	6	0
Porter, c	4	0	0	0	3	0
Otis, cf	3	1	0	0	4	0
Patek, ss	4	2	3	1	0	4
F. White, 2b	3	0	1	2	4	4
Gura, p	0	0	0	0	0	0
Pattin, p	0	0	0	0	1	2
Mingori, p	0	0	0	0	0	0
Bird, p	0	0	0	0	0	0
Totals	33	4	8	4	27	13

New York 1 2 1 1 0 0 0 0 1—6
Kansas City 0 0 2 2 0 0 0 0 0—4

New York	IP.	H.	R.	ER.	BB.	SO.
Figueroa	3⅓	5	4	4	2	3
Tidrow	⅓	1	0	0	1	0
Lyle (W)	5⅓	2	0	0	0	1

Kansas City	IP.	H.	R.	ER.	BB.	SO.
Gura (L)	2*	6	4	4	1	2
Pattin	6†	6	2	1	0	0
Mingori	⅓	0	0	0	0	0
Bird	⅔	1	0	0	0	0

*Pitched to two batters in third.
†Pitched to one batter in ninth.

E—Patek, Mayberry. DP—New York 1, Kansas City 1. LOB—New York 8, Kansas City 6. 2B—Rivers, Dent, Munson, Patek, F. White, Piniella. 3B—Patek, Brett. SH—Dent. SF—F. White, Munson. Wild pitch—Mingori. U—Springstead, Bremigan, Deegan, Neudecker, Goetz and McKean. T—3:08. A—41,135.

Game 5

Sunday, October 9, At Kansas City

New York	AB.	R.	H.	RBI.	PO.	A.
Rivers, cf	5	2	2	1	2	0
Randolph, 2b	3	1	1	1	3	2
Munson, c	5	0	1	1	7	1
Piniella, lf	5	0	2	0	3	1
Johnson, dh	2	0	1	0	0	0
Jackson, ph-dh	2	0	1	1	0	0
Nettles, 3b	4	0	0	0	0	4
Chambliss, 1b	4	0	0	0	8	1
Blair, rf	4	1	1	0	1	0
Dent, ss	3	0	1	0	1	3
R. White, ph	0	1	0	0	0	0
Stanley, ss	0	0	0	0	1	0
Guidry, p	0	0	0	0	1	0
Torrez, p	0	0	0	0	0	0
Lyle, p	0	0	0	0	0	0
Totals	37	5	10	4	27	12

Kansas City	AB.	R.	H.	RBI.	PO.	A.
Patek, ss	5	0	0	0	1	6
McRae, lf	4	2	3	0	0	0
Brett, 3b	3	1	1	1	1	3
Cowens, rf	4	0	2	2	5	0
Otis, cf	3	0	1	0	1	0
Wathan, 1b	2	0	0	0	11	0
LaCock, ph-1b	1	0	0	0	4	0
Rojas, dh	4	0	1	0	0	0
Porter, c	4	0	1	0	3	0
F. White, 2b	4	0	1	0	1	6
Splittorff, p	0	0	0	0	0	1
Bird, p	0	0	0	0	0	0
Mingori, p	0	0	0	0	0	0
Leonard, p	0	0	0	0	0	0
Gura, p	0	0	0	0	0	0
Littell, p	0	0	0	0	0	0
Totals	34	3	10	3	27	16

New York 0 0 1 0 0 0 0 1 3—5
Kansas City 2 0 1 0 0 0 0 0 0—3

New York	IP.	H.	R.	ER.	BB.	SO.
Guidry	2⅓	6	3	3	0	1
Torrez	5⅓	3	0	0	3	4
Lyle (W)	1⅓	1	0	0	0	1

Kansas City	IP.	H.	R.	ER.	BB.	SO.
Splittorff	7*	6	2	2	2	2
Bird	⅓	2	0	0	0	1
Mingori	⅔	0	0	0	0	0
Leonard (L)	0‡	1	2	2	1	0
Gura	0‡	1	1	0	0	0
Littell	1	0	0	0	0	0

*Pitched to one batter in eighth.
†Pitched to two batters in ninth.
‡Pitched to one batter in ninth.

E—Brett. DP—New York 1. Left on base—New York 9, Kansas City 7. 2B—Piniella, McRae, Johnson. 3B—Brett. Stolen bases—Rivers, Rojas, Otis. SF—Randolph. U—Bremigan, Deegan, Neudecker, Springstead, Goetz and McKean. T—3:04. A—41,133.

COMPOSITE BATTING AVERAGES

New York Yankees

Player-Position	G.	AB.	R.	H.	2B.	3B.	HR.	RBI.	BA.
Johnson, dh-ph	5	15	2	6	2	0	1	2	.400
Blair, rf	3	5	1	2	0	0	0	0	.400
R. White, ph-lf-pr-dh	4	5	2	2	2	0	0	0	.400
Rivers, cf	5	23	5	9	2	0	0	2	.391
Piniella, lf-dh	5	21	1	7	3	0	0	2	.333
Munson, c	5	21	3	6	1	0	1	5	.286
Randolph, 2b	5	18	4	5	1	0	0	2	.278
Dent, ss	5	14	1	3	1	0	0	2	.214
Nettles, 3b	5	20	1	3	0	0	0	1	.150
Jackson, rf-ph-dh	5	16	1	2	0	0	0	1	.125
Chambliss, 1b	5	17	0	1	0	0	0	0	.059
Figueroa, p	1	0	0	0	0	0	0	0	.000
Guidry, p	2	0	0	0	0	0	0	0	.000
Gullett, p	1	0	0	0	0	0	0	0	.000
Lyle, p	4	0	0	0	0	0	0	0	.000
Stanley, ss	2	0	0	0	0	0	0	0	.000
Tidrow, p	2	0	0	0	0	0	0	0	.000
Torrez, p	2	0	0	0	0	0	0	0	.000
Totals	5	175	21	46	12	0	2	17	.263

Kansas City Royals

Player-Position	G.	AB.	R.	H.	2B.	3B.	HR.	RBI.	BA.
McRae, dh-lf	5	18	6	8	3	0	1	2	.444
Patek, ss	5	18	4	7	3	1	0	5	.389
Porter, c	5	15	3	5	0	0	0	0	.333
Brett, 3b	5	20	2	6	0	2	0	2	.300
F. White, 2b	5	18	1	5	1	0	0	2	.278
Cowens, rf-cf	5	19	2	5	0	0	1	5	.263
Rojas, dh	1	4	0	1	0	0	0	0	.250
Mayberry, 1b	4	12	1	2	1	0	1	3	.167
Poquette, rf-lf	2	6	0	1	0	0	0	0	.167
Otis, cf-ph	5	16	1	2	1	0	0	2	.125
Bird, p	3	0	0	0	0	0	0	0	.000
Gura, p	2	0	0	0	0	0	0	0	.000
Hassler, p	1	0	0	0	0	0	0	0	.000
Leonard, p	2	0	0	0	0	0	0	0	.000
Littell, p	2	0	0	0	0	0	0	0	.000
Mingori, p	3	0	0	0	0	0	0	0	.000
Pattin, p	1	0	0	0	0	0	0	0	.000
Splittorff, p	2	0	0	0	0	0	0	0	.000
LaCock, ph-1b	1	1	0	0	0	0	0	0	.000
Lahoud, dh	1	1	2	0	0	0	0	0	.000
Wathan, ph-c-dh-1b	4	6	0	0	0	0	0	0	.000
Zdeb, lf-ph	4	9	0	0	0	0	0	0	.000
Totals	5	163	22	42	9	3	3	21	.258

COMPOSITE PITCHING AVERAGES

New York Yankees

Pitcher	G.	IP.	H.	R.	ER.	BB.	SO.	W.	L.	ERA.
Lyle	4	9⅓	7	1	1	0	3	2	0	0.96
Tidrow	2	7	6	3	3	3	3	0	0	3.86
Guidry	2	11⅓	9	5	5	3	8	1	0	3.97
Torrez	2	11	11	5	5	5	5	0	1	4.09
Figueroa	1	3⅓	5	4	4	2	3	0	0	10.80
Gullett	1	2	4	4	4	2	0	0	1	18.00
Totals	5	44	42	22	22	15	22	3	2	4.50

Kansas City Royals

Pitcher	G.	IP.	H.	R.	ER.	BB.	SO.	W.	L.	ERA.
Bird	3	2	4	0	0	0	1	0	0	0.00
Mingori	3	1⅓	0	0	0	0	1	0	0	0.00
Pattin	1	6	6	2	1	0	0	0	0	1.50
Splittorff	2	15	14	4	4	3	4	1	0	2.40
Leonard	2	9	5	4	3	2	4	1	1	3.00
Littell	2	3	5	3	1	3	1	0	0	3.00
Hassler	1	5⅔	5	3	3	0	3	0	1	4.76
Gura	2	2	7	5	4	1	2	0	1	18.00
Totals	5	44	46	21	16	9	16	2	3	3.27

1977
LOS ANGELES DODGERS
VS.
PHILADELPHIA PHILLIES

The Los Angeles Dodgers returned to their second World Series in four seasons after subduing the Philadelphia Phillies in four games, one of which pivoted on a controversial call—a decision which, accurate or not, heavily influenced the outcome of an entire season.

In winning the title, the Dodgers became the first club in the nine-year history of the Championship Series to lose the first game at home and then come back to win the series. That initial game featured a pitching matchup of two of the league's outstanding lefthanders, Steve Carlton and Tommy John, each a prominent contender for the Cy Young Award later won by Carlton. Neither fared well, however. John, in large part due to poor defensive play, and Carlton, because of control problems.

John exited in the fifth inning after allowing four runs, all unearned. With two out in the first inning a poor throw by shortstop Bill Russell allowed Mike Schmidt to reach base. Greg Luzinski capitalized on the miscue, driving a 1-2 pitch over the center-field wall for a 2-0 Philadelphia lead. In the fourth inning, it was again a Russell mistake, this time a failure to touch second on a forceout, that opened the gates for two more runs. A tally off reliever Elias Sosa an inning later brought the count to 5-1 going into the home seventh.

In that inning, walks to pinch-hitter Jerry Grote and Reggie Smith, sandwiched around a Davey Lopes single, loaded the bases. After fouling away three full-count deliveries, Ron Cey, one of four Dodgers to hit 30 or more home runs in 1977, belted a game-tying grand slam.

But Gene Garber and Tug

Los Angeles Manager Tommy Lasorda enjoys the fruits of his labor after watching his Dodgers defeat Philadelphia in the 1977 N.L. title series.

McGraw blanked the Dodgers the rest of the way, and when Bake McBride, Larry Bowa and Schmidt singled in the ninth, the Phillies had captured at least a split at Dodger Stadium.

Los Angeles prevailed in Game 2, 7-1, on the strength of the second Dodger grand slam in as many nights. This time it was Dusty Baker, also a member of the 30-home run club. The fourth-inning blast broke a 1-1 tie.

Righthander Don Sutton scattered nine hits and did not walk a batter in going the route.

The season had come down to a best-of-three series, and the Phillies had ample reason for their swagger. They had won 60 of 81 games at the Vet during the regular season. Four of the six encounters with their playoff opponent had gone their way. And for a time it did seem that this advantage might tip the scales. Dodger starter Burt Hooton was visibly unnerved by the crowd's incessant hooting which accompanied his every delivery. With the bases loaded, plate umpire Harry Wen-

delstedt waved Larry Christenson, McBride and Bowa to first with free passes. What had been a 2-0 deficit had become a 3-2 lead. After eight innings, the Phils had stretched their lead to 5-3.

With two outs in the ninth inning, no one on base and the dependable Garber having retired on ground balls all eight batters he had faced, Dodger Manager Tommy Lasorda was but one out from falling into a Dodger Blue trance.

But then it happened. In the space of a few short minutes, the Phillies' season unraveled. Ironically, it was the Dodgers' bench, considered inferior in pre-series analyses, that did the damage. Aging Vic Davalillo, obtained from the Mexican League in August, beat out a drag bunt. Then Manny Mota sent a two-strike pitch to deep left field. Luzinski, oddly unreplaced by Jerry Martin, a more capable fielder, got his glove on it but could not hang on as he bulled into the wall. Mota had a double, scoring Davalillo, and when the relay escaped second baseman Sizemore, Mota

took third.

Lopes followed with a shot off the glove of third baseman Schmidt that Bowa alertly rebounded and threw to first. Bruce Froemming ruled Lopes safe and the game was tied. The Phillies insisted otherwise.

Lopes became the game-winning run when, after moving up a base on an errant Garber pickoff attempt, he scored on a Bill Russell bouncer through the middle.

Game 5 was played before 64,924 fans in a steady downpour. Los Angeles took a third straight win and with it the title. Baker's two-run homer in the second inning was more than enough for John. Stranding nine runners, he bested Carlton, 4-1.

Game 1

Tuesday, October 4, At Los Angeles

Philadelphia	AB.	R.	H.	RBI.	PO.	A.
McBride, cf	5	1	2	0	3	0
Bowa, ss	5	2	1	0	0	5
Schmidt, 3b	5	2	1	1	1	5
Luzinski, lf	3	1	1	2	1	0
Johnson, 1b	4	0	1	2	8	0
Hutton, 1b	1	0	0	0	5	0
Martin, rf	3	0	0	0	1	0
Johnstone, ph-rf	1	0	0	0	0	0
McCarver, c	3	1	1	0	4	0
Boone, c	0	0	0	0	1	0
Sizemore, 2b	3	0	0	0	3	2
Carlton, p	2	0	2	1	0	0
Garber, p	0	0	0	0	0	1
Hebner, ph	1	0	0	0	0	0
McGraw, p	0	0	0	0	0	0
Totals	36	7	9	6	27	13

Los Angeles	AB.	R.	H.	RBI.	PO.	A.
Lopes, 2b	5	1	2	1	3	3
Russell, ss	5	1	0	0	2	3
Smith, rf	4	1	0	0	1	0
Cey, 3b	4	1	2	4	2	4
Garvey, 1b	4	0	3	0	12	0
Baker, lf	3	0	1	0	0	0
Burke, cf	3	0	0	0	1	0
Monday, ph-cf	1	0	0	0	0	0
Yeager, c	4	0	0	0	6	1
John, p	1	0	0	0	0	1
Garman, p	0	0	0	0	0	0
Lacy, ph	1	1	1	0	0	0
Hough, p	0	0	0	0	0	1
Grote, ph	0	0	0	0	0	0
Sosa, p	1	0	0	0	0	0
Totals	36	5	9	5	27	13

Philadelphia	2 0 0 0 2 1 0 0 2—7
Los Angeles	0 0 0 0 1 0 4 0 0—5

Philadelphia	IP.	H.	R.	ER.	BB.	SO.
Carlton	6⅔	9	5	5	3	3
Garber (W)	1⅓	0	0	0	0	2
McGraw (S)	1	0	0	0	0	0

Los Angeles	IP.	H.	R.	ER.	BB.	SO.
John	4⅔	4	4	0	3	3
Garman	⅓	0	0	0	0	1
Hough	2	2	1	1	0	3
Sosa (L)	2	3	2	2	0	0

E—Russell 2. DP—Los Angeles 1. LOB—Philadelphia 7, Los Angeles 7. HR—Luzinski, Cey. SB—Luzinski, Garvey. SH—Sizemore. HBP—By John (Carlton). Balks—Carlton, Sosa. U—Pryor, Engel, Wendelstedt, Froemming, Rennert and Runge. T—2:35. A—55,968.

Game 2

Wednesday, October 5, At Los Angeles

Philadelphia	AB.	R.	H.	RBI.	PO.	A.
McBride, cf	4	1	2	1	0	1
Bowa, ss	4	0	1	0	0	5
Schmidt, 3b	4	0	0	0	1	1
Luzinski, lf	4	0	1	0	0	0
Hebner, 1b	4	0	2	0	11	0
Johnstone, rf	4	0	1	0	4	0
Boone, c	4	0	1	0	6	1
Sizemore, 2b	4	0	1	0	2	1
Lonborg, p	1	0	0	0	0	2
Hutton, ph	1	0	0	0	0	0
Reed, p	0	0	0	0	0	0
Brown, ph	1	0	0	0	0	0
Brusstar, p	0	0	0	0	0	0
Totals	35	1	9	1	24	11

Los Angeles	AB.	R.	H.	RBI.	PO.	A.
Lopes, 2b	4	0	1	1	2	1
Russell, ss	4	2	2	0	3	2
Smith, rf	4	1	2	1	2	0
Cey, 3b	3	1	1	0	2	1
Garvey, 1b	3	1	0	0	7	1
Baker, lf	4	1	1	4	3	0
Monday, cf	3	1	1	0	3	0
Burke, cf	0	0	0	0	0	0
Yeager, c	3	0	1	1	5	0
Sutton, p	3	0	0	0	0	2
Totals	31	7	9	7	27	7

Philadelphia	0 0 1 0 0 0 0 0 0—1
Los Angeles	0 0 1 4 0 1 1 0 x—7

Philadelphia	IP.	H.	R.	ER.	BB.	SO.
Lonborg (L)	4	5	5	5	1	1
Reed	2	2	1	1	1	2
Brusstar	2	2	1	1	0	2

Los Angeles	IP.	H.	R.	ER.	BB.	SO.
Sutton (W)	9	9	1	1	0	4

E—Sizemore, Lopes. DP—Los Angeles 2. LOB—Philadelphia 7, Los Angeles 3. 2B—Luzinski, Monday. 3B—Smith. HR—McBride, Baker. SB—Cey. SH—Cey. U—Engel, Wendelstedt, Froemming, Rennert, Runge and Pryor. T—2:14. A—55,973.

Game 3

Friday, October 7, At Philadelphia

Los Angeles	AB.	R.	H.	RBI.	PO.	A.
Lopes, 2b	5	1	1	1	3	3
Russell, ss	5	0	2	1	5	2
Smith, rf	5	0	0	0	2	0
Cey, 3b	4	1	1	0	1	4
Garvey, 1b	4	1	1	0	9	0
Baker, lf	4	1	2	2	0	0
Monday, cf	3	0	1	0	3	0
Grote, c	0	0	0	0	0	0
Yeager, c	2	0	1	1	3	0
Davalillo, ph	1	1	1	0	0	0
Burke, cf	0	0	0	0	1	0
Hooton, p	1	0	1	0	0	1
Rhoden, p	1	0	0	0	0	0
Goodson, ph	1	0	0	0	0	0
Rau, p	0	0	0	0	0	0
Sosa, p	0	0	0	0	0	1
Rautzhan, p	0	0	0	0	0	0
Mota, ph	1	1	1	0	0	0
Garman, p	0	0	0	0	0	0
Totals	37	6	12	5	27	11

Philadelphia	AB.	R.	H.	RBI.	PO.	A.
McBride, rf	4	0	0	1	1	1
Bowa, ss	4	0	0	1	0	5
Schmidt, 3b	4	0	0	0	1	6
Luzinski, lf	3	0	1	0	0	1
Martin, pr	0	0	0	0	0	0
Hebner, 1b	5	2	1	0	14	0
Maddox, cf	4	1	1	1	3	0
Boone, c	4	1	2	0	6	0
Sizemore, 2b	3	1	1	0	2	3
Christenson, p	0	0	0	1	0	0
Brusstar, p	0	0	0	0	0	0
Hutton, ph	1	0	0	0	0	0
Reed, p	0	0	0	0	0	0
McCarver, ph	1	0	0	0	0	0
Garber, p	0	0	0	0	0	1
Totals	33	5	6	4	27	17

Los Angeles	0 2 0 1 0 0 0 0 3—6
Philadelphia	0 3 0 0 0 0 0 2 0—5

Los Angeles	IP.	H.	R.	ER.	BB.	SO.
Hooton	1⅔	2	3	3	4	1
Rhoden	4⅓	2	0	0	2	0
Rau	1	0	0	0	0	1
Sosa	⅔	2	2	1	0	0
Rautzhan (W)	⅓	0	0	0	0	0
Garman (S)	1	0	0	0	0	0

Philadelphia	IP.	H.	R.	ER.	BB.	SO.
Christenson	3⅓	7	3	3	0	2
Brusstar	⅔	0	0	0	1	0
Reed	2	1	0	0	1	2
Garber (L)	3	4	3	2	0	0

E—Cey, Sizemore, Garber, Smith. DP—Philadelphia 1. LOB—Los Angeles 6, Philadelphia 9. 2B—Baker, Hooton, Cey, Russell, Hebner, Mota. SH—Garber. HBP—By Garman (Luzinski). PB—Boone. U—Wendelstedt, Froemming, Rennert, Runge, Pryor and Engel. T—2:51. A—63,719.

Game 4

Saturday, October 8, At Philadelphia

Los Angeles	AB.	R.	H.	RBI.	PO.	A.
Lopes, 2b	3	0	0	0	1	3
Russell, ss	4	0	1	1	1	5
Smith, rf	3	0	1	0	2	0
Cey, 3b	2	1	0	0	2	5
Garvey, 1b	2	0	0	0	12	0
Baker, lf	3	2	1	2	0	0
Burke, cf	4	0	0	0	1	0
Yeager, c	4	1	1	0	8	0
John, p	4	0	1	0	0	0
Totals	29	4	5	3	27	13

Philadelphia	AB.	R.	H.	RBI.	PO.	A.
McBride, rf	5	0	0	0	2	0
Bowa, ss	4	0	0	0	0	2
Schmidt, 3b	3	0	0	0	1	3
Luzinski, lf	4	1	1	0	3	0
Hebner, 1b	4	0	2	0	7	0
Maddox, cf	3	0	2	1	3	0
McCarver, c	2	0	0	0	3	0
Reed, p	0	0	0	0	0	0
Brown, ph	1	0	0	0	0	0
McGraw, p	0	0	0	0	0	0
Martin, ph	1	0	0	0	0	0
Garber, p	0	0	0	0	0	0
Sizemore, 2b	3	0	1	0	3	2
Carlton, p	2	0	0	0	0	0
Boone, c	2	0	1	0	5	1
Totals	34	1	7	1	27	8

Los Angeles	0 2 0 0 2 0 0 0 0—4
Philadelphia	0 0 0 1 0 0 0 0 0—1

Los Angeles	IP.	H.	R.	ER.	BB.	SO.
John (W)	9	7	1	1	2	8

Philadelphia	IP.	H.	R.	ER.	BB.	SO.
Carlton (L)	5*	4	4	4	5	3
Reed	1	0	0	0	0	1
McGraw	2	1	0	0	2	3
Garber	1	0	0	0	0	1

*Pitched to one batter in sixth.

DP—Philadelphia 2. LOB—Los Angeles 6, Philadelphia 9. 2B—Hebner. HR—Baker. SB—Smith. SH—Garvey. HBP—By John (Maddox). WP—Carlton. U—Froemming, Rennert, Runge, Pryor, Engel and Wendelstedt. T—2:39. A—64,924.

COMPOSITE BATTING AVERAGES

Los Angeles Dodgers

Player-Position	G.	AB.	R.	H.	2B.	3B.	HR.	RBI.	BA.
Davalillo, ph	1	1	1	1	0	0	0	0	1.000
Hooton, p	1	1	0	1	1	0	0	0	1.000
Lacy, ph	1	1	1	1	0	0	0	0	1.000
Mota, ph	1	1	1	1	1	0	0	0	1.000
Baker, lf	4	14	4	5	1	0	2	8	.357
Cey, 3b	4	13	4	4	1	0	1	4	.308
Garvey, 1b	4	13	2	4	0	0	0	0	.308
Monday, ph-cf	3	7	1	2	1	0	0	0	.286
Russell, ss	4	18	3	5	1	0	0	2	.278
Lopes, 2b	4	17	2	4	0	0	0	3	.235
Yeager, c	4	13	1	3	0	0	0	2	.231
John, p	2	5	0	1	0	0	0	0	.200
Smith, rf	4	16	2	3	0	1	0	1	.188
Garman, p	2	0	0	0	0	0	0	0	.000
Grote, ph-c	2	0	0	0	0	0	0	0	.000
Hough, p	1	0	0	0	0	0	0	0	.000
Rau, p	1	0	0	0	0	0	0	0	.000
Rautzhan, p	1	0	0	0	0	0	0	0	.000
Goodson, ph	1	1	0	0	0	0	0	0	.000
Rhoden, p	1	1	0	0	0	0	0	0	.000
Sosa, p	2	1	0	0	0	0	0	0	.000
Sutton, p	1	3	0	0	0	0	0	0	.000
Burke, cf	4	7	0	0	0	0	0	0	.000
Totals	4	133	22	35	6	1	3	20	.263

Philadelphia Phillies

Player-Position	G.	AB.	R.	H.	2B.	3B.	HR.	RBI.	BA.
Carlton, p	2	4	0	2	0	0	0	1	.500
Maddox, cf	2	7	1	3	0	0	0	2	.429
Boone, c	4	10	1	4	0	0	0	0	.400
Hebner, ph-1b	4	14	2	5	2	0	0	0	.357
Luzinski, lf	4	14	2	4	1	0	1	2	.286
Johnson, 1b	1	4	0	1	0	0	0	2	.250
Sizemore, 2b	4	13	1	3	0	0	0	0	.231
McBride, cf-rf	4	18	2	4	0	0	1	2	.222
Johnstone, ph-rf	2	5	0	1	0	0	0	0	.200
McCarver, c-ph	3	6	1	1	0	0	0	0	.167
Bowa, ss	4	17	2	2	0	0	0	1	.118
Schmidt, 3b	4	16	2	1	0	0	0	1	.063
Brusstar, p	2	0	0	0	0	0	0	0	.000
Christenson, p	1	0	0	0	0	0	0	1	.000
Garber, p	3	0	0	0	0	0	0	0	.000
McGraw, p	2	0	0	0	0	0	0	0	.000
Reed, p	3	0	0	0	0	0	0	0	.000
Lonborg, p	1	1	0	0	0	0	0	0	.000
Brown, ph	2	2	0	0	0	0	0	0	.000
Hutton, 1b-ph	3	3	0	0	0	0	0	0	.000
Martin, rf-pr-ph	3	4	0	0	0	0	0	0	.000
Totals	4	138	14	31	3	0	2	12	.225

COMPOSITE PITCHING AVERAGES

Los Angeles Dodgers

Pitcher	G.	IP.	H.	R.	ER.	BB.	SO.	W.	L.	ERA.
Rhoden	1	4⅓	2	0	0	2	0	0	0	0.00
Garman	2	1⅓	0	0	0	0	1	0	0	0.00
Rau	1	1	0	0	0	0	1	0	0	0.00
Rautzhan	1	⅓	0	0	0	0	0	1	0	0.00
John	2	13⅔	11	5	1	5	11	1	0	0.66
Sutton	1	9	9	1	1	0	4	1	0	1.00
Hough	1	2	2	1	1	0	3	0	0	4.50
Sosa	2	2⅔	5	4	3	0	0	0	1	10.13
Hooton	1	1⅔	2	3	3	4	1	0	0	16.20
Totals	4	36	31	14	9	11	21	3	1	2.25

Philadelphia Phillies

Pitcher	G.	IP.	H.	R.	ER.	BB.	SO.	W.	L.	ERA.
McGraw	2	3	1	0	0	2	3	0	0	0.00
Reed	3	5	3	1	1	2	5	0	0	1.80
Garber	3	5⅓	4	3	2	0	3	1	1	3.38
Brusstar	2	2⅔	2	1	1	1	2	0	0	3.38
Carlton	2	11⅔	13	9	9	8	6	0	1	6.94
Christenson	1	3⅓	7	3	3	0	2	0	0	8.10
Lonborg	1	4	5	5	5	1	1	0	1	11.25
Totals	4	35	35	22	21	14	22	1	3	5.40

1978
NEW YORK YANKEES
VS.
KANSAS CITY ROYALS

If you listened to the Royals, things had fallen just right for them in this third try at stopping the Yankees in the American League Championship Series. Kansas City would have its ace, Dennis Leonard, facing New York and virtually untested Jim Beattie, since Ron Guidry had been forced to pitch in the Yankees' one-game playoff against the Boston Red Sox. But as is often the case, things just didn't work out the way they were planned, with the Yankees winning the A.L. pennant three games to one.

New York ripped Leonard and three other Royals' pitchers for 16 hits and the 7-1 score could have been worse as the Yanks stranded 12 runners. While the Yankees were busy circling the base paths, Beattie, with help from Ken Clay, was limiting the Royals to just two hits.

New York went in front 1-0 in the second on a Bucky Dent single after a Roy White double. A double by Reggie Jackson and a triple by Graig Nettles increased the lead to 2-0 in the third. Leonard exited in the fifth after a leadoff single by Lou Piniella and was relieved by Steve Mingori. Jackson walked after a passed ball moved Piniella to second, and Chris Chambliss and Brian Doyle followed with run-scoring singles for a 4-0 Yankee lead.

In the Kansas City sixth, Beattie's control deserted him. After George Brett doubled to start the inning, Beattie walked Amos Otis and Pete LaCock to load the bases. Enter Clay with one out. He pitched out of trouble allowing one run on a sacrifice fly by Hal McRae and ending the inning on an Al Cowens ground out. Clay, in his relief role, did not allow a hit over the last 3⅔ innings.

Meanwhile, Jackson, who was

Yankee shortstop Bucky Dent douses teammate Reggie Jackson after New York's pennant-clinching 2-1 victory over Kansas City.

on base five times, put the game out of reach in the eighth. Royals' reliever Al Hrabosky was summoned with two runners on. The "Mad Hungarian" went through his usual psyching routine but Jackson wasn't impressed. He blasted a three-run homer to right-center, clinching the verdict.

With the Yankees now relaxed entering Game 2, the Royals lowered the boom with a hitting barrage of their own. Kansas City jumped to a 5-0 lead after just two innings, knocking out New York starter Ed Figueroa. Singles by George Brett and Amos Otis and a sacrifice fly by Darrell Porter gave the Royals their run in the first, and four runs in the second came by way of five singles and a Bucky Dent error. The Yankees cut the lead to 5-2 off Royal starter Larry Gura in the seventh,

knocking Gura out, but Freddie Patek enlisted some unexpected power in the bottom of the inning, crashing a two-run homer in the three-run inning as the Royals went on to a 10-4 win.

All George Brett did in game three was hit three homers, all off Catfish Hunter, but it was a Thurman Munson blow that decided the contest in favor of New York. Brett's first homer led off the game. But Jackson matched the clout in the New York second. No. 2 for Brett came in the third for a 2-1 Royal lead, but singles by Jackson and Pinella, following a Munson double, gave the Yankees a 3-2 lead in the fourth.

Brett's third homer tied the game leading off the fifth. But the Yankees went ahead again in the sixth on singles by White and Munson and a sacrifice fly by Jackson. In the eighth, Kansas City regained the lead, 5-4, and it was done without the aid of Brett. Porter scored Otis with a single, after Otis had doubled, and Porter scored the go-ahead run on a force out by Cowens. But the bottom of the eighth was the Royals' undoing. With one out, White singled off Royals' starter Paul Splittorff and with the righthanded-hitting Munson coming up, Manager Whitey Herzog called in reliever Doug Bird.

On the third delivery, Munson rocketed a home run into the left-center field bullpen. Rich Gossage stopped the Royals in the ninth.

With a 2-1 lead in the series, the Yankees now would be hard to beat. Guidry would be the pitcher in the crucial fourth game, while the Royals would come back with Leonard. It turned out to be a masterful pitching exhibition by both hurlers.

Brett greeted Guidry with a triple leading off the game and

scored on a McRae single. McRae promptly stole second but was left there as Guidry retired the side. It was to be the only run yielded by Guidry in eight-plus innings.

Nettles tied the game for the Yankees with a leadoff homer in the second. Leonard then settled down to retire 10 consecutive batters, five on strikeouts, until one man was out in the sixth. It was then he made his final mistake, White hitting it for a homer and a 2-1 Yankee lead.

Guidry was also sailing along and escaped a two-out, first and third situation in the fourth by fanning Patek. However, when Otis led off the ninth with a double, Manager Bob Lemon called on Gossage. He didn't disappoint Lemon. Throwing nothing but bullets, Gossage struck out pinch-hitter Clint Hurdle and retired Porter and pinch-hitter Pete LaCock on fly balls to seal the New York victory.

Game 1

Tuesday, October 3, At Kansas City

New York	AB.	R.	H.	RBI.	PO.	A.
Rivers, cf	5	0	2	0	3	0
Blair, pr-cf	1	1	0	0	2	0
Munson, c	5	0	1	0	6	0
Piniella, rf	5	2	2	0	6	0
Jackson, dh	3	2	3	3	0	0
Nettles, 3b	5	1	2	1	1	1
Chambliss, 1b	5	0	2	1	4	0
R. White, lf	4	1	1	0	1	0
Doyle, 2b	5	0	2	1	2	4
Dent, ss	5	0	1	1	0	1
Beattie, p	0	0	0	0	2	0
Clay, p	0	0	0	0	0	0
Totals	43	7	16	7	27	6

Kansas City	AB.	R.	H.	RBI.	PO.	A.
Braun, lf	4	0	0	0	5	0
Brett, 3b	4	1	1	0	2	4
Otis, cf	2	0	0	0	1	0
Porter, c	3	0	0	0	4	1
LaCock, 1b	2	0	0	0	9	0
McRae, dh	2	0	0	1	0	0
Cowens, rf	4	0	1	0	1	0
Patek, ss	3	0	0	0	4	3
Hurdle, ph	0	0	0	0	0	0
F. White, 2b	3	0	0	0	1	3
Poquette, ph	1	0	0	0	0	0
Leonard, p	0	0	0	0	0	0
Mingori, p	0	0	0	0	0	0
Hrabosky, p	0	0	0	0	0	0
Bird, p	0	0	0	0	0	1
Totals	28	1	2	1	27	12

New York	0 1 1	0 2 0	0 3 0	—7
Kansas City	0 0 0	0 0 1	0 0 0	—1

New York	IP.	H.	R.	ER.	BB.	SO.
Beattie (W)	5⅓	2	1	1	5	3
Clay (S)	3⅔	0	0	0	3	2

Kansas City	IP.	H.	R.	ER.	BB.	SO.
Leonard (L)	4*	9	3	3	0	2
Mingori	3⅔	5	3	3	3	0
Hrabosky	⅓	1	1	1	0	0
Bird	1	1	0	0	0	1

*Pitched to one batter in fifth.

E—Otis, Brett. LOB—New York 12, Kansas City 9. 2B—R. White, Jackson, Brett. 3B—Nettles. HR—Jackson. SB—LaCock, Otis. SF—McRae. PB—Porter. U—DiMuro, Garcia, Luciano, Kunkel, Phillips and Cooney. T—2:57. A—41,143.

Game 2

Wednesday, October 4, At Kansas City

New York	AB.	R.	H.	RBI.	PO.	A.
Rivers, cf	3	0	2	0	1	0
Thomasson, ph-cf	1	0	0	0	0	0
Munson, c	5	0	0	0	2	1
Piniella, lf	5	0	0	0	3	0
Jackson, rf	4	1	1	0	4	0
Nettles, 3b	4	1	1	0	1	2
Chambliss, 1b	4	1	4	1	10	1
R. White, dh	4	1	1	0	0	0
Stanley, 2b	2	0	1	0	1	2
Johnson, ph	1	0	0	0	0	0
Doyle, 2b	0	0	0	0	0	0
Blair, ph-2b	1	0	0	0	1	0
Dent, ss	4	0	2	3	0	4
Figueroa, p	0	0	0	0	0	0
Tidrow, p	0	0	0	0	0	2
Lyle, p	0	0	0	0	1	1
Totals	38	4	12	4	24	13

Kansas City	AB.	R.	H.	RBI.	PO.	A.
Brett, 3b	5	2	2	0	0	1
McRae, dh	3	0	2	0	0	0
Otis, cf	5	1	3	1	3	0
Porter, c	4	0	2	2	3	0
LaCock, 1b	5	1	2	1	11	1
Hurdle, lf	3	1	2	1	0	0
Wilson, pr-lf	1	0	0	0	1	0
Cowens, rf	4	2	1	0	0	0
Patek, ss	4	2	1	2	2	1
F. White, 2b	4	1	1	2	6	5
Gura, p	0	0	0	0	1	4
Pattin, p	0	0	0	0	0	0
Hrabosky, p	0	0	0	0	0	0
Totals	38	10	16	9	27	12

New York	0 0 0	0 0 0	2 2 0	— 4
Kansas City	1 4 0	0 0 0	3 2 x	—10

New York	IP.	H.	R.	ER.	BB.	SO.
Figueroa (L)	1*	5	5	3	0	0
Tidrow	5⅔	8	3	3	2	1
Lyle	1⅓	3	2	2	0	0

Kansas City	IP.	H.	R.	ER.	BB.	SO.
Gura (W)	6⅓	8	2	2	2	2
Pattin	⅔†	2	2	2	0	0
Hrabosky	2	2	0	0	0	1

*Pitched to four batters in second.
†Pitched to two batters in seventh.

E—Patek, Dent. DP—Kansas City 2. LOB—New York 9, Kansas City 8. 2B—LaCock. 3B—Hurdle. HR—Patek. SB—Otis 2. SH—McRae. SF—Porter. U—Garcia, Luciano, Kunkel, Phillips, Cooney and DiMuro. T—2:42. A—41,158.

Game 3

Friday, October 6, At New York

Kansas City	AB.	R.	H.	RBI.	PO.	A.
Brett, 3b	5	3	3	3	0	1
McRae, dh	5	0	0	0	0	0
Otis, cf	3	1	2	0	2	0
Porter, c	4	1	2	1	4	0
LaCock, 1b	3	0	2	0	5	0
Hurdle, lf	4	0	1	0	6	1
Wilson, pr-lf	0	0	0	0	1	0
Cowens, rf	4	0	0	1	4	0
Patek, ss	3	0	0	0	1	2
F. White, 2b	3	0	0	0	1	2
Braun, ph	1	0	0	0	0	0
Splittorff, p	0	0	0	0	0	0
Bird, p	0	0	0	0	0	0
Hrabosky, p	0	0	0	0	0	0
Totals	35	5	10	5	24	6

New York	AB.	R.	H.	RBI.	PO.	A.
Rivers, cf	1	0	1	0	2	1
Blair, ph-cf	3	0	0	0	3	0
R. White, lf	4	2	2	0	1	0
Thomasson, lf	0	0	0	0	1	0
Munson, c	4	2	3	2	7	1
Jackson, dh	3	2	2	3	0	0
Piniella, rf	4	0	2	0	2	0
Nettles, 3b	3	0	0	0	1	1
Chambliss, 1b	3	0	0	0	6	0
Stanley, 2b	3	0	0	0	2	1
Dent, ss	3	0	0	0	2	2
Hunter, p	0	0	0	0	0	1
Gossage, p	0	0	0	0	0	1
Totals	31	6	10	5	27	8

Kansas City	1 0 1	0 1 0	0 2 0	—5
New York	0 1 0	2 0 1	0 2 x	—6

Kansas City	IP.	H.	R.	ER.	BB.	SO.
Splittorff	7⅓	9	5	4	0	2
Bird (L)	0*	1	1	1	0	0
Hrabosky	⅔	0	0	0	0	1

New York	IP.	H.	R.	ER.	BB.	SO.
Hunter	6	7	3	3	3	5
Gossage (W)	3	3	2	2	0	2

*Pitched to one batter in eighth.

E—Patek. DP—Kansas City 2, New York 1. LOB—Kansas City 6, New York 2. 2B—LaCock, Porter, Munson, Otis. 3B—LaCock. HR—Brett 3, Jackson, Munson. SB—Otis. SF—Jackson. PB—Munson. U—Luciano, Kunkel, Phillips, Cooney, DiMuro and Garcia. T—2:13. A—55,535.

Game 4

Saturday, October 7, At New York

Kansas City	AB.	R.	H.	RBI.	PO.	A.
Brett, 3b	4	1	1	0	1	2
McRae, dh	4	0	1	1	0	0
Otis, cf	4	0	1	0	2	0
Cowens, rf	3	0	0	0	0	0
Hurdle, ph	1	0	0	0	0	0
Porter, c	3	0	1	0	10	0
Wathan, 1b	3	0	0	0	7	0
LaCock, ph	1	0	0	0	0	0
F. White, 2b	3	0	2	0	1	2
Patek, ss	3	0	0	0	2	2
Wilson, lf	3	0	1	0	0	0
Leonard, p	0	0	0	0	1	0
Totals	32	1	7	1	24	6

New York	AB.	R.	H.	RBI.	PO.	A.
Rivers, cf	2	0	0	0	2	0
Blair, cf	1	0	0	0	2	0
R. White, lf	4	1	1	1	1	0
Thomasson, lf	0	0	0	0	1	0
Munson, c	4	0	1	0	7	2
Jackson, dh	3	0	0	0	0	0
Piniella, rf	3	0	0	0	2	0
Nettles, 3b	3	1	2	1	3	3
Chambliss, 1b	3	0	0	0	8	0
Doyle, 2b	2	0	0	0	1	2
Dent, ss	3	0	0	0	0	1
Guidry, p	0	0	0	0	0	0
Gossage, p	0	0	0	0	0	0
Totals	28	2	4	2	27	8

Kansas City	1 0 0	0 0 0	0 0 0	—1
New York	0 1 0	0 0 1	0 0 x	—2

Kansas City	IP.	H.	R.	ER.	BB.	SO.
Leonard (L)	8	4	2	2	2	9

New York	IP.	H.	R.	ER.	BB.	SO.
Guidry (W)	8*	7	1	1	1	7
Gossage (S)	1	0	0	0	0	1

*Pitched to one batter in ninth.

DP—New York 1. LOB—Kansas City 5, New York 4. 2B—Otis. 3B —Brett. HR—Nettles, R. White. SB—McRae. WP—Leonard. U—Kunkel, Phillips, Cooney, DiMuro, Garcia and Luciano. T—2:20. A—56,356.

COMPOSITE BATTING AVERAGES

New York Yankees

Player-Position	G.	AB.	R.	H.	2B.	3B.	HR.	RBI.	BA.
Jackson, dh-rf	4	13	5	6	1	0	2	6	.462
Rivers, cf	4	11	0	5	0	0	0	0	.455
Chambliss, 1b	4	15	1	6	0	0	0	2	.400
Nettles, 3b	4	15	3	5	0	1	1	2	.333
R. White, lf-dh	4	16	5	5	1	0	1	1	.313
Doyle, 2b	3	7	0	2	0	0	0	1	.286
Munson, c	4	18	2	5	1	0	1	2	.278
Piniella, rf-lf	4	17	2	4	0	0	0	0	.235
Dent, ss	4	15	0	3	0	0	0	4	.200
Stanley, 2b	2	5	0	1	0	0	0	0	.200
Beattie, p	1	0	0	0	0	0	0	0	.000
Clay, p	1	0	0	0	0	0	0	0	.000
Figueroa, p	1	0	0	0	0	0	0	0	.000
Guidry, p	1	0	0	0	0	0	0	0	.000
Hunter, p	1	0	0	0	0	0	0	0	.000
Lyle, p	1	0	0	0	0	0	0	0	.000
Tidrow, p	1	0	0	0	0	0	0	0	.000
Gossage, p	2	0	0	0	0	0	0	0	.000
Johnson, ph	1	1	0	0	0	0	0	0	.000
Thomasson, ph-cf-lf	3	1	0	0	0	0	0	0	.000
Blair, pr-cf-ph-2b	4	6	1	0	0	0	0	0	.000
Totals	4	140	19	42	3	1	5	18	.300

Kansas City Royals

Player-Position	G.	AB.	R.	H.	2B.	3B.	HR.	RBI.	BA.
Otis, cf	4	14	2	6	2	0	0	1	.429
Brett, 3b	4	18	7	7	1	1	3	3	.389
Hurdle, ph-lf	4	8	1	3	0	1	0	1	.375
LaCock, 1b-ph	4	11	1	4	2	1	0	1	.364
Porter, c	4	14	1	5	1	0	0	3	.357
Wilson, pr-lf	3	4	0	1	0	0	0	0	.250
F. White, 2b	4	13	1	3	0	0	0	2	.231
McRae, dh	4	14	0	3	0	0	0	2	.214
Cowens, rf	4	15	2	2	0	0	0	1	.133
Patek, ss	4	13	2	1	0	0	1	2	.077
Gura, p	1	0	0	0	0	0	0	0	.000
Mingori, p	1	0	0	0	0	0	0	0	.000
Pattin, p	1	0	0	0	0	0	0	0	.000
Splittorff, p	1	0	0	0	0	0	0	0	.000
Bird, p	2	0	0	0	0	0	0	0	.000
Leonard, p	2	0	0	0	0	0	0	0	.000
Hrabosky, p	3	0	0	0	0	0	0	0	.000
Poquette, ph	1	1	0	0	0	0	0	0	.000
Wathan, 1b	1	3	0	0	0	0	0	0	.000
Braun, lf-ph	2	5	0	0	0	0	0	0	.000
Totals	4	133	17	35	6	3	4	16	.263

COMPOSITE PITCHING AVERAGES

New York Yankees

Pitcher	G.	IP.	H.	R.	ER.	BB.	SO.	W.	L.	ERA.
Clay	1	3⅔	0	0	0	3	2	0	0	0.00
Guidry	1	8	7	1	1	1	7	1	0	1.13
Beattie	1	5⅓	2	1	1	5	3	1	0	1.69
Hunter	1	6	7	3	3	3	5	0	0	4.50
Gossage	2	4	3	2	2	0	3	1	0	4.50
Tidrow	1	5⅔	8	3	3	2	1	0	0	4.76
Lyle	1	1⅓	3	2	2	0	0	0	0	13.50
Figueroa	1	1	5	5	3	0	0	0	1	27.00
Totals	4	35	35	17	15	14	21	3	1	3.86

Kansas City Royals

Pitcher	G.	IP.	H.	R.	ER.	BB.	SO.	W.	L.	ERA.
Gura	1	6⅓	8	2	2	2	2	1	0	2.84
Hrabosky	3	3	3	1	1	0	2	0	0	3.00
Leonard	2	12	13	5	5	2	11	0	2	3.75
Splittorff	1	7⅓	9	5	4	0	2	0	0	4.91
Mingori	1	3⅔	5	3	3	3	0	0	0	7.36
Bird	2	1	2	1	1	0	1	0	1	9.00
Pattin	1	⅔	2	2	2	0	0	0	0	27.00
Totals	4	34	42	19	18	7	18	1	3	4.76

1978
LOS ANGELES DODGERS
VS.
PHILADELPHIA PHILLIES

As he made the long run from center field to the dugout, with Dodgers celebrating around him, Garry Maddox must have been in a daze. Two plays earlier, Maddox had dropped a two-out line drive off the bat of Dusty Baker, prolonging Los Angeles' 10th inning. And when Bill Russell followed with a single that scored Ron Cey from second base, the Dodgers had wrapped up their second consecutive National League title and handed the Phillies their third straight loss.

The series began in Philadelphia with Phils' Manager Danny Ozark proclaiming a three-game sweep. However, after the Dodgers shelled four Phillies' pitchers for four home runs in the opener, Ozark amended his statement.

In the 9-5 Dodger victory, Steve Garvey's three-run homer followed a Davey Lopes double, a Mike Schmidt error on Russell's grounder and a run-scoring single by Reggie Smith. One inning later, Rick Monday blasted a triple to deep center field and Lopes cracked a two-run homer for a 6-1 Los Angeles lead against battered Phillies starter Larry Christenson.

In Game 2, the Phillies sent Dick Ruthven to face the Dodgers' Tommy John. Ruthven had been the ace of the staff during the second half of the season after being acquired from the Atlanta Braves, having won 11 of 15 decisions. And after pitching perfect ball against Los Angeles for the first three innings, it looked as though Ruthven and the Phillies might be ready to get back at the Dodgers.

But Los Angeles turned to the long ball once again. Lopes greeted Ruthven with a home run leading off the fourth and that

Davey Lopes returns to the dugout after hitting his 1978 Game 1 home run that helped the Dodgers build a commanding lead.

was to be all John needed in his 4-0 victory. The Dodger lefty allowed only four singles, induced hard-hitting Philadelphia to bounce into three double plays and watched as his fielders gobbled up the 18 ground balls that came weakly off the Phillies' bats.

When the scene shifted to Dodger Stadium for Game 3, Steve Carlton stopped the Dodgers with his bat and his arm. He staked the Phils to a 4-0 second-inning lead with a cannon-like three-run homer to center field off Don Sutton. The blast had followed a run-scoring single by Ted Sizemore. When the Dodgers crawled to within 4-3 after three innings, Carlton let his bat do the talking again.

Lopes opened the gates for the Phils' three-run sixth with a two-out error on Tim McCarver's grounder. Sizemore followed with a single and Carlton knocked in McCarver with another single. Sizemore scored when

Smith's throw from right field sailed past third base, and Carlton scored on Jerry Martin's pinch-double. That was to be all the Phillies needed, though Greg Luzinski added a homer in the ninth for good measure and a 9-4 victory, paving the way for Game 4 —one of the most exciting in Championship Series history.

Barring Maddox's error, the game was probably lost by the Phillies in the first inning. Schmidt doubled down the left-field line to start the game off Doug Rau. Larry Bowa walked and Maddox singled, loading the bases with none out. But Rau escaped with no runs scored. He struck out the dangerous Luzinski and retired Jose Cardenal on a liner to short and Martin on a foul pop to the catcher.

Los Angeles jumped to a 1-0 lead in the second when Baker scored Ron Cey with a single off Randy Lerch. But the Phillies came right back in the third, tak-

ing a 2-1 lead on a two-run homer by Luzinski. Cey evened matters with a homer of his own in the fourth, and Garvey gave the Dodgers the lead again with a homer in the sixth, knocking out Lerch.

Rau had given way to Rick Rhoden in the sixth and Bake McBride, hitting for Phillie reliever Warren Brusstar, tied the game again with a homer in the seventh. And that's the way it stayed until the memorable 10th.

Tug McGraw had relieved Ron Reed in the ninth and appeared in command, retiring five straight batters. But with two down in the 10th, McGraw walked Cey on four pitches and Baker followed with the liner that Maddox mishandled, Cey stopping at second. It was now McGraw against Russell. And on the second pitch, Russell singled to center, scoring Cey and giving the Dodgers the game and series.

Game 1

Wednesday, October 4, At Philadelphia

Los Angeles	AB.	R.	H.	RBI.	PO.	A.
Lopes, 2b	5	2	3	2	3	3
Russell, ss	5	1	1	0	1	2
Smith, rf	3	1	1	1	1	0
North, cf	1	0	0	0	0	0
Garvey, 1b	5	3	3	4	6	1
Cey, 3b	5	0	2	1	0	1
Baker, lf	3	0	1	0	1	0
Monday, cf-rf	4	1	1	0	4	0
Yeager, c	4	1	1	1	10	0
Hooton, p	2	0	0	0	1	0
Welch, p	2	0	0	0	0	1
Totals	39	9	13	9	27	8

Philadelphia	AB.	R.	H.	RBI.	PO.	A.
McBride, rf	5	1	1	0	1	0
Bowa, ss	5	1	3	0	0	4
Maddox, cf	5	0	2	2	4	0
Luzinski, lf	4	1	1	0	1	1
Hebner, 1b	4	0	1	1	11	0
Schmidt, 3b	3	0	0	1	2	4
Boone, c	4	0	1	0	6	1
Sizemore, 2b	4	1	2	0	2	3
Christenson, p	1	0	0	0	0	0
Brusstar, p	0	0	0	0	0	0
Gonzalez, ph	1	0	0	0	0	0
Eastwick, p	0	0	0	0	0	0
McCarver, ph	1	0	0	0	0	0
McGraw, p	0	0	0	0	0	0
Martin, ph	1	1	1	1	0	0
Totals	38	5	12	5	27	13

Los Angeles	0 0 4	2 1 1	0 0 1	—9
Philadelphia	0 1 0	0 3 0	0 0 1	—5

Los Angeles	IP.	H.	R.	ER.	BB.	SO.
Hooton	4⅔	10	4	4	0	5
Welch (W)	4⅓	2	1	1	0	5

Philadelphia	IP.	H.	R.	ER.	BB.	SO.
Christenson (L)	4⅓	7	7	6	1	3
Brusstar	⅔	1	0	0	0	0
Eastwick	1	3	1	1	0	1
McGraw	3	2	1	1	3	3

E—Lopes, Schmidt. DP—Los Angeles 1, Philadelphia 1. LOB—Los Angeles 8, Philadelphia 7. 2B—Lopes. 3B—Luzinski, Monday, Garvey. HR—Garvey 2, Lopes, Yeager, Martin. SF—Schmidt. HBP—By Eastwick (Smith). U—Weyer, Colosi, Olsen, Davidson, W. Williams and McSherry. T—2:37. A—63,460.

Game 2

Thursday, October 5, At Philadelphia

Los Angeles	AB.	R.	H.	RBI.	PO.	A.
Lopes, 2b	4	1	3	3	4	4
Russell, ss	4	0	1	0	1	9
Smith, rf	4	0	1	0	0	0
North, cf	0	0	0	0	0	0
Garvey, 1b	4	0	0	0	16	0
Cey, 3b	4	0	0	0	0	7
Baker, lf	4	1	1	0	0	0
Monday, cf-rf	4	1	1	0	2	0
Yeager, c	3	1	1	1	4	1
John, p	3	0	0	0	0	0
Totals	34	4	8	4	27	21

Philadelphia	AB.	R.	H.	RBI.	PO.	A.
Schmidt, 3b	4	0	1	0	0	4
Bowa, ss	4	0	0	0	1	4
Maddox, cf	4	0	1	0	5	0
Luzinski, lf	3	0	1	0	2	0
Cardenal, 1b	2	0	0	0	10	0
Boone, c	3	0	1	0	5	0
Martin, rf	2	0	0	0	1	0
Sizemore, 2b	3	0	0	0	3	1
Ruthven, p	1	0	0	0	0	0
Brusstar, p	0	0	0	0	0	0
Morrison, ph	1	0	0	0	0	0
Reed, p	0	0	0	0	0	0
Foote, ph	1	0	0	0	0	0
McGraw, p	0	0	0	0	0	0
Totals	28	0	4	0	27	9

Los Angeles	0 0 0	1 2 0	1 0 0	—4
Philadelphia	0 0 0	0 0 0	0 0 0	—0

Los Angeles	IP.	H.	R.	ER.	BB.	SO.
John (W)	9	4	0	0	2	4

Philadelphia	IP.	H.	R.	ER.	BB.	SO.
Ruthven (L)	4⅔	6	3	3	0	3
Brusstar	1⅓	0	0	0	0	0
Reed	2	2	1	1	0	1
McGraw	1	0	0	0	1	0

DP—Los Angeles 3. LOB—Los Angeles 5, Philadelphia 3. 2B—Smith, Baker. 3B—Lopes. HR—Lopes. SB—Yeager. SH—John. U—Colosi, Olsen, Davidson, W. Williams, McSherry and Weyer. T—2:06. A—60,642.

Game 3

Friday, October 6, At Los Angeles

Philadelphia	AB.	R.	H.	RBI.	PO.	A.
McBride, rf	3	0	0	0	0	0
Martin, ph-rf	2	0	1	1	1	0
Bowa, ss	5	0	1	0	2	5
Maddox, cf	5	1	1	0	3	0
Luzinski, lf	5	1	3	1	1	0
Hebner, 1b	4	0	0	0	10	0
Schmidt, 3b	4	1	1	0	1	5
McCarver, c	3	2	0	1	8	0
Sizemore, 2b	2	2	2	1	1	2
Carlton, p	4	2	2	4	0	0
Totals	37	9	11	8	27	12

Los Angeles	AB.	R.	H.	RBI.	PO.	A.
Lopes, 2b	4	0	0	0	2	2
North, cf	4	0	0	0	2	0
Smith, rf	4	1	1	0	2	0
Garvey, 1b	4	2	2	2	16	2
Cey, 3b	3	1	1	1	2	3
Baker, lf	3	0	1	0	0	0
Russell, ss	4	0	2	1	0	2
Yeager, c	3	0	0	0	2	0
Lacy, ph	1	0	0	0	0	0
Sutton, p	2	0	0	0	0	1
Rautzhan, p	0	0	0	0	0	1
Mota, ph	1	0	1	0	0	0
Hough, p	0	0	0	0	1	1
Ferguson, ph	1	0	0	0	0	0
Totals	34	4	8	4	27	12

Philadelphia	0 4 0	0 0 3	1 0 1	—9
Los Angeles	0 1 2	0 0 0	0 1 0	—4

Philadelphia	IP.	H.	R.	ER.	BB.	SO.
Carlton (W)	9	8	4	4	2	8

Los Angeles	IP.	H.	R.	ER.	BB.	SO.
Sutton (L)	5⅔	7	7	4	2	0
Rautzhan	1⅓	3	1	1	2	0
Hough	2	1	1	1	0	1

E—Lopes, Smith, Schmidt. DP—Philadelphia 2. LOB—Philadelphia 7, Los Angeles 5. 2B—Schmidt, Martin, Russell, Garvey, Mota. HR—Carlton, Luzinski, Garvey. SH—Sizemore, Hebner. U—Olsen, Davidson, W. Williams, McSherry, Weyer and Colosi. T—2:18. A—55,043.

Game 4

Saturday, October 7, At Los Angeles

Philadelphia	AB.	R.	H.	RBI.	PO.	A.
Schmidt, 3b	4	0	1	0	0	5
Bowa, ss	4	1	2	0	2	3
Maddox, cf	5	0	1	0	4	0
Luzinski, lf	4	1	1	2	1	0
Cardenal, 1b	4	0	1	0	11	0
Martin, rf	4	0	0	0	5	0
Boone, c	4	0	0	0	5	1
Sizemore, 2b	4	0	1	0	1	2
Lerch, p	2	0	0	0	0	1
Brusstar, p	0	0	0	0	0	0
McBride, ph	1	1	1	1	0	0
Reed, p	0	0	0	0	0	0
Hebner, ph	1	0	0	0	0	0
McGraw, p	0	0	0	0	0	0
Totals	37	3	8	3	29	12

Los Angeles	AB.	R.	H.	RBI.	PO.	A.
Lopes, 2b	5	0	1	0	1	1
North, cf	3	0	0	0	7	0
Monday, ph-cf	2	0	0	0	0	0
Smith, rf	5	0	0	0	2	0
Garvey, 1b	5	1	2	1	6	2
Cey, 3b	4	3	2	1	0	2
Baker, lf	5	0	4	1	4	0
Russell, ss	4	0	3	1	2	1
Yeager, c	3	0	1	0	5	1
Lacy, ph	1	0	0	0	0	0
Grote, c	0	0	0	0	2	0
Rau, p	1	0	0	0	1	0
Mota, ph	0	0	0	0	0	0
Rhoden, p	1	0	0	0	0	2
Ferguson, ph	1	0	0	0	0	0
Forster, p	0	0	0	0	0	0
Totals	40	4	13	4	30	9

Philadelphia	0 0 2	0 0 0	1 0 0	0	—3
Los Angeles	0 1 0	1 0 1	0 0 0	1	—4

Two out when winning run scored.

Philadelphia	IP.	H.	R.	ER.	BB.	SO.
Lerch	5⅓	7	3	3	0	0
Brusstar	⅔	1	0	0	1	0
Reed	2	4	0	0	0	1
McGraw (L)	1⅔	1	1	0	1	2

Los Angeles	IP.	H.	R.	ER.	BB.	SO.
Rau	5	5	2	2	2	1
Rhoden	4	2	1	1	1	3
Forster (W)	1	1	0	0	0	2

E—Boone, Maddox. DP—Philadelphia 1. LOB—Philadelphia 7, Los Angeles 10. 2B—Schmidt, Cey, Baker. 3B—Sizemore. HR—Luzinski, Cey, Garvey, McBride. SB—Lopes. SH—Mota. U—Davidson, W. Williams, McSherry, Weyer, Colosi and Olsen. T—2:53. A—55,124.

COMPOSITE BATTING AVERAGES

Los Angeles Dodgers

Player-Position	G.	AB.	R.	H.	2B.	3B.	HR.	RBI.	BA.
Mota, ph	2	1	0	1	1	0	0	0	1.000
Baker, lf	4	15	1	7	2	0	0	1	.467
Russell, ss	4	17	1	7	1	0	0	2	.412
Garvey, 1b	4	18	6	7	1	1	4	7	.389
Lopes, 2b	4	18	3	7	1	1	2	5	.389
Cey, 3b	4	16	4	5	1	0	1	3	.313
Yeager, c	4	13	2	3	0	0	1	2	.231
Monday, cf-rf-ph	3	10	2	2	0	1	0	0	.200
Smith, rf	4	16	2	3	1	0	0	1	.188
Grote, c	1	0	0	0	0	0	0	0	.000
Hough, p	1	0	0	0	0	0	0	0	.000
Forster, p	1	0	0	0	0	0	0	0	.000
Rautzhan, p	1	0	0	0	0	0	0	0	.000
Rau, p	1	1	0	0	0	0	0	0	.000
Rhoden, p	1	1	0	0	0	0	0	0	.000
Hooton, p	1	2	0	0	0	0	0	0	.000
Sutton, p	1	2	0	0	0	0	0	0	.000
Welch, p	1	2	0	0	0	0	0	0	.000
Ferguson, ph	2	2	0	0	0	0	0	0	.000
Lacy, ph	2	2	0	0	0	0	0	0	.000
John, p	1	3	0	0	0	0	0	0	.000
North, cf	4	8	0	0	0	0	0	0	.000
Totals	4	147	21	42	8	3	8	21	.286

Philadelphia Phillies

Player-Position	G.	AB.	R.	H.	2B.	3B.	HR.	RBI.	BA.
Carlton, p	1	4	2	2	0	0	1	4	.500
Sizemore, 2b	4	13	3	5	0	1	0	1	.385
Luzinski, lf	4	16	3	6	0	1	2	3	.375
Bowa, ss	4	18	2	6	0	0	0	0	.333
Maddox, cf	4	19	1	5	0	0	0	2	.263
McBride, rf-ph	3	9	2	2	0	0	1	1	.222
Martin, ph-rf	4	9	1	2	1	0	1	2	.222
Schmidt, 3b	4	15	1	3	2	0	0	1	.200
Boone, c	3	11	0	2	0	0	0	0	.182
Cardenal, 1b	2	6	0	1	0	0	0	0	.167
Hebner, 1b-ph	3	9	0	1	0	0	0	1	.111
Christenson, p	1	1	0	0	0	0	0	0	.000
Eastwick, p	1	0	0	0	0	0	0	0	.000
Reed, p	2	0	0	0	0	0	0	0	.000
Brusstar, p	3	0	0	0	0	0	0	0	.000
McGraw, p	3	0	0	0	0	0	0	0	.000
Foote, ph	1	1	0	0	0	0	0	0	.000
Gonzalez, ph	1	1	0	0	0	0	0	0	.000
Morrison, ph	1	1	0	0	0	0	0	0	.000
Ruthven, p	1	1	0	0	0	0	0	0	.000
Lerch, p	1	2	0	0	0	0	0	0	.000
McCarver, ph-c	2	4	2	0	0	0	0	1	.000
Totals	4	140	17	35	3	2	5	16	.250

COMPOSITE PITCHING AVERAGES

Los Angeles Dodgers

Pitcher	G.	IP.	H.	R.	ER.	BB.	SO.	W.	L.	ERA.
John	1	9	4	0	0	2	4	1	0	0.00
Forster	1	1	1	0	0	0	2	1	0	0.00
Welch	1	4⅓	2	1	1	0	5	1	0	2.08
Rhoden	1	4	2	1	1	1	3	0	0	2.25
Rau	1	5	5	2	2	2	1	0	0	3.60
Hough	1	2	1	1	1	0	1	0	0	4.50
Sutton	1	5⅔	7	7	4	2	0	0	1	6.35
Rautzhan	1	1⅓	3	1	1	2	0	0	0	6.75
Hooton	1	4⅔	10	4	4	0	5	0	0	7.71
Totals	4	37	35	17	14	9	21	3	1	3.41

Philadelphia Phillies

Pitcher	G.	IP.	H.	R.	ER.	BB.	SO.	W.	L.	ERA.
Brusstar	3	2⅔	2	0	0	1	0	0	0	0.00
McGraw	3	5⅔	3	2	1	5	5	0	1	1.59
Reed	2	4	6	1	1	0	2	0	0	2.25
Carlton	1	9	8	4	4	2	8	1	0	4.00
Lerch	1	5⅓	7	3	3	0	0	0	0	5.06
Ruthven	1	4⅔	6	3	3	0	3	0	1	5.79
Eastwick	1	1	3	1	1	0	1	0	0	9.00
Christenson	1	4⅓	7	7	6	1	3	0	1	12.46
Totals	4	36⅔	42	21	19	9	22	1	3	4.66

1979
BALTIMORE ORIOLES VS. CALIFORNIA ANGELS

"I've seen that play a hundred times before," said Baltimore shortstop Mark Belanger. "But by another third baseman."

"I thought of Brooks Robinson," said Brooks Robinson.

Memories. Of diving stops. Of World Series gems. Of Brooks Robinson.

But Brooks was retired and those sparkling plays were now only memories.... The California Angels had the bases loaded with one out in the fifth inning, trailing the Baltimore Orioles, 3-0, in the fourth game of the American League Championship Series. The Orioles led the Series two games to one, but the potential tying runs were on the bases.

Shortstop Jim Anderson was at the plate against Scott McGregor with 43,199 Anaheim Stadium fans on their feet, sensing their Angels were going to turn things around.

Anderson swung at the second pitch and hit a vicious one-hopper down the third-base line. It looked like at least a double as the ball sped over the bag. Two runs would have scored for sure, maybe three. Doug DeCinces, who had never really escaped the shadow of Brooks Robinson at third base in the eyes of Orioles' rooters, dived to his right and somehow snared the ball. He recovered, straightened up and, while standing on third, threw to first to complete the double play and end the Angels' threat.

McGregor went on to hurl a six-hit shutout and the Orioles won 8-0 for a 3-1 Series triumph and their first visit to the World Series since 1971.

Pat Kelly's seventh-inning homer closed out the scoring and was the second three-run blast off California reliever John Montague. However, it was far less dra-

California shortstop Jim Anderson looks on as Baltimore's Al Bumbry gets to his feet after stealing second base in Game 2 of the 1979 Championship Series.

matic than the first one.

With two out in the 10th inning of the first game, the score deadlocked, 3-3, and DeCinces and Al Bumbry aboard via a single and intentional walk, respectively, pinch-hitter John Lowenstein strolled to the plate against Montague.

Lowenstein, sidelined for much of the latter part of the season because of a severely sprained ankle, sliced a two-strike pitch to the opposite field, just over the left-field wall, to break up the game before 52,787 at Baltimore's Memorial Stadium.

Jim Palmer hurled the first nine innings, yielding seven hits, including a homer and double by Dan Ford, before Don Stanhouse pitched a perfect 10th inning to

gain credit for the victory.

The Orioles sent 23-game winner Mike Flanagan to the mound in Game 2 and, after Ford connected off Flanagan in the first inning for his second homer in as many games, the A.L. Cy Young Award winner was given a 9-1 cushion in the first three innings, only to see it dwindle to one run before Stanhouse slowed the game down to his pace and saved a 9-8 victory.

The Orioles had scored four runs in their half of the first and added four more in the second, highlighted by first baseman Eddie Murray's 400-foot homer. Kiko Garcia's RBI single in the third made the score 9-1.

After the Angels cuffed Flanagan for single runs in the sixth and seventh, they knocked the lefthander from the mound in the eighth, scoring three more runs, aided by a Murray error.

Stanhouse put gasoline on the fire for Flanagan in the eighth when he yielded a run-scoring single by Don Baylor and a sacrifice fly, reducing Baltimore's lead to 9-6.

In the ninth, Stanhouse permitted a walk, a pinch-double by Willie Davis, an infield out for one run and an RBI single by Carney Lansford, sending Baltimore skipper Earl Weaver to the mound.

"I was going to leave him (Stanhouse) in there until they tied the score," Weaver said later, after watching the Angels load the bases on a single by Ford and an intentional walk to Baylor, before Brian Downing grounded into a forceout to put a halt to the nail-biting.

With no days off for travel, the scene shifted to Anaheim Stadium for Game 3, where high drama once again dominated.

The Orioles were only two outs away from sweeping the series when the Angels struck back for a 4-3 victory.

Dennis Martinez spaced seven hits in the first eight innings prior to permitting a one-out double to Rod Carew in the ninth, bringing Stanhouse to the mound for the third straight game.

A walk to Downing preceded Bobby Grich's liner to center field where Al Bumbry, unable to hear the crack of the bat because of the roar of the crowd, got a late jump on the ball and dropped it for an error. Carew scored to tie the game, 3-3, with Downing stopping at second.

When Larry Harlow followed with a looping double down the left-field line, Downing raced home with the winning run.

The ecstasy was short-lived for the Angels, who finally made it to the playoffs after 19 years of trying.

Game 1

Wednesday, October 3, At Baltimore

California	AB.	R.	H.	RBI.	PO.	A.
Miller, cf	5	1	1	0	2	1
Lansford, 3b	4	0	0	0	0	3
Ford, rf	4	1	2	2	3	0
Baylor, dh	4	0	0	0	0	0
Carew 1b	4	1	3	0	8	1
Downing, c	4	0	0	0	9	0
Grich, 2b	3	0	1	1	1	3
Harlow, lf	4	0	0	0	4	0
Anderson, ss	3	0	0	0	1	2
Davis, ph	1	0	0	0	0	0
Campaneris, ss	0	0	0	0	0	0
Ryan, p	0	0	0	0	0	0
Montague, p	0	0	0	0	1	1
Totals	36	3	7	3	29	11

Baltimore	AB.	R.	H.	RBI.	PO.	A.
Bumbry, cf	4	1	0	0	3	0
Belanger, ss	4	0	1	1	0	5
Lowenstein, ph	1	1	1	3	0	0
Singleton, rf	3	0	0	0	1	0
Murray, 1b	2	0	0	0	13	1
Kelly, lf	3	1	1	0	3	0
May, dh	4	0	0	0	0	0
DeCinces, 3b	3	2	1	1	2	3
Dauer, 2b	3	0	1	0	3	3
Dempsey, c	3	1	1	1	4	1
Crowley, ph	1	0	0	0	0	0
Palmer, p	0	0	0	0	1	1
Stanhouse, p	0	0	0	0	0	0
Totals	31	6	6	6	30	14

California	1 0 1 0 0 1 0 0 0 0—3
Baltimore	0 0 2 1 0 0 0 0 0 3—6

Two out when winning run scored.

California	IP.	H.	R.	ER.	BB.	SO.
Ryan	7	4	3	1	3	8
Montague (L)	2⅔	2	3	3	2	1

Baltimore	IP.	H.	R.	ER.	BB.	SO.
Palmer	9	7	3	3	2	3
Stanhouse (W)	1	0	0	0	0	0

E—Grich. DP—California 2. LOB—California 5, Baltimore 3. 2B—Ford, Dempsey, Carew, Grich. HR—Ford, Lowenstein. SB—Kelly. SH—Dauer. SF—DeCinces. WP—Ryan. PB—Dempsey. U—Barnett, Ford, Evans, Denkinger, Clark and Kosc. T—3:10. A—52,787.

Game 2

Thursday, October 4, At Baltimore

California	AB.	R.	H.	RBI.	PO.	A.
Carew, 1b	5	2	1	1	10	0
Lansford, 3b	5	1	3	3	0	1
Ford, rf	5	1	2	1	0	0
Baylor, dh	4	1	2	1	0	0
Downing, c	4	0	1	1	6	0
Grich, 2b	3	0	0	1	1	3
Clark, lf	3	0	0	0	3	0
Harlow, ph	0	0	0	0	0	0
Miller, cf	4	1	0	0	2	0
Anderson, ss	2	0	0	0	2	3
Rettenmund, ph	0	0	0	0	0	0
Thon, pr-ss	0	1	0	0	0	0
Davis, ph	1	1	1	0	0	0
Frost, p	0	0	0	0	0	0
Clear, p	0	0	0	0	0	0
Aase, p	0	0	0	0	0	0
Totals	36	8	10	8	24	7

Baltimore	AB.	R.	H.	RBI.	PO.	A.
Bumbry, cf	4	2	3	0	3	0
Garcia, ss	3	1	2	2	2	9
Singleton, rf	5	1	1	0	0	0
Murray, 1b	4	2	2	4	13	0
Lowenstein, lf	3	1	0	0	3	0
Kelly, dh	4	1	1	1	0	0
DeCinces, 3b	3	1	1	1	1	2
Dauer, 2b	4	0	0	0	3	5
Dempsey, c	4	0	1	0	2	0
Flanagan, p	0	0	0	0	0	0
Stanhouse, p	0	0	0	0	0	0
Totals	34	9	11	8	27	16

California	1 0 0 0 0 1 1 3 2—8
Baltimore	4 4 1 0 0 0 0 0 x—9

California	IP.	H.	R.	ER.	BB.	SO.
Frost (L)	1⅓	5	6	5	3	0
Clear	5⅔	4	3	3	2	3
Aase	1	2	0	0	0	2

Baltimore	IP.	H.	R.	ER.	BB.	SO.
Flanagan (W)	7*	6	6	4	1	2
Stanhouse	2	4	2	2	2	0

*Pitched to three batters in eighth.

E—Ford, Murray. DP—California 1. LOB—California 6, Baltimore 6. 2B—Carew, Davis. HR—Ford, Murray. SB—Bumbry 2. SF—Grich, Downing. WP—Clear. U—Ford, Evans, Denkinger, Clark, Kosc and Barnett. T—2:51. A—52,108.

Game 3

Friday, October 5, At California

Baltimore	AB.	R.	H.	RBI.	PO.	A.
Bumbry, cf	5	1	1	0	1	0
Garcia, ss	3	0	0	0	2	2
Crowley, ph	1	0	1	1	0	0
Belanger, pr-ss	1	0	0	0	0	0
Singleton, rf	4	2	2	0	2	1
Murray, 1b	2	0	2	0	8	2
May, dh	3	0	1	1	0	0
DeCinces, 3b	3	0	0	1	0	1
Roenicke, lf	1	0	0	0	2	1
Lowenstein, ph-lf	1	0	0	0	2	0
Dauer, 2b	4	0	1	0	3	4
Skaggs, c	4	0	0	0	3	1
D. Martinez, p	0	0	0	0	2	0
Stanhouse, p	0	0	0	0	0	0
Totals	32	3	8	3	25	12

California	AB.	R.	H.	RBI.	PO.	A.
Miller, cf	4	0	1	0	7	1
Lansford, 3b	4	1	1	0	0	3
Ford, rf	4	0	1	1	2	0
Baylor, dh	4	1	1	1	0	0
Carew, 1b	4	1	2	0	7	0
Downing, c	3	1	1	0	8	0
Grich, 2b	4	0	0	0	1	1
Harlow, lf	4	0	1	1	2	0
Anderson, ss	3	0	1	0	0	3
Tanana, p	0	0	0	0	0	0
Aase, p	0	0	0	0	0	1
Totals	34	4	9	3	27	9

Baltimore	0 0 0 1 0 1 1 0 0—3
California	1 0 0 1 0 0 0 0 2—4

One out when winning run scored.

Baltimore	IP.	H.	R.	ER.	BB.	SO.
D. Martinez	8⅓	8	3	3	0	4
Stanhouse (L)	0†	1	1	0	1	0

California	IP.	H.	R.	ER.	BB.	SO.
Tanana	5*	6	2	2	2	3
Aase (W)	4	2	1	1	2	4

*Pitched to three batters in sixth.
†Pitched to three batters in ninth.

E—Garcia, Murray, Bumbry. DP—Baltimore 2, California 2. LOB—Baltimore 8, California 6. 2B—Singleton, Carew, Harlow. 3B—Bumbry. HR —Baylor. SB—Lansford, Carew. SF—DeCinces. HBP—By Tanana (Roenicke). U—Evans, Denkinger, Clark, Kosc, Barnett and Ford. T—2:59. A—43, 199.

Game 4

Saturday, October 6, At California

Baltimore	AB.	R.	H.	RBI.	PO.	A.
Bumbry, cf	3	1	0	0	3	0
Garcia, ss	5	0	1	0	2	5
Belanger, ss	0	0	0	0	0	1
Singleton, rf	4	1	3	2	2	0
Murray, 1b	4	1	1	1	10	0
Lowenstein, lf	1	0	0	0	1	0
Roenicke, ph-lf	4	1	1	1	1	0
Kelly, dh	4	1	2	3	0	0
DeCinces, 3b	4	1	2	0	2	2
Smith, 2b	4	0	0	0	1	2
Dauer, 2b	0	0	0	0	1	0
Dempsey, c	3	2	2	1	4	0
McGregor, p	0	0	0	0	0	0
Totals	36	8	12	8	27	10

California	AB.	R.	H.	RBI.	PO.	A.
Carew, 1b	4	0	1	0	9	0
Lansford, 3b	4	0	1	0	4	1
Ford, rf	4	0	0	0	1	0
Baylor, lf	4	0	0	0	4	0
Downing, c	4	0	1	0	4	0
Grich, 2b	3	0	1	0	1	5
Rettenmund, dh	2	0	0	0	0	0
Miller, cf	3	0	2	0	3	0
Anderson, ss	3	0	0	0	1	3
Knapp, p	0	0	0	0	0	0
LaRoche, p	0	0	0	0	0	0
Frost, p	0	0	0	0	0	0
Montague, p	0	0	0	0	0	1
Barlow, p	0	0	0	0	0	0
Totals	31	0	6	0	27	10

Baltimore	0 0 2 1 0 0 5 0 0—8
California	0 0 0 0 0 0 0 0 0—0

Baltimore	IP.	H.	R.	ER.	BB.	SO.
McGregor (W)	9	6	0	0	1	4

California	IP.	H.	R.	ER.	BB.	SO.
Knapp (L)	2⅓	5	2	2	1	0
LaRoche	1⅓	2	1	1	1	1
Frost	3	3	4	4	2	1
Montague	1⅓	2	1	1	0	1
Barlow	1	0	0	0	0	0

E—Garcia. DP—Baltimore 3, California 2. LOB —Baltimore 6, California 5. 2B—DeCinces, Dempsey, Singleton. HR—Kelly. SB—Kelly, Dempsey. SF—Singleton. WP—Frost. U—Denkinger, Clark, Kosc, Barnett, Ford and Evans. T—2:56. A—43,199.

COMPOSITE BATTING AVERAGES

Baltimore Orioles

Player-Position	G.	AB.	R.	H.	2B.	3B.	HR.	RBI.	BA.
Crowley, ph	2	2	0	1	0	0	0	1	.500
Murray, 1b	4	12	3	5	0	0	1	5	.417
Dempsey, c	3	10	3	4	2	0	0	2	.400
Singleton, rf	4	16	4	6	2	0	0	2	.375
Kelly, lf-dh	3	11	3	4	0	0	1	4	.364
DeCinces, 3b	4	13	4	4	1	0	0	3	.308
Garcia, ss	3	11	1	3	0	0	0	2	.273
Bumbry, cf	4	16	5	4	0	1	0	0	.250
Roenicke, lf-ph	2	5	1	1	0	0	0	1	.200
Belanger, ss-pr	3	5	0	1	0	0	0	1	.200
Dauer, 2b	4	11	0	2	0	0	0	0	.182
Lowenstein, ph-lf	4	6	2	1	0	0	1	3	.167
May, dh	2	7	0	1	0	0	0	1	.143
D. Martinez, p	1	0	0	0	0	0	0	0	.000
Palmer, p	1	0	0	0	0	0	0	0	.000
Flanagan, p	1	0	0	0	0	0	0	0	.000
McGregor, p	1	0	0	0	0	0	0	0	.000
Stanhouse, p	3	0	0	0	0	0	0	0	.000
Skaggs, c	1	4	0	0	0	0	0	0	.000
Smith, 2b	1	4	0	0	0	0	0	0	.000
Totals	4	133	26	37	5	1	3	25	.278

California Angels

Player-Position	G.	AB.	R.	H.	2B.	3B.	HR.	RBI.	BA.
Davis, ph	2	2	1	1	1	0	0	0	.500
Carew, 1b	4	17	4	7	3	0	0	1	.412
Ford, rf	4	17	2	5	1	0	2	4	.294
Lansford, 3b	4	17	2	5	0	0	0	3	.294
Miller, cf	4	16	2	4	0	0	0	0	.250
Downing, c	4	15	1	3	0	0	0	1	.200
Baylor, dh-lf	4	16	2	3	0	0	1	2	.188
Grich, 2b	4	13	0	2	1	0	0	2	.154
Harlow, lf-ph	3	8	0	1	1	0	0	1	.125
Anderson, ss	4	11	0	1	0	0	0	0	.091
Thon, pr-ss	1	0	1	0	0	0	0	0	.000
Barlow, p	1	0	0	0	0	0	0	0	.000
Campaneris, ss	1	0	0	0	0	0	0	0	.000
Clear, p	1	0	0	0	0	0	0	0	.000
Knapp, p	1	0	0	0	0	0	0	0	.000
LaRoche, p	1	0	0	0	0	0	0	0	.000
Ryan, p	1	0	0	0	0	0	0	0	.000
Tanana, p	1	0	0	0	0	0	0	0	.000
Montague, p	2	0	0	0	0	0	0	0	.000
Aase, p	2	0	0	0	0	0	0	0	.000
Frost, p	2	0	0	0	0	0	0	0	.000
Rettenmund, ph-dh	2	2	0	0	0	0	0	0	.000
Clark, lf	1	3	0	0	0	0	0	0	.000
Totals	4	137	15	32	7	0	3	14	.234

COMPOSITE PITCHING AVERAGES

Baltimore Orioles

Pitcher	G.	IP.	H.	R.	ER.	BB.	SO.	W.	L.	ERA.
McGregor	1	9	6	0	0	1	4	1	0	0.00
Palmer	1	9	7	3	3	2	3	0	0	3.00
D. Martinez	1	8⅓	8	3	3	0	4	0	0	3.24
Flanagan	1	7	6	6	4	1	2	1	0	5.14
Stanhouse	3	3	5	3	2	3	0	1	1	6.00
Totals	4	36⅓	32	15	12	7	13	3	1	2.97

California Angels

Pitcher	G.	IP.	H.	R.	ER.	BB.	SO.	W.	L.	ERA.
Barlow	1	1	0	0	0	0	0	0	0	0.00
Ryan	1	7	4	3	1	3	8	0	0	1.29
Aase	2	5	4	1	1	2	6	1	0	1.80
Tanana	1	5	6	2	2	2	3	0	0	3.60
Clear	1	5⅔	4	3	3	2	3	0	0	4.76
LaRoche	1	1⅓	2	1	1	1	1	0	0	6.75
Knapp	1	2⅓	5	2	2	1	0	0	1	7.71
Montague	2	4	4	4	4	2	2	0	1	9.00
Frost	2	4⅓	8	10	9	5	1	0	1	18.69
Totals	4	35⅔	37	26	23	18	24	1	3	5.80

The 1979 National League Championship Series belonged to the Pittsburgh Pirates and Willie Stargell.

Stargell's contributions were headline material in papers across the country: A three-run, 11th-inning homer that decided a 5-2 win in the opener; a single and double in the Pirates' 10-inning 3-2 triumph in Game 2; a homer and two-run double in the 7-1 clinching victory.

It was sweet revenge for the Pirates' dauntless 38-year-old captain and main inspirational force. The Pirates had been swept by the Reds in the N.L. playoffs in 1970 and 1975.

After a 45-minute delay by rain at the start of Game 1, the Pirates, losers in eight of 12 games with the Reds in '79, bolted to a 2-0 lead in the third inning. Phil Garner sliced a homer to right field, Omar Moreno tripled on a drive that eluded the diving Dave Collins in right and Tim Foli contributed a sacrifice fly.

But the Reds rebounded with a pair in the fourth on a single by Dave Concepcion and a homer by George Foster off Pittsburgh starting pitcher John Candelaria.

The deadlock persisted until the top half of the 11th. For two innings in relief of starter Tom Seaver, righthander Tom Hume was in command. But Foli and Dave Parker singled before Stargell's first-pitch homer settled the issue and sent flocks of the 55,006 spectators streaming for the exits.

A single by Concepcion and walks to Foster and Johnny Bench gave Reds' diehards one last hope in their half, before Don Robinson fanned Ray Knight to end the threat.

After using five pitchers in the first game, Pittsburgh Manager Chuck Tanner came right back

Pittsburgh righthander Bert Blyleven greets catcher Ed Ott after pitching the 1979 pennant-clinching victory over Cincinnati.

with six hurlers for a 3-2 verdict in 10 innings in Game 2.

Controversy surrounded the victory, however.

With the score tied 1-1 in the Pirates' half of the fifth, Garner lashed a liner to right field. Collins dived for the ball, but second base umpire Frank Pulli ruled a trap. Television replays showed that Collins had made a clean grab.

Garner advanced on a sacrifice by pitcher Jim Bibby and scored on Foli's double, giving the Pirates a 2-1 lead.

The Reds knotted the score with one out in the ninth on a pinch-double by Hector Cruz and another two-bagger by Collins.

The rally continued when Dave Roberts walked Joe Morgan. Don Robinson was summoned by Tanner and proceeded to strike out Concepcion and retire Foster on a groundout.

Then Moreno and Parker singled around a Foli sacrifice in the 10th to make Robinson the winner and saddle Doug Bair with the loss.

A 30-minute rain delay preceded Game 3 as the scene shifted upriver to Pittsburgh on October 5.

Robinson, who saved Game 1, was extremely impressive as he set down five straight batters in the second game.

While Stargell was providing the slugging feats, the Pirates' pitching staff was limiting the once-feared Cincinnati offense to five runs in three games, climaxed by Bert Blyleven's route-going performance, only his fifth complete game of the year and first since August 15.

Blyleven put to rest frequent reports that he couldn't win the big games by becoming the only starter to go the distance. He scattered eight hits and fanned nine, losing his shutout bid in the sixth inning when Bench tagged him for a home run.

And the Bucs' bats went to work early, getting single runs in the first and second and two runs each in the third and fourth. Stargell and Bill Madlock socked homers in the third.

Game 1

Tuesday, October 2, At Cincinnati

Pittsburgh	AB.	R.	H.	RBI.	PO.	A.
Moreno, cf	5	1	1	0	2	0
Foli, ss	4	0	2	1	1	6
Alexander, pr	0	1	0	0	0	0
B. Robinson, lf	0	0	0	0	0	0
Parker, rf	4	1	1	0	2	0
Stargell, 1b	4	1	1	3	17	0
Milner, lf	5	0	0	0	1	0
Stennett, 2b	0	0	0	0	0	0
Madlock, 3b	5	0	2	0	0	4
Ott, c	5	0	1	0	7	2
Garner, 2b-ss	4	1	2	1	3	5
Candelaria, p	3	0	0	0	0	1
Romo, p	0	0	0	0	0	0
Tekulve, p	0	0	0	0	0	1
Easler, ph	1	0	0	0	0	0
Jackson, p	1	0	0	0	0	0
D. Robinson, p	0	0	0	0	0	0
Totals	41	5	10	5	33	19

Cincinnati	AB.	R.	H.	RBI.	PO.	A.
Collins, rf	5	0	2	0	3	0
Morgan, 2b	4	0	0	0	3	4
Concepcion, ss	5	1	2	0	1	6
Foster, lf	3	1	1	2	1	0
Bench, c	3	0	2	0	7	0
Knight, 3b	5	0	0	0	0	0
Driessen, 1b	4	0	0	0	14	0
Cruz, cf	4	0	0	0	3	0
Seaver, p	2	0	0	0	0	0
Auerbach, ph	1	0	0	0	0	0
Hume, p	1	0	0	0	0	2
Tomlin, p	0	0	0	0	1	0
Totals	37	2	7	2	33	13

Pittsburgh.....0 0 2 0 0 0 0 0 0 3—5
Cincinnati......0 0 0 2 0 0 0 0 0 0—2

Pittsburgh	IP.	H.	R.	ER.	BB.	SO.
Candelaria	7	5	2	2	1	4
Romo	⅓	1	0	0	1	0
Tekulve	1⅔	0	0	0	1	0
Jackson (W)	1⅔	1	0	0	1	2
D. Robinson (S)	⅓	0	0	0	1	1

Cincinnati	IP.	H.	R.	ER.	BB.	SO.
Seaver	8	5	2	2	2	5
Hume (L)	2⅓	5	3	3	0	1
Tomlin	⅔	0	0	0	1	1

DP—Pittsburgh 2, Cincinnati 1. LOB—Pittsburgh 7, Cincinnati 7. 3B—Bench, Moreno. HR—Garner, Foster, Stargell. SB—Madlock 2, Collins. SF—Foli. U—Kibler, Montague, Dale, Pulli, Stello and Quick. T—3:14. A—55,006.

Game 2

Wednesday, October 3, At Cincinnati

Pittsburgh	AB.	R.	H.	RBI.	PO.	A.
Moreno, cf	5	1	2	0	4	0
Foli, ss	4	1	2	1	2	1
Parker, rf	5	0	2	1	4	0
Stargell, 1b	3	0	2	0	6	1
Milner, lf	2	0	0	0	1	0
B. Robinson, lf	2	0	0	0	3	0
Madlock, 3b	5	0	1	1	0	0
Ott, c	4	0	2	0	9	1
Garner, 2b	4	1	1	0	1	3
Bibby, p	0	0	0	0	0	1
Jackson, p	0	0	0	0	0	0
Romo, p	0	0	0	0	0	0
Tekulve, p	1	0	0	0	0	0
Roberts, p	0	0	0	0	0	0
D. Robinson, p	0	0	0	0	0	0
Totals	35	3	11	3	30	7

Cincinnati	AB.	R.	H.	RBI.	PO.	A.
Collins, rf	5	0	1	1	0	0
Morgan, 2b	3	0	0	0	6	6
Concepcion, ss	5	0	2	0	1	8
Foster, lf	3	0	1	0	3	2
Bench, c	5	0	0	0	5	1
Driessen, 1b	4	1	1	0	12	0
Knight, 3b	5	0	2	0	0	2
Geronimo, cf	3	0	0	0	3	0
Pastore, p	0	0	0	1	0	0
Spilman, ph	1	0	0	0	0	0
Tomlin, p	0	0	0	0	0	0
Hume, p	0	0	0	0	0	0
Cruz, ph	1	1	1	0	0	0
Bair, p	0	0	0	0	0	1
Totals	35	2	8	2	30	20

Pittsburgh......0 0 0 1 1 0 0 0 0 1—3
Cincinnati......0 1 0 0 0 0 0 0 1 0—2

Pittsburgh	IP.	H.	R.	ER.	BB.	SO.
Bibby	7	4	1	1	4	5
Jackson	⅓	0	0	0	0	0
Romo	0*	2	0	0	0	0
Tekulve	1	2	1	1	1	2
Roberts	0†	0	0	0	1	0
D. Robinson (W)	1⅔	0	0	0	0	2

Cincinnati	IP.	H.	R.	ER.	BB.	SO.
Pastore	7	7	2	2	3	1
Tomlin	⅔	1	0	0	0	1
Hume	1⅓	1	0	0	1	0
Bair (L)	1	2	1	1	1	0

*Pitched to two batters in eighth.
†Pitched to one batter in ninth.

DP—Cincinnati 1. LOB—Pittsburgh 9, Cincinnati 11. 2B—Concepcion, Foli, Stargell, Cruz, Collins. SB—Morgan, Knight, Collins. SH—Bibby 2, Geronimo, Foli. SF—Pastore. WP—Tekulve. U—Montague, Dale, Pulli, Stello, Quick and Kibler. T—3:24. A—55,000.

Game 3

Friday, October 5, At Pittsburgh

Cincinnati	AB.	R.	H.	RBI.	PO.	A.
Collins, rf	4	0	2	0	2	0
Morgan, 2b	4	0	0	0	3	1
Concepcion, ss	4	0	2	0	1	0
Foster, lf	4	0	0	0	2	0
Bench, c	4	1	1	1	5	1
Driessen, 1b	4	0	0	0	6	0
Knight, 3b	4	0	2	0	0	2
Geronimo, cf	4	0	1	0	5	0
LaCoss, p	2	0	0	0	0	0
Norman, p	0	0	0	0	0	0
Leibrandt, p	0	0	0	0	0	0
Auerbach, ph	1	0	0	0	0	0
Soto, p	0	0	0	0	0	0
Spilman, ph	1	0	0	0	0	0
Tomlin, p	0	0	0	0	0	1
Hume, p	0	0	0	0	0	1
Totals	35	1	8	1	24	6

Pittsburgh	AB.	R.	H.	RBI.	PO.	A.
Moreno, cf	2	1	0	0	1	0
Foli, ss	4	0	1	0	0	2
Parker, rf	3	1	1	1	3	0
Stargell, 1b	4	1	2	3	9	1
Milner, lf	2	0	0	0	0	0
B. Robinson, lf	1	0	0	0	0	0
Madlock, 3b	2	1	1	1	0	3
Ott, c	4	0	0	0	9	0
Garner, 2b	4	2	2	0	4	1
Blyleven, p	3	1	1	0	1	1
Totals	29	7	7	6	27	8

Cincinnati.....0 0 0 0 0 0 1 0 0—1
Pittsburgh.....1 1 2 2 0 0 0 1 x—7

Cincinnati	IP.	H.	R.	ER.	BB.	SO.
LaCoss (L)	1⅔	2	2	2	4	0
Norman	2	4	4	4	1	1
Leibrandt	⅓	0	0	0	0	0
Soto	2	0	0	0	0	1
Tomlin	1⅔	2	1	0	1	1
Hume	⅓	0	0	0	0	0

Pittsburgh	IP.	H.	R.	ER.	BB.	SO.
Blyleven (W)	9	8	1	1	0	9

E—Geronimo. LOB—Cincinnati 7, Pittsburgh 8. 2B—Knight, Stargell. 3B—Garner. HR—Stargell, Madlock, Bench. SB—Morgan, Parker. SH—Moreno, Blyleven. SF—Parker, Foli. Balk—Leibrandt. U—Dale, Pulli, Stello, Quick, Kibler and Montague. T—2:45. A—42,240.

COMPOSITE BATTING AVERAGES
Pittsburgh Pirates

Player-Position	G.	AB.	R.	H.	2B.	3B.	HR.	RBI.	BA.
Stargell, 1b	3	11	2	5	2	0	2	6	.455
Garner, 2b-ss	3	12	4	5	0	1	1	1	.417
Foli, ss	3	12	1	4	1	0	0	3	.333
Parker, rf	3	12	2	4	0	0	0	3	.333
Blyleven, p	1	3	1	1	0	0	0	0	.333
Madlock, 3b	3	12	1	3	0	0	1	2	.250
Moreno, cf	3	12	3	3	0	1	0	0	.250
Ott, c	3	13	0	3	0	0	0	0	.231
Alexander, pr	1	0	1	0	0	0	0	0	.000
Bibby, p	1	0	0	0	0	0	0	0	.000
Stennett, 2b	1	0	0	0	0	0	0	0	.000
Roberts, p	1	0	0	0	0	0	0	0	.000
D. Robinson, p	2	0	0	0	0	0	0	0	.000
Romo, p	2	0	0	0	0	0	0	0	.000
Easler, ph	1	1	0	0	0	0	0	0	.000
Tekulve, p	2	1	0	0	0	0	0	0	.000
Jackson, p	2	1	0	0	0	0	0	0	.000
Candelaria, p	1	3	0	0	0	0	0	0	.000
B. Robinson, lf	3	3	0	0	0	0	0	0	.000
Milner, lf	3	9	0	0	0	0	0	0	.000
Totals	3	105	15	28	3	2	4	14	.267

Cincinnati Reds

Player-Position	G.	AB.	R.	H.	2B.	3B.	HR.	RBI.	BA.
Concepcion, ss	3	14	1	6	1	0	0	0	.429
Collins, rf	3	14	0	5	1	0	0	1	.357
Knight, 3b	3	14	0	4	1	0	0	0	.286
Bench, c	3	12	1	3	0	1	1	1	.250
Foster, lf	3	10	1	2	0	0	1	2	.200
Cruz, cf-ph	2	5	1	1	1	0	0	0	.200
Geronimo, cf	2	7	0	1	0	0	0	0	.143
Driessen, 1b	3	12	1	1	0	0	0	0	.083
Pastore, p	1	0	0	0	0	0	0	1	.000
Bair, p	1	0	0	0	0	0	0	0	.000
LaCoss, p	1	0	0	0	0	0	0	0	.000
Leibrandt, p	1	0	0	0	0	0	0	0	.000
Soto, p	1	0	0	0	0	0	0	0	.000
Tomlin, p	3	0	0	0	0	0	0	0	.000
Norman, p	1	1	0	0	0	0	0	0	.000
Hume, p	3	1	0	0	0	0	0	0	.000
Seaver, p	1	2	0	0	0	0	0	0	.000
Auerbach, ph	2	2	0	0	0	0	0	0	.000
Spilman, ph	2	2	0	0	0	0	0	0	.000
Morgan, 2b	3	11	0	0	0	0	0	0	.000
Totals	3	107	5	23	4	1	2	5	.215

COMPOSITE PITCHING AVERAGES
Pittsburgh Pirates

Pitcher	G.	IP.	H.	R.	ER.	BB.	SO.	W.	L.	ERA.
D. Robinson	2	2	0	0	0	1	3	1	0	0.00
Jackson	2	2	1	0	0	2	1	0	0	0.00
Romo	2	⅓	3	0	0	1	0	0	0	0.00
Roberts	1	0	0	0	0	1	0	0	0	0.00
Blyleven	1	9	8	1	1	0	9	1	0	1.00
Bibby	1	7	4	1	1	4	5	0	0	1.29
Candelaria	1	7	5	2	2	1	4	0	0	2.57
Tekulve	2	2⅔	2	1	1	2	2	0	0	3.38
Totals	3	30	23	5	5	11	26	3	0	1.50

Cincinnati Reds

Pitcher	G.	IP.	H.	R.	ER.	BB.	SO.	W.	L.	ERA.
Tomlin	3	3	3	1	0	2	3	0	0	0.00
Soto	1	2	0	0	0	0	1	0	0	0.00
Leibrandt	1	⅓	0	0	0	0	0	0	0	0.00
Seaver	1	8	5	2	2	2	5	0	0	2.25
Pastore	1	7	7	2	2	3	1	0	0	2.57
Hume	3	4	6	3	3	1	1	0	1	6.75
Bair	1	1	2	1	1	1	0	0	1	9.00
LaCoss	1	1⅔	2	2	2	4	0	0	1	10.80
Norman	1	2	4	4	4	1	1	0	0	18.00
Totals	3	29	28	15	14	13	13	0	3	4.34

1980
KANSAS CITY ROYALS
VS.
NEW YORK YANKEES

The Kansas City Royals were driven by the idea of beating the New York Yankees. Yes, beating those same Big Apple brutes who had sent the Royals away unhappy with playoff losses in 1976, '77 and '78.

The idea of beating the Yankees was almost haunting to the Royals, even to a player like The Sporting News 1980 American League Fireman of the Year, Dan Quisenberry, who wasn't with Kansas City during those second-best seasons.

"I thought to myself, 'Hey, you know all the years the Royals had short relief problems and they blew leads—that's how they lost all those playoff games. You're the guy who is supposed to turn all that around this year. What are you walking all these guys

for?'" Quisenberry commented before he set down the Yankees to extinguish an eighth-inning threat and preserve a 4-2 victory in Game 3, enabling the Royals to sweep the A.L. Championship Series from the Yanks.

"Our fans think we've already won the World Series by beating the Yankees," said George Brett, whose towering three-run homer into the third tier of seats at Yankee Stadium off ace reliever Rich Gossage erased a 2-1 deficit and provided the winning touch to the third-game triumph.

Gossage, unhittable for the final eight weeks of the season, entered the contest after Tommy John yielded a two-out double by Willie Wilson. U.L. Washington greeted Gossage by beating out an infield chopper.

The stage was set. As Gossage put it: "It was power versus power."

In one classic swipe of the bat, Brett slayed the giants.

The Royals didn't begin the series with the glee that climaxed it. In fact, there was doubt in the mind of their starting pitcher, Larry Gura, after Rick Cerone and Lou Piniella hit back-to-back homers for a 2-0 lead in the second inning of Game 1.

Gura didn't exactly dazzle the Yanks but he did manage to scatter 10 hits and pitch the Royals to a 7-2 verdict and a one-game edge.

Frank White began the Kansas City comeback with a two-out, two-run double in the second and Willie Aikens sent two more runs home with a third-inning single. Brett blasted a homer in the seventh and Wilson doubled in the final two tallies in the eighth.

The Royals put together four straight hits for all their runs in the third inning and shaded the Yanks, 3-2, in Game 2. Darrell Porter and White singled before Wilson cleared the sacks with a triple and Washington completed the outburst with a two-base hit.

The Yankees had an inside-the-park homer by Graig Nettles and a run-scoring double by Willie Randolph for their only runs.

However, the most talked about New York play occurred in the eighth when Randolph was thrown out at the plate attempting to score from first on a two-out double by Bob Watson. Blustery Yankees Owner George Steinbrenner wanted third base coach Mike Ferraro fired. The consensus: when left fielder Wilson overthrew the relay man the runner had to score. Brett, backing up Washington, snared the throw and gunned Randolph out at the plate with a perfect peg.

Kansas City catcher Darrell Porter blocks the plate and tags out New York's Willie Randolph on the key play in the Royals' Game 2 victory.

George Brett gets a warm welcome from his Kansas City teammates after hitting a Game 1 homer in the 1980 title series against the Yankees.

White, who was voted MVP of the series with his 6-for-11 hitting and several outstanding plays in the field, staked the Royals to a 1-0 lead in Game 3 before the Yanks rallied for two runs in the sixth—one coming off starter Paul Splittorff and the other coming off Quisenberry.

Center stage was set for the Brett-Gossage confrontation.

"We all kept hollering, 'It's going to happen, it's going to happen,'" said White. "We just knew they couldn't keep getting George (0 for his last 7) out like that."

The rest is history.

Game 1

Wednesday, October 8, At Kansas City

New York	AB.	R.	H.	RBI.	PO.	A.
Randolph, 2b	5	0	2	0	0	5
Dent, ss	4	0	2	0	3	3
Watson, 1b	4	0	2	0	11	2
Jackson, rf	4	0	0	0	1	0
Soderholm, dh	4	0	1	0	0	0
Cerone, c	4	1	1	1	6	1
Piniella, lf	3	1	1	1	1	0
Rodriguez, 3b	4	0	1	0	1	2
Brown, cf	4	0	0	0	1	0
Guidry, p	0	0	0	0	0	1
Davis, p	0	0	0	0	0	2
Underwood, p	0	0	0	0	0	0
Totals	36	2	10	2	24	17

Kansas City	AB.	R.	H.	RBI.	PO.	A.
Wilson, lf	5	0	1	2	2	0
Washington, ss	4	0	1	0	1	3
G. Brett, 3b	3	2	2	1	1	2
McRae, dh	3	0	0	0	0	0
Otis, cf	4	2	2	0	5	0
Wathan, rf	1	1	0	0	4	0
Hurdle, rf	0	0	0	0	0	0
Aikens, 1b	4	0	1	2	7	0
LaCock, 1b	0	0	0	0	0	0
Porter, c	4	1	0	0	5	0
White, 2b	4	1	3	2	2	3
Gura, p	0	0	0	0	0	1
Totals	32	7	10	7	27	9

New York .... 0 2 0 0 0 0 0 0 0—2
Kansas City .... 0 2 2 0 0 0 1 2 x—7

New York	IP.	H.	R.	ER.	BB.	SO.
Guidry (L)	3	5	4	4	4	2
Davis	4	3	1	1	1	3
Underwood	1	2	2	0	2	0

Kansas City	IP.	H.	R.	ER.	BB.	SO.
Gura (W)	9	10	2	2	1	4

Game-winning RBI—Aikens.
E—Watson. DP—New York 1. LOB—New York 9, Kansas City 7. 2B—Randolph, G. Brett, Rodriguez, White, Watson, Otis, Wilson. HR—Cerone, Piniella, G. Brett. SB—Otis, White. SH—Dent. HBP—By Davis (McRae). WP—Guidry. U—Palermo, Brinkman, McCoy, Haller, Kaiser and Maloney. T—3:00. A—42,598.

Game 2

Thursday, October 9, At Kansas City

New York	AB.	R.	H.	RBI.	PO.	A.
Randolph, 2b	4	0	2	1	1	1
Murcer, dh	4	0	0	0	0	0
Watson, 1b	4	0	1	0	6	2
Jackson, rf	4	0	2	0	2	0
Gamble, lf	4	0	0	0	0	0
Cerone, c	4	0	2	0	4	1
Nettles, 3b	4	1	1	1	0	1
Dent, ss	3	0	0	0	3	2
Brown, cf	2	1	0	0	5	0
May, p	0	0	0	0	0	2
Totals	33	2	8	2	24	9

Kansas City	AB.	R.	H.	RBI.	PO.	A.
Wilson, lf	3	1	1	2	2	1
Washington, ss	3	0	1	1	3	1
G. Brett, 3b	4	0	0	0	0	3
McRae, dh	3	0	0	0	0	0
Otis, cf	4	0	1	0	3	0
Wathan, rf	3	0	0	0	3	0
Hurdle, rf	0	0	0	0	0	0
Aikens, 1b	3	0	0	0	7	0
Porter, c	3	1	1	0	8	0
White, 2b	3	1	2	0	1	2
Leonard, p	0	0	0	0	0	0
Quisenberry, p	0	0	0	0	0	0
Totals	29	3	6	3	27	8

New York .... 0 0 0 0 2 0 0 0 0—2
Kansas City .... 0 0 3 0 0 0 0 0 x—3

New York	IP.	H.	R.	ER.	BB.	SO.
May (L)	8	6	3	3	3	4

Kansas City	IP.	H.	R.	ER.	BB.	SO.
Leonard (W)	8*	7	2	2	1	8
Quisenberry (S)	1	1	0	0	0	0

*Pitched to one batter in ninth.
Game-winning RBI—Wilson.
DP—Kansas City 1. LOB—New York 5, Kansas City 5. 2B—Washington, Randolph, Watson. 3B—Wilson. HR—Nettles. SB—Otis. U—Brinkman, McCoy, Haller, Kaiser, Maloney and Palermo. T—2:51. A—42,633.

Game 3

Friday, October 10, At New York

Kansas City	AB.	R.	H.	RBI.	PO.	A.
Wilson, lf	5	1	2	0	2	0
Washington, ss	4	1	2	0	1	3
G. Brett, 3b	4	1	1	3	1	2

	AB.	R.	H.	RBI.	PO.	A.
McRae, dh	4	0	2	0	0	0
Otis, cf	4	0	1	0	3	0
Aikens, 1b	4	0	3	0	8	1
Porter, c	3	0	0	0	4	0
Hurdle, rf	2	0	0	0	1	0
Wathan, ph-rf	2	0	0	0	0	0
White, 2b	4	1	1	1	6	5
Splittorff, p	0	0	0	0	0	1
Quisenberry, p	0	0	0	0	1	0
Totals	36	4	12	4	27	12

New York	AB.	R.	H.	RBI.	PO.	A.
Randolph, 2b	4	0	1	0	1	3
Dent, ss	4	0	0	0	3	7
Watson, 1b	4	0	3	0	11	1
Jackson, rf	3	1	1	0	2	0
Soderholm, dh	2	0	0	0	0	0
Gamble, ph-dh	1	1	1	0	0	0
Cerone, c	4	0	1	1	4	2
Piniella, lf	2	0	0	0	4	0
Spencer, ph	1	0	0	0	0	0
Lefebvre, lf	0	0	0	0	0	0
Rodriguez, 3b	2	0	1	0	1	0
Nettles, ph-3b	2	0	0	0	1	0
Brown, cf	4	0	0	0	1	0
John, p	0	0	0	0	0	0
Gossage, p	0	0	0	0	0	0
Underwood, p	0	0	0	0	0	1
Totals	33	2	8	1	27	16

Kansas City .... 0 0 0 0 1 0 3 0 0—4
New York .... 0 0 0 0 0 2 0 0 0—2

Kansas City	IP.	H.	R.	ER.	BB.	SO.
Splittorff	5⅓	5	1	1	2	3
Quisenberry (W)	3⅔	3	1	0	2	1

New York	IP.	H.	R.	ER.	BB.	SO.
John	6⅔	8	2	2	1	3
Gossage (L)	⅓	3	2	2	0	0
Underwood	2	1	0	0	0	1

Game-winning RBI—G. Brett.
E—White. DP—Kansas City 2, New York 1. LOB—Kansas City 6, New York 8. 2B—Watson, Jackson, Wilson. 3B—Watson. HR—White, G. Brett. WP—John. Balk—Splittorff. U—McCoy, Haller, Kaiser, Maloney, Palermo and Brinkman. T—2:59. A—56,588.

COMPOSITE BATTING AVERAGES

Kansas City Royals

Player-Position	G.	AB.	R.	H.	2B.	3B.	HR.	RBI.	BA.
White, 2b	3	11	3	6	1	0	1	3	.545
Washington, ss	3	11	1	4	1	0	0	1	.364
Aikens, 1b	3	11	0	4	0	0	0	2	.364
Otis, cf	3	12	2	4	1	0	0	0	.333
Wilson, lf	3	13	4	4	2	1	0	4	.308
G. Brett, 3b	3	11	3	3	1	0	2	4	.273
McRae, dh	3	10	0	2	0	0	0	0	.200
Porter, c	3	10	2	1	0	0	0	0	.100
Quisenberry, p	2	0	0	0	0	0	0	0	.000
Gura, p	1	0	0	0	0	0	0	0	.000
LaCock, 1b	1	0	0	0	0	0	0	0	.000
Leonard, p	1	0	0	0	0	0	0	0	.000
Splittorff, p	1	0	0	0	0	0	0	0	.000
Hurdle, rf	3	2	0	0	0	0	0	0	.000
Wathan, rf-ph	3	6	1	0	0	0	0	0	.000
Totals	3	97	14	28	6	1	3	14	.289

New York Yankees

Player-Position	G.	AB.	R.	H.	2B.	3B.	HR.	RBI.	BA.
Watson, 1b	3	12	0	6	3	1	0	0	.500
Randolph, 2b	3	13	0	5	2	0	0	1	.385
Cerone, c	3	12	1	4	0	0	1	2	.333
Rodriguez, 3b	2	6	0	2	1	0	0	0	.333
Jackson, rf	3	11	1	3	1	0	0	0	.273
Piniella, lf	2	5	1	1	0	1	1	1	.200
Gamble, lf-ph-dh	2	5	1	1	0	0	0	0	.200
Dent, ss	3	11	0	2	0	0	0	0	.182
Nettles, 3b-ph	2	6	1	1	0	0	1	1	.167
Soderholm, dh	2	6	0	1	0	0	0	0	.167
Underwood, p	2	0	0	0	0	0	0	0	.000
Davis, p	1	0	0	0	0	0	0	0	.000
Gossage, p	1	0	0	0	0	0	0	0	.000
Guidry, p	1	0	0	0	0	0	0	0	.000
John, p	1	0	0	0	0	0	0	0	.000
Lefebvre, lf	1	0	0	0	0	0	0	0	.000
May, p	1	0	0	0	0	0	0	0	.000
Spencer, ph	1	1	0	0	0	0	0	0	.000
Murcer, dh	1	4	0	0	0	0	0	0	.000
Brown, cf	3	10	1	0	0	0	0	0	.000
Totals	3	102	6	26	7	1	3	5	.255

COMPOSITE PITCHING AVERAGES

Kansas City Royals

Pitcher	G.	IP.	H.	R.	ER.	BB.	SO.	W.	L.	ERA.
Quisenberry	2	4⅔	4	1	0	2	1	1	0	0.00
Splittorff	1	5⅓	5	1	1	2	3	0	0	1.69
Gura	1	9	10	2	2	1	4	1	0	2.00
Leonard	1	8	7	2	2	1	8	1	0	2.25
Totals	3	27	26	6	5	6	16	3	0	1.67

New York Yankees

Pitcher	G.	IP.	H.	R.	ER.	BB.	SO.	W.	L.	ERA.
Underwood	2	3	2	0	0	0	3	0	0	0.00
Davis	1	4	3	1	1	1	3	0	0	2.25
John	1	6⅔	8	2	2	1	3	0	0	2.70
May	1	8	6	3	3	3	4	0	1	3.38
Guidry	1	3	5	4	4	4	2	0	1	12.00
Gossage	1	⅓	3	2	2	0	0	0	1	54.00
Totals	3	25	28	14	12	9	15	0	3	4.32

1980
PHILADELPHIA PHILLIES
VS.
HOUSTON ASTROS

The 1980 National League Championship Series had a little of everything. It had controversy. It had rallies. It had drama. It had heartbreak. Most of all, it had two teams that wouldn't give up.

Not until Garry Maddox cradled that final fly ball by Enos Cabell in the 10th inning of the fifth game October 12 did the Philadelphia Phillies finally gain an edge for an 8-7 victory and a three games to two elimination of the West Division-champion Houston Astros.

The Phillies rebounded from a 1-0 deficit in the first game when Greg Luzinski slammed a two-run homer to left field in the seventh inning and Greg Gross plated Maddox with a pinch-single in the eighth for a 3-1 verdict.

The Phils were on the threshold of a second consecutive victory at Veterans Stadium after Steve Carlton and Tug McGraw had collaborated in the opener. However, Bake McBride's baserunning blunder cost them a chance to win in the ninth and the Astros rallied with a four-run outburst in the 10th inning to take a 7-4 decision, sending the series to Houston tied at one game apiece.

Joe Niekro, Houston's two-time 20-game winner, and injury-plagued Larry Christenson of the Phillies threw zeroes at one another in Game 3. The Phils fired 10 blanks at Niekro while Christenson was shutting out the Astros for six frames and McGraw for three more.

In the 11th, Joe Morgan crashed a leadoff triple and Jose Cruz and Art Howe were walked intentionally, before Dennis Walling's sacrifice fly scored pinch-runner Rafael Landestoy and made a winner of Dave Smith for one inning of work.

The victory was costly, howev-er, as outfielder Cesar Cedeno dislocated his right ankle when he stepped awkwardly on first base while trying to beat a double-play relay.

Game 4 abounded in controversy, was protested by both clubs and ended up in a 5-3, 10-inning triumph by the Phillies to tie the series at two games each.

McBride and Trillo started the confusion in the fourth inning with singles off Vern Ruhle. When Maddox stroked a soft liner back to the mound controversy turned to chaos.

Ruhle fielded the ball and threw to first base for an apparent double play. Philadelphia players streamed from the dugout, insisting that Ruhle had trapped the ball. Houston players maintained the ball had been caught. Slow-motion replays from numerous angles were inconclusive.

During the confusion, Houston first baseman Howe strolled over to second base and claimed a triple play.

Plate umpire Doug Harvey, with nearly two decades of National League experience, reset the play after conferring with fellow umpires and meeting with N.L. President Chub Feeney, who was in a first base box seat.

The play was ruled as a catch. Inasmuch as time had been called before Howe tagged second base, Harvey disallowed the putout, returned McBride to second and ordered the game to go on. The rhubarb consumed 20 minutes and prompted an official protest by each club before the Phillies were retired without any scoring.

After the Astros had taken a 2-0 lead with single runs in the fourth and fifth, the Phillies fought back, taking a 3-2 lead in the eighth when Gross, pinch-hitting for Carlton, singled and scored on singles by Smith and Pete Rose. Schmidt's infield single scored Smith and Trillo followed with a sacrifice fly.

After the Astros once again tied the score in the ninth on a run-scoring single by Terry Puhl, Rose singled and raced home, bowling over catcher Bruce Bochy when pinch-hitter Luzinski doubled in the 10th. Trillo also doubled, driving in Luzinski.

Bochy was in the game only because Alan Ashby suffered a rib separation in the West Division playoff with Los Angeles and Pujols was sidelined with an ankle injury when struck by an eighth-inning foul tip.

The topsy-turvy fifth game saw the Astros' 5-2 lead evaporate into a 7-5 deficit before they staged a rally in the eighth inning to force extra innings.

Game 1

Tuesday, October 7, At Philadelphia

Houston	AB.	R.	H.	RBI.	PO.	A.
Landestoy, 2b	5	0	0	0	1	2
Cabell, 3b	4	0	1	0	0	2
Cruz, lf	3	1	1	0	5	0
Cedeno, cf	3	0	1	0	1	0
Howe, 1b	4	0	0	0	8	1
Woods, rf	4	0	2	1	1	0
Pujols, c	3	0	0	0	5	1
Bergman, pr	0	0	0	0	0	0
Reynolds, ss	2	0	0	0	2	4
Puhl, ph	1	0	0	0	0	0
Forsch, p	2	0	1	0	1	0
Leonard, ph	1	0	0	0	0	0
Totals	32	1	7	1	24	10

Philadelphia	AB.	R.	H.	RBI.	PO.	A.
Rose, 1b	4	1	2	0	11	1
McBride, rf	4	0	1	0	2	0
Schmidt, 3b	3	0	0	0	0	4
Luzinski, lf	4	1	1	2	0	0
Unser, lf	0	0	0	0	1	0
Trillo, 2b	4	0	0	0	5	8
Maddox, cf	3	1	1	0	3	0
Bowa, ss	2	0	1	0	1	1
Boone, c	3	0	1	0	4	1
Carlton, p	2	0	0	0	0	0
Gross, ph	1	0	1	1	0	0
McGraw, p	0	0	0	0	0	0
Totals	30	3	8	3	27	15

Houston ....0 0 1 0 0 0 0 0 0—1
Philadelphia ....0 0 0 0 0 2 1 0 x—3

Houston	IP.	H.	R.	ER.	BB.	SO.
Forsch (L)	8	8	3	3	1	5

Philadelphia	IP.	H.	R.	ER.	BB.	SO.
Carlton (W)	7	7	1	1	3	3
McGraw (S)	2	0	0	0	1	1

Game-winning RBI—Luzinski.
E—Bowa. DP—Philadelphia 1. LOB—Houston 9, Philadelphia 5. HR—Luzinski. SB—McBride, Maddox. SH—Forsch, Bowa. U—Engel, Tata, Froemming, Harvey, Vargo and Crawford. T—2:35. A—65,277.

Game 2

Wednesday, October 8, At Philadelphia

Houston	AB.	R.	H.	RBI.	PO.	A.
Puhl, rf	5	1	3	2	3	0
Cabell, 3b	4	0	0	0	0	0
Morgan, 2b	2	1	1	0	4	0
Landestoy, pr-2b	0	1	0	0	0	1
Cruz, lf	4	1	2	2	4	0
Cedeno, cf	5	1	1	1	3	0
Howe, 1b	4	0	0	0	5	1
Bergman, 1b	1	0	1	2	1	1
Ashby, c	5	0	0	0	9	2
Reynolds, ss	3	1	0	0	1	1
Ryan, p	1	1	0	0	0	2
Sambito, p	0	0	0	0	0	0
D. Smith, p	0	0	0	0	0	0
Leonard, ph	1	0	0	0	0	0
LaCorte, p	1	0	0	0	0	0
Andujar, p	0	0	0	0	0	0
Totals	36	7	8	7	30	8

Philadelphia	AB.	R.	H.	RBI.	PO.	A.
Rose, 1b	4	0	2	0	14	2
McBride, rf	5	0	1	0	2	0
Schmidt, 3b	6	1	2	0	0	3
Luzinski, lf	4	1	2	1	3	0
L. Smith, pr-lf	1	1	1	0	0	0
Trillo, 2b	3	0	1	0	2	7
Maddox, cf	5	0	2	2	2	0
Bowa, ss	4	1	2	0	0	4
Boone, c	4	0	1	0	5	0
Ruthven, p	2	0	0	0	2	0
Gross, ph	0	0	0	0	0	0
McGraw, p	0	0	0	0	0	0
Unser, ph	1	0	0	0	0	0
Reed, p	0	0	0	0	0	0
Saucier, p	0	0	0	0	0	0
G. Vukovich, ph	1	0	0	0	0	0
Totals	40	4	14	3	30	16

Houston 0 0 1 0 0 0 1 1 0 4—7
Philadelphia 0 0 0 2 0 0 0 1 0 1—4

Houston	IP.	H.	R.	ER.	BB.	SO.
Ryan	6⅓	8	2	2	1	6
Sambito	⅓	0	0	0	1	1
D. Smith	1⅓	2	1	1	1	2
LaCorte (W)	1*	4	1	0	1	1
Andujar (S)	1	0	0	0	1	0

Philadelphia	IP.	H.	R.	ER.	BB.	SO.
Ruthven	7	3	2	2	5	4
McGraw	1	2	1	1	0	0
Reed (L)	1⅓	2	4	4	1	1
Saucier	⅔	1	0	0	1	0

*Pitched to two batters in tenth.

Game-winning RBI—Cruz.

E—Schmidt, McBride, Reynolds. DP—Philadelphia 1. LOB—Houston 8, Philadelphia 14. 2B—Schmidt, Luzinski, Puhl, Morgan. 3B—Bergman. SH—Trillo 2, Ryan, Gross, Cabell. U—Tata, Froemming, Harvey, Vargo, Crawford and Engel. T—3:34. A—65,476.

Game 3

Friday, October 10, At Houston

Philadelphia	AB.	R.	H.	RBI.	PO.	A.
Rose, 1b	5	0	1	0	13	0
McBride, rf	5	0	1	0	1	0
Schmidt, 3b	5	0	1	0	0	2
Luzinski, lf	5	0	0	0	2	0
Trillo, 2b	5	0	2	0	4	5
Maddox, cf	4	0	2	0	6	0
Bowa, ss	3	0	0	0	2	4
Boone, c	4	0	0	0	3	1
Unser, ph	1	0	0	0	0	0
Moreland, c	0	0	0	0	0	0
Christenson, p	2	0	0	0	0	1
G. Vukovich, ph	1	0	0	0	0	0
Noles, p	0	0	0	0	0	1
McGraw, p	1	0	0	0	0	0
Totals	41	0	7	0	31	14

Houston	AB.	R.	H.	RBI.	PO.	A.
Puhl, rf-cf	4	0	2	0	5	0
Cabell, 3b	4	0	2	0	1	4
Morgan, 2b	4	0	1	0	0	2
Landestoy, pr	0	1	0	0	0	0
Cruz, lf	2	0	1	0	7	0
Cedeno, cf	3	0	0	0	1	0
Bergman, 1b	1	0	0	0	5	0
Howe, ph	0	0	0	0	0	0
Walling, 1b-rf	3	0	0	1	5	0
Pujols, c	3	0	0	0	5	0
Reynolds, ss	3	0	0	0	3	5
Niekro, p	3	0	0	0	1	0
Woods, ph	1	0	0	0	0	0
Smith, p	0	0	0	0	0	0
Totals	31	1	6	1	33	11

Philadelphia 0 0 0 0 0 0 0 0 0 0 0—0
Houston 0 0 0 0 0 0 0 0 0 0 1—1
One out when winning run scored.

Philadelphia	IP.	H.	R.	ER.	BB.	SO.
Christenson	6	3	0	0	4	2
Noles	1⅓	1	0	0	1	0
McGraw (L)	3	2	1	1	3	1

Houston	IP.	H.	R.	ER.	BB.	SO.
Niekro	10	6	0	0	1	2
Smith (W)	1	1	0	0	1	2

Game-winning RBI—Walling.

E—Christenson, Bergman. DP—Philadelphia 2. LOB—Philadelphia 11, Houston 10. 2B—Puhl, Trillo, Maddox. 3B—Cruz, Morgan. SB—Schmidt, Maddox. SH—Reynolds, Cabell. SF—Walling. HBP—By Niekro (Maddox). PB—Pujols. U—Froemming, Harvey, Vargo, Crawford, Engel and Tata. T—3:22. A—44,443.

Game 4

Saturday, October 11, At Houston

Philadelphia	AB.	R.	H.	RBI.	PO.	A.
L. Smith, lf	4	1	2	0	2	1
Unser, lf-rf	1	0	0	0	1	0
Rose, 1b	4	2	2	1	6	2
Schmidt, 3b	5	0	2	1	3	5
McBride, rf	4	0	2	0	3	2
Luzinski, ph	1	1	1	1	0	0
McGraw, p	0	0	0	0	0	0
Trillo, 2b	4	0	2	2	3	0
Maddox, cf	4	0	0	0	6	0
Bowa, ss	5	0	1	0	0	0
Boone, c	4	0	0	0	4	1
Carlton, p	2	0	0	0	0	1
Noles, p	0	0	0	0	1	1
Saucier, p	0	0	0	0	0	0
Reed, p	0	0	0	0	1	0
Gross, ph	1	1	1	0	0	0
Brusstar, p	1	0	0	0	0	0
G. Vukovich, lf	0	0	0	0	0	0
Totals	40	5	13	5	30	13

Houston	AB.	R.	H.	RBI.	PO.	A.
Puhl, cf	3	0	1	1	2	0
Cabell, 3b	4	1	1	0	0	2
Morgan, 2b	3	0	0	0	1	4
Woods, rf	2	0	0	0	0	0
Walling, ph	1	0	0	0	0	0
Leonard, rf	1	0	0	0	2	1
Howe, 1b	3	0	1	1	12	1
Cruz, lf	3	0	0	0	2	0
Pujols, c	3	1	1	0	3	0
Bochy, c	1	0	0	0	5	1
Landestoy, ss	3	1	1	1	2	4
Ruhle, p	3	0	0	0	1	1
D. Smith, p	0	0	0	0	0	0
Sambito, p	0	0	0	0	0	0
Totals	30	3	5	3	30	14

Philadelphia 0 0 0 0 0 0 0 3 0 2—5
Houston 0 0 0 1 1 0 0 0 1 0—3

Philadelphia	IP.	H.	R.	ER.	BB.	SO.
Carlton	5⅓	4	2	2	5	3
Noles	1⅓	0	0	0	2	0
Saucier	0*	0	0	0	1	0
Reed	⅓	0	0	0	0	0
Brusstar (W)	2	1	1	1	1	0
McGraw (S)	1	0	0	0	0	1

Houston	IP.	H.	R.	ER.	BB.	SO.
Ruhle	7†	8	3	3	1	3
D. Smith	0‡	1	0	0	0	0
Sambito (L)	3	4	2	2	1	5

*Pitched to one batter in seventh.
†Pitched to three batters in eighth.
‡Pitched to one batter in eighth.

Game-winning RBI—Luzinski.

E—Landestoy. DP—Philadelphia 3, Houston 2. LOB—Philadelphia 8, Houston 8. 2B—Howe, Cabell, Luzinski, Trillo. 3B—Pujols. SB—McBride, L. Smith, Landestoy, Woods, Puhl, Bowa. SH—Sambito. SF—Howe, Trillo. U—Harvey, Vargo, Crawford, Engel, Tata and Froemming. T—3:55. A—44,952.

Game 5

Sunday, October 12, At Houston

Philadelphia	AB.	R.	H.	RBI.	PO.	A.
Rose, 1b	3	0	1	1	9	2
McBride, rf	3	0	0	0	3	1
Moreland, ph	1	0	0	1	0	0
Aviles, pr	0	1	0	0	0	0
McGraw, p	0	0	0	0	0	0
G. Vukovich, ph	1	0	0	0	0	0
Ruthven, p	0	0	0	0	0	0
Schmidt, 3b	5	0	0	0	0	3
Luzinski, lf	3	0	1	0	0	0
Smith, pr	0	0	0	0	0	0
Christenson, p	0	0	0	0	0	0
Reed, p	0	0	0	0	0	0
Unser, ph-rf	2	2	2	1	0	0
Trillo, 2b	5	1	3	2	4	5
Maddox, cf	4	1	1	1	6	0
Bowa, ss	5	1	2	0	1	2
Boone, c	3	1	2	2	6	0
Bystrom, p	2	0	0	0	0	0
Brusstar, p	0	0	0	0	0	0
Gross, lf	2	1	1	0	1	0
Totals	39	8	13	8	30	13

Houston	AB.	R.	H.	RBI.	PO.	A.
Puhl, cf	6	3	4	0	3	0
Cabell, 3b	5	0	1	0	0	1
Morgan, 2b	4	0	0	0	4	2
Landestoy, 2b	1	0	1	1	2	1
Cruz, lf	3	1	2	2	1	0
Walling, rf	5	2	1	1	1	0
LaCorte, p	0	0	0	0	0	0
Howe, 1b	4	0	2	1	4	0
Bergman, pr-1b	1	0	0	0	2	1
Pujols, c	1	0	0	0	8	1
Ashby, ph-c	3	0	1	1	2	0
Reynolds, ss	5	1	2	0	2	2
Ryan, p	3	0	0	0	1	1
Sambito, p	0	0	0	0	0	0
Forsch, p	0	0	0	0	0	0
Woods, ph-rf	1	0	0	0	0	0
Heep, ph	1	0	0	0	0	0
Totals	43	7	14	6	30	9

Philadelphia 0 2 0 0 0 0 0 5 0 1—8
Houston 1 0 0 0 0 1 3 2 0 0—7

Philadelphia	IP.	H.	R.	ER.	BB.	SO.
Bystrom	5⅓	7	2	1	2	1
Brusstar	⅔	0	0	0	0	0
Christenson	⅔	2	3	3	1	0
Reed	⅓	1	0	0	0	0
McGraw	1	4	2	2	0	2
Ruthven (W)	2	0	0	0	0	0

Houston	IP.	H.	R.	ER.	BB.	SO.
Ryan	7*	8	6	6	2	8
Sambito	⅓	0	0	0	0	0
Forsch	⅔	2	1	1	0	1
LaCorte (L)	2	3	1	1	1	1

*Pitched to four batters in eighth.

Game-winning RBI—Maddox.

E—Trillo, Luzinski. DP—Houston 2. LOB—Philadelphia 5, Houston 10. 2B—Cruz, Reynolds, Unser, Maddox. 3B—Howe, Trillo. SB—Puhl. SH—Cabell, Boone. WP—Christenson. U—Vargo, Crawford, Engel, Tata, Froemming and Harvey. T—3:38. A—44,802.

COMPOSITE BATTING AVERAGES

Philadelphia Phillies

Player-Position	G.	AB.	R.	H.	2B.	3B.	HR.	RBI.	BA.
Gross, ph-lf	4	4	2	3	0	0	0	1	.750
L. Smith, pr-lf	3	5	2	3	0	0	0	0	.600
Rose, 1b	5	20	3	8	0	0	0	2	.400
Unser, lf-ph-rf	5	5	2	2	1	0	0	1	.400
Trillo, 2b	5	21	1	8	2	1	0	4	.381
Bowa, ss	5	19	2	6	0	0	0	0	.316
Maddox, cf	5	20	2	6	2	0	0	3	.300
Luzinski, lf-ph	5	17	3	5	2	0	1	4	.294
McBride, rf	5	21	0	5	0	0	0	0	.238
Boone, c	5	18	1	4	0	0	0	2	.222
Schmidt, 3b	5	24	1	5	1	0	0	1	.208
Reed, p	3	0	0	0	0	0	0	0	.000
Noles, p	2	0	0	0	0	0	0	0	.000
Saucier, p	2	0	0	0	0	0	0	0	.000
Aviles, pr	1	0	1	0	0	0	0	0	.000
McGraw, p	5	1	0	0	0	0	0	0	.000
Brusstar, p	2	1	0	0	0	0	0	0	.000
Moreland, c-ph	2	1	0	0	0	0	0	1	.000
Christenson, p	2	2	0	0	0	0	0	0	.000
Ruthven, p	2	2	0	0	0	0	0	0	.000
Bystrom, p	1	2	0	0	0	0	0	0	.000
G. Vukovich, ph-lf	4	3	0	0	0	0	0	0	.000
Carlton, p	2	4	0	0	0	0	0	0	.000
Totals	5	190	20	55	8	1	1	19	.290

Houston Astros

Player-Position	G.	AB.	R.	H.	2B.	3B.	HR.	RBI.	BA.
Forsch, p	2	2	0	2	0	0	0	0	1.000
Puhl, ph-rf-cf	5	19	4	10	2	0	0	3	.526
Cruz, lf	5	15	3	6	1	1	0	4	.400
Bergman, pr-1b	4	3	0	1	0	1	0	2	.333
Woods, rf-ph	4	8	0	2	0	0	0	1	.250
Cabell, 3b	5	21	1	5	1	0	0	0	.238
Landestoy, 2b-pr-ss	5	9	3	2	0	0	0	2	.222
Howe, 1b-ph	5	15	0	3	1	1	0	2	.200
Cedeno, cf	3	11	1	2	0	0	0	1	.182
Morgan, 2b	4	13	1	2	1	1	0	0	.154
Reynolds, ss	4	13	2	2	1	0	0	0	.154
Ashby, c-ph	2	8	0	1	0	0	0	1	.125
Walling, 1b-rf-ph	3	9	2	1	0	0	0	2	.111
Pujols, c	4	10	1	1	0	1	0	0	.100
Sambito, p	3	0	0	0	0	0	0	0	.000
D. Smith, p	3	0	0	0	0	0	0	0	.000
Andujar, p	1	0	0	0	0	0	0	0	.000
LaCorte, p	2	1	0	0	0	0	0	0	.000
Bochy, c	1	1	0	0	0	0	0	0	.000
Heep, ph	1	1	0	0	0	0	0	0	.000
Leonard, ph-rf	3	3	0	0	0	0	0	0	.000
Niekro, p	1	3	0	0	0	0	0	0	.000
Ruhle, p	1	3	0	0	0	0	0	0	.000
Ryan, p	2	4	1	0	0	0	0	0	.000
Totals	5	172	19	40	7	5	0	18	.233

COMPOSITE PITCHING AVERAGES

Philadelphia Phillies

Pitcher	G.	IP.	H.	R.	ER.	BB.	SO.	W.	L.	ERA.
Noles	2	2⅔	1	0	0	3	0	0	0	0.00
Saucier	2	⅔	1	0	0	2	0	0	0	0.00
Bystrom	1	5⅓	7	2	1	2	1	0	0	1.69
Ruthven	2	9	3	2	2	5	4	1	0	2.00
Carlton	2	12⅓	11	3	3	8	6	1	0	2.19
Brusstar	2	2⅔	1	1	1	1	0	1	0	3.38
Christenson	2	6⅔	5	3	3	5	2	0	0	4.05
McGraw	5	8	8	4	4	4	5	0	1	4.50
Reed	3	2	3	4	4	1	1	0	1	18.00
Totals	5	49⅓	40	19	18	31	19	3	2	3.28

Houston Astros

Pitcher	G.	IP.	H.	R.	ER.	BB.	SO.	W.	L.	ERA.
Niekro	1	10	6	0	0	1	2	0	0	0.00
Andujar	1	1	0	0	0	1	0	0	0	0.00
LaCorte	2	3	7	2	1	2	2	1	1	3.00
Ruhle	1	7	8	3	3	1	3	0	0	3.86
D. Smith	3	2⅓	4	1	1	2	4	1	0	3.86
Forsch	2	8⅔	10	4	4	1	6	0	1	4.15
Sambito	3	3⅔	4	2	2	2	6	0	1	4.91
Ryan	2	13⅓	16	8	8	3	14	0	0	5.40
Totals	5	49	55	20	19	13	37	2	3	3.49

1981
NEW YORK YANKEES
VS.
OAKLAND A's

While everyone was concentrating on the war of words between Billy Martin and George Steinbrenner as the Oakland A's and New York Yankees prepared to square off in the American League Championship Series, Graig Nettles quietly went about his business.

The 37-year-old Nettles started the series with a three-run double, keying the Yankees' 3-1 victory in Game 1. He went 4-for-4, including a three-run homer, to lead the Yanks in a 13-3 rout in Game 2. Then he ended the series the way he started it—with a three-run double that climaxed a 4-0 triumph and a three-game Yankee sweep.

"This series was a victory for the veterans," said Nettles. He added that it was an inside joke. But everyone knew Steinbrenner had issued a win-or-else ultimatum to the club during the A.L. East Division Series against Milwaukee. The "or else" meant that the veteran New York club would be broken up.

Nettles' 6-for-12 performance with a Championship Series-record nine RBIs was a dramatic contrast to his 1-for-17 batting mark in the division series against the Brewers.

"George made his big speech before we eliminated Milwaukee in the division series," Nettles said. "He said we'd better win or a lot of the veterans would be gone. We joked about it later."

Joke or no joke, the Yankees were laced with veteran players. Six of their eight starters were over 30 as were seven of their pitchers. Someone suggested in jest that the proud Yankee pinstripes had been erased and replaced by varicose veins.

Martin tried to pull a psyche job on the Yankees before the se-

Third baseman Graig Nettles is greeted at the plate after hitting a three-run homer that helped New York to a 13-3 Game 2 win over Oakland.

ries, saying that his youthful A's were "awesome against lefthanders." He also pointed out that the Yanks had to use their top two pitchers, Ron Guidry and Dave Righetti, to finish off the Brewers.

"If I'm only the No. 3 man in the Yankee rotation, then we must be in pretty good shape because we still have No. 1 and No. 2 waiting to pitch," growled 35-year-old Tommy John after he, Ron Davis and Goose Gossage had stymied the A's on six hits in Game 1.

The victory was secured in the first inning when Larry Milbourne stroked a one-out single, Dave Winfield and Oscar Gamble walked, and Nettles drilled an 0-2

pitch into the left-center field gap to clear the bases.

The A's held a 3-1 lead in Game 2 behind Steve McCatty after they pushed across two runs in the top of the fourth inning. But the Yanks responded with seven runs in their half and rolled to a 13-3 win.

Nettles opened the inning with a single and later set another Championship Series record by becoming the first player to get two hits in one inning. After Bob Watson flied out, Cerone was hit by a pitch and Willie Randolph stroked an RBI single. Jerry Mumphrey walked to load the bases and Dave Beard replaced McCatty on the mound for Oak-

land. Milbourne tied the game with a single before Winfield provided a two-run double and Lou Piniella blasted a three-run homer.

George Frazier hurled 5⅔ innings of scoreless relief for the victory. The Yankees' 13 runs and 19 hits also were records.

Game 3 was a pitchers battle. Oakland's Matt Keough and Righetti of New York threw zeros for the first five innings. Then Randolph broke up the scoreless tie with a two-out homer in the sixth to back the five-hit pitching by Righetti, Davis and Gossage as the Yankees captured their 33rd A.L. pennant.

The Yanks had stranded nine runners in the first five innings before Randolph slugged his first homer since April 28 and his first in postseason play since 1977. New York put the game out of reach in the ninth on Nettles' three-run double.

The Yankees finished off the A's in three straight games, but to borrow a line from Yogi Berra, a coach for the Yankees, "It isn't over 'til it's over." Not when the Yanks are involved at least.

A team party was held at an Oakland restaurant the night of October 15. Friends and family were present and what was billed as a celebration turned into a shoving match when Nettles' family was allegedly mistreated by some of Reggie Jackson's friends. Before order could be restored, Nettles had popped Jackson with a right hand and Mr. October was seeing stars.

It was just another chapter in the wacky world of the Yankees.

Game 1

Tuesday, October 13, At New York

Oakland	AB.	R.	H.	RBI.	PO.	A.
Henderson, lf	4	0	2	0	1	0
Murphy, cf	2	0	0	1	6	0
Johnson, dh	3	0	0	0	0	0
Armas, rf	4	0	1	0	2	1
Klutts, 3b	3	0	2	0	1	1
Gross, ph-3b	1	0	0	0	0	0
Moore, 1b	4	0	0	0	4	1
Newman, c	2	0	0	0	4	1
Drumright, ph	1	0	0	0	0	0
Heath, c	1	0	0	0	1	0
McKay, 2b	4	0	0	0	1	2
Picciolo, ss	3	1	1	0	3	1
Norris, p	0	0	0	0	1	2
Underwood, p	0	0	0	0	0	0
Totals	32	1	6	1	23	7

New York	AB.	R.	H.	RBI.	PO.	A.
Mumphrey, cf	4	0	1	0	1	0
Milbourne, ss	4	1	3	0	2	4
Winfield, lf	3	0	0	0	2	0
Jackson, rf	3	1	0	0	1	0
Gamble, dh	2	1	0	0	0	0
Piniella, ph-dh	1	0	1	0	0	0
Nettles, 3b	3	0	1	3	0	2
Watson, 1b	3	0	1	0	8	0
Brown, pr	0	0	0	0	0	0
Revering, 1b	1	0	0	0	3	0
Cerone, c	2	0	0	0	6	0
Randolph, 2b	3	0	0	0	4	7
John, p	0	0	0	0	0	0
Davis, p	0	0	0	0	0	0
Gossage, p	0	0	0	0	0	0
Totals	29	3	7	3	27	13

Oakland .... 0 0 0 0 1 0 0 0 0—1
New York .... 3 0 0 0 0 0 0 0 x—3

Oakland	IP.	H.	R.	ER.	BB.	SO.
Norris (L)	7⅓	6	3	3	2	4
Underwood	⅔	1	0	0	2	0

New York	IP.	H.	R.	ER.	BB.	SO.
John (W)	6	6	1	1	1	3
Davis	1⅓	0	0	0	2	3
Gossage (S)	1⅔	0	0	0	0	0

Game-winning RBI—Nettles.

E—Nettles, Henderson. DP—New York 2. LOB—Oakland 7, New York 7. 2B—Nettles, Henderson 2. SB—Jackson. SH—Cerone. U—Bremigan, Goetz, Neudecker, Springstead, Merrill and Voltaggio. T—2:52. A—55,740.

Game 2

Wednesday, October 14, At New York

Oakland	AB.	R.	H.	RBI.	PO.	A.
Henderson, lf	5	0	1	1	3	0
Murphy, cf	5	0	2	0	3	0
Moore, 1b	2	0	0	0	3	2
Spencer, ph-1b	2	0	0	0	3	2
Armas, rf	4	0	0	0	1	1
Klutts, 3b	2	1	1	0	0	2
Gross, ph-3b	2	0	0	0	1	0
Heath, c	4	1	2	0	2	0
McKay, 2b	4	0	2	1	2	3
Bosetti, dh	1	1	1	0	0	0
Drumright, ph-dh	2	0	0	0	0	0
Stanley, ss	3	0	1	1	4	2
Davis, ph	1	0	1	0	0	0
McCatty, p	0	0	0	0	1	1
Beard, p	0	0	0	0	0	1
Jones, p	0	0	0	0	1	0
Kingman, p	0	0	0	0	0	0
Owchinko, p	0	0	0	0	0	1
Totals	37	3	11	3	22	12

New York	AB.	R.	H.	RBI.	PO.	A.
Mumphrey, cf	5	2	4	0	3	0
Milbourne, ss	5	2	2	1	0	1
Robertson, ph-ss	1	0	0	0	2	1
Winfield, lf	5	2	2	2	2	0
Jackson, rf	1	0	0	1	0	0
Piniella, rf	3	1	1	3	0	0
Brown, rf	1	1	1	0	0	0
Gamble, dh	3	1	1	1	0	0
Nettles, 3b	4	2	4	3	3	0
Rodriguez, 3b	0	0	0	0	0	0
Watson, 1b	4	0	1	1	2	0
Revering, 1b	1	0	1	0	3	1
Cerone, c	4	1	0	0	10	2
Foote, c	0	0	0	0	0	0
Randolph, 2b	5	1	2	1	2	3
May, p	0	0	0	0	0	0
Frazier, p	0	0	0	0	0	2
Totals	42	13	19	13	27	8

Oakland .... 0 0 1 2 0 0 0 0 0— 3
New York .... 1 0 0 7 0 1 4 0 x—13

Oakland	IP.	H.	R.	ER.	BB.	SO.
McCatty (L)	3⅓	6	5	5	2	2
Beard	⅔	5	3	3	0	0
Jones	2	2	1	1	1	0
Kingman	⅓	3	3	3	0	0
Owchinko	1⅔	3	1	1	0	0

New York	IP.	H.	R.	ER.	BB.	SO.
May	3⅓	6	3	3	0	5
Frazier (W)	5⅔	5	0	0	1	5

Game-winning RBI—Winfield.

E—Klutts. DP—New York 2. LOB—Oakland 8, New York 11. 2B—Mumphrey, Bosetti, Winfield, Murphy. 3B—Henderson. HR—Piniella, Nettles. SB—Winfield. SF—Gamble. HBP—By McCatty (Cerone), by Jones (Nettles). WP—Frazier. PB—Cerone. U—Goetz, Neudecker, Springstead, Merrill, Voltaggio and Bremigan. T—3:08. A—48,497.

Game 3

Thursday, October 15, At Oakland

New York	AB.	R.	H.	RBI.	PO.	A.
Mumphrey, cf	3	0	1	0	0	0
Milbourne, ss	4	1	1	0	0	2
Winfield, lf	5	0	0	0	2	0
Murcer, dh	3	0	1	0	0	0
Piniella, ph-dh	1	1	1	0	0	0
Gamble, rf	1	0	0	0	4	0
Foote, ph	1	0	1	0	0	0
Brown, pr-rf	0	1	0	0	0	0
Nettles, 3b	5	0	1	3	1	2
Watson, 1b	5	0	1	0	7	0
Cerone, c	4	0	1	0	7	0
Randolph, 2b	4	1	2	1	6	2
Righett, p	0	0	0	0	0	1
Davis, p	0	0	0	0	0	0
Gossage, p	0	0	0	0	0	0
Totals	36	4	10	4	27	6

Oakland	AB.	R.	H.	RBI.	PO.	A.
Henderson, lf	2	0	1	0	2	0
Heath, lf	1	0	0	0	0	1
Murphy, cf	1	0	0	0	0	0
Bosetti, ph-cf	3	0	0	0	2	0
Johnson, dh	3	0	0	0	0	0
Armas, rf	4	0	1	0	2	0
Klutts, 3b	2	0	0	0	2	2
Gross, ph-3b	2	0	0	0	1	0
Moore, 1b	2	0	2	0	6	0
Spencer, ph-1b	1	0	0	0	1	0
McKay, 2b	3	0	1	0	4	1
Newman, c	3	0	0	0	5	0
Picciolo, ss	2	0	0	0	2	4
Drumright, ph	1	0	0	0	0	0
Stanley, ss	0	0	0	0	0	0
Keough, p	0	0	0	0	0	1
Underwood, p	0	0	0	0	0	0
Totals	30	0	5	0	27	8

New York .... 0 0 0 0 0 1 0 0 3—4
Oakland .... 0 0 0 0 0 0 0 0 0—0

New York	IP.	H.	R.	ER.	BB.	SO.
Righetti (W)	6	4	0	0	2	4
Davis	2	0	0	0	0	1
Gossage	1	1	0	0	0	2

Oakland	IP.	H.	R.	ER.	BB.	SO.
Keough (L)	8⅓	7	2	1	6	4
Underwood	⅔	3	2	2	0	0

Game-winning RBI—Randolph.

E—Picciolo, McKay. DP—New York 2, Oakland 1. LOB—New York 12, Oakland 5. 2B—Nettles. HR—Randolph. SB—Henderson 2. SH—Milbourne. WP—Keough. U—Neudecker, Springstead, Merrill, Voltaggio, Bremigan and Goetz. T—3:19. A—47,302.

COMPOSITE BATTING AVERAGES

New York Yankees

Player-Position	G.	AB.	R.	H.	2B.	3B.	HR.	RBI.	BA.
Brown, pr-rf	3	1	2	1	0	0	0	0	1.000
Foote, c-ph	2	1	0	1	0	0	0	0	1.000
Piniella, ph-dh-rf	3	5	2	3	0	0	1	3	.600
Nettles, 3b	3	12	2	6	2	0	1	9	.500
Mumphrey, cf	3	12	2	6	1	0	0	0	.500
Revering, 1b	2	2	0	1	0	0	0	0	.500
Milbourne, ss	3	13	4	6	0	0	0	1	.462
Randolph, 2b	3	12	2	4	0	0	1	2	.333
Murcer, dh	1	3	0	1	0	0	0	0	.333
Watson, 1b	3	12	0	3	0	0	0	1	.250
Gamble, dh-rf	3	6	2	1	0	0	0	1	.167
Winfield, lf	3	13	2	2	1	0	0	2	.154
Cerone, c	3	10	1	1	0	0	0	0	.100
Davis, p	2	0	0	0	0	0	0	0	.000
Gossage, p	2	0	0	0	0	0	0	0	.000
Frazier, p	1	0	0	0	0	0	0	0	.000
John, p	1	0	0	0	0	0	0	0	.000
May, p	1	0	0	0	0	0	0	0	.000
Righetti, p	1	0	0	0	0	0	0	0	.000
Rodriguez, 3b	1	0	0	0	0	0	0	0	.000
Robertson, ph-ss	1	1	0	0	0	0	0	0	.000
Jackson, rf	2	4	1	0	0	0	0	1	.000
Totals	3	107	20	36	4	0	3	20	.336

Oakland Athletics

Player-Position	G.	AB.	R.	H.	2B.	3B.	HR.	RBI.	BA.
Davis, ph	1	1	0	1	0	0	0	0	1.000
Klutts, 3b	3	7	1	3	0	0	0	0	.429
Henderson, lf	3	11	0	4	2	1	0	1	.364
Heath, c-lf	3	6	1	2	0	0	0	0	.333
Stanley, ss	2	3	0	1	0	0	0	1	.333
McKay, 2b	3	11	0	3	0	0	0	1	.273
Murphy, cf	3	8	0	2	1	0	0	1	.250
Moore, 1b	3	8	0	2	0	0	0	0	.250
Bosetti, dh-ph-cf	2	4	1	1	1	0	0	0	.250
Picciolo, ss	2	5	1	1	0	0	0	0	.200
Armas, rf	3	12	0	2	0	0	0	0	.167
Underwood, p	2	0	0	0	0	0	0	0	.000
Beard, p	1	0	0	0	0	0	0	0	.000
Jones, p	1	0	0	0	0	0	0	0	.000
Keough, p	1	0	0	0	0	0	0	0	.000
Kingman, p	1	0	0	0	0	0	0	0	.000
McCatty, p	1	0	0	0	0	0	0	0	.000
Norris, p	1	0	0	0	0	0	0	0	.000
Owchinko, p	1	0	0	0	0	0	0	0	.000
Spencer, ph-1b	2	3	0	0	0	0	0	0	.000
Drumright, ph-dh	3	4	0	0	0	0	0	0	.000
Gross, ph-3b	3	5	0	0	0	0	0	0	.000
Newman, c	2	5	0	0	0	0	0	0	.000
Johnson, dh	2	6	0	0	0	0	0	0	.000
Totals	3	99	4	22	4	1	0	4	.222

COMPOSITE PITCHING AVERAGES

New York Yankees

Pitcher	G.	IP.	H.	R.	ER.	BB.	SO.	W.	L.	ERA.
Righetti	1	6	4	0	0	2	4	1	0	0.00
Frazier	1	5⅔	5	0	0	1	5	1	0	0.00
Davis	2	3⅓	0	0	0	2	4	0	0	0.00
Gossage	2	2⅔	1	0	0	0	2	0	0	0.00
John	1	6	6	1	1	1	3	1	0	1.50
May	1	3⅓	6	3	3	0	5	0	0	8.10
Totals	3	27	22	4	4	6	23	3	0	1.33

Oakland Athletics

Pitcher	G.	IP.	H.	R.	ER.	BB.	SO.	W.	L.	ERA.
Keough	1	8⅓	7	2	1	6	4	0	1	1.08
Norris	1	7⅓	6	3	3	2	4	0	1	3.68
Jones	1	2	2	1	1	1	0	0	0	4.50
Owchinko	1	1⅔	3	1	1	0	0	0	0	5.40
McCatty	1	3⅓	6	5	5	2	2	0	1	13.50
Underwood	2	1⅓	4	2	2	2	0	0	0	13.50
Beard	1	⅔	5	3	3	0	0	0	0	40.50
Kingman	1	⅓	3	3	3	0	0	0	0	81.00
Totals	3	25	36	20	19	13	10	0	3	6.84

1981
LOS ANGELES DODGERS
VS.
MONTREAL EXPOS

"I don't know what to think. I'm just numb. I didn't make the pitch where I wanted. Mechanically, I made a mistake. I was called on to do the job and I came up one pitch short."

Montreal ace righthander Steve Rogers was being a little hard on himself October 19 after Rick Monday's two-out, ninth-inning home run had given the Los Angeles Dodgers a 2-1 victory over the Expos and a fifth-game triumph in the National League Championship Series.

There was a chill in the air. The rain that had postponed Game 5 one day earlier also had delayed the start of this game by some 26 minutes. Snow was even in the Montreal forecast.

But by mid-afternoon the sun had broken through and Montreal's Ray Burris and rookie sensation Fernando Valenzuela of the Dodgers had dueled on even terms for eight innings.

When Montreal Manager Jim Fanning summoned Rogers from his bullpen, he was calling on his late-season ace. Rogers had won four straight games and had permitted just two runs in 42 innings. But those statistics were compiled in starting roles.

The relief appearance was only the third in Rogers' nine-year major league career and the first since July 3, 1978.

Lightning struck in the form of the 35-year-old Monday, who was finishing off the final year of a five-year contract with the Dodgers. Monday had batted .315 during the season, including a great month of September when he belted six home runs, but he was on the bench when the Championship Series began. Though he started Game 4 in place of a slumping Ken Landreaux, Monday was 1 for 5 in the

Dejected Montreal Manager Jim Fanning removes pitcher Bill Gullickson after Steve Garvey's Game 4 eighth-inning homer.

series and had struck out four times.

After the Expos took a 1-0 lead in Game 5, it was Monday who started the Dodgers' fifth inning with a single and eventually came home on Valenzuela's groundout. Then, Monday's clout in the ninth turned the 40-degree chill into a warm wonderful day for Lasorda's Dodger Blue.

The series opened in warm, sunny Los Angeles, where the Dodgers had beaten the Expos in 18 of their previous 19 meetings.

The Dodgers were aided by the return of third baseman Ron Cey, while the Expos were boosted by the return of fleet left fielder Tim Raines, who broke a bone in his hand September 12 and was relegated to pinch-running activity.

Cey, who had missed 28 games with a broken bone in his left forearm, celebrated his return to action with a double into the right-field corner to drive home Steve Garvey for the game's first

run in the second inning. Mike Scioscia's single moved Cey to third and he scored on Bill Russell's perfectly placed squeeze bunt.

With two out in the eighth, Cey singled and Pedro Guerrero and Scioscia hit back-to-back home runs to insure the verdict.

Game 2 pitted Valenzuela against Burris. Advantage Dodgers?

Burris proved differently, stopping the Dodgers, 3-0, on five singles to even the series at one game apiece. Burris, who said he tried to throw the ball by the Dodgers earlier in the season when he was shelled for six runs in one start and two in another, kept them off balance all night and was never in serious trouble.

"From Burris to B-R-R-R!!!" read one headline as the series shifted to chilly Montreal for Game 3.

Rogers went the route on a seven-hitter, yielding only one run when the Dodgers put together singles by Dusty Baker and Garvey and a run-scoring groundout by Cey. The Dodgers' Jerry Reuss held a 1-0 lead going into the bottom of the sixth.

Dawson touched him for a seemingly harmless two-out single and the tall, blond lefthander walked Gary Carter. Larry Parrish tied the game with an RBI single and Jerry White turned from anonymous outfielder (.218 with three homers in '81) into a Canadian national hero when he sent one of Reuss' fastballs over the left-field wall for a 4-1 victory.

The script for Game 4 was similar. With the score knotted at 1-1 going into the eighth inning, it was Dodgers first baseman Garvey who stepped into the spotlight.

Baker opened the eighth with a

single off Bill Gullickson and Garvey followed with a two-run homer. The Dodgers sent 10 men to the plate and added four runs in the ninth, coasting home with a 7-1 triumph.

Game 1

Tuesday, October 13, At Los Angeles

Montreal	AB.	R.	H.	RBI.	PO.	A.
Raines, lf	4	0	1	0	5	0
Scott, 2b	3	0	2	0	1	1
Dawson, cf	4	0	0	0	1	0
Carter, c	3	1	2	0	7	1
Parrish, 3b	4	0	1	1	0	0
Cromartie, 1b	4	0	1	0	8	0
White, rf	4	0	2	0	0	0
Speier, ss	4	0	0	0	2	2
Gullickson, p	1	0	0	0	0	1
Francona, ph	1	0	0	0	0	0
Reardon, p	0	0	0	0	0	0
Totals	32	1	9	1	24	5

Los Angeles	AB.	R.	H.	RBI.	PO.	A.
Lopes, 2b	3	0	1	0	6	4
Landreaux, cf	4	0	1	0	0	0
Baker, lf	3	0	0	0	3	0
Garvey, 1b	4	1	1	0	9	0
Cey, 3b	4	1	2	1	2	2
Thomas, pr-3b	0	1	0	0	0	0
Guerrero, rf	4	1	1	2	2	1
Scioscia, c	3	1	2	1	4	1
Russell, ss	3	0	0	1	1	3
Hooton, p	3	0	0	0	0	0
Welch, p	0	0	0	0	0	0
Howe, p	0	0	0	0	0	0
Totals	31	5	8	5	27	11

Montreal	0 0 0 0 0 0 0 0 1—1
Los Angeles	0 2 0 0 0 0 0 3 x—5

Montreal	IP.	H.	R.	ER.	BB.	SO.
Gullickson (L)	7	5	2	2	2	6
Reardon	1	3	3	3	0	0

Los Angeles	IP.	H.	R.	ER.	BB.	SO.
Hooton (W)	7⅓	6	0	0	3	2
Welch	⅔*	2	1	1	0	1
Howe	1	1	0	0	0	0

*Pitched to two batters in the ninth.

Game-winning RBI—Cey.

DP—Los Angeles 4. LOB—Montreal 7, Los Angeles 6. 2B—Carter, White, Cey, Landreaux, Parrish. HR—Guerrero, Scioscia. SB—White, Scott, Lopes 2. SH—Russell. HBP—By Gullickson (Baker). U—Pryor, Gregg, Runge, Rennert, Wendelstedt and West. T—2:47. A—51,273.

Game 2

Wednesday, October 14, At Los Angeles

Montreal	AB.	R.	H.	RBI.	PO.	A.
Raines, lf	5	0	3	1	1	0
Francona, lf	0	0	0	0	0	0
Scott, 2b	4	0	0	0	3	3
Dawson, cf	4	1	1	0	4	0
Carter, c	4	0	2	0	4	0
Parrish, 3b	4	1	1	0	0	3
White, rf	3	1	1	0	1	0
Cromartie, 1b	4	0	1	1	8	1
Speier, ss	3	0	1	0	6	3
Burris, p	4	0	0	0	0	0
Totals	35	3	10	2	27	10

Los Angeles	AB.	R.	H.	RBI.	PO.	A.
Lopes, 2b	3	0	0	0	0	3
Monday, ph	1	0	0	0	0	0
Castillo, p	0	0	0	0	0	1
Landreaux, cf	3	0	0	0	1	0
Baker, lf	4	0	2	0	2	0
Garvey, 1b	4	0	1	0	11	1
Cey, 3b	4	0	0	0	1	4
Guerrero, rf	3	0	0	0	1	1
Scioscia, c	3	0	0	0	7	0
Russell, ss	3	0	2	0	4	3
Valenzuela, p	2	0	0	0	0	1
Niedenfuer, p	0	0	0	0	0	1
Forster, p	0	0	0	0	0	0
Pena, p	0	0	0	0	0	0
Johnstone, ph	1	0	0	0	0	0
Sax, 2b	0	0	0	0	0	1
Totals	31	0	5	0	27	16

Montreal	0 2 0 0 0 1 0 0 0—3
Los Angeles	0 0 0 0 0 0 0 0 0—0

Montreal	IP.	H.	R.	ER.	BB.	SO.
Burris (W)	9	5	0	0	2	3

Los Angeles	IP.	H.	R.	ER.	BB.	SO.
Valenzuela (L)	6	7	3	3	2	4
Niedenfuer	⅓	2	0	0	0	0
Forster	⅓	0	0	0	0	1
Pena	1⅓	1	0	0	0	0
Castillo	1	0	0	0	0	1

Game-winning RBI—Cromartie.

E—Baker, Speier. DP—Montreal 2. LOB—Montreal 7, Los Angeles 6. 2B—Cromartie, Raines. WP—Valenzuela. U—Gregg, Runge, Rennert, Wendelstedt, West and Pryor. T—2:48. A—53,463.

Game 3

Friday, October 16, At Montreal

Los Angeles	AB.	R.	H.	RBI.	PO.	A.
Lopes, 2b	4	0	2	0	2	1
Landreaux, cf	3	0	0	0	2	0
Baker, lf	4	1	1	0	1	0
Garvey, 1b	4	0	2	0	14	1
Cey, 3b	4	0	1	1	2	8
Guerrero, rf	4	0	0	0	0	0
Scioscia, c	4	0	0	0	2	0
Russell, ss	3	0	1	0	1	3
Reuss, p	2	0	0	0	0	0
Johnstone, ph	1	0	0	0	0	0
Pena, p	0	0	0	0	0	0
Totals	33	1	7	1	24	13

Montreal	AB.	R.	H.	RBI.	PO.	A.
Raines, lf	4	0	0	0	1	0
Scott, 2b	4	0	0	0	2	4
Dawson, cf	4	1	2	0	0	0
Carter, c	3	1	1	0	5	1
Parrish, 3b	4	1	2	1	1	6
White, rf	3	1	1	3	0	0
Cromartie, 1b	3	0	0	0	15	0
Speier, ss	3	0	1	0	3	4
Rogers, p	2	0	0	0	0	1
Totals	30	4	7	4	27	16

Los Angeles	0 0 0 1 0 0 0 0 0—1
Montreal	0 0 0 0 0 4 0 0 x—4

Los Angeles	IP.	H.	R.	ER.	BB.	SO.
Reuss (L)	7	7	4	4	1	2
Pena	1	0	0	0	0	0

Montreal	IP.	H.	R.	ER.	BB.	SO.
Rogers (W)	9	7	1	1	1	5

Game-winning RBI—White.

E—Scott. DP—Montreal 3. LOB—Los Angeles 6, Montreal 4. HR—White. SB—Lopes. SH—Rogers. WP—Rogers. PB—Scioscia. U—Runge, Rennert, Wendelstedt, West, Pryor and Gregg. T—2:27. A—54,372.

Game 4

Saturday, October 17, At Montreal

Los Angeles	AB.	R.	H.	RBI.	PO.	A.
Lopes, 2b	4	0	1	0	2	2
Russell, ss	3	2	0	0	2	1
Baker, lf	4	2	3	3	4	0
Garvey, 1b	5	1	2	2	5	0
Cey, 3b	3	0	2	1	0	0
Monday, rf	4	0	1	0	2	0
Landreaux, cf	0	0	0	0	1	0
Guerrero, cf-rf	4	0	0	0	1	0
Welch, p	0	0	0	0	0	0
Smith, ph	1	0	1	1	0	0
Howe, p	0	0	0	0	0	0
Scioscia	2	0	0	0	7	0
Yeager, ph-c	2	1	1	0	2	0
Hooton, p	2	0	0	0	0	1
Thomas, rf	1	1	1	0	1	0
Totals	35	7	12	7	27	4

Montreal	AB.	R.	H.	RBI.	PO.	A.
Raines, lf	4	0	0	0	0	0
Scott, 2b	4	0	1	0	2	2
Dawson, cf	4	0	0	0	3	0
Carter, c	3	1	1	0	8	0
Parrish, 3b	4	0	0	0	2	3
White, rf	3	0	1	0	3	0
Cromartie, 1b	4	0	1	1	5	1
Speier, ss	3	0	1	0	4	2
Gullickson, p	2	0	0	0	0	1
Fryman, p	0	0	0	0	0	0
Sosa, p	0	0	0	0	0	0
Lee, p	0	0	0	0	0	0
Milner, ph	1	0	0	0	0	0
Totals	32	1	5	1	27	9

Los Angeles	0 0 1 0 0 0 0 2 4—7
Montreal	0 0 0 1 0 0 0 0 0—1

Los Angeles	IP.	H.	R.	ER.	BB.	SO.
Hooton (W)	7⅓	5	1	0	3	5
Welch	⅔	0	0	0	0	1
Howe	1	0	0	0	0	2

Montreal	IP.	H.	R.	ER.	BB.	SO.
Gullickson (L)	7⅓	7	3	2	4	6
Fryman	1	3	4	4	1	1
Sosa	⅓	1	0	0	1	0
Lee	⅓	1	0	0	0	0

Game-winning RBI—Garvey.

E—Parrish, Cey. DP—Montreal 2. LOB—Los Angeles 10, Montreal 8. 2B—Baker. HR—Garvey. SB—Lopes. SH—Russell, Gullickson, Hooton, Lopes. U—Rennert, Wendelstedt, West, Pryor, Gregg and Runge. T—3:14. A—54,499.

Game 5

Monday, October 19, At Montreal

Los Angeles	AB.	R.	H.	RBI.	PO.	A.
Lopes, 2b	4	0	1	0	3	3
Russell, ss	4	0	2	0	2	3
Baker, lf	4	0	0	0	0	0
Garvey, 1b	4	0	0	0	10	0
Cey, 3b	3	0	0	0	0	2
Monday, rf	4	2	2	1	0	0
Landreaux, cf	0	0	0	0	0	0
Guerrero, cf-rf	4	0	1	0	5	0
Scioscia, c	3	0	0	0	7	0
Valenzuela, p	3	0	0	1	0	1
Welch, p	0	0	0	0	0	0
Totals	33	2	6	2	27	9

Montreal	AB.	R.	H.	RBI.	PO.	A.
Raines, lf	4	1	1	0	2	0
Scott, 2b	3	0	0	0	4	4
Dawson, cf	4	0	0	0	4	0
Carter, c	3	0	1	0	3	1
Manuel, pr	0	0	0	0	0	0
Parrish, 3b	3	0	1	0	0	1
White, rf	3	0	0	0	2	0
Cromartie, 1b	3	0	0	0	12	0
Speier, ss	3	0	0	0	0	5
Burris, p	2	0	0	0	0	1
Wallach, ph	1	0	0	0	0	0
Rogers, p	0	0	0	0	0	0
Totals	29	1	3	0	27	12

Los Angeles	0 0 0 0 1 0 0 0 1—2
Montreal	1 0 0 0 0 0 0 0 0—1

Los Angeles	IP.	H.	R.	ER.	BB.	SO.
Valenzuela (W)	8⅔	3	1	1	3	6
Welch (S)	⅓	0	0	0	0	0

Montreal	IP.	H.	R.	ER.	BB.	SO.
Burris	8	5	1	1	1	1
Rogers (L)	1	1	1	1	0	1

Game-winning RBI—Monday.

E—Speier. DP—Los Angeles 1, Montreal 1. LOB—Los Angeles 5, Montreal 5. 2B—Raines, Parrish. 3B—Russell. HR—Monday. SB—Lopes. SH—Scott. WP—Burris. U—Wendelstedt, West, Pryor, Gregg, Runge and Rennert. T—2:41. A—36,491.

COMPOSITE BATTING AVERAGES

Los Angeles Dodgers

Player-Position	G.	AB.	R.	H.	2B.	3B.	HR.	RBI.	BA.
Thomas, pr-3b-rf	2	1	2	1	0	0	0	0	1.000
Smith, ph	1	1	0	1	0	0	0	1	1.000
Yeager, ph-c	1	2	1	1	0	0	0	0	.500
Monday, ph-rf	3	9	2	3	0	0	1	1	.333
Baker, lf	5	19	3	6	1	0	0	3	.316
Russell, ss	5	16	2	5	0	1	0	1	.313
Garvey, 1b	5	21	2	6	0	0	1	2	.286
Cey, 3b	5	18	1	5	1	0	0	3	.278
Lopes, 2b	5	18	0	5	0	0	0	0	.278
Scioscia, c	5	15	1	2	0	0	1	1	.133
Guerrero, rf-cf	5	19	1	2	0	0	1	2	.105
Landreaux, cf	5	10	0	1	1	0	0	0	.100
Welch, p	3	0	0	0	0	0	0	0	.000
Howe, p	2	0	0	0	0	0	0	0	.000
Pena, p	2	0	0	0	0	0	0	0	.000
Castillo, p	1	0	0	0	0	0	0	0	.000
Forster, p	1	0	0	0	0	0	0	0	.000
Niedenfuer, p	1	0	0	0	0	0	0	0	.000
Sax, 2b	1	0	0	0	0	0	0	0	.000
Johnstone, ph	2	2	0	0	0	0	0	0	.000
Reuss, p	1	2	0	0	0	0	0	0	.000
Hooton, p	2	5	0	0	0	0	0	0	.000
Valenzuela, p	2	5	0	0	0	0	0	1	.000
Totals	5	163	15	38	3	1	4	15	.233

Montreal Expos

Player-Position	G.	AB.	R.	H.	2B.	3B.	HR.	RBI.	BA.
Carter, c	5	16	3	7	1	0	0	0	.438
White, rf	5	16	2	5	1	0	1	3	.313
Parrish, 3b	5	19	2	5	2	0	0	2	.263
Raines, lf	5	21	1	5	2	0	0	1	.238
Speier, ss	5	16	0	3	0	0	0	0	.188
Cromartie, 1b	5	18	0	3	1	0	0	2	.167
Scott, 2b	5	18	0	3	0	0	0	0	.167
Dawson, cf	5	20	2	3	0	0	0	0	.150
Fryman, p	1	0	0	0	0	0	0	0	.000
Lee, p	1	0	0	0	0	0	0	0	.000
Manuel, pr	1	0	0	0	0	0	0	0	.000
Reardon, p	1	0	0	0	0	0	0	0	.000
Sosa, p	1	0	0	0	0	0	0	0	.000
Francona, ph-lf	2	1	0	0	0	0	0	0	.000
Milner, ph	1	1	0	0	0	0	0	0	.000
Wallach, ph	1	1	0	0	0	0	0	0	.000
Rogers, p	2	2	0	0	0	0	0	0	.000
Gullickson, p	2	3	0	0	0	0	0	0	.000
Burris, p	2	6	0	0	0	0	0	0	.000
Totals	5	158	10	34	7	0	1	8	.215

COMPOSITE PITCHING AVERAGES

Los Angeles Dodgers

Pitcher	G.	IP.	H.	R.	ER.	BB.	SO.	W.	L.	ERA.
Hooton	2	14⅔	11	1	0	6	7	2	0	0.00
Pena	2	2⅓	1	0	0	0	0	0	0	0.00
Howe	2	2	1	0	0	0	2	0	0	0.00
Castillo	1	1	0	0	0	0	1	0	0	0.00
Forster	1	⅓	0	0	0	0	1	0	0	0.00
Niedenfuer	1	⅓	2	0	0	0	0	0	0	0.00
Valenzuela	2	14⅔	10	4	4	5	10	1	1	2.45
Reuss	1	7	7	4	4	1	2	0	1	5.14
Welch	3	1⅔	2	1	1	0	2	0	0	5.40
Totals	5	44	34	10	9	12	25	3	2	1.84

Montreal Expos

Pitcher	G.	IP.	H.	R.	ER.	BB.	SO.	W.	L.	ERA.
Lee	1	⅓	1	0	0	0	0	0	0	0.00
Sosa	1	⅓	1	0	0	1	0	0	0	0.00
Burris	2	17	10	1	1	3	4	1	0	0.53
Rogers	2	10	8	2	2	1	6	1	1	1.80
Gullickson	2	14⅓	12	5	4	6	12	0	2	2.51
Reardon	1	1	3	3	3	0	0	0	0	27.00
Fryman	1	1	3	4	4	1	1	0	0	36.00
Totals	5	44	38	15	14	12	23	2	3	2.86

1982
MILWAUKEE BREWERS
VS.
CALIFORNIA ANGELS

In many postseason games in the American League over the past decade, the man you expected to see celebrating was Reggie Jackson. But it didn't happen in 1982.

Jackson didn't have a chance to wave his magic wand in the ninth inning with California trailing Milwaukee, 4-3, in the fifth and decisive game of the A.L. Championship Series. Instead, he was left in the on-deck circle watching Peter Ladd retire Rod Carew for the final out as the Brewers captured the first A.L. pennant in the franchise's 14 years.

History confronted Manager Harvey Kuenn's Brewers with at least 15 good reasons why they should fail in their bid for a comeback triumph in the series. Entering the 1982 playoffs, 15 teams had fallen behind two games to none in Championship Series play and then dropped into oblivion.

But the Brewers had beaten the odds after losing the first two games of the series at Anaheim and then trailing late in Game 5. In Game 1, the Angels looked like the champions, devastating Mike Caldwell and the Brewers, 8-3, behind five runs batted in by Don Baylor and a complete-game effort by 39-year-old lefthander Tommy John.

Baylor drove home the game's first run with a sacrifice fly in the opening inning. But Milwaukee bolted to a 3-1 advantage on a towering two-run homer by Gorman Thomas in the second and a run-scoring groundout by Cecil Cooper in the third.

Baylor, who set a league record with 21 game-winning RBIs during the season, followed an RBI single by Bobby Grich with a two-run triple in the third to put the Angels ahead, 4-3. In the fourth,

he singled home two more runs. The five RBIs matched a Championship Series record established by Paul Blair of Baltimore in 1969 and equaled by Bob Robertson of Pittsburgh in 1971.

California's Bruce Kison limited the Brewers to five hits in Game 2, struck out eight, issued no walks and induced 14 Milwaukee batters to ground out as the Angels gained a 2-0 cushion in the series with a 4-2 triumph.

The change of scenery seemed to agree with the Brewers when the series shifted to Milwaukee. The Brewers roared to a 5-0 cushion after seven innings in Game 3 and had veteran Don Sutton on the mound.

After Robin Yount walked to lead off the fourth inning, Cooper doubled him home. Ted Simmons singled Cooper to third before Thomas produced the second run with a sacrifice fly to center. A single by Ben Oglivie preceded another sacrifice fly, this one by Don Money. The Brewers added to that 3-0 lead when Paul Molitor collected his second two-run homer in as many games in the seventh inning.

The Brewers, with Ladd closing the door, held on for a 5-3 victory.

The next afternoon, following a rain delay at the start, pitcher Moose Haas got the call for the Brewers and John was back for the Angels after only three days rest.

But the name to remember in Game 4 was Mark Brouhard, a substitute left fielder for Oglivie, who was bothered by a rib injury. Brouhard hadn't played since September 11 but scored four times, had a single, double and homer and drove in three runs to key the Brewers' 9-5 victory that evened the series at two games

apiece.

The Angels opened Game 5 with a double by Brian Downing, who later scored on a single by Fred Lynn. But the Brewers scored in their half of the first on a double by Molitor, a grounder and a sacrifice fly by Simmons.

Lynn, who had 11 hits in the playoffs and was the series' Most Valuable Player, drove home the second California run with a single in the third. Bob Boone extended the Angels' lead to 3-1 in the fourth with an RBI single.

But Oglivie, back in the lineup, belted a long home run over the right-field wall in the Brewers' fourth.

Kison, who had a lifetime September-October record of 32-8, pitched five innings before giving way to hard-throwing Luis Sanchez. Sanchez mowed down the Brewers in the sixth and then retired Money to lead off the seventh before running into trouble.

Moore's bloop hit dropped in the middle of the infield, just out of the reach of a diving Grich at second base. First-base umpire Al Clark ruled that Grich had caught the ball, but was overruled by home-plate umpire Don Denkinger.

Gantner followed with a single up the middle and, after Molitor fouled out for the second out, Yount coaxed a walk.

Cooper, who had gone 2 for 19 and was hitless in his previous nine at-bats, strolled to the plate. He had been a .313 hitter during the regular season. Nearly everyone expected California Manager Gene Mauch to bring in lefthander Andy Hassler, but the veteran skipper stayed with Sanchez.

The 1-and-1 pitch to Cooper was a fastball, tailing away but slightly up in the strike zone, and Cooper stroked it to left field.

Two runs scored and the Brewers were on their way to the World Series.

Game 1

Tuesday, October 5, At California

Milwaukee	AB.	R.	H.	RBI.	PO.	A.
Molitor, 3b	4	1	1	0	0	0
Yount, ss	4	0	1	0	4	1
Cooper, 1b	4	0	1	1	6	0
Simmons, c	4	1	2	0	7	0
Thomas, cf	4	1	1	2	3	0
Oglivie, lf	4	0	0	0	2	0
Money, dh	3	0	0	0	0	0
Moore, rf	3	0	1	0	1	0
Gantner, 2b	4	0	0	0	0	3
Caldwell, p	0	0	0	0	0	2
Slaton, p	0	0	0	0	1	0
Ladd, p	0	0	0	0	0	0
Bernard, p	0	0	0	0	0	0
Totals	34	3	7	3	24	6

California	AB.	R.	H.	RBI.	PO.	A.
Downing, lf	4	2	1	0	1	0
Beniquez, lf	0	0	0	0	1	0
DeCinces, 3b	4	2	1	0	2	5
Grich, 2b	3	1	2	1	1	3
Baylor, dh	3	1	2	5	0	0
Re. Jackson, rf	4	0	0	1	0	0
Clark, rf	0	0	0	0	1	0
Lynn, cf	4	1	3	1	4	0
Carew, 1b	4	0	0	0	8	2
Foli, ss	4	0	0	0	1	1
Boone, c	4	1	1	0	5	0
John, p	0	0	0	0	3	1
Totals	34	8	10	8	27	12

Milwaukee	0 2 1	0 0 0	0 0 0	—3
California	1 0 4	2 1 0	0 0 x	—8

Milwaukee	IP.	H.	R.	ER.	BB.	SO.
Caldwell (L)	3*	7	6	5	1	2
Slaton	3	3	2	1	1	2
Ladd	1	0	0	0	0	3
Bernard	1	0	0	0	0	0

California	IP.	H.	R.	ER.	BB.	SO.
John (W)	9	7	3	3	1	5

*Pitched to one batter in fourth.

Game-winning RBI—Baylor.

E—Caldwell, Molitor. DP—Milwaukee 1. LOB—Milwaukee 6, California 5. 2B—Cooper, Grich. 3B—Baylor. HR—Thomas, Lynn. SF—Baylor. HBP—By John (Moore). WP—Caldwell. U—Barnett, Kunkel, Garcia, Palermo, Denkinger and Clark. T—2:31. A—64,406.

Game 2

Wednesday, October 6, At California

Milwaukee	AB.	R.	H.	RBI.	PO.	A.
Molitor, 3b	4	1	2	2	1	1
Yount, ss	4	0	1	0	2	3
Cooper, 1b	4	0	0	0	5	1
Simmons, c	4	0	0	0	5	0
Oglivie, lf	4	0	0	0	1	0
Thomas, cf	3	0	0	0	3	0
Howell, dh	3	0	0	0	0	0
Moore, rf	3	1	2	0	3	0
Gantner, 2b	3	0	0	0	4	2
Vuckovich, p	0	0	0	0	0	1
Totals	32	2	5	2	24	8

California	AB.	R.	H.	RBI.	PO.	A.
Downing, lf	3	0	0	0	1	0
Beniquez, lf	0	0	0	0	0	0
Carew, 1b	4	0	0	0	14	0
Re. Jackson, rf	3	1	1	1	1	0
Clark, rf	0	0	0	0	0	0
Lynn, cf	4	1	2	0	1	0
Baylor, dh	3	0	0	0	0	0
DeCinces, 3b	3	2	1	0	1	1
Grich, 2b	2	0	1	0	1	5
Foli, ss	2	0	1	1	0	2
Boone, c	1	0	0	2	8	1
Kison, p	0	0	0	0	0	0
Totals	25	4	6	4	27	9

Milwaukee	0 0 0	0 2 0	0 0 0	—2
California	0 2 1	1 0 0	0 0 x	—4

Milwaukee	IP.	H.	R.	ER.	BB.	SO.
Vuckovich (L)	8	6	4	4	4	4

California	IP.	H.	R.	ER.	BB.	SO.
Kison (W)	9	5	2	2	0	8

Game-winning RBI—Foli.

DP—Milwaukee 2. LOB—Milwaukee 3, California 5. 2B—DeCinces. HR—Re. Jackson, Molitor. SH—Boone, Foli. SF—Boone. HBP—By Vuckovich (Grich). U—Kunkel, Garcia, Palermo, Denkinger, Clark and Barnett. T—2:06. A—64,179.

Game 3

Friday, October 8, At Milwaukee

California	AB.	R.	H.	RBI.	PO.	A.
Downing, lf	4	0	0	0	2	0
Carew, 1b	4	1	2	0	4	0
Re. Jackson, rf	4	0	1	0	0	0
Lynn, cf	3	1	2	1	4	0
Baylor, dh	3	0	1	1	0	0
DeCinces, 3b	4	0	1	0	3	1
Grich, 2b	4	0	0	0	2	2
Foli, ss	3	0	0	0	3	1
Wilfong, ph	1	0	0	0	0	0
Boone, c	4	1	1	1	6	0
Zahn, p	0	0	0	0	0	0
Witt, p	0	0	0	0	0	1
Hassler, p	0	0	0	0	0	0
Totals	34	3	8	3	24	5

Milwaukee	AB.	R.	H.	RBI.	PO.	A.
Molitor, 3b	4	1	1	2	1	4
Yount, ss	2	1	1	0	0	4
Cooper, 1b	4	1	1	1	12	0
Simmons, c	4	1	1	0	11	0
Thomas, cf	3	0	0	1	2	0
Oglivie, lf	3	0	1	0	0	0
Money, dh	1	0	0	1	0	0
Edwards, pr-dh	0	1	0	0	0	0
Moore, rf	2	0	1	0	0	0
Gantner, 2b	3	0	0	0	1	1
Sutton, p	0	0	0	0	0	1
Ladd, p	0	0	0	0	0	0
Totals	26	5	6	5	27	10

California	0 0 0	0 0 0	0 3 0	—3
Milwaukee	0 0 0	3 0 0	2 0 x	—5

California	IP.	H.	R.	ER.	BB.	SO.
Zahn (L)	3$\frac{2}{3}$	4	3	3	1	2
Witt	3	2	2	2	2	3
Hassler	1$\frac{1}{3}$	0	0	0	0	1

Milwaukee	IP.	H.	R.	ER.	BB.	SO.
Sutton (W)	7$\frac{2}{3}$	8	3	3	2	9
Ladd (S)	1$\frac{1}{3}$	0	0	0	0	2

Game-winning RBI—Cooper.

DP—California 1, Milwaukee 1. LOB—California 6, Milwaukee 4. 2B—Lynn, Baylor, Cooper. HR—Molitor, Boone. SB—Carew. SH—Moore. SF—Thomas, Money. HBP—By Zahn (Oglivie). U—Garcia, Palermo, Denkinger, Clark, Barnett and Kunkel. T—2:41. A—50,135.

Game 4

Saturday, October 9, At Milwaukee

California	AB.	R.	H.	RBI.	PO.	A.
Downing, lf	4	1	1	0	0	0
Carew, 1b	2	1	1	0	10	2
Re. Jackson, rf	4	1	0	0	0	0
Lynn, cf	3	1	1	1	4	0
Baylor, dh	4	1	1	4	0	0
DeCinces, 3b	4	0	0	0	1	3
Grich, 2b	3	0	0	0	3	5
Foli, ss	4	0	1	0	2	3
Boone, c	4	0	0	0	4	2
John, p	0	0	0	0	0	0
Goltz, p	0	0	0	0	0	0
Sanchez, p	0	0	0	0	0	0
Totals	32	5	5	5	24	15

Milwaukee	AB.	R.	H.	RBI.	PO.	A.
Molitor, 3b	4	0	0	1	0	3
Yount, ss	4	0	1	0	2	2
Cooper, 1b	4	0	0	0	5	1
Simmons, c	3	1	0	0	9	1
Thomas, cf	2	0	0	0	5	0
Money, dh	3	2	2	0	0	0
Edwards, pr-dh	0	1	0	0	0	0
Brouhard, lf	4	4	3	3	1	0
Moore, rf	2	1	1	0	2	0
Gantner, 2b	4	0	2	2	3	0
Haas, p	0	0	0	0	0	0
Slaton, p	0	0	0	0	0	0
Totals	30	9	9	6	27	7

California	0 0 0	0 0 1	0 4 0	—5
Milwaukee	0 3 0	3 0 1	0 2 x	—9

California	IP.	H.	R.	ER.	BB.	SO.
John (L)	3$\frac{1}{3}$	4	6	4	5	1
Goltz	3$\frac{2}{3}$	4	3	3	2	2
Sanchez	1	1	0	0	0	0

Milwaukee	IP.	H.	R.	ER.	BB.	SO.
Haas (W)	7$\frac{1}{3}$	5	5	4	5	7
Slaton (S)	1$\frac{2}{3}$	0	0	0	0	1

*Pitched to two batters in eighth.

Game-winning RBI—Brouhard.

E—Lynn, DeCinces 2, Yount, Cooper. DP—California 1. LOB—California 5, Milwaukee 5. 2B—Lynn, Carew, Brouhard. HR—Baylor, Brouhard. SB—Edwards. SH—Moore. WP—John 3. PB—Boone. U—Palermo, Denkinger, Clark, Barnett, Kunkel and Garcia. T—3:10. A—51,003.

Game 5

Sunday, October 10, At Milwaukee

California	AB.	R.	H.	RBI.	PO.	A.
Downing, lf	4	1	1	0	1	0
Carew, 1b	3	0	0	0	7	0
Re. Jackson, rf	3	0	0	0	1	0
Lynn, cf	4	0	3	2	3	0
Baylor, dh	4	0	1	0	0	0
DeCinces, 3b	4	1	3	0	2	2
Grich, 2b	3	0	0	0	3	2
Foli, ss	3	0	0	0	0	0
Ro. Jackson, ph	1	0	1	0	0	0
Wilfong, pr	0	0	0	0	0	0
Boone, c	3	1	2	1	7	0
Kison, p	0	0	0	0	0	0
Sanchez, p	0	0	0	0	0	0
Hassler, p	0	0	0	0	0	1
Totals	32	3	11	3	24	5

Milwaukee	AB.	R.	H.	RBI.	PO.	A.
Molitor, 3b	3	1	2	0	2	3
Yount, ss	2	0	0	0	3	2
Cooper, 1b	4	0	1	2	9	1
Simmons, c	3	0	0	1	4	2
Oglivie, lf	4	1	1	1	2	0
Thomas, cf	3	0	0	0	0	0
Edwards, cf	1	0	0	0	2	0
Money, dh	4	0	0	0	0	0
Moore, rf	3	1	1	0	1	1
Gantner, 2b	2	1	1	0	4	2
Vuckovich, p	0	0	0	0	0	2
McClure, p	0	0	0	0	0	0
Ladd, p	0	0	0	0	0	1
Totals	29	4	6	4	27	14

California	1 0 1	1 0 0	0 0 0	—3
Milwaukee	1 0 0	1 0 0	2 0 x	—4

California	IP.	H.	R.	ER.	BB.	SO.
Kison	5	3	2	1	3	4
Sanchez (L)	1$\frac{2}{3}$	3	2	2	1	1
Hassler	1$\frac{1}{3}$	0	0	0	0	1

Milwaukee	IP.	H.	R.	ER.	BB.	SO.
Vuckovich	6$\frac{1}{3}$	9	3	3	3	4
McClure (W)	1$\frac{2}{3}$*	2	0	0	0	0
Ladd (S)	1	0	0	0	0	0

*Pitched to one batter in ninth.

Game-winning RBI—Cooper.

E—Oglivie 2, Molitor, Cooper, DeCinces. DP—California 1, Milwaukee 2. LOB—California 8, Milwaukee 6. 2B—Downing, DeCinces, Molitor. HR—Oglivie. SB—Molitor. SH—Downing, Grich, Boone. SF—Simmons. U—Denkinger, Clark, Barnett, Kunkel, Garcia and Palermo. T—3:01. A—54,968.

COMPOSITE BATTING AVERAGES

Milwaukee Brewers

Player-Position	G.	AB.	R.	H.	2B.	3B.	HR.	RBI.	BA.
Brouhard, lf	1	4	4	3	1	0	1	3	.750
Moore, rf	5	13	3	6	0	0	0	0	.462
Molitor, 3b	5	19	4	6	1	0	2	5	.316
Yount, ss	5	16	1	4	0	0	0	0	.250
Gantner, 2b	5	16	1	3	0	0	0	2	.188
Money, dh	4	11	2	2	0	0	0	1	.182
Simmons, c	5	18	3	3	0	0	0	1	.167
Cooper, 1b	5	20	1	3	2	0	0	4	.150
Oglivie, lf	4	15	1	2	0	0	1	1	.133
Thomas, cf	5	16	1	1	0	0	1	3	.063
Edwards, pr-dh-cf	3	0	2	0	0	0	0	0	.000
Ladd, p	3	0	0	0	0	0	0	0	.000
Slaton, p	2	0	0	0	0	0	0	0	.000
Vuckovich, p	2	0	0	0	0	0	0	0	.000
Bernard, p	1	0	0	0	0	0	0	0	.000
Caldwell, p	1	0	0	0	0	0	0	0	.000
Haas, p	1	0	0	0	0	0	0	0	.000
McClure, p	1	0	0	0	0	0	0	0	.000
Sutton, p	1	0	0	0	0	0	0	0	.000
Howell, dh	1	3	0	0	0	0	0	0	.000
Totals	5	151	23	33	4	0	5	20	.219

California Angels

Player-Position	G.	AB.	R.	H.	2B.	3B.	HR.	RBI.	BA.
Ro. Jackson, ph	1	1	0	1	0	0	0	0	1.000
Lynn, cf	5	18	5	11	2	0	1	5	.611
DeCinces, 3b	5	19	5	6	2	0	0	0	.316
Baylor, dh	5	17	2	5	1	1	1	10	.294
Boone, c	5	16	3	4	0	0	1	4	.250
Grich, 2b	5	15	1	3	1	0	0	1	.200
Carew, 1b	5	17	2	3	1	0	0	0	.176
Downing, lf	5	19	3	3	1	0	0	0	.158
Foli, ss	5	16	0	2	0	0	0	1	.125
Re. Jackson, rf	5	18	2	2	0	0	1	2	.111
Beniquez, lf	2	0	0	0	0	0	0	0	.000
Clark, rf	2	0	0	0	0	0	0	0	.000
Hassler, p	2	0	0	0	0	0	0	0	.000
John, p	2	0	0	0	0	0	0	0	.000
Kison, p	2	0	0	0	0	0	0	0	.000
Sanchez, p	2	0	0	0	0	0	0	0	.000
Goltz, p	1	0	0	0	0	0	0	0	.000
Witt, p	1	0	0	0	0	0	0	0	.000
Zahn, p	1	0	0	0	0	0	0	0	.000
Wilfong, ph-pr	2	1	0	0	0	0	0	0	.000
Totals	5	157	23	40	8	1	4	23	.255

COMPOSITE PITCHING AVERAGES

Milwaukee Brewers

Pitcher	G.	IP.	H.	R.	ER.	BB.	SO.	W.	L.	ERA.
Ladd	3	3$\frac{1}{3}$	0	0	0	0	5	0	0	0.00
McClure	1	1$\frac{2}{3}$	2	0	0	0	0	1	0	0.00
Bernard	1	1	0	0	0	0	0	0	0	0.00
Slaton	2	4$\frac{2}{3}$	3	2	1	1	3	0	0	1.93
Sutton	1	7$\frac{2}{3}$	8	3	3	2	9	1	0	3.52
Vuckovich	2	14$\frac{1}{3}$	15	7	7	7	8	0	1	4.40
Haas	1	7$\frac{1}{3}$	5	5	4	5	7	1	0	4.91
Caldwell	1	3	7	6	5	1	2	0	1	15.00
Totals	5	43	40	23	20	16	34	3	2	4.19

California Angels

Pitcher	G.	IP.	H.	R.	ER.	BB.	SO.	W.	L.	ERA.
Hassler	2	2$\frac{2}{3}$	0	0	0	0	2	0	0	0.00
Kison	2	14	8	4	3	3	12	1	0	1.93
John	2	12$\frac{1}{3}$	11	9	7	6	6	1	1	5.11
Witt	1	3	2	2	2	2	3	0	0	6.00
Sanchez	2	2$\frac{2}{3}$	4	2	2	1	1	0	1	6.75
Goltz	1	3$\frac{2}{3}$	4	3	3	2	2	0	0	7.36
Zahn	1	3$\frac{2}{3}$	4	3	3	1	2	0	1	7.36
Totals	5	42	33	23	20	15	28	2	3	4.29

1982
ST. LOUIS CARDINALS
VS.
ATLANTA BRAVES

Darrell Porter was finally back in the baseball limelight as reporters approached him in the locker room at Atlanta Stadium. The veteran catcher had just helped the St. Louis Cardinals sweep the Atlanta Braves in the 1982 National League Championship Series.

Porter turned in his best offensive showing since leaving Kansas City following the 1980 season to sign a huge free-agent contract with the Cardinals. He reached base safely 10 times (five hits and five walks) in 14 plate appearances. He drove in a run, scored once in each of the three games and tied a Championship Series record (for a three-game series) with three doubles.

Porter, who had set his life straight after years of alcohol and drug abuse, batted .231 during the 1982 season after hitting .224 in 1981 for the Cardinals. But he was the driving force in the Cardinals' first Championship Series appearance.

Rain aborted Game 1 in which the Braves, behind pitching ace Phil Niekro, were leading the Cardinals 1-0 after 4½ innings. The postponement erased Niekro and Joaquin Andujar of the Cardinals as the opening-game pitchers. Bob Forsch then treated the St. Louis fans to a dazzling three-hit shutout one night later as the Cardinals jumped in front in the series with a 7-0 victory.

Forsch, who struck out six batters and walked none, became the third man to pitch a shutout in the first game of a league Championship Series. The others were Baltimore's Jim Palmer in 1973 and Don Sutton of Los Angeles in 1974.

Forsch helped offensively, too. He had two singles, hit a sacrifice fly in a five-run sixth inning that

St. Louis third baseman Ken Oberkfell and relief ace Bruce Sutter prepare to celebrate after the Cardinals' 1982 three-game sweep of Atlanta.

spelled the exit of starter-loser Pascual Perez and scored the game's final run in the eighth.

The Cardinals broke it open in the sixth, setting a Championship Series record for most hits in an inning (six) and tying the mark for most runs (five). George Hendrick, Willie McGee and Ozzie Smith produced run-scoring singles to highlight the outburst.

Prior to the series there hadn't been a rainout at Busch Memorial Stadium since August of 1976, but Game 2 also was delayed a day.

Though the Cardinals scored a run off Niekro in the first inning

of the second contest, the Braves took command in the third. Rafael Ramirez singled home Bruce Benedict, who had walked and advanced to second on a sacrifice, and then came all the way around himself when the ball got past McGee in center field and went to the wall for a three-base error.

With knuckleballer Niekro pitching well after his washed-out effort of three days earlier, the Braves increased their lead to 3-1 in the fifth on a single by Glenn Hubbard, Benedict's double and a sacrifice fly by Niekro.

The Cardinals pecked away at

the lead, getting a sixth-inning run on Porter's second double of the game, which chased Keith Hernandez home from first base. And with Gene Garber pitching in the eighth for the Braves, Porter drew a one-out walk, went to third on a single by Hendrick and scored the tying run on McGee's high bounder up the middle. Atlanta shortstop Ramirez got to the ball, but the only man he could retire was Hendrick at second base.

Momentum seemingly had swung to the Cardinals.

David Green, who went in to play left field in the eighth inning, opened the ninth with a single to left. Tom Herr sacrificed Green to second, bringing Ken Oberkfell to the plate.

Oberkfell, who had a .289 average during the regular season but a .600 mark over his career against Garber (6 for 10), was given a chance to bat even though Cardinal reliever Bruce Sutter was scheduled next.

When Oberkfell lashed a liner just over the glove of a leaping Brett Butler in center field, the Cardinals had themselves a 4-3 victory and a 2-0 lead in the series.

If the come-from-behind effort by the Cardinals in Game 2 hadn't finished off the Braves, then a four-run outburst in the second inning of Game 3 at Atlanta did.

Hernandez began the uprising with a single to left. Porter walked. Hendrick lined a single to right-center field to score Hernandez. McGee then split the gap in right-center for a triple, making the score 3-0. Ozzie Smith boosted the lead to four runs with a single to left-center. Exit Atlanta starter Rick Camp.

The Redbirds added a run in the fifth on a leadoff double by Herr and a two-out single by Hernandez. And McGee hit a bases-empty homer in the ninth.

The only runs the Braves could manage against Andujar came in the seventh when Atlanta had four singles, scoring on a double-play grounder by Chris Chambliss and a single by Hubbard. Sutter quelled that rally, and retired the last seven batters for a 6-2 triumph.

Game 1

Thursday, October 7, At St. Louis

Atlanta	AB.	R.	H.	RBI.	PO.	A.
Washington, rf	4	0	2	0	3	0
Ramirez, ss	4	0	0	1	2	
Murphy, cf	4	0	0	0	4	0
Chambliss, 1b	3	0	0	0	8	1
Horner, 3b	3	0	0	0	0	2
Royster, lf	3	0	0	0	2	0
Hubbard, 2b	3	0	0	0	0	3
Benedict, c	3	0	1	0	5	0
Perez, p	2	0	0	0	0	0
Bedrosian, p	0	0	0	0	0	0
Moore, p	0	0	0	0	1	0
Whisenton, ph	1	0	0	0	0	0
Walk, p	0	0	0	0	0	0
Totals	30	0	3	0	24	9

St. Louis	AB.	R.	H.	RBI.	PO.	A.
Herr, 2b	5	0	2	0	2	2
Oberkfell, 3b	5	0	1	1	0	3
L. Smith, lf	3	1	1	1	0	0
Green, lf	0	0	0	0	0	0
Hernandez, 1b	4	1	1	0	10	0
Hendrick, rf	4	1	1	1	3	0
Porter, c	4	1	2	0	6	1
McGee, cf	4	2	2	1	3	0
O. Smith, ss	3	0	1	2	3	4
Forsch, p	3	1	2	1	0	2
Totals	35	7	13	7	27	12

Atlanta ....0 0 0 0 0 0 0 0 0—0
St. Louis ....0 0 1 0 0 5 0 1 x—7

Atlanta	IP.	H.	R.	ER.	BB.	SO.
Perez (L)	5*	4	4	1	2	0
Bedrosian	2/3	3	2	2	1	1
Moore	1 1/3	1	0	0	0	1
Walk	1	2	1	1	1	1

St. Louis	IP.	H.	R.	ER.	BB.	SO.
Forsch (W)	9	3	0	0	0	6

*Pitched to three batters in sixth.

Game-winning RBI—O. Smith.

E—Oberkfell. LOB—Atlanta 3, St. Louis 11. 2B—Porter. 3B—McGee. SF—O. Smith, Forsch, L. Smith. HBP—By Moore (L. Smith). WP—Bedrosian. U—Williams, Engel, Wendelstedt, Froemming, Rennert and Runge. T—2:25. A—53,008.

Game 2

Saturday, October 9, At St. Louis

Atlanta	AB.	R.	H.	RBI.	PO.	A.
Washington, rf	3	0	0	0	2	1
Ramirez, ss	4	1	1	1	2	5
Murphy, cf-lf	4	0	1	0	1	0
Chambliss, 1b	3	0	0	0	12	1
Horner, 3b	4	0	0	0	1	0
Butler, cf	0	0	0	0	0	0
Royster, lf-3b	4	0	2	0	0	0
Hubbard, 2b	3	1	1	0	1	4
Benedict, c	2	1	1	0	5	2
Niekro, p	0	0	0	0	1	1
Pocoroba, ph	1	0	0	0	0	0
Garber, p	1	0	0	0	0	1
Totals	29	3	6	2	25	15

St. Louis	AB.	R.	H.	RBI.	PO.	A.
Herr, 2b	3	0	0	0	2	2
Oberkfell, 3b	5	1	1	1	1	0
L. Smith, lf	4	0	1	0	1	0
Sutter, p	0	0	0	0	0	2
Hernandez, 1b	4	1	1	0	11	1
Porter, c	2	1	2	1	5	1
Hendrick, rf	4	0	2	0	1	0
McGee, cf	4	0	0	1	6	0
O. Smith, ss	2	0	1	0	0	3
Stuper, p	1	0	0	0	0	0
Braun, ph	1	0	0	0	0	0
Bair, p	0	0	0	0	0	1
Green, lf	1	1	1	0	0	0
Totals	31	4	9	3	27	10

Atlanta ....0 0 2 0 1 0 0 0 0—3
St. Louis ....1 0 0 0 0 1 0 1 1—4

One out when winning run scored.

Atlanta	IP.	H.	R.	ER.	BB.	SO.
Niekro	6	6	2	2	4	5
Garber (L)	2 1/3	3	2	2	1	2

St. Louis	IP.	H.	R.	ER.	BB.	SO.
Stuper	6	4	3	2	1	4
Bair	1*	2	0	0	3	0
Sutter (W)	2	0	0	0	0	1

*Pitched to two batters in eighth.

Game-winning RBI—Oberkfell.

E—McGee. LOB—Atlanta 6, St. Louis 9. 2B—Porter 2, Benedict. SB—O. Smith, Murphy. SH—Stuper, Niekro, Hubbard, Herr. SF—Niekro. WP—Niekro. PB—Benedict. U—Engel, Wendelstedt, Froemming, Rennert, Runge and Williams. T—2:46. A—53,408.

Game 3

Sunday, October 10, At Atlanta

St. Louis	AB.	R.	H.	RBI.	PO.	A.
Herr, 2b	5	1	1	0	2	6
Oberkfell, 3b	5	0	1	0	1	1
L. Smith, lf	5	0	1	0	1	0
Hernandez, 1b	4	1	2	1	14	0
Porter, c	3	1	1	0	4	1
Hendrick, rf	5	1	1	1	4	0
McGee, cf	5	2	2	3	3	0
O. Smith, ss	4	0	3	1	4	4

	AB.	R.	H.	RBI.	PO.	A.
Andujar, p	1	0	0	0	0	1
Sutter, p	1	0	0	0	0	0
Totals	37	6	12	6	27	13

Atlanta	AB.	R.	H.	RBI.	PO.	A.
Ramirez, ss	3	0	1	0	2	4
Royster, lf	4	0	0	0	2	0
Washington, rf	2	0	1	0	0	0
Harper, pr-rf	1	1	0	0	0	0
Horner, 3b	4	0	1	0	1	3
Chambliss, 1b	4	0	0	1	10	3
Murphy, cf	3	1	2	0	3	0
Hubbard, 2b	3	0	1	1	3	4
Benedict, c	3	0	0	0	6	0
Camp, p	0	0	0	0	0	0
Perez, p	1	0	0	0	0	0
Moore, p	0	0	0	0	0	0
Whisenton, ph	1	0	0	0	0	0
Mahler, p	0	0	0	0	0	0
Bedrosian, p	0	0	0	0	0	0
Butler, ph	1	0	0	0	0	0
Garber, p	0	0	0	0	0	0
Totals	30	2	6	1	27	15

St. Louis ....0 4 0 0 0 3 0 0 0—6
Atlanta ....0 0 0 0 0 0 2 0 0—2

St. Louis	IP.	H.	R.	ER.	BB.	SO.
Andujar (W)	6 2/3	6	2	2	2	4
Sutter (S)	2 1/3	0	0	0	0	0

Atlanta	IP.	H.	R.	ER.	BB.	SO.
Camp (L)	1*	4	4	4	1	0
Perez	3 2/3	3	1	1	1	2
Moore	1 1/3	0	0	0	0	0
Mahler	1 2/3	3	0	0	2	0
Bedrosian	1/3	0	0	0	0	1
Garber	1	1	1	1	1	0

*Pitched to five batters in second.

Game-winning RBI—Hendrick.

E—Ramirez. DP—St. Louis 3. LOB—St. Louis 11, Atlanta 3. 2B—Herr. 3B—McGee. HR—McGee. SH—Andujar 2, L. Smith. WP—Andujar 2. Balk—Andujar. U—Wendelstedt, Froemming, Rennert, Runge, Williams and Engel. T—2:51. A—52,173.

COMPOSITE BATTING AVERAGES

St. Louis Cardinals

Player-Position	G.	AB.	R.	H.	2B.	3B.	HR.	RBI.	BA.
Green, lf	2	1	1	1	0	0	0	0	1.000
Forsch, p	1	3	1	2	0	0	0	1	.667
Porter, c	3	9	3	5	3	0	0	1	.556
O. Smith, ss	3	9	0	5	0	0	0	3	.556
Hernandez, 1b	3	12	3	4	0	0	0	1	.333
McGee, cf	3	13	4	4	0	2	1	5	.308
Hendrick, rf	3	13	2	4	0	0	0	2	.308
L. Smith, lf	3	11	1	3	0	0	0	1	.273
Herr, 2b	3	13	1	3	1	0	0	0	.231
Oberkfell, 3b	3	15	1	3	0	0	0	2	.200
Bair, p	1	0	0	0	0	0	0	0	.000
Sutter, p	2	1	0	0	0	0	0	0	.000
Andujar, p	1	2	0	0	0	0	0	0	.000
Braun, ph	1	1	0	0	0	0	0	0	.000
Stuper, p	1	1	0	0	0	0	0	0	.000
Totals	3	103	17	34	4	2	1	16	.330

Atlanta Braves

Player-Position	G.	AB.	R.	H.	2B.	3B.	HR.	RBI.	BA.
Washington, rf	3	9	0	3	0	0	0	0	.333
Murphy, cf-lf	3	11	1	3	0	0	0	0	.273
Benedict, c	3	8	1	2	1	0	0	0	.250
Hubbard, 2b	3	9	1	2	0	0	0	1	.222
Ramirez, ss	3	11	1	2	0	0	0	1	.182
Royster, lf-3b	3	11	0	2	0	0	0	0	.182
Horner, 3b	3	11	0	1	0	0	0	0	.091
Bedrosian, p	2	0	0	0	0	0	0	0	.000
Moore, p	2	0	0	0	0	0	0	0	.000
Camp, p	1	0	0	0	0	0	0	0	.000
Mahler, p	1	0	0	0	0	0	0	0	.000
Niekro, p	1	0	0	0	0	0	0	1	.000
Walk, p	1	0	0	0	0	0	0	0	.000
Butler, cf-ph	2	1	0	0	0	0	0	0	.000
Garber, p	2	1	0	0	0	0	0	0	.000
Pocoroba, ph	1	1	0	0	0	0	0	0	.000
Harper, pr-rf	1	1	1	0	0	0	0	0	.000
Whisenton, ph	2	2	0	0	0	0	0	0	.000
Perez, p	2	3	0	0	0	0	0	0	.000
Chambliss, 1b	3	10	0	0	0	0	0	0	.000
Totals	3	89	5	15	1	0	0	3	.169

COMPOSITE PITCHING AVERAGES

St. Louis Cardinals

Pitcher	G.	IP.	H.	R.	ER.	BB.	SO.	W.	L.	ERA.
Forsch	1	9	3	0	0	0	6	1	0	0.00
Sutter	2	4 1/3	0	0	0	0	1	1	0	0.00
Bair	1	1	2	0	0	3	0	0	0	0.00
Andujar	1	6 2/3	6	2	2	2	4	1	0	2.70
Stuper	1	6	4	3	2	1	4	0	0	3.00
Totals	3	27	15	5	4	6	15	3	0	1.33

Atlanta Braves

Pitcher	G.	IP.	H.	R.	ER.	BB.	SO.	W.	L.	ERA.
Moore	2	2 2/3	2	0	0	0	1	0	0	0.00
Mahler	1	1 2/3	3	0	0	2	0	0	0	0.00
Niekro	1	6	6	2	2	4	5	0	0	3.00
Perez	2	8 2/3	10	5	5	2	4	0	1	5.19
Garber	2	3 1/3	4	3	3	1	0	0	1	8.10
Walk	1	1	2	1	1	1	1	0	0	9.00
Bedrosian	2	1	3	2	2	1	2	0	0	18.00
Camp	1	1	4	4	4	1	0	0	1	36.00
Totals	3	25 1/3	34	17	17	12	16	0	3	6.04

1983
BALTIMORE ORIOLES
VS.
CHICAGO WHITE SOX

After watching Chicago right-hander LaMarr Hoyt mow down his Baltimore teammates, 2-1, on five hits in Game 1 of the 1983 American League Championship Series, Orioles designated hitter Ken Singleton suggested: "We had better win the next three games, guys, because I don't think any of us wants to face Hoyt again in Game 5."

The Orioles took Singleton's suggestion to heart, prevailing by 4-0, 11-1 and 3-0 scores in the next three games to earn the right to face the Philadelphia Phillies in the World Series.

Baltimore pitchers made sure Hoyt wouldn't take the mound again, limiting the White Sox to one run in the final 31 innings of the playoff series. The Orioles' staff combined for a 0.49 earned-run average overall and stymied the heart of the Chicago batting order, holding Carlton Fisk, Greg Luzinski, Ron Kittle, Harold Baines and Tom Paciorek to a combined .183 average on 13 hits in 71 at-bats.

As dominant as Hoyt was in Game 1, Baltimore rookie right-hander Mike Boddicker was even more masterful in the second game as he blanked the Sox on five hits and struck out a Championship Series record-tying 14 batters. Boddicker, who went 16-8 after being recalled from Rochester (International) in early May to replace the injured Jim Palmer, tied Detroit's Joe Coleman, who fanned 14 Oakland hitters in 1972, and Pittsburgh's John Candelaria, who had 14 strikeouts against Cincinnati in 1975. The performance led to Boddicker's selection as the A.L. playoffs' Most Valuable Player.

Gary Roenicke was the offensive star in Game 2, scoring three runs and driving in two with a

Baltimore relief ace Tippy Martinez hugs catcher Rick Dempsey after recording the final Chicago out in the Orioles' 1983 pennant clincher.

homer in the sixth inning. Half of Baltimore's left-field combination (he platooned with John Lowenstein), Roenicke doubled and scored on Julio Cruz's error in the second, walked and scored on Singleton's double in the fourth and then belted his homer to climax the scoring.

The scene shifted to Chicago for Game 3, and the Orioles brought out all of their artillery. The Orioles jumped on 22-game winner Richard Dotson in the first inning as Eddie Murray slugged a three-run homer. Murray, held hitless in his previous 29 postseason at-bats (21 in the 1979 World Series and eight in the first two games of this playoff), connected after a

double by Jim Dwyer and a single by Cal Ripken.

Al Bumbry's double scored another run in the second, and there was no stopping the Orioles. Baltimore had only eight hits off four Chicago hurlers, but the Sox pitchers walked nine batters. Murray, who drew three bases on balls, scored four runs.

Mike Flanagan pitched five innings before his knee stiffened and Sammy Stewart came on to limit the Sox to one hit and no runs over the final four frames to record the save.

Though the Orioles led the series, two games to one, the Sox figured they had the edge in the Britt Burns-Storm Davis pitching pairing in Game 4. The matchup turned out to be a dandy.

Davis hurled six innings of scoreless ball before Tippy Martinez took over after Greg Walker singled to open the Chicago seventh. Burns matched zeroes with both as the scoreless duel extended into the 10th inning.

When a game of such importance goes down to the wire, a player least expected to produce often becomes the hero. The name to go down in history this time was Tito Landrum.

Ticketed for the minor leagues in spring training by the St. Louis Cardinals but given a reprieve because of an injury to outfielder Willie McGee, Landrum had only five at-bats with the Cards when he finally was sent to Triple-A in late April. He batted .292 with 18 homers and 77 RBIs at Louisville (American Association), but was frozen in the minors until being obtained by the Orioles on August 31.

Landrum, 0 for 5 in the first three games of the playoffs, was in the starting lineup in Games 2 and 4 because right fielder Dan

Ford had come up lame in Game 1. Having a 1-for-4 day when he strode to the plate in the 10th inning of the fourth game, the 28-year-old Landrum belted a home run against a brisk wind that had held up numerous long blasts earlier in the game.

As heartwarming as the story had become for Landrum, a veteran of 11 seasons in the Cardinals' organization, it had evolved into a nightmare for Burns, who was brilliant in holding the Orioles at bay while awaiting the one run that would have made him a winner. Instead, Burns' 147 pitches resulted only in a losing effort.

After Burns departed, the Orioles added two more runs against Salome Barojas.

Game 1

Wednesday, October 5, At Baltimore

Chicago	AB.	R.	H.	RBI.	PO.	A.
R. Law, cf	5	1	3	0	3	0
Fisk, c	5	0	1	0	5	0
Paciorek, 1b-lf	4	1	2	1	9	2
Luzinski, dh	3	0	1	0	0	0
Kittle, lf	3	0	0	0	1	0
Squires, 1b	1	0	0	0	2	0
Baines, rf	4	0	0	0	2	0
V. Law, 3b	3	0	0	0	0	2
Fletcher, ss	2	0	0	0	2	2
J. Cruz, 2b	2	0	0	0	1	6
Hoyt, p	0	0	0	0	2	1
Totals	32	2	7	1	27	13

Baltimore	AB.	R.	H.	RBI.	PO.	A.
Bumbry, cf	4	0	0	0	0	0
Ford, rf	4	0	1	0	1	0
Landrum, pr	0	1	0	0	0	0
Ripken, ss	4	0	1	1	2	2
Murray, 1b	4	0	0	0	10	1
Lowenstein, lf	3	0	0	0	1	0
Singleton, dh	3	0	1	0	0	0
Dauer, 2b	3	0	0	0	5	3
T. Cruz, 3b	3	0	1	0	3	6
Dempsey, c	2	0	1	0	4	2
Dwyer, ph	1	0	0	0	0	0
McGregor, p	0	0	0	0	1	1
Stewart, p	0	0	0	0	0	0
T. Martinez, p	0	0	0	0	0	1
Totals	31	1	5	1	27	16

Chicago 0 0 1 0 0 1 0 0 0—2
Baltimore 0 0 0 0 0 0 0 0 1—1

Chicago	IP.	H.	R.	ER.	BB.	SO.
Hoyt (W)	9	5	1	1	0	4

Baltimore	IP.	H.	R.	ER.	BB.	SO.
McGregor (L)	6⅔	6	2	1	3	2
Stewart	⅓*	1	0	0	1	1
T. Martinez	2	0	0	0	2	1

*Pitched to two batters in eighth.

Game-winning RBI—Paciorek.

E—Murray. DP—Chicago 1, Baltimore 1. LOB—Chicago 10, Baltimore 3. 2B—Luzinski, Singleton, R. Law, Ford. SH—Fletcher. WP—T. Martinez. Balk—McGregor. U—McKean, Merrill, Bremigan, Evans, Phillips and Reilly. T—2:38. A—51,289.

Game 2

Thursday, October 6, At Baltimore

Chicago	AB.	R.	H.	RBI.	PO.	A.
R. Law, cf	4	0	2	0	2	0
Fisk, c	3	0	0	0	6	0
Baines, rf	4	0	0	0	1	0
Dybzinski, ss	0	0	0	0	1	1
Luzinski, dh	3	0	0	0	0	0
Paciorek, 1b	3	0	1	0	9	0
Kittle, lf	3	0	1	0	2	0
V. Law, 3b	2	0	0	0	0	3
Walker, ph	1	0	0	0	0	0
Rodriguez, 3b	0	0	0	0	0	0
Squires, ph	1	0	0	0	0	0
Fletcher, ss	2	0	0	0	1	3
Hairston, ph-rf	1	0	0	0	0	0
J. Cruz, 2b	4	0	1	0	2	1
Bannister, p	0	0	0	0	0	0
Barojas, p	0	0	0	0	0	1
Lamp, p	0	0	0	0	0	0
Totals	31	0	5	0	24	9

Baltimore	AB.	R.	H.	RBI.	PO.	A.
Shelby, cf	4	0	1	0	0	0
Landrum, rf	4	0	0	0	2	0
Ripken, ss	4	1	2	0	0	0
Murray, 1b	4	0	0	0	6	0
Roenicke, lf	2	3	2	2	1	0
Singleton, dh	4	0	1	1	0	0
Dauer, 2b	3	0	0	0	2	3
T. Cruz, 3b	3	0	0	0	1	3
Dempsey, c	3	0	0	0	15	1
Boddicker, p	0	0	0	0	0	1
Totals	31	4	6	3	27	8

Chicago 0 0 0 0 0 0 0 0 0—0
Baltimore 0 1 0 1 0 2 0 0 x—4

Chicago	IP.	H.	R.	ER.	BB.	SO.
Bannister (L)	6	5	4	3	1	5
Barojas	1	1	0	0	0	0
Lamp	1	0	0	0	1	0

Baltimore	IP.	H.	R.	ER.	BB.	SO.
Boddicker (W)	9	5	0	0	3	14

Game-winning RBI—None.

E—V. Law, Rodriguez. DP—Chicago 1, Baltimore 1. LOB—Chicago 9, Baltimore 5. 2B—Roenicke, Singleton, Ripken. HR—Roenicke. SB—R. Law 2, Shelby. HBP—By Boddicker (Paciorek, Luzinski). U—Merrill, Bremigan, Evans, Phillips, Reilly and McKean. T—2:51. A—52,347.

Game 3

Friday, October 7, At Chicago

Baltimore	AB.	R.	H.	RBI.	PO.	A.
Bumbry, cf	4	0	1	1	3	0
Shelby, ph-cf	0	1	0	0	0	0
Dwyer, rf	3	1	1	0	4	0
Landrum, ph-rf	1	0	0	0	2	0
Ripken, ss	4	3	2	0	2	4
Murray, 1b	2	4	1	3	7	2
Lowenstein, lf	3	0	1	2	3	0
Roenicke, ph-lf	0	1	0	1	0	0
Singleton, dh	3	0	1	0	0	0
Palmer, pr	0	0	0	0	0	0
Nolan, ph	0	0	0	1	0	0
Dauer, 2b	4	0	0	1	1	4
T. Cruz, 3b	5	0	1	1	1	1
Dempsey, c	3	1	0	0	2	0
Flanagan, p	0	0	0	0	0	0
Stewart, p	0	0	0	0	2	0
Totals	32	11	8	10	27	11

Chicago	AB.	R.	H.	RBI.	PO.	A.
R. Law, cf	4	0	2	0	3	0
Fisk, c	4	0	1	0	8	2
Paciorek, 1b	4	0	0	0	11	1
Luzinski, dh	4	0	1	0	0	0
Kittle, lf	1	1	1	0	0	0
Hairston, ph-lf	2	0	0	0	0	0
Baines, rf	4	0	0	0	2	1
V. Law, 3b	2	0	1	1	1	1
Squires, ph	1	0	0	0	0	0
Rodriguez, 3b	0	0	0	0	0	0
Fletcher, ss	3	0	0	0	0	3
J. Cruz, 2b	3	0	0	0	1	5
Dotson, p	0	0	0	0	1	1
Tidrow, p	0	0	0	0	0	0
Koosman, p	0	0	0	0	0	0
Lamp, p	0	0	0	0	0	0
Totals	32	1	6	1	27	14

Baltimore 3 1 0 0 2 0 0 1 4—11
Chicago 0 1 0 0 0 0 0 0 0— 1

Baltimore	IP.	H.	R.	ER.	BB.	SO.
Flanagan (W)	5	5	1	1	0	1
Stewart (S)	4	1	0	0	0	1

Chicago	IP.	H.	R.	ER.	BB.	SO.
Dotson (L)	5	6	6	6	3	3
Tidrow	3	1	1	1	3	3
Koosman	⅓	1	3	2	2	0
Lamp	⅔	0	1	0	1	1

Game-winning RBI—Murray.

E—Dempsey, Hairston. DP—Baltimore 1, Chicago 1. LOB—Baltimore 6, Chicago 5. 2B—Dwyer, Bumbry, Kittle, Fisk, Lowenstein, Ripken. HR—Murray. SB—Murray. SF—Nolan, Dauer. HBP—By Flanagan (Kittle); by Dotson (Ripken). U—Bremigan, Evans, Phillips, Reilly, McKean and Merrill. T—2:58. A—46,635.

Game 4

Saturday, October 8, At Chicago

Baltimore	AB.	R.	H.	RBI.	PO.	A.
Shelby, cf	5	0	1	0	3	0
Landrum, rf	5	1	2	1	1	0
Ripken, ss	3	1	1	0	3	5
Murray, 1b	5	1	3	0	11	0
Roenicke, lf	2	0	1	1	3	1
Singleton, dh	2	0	0	0	0	0
Bumbry, pr	0	0	0	0	0	0
Ford, ph	1	0	0	0	0	0
Lowenstein, ph	0	0	0	0	0	0
Ayala, ph	0	0	0	1	0	0
Dauer, 2b	4	0	0	0	0	2
T. Cruz, 3b	4	0	0	0	1	3
Dempsey, c	4	0	1	0	8	2
Davis, p	0	0	0	0	0	0
T. Martinez, p	0	0	0	0	0	1
Totals	35	3	9	3	30	14

Chicago	AB.	R.	H.	RBI.	PO.	A.
R. Law, cf	5	0	0	0	2	0
Fisk, c	5	0	1	0	8	1
Baines, rf	4	0	2	0	0	0
Luzinski, dh	5	0	0	0	0	0
Paciorek, lf	5	0	1	0	1	0
Walker, 1b	2	0	1	0	7	1
Squires, pr-1b	1	0	0	0	4	0
V. Law, 3b	4	0	1	0	0	3
Dybzinski, ss	4	0	1	0	2	7
J. Cruz, 2b	3	0	3	0	6	2
Burns, p	0	0	0	0	0	1
Barojas, p	0	0	0	0	0	0
Agosto, p	0	0	0	0	0	0
Lamp, p	0	0	0	0	0	0
Totals	38	0	10	0	30	15

Baltimore 0 0 0 0 0 0 0 0 0 3—3
Chicago 0 0 0 0 0 0 0 0 0 0—0

Baltimore	IP.	H.	R.	ER.	BB.	SO.
Davis	6*	5	0	0	2	2
T. Martinez (W)	4	5	0	0	1	4

Chicago	IP.	H.	R.	ER.	BB.	SO.
Burns (L)	9⅓	6	1	1	5	8
Barojas	0†	3	2	2	0	0
Agosto	⅓	0	0	0	0	0
Lamp	⅓	0	0	0	0	0

*Pitched to one batter in seventh.
†Pitched to three batters in tenth.

Game-winning RBI—Landrum.

DP—Baltimore 1, Chicago 2. LOB—Baltimore 10, Chicago 11. HR—Landrum. SB—J. Cruz 2. SH—Dauer. SF—Ayala. HBP—By Burns (Roenicke). Balk—T. Martinez. U—Evans, Phillips, Reilly, McKean, Merrill and Bremigan. T—3:41. A—45,477.

COMPOSITE BATTING AVERAGES

Baltimore Orioles

Player-Position	G.	AB.	R.	H.	2B.	3B.	HR.	RBI.	BA.
Roenicke, lf-ph	3	4	4	3	1	0	1	4	.750
Ripken, ss	4	15	5	6	2	0	0	1	.400
Murray, 1b	4	15	5	4	0	0	1	3	.267
Singleton, dh	4	12	0	3	2	0	0	1	.250
Dwyer, ph-rf	2	4	1	1	1	0	0	0	.250
Shelby, cf-ph	3	9	1	2	0	0	0	0	.222
Landrum, pr-rf-ph	4	10	2	2	0	0	1	1	.200
Ford, rf-ph	2	5	0	1	1	0	0	0	.200
Dempsey, c	4	12	1	2	0	0	0	0	.167
Lowenstein, lf-ph	3	6	0	1	1	0	0	2	.167
T. Cruz, 3b	4	15	0	2	0	0	0	1	.133
Bumbry, cf-pr	3	8	0	1	1	0	0	1	.125
T. Martinez, p	2	0	0	0	0	0	0	0	.000
Stewart, p	2	0	0	0	0	0	0	0	.000
Ayala, ph	1	0	0	0	0	0	0	1	.000
Boddicker, p	1	0	0	0	0	0	0	0	.000
Davis, p	1	0	0	0	0	0	0	0	.000
Flanagan, p	1	0	0	0	0	0	0	0	.000
McGregor, p	1	0	0	0	0	0	0	0	.000
Nolan, ph	1	0	0	0	0	0	0	1	.000
Palmer, pr	1	0	0	0	0	0	0	0	.000
Dauer, 2b	4	14	0	0	0	0	0	1	.000
Totals	4	129	19	28	9	0	3	17	.217

Chicago White Sox

Player-Position	G.	AB.	R.	H.	2B.	3B.	HR.	RBI.	BA.
R. Law, cf	4	18	1	7	1	0	0	0	.389
J. Cruz, 2b	4	12	0	4	0	0	0	0	.333
Walker, ph-1b	2	3	0	1	0	0	0	0	.333
Kittle, lf	3	7	1	2	1	0	0	0	.286
Paciorek, 1b-lf	4	16	1	4	0	0	0	1	.250
Dybzinski, ss	2	4	0	1	0	0	0	0	.250
V. Law, 3b	4	11	0	2	0	0	0	1	.182
Fisk, c	4	17	0	3	1	0	0	0	.176
Luzinski, dh	4	15	0	2	1	0	0	0	.133
Baines, rf	4	16	0	2	0	0	0	0	.125
Lamp, p	3	0	0	0	0	0	0	0	.000
Barojas, p	2	0	0	0	0	0	0	0	.000
Rodriguez, 3b	2	0	0	0	0	0	0	0	.000
Agosto, p	1	0	0	0	0	0	0	0	.000
Bannister, p	1	0	0	0	0	0	0	0	.000
Burns, p	1	0	0	0	0	0	0	0	.000
Dotson, p	1	0	0	0	0	0	0	0	.000
Hoyt, p	1	0	0	0	0	0	0	0	.000
Koosman, p	1	0	0	0	0	0	0	0	.000
Tidrow, p	1	0	0	0	0	0	0	0	.000
Hairston, ph-rf-lf	2	3	0	0	0	0	0	0	.000
Squires, 1b-ph-pr	4	4	0	0	0	0	0	0	.000
Fletcher, ss	3	7	0	0	0	0	0	0	.000
Totals	4	133	3	28	4	0	0	2	.211

COMPOSITE PITCHING AVERAGES

Baltimore Orioles

Pitcher	G.	IP.	H.	R.	ER.	BB.	SO.	W.	L.	ERA.
Boddicker	1	9	5	0	0	3	14	1	0	0.00
Davis	1	6	5	0	0	2	2	0	0	0.00
T. Martinez	2	6	5	0	0	3	5	1	0	0.00
Stewart	2	4⅓	2	0	0	1	2	0	0	0.00
McGregor	1	6⅔	6	2	1	3	2	0	1	1.35
Flanagan	1	5	5	1	1	0	1	1	0	1.80
Totals	4	37	28	3	2	12	26	3	1	0.49

Chicago White Sox

Pitcher	G.	IP.	H.	R.	ER.	BB.	SO.	W.	L.	ERA.
Lamp	3	2	0	1	0	2	1	0	0	0.00
Agosto	1	⅓	0	0	0	0	0	0	0	0.00
Burns	1	9⅓	6	1	1	5	8	0	1	0.96
Hoyt	1	9	5	1	1	0	4	1	0	1.00
Tidrow	1	3	1	1	1	3	3	0	0	3.00
Bannister	1	6	5	4	3	1	5	0	1	4.50
Dotson	1	5	6	6	6	3	3	0	1	10.80
Barojas	2	1	4	2	2	0	0	0	0	18.00
Koosman	1	⅓	1	3	2	2	0	0	0	54.00
Totals	4	36	28	19	16	16	24	1	3	4.00

When he strolled to the plate in the second inning of the second game of the 1983 National League Championship Series, Gary Matthews did so with considerable trepidation.

Matthews, a .284 career hitter entering the 1983 season and a man who normally produced 15-20 homers and more than 70 runs batted in per year, had fallen off to a .258 average in '83 with only 10 homers and 50 RBIs. He had become a platoon player shortly after Phillies General Manager Paul Owens took over as field manager July 18.

Matthews, a righthanded batter, knew very well that many platoon players never become regulars again. And at age 33, he wasn't pleased with the outlook.

The Championship Series, Matthews figured, offered the perfect setting for regaining his starting left-field job. The fact that he was 0 for 4 in Game 1 against Los Angeles lefthander Jerry Reuss hadn't set well with Matthews. And he knew the Dodgers were talking about starting righthanders Bob Welch and Alejandro Pena in Games 3 and 4 when the playoffs shifted from Los Angeles to Philadelphia. If he was going to produce, now was the time.

To that end, Matthews ended a personal 1-for-25 slump in great fashion against lefthander Fernando Valenzuela by blasting a home run into the left-field seats. He wound up with a 2-for-4 game, and his homer was the only offense for the Phillies as they dropped a 4-1 decision to even the Championship Series at one game apiece.

When the playoff resumed two days later, Owens again had penciled Matthews' name into the lineup, even though Welch was on the mound. He responded

Philadelphia players congratulate Gary Matthews after his Game 2 home run, the first of three he hit in the 1983 Championship Series.

with a 3-for-3 day, including another homer and four RBIs, as the Phillies downed the Dodgers, 7-2.

Now, Matthews was on a roll.

In the first inning of Game 4, he clubbed a three-run homer off Reuss (Pena had pitched in relief the day before) and, behind lefthander Steve Carlton, the Phillies won another 7-2 decision to advance to the World Series against the Baltimore Orioles.

Matthews had five straight hits to set an N.L. Championship Series record. His eight RBIs tied a league playoff mark set by the Dodgers' Dusty Baker in 1977, and his homers in three consecutive games equalled Hank Aaron's Championship Series record established in 1969.

The Phillies also wouldn't have made it to the World Series without the strong pitching of Carlton and Al Holland, who combined for victories in the Championship Series opener and in the clincher. Reliever Ron Reed also helped

out in the finale.

Mike Schmidt's first-inning homer was all the offense the Phillies needed behind Carlton and Holland in Game 1. When Carlton (who permitted only seven hits in 7⅔ innings) loaded the bases on singles by Steve Sax and Baker and a walk to Pedro Guerrero in the eighth inning, Holland bailed out the veteran by getting Mike Marshall to fly out. Holland then set down the Dodgers in the ninth to preserve the Phils' 1-0 victory.

The Phillies' bats were unproductive in Game 2 against Valenzuela and reliever Tom Niedenfuer, the Dodgers knotting the playoffs on the strength of Guerrero's two-run triple in the fifth inning and a run-scoring single by Jack Fimple in the eighth.

The Phillies got their first two runs in Game 3 without a hit, scoring on a passed ball and on a groundout by Ivan DeJesus in the second inning. They added another run in the third on Le-

febvre's sacrifice fly. Then, after Marshall belted a two-run homer for the Dodgers in the fourth, Matthews took over. He hit a solo homer in the bottom of the fourth, drove in two more runs with a single in the fifth and climaxed the victory with another run-scoring single in the seventh. Meanwhile, rookie Charles Hudson shackled the Dodgers on four hits.

Schmidt and Sixto Lezcano had two-out singles preceding Matthews' three-run blast in the first inning of Game 4. Schmidt, who had three hits in the final game and batted .467 (7 for 15) in the four games, doubled home a run and scored on a groundout by Garry Maddox in the fifth, making the score 5-1. Lezcano increased the lead to 7-1 with a two-run homer in the sixth.

Carlton, Reed and Holland scattered 10 hits in the clincher.

Game 1

Tuesday, October 4, At Los Angeles

Philadelphia	AB.	R.	H.	RBI.	PO.	A.
Morgan, 2b	4	0	0	0	3	1
Rose, 1b	4	0	1	0	8	1
Schmidt, 3b	3	1	2	1	0	2
Lezcano, rf	3	0	1	0	2	0
Matthews, lf	4	0	0	0	2	0
Holland, p	0	0	0	0	0	0
Maddox, cf	4	0	1	0	4	0
Diaz, c	3	0	0	0	6	0
DeJesus, ss	3	0	0	0	1	2
Carlton, p	3	0	0	0	1	3
G. Gross, lf	1	0	0	0	0	0
Totals	32	1	5	1	27	9

Los Angeles	AB.	R.	H.	RBI.	PO.	A.
Sax, 2b	4	0	3	0	1	5
Russell, ss	3	0	1	0	0	3
Baker, lf	4	0	1	0	3	0
Guerrero, 3b	2	0	0	0	0	1
Marshall, 1b	4	0	0	0	11	0
Niedenfuer, p	0	0	0	0	0	1
Yeager, c	4	0	0	0	4	0
Landreaux, cf	3	0	0	0	3	0
Morales, ph	1	0	0	0	0	0
Thomas, rf	4	0	2	0	4	0
Reuss, p	1	0	0	0	0	1
Maldonado, ph	1	0	0	0	0	0
Brock, 1b	1	0	0	0	1	0
Totals	32	0	7	0	27	11

Philadelphia..........1 0 0 0 0 0 0 0 0—1
Los Angeles..........0 0 0 0 0 0 0 0 0—0

Philadelphia	IP.	H.	R.	ER.	BB.	SO.
Carlton (W)	7⅔	7	0	0	2	6
Holland (S)	1⅓	0	0	0	0	0

Los Angeles	IP.	H.	R.	ER.	BB.	SO.
Reuss (L)	8	5	1	1	3	3
Niedenfuer	1	0	0	0	1	1

Game-winning RBI—Schmidt.

E—Schmidt. LOB—Philadelphia 8, Los Angeles 9. HR—Schmidt. SB—Thomas. SH—Reuss, Russell. WP—Carlton, Reuss. U—Tata, Stello, McSherry, Weyer, Harvey and Crawford. T—2:17. A—49,963.

Game 2

Wednesday, October 5, At Los Angeles

Philadelphia	AB.	R.	H.	RBI.	PO.	A.
Morgan, 2b	3	0	0	0	4	3
Rose, 1b	3	0	0	0	7	0
Schmidt, 3b	4	0	1	0	1	3
Lezcano, rf	4	0	0	0	1	0
Matthews, lf	4	1	2	1	1	0
Maddox, cf	3	0	2	0	4	0
G. Gross, ph	0	0	0	0	0	0
Diaz, c	3	0	0	0	5	1
Lefebvre, ph	1	0	0	0	0	0
DeJesus, ss	2	0	1	0	1	3
Hayes, ph	1	0	0	0	0	0
Denny, p	1	0	0	0	0	0
Perez, ph	1	0	1	0	0	0
Samuel, pr	0	0	0	0	0	0
Reed, p	0	0	0	0	0	1
Virgil, ph	1	0	0	0	0	0
Totals	31	1	7	1	24	11

Los Angeles	AB.	R.	H.	RBI.	PO.	A.
Sax, 2b	4	0	0	0	4	4
Brock, 1b	4	1	0	0	7	0
Thomas, rf	0	0	0	0	0	0
Baker, lf	3	2	0	0	3	0
Guerrero, 3b	3	0	1	2	0	2
Landreaux, cf	3	0	2	1	3	0
Marshall, rf-1b	4	0	0	0	2	0
Russell, ss	3	1	2	0	1	5
Fimple, c	4	0	1	1	6	1
Valenzuela, p	3	0	0	0	1	0
Niedenfuer, p	0	0	0	0	0	0
Totals	31	4	6	4	27	12

Philadelphia..........0 1 0 0 0 0 0 0 0—1
Los Angeles..........1 0 0 0 2 0 0 1 x—4

Philadelphia	IP.	H.	R.	ER.	BB.	SO.
Denny (L)	6	5	3	0	3	3
Reed	2	1	1	1	1	1

Los Angeles	IP.	H.	R.	ER.	BB.	SO.
Valenzuela (W)	8*	7	1	1	4	5
Niedenfuer (S)	1	0	0	0	0	2

*Pitched to two batters in ninth.

Game-winning RBI—Guerrero.

E—DeJesus, Maddox, Russell. DP—Los Angeles 3. LOB—Philadelphia 8, Los Angeles 8. 2B—Maddox. 3B—Guerrero. HR—Matthews. SB—Rose, Russell. SH—Denny. HBP—By Denny (Guerrero). WP—Valenzuela. U—Stello, McSherry, Weyer, Harvey, Crawford and Tata. T—2:44. A—55,967.

Game 3

Friday, October 7, At Philadelphia

Los Angeles	AB.	R.	H.	RBI.	PO.	A.
Sax, 2b	3	0	0	0	1	0
Brock, 1b	4	0	0	0	5	0
Baker, lf	4	1	2	0	2	0
Guerrero, 3b	4	0	0	0	0	4
Landreaux, cf	4	0	0	0	5	0
Marshall, rf	3	1	1	2	4	0
Russell, ss	4	0	0	0	0	0
Fimple, c	3	0	0	0	7	1
Welch, p	0	0	0	0	0	0
Pena, p	1	0	1	0	0	0
Landestoy, ph	1	0	0	0	0	0
Honeycutt, p	0	0	0	0	0	0
Beckwith, p	0	0	0	0	0	0
Thomas, ph	1	0	0	0	0	0
Zachry, p	0	0	0	0	0	0
Totals	32	2	4	2	24	5

Philadelphia	AB.	R.	H.	RBI.	PO.	A.
Morgan, 2b	4	1	1	0	0	2
Rose, 1b	4	2	3	0	7	0
Schmidt, 3b	3	1	1	0	3	1
Lefebvre, rf	1	0	0	1	2	0
Lezcano, ph-rf	2	0	0	0	0	0
Matthews, lf	3	2	3	4	2	0
Dernier, cf	0	0	0	0	0	0
G. Gross, cf-lf	3	1	0	0	4	0
Diaz, c	3	0	0	0	9	0
DeJesus, ss	4	0	1	1	0	2
Hudson, p	4	0	0	0	0	0
Totals	31	7	9	6	27	5

Los Angeles..........0 0 0 2 0 0 0 0 0—2
Philadelphia..........0 2 1 1 2 0 1 0 x—7

Los Angeles	IP.	H.	R.	ER.	BB.	SO.
Welch (L)	1⅓	0	2	1	2	0
Pena	2⅔	4	2	2	1	3
Honeycutt	⅓	2	2	2	0	0
Beckwith	1⅔	1	0	0	0	3
Zachry	2	2	1	1	1	1

Philadelphia	IP.	H.	R.	ER.	BB.	SO.
Hudson (W)	9	4	2	2	2	9

Game-winning RBI—None.

E—DeJesus. LOB—Los Angeles 5, Philadelphia 5. 2B—Baker, Schmidt. HR—Marshall, Matthews. SB—Sax, Matthews. SF—Lefebvre. WP—Pena 2. PB—Fimple. U—McSherry, Weyer, Harvey, Crawford, Tata and Stello. T—2:51. A—53,490.

Game 4

Saturday, October 8, At Philadelphia

Los Angeles	AB.	R.	H.	RBI.	PO.	A.
Sax, 2b	5	0	1	0	5	3
Russell, ss	4	0	1	0	3	2
Guerrero, 3b	3	1	2	0	0	2
Baker, lf	3	1	2	1	1	0
Marshall, 1b	4	0	1	0	5	2
Yeager, c	2	0	1	0	3	1
Monday, ph	0	0	0	0	0	0
Morales, ph	1	0	0	0	0	0
Fimple, c	0	0	0	0	1	0
Landreaux, cf	4	0	0	0	1	0
Thomas, rf	4	0	2	0	3	0
Reuss, p	2	0	0	0	0	0
Beckwith, p	0	0	0	0	0	0
Honeycutt, p	0	0	0	0	1	0
Landestoy, ph	1	0	0	0	0	0
Zachry, p	0	0	0	0	1	0
Maldonado, ph	1	0	0	0	0	0
Totals	34	2	10	1	24	10

Philadelphia	AB.	R.	H.	RBI.	PO.	A.
Morgan, 2b	4	0	0	0	1	1
Rose, 1b	5	1	2	0	7	1
Schmidt, 3b	5	3	3	1	2	1
Lezcano, rf-lf	4	2	3	2	2	1
Matthews, lf	3	1	1	3	1	0
Reed, p	0	0	0	0	0	0
Hayes, rf	1	0	0	0	0	0
Maddox, cf	4	0	0	1	0	0
Diaz, c	4	0	2	0	12	1
DeJesus, ss	3	0	1	0	2	4
Carlton, p	2	0	1	0	0	2
G. Gross, lf	1	0	0	0	0	0
Holland, p	0	0	0	0	0	0
Totals	36	7	13	7	27	11

Los Angeles..........0 0 0 1 0 0 0 1 0—2
Philadelphia..........3 0 0 0 2 2 0 0 x—7

Los Angeles	IP.	H.	R.	ER.	BB.	SO.
Reuss (L)	4*	9	5	5	0	1
Beckwith	⅔	0	0	0	2	0
Honeycutt	1⅓	2	2	2	0	2
Zachry	2	2	0	0	1	1

Philadelphia	IP.	H.	R.	ER.	BB.	SO.
Carlton (W)	6	6	1	1	3	7
Reed	1⅓	3	1	0	0	2
Holland	1⅔	1	0	0	0	3

*Pitched to two batters in fifth.

Game-winning RBI—Matthews.

E—Lezcano. LOB—Los Angeles 9, Philadelphia 10. 2B—Guerrero, Marshall, Schmidt, Yeager, Diaz, Thomas. HR—Matthews, Baker, Lezcano. SH—Carlton, Lezcano. HBP—By Carlton (Yeager). WP—Carlton. U—Weyer, Harvey, Crawford, Tata, Stello and McSherry. T—2:50. A—64,494.

COMPOSITE BATTING AVERAGES

Philadelphia Phillies

Player-Position	G.	AB.	R.	H.	2B.	3B.	HR.	RBI.	BA.
Perez, ph	1	1	0	1	0	0	0	0	1.000
Schmidt, 3b	4	15	5	7	2	0	1	2	.467
Matthews, lf	4	14	4	6	0	0	3	8	.429
Rose, 1b	4	16	3	6	0	0	0	0	.375
Lezcano, rf-ph-lf	4	13	2	4	0	0	1	2	.308
Maddox, cf	3	11	0	3	1	0	0	1	.273
DeJesus, ss	4	12	0	3	0	0	0	1	.250
Carlton, p	2	5	0	1	0	0	0	0	.200
Diaz, c	4	13	0	2	1	0	0	0	.154
Morgan, 2b	4	15	1	1	0	0	0	0	.067
Dernier, cf	1	0	0	0	0	0	0	0	.000
Holland, p	2	0	0	0	0	0	0	0	.000
Reed, p	2	0	0	0	0	0	0	0	.000
Samuel, pr	1	0	0	0	0	0	0	0	.000
Denny, p	1	1	0	0	0	0	0	0	.000
Virgil, ph	1	1	0	0	0	0	0	0	.000
Hayes, ph-rf	2	2	0	0	0	0	0	0	.000
Lefebvre, ph-rf	2	2	0	0	0	0	0	1	.000
Hudson, p	1	4	0	0	0	0	0	0	.000
G. Gross, lf-ph-cf	4	5	1	0	0	0	0	0	.000
Totals	4	130	16	34	4	0	5	15	.262

Los Angeles Dodgers

Player-Position	G.	AB.	R.	H.	2B.	3B.	HR.	RBI.	BA.
Pena, p	1	1	0	1	0	0	0	0	1.000
Thomas, rf-ph	4	9	0	4	1	0	0	0	.444
Baker, lf	4	14	4	5	1	0	1	1	.357
Russell, ss	4	14	1	4	0	0	0	0	.286
S. Sax, 2b	4	16	0	4	0	0	0	0	.250
Guerrero, 3b	4	12	1	3	1	1	0	2	.250
Yeager, c	2	6	0	1	1	0	0	0	.167
Landreaux, cf	4	14	0	2	0	0	0	1	.143
Fimple, c	3	7	0	1	0	0	0	1	.143
Marshall, 1b-rf	4	15	1	2	1	0	1	2	.133
Beckwith, p	2	0	0	0	0	0	0	0	.000
Honeycutt, p	2	0	0	0	0	0	0	0	.000
Niedenfuer, p	2	0	0	0	0	0	0	0	.000
Zachry, p	2	0	0	0	0	0	0	0	.000
Monday, ph	1	0	0	0	0	0	0	0	.000
Welch, p	1	0	0	0	0	0	0	0	.000
Landestoy, ph	2	2	0	0	0	0	0	0	.000
Maldonado, ph	2	2	0	0	0	0	0	0	.000
Morales, ph	2	2	0	0	0	0	0	0	.000
Reuss, p	2	3	0	0	0	0	0	0	.000
Valenzuela, p	1	3	0	0	0	0	0	0	.000
Brock, 1b	3	9	1	0	0	0	0	0	.000
Totals	4	129	8	27	5	1	2	7	.209

COMPOSITE PITCHING AVERAGES

Philadelphia Phillies

Pitcher	G.	IP.	H.	R.	ER.	BB.	SO.	W.	L.	ERA.
Denny	1	6	5	3	0	3	3	0	1	0.00
Holland	2	3	1	0	0	0	3	0	0	0.00
Carlton	2	13⅔	13	1	1	5	13	2	0	0.66
Hudson	1	9	4	2	2	2	9	1	0	2.00
Reed	2	3⅓	4	2	1	1	3	0	0	2.70
Totals	4	35	27	8	4	11	31	3	1	1.03

Los Angeles Dodgers

Pitcher	G.	IP.	H.	R.	ER.	BB.	SO.	W.	L.	ERA.
Beckwith	2	2⅓	1	0	0	2	3	0	0	0.00
Niedenfuer	2	2	0	0	0	1	3	0	0	0.00
Valenzuela	1	8	7	1	1	4	5	1	0	1.13
Zachry	2	4	4	1	1	2	2	0	0	2.25
Reuss	2	12	14	6	6	3	4	0	2	4.50
Pena	1	2⅔	4	2	2	1	3	0	0	6.75
Welch	1	1⅓	0	2	1	2	0	0	1	6.75
Honeycutt	2	1⅔	4	4	4	0	2	0	0	21.60
Totals	4	34	34	16	15	15	22	1	3	3.97

1984
DETROIT TIGERS
vs.
KANSAS CITY ROYALS

Prior to starting Game 3 of the 1984 A.L. Championship Series against the Kansas City Royals, Milt Wilcox said one of his first big thrills in baseball was when Cincinnati Manager Sparky Anderson brought him in to pitch in the third game of the 1970 N.L. Championship Series. He hurled three shutout innings and was credited with a 3-2 victory over the Pittsburgh Pirates that clinched the pennant for the Reds.

On October 5, 1984, 14 years to the day after he had been summoned from the bullpen to help wrap up the Reds' title, Anderson again showed confidence in Wilcox, sending him to the mound against the Royals with a chance to clinch the A.L. pennant for the Detroit Tigers. When the results were in, Wilcox had become the first pitcher to record clinching victories in the Championship Series in each league.

Wilcox was the beneficiary of a single run that night in Detroit. Designated hitter Barbaro Garbey opened the second inning with a single up the middle. Center fielder Chet Lemon forced Garbey at second, but Lemon went to third on an ensuing single by Darrell Evans. Third baseman Marty Castillo then hit a two-hopper to Kansas City shortstop Onix Concepcion, who flipped to Frank White for the force on Evans at second. White's relay to first, however, was an instant late, and Castillo was safe as Lemon scored. That was to be the only run surrendered by Kansas City lefthander Charlie Leibrandt, who allowed the Tigers just three hits while starting and finishing for the Royals.

But Wilcox made that one run look monumental. He struck out eight batters, walked two and al-

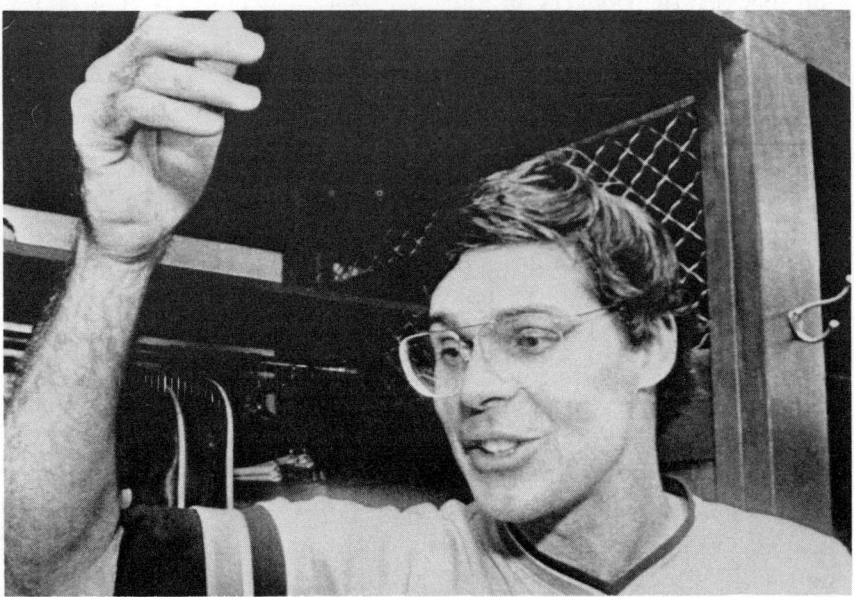

Detroit designated hitter Johnny Grubb describes his 11th-inning game-winning double in the Tigers' Game 2 victory over Kansas City.

lowed only a single by third baseman George Brett in the fourth and another by catcher Don Slaught in the eighth.

Wilcox, who completed none of his 33 starts during the regular season, gave way to Willie Hernandez at the start of the ninth. The lefthander preserved the 1-0 decision that gave the Tigers a three-game sweep over the Royals.

Before the playoffs, Detroit had become the fourth team in major league history to be in first place from the start of its season to the end of the year, joining the 1923 New York Giants, 1927 New York Yankees and 1955 Brooklyn Dodgers in that category. The Tigers started the season at a 35-5 pace and finished with 104 regular-season victories.

The Tigers proved they were no fluke right from the start against the Royals. In the first inning of the opener in Kansas City, they exploded for two runs, the 62nd time in 1984 they had scored in the first inning. This time, second

baseman Lou Whitaker stroked a leadoff single to right and shortstop Alan Trammell followed with a run-scoring triple over the head of left fielder Darryl Motley. Trammell scored one out later on a sacrifice fly by catcher Lance Parrish.

The Tigers slowly started to pull away as left fielder Larry Herndon hit a leadoff homer off loser Bud Black in the fourth inning. Trammell opened the fifth with a home run off Black and two innings later delivered a run-scoring single off reliever Mark Huismann to make the score 5-0. Evans and Castillo drove in one run each in the eighth before Parrish pounded out the Tigers' third homer (all leadoff shots) of the game in the ninth.

The Royals managed only five hits off winner Jack Morris and none off Hernandez, who worked the final two innings to wrap up Detroit's 8-1 victory.

In Game 2, the Tigers were to win the eighth of eight games be-

tween the two clubs at Royals Stadium in '84, but not without a struggle.

In yet another first-inning explosion, the Tigers scored two runs. Whitaker opened the game by reaching first base on an error by Concepcion. One out later, Kirk Gibson and Parrish smacked back-to-back run-scoring doubles. Gibson made it 3-0 in the third when he slugged a home run over the center-field wall.

The Royals got to starter Dan Petry for a run in the fourth on a walk to right fielder Pat Sheridan, a single by Brett and a fielder's-choice grounder by Jorge Orta. Then they turned to their bench. Dane Iorg drove in a run with a two-out pinch-hit single in the seventh. Lynn Jones, batting for Sheridan, greeted Hernandez with another pinch single to open the eighth. After Brett struck out, Hal McRae ripped a pinch double into the left-field corner, scoring Jones and tying the game, 3-3.

Entering the ninth, Kansas City Manager Dick Howser removed starter Bret Saberhagen, a 20-year-old rookie. Saberhagen had gotten off to a shaky start and was behind, 3-0, after three innings, but he yielded only a pair of singles in the next five innings to keep the Royals in the game.

After Hernandez was touched for the tying run in the eighth, the game came down to a duel of relievers: Kansas City's Dan Quisenberry vs. Detroit's Aurelio Lopez.

Parrish singled sharply off the glove of third baseman Greg Pryor to open the winning uprising for the Tigers in the 11th. Evans sacrificed, but both runners were safe when catcher Slaught fumbled the ball. After left fielder Ruppert Jones failed in his bunt attempt and forced Parrish at third, designated hitter Johnny Grubb belted a high sinker from Quisenberry into right-center, scoring Evans and Jones and giving the Tigers a 5-3 margin.

Game 1

Tuesday, October 2, At Kansas City

Detroit	AB.	R.	H.	RBI.	PO.	A.
Whitaker, 2b	5	2	1	0	0	1
Brookens, 2b	0	0	0	0	0	0
Trammell, ss	3	2	3	3	1	5
Baker, ss	0	0	0	0	0	0
Gibson, rf	5	0	2	0	3	0
Parrish, c	4	1	1	2	6	0
Herndon, lf	3	1	1	1	3	0
R. Jones, ph-lf	1	0	0	0	2	0
Kuntz, ph-lf	1	0	0	0	0	0
Garbey, dh	5	1	2	0	0	0
Lemon, cf	5	0	0	0	2	0
Evans, 1b	4	0	2	1	8	1
Bergman, pr-1b	0	1	0	0	1	0
Castillo, 3b	4	0	2	1	0	1
Morris, p	0	0	0	0	1	1
Hernandez, p	0	0	0	0	0	0
Totals	40	8	14	8	27	9

Kansas City	AB.	R.	H.	RBI.	PO.	A.
Wilson, cf	4	0	1	0	4	0
Sheridan, rf	2	0	0	0	3	0
L. Jones, ph-rf	1	0	0	0	1	0
Brett, 3b	4	0	0	0	2	1
Orta, dh	4	1	1	0	0	0
Motley, lf	4	0	0	1	4	0
Balboni, 1b	4	0	0	0	6	1
White, 2b	3	0	1	0	1	2
Slaught, c	3	0	2	0	5	0
Concepcion, ss	3	0	0	0	0	2
Black, p	0	0	0	0	1	1
Huismann, p	0	0	0	0	0	0
M. Jones, p	0	0	0	0	0	0
Totals	32	1	5	1	27	7

Detroit .... 2 0 0 1 1 0 1 2 1—8
Kansas City .... 0 0 0 0 0 0 1 0 0—1

Detroit	IP.	H.	R.	ER.	BB.	SO.
Morris (W)	7	5	1	1	4	
Hernandez	2	0	0	0	0	2

Kansas City	IP.	H.	R.	ER.	BB.	SO.
Black (L)	5	7	4	4	1	3
Huismann	2⅔	6	3	2	1	2
M. Jones	1⅓	1	1	1	0	0

Game-winning RBI—Trammell.

E—Sheridan. DP—Kansas City 1. LOB—Detroit 8, Kansas City 5. 2B—Evans. 3B—Trammell, Orta. HR—Herndon, Trammell, Parrish. SF—Parrish. WP—Huismann. U—Deegan, Bible, Christal, Zirbel, Jordan and O'Dell. T—2:42. A—41,973.

Game 2

Wednesday, October 3, At Kansas City

Detroit	AB.	R.	H.	RBI.	PO.	A.
Whitaker, 2b	5	1	1	0	5	5
Trammell, ss	5	0	1	0	3	2
Gibson, rf	4	2	2	3	2	0
Parrish, c	5	0	2	1	7	2
Evans, 3b-1b	4	1	0	0	7	1
R. Jones, lf	4	1	0	0	3	0
Grubb, dh	4	0	1	2	0	0
Lemon, cf	5	0	0	0	4	0
Bergman, 1b	1	0	1	0	4	0
Brookens, 3b	2	0	0	0	0	2
Garbey, ph	1	0	0	0	0	0
Castillo, 3b	1	0	0	0	0	0
Petry, p	0	0	0	0	0	0
Hernandez, p	0	0	0	0	0	0
Lopez, p	0	0	0	0	0	0
Totals	41	5	8	5	33	12

Kansas City	AB.	R.	H.	RBI.	PO.	A.
Wilson, cf	5	0	1	0	4	0
Sheridan, rf	2	1	0	0	6	0
L. Jones, ph-rf	3	1	1	0	1	0
Brett, 3b	5	0	2	0	0	2
Pryor, pr-3b	0	0	0	0	1	0
Orta, dh	3	0	0	1	0	0
McRae, ph	1	0	1	1	0	0
Wathan, pr-dh	1	0	0	0	0	0
Motley, lf	4	0	2	0	4	0
Balboni, 1b	5	0	1	0	7	1
White, 2b	5	1	0	0	1	0
Slaught, c	5	0	1	0	6	0
Concepcion, ss	2	0	0	0	0	2
Iorg, ph	1	0	1	1	0	0
Biancalana, pr-ss	1	0	0	0	1	2
Washington, ph	1	0	0	0	0	0
Saberhagen, p	0	0	0	0	1	1
Quisenberry, p	0	0	0	0	1	1
Totals	44	3	10	3	33	9

Detroit .... 2 0 1 0 0 0 0 0 0 2—5
Kansas City .... 0 0 0 1 0 0 1 1 0 0—3

Detroit	IP.	H.	R.	ER.	BB.	SO.
Petry	7	4	2	2	1	4
Hernandez	1	2	1	1	1	1
Lopez (W)	3	4	0	0	1	2

Kansas City	IP.	H.	R.	ER.	BB.	SO.
Saberhagen	8	6	3	2	1	5
Quisenberry (L)	3	2	2	1	1	1

Game-winning RBI—Grubb.

E—Concepcion, Saberhagen, Brookens, Slaught. LOB—Detroit 7, Kansas City 11. 2B—Gibson, Parrish, McRae, Grubb. HR—Gibson. SB—Bergman. SH—Grubb, Evans. U—Deegan, Bible, Christal, Jones, Denny and Nothnagel. T—3:37. A—42,019.

Game 3

Friday, October 5, At Detroit

Kansas City	AB.	R.	H.	RBI.	PO.	A.
Wilson, cf	4	0	0	0	2	0
Sheridan, rf	2	0	0	0	0	0
L. Jones, ph	1	0	0	0	0	0
Brett, 3b	4	0	1	0	0	4
Orta, dh	3	0	0	0	0	0
McRae, ph	1	0	1	0	0	0
Washington, pr	0	0	0	0	0	0
Motley, lf	4	0	0	0	3	0
Balboni, 1b	2	0	0	0	7	1
White, 2b	3	0	0	0	5	1
Slaught, c	3	0	1	0	6	0
Concepcion, ss	2	0	0	0	0	2
Iorg, ph	1	0	0	0	0	0
Biancalana, ss	0	0	0	0	0	0
Leibrandt, p	0	0	0	0	1	2
Totals	30	0	3	0	24	10

Detroit	AB.	R.	H.	RBI.	PO.	A.
Whitaker, 2b	4	0	0	0	0	1
Trammell, ss	3	0	0	0	0	1
Gibson, rf	3	0	1	0	1	0
Parrish, c	3	0	0	0	8	0
Herndon, lf	2	0	0	0	3	0
Garbey, dh	3	0	1	0	0	0
Lemon, cf	3	1	0	0	3	0
Evans, 1b	2	0	1	0	7	2
Castillo, 3b	3	0	1	1	3	3
Wilcox, p	0	0	0	0	2	0
Hernandez, p	0	0	0	0	0	0
Totals	26	1	3	1	27	6

Kansas City .... 0 0 0 0 0 0 0 0 0—0
Detroit .... 0 1 0 0 0 0 0 0 x—1

Kansas City	IP.	H.	R.	ER.	BB.	SO.
Leibrandt (L)	8	3	1	1	4	6

Detroit	IP.	H.	R.	ER.	BB.	SO.
Wilcox (W)	8	2	0	0	2	8
Hernandez (S)	1	1	0	0	0	0

Game-winning RBI—Castillo.

E—Slaught 2, Balboni. DP—Kansas City 1. LOB—Kansas City 5, Detroit 5. SB—Castillo, Gibson, Evans. U—Deegan, Bible, Christal, Cossey, Runchey and Zivic. T—2:39. A—52,168.

COMPOSITE BATTING AVERAGES

Detroit Tigers

Player-Position	G.	AB.	R.	H.	2B.	3B.	HR.	RBI.	BA.
Bergman, pr-1b	2	1	1	1	0	0	0	0	1.000
Gibson, rf	3	12	2	5	1	0	1	2	.417
Trammell, ss	3	11	2	4	0	1	1	3	.364
Garbey, dh-ph	3	9	1	3	0	0	0	0	.333
Evans, 1b-3b	3	10	1	3	1	0	0	1	.300
Parrish, c	3	12	1	3	1	0	1	3	.250
Castillo, 3b	3	8	0	2	0	0	0	2	.250
Grubb, dh	1	4	0	1	1	0	0	2	.250
Herndon, lf	2	5	1	1	0	0	1	1	.200
Whitaker, 2b	3	14	3	2	0	0	0	0	.143
Hernandez, p	3	0	0	0	0	0	0	0	.000
Baker, ss	1	0	0	0	0	0	0	0	.000
Lopez, p	1	0	0	0	0	0	0	0	.000
Morris, p	1	0	0	0	0	0	0	0	.000
Petry, p	1	0	0	0	0	0	0	0	.000
Wilcox, p	1	0	0	0	0	0	0	0	.000
Kuntz, ph-lf	1	1	0	0	0	0	0	0	.000
Brookens, 2b-3b	2	2	0	0	0	0	0	0	.000
R. Jones, ph-lf	2	5	1	0	0	0	0	0	.000
Lemon, cf	3	13	1	0	0	0	0	0	.000
Totals	3	107	14	25	4	1	4	14	.234

Kansas City Royals

Player-Position	G.	AB.	R.	H.	2B.	3B.	HR.	RBI.	BA.
McRae, ph	2	2	0	2	1	0	0	1	1.000
Iorg, ph	2	2	0	1	0	0	0	1	.500
Slaught, c	3	11	0	4	0	0	0	0	.364
Brett, 3b	3	13	0	3	0	0	0	0	.231
L. Jones, ph-rf	3	5	1	1	0	0	0	0	.200
Motley, lf	3	12	0	2	0	0	0	1	.167
Wilson, cf	3	13	0	2	0	0	0	0	.154
Orta, dh	3	10	1	1	0	1	0	1	.100
Balboni, 1b	3	11	0	1	0	0	0	0	.091
White, 2b	3	11	1	1	0	0	0	0	.091
Black, p	1	0	0	0	0	0	0	0	.000
Huismann, p	1	0	0	0	0	0	0	0	.000
M. Jones, p	1	0	0	0	0	0	0	0	.000
Leibrandt, p	1	0	0	0	0	0	0	0	.000
Pryor, pr-3b	1	0	0	0	0	0	0	0	.000
Quisenberry, p	1	0	0	0	0	0	0	0	.000
Saberhagen, p	1	0	0	0	0	0	0	0	.000
Biancalana, pr-ss	2	1	0	0	0	0	0	0	.000
Washington, ph-pr	2	1	0	0	0	0	0	0	.000
Wathan, pr-dh	1	1	0	0	0	0	0	0	.000
Sheridan, rf	3	6	1	0	0	0	0	0	.000
Concepcion, ss	3	7	0	0	0	0	0	0	.000
Totals	3	106	4	18	1	1	0	4	.170

COMPOSITE PITCHING AVERAGES

Detroit Tigers

Pitcher	G.	IP.	H.	R.	ER.	BB.	SO.	W.	L.	ERA.
Wilcox	1	8	2	0	0	2	8	1	0	0.00
Lopez	1	3	4	0	0	1	2	1	0	0.00
Morris	1	7	5	1	1	4	1	1	0	1.29
Hernandez	3	4	3	1	1	1	3	0	0	2.25
Petry	1	7	4	2	2	1	4	0	0	2.57
Totals	3	29	18	4	4	6	21	3	0	1.24

Kansas City Royals

Pitcher	G.	IP.	H.	R.	ER.	BB.	SO.	W.	L.	ERA.
Leibrandt	1	8	3	1	1	4	6	0	1	1.13
Saberhagen	1	8	6	3	2	1	5	0	0	2.25
Quisenberry	1	3	2	2	1	1	1	0	1	3.00
Huismann	1	2⅔	6	3	2	1	2	0	0	6.75
M. Jones	1	1⅓	1	1	1	0	0	0	0	6.75
Black	1	5	7	4	4	1	3	0	1	7.20
Totals	3	28	25	14	11	8	17	0	3	3.54

1984
SAN DIEGO PADRES
VS.
CHICAGO CUBS

All of America, it seemed, was behind them. Two victories in two games—the first by a 13-0 score, the second a 4-2 margin—also were behind them. Needing just one more win, the Chicago Cubs appeared to be on their way to ending their 39-year World Series famine.

But a funny thing happened to the Cubs en route to the Fall Classic. The San Diego Padres, given up for dead after losing the first two games in Chicago, came back to life, won the next three games and became the first team ever to recover from a 2-0 deficit and win the National League Championship Series.

Numerous Championship Series batting records were broken or tied as the Cubs thrashed the Padres in the opener. They banged out 16 hits, including five home runs, and scored 13 runs, all N.L. playoff records. That cushion made it easy on starter Rick Sutcliffe, who allowed only two hits—a bunt single by first baseman Steve Garvey and a bloop single by shortstop Garry Templeton—while striking out eight and walking five over seven innings. As if that wasn't enough, Sutcliffe flexed his muscles and joined teammates Bob Dernier, Gary Mathews and Ron Cey in the Cubs' home run-hitting parade.

Every player in the Cubs' starting lineup had at least one hit and one run batted in. Matthews' two home runs extended his streak of Championship Series homers to four (a major league record), having hit one in each of the last three games of the 1983 playoffs when he led the Philadelphia Phillies to the league pennant.

The Cubs showed a different side of their attack in Game 2, using speed and timely hitting to

defeat the Padres. Dernier and Ryne Sandberg were the architects of the 4-2 victory, with left-hander Steve Trout and relief ace Lee Smith limiting the Padres to five hits.

When the Cubs took a 1-0 lead in the second inning of Game 3 on a double by Keith Moreland and an RBI single by Cey, they appeared to be on the verge of a three-game sweep. But the Padres were to have none of that script.

Terry Kennedy and Kevin McReynolds opened the Padres' fifth with singles, and one out later, Templeton came to the plate for the biggest hit of his career, a two-run double to the wall in left-center. That gave the Padres a 2-1 edge, their first lead of the series. Templeton scored the third run of the inning on a single by second baseman Alan Wiggins and the Pirates added four more runs in the sixth, three coming on a McReynolds homer.

Game 4 was, by far, the most competitive and dramatic of the playoffs. It also was a showcase for San Diego's Garvey.

Garvey had four hits and five RBIs in Game 4, including a run-scoring double that capped a two-run third, marking the first time the Padres had scored first in the series. Garvey's hit followed a single and stolen base by Templeton, a single by Wiggins and a sacrifice fly by Gwynn. But he saved his best for last.

With the score tied, 5-5, in the bottom of the ninth, Gwynn singled and Garvey burned Smith with a game-winning home run to right-center field.

The Padres had met the challenge of evening the series at two games each. But in the decisive fifth game, they still had to beat the Cy Young Award winner Sutcliffe, who finished the season

with 15 straight victories (including Game 1 of the playoffs).

The Padres managed just two weak infield hits in the first five innings against Sutcliffe. Meanwhile, Leon Durham had belted a two-run homer in the first inning and Jody Davis had contributed a leadoff blast in the second for a 3-0 Chicago lead.

The San Diego bullpen stopped the Cubs right there, however, while the Padres fought back.

The Padres scored twice in the sixth to make the score 3-2, and Sutcliffe was back in trouble in the seventh after he walked Carmelo Martinez, the first batter of the inning, on four straight pitches. Templeton sacrificed Martinez to second, and pinch-hitter Tim Flannery followed with a sharp grounder to Durham at first. The ball went between Durham's legs for an error, and Martinez scored to tie the game, 3-3.

The Cubs' only luck in that inning was bad luck. The next batter, Wiggins, punched a check-swing single into short left field. Gwynn then delivered the key blow, a smash at Sandberg that took a bad hop and rocketed over the second baseman's shoulder and into right-center for a double, scoring Flannery and Wiggins. Gwynn took third on the throw home and scored on Garvey's single, giving San Diego its final 6-3 edge.

Game 1
Tuesday, October 2, At Chicago

San Diego	AB.	R.	H.	RBI.	PO.	A.
Wiggins, 2b	5	0	0	0	2	3
Gwynn, rf	4	0	0	0	1	0
Garvey, 1b	4	0	2	0	6	0
Nettles, 3b	4	0	1	0	1	1
Kennedy, c	3	0	0	0	6	0
McReynolds, cf	2	0	0	0	3	0
Martinez, lf	3	0	1	0	1	0
Templeton, ss	3	0	2	0	4	1
Show, p	1	0	0	0	0	0
Flannery, ph	0	0	0	0	0	0
Harris, p	0	0	0	0	0	0
Brown, ph	1	0	0	0	0	0
Booker, p	0	0	0	0	0	0
Summers, ph	1	0	0	0	0	0
Totals	31	0	6	0	24	5

Chicago	AB.	R.	H.	RBI.	PO.	A.
Dernier, cf	3	3	2	1	6	0
Sandberg, 2b	4	2	2	1	2	3
Matthews, lf	4	2	2	4	0	0
Cotto, lf	1	0	1	0	0	0
Durham, 1b	5	0	1	1	4	0
Moreland, rf	3	1	1	1	1	0
Woods, ph-rf	1	0	0	0	1	0
Cey, 3b	3	2	1	1	0	0
Veryzer, 3b	0	0	0	0	0	0
Davis, c	4	1	2	1	8	0
Lake, c	1	0	1	0	0	0
Bowa, ss	4	1	1	1	5	2
Sutcliffe, p	4	1	2	1	0	0
Brusstar, p	1	0	0	0	0	0
Totals	38	13	16	12	27	5

San Diego	0 0 0	0 0 0	0 0 0	— 0
Chicago	2 0 3	0 6 2	0 0 x	—13

San Diego	IP.	H.	R.	ER.	BB.	SO.
Show (L)	4	5	5	5	2	2
Harris	2	9	8	7	3	2
Booker	2	2	0	0	1	2

Chicago	IP.	H.	R.	ER.	BB.	SO.
Sutcliffe (W)	7	2	0	0	5	8
Brusstar	2	4	0	0	0	0

Game-winning RBI—Dernier.

E—Templeton. DP—San Diego 1, Chicago 2. LOB—San Diego 10, Chicago 8. 2B—Dernier, Davis, Lake. HR—Dernier, Matthews 2, Sutcliffe, Cey. SF—Moreland. HBP—By Sutcliffe (Flannery). U—Cavanaugh, Slickenmeyer, Pomponi and Maher. T—2:49. A—36,282.

Game 2

Wednesday, October 3, At Chicago

San Diego	AB.	R.	H.	RBI.	PO.	A.
Wiggins, 2b	3	1	1	0	3	1
Gwynn, rf	4	1	1	0	4	0
Garvey, 1b	4	0	1	1	9	2
McReynolds, cf	2	0	0	1	2	0
Martinez, lf	4	0	1	0	2	0
Kennedy, c	4	0	0	0	1	1
Salazar, 3b	3	0	0	0	1	3
Templeton, ss	2	0	0	0	1	3
Thurmond, p	1	0	1	0	0	1
Hawkins, p	0	0	0	0	0	0
Ramirez, ph	1	0	0	0	0	0
Dravecky, p	0	0	0	0	1	1
Bevacqua, ph	1	0	0	0	0	0
Lefferts, p	0	0	0	0	0	0
Totals	29	2	5	2	24	12

Chicago	AB.	R.	H.	RBI.	PO.	A.
Dernier, cf	3	2	1	0	0	0
Sandberg, 2b	4	0	2	1	2	5
Matthews, lf	3	0	0	1	3	0
Cotto, lf	0	0	0	0	2	0
Moreland, rf	4	1	2	0	2	0
Smith, p	0	0	0	0	0	0
Cey, 3b	3	1	1	1	0	2
Davis, c	3	0	0	1	3	0
Durham, 1b	4	0	0	0	14	0
Bowa, ss	3	0	1	0	1	7
Trout, p	2	0	1	0	0	1
Lopes, lf	0	0	0	0	0	0
Totals	29	4	8	4	27	15

San Diego	0 0 0	1 0 1	0 0 0	—2
Chicago	1 0 2	1 0 0	0 0 x	—4

San Diego	IP.	H.	R.	ER.	BB.	SO.
Thurmond (L)	3⅔	7	4	4	2	1
Hawkins	1⅓	0	0	0	1	0
Dravecky	2	1	0	0	0	1
Lefferts	1	0	0	0	0	0

Chicago	IP.	H.	R.	ER.	BB.	SO.
Trout (W)	8⅓	5	2	2	3	2
Smith (S)	⅔	0	0	0	0	1

Game-winning RBI—Matthews.

E—Trout. DP—Chicago 2. LOB—San Diego 4, Chicago 6. 2B—Moreland, Cey, Gwynn, Sandberg. SB—Dernier. SH—Trout. SF—Davis, McReynolds. U—Slickenmeyer, Pomponi, Maher and Cavanaugh. T—2:18. A—36,282.

Game 3

Thursday, October 4, At San Diego

Chicago	AB.	R.	H.	RBI.	PO.	A.
Dernier, cf	3	0	0	0	3	1
Sandberg, 2b	4	0	1	0	4	5
Matthews, lf	3	0	1	0	2	0
Durham, 1b	4	0	0	0	11	2
Moreland, rf	4	1	1	0	0	0
Cey, 3b	4	0	1	1	0	1
Davis, c	3	0	1	0	2	2
Bowa, ss	3	0	0	0	1	2
Eckersley, p	2	0	0	0	0	0
Frazier, p	0	0	0	0	0	0
Bosley, ph	1	0	0	0	0	0
Stoddard, p	0	0	0	0	1	0
Totals	31	1	5	1	24	13

San Diego	AB.	R.	H.	RBI.	PO.	A.
Wiggins, 2b	4	0	2	1	0	4
Gwynn, rf	4	1	3	0	0	0
Garvey, 1b	4	0	0	0	8	0
Nettles, 3b	4	1	1	1	0	2
Kennedy, c	4	2	2	0	8	1
McReynolds, cf	3	2	2	3	3	0
Martinez, lf	3	0	0	0	0	0
Templeton, ss	3	1	1	2	7	2
Whitson, p	3	0	0	0	1	0
Gossage, p	0	0	0	0	0	0
Totals	32	7	11	7	27	9

Chicago	0 1 0	0 0 0	0 0 0	—1
San Diego	0 0 0	0 3 4	0 0 x	—7

Chicago	IP.	H.	R.	ER.	BB.	SO.
Eckersley (L)	5⅓	9	5	5	0	0
Frazier	1⅔	2	2	2	0	1
Stoddard	1	0	0	0	0	2

San Diego	IP.	H.	R.	ER.	BB.	SO.
Whitson (W)	8	5	1	1	2	6
Gossage	1	0	0	0	0	2

Game-winning RBI—Templeton.

DP—Chicago 1, San Diego 1. LOB—Chicago 5, San Diego 1. 2B—Gwynn, Moreland, Templeton, Sandberg. HR—McReynolds. SB—Sandberg. U—Bovey, Campagna, Fisher and Stewart. T—2:19. A—58,346.

Game 4

Saturday, October 6, At San Diego

Chicago	AB.	R.	H.	RBI.	PO.	A.
Dernier, cf	4	0	1	0	0	0
Sandberg, 2b	3	1	1	0	3	2
Matthews, lf	3	1	0	0	3	0
Moreland, rf	4	0	1	1	4	0
Cotto, pr-rf	0	1	0	0	0	0
Cey, 3b	5	0	0	0	1	1
Davis, c	4	1	3	3	4	0
Durham, 1b	3	1	1	1	10	1
Bowa, ss	3	0	1	0	0	4
Hebner, ph	1	0	0	0	0	0
Smith, p	0	0	0	0	0	0
Sanderson, p	2	0	0	0	0	1
Brusstar, p	0	0	0	0	0	0
Lopes, ph	1	0	0	0	0	0
Stoddard, p	0	0	0	0	0	1
Veryzer, ss	1	0	0	0	0	0
Totals	34	5	8	5	25	10

San Diego	AB.	R.	H.	RBI.	PO.	A.
Wiggins, 2b	4	1	1	0	1	1
Gwynn, rf	3	2	1	1	2	0
Garvey, 1b	5	1	4	5	8	0
Nettles, 3b	3	0	0	0	3	3
Kennedy, c	4	0	1	0	7	0
McReynolds, cf	3	0	1	0	2	0
Salazar, ph-cf	1	0	0	0	0	0
Martinez, lf	4	0	1	0	0	0
Templeton, ss	4	1	1	0	4	3
Lollar, p	1	0	0	0	0	0
Hawkins, p	0	0	0	0	0	1
Flannery, ph	1	1	1	0	0	0
Dravecky, p	0	0	0	0	0	0
Brown, ph	0	1	0	0	0	0
Gossage, p	0	0	0	0	0	0
Summers, ph	1	0	0	0	0	0
Lefferts, p	0	0	0	0	0	0
Totals	34	7	11	6	27	8

Chicago	0 0 0	3 0 0	0 2 0	—5
San Diego	0 0 2	0 1 0	2 0 2	—7

One out when winning run scored.

Chicago	IP.	H.	R.	ER.	BB.	SO.
Sanderson	4⅔	6	3	3	1	2
Brusstar	1⅓	1	0	0	0	0
Stoddard	1	1	2	1	2	0
Smith (L)	1⅓	3	2	2	0	2

San Diego	IP.	H.	R.	ER.	BB.	SO.
Lollar	4⅓	3	3	3	4	3
Hawkins	⅔	0	0	0	0	0
Dravecky	2	1	0	0	0	2
Gossage	1	3	2	2	1	1
Lefferts (W)	1	1	0	0	1	0

Game-winning RBI—Garvey.

E—Sandberg. DP—Chicago 1, San Diego 1. LOB—Chicago 9, San Diego 7. 2B—Bowa, Garvey, Dernier, Davis. HR—Davis, Durham, Garvey. SB—Templeton, Dernier, Brown, Sandberg. SH—Wiggins. SF—Gwynn. HBP—By Lefferts (Cotto). PB—Davis. U—Bovey, Campagna, Fisher and Stewart. T—3:13. A—58,354.

Game 5

Sunday, October 7, At San Diego

Chicago	AB.	R.	H.	RBI.	PO.	A.
Dernier, cf	4	0	0	0	3	0
Sandberg, 2b	4	0	1	0	2	3
Matthews, lf	2	1	0	0	2	0
Durham, 1b	4	1	1	2	8	0
Moreland, lf	3	0	1	0	2	0
Cey, 3b	4	0	0	0	0	2
Davis, c	4	1	1	1	6	0
Bowa, ss	2	0	0	0	1	0
Bosley, ph	1	0	0	0	0	0
Veryzer, ss	0	0	0	0	0	0
Sutcliffe, p	2	0	1	0	0	0
Trout, p	0	0	0	0	0	0
Hebner, ph	0	0	0	0	0	0
Brusstar, p	0	0	0	0	0	1
Totals	30	3	5	3	24	6

San Diego	AB.	R.	H.	RBI.	PO.	A.
Wiggins, 2b	3	2	2	0	5	2
Gwynn, rf	4	2	2	2	2	0
Garvey, 1b	3	0	1	1	4	1
Nettles, 3b	3	0	0	1	1	2
Kennedy, c	3	0	1	1	6	2
Brown, cf	3	0	0	0	3	0
Salazar, cf	1	0	1	0	0	0
Martinez, lf	3	1	0	0	3	0
Templeton, ss	3	0	1	0	3	2
Show, p	0	0	0	0	0	0
Hawkins, p	0	0	0	0	0	0
Ramirez, ph	1	0	0	0	0	0
Dravecky, p	0	0	0	0	0	0
Bevacqua, ph	1	0	0	0	0	0
Lefferts, p	0	0	0	0	0	0
Flannery, ph	1	1	0	0	0	0
Gossage, p	0	0	0	0	0	0
Totals	29	6	8	5	27	9

Chicago	2 1 0	0 0 0	0 0 0	—3
San Diego	0 0 0	0 0 2	4 0 x	—6

Chicago	IP.	H.	R.	ER.	BB.	SO.
Sutcliffe (L)	6⅓	7	6	5	3	2
Trout	⅔	0	0	0	0	1
Brusstar	1	1	0	0	0	1

San Diego	IP.	H.	R.	ER.	BB.	SO.
Show	1⅓	3	3	3	2	0
Hawkins	1⅔	0	0	0	1	1
Dravecky	2	0	0	0	0	2
Lefferts (W)	2	0	0	0	0	1
Gossage (S)	2	2	0	0	0	2

Game-winning RBI—Gwynn.

E—Durham. DP—San Diego 1. LOB—Chicago 4, San Diego 5. 2B—Gwynn. 3B—Salazar. HR—Durham, Davis. SB—Matthews, Sandberg. SH—Templeton. SF—Nettles, Kennedy. HBP—By Gossage (Hebner). U—Kibler, Runge, McSherry and Harvey. T—2:41. A—58,359.

COMPOSITE BATTING AVERAGES

San Diego Padres

Player-Position	G.	AB.	R.	H.	2B.	3B.	HR.	RBI.	BA.
Thurmond, p	1	1	0	1	0	0	0	0	1.000
Flannery, ph	3	2	2	1	0	0	0	0	.500
Garvey, 1b	5	20	1	8	1	0	1	7	.400
Gwynn, rf	5	19	6	7	3	0	0	3	.368
Templeton, ss	5	15	2	5	1	0	0	2	.333
Wiggins, 2b	5	19	4	6	0	0	0	1	.316
McReynolds, cf	4	10	2	3	0	0	1	4	.300
Kennedy, c	5	18	2	4	0	0	0	1	.222
Salazar, 3b-ph-cf	3	5	0	1	0	1	0	0	.200
Martinez, lf	5	17	1	3	0	0	0	0	.176
Nettles, 3b	4	14	1	2	0	0	0	2	.143
Dravecky, p	3	0	0	0	0	0	0	0	.000
Gossage, p	3	0	0	0	0	0	0	0	.000
Hawkins, p	3	0	0	0	0	0	0	0	.000
Lefferts, p	3	0	0	0	0	0	0	0	.000
Booker, p	1	0	0	0	0	0	0	0	.000
Harris, p	1	0	0	0	0	0	0	0	.000
Show, p	2	1	0	0	0	0	0	0	.000
Lollar, p	1	1	0	0	0	0	0	0	.000
Bevacqua, ph	2	2	0	0	0	0	0	0	.000
Ramirez, ph	2	2	0	0	0	0	0	0	.000
Summers, ph	2	2	0	0	0	0	0	0	.000
Whitson, p	1	3	0	0	0	0	0	0	.000
Brown, ph-cf	3	4	1	0	0	0	0	0	.000
Totals	5	155	22	41	5	1	2	20	.265

Chicago Cubs

Player-Position	G.	AB.	R.	H.	2B.	3B.	HR.	RBI.	BA.
Cotto, lf-pr-rf	3	1	1	1	0	0	0	0	1.000
Lake, c	1	1	0	1	1	0	0	0	1.000
Sutcliffe, p	2	6	1	3	0	0	1	1	.500
Trout, p	2	2	0	1	0	0	0	0	.500
Davis, c	5	18	3	7	2	0	2	6	.389
Sandberg, 2b	5	19	3	7	2	0	0	2	.368
Moreland, rf	5	18	3	6	2	0	0	2	.333
Dernier, cf	5	17	5	4	2	0	1	1	.235
Bowa, ss	5	15	1	3	1	0	0	1	.200
Matthews, lf	5	15	4	3	0	0	2	5	.200
Cey, 3b	5	19	3	3	1	0	1	3	.158
Durham, 1b	5	20	2	3	0	0	2	4	.150
Smith, p	2	0	0	0	0	0	0	0	.000
Stoddard, p	2	0	0	0	0	0	0	0	.000
Frazier, p	1	0	0	0	0	0	0	0	.000
Brusstar, p	3	1	0	0	0	0	0	0	.000
Veryzer, 3b-ss	3	1	0	0	0	0	0	0	.000
Hebner, ph	2	1	0	0	0	0	0	0	.000
Lopes, rf-ph	2	1	0	0	0	0	0	0	.000
Woods, ph-rf	1	1	0	0	0	0	0	0	.000
Bosley, ph	2	2	0	0	0	0	0	0	.000
Eckersley, p	1	2	0	0	0	0	0	0	.000
Sanderson, p	1	2	0	0	0	0	0	0	.000
Totals	5	162	26	42	11	0	9	25	.259

COMPOSITE PITCHING AVERAGES

San Diego Padres

Pitcher	G.	IP.	H.	R.	ER.	BB.	SO.	W.	L.	ERA.
Dravecky	3	6	2	0	0	0	5	0	0	0.00
Lefferts	3	4	1	0	0	1	1	2	0	0.00
Hawkins	3	3⅔	0	0	0	2	1	0	0	0.00
Booker	1	2	2	0	0	1	2	0	0	0.00
Whitson	1	8	5	1	1	2	6	1	0	1.13
Gossage	3	4	5	2	2	1	5	0	0	4.50
Lollar	1	4⅓	3	3	3	4	3	0	0	6.23
Thurmond	1	3⅔	7	4	4	2	1	0	1	9.82
Show	2	5⅓	8	8	8	4	2	0	1	13.50
Harris	1	2	9	8	7	3	2	0	0	31.50
Totals	5	43	42	26	25	20	28	3	2	5.23

Chicago Cubs

Pitcher	G.	IP.	H.	R.	ER.	BB.	SO.	W.	L.	ERA.
Brusstar	3	4⅓	6	0	0	0	1	0	0	0.00
Trout	2	9	5	2	2	3	3	1	0	2.00
Sutcliffe	2	13⅓	9	6	5	8	10	1	1	3.38
Stoddard	2	2	1	2	1	2	2	0	0	4.50
Sanderson	1	4⅔	6	3	3	1	2	0	0	5.79
Eckersley	1	5⅓	9	5	5	0	0	0	1	8.44
Smith	2	2	3	2	2	0	3	0	1	9.00
Frazier	1	1⅔	2	2	2	0	1	0	0	10.80
Totals	5	42⅓	41	22	20	14	22	2	3	4.25

KANSAS CITY ROYALS
VS.
TORONTO BLUE JAYS

Some players go through an entire career without experiencing that sweet smell of success. They give it their all, day in and day out, but never get a chance to play in a League Championship Series or World Series. Give them their chance, however, and they produce.

Take Jim Sundberg, for example. For 10 years, the veteran catcher punched his time card for some weak Texas Rangers clubs. Then he spent a season with a slumping Milwaukee Brewers club. Finally he was traded to Kansas City Royals prior to the 1985 season.

"I thought it was never going to happen," Sundberg said after driving in four runs to lead the Royals to a 6-2 victory over the Toronto Blue Jays in Game 7 of the American League Championship Series.

A six-time Gold Glove winner for his fielding excellence, Sundberg wasn't exactly tearing up the Blue Jays offensively through the first six playoff games. He had only two hits in 20 at-bats.

But Sundberg wasn't about to blow his Game 7 opportunity. He drove in Kansas City's first run with a second-inning single. After right fielder Pat Sheridan added to the Royals' lead with a long solo home run in the fourth, Sundberg provided the game's biggest blow when he tripled off the top of the right-field fence with the bases loaded in the sixth, extending Kansas City's lead to 5-1. He then scored the Royals' sixth and final run on second baseman Frank White's single.

Sundberg's big game allowed the Royals to take full advantage of the new best-of-seven format for the League Championship Series, previously a best-of-five affair. After dropping the first two

Championship Series Most Valuable Player George Brett gets a champagne shower after Kansas City's 1985 victory over Toronto.

games of the playoffs in Toronto, the Royals split the next two games with the Blue Jays in Kansas City. While that 3-1 edge in games would have given Toronto the pennant in previous years, it still gave Kansas City a chance in 1985. The Royals responded by winning the last three games—including the final two in Toronto—to earn their second ticket to the World Series in the 17-year history of the franchise.

Toronto ace Dave Stieb was much sharper in Game 1 of the playoffs than in Game 7. The righthander struck out eight batters and scattered three hits over eight innings in leading the Blue

Jays to a 6-1 triumph in the opener.

The setback stretched Kansas City's losing streak in postseason play (dating to the 1980 World Series) to nine games. And for Royals Manager Dick Howser, whose Yankees had been swept by Kansas City in the A.L. playoffs in '80, it was 10 straight postseason defeats.

Things didn't get any better for Howser or the Royals in Game 2 as Kansas City fell, 6-5, in a gut-wrenching, 10-inning loss.

The Royals built a 3-0 lead in Game 2 against Blue Jay starter Jimmy Key, but Dennis Lamp came on to throw 3⅔ innings of scoreless relief. Meanwhile, the Blue Jays inched back and finally took a 4-3 lead in the eighth inning.

Then the game really got weird.

Sheridan, who had hit only three homers in 206 at-bats during the regular season, slugged a pinch homer off reliever Tom Henke in the ninth inning, tying the game, 4-4, and sending it into extra innings. In the top of the 10th, Willie Wilson, who had homered earlier in the game, spanked a single to center and stole second base as Henke fanned Hal McRae for the second out. White followed with a sinking liner to center, where Lloyd Moseby galloped in and went down for the scoop. Second base umpire Ted Hendry was out of position and made no call. When right-field umpire Dave Phillips ruled that Moseby had played the ball on one hop, allowing Wilson to cross the plate with the go-ahead run, bedlam arose in the friendly confines of Exhibition Stadium.

At this point, Royals reliever Dan Quisenberry was shaping up as the eventual winner and Henke

as the goat. But in Toronto's half of the 10th, Tony Fernandez legged out an infield hit as Royals shortstop Onix Concepcion had trouble getting the ball out of his glove. Fernandez went to second on a groundout by second baseman Damaso Garcia and scored on Moseby's single to right, tying the game. Moseby reached second when first baseman Steve Balboni couldn't handle Quisenberry's pickoff attempt for an error. After George Bell flied out, pinch-hitter Al Oliver singled to left to make Henke the winner and Quisenberry the loser.

Kansas City third baseman George Brett could do no wrong in Game 3 as the scene shifted to Kansas City. The Royals' All-Star slugger and Gold Glove fielder took the Series into his own hands, leading the Royals to a 6-5 triumph with a 4-for-4 performance, including two homers.

In Game 4, the Blue Jays stole another late-inning decision from Kansas City in a 3-1 game that bore a striking resemblance to Game 2. Just like before, Moseby and Oliver provided the game-tying and -winning hits, Henke was the winner for Toronto and Quisenberry was the victim for Kansas City.

But not the loser. That distinction went to Charlie Leibrandt, the Game 1 loser who pitched effectively for eight innings and took a 1-0 lead into the ninth. But he walked Garcia to open Toronto's half of the ninth and Moseby followed with a run-scoring double to right-center, bringing Quisenberry to the mound with the game tied.

Bell greeted Quiz with a bloop single to center, Moseby stopping at third. That's when Toronto Manager Bobby Cox sent Oliver in to bat for Cliff Johnson. Oliver laced a double to right field, scoring Moseby and Bell and clinching a 3-1 lead in the series for the Blue Jays.

One more victory is all Toronto needed to make the trip to the World Series. But Kansas City lefthander Danny Jackson had other thoughts, limiting the Blue Jays to eight hits and shutting them out, 2-0, in Game 5.

When the series went back to Toronto for Game 6, the Royals once again dodged the executioner's blade, winning 5-3. The Royals jumped on top in the first when McRae singled home Wilson. After the Blue Jays tied it in their half of the first on Rance Mulliniks' double-play grounder, Kansas City went in front again in the third on McRae's RBI double. Toronto quickly produced a 2-2 deadlock with one run in their half of the third on Moseby's run-scoring groundout. Enter Brett, the reigning Mr. October once again.

With one out in the fifth, Brett touched starter and loser Doyle Alexander for his third home run of the series, giving the Royals a 3-2 cushion. It was Brett's ninth career home run in League Championship Series play, breaking Steve Garvey's major league record of eight.

One inning later, the Royals padded their lead with run-scoring doubles by shorstop Buddy Biancalana and Smith. The Blue Jays' final tally came on Johnson's pinch single in the sixth. The victory went to righthanded starter Mark Gubicza, who went 5⅓ innings, with Bud Black and Quisenberry combining for shutout relief for the final 3⅔ innings.

Kansas City's Bret Saberhagen and Toronto's Stieb, were matched in the decisive Game 7.

The odds appeared to be in the Blue Jays' favor and they grew even larger when Willie Upshaw smashed a first-inning line drive off Saberhagen's pitching hand, necessitating his removal after three scoreless innings. But Leibrandt, the hard-luck loser of Game 4, made his first relief appearance of the season and rose to the occasion. A run-scoring double by Upshaw in the fifth and an RBI groundout by Garcia in the ninth were charged to the veteran lefty, but he earned the victory while allowing only five hits in 5⅓ innings.

	AB.	R.	H.	RBI.	PO.	A.
Balboni, 1b	3	0	0	0	8	1
Sundberg, c	3	0	0	0	3	0
Biancalana, ss	2	0	0	0	1	7
D. Iorg, ph	1	0	1	0	0	0
Concepcion, pr-ss	0	0	0	0	0	0
Leibrandt, p	0	0	0	0	0	0
Farr, p	0	0	0	0	0	0
Gubicza, p	0	0	0	0	0	0
Jackson, p	0	0	0	0	1	0
Totals	32	1	5	0	24	10
Toronto	AB.	R.	H.	RBI.	PO.	A.
Garcia, 2b	5	0	2	0	0	2
Lee, pr-2b	0	0	0	0	0	0
Moseby, cf	5	0	0	0	4	0
Bell, lf	5	1	2	0	3	0
Johnson, dh	4	1	1	0	0	0
Barfield, rf	2	1	1	0	1	0
Upshaw, 1b	3	2	1	0	8	1
G. Iorg, 3b	1	1	0	0	1	1
Mulliniks, ph-3b	3	0	1	1	1	0
Whitt, c	3	0	1	2	8	0
Fernandez, ss	3	0	2	2	1	0
Stieb, p	0	0	0	0	0	0
Henke, p	0	0	0	0	0	0
Totals	34	6	11	5	27	5

Kansas City .... 0 0 0 0 0 0 0 0 1—1
Toronto .... 0 2 3 1 0 0 0 0 x—6

Kansas City	IP.	H.	R.	ER.	BB.	SO.
Leibrandt (L)	2*	7	5	5	1	0
Farr	2	2	1	1	1	0
Gubicza	3	0	0	0	1	2
Jackson	1	2	0	0	0	1
Toronto	IP.	H.	R.	ER.	BB.	SO.
Stieb (W)	8	3	0	0	1	8
Henke	1	2	1	1	0	0

*Pitched to three batters in third.
Game-winning RBI—Whitt.
E—Balboni. LOB—Kansas City 5, Toronto 9. 2B—Brett, Bell, Johnson, D. Iorg. SB—Barfield. SF—Fernandez. HBP—By Leibrandt (Upshaw). U—Phillips, Ford, Evans, Hendry, Voltaggio and Cousins. T—2:24. A—39,115.

Game 2

Wednesday, October 9, At Toronto

Kansas City	AB.	R.	H.	RBI.	PO.	A.
Smith, lf	5	0	0	0	0	1
Wilson, cf	5	2	3	2	3	0
Brett, 3b	4	0	0	0	1	2
McRae, dh	5	0	2	0	0	0
White, 2b	4	0	2	1	1	6
Balboni, 1b	5	0	0	0	8	1
Motley, rf	2	1	0	0	4	0
Sheridan, ph-rf	1	1	1	1	0	0
Sundberg, c	4	0	1	1	8	1
Biancalana, ss	2	1	1	0	1	1
D. Iorg, ph	0	0	0	0	0	0
Concepcion, pr-ss	0	0	0	0	0	0
Black, p	0	0	0	0	2	2
Quisenberry, p	0	0	0	0	1	0
Totals	37	5	10	5	29	14
Toronto	AB.	R.	H.	RBI.	PO.	A.
Garcia, 2b	5	0	0	0	1	2
Moseby, cf	5	2	2	1	1	0
Bell, lf	3	2	1	0	0	0
Johnson, dh	3	0	2	1	0	0
Thornton, pr	0	1	0	0	0	0
Oliver, dh	2	0	1	1	0	0
Barfield, rf	4	0	1	2	3	0
Upshaw, 1b	4	0	1	0	10	1
G. Iorg, 3b	3	0	1	0	2	3
Mulliniks, ph-3b	1	1	0	0	0	0
Whitt, c	4	0	0	0	9	2
Fernandez, ss	3	1	1	0	3	5
Key, p	0	0	0	0	0	0
Lamp, p	0	0	0	0	1	0
Lavelle, p	0	0	0	0	0	0
Henke, p	0	0	0	0	0	0
Totals	37	6	10	6	30	13

Kansas City .... 0 0 2 1 0 0 0 0 1—5
Toronto .... 0 0 0 1 0 2 0 0 2—6

Two out when winning run scored.

Kansas City	IP.	H.	R.	ER.	BB.	SO.
Black	7	5	3	2	1	5
Quisenberry (L)	2⅔	5	3	1	0	2
Toronto	IP.	H.	R.	ER.	BB.	SO.
Key	3⅓	7	3	3	1	2
Lamp	3⅔	0	0	0	0	3
Lavelle	0*	0	0	0	1	0
Henke (W)	3	3	2	2	4	4

*Pitched to one batter in eighth.
Game-winning RBI—Oliver.
E—Brett, Sundberg, Balboni. DP—Kansas City 1, Toronto 1. LOB—Kansas City 7, Toronto 5. 2B—Sundberg, Johnson. HR—Wilson, Sheridan. SB—Moseby, Wilson. SH—Biancalana. SF—Bell. HBP—By Black (Bell). WP—Black. U—Ford, Evans, Voltaggio, Hendry, Cousins and Phillips. T—3:39. A—34,029.

Game 3

Friday, October 11, At Kansas City

Toronto	AB.	R.	H.	RBI.	PO.	A.
Garcia, 2b	5	1	2	0	1	1
Moseby, cf	4	1	1	1	1	0
Mulliniks, 3b	4	1	1	2	0	0

Game 1

Tuesday, October 8, At Toronto

Kansas City	AB.	R.	H.	RBI.	PO.	A.
Smith, lf	4	0	0	0	0	1
Wilson, cf	4	1	1	0	2	0
Brett, 3b	4	0	3	0	3	0
Orta, dh	4	0	0	0	0	0
Sheridan, rf	3	0	0	1	6	0
White, 2b	4	0	0	0	0	1

	AB.	R.	H.	RBI.	PO.	A.
Upshaw, 1b	4	0	1	0	4	1
Oliver, dh	2	0	1	0	0	0
Johnson, dh	2	0	1	0	0	0
Bell, lf	4	0	3	0	2	0
Whitt, c	3	1	1	0	5	1
Barfield, rf	4	1	1	2	9	0
Fernandez, ss	4	0	1	0	1	2
Alexander, p	0	0	0	0	1	0
Lamp, p	0	0	0	0	0	1
Clancy, p	0	0	0	0	0	1
Totals	36	5	13	5	24	7

Kansas City	AB.	R.	H.	RBI.	PO.	A.
Smith, lf	4	0	1	0	3	0
L. Jones, lf	0	0	0	0	0	0
Wilson, cf	4	1	2	0	0	0
Brett, 3b	4	4	4	3	1	1
McRae, dh	3	0	1	0	0	0
White, 2b	3	0	0	1	2	4
Sheridan, rf	3	0	0	0	0	0
Balboni, 1b	4	0	1	1	10	0
Sundberg, c	4	1	1	1	8	1
Biancalana, ss	1	0	0	0	1	2
D. Iorg, ph	1	0	0	0	0	0
Concepcion, ss	1	0	0	0	2	4
Saberhagen, p	0	0	0	0	0	1
Black, p	0	0	0	0	0	0
Farr, p	0	0	0	0	0	1
Totals	32	6	10	6	27	14

Toronto 0 0 0 0 5 0 0 0 0—5
Kansas City 1 0 0 1 1 2 0 1 x—6

Toronto	IP.	H.	R.	ER.	BB.	SO.
Alexander	5*	7	5	5	0	3
Lamp	2	1	0	0	0	2
Clancy (L)	1	2	1	1	1	0

Kansas City	IP.	H.	R.	ER.	BB.	SO.
Saberhagen	4⅓	9	5	5	1	4
Black	⅓	2	0	0	1	0
Farr (W)	4⅓	2	0	0	0	3

*Pitched to three batters in sixth.

Game-winning RBI—Balboni.

E—Upshaw, Smith. DP—Kansas City 3. LOB—Toronto 6, Kansas City 5. 2B—Garcia 2, Upshaw, Brett, McRae. HR—Brett 2, Barfield, Mulliniks, Sundberg. SH—McRae. SF—White. U—Evans, Hendry, Voltaggio, Cousins, Phillips and Ford. T—2:51. A—40,224.

Game 4

Saturday, October 12, At Kansas City

Toronto	AB.	R.	H.	RBI.	PO.	A.
Garcia, 2b	3	1	1	0	2	2
Moseby, cf	4	1	1	1	4	0
Bell, lf	4	1	1	0	2	0
Johnson, dh	2	0	0	0	0	0
Oliver, ph	1	0	1	2	0	0
Barfield, rf	4	0	2	0	1	0
Upshaw, 1b	4	0	0	0	6	2
G. Iorg, 3b	4	0	0	0	1	2
Whitt, c	2	0	0	0	6	0
Fielder, ph	1	0	1	0	0	0
Thornton, pr	0	0	0	0	0	0
Hearron, c	0	0	0	0	0	0
Fernandez, ss	3	0	0	0	3	2
Stieb, p	0	0	0	0	1	1
Henke, p	0	0	0	0	1	0
Totals	32	3	7	3	27	9

Kansas City	AB.	R.	H.	RBI.	PO.	A.
Smith, lf	1	1	0	0	3	0
L. Jones, lf	0	0	0	0	2	0
Quirk, ph	1	0	0	0	0	0
Wilson, cf	3	0	2	0	2	0
Brett, 3b	2	0	0	0	0	1
McRae, dh	3	0	0	1	0	0
Sheridan, rf	4	0	0	0	1	0
White, 2b	4	0	0	0	0	3
Balboni, 1b	3	0	0	0	12	4
Sundberg, c	3	0	0	0	1	0
Orta, ph	1	0	0	0	0	0
Biancalana, ss	2	0	0	0	3	3
D. Iorg, ph	0	0	0	0	0	0
Concepcion, pr-ss	0	0	0	0	0	0
Leibrandt, p	0	0	0	0	3	5
Quisenberry, p	0	0	0	0	0	0
Totals	27	1	2	1	27	16

Toronto 0 0 0 0 0 0 0 0 3—3
Kansas City 0 0 0 0 0 1 0 0 0—1

Toronto	IP.	H.	R.	ER.	BB.	SO.
Stieb	6⅔	2	1	1	7	6
Henke (W)	2⅓	0	0	0	2	0

Kansas City	IP.	H.	R.	ER.	BB.	SO.
Leibrandt (L)	8*	5	2	2	2	1
Quisenberry	1	2	1	1	0	0

*Pitched to two batters in ninth.

Game-winning RBI—Oliver.

DP—Toronto 1, Kansas City 1. LOB—Toronto 4, Kansas City 9. 2B—Barfield, Garcia, Fielder, Moseby, Oliver. SH—Wilson. U—Hendry, Voltaggio, Cousins, Phillips, Ford and Evans. T—3:02. A—41,112.

Game 5

Sunday, October 13, At Kansas City

Toronto	AB.	R.	H.	RBI.	PO.	A.
Garcia, 2b	4	0	0	0	3	2
Moseby, cf	4	0	0	0	1	0
Bell, lf	4	0	2	0	0	0
Johnson, dh	4	0	1	0	0	0
Barfield, rf	4	0	1	0	3	0
Upshaw, 1b	4	0	1	0	11	1
G. Iorg, 3b	3	0	1	0	0	2
Whitt, c	3	0	1	0	5	0
Fielder, ph	1	0	0	0	0	0
Fernandez, ss	3	0	1	0	1	2
Key, p	0	0	0	0	0	3
Acker, p	0	0	0	0	0	1
Totals	34	0	8	0	24	11

Kansas City	AB.	R.	H.	RBI.	PO.	A.
Smith, lf	4	1	3	0	0	1
L. Jones, lf	0	0	0	0	0	0
Wilson, cf	4	0	0	0	1	0
Brett, 3b	3	0	0	1	1	4
McRae, dh	4	0	0	0	0	0
White, 2b	3	1	2	0	3	3
Balboni, 1b	3	0	2	0	13	0
Motley, rf	1	0	1	1	0	0
Sheridan, ph-rf	1	0	0	0	3	0
Sundberg, c	3	0	0	0	6	0
Biancalana, ss	3	0	0	0	0	2
Jackson, p	0	0	0	0	0	1
Totals	29	2	8	2	27	11

Toronto 0 0 0 0 0 0 0 0 0—0
Kansas City 1 1 0 0 0 0 0 0 x—2

Toronto	IP.	H.	R.	ER.	BB.	SO.
Key (L)	5⅓	8	2	2	1	3
Acker	2⅔	0	0	0	0	2

Kansas City	IP.	H.	R.	ER.	BB.	SO.
Jackson (W)	9	8	0	0	1	6

Game-winning RBI—Brett.

DP—Toronto 1. LOB—Toronto 8, Kansas City 5. 2B—Bell, Smith, Whitt. SB—Smith. SF—Motley. U—Voltaggio, Cousins, Phillips, Ford, Evans and Hendry. T—2:21. A—40,046.

Game 6

Tuesday, October 15, At Toronto

Kansas City	AB.	R.	H.	RBI.	PO.	A.
Smith, lf	5	0	1	1	0	0
L. Jones, lf	0	0	0	0	0	0
Wilson, cf	4	1	1	0	2	0
Brett, 3b	3	2	1	1	0	0
McRae, dh	5	0	3	2	0	0
Sheridan, rf	4	0	0	0	2	0
Balboni, 1b	4	0	0	0	11	0
Sundberg, c	3	1	0	0	8	0
White, 2b	3	0	0	0	1	6
Biancalana, ss	4	1	2	1	3	4
Gubicza, p	0	0	0	0	0	1
Black, p	0	0	0	0	0	1
Quisenberry, p	0	0	0	0	0	0
Totals	35	5	8	5	27	12

Toronto	AB.	R.	H.	RBI.	PO.	A.
Garcia, 2b	3	1	1	0	2	1
Moseby, cf	4	1	3	1	1	0
Mulliniks, 3b	2	0	0	0	0	2
G. Iorg, ph-3b	2	0	0	0	0	0
Upshaw, 1b	3	0	0	0	5	1
Oliver, dh	2	0	0	0	0	0
Johnson, dh	2	0	2	1	0	0
Bell, lf	4	0	0	0	3	0
Whitt, c	3	0	0	0	10	0
Fielder, ph	1	0	0	0	0	0
Hearron, c	0	0	0	0	2	0
Barfield, rf	4	0	0	0	3	0
Fernandez, ss	4	1	2	0	1	1
Alexander, p	0	0	0	0	0	0
Lamp, p	0	0	0	0	0	1
Totals	34	3	8	2	27	6

Kansas City 1 0 1 0 1 2 0 0 0—5
Toronto 1 0 1 0 0 1 0 0 0—3

Kansas City	IP.	H.	R.	ER.	BB.	SO.
Gubicza (W)	5⅓	4	3	3	3	2
Black	3⅓	4	0	0	2	3
Quisenberry (S)	⅓	0	0	0	0	1

Toronto	IP.	H.	R.	ER.	BB.	SO.
Alexander (L)	5⅓	7	5	5	3	6
Lamp	3⅔	1	0	0	1	5

Game-winning RBI—Brett.

E—Fernandez, Barfield, Brett. DP—Kansas City 2. LOB—Kansas City 8, Toronto 9. 2B—Garcia, McRae, Fernandez, Biancalana, Smith. HR—Brett. SH—White. WP—Alexander, Gubicza, Black. U—Cousins, Phillips, Ford, Evans, Hendry and Voltaggio. T—3:12. A—37,557.

Game 7

Wednesday, October 16, At Toronto

Kansas City	AB.	R.	H.	RBI.	PO.	A.
Smith, lf	5	0	2	0	2	0
L. Jones, lf	0	0	0	0	0	0
Wilson, cf	5	0	0	0	2	0
Brett, 3b	3	0	0	0	1	0
McRae, dh	3	1	0	0	0	0
Sheridan, rf	4	3	2	1	1	0
Balboni, 1b	3	1	0	0	10	1
Sundberg, c	4	1	2	4	7	0
White, 2b	4	0	1	1	2	5
Biancalana, ss	4	0	1	0	0	1
Saberhagen, p	0	0	0	0	2	0
Leibrandt, p	0	0	0	0	0	2
Quisenberry, p	0	0	0	0	0	1
Totals	35	6	8	6	27	10

Toronto	AB.	R.	H.	RBI.	PO.	A.
Garcia, 2b	5	1	1	1	1	2
Moseby, cf	5	0	0	0	4	0
Mulliniks, 3b	1	0	1	0	0	2
G. Iorg, ph-3b	2	0	0	0	1	2
Upshaw, 1b	4	0	2	1	9	0
Oliver, dh	1	0	0	0	0	0
Johnson, dh	2	0	0	0	0	0
Bell, lf	4	0	1	0	3	0
Whitt, c	3	0	1	0	7	0
Burroughs, ph	1	0	0	0	0	0
Barfield, rf	3	1	1	0	1	0
Fernandez, ss	4	0	1	0	1	3
Stieb, p	0	0	0	0	0	1
Acker, p	0	0	0	0	0	0
Totals	35	2	8	2	27	10

Kansas City 0 1 0 1 0 4 0 0 0—6
Toronto 0 0 0 0 1 0 0 0 1—2

Kansas City	IP.	H.	R.	ER.	BB.	SO.
Saberhagen	3	3	0	0	1	2
Leibrandt (W)	5⅓	5	2	2	1	5
Quisenberry	⅔	0	0	0	0	0

Toronto	IP.	H.	R.	ER.	BB.	SO.
Stieb (L)	5⅔	6	6	6	2	4
Acker	3⅓	2	0	0	0	3

Game-winning RBI—Sundberg.

E—Fernandez. DP—Toronto 1. LOB—Kansas City 5, Toronto 9. 2B—Mulliniks, Bell, Upshaw, Fernandez. 3B—Sundberg. HR—Sheridan. HBP—By Saberhagen (Oliver), by Stieb (McRae). U—Phillips, Ford, Evans, Hendry, Voltaggio and Cousins. T—2:49. A—32,084.

COMPOSITE BATTING AVERAGES

Kansas City Royals

Player-Position	G.	AB.	R.	H.	2B.	3B.	HR.	RBI.	BA.
D. Iorg, ph	4	2	0	1	1	0	0	0	.500
Brett, 3b	7	23	6	8	2	0	3	5	.348
Motley, rf	2	3	1	1	0	0	0	1	.333
Wilson, cf	7	29	5	9	0	0	1	2	.310
McRae, dh	6	23	1	6	2	0	0	3	.261
Smith, lf	7	28	2	7	2	0	0	1	.250
Biancalana, ss	7	18	2	4	1	0	0	1	.222
White, 2b	7	25	1	5	0	0	0	3	.200
Sundberg, c	7	24	3	4	1	1	1	6	.167
Sheridan, rf-ph	7	20	4	3	0	0	2	3	.150
Balboni, 1b	7	25	1	3	0	0	0	1	.120
Jones, lf	5	0	0	0	0	0	0	0	.000
Quisenberry, p	4	0	0	0	0	0	0	0	.000
Black, p	3	0	0	0	0	0	0	0	.000
Leibrandt, p	3	0	0	0	0	0	0	0	.000
Farr, p	2	0	0	0	0	0	0	0	.000
Gubicza, p	2	0	0	0	0	0	0	0	.000
Jackson, p	2	0	0	0	0	0	0	0	.000
Saberhagen, p	2	0	0	0	0	0	0	0	.000
Quirk, ph	1	1	0	0	0	0	0	0	.000
Concepcion, ss-pr	4	1	0	0	0	0	0	0	.000
Orta, dh-ph	2	5	0	0	0	0	0	0	.000
Totals	7	227	26	51	9	1	7	26	.225

Toronto Blue Jays

Player-Position	G.	AB.	R.	H.	2B.	3B.	HR.	RBI.	BA.
Oliver, ph-dh	5	8	0	3	1	0	0	3	.375
Johnson, dh-ph	7	19	1	7	2	0	0	2	.368
Mulliniks, ph-3b	5	11	1	4	1	0	1	3	.364
Fernandez, ss	7	24	2	8	2	0	0	2	.333
Fielder, ph	3	3	0	1	1	0	0	0	.333
Bell, lf	7	28	4	9	3	0	0	1	.321
Barfield, rf	7	25	3	7	1	0	1	4	.280
Garcia, 2b	7	30	4	7	4	0	0	1	.233
Upshaw, 1b	7	26	2	6	2	0	0	1	.231
Moseby, cf	7	31	5	7	1	0	0	4	.226
Whitt, c	7	21	1	4	1	0	0	2	.190
G. Iorg, 3b-ph	6	15	1	2	0	0	0	0	.133
Henke, p	3	0	0	0	0	0	0	0	.000
Lamp, p	3	0	0	0	0	0	0	0	.000
Stieb, p	3	0	0	0	0	0	0	0	.000
Thornton, pr	2	0	1	0	0	0	0	0	.000
Acker, p	2	0	0	0	0	0	0	0	.000
Alexander, p	2	0	0	0	0	0	0	0	.000
Hearron, c	2	0	0	0	0	0	0	0	.000
Key, p	2	0	0	0	0	0	0	0	.000
Clancy, p	1	0	0	0	0	0	0	0	.000
Lavelle, p	1	0	0	0	0	0	0	0	.000
Lee, pr-2b	1	0	0	0	0	0	0	0	.000
Burroughs, ph	1	1	0	0	0	0	0	0	.000
Totals	7	242	25	65	19	0	2	23	.269

COMPOSITE PITCHING AVERAGES

Kansas City Royals

Pitcher	G.	IP.	H.	R.	ER.	BB.	SO.	W.	L.	ERA.
Jackson	2	10	10	0	0	1	7	1	0	0.00
Farr	2	6⅓	4	1	1	1	3	1	0	1.42
Black	3	10⅔	11	3	2	4	8	0	0	1.69
Gubicza	2	8⅓	4	3	3	4	4	1	0	3.24
Quisenberry	4	4⅔	7	4	2	0	3	0	1	3.86
Leibrandt	3	15⅓	17	9	9	4	6	1	2	5.28
Saberhagen	2	7⅓	12	5	5	2	6	0	0	6.14
Totals	7	62⅔	65	25	22	16	37	4	3	3.16

Toronto Blue Jays

Pitcher	G.	IP.	H.	R.	ER.	BB.	SO.	W.	L.	ERA.
Lamp	3	9⅓	2	0	0	1	10	0	0	0.00
Acker	2	6	2	0	0	0	5	0	0	0.00
Lavelle	1	*0	0	0	0	1	0	0	0	0.00
Stieb	3	20⅓	11	7	7	10	18	1	1	3.10
Henke	3	6⅓	5	3	3	4	4	2	0	4.26
Key	2	8⅔	15	5	5	2	5	0	1	5.19
Alexander	2	10⅓	14	10	10	3	9	0	1	8.71
Clancy	1	1	2	1	1	1	0	0	1	9.00
Totals	7	62	51	26	26	22	51	3	4	3.77

*Pitched to one batter in eighth inning of Game 2.

1985
ST. LOUIS CARDINALS
VS.
LOS ANGELES DODGERS

Baseball has produced its share of dramatic home runs, but the 1985 St. Louis Cardinals picked the National League Championship Series to redefine the word "dramatic."

First, light-hitting shortstop Ozzie Smith shocked the Los Angeles Dodgers and the rest of the baseball world by hitting his first-ever home run from the left side of the plate (he's a switch-hitter) in the ninth inning of Game 5, giving the Cardinals a 3-2 decision and a sweep of the three games played in St. Louis after the Dodgers had won the first two games of the series in Los Angeles.

First baseman Jack Clark then shocked the Dodgers in Game 6 when he crushed a 450-foot homer into the left-field bleachers with two on and two out in the ninth inning and the Cardinals trailing, 5-4. The Redbirds' 7-5 triumph bought them a ticket to the World Series.

What made these home runs even more special is that the Cardinals were not a power-hitting team. They won a major league-leading 101 games in 1985 with speed (a club-record 314 stolen bases), pitching (two 20-game winners in John Tudor and Joaquin Andujar) and timely hitting (a league-leading .264 average). Home runs? The Cardinals hit 87, the second lowest total in the major leagues.

"I guess you'd have to say I'm an unlikely hero," Smith said after his blast. Unlikely is an understatement. Entering the Championship Series, Smith was a .243 lifetime switch-hitter who had never hit a lefthanded homer in more than 4,000 career at-bats.

Clark's Game 6 homer didn't carry the element of surprise. The former Giant is a bona fide power hitter. But his blow was even

St. Louis shortstop Ozzie Smith makes a triumphant trot around the bases after shocking the Dodgers with a ninth-inning, Game 5-winning home run in the 1985 title series.

more devastating. After the game, observers were second-guessing Dodgers Manager Tommy Lasorda for not walking Clark when he had a base open and Andy Van Slyke coming up next.

When the series began, it looked like a Hollywood writer had produced a tidy little script for the Dodgers. Ace lefthander Fernando Valenzuela and bullpen ace Tom Niedenfuer combined to limit the Cardinals to eight hits in a 4-1 Dodger triumph in Game 1.

The Dodgers routed Andujar the next day for eight hits and six runs in 4⅓ innings and went on to an 8-2 triumph and a 2-0 series lead behind the eight-hit pitching

of Orel Hershiser.

Dodgers catcher Mike Scioscia served notice to the Cardinals that he wasn't going to be an easy mark for their base thiefs, throwing out both Vince Coleman and Willie McGee attempting to steal in the first inning.

The Cardinals averted disaster in Game 3, recording a 4-2 victory to cut the Dodgers' lead to 2-1.

Coleman singled to left and stole second to start the first inning. After McGee drew a walk, the Cardinals' speedsters went to work on Dodgers starter Bob Welch. Welch made a wild pickoff attempt to second base, Coleman scoring easily and McGee going to third. Tom Herr walked and stole second. Then, after Clark struck out, Welch walked Van Slyke to load the bases before Terry Pendleton's grounder plated McGee, giving the Cardinals a 2-0 lead.

The pesky Coleman walked with one out in the second. This time, he went to third on an errant pickoff attempt by Scioscia. After McGee singled to score Coleman, he was caught stealing. But Herr followed with a home run, increasing the Cardinals' lead to 4-0.

Danny Cox limited the Dodgers to only four hits in six-plus innings, yielding two runs.

Just when the Cardinals appeared to have their running game in gear, Coleman was lost in a freak accident prior to Game 4. The rookie sensation was disabled when an automatic tarp rolled over his left leg. But as so often happens when a team loses a key player, somebody comes off the bench and provides an Emmy-winning performance.

That role belonged to Tito Landrum, who went 4 for 5 with three RBIs in the Cardinals' 12-2 Game 4 rout of the Dodgers.

That game featured the Cardinals' Championship Series-record nine-run second inning. That came at the expense of Dodger starter and St. Louis native Jerry Reuss and helped the Redbirds even the series at two games apiece.

The Dodgers sent Valenzuela to the mound in Game 5, while the

Cardinals countered with Bob Forsch.

Again the Cardinals struck first. McGee and Smith drew leadoff walks in the first. Both came home when Herr doubled to left. After that, however, Valenzuela found his good stuff and shut the Cardinals down.

The Dodgers scored the tying runs in the fourth when Ken Landreaux led off with a single and scored ahead of Bill Madlock's long home run to left.

The score remained knotted until Niedenfuer relieved Valenzuela in the ninth. The big reliever retired McGee on a foul pop to third base to start the inning and then got ahead in the count (1 and 2) to Smith. But the slick-fielding shortstop shocked the capacity Busch Stadium crowd by lashing a screamer down the right-field line for only the 14th homer of his major league career.

Smith leaped for joy when he rounded first and saw the ball hit off the cement pillar above the right-field wall and then literally danced around the base.

Hershiser was asked to stop the Cardinals' momentum two days later against Andujar at Dodger Stadium. The Dodgers held the edge most of the way, until Clark found another one of those Niedenfuer fastballs to his liking in the ninth.

Madlock singled home Mariano Duncan, who had doubled to lead off the first, giving the Dodgers a 1-0 lead. They made it 2-0 in the second on Duncan's two-out RBI single.

The Cardinals got on the board in the third when Andujar hit a leadoff double and scored on Herr's two-out single. But the Dodgers rallied for two more runs in the fifth when Duncan, who had reached on an error by Andujar and stolen second, scored on a sacrifice fly by Pedro Guerrero and Madlock followed with his third home run of the series.

Hershiser scattered six hits and walked one, but he managed to hold the Dodgers' 4-1 lead until the seventh. That's when the Cardinals scored three times to tie the score and send Hershiser to the

showers.

The Dodgers appeared to have weathered the storm when Mike Marshall sent a Todd Worrell delivery over the right-center field fence in the bottom half of the eighth to put Los Angeles on top, 5-4.

But Niedenfuer couldn't stand prosperity, surrendering a one-out single to McGee. After McGee stole second and Smith drew a walk, Herr tapped easily to first baseman Brock, with the runners moving to second and third. That set the stage for the Clark-Niedenfuer matchup. And the Cardinals were on their way to the World Series.

Game 1

Wednesday, October 9, At Los Angeles

St. Louis	AB.	R.	H.	RBI.	PO.	A.
Coleman, lf	4	0	0	0	4	0
McGee, cf	4	0	0	0	2	0
Herr, 2b	3	0	1	0	1	2
Clark, 1b	3	0	1	0	10	0
Cedeno, rf	4	0	0	0	2	0
Worrell, p	0	0	0	0	0	0
Pendleton, 3b	4	1	2	0	0	4
Porter, c	4	0	1	0	3	1
Smith, ss	4	0	2	0	1	1
Tudor, p	2	0	0	0	0	1
Dayley, p	0	0	0	0	0	0
Landrum, ph	1	0	1	1	0	0
Campbell, p	0	0	0	0	0	0
Van Slyke, rf	0	0	0	0	1	0
Totals	33	1	8	1	24	9

Los Angeles	AB.	R.	H.	RBI.	PO.	A.
Duncan, ss	4	0	0	0	2	3
Cabell, 1b	4	0	0	0	9	1
Madlock, 3b	4	2	1	0	0	3
Guerrero, lf	3	1	2	1	1	0
Marshall, rf	4	0	0	0	0	0
Scioscia, c	4	1	1	1	8	0
Maldonado, cf	3	0	1	1	2	0
Landreaux, ph-cf	1	0	0	0	0	0
Sax, 2b	3	0	2	1	5	2
Valenzuela, p	2	0	1	0	0	1
Niedenfuer, p	0	0	0	0	0	0
Totals	32	4	8	4	27	10

St. Louis.................0 0 0 0 0 0 1 0 0—1
Los Angeles.............0 0 0 1 0 3 0 0 x—4

St. Louis	IP.	H.	R.	ER.	BB.	SO.
Tudor (L)	5⅔	7	4	3	1	3
Dayley	⅓	0	0	0	0	0
Campbell	1*	1	0	0	0	0
Worrell	1	0	0	0	0	0

Los Angeles	IP.	H.	R.	ER.	BB.	SO.
Valenzuela (W)	6⅓	7	1	1	2	6
Niedenfuer (S)	2⅔	1	0	0	0	2

*Pitched to one batter in eighth.

Game-winning RBI—Guerrero.
E—Pendleton. DP—Los Angeles 1. LOB—St. Louis 7, Los Angeles 6. 2B—Herr, Madlock, Sax. SB—Smith, Madlock, Guerrero 2. SH—Valenzuela. WP—Worrell. U—Stello, Froemming, McSherry, Tata, Runge and Crawford. T—2:42. A—55,270.

Game 2

Thursday, October 10, At Los Angeles

St. Louis	AB.	R.	H.	RBI.	PO.	A.
Coleman, lf	5	0	2	1	1	0
McGee, cf	5	1	1	0	5	0
Herr, 2b	3	0	1	0	1	1
Clark, 1b	3	0	1	0	6	0
Van Slyke, rf	3	0	0	0	1	0
Pendleton, 3b	4	1	1	0	1	2
Porter, c	2	0	0	0	8	0
Smith, ss	4	0	2	0	0	1
Andujar, p	2	0	0	0	0	0
Horton, p	0	0	0	0	1	2
Campbell, p	0	0	0	0	0	0
Braun, ph	1	0	0	0	0	0
Dayley, p	0	0	0	0	0	0
Lahti, p	0	0	0	0	0	0
Jorgensen, ph	1	0	0	0	0	0
Totals	33	2	8	1	24	6

Los Angeles	AB.	R.	H.	RBI.	PO.	A.
Duncan, ss	4	0	1	0	2	2
Anderson, pr-ss	1	1	0	0	0	2
Landreaux, cf	4	3	3	1	0	0

Los Angeles	AB.	R.	H.	RBI.	PO.	A.
Madlock, 3b	5	0	3	2	0	3
Bailor, pr-3b	0	0	0	0	0	0
Guerrero, lf	3	0	1	1	1	0
Maldonado, lf	0	0	0	0	0	0
Marshall, rf	4	0	1	1	3	0
Scioscia, c	3	1	1	0	4	2
Brock, 1b	4	1	1	2	15	1
Sax, 2b	4	1	1	0	1	7
Hershiser, p	4	1	1	1	0	1
Totals	36	8	13	8	27	16

St. Louis 0 0 1 0 0 0 0 0 1—2
Los Angeles 0 0 3 2 1 2 0 0 x—8

St. Louis	IP.	H.	R.	ER.	BB.	SO.
Andujar (L)	4⅓	8	6	6	2	6
Horton	1⅓	1	2	2	2	0
Campbell	⅓	2	0	0	0	1
Dayley	1	0	0	0	0	0
Lahti	1	2	0	0	0	1

Los Angeles	IP.	H.	R.	ER.	BB.	SO.
Hershiser (W)	9	8	2	2	5	4

Game-winning RBI—Landreaux.

E—Duncan, Andujar. DP—St. Louis 1, Los Angeles 1. LOB—St. Louis 9, Los Angeles 8. 2B—Herr, Landreaux 2, Duncan. HR—Brock. WP—Hershiser. PB—Porter. U—Froemming, McSherry, Tata, Runge, Crawford and Stello. T—3:04. A—55,222.

Game 3

Saturday, October 12, At St. Louis

Los Angeles	AB.	R.	H.	RBI.	PO.	A.
Anderson, ss	3	0	0	0	1	2
Landreaux, cf	5	0	2	1	3	0
Madlock, 3b	4	0	0	0	1	0
Guerrero, lf	3	1	1	0	2	0
Marshall, rf	4	0	2	1	1	0
Scioscia, c	3	0	0	0	6	1
Brock, 1b	4	0	0	0	7	0
Sax, 2b	3	0	2	0	2	6
Welch, p	1	0	0	0	0	0
Honeycutt, p	0	0	0	0	0	1
Johnstone, ph	1	0	0	0	0	0
Diaz, p	0	0	0	0	1	0
Matuszek, ph	0	0	0	0	0	0
Cabell, ph	1	1	0	0	0	0
Howell, p	0	0	0	0	0	1
Whitfield, ph	0	0	0	0	0	0
Maldonado, ph	1	0	0	0	0	0
Totals	33	2	7	2	24	11

St. Louis	AB.	R.	H.	RBI.	PO.	A.
Coleman, lf	5	2	2	0	3	0
McGee, cf	4	1	2	1	2	0
Herr, 2b	4	1	2	1	3	4
Clark, 1b	2	0	0	0	10	0
Van Slyke, rf	1	0	0	0	1	0
Cedeno, ph-rf	2	0	0	0	0	0
Worrell, p	0	0	0	0	0	0
Dayley, p	0	0	0	0	0	0
Pendleton, 3b	4	0	0	1	2	3
Porter, c	3	0	1	0	4	1
Smith, ss	3	0	1	0	2	1
Cox, p	2	0	0	0	0	0
Horton, p	0	0	0	0	0	0
Landrum, rf	1	0	0	0	0	0
Totals	31	4	8	3	27	9

Los Angeles 0 0 0 1 0 0 1 0 0—2
St. Louis 2 2 0 0 0 0 0 0 x—4

Los Angeles	IP.	H.	R.	ER.	BB.	SO.
Welch (L)	2⅔	5	4	2	6	2
Honeycutt	1⅓	1	0	0	1	1
Diaz	2	2	0	0	1	1
Howell	2	0	0	0	0	2

St. Louis	IP.	H.	R.	ER.	BB.	SO.
Cox (W)	6*	4	2	2	5	4
Horton	⅔	1	0	0	0	0
Worrell	1⅓†	2	0	0	0	0
Dayley (S)	1	0	0	0	0	0

*Pitched to one batter in seventh.
†Pitched to one batter in ninth.

Game-winning RBI—None.

E—Welch, Scioscia. LOB—Los Angeles 9, St. Louis 11. 2B—Landreaux, Porter, Guerrero, Marshall 2, Smith, Herr, Sax. HR—Herr. SB—Coleman, Herr, McGee. WP—Worrell. U—McSherry, Tata, Runge, Crawford, Stello and Froemming. T—3:21. A—53,708.

Game 4

Sunday, October 13, At St. Louis

Los Angeles	AB.	R.	H.	RBI.	PO.	A.
Duncan, ss	2	0	0	0	0	2
Anderson, ss	1	0	0	0	1	2
Cabell, 1b	4	0	0	0	8	1
Guerrero, lf	4	0	1	1	2	0
Diaz, p	0	0	0	0	0	0
Madlock, 3b	3	1	1	1	2	0
Bailor, 3b	1	0	0	0	0	1
Marshall, rf	4	0	1	0	3	0
Scioscia, c	1	0	0	0	1	0
Yeager, ph-c	2	0	0	0	4	0
Maldonado, cf	3	0	0	0	2	0
Brock, ph	1	0	0	0	0	0
Sax, 2b	3	0	1	0	0	1
Reuss, p	0	0	0	0	0	0
Honeycutt, p	0	0	0	0	0	0
Castillo, p	2	0	0	0	1	3
Matuszek, ph-lf	1	1	1	0	0	0
Totals	32	2	5	2	24	10

St. Louis	AB.	R.	H.	RBI.	PO.	A.
McGee, cf	5	1	1	0	2	0
Smith, ss	5	1	2	1	2	7
Herr, 2b	4	1	1	2	2	2
Clark, 1b	5	3	3	1	11	0
Cedeno, rf	2	2	2	0	0	0
Van Slyke, pr-rf	2	1	1	1	1	0
Landrum, lf	5	1	4	3	1	0
Pendleton, 3b	4	0	1	3	1	4
Nieto, c	3	1	0	0	7	0
Tudor, p	2	1	0	0	0	0
Jorgensen, ph	1	0	0	0	0	0
Horton, p	0	0	0	0	0	0
Campbell, p	0	0	0	0	0	0
Totals	38	12	15	11	27	13

Los Angeles 0 0 0 0 0 0 1 1 0— 2
St. Louis 0 9 0 1 1 0 0 1 x—12

Los Angeles	IP.	H.	R.	ER.	BB.	SO.
Reuss (L)	1⅔	5	7	2	1	0
Honeycutt	0*	3	2	2	1	0
Castillo	5⅓	4	2	2	2	4
Diaz	1	3	1	1	0	1

St. Louis	IP.	H.	R.	ER.	BB.	SO.
Tudor (W)	7	3	1	1	2	5
Horton	1	2	1	1	0	1
Campbell	1	0	0	0	0	1

*Pitched to four batters in second.

Game-winning RBI—Landrum.

E—Reuss, Maldonado. DP—Los Angeles 1. LOB—Los Angeles 5, St. Louis 7. 2B—Cedeno, McGee, Sax. HR—Madlock. SF—Herr. U—Tata, Runge, Crawford, Stello, Froemming and McSherry. T—2:47. A—53,708.

Game 5

Monday, October 14, At St. Louis

Los Angeles	AB.	R.	H.	RBI.	PO.	A.
Duncan, ss	3	0	0	0	1	3
Landreaux, cf	4	1	2	0	2	0
Guerrero, lf	4	0	0	0	4	0
Madlock, 3b	4	1	1	2	3	1
Marshall, rf	3	0	0	0	0	0
xScioscia, c	2	0	1	0	7	0
Brock, 1b	1	0	0	0	2	0
Cabell, ph-1b	3	0	1	0	3	1
Niedenfuer, p	0	0	0	0	0	0
Sax, 2b	3	0	0	0	2	0
Valenzuela, p	3	0	0	0	1	2
Matuszek, 1b	0	0	0	0	0	0
Totals	30	2	5	2	25	7

St. Louis	AB.	R.	H.	RBI.	PO.	A.
McGee, cf	3	1	0	0	3	0
Smith, ss	3	2	1	1	1	3
Herr, 2b	4	0	1	2	2	2
Clark, 1b	3	0	1	0	12	0
Cedeno, rf	3	0	0	0	3	0
Landrum, lf	3	0	0	0	2	0
Pendleton, 3b	4	0	1	0	1	3
Porter, c	2	0	0	0	3	0
Forsch, p	0	0	0	0	0	1
Dayley, p	2	0	1	0	0	1
Worrell, p	0	0	0	0	0	1
Harper, ph	1	0	0	0	0	0
Lahti, p	0	0	0	0	0	0
Totals	28	3	5	3	27	11

Los Angeles 0 0 0 2 0 0 0 0 0—2
St. Louis 2 0 0 0 0 0 0 0 1—3
One out when winning run scored.

Los Angeles	IP.	H.	R.	ER.	BB.	SO.
Valenzuela	8	4	2	2	8	7
Niedenfuer (L)	⅓	1	1	1	0	0

St. Louis	IP.	H.	R.	ER.	BB.	SO.
Forsch	3⅓	3	2	2	2	0
Dayley	2⅔*	2	0	0	1	1
Worrell	2	0	0	0	0	1
Lahti (W)	1	0	0	0	0	0

*Pitched to two batters in seventh.

Game-winning RBI—Smith.

xAwarded first base on catcher's interference. E—Valenzuela, Porter. DP—St. Louis 2. LOB—Los Angeles 5, St. Louis 10. 2B—Herr, Pendleton. HR—Madlock, Smith. SB—Landrum. SH—Forsch, Smith. WP—Valenzuela. U—Runge, Crawford, Stello, Froemming, McSherry and Tata. T—2:56. A—53,708.

Game 6

Wednesday, October 16 At Los Angeles

St. Louis	AB.	R.	H.	RBI.	PO.	A.
McGee, cf	5	2	3	2	4	0
Smith, ss	4	1	2	1	0	3
Herr, 2b	3	0	1	1	4	1
Clark, 1b	5	1	2	3	6	0
Van Slyke, rf	5	0	0	0	2	0
Pendleton, 3b	4	0	0	0	1	2
Porter, c	4	1	2	0	7	0
Landrum, lf	4	1	1	0	3	0
Andujar, p	2	1	1	0	0	0
Braun, ph	1	0	0	0	0	0
Worrell, p	0	0	0	0	0	0
Cedeno, ph	1	0	0	0	0	0
Dayley, p	0	0	0	0	0	0
Totals	38	7	12	7	27	6

Los Angeles	AB.	R.	H.	RBI.	PO.	A.
Duncan, ss	5	2	3	1	2	6
Landreaux, cf	4	0	0	0	2	0
Cabell, ph	1	0	0	0	0	0
Guerrero, lf	3	0	0	1	1	0
Madlock, 3b	4	1	2	2	0	2
Anderson, 3b	0	0	0	0	0	0
Marshall, rf	4	1	1	1	1	0
Scioscia, c	3	0	1	0	5	1
Brock, 1b	2	1	0	0	11	3
Sax, 2b	4	0	0	0	1	5
Hershiser, p	3	0	1	0	2	1
Niedenfuer, p	1	0	0	0	2	0
Totals	34	5	8	5	27	18

St. Louis 0 0 1 0 0 0 3 0 3—7
Los Angeles 1 1 0 0 2 0 0 1 0—5

St. Louis	IP.	H.	R.	ER.	BB.	SO.
Andujar	6	6	4	2	2	3
Worrell (W)	2	2	1	1	2	2
Dayley (S)	1	0	0	0	0	2

Los Angeles	IP.	H.	R.	ER.	BB.	SO.
Hershiser	6⅓	9	4	4	1	1
Niedenfuer (L)	2⅔	3	3	3	2	3

Game-winning RBI—Clark.

E—Andujar. DP—St. Louis 1. LOB—St. Louis 7, Los Angeles 7. 2B—Duncan, Andujar. 3B—Smith, Duncan. HR—Madlock, Marshall, Clark. SB—Duncan, McGee. SF—Guerrero. U—Crawford, Stello, Froemming, McSherry, Tata and Runge. Time—3:32. A—55,208.

COMPOSITE BATTING AVERAGES

St. Louis Cardinals

Player-Position	G.	AB.	R.	H.	2B.	3B.	HR.	RBI.	BA.
Dayley, p	5	2	0	1	0	0	0	0	.500
Smith, ss	6	23	4	10	1	1	1	3	.435
Landrum, ph-rf-lf	5	14	2	6	0	0	0	4	.429
Clark, 1b	6	21	4	8	0	0	1	4	.381
Herr, 2b	6	21	2	7	4	0	1	6	.333
Coleman, lf	3	14	2	4	0	0	0	1	.286
McGee, cf	6	26	6	7	1	0	0	3	.269
Porter, c	5	15	1	4	1	0	0	0	.267
Andujar, p	2	4	1	1	1	0	0	0	.250
Pendleton, 3b	6	24	2	5	1	0	0	4	.208
Cedeno, rf-ph	5	12	2	2	1	0	0	0	.167
Van Slyke, rf-pr	5	11	1	1	0	0	0	1	.091
Worrell, p	4	0	0	0	0	0	0	0	.000
Campbell, p	3	0	0	0	0	0	0	0	.000
Horton, p	3	0	0	0	0	0	0	0	.000
Lahti, p	2	0	0	0	0	0	0	0	.000
Forsch, p	1	0	0	0	0	0	0	0	.000
Harper, ph	1	1	0	0	0	0	0	0	.000
Braun, ph	2	2	0	0	0	0	0	0	.000
Jorgensen, ph	2	2	0	0	0	0	0	0	.000
Cox, p	1	2	0	0	0	0	0	0	.000
Nieto, c	1	3	1	0	0	0	0	0	.000
Tudor, p	2	4	1	0	0	0	0	0	.000
Totals	6	201	29	56	10	1	3	26	.279

Los Angeles Dodgers

Player-Position	G.	AB.	R.	H.	2B.	3B.	HR.	RBI.	BA.
Matuszek, ph-lf-1b	3	1	1	1	0	0	0	0	1.000
Landreaux, ph-cf	5	18	4	7	3	0	0	2	.389
Madlock, 3b	6	24	5	8	1	0	3	7	.333
Sax, 2b	6	20	1	6	3	0	0	1	.300
Hershiser, p	2	7	1	2	0	0	0	1	.286
Guerrero, lf	6	20	2	5	1	0	0	4	.250
Scioscia, c	6	16	2	4	0	0	0	1	.250
Duncan, ss	5	18	2	4	2	1	0	1	.222
Marshall, rf	6	23	1	5	2	0	1	3	.217
Valenzuela, p	2	5	0	1	0	0	0	0	.200
Maldonado, cf-lf-ph	4	7	0	1	0	0	0	1	.143
Brock, 1b-ph	5	12	2	1	0	0	1	2	.083
Cabell, 1b-ph	5	13	1	1	0	0	0	0	.077
Diaz, p	2	0	0	0	0	0	0	0	.000
Honeycutt, p	2	0	0	0	0	0	0	0	.000
Howell, p	1	0	0	0	0	0	0	0	.000
Reuss, p	1	0	0	0	0	0	0	0	.000
Whitfield, ph	1	0	0	0	0	0	0	0	.000
Niedenfuer, p	3	1	0	0	0	0	0	0	.000
Bailor, pr-3b	2	1	0	0	0	0	0	0	.000
Johnstone, ph	1	1	0	0	0	0	0	0	.000
Welch, p	1	1	0	0	0	0	0	0	.000
Castillo, p	1	2	0	0	0	0	0	0	.000
Yeager, ph-c	1	2	0	0	0	0	0	0	.000
Anderson, pr-ss-3b	4	5	1	0	0	0	0	0	.000
Totals	6	197	23	46	12	1	5	23	.234

COMPOSITE PITCHING AVERAGES

St. Louis Cardinals

Pitcher	G.	IP.	H.	R.	ER.	BB.	SO.	W.	L.	ERA.
Dayley	5	6	2	0	0	1	3	0	0	0.00
Campbell	3	2⅓	3	0	0	0	2	0	0	0.00
Lahti	2	2	2	0	0	0	1	1	0	0.00
Worrell	4	6⅓	4	1	1	2	3	1	0	1.42
Cox	1	6	4	1	1	5	4	1	0	1.50
Tudor	2	12⅔	10	5	4	3	8	1	1	2.84
Forsch	1	3⅓	3	2	2	2	0	0	0	5.40
Andujar	2	10⅓	14	10	8	4	9	0	1	6.97
Horton	3	3	4	4	4	2	1	0	0	12.00
Totals	6	52	46	23	20	19	31	4	2	3.46

Los Angeles Dodgers

Pitcher	G.	IP.	H.	R.	ER.	BB.	SO.	W.	L.	ERA.
Howell	1	2	0	0	0	0	2	0	0	0.00
Valenzuela	2	14⅓	11	3	3	10	13	1	0	1.88
Diaz	2	3	5	1	1	1	2	0	0	3.00
Castillo	1	5⅓	4	2	2	2	4	0	0	3.38
Hershiser	2	15⅓	17	6	6	6	5	1	0	3.52
Niedenfuer	3	5⅔	5	4	4	2	5	0	2	6.35
Welch	1	2⅔	5	4	2	6	2	0	1	6.75
Reuss	1	1⅔	5	7	2	1	0	0	1	10.80
Honeycutt	2	1⅓	4	2	2	2	1	0	0	13.50
Totals	6	51⅓	56	29	*20	30	34	2	4	3.51

*Individual earned runs do not add up to team total because of rule 10.18 (i) being applied in Game 4.

1986
BOSTON RED SOX
VS.
CALIFORNIA ANGELS

More than 64,000 people were on their feet, ready to rejoice at a historic moment—the first California Angels pennant in the 26 years of the club's existence and Gene Mauch's first pennant in 25 years of managing.

One more strike. That's all the Angels needed.

The Angels held a three-games-to-one lead over the Boston Red Sox in the 1986 American League Championship Series. Mauch's team also held a 5-4 lead on this October 12 afternoon with one man on base and two out in the top of the ninth inning at Anaheim Stadium.

Angels ace reliever Donnie Moore was pitching to Dave Henderson with a 1-2 count.

Moore's next pitch was low. Ball two. The crowd gasped. The Angels' players, poised on the top step of the dugout and ready to race onto the field, gestured for Moore to get that final out.

Henderson fouled the next pitch to the left of the plate. More suspense. More noise. Then there was another foul ball. Still 2-and-2.

When Moore sent his third 2-2 delivery to the plate, Henderson took a mighty swing. In a matter of seconds, players were joyously jumping all over the field. But the happy players weren't wearing a halo on their caps.

Henderson had belted a two-run home run into the left-field seats, giving the Red Sox a 6-5 lead. It was poetic justice for Henderson, who had inadvertently knocked Bobby Grich's long drive over the center-field wall to give the Angels a 3-2 lead three innings earlier.

As Henderson did a leaping pirouette before going into his home run trot, you somehow had the feeling this wild and wonderful game was far from over.

Catcher Bob Boone singled off reliever Bob Stanley to start the bottom of the ninth for the Angels. Then pinch-runner Ruppert Jones was sacrificed to second by Gary Pettis. Joe Sambito replaced Stanley on the mound for Boston, but second baseman Rob Wilfong followed with a line single to right, scoring Jones and tying the game. Red Sox Manager John McNamara then called on righthander Steve Crawford, who worked out of a bases-loaded, one-out jam by retiring Doug DeCinces on a fly ball to right field and Grich on a soft liner back to the mound.

Moore was still pitching for California when the game went into the 11th inning. Leading off, designated hitter Don Baylor was hit by a pitch. Dwight Evans followed with a single to center. Rich Gedman, trying to sacrifice, was credited with a bunt single, loading the bases. That's when Henderson stepped up to the plate again.

Once more, Henderson wielded his magic wand, lofting Moore's first pitch into center field for a sacrifice fly. The heavens had frowned on the Angels and smiled on the Red Sox in this 7-6 victory.

By all rights, the Red Sox should have died that day. But they didn't. In fact, they needed no more late-inning heroics in capturing Game 6, 10-4, and Game 7, 8-1, to complete their dramatic comeback.

This unpredictable series began in Boston's Fenway Park with a dream pitching matchup—Roger Clemens (24-4) for the Red Sox vs. Mike Witt (18-10) for the Angels. Instead of seeing a low-scoring affair, however, the Boston faithful were knocked for a loop when the Angels hammered Clemens for 10 hits and eight runs in 7⅓ innings. Meanwhile, Witt pitched almost perfect baseball for six innings, retiring 16 batters in succession and not allowing a hit until two were out in the sixth. He finished with a five-hitter and the Angels had claimed an 8-1 victory.

The Red Sox tied the series with a 9-2 triumph in an error-filled Game 2.

Bruce Hurst scattered 11 hits over nine innings while raising his record to 9-3 at home in '86, an unbelievable mark considering that Fenway Park's left-field wall normally gives lefthanders fits.

When the scene shifted to Anaheim Stadium for Game 3, righthander Dennis (Oil Can) Boyd sang much the same tune that Clemens did in Game 1. Boyd held a 1-0 lead going into the bottom of the sixth, but it wasn't the big guys who inflicted the damage in California's 5-3 victory.

After Reggie Jackson's run-scoring single tied the contest, 1-1, in the sixth, the Angels scored three more runs in the seventh. With two out, Dick Schofield blasted Boyd's first pitch over the fence in left-center field to give California the lead. After Boone singled to right, Pettis smashed a 2-1 delivery from Boyd into the right-field seats for another home run. The Angels were in control.

In Game 4, which featured Clemens starting for the first time in his career on three days' rest against veteran Don Sutton, the Angels pulled off a stunning comeback to take a 3-1 lead in the series.

Thanks to Bill Buckner's run-scoring double in the sixth and Marty Barrett's RBI single and some costly California errors in the eighth, Clemens had a 3-0 lead

Boston's Dave Henderson gets a hug from teammate Bill Buckner after hitting a dramatic Game 5 home run that kept his team alive in the 1986 playoffs against California.

heading into the bottom of the ninth. The righthander was working on a five-hit shutout when De-Cinces opened the frame with a towering homer to left-center field. Schofield and Boone then hit consecutive one-out singles to left. With the tying runs on base, McNamara called on his relief ace, rookie Calvin Schiraldi.

Pettis greeted the righthander with a double off the left-field wall that Jim Rice lost in the lights, scoring Schofield and sending Devon White, who was running for Boone, to third. After Jones was walked intentionally to load the bases, Schiraldi fanned Grich for the second out of the inning. Then, when the count reached 1 and 2 on Brian Downing, Schiraldi heaved a pitch that hit Downing in the side, forcing home White with the tying run.

Reserve catcher Jerry Narron opened the Angels' 11th with a single and went to second on a sacrifice by Pettis. Jones again was walked intentionally, bringing up Grich. The Angels' second baseman hit a drive into the left-field corner to score Narron and give the Angels a 4-3 victory.

Less than 24 hours later, the Angels were all set to wrap up the series before Henderson pulled off his heroics to rally the Red Sox to a 7-6, 11-inning victory in the pivotal fifth game.

In Game 6, the Angels jumped on Boyd in the first inning with consecutive run-scoring doubles by Jackson and DeCinces. But the Red Sox, back in the friendly confines of Fenway Park, rallied against McCaskill in their half of the first to tie the game without the benefit of a hit. Wade Boggs and Barrett led off with walks and scored on Boone's passed ball and a run-scoring groundout by Rice.

Boston added five runs on six hits in the third to knock out McCaskill and put the game out of reach.

With the momentum clearly on their side and Clemens on the mound for the third time, the Red Sox bombed the Angels, 8-1, in Game 7.

Game 1

Tuesday, October 7, At Boston

California	AB.	R.	H.	RBI.	PO.	A.
Jones, rf	4	1	1	1	2	0
Burleson, ph	1	0	0	0	0	0
White, rf	0	0	0	0	0	0
Joyner, 1b	4	1	2	1	8	0
Downing, lf	5	0	2	4	5	0
Jackson, dh	4	0	0	0	0	0
DeCinces, 3b	5	0	1	0	0	4
Wilfong, 2b	5	1	0	0	1	1
Schofield, ss	5	1	1	0	0	1
Boone, c	3	2	2	1	5	0
Pettis, cf	3	2	2	1	4	0
Witt, p	0	0	0	0	0	1
Totals	39	8	11	8	27	7

Boston	AB.	R.	H.	RBI.	PO.	A.
Boggs, 3b	3	0	1	0	2	0
Barrett, 2b	4	0	2	1	0	3
Buckner, 1b	4	0	0	0	9	2
Rice, lf	4	0	0	0	3	0
Baylor, dh	4	0	1	0	0	0
Evans, rf	4	0	0	0	1	0
Gedman, c	3	0	0	0	5	0
Armas, cf	3	0	0	0	4	0
Owen, ss	2	1	1	0	2	4
Clemens, p	0	0	0	0	1	0
Sambito, p	0	0	0	0	0	0
Stanley, p	0	0	0	0	0	0
Totals	31	1	5	1	27	9

California ..... 0 4 1 0 0 0 0 3 0—8
Boston ..... 0 0 0 0 0 1 0 0 0—1

California	IP.	H.	R.	ER.	BB.	SO.
Witt (W)	9	5	1	1	2	3

Boston	IP.	H.	R.	ER.	BB.	SO.
Clemens (L)	7⅓	10	8	7	3	5
Sambito	⅓	0	0	0	1	0
Stanley	1⅓	1	0	0	0	0

Game-winning RBI—Jones.
E—Owen. DP—California 1. LOB—California 8, Boston 5. 2B—Joyner 2, Baylor. SB—Schofield. U—Barnett, McCoy, Cooney, Bremigan, Roe and Garcia. T—2:52. A—32,993.

Game 2

Wednesday, October 8, At Boston

California	AB.	R.	H.	RBI.	PO.	A.
Burleson, dh	5	0	1	0	0	0
Joyner, 1b	4	1	2	1	8	1
Downing, lf	4	1	1	0	1	0
DeCinces, 3b	4	0	1	0	1	4
Hendrick, rf	4	0	0	0	1	0
Grich, 2b	4	0	2	0	2	1
Schofield, ss	4	0	2	1	3	3
Boone, c	4	0	1	0	5	1
Pettis, cf	4	0	1	0	2	0
McCaskill, p	0	0	0	0	1	0
Lucas, p	0	0	0	0	0	0
Corbett, p	0	0	0	0	0	0
Totals	37	2	11	2	24	10

Boston	AB.	R.	H.	RBI.	PO.	A.
Boggs, 3b	4	1	2	0	1	4
Barrett, 2b	5	1	3	2	5	1
Buckner, 1b	4	2	1	0	7	1
Stapleton, 1b	0	0	0	0	0	0
Rice, lf	5	2	2	2	0	1
Baylor, dh	2	1	2	0	0	0
Evans, rf	5	0	1	2	4	0
Gedman, c	4	1	1	0	4	0
Armas, cf	4	0	0	0	2	0
Henderson, cf	0	0	0	0	1	0
Owen, ss	3	1	1	0	2	4
Hurst, p	0	0	0	0	0	0
Totals	36	9	13	8	27	11

California ..... 0 0 0 1 1 0 0 0 0—2
Boston ..... 1 1 0 0 1 0 3 3 x—9

California	IP.	H.	R.	ER.	BB.	SO.
McCaskill (L)	7	10	6	3	3	6
Lucas	⅔	1	2	2	0	1
Corbett	⅓	2	1	1	0	0

Boston	IP.	H.	R.	ER.	BB.	SO.
Hurst (W)	9	11	2	1	0	4

Game-winning RBI—Evans.
E—Owen, Boggs, Grich, DeCinces, Schofield. DP—California 1, Boston 1. LOB—California 8, Boston 9. 2B—Barrett, Evans. 3B—Boggs. HR—Joyner, Rice. SH—Boggs. SF—Buckner. U—McCoy, Cooney, Bremigan, Roe, Garcia and Barnett. T—2:47. A—32,786.

Game 3

Friday, October 10, At California

Boston	AB.	R.	H.	RBI.	PO.	A.
Boggs, 3b	4	0	0	0	2	2
Barrett, 2b	5	1	2	0	1	5
Buckner, 1b	5	0	0	0	8	1
Rice, lf	3	2	1	0	3	0
Baylor, dh	3	0	1	0	0	0
Evans, rf	3	0	1	0	0	0
Gedman, c	4	0	3	2	4	1
Armas, cf	4	0	1	0	2	0
Owen, ss	3	0	0	0	3	1
Greenwell, ph	1	0	0	0	0	0
Boyd, p	0	0	0	0	1	2
Sambito, p	0	0	0	0	0	0
Schiraldi, p	0	0	0	0	0	0
Totals	35	3	9	2	24	12

California	AB.	R.	H.	RBI.	PO.	A.
Pettis, cf	3	1	1	2	9	0
Joyner, 1b	3	1	1	0	8	0
Downing, lf	4	0	1	0	3	0

California	AB.	R.	H.	RBI.	PO.	A.
Jackson, dh	3	1	1	1	0	0
DeCinces, 3b	4	0	1	0	0	1
Jones, rf	3	0	0	1	1	0
White, rf	0	0	0	0	0	0
Grich, 2b	4	0	0	0	0	0
Schofield, ss	3	1	2	1	1	1
Boone, c	3	1	1	0	5	1
Candelaria, p	0	0	0	0	0	1
Moore, p	0	0	0	0	0	0
Totals	30	5	8	5	27	4

Boston .... 0 1 0 0 0 0 0 2 0—3
California .... 0 0 0 0 0 1 3 1 x—5

Boston	IP.	H.	R.	ER.	BB.	SO.
Boyd (L)	6⅔	8	4	4	2	3
Sambito	⅓	0	0	0	0	0
Schiraldi	1	0	1	0	1	0

California	IP.	H.	R.	ER.	BB.	SO.
Candelaria (W)	7	5	1	1	3	5
Moore (S)	2	4	2	2	1	0

Game-winning RBI—Schofield.

E—Boggs. DP—Boston 1. LOB—Boston 9, California 5. 2B—Armas, Schofield, Rice. HR—Schofield, Pettis. SF—Jones. Balk—Moore. U—Cooney, Bremigan, Roe, Garcia, Barnett, and McCoy. T—2:48. A—64,206.

Game 4

Saturday, October 11 At California

Boston	AB.	R.	H.	RBI.	PO.	A.
Boggs, 3b	5	0	1	0	1	2
Barrett, 2b	3	1	1	1	1	2
Buckner, 1b	5	0	1	1	10	1
Rice, lf	5	0	0	0	0	0
Baylor, dh	5	0	1	0	0	0
Evans, rf	4	0	0	0	2	0
Gedman, c	5	0	0	0	11	1
Armas, cf	3	1	1	0	2	0
Henderson, cf	1	0	0	0	2	0
Owen, ss	3	1	1	0	2	5
Clemens, p	0	0	0	0	0	1
Schiraldi, p	0	0	0	0	0	0
Totals	39	3	6	2	31	12

California	AB.	R.	H.	RBI.	PO.	A.
Jones, rf	2	0	1	0	2	0
Grich, 2b	6	0	1	1	1	6
Downing, lf	3	0	0	1	1	0
Jackson, dh	5	0	0	0	0	0
DeCinces, 3b	5	1	2	1	2	2
Hendrick, 1b	5	0	0	0	14	2
Schofield, ss	5	1	1	0	3	4
Boone, c	4	0	2	0	4	0
White, pr	0	1	0	0	0	0
Narron, c	1	1	1	0	0	0
Pettis, cf	4	0	3	1	5	0
Sutton, p	0	0	0	0	1	1
Lucas, p	0	0	0	0	0	0
Ruhle, p	0	0	0	0	0	0
Finley, p	0	0	0	0	0	0
Corbett, p	0	0	0	0	0	1
Totals	40	4	11	4	33	16

Boston .... 0 0 0 0 0 1 0 2 0 0 0—3
California .... 0 0 0 0 0 0 0 0 3 0 1—4

One out when winning run scored.

Boston	IP.	H.	R.	ER.	BB.	SO.
Clemens	8⅓	8	3	3	3	9
Schiraldi (L)	2	3	1	1	2	2

California	IP.	H.	R.	ER.	BB.	SO.
Sutton	6⅓	4	1	1	1	2
Lucas	⅓	0	0	0	0	1
Ruhle	⅔	2	2	1	0	0
Finley	0*	0	0	0	0	0
Corbett (W)	3⅔	0	0	0	1	1

*Pitched to one batter in eighth.

Game-winning RBI—Grich.

E—Owen, Grich, DeCinces. DP—Boston 1. LOB—Boston 7, California 12. 2B—Boggs, Buckner, Baylor, Jones, Pettis. HR—DeCinces. SH—Barrett, Owen, Pettis. HBP—By Schiraldi (Downing). WP—Ruhle. PB—Boone. U—Bremigan, Roe, Garcia, Barnett, McCoy and Cooney. T—3:50. A—64,223.

Game 5

Sunday, October 12, At California

Boston	AB.	R.	H.	RBI.	PO.	A.
Boggs, 3b	5	0	1	0	1	2
Barrett, 2b	5	0	0	0	7	4
Buckner, 1b	4	0	1	0	4	0
Stapleton, pr-1b	1	1	1	0	2	1
Rice, lf	5	1	1	0	3	0
Baylor, dh	4	2	1	2	0	0
Evans, rf	5	0	1	0	1	0
Gedman, c	4	2	4	2	8	2
Armas, cf	2	0	0	0	2	0
Henderson, cf	2	1	1	3	3	0
Owen, ss	2	0	0	0	1	0
Greenwell, ph	1	0	1	0	0	0
Romero, pr-ss	2	0	0	0	0	0
Hurst, p	0	0	0	0	0	2
Stanley, p	0	0	0	0	0	1
Sambito, p	0	0	0	0	0	0
Crawford, p	0	0	0	0	1	0
Schiraldi, p	0	0	0	0	0	0
Totals	42	7	12	7	33	12

California	AB.	R.	H.	RBI.	PO.	A.
Burleson, 2b	2	0	0	0	1	3
Wilfong, ph-2b	3	0	2	2	3	3
Schofield, ss	5	0	1	0	3	5
Downing, lf	3	0	0	1	4	0
DeCinces, 3b	5	1	2	0	1	0
Grich, 1b	5	1	1	2	10	2
Jackson, dh	5	0	1	0	0	0
Hendrick, rf	3	0	1	0	1	0
White, pr-rf	2	1	1	0	1	0
Boone, c	3	1	3	1	6	0
Jones, pr	0	1	0	0	0	0
Narron, c	0	0	0	0	0	0
Pettis, cf	3	1	1	0	1	0
Witt, p	0	0	0	0	2	3
Lucas, p	0	0	0	0	0	0
Moore, p	0	0	0	0	0	0
Finley, p	0	0	0	0	0	0
Totals	39	6	13	6	33	16

Boston .... 0 2 0 0 0 0 0 0 4 0 1—7
California .... 0 0 1 0 0 2 2 0 1 0 0—6

Boston	IP.	H.	R.	ER.	BB.	SO.
Hurst	6	7	3	3	1	4
Stanley	2⅓	4	3	3	2	1
Sambito	0*	1	0	0	0	0
Crawford (W)	1⅔	1	0	0	2	1
Schiraldi (S)	1	0	0	0	0	2

California	IP.	H.	R.	ER.	BB.	SO.
Witt	8⅔	8	4	4	0	5
Lucas	0*	0	1	1	0	0
Moore (L)	2	4	2	2	1	0
Finley	⅓	0	0	0	0	0

*Pitched to one batter in ninth.

Game-winning RBI—Henderson.

DP—California 2. LOB—Boston 6, California 9. 2B—DeCinces 2, Gedman, Wilfong. HR—Gedman, Boone, Grich, Baylor, Henderson. SH—Burleson, Boone, Pettis. SF—Downing, Henderson. HBP—By Lucas (Gedman), by Moore (Baylor). U—Roe, Garcia, Barnett, McCoy, Cooney and Bremigan. T—3:54. A—64,223.

Game 6

Tuesday, October 14, At Boston

California	AB.	R.	H.	RBI.	PO.	A.
Pettis, cf	5	0	1	0	2	0
Jones, rf	4	1	0	0	1	0
Downing, lf	5	1	1	1	1	0
Jackson, dh	5	1	3	1	0	0
DeCinces, 3b	5	0	1	1	1	4
Schofield, ss	4	1	2	0	2	5
Grich, 1b	3	0	1	0	8	0
Wilfong, 2b	4	0	2	0	4	5
Boone, c	3	0	0	0	4	1
Howell, ph	0	0	0	0	0	0
Narron, c	0	0	0	0	1	0
McCaskill, p	0	0	0	0	0	0
Lucas, p	0	0	0	0	0	0
Corbett, p	0	0	0	0	0	0
Finley, p	0	0	0	0	0	0
Totals	38	4	11	3	24	15

Boston	AB.	R.	H.	RBI.	PO.	A.
Boggs, 3b	4	2	1	0	0	1
Barrett, 2b	4	1	3	1	2	1
Buckner, 1b	4	1	2	1	6	0
Stapleton, pr-1b	1	0	1	0	4	0
Rice, lf	5	1	0	1	3	0
Baylor, dh	4	2	1	0	0	0
Evans, rf	4	0	2	1	2	0
Gedman, c	4	1	2	0	5	0
Henderson, cf	3	1	0	1	3	0
Owen, ss	4	1	4	2	1	5
Boyd, p	0	0	0	0	1	0
Stanley, p	0	0	0	0	0	0
Totals	37	10	16	7	27	7

California .... 2 0 0 0 0 0 1 1 0— 4
Boston .... 2 0 5 0 1 0 2 0 x—10

California	IP.	H.	R.	ER.	BB.	SO.
McCaskill (L)	2⅓	6	7	5	2	1
Lucas	1⅓	2	0	0	0	1
Corbett	2⅔	7	3	3	1	1
Finley	1⅔	1	0	0	0	1

Boston	IP.	H.	R.	ER.	BB.	SO.
Boyd (W)	7	9	3	3	1	5
Stanley	2	2	1	0	1	0

Game-winning RBI—Barrett.

E—Grich, Owen. DP—Boston 1, California 3. LOB—California 10, Boston 7. 2B—Jackson 2, DeCinces, Barrett. 3B—Owen. HR—Downing. HBP—By Boyd (Grich), by Corbett (Baylor). PB—Boone. U—Garcia, Barnett, McCoy, Cooney, Bremigan and Roe. T—3:23. A—32,998.

Game 7

Wednesday, October 15, At Boston

California	AB.	R.	H.	RBI.	PO.	A.
Jones, rf	4	1	1	0	0	0
Wilfong, 2b	1	0	0	0	0	1
Burleson, 2b	3	0	2	0	2	2
Downing, lf	3	0	1	0	3	0
Jackson, dh	4	0	0	0	0	0
DeCinces, 3b	4	0	1	1	1	3
Schofield, ss	4	0	0	0	1	4
Pettis, cf	4	0	0	0	5	0
Grich, 1b	2	0	0	0	8	0
Howell, ph	1	0	0	0	0	0
Boone, c	2	0	1	0	4	0
Narron, ph	1	0	0	0	0	0
Candelaria, p	0	0	0	0	0	0
Sutton, p	0	0	0	0	0	0
Moore, p	0	0	0	0	0	0
Totals	33	1	6	1	24	10

Boston	AB.	R.	H.	RBI.	PO.	A.
Boggs, 3b	5	0	1	2	0	2
Barrett, 2b	4	0	0	0	3	5
Buckner, 1b	2	0	1	0	5	0
Stapleton, pr-1b	1	1	0	0	6	0
Rice, lf	4	2	1	3	1	0
Baylor, dh	4	1	2	0	0	0
Evans, rf	3	2	1	1	1	0
Gedman, c	4	0	0	1	8	0
Henderson, cf	3	1	0	0	2	0
Owen, ss	4	1	2	1	1	2
Clemens, p	0	0	0	0	0	1
Schiraldi, p	0	0	0	0	0	0
Totals	34	8	8	8	27	10

California .... 0 0 0 0 0 0 0 1 0—1
Boston .... 0 3 0 4 0 0 1 0 x—8

California	IP.	H.	R.	ER.	BB.	SO.
Candelaria (L)	3⅔	6	7	0	3	2
Sutton	3⅓	2	1	1	0	2
Moore	1	0	0	0	0	0

Boston	IP.	H.	R.	ER.	BB.	SO.
Clemens (W)	7*	4	1	1	1	3
Schiraldi	2	2	0	0	0	5

*Pitched to one batter in eighth.

Game-winning RBI—Gedman.

E—Schofield, Pettis, Owen. DP—Boston 1. LOB—California 8, Boston 5. 2B—Baylor. HR—Rice, Evans. SB—Owen. HBP—By Clemens (Boone, Grich). U—Barnett, McCoy, Garcia, Bremigan and Roe. T—2:39. A—33,001.

COMPOSITE BATTING AVERAGES

Boston Red Sox

Player-Position	G.	AB.	R.	H.	2B.	3B.	HR.	RBI.	BA.
Stapleton, 1b-pr	4	3	2	2	0	0	0	0	.667
Greenwell, ph	2	2	0	1	0	0	0	0	.500
Owen, ss	7	21	5	9	0	1	0	3	.429
Barrett, 2b	7	30	4	11	2	0	0	5	.367
Gedman, c	7	28	4	10	1	0	1	6	.357
Baylor, dh	7	26	6	9	3	0	1	2	.346
Boggs, 3b	7	30	3	7	1	1	0	2	.233
Evans, rf	7	28	2	6	1	0	1	4	.214
Buckner, 1b	7	28	3	6	1	0	0	3	.214
Rice, lf	7	31	8	5	1	0	2	6	.161
Armas, cf	5	16	1	2	1	0	0	0	.125
Henderson, cf	5	9	3	1	0	0	1	4	.111
Schiraldi, p	4	0	0	0	0	0	0	0	.000
Clemens, p	3	0	0	0	0	0	0	0	.000
Sambito, p	3	0	0	0	0	0	0	0	.000
Stanley, p	3	0	0	0	0	0	0	0	.000
Boyd, p	2	0	0	0	0	0	0	0	.000
Crawford, p	1	0	0	0	0	0	0	0	.000
Hurst, p	2	0	0	0	0	0	0	0	.000
Romero, pr-ss	1	2	0	0	0	0	0	0	.000
Totals	7	254	41	69	11	2	6	35	.272

California Angels

Player-Position	G.	AB.	R.	H.	2B.	3B.	HR.	RBI.	BA.
White, rf-pr	4	2	2	1	0	0	0	0	.500
Narron, c-ph	4	2	1	1	0	0	0	0	.500
Boone, c	7	22	4	10	0	0	1	2	.455
Joyner, 1b	3	11	3	5	2	0	1	2	.455
Pettis, cf	7	26	4	9	1	0	1	4	.346
Wilfong, 2b-ph	4	13	1	4	1	0	0	2	.308
Schofield, ss	7	30	4	9	1	0	1	2	.300
DeCinces, 3b	7	32	2	9	3	0	1	3	.281
Burleson, ph-dh-2b	4	11	0	3	0	0	0	0	.273
Downing, lf	7	27	2	6	0	0	1	7	.222
Grich, 2b-1b	6	24	1	5	0	0	1	3	.208
Jackson, dh	6	26	2	5	2	0	0	2	.192
Jones, rf-pr	6	17	4	3	1	0	0	2	.176
Hendrick, rf-1b	3	12	0	1	0	0	0	0	.083
Lucas, p	4	0	0	0	0	0	0	0	.000
Corbett, p	3	0	0	0	0	0	0	0	.000
Finley, p	3	0	0	0	0	0	0	0	.000
Moore, p	3	0	0	0	0	0	0	0	.000
Candelaria, p	2	0	0	0	0	0	0	0	.000
McCaskill, p	2	0	0	0	0	0	0	0	.000
Sutton, p	2	0	0	0	0	0	0	0	.000
Witt, p	2	0	0	0	0	0	0	0	.000
Ruhle, p	1	0	0	0	0	0	0	0	.000
Howell, ph	2	1	0	0	0	0	0	0	.000
Totals	7	256	30	71	11	0	7	29	.277

COMPOSITE PITCHING AVERAGES

Boston Red Sox

Pitcher	G.	IP.	H.	R.	ER.	BB.	SO.	W.	L.	ERA.
Crawford	1	1⅔	1	0	0	2	1	1	0	0.00
Sambito	3	⅔	1	0	0	1	0	0	0	0.00
Schiraldi	4	6	5	2	1	3	9	0	1	1.50
Hurst	2	15	18	5	4	1	8	1	0	2.40
Clemens	3	22⅔	22	12	11	7	17	1	1	4.37
Boyd	2	13⅔	17	7	7	3	8	1	1	4.61
Stanley	3	5⅔	7	4	3	3	1	0	0	4.76
Totals	7	65⅓	71	30	26	20	44	4	3	3.58

California Angels

Pitcher	G.	IP.	H.	R.	ER.	BB.	SO.	W.	L.	ERA.
Finley	3	2	1	0	0	0	1	0	0	0.00
Candelaria	2	10⅔	11	8	1	6	7	1	1	0.84
Sutton	2	9⅔	6	2	2	1	4	0	0	1.86
Witt	2	17⅔	13	5	5	2	8	1	0	2.55
Corbett	3	6⅔	9	4	4	2	2	1	0	5.40
Moore	3	5	8	4	4	2	0	0	1	7.20
McCaskill	2	9⅓	16	13	8	5	7	0	2	7.71
Lucas	4	2⅓	3	3	3	1	2	0	0	11.57
Ruhle	1	⅔	2	2	1	0	0	0	0	13.50
Totals	7	64	69	41	28	19	31	3	4	3.94

1986
NEW YORK METS
VS.
HOUSTON ASTROS

The scene was dramatic and the players were fighting for their lives. There was Houston's Kevin Bass facing near-exhausted Mets relief ace Jesse Orosco. The tying run was on base, the lead run was on base. The Mets, leading the 1986 Championship Series three games to two, were clinging to a 7-6 lead in the bottom of the 16th inning of Game 6. Everything was on the line.

When Orosco finally struck out Bass to clinch the N.L. pennant for the Mets, the longest game in postseason history was over. And after 16 innings and four hours, 42 minutes, the Mets breathed a collective sigh of relief.

The players knew they would not have to face Astros righthander Mike Scott, who had pitched a five-hit shutout in Game 1 and permitted only one run on three hits in Game 4. Scott, who was named the Most Valuable Player of the playoffs even though the Astros lost, was scheduled to pitch Game 7.

"I feel like I've been pardoned," Mets Manager Davey Johnson said. "We'd have no bullpen left for a seventh game, and I really don't want to see Scott again until next April."

The bullpen was the key for the Mets in the pennant-clinching affair. Starter Bob Ojeda, who yielded the Astros three runs in the first inning on a run-scoring double by third baseman Phil Garner and RBI singles by Davis and left fielder Jose Cruz, departed after five innings. Righthander Rick Aguilera then hurled one-hit, shutout relief from the sixth through the eighth innings, and righthander Roger McDowell permitted just one hit over five innings before Orosco entered the game in the 14th.

Astros starter Bob Knepper al-

New York catcher Gary Carter enjoys his triumph after producing the winning hit in Game 5 of the 1986 title series against Houston.

lowed only two hits and had the Mets shut out until the ninth. But pesky Lenny Dykstra opened that inning with a pinch-hit triple and scored on a single by Mookie Wilson. After Knepper retired Kevin Mitchell on a grounder, Hernandez doubled home another run. It was at that point that Astros Manager Hal Lanier called for re-

lief ace Dave Smith.

Smith walked Carter and right fielder Darryl Strawberry before Knight hit a fly ball to right field. Hernandez scored after Bass' catch to send the 3-3 game into extra innings.

Smith and righthander Larry Andersen held the Mets scoreless through the 13th inning. New York then went ahead in the 14th when righthander Aurelio Lopez took the mound for the Astros. A single by Carter, a walk to Strawberry and second baseman Wally Backman's single put New York on top, 4-3. But the Astros came right back to tie the game in their half of the inning when Billy Hatcher belted an Orosco delivery off the screen attached to the left-field foul pole.

Strawberry, who was hitless in four previous at-bats in the game, opened the fateful 16th with a pop-fly double that fell between center fielder Hatcher and second baseman Bill Doran. Knight singled to right to drive in Strawberry and took second on Bass' throw home, then went to third on reliever Jeff Calhoun's wild pitch. After Calhoun walked Backman, both runners advanced on another wild pitch, giving the Mets a 6-4 lead. Dykstra's single provided the Mets with the eventual winning run.

Orosco was to earn his third victory of the playoffs, but not before a scare in the bottom of the 16th.

The threat began when pinch-hitter Davey Lopes drew a one-out walk and went to second on a single by Doran. Hatcher singled to left-center, scoring Lopes. After Denny Walling forced Hatcher at second, Davis pulled the Astros to within one run with his single and set the stage for the Orosco-Bass confrontation and the game-ending strikeout.

The Mets were completely befuddled by Scott's split-finger fastball in the playoff opener, a 1-0 Houston victory.

The only run of the game came when Davis crushed a 1-0 pitch from Dwight Gooden, the previous year's N.L. Cy Young Award winner, over the center-field wall to open the second inning. But

Scott made that slim lead stand by allowing only five hits and fanning 14 batters, matching the major league Championship Series record for strikeouts.

Pitching continued to dominate the series in Game 2 as Ojeda and Nolan Ryan tossed zeroes through the first three innings. Ryan retired the first 10 batters he faced, including five on strikeouts, but the Mets reached him for two runs in the fourth and added three more while knocking him out in the fifth en route to a 5-1 victory.

The Astros looked like they were off to a cakewalk in Game 3 when they scored two runs in each of the first two innings against starter Ron Darling. But the Mets, who had been held to four singles in the first five innings by Knepper, rallied for four runs in the sixth to tie the contest, the big blow a three-run homer by Strawberry.

The Astros, however, retaliated in the seventh without getting a hit. Doran walked, ran to third when Knight made a throwing error on Hatcher's bunt and scored on Walling's grounder to second.

After Houston reliever Charlie Kerfeld set the Mets down in order in the eighth, Lanier called on his No. 1 reliever, Smith, to protect the Astros' 5-4 lead.

Leading off, Backman dragged a bunt down the first-base line that was fielded by Davis, but Backman avoided the tag with a sweeping slide. One out and a passed ball later, Dykstra sent shock waves through Houston, blasting a game-winning homer into the Mets' bullpen to give his team a 2-1 advantage.

Houston catcher Alan Ashby combined with Scott in Game 4 to get the Astros even again. Ashby's two-run homer was all Scott needed en route to a 3-1 victory.

It was another exercise in futility for the Mets against Scott, who permitted only three hits and struck out five.

Rain forced postponement of Game 5 and Lanier switched his scheduled starter from rookie Jim Deshaies to Ryan, baseball's all-time strikeout king. But neither

Ryan's two-hit, 12-strikeout performance over nine innings nor Gooden's 10 solid innings was good enough to decide this contest. The game ended in the 12th inning when Carter ended a personal 1-for-21 slump with an RBI single that gave the Mets a 2-1 victory and a 3-2 lead in the series.

The Astros jumped on top when Backman took too long to complete a double play with one out in the fifth. Ashby stroked a leadoff double, went to third on a single by Reynolds and scored on a one-out, fielder's-choice grounder to second by Doran. But the Mets tied the game, 1-1, in their half of the fifth on Strawberry's homer.

Until that hit, Ryan was pitching a perfect game, and the right-hander surrendered only one more single and one walk before giving way to Kerfeld in the 10th. Orosco relieved Gooden in the 11th and recorded his second series victory when New York rallied in the bottom of the 12th, finally winning when Carter snapped a 1-for-21 skid with his game-winning single and thus set the stage for a dramatic Game 6.

Game 1

Wednesday, October 8, At Houston

New York	AB.	R.	H.	RBI.	PO.	A.
Dykstra, cf	3	0	1	0	1	0
Backman, 2b	4	0	0	0	1	1
Hernandez, 1b	4	0	1	0	5	2
Carter, c	4	0	0	0	7	0
Strawberry, rf	4	0	1	0	3	0
Wilson, lf	4	0	0	0	4	0
Knight, 3b	4	0	0	0	1	2
Santana, ss	2	0	1	0	0	2
Mazzilli, ph	1	0	0	0	0	0
Orosco, p	0	0	0	0	0	0
Gooden, p	2	0	0	0	2	0
Heep, ph	1	0	1	0	0	0
Elster, pr-ss	0	0	0	0	0	0
Totals	33	0	5	0	24	7

Houston	AB.	R.	H.	RBI.	PO.	A.
Hatcher, cf	3	0	0	0	1	0
Doran, 2b	4	0	0	0	1	3
Walling, 3b	4	0	0	0	0	1
Davis, 1b	4	1	1	1	6	1
Bass, rf	4	0	2	0	1	0
Cruz, lf	4	0	1	0	2	0
Ashby, c	1	0	1	0	14	0
Reynolds, ss	3	0	2	0	1	0
Thon, ss	0	0	0	0	0	0
Scott, p	3	0	0	0	1	2
Totals	30	1	7	1	27	7

New York.........0 0 0　0 0 0　0 0 0—0
Houston..........0 1 0　0 0 0　0 0 x—1

New York	IP.	H.	R.	ER.	BB.	SO.
Gooden (L)	7	7	1	1	3	5
Orosco	1	0	0	0	0	1

Houston	IP.	H.	R.	ER.	BB.	SO.
Scott (W)	9	5	0	0	1	14

Game-winning RBI—Davis.

E—Reynolds. DP—New York 1. LOB—New York 7, Houston 8. 2B—Bass. HR—Davis. SB—Hatcher, Dykstra, Bass, Strawberry. U—Harvey, Weyer, Pulli, Rennert, West and Brocklander. T—2:56. A—44,131.

Game 2

Thursday, October 9, At Houston

New York	AB.	R.	H.	RBI.	PO.	A.
Dykstra, cf	5	1	2	0	2	0
Backman, 2b	5	2	2	1	5	2
Hernandez, 1b	3	1	2	2	9	0

	AB.	R.	H.	RBI.	PO.	A.
Carter, c	5	0	1	1	6	0
Strawberry, rf	3	0	0	1	1	0
Wilson, lf	4	0	1	0	1	0
Knight, 3b	3	0	1	0	1	3
Santana, ss	4	0	1	0	1	5
Ojeda, p	4	1	0	0	1	2
Totals	36	5	10	5	27	12

Houston	AB.	R.	H.	RBI.	PO.	A.
Hatcher, cf	5	1	1	0	3	0
Doran, 2b	4	0	1	0	3	2
Garner, 3b	3	0	1	1	1	1
Davis, 1b	4	0	1	0	4	1
Bass, rf	3	0	2	0	1	0
Cruz, lf	4	0	1	0	3	0
Ashby, c	4	0	0	0	9	0
Thon, ss	4	0	2	0	2	2
Ryan, p	1	0	0	0	0	1
Pankovits, ph	1	0	0	0	0	0
Andersen, p	0	0	0	0	1	0
Puhl, ph	1	0	1	0	0	0
Lopez, p	0	0	0	0	0	0
Kerfeld, p	0	0	0	0	0	0
Lopes, ph	1	0	0	0	0	0
Totals	35	1	10	1	27	7

New York ....0 0 0 2 3 0 0 0 0—5
Houston ....0 0 0 0 0 0 1 0 0—1

New York	IP.	H.	R.	ER.	BB.	SO.
Ojeda (W)	9	10	1	1	2	5

Houston	IP.	H.	R.	ER.	BB.	SO.
Ryan (L)	5	7	5	5	0	5
Andersen	2	1	0	0	1	2
Lopez	1⅓	2	0	0	2	1
Kerfeld	⅔	0	0	0	0	0

Game-winning RBI—Carter.

E—Hatcher, Davis. DP—New York 2, Houston 1. LOB—New York 8, Houston 9. 2B—Bass, Carter, Dykstra. 3B—Hernandez. SB—Wilson. SF—Strawberry. U—Weyer, Pulli, Rennert, West, Brocklander and Harvey. T—2:40. A—44,391.

Game 3

Saturday, October 11, At New York

Houston	AB.	R.	H.	RBI.	PO.	A.
Doran, 2b	4	2	2	2	1	1
Hatcher, cf	3	1	2	0	3	0
Walling, 3b	5	1	1	2	0	2
Davis, 1b	3	0	1	0	9	0
Bass, rf	3	0	0	0	4	0
Cruz, lf	3	0	1	1	2	0
Ashby, c	4	0	0	0	4	0
Reynolds, ss	2	1	1	0	2	3
Lopes, ph	1	0	0	0	0	0
Kerfeld, p	0	0	0	0	0	1
Smith, p	0	0	0	0	0	0
Knepper, p	3	0	0	0	0	1
Thon, ss	1	0	0	0	0	0
Totals	32	5	8	5	25	8

New York	AB.	R.	H.	RBI.	PO.	A.
Wilson, cf-lf	4	0	0	0	2	0
Mitchell, lf	4	1	2	0	1	0
Orosco, p	0	0	0	0	0	0
Hernandez, 1b	4	1	2	0	10	2
Carter, c	4	1	0	0	8	1
Strawberry, rf	4	1	2	3	1	0
Knight, 3b	4	0	1	0	0	3
Teufel, 2b	3	0	0	0	2	3
Backman, 2b	1	1	1	0	0	1
Santana, ss	3	0	0	0	2	4
Heep, ph	1	0	0	0	0	0
Darling, p	1	0	0	0	1	2
Mazzilli, ph	1	0	1	0	0	0
Aguilera, p	0	0	0	0	0	0
Dykstra, ph-cf	2	1	1	2	0	0
Totals	36	6	10	5	27	16

Houston ....2 2 0 0 0 0 1 0 0—5
New York ....0 0 0 0 0 4 0 0 2—6
One out when winning run scored.

Houston	IP.	H.	R.	ER.	BB.	SO.
Knepper	7	8	4	3	0	3
Kerfeld	1	0	0	0	0	1
Smith (L)	⅓	2	2	2	0	0

New York	IP.	H.	R.	ER.	BB.	SO.
Darling	5	6	4	4	2	5
Aguilera	2	1	1	0	2	1
Orosco (W)	2	1	0	0	1	2

Game-winning RBI—Dykstra.

E—Reynolds, Knight. DP—New York 1. LOB—Houston 7, New York 5. HR—Doran, Strawberry, Dykstra. SB—Hatcher 2, Bass. SH—Hatcher. HBP—By Darling (Davis). WP—Darling. PB—Ashby 2. U—Pulli, Rennert, West, Brocklander, Harvey and Weyer. T—2:55. A—55,052.

Game 4

Sunday, October 12, At New York

Houston	AB.	R.	H.	RBI.	PO.	A.
Doran, 2b	4	0	0	0	2	3
Hatcher, cf	4	0	0	0	2	0
Garner, 3b	3	0	0	0	0	3
Walling, ph-3b	1	0	1	0	0	0
Davis, 1b	3	1	1	0	14	1
Bass, rf	3	0	0	0	1	0
Cruz, lf	4	0	0	0	1	0
Ashby, c	3	1	1	2	5	0
Thon, ss	3	1	1	1	1	4
Scott, p	3	0	0	0	1	2
Totals	31	3	4	3	27	13

New York	AB.	R.	H.	RBI.	PO.	A.
Dykstra, cf	4	0	1	0	5	0
Backman, 2b	4	0	0	0	2	2
Hernandez, 1b	4	0	0	0	9	0
Carter, c	4	0	0	0	7	0
Strawberry, rf	3	0	0	0	1	0
Wilson, lf	3	1	1	0	2	0
Knight, 3b	3	0	1	0	1	3
Santana, ss	2	0	0	0	0	3
Heep, ph	0	0	0	1	0	0
Sisk, p	0	0	0	0	0	0
Fernandez, p	1	0	0	0	0	0
Mazzilli, ph	1	0	0	0	0	0
McDowell, p	0	0	0	0	0	0
Johnson, ph	1	0	0	0	0	0
Elster, ss	0	0	0	0	0	1
Totals	30	1	3	1	27	9

Houston ....0 2 0 0 1 0 0 0 0—3
New York ....0 0 0 0 0 0 0 1 0—1

Houston	IP.	H.	R.	ER.	BB.	SO.
Scott (W)	9	3	1	1	0	5

New York	IP.	H.	R.	ER.	BB.	SO.
Fernandez (L)	6	3	3	3	1	5
McDowell	2	0	0	0	0	1
Sisk	1	1	0	0	1	0

Game-winning RBI—Ashby.

E—Scott. LOB—Houston 3, New York 3. 2B—Walling. HR—Ashby, Thon. SB—Backman. SF—Heep. U—Rennert, West, Brocklander, Harvey, Weyer and Pulli. T—2:23. A—55,038.

Game 5

Tuesday, October 14, At New York

Houston	AB.	R.	H.	RBI.	PO.	A.
Doran, 2b	4	0	1	1	1	2
Hatcher, cf	3	0	1	0	0	0
Walling, 3b	5	0	1	0	1	1
Davis, 1b	5	0	0	0	8	0
Bass, rf	5	0	2	0	6	0
Cruz, lf	5	0	1	0	2	0
Ashby, c	5	1	1	0	15	0
Reynolds, ss	4	0	1	0	1	2
Thon, ph-ss	1	0	0	0	0	0
Ryan, p	3	0	0	0	0	1
Puhl, ph	1	0	1	0	0	0
Kerfeld, p	0	0	0	0	0	0
Totals	41	1	9	1	34	6

New York	AB.	R.	H.	RBI.	PO.	A.
Dykstra, cf	5	0	0	0	1	0
Backman, 2b	5	1	1	0	0	9
Hernandez, 1b	4	0	1	0	14	1
Carter, c	5	0	1	1	6	1
Strawberry, rf	3	1	1	1	2	0
Wilson, lf	4	0	0	0	5	1
Orosco, p	0	0	0	0	0	1
Knight, 3b	4	0	0	0	1	1
Santana, ss	3	0	0	0	6	3
Mazzilli, ph	1	0	0	0	0	0
Elster, ss	0	0	0	0	0	0
Gooden, p	3	0	0	0	1	2
Heep, lf	1	0	0	0	0	0
Totals	38	2	4	2	36	19

Houston ....0 0 0 0 1 0 0 0 0 0 0 0—1
New York ....0 0 0 0 1 0 0 0 0 0 0 1—2
One out when winning run scored.

Houston	IP.	H.	R.	ER.	BB.	SO.
Ryan	9	2	1	1	1	12
Kerfeld (L)	2⅓	2	1	1	1	3

New York	IP.	H.	R.	ER.	BB.	SO.
Gooden	10	9	1	1	2	4
Orosco (W)	2	0	0	0	0	2

Game-winning RBI—Carter.

E—Kerfeld. DP—New York 2. LOB—Houston 7, New York 4. 2B—Ashby. HR—Strawberry. SB—Doran, Puhl. SH—Hatcher. U—West, Brocklander, Harvey, Weyer, Pulli and Rennert. T—3:45. A—54,986.

Game 6

Wednesday, October 15, At Houston

New York	AB.	R.	H.	RBI.	PO.	A.
Wilson, cf-lf	7	1	1	1	2	0
Mitchell, lf	4	0	0	0	2	0
Elster, ss	3	0	0	0	2	2
Hernandez, 1b	7	1	1	1	20	7
Carter, c	5	0	2	0	8	3
Strawberry, rf	5	2	1	0	1	0
Knight, 3b	6	1	1	2	1	7
Teufel, 2b	3	0	1	0	0	5
Backman, ph-2b	2	1	1	1	1	2
Santana, ss	3	0	1	0	4	1
Heep, ph	1	0	0	0	0	0
McDowell, p	1	0	0	0	3	1
Johnson, ph	1	0	0	0	0	0
Orosco, p	0	0	0	0	1	0
Ojeda, p	1	0	0	0	1	2
Mazzilli, ph	1	0	0	0	0	0
Aguilera, p	0	0	0	0	1	1
Dykstra, ph-cf	4	1	2	1	1	0
Totals	54	7	11	6	48	31

Houston	AB.	R.	H.	RBI.	PO.	A.
Doran, 2b	7	1	2	0	1	6
Hatcher, cf	7	2	3	2	2	0
Garner, 3b	3	1	1	1	0	5
Walling, ph-3b	4	0	0	0	2	2
Davis, 1b	7	1	3	2	21	0
Bass, rf	6	0	1	0	3	0
Cruz, lf	6	0	1	1	1	0
Ashby, c	6	0	0	0	12	1
Thon, ss	3	0	0	0	3	3
Reynolds, ph-ss	3	0	0	0	3	3
Knepper, p	2	0	0	0	0	2
Smith, p	0	0	0	0	0	0
Puhl, ph	1	0	0	0	0	0
Andersen, p	0	0	0	0	0	2
Pankovits, ph	1	0	0	0	0	0
Lopez, p	0	0	0	0	0	1
Calhoun, p	0	0	0	0	0	0
Lopes, ph	0	1	0	0	0	0
Totals	56	6	11	6	48	25

New York ....000 000 003 000 010 3—7
Houston ....300 000 000 000 010 2—6

New York	IP.	H.	R.	ER.	BB.	SO.
Ojeda	5	5	3	3	2	1
Aguilera	3	1	0	0	0	1
McDowell	5	1	0	0	0	2
Orosco (W)	3	4	3	3	1	5

Houston	IP.	H.	R.	ER.	BB.	SO.
Knepper	8⅓	5	3	3	1	6
Smith	1⅔	0	0	0	3	2
Andersen	3	0	0	0	1	1
Lopez (L)	2*	5	3	3	2	2
Calhoun	1	1	1	1	1	0

*Pitched to two batters in sixteenth.

Game-winning RBI—Knight.

E—Bass. DP—Houston 2. LOB—New York 9, Houston 5. 2B—Garner, Davis, Hernandez, Strawberry. 3B—Dykstra. HR—Hatcher. SB—Doran. SH—Orosco. SF—Knight. WP—Calhoun 2. U—Brocklander, Harvey, Weyer, Pulli, Rennert and West. T—4:42. A—45,718.

COMPOSITE BATTING AVERAGES

New York Mets

Player-Position	G.	AB.	R.	H.	2B.	3B.	HR.	RBI.	BA.
Dykstra, cf-ph	6	23	3	7	1	1	1	3	.304
Hernandez, 1b	6	26	3	7	1	1	0	3	.269
Mitchell, lf	2	8	1	2	0	0	0	0	.250
Heep, ph-lf	5	4	0	1	0	0	0	1	.250
Backman, 2b-ph	6	21	5	5	0	0	0	2	.238
Strawberry, rf	6	22	4	5	1	0	2	5	.227
Mazzilli, ph	5	5	0	1	0	0	0	0	.200
Santana, ss	6	17	0	3	0	0	0	0	.176
Knight, 3b	6	24	1	4	0	0	0	2	.167
Teufel, 2b	2	6	0	1	0	0	0	0	.167
Carter, c	6	27	1	4	1	0	0	2	.148
Wilson, lf-cf	6	26	2	3	0	0	0	1	.115
Aguilera, p	2	0	0	0	0	0	0	0	.000
Orosco, p	4	0	0	0	0	0	0	0	.000
Sisk, p	1	0	0	0	0	0	0	0	.000
Darling, p	1	1	0	0	0	0	0	0	.000
Fernandez, p	1	1	0	0	0	0	0	0	.000
McDowell, p	2	1	0	0	0	0	0	0	.000
Johnson, ph	2	2	0	0	0	0	0	0	.000
Elster, pr-ss	4	3	0	0	0	0	0	0	.000
Gooden, p	2	5	0	0	0	0	0	0	.000
Ojeda, p	2	5	1	0	0	0	0	0	.000
Totals	6	227	21	43	4	2	3	19	.189

Houston Astros

Player-Position	G.	AB.	R.	H.	2B.	3B.	HR.	RBI.	BA.
Puhl, ph	3	3	0	2	0	0	0	0	.667
Reynolds, ss-ph	4	12	1	4	0	0	0	0	.333
Bass, rf	6	24	0	7	2	0	0	0	.292
Hatcher, cf	6	25	4	7	0	0	1	2	.280
Davis, 1b	6	26	3	7	1	0	1	3	.269
Thon, ss-ph	6	12	1	3	0	0	1	1	.250
Doran, 2b	6	27	3	6	0	0	1	3	.222
Garner, 3b	3	9	1	2	1	0	0	2	.222
Cruz, lf	6	26	0	5	0	0	0	2	.192
Walling, 3b-ph	5	19	1	3	1	0	0	2	.158
Ashby, c	6	23	2	3	1	0	1	2	.130
Andersen, p	2	0	0	0	0	0	0	0	.000
Calhoun, p	1	0	0	0	0	0	0	0	.000
Lopez, p	2	0	0	0	0	0	0	0	.000
Kerfeld, p	3	0	0	0	0	0	0	0	.000
Smith, p	2	0	0	0	0	0	0	0	.000
Lopes, ph	3	2	1	0	0	0	0	0	.000
Pankovits, ph	2	2	0	0	0	0	0	0	.000
Ryan, p	2	4	0	0	0	0	0	0	.000
Knepper, p	2	5	0	0	0	0	0	0	.000
Scott, p	2	6	0	0	0	0	0	0	.000
Totals	6	225	17	49	6	0	5	17	.218

COMPOSITE PITCHING AVERAGES

New York Mets

Pitcher	G.	IP.	H.	R.	ER.	BB.	SO.	W.	L.	ERA.
McDowell	2	7	1	0	0	0	3	0	0	0.00
Aguilera	2	5	2	1	0	2	2	0	0	0.00
Sisk	1	1	1	0	0	1	0	0	0	0.00
Gooden	2	17	16	2	2	5	9	0	1	1.06
Ojeda	2	14	15	4	4	4	6	1	0	2.57
Orosco	4	8	5	3	3	2	10	3	0	3.38
Fernandez	1	6	3	3	3	1	5	0	1	4.50
Darling	1	5	6	4	4	2	5	0	0	7.20
Totals	6	63	49	17	16	17	40	4	2	2.29

Houston Astros

Pitcher	G.	IP.	H.	R.	ER.	BB.	SO.	W.	L.	ERA.
Andersen	2	5	1	0	0	2	3	0	0	0.00
Scott	2	18	8	1	1	1	19	2	0	0.50
Kerfeld	3	4	2	1	1	1	4	0	1	2.25
Knepper	2	15⅓	13	7	6	1	9	0	0	3.52
Ryan	2	14	9	6	6	1	17	0	1	3.86
Lopez	2	3⅓	7	3	3	4	3	0	1	8.10
Smith	2	2	2	2	2	3	2	0	1	9.00
Calhoun	1	1	1	1	1	1	0	0	0	9.00
Totals	6	62⅔	43	21	20	14	57	2	4	2.87

1987 MINNESOTA TWINS VS. DETROIT TIGERS

When Matt Nokes grounded back to the mound with two out in the ninth inning of Game 5 of the 1987 American League Championship Series, Minnesota reliever Jeff Reardon made the easy toss to first baseman Kent Hrbek and the Twins were A.L. champions. The Detroit Tigers were down and out after compiling the best regular-season record of any of the four division winners.

It was fitting that Reardon would be involved in the 9-5 victory that put Minnesota into the World Series for the first time since 1965.

Reardon, acquired during the off-season from Montreal, was the puzzle piece that helped reshape the Twins' mediocre pitching staff. The hard-throwing right-hander posted 31 saves during the regular season. He also was credited with a victory in relief of Frank Viola in Game 1 of the Championship Series and had saves in Games 4 and 5.

Even with the addition of Reardon, however, most observers fell short in their assessment of the 1987 Twins. That the Twins could contend in the American League West was generally accepted. But most baseball followers were quick to concede that anything beyond a division title was wishful thinking.

After all, the Tigers had won 98 games, the Twins 85. In fact, the Twins' 85-77 record would have placed them no better than fifth in the A.L. East.

"We were the champions in the A.L. West, but everybody said, 'So what?'" said Viola.

The odds clearly were stacked against the Twins, who tackled them one by one.

First, the Tigers had righthander Doyle Alexander primed for Game 1 of the Championship Se-

Minnesota third baseman Gary Gaetti hugs the trophy that he earned as the Most Valuable Player in the 1987 A.L. Championship Series.

ries. Alexander had compiled a sparkling 9-0 record with Detroit after being obtained from Atlanta in September. Even more impressive was the 11-0 mark recorded by the Tigers in games that Alexander started.

Second, Detroit's Game 2 starter, Jack Morris, a St. Paul native, boasted a career record of 11-0 in games he had pitched in Minnesota.

And third, Game 3 starter Walt Terrell boasted a 32-7 career mark, including 13-2 in 1987, at Tiger Stadium.

But a funny thing happened on the way to the World Series. . . .

"There were a lot of things that were against us when you looked at this series on paper—the win-

ning streaks by their starting pitchers and our lousy record on the road—but those things actually helped to drive us," said Twins third baseman Gary Gaetti, who batted .300 with two home runs and five RBIs en route to Most Valuable Player honors in the Championship Series.

Who would have thought that Gaetti would set a Championship Series record by connecting for homers in his first two at-bats against Alexander? Who would have thought that Twins catcher Tim Laudner, a .191 hitter, would find a magic wand in Game 2 and provide the game-winning hit? Who would have thought that the Twins would win while Kent Hrbek and Kirby Puckett were

struggling to a combined .182 (8 for 44) average? And who would have dreamed that Twins shortstop Greg Gagne would outhit (.278 to .200) his Detroit counterpart, Alan Trammell, and drive in more runs (3-2)?

Though the Twins had compiled the best home record (56-25) in the majors, they had lost four of six meetings against the Tigers at the Metrodome. But, as Gaetti pointed out, paper lions don't always have the sharpest claws.

Though the Twins had never won a Championship Series contest before (they were swept three straight by Baltimore in 1969 and 1970), they jumped on the Tigers and Alexander quickly, made good use of the experience of 38-year-old veteran Don Baylor and took advantage of the Tigers' shaky relief pitching to rally from a 5-4 deficit in the bottom of the eighth inning and post their 8-5 Game 1 triumph.

Dan Gladden led off the decisive eighth with a single. After Gagne popped up attempting to sacrifice, Puckett doubled to left-center and Gladden scored the tying run.

Rookie Mike Henneman replaced Alexander and added gasoline to the fire by walking Hrbek and Gaetti to load the bases. With the crowd of 53,269 in a frenzy, veteran lefthander Willie Hernandez replaced Henneman and Baylor batted for Randy Bush.

Baylor, who had been obtained from Boston on August 31 for pennant insurance, paid a big dividend when he lined a 2-2 offering to left field to give the Twins a 6-5 lead. Tom Brunansky then added a pair of insurance runs with his second double of the game.

The Championship Series defeat was the first for Detroit Manager Sparky Anderson in 10 games.

Things were supposed to get better for Anderson in Game 2 with Morris on the mound. But the Twins struck for three runs in the second inning, two coming on Laudner's double, and two more in the fourth as they rallied from a 2-0 deficit for a 6-3 victory and a commanding 2-0 series lead.

Surprisingly, the Twins came within five outs of taking a 3-0 lead when the series shifted to Detroit. Yes, the same Twins who posted a miserable 29-52 road record in 1987 and won only nine road games after the All-Star break. But with Minnesota holding a 6-5 lead with Reardon on the mound in the eighth inning, Detroit's Pat Sheridan spoiled that plan by hitting a two-run homer to lift the Tigers to victory.

Sheridan had triggered a five-run third-inning explosion with a double. After Lou Whitaker singled and Darrell Evans walked to load the bases, Kirk Gibson forced Evans at second as the first run crossed the plate. Gibson then stole second and, when Minnesota starter Les Straker committed a balk, Whitaker scored and Gibson went to third. Before the inning had ended, Trammell had singled home one run and Herndon had connected for a two-run pinch double.

Minnesota chipped away at that lead, scoring twice in the fourth on a solo homer by Gagne and an RBI single by Bush. Brunansky smashed a two-run homer in the sixth and the Twins went ahead in the seventh on Gaetti's two-out, two-run single.

Though no team had ever come back from a five-run deficit to win a Championship Series contest, the Twins were headed in that direction before Sheridan's heroics capped a three-hour, 29-minute thriller, the longest nine-inning game in A.L. Championship Series history.

In Game 4, Puckett and Gagne ended slumps with home runs and a couple of blunders by Detroit veteran Evans helped the Twins register a 5-3 victory and take a 3-1 series lead.

Puckett, who had managed just one hit in 14 at-bats, hit a solo homer in the third inning. Gagne, who was 1 for 11, put the Twins ahead, 2-1, with a fourth-inning homer. The Twins added single runs in the fifth and sixth on Gaetti's sacrifice fly and Gene Larkin's RBI pinch double.

Detroit closed to 4-3 with one run in the sixth, but Evans' base-running gaffe cost the Tigers at least one run. Leadoff singles by

Lemon and Evans knocked out Viola and placed runners on first and third. Bergman's pinch single off Keith Atherton scored Lemon and Mike Heath's sacrifice advanced both runners.

At this point, Juan Berenguer replaced Atherton and, on the first pitch to Whitaker, Laudner's throw to Gaetti picked Evans off third base. But the horrifying night wasn't over for the 40-year-old slugger.

In the eighth, Evans, who had been switched from first base to third, failed to come up with Laudner's grounder. After reaching first base on Evans' error, Laudner went to second on a wild pitch and to third on a groundout. Lombardozzi plated him with a single past Evans' glove.

The Twins, who trailed in each of the first four games, jumped on Alexander for four runs in the second inning of Game 5 and went on to post a 9-5 victory.

Brunansky, who had seven hits in 17 at-bats in the series, including four doubles, a pair of home runs and nine RBIs, highlighted the Twins' four-run second with a two-run double and then homered in the ninth. His nine RBIs were one short of Baylor's Championship Series record set in 1982 when Baylor was with California.

Homers by Nokes, Lemon and Brunansky in Game 5 gave the teams 15 for the series, breaking the playoff record of 13 set by Los Angeles and Philadelphia in 1978 and equalled by California and Boston in 1986.

In eliminating the Tigers in five games, the Twins joined the 1973 New York Mets as the only division winner with fewer than 90 wins to advance to the World Series.

Game 1

Wednesday, October 7, At Minnesota

Detroit	AB.	R.	H.	RBI.	PO.	A.
Whitaker, 2b	4	0	0	0	2	2
Madlock, dh	5	0	0	0	0	0
Gibson, lf	4	2	1	1	3	1
Trammell, ss	4	1	1	0	0	3
Herndon, rf	3	1	0	0	0	0
Bergman, ph	0	0	0	1	0	0
Sheridan, lf	0	0	0	0	0	0
Lemon, cf	3	0	2	1	3	0
Evans, 1b	4	0	2	0	10	0
Brookens, 3b	3	0	0	0	0	2
Grubb, ph	1	0	1	0	0	0
Heath, c	3	1	2	2	6	0
Nokes, ph	1	0	0	0	0	0
Alexander, p	0	0	0	0	0	1
Henneman, p	0	0	0	0	0	0
Hernandez, p	0	0	0	0	0	0
King, p	0	0	0	0	0	0
Totals	35	5	10	5	24	9

Minnesota	AB.	R.	H.	RBI.	PO.	A.
Gladden, lf	4	1	2	1	2	0
Gagne, ss	4	0	0	0	0	2
Puckett, cf	4	1	1	1	1	0
Hrbek, 1b	3	1	0	0	9	1
Gaetti, 3b	3	3	2	2	0	2
Bush, dh	3	1	1	0	0	0
Baylor, ph	1	0	1	1	0	0
Brunansky, rf	4	1	2	3	3	0
Lombardozzi, 2b	3	0	1	0	2	0
Laudner, c	3	0	0	0	10	0
Viola, p	0	0	0	0	0	1
Reardon, p	0	0	0	0	0	0
Totals	32	8	10	8	27	6

Detroit 0 0 1 0 0 1 1 2 0—5
Minnesota 0 1 0 0 3 0 0 4 x—8

Detroit	IP.	H.	R.	ER.	BB.	SO.
Alexander (L)	7⅓	8	6	6	0	5
Henneman	0*	0	2	2	2	0
Hernandez	⅓	2	0	0	0	0
King	⅓	0	0	0	0	0

Minnesota	IP.	H.	R.	ER.	BB.	SO.
Viola	7*	9	5	5	1	6
Reardon (W)	2	1	0	0	1	3

*Pitched to two batters in eighth.

Game-winning RBI—Baylor.

LOB—Detroit 7, Minnesota 3. 2B—Brunansky 2, Trammell, Puckett. 3B—Bush. HR—Gaetti 2, Heath, Gibson. SH—Lombardozzi. SF—Bergman, Lemon. U—Brinkman, Merrill, Coble, Clark, Reilly and McKean. T—2:46. A—53,269.

Game 2

Thursday, October 8, At Minnesota

Detroit	AB.	R.	H.	RBI.	PO.	A.
Whitaker, 2b	3	1	2	1	2	4
Evans, 1b	4	0	2	0	6	0
Gibson, lf	4	0	0	0	0	0
Trammell, ss	4	0	0	0	2	1
Nokes, dh-c	4	1	1	0	1	0
Lemon, cf	4	1	1	2	2	0
Sheridan, rf	4	0	1	0	4	0
Brookens, 3b	2	0	0	0	0	3
Heath, c	2	0	0	0	6	0
Grubb, ph	1	0	0	0	0	0
Morris, p	0	0	0	0	0	0
Totals	32	3	7	3	24	8

Minnesota	AB.	R.	H.	RBI.	PO.	A.
Gladden, lf	4	0	1	2	1	0
Lombardozzi, 2b	4	0	0	0	3	3
Puckett, cf	4	0	0	0	2	0
Hrbek, 1b	4	1	1	1	8	0
Gaetti, 3b	4	1	1	0	1	1
Bush, dh	4	1	1	0	0	0
Brunansky, rf	2	2	1	1	1	0
Gagne, ss	1	1	0	0	1	3
Laudner, c	3	0	1	2	10	1
Blyleven, p	0	0	0	0	0	1
Berenguer, p	0	0	0	0	0	0
Totals	30	6	6	6	27	9

Detroit 0 2 0 0 0 0 0 1 0—3
Minnesota 0 3 0 2 1 0 0 0 x—6

Detroit	IP.	H.	R.	ER.	BB.	SO.
Morris (L)	8	6	6	6	3	7

Minnesota	IP.	H.	R.	ER.	BB.	SO.
Blyleven (W)	7⅓	7	3	3	1	6
Berenguer (S)	1⅔	0	0	0	0	4

Game-winning RBI—Laudner.

E—Trammell. DP—Detroit 1, Minnesota 1. LOB—Detroit 4, Minnesota 3. 2B—Gaetti, Brunansky, Laudner. HR—Lemon, Hrbek, Whitaker. SB—Whitaker, Sheridan, Bush 2. SH—Brookens. U—Merrill, Coble, Clark, Reilly, McKean and Brinkman. T—2:54. A—55,245.

Game 3

Saturday, October 10, At Detroit

Minnesota	AB.	R.	H.	RBI.	PO.	A.
Gladden, lf	3	1	1	0	2	0
Gagne, ss	5	2	1	1	3	1
Puckett, cf	5	0	0	0	1	0
Hrbek, 1b	3	1	0	0	5	2
Gaetti, 3b	5	0	2	2	2	0
Bush, dh	3	1	1	1	0	0
Brunansky, rf	3	1	1	2	2	0
Lombardozzi, 2b	3	0	0	0	1	1
Butera, c	3	0	2	0	6	0
Davidson, pr	0	0	0	0	0	0
Laudner, c	1	0	0	0	1	0
Straker, p	0	0	0	0	0	2
Schatzeder, p	0	0	0	0	0	0
Berenguer, p	0	0	0	0	0	0
Reardon, p	0	0	0	0	0	0
Totals	34	6	8	6	24	6

Detroit	AB.	R.	H.	RBI.	PO.	A.
Whitaker, 2b	4	1	1	0	1	3
Evans, 1b	1	0	0	0	11	1
Gibson, lf	5	1	1	1	1	0
Trammell, ss	4	1	1	1	2	0
Nokes, c	3	0	0	0	5	2
Lemon, cf	3	1	1	0	4	0
Bergman, dh	1	0	0	0	0	0
Herndon, dh	3	0	2	2	0	0
Morris, pr	0	1	0	0	0	0
Brookens, 3b	4	0	0	0	0	4
Sheridan, rf	4	2	2	2	3	0
Terrell, p	0	0	0	0	0	1
Henneman, p	0	0	0	0	0	1
Totals	32	7	7	6	27	12

Minnesota 0 0 0 2 0 2 2 0 0—6
Detroit 0 0 5 0 0 0 0 2 x—7

Minnesota	IP.	H.	R.	ER.	BB.	SO.
Straker	2⅔	3	5	5	4	1
Schatzeder	3⅓†	2	0	0	0	5
Berenguer	1	0	0	0	1	1
Reardon (L)	1	2	2	2	1	0

Detroit	IP.	H.	R.	ER.	BB.	SO.
Terrell	6*	7	6	6	4	4
Henneman (W)	3	1	0	0	3	1

*Pitched to two batters in seventh.
†Pitched to one batter in seventh.

Game-winning RBI—Sheridan.

E—Lombardozzi. LOB—Minnesota 8, Detroit 8. 2B—Sheridan, Herndon. HR—Gagne, Brunansky, Sheridan. SB—Gibson 2. HBP—By Schatzeder (Evans). Balk—Straker. U—Coble, Clark, Reilly, McKean, Brinkman and Merrill. T—3:29. A—49,730.

Game 4

Sunday, October 11, At Detroit

Minnesota	AB.	R.	H.	RBI.	PO.	A.
Gladden, lf	3	0	0	0	3	0
Newman, 2b	2	0	0	0	0	1
Larkin, ph	1	0	1	1	0	0
Lombardozzi, pr-2b	1	0	1	1	2	1
Puckett, cf	5	2	2	1	1	0
Gaetti, 3b	4	0	0	1	3	4
Baylor, dh	4	0	1	0	0	0
Brunansky, rf	3	0	0	0	1	0
Hrbek, 1b	5	0	0	0	8	0
Gagne, ss	4	2	2	1	2	4
Laudner, c	2	1	0	0	7	1
Viola, p	0	0	0	0	0	0
Atherton, p	0	0	0	0	0	0
Berenguer, p	0	0	0	0	0	0
Reardon, p	0	0	0	0	0	0
Totals	34	5	7	5	27	11

Detroit	AB.	R.	H.	RBI.	PO.	A.
Whitaker, 2b	2	2	0	0	3	2
Morrison, dh	4	0	1	0	0	0
Nokes, ph	1	0	0	0	0	0
Gibson, lf	4	0	1	1	3	0
Trammell, ss	3	0	1	0	1	3
Herndon, rf	3	0	0	0	2	0
Lemon, cf	4	1	1	0	2	0
Evans, 1b-3b	4	0	1	0	7	1
Brookens, 3b	2	0	0	0	1	6
Bergman, ph-1b	2	0	1	1	6	0
Heath, c	2	0	0	0	2	0
Grubb, ph	1	0	1	0	0	0
Sheridan, pr	0	0	0	0	0	0
Tanana, p	0	0	0	0	0	1
Petry, p	0	0	0	0	0	1
Thurmond, p	0	0	0	0	0	0
Totals	32	3	7	2	27	14

Minnesota 0 0 1 1 1 1 0 1 0—5
Detroit 1 0 0 0 1 1 0 0 0—3

Minnesota	IP.	H.	R.	ER.	BB.	SO.
Viola (W)	5*	5	3	2	4	3
Atherton	⅓	1	0	0	0	0
Berenguer	2⅔	0	0	0	2	1
Reardon (S)	1	1	0	0	0	2

Detroit	IP.	H.	R.	ER.	BB.	SO.
Tanana (L)	5⅓	6	4	3	4	1
Petry	3⅓	1	1	0	0	1
Thurmond	⅓	0	0	0	0	0

*Pitched to two batters in sixth.

Game-winning RBI—Gagne.

E—Gagne, Herndon, Evans 2. DP—Minnesota 1. LOB—Minnesota 11, Detroit 9. 2B—Gagne, Larkin. HR—Puckett, Gagne. SH—Newman, Heath. SF—Gaetti. HBP—By Tanana (Gladden 2, Baylor). WP—Tanana, Berenguer, Petry. U—Clark, Reilly, McKean, Brinkman, Merrill and Coble. T—3:24. A—51,939.

Game 5

Monday, October 12, At Detroit

Minnesota	AB.	R.	H.	RBI.	PO.	A.
Gladden, lf	6	3	3	2	4	0
Gagne, ss	4	0	2	1	3	3
Puckett, cf	6	0	2	1	2	0
Hrbek, 1b	5	1	2	0	10	0
Gaetti, 3b	4	1	1	0	2	0
Bush, dh	2	1	0	1	0	0
Brunansky, rf	5	1	3	3	3	0
Lombardozzi, 2b	4	2	2	0	0	4
Laudner, c	5	0	0	0	3	0
Blyleven, p	0	0	0	0	0	0
Schatzeder, p	0	0	0	0	0	1
Berenguer, p	0	0	0	0	0	0
Reardon, p	0	0	0	0	0	1
Totals	41	9	15	8	27	9

Detroit	AB.	R.	H.	RBI.	PO.	A.
Whitaker, 2b	4	0	0	0	3	3
Evans, 1b	4	0	0	0	9	2
Gibson, lf	4	1	3	1	3	0
Trammell, ss	5	1	1	1	1	2
Nokes, c	5	1	1	2	5	0
Lemon, cf	4	1	1	1	2	0
Grubb, dh	4	0	2	0	0	0
Sheridan, rf	2	0	0	0	0	1
Brookens, 3b	2	0	0	0	1	0
Bergman, ph	1	0	0	0	0	0
Morrison, 3b	1	1	1	0	1	2
Alexander, p	0	0	0	0	1	0
King, p	0	0	0	0	0	1
Henneman, p	0	0	0	0	0	1
Robinson, p	0	0	0	0	0	1
Totals	36	5	9	5	27	13

Minnesota 0 4 0 0 0 0 1 1 3—9
Detroit 0 0 0 3 0 0 0 1 1—5

Minnesota	IP.	H.	R.	ER.	BB.	SO.
Blyleven (W)	6	5	3	3	2	3
Schatzeder	1	0	0	0	0	0
Berenguer	⅔	1	1	1	0	0
Reardon (S)	1⅓	3	1	1	1	0

Detroit	IP.	H.	R.	ER.	BB.	SO.
Alexander (L)	1⅔	6	4	4	1	0
King	5	3	1	1	2	4
Henneman	2	5	4	4	1	2
Robinson	⅓	1	0	0	0	0

Game-winning RBI—Brunansky.

E—Gagne, Evans. DP—Minnesota 1. LOB—Minnesota 12, Detroit 9. 2B—Gagne 2, Brunansky, Gibson, Gladden 2. HR—Nokes, Lemon, Brunansky. SB—Bush, Puckett, Gibson. SF—Bush. HBP—By Alexander (Gagne), by Blyleven (Sheridan 2), by King (Gaetti). WP—King, Reardon. PB—Nokes. U—Reilly, McKean, Brinkman, Merrill, Coble and Clark. T—3:14. A—47,448.

COMPOSITE BATTING AVERAGES

Minnesota Twins

Player-Position	G.	AB.	R.	H.	2B.	3B.	HR.	RBI.	BA.
Larkin, ph	1	1	0	1	1	0	0	1	1.000
Butera, c	1	3	0	2	0	0	0	0	.667
Brunansky, rf	5	17	5	7	4	0	2	9	.412
Baylor, ph-dh	2	5	0	2	0	0	0	1	.400
Gladden, lf	5	20	5	7	2	0	0	5	.350
Gaetti, 3b	5	20	5	6	1	0	2	5	.300
Gagne, ss	5	18	5	5	3	0	2	3	.278
Lombardozzi, 2b-pr	5	15	2	4	7	0	0	1	.267
Bush, dh	4	12	4	3	0	1	0	2	.250
Puckett, cf	5	24	3	5	1	0	1	3	.208
Hrbek, 1b	5	20	4	3	0	0	1	1	.150
Laudner, c	5	14	1	1	1	0	0	2	.071
Berenguer, p	4	0	0	0	0	0	0	0	.000
Reardon, p	4	0	0	0	0	0	0	0	.000
Blyleven, p	2	0	0	0	0	0	0	0	.000
Schatzeder, p	2	0	0	0	0	0	0	0	.000
Viola, p	2	0	0	0	0	0	0	0	.000
Atherton, p	1	0	0	0	0	0	0	0	.000
Davidson, pr	1	0	0	0	0	0	0	0	.000
Straker, p	1	0	0	0	0	0	0	0	.000
Newman, 2b	1	2	0	0	0	0	0	0	.000
Totals	5	171	34	46	13	1	8	33	.269

Detroit Tigers

Player-Position	G.	AB.	R.	H.	2B.	3B.	HR.	RBI.	BA.
Grubb, ph-dh	4	7	0	4	0	0	0	0	.571
Morrison, dh-3b	2	5	1	2	0	0	0	0	.400
Herndon, rf-ph-dh	3	9	1	3	1	0	0	2	.333
Sheridan, rf-pr	5	10	2	3	1	0	1	2	.300
Evans, 1b-3b	5	17	0	5	0	0	0	0	.294
Gibson, lf	5	21	4	6	1	0	1	4	.286
Heath, c	3	7	1	2	0	0	1	2	.286
Lemon, cf	5	18	4	5	0	0	2	4	.278
Bergman, ph-dh-1b	4	4	0	1	0	0	0	2	.250
Trammell, ss	5	20	3	4	1	0	0	2	.200
Whitaker, 2b	5	17	4	3	0	0	1	1	.176
Nokes, ph-dh-c	5	14	2	2	0	0	1	2	.143
Henneman, p	3	0	0	0	0	0	0	0	.000
Alexander, p	2	0	0	0	0	0	0	0	.000
King, p	2	0	0	0	0	0	0	0	.000
Morris, p-pr	2	0	1	0	0	0	0	0	.000
Hernandez, p	1	0	0	0	0	0	0	0	.000
Petry, p	1	0	0	0	0	0	0	0	.000
Robinson, p	1	0	0	0	0	0	0	0	.000
Tanana, p	1	0	0	0	0	0	0	0	.000
Terrell, p	1	0	0	0	0	0	0	0	.000
Thurmond, p	1	0	0	0	0	0	0	0	.000
Madlock, dh	1	5	0	0	0	0	0	0	.000
Brookens, 3b	5	13	0	0	0	0	0	0	.000
Totals	5	167	23	40	4	0	7	21	.240

COMPOSITE PITCHING AVERAGES

Minnesota Twins

Pitcher	G.	IP.	H.	R.	ER.	BB.	SO.	W.	L.	ERA.
Schatzeder	2	4⅓	2	0	0	0	5	0	0	0.00
Atherton	1	⅓	1	0	0	0	0	0	0	0.00
Berenguer	4	6	1	1	1	3	6	0	0	1.50
Blyleven	2	13⅓	12	6	6	3	9	2	0	4.05
Reardon	4	5⅓	7	3	3	3	5	1	1	5.06
Viola	2	12	14	8	7	5	9	1	0	5.25
Straker	1	2⅔	3	5	5	4	1	0	0	16.88
Totals	5	44	40	23	22	18	35	4	1	4.50

Detroit Tigers

Pitcher	G.	IP.	H.	R.	ER.	BB.	SO.	W.	L.	ERA.
Petry	1	3⅓	1	1	0	0	1	0	0	0.00
Hernandez	1	⅓	2	0	0	0	0	0	0	0.00
Robinson	1	⅓	1	0	0	0	0	0	0	0.00
Thurmond	1	⅓	0	0	0	0	0	0	0	0.00
King	2	5⅓	3	1	1	2	4	0	0	1.69
Tanana	1	5⅓	6	4	3	4	1	0	1	5.06
Morris	1	8	6	6	6	3	7	0	1	6.75
Terrell	1	6	7	6	6	4	4	0	0	9.00
Alexander	2	9	14	10	10	1	5	0	2	10.00
Henneman	3	5	6	6	6	6	3	1	0	10.80
Totals	5	43	46	34	32	20	25	1	4	6.70

1987
ST. LOUIS CARDINALS
VS.
SAN FRANCISCO GIANTS

Jose Oquendo was faced with a challenge. October 14, 1987, was his daughter Adianez's third birthday and Zenaida Oquendo, Jose's wife, had made a special request.

"My wife asked me to do something special for my daughter," Oquendo said after hitting the third home run of his major league career in Game 7 of the 1987 National League Championship Series. "So when I hit the home run, I was thinking about Adianez."

The home run was indeed memorable.

Oquendo's unlikely three-run blast highlighted a four-run second inning and powered the St. Louis Cardinals to a 6-0 victory over the San Francisco Giants. And it enabled the Cardinals to go to the World Series for the third time in six years.

Oquendo, the Cardinals' utility man supreme, came into the playoffs with just two career home runs in 903 at-bats before connecting against San Francisco lefthander Atlee Hammaker.

Ironically, Oquendo's other two big league homers also came against Giants' lefthanders—August 21, 1983, as a pinch-hitter against Gary Lavelle (when Oquendo was a member of the New York Mets) and July 25, 1987, against Craig Lefferts.

While Oquendo's surprising display of power highlighted the Cardinals' comeback from a 3-2 series deficit, it was the St. Louis pitching that really saved the day.

The Giants had pulled within one victory of their first World Series appearance since 1962 by hitting nine homers and scoring 23 runs in the first five games. But when the scene shifted back to St. Louis, the Cardinals recorded a Championship Series-record two straight shutouts.

John Tudor combined with Todd Worrell and Ken Dayley for a 1-0 decision in Game 6 and Danny Cox stymied the Giants on eight hits in a 6-0 finale.

In all, Cardinals' pitchers strung together 22 consecutive shutout innings, another Championship Series record. The Giants got only one runner as far as third in the final two games.

"We came in here needing just one win and we didn't even score a run," said San Francisco Manager Roger Craig. "I wouldn't have believed it."

Cox, who also pitched the regular-season division-clinching victory, was scheduled to start Game 1, but was sidelined with a stiff neck. Lefthander Greg Mathews, however, proved a capable substitute, allowing only four hits over 7⅓ innings and singling home two runs to help the Cardinals record a 5-3 victory.

The Cardinals' sixth-inning uprising turned out to be the difference. With runners on second and third and one out, Terry Pendleton broke a 2-2 tie with a bloop single just inside the foul line in left field. Curt Ford singled to load the bases, but catcher Tony Pena fouled out. That brought Mathews to the plate.

Mathews, a .191 hitter in the regular season, looped Rick Reuschel's 1-2 delivery to center, scoring Willie McGee and Pendleton.

After Mathews walked Robby Thompson with one out in the eighth, Worrell came in and retired only one of the four batters he faced. However, Dayley came in to put out the fire, retiring Will Clark on a long fly to right-center with the bases loaded. He also induced Bob Melvin to hit into a game-ending double play.

The Cardinals had entered the series without the services of first baseman-slugger Jack Clark (tendon tear in his ankle), who had been ailing since early September. The Cardinals were 20-16 without Clark in the lineup through the end of the season, but their run production fell from 5.31 per game to 3.61.

The Cardinals' meager attack was notable in Game 2 as Will Clark and Jeffrey Leonard flexed their home-run muscles and Dave Dravecky pitched a record-tying two-hitter in leading the Giants to a 5-0 victory. It was the first Championship Series home loss in seven games for the Cardinals.

Clark slugged a two-run homer in the second inning and Leonard added a leadoff round-tripper in the fourth, his second homer in as many games. The Giants' victory sent the best-of-seven series to Candlestick Park tied at one victory apiece.

The Giants appeared to be in control of Game 3 after bolting to a 4-0 lead. Three second-inning runs and Leonard's record-tying third homer in as many games provided the cushion. The Giants almost broke the game open in the fifth, but St. Louis reliever Bob Forsch wriggled out of a bases-loaded jam.

The Giants would later have reason to look back and lament that failure to score. Jim Lindeman, a .208 regular-season hitter who was replacing Jack Clark in the cleanup spot, got the Cardinals back in the game with a two-run, sixth-inning home run. And suddenly the momentum was on the Cardinals' side.

With their 17-inning scoreless streak a thing of the past, the Cardinals added a seventh-inning run on Dan Driessen's single and scored four more times in the eighth, two runs coming on Vince

Coleman's single and another on Lindeman's sacrifice fly. Forsch held off the Giants and was credited with his first victory at Candlestick Park since August 1979.

But even with their dramatic comeback victory the Cardinals had reason for concern. Third baseman Pendleton sprained his ankle during an off-day workout and was relegated to limited duty.

Cox finally made his first start in Game 4, facing Mike Krukow, the first San Francisco starter in the series who was a member of the Giants' opening-day roster. Krukow won the battle of right-handers, 4-2.

While Krukow was scattering nine hits and benefitting from four double plays, Thompson, Leonard and Bob Brenly all hit homers as the Giants erased a 2-0 second-inning St. Louis lead.

Thompson broke an 0-for-11 slump with a two-out solo homer in the fourth, Leonard put the Giants in front for good with a two-out, two-run homer in the fifth and Brenly's homer put icing on the cake in the eighth. Leonard set a playoff record by slugging four homers in as many games, equaling the Championship Series mark of four homers in one series set by Pittsburgh's Bob Robertson in 1971 and tied by San Diego's Steve Garvey in 1978.

The Cardinals took a 3-2 lead into the bottom of the fourth inning in Game 5, but lost Mathews with a thigh injury and wound up losing, 6-3.

Bullpens were the key in this contest. Veteran San Francisco lefthander Joe Price replaced Reuschel in the fifth and retired 15 of the 17 batters he faced, allowing only one hit. Meanwhile, Forsch replaced Mathews to open the fourth and failed to get a batter out.

Chili Davis singled on Forsch's first delivery and went to third on Clark's hit-and-run single. After Brenly walked to load the bases, Jose Uribe, who was sent by the Cardinals to San Francisco in 1985 as part of the five-player deal involving Jack Clark, lined Forsch's first pitch to right for a two-run single. Pinch-hitter Mike Aldrete then delivered a sacrifice fly and Thompson capped the uprising with an triple.

The Giants returned to St. Louis with high hopes that Dravecky could perform a replay of his Game 2 masterpiece. Lefthanders had been poison to the Cardinals in the first five games of the series, combining for an earned-run average of 1.23 while holding the Redbirds to a woeful .171 batting average. But. . . .

The Cardinals, playing on the brink for most of September while fighting the Mets and Montreal Expos for first place in the N.L. East, rebounded, winning by the barest of margins, 1-0.

In a tense matchup that began with lefthanders Dravecky and Tudor trading changeups and strikeouts, the Cardinals touched Dravecky for a tainted run when Pena led off the St. Louis second inning with a triple, a hit that Giants right fielder Candy Maldonado misplayed when he lost the ball in the lights.

One out later, Oquendo hit a short fly ball down the right-field line. Maldonado caught it, but his throw home was up the third-base line, Pena stepping around Melvin's tag. It was the first run off Dravecky, ending his playoff record scoreless streak at 16⅓ innings.

Tudor worked around six hits and two walks in 7⅓ innings. Worrell came in to finish off the eighth and struck out Will Clark leading off the ninth.

But when Craig sent Harry Spilman up to pinch hit, Herzog remembered a regular-season homer Spilman had hit off Worrell in San Francisco. In came the lefthanded Dayley, with Worrell moving to right field in case he was needed for one more batter. He wasn't.

The Cardinals didn't leave anything to chance in the decisive seventh game, scoring four times in the second inning and riding Cox's pitching to a 6-0 victory.

After Pena and Pendleton singled with one out in the second, McGee staked Cox to the only run he would need with a single past Giants shortstop Uribe. That's when Oquendo sent Hammaker's 3-2 pitch over the left-field wall.

Tommy Herr added a two-run single in the sixth.

Game 1

Tuesday, October 6, At St. Louis

San Francisco	AB.	R.	H.	RBI.	PO.	A.
Thompson, 2b	3	2	0	0	3	4
Mitchell, 3b	4	0	1	0	1	1
Leonard, lf	4	1	2	1	3	0
Maldonado, rf	4	0	1	2	3	0
C. Davis, cf	3	0	0	0	2	0
W. Clark, 1b	4	0	1	0	7	1
Brenly, c	4	0	0	0	3	1
Uribe, ss	4	0	2	0	1	2
Reuschel, p	1	0	0	0	0	2
Lefferts, p	0	0	0	0	0	1
Speier, ph	1	0	0	0	0	0
Garrelts, p	0	0	0	0	1	0
Melvin, ph	1	0	0	0	0	0
Totals	33	3	7	3	24	12

St. Louis	AB.	R.	H.	RBI.	PO.	A.
Coleman, lf	3	0	1	1	2	0
Smith, ss	3	1	1	0	0	4
Herr, 2b	4	0	0	0	4	2
Driessen, 1b	4	1	2	0	8	0
McGee, cf	4	1	2	1	2	0
Pendleton, 3b	4	1	1	1	0	2
Ford, rf	4	0	1	0	3	0
Pena, c	3	1	1	0	8	1
Mathews, p	1	0	1	2	0	0
Worrell, p	0	0	0	0	0	0
Dayley, p	0	0	0	0	0	0
Totals	30	5	10	5	27	9

San Francisco ....1 0 0 1 0 0 0 1 0—3
St. Louis ....0 0 1 1 0 3 0 0 x—5

San Francisco	IP.	H.	R.	ER.	BB.	SO.
Reuschel (L)	6	9	5	5	2	1
Lefferts	1	0	0	0	1	0
Garrelts	1	0	0	0	0	2

St. Louis	IP.	H.	R.	ER.	BB.	SO.
Mathews (W)	7⅓	4	3	2	1	7
Worrell	⅓	2	0	0	1	0
Dayley (S)	1⅓	1	0	0	0	1

Game-winning RBI—Pendleton.
E—Driessen, Uribe. DP—San Francisco 1, St. Louis 1. LOB—San Francisco 6, St. Louis 6. 2B—Maldonado, Driessen 2. 3B—Smith. HR—Leonard. SB—W. Clark. SH—Mathews 2, Reuschel. U—Kibler, Montague, Pallone, Gregg, Quick and Engel. T—2:34. A—55,331.

Game 2

Wednesday, October 7, At St. Louis

San Francisco	AB.	R.	H.	RBI.	PO.	A.
Thompson, 2b	5	0	0	0	3	3
Mitchell, 3b	5	0	0	0	0	4
Leonard, lf	4	2	3	1	4	0
Maldonado, rf	4	2	2	0	2	0
C. Davis, cf	3	0	1	0	0	0
Milner, pr-cf	0	0	0	0	3	0
W. Clark, 1b	3	1	2	2	7	0
Melvin, c	3	0	0	0	6	1
Uribe, ss	4	0	1	0	2	1
Dravecky, p	4	0	1	0	0	0
Totals	35	5	10	3	27	9

St. Louis	AB.	R.	H.	RBI.	PO.	A.
Coleman, lf	3	0	0	0	1	0
Smith, ss	3	0	0	0	0	2
Herr, 2b	4	0	1	0	3	1
Pendleton, 3b	3	0	0	0	1	1
McGee, cf	3	0	0	0	1	0
Lindeman, 1b	3	0	1	0	8	1
Oquendo, rf	2	0	0	0	3	0
Pena, c	2	0	0	0	10	0
Tudor, p	2	0	0	0	0	3
Pagnozzi, ph	1	0	0	0	0	0
Forsch, p	0	0	0	0	0	0
Totals	26	0	2	0	27	8

San Francisco ....0 2 0 1 0 0 0 2 0—5
St. Louis ....0 0 0 0 0 0 0 0 0—0

San Francisco	IP.	H.	R.	ER.	BB.	SO.
Dravecky (W)	9	2	0	0	4	6

St. Louis	IP.	H.	R.	ER.	BB.	SO.
Tudor (L)	8	10	5	3	2	6
Forsch	1	0	0	0	0	2

Game-winning RBI—W. Clark.
E—Smith. DP—San Francisco 2. LOB—San Francisco 6, St. Louis 3. 2B—Uribe. HR—W. Clark, Leonard. SH—Milner. U—Montague, Pallone, Gregg, Quick, Engel and Kibler. T—2:33. A—55,331.

Game 3

Friday, October 9, At San Francisco

St. Louis	AB.	R.	H.	RBI.	PO.	A.
Coleman, lf	4	1	1	1	2	0
Smith, ss	5	1	3	0	1	4
Herr, 2b	4	0	0	0	0	0
Lindeman, 1b	3	1	3	11	0	0
McGee, cf	4	0	1	0	3	0
Pena, c	4	0	1	0	9	1
Oquendo, rf-3b	4	1	1	0	1	0

St. Louis	AB.	R.	H.	RBI.	PO.	A.
Lawless, 3b	2	0	1	0	0	3
Ford, ph-rf	1	1	1	0	1	0
Magrane, p	1	0	0	0	0	1
J. Clark, ph	1	0	0	0	0	0
Forsch, p	0	0	0	0	0	1
Driessen, ph	1	0	1	1	0	0
Johnson, pr	0	1	0	0	0	0
Worrell, p	1	0	0	0	0	0
Totals	35	6	11	6	27	10

San Francisco	AB.	R.	H.	RBI.	PO.	A.
Thompson, 2b	2	0	0	0	3	3
Spilman, ph	1	1	1	1	0	0
Mitchell, 3b	5	0	1	0	0	2
Leonard, lf	3	1	1	1	2	0
Maldonado, rf	4	0	0	0	0	0
C. Davis, cf	3	1	1	0	3	1
Milner, cf	1	0	0	0	1	0
W. Clark, 1b	4	1	2	1	13	0
Brenly, c	4	1	1	1	5	0
Uribe, ss	4	0	0	0	0	5
Hammaker, p	3	0	0	0	0	0
D. Robinson, p	0	0	0	0	0	0
Lefferts, p	0	0	0	0	0	1
LaCoss, p	0	0	0	0	0	1
Aldrete, ph	1	0	0	0	0	0
Totals	35	5	7	4	27	13

St. Louis 0 0 0 0 0 2 4 0 0—6
San Francisco 0 3 1 0 0 0 0 0 1—5

St. Louis	IP.	H.	R.	ER.	BB.	SO.
Magrane	4	4	4	4	2	3
Forsch (W)	2	1	0	0	0	1
Worrell (S)	3	2	1	1	0	4

San Francisco	IP.	H.	R.	ER.	BB.	SO.
Hammaker	6*	7	3	3	0	4
D. Robinson (L)	0†	3	3	3	0	0
Lefferts	1	1	0	0	0	0
LaCoss	2	0	0	0	2	1

*Pitched to one batter in seventh.
†Pitched to three batters in seventh.

Game-winning RBI—Coleman.

E—Mitchell, Herr. DP—San Francisco 2. LOB—St. Louis 6, San Francisco 6. 2B—C. Davis, Brenly, W. Clark. 3B—McGee. HR—Leonard, Lindeman, Spilman. SB—Thompson, Herr, Johnson. SH—Herr. SF—Lindeman. HBP—By Forsch (Leonard). WP—Magrane. U—Pallone, Gregg, Quick, Engel, Kibler and Montague. T—3:27. A—57,913.

Game 4

Saturday, October 10, At San Francisco

St. Louis	AB.	R.	H.	RBI.	PO.	A.
Coleman, lf	4	0	2	1	1	1
Smith, ss	4	0	0	0	0	4
Herr, 2b	4	0	1	0	1	1
Driessen, 1b	3	0	0	0	9	2
McGee, cf	4	0	1	0	1	0
Pendleton, 3b	4	0	1	0	0	1
Ford, rf	4	1	1	0	2	0
Pena, c	3	1	2	0	8	0
Cox, p	3	0	1	1	2	3
Totals	33	2	9	2	24	12

San Francisco	AB.	R.	H.	RBI.	PO.	A.
Milner, cf	4	0	0	0	3	0
Mitchell, 3b	4	1	2	0	0	1
Leonard, lf	2	1	1	2	0	0
W. Clark, 1b	4	0	2	0	12	3
Aldrete, rf	4	0	1	0	3	0
Brenly, c	4	1	2	1	3	0
Thompson, 2b	4	1	1	1	1	4
Uribe, ss	4	0	0	0	3	3
Krukow, p	2	0	0	0	2	2
Totals	32	4	9	4	27	13

St. Louis 0 2 0 0 0 0 0 0 0—2
San Francisco 0 0 0 1 2 0 0 1 x—4

St. Louis	IP.	H.	R.	ER.	BB.	SO.
Cox (L)	8	9	4	4	3	6

San Francisco	IP.	H.	R.	ER.	BB.	SO.
Krukow (W)	9	9	2	2	1	3

Game-winning RBI—Leonard.

E—Thompson, W. Clark. DP—San Francisco 4. LOB—St. Louis 5, San Francisco 7. 2B—Mitchell, W. Clark. HR—Thompson, Leonard, Brenly. U—Gregg, Quick, Engel, Kibler, Montague and Pallone. T—2:23. A—57,997.

Game 5

Sunday, October 11, At San Francisco

St. Louis	AB.	R.	H.	RBI.	PO.	A.
Coleman, lf	4	1	2	0	1	0
Smith, ss	2	0	0	1	0	0
Herr, 2b	3	0	0	1	3	1
Driessen, 1b	3	0	0	0	5	0
Lindeman, ph-1b	1	0	0	0	1	0
McGee, cf	4	0	2	0	4	0
Pendleton, 3b	4	1	1	0	1	5
Morris, rf	2	0	0	0	1	0
Forsch, p	0	0	0	0	0	0
Horton, p	0	0	0	0	0	0
Lawless, ph-rf	2	0	0	0	1	0
Pena, c	2	1	1	0	6	2
Mathews, p	1	0	1	0	0	0
Ford, rf	0	0	0	0	0	0
Oquendo, ph-rf	2	0	0	0	1	0
Dayley, p	0	0	0	0	0	0
Totals	30	3	7	2	24	8

San Francisco	AB.	R.	H.	RBI.	PO.	A.
Thompson, 2b	2	1	1	1	1	4
Mitchell, 3b	4	1	2	2	1	1
Leonard, lf	4	0	0	0	1	0
Maldonado, rf	4	0	1	0	0	0
C. Davis, cf	3	1	1	0	3	0
Milner, cf	1	0	0	0	1	0
W. Clark, 1b	3	1	1	0	9	2
Brenly, c	1	1	0	0	7	1
Uribe, ss	4	1	1	2	4	2
Reuschel, p	1	0	0	0	0	1
Aldrete, ph	0	0	0	1	0	0
Price, p	1	0	0	0	0	0
Totals	28	6	7	6	27	11

St. Louis 1 0 1 1 0 0 0 0 0—3
San Francisco 1 0 1 4 0 0 0 0 x—6

St. Louis	IP.	H.	R.	ER.	BB.	SO.
Mathews	3	2	2	2	2	3
Forsch (L)	0*	3	4	4	1	0
Horton	3	2	0	0	0	2
Dayley	2	0	0	0	2	2

San Francisco	IP.	H.	R.	ER.	BB.	SO.
Reuschel	4	6	3	2	0	1
Price (W)	5	1	0	0	1	6

*Pitched to four batters in fourth.

Game-winning RBI—Uribe.

E—Reuschel. DP—St. Louis 1, San Francisco 1. LOB—St. Louis 4, San Francisco 5. 2B—Coleman. 3B—Pendleton, Thompson. HR—Mitchell. SB—Thompson, Mitchell, Uribe. SH—Smith. SF—Herr, Smith, Aldrete. HBP—By Dayley (Thompson). WP—Reuschel. U—Quick, Engel, Kibler, Montague, Pallone and Gregg. T—2:48. A—59,363.

Game 6

Tuesday, October 13, At St. Louis

San Francisco	AB.	R.	H.	RBI.	PO.	A.
Thompson, 2b	3	0	0	0	0	1
Mitchell, 3b	4	0	1	0	0	1
Leonard, lf	3	0	1	0	3	0
Maldonado, rf	3	0	0	0	2	0
Aldrete, ph-rf	1	0	0	0	0	0
C Davis, cf	4	0	0	0	1	0
W. Clark, 1b	3	0	0	0	9	0
Melvin, c	3	0	3	0	8	0
Milner, pr	0	0	0	0	0	0
D. Robinson, p	0	0	0	0	0	0
Spilman, ph	0	0	0	0	0	0
Speier, ph	1	0	0	0	0	0
Uribe, ss	3	0	1	0	0	4
Dravecky, p	2	0	0	0	0	2
Brenly, ph-c	1	0	0	0	1	0
Totals	31	0	6	0	24	8

St. Louis	AB.	R.	H.	RBI.	PO.	A.
Coleman, lf	4	0	0	0	1	0
Smith, ss	4	0	0	0	3	0
Herr, 2b	3	0	2	0	1	2
Lindeman, 1b	3	0	2	0	6	0
Pendleton, 3b	3	0	0	0	1	2
Pena, c	3	1	1	0	9	1
McGee, cf	3	0	0	0	5	0
Oquendo, rf	2	0	0	1	1	0
Worrell, p-rf	0	0	0	0	0	0
Tudor, p	2	0	0	0	0	1
Morris, rf	1	0	0	0	0	0
Dayley, p	0	0	0	0	0	0
Totals	28	1	5	1	27	6

San Francisco 0 0 0 0 0 0 0 0 0—0
St. Louis 0 1 0 0 0 0 0 0 x—1

San Francisco	IP.	H.	R.	ER.	BB.	SO.
Dravecky (L)	6	5	1	1	0	8
D. Robinson	2	0	0	0	0	1

St. Louis	IP.	H.	R.	ER.	BB.	SO.
Tudor (W)	7⅓	6	0	0	3	6
Worrell	1	0	0	0	0	2
Dayley (S)	⅔	0	0	0	0	1

Game-winning RBI—Oquendo.

LOB—San Francisco 8, St. Louis 4. 3B—Pena. SH—Uribe. SF—Oquendo. U—Engel, Kibler, Montague, Pallone, Gregg and Quick. T—3:09. A—55,331.

Game 7

Wednesday, October 14, At St. Louis

San Francisco	AB.	R.	H.	RBI.	PO.	A.
Aldrete, rf	4	0	0	0	2	0
Mitchell, 3b	4	0	1	0	2	1
Leonard, lf	4	0	2	0	1	1
W. Clark, 1b	4	0	1	0	6	1
C. Davis, cf	4	0	0	0	2	0
Brenly, c	3	0	1	0	9	0
Speier, 2b	3	0	0	0	1	3
Uribe, ss	3	0	2	0	1	3
Hammaker, p	0	0	0	0	0	1
Milner, ph	1	0	1	0	0	0
Price, p	0	0	0	0	0	0
Downs, p	0	0	0	0	0	0
Thompson, ph	1	0	0	0	0	0
Garrelts, p	0	0	0	0	0	0
Lefferts, p	0	0	0	0	0	0
LaCoss, p	0	0	0	0	0	1
Spilman, ph	1	0	0	0	0	0
D. Robinson, p	0	0	0	0	0	0
Totals	32	0	8	0	24	11

St. Louis	AB.	R.	H.	RBI.	PO.	A.
Coleman, lf	4	1	1	0	2	0
Smith, ss	4	0	1	0	6	5
Herr, 2b	5	0	2	2	0	4
Lindeman, 1b	3	0	0	0	7	1
Driessen, ph-1b	1	0	0	0	4	1
Pendleton, 3b	1	1	1	0	0	0
Lawless, ph-3b	2	0	1	0	0	1
Pena, c	4	1	2	0	5	0
McGee, cf	4	1	2	1	0	0
Oquendo, rf	2	2	1	3	1	0
Cox, p	3	0	1	0	2	2
Totals	33	6	12	6	27	14

San Francisco 0 0 0 0 0 0 0 0 0—0
St. Louis 0 4 0 0 0 2 0 0 x—6

San Francisco	IP.	H.	R.	ER.	BB.	SO.
Hammaker (L)	2	5	4	4	0	3
Price	⅔	2	0	0	0	1
Downs	1⅓	1	0	0	0	0
Garrelts	1⅔	2	2	2	4	2
Lefferts	0*	1	0	0	0	0
LaCoss	1⅓	1	0	0	1	1
D. Robinson	1	0	0	0	0	2

St. Louis	IP.	H.	R.	ER.	BB.	SO.
Cox (W)	9	8	0	0	0	5

*Pitched to one batter in sixth.

Game-winning RBI—McGee.

E—C. Davis. DP—St. Louis 3. LOB—San Francisco 5, St. Louis 9. 2B—McGee. HR—Oquendo. SB—Coleman, Pena. SH—Cox. WP—Garrelts. PB—Brenly. U—Kibler, Montague, Pallone, Gregg, Quick and Engel. T—2:59. A—55,331.

COMPOSITE BATTING AVERAGES

St. Louis Cardinals

Player-Position	G.	AB.	R.	H.	2B.	3B.	HR.	RBI.	BA.
Mathews, p	2	2	0	2	0	0	0	2	1.000
Pena, c	7	21	5	8	0	1	0	0	.381
Ford, rf-ph	4	9	2	3	0	0	0	0	.333
Cox, p	2	6	0	2	0	0	0	1	.333
Lawless, 3b-ph-rf	3	6	0	2	0	0	0	0	.333
McGee, cf	7	26	2	8	1	1	0	2	.308
Lindeman, 1b-ph	5	13	1	4	0	0	1	3	.308
Coleman, lf	7	26	3	7	1	0	0	4	.269
Driessen, 1b-ph	5	12	1	3	2	0	0	1	.250
Herr, 2b	7	27	0	6	0	0	0	3	.222
Pendleton, 3b	6	19	3	4	0	1	0	1	.211
Smith, ss	7	25	2	5	0	1	0	1	.200
Oquendo, rf-3b-ph	5	12	3	2	0	0	1	4	.167
Dayley, p	3	0	0	0	0	0	0	0	.000
Forsch, p	3	0	0	0	0	0	0	0	.000
Horton, p	1	0	0	0	0	0	0	0	.000
Johnson, pr	1	0	1	0	0	0	0	0	.000
Clark, ph	1	1	0	0	0	0	0	0	.000
Magrane, p	1	1	0	0	0	0	0	0	.000
Pagnozzi, ph	1	1	0	0	0	0	0	0	.000
Worrell, p-rf	3	1	0	0	0	0	0	0	.000
Morris, rf	2	3	0	0	0	0	0	0	.000
Tudor, p	2	4	0	0	0	0	0	0	.000
Totals	7	215	23	56	4	4	2	22	.260

San Francisco Giants

Player-Position	G.	AB.	R.	H.	2B.	3B.	HR.	RBI.	BA.
Spilman, ph	3	2	1	1	0	0	1	1	.500
Melvin, ph-c	3	7	0	3	0	0	0	0	.429
Leonard, lf	7	24	5	10	0	0	4	5	.417
Clark, 1b	7	25	3	9	2	0	1	3	.360
Uribe, ss	7	26	1	7	1	0	0	2	.269
Mitchell, 3b	7	30	2	8	1	0	1	2	.267
Brenly, c-ph	6	17	3	4	1	0	1	2	.235
Maldonado, rf	5	19	2	4	1	0	0	2	.211
Dravecky, p	2	6	0	1	0	0	0	0	.167
Davis, cf	6	20	2	3	1	0	0	0	.150
Milner, pr-cf-ph	6	7	0	1	0	0	0	0	.143
Thompson, 2b-ph	7	20	4	2	0	1	1	2	.100
Aldrete, ph-rf	5	10	0	1	0	0	0	1	.100
Downs, p	1	0	0	0	0	0	0	0	.000
Garrelts, p	2	0	0	0	0	0	0	0	.000
Lefferts, p	3	0	0	0	0	0	0	0	.000
Robinson, p	3	0	0	0	0	0	0	0	.000
LaCoss, p	2	0	0	0	0	0	0	0	.000
Price, p	2	1	0	0	0	0	0	0	.000
Krukow, p	1	2	0	0	0	0	0	0	.000
Reuschel, p	2	2	0	0	0	0	0	0	.000
Hammaker, p	2	2	0	0	0	0	0	0	.000
Speier, ph-2b	3	5	0	0	0	0	0	0	.000
Totals	7	226	23	54	7	1	9	20	.239

COMPOSITE PITCHING AVERAGES

St. Louis Cardinals

Pitcher	G.	IP.	H.	R.	ER.	BB.	SO.	W.	L.	ERA.
Dayley	3	4	1	0	0	2	4	0	0	0.00
Horton	1	3	2	0	0	0	2	0	0	0.00
Tudor	2	23⅓	16	5	3	5	12	1	1	1.76
Worrell	3	7⅔	4	1	1	1	6	0	0	2.08
Cox	2	17	17	4	4	3	11	1	1	2.12
Mathews	2	17⅔	6	5	4	3	10	1	0	3.48
Magrane	1	4	4	4	4	2	3	0	0	9.00
Forsch	3	3	4	4	4	1	3	1	1	12.00
Totals	7	61	54	23	20	17	51	4	3	2.95

San Francisco Giants

Pitcher	G.	IP.	H.	R.	ER.	BB.	SO.	W.	L.	ERA.
Price	2	5⅔	3	0	0	1	7	1	0	0.00
LaCoss	2	3⅓	1	0	0	3	2	0	0	0.00
Lefferts	3	2	3	0	0	1	0	0	0	0.00
Downs	1	1⅓	1	0	0	0	0	0	0	0.00
Dravecky	2	15	7	1	1	4	14	1	1	0.60
Krukow	1	9	9	2	2	1	3	1	0	2.00
Reuschel	2	10	15	8	7	2	2	0	1	6.30
Garrelts	2	2⅔	2	2	2	4	4	0	0	6.75
Hammaker	2	8	12	7	7	0	7	0	1	7.88
Robinson	3	3	3	3	3	0	3	0	1	9.00
Totals	7	60	56	23	22	16	42	3	4	3.30

Championship Series Player Roster

Players Appearing in One or More Games

A

Aaron, Henry L.—Atlanta NL 1969.
Aaron, Tommie L.—Atlanta NL 1969.
Aase, Donald W.—California AL 1979.
Abbott, W. Glenn—Oakland AL 1975.
Acker, James J.—Toronto AL 1985.
Agee, Tommie L.—New York NL 1969.
Agosto, Juan R.—Chicago AL 1983.
Aguilera, Richard W.—New York NL 1986.
Aikens, Willie M.—Kansas City AL 1980.
Aldrete, Michael P.—San Francisco NL 1987.
Alexander, Doyle L.—Baltimore AL 1973; Toronto AL 1985; Detroit AL 1987.
Alexander, Matthew—Pittsburgh NL 1979.
Allen, Richard A.—Philadelphia NL 1976.
Alley, L. Eugene—Pittsburgh NL 1970-71-72.
Allison, W. Robert—Minnesota AL 1969-70.
Alomar, Santos—New York AL 1976.
Alou, Felipe R.—Atlanta NL 1969.
Alou, Jesus M.—Oakland AL 1973-74.
Alou, Mateo R.—Pittsburgh NL 1970; Oakland AL 1972.
Alyea, Garrabrant R.—Minnesota AL 1970.
Andersen, Larry E.—Houston NL 1986.
Anderson, David C.—Los Angeles NL 1985.
Anderson, James L.—California AL 1979.
Andrews, Michael J.—Oakland AL 1973.
Andujar, Joaquin—Houston NL 1980; St. Louis NL 1982-85.
Armas, Antonio R.—Oakland AL 1981; Boston AL 1986.
Armbrister, Edison R.—Cincinnati NL 1973-75-76.
Ashby, Alan D.—Houston NL 1980-86.
Aspromonte, Robert T.—Atlanta NL 1969.
Atherton, Keith R.—Minnesota AL 1987.
Auerbach, Frederick S.—Los Angeles NL 1974; Cincinnati NL 1979.
Aviles, Ramon A.A.—Philadelphia NL 1980.
Ayala, Benigno F.—Baltimore AL 1983.

B

Backman, Walter W.—New York NL 1986.
Bailor, Robert M.—Los Angeles NL 1986.
Baines, Harold D.—Chicago AL 1983.
Bair, C. Douglas—Cincinnati NL 1979; St. Louis NL 1982.
Baker, Douglas L.—Detroit AL 1984.
Baker, Frank W.—Baltimore AL 1973-74.
Baker, Johnnie B.—Los Angeles NL 1977-78-81-83.
Balboni, Stephen C.—Kansas City AL 1984-85.
Bando, Salvatore L.—Oakland AL 1971-72-73-74-75.
Bannister, Floyd F.—Chicago AL 1983.
Barfield, Jesse L.—Toronto AL 1985.
Barlow, Michael R.—California AL 1979.
Barojas, Salome—Chicago AL 1983.
Barr, James L.—San Francisco NL 1971.
Barrett, Martin G.—Boston AL 1986.
Bass, Kevin C.—Houston NL 1986.
Baylor, Donald E.—Baltimore AL 1973-74; California AL 1979-82; Boston AL 1986; Minnesota AL 1987.
Beard, C. David—Oakland AL 1981.
Beattie, James L.—New York AL 1978.
Beckwith, T. Joseph—Los Angeles NL 1983.
Bedrosian, Stephen W.—Atlanta NL 1982.
Belanger, Mark H.—Baltimore AL 1969-70-71-73-74-79.
Bell, George A.—Toronto AL 1985.
Bench, Johnny L.—Cincinnati NL 1970-72-73-75-76-79.
Benedict, Bruce E.—Atlanta NL 1982.
Beniquez, Juan J.—Boston AL 1975; California AL 1982.
Berenguer, Juan B.—Minnesota AL 1987.
Bergman, David B.—Houston NL 1980; Detroit AL 1984-87.
Bernard, Dwight V.—Milwaukee AL 1982.
Bevacqua, Kurt A.—San Diego NL 1984.
Biancalana, Roland A.—Kansas City AL 1984-85.
Bibby, James B.—Pittsburgh NL 1979.
Billingham, John E.—Cincinnati NL 1972-73.

Bird, J. Douglas—Kansas City AL 1976-77-78.
Black, Harry R.—Kansas City AL 1984-85.
Blair, Paul L.—Baltimore AL 1969-70-71-73-74; New York AL 1977-78.
Blass, Stephen R.—Pittsburgh NL 1971-72.
Blefary, Curtis L.—Oakland AL 1971.
Blue, Vida R.—Oakland AL 1971-72-73-74-75.
Blyleven, Rikalbert—Minnesota AL 1970-87; Pittsburgh NL 1979.
Bochy, Bruce D.—Houston NL 1980.
Boddicker, Michael J.—Baltimore AL 1983.
Boggs, Wade A.—Boston AL 1986.
Bonds, Bobby L.—San Francisco NL 1971.
Booker, Gregory S.—San Diego NL 1984.
Boone, Robert R.—Philadelphia NL 1976-77-78-80; California AL 1982-86.
Borbon, Pedro R.—Cincinnati NL 1972-73-75-76.
Bosetti, Richard A.—Oakland AL 1981.
Bosley, Thaddis—Chicago NL 1984.
Bosman, Richard A.—Oakland AL 1975.
Boswell, David W.—Minnesota AL 1969.
Boswell, Kenneth G.—New York NL 1969-73.
Bourque, Patrick D.—Oakland AL 1973.
Bowa, Lawrence R.—Philadelphia NL 1976-77-78-80; Chicago NL 1984.
Boyd, Dennis R.—Boston AL 1986.
Boyer, Cletis L.—Atlanta NL 1969.
Braun, Stephen R.—Kansas City AL 1978; St. Louis NL 1982-85.
Bravo, Angel A.—Cincinnati NL 1970.
Brenly, Robert E.—San Francisco NL 1987.
Brett, George H.—Kansas City AL 1976-77-78-80-84-85.
Brett, Kenneth A.—Pittsburgh NL 1974-75.
Briles, Nelson K.—Pittsburgh NL 1972.
Brinkman, Edwin A.—Detroit AL 1972.
Britton, James A.—Atlanta NL 1969.
Brock, Gregory A.—Los Angeles NL 1983-85.
Brookens, Thomas D.—Detroit AL 1984-87.
Brouhard, Mark S.—Milwaukee AL 1982.
Brown, Isaac—Detroit AL 1972.
Brown, Larry L.—Baltimore AL 1973.
Brown, Ollie L.—Philadelphia NL 1976-77.
Brown, R.L. Bobby—New York AL 1980-81; San Diego NL 1984.
Brown, W. Gates—Detroit AL 1972.
Brunansky, Thomas A.—Minnesota AL 1987.
Brusstar, Warren S.—Philadelphia NL 1977-78-80; Chicago NL 1984.
Bryant, Ronald R.—San Francisco NL 1971.
Buckner, William J.—Los Angeles NL 1974; Boston AL 1986.
Buford, Donald A.—Baltimore AL 1969-70-71.
Bumbry, Alonza B.—Baltimore AL 1973-74-79-83.
Burke, Glenn L.—Los Angeles NL 1977.
Burleson, Richard P.—Boston AL 1975; California AL 1986.
Burns, R. Britt—Chicago AL 1983.
Burris, B. Ray—Montreal NL 1981.
Burroughs, Jeffrey A.—Toronto AL 1985.
Bush, R. Randall—Minnesota AL 1987.
Butera, Salvatore P.—Minnesota AL 1987.
Butler, Brett M.—Atlanta NL 1982.
Bystrom, Martin E.—Philadelphia NL 1980.

C

Cabell, Enos M.—Baltimore AL 1974; Houston NL 1980; Los Angeles NL 1985.
Caldwell, R. Michael—Milwaukee AL 1982.
Calhoun, Jeffrey W.—Houston NL 1986.
Camp, Rick L.—Atlanta NL 1982.
Campaneris, Dagoberto B.—Oakland AL 1971-72-73-74-75; California AL 1982.
Campbell, William R.—St. Louis NL 1985.
Candelaria, John R.—Pittsburgh NL 1975-79; California AL 1986.
Carbo, Bernardo—Cincinnati NL 1970.
Cardenal, Jose D.—Philadelphia NL 1978.
Cardenas, Leonardo A.—Minnesota AL 1969-70.
Carew, Rodney C.—Minnesota AL 1969-70; California AL 1979-82.

Carlton, Steven N.—Philadelphia NL 1976-77-78-80-83.
Carrithers, Donald G.—San Francisco NL 1971.
Carroll, Clay P.—Cincinnati NL 1970-72-73-75.
Carter, Gary E.—Montreal NL 1981; New York NL 1986.
Carty, Ricardo A. J.—Atlanta NL 1969.
Cash, David—Pittsburgh NL 1970-71-72; Philadelphia NL 1976.
Cash, Norman D.—Detroit AL 1972.
Castillo, Martin H.—Detroit AL 1984.
Castillo, Robert E.—Los Angeles NL 1981-85.
Cedeno, Cesar—Houston NL 1980; St. Louis NL 1985.
Cepeda, Orlando M.—Atlanta NL 1969.
Cerone, Richard A.—New York AL 1980-81.
Cey, Ronald C.—Los Angeles NL 1974-77-78-81; Chicago NL 1984.
Chambliss, C. Christopher—New York AL 1976-77-78; Atlanta NL 1982.
Chance, W. Dean—Minnesota AL 1969.
Chaney, Darrel L.—Cincinnati NL 1972-73.
Christenson, Larry R.—Philadelphia NL 1977-78-80.
Clancy, James—Toronto AL 1985.
Clark, Jack A.—St. Louis NL 1985-87.
Clark, Robert C.—California AL 1979-82.
Clark, William N.—San Francisco NL 1987.
Clay, Kenneth E.—New York AL 1978.
Clear, Mark A.—California AL 1979.
Clemens, W. Roger—Boston AL 1986.
Clemente, Roberto W.—Pittsburgh NL 1970-71-72.
Cleveland, Reginald L.—Boston AL 1975.
Cline, Tyrone K.—Cincinnati NL 1970.
Clines, Eugene A.—Pittsburgh NL 1971-72-74.
Cloninger, Tony L.—Cincinnati NL 1970.
Coggins, Richard A.—Baltimore AL 1973-74.
Coleman, Joseph H.—Detroit AL 1972.
Coleman, Vincent M.—St. Louis NL 1985-87.
Collins, David S.—Cincinnati NL 1979.
Concepcion, David I.—Cincinnati NL 1970-72-75-76-79.
Concepcion, Onix—Kansas City AL 1984-85.
Conigliaro, William M.—Oakland AL 1973.
Cooper, Cecil C.—Boston AL 1975; Milwaukee AL 1982.
Corbett, Douglas M.—California AL 1986.
Cotto, Henry—Chicago NL 1984.
Cowens, Alfred E.—Kansas City AL 1976-77-78.
Cox, Danny B.—St. Louis NL 1985-87.
Crawford, Willie M.—Los Angeles NL 1974.
Crawford, Steven R.—Boston AL 1986.
Cromartie, Warren L.—Montreal NL 1981.
Crosby, Edward C.—Cincinnati NL 1973.
Crowley, Terrence M.—Baltimore AL 1973-79; Cincinnati NL 1975.
Cruz, Hector—Cincinnati NL 1979.
Cruz, Jose—Houston NL 1980-86.
Cruz, Julio L.—Chicago AL 1983.
Cruz, Todd R.—Baltimore AL 1983.
Cuellar, Miguel—Baltimore AL 1969-70-71-73-74.
Cullen Timothy L.—Oakland AL 1972.
Cumberland, John S.—San Francisco NL 1971.

D

Darling, Ronald M.—New York NL 1986.
Dauer, Richard F.—Baltimore AL 1979-83.
Davalillo, Victor J.—Pittsburgh NL 1971-72; Oakland AL 1973; Los Angeles NL 1977.
Davidson, J. Mark—Minnesota AL 1987.
Davis, Charles T.—San Francisco NL 1987.
Davis, George E.—Baltimore AL 1983.
Davis, Glenn E.—Houston NL 1986.
Davis, H. Thomas—Oakland AL 1971; Baltimore AL 1973-74.
Davis, Jody R.—Chicago NL 1984.
Davis, Michael O.—Oakland AL 1981.
Davis, Ronald G.—New York AL 1980-1981.
Davis, William H.—California AL 1979.

Dawson, Andre F.—Montreal NL 1981.
Dayley, Kenneth G.—St. Louis NL 1985-87.
DeCinces, Douglas V.—Baltimore AL 1979; California AL 1982-86.
DeJesus, Ivan—Philadelphia NL 1983.
Demery, Lawrence C.—Pittsburgh NL 1974-75.
Dempsey, J. Rikard—Baltimore AL 1979-83.
Denny, John A.—Philadelphia NL 1983.
Dent, Russell E.—New York AL 1977-78-80.
Dernier, Robert E.—Philadelphia NL 1983; Chicago NL 1984.
Diaz, Baudilio J.—Philadelphia NL 1983.
Diaz, Carlos A.—Los Angeles NL 1985.
Didier, Robert D.—Atlanta NL 1969.
Dietz, Richard A.—San Francisco NL 1971.
Doran, William D.—Houston NL 1986.
Dotson, Richard E.—Chicago AL 1983.
Downing, Alphonso E.—Los Angeles NL 1974.
Downing, Brian J.—California AL 1979-82-86.
Downs, Kelly R.—San Francisco NL 1987.
Doyle, Brian R.—New York AL 1978.
Doyle, Paul S.—Atlanta NL 1969.
Doyle, R. Dennis—Boston AL 1975.
Drago, Richard A.—Boston AL 1975.
Dravecky, David F.—San Diego NL 1984; San Francisco NL 1987.
Driessen, Daniel D.—Cincinnati NL 1973-76-79; St. Louis NL 1987.
Drumright, Keith A.—Oakland AL 1981.
Duffy, Frank T.—San Francisco NL 1971.
Duncan, David E.—Oakland AL 1971-72.
Duncan, Mariano—Los Angeles NL 1985.
Durham, Leon—Chicago NL 1984.
Dwyer, James E.—Baltimore AL 1983.
Dybzinski, Jerome M.—Chicago AL 1983.
Dyer, Don R.—Pittsburgh NL 1975.
Dykstra, Leonard K.—New York NL 1986.

E

Easler, Michael A.—Pittsburgh NL 1979.
Eastwick, Rawlins J.—Cincinnati NL 1975-76; Philadelphia NL 1978.
Eckersley, Dennis L.—Chicago NL 1984.
Edwards, Marshall L.—Milwaukee AL 1982.
Ellis, Dock P.—Pittsburgh NL 1970-71-72-75; New York AL 1976.
Elster, Kevin D.—New York NL 1986.
Epstein, Michael P.—Oakland AL 1971-72.
Etchebarren, Andrew A.—Baltimore AL 1969-70-71-73-74.
Evans, Darrell W.—Detroit AL 1984-87.
Evans, Dwight W.—Boston AL 1975-86.

F

Farr, Steven M.—Kansas City AL 1985.
Ferguson, Joseph V.—Los Angeles NL 1974-78.
Fernandez, C. Sidney—New York NL 1986.
Fernandez, O. Antonio—Toronto AL 1985.
Fielder, Cecil G.—Toronto AL 1985.
Figueroa, Eduardo—New York AL 1976-77-78.
Fimple, John J.—Los Angeles NL 1983.
Fingers, Roland G.—Oakland AL 1971-72-73-74-75.
Finley, Charles E.—California AL 1986.
Fisk, Carlton E.—Boston AL 1975; Chicago AL 1983.
Flanagan, Michael K.—Baltimore AL 1979-83.
Flannery, Timothy E.—San Diego NL 1984.
Fletcher, Scott B.—Chicago AL 1983.
Flynn, R. Douglas—Cincinnati NL 1976.
Foli, Timothy J.—Pittsburgh NL 1979; California AL 1982.
Foote, Barry C.—Philadelphia NL 1978; New York AL 1981.
Ford, Curtis G.—St. Louis NL 1987.
Ford, Darnell G.—California AL 1979; Baltimore AL 1983.
Forsch, Kenneth R.—Houston NL 1980.
Forsch, Robert H.—St. Louis NL 1982-85-87.
Forster, Terry J.—Los Angeles NL 1978-81.
Fosse, Raymond E.—Oakland AL 1973-74-75.
Foster, George A.—Cincinnati NL 1972-75-76-79.
Francona, Terry J.—Montreal NL 1981.
Frazier, George A.—New York AL 1981;

Chicago NL 1984.
Freehan, William A.—Detroit AL 1972.
Frost, C. David—California AL 1979.
Fryman, Woodrow T.—Detroit AL 1972; Montreal NL 1981.
Fuentes, Rigoberto—San Francisco NL 1971.

G

Gaetti, Gary J.—Minnesota AL 1987.
Gagliano, Philip J.—Cincinnati NL 1973.
Gagne, Gregory C.—Minnesota AL 1987.
Gallagher, Alan M.—San Francisco NL 1971.
Gamble, Oscar C.—New York AL 1976-80-81.
Gantner, James E.—Milwaukee AL 1982.
Garber, H. Eugene—Philadelphia NL 1976-77; Atlanta NL 1982.
Garbey, Barbaro G.—Detroit AL 1984.
Garcia, Alfonso R.—Baltimore AL 1979.
Garcia, Damaso D.—Toronto AL 1985.
Garland, M. Wayne—Baltimore AL 1974.
Garman, Michael D.—Los Angeles NL 1977.
Garner, Philip M.—Oakland AL 1975; Pittsburgh NL 1979; Houston NL 1986.
Garrelts, Scott W.—San Francisco NL 1987.
Garrett, R. Wayne—New York NL 1969-73.
Garrido, Gil G.—Atlanta NL 1969.
Garvey, Steven P.—Los Angeles NL 1974-77-78-81; San Diego NL 1984.
Gaspar, Rodney E.—New York NL 1969.
Gedman, Richard L.—Boston AL 1986.
Gentry, Gary E.—New York NL 1969.
Geronimo, Cesar F.—Cincinnati NL 1972-73-75-76-79.
Gibbon, Joseph C.—Pittsburgh NL 1970.
Gibson, Kirk H.—Detroit AL 1984-87.
Giusti, J. David—Pittsburgh NL 1970-71-72-74-75.
Gladden, C. Daniel—Minnesota AL 1987.
Goltz, David A.—California AL 1982.
Gonzalez, A. Antonio—Atlanta NL 1969.
Gonzalez, Julio C.—Philadelphia NL 1978.
Gooden, Dwight L.—New York NL 1986.
Goodson, J. Edward—Los Angeles NL 1977.
Gossage, Richard M.—New York AL 1978-80-81; San Diego NL 1984.
Granger, Wayne A.—Cincinnati NL 1970.
Grant, James T.—Oakland AL 1971.
Green, David A.—St. Louis NL 1982.
Green, Richard L.—Oakland AL 1971-72-73-74.
Greenwell, Michael L.—Boston AL 1986.
Grich, Robert A.—Baltimore AL 1973-74; California AL 1979-82-86.
Griffey, G. Kenneth—Cincinnati NL 1973-75-76.
Grimsley, Ross A.—Cincinnati NL 1972-73; Baltimore AL 1974.
Gross, Gregory E.—Philadelphia NL 1980-83.
Gross, Wayne D.—Oakland AL 1981.
Grote, Gerald W.—New York NL 1969-73; Los Angeles NL 1977-78.
Grzenda, Joseph C.—Minnesota AL 1969.
Gubicza, Mark S.—Kansas City AL 1985.
Guerrero, Pedro—Los Angeles NL 1981-83-85.
Guidry, Ronald A.—New York AL 1976-77-78-80.
Gullett, Donald E.—Cincinnati NL 1970-72-73-75-76; New York AL 1977.
Gullickson, William L.—Montreal NL 1981.
Gura, Lawrence C.—Kansas City AL 1976-77-78-80.
Gwynn, Anthony K.—San Diego NL 1984.

H

Haas, Bryan E.—Milwaukee AL 1982.
Hague, Joe C.—Cincinnati NL 1972.
Hahn, Donald A.—New York NL 1973.
Hairston, Jerry W.—Chicago AL 1983.
Hall, Richard W.—Baltimore AL 1969-70.
Hall, Thomas E.—Minnesota AL 1969-70; Cincinnati NL 1972-73; Kansas City AL 1976.
Haller, Thomas F.—Detroit AL 1972.
Hamilton, David E.—Oakland AL 1972.
Hamilton, Steve A.—San Francisco NL 1971.
Hammaker, C. Atlee—San Francisco NL

1987.
Harlow, Larry D.—California AL 1979.
Harmon, Terry W.—Philadelphia NL 1976.
Harper, Brian D.—St. Louis NL 1985.
Harper, Terry J.—Atlanta NL 1982.
Harper, Tommy—Oakland AL 1975.
Harrelson, Derrel M.—New York NL 1969-73.
Harris, Greg A.—San Diego NL 1984.
Hart, James R.—San Francisco NL 1971.
Hassler, Andrew E.—Kansas City AL 1976-77; California AL 1982.
Hatcher, William A.—Houston NL 1986.
Hawkins, M. Andrew—San Diego NL 1984.
Hayes, Von F.—Philadelphia NL 1983.
Hearron, Jeffrey V.—Toronto AL 1985.
Heath, Michael T.—Oakland AL 1981; Detroit AL 1987.
Hebner, Richard J.—Pittsburgh NL 1970-71-72-74-75; Philadelphia NL 1977-78; Chicago NL 1984.
Heep, Daniel W.—Houston NL 1980; New York NL 1986.
Hegan, J. Michael—Oakland AL 1971-72.
Helms, Tommy V.—Cincinnati NL 1970.
Henderson, David L.—Boston AL 1986.
Henderson, Kenneth J.—San Francisco NL 1971.
Henderson, Rickey H.—Oakland AL 1981.
Hendrick, George A.—Oakland AL 1972; St. Louis NL 1982; California AL 1986.
Hendricks, Elrod J.—Baltimore AL 1969-70-71-74; New York AL 1976.
Henke, Thomas A.—Toronto AL 1985.
Henneman, Michael A.—Detroit AL 1987.
Hernandez, Guillermo—Detroit AL 1984-87.
Hernandez, Jacinto—Pittsburgh NL 1971.
Hernandez, Keith—St. Louis NL 1982; New York NL 1986.
Hernandez, Ramon G.—Pittsburgh NL 1972-74-75.
Herndon, Larry D.—Detroit AL 1984-87.
Herr, Thomas M.—St. Louis NL 1982-85-87.
Hershiser, Orel L.—Los Angeles NL 1985.
Hiller, John F.—Detroit AL 1972.
Holland, Alfred W.—Philadelphia NL 1983.
Holt, James W.—Minnesota AL 1970; Oakland AL 1974-75.
Holtzman, Kenneth D.—Oakland AL 1972-73-74-75.
Honeycutt, Frederick W.—Los Angeles NL 1983-85.
Hood, Donald H.—Baltimore AL 1973.
Hooton, Burt C.—Los Angeles NL 1977-78-81.
Hopkins, Donald—Oakland AL 1975.
Horlen, Joel E.—Oakland AL 1972.
Horner, J. Robert—Atlanta NL 1982.
Horton, Ricky N.—St. Louis NL 1985-87.
Horton, William W.—Detroit AL 1972.
Hough, Charles O.—Los Angeles NL 1974-77-78.
Howe, Arthur H.—Pittsburgh NL 1974; Houston NL 1980.
Howe, Steven R.—Los Angeles NL 1981.
Howell, Jack R.—California AL 1986.
Howell, Kenneth—Los Angeles NL 1985.
Howell, Roy L.—Milwaukee AL 1982.
Hoyt, D. LaMarr—Chicago AL 1983.
Hrabosky, Alan T.—Kansas City AL 1978.
Hrbek, Kent A.—Minnesota AL 1987.
Hubbard, Glenn D.—Atlanta NL 1982.
Hudson, Charles L.—Philadelphia NL 1983.
Huismann, Mark L.—Kansas City AL 1984.
Hume, Thomas H.—Cincinnati NL 1979.
Hunter, James A.—Oakland AL 1971-72-73-74; New York AL 1976-78.
Hurdle, Clinton M.—Kansas City AL 1978-80.
Hurst, Bruce V.—Boston AL 1986.
Hutton, Thomas G.—Philadelphia NL 1976-77.

I

Iorg, Dane C.—Kansas City AL 1984-85.
Iorg, Garth R.—Toronto AL 1985.

J

Jackson, Danny L.—Kansas City AL 1985.
Jackson, Grant D.—Baltimore AL 1973-74; New York AL 1976; Pittsburgh NL 1979.
Jackson, Reginald M.—Oakland AL 1971-72-73-74-75; New York AL 1977-78-80-81; California AL 1982-86.
Jackson, Ronnie D.—California AL 1982.

Thompson, Danny L.—Minnesota AL 1970.
Thompson, Robert R.—San Francisco NL 1987.
Thon, Richard W.—California AL 1979; Houston NL 1986.
Thornton, Louis—Toronto AL 1985.
Thurmond, Mark A.—San Diego NL 1984; Detroit AL 1987.
Tiant, Luis C.—Minnesota AL 1970; Boston AL 1975.
Tidrow, Richard W.—New York AL 1976-77-78; Chicago AL 1983.
Tillman, J. Robert—Atlanta NL 1969.
Todd, James R.—Oakland AL 1975.
Tolan, Robert—Cincinnati NL 1970-72; Philadelphia NL 1976.
Tomlin, David A.—Cincinnati NL 1973-79.
Torrez, Michael A.—New York AL 1977.
Tovar, Cesar L.—Minnesota AL 1969-70; Oakland AL 1975.
Trammell, Alan S.—Detroit AL 1984-87.
Trillo, J. Manuel—Oakland AL 1974; Philadelphia NL 1980.
Trout, Steven R.—Chicago NL 1984.
Tudor, John T.—St. Louis NL 1985-87.

U

Uhlaender, Theodore O.—Minnesota AL 1969; Cincinnati NL 1972.
Underwood, Thomas G.—Philadelphia NL 1976; New York AL 1980; Oakland AL 1981.
Unser, Delbert B.—Philadelphia NL 1980.
Upshaw, Cecil L.—Boston AL 1969.
Upshaw, Willie C.—Toronto AL 1985.
Uribe, Jose A.—San Francisco NL 1987.

V

Valenzuela, Fernando—Los Angeles NL 1981-83-85.
Van Slyke, Andrew J.—St. Louis NL 1985.
Velez, Otoniel—New York AL 1976.
Veryzer, Thomas M.—Chicago NL 1984.
Viola, Frank J.—Minnesota AL 1987.
Virgil, Osvaldo J.—Philadelphia NL 1983.
Vuckovich, Peter D.—Milwaukee AL 1982.
Vukovich, George S.—Philadelphia NL 1980.

W

Walk, Robert V.—Atlanta NL 1982.
Walker, Gregory L.—Chicago AL 1983.
Walker, J. Luke—Pittsburgh NL 1970-72.
Wallach, Timothy C.—Montreal NL 1981.
Walling, Dennis M.—Houston NL 1980-86.
Washington, Claudell—Oakland AL 1974-75; Atlanta NL 1982.

Washington, Herbert L.—Oakland AL 1974.
Washington, U. L.—Kansas City AL 1980-84.
Wathan, John D.—Kansas City AL 1976-77-78-80-84.
Watson, Robert J.—New York AL 1980-81.
Watt, Eddie D.—Baltimore AL 1969-71-73.
Weis, Albert J.—New York NL 1969.
Welch, Robert L.—Los Angeles NL 1978-81-83-85.
Whisenton, Larry—Atlanta NL 1982.
Whitaker, Louis R.—Detroit AL 1984-87.
White, Devon M.—California AL 1986.
White, Frank—Kansas City AL 1976-77-78-80-84.
White, Jerome C.—Montreal NL 1981.
White, Roy H.—New York AL 1976-77-78.
Whitfield, Terry B.—Los Angeles NL 1985.
Whitson, Eddie L.—San Diego NL 1984.
Whitt, L. Ernest—Toronto AL 1985.
Wiggins, Alan A.—San Diego NL 1984.
Wilcox, Milton E.—Cincinnati NL 1970; Detroit AL 1984.
Wilfong, Robert D.—California AL 1982-86.
Williams, Billy L.—Oakland AL 1975.
Williams, Earl C.—Baltimore AL 1973-74.
Williams, Stanley W.—Minnesota AL 1970.
Wilson, William H.—New York NL 1986.
Wilson, Willie J.—Kansas City AL 1978-80-84-85.
Winfield, David M.—New York AL 1981.
Wise, Richard C.—Boston AL 1975.
Witt, Michael A.—California AL 1982-86.
Wohlford, James E.—Kansas City AL 1976.
Woods, Gary L.—Houston NL 1980; Chicago NL 1984.
Woodson, Richard L.—Minnesota AL 1969-70.
Woodward, William F.—Cincinnati NL 1970.
Worrell, Todd R.—St. Louis NL 1985-87.
Worthington, Allan F.—Minnesota AL 1969.
Wynn, James S.—Los Angeles NL 1974.

Y

Yastrzemski, Carl M.—Boston AL 1975.
Yeager, Stephen W.—Los Angeles NL 1974-77-78-81-83-85.
Yount, Robin R.—Milwaukee AL 1982.

Z

Zachary, W. Chris—Detroit AL 1972.
Zachry, Patrick P.—Cincinnati NL 1976; Los Angeles NL 1983.

Zahn, Geoffrey C.—California AL 1982.
Zdeb, Joseph E.—Kansas City AL 1977.
Zepp, William C.—Minnesota AL 1970.
Zisk, Richard W.—Pittsburgh NL 1974-75.

Managers

Alston, Walter E.—Los Angeles NL 1974.
Altobelli, Joseph S.—Baltimore AL 1983.
Anderson, George L.—Cincinnati NL 1970-72-73-75-76; Detroit AL 1984-87.
Berra, Lawrence P.—New York NL 1973.
Cox, Robert J.—Toronto AL 1985.
Craig, Roger L.—San Francisco NL 1987.
Dark, Alvin R.—Oakland AL 1974-75.
Fanning, W. James—Montreal NL 1981.
Fox, Charles F.—San Francisco NL 1971.
Fregosi, James L.—California AL 1979.
Frey, James G.—Kansas City AL 1980; Chicago NL 1984.
Green, G. Dallas—Philadelphia NL 1980.
Harris, C. Luman—Atlanta NL 1969.
Herzog, Dorrell N. E.—Kansas City AL 1976-77-78; St. Louis NL 1982-85-87.
Hodges, Gilbert R.—New York NL 1969.
Howser, Richard D.—New York AL 1980; Kansas City AL 1984-85.
Johnson, Darrell D.—Boston AL 1975.
Johnson, David A.—New York NL 1986.
Kelly, J. Thomas—Minnesota AL 1987.
Kuenn, Harvey E.—Milwaukee AL 1982.
Lanier, Harold C.—Houston NL 1986.
LaRussa, Anthony—Chicago AL 1983.
Lasorda, Thomas C.—Los Angeles NL 1977-78-81-83-85.
Lemon, Robert G.—New York AL 1978-81.
Martin, Alfred M.—Minnesota AL 1969; Detroit AL 1972; New York AL 1976-77; Oakland AL 1981.
Mauch, Gene W.—California AL 1982-86.
McNamara, John F.—Cincinnati NL 1979; Boston AL 1986.
Murtaugh, Daniel E.—Pittsburgh NL 1970-71-74-75.
Owens, Paul F.—Philadelphia NL 1983.
Ozark, Daniel L.—Philadelphia NL 1976-77-78.
Rigney, William J.—Minnesota AL 1970.
Tanner, Charles W.—Pittsburgh NL 1979.
Torre, Joseph P.—Atlanta NL 1982.
Virdon, William C.—Pittsburgh NL 1972; Houston NL 1980.
Weaver, Earl S.—Baltimore AL 1969-70-71-73-74-79.
Williams, Richard H.—Oakland AL 1971-72-73; San Diego NL 1984.

CHAMPIONSHIP SERIES TOP 20
BATTING

Series (Pitchers Excluded)

Player	S.
Reggie Jackson	11
Richie Hebner	8
Hal McRae	8
Paul Blair	7
Joe Morgan	7
Graig Nettles	7
Pete Rose	7
Many tied with	6

Games

Player	G.
Reggie Jackson	45
Hal McRae	28
Pete Rose	28
Bob Boone	27
George Brett	27
Richie Hebner	27
Joe Morgan	27
Don Baylor	26
Frank White	26
Paul Blair	25
Bobby Grich	24
Graig Nettles	24
Al Oliver	23
Johnny Bench	22
Ron Cey	22
Steve Garvey	22
Dave Lopes	22
Willie Stargell	22
Three tied with	21

Batting Average (50+ AB)

Player	AB.	BA.
Mickey Rivers	57	.386
Pete Rose	118	.381
Dusty Baker	62	.371
Steve Garvey	90	.356
Ozzie Smith	57	.351
Brooks Robinson	69	.348
George Brett	103	.340
Thurman Munson	62	.339
Bill Russell	83	.337
Darrell Porter	63	.317
Bob Boone	84	.310
Lou Piniella	59	.305
Doug DeCinces	64	.297
Willie McGee	65	.292
Don Baylor	90	.289
Fred Patek	52	.288
Dave Cash	59	.288
Chris Chambliss	63	.286
Garry Maddox	70	.286
Richie Hebner	88	.284

Slugging Average (50+ AB)

Player	AB.	SLG.
George Brett	103	.728
Steve Garvey	90	.678
Dusty Baker	62	.597
Greg Luzinski	73	.589
Pete Rose	118	.534
Johnny Bench	83	.530
Sal Bando	74	.527
Brooks Robinson	69	.522
Ron Cey	82	.500
Thurman Munson	62	.500
Graig Nettles	85	.494
Ozzie Smith	57	.491
Fred Patek	52	.481
Lou Piniella	59	.475
Willie Stargell	79	.468
Richie Hebner	88	.466
Willie McGee	65	.462
Mickey Rivers	57	.456
Don Baylor	90	.456
Doug DeCinces	64	.438

At-Bats

Player	AB.
Reggie Jackson	163
Pete Rose	118
George Brett	103
Joe Morgan	96
Don Baylor	90
Steve Garvey	90
Bobby Grich	88
Richie Hebner	88
Hal McRae	88
Frank White	86
Graig Nettles	85
Bob Boone	84
Johnny Bench	83
Bill Russell	83
Mike Schmidt	83
Ron Cey	82
Paul Blair	80
Willie Stargell	79
Larry Bowa	77
Tony Perez	77

Runs

Player	R.
George Brett	22
Pete Rose	17
Reggie Jackson	16
Steve Garvey	15
Ron Cey	14
Don Baylor	13
Dusty Baker	12
Willie McGee	12
Joe Morgan	12
Johnny Bench	11
Doug DeCinces	11
Roy White	11
Many tied with	10

Hits

Player	H.
Pete Rose	45
Reggie Jackson	37
George Brett	35
Steve Garvey	32
Bill Russell	28
Don Baylor	26
Bob Boone	26
Richie Hebner	25
Brooks Robinson	24
Dusty Baker	23
Hal McRae	23
Ron Cey	22
Graig Nettles	22
Mickey Rivers	22
Johnny Bench	21
Thurman Munson	21
Frank White	21
Many tied with	20

Total Bases

Player	TB.
George Brett	75
Pete Rose	63
Reggie Jackson	62
Steve Garvey	61
Johnny Bench	44
Greg Luzinski	43
Graig Nettles	42
Don Baylor	41
Ron Cey	41
Richie Hebner	41
Sal Bando	39
Dusty Baker	37
Willie Stargell	37
Brooks Robinson	36
Hal McRae	35
Bob Boone	32
Bill Russell	32
Dave Lopes	31
Thurman Munson	31
Al Oliver	31

Doubles

Player	2B.
Ron Cey	7
Richie Hebner	7
Reggie Jackson	7
Hal McRae	7
Pete Rose	7
Mike Schmidt	7
Doug DeCinces	6
Greg Luzinski	6
Brooks Robinson	6
Roy White	6
Matty Alou	5
Dusty Baker	5
George Brett	5
Tommy Herr	5
Joe Morgan	5
Fred Patek	5
Darrell Porter	5
Willie Stargell	5
Many tied with	4

Triples

Player	3B.
George Brett	4
Willie McGee	3
Johnny Bench	2
Dave Lopes	2
Ozzie Smith	2
Many tied with	1

Home Runs

Player	HR.
George Brett	9
Steve Garvey	8
Reggie Jackson	6
Sal Bando	5
Johnny Bench	5
Greg Luzinski	5
Gary Matthews	5
Graig Nettles	5
Ron Cey	4
Jeff Leonard	4
Bill Madlock	4
Boog Powell	4
Bob Robertson	4
Willie Stargell	4
Many tied with	3

Runs Batted In

Player	RBI.
Steve Garvey	21
Reggie Jackson	20
George Brett	19
Graig Nettles	19
Don Baylor	16
Al Oliver	15
Ron Cey	13
Dusty Baker	13
Gary Matthews	13
Tony Perez	13
Richie Hebner	12
Greg Luzinski	12
Willie Stargell	12
Dave Lopes	11
Fred Patek	11
Boog Powell	11
Pete Rose	11
Five tied with	10

Game-Winning RBIs (1980—Present)

Player	GW.
George Brett	3
Don Baylor	2
Gary Carter	2
Cecil Cooper	2
Pedro Guerrero	2
Tito Landrum	2
Greg Luzinski	2
Gary Matthews	2
Al Oliver	2
Ozzie Smith	2
Many tied with	1

Bases on Balls

Player	BB.
Joe Morgan	23
Reggie Jackson	17
Darrell Porter	16
Ron Cey	13
Gene Tenace	13
George Brett	11
Don Baylor	10
Johnny Bench	10
Pete Rose	10
Willie Stargell	10
Larry Bowa	9
Jose Cruz	9
Pedro Guerrero	9
Dave Lopes	9
Frank Robinson	9
Ozzie Smith	9
Jim Wynn	9
Many tied with	8

Strikeouts

Player	SO.
Reggie Jackson	41
Cesar Geronimo	24
Bobby Grich	22
Greg Luzinski	20
Willie Stargell	19
Hal McRae	18
Johnny Bench	17
Paul Blair	17
Willie McGee	16
Tony Perez	16
Gene Tenace	16
Ron Cey	15
Roberto Clemente	15
Mike Schmidt	15
Don Baylor	14
Richie Hebner	14
Steve Balboni	12
Sal Bando	12
Rick Monday	12
Darryl Strawberry	12

Stolen Bases

Player	SB.
Dave Lopes	9
Joe Morgan	8
Amos Otis	8
Bert Campaneris	6
Ken Griffey	5
Johnny Bench	4
Kirk Gibson	4
Reggie Jackson	4
Al Bumbry	3
Randy Bush	3
Vince Coleman	3
Billy Hatcher	3
Bill Madlock	3
Terry Puhl	3
Ryne Sandberg	3
Many tied with	2

CHAMPIONSHIP SERIES TOP 20
PITCHING

Series

Pitcher	S.
Don Gullett	6
Jim Hunter	6
Tug McGraw	6
Jim Palmer	6
Ron Reed	6
Vida Blue	5
Steve Carlton	5
Mike Cuellar	5
Dock Ellis	5
Rollie Fingers	5
Dave Giusti	5
Tom Hall	5
Tommy John	5
Bruce Kison	5
Dave McNally	5
Jerry Reuss	5
Don Sutton	5
Many tied with	4

Games

Pitcher	G.
Tug McGraw	15
Dave Giusti	13
Ron Reed	13
Rollie Fingers	11
Pedro Borbon	10
Warren Brusstar	10
Don Gullett	10
Jim Hunter	10
Vida Blue	9
Tom Hall	9
Steve Carlton	8
Clay Carroll	8
Ken Dayley	8
Rich Gossage	8
Jim Palmer	8
Many tied with	7

Innings

Pitcher	IP.
Jim Hunter	69⅓
Jim Palmer	59⅔
Steve Carlton	53⅔
Don Sutton	49
Tommy John	47⅔
Mike Cuellar	44
Nolan Ryan	41⅓
Don Gullett	40⅔
Dave McNally	40⅓
Paul Splittorff	37
Fernando Valenzuela	37
Ken Holtzman	35
Jerry Reuss	33
Tom Seaver	31⅔
Vida Blue	31⅓
Dennis Leonard	31⅓
Dock Ellis	29⅔
Bruce Kison	29⅔
Larry Gura	28
John Tudor	28

ERA (20+ Innings)

Pitcher	IP.	ERA.
John Odom	22⅓	0.40
Dave Dravecky	21	0.43
Bruce Kison	29⅔	1.21
Gary Nolan	26⅔	1.35
Fernando Valenzuela	37	1.95
Jim Palmer	59⅔	1.96
Danny Cox	23	1.96
Don Sutton	49	2.02
Ken Holtzman	35	2.06
Tommy John	47⅔	2.08
John Candelaria	25⅓	2.13
John Tudor	28	2.25
Dock Ellis	29⅔	2.43
Bert Blyleven	24⅓	2.59
Tug McGraw	27	2.67
Dave McNally	40⅓	2.68
Paul Splittorff	37	2.68
Tom Seaver	31⅔	2.84
Burt Hooton	21	3.00
Mike Witt	20⅔	3.05

Games Started

Pitcher	GS.
Jim Hunter	10
Steve Carlton	8
Tommy John	7
Dennis Leonard	7
Jim Palmer	7
Jerry Reuss	7
Mike Cuellar	6
Don Gullett	6
Don Sutton	6
Doyle Alexander	5
Vida Blue	5
Larry Gura	5
Ken Holtzman	5
Dave McNally	5
Nolan Ryan	5
Fernando Valenzuela	5
Many tied with	4

Wins

Pitcher	W.
Steve Carlton	4
Jim Hunter	4
Tommy John	4
Bruce Kison	4
Jim Palmer	4
Don Sutton	4
Bert Blyleven	3
Dave McNally	3
Jesse Orosco	3
Fernando Valenzuela	3
Many tied with	2

Losses

Player	L.
Jerry Reuss	7
Doyle Alexander	4
Gene Garber	3
Don Gullett	3
Ken Holtzman	3
Jim Hunter	3
Charlie Leibrandt	3
Dennis Leonard	3
Many tied with	2

Winning Pct. (2+ Dec.)

Pitcher	W-L	PCT.
Bruce Kison	4-0	1.000
Bert Blyleven	3-0	1.000
Jesse Orosco	3-0	1.000
Rawley Eastwick	2-0	1.000
Mike Flanagan	2-0	1.000
Dick Hall	2-0	1.000
Tom Henke	2-0	1.000
Burt Hooton	2-0	1.000
Grant Jackson	2-0	1.000
Craig Lefferts	2-0	1.000
Sparky Lyle	2-0	1.000
John Odom	2-0	1.000
Mike Scott	2-0	1.000
Paul Splittorff	2-0	1.000
Milt Wilcox	2-0	1.000
Tommy John	4-1	.800
Jim Palmer	4-1	.800
Don Sutton	4-1	.800
Fernando Valenzuela	3-1	.750
Many tied with	4-2 or 2-1	.667

Complete Games

Pitcher	CG.
Jim Palmer	5
Jim Hunter	3
Tommy John	3
Danny Cox	2
Mike Cuellar	2
Ken Holtzman	2
Dennis Leonard	2
Dave McNally	2
Mike Scott	2
Don Sutton	2
Many tied with	1

Hits

Pitcher	H.
Jim Hunter	57
Steve Carlton	53
Jim Palmer	46
Larry Gura	43
Tommy John	40
Jerry Reuss	37
Don Sutton	37
Paul Splittorff	35
Dennis Leonard	34
Doyle Alexander	33
Mike Cuellar	32
Nolan Ryan	32
Don Gullett	31
Dave McNally	29
Dock Ellis	28
Fernando Valenzuela	28
Vida Blue	27
Ron Reed	27
Three tied with	26

Runs

Pitcher	R.
Jim Hunter	25
Jerry Reuss	25
Doyle Alexander	23
Steve Carlton	22
Nolan Ryan	19
Don Gullett	18
Ed Figueroa	17
Tommy John	17
Vida Blue	16
Mike Cuellar	16
Dennis Leonard	16
Ron Reed	16
Larry Gura	15
Don Sutton	14
Steve Blass	13
John Candelaria	13
Larry Christenson	13
Kirk McCaskill	13
Dave McNally	13
Jim Palmer	13

Earned Runs

Pitcher	ER.
Jim Hunter	25
Doyle Alexander	22
Steve Carlton	21
Jerry Reuss	20
Don Gullett	18
Nolan Ryan	17
Vida Blue	16
Mike Cuellar	15
Ed Figueroa	15
Dennis Leonard	15
Ron Reed	15
Larry Gura	13
Jim Palmer	13
Steve Blass	12
Larry Christenson	12
Dave McNally	12
Many tied with	11

Bases on Balls

Pitcher	BB.
Steve Carlton	28
Mike Cuellar	19
Jim Palmer	19
Fernando Valenzuela	19
Jim Hunter	18
Jerry Reuss	17
Tug McGraw	16
Tommy John	15
Dave McNally	15
Don Gullett	12
Bruce Kison	12
Dick Tidrow	12
Dock Ellis	11
Tom Hall	11
Burt Hooton	10
Tom Seaver	10
Paul Splittorff	10
Dave Stieb	10
Four tied with	9

Strikeouts

Pitcher	SO.
Jim Palmer	46
Nolan Ryan	46
Steve Carlton	39
Jim Hunter	37
Dave McNally	30
Don Sutton	30
Mike Cuellar	28
Fernando Valenzuela	28
Tommy John	27
Vida Blue	25
John Candelaria	25
Bruce Kison	24
Tom Seaver	24
Don Gullett	23
Dennis Leonard	23
Tug McGraw	22
Bert Blyleven	20
John Tudor	20
Three tied with	19

Saves (1969—Present)

Pitcher	SV.
Tug McGraw	5
Ken Dayley	4
Dave Giusti	4
Pedro Borbon	3
Rich Gossage	3
Dick Drago	2
Rollie Fingers	2
Don Gullett	2
Pete Ladd	2
Tom Niedenfuer	2
Dan Quisenberry	2
Jeff Reardon	2
Many tied with	1

Shutouts

Pitcher	SHO.
Vida Blue	1
Mike Boddicker	1
Ray Burris	1
Joe Coleman	1
Danny Cox	1
Dave Dravecky	1
Bob Forsch	1
Ken Holtzman	1
Jim Hunter	1
Danny Jackson	1
Tommy John	1
Jon Matlack	1
Scott McGregor	1
Dave McNally	1
John Odom	1
Jim Palmer	1
Mike Scott	1
Don Sutton	1